IMMIGRATION AND CITIZENSHIP

PROCESS AND POLICY

Seventh Edition

■ ■ ■

By

Thomas Alexander Aleinikoff

United Nations Deputy High Commissioner for Refugees
Professor of Law (on leave)
Georgetown University Law Center

David A. Martin

Warner–Booker Distinguished Professor
of International Law
University of Virginia

Hiroshi Motomura

Susan Westerberg Prager Professor of Law
University of California, Los Angeles, School of Law

Maryellen Fullerton

Professor of Law
Brooklyn Law School

AMERICAN CASEBOOK SERIES®

WEST®

A Thomson Reuters business

Mat # 41057222

COPYRIGHT © 1985, 1990, 1991, 1995 WEST PUBLISHING CO.
© West, a Thomson business, 1998, 2003
© 2008 Thomson/West
© 2012 Thomson Reuters
 610 Opperman Drive
 St. Paul, MN 55123
 1–800–313–9378
Printed in the United States of America

ISBN: 978–0–314–26709–2

To the Aleinikoffs, Marrows, Mays, and Wises
And for Rachel, Shoshana, Sam, and Eli

To the Martins, Meekers, Johnstons, and Bowmans
And for Cyndy; Amy, Drew, Webb, Isa, and Doran; Jeff and Aggie

To the Motomuras, Sakumas, Kishis, and Katos
And for Linda and Amy

To the Fullertons, McDonnells, Roberts, and Ingersolls
And for Tom, Owen, Cullen, and Eleanor

PREFACE TO THE SEVENTH EDITION

This casebook was first published 27 years ago. The intervening years have seen remarkable changes in the field of immigration—to statutes, administrative policies, case law, and even to the tone and content of political debate. Our various editions have traced these changes, sometimes resulting in major revisions from edition to edition. Three major pieces of legislation enacted in 1996, for example, significantly restructured both substantive provisions and procedures, and also altered terminology and categories to which immigration lawyers and scholars had become accustomed. Despite Congress' attempted restrictions on judicial review, the 1996 amendments also generated a torrent of judicial decisions, often reaching conflicting results, addressing both the new substantive provisions and the shape of remaining judicial authority. Again, after the terrorist attacks of September 11, 2011, both Congress and the executive branch restructured statutory provisions, administrative practices, and screening procedures. Major efforts to enact comprehensive immigration reform in 2005–2007 then presented for our Sixth Edition new material to use in considering the difficult state of our immigration management regime and proposals on how to change it, even though all such bills fell short of enactment. States and local jurisdictions also became more active with their own efforts to participate in immigration enforcement—or occasionally to offer greater assistance to immigrants, both authorized and unauthorized.

The four years since our last edition, in contrast, have been largely a time of consolidation and incremental change. Many—but far from all—of the challenging and complex legal questions generated by the 1996 laws and the post-September 11 changes are beginning to find resolution through case law or administrative adaptation. An ailing economy, apparently coupled with increased federal enforcement efforts, has resulted in a slight decline and then a leveling off of the unauthorized immigrant population. Despite high hopes for comprehensive statutory reform after the elections of 2008, new legislation has made little headway. Some states have passed more restrictive legislation meant to get their officers or agencies involved in enforcing the immigration laws or at least to deter the settlement of unauthorized migrants within their boundaries. The federal government has responded with lawsuits claiming that many such provisions are preempted by federal law, blocking, at least temporarily, the full implementation of these measures.

This edition, therefore, does not reflect major ferment in the law and policies governing immigration—though an instructor who has taught from the Sixth Edition will recognize a host of subtle and important refinements reflected in our choice of new materials, and a few areas in which the law or policy has unfolded in surprising ways. Nonetheless, we have used this occasion to adopt a few modest but important changes to the organization of the book—changes that should provide a better flow of coverage for classroom use.

We now begin with a new, brief first chapter containing an overview of the history of U.S. immigration regulation and a snapshot of the current situation. From there we move, as with the Sixth Edition, to chapters that consider citizenship; the foundations of the immigration control power, including theoretical perspectives on both its effective and its moral use; and a survey of the agencies and courts involved in the immigration process. With Chapter Five comes something of a change. As before, this chapter covers in detail the basic admission categories for immigrants and nonimmigrants, but it now includes as well a broad look at the unauthorized migrant population within the United States. Chapter Six surveys the procedures governing admission.

Then comes another significant reordering. Inadmissibility grounds have been separated from the admission categories material, where they have been covered in our earlier editions, and are now included in a new Chapter Seven that addresses those grounds along with deportability grounds, followed by the provisions for relief from removal. We have found that this consolidation allows for a more logical and unified approach to several themes that run throughout the removal grounds and the provisions for relief—among others, consideration of the interplay between immigration law and criminal law, including the Supreme Court's 2010 decision in *Padilla v. Kentucky*. Chapter Eight covers asylum and protection under the Convention Against Torture. But as with the previous edition, we have considerably abbreviated the treatment here, as compared with the first five editions of this book, in view of the increasing tendency within law schools to offer detailed treatment of refugee law in a separate course offering. Our companion casebook, *Forced Migration: Law and Policy,* provides more extensive and detailed teaching materials that can be used in such a course, or indeed to augment this chapter.

Chapter Nine pulls together materials on enforcement, addressing both federal government mechanisms and the efforts by states and localities. We also place in Chapter Nine an overview of proposals to reform the immigration system, including proposals to legalize much of the current undocumented population, and thus to develop a more effective overall regime to enforce the immigration laws. We include consideration of the 2005–2007 reform bills, as well as more recent proposals for comprehensive immigration reform or for more focused changes, such as the DREAM Act. Chapter Ten treats removal proceedings, detention, and selected issues of judicial review. We close our consideration with a chapter on constitutional protection of noncitizens within the United States.

We do not expect that any instructor will use all this material in the space of a one-semester course. Instead, the book is meant to offer a wide range of coverage choices for teachers of immigration and citizenship law.

During some of the time covered by this casebook (in the mid–1990s), both Alex Aleinikoff and David Martin served as policy-level officials of the Immigration and Naturalization Service—the former as General Counsel and later as Executive Associate Commissioner for Programs, the latter as Aleinikoff's successor in the General Counsel position. Martin returned to government service from January 2009 to December 2010, as Principal Deputy General Counsel for the Department of Homeland Security. Both of these coauthors took part in developing regulations and in crafting positions for the INS or DHS on many of the issues addressed in the book. Of course, none of the opinions expressed or implied in this book should be taken as representing the views of INS, DHS, or the U.S. government. Hiroshi Motomura served as co-counsel or volunteer consultant on behalf of the noncitizen respondent or detainee in several principal cases or cases mentioned in the Notes, including *INS v. Aguirre–Aguirre, Zadvydas v. Davis,* and the early stages of what became *INS v. St. Cyr.* Because of his current position as United Nations Deputy High Commissioner for Refugees, Alex Aleinikoff has not participated in the preparation of this edition; and nothing in this edition should be understood as reflecting the views of UNHCR or the United Nations.

Acknowledgments. This book owes a great deal to the advice, reactions, and helpful suggestions received from colleagues and users—both instructors and students. With particular reference to this edition (and at the risk of omitting some who have certainly contributed to the coauthors' understanding and perspective on the field), we gratefully acknowledge comments, suggestions, or stimulating conversations from Kerry Abrams, Lenni Benson, Stacy Caplow, Tino Cuellar, William Dailey, Ingrid Eagly, Doug Ford, Brianna Fuller, Deep Gulasekaram, Lucas Guttentag, Alan Hyde, Dan Kanstroom, Gerry Neuman, Michael Olivas, Juan Osuna, Nicholas Perry, Judy Rabinovitz, Peter Schuck, Rebecca Sharpless, Juliet Stumpf, Margaret Taylor, Norton Tooby, Nadine Wettstein, and Art Wolf.

We have benefited greatly from excellent research assistance by Peter Hilton, Diane Rish, and Eve Aguilar at Virginia; Laura Hernandez, Maya Ingram, Jennifer Lin, Alex Pauley, and Kate Raven at UCLA; and Brendan Cranna, Danielle Coleman, Margaret Garrett, William Hine–Ramsberger, David Montgomery, Stephen Popernick, and Riti Singh at Brooklyn. We also express our gratitude for help with proofing, copying, preparation of tables, assembling and transmission of drafts and documents, and for a range of other indispensable administrative attention, to our faculty assistants Shannon Foreman, Pennie Newell, Beth Pollastro, and Kasse Reyes. And we extend a special word of thanks to Roxy Birkel of Thomson Reuters/West for her patience in dealing with sometimes belated submissions, her creativity in dealing with the occasional production snag, and her determination to keep us on course for timely publication.

Finally, we gratefully acknowledge research support for this edition provided by Brooklyn Law School, the UCLA School of Law, the UCLA Academic Senate, the University of Virginia School of Law, and the Virginia

Law School Foundation. Responsibility for any errors rests with the authors alone. We welcome ongoing suggestions and corrections from any of the book's users.

DAVID MARTIN
HIROSHI MOTOMURA
MARYELLEN FULLERTON

November 2011

Preface to the First Edition

For decades, immigration and nationality law has been something of a neglected stepchild in the law schools. Most schools offer no immigration course at all. Where courses exist, they typically focus on the practical business of learning a complex statute and preparing students for careers as immigration attorneys, often finding little time to devote to larger issues of policy and principle.

Immigration law has suffered from the lack of sustained academic attention. All too often, instead of measured policy debate, one encounters in this field merely the polarized confrontation of charge and countercharge: government supporters reflexively advocating a hardline response; government opponents reflexively assuming that maximum advocacy for the particular aliens involved will bring about the best public policy. We don't deny that the issues are the kind that stir—and ought to stir—deep feelings. But we believe there is far more room for careful and balanced study of long-term policy options, even among those who care passionately about the ultimate values at stake. Law schools should serve as one important forum for such exploration.

As law students, we too enjoyed little exposure to the subject. Later, during stints in government service in Washington, each of us found himself dealing occasionally with immigration matters, but we discovered our mutual interest in the subject only when the Cuban boatlift of 1980 brought lawyers from the Departments of Justice and State together. There is nothing like a full-fledged crisis—especially one offering no satisfactory solutions—to cement an appreciation of the subject's fascinations and frustrations. We carried that interest with us when we moved into the academy, along with vague intentions to teach immigration law, but with little idea of just what was in store.

Now, after teaching and writing in the field for several years, we have come to wonder how the intrinsic attractions of the subject for classroom teaching have gone so widely unnoticed. Immigration law, we have learned, can be one of the richest and most rewarding subjects for both students and professors. It is redolent of our national history, reflecting both successes that are the legitimate source of national pride, and dispiriting failures. Major public policy issues appear repeatedly, posing deeper questions concerning national identity, membership, moral philosophy, constitutional interpretation, public law, public administration, international relations, and the limits of practical politics. Immigration law also furnishes a vital setting for studying the interaction of our three branches of government. Indeed, we have been struck by how many major Supreme Court decisions on larger questions of administrative and constitutional law have been decided in immigration cases—the legislative veto case, *INS v. Chadha*, 103 S.Ct. 2764 (1983), being only the latest example.

An immigration course, however, need not always keep the student at the heights occupied by great questions of philosophy, public policy, and constitutional interpretation. Immigration law also provides a worthy vehicle for refining basic lawyering skills, especially the capacity for close reading of an intricate statute and the discipline of mastering a specialized technical vocabulary. One judge who had just struggled through a complex interpretive task reflected on his experience:

> Whatever guidance the regulations furnish to those cognoscenti familiar with [immigration] procedures, this court, despite many years of legal experience, finds that they yield up meaning only grudgingly and that morsels of comprehension must be pried from mollusks of jargon.

Dong Sik Kwon v. INS, 646 F.2d 909, 919 (5th Cir.1981). Students ought to learn how to wield their *escargot* forks expertly, and then they should be inspired to ask whether the food could not be prepared in a more sensible way.

Beyond this, the student of immigration law must develop an awareness of how legislation evolves and an ability to make use of the materials of legislative history—for today's Immigration and Nationality Act (INA) is the product of over a hundred years of congressional efforts to fashion laws that regulate immigration. There are also thousands of administrative and judicial precedents, often in remarkable conflict with one another in both holding and spirit. These provide excellent raw materials for practice in the art of advocacy, hypothetically representing either a private client or a government agency.

There may be many reasons for immigration law's historical insularity. But we wrote this book with the conviction that a lack of good teaching materials has played a role—materials with which nonspecialists might feel comfortable but which specialists might also find challenging. (In this respect, we remember well our own problems when we first taught the course.) When we began our work on this book, there was no casebook at all on the subject of immigration law. Treatises existed, and various kinds of manuals that have been used as the basis for the course by practitioners of many years' experience. But it is a daunting prospect for nonspecialists to put together workable supplemental materials on their own, especially if they aspire to teaching more than just the technical details.

We hope this book will contribute toward ending the law schools' neg-lect and the subject's insularity. We have consciously sought to make the reader aware of the broader dimensions of the subject, but without ignoring the nuts-and-bolts foundation that a novice practitioner in the field would find necessary. We don't spend time, for example, exploring all 19 grounds for deportation appearing in INA § 241(a). We do devote enough attention to selected grounds, however, as well as the basic structure of those provisions, so that a student would know where to turn for answers to the detailed questions that might arise in practice. We have aimed, above all, at recapturing immigration law as a worthy and exciting area for academic study, without losing sight of the basic learning a student must master if he or she chooses to open an immigration practice the following year. Whether we have succeeded in these aims remains to be seen, but we invite users of this book—instructors and students—to write us with their reactions and suggestions for expanded or reduced coverage.

We have also consciously tried to avoid the polarities that often beset the field. It is easy to develop sympathy for the individual alien involved in a particular case, and to strive to mold the legal doctrine to bring about a warm-hearted result for that person. Too many law review notes, and often judges as well, succumb to this temptation, neglecting to take adequate account of the long-term implications for an immigration system that must cope with millions of applications each year. We try to keep the reader aware of that larger systemic perspective—without suggesting that systems should always prevail over warm-heartedness, of course.

ALEX ALEINIKOFF
DAVID MARTIN

November 30, 1984

TECHNICAL MATTERS

Editing Style

In editing cases and other materials reprinted here, we have marked textual deletions with triple asterisks, but we have often omitted simple citations to cases or other authorities without any printed indication. Similarly, we have deleted footnotes from reprinted materials without signaling the omission. Where we chose to retain a footnote, however, we have maintained the original numbering. Our own footnotes appearing in the midst of reprinted materials are marked with alphabetical superscripts; they also end with the notation "—eds." When we drop footnotes to text that we wrote ourselves, we have used the ordinary numerical designations.

INA Citations

How to cite the sections of the Immigration and Nationality Act (INA) has posed an ongoing problem for teachers and writers in this field. Most court decisions refer to INA provisions by means of the numbers employed in Title 8 of the U.S. Code, where the Act is codified. This is understandable as a matter of convenience, even though technically incorrect, because Title 8 has not been codified—that is, directly enacted by Congress to serve as the official version of the legislation. Citation to the INA, not the U.S. code is the correct method. But perhaps more importantly as a practical matter, specialists in the field almost religiously employ the INA section numbers and are not always familiar with references to the U.S. Code enumeration (in part because the system used to translate Act numbers into U.S. Code numbers appears to us to be eccentric and unpredictable). Moreover, the administrative framework for regulations and certain other manuals and instructions is closely linked to the numbering scheme of the original Act. For example, the regulations of the Department of Homeland Security implementing the asylum provision, § 208 of the INA, appear in Part 208 of 8 C.F.R., while the equivalent asylum-related regulations of the Executive Office for Immigration Review (in the Department of Justice) appear in Part 1208.

For these reasons, we have decided to use the section numbers of the Act consistently throughout this book, to the exclusion of the U.S. Code numbers. This means that we have excised references to the Act using the U.S. Code numbering system from all cases and materials, and substituted direct INA section references, without expressly indicating where such substitutions have occurred. Readers who must know the corresponding U.S. Code number will find a conversion chart in the opening pages of our Statutory Supplement, *Immigration and Nationality Laws of the United States: Selected Statutes, Regulations, and Forms*. The supplement also indicates with each section what its U.S. Code citation would be.

Citations and Abbreviations

Most citations in the book conform generally to *A Uniform System of Citation*, customarily used by law journals, but without giving full names of authors. For a few items that are cited frequently, however, we have abbreviated even further. Abbreviations that appear frequently, either in our material or in cases, are also set forth below.

1990 Act   Immigration Act of 1990, Pub.L. 101–649, 104 Stat. 4978.

1996 Act   Illegal Immigration Reform and Immigrant Responsibility Act of 1996, Pub.L. 104–208, Div.C., 110 Stat. 3009–546. Also sometimes referred to as IIRIRA.

AAO   Administrative Appeals Office of the U.S. Citizenship and Immigration Services, an office that handles specified types of administrative appeals. Also sometimes called the Administrative Appeals Unit (AAU)

AEDPA   Antiterrorism and Effective Death Penalty Act of 1996, Pub.L. 104–132, 110 Stat. 1214. It contained many provisions relating to immigration, particularly with respect to criminal and terrorist grounds of removal. Many of those provisions were further modified by the 1996 Act.

AG   Attorney General, the Cabinet officer who heads the U.S. Department of Justice.

Bender's Imm. Bull.

Bender's Immigration Bulletin. A leading reporting service on administrative, legislative and judicial developments in the immigration field, published twice monthly by LexisNexis.

BIA   Board of Immigration Appeals, a component of the Executive Office for Immigration Review within the U.S. Department of Justice.

CBP   U.S. Customs and Border Protection, U.S. Department of Homeland Security. Created in 2003, CBP houses border inspection functions and the Border Patrol.

DHS   U.S. Department of Homeland Security. Created by a 2003 reorganization spurred by the September 11 terrorist attacks, this department inherited most of the functions formerly carried out by the Immigration and Naturalization Service. Those functions are distributed, primarily, among three DHS components: CBP, ICE, and USCIS.

DHS Statistical Yearbook

Office of Immigration Statistics, U.S. Department of Homeland Security, Yearbook of Immigration Statistics.

EOIR   Executive Office for Immigration Review. This unit of the Department of Justice houses both the Board of Immigration Appeals and the corps of immigration judges.

EWI   Entrant without inspection.

FY   Fiscal year.

GM & Y   C. Gordon, S. Mailman, and S. Yale–Loehr, Immigration Law and Procedure (rev. ed. 2011). A leading treatise in the field, now published as a multi-volume looseleaf set, including several volumes containing primary materials (including the INA, implementing regulations, Operations Instructions, INS manuals and handbooks, and the visa-related portions of the Foreign Affairs Manual).

ICE   U.S. Immigration and Customs Enforcement, U.S. Department of Homeland Security. Created in 2003, ICE houses interior enforcement functions transferred from the former Immigration and Naturalization Service, including investigations, detention and removal, and the trial attorneys who represent the government in immigration court.

IIRIRA   Illegal Immigration Reform and Immigrant Responsibility Act of 1996, Pub.L. 104–208, Div.C., 110 Stat. 3009–546. We sometimes refer to it as the 1996 Act or the 1996 Immigration Act.

IJ   Immigration judge. The corps of immigration judges is a component of the Executive Office for Immigration Review within the U.S. Department of Justice.

IMFA   Immigration Marriage Fraud Amendments of 1986, Pub.L. 99–639, 100 Stat. 3537.

INA   The Immigration and Nationality Act. Pub.L. 82–414, 66 Stat. 163. Passed in 1952 as a comprehensive codification replacing earlier immigration and nationality laws, it has been frequently amended since then. The Act itself is unofficially codified, according to an idiosyncratic numbering scheme, in Title 8 of the United States Code; a conversion chart, showing corresponding section numbers, appears in our Statutory Supplement. In this book we cite by INA section number, not U.S.C. section number, to the current amended statute.

INS   Immigration and Naturalization Service. Until 2003, as a component of the Department of Justice, INS was the lead federal agency on immigration policy and operations. In 2003, INS was abolished and its functions were transferred to three separate units of the new Department of Homeland Security (see CBP, ICE, USCIS).

IRCA   Immigration Reform and Control Act of 1986, Pub.L. 99–603, 100 Stat. 3359.

Interp.Rel.   Interpreter Releases. A leading reporting service on administrative, legislative and judicial developments in the immigration field, published weekly by Thomson Reuters/West and available on Westlaw.

O.I.   Operations Instructions. The manual of detailed guidelines and policy statements issued by the Immigration and Naturalization Service and used by immigration officers in implementing the statute and the regulations. Those Instructions that have been released to the public are reprinted in an appendix volume of the GM & Y treatise. The Operations Instructions are now being phased out, as they are gradually replaced by newly issued DHS field manuals.

UNHCR   United Nations High Commissioner for Refugees.

USCIS   U.S. Citizenship and Immigration Services, Department of Homeland Security. Created in 2003, USCIS houses the principal services and adjudications functions inherited from the Immigration and Naturalization Service. Sometimes also referred to as CIS.

ACKNOWLEDGEMENTS

The authors wish to express their thanks to copyright holders and authors for permission to reprint excerpts from the following materials.

Abrams, Kerry, Immigration Law and the Regulation of Marriage, 91 Minnesota Law Review 1625 (2007). Reprinted by permission.

Ackerman, Bruce, Social Justice in the Liberal State. Copyright © 1980 by the Yale University Press. Reprinted by permission of the publisher.

Alden, Edward, America's 'National Suicide.' From Newsweek, April 10, 2011 © 2011 The Newsweek/Daily Beast Company LLC. All rights reserved. Used by permission and protected by the Copyright Laws of the United States. The printing, copying, redistribution, or retransmission of the Material without express written permission is prohibited.

Aleinikoff, T. Alexander, & Klusmeyer, Douglas, eds., From Migrants to Citizens: Membership in a Changing World (2000). Copyright © 2000 by Carnegie Endowment for International Peace. Reprinted by permission of the publisher from From Migrants to Citizens: Membership in a Changing World (Washington, DC: Carnegie Endowment for International Peace, 2000), pp. 137–141.

Aleinikoff, T. Alexander, Protected Characteristics and Social Perceptions: An Analysis of the Meaning of "Membership of a Particular Social Group", in Refugee Protection in International Law 263 (E. Feller, V. Türk, & F. Nicholson eds., 2003). © 2003 UNHCR. All worldwide rights reserved. Reprinted by permission.

Andreas, Peter, Border Games: Policing the U.S.-Mexico Divide (2000). Reprinted by permission from Political Science Quarterly, 113 (Winter 1998–99): 591–615.

Borjas, George J., Heaven's Door: Immigration Policy and the American Economy. Copyright © 1999 Princeton University Press. Reprinted by permission of Princeton University Press.

Bosniak, Linda S., Membership, Equality, and the Difference That Alienage Makes, 69 New York University Law Review 1047 (1994). Reprinted by permission.

Bosniak, Linda S., Opposing Prop. 187: Undocumented Immigrants and the National Imagination, 28 Connecticut Law Review 555 (1996). Reprinted by permission.

Bosniak, Linda, Being Here: Ethical Territoriality and the Rights of Immigrants, 8 Theoretical Inquiries in Law 389 (2007). Reprinted by permission.

83 Interpreter Releases 1597 (July 31, 2006). Reprinted by permission of Thomson West.

Clark, David. "It is better to have one child only." Photo of billboard in China reprinted by permission.

Cornelius, Wayne A., Mexican Migration to the United States: Introduction, in Mexican Migration to the United States: Origins, Consequences, and Policy Options 1 (W. Cornelius & J. Bustamante eds., 1989). Copyright © 1989 by the Center for U.S.-Mexican Studies, University of California, San Diego. Reprinted by permission.

Cumulative Growth in the Foreign–Born Population, New and Traditional Destination States, 1960 to 2009, MPI Data Hub, http://www.migration information.org/usfocus/vdisplay.cfm?ID=826. Reprinted by permission.*

Daniels, Roger, "No Lamps Were Lit for Them: Angel Island and the Historiography of Asian American Immigration," Journal of American Ethnic History 17, no. 1 (Fall 1997): 3–18. Copyright 1997 by the Immigration and Ethnic History Society. Reprinted by permission.

De la Garza, Rodolfo O. & DeSipio, Louis, Save the Baby, Change the Bathwater, and Scrub the Tub: Latino Electoral Participation After Seventeen Years of Voting Rights Act Coverage, 71 Texas Law Review 1479 (1993). Reprinted by permission.

Dingeman, M. Kathleen & Rumbaut, Rubén G. The Immigration–Crime Nexus and Post–Deportation Experiences: En/Countering Stereotypes in Southern California and El Salvador, 31 University of La Verne Law Review 363 (2010). Reprinted by permission.

Durand, Jorge, and Massey, Douglas S., Borderline Sanity. Reprinted with permission from The American Prospect: September 2001. Volume 12, Issue 17. http://www.prospect.org. The American Prospect, 1710 Rhode Island Avenue, NW, 12th Floor, Washington, DC 20036. All rights reserved.

Duvall, Donald, Expatriation under United States Law, Perez to Afroyim: The Search for a Philosophy of American Citizenship, 56 Virginia Law Review 408 (1970). Copyright © 1970. Reprinted by permission of the Virginia Law Review and Fred B. Rothman & Co.

Eagly, Ingrid V., Prosecuting Immigration, 104 Northwestern University Law Review 1281 (2009). Reprinted by permission.

Epps, Garrett, The Citizenship Clause: A "Legislative History," 60 American University Law Review 331 (2010). Reprinted by permission.

Estimates of the Top Diaspora Groups and Top Foreign–Born Groups, 2009, MPI Data Hub, http://www.migrationinformation.org/datahub/charts/diaspora1.cfm. Reprinted by permission.*

Ethical Considerations in Immigration Cases, 4 Immigration Law Report 169 (Dec. 1985). Reprinted by permission of Thomson West.

Fallows, James, Immigration: How It's Affecting Us, The Atlantic Monthly, Nov. 1983, at 88. Copyright © 1983 The Atlantic Monthly. Reprinted by permission.

Fein, Bruce. Divided Loyalties, Washington Times, Dec. 13, 2005, p. A19. Copyright © 2005 by The Washington Times LLC. Reprinted by permission.

Fitz, Marshall, Martinez, Gebe, & Wijewardena, Madura, The Costs of Mass Deportation: Impractical, Expensive, and Ineffective. Center for American Progress (March 2010). Reprinted by permission.

Fry, Brian N., Responding to Immigration: Perceptions of Promise and Threat, in The New Americans: Recent Immigration and American Society, Carola Suarez–Orozco and Marcelo Suarez–Orozco, editors. New York: LFB Scholarly Publishing LLC, 2001. Reprinted by permission.

Gates, Bill, How to Keep America Competitive, Washington Post, February 25, 2007, at B7. Reprinted by permission.

Gordon, Charles, Mailman, Stanley, and Yale–Loehr, Stephen, Immigration Law and Procedure, §§ 17.01, 17.03, 17.05–17.06, 94.01[2]. Reprinted from Immigration Law and Procedure with permission. Copyright © 2003, 2007 by Matthew Bender & Company, Inc., a member of the LexisNexis® Group. All rights reserved.

Griswold, Daniel T., "Willing Workers: Fixing the Problem of Illegal Mexican Migration to the United States," in Trade Policy Analysis no. 19, Oct. 15, 2002. © Cato Institute. Reprinted by permission.

Gross, Samuel R., & Livingston, Debra, Racial Profiling Under Attack, 102 Columbia Law Review 1413 (2002). Reprinted by permission.

Haney López, Ian F., White by Law: The Legal Construction of Race (1996). Copyright © 1996 by the New York University Press. Reprinted by permission of the publisher.

Hanson, Gordon H., The Economics and Policy of Illegal Immigration in the United States 1–2 (MPI Dec. 2009) http://www.migrationpolicy.org/pubs/Hanson–Dec09.pdf. Reprinted by permission.*

Hart, Henry, The Power of Congress to Limit the Jurisdiction of the Federal Courts: An Exercise in Dialectic, 66 Harvard Law Review 1362 (1953). Copyright © 1953 by the Harvard Law Review Association. Reprinted by permission.

Henkin, Louis, Foreign Affairs and the Constitution. Copyright © 1972 by The Foundation Press, Inc. Reprinted by permission of Foundation Press.

Henkin, Louis, The Constitution and United States Sovereignty: A Century of Chinese Exclusion and Its Progeny, 100 Harvard Law Review 853 (1987). Copyright © 1987 by the Harvard Law Review Association. Reprinted by permission.

Higham, John, Strangers in the Land: Patterns of American Nativism. Copyright © 1955 The Trustees of Rutgers College in New Jersey. Reprinted by permission of Rutgers University Press.

Hira, Ron, The H–1B and L–1 Visa Programs: Out of Control, Economic Policy Institute, Briefing Paper #280 (2010). Reprinted with permission of the Economic Policy Institute.

Jacoby, Tamar, An Idea Whose Time Has Finally Come?: The Case for Employment Verification, Migration Policy Institute Policy Brief No. 9 (2005). Reprinted by permission.*

Jacoby, Tamar, Immigration Nation, 85 Foreign Affairs 50 (2006). Reprinted by permission of FOREIGN AFFAIRS, Volume 85, Issue no. 6, November/December 2006. Copyright 2006 by the Council on Foreign Relations, Inc.

Johnson, Kevin, The Case Against Racial Profiling in Immigration Enforcement, 78 Washington University Law Quarterly 875 (2000). Reprinted by permission.

Kanstroom, Daniel, Deportation Nation: Outsiders in American History (2007). Reprinted by permission of the publisher from DEPORTATION NATION: OUTSIDERS IN AMERICAN HISTORY by Daniel Kanstroom, pp. 5–6, 231–232, Cambridge, Mass.: Harvard University Press, Copyright © 2007 by the President and Fellows of Harvard College.

Krikorian, Mark, Downsizing Illegal Immigration: A Strategy of Attrition Through Enforcement, Center for Immigration Studies Backgrounder, May 2005. Reprinted by permission.

Martin, David A., Eight Myths about Immigration Enforcement, 10 New York University Journal of Legislation and Public Policy 525 (2006–07). Reprinted by permission.

Martin, David A., Membership and Consent: Abstract or Organic?, 11 Yale Journal of International Law 278 (1985). Reprinted by permission.

Martin, David A., Refining Immigration Law's Role in Counterterrorism, from Legislating the War on Terror: An Agenda for Reform (B. Wittes ed. 2009). Reprinted by permission.

Martin, David A., The Refugee Concept: On Definitions, Politics, and the Careful Use of a Scarce Resource, from Refugee Policy: Canada and the United States (Howard Adelman ed. 1991). Reprinted by permission.

Martin, David A., Waiting for Solutions, Legal Times, May 29, 2001, at 66. Reprinted with permission from the May 29, 2001 edition of the Legal Times. © 2011 ALM Media Properties, LLC. All rights reserved. Further duplication without permission is prohibited. For information, contact 877–257–3382 or reprints@alm.com or visit www.almreprints.com.

Martin, Philip L. & Teitelbaum, Michael S., The Mirage of Mexican Guest Workers, 80 Foreign Affairs 117 (2001). Reprinted by permission of FOREIGN AFFAIRS, Volume 80, Issue no. 6, November/December 2001. Copyright 2001 by the Council on Foreign Relations, Inc.

Martin, Philip, & Midgley, Elizabeth, Immigration: Shaping and Reshaping America. (2d edition). © 2006 by the Population Reference Bureau. Reprinted by permission.

Martin, Susan F., A Nation of Immigrants. New York, NY: Cambridge University Press, 2010. Reprinted with permission of the author.

Massey, Douglas S., "Backfire at the Border: Why Enforcement Without Legalization Cannot Stop Illegal Migration," in Trade Policy Analysis no. 29 (June 13, 2005). © Cato Institute. Reprinted by permission.

Massey, Douglas S., Goldring, Luin, and Durand, Jorge, Continuities in Transnational Migration: An Analysis of Nineteen Mexican Communities, 99 American Journal of Sociology 1492 (1994). Copyright © 1994 by the University of Chicago Press. Reprinted by permission.

Massey, Douglas S., Jorge Durand, and Nolan J. Malone. "Principles of Operation: Theories of International Migration," in Beyond Smoke and Mirrors: Mexican Immigration in an Era of Economic Integration. © 2002 Russell Sage Foundation, 112 East 64th Street, New York, NY 10065. Reprinted by permission.

Matza, Michael, House of Dreams, Philadelphia Inquirer, Dec. 19, 2010, at A1. Used with permission of Philadelphia Inquirer Permissions. Copyright© 2010. All rights reserved.

McNew, David. U.S. Population Passes 300 Million. David McNew/Getty Images News/Getty Images. Photo of San Diego border station reprinted by permission.

Medige, Patricia, The Labyrinth: Pursuing a Human Trafficking Case in Middle America, 10 Journal of Gender, Race and Justice 269 (2007). Reprinted by permission.

Meissner, Doris, Myers, Deborah W., Papademetriou, Demetrios, & Fix, Michael, Immigration and America's Future: A New Chapter, Report of the Independent Task Force on Immigration and America's Future (2006). Copyright 2006, Migration Policy Institute. Reprinted by permission.*

Meyer, Brandon & Caco, Karen, Now for the Hard Part: Attracting Investors to EB–5 Regional Centers, 10–03 Immigration Briefings (March 2010). Reprinted by permission of Thomson West.

Motomura, Hiroshi, Americans in Waiting: The Lost Story of Immigration and Citizenship in the United States, copyright © 2006 by Oxford University Press, Inc. Used by permission of Oxford University Press, Inc.

Motomura, Hiroshi, Comment—Choosing Immigrants, Making Citizens, 59 Stanford Law Review 857 (2007). Reprinted by permission.

Motomura, Hiroshi, Immigration and Alienage, Federalism and Proposition 187, 35 Virginia Journal of International Law 201 (1994). Reprinted by permission.

Motomura, Hiroshi, The Rights of Others: Legal Claims and Immigration Outside the Law, 59 Duke Law Journal 1723 (2010). Reprinted with permission of the author.

Motomura, Immigration Outside the Law, 108 Columbia Law Review 2037 (2008). Reprinted by permission.

Muller, Eric L., 12/7 and 9/11: War, Liberties, and the Lessons of History. Originally published in the West Virginia Law Review, 104 W. Va. L.Rev. 571 (2002). Reprinted by permission.

Murguia, Janet, A Change of Heart on Guest Workers, Washington Post, February 11, 2007, at B7. Reprinted by permission.

Neuman, Gerald L., Terrorism, Selective Deportation and the First Amendment after Reno v. AADC, 14 Georgetown Immigration Law Journal 313 (2000). Reprinted with permission of the publisher, Georgetown Immigration Law Journal © 2000.

Ngai, Mae, We Need a Deportation Deadline, Washington Post, June 14, 2005, at A21. Reprinted by permission.

Novotny, Ann, Strangers at the Door: Ellis Island, Castle Garden, and the Great Migration to America. Copyright © 1971 by Devin–Adair Publishing Co. Reprinted by permission.

Papademetriou, Demetrious G. and Sumption, Madeline, Rethinking Points Systems and Employer–Selected Immigration (June 2011) http://www. migrationpolicy.org/pubs/rethinkingpointssystem.pdf. Reprinted by permission.*

Passel, Jeffrey S. & Cohn, D'Vera, A Portrait of Unauthorized Immigrants in the United States (Pew Hispanic Center, Apr. 14, 2009). http:// pewhispanic.org/reports/report.php?ReportID=107. Reprinted by permission.

Passel, Jeffrey S. & Cohn, D'Vera, Unauthorized Immigrant Population: National and State Trends, 2010 (Pew Hispanic Center, Feb. 1, 2011). http://pewhispanic.org/reports/report.php?ReportID=133. Reprinted by permission.

Percent Admitted LPRs by State or Territory of Intended Residence, MPI Data Hub, http://www.migrationinformation.org/Feature/print.cfm?ID= 730#12. Reprinted by permission.*

Portes, Alejandro, and Böröscz, József, Contemporary Immigration: Theoretical Perspectives on Its Determinants and Modes of Incorporation, 23 International Migration Review 606 (1989). Copyright © 1989 by the Center for Migration Studies of New York, Inc. Reprinted by permission.

Ramadan, Tariq, Why I'm Banned in the USA, Washington Post, Oct. 1, 2006, at B1. Reprinted by permission.

Raskin, Jamin B., Legal Aliens, Local Citizens: The Historical, Constitutional, and Theoretical Meanings of Alien Suffrage, 141 University of Pennsylvania Law Review, 1391 (1993). Reprinted by permission.

Roberts, Maurice, The Exercise of Administrative Discretion Under the Immigration Laws, 13 San Diego Law Review 144 (1975). Copyright 1975 San Diego Law Review. Reprinted with permission of the San Diego Law Review.

Rodríguez, Cristina M., Guest Workers and Integration: Toward a Theory of What Immigrants and Americans Owe One Another, 2007 University of Chicago Legal Forum 219 (2007). Reprinted by permission.

Rosberg, Gerald M., Aliens and Equal Protection: Why Not the Right to Vote?, 75 Michigan Law Review 1092 (1977). Reprinted from Michigan Law Review, April–May 1977, Vol. 75, Nos. 5 & 6. Copyright 1977 by The Michigan Law Review Association. Reprinted with permission of the author.

Rosenblum, Marc R., E–Verify: Strengths, Weaknesses, and Proposals for Reform, Migration Policy Institute Insight (February 2011). http://www.migrationpolicy.org/pubs/E–Verify–Insight.pdf. Reprinted by permission.*

Scherner–Kim, Karin, The Role of the Oath of Renunciation in Current U.S. Nationality Policy—To Enforce, To Omit, or Maybe to Change?, 88 Georgetown Law Journal 329 (2000). Reprinted with permission of the publisher, Georgetown Law Journal © 2000.

Schuck, Peter H., and Smith, Rogers M., Citizenship Without Consent: Illegal Aliens in the American Polity (1985). Copyright © 1985 by The Yale University Press. Reprinted by permission of the publisher.

Sharpless, Rebecca, Toward a True Elements Test: Taylor and the Categorical Analysis of Crimes in Immigration Law, 62 University of Miami Law Review 979 (2008). Reprinted by permission.

Spiro, Peter J., Dual Nationality and the Meaning of Citizenship, 46 Emory Law Journal 1411 (1997). Reprinted by permission.

Stern, Marcus, Jobs Magnet, San Diego Union–Tribune, Nov. 2, 1997. Reprinted by permission of the San Diego Union–Tribune.

Ten Source Countries with the Largest Populations in the United States as Percentages of the Total Foreign–Born Population: 2009, MPI Data Hub, http://www.migrationinformation.org/datahub/charts/10.2009.shtml. Reprinted by permission.*

Trillin, Calvin, Making Adjustments. Copyright © 1984 by Calvin Trillin. Originally appeared in The New Yorker, May 28, 1984. Reprinted by permission of Lescher & Lescher, Ltd. All rights reserved.

Volpp, Leti, The Citizen and the Terrorist. Originally published in 49 UCLA Law Review 1575 (2002). Reprinted by permission.

Walzer, Michael, Spheres of Justice: A Defense of Pluralism and Equality. Copyright © 1984 Michael Walzer. Reprinted by permission of Basic Books, a member of the Perseus Books Group.

Weiss, Elaine, A Day in the Life of an Immigration Practitioner, The Florida Bar Journal, May 1992, at 74. Copyright © 1992. Reprinted by permission.

Zolberg, Aristide R., Suhrke, Astri, and Aguayo, Sergio, from Escape from Violence: Conflict and the Refugee Crisis in the Developing World, copyright © 1989 by Oxford University Press, Inc. Used by permission of Oxford University Press, Inc.

---

* Originally published by the Migration Policy Institute, an independent, nonpartisan, nonprofit think tank dedicated to the study of the movement of people worldwide.

SUMMARY OF CONTENTS

TABLE OF CONTENTS

TABLE OF CASES

The principal cases are in bold type. Cases cited or discussed in the text are in roman type. References are to pages. Cases cited in principal cases and within other quoted materials are not included.

TABLE OF AUTHORITIES

TABLE OF STATUTES, RULES AND REGULATIONS

POPULAR NAME ACTS

CIVIL RIGHTS ACT OF 1964

IMMIGRATION AND CITIZENSHIP
PROCESS AND POLICY

Seventh Edition

CHAPTER ONE

IMMIGRATION AND CITIZENSHIP LAW
IN HISTORICAL CONTEXT

■ ■ ■

Welcome to the study of immigration and citizenship law, an area of complex laws, fundamental humanitarian concerns, major economic importance, and passionate debate. The immigration and citizenship laws define who we are as a society: who are full members of our society; who can become members; which nonmembers can enter; and the conditions upon which nonmembers can remain. These decisions by the United States do not exist in a vacuum, but rather in a contemporary world of nation states. For the most part, each nation state's population consists of its citizens—a term generally understood to mean full members of the state, entitled to the basic rights and opportunities afforded by the state. Virtually all states have laws regulating the entry and stay of noncitizens, and these laws affect very large numbers of people. As of 2010, according to UN data, over 175 million persons reside in states of which they are not citizens. Most immigrants follow prescribed procedures in obtaining admission to state territory, but many individuals cross state borders or remain in state territory in violation of domestic law. We will refer to such persons as undocumented or unauthorized migrants or aliens.

This book concerns the law regarding citizenship, immigration, and the treatment of immigrants in the United States. The primary federal immigration statute is the Immigration and Nationality Act (INA), which is codified in Title 8 of the United States Code. The primary federal agency charged with administering and enforcing the INA is the Department of Homeland Security (DHS), with lesser roles for the Department of Justice, the Department of State, and the Department of Labor. Until 2003, the key agency was the Immigration and Naturalization Service (INS), located within the Justice Department, and many of the cases and materials here will still speak of INS. (Chapter Four explains the agency structure in more detail.) We will examine the basic categories for entry and residence of immigrants and the procedures for admission and removal; and we will identify and elaborate themes of due process, fair treatment of immigrants, and the social, economic and political implications of immigration. In so doing, we will be concerned with fundamental issues of

1

membership—what it means, how it is attained (and lost), and what rights and opportunities accompany it. Thus, throughout the course we will ask what particular understandings of membership inform societal decisions about immigration, immigrants, and citizens, and to what extent U.S. law—embodied in the Constitution, statutes, administrative policies and judicial decisions—establishes varying degrees of membership.

First, though, we think it important to provide historical and political context to your study of U.S. citizenship and immigration law. Writing in the Federalist Papers, John Jay observed: "Providence has been pleased to give this one connected country to one united people—a people descended from the same ancestors, speaking the same language, professing the same religion, attached to the same principles of government, very similar in their manners and customs." The Federalist No. 2. This statement, clearly false when written in 1787, cannot begin to describe the ethnic, racial, religious and political richness that two hundred years of immigration have brought the United States.

Our immigration history has shown America at its best and worst. Tens of millions of noncitizens have been welcomed to our shores. The United States has accepted more refugees for permanent settlement than any other country in the world. And in a time of growing restrictionism in most of the countries of the world, the United States currently admits for permanent residence more than three-quarters of a million noncitizens a year. Unlike many of the Western industrialized nations, the United States makes it relatively easy for lawfully admitted immigrants to attain citizenship; and virtually any person born in the United States is an American citizen, irrespective of the nationality of her parents.

But there is also a less welcoming side to the history of American immigration policy—one that often has overshadowed the national symbol of the Statue of Liberty. Some federal laws have been blatantly racist, prohibiting immigration and naturalization of noncitizens from China and Japan and favoring northern and western Europeans over southern and eastern Europeans. Persons have been excluded or deported for their political beliefs. Enforcement of the immigration laws has, at times, violated fundamental notions of fairness and decency. Noncitizens continue to be scapegoats for some of the problems of American society.

To provide a summary of the major legal and political developments in U.S. immigration policy, we have selected two sketches of American immigration history. The first, part of a report issued by the Select Commission on Immigration and Refugee Policy, surveys the evolving U.S. immigration policy up to 1980. The second, excerpted from a new study of immigration history, takes us up to the second decade of the twenty-first century. As you read these summaries, focus not on the details but on the general trends that the various developments embody. Note particularly the role that economic, political, and international events have played in the evolution of immigration policy. Later during the course you may wish to return from time to time to these background sketches as you encounter discussions of the historical periods or successive laws mentioned here.

SELECT COMMISSION ON IMMIGRATION AND REFUGEE POLICY, U.S. IMMIGRATION POLICY AND THE NATIONAL INTEREST

Staff Report 161–216 (1981).

IMMIGRATION AND U.S. HISTORY—THE EVOLUTION OF THE OPEN SOCIETY[a]

* * * The first inhabitants to the New World, scientists believe, came when the last great Ice Age lowered the level of the Pacific Ocean sufficiently to expose a land bridge between Asia and North America, enabling people to cross the ocean from Asia. Recent evidence suggests that the ancestors of the present-day native Americans settled in North America more than 30,000 years ago and by about 10,000 B.C. had expanded their settlement as far as the tip of South America.

Some 116 centuries later, migration to America occurred again, this time coming from the opposite direction. European monarchs and merchants—whether Spanish, Portuguese, French, English or Dutch—encouraged exploration and then settlement of the newly "discovered" lands of the Americas. The descendants of the occupants of these lands, native American Indians, sometimes joke that the "Indians had bad immigration laws." In fact, there were a variety of responses. In some cases, Indian tribes welcomed the new settlers, negotiating treaties, many of which were abrogated by the colonists. In other instances, the Indians fought newcomers who encroached upon their lands. Whatever the response, though, most tribes found themselves overwhelmed by the better-armed Europeans.

The continents of the Western Hemisphere soon became a microcosm of the European continent, peopled in the north by northern and western Europeans and in the south by the Spanish and Portuguese.

Because of the diversity of national origins, it was by no means certain at the time of English settlement that those who spoke the English language would dominate the development of the area that eventually became the United States. To the south of the British-occupied territories were Spanish colonies, to the north were the French, between were Dutch and Swedish settlements. By the second half of the eighteenth century, though, the French had been defeated and had withdrawn from Canada, a modus vivendi of sorts had been established with Spain and the small Dutch and Swedish settlements had been incorporated into the middle colonies of New York, New Jersey, Pennsylvania and Delaware. Hence, it was a certainty by the time of the Revolution that the newly formed republic would be one in which the English influence would prevail.

---

a. Lawrence H. Fuchs and Susan Forbes Martin, principal authors. [The footnotes have been renumbered—eds.]

Despite Anglo–American dominance, however, the colonial period saw the establishment of a tendency towards ethnic pluralism that also was to become a vital part of U.S. life. At least a dozen national groups found homes in the area. Most came in search of religious toleration, political freedom and/or economic opportunity. Many, particularly some ancestors of those who later thought of themselves as "the best people," came as paupers, or as bond servants and laborers who paid for their passage by promising to serve employers, whom they could not leave for a specified number of years. Not all came of their own free will. Convicts and vagrants were shipped from English jails in the seventeenth century. Beginning in Virginia in 1619, some 350,000 slaves were brought from Africa until the end of the slave trade in 1807.

Non–English arrivals were treated with ambivalence, whether they were Dutch, German or even Scotch–Irish Presbyterians from Great Britain. The Germans who came to Pennsylvania, for example, had first learned of the colony through an advertising campaign designed by William Penn to attract their attention and migration. The earliest German settlers came in the hopes of finding liberty of conscience, and once their glowing reports were sent back to Germany, others of their nationality—seeking not only religious toleration but economic opportunity—followed. They were welcomed by many English colonists who applauded their industry and piety. Yet, they were attacked by others who questioned if they would ever assimilate.

This question asked about each successive wave of immigrants was to become a familiar refrain in U.S. history, but the ambivalence towards foreigners was by no means great enough during the colonial period to cause restrictions on immigration. In fact, the Declaration of Independence cites as one of the failings of King George III, and thus a justification for revolution, that "He has endeavored to prevent the Population of these States; for that purpose obstructing the Laws for Naturalization of Foreigners; refusing to pass others to encourage their migrations hither, and raising the conditions of new Appropriations of Lands."

After the revolution and the creation of a new government, Americans kept the gates of their new country open for several reasons. The land was vast, relatively rich and sparsely settled. At the time of the first census, taken in 1790, America had a recorded population of 3,227,000—all immigrants or descendants of seventeenth and eighteenth century arrivals.[1] The population density at that time was about 4.5 persons per square mile. Labor was needed to build communities as well as to clear farms on the frontier and push back the Indians. People were needed to build a strong country, strong enough to avoid coming once again under the rule of a foreign power. Moreover, many U.S. citizens thought of their new

---

1. More than 75 percent of this population was of British origin, another eight percent was German and the rest were mainly Dutch, French or Spanish. In addition, approximately a half million black slaves and perhaps as many Native Americans lived within the borders of the United States.

nation as an experiment in freedom—to be shared by all people, regardless of former nationality, who wished to be free.

Despite all of these reasons for a liberal immigration policy, some doubts still remained about its wisdom. Although people were needed to build the new nation, some feared that the entry of too many aliens would cause disruptions and subject the United States to those foreign influences that the nation sought to escape in independence.

With the signing of the Treaty of Paris in 1783, the United States was officially recognized as an independent nation and the history of official U.S. immigration policy began. * * *

Beginning in 1790, Congress passed a series of acts regulating naturalization. The first act permitted the liberal granting of citizenship to immigrants. After a heated debate—in which the losing side argued not only for strict naturalization requirements but also for barriers against the admission of "the common class of vagrants, paupers and other outcasts of Europe"—Congress required a two-year period of residence and the renunciation of former allegiances before citizenship could be claimed.

By 1795, though, the French Revolution, and the ensuing turmoil in Europe, had raised new fears about foreign political intrigue and influence. A new naturalization act, passed in 1795, imposed more stringent requirements including a five-year residency requirement for citizenship and the renunciation of not only allegiances but titles of nobility. Still, some thought U.S. standards for naturalization were too liberal, and, in 1798, another law was passed that raised the residency requirement to fourteen years. At the same time, the Alien Enemies Act and the Alien Friends Act gave the president powers to deport any alien whom he considered dangerous to the welfare of the nation. One proponent of these laws explained his support: "If no law of this kind was passed, it would be in the power of an individual State to introduce such a number of aliens into the country, as might not only be dangerous, but as might be sufficient to overturn the Government, and introduce the greatest confusion in the country."

The xenophobia that gave rise to the Alien Acts of 1798 passed with the transfer of power from the Federalist to the Republican Party in 1800. The [Alien Friends Act was] permitted to expire,[b] and, in 1802, a new Naturalization Act re-established the provisions of the 1795 Act—what was to become a permanent five-year residency requirement for citizenship. While the Republicans were by no means free of suspicion of foreigners, they were not sufficiently fearful of the consequences of immigration to impose any restraints on the entry or practices of the foreign born. Instead, they pursued a policy that has been aptly described by Maldwyn Allen Jones in his history, *American Immigration*:

---

b. The Alien Enemies Act is still on the books. 50 U.S.C.A. §§ 21–23.—eds.

Americans had to some degree reconciled the contradictory ideas that had influenced the thinking of the Revolutionary generation and had developed a clearly defined immigration policy. All who wished to come were welcome to do so; but no special inducements or privileges would be offered them.

For the next 75 years, the federal government did little about the regulation of immigration. It did establish procedures that made the counting of a portion of all immigrants possible. In 1819 Congress passed a law requiring ship captains to supply to the Collector of Customs a list of all passengers on board upon arrival at U.S. ports. This list was to indicate their sex, occupation, age and "country to which they severally belonged." At first only Atlantic and Gulf port information was collected; Pacific ports were added after 1850. Immigration information from Hawaii, Puerto Rico and Alaska dates only from the beginning of the twentieth century, as does the recording of information across land borders with Canada and Mexico.

Although a fully accurate picture of the level of all immigration cannot be made, the data available have enabled historians to sketch the general composition and trend of U.S. immigration. These data show a steadily increasing level of immigration. Immigrants arriving between the end of the Revolutionary War and the passage of the 1819 act are estimated to have totaled about 250,000. During the next ten years, over 125,000 came, and between 1830 and 1860, almost 4.5 million European immigrants arrived in the United States. Never before had the United States had to incorporate so large a number of newcomers into its midst. At first, the new arrivals were greeted with enthusiasm. With a nation to be built, peasants from Norway were as welcome as skilled craftsmen from Great Britain and experienced farmers from western, Protestant Germany. The novelist Herman Melville characterized this spirit:

> There is something in the contemplation of the mode in which America has been settled, that, in a noble breast, should forever extinguish the prejudices of national dislikes.

> Settled by the people of all nations, all nations may claim her for their own. You cannot spill a drop of American blood without spilling the blood of the whole world....

> We are the heirs of all time, and with all nations, we divide our inheritance. On this Western Hemisphere all tribes and people are forming into one federate whole; and there is a future which shall see the estranged children of Adam restored as to the old hearthstone in Eden.

Beginning in the 1830s, though, the composition of the groups entering the United States began to change, and few U.S. residents thought so romantically about the new immigrants.

Waves of Irish during the potato famines and German Catholic immigrants flowed into the country during the European depressions of the 1840s. These Catholics entered a country that was not only overwhelmingly Protestant, but that had been settled by some of the most radical sectarians, who prided themselves on their independence from the Pope's authority as well as from any king's. To begin with, U.S. residents had brought with them from Europe centuries of memories of the Catholic–Protestant strife that had so long dominated that continent's social and political life. Much anti-Irish feeling arose from these roots and was nourished by an oversimplified view of Catholicism which saw Catholics as unable to become good citizens—that is, independent and self-reliant— since they were subject to orders from the church. Even before the mass immigration of Catholics during the 1840s and 1850s, the xenophobic inventor Samuel F.B. Morse warned his fellow Americans:

> How is it possible that foreign turbulence imported by shiploads, that riot and ignorance in hundreds of thousands of human priest-controlled machines should suddenly be thrown into our society and not produce turbulence and excess? Can one throw mud into pure water and not disturb its clearness?

It was easy to blame these new immigrants for many of the problems of the rapidly changing, increasingly urban nineteenth century U.S. society. Hostility against immigrants grew as they were accused of bringing intemperance, crime and disease to the new world. The first Select Committee of the House of Representatives to study immigration concluded:

> that the number of emigrants from foreign countries into the United States is increasing with such rapidity as to jeopardize the peace and tranquility of our citizens, if not the permanency of the civil, religious, and political institutions of the United States.... Many of them are the outcasts of foreign countries; *paupers*, *vagrants*, and *malefactors* ... sent hither at the expense of foreign governments, to relieve them from the burden of their maintenance.

A Protestant magazine sounded a further alarm by suggesting that "the floodgates of intemperance, pauperism and crime are thrown open by [immigrants], and if nothing be done to close them, they will carry us back to all of the drunkenness and evil of former times.["]

Out of these fears arose an alliance of those committed to saving the United States from the alleged dangers of immigration. Composed of social reformers who hoped to preserve the nation's institutions, some Protestant evangelicals who hoped to preserve the nation's morals and nativists who hoped to preserve the nation's ethnic purity, they formed associations, such as the secret Order of the Star–Spangled Banner, and political parties, such as the Know–Nothing Party.

These groups were committed to placing a curb on immigration itself and to ensuring that foreigners not be permitted to participate in the nation's political affairs. The naturalization statutes were a principal target of their concern. A pamphlet of the Know–Nothing Party warned of the inadequacy of these laws in protecting the nation against fraud:

It is notorious that the grossest frauds have been practiced on our naturalization laws, and that thousands and tens of thousands have every year deposited votes in the ballot box, who could not only not read them, and knew nothing of the nature of the business in which they were engaged, but who had not been six months in the country, and, in many cases, hardly six days.

The party hoped to avoid these problems by eliminating the participation of even naturalized immigrants in the political process.

At its most vitriolic, nativism manifested itself in anti-Catholic riots against the Irish. New York, Philadelphia and Boston all saw such violence. Exposes revealing the "truth" about Catholic nunneries—that they were dens of iniquity and vice—precipitated the burning of convents and Catholic churches.[2] Although strident, nativist voices did not prevail. Attacks on ethnic groups usually came from a small, but vocal portion of the population that by no means represented the wishes of all Americans. Even during the times in which nativism reached its peak, there continued to be a variety of potent support for unlimited immigration. Economic needs, reinforced by the ideals of opportunity and freedom that were more deeply rooted in the country than was the anti-Catholic heritage or fears of foreign takeover, worked against restricting immigration or making requirements for citizenship or voting more stringent.

After the Civil War, the country's desire for immigrants seemed insatiable * * *. Railroads were being laid across the nation, thus opening vast lands for settlement. Labor was needed to gouge the earth for coal and iron, to work in rapidly developing mills and to build cities.

As demand for labor increased, so too did the number of immigrants. From 1860 to 1880, about 2.5 million Europeans entered this country each decade; during the 1880s the number more than doubled to 5.25 million. Another 16 million immigrants entered during the next quarter century, with 1.25 million entering in 1908.

Because the numbers of immigrants were so large, it appeared as if the United States had never before experienced immigration of this sort. Not only was there a change in the size of the flow, there was also a change, once more, in the source of immigration. The migration before the 1880s had been overwhelmingly from northern and western Europe. Even the hated Irish Catholics had come from a country where English was generally spoken and Irish immigration was now traditional. Less than three percent of the foreign-born population of the country had come from eastern or southern Europe. During the 1890s that pattern began to reverse itself, and during the first decade of the twentieth century, about 70 percent came from the new areas.

Just as the Irish and Germans had appeared to Americans to be more "foreign" than English Protestants, so too did the new immigrants appear

---

2. Not all convent-burning was indicative of anti-Catholicism per se. The burning of the Ursuline Convent at Charlestown, Massachusetts was due mainly to the local brickmakers' resentment of Irish economic competition.

to be more "foreign" than the old ones. In what may be an inevitable process, the old immigrants had become familiar and, therefore, respectable while the new ones were put under the closest possible scrutiny for signs of dissimilitude. And, alien characteristics are exactly what many Americans found—strange coloring, strange physiques, strange customs and strange languages.

The new immigrants were disliked and feared. They were considered culturally different and incapable of this country's version of self-government, and not because of their backgrounds but because they were thought to be biologically and inherently inferior. Influential professors of history, sociology and eugenics taught that some races could never become what came to be called "100 percent American."

A leading academic proponent of nativism, Edward Ross, wrote of Jews that they are "the polar opposite of our pioneer breed. Undersized and weak muscled, they shun bodily activity and are exceedingly sensitive to pain." He also lamented that it was impossible to make Boy Scouts out of them. Italians, he noted, "possess a distressing frequency of low foreheads, open mouths, weak chins, poor features, skewed faces, small or knobby crania and backless heads." According to Ross, Italians "lack the power to take rational care of themselves." * * *

Even though * * * mortality statistics do not support the contention that the new immigrants were inherently diseased or biologically inferior, such sentiments began to take their toll. In 1882 the United States passed its first racist, restrictionist immigration law, the Chinese Exclusion Act. From 1860 to 1880, Chinese immigration had grown from 40,000 to over 100,000. Chinese labor had been welcomed to lay railway lines and work in mining. However, with the completion of the transcontinental railroad, which was followed by a depression in the 1870s, intense anti-Chinese feelings developed, particularly in the West, where hard-working and ambitious Chinese had made lives for themselves.

The attacks upon the Chinese often focused upon their inability, in the eyes of their opponents, to assimilate. In 1876, a California State Senate Committee described the Chinese as follows:

> They fail to comprehend our system of government; they perform no duties of citizenship.... They do not comprehend or appreciate our social ideas.... The great mass of the Chinese ... are not amenable to our laws.... They do not recognize the sanctity of an oath.

The supposed criminality of the Chinese was of particular concern. Although the crime statistics of the period do not bear out the accusations, the Chinese were believed to be criminals nevertheless. The state senate committee complained that "the Pacific Coast has become a Botany Bay to which the criminal classes of China are brought in large numbers and the people of this coast are compelled to endure this affliction." The Chinese were especially accused of bringing gambling and prostitution to the region. In 1876, *Scribner's Magazine* noted that "no matter how good a

Chinaman may be, ladies never leave their children with them, especially little girls." The legislative committee concluded that "the Chinese are inferior to any race God ever made ... [and] have no souls to save, and if they have, they are not worth saving."

Restrictionists—looking for justifications for closing other types of immigration—also eyed European immigrants as criminally inclined. The Police Commissioner of New York, Theodore Bingham, wrote in the *North American Review* that ["]85 percent of New York criminals were of exotic origin and half of them were Jewish." The author of an article in *Collier's Magazine* labeled Italians as "the most vicious and dangerous" criminals, and he suggested that "80 percent of the limited number of clever thieves" were Jewish.

Again, the crime statistics do not bear out the accusations. * * * The majority of immigrants were arrested for the petty crimes—vagrancy, disorderly conduct, breach of the peace, drunkenness—associated with poverty and difference in values. Immigrants were statistically more likely to commit minor offenses than were the native born who tended to commit property crimes and crimes of personal violence. According to the statistics, there was only one real cause for concern as far as immigrant crime was concerned. The children of the foreign born were the most likely group of all to commit crimes. Their crimes more often resembled those of the native born, though, than those of immigrants. This pattern indicates, more than anything else, that acculturation occurred even in the area of crime.

Despite the known evidence that immigrants were neither inherently criminal nor diseased, nativist arguments emphasizing the inferiority of immigrants were widely accepted. Restrictionists called for legislation that would decide whether the United States would be, as some put it, peopled by British, German and Scandinavian stock, or the new immigrants, "beaten men from beaten races; representing the worst failures in the struggle for existence."

Earlier, nativism had been offset by confidence that the United States had room for all, by a tradition of welcoming the poor and the oppressed and by belief that life in the New World would transform all comers into new Adams and Eves in the American Eden. At the end of the century, however, these ideas were affected by four historical developments:

- The official closing of the U.S. frontier;
- Burgeoning cities and increasing industrialization;
- The persistence of immigrants from southern and eastern Europe in maintaining their traditions; and
- The Catholic or Jewish religion of most of the new immigrants.

In the light of these developments, many Americans began to doubt the country's capacity to welcome and absorb the ever-increasing waves of new immigrants.

Evidence of this new feeling about European immigration could be seen as early as 1891. There had been earlier attempts at controlling the entry of immigrants to the United States—in the Act of 1875 that excluded prostitutes and alien convicts and in the Act of 1882 that barred the entry of lunatics, idiots, convicts and those liable to become a public charge—but these were not as comprehensive as the measure debated that year. One of the principal spokesmen for the bill, Henry Cabot Lodge, of Massachusetts, urged his fellow congressmen to establish new categories of admission to the United States in order to "sift . . . the chaff from the wheat" and prevent "a decline in the quality of American citizenship." The 1891 bill added new categories of exclusion that mirrored the concerns about the biological inferiority of immigrants. Those suffering from loathsome or contagious diseases and aliens convicted of crimes involving moral turpitude were barred from entry. The bill also provided for the medical inspection of all arrivals.[3]

Both houses of Congress quickly passed the measure; in the Senate, noted the *New York Times*, "the matter did not even occupy ten minutes." The measure did not go far enough for the quantitative restrictionists, though, since it did not succeed in stemming the flow of new entrants. In their efforts to change immigration policy, these restrictionists began to center their arguments upon one area of regulation—literacy.

As early as 1887, economist Edward W. Bemis gave a series of lectures in which he proposed that the United States prevent the entry of all male adults who were unable to read and write their own language. He argued that such a regulation would reduce by half or more those who were poor and undereducated. As awareness of the nature of the new immigration grew, nativists realized that a literacy test would also discriminate between desirable and undesirable nationalities, not just individuals. The proponents of the test saw it as an effective method of nationality restriction because, unlike the other "proofs" of cultural inferiority, literacy could easily and readily be measured.

The new immigrants were often attacked for their attachments to their native languages and what was perceived to be a failure to learn English. In an editorial, the *Nation* magazine proposed that a literacy test was insufficient and that English-language ability should be a requirement of entry. Recognizing that a proposal to make English a requirement of entry would effectively limit immigration to residents of the British Isles, the *Nation* declared in 1891 what other restrictionists believed—that "we are under no obligation to see that all races and nations enjoy an equal chance of getting here."

A literacy bill was first introduced in the Congress in 1895, and under the leadership of Senator Lodge passed both houses. In the last days of his administration, President Cleveland vetoed it, suggesting that the test was hypocritical. The House overrode his veto, but the Senate took no action and the proposal died. In a new wave of xenophobia that followed the

---

3.   Further grounds of exclusion similar in intent were added in 1903 and 1907.

assassination of President McKinley by an anarchist mistakenly believed to be an immigrant, a new bill passed the House. Despite the support of the new president, Theodore Roosevelt, the bill's sponsors were unable to gain a favorable vote in the Senate, and it too died.

In 1906, new, comprehensive legislation was proposed that included a literacy test for admission and both a literacy and an English-language requirement for naturalization. The restrictionists, now aided by labor unions wary of competition, were opposed in their endeavors by newly organized ethnic groups as well as business leaders opposed to any elimination of new labor sources. In all but one area, the restrictionists were triumphant. Once again, though, they were unsuccessful in gaining passage of a literacy requirement for either entry or naturalization. English-language proficiency was made a basis for citizenship, though, since most congressmen agreed with Representative Bonynge that "history and reason alike demonstrate that you cannot make a homogeneous people out of those who are unable to communicate with each other in one common language."

In 1907, after the restrictionist attempt to impose a literacy requirement failed, immigration to the United States reached a new high—with the arrival of 1,285,000 immigrants—and an economic depression hit the country. That same year, Congress passed legislation to establish a joint congressional presidential Commission to study the impact of immigrants on the United States. Its members appointed in 1909, the Dillingham Commission, as it is usually known, began its work convinced that the pseudoscientific racist theories of superior and inferior peoples were correct and that the more recent immigrants from southern and eastern Europe were not capable of becoming successful Americans. Although their own data contradicted these ideas, the Commission nevertheless held on to them. The Commission's recommendations were published in 1911 with 41 volumes of monographs on specific subjects, including discussions of immigrants and crime, changes in the bodily form of immigrants and the industrial impact of immigration. In the view of the Commission, their findings all pointed to the same conclusions:

- Twentieth century immigration differed markedly from earlier movements of people to the United States;

- The new immigration was dominated by the so-called inferior peoples—those who were physically, mentally and linguistically different, and, therefore, less desirable than either the native-born or early immigrant groups; and

- Because of the inferiority of these people, the United States no longer benefited from a liberal immigration admissions policy and should, therefore, impose new restrictions on entry.

The Commission endorsed the literacy test as an appropriate mechanism to accomplish its ends.

The demand for large-scale restriction still did not succeed, though, because of the continuing demand for labor, the growing political power of the new immigrant groups and the commitment of the nation's leaders to preserving the tradition of free entry. In 1912, Congress once more passed a literacy test, but President Taft successfully vetoed it, extolling the "sturdy but uneducated peasantry brought to this country and raised in an atmosphere of thrift and hard work" where they have "contributed to the strength of our people and will continue to do so." Another veto, this time by President Woodrow Wilson, defeated the work of the restrictionists in 1915. According to Wilson, the literacy test "seeks to all but close entirely the gates of asylum which have always been open to those who could find nowhere else the right and opportunity of constitutional agitation for what they conceived to be the natural and inalienable rights of men."

After the United States entered World War I in 1917, Congress finally overrode the presidential veto and enacted legislation that made literacy a requirement for entry. The bill also codified the list of aliens to be excluded, and it virtually banned all immigration from Asia. The efforts of the restrictionists were finally successful, in large measure because World War I brought nervousness about the loyalty and assimilability of the foreign born to a fever pitch. The loyalty of immigrants became a hot political issue. Theodore Roosevelt, for example, stormed against "hyphenated Americans," as he voiced his concern that the country was becoming little more than a "poly-glot boarding house." A frenzy of activity against German Americans (who only a short while before were thought, along with the English, Scots and Scandinavians to be the best qualified to enter) led to the closing of thriving German-language schools, newspapers and social clubs. The Governor of Iowa took what may have been the strongest measures; he decreed that the use of any language other than English in public places or over the telephone would be prohibited.

This agitation against the foreign born culminated in two efforts: a movement to "Americanize" immigrants and the development of immigration restrictions based on national origins quotas. The Americanization movement had had its start in 1915 when two government agencies, operating independently of each other, began assessing the number and efficacy of immigrant education programs operating in the country. One of these agencies, the Bureau of Naturalization, undertook a letter-writing campaign aimed at learning the degree to which such programs existed. The following summer, the Bureau held a conference in Washington to discuss the information it collected and propose plans for speeding the acculturation of immigrants. In the meantime, though, the Bureau of Education convened its own conference, out of which came the National Committee of One Hundred—prominent citizens organized "for the purpose of assisting in a national campaign for the education of immigrants to fit them for American life and citizenship." With the efforts of these two agencies for guidance, hundreds of communities, private organizations and businesses embarked upon their own programs of Americanization. * * *

Lobbying efforts by the Bureau of Education led many states—twenty between 1919 and 1921—to pass legislation establishing Americanization programs to ensure that all immigrants would learn English, the "language of America," as a California commission called it.

Industry also joined the movement. It was frequently asserted that "ignorance of English is a large factor in [job] turnover" and similarly that "there is an important connection between ignorance of English and illiteracy to economic loss." The National Association of Manufacturers encouraged Americanization programs among its members. Henry Ford set up classes within his plants and required attendance of his 5,000 non-English-speaking employees. The International Harvester Company produced its own lesson plans for the non-English-speaking workers in its plants. They clearly taught more than English itself. The first plan read:

I hear the whistle. I must hurry.

I hear the five minute whistle.

It is time to go into the shop. . . .

I change my clothes and get ready to work. . . .

I work until the whistle blows to quit.

I leave my place nice and clean.

I put all my clothes in the locker.

I must go home.

By 1923, the Bureau of Naturalization announced it had 252,808 immigrants in 6,632 citizenship-training courses around the nation. Of these, 4,132 were conducted in public school buildings, 1,256 in homes, 371 in factories and 873 at other locations.

The success of the Americanization program in enrolling immigrants was not enough to satisfy the opponents of immigration. Still convinced that racial differences precluded the full assimilation of the new immigrants, some nativists doubted the ability of Americanization classes to transform immigrants into "100 percent Americans." Some were convinced that all immigrants should be compelled to learn English, and if they could not, should be subject to deportation. Theodore Roosevelt proclaimed that "I would have the government provide that every immigrant be required to learn English, with instruction furnished free. If after five years he has not learned it let him be returned to the country from which he came." To Roosevelt and other nativists, failure to learn English represented some sort of disloyalty or a failure of will; both were clearly reasons for expelling the alien.

As the movement to compel assimilation of those already here progressed, those fearful of the consequences of immigration also sought new restrictions on entry. Restrictionists had learned that the literacy requirement which they believed held so much promise was not succeeding as had been expected. Immigration from southern and eastern Europe continued. The literacy rates of European countries showed increasing numbers eligible for entry; Italy even established schools in areas of high emigration to teach peasants to be literate so that they could pass the new U.S. test for entry.

To quantitative restrictionists, new measures were needed. The suspension of all immigration—an idea never before of any great appeal in U.S. immigration history—began to gain support. The two groups most associated with it, organized labor and "100 percenters," had little else in common. Labor supported suspension of immigration because of the competition for jobs that occurred with the entry of aliens.

The 100 percenters feared that European people and ideas—whether "bestial hordes" from conquered Germany or the "red menace" of Bolshevism—would contaminate U.S. institutions and culture.

The extreme form of restrictionism proposed by those wishing to ban all immigration gained some support in the House of Representatives, where arguments that postwar immigration was composed largely of Jews who were "filthy, un-American, and often dangerous in their habits" were particularly effective, but failed to pass the Senate Committee on Immigration, which was dominated by easterners with large businesses and ethnic constituencies favorable to immigration.

Instead, the Senate proposed its own legislation to reduce overall immigration and to change the ethnic composition of those permitted entry. The goal of the bill—similar to one originally proposed by Senator Dillingham of the earlier Immigration Commission—was to ensure that northern and western Europeans still had access to the United States while southern and eastern European immigration would be restricted. In 1921, Congress passed and President Harding signed into law the Senate-proposed legislation—a provisional measure which introduced the concept of national origins quotas. This act established a ceiling on European immigration and limited the number of immigrants of each nationality to three percent of the number of foreign-born persons of that nationality resident in the United States at the time of the 1910 census.

This first quota act was extended for two more years, but in 1924 came the passage of what was heralded as a permanent solution to U.S. immigration problems. The Johnson–Reed measure, more commonly known as the National Origins Act, provided for an annual limit of 150,000 Europeans, a complete prohibition on Japanese immigration, the issuance and counting of visas against quotas abroad rather than on arrival, and the development of quotas based on the contribution of each nationality to the overall U.S. population rather than on the foreign-born population.[c] This law was designed to preserve, even more effectively than the 1921 law, the racial and ethnic status quo of the United States. The

---

c. For purposes of calculating the national quotas, the 1924 legislation excluded the descendants of slaves from its definition of the population of the United States. Act of May 26, 1924, ch. 190, § 11(d), 43 Stat. 153, 159. African Americans constituted nine percent of the U.S. population, and European countries received the proportion of the quota that should have gone to Africa. For further discussion of the racial ramifications of the National Origins Act, see M. Ngai, *Impossible Subjects: Illegal Aliens and the Making of Modern America* 21–55 (2004).—eds.

national origins concept was also designed, as John Higham wrote in his study of U.S. nativism, *Strangers in the Land*, to give "comfort to the democratic conscience" by counting everyone's ancestors and not just the foreign born themselves.

Recognizing that it would take some time to develop the new quotas, as a stopgap measure the bill provided for the admission of immigrants according to annual quotas of two percent of each nationality's proportion of the foreign-born U.S. population in 1890 until 1927—amended to 1929—when the national origins quotas were established. The use of the 1890 census had been criticized as a discriminatory measure since it seemed to change the rules of European entry solely to lower the number of the so-called "new" immigrants. Use of the 1890 census instead of that of 1910 meant a reduction in the Italian quota from 42,000 to about 4,000, in the Polish quota from 31,000 to 6,000 and in the Greek quota from 3,000 to 100. The proponents of the new legislation argued, however, that use of the 1910 Census was what was really discriminatory since it underestimated the number of visas that should go to those from northern and western Europe.

In preparing its report on the new legislation, the House Committee on Immigration relied heavily on an analysis prepared by John B. Trevor, an aide to Representative Johnson, which gave an estimated, statistical breakdown of the origins of the U.S. population. Trevor also calculated the quotas that would be derived from the use of the 1890 and 1910 census figures on the foreign born. He found that the 1890 census better approximated the national origins of the overall population. Trevor argued that about 12 percent of the U.S. population in 1890 derived from eastern and southern Europe, but on the basis of the 1910 census they were given about 44 percent of the total quota. Using the 1890 census they would have 15 percent of the immigrant numbers. The restrictionists were thus able to turn around the criticism aimed against them by arguing that previous policy favored the "new" immigrants at the expense of the older U.S. stock.

Despite the rhetoric of its supporters—and the exemption of members of the Western Hemisphere from its quotas—the Immigration Act of 1924 clearly represented a rejection of one of [the] longest-lived democratic traditions of the United States, represented by George Washington's view that the United States should ever be "an asylum to the oppressed and the needy of the earth." It also represented a rejection of cultural pluralism as a U.S. ideal. The Commissioner of Immigration could report, one year after this legislation took effect, that virtually all immigrants now "looked" exactly like Americans. Abraham Lincoln's fear that when the nativists gained control of U.S. policy they would rewrite the Declaration of Independence to read: "All men are created equal, except Negroes, and foreigners, and Catholics" seemed to be coming true.

Immigration to the United States suffered still another blow with the Great Depression. During the 1930s, only 500,000 immigrants came to the

United States, less than one-eighth of the number that had arrived in the previous decade. Most reduced in number were members of those nations jointly affected by the national origins quotas, and by economic conditions that made impossible their usual pattern of temporary migration for the purposes of work. Temporary migration was a familiar pattern before the imposition of the new legislation. In fact, the prevalence among the "new" immigrants of "birds of passage"—accused of being unstable forces in society, prone to crime and disease and displacing U.S. citizens from jobs—had been one reason for passing restrictive legislation. Temporary migration can be measured through data on emigration, the number of immigrants who leave the country some time after arrival. Throughout most of the early twentieth century, according to official statistics that were collected beginning in 1908, emigration stood at a minimum of 20 percent of immigration and, more commonly, at 30 to 40 percent. In times of depression, the proportion of those who left the country as opposed to those who arrived increased still further; the temporary migrants returned home until conditions in this country improved. In 1932, at the height of the Great Depression, the emigration figure stood at 290 percent of legal immigration. While 35,576 entered the country, over 100,000 left.

Those most tragically affected by the U.S. policy of restrictive immigration (and the economic problems that made U.S. citizens unwilling to alter it) were the refugees who tried to flee Europe before the outbreak of World War II. Although some efforts were made to accommodate them—in 1940 the State Department permitted consuls outside of Germany to issue visas to German refugees because the German quota sometimes remained unfilled—these measures were too few and came too late to help most of the victims of Nazi persecution. In what may be the cruelest single action in U.S. immigration history, the U.S. Congress in 1939 defeated a bill to rescue 20,000 children from Nazi Germany, despite the willingness of U.S. families to sponsor them, on the grounds that the children would exceed the German quota. Those refugees who were able to come in under existing quotas were still subject to all of the other requirements of entry, and a significant number were refused visas because of the public charge provisions in the grounds for exclusion.

Although the quota system of the 1920s stood substantially intact until 1965, U.S. immigration policy was affected by the events of World War II—in particular the shock this country received when it learned most graphically of the fate of the refugees refused entry. Even before that knowledge came, the war challenged long-held notions about U.S. traditions and needs. The United States realized that it once more needed the labor of aliens, for example. This country and Mexico then negotiated a large-scale temporary worker program—the bracero program—designed to fill the wartime employment needs of the United States. Also, in large part because of the alliance of the United States with China, Congress repealed the ban on all Chinese immigration, making it possible for a small number of Chinese once again to enter the country as legal immigrants. Notions of the inherent inferiority of certain groups [were] dispelled when those same groups became allies in the fight against other groups that were proving to be much stronger enemies than expected.

For a short period, the atmosphere was right for a liberalization of immigration policy. At the close of the war, especially after Americans learned of the Nazi atrocities, they seemed united in their appreciation of democracy and their commitment to renewing the U.S. role as a haven for the oppressed. An important first step was taken by President Harry S. Truman who issued a directive in December 1945 admitting 40,000 war refugees. Responding to the plight of U.S. soldiers who had married overseas, Congress passed the "War Brides Act" in 1946, which permitted 120,000 alien wives, husbands and children of members of the armed forces to immigrate to the United States.

In the years following the war, the executive branch continued to take an active role in reshaping immigration policy, even after the advent of the Cold War when public attitudes towards the issue turned more conservative. Most of these efforts, though, were in the area of refugee admissions and did not change the basic structure of U.S. immigration law. President Truman prodded the Congress to pass the Displaced Persons Act in 1948. After its expiration, Congress passed the Refugee Relief Act, under which 214,000 persons were admitted. Designed principally to expedite the admission of refugees fleeing Iron Curtain countries, the Act incorporated safeguards to prevent the immigration of undesirable aliens. Additional measures were passed in 1956 and 1957 to facilitate the entry of Hungarians displaced by the revolution in that country and "refugee-escapees" fleeing Communist or Communist-occupied or dominated countries and countries in the Middle East. In 1960, the Refugee Fair Share Law was passed to provide a temporary program for the admission of World War II refugees and displaced persons who remained in camps under the mandate of the United Nations High Commissioner for Refugees. This legislation gave the Attorney General a specific mandate to use his parole authority to admit eligible refugee-escapees. Although the statute was for a limited period of time, it was more comprehensive than other refugee admission programs and provided an ongoing mechanism to assist refugees.

Despite these strides in developing a policy that permitted refugees to escape from some of the restrictions of the national origins quota requirements, little else in the way of progress occurred in the immigration area until the 1960s. In fact the determination to preserve the quota system was so strong that the refugee measures provided that those entering under those provisions were to be charged to future quotas of their country of origin, as long as these did not exceed 50 percent of the quota of any one year. The refugee acts were seen as complements to the national origins policy; they made the 1924 law more responsive to emergencies but did not significantly alter immigration policy itself.

During the early 1950s, the climate was not ripe for any major liberalizing changes. Concern with communist expansion dominated U.S.

thinking in the early 1950s, and the stand against communism often took the form of opposition to anything foreign. It was a period in which ethnic customs and values could easily be defined as "un-American."

It was in such an atmosphere that congressional hearings on a new immigration law took place. They were conducted under the leadership of Senator Patrick A. McCarran who, with his followers, believed that there were in the United States what he called "indigestible blocks" which would not assimilate into the American way of life. In 1952, the McCarran–Walter bill—passed into law as the Immigration and Nationality Act—consolidated previous immigration laws into one statute, but, in so doing, it preserved the national origins quota system. The Act also established a system of preferences for skilled workers and the relatives of U.S. citizens and permanent resident aliens, and tightened security and screening procedures.

It established a 150,000 numerical limitation on immigration from the Eastern Hemisphere; most Western Hemisphere immigration remained unrestricted, although it established a subquota for immigrants born in the colonies or dependent areas of the Western Hemisphere. Finally, the Act repealed Japanese exclusion and established a small quota for the Asia–Pacific Triangle under which Orientals would be charged.

Congress passed the McCarran–Walter Act over the veto of President Truman who favored the liberalization of the immigration statutes and the elimination of national origins quotas. In his veto message, he strongly reaffirmed U.S. ideals.

> Such a concept [national origins quota] is utterly unworthy of our traditions and ideals. It violates the great political doctrine of the Declaration of Independence that "all men are created equal." It denies the humanitarian creed inscribed beneath the Statue of Liberty proclaiming to all nations: "Give me your tired your poor, your huddled masses, yearning to breathe free...."

President Truman on September 4, 1952 appointed a commission to study and evaluate the immigration and naturalization policies of the United States. On January 1, 1953 the Commission issued its report, *Whom We Shall Welcome*, a statement of support for a nondiscriminatory, liberal immigration policy. The Commission summarized its findings:

> The Commission believes that our present immigration laws flout fundamental American traditions and ideals, display a lack of faith in America's future, damage American prestige and position among other nations, ignore the lessons of the American way of life.

> The Commission believes that laws which fail to reflect the American spirit must sooner or later disappear from the statute books.

> The Commission believes that our present immigration laws should be completely rewritten.

It was not until 1965 that major changes—some urged as early as the Truman Commission—were actually made in the Immigration and Nationality Act. The election of John F. Kennedy, a descendent of Irish immigrants and the first Catholic president of the United States, marked a turning point in immigration history and focused attention again on immigration policy. As a senator, Kennedy had written *A Nation of Immigrants*, a book denouncing the national origins quota system. Now, as President, he introduced legislation to abolish the 40–year–old formula.

That a Catholic could be elected president signified the extent to which the United States had changed since the 1920s. Across the country came a lessening in anti-Catholic, anti-Asian and anti-Semitic sentiment, in part the result of a new tolerance of racial and ethnic differences stimulated by the civil rights movement. By the mid–1960s, Congress was ready for proposals to liberalize immigration policy, particularly after the assassination of President Kennedy and the Lyndon Johnson presidential landslide of 1964. The effort to eliminate the national origins quotas—begun many years earlier—culminated in the passage of the Immigration and Nationality Act Amendments of 1965.

The amendments accomplished the following:

- Abolished the national origins formula, replacing it with a per-country limit of 20,000 on every country outside the Western Hemisphere, and an overall ceiling of 160,000 for those countries;
- Placed a ceiling of 120,000 on immigration from the Western Hemisphere with no country limits; and
- Established Eastern Hemisphere preferences for close relatives, as well as those who had occupational skills needed in the United States under a seven-category preference system.

In signing the new bill, President Lyndon Johnson said:

from this day forth, those wishing to emigrate into America shall be admitted on the basis of their skills and their close relationship to those already here.

The fairness of this standard is so self-evident . . . yet the fact is that for over four decades the immigration policy of the United States has been twisted and has been distorted like a harsh injustice of the national origins quota system . . . families were kept apart because a husband or a wife or a child had been born in the wrong place. Men of needed skill and talent were denied entrance because they came from southern or eastern Europe or from one of the developing continents. The system violated the basic principle of American democracy—the principle that values and rewards each man on the basis of his merit . . . it has been un-American.

The new amendments, as the President suggested, heralded in a new era in U.S. immigration policy. No longer would one nationality be given a larger quota than another in the Eastern Hemisphere. Preference would be given to reuniting families and to bringing those who had certain desirable or needed abilities. These were to be the goals of immigration policy, and the goal of preserving the racial and ethnic domination of northern and western Europe would no longer be an explicit part of U.S. immigration law.

The United States was, of course, far from free of prejudice at that time, and one part of the 1965 law reflected a change in policy that was in part due to antiforeign sentiments. Prejudice against dark-skinned people, particularly in social and economic life, remained strong. In the years after World War II, as the proportion of Spanish-speaking residents increased, much of the lingering nativism in the United States was directed against those from Mexico and Central and South America. The 1952 law—in keeping with the "Good Neighbor" policy, as it was described by Franklin Delano Roosevelt—had not placed any limitations on immigration from these regions, but by 1965 the pressure for such restrictions had mounted. Giving in to these pressures as a price to be paid for abolishing the national origins system, Congress put into the 1965 amendments a ceiling on immigration from the Western Hemisphere that was designed to close the last remaining open door of U.S. policy. This provision went into effect on July 1, 1968.

The legislation did not accomplish its goal regarding Western Hemisphere immigration without substantial costs. In 1976, the House Judiciary Committee reported on the effect of ending the Good Neighbor open door: a steadily increasing backlog of applicants from Latin America, with prospective immigrants waiting two years for a visa. The Committee, recognizing that the ceiling on Western Hemisphere migration had been part of a compromise in the passage of the 1965 amendments, noted:

> When repealing the national origins quota system, the 89th Congress did not provide an adequate mechanism for implementing the Western Hemisphere ceiling.... The result, completely unforeseen and unintended, has been considerable hardship for intending immigrants from this hemisphere who until 1968 enjoyed the privilege of unrestricted immigration.

In 1976 a new law was passed to make regulations regarding immigration the same for both hemispheres, applying to countries of the Western Hemisphere the 20,000–per–country limit and the preference system that was in effect in the Eastern Hemisphere. The only provision to cause any controversy in the 1976 Act was the application of the per-country ceiling provision to Mexico, which had exceeded the 20,000 limit every year since the enactment of the 1965 amendments. There was considerable support for the idea that special provisions should be permitted for contiguous countries, particularly Mexico, because of the special relationship that had developed as a result of shared borders. President Gerald Ford noted in his statement on signing the 1976 amendments into law that he would submit legislation to Congress to increase the immigration quotas for Mexicans desiring to come to the United States, and

President Jimmy Carter endorsed similar legislation in 1977. No action, however, was taken to provide this special treatment for Mexico.

The 1976 law maintained two last vestiges of differential geographic treatment—the separate annual ceilings of 170,000 for the Eastern and 120,000 for the Western Hemisphere and the special ceiling (600 visas per year) assigned to colonies and dependencies. In 1978, new legislation combined the ceilings for both hemispheres into a worldwide total of 290,000 with the same seven-category preference system and per-country limits applied to both. Senator Edward Kennedy described the benefits accruing from the 1978 legislation:

> The establishment of a worldwide ceiling corrects an anomaly in the law, and is a logical step in consequence of the major immigration reforms Congress enacted in 1965—on which I served as floor manager at the time.

> In the long term, this reform makes more flexible the provisions of the preference system, and in the short run it has the likely effect of allowing the use of more nonpreference visas next year for the backlog in the Western Hemisphere and the use of more conditional entry visas for Indochina refugees—a need that is extraordinarily urgent in Southeast Asia today. All this will not involve, however, any increase in the total annual immigration authorized under the law.

Concern about Indochinese conditional entries was an important consideration in the establishment of a worldwide ceiling. The 1965 amendments to the Immigration and Nationality Act had included a permanent statutory authority for the admission of refugees, called the conditional entry provision, patterned after earlier legislation, especially the Fair Share Refugee Act of 1960. The seventh preference category was designated for these admissions and was allocated six percent of the Eastern Hemisphere ceiling of 170,000 visas, one-half of which could be used for aliens in the United States who were adjusting their status. In 1976 the preference system was extended to the Western Hemisphere, under a separate numerical ceiling with its own proportion of seventh-preference slots. At the time of Senator Kennedy's remarks, it was apparent that Western Hemisphere seventh-preference numbers—applicable only to Cubans who were then unable to leave in sizable numbers—were unused whereas Eastern Hemisphere demand was great. A worldwide ceiling would permit the visas to go where the refugee need was greatest without reference to hemisphere.

The 1978 amendments did not address the full range of issues raised by U.S. refugee policy, nor were they intended to do so. The working definition of a refugee—originally developed during the Cold War—still included considerations of national origins, even though the rest of immigration policy had dismissed this criteria.

In the Immigration and Nationality Act of 1952, a refugee was defined as a person [sic] who:

(i) because of persecution or fear of persecution on account of race, religion, or political opinion * * * have fled (I) from any Communist or Communist-dominated country or area, or (II) from any country within the general area of the Middle East, and (ii) are unable or unwilling to return to such country or area on account of race, religion, or political opinion, and (iii) are not nationals of the countries or areas in which their application for conditional entry is made; or (B) that they are persons uprooted by catastrophic natural calamity as defined by the President who are unable to return to their usual place of abode.

This definition did not permit the entry of those fleeing noncommunist persecution unless they came from the Middle East.

Problems also arose because of the inadequacy of the conditional-entry provisions in dealing with large-scale emergencies. Although when these provisions were enacted Congress intended that they would be the means through which most refugees would be admitted, the parole provision of the Immigration and Nationality Act was actually the major authority for the entrance of large groups of refugees. Under the parole authority, the Attorney General has the discretion to parole any alien into the United States temporarily, under such conditions as the Attorney General may prescribe, in emergencies or for reasons deemed strictly in the public interest. During the 1960s, Cuban refugees were paroled into the United States; between 1962 and the end of May 1979, over 690,000 Cubans entered this country under that authority. In 1975, two parole programs were adopted to aid the resettlement of refugees from Indochina. Other major programs permitted the parole of still more Indochinese between 1976 and 1979. In June 1979 President Carter announced that the number of Indochinese paroled into the country would be set at 14,000 per month. During the same period, the parole of about 35,000 Soviet refugees for the year was also authorized as was the entry of slightly more than a thousand Chilean and Lebanese parolees.

The parole authority had been used in these cases because the conditional entry provisions were too limited to deal with emergencies. Yet reliance on the parole authority seemed to be an inappropriate response to what were recurring situations. Attorney General Griffin B. Bell described one of the major problems with the use of the parole authority in refugee crises: "This ... has the practical effect of giving the Attorney General more power than the Congress in determining limits on the entry of refugees into the country." He also noted that the use of parole authority prevented the country from giving clear signals to other nations about the extent of U.S. willingness and ability to respond to world refugee needs. Because of the absence of an ongoing policy for refugee admissions, the United States was unable to plan effectively, and, as Bell concluded, "individual refugees [were] hostage to a system that necessitates that their plight build to tragic proportions so as to establish the imperative to act."

The concerns about refugees led to legislative action in 1979 and 1980. The Refugee Act of 1980 was designed to correct the deficiencies of U.S. refugee policy by providing ongoing mechanisms for the admission and aid of refugees. The legislation broadened the definition of refugee by removing the geographic and ideological limitations of the earlier conditional-entry provisions. It also established an allocation of 50,000 for normal refugee admissions, through 1982, and provided procedures through which the President in consultation with Congress could increase this number annually in response to unforeseen circumstances. It further provided for a special conditional entry status with adjustment to permanent resident alien status after one year in the United States.

In addition to making changes in admissions policy, the Refugee Act of 1980 also established the ongoing responsibility of the federal government for the resettlement of refugees accepted under the Act. The legislation included provision for up to 100 percent reimbursement to states for cash and medical assistance provided to refugees during their first 36 months in this country and for grants to voluntary agencies for some of their costs incurred in resettlement.

SUSAN F. MARTIN, A NATION OF IMMIGRANTS
1–2, 213–16, 218–19, 253–54, 265–68, 271–78, 280–81, 284–86 (2010)

The United States is in the midst of its fourth major wave of immigration. Today's wave is the largest in absolute numbers, although not as a proportion of the total population. Unlike in previous waves, today's immigrants come from every inhabited continent and represent just about every country in the United Nations. As in previous waves, there is a profound ambivalence about immigration among the American public.

* * *

Immigration has indeed been formative in making America what it is and what it will become. The phrase "a nation of immigrants," however, hides as much as it illuminates in lumping together all immigrants and all forms of immigration. In fact, [I argue], America has been settled from its very origins by three different models of immigration, all of which persist through the four waves * * *. Lawrence Fuchs[d] described each model in relationship to the colony in which it most thrived:

> * * * Pennsylvania sought immigrants who would be good citizens regardless of their religious background; Massachusetts wanted as members only those who were religiously pure; and Virginia, with its increasing reliance on a plantation economy, wanted workers as cheaply as it could get them, without necessarily welcoming them to membership in the community.

* * *

---

d. Lawrence Fuchs, *The American Kaleidoscope: Race, Ethnicity, and the Civil Culture*, Wesleyan University Press 8 (1990)—eds.

[Martin argues that the 1965 amendments abolishing the national origins quotas restored the Pennsylvania model by reopening immigration to those—no matter where they originated—who sought to make the United States their permanent home. She emphasizes that total immigration increased dramatically in the wake of the 1965 legislation, and that it shifted noticeably to immigrants from Asia and from the Caribbean. She then discusses the growth of undocumented migration in the 1970s and 1980s, and the legislative efforts to respond to this situation.]

[In 1986] the Immigration Reform and Control Act (IRCA) was signed into law. * * * [T]he intent was to reduce future illegal immigration through a combination of improved border enforcement and sanctions against employers who knowingly hired person without a work authorization, while bringing those who were illegally in the country out of the shadows and onto a path to citizenship. For the first time, IRCA made it illegal to hire an illegal alien but imposed sanctions[e] only if the employer knew the worker was in the country illegally. * * *

To address concerns about discrimination, IRCA authorized a new office within the Justice Department to investigate "unfair immigration-related employment practices." IRCA prohibited employers from discriminating * * * because of [an] individual's national origin, or * * * citizenship status. It was considered an unfair practice to seek different or additional documents from any newly hired employees, a provision designed to dissuade employers from setting up special procedures for foreign-appearing workers.

The legalization provisions included two separate programs. One program focused on undocumented immigrants who had been in the country since January 1, 1982. Initially, they obtained conditional legal status upon demonstrating their continued presence in the United States. After eighteen months, they could apply for legal permanent resident status upon showing that they had successfully completed a course in the English language and civics or had passed an examination that was comparable with the naturalization tests. * * *. The second program was the SAW (Special Agricultural Workers) program. Under its terms, persons who could demonstrate that they had worked unlawfully in agriculture for ninety days during the twelve month period ending on May 1, 1986, were eligible to be legalized. After demonstrating that they continued to work in agriculture during the following three years, they could become permanent residents. * * *

IRCA barred the newly legalized from most public benefit programs for the first five years after they received legal status. Exceptions were made for education and training programs, especially those, like Head Start, that helped children. * * *

In the years after enactment of IRCA, 1.6 million immigrants who were in the United States illegally were found eligible for legalization under the pre–1982 program and 1.1 million were found eligible under the

---

e. We will describe in Chapter Nine the other sanctions for failing to verify properly.—eds.

SAW program. These numbers represented 90 percent of pre–1982 applicants and 86 percent of SAW applicants. * * * The number of [SAW] applications far exceeded estimates of the seasonal agricultural workforce. Several explanations have been offered for the wide discrepancy. SAW applications could be made from outside the country, meaning that people who had worked previously in agriculture (perhaps not during the period included in the law) could apply even if they had left the country. More seriously, there appeared to be many fraudulent applications by people who had never worked in agriculture but found someone to provide an affidavit or counterfeit documents showing that they had put in ninety days in the fields.

* * *

Two immediate issues were raised by the IRCA legalization program. First, it did not cover undocumented immigrants who had entered after January 1, 1982, unless they were seasonal agricultural workers. IRCA thus led to a large residual population that was still in the country illegally. Second, IRCA made no accommodations for the admission of the families of legalized immigrants. Once legalized immigrants had the opportunity, they began to petition for their spouses and children to obtain permanent residence. Some of these family members were in the home country while others were in the United States but did not meet the IRCA requirements for legalization or had entered after their "anchor" relative gained legalized status. Because the immigrants whose status was legalized under IRCA came from so few countries, and the per-country limits applied to immediate relatives of legal permanent residents, the backlog of applicants began to grow exponentially.

* * *

In 1988, action began on reform of the legal admissions system. [The Immigration Act of 1990 increased the number of immigrant visas, setting a nominal annual ceiling of 480,000 on family admissions, but actually allowing them to go much higher, because there is no cap on admission of spouses and children of U.S. citizens. In addition, the Act set annual quotas of 140,000 visas for employment-based immigration and 55,000 for diversity immigration. The statute also streamlined naturalization, but still allowed judicial ceremonies.]

* * *

[In sum, the] Immigration Act of 1990, and the massive legalization program under IRCA, [together with] the Refugee Act of 1980, * * * culminated a 25–year period in which there was a substantial return to the Pennsylvania model of immigration. The 1965 Amendments reversed the discriminatory national origins quotas, but the architects of the reform did not extol the benefits of immigration. Rather, they argued that national origins quotas were an anachronism in a period in which civil rights were flourishing. Eliminating the discriminatory provisions would enhance American prestige around the world, but they would not necessarily open the United States to increased immigration. By contrast, the 1990 legislation was promoted precisely because its supporters thought an expansion in immigration was in the national interest. Even those who favored controls on overall numbers, such as Senator Alan Simpson, were persuaded by the need to expand highly skilled immigration to meet the needs of a global economy. Moreover, Congress chose permanent admissions over temporary workers. In the spirit of the Pennsylvania model, immigrants would be welcomed as proto-citizens rather than as indentured laborers. IRCA had legalized millions of undocumented immigrants, putting them on a road to citizenship if they learned English and civics.

The 1990 legislation was intended to facilitate family reunification, with family unity visas and the lifting of per-country limits on spouses and minor children of legal permanent residents. This is not to say that everything about the 1990 legislation should be seen within this context. The legislation also expanded the grounds for deportation, including the creation of a category of aggravated felons that would become problematic in later years. On balance, though, the Immigration Act of 1990 favored a form of immigration that valued family, skills, and humanitarian interests and provided immigrants the opportunity to join the American community.

The consensus that led to passage of the Immigration Act of 1990 was short-lived. Within a few years of its passage, the reemergence of illegal immigration and concerns about the fiscal impact of legal immigration challenged the Pennsylvania model. * * *

By the early 1990s, unauthorized immigration was indeed on the rise.[f] In California, the concerns about illegal immigration were taking the shape of a political movement. The United States–Mexico border appeared to be a free entry zone with no controls over illegal migration. Photos of large numbers of migrants racing by foot up Interstate Highway 5, the major route which runs from the Mexican to the Canadian border, became stock footage on U.S. news reports. Reflecting growing dissatisfaction with the federal government's apparent inability to control the border, California activists responded by introducing Proposition 187. The preamble summarized their concerns: "The People of California find and declare as follows: That they have suffered and are suffering economic hardship caused by the presence of illegal aliens in this state. That they have suffered and are suffering personal injury and damage caused by the criminal conduct of illegal aliens in this state. That they have a right to the protection of their government from any person or persons entering this country unlawfully." Proposition 187 required state and local law enforcement agencies to cooperate with federal authorities in administering immigration law.* * *

Proposition 187 also barred undocumented immigrants from a range of public services, with the exception of emergency medical assistance. In what may have been the most controversial provision, the bar extended to

---

f. Relocated sentence—eds.

public primary and secondary education. A 1982 Supreme Court decision, *Plyler v. Doe*, guaranteed the right of all children, including undocumented immigrants, to public education. The Supreme Court had determined that children should not be punished for the decisions of their parents to come to the United States illegally. Supporters of Proposition 187 felt they were sending a powerful message to the federal government to gain control over illegal immigration. Opponents saw the proposition as a mean-spirited assault on undocumented immigrants but not a serious effort to get at the underlying factors at work.

* * *

During the 1990s, as is the case today, unauthorized entry occurred in a number of different ways. Most of those illegally in the United States were believed to have entered clandestinely, largely across the land border with Mexico although others arrived by sea, often in makeshift boats or rafts. A sizable minority (estimated as high as 40–45 percent) entered through recognized ports of entry. Many did so having obtained legitimate visas, often as tourists, and then overstayed the period that the visa covered. Some obtained a border crossing card or longer-term visa that did not permit employment, and then worked in contravention of the terms of their admission. In still other cases, migrants entered as temporary workers but failed to leave when their period of work authorization ended. In some cases, migrants sought visas knowing that they planned to violate the terms. In other cases, the migrants had no initial intention of overstaying or working illegally, but circumstances changed, their stay was prolonged, and they entered into irregular status.

* * *

IRCA had attempted to deal with all of these forms of illegal migration, focusing on the one common element—the employment magnet. Employer sanctions had done little to curb employment of undocumented workers, however, because of a faulty employment verification system [that is easily defeated by false documents]. * * *

[In 1996 Congress enacted three laws, the Illegal Immigration Reform and Immigrant Responsibility Act (IIRIRA), the Anti–Terrorism and Effective Death Penalty Act (AEDPA), and the Personal Responsibility and Work Opportunity Reconciliation Act of 1996 (better known as welfare reform), that represent a distinct shift in U.S. law on the rights of legal immigrants.]

IIRIRA, in combination with the Anti–Terrorism Act, included provisions that weakened the due process rights of legal permanent residents. Passed in the aftermath of the Oklahoma City bombing, with the 1993 bombings of the World Trade Center still fresh in memory, the law went well beyond terrorism, including sections on the removal of immigrants who committed crimes. * * *

The Anti–Terrorism law redefined crimes of "moral turpitude" to include those punishable by imprisonment for one year or more, rather than those for which the aliens is actually sentenced to imprisonment for one year or more, and expanded the list of crimes that could be considered aggravated felonies. IIRIRA revised the definition of an aggravated felony to include far less serious crimes than those covered by the 1990 legislation or the Anti–Terrorism Act. Just about any offense that could result in a potential—not necessarily actual—custodial sentence of one year or more could render the alien deportable. The new rule was applied retroactively; crimes committed many years ago, even if there was no evidence of subsequent criminality, qualified as grounds for removal. * * *

Some of the most profound changes to occur in immigrant policy found their way into law through the welfare reform legislation passed in 1996. The Welfare Reform Act, in combination with IIRIRA, reduced substantially the access of legal immigrants to public benefit programs available to citizens. * * *

Until 1996, no federal benefit program denied eligibility to permanent resident aliens solely on the basis of alien status. * * * [In the past distinctions had been] made between aliens residing permanently and legally in this country and undocumented aliens. The former were generally determined eligible for federal assistance; the latter were generally barred from these programs.

The welfare reform bill moved the line. Now, the major distinction was between immigrants, regardless of their status, and citizens. The welfare act made legal immigrants ineligible for Supplementary Security Income (SSI) and food stamps until citizenship * * *.

Legal immigrants were made ineligible for federal, means-tested benefits during their first five years after entry. * * *

Under IIRIRA, all immigrants admitted under family-based categories must be sponsored by a relative who signs an affidavit of support and who can demonstrate an ability to support the immigrant and members of his or her immediate family at 125 percent of poverty level. The affidavits would be legally enforceable against the sponsor * * *.

In effect, 1996 legislative activities turned out to be pro-immigration but anti-immigrant, in the best tradition of the Virginia model. At a time when the United States was admitting record numbers of immigrants, and a sizable proportion lived and worked in poverty, restricting eligibility for safety-net programs made it clear that immigrants were welcomed as workers, but not as full members of the community. The welfare reforms said, in effect, that all obligations were one-sided: immigrants must continue to pay taxes, contribute to the U.S. economy, obey U.S. laws, and otherwise contribute to the public weal, but the broader society had no reciprocal obligations toward them. * * *

When President George W. Bush had his first meeting with President Vincente Fox of Mexico early in 2001, the two leaders pledged cooperation in solving the problem of unauthorized migration from Mexico to the United States. A series of high-level meetings, including presidential summits, began to outline a set of policies to be adopted by both countries. Mexico would enhance border controls to dissuade its nationals from exiting the country illegally, while the United States would provide a mechanism through which Mexicans could enter as temporary workers or regularize their status within the United States or both. Called "earned legalization," the idea was that Mexicans who had been working in the United States and paying their taxes had proven themselves worthy of regularization.

* * *

The negotiations between the United States and Mexico came to an almost complete halt after the terrorist attacks of September 11. * * * Attention turned instead to legislative and administrative actions to ensure that foreign terrorists did not pose a danger to the United States. Action focused on four principal issues: issuance of visas to terrorists, tracking foreign nationals in the United States, bars on entry and removal of suspected terrorists, and organizational roles and responsibilities.

* * *

In the aftermath of the attacks, the State Department took steps to tighten issuance of visas. All applicants from countries where visas were required had to come to embassies and consulates for a hearing. Most of the terrorists had obtained their visas in Saudi Arabia, where an expedited process had waived an interview for many applicants. * * *

A second prong of the response to 9/11 focused on identifying terrorists who might still be in the country. In the days following September 11, the government detained more than one thousand foreign nationals from Arab and other Muslim countries that have been linked to terrorism. Most of the detainees were found to have no ties to terrorist organizations. More than 750 were turned over to the Immigration and Nationalism Service, though, because they were found to have violated immigration laws. * * *

The administration then introduced a new registration system for nationals of more than 30 countries that are largely Arabic or Muslim, the National Security Entry–Exit Registration System (NSEERS). NSEERS was composed of a registration program conducted at various ports of entry and a special registration program for certain foreign nationals already in the county.

* * * Critics of the program were especially concerned about the targeting of Arab and Muslim foreign nationals for registration. * * *

Recognizing the controversy surrounding the special registration provisions, the administration moved forward with a universal entry-exit program, which had been mandated in IIRIRA but postponed because of the fears of businesses along the border between the United States and Canada that it would impede commerce. US–Visit (United States Visitor and Immigrant Status Indicator Technology) allowed the automated capture of basic information about each arriving and departing passenger. All arriving foreign visitors would have their photograph and fingerprints taken upon arrival and departure. The system would be introduced at air and sea ports of entry and then extended to the land ports of entry, which had far more crossing each day. As of this writing, US–Visit is operational on entry but exit controls have still not been introduced.

Because several hijackers had received student visas, movement in introducing a tracking system of foreign students and exchange visitors also accelerated. The Student and Exchange Visitor Information System (SEVIS) became operational in 2003. Schools report electronically to the Department of Homeland Security on the arrival of foreign students and exchange visitors and on the students' and visitors' change of address, changes in program of study, and other pertinent information.

The third area receiving post 9/11 attention related to bars on entry and grounds for removal of persons suspected of being foreign terrorists. * * *

The USA Patriot Act, passed after September 11, expanded the definition of terrorist activity [and] * * * expanded the grounds for detaining aliens who were barred from entering or could be removed because of suspected terrorist activities or membership.

* * *

Complicating the situation was the bar imposed by the USA Patriot Act on the admission of foreign nationals who provided material support to terrorist organizations. Terrorist organizations are defined broadly to include "groups of two or more individuals, whether organized or not," which engage in proscribed activities. There is no exception for providing material support under duress, which is particularly problematic for refugees. Even minimal support is prohibited. * * * The legislation permits admission only if the secretary of state and secretary of homeland security specifically waive the application of the material support bar.[g]

As applied, the law has had an unintended effect. The bar also applies to organizations that are working to overthrow governments that the United States has opposed militarily. * * *

In the aftermath of September 11, serious discussion of immigration reform languished in the United States although some progress was made in achieving agreements with Canada and Mexico on border security strategies. The summit of the Americas held in Monterrey, Mexico, January 12–13, 2004, provided the opportunity for President Bush to return to the issue of immigration reform. Less than a week before the summit, he unveiled his proposal for a new temporary worker program, titled the "Fair and Secure Immigration Reform." * * *

---

g. Either official can grant the waiver, after appropriate interagency consultation.—eds.

* * * Harsh public criticism of his plan came from both liberal and conservative camps, effectively blocking any comprehensive immigration reform.

* * *

Several legislative alternatives to President Bush's temporary worker proposal were introduced but not enacted. * * * Two bills, had bipartisan sponsorship in Congress. AgJOBS, was the principal legislative effort to reform the system for admitting temporary agricultural workers. * * *

The DREAM Act (Development, Relief, and Education for Alien Minors Act), * * * sought to facilitate the entry into institutions of higher education of those illegal immigrant minors who have obtained a high-school diploma. * * *

Despite their bipartisan support, AgJOBS and the DREAM Act languished as Congress considered more far-reaching reform. In the 109th Congress, the Senate and the House of Representatives took very different approaches to the issue. The House focused primarily on enhanced enforcement while the Senate tried for comprehensive reform. * * *

As the prospects for federal reform diminished, a number of states and localities took action to address what they perceived as the growing problem of illegal immigration. The National Council of State Legislators documented the trend: "State laws related to immigration have increased dramatically in recent years: In 2005, 300 bills were introduced and 38 laws were enacted. In 2006, activity doubled: 570 bills were introduced and 84 laws were enacted. In 2007, activity tripled: 1,562 bills were introduced and 240 laws were enacted." Some of these laws attempt to implement at the state level provisions that were debated at the federal level. For example, in 2008, nineteen laws were enacted in thirteen states to enforce sanctions against employers who hire unauthorized workers and to impose employment eligibility verification requirements and penalties.

Perhaps the most controversy was generated by an Arizona law (S.B. 1070) "requiring that a [law enforcement] officer make a reasonable attempt to determine the immigration status of a person stopped, detained or arrested if there is a reasonable suspicion that the person is unlawfully present in the United States, and requiring verification of the immigration status of any person arrested prior to releasing that person." The law, enacted in April 2010, further made it a criminal act if an unauthorized immigrant sought employment or failed to carry federal alien registration documents. It also allowed warrantless arrests "where there is probable cause to believe the person has committed a public offense that makes the person removable from the United States." And the legislation allowed people to sue local government or agencies if they believe the law is not being enforced. S.B. 1070 followed other Arizona initiatives to curb illegal immigration, including legislation that required employers in the state to use the E–Verify program[h] to determine authorization to work and made it a state offense to knowingly hire an unauthorized immigrant.

In signing the law, the Arizona governor called it a "tool for our state to use as we work to solve a crisis we did not create and the federal government has refused to fix." Proponents of the legislation cited what they described as increasing crime and border violence related to illegal immigration. The law was condemned immediately by civil rights and other groups that feared it would lead to racial and ethnic profiling. The governor's assurances that law enforcement could be trusted to implement the law in a nondiscriminatory manner did little to quell these concerns. The law was also criticized as an overreaction to concerns about border violence and crime, with opponents pointing out the crime rates had actually gone down in Arizona. Law enforcement officials were split, some favoring the legislation and others concerned that it would drive a wedge between the police and the communities they served. A number of legal suits followed, * * * [and] a federal judge enjoined Arizona from implementing several provisions of law * * *.

Just a few years after the liberalizing reforms of the Immigration Act of 1990 were enacted, immigration was in crisis. The country reacted with ambivalence. Public backlash against illegal immigration fueled efforts such as Proposition 187, but economic and humanitarian interests kept the back door open. The tension inherent in these two positions led to a return to the Virginia model. Foreign workers would be tolerated, even encouraged, but within restrictive frameworks that often precluded full membership in American society. An underclass of undocumented immigrants would pick the crops, process the food, garden and landscape, construct homes, manufacture garments, clean homes, take care of children and the elderly, and provide myriad other services. The immigrants benefited from higher wages than they could expect at home but were without the legal protections afforded to citizens in the labor market. Middle-and upper-class Americans benefited from having a workforce willing and able to do these jobs at low wages and under working conditions that most Americans would not accept.

At the same time, industries employing highly skilled workers benefited from the growth in temporary worker programs. A broken permanent immigration system could not keep up with demand for foreign science, information technology, and engineering professions. Rather than fix the permanent program to benefit from this human capital, Congress repeatedly tinkered with the H–1B program, increasing numbers and allowing workers to remain tied to an employer for longer and longer periods. As of July 2010, second-preference applicants (that is, persons with advanced degrees) from India and China must have applied before October 2005 because of large backlogs. The waiting times for family reunification

---

h. Employers use an internet link to a federal database to determine whether a new employee is authorized to work.—eds.

for adult children of U.S. citizens, spouses, and minor children of Mexican legal permanent residents, and siblings of U.S. citizens, were even longer.

The Massachusetts model also had a resurgence in the aftermath of the World Trade Center bombings in 1993 and 2001. Although most of the impetus for the 1996 Anti–Terrorism legislation was the Oklahoma bombings that were carried out by native-born U.S. citizens, Congress took the opportunity to institute restrictive measures affecting the rights of immigrants. September 11 quickly led to ethnic and religious profiling in the form of the NSEERs program. With passage of the USA Patriot Act, new ideological bars to admission were adopted, the most problematic being the provisions on persons providing material support to terrorist organizations even under significant duress. With an end to the Cold War, the ideological underpinnings of the refugee program disappeared, making it the first victim of the new preoccupation with terrorism.

The Pennsylvania model is not dead, but it is under severe challenge. Permanent immigration, with a route to citizenship, remains substantial but during the first half of the 2000 decade, the increase in unauthorized migrants exceeded the net increase in legal immigrants. This situation appears to be shifting as a result of the economic recession. In 2008, net growth in the unauthorized migrant population slowed down considerably because of fewer new arrivals. Demographers have found no evidence, as of the time of this writing, that returns to Mexico (the largest sources of unauthorized migration) have increased significantly.

Public concerns about immigration have not disappeared, however. [R]ecent years have seen a proliferation of initiatives at the state and local level to curb illegal immigration. Proponents argue that the federal government has abdicated its responsibility to manage movements of people into the country, creating a vacuum to be replaced by state and local efforts to deal with unresolved issues. Moreover, systemic problems in U.S. immigration policy remain, as do the underlying causes of migration. With economic recovery, illegal immigration is likely to resume at least at the same levels as were reached in the past decade. The question will be whether the country will resume the pro-immigration, fundamentally anti-immigrant, policies of the past fifteen years or renew the covenant with immigrants, with mutual obligations, that long characterized the Pennsylvania model.

NOTES AND QUESTIONS

1.   Based on these readings, list the factors that have most shaped the immigration policy of the United States. What role do you think the economy has played? What about political ideas? Race, religion, and ethnic background? National security concerns? To what extent are the factors affecting migration different today from those a century ago?

2.   The excerpts indicate that throughout the history of immigration to the United States, economic and social considerations have motivated many

policy decisions. Frequently, however, their influences have been diametrically opposed, as when the economic need for labor conflicted with restrictionist social concerns. How has the United States generally responded to these opposing perspectives on immigration?

3. The last paragraph of the Martin reading describes the Pennsylvania model as a covenant with immigrants, embodying mutual obligations. How do undocumented migrants fit that model? One can imagine many different versions of the respective obligations, but if a particular polity so chose, wouldn't the Pennsylvania model be consistent with a strong insistence that newcomers observe the nation's laws?

4. If the Pennsylvania model emphasizes the mutual agreement between the would-be immigrant and the United States, what is (or should be) the content of the agreement? Does the immigrant agree to anything more than observing the laws of the United States? Is there an implicit assumption, though no explicit requirement, that the immigrant will eventually become an American citizen? Is there an assumption that current citizens are free at any time to revoke the right of noncitizens to remain?

5. In order to become citizens, immigrants have historically been required to show some level of assimilation, by demonstrating proficiency in English and general civic knowledge. Should a showing of assimilation be required before an individual naturalizes? What about before a person is granted permanent residence? What are the justifications for a focus on assimilation in the naturalization process? What, if any, negative consequences might flow from a decision to de-emphasize assimilation?

6. As described further in Chapter Five, the terminology used to describe people who migrate from one society to another can be confusing, inconsistent, and offensive. The Immigration and Nationality Act uses the term "alien" to refer to all individuals, including those who live here permanently and lawfully, who are not citizens or nationals of the United States. We prefer the term "noncitizen," and will use that instead. In addition to being a less emotionally laden term, it emphasizes the importance of the concept of citizenship, the topic we turn to in Chapter Two.

7. Interested readers will find a wealth of additional informative and insightful treatments of American immigration history and policy in S. Martin, A Nation of Immigrants (2010); M. Waters & R. Ueda (eds.), The New Americans: A Guide to Immigration Since 1965 (2007); D. Kanstroom, Deportation Nation: Outsiders in American History (2007); H. Motomura, Americans in Waiting: The Lost Story of Immigration and Citizenship in the United States (2006); A. Zolberg, A Nation by Design: Immigration Policy in the Fashioning of America (2006); M. Ngai, Impossible Subjects: Illegal Aliens and the Making of Modern America (2004); R. Daniels, Guarding the Golden Door: American Immigration Policy and Immigrants Since 1882 (2004); D. King, Making Americans: Immigration, Race, and the Origins of the Diverse Democracy (2002); D. Massey, J. Durand, & N. Malone, Beyond Smoke And Mirrors: Mexican Immigration In An Era Of Economic Integration (2002); D. Tichenor, Dividing Lines: The Politics of Immigration Control in America (2002); R. Daniels, Coming to America: History of Immigration and Ethnicity in American Life (2d ed. 2002); C. Hirschman, P. Kasinitz, & J. DeWind (eds.), The

Handbook of International Migration: The American Experience (1999); D. Reimers, Still the Golden Door: The Third World Comes to America (2d ed. 1992); M. LeMay, From Open Door to Dutch Door: An Analysis of U.S. Immigration Policy Since 1820 (1987); T. Miller & M. Espenshade, The Fourth Wave: California's Newest Immigrants (1985); O. Handlin, The Uprooted (2d ed. 1973); M. Jones, American Immigration (1960); J. Higham, Strangers in the Land: Patterns of American Nativism, 1860–1925 (1955).

CHAPTER TWO

CITIZENSHIP

■ ■ ■

Membership in a nation state is fundamental to protection under international law. States have laws defining who are full members—citizens—and who are not. The populations of states, of course, include many who are not citizens. These individuals, particularly if they are long-time residents, may also have large stakes in the society. Although not full members, they also claim legal rights and opportunities. Thus, the laws of immigration necessarily raise questions of membership and are inextricably linked to laws defining citizenship.

In this book we use two different schemes to represent membership. One model is represented by concentric circles: citizens form the innermost membership ring, with categories of noncitizens (residents, visitors, unauthorized migrants, aliens seeking entry) filling in outer rings. Under this representation, membership rights are assigned by category. The other model is chronological (or horizontal): immigrants begin the process (usually) by receiving a visa overseas, entering the United States, establishing residence and ultimately obtaining citizenship. Rights and opportunities (the privileges of membership) might be understood to accumulate over time as one moves along the process.

In identifying these two perspectives, we do not mean to imply that they necessarily define different conceptions of membership; we present them simply as heuristics. We think they help explain the basic themes and organization of this book. In a number of chapters, we will be looking at the concentric circles, asking what follows from being in one circle or another in terms of rights, benefits, and obligations. In other chapters we will be pursuing the chronological model by examining the rules for entry, residence, and removal of immigrants.

We start in this chapter with the topic at the core of the first model: the question of citizenship. We consider first the various ways by which individuals become citizens.

SECTION A. ACQUISITION OF NATIONALITY BY BIRTH

Two basic principles for the acquisition of nationality at birth are known to international practice: the *jus soli,* literally right of land or ground—conferral of nationality based on birth within the national territory; and the *jus sanguinis,* or right of blood—the conferral of nationality based on descent, irrespective of the place of birth. Anglo–American nationality law is fundamentally based on the *jus soli,* although both principles have played a role in the transmission of United States citizenship ever since the first nationality statute was passed. Act of March 26, 1790, Ch. 3, 1 Stat. 103.

Virtually all persons in the world possess citizenship of some state, and the vast majority acquired their citizenship at birth. In establishing birthright citizenship, polities effectively yield basic decisions about membership to the private decisions and acts of their populations. It might be thought sensible for a political community to grant children of citizens a provisional citizenship that ripens into full membership at the age of majority if certain criteria are met. But we are aware of no country that has taken this route. Why might this be so?

1. *JUS SANGUINIS*

a. Overview

We normally think of citizenship as a status of enormous significance. Chief Justice Warren described citizenship as "nothing less than the right to have rights." *Perez v. Brownell,* 356 U.S. 44, 64, 78 S.Ct. 568, 2 L.Ed.2d 603 (1958) (dissenting opinion). And the Supreme Court has stated that "[i]t would be difficult to exaggerate [the] value and importance" of American citizenship: "by many it is regarded as the highest hope of civilized men." *Schneiderman v. United States,* 320 U.S. 118, 122, 63 S.Ct. 1333, 87 L.Ed. 1796 (1943).

Yet the Constitution, as initially drafted, included no definition of citizenship. It is clear that the framers believed that the status had some significance: citizenship was made a qualification for the Presidency and election to Congress; and Congress was given the authority to adopt "an uniform Rule of Naturalization." But the original Constitution left unanswered basic questions about the acquisition, distribution and loss of citizenship and what rights pertained to citizenship. The *jus soli* principle, embodied in common law, statutes, and ultimately in the Fourteenth Amendment to the U.S. Constitution, has been the major mode of birthright citizenship in the United States, and will be discussed in greater detail below. Less noticed, U.S. law has also adopted the *jus sanguinis* approach to transmitting citizenship at birth.

The first Congress, at its second session, adopted legislation extending U.S. citizenship to children born abroad to U.S. citizen fathers. Act of

March 26, 1790, Ch. 3, 1 Stat. 103. This transmission of U.S. nationality *jure sanguinis* to children born abroad to American parents can be considered a form of birthright citizenship; the children do not apply for naturalization or go through a naturalization proceeding because they are citizens at birth. In light of the absence of any definition of citizenship in the U.S. Constitution ratified in 1789, what authority did Congress have to adopt *jus sanguinis* rules for children born abroad? *See Rogers v. Bellei*, 401 U.S. 815, 823, 827–31, 91 S.Ct. 1060, 28 L.Ed.2d 499 (1971).

The current *jus sanguinis* rules are set forth in INA §§ 301(c), (d), (e), (g), (h); 308(2), (4); and 309. The most important relate to children born outside U.S. territory to parents either one or both of whom are U.S. citizens. If both are citizens, the child acquires citizenship at birth, provided only that one of the parents had a residence in the United States at some time prior thereto. INA § 301(c).[1] *See Weedin v. Chin Bow*, 274 U.S. 657, 47 S.Ct. 772, 71 L.Ed. 1284 (1927) (parental residence must precede birth of the child). If one parent is a noncitizen, however, then the citizen parent must have been physically present in the United States for a total of five years before the birth, including at least two years after the age of fourteen. Certain kinds of government and military service abroad count as physical presence in the United States for these purposes. INA § 301(g).

Congress has amended the *jus sanguinis* statutes on multiple occasions, and, in general, the law at the time of birth is the one that governs. To determine whether a person born outside the territorial jurisdiction is a United States citizen, therefore, it is not enough to consult the present INA, unless of course the birth occurred after enactment of the latest amendments. One must check carefully the precise requirements in effect at the time of the birth of the individual in question, and also see whether any requirements for later residence in the United States have been fulfilled. *See, e.g., Runnett v. Shultz*, 901 F.2d 782 (9th Cir.1990). For summaries of the relevant rules, broken down by date of birth, *see* C. Gordon, S. Mailman & S. Yale–Loehr, Immigration Law and Procedure (GM & Y) § 93.02[5][c]; 66 Interp.Rel. 444 (1989) (reprinting charts used by the State Department, showing the different rules that apply for legitimate and illegitimate children born during the various time periods).

b. Physical Presence in the United States

These current rules are fairly straightforward, but until 1978 the statute included several other provisos, rendered even more complicated for ready application by the fact that the rules had been modified frequently over the years. *See* GM & Y § 93.03. The complexities result from evolving congressional views about how a fairly consistent aim should be

---

1. The statute provides that the term "residence" means "the place of general abode; the place of general abode of a person means his principal, actual dwelling place in fact, without regard to intent." INA § 101(a)(33). This objective test of residence was adopted in reaction to administrative rulings which had found that even temporary sojourn in the United States, lasting no more than a few days, might fulfill the parental residence requirements of earlier statutes. *See, e.g., Matter of E–*, 1 I. & N. Dec. 40 (AG 1941); *Matter of V–*, 6 I. & N. Dec. 1 (AG 1953).

achieved. From the beginning, Congress has sought to avoid the creation of a class of expatriates who may transmit U.S. citizenship to their children indefinitely, even though the family has had no close contact with actual life in the United States for generations. The issue has been what type of contact, on the part of the parents or the child, should be required.

Congress has employed two principal means toward this end. First, U.S. citizen parents lacking a specified period of historical residence in the United States have been unable to transmit citizenship to their children. Second, from 1934 until 1978, the child had to establish his or her own residence or extended physical presence in the United States for a specified number of years within stated periods, or else lose the citizenship acquired at birth. The length of residence and the ages during which residence had to be established—for parent or child—have been altered several times.

The first type of limitation, concerning parental residence before the child's birth, has raised few constitutional issues, and, as noted, remains part of current law. The second came under attack after *Afroyim v. Rusk,* 387 U.S. 253, 87 S.Ct. 1660, 18 L.Ed.2d 757 (1967), imposed strict constitutional limits on the power of Congress to deprive persons of U.S. citizenship involuntarily. But the Supreme Court, by a vote of five to four, eventually held that Congress retained the power to impose such a residence requirement as a "condition subsequent" on persons who are U.S. citizens by virtue of their birth to U.S. nationals abroad. *Rogers v. Bellei,* 401 U.S. 815, 91 S.Ct. 1060, 28 L.Ed.2d 499 (1971). At the time of *Bellei,* the statute required the citizen *jure sanguinis* to be physically present in the United States for five years between the ages of 14 and 28, or else lose U.S. citizenship.

Despite the judicial endorsement of this type of post-acquisition residence requirement, Congress chose in 1978 to remove all such provisions from the immigration laws. Current law therefore relies solely on *parental* residence requirements to avoid the indefinite perpetuation of U.S. citizenship *jure sanguinis* within families that realistically have lost touch with their American roots. This change has considerably simplified the operation of current *jus sanguinis* rules, but Congress, as has been its usual (though not universal) practice when amending the citizenship rules, did not make its amendment retroactive. Persons who had already lost their citizenship under the earlier residency requirements thus remain denationalized, and those who did not acquire citizenship under the rules extant on the date of birth usually cannot benefit from later statutory liberalization.

Congress clearly aims to forestall the transmission of U.S. citizenship to multiple generations of families who have not maintained some physical connection with the territory of the United States. Do you think this is an appropriate goal?

If you think that there may be valid reasons to limit the role of *jus sanguinis* in some instances when children are born abroad, would you change the statutory scheme? Here are a few alternatives to consider:

- a rule that citizenship can be transmitted only to the first generation of persons born to U.S. citizens outside the United States (this is the rule in Mexico);

- a rule re-establishing the requirement that a person born outside the United States reside for some period of time in the United States in order to retain U.S. citizenship;

- a rule requiring that persons born to U.S. citizens abroad register with U.S. authorities at the age of majority in order to maintain (or attain?) U.S. citizenship;

- a rule mandating that a person having two nationalities based on birth abroad to U.S. citizen parents elect one or the other citizenship at the age of majority.

Turning from the rules adopted by some other countries, take a look at the INA provisions establishing citizenship *jure sanguinis*, INA §§ 301(c), (d), (g), (h), and at the provision detailing transmission of U.S. citizenship at birth to children born out of wedlock, INA § 309. These will help you analyze the problems below.

PROBLEMS

1.   Your clients, a married couple, are Presbyterian missionaries in Ukraine. They are both children of missionaries; the husband was born in Poland and the wife in the Philippines, but both acquired U.S. citizenship at birth. They are expecting a baby next month, and it will be born in Ukraine. Will the child have U.S. citizenship?

a.   Would it matter if neither of your clients has ever spent more than one academic semester in the United States? One summer vacation?

b.   If you learn that one of your clients went to high school in the United States but the other has never been in the country, does it matter whether it is the husband or the wife?

2.   Your client was born in the United States, but his parents moved to Switzerland when he was two, and he has spent most of his life in Europe. He has been living with a French woman in Paris for the past three years, and she recently discovered that she is pregnant. The child is due in five months. This event has prompted the couple to talk more earnestly about a subject they have discussed for a long time but never acted upon: whether they should get married. They haven't yet decided. In any event he wants to make sure that the child has U.S. citizenship.

a.   He asks whether he has to move to the United States with his fiancée to accomplish this aim. He is not sure he could even arrange this in time because she has no passport and no U.S. visa. What do you advise?

b. The couple may decide anyway to stay in France, "to be absolutely certain," he says, "that the baby has French citizenship too." Is there any way that he can arrange for the child also to have U.S. nationality if it is born in Paris? Does he have to marry the mother to accomplish this? (Think about other factual information you might have to obtain to answer his questions.)

c. How, if at all, would your analysis change if the U.S. citizen in this problem were the mother, not the father?

c. Gender Discrimination and *Jus Sanguinis*

In addition to requirements of physical presence in the United States, the *jus sanguinis* statutes have had, and continue to have, gender-based elements. Frequently these rules have disadvantaged women, sometimes they have a discriminatory impact on men. Until 1934, federal statutes explicitly discriminated against women by allowing the transmission of citizenship *jure sanguinis* only by U.S. citizen fathers, not by U.S. citizen mothers.

This was but one form of gender discrimination in citizenship law. Congress adopted legislation in 1907 providing that U.S. citizen women who married non-citizen men lost their citizenship for so long as the marriage lasted. The Supreme Court expressly approved the constitutionality of these provisions. *Mackenzie v. Hare*, 239 U.S. 299, 36 S.Ct. 106, 60 L.Ed. 297 (1915) discussed in Section D.2 *infra*. The statute was partially repealed in the 1920s, but the result persisted for some women until 1934. Importantly, the 1920s legislation did not apply to U.S. citizen women who married Asian men ineligible for naturalization; they continued to lose their citizenship upon marriage. Furthermore, women who lost their citizenship through marriage could not regain citizenship under the later law if they were racially ineligible to naturalize.

Unfortunately, although this discriminatory aspect of *jus sanguinis* rules is long gone, its impact lives on. Consider the case of Valerie Wauchope. Wauchope was born in Canada in 1911. Her mother was a U.S. citizen; her father was a Canadian citizen. In 1989, she applied to the State Department for a U.S. passport. If born today, Wauchope would be a U.S. citizen (provided her mother had met the requirements of residence in the United States). But under the rules in place in 1911, she was not a citizen at birth. And when Congress eliminated the gender-based rule in 1934, it did not make the change retroactive. Accordingly, she was denied a passport. Wauchope sued and won. *Wauchope v. U.S. Dep't of State*, 985 F.2d 1407 (9th Cir.1993). The court held that the gender discrimination violated modern equal protection principles in the Fifth Amendment's due process clause, and it ruled that its holding should be applied retroactively—that is, persons who could demonstrate that they would have been citizens prior to 1934 if the *jus sanguinis* rules had been written in gender-neutral terms would be deemed to have acquired U.S. citizenship at birth.

The United States chose not to appeal the court of appeals' decision. (Solicitor General Drew S. Days later explained that the United States did not seek Supreme Court review because it was convinced that the court's decision was "consistent with modern developments in the Supreme Court's jurisprudence concerning statutory distinctions based on gender." Days, *The Solicitor General and the American Legal Ideal*, 49 S.M.U.L.Rev. 73, 81 (1995).) In 1994, Congress accepted the ruling and adopted rules for implementing *Wauchope. See* INA § 301(h). The statute allows the children of the disadvantaged U.S. citizen mothers to take advantage of the retroactive change in the rules. Citizenship can be transmitted to future generations if the first generation mother has met the usual U.S. residence requirements.

In contrast to the *Wauchope* case, most of the more recent *jus sanguinis* litigation attacks statutory provisions that disadvantage men. Section 309 of the INA extends citizenship at birth to a child born out of wedlock outside of the United States to a U.S. citizen mother (provided the mother has at some point been physically present in the U.S. for a continuous period of 1 year); but a child born abroad and out of wedlock to a U.S. citizen father attains citizenship at birth only if a number of additional conditions are met: (1) a blood relationship between the person and the father must be established by clear and convincing evidence; (2) the father must have had U.S. nationality at the time of the child's birth; (3) the father must have agreed in writing to provide financial support until the child reaches 18; and (4) while the child is under 18, (a) he or she must be legitimated under the law of his or her residence or domicile; (b) the father must acknowledge paternity of the child in writing under oath; or (c) the paternity of the child must be established by court adjudication. INA § 309(a).

During the past fifteen years the Supreme Court has reviewed three cases involving children born overseas out of wedlock to U.S. citizen fathers and noncitizen mothers. *Miller v. Albright*, 523 U.S. 420, 118 S.Ct. 1428, 140 L.Ed.2d 575 (1998) (rejecting on justiciability grounds a challenge to requirement of legitimation before child reaches age of 18); *Nguyen v. INS*, 533 U.S. 53, 121 S.Ct. 2053, 150 L.Ed.2d 115 (2001) (requirement that father acknowledges paternity before child reaches 18); *Flores–Villar v. United States*, ___ U.S. ___, 131 S.Ct. 2312, 180 L.Ed.2d 222 (2011). In *Flores–Villar*, the most recent case to reach the Supreme Court, Justice Kagan did not participate, which resulted in a 4–4 split. The per curiam affirmance of the lower court decision upheld the statute's imposition of lengthier U.S. residency requirements on U.S. citizen fathers who wish to transmit citizenship to their out of wedlock children at birth. This leaves Justice Kennedy's *Nguyen* opinion as the most recent Supreme Court analysis of the constitutionality of the legitimation or proof of paternity requirement set forth in § 309(a)(4). Writing for a 5–4 majority,

Justice Kennedy stated that the statutory provision must be substantially related to the achievement of important governmental objectives, in order to prevail under the appropriate standard that applies in equal protection challenges based on gender discrimination. He identified two such objectives:

> The first governmental interest to be served is the importance of assuring that a biological parent-child relationship exists. In the case of the mother, the relation is verifiable from the birth itself. The mother's status is documented in most instances by the birth certificate or hospital records and the witnesses who attest to her having given birth.

> In the case of the father, the uncontestable fact is that he need not be present at the birth. If he is present, furthermore, that circumstance is not incontrovertible proof of fatherhood. Fathers and mothers are not similarly situated with regard to the proof of biological parenthood. The imposition of a different set of rules for making that legal determination with respect to fathers and mothers is neither surprising nor troublesome from a constitutional perspective. Section 309(a)(4)'s provision of three options for a father seeking to establish paternity—legitimation, paternity oath, and court order of paternity—is designed to ensure an acceptable documentation of paternity.

* * *

> The second important governmental interest furthered in a substantial manner by § 309(a)(4) is the determination to ensure that the child and the citizen parent have some demonstrated opportunity or potential to develop not just a relationship that is recognized, as a formal matter, by the law, but one that consists of the real, everyday ties that provide a connection between child and citizen parent and, in turn, the United States. In the case of a citizen mother and a child born overseas, the opportunity for a meaningful relationship between citizen parent and child inheres in the very event of birth, an event so often critical to our constitutional and statutory understandings of citizenship. The mother knows that the child is in being and is hers and has an initial point of contact with him. There is at least an opportunity for mother and child to develop a real, meaningful relationship.

> The same opportunity does not result from the event of birth, as a matter of biological inevitability, in the case of the unwed father. Given the 9–month interval between conception and birth, it is not always certain that a father will know that a child was conceived, nor is it always clear that even the mother will be sure of the father's identity. This fact takes on particular significance in the case of a child born overseas and out of wedlock. One concern in this context has always been with young people, men for the most part, who are on duty with the Armed Forces in foreign countries. *See* Department

of Defense, Selected Manpower Statistics 48, 74 (1999) (reporting that in 1969, the year in which Nguyen was born, there were 3,458,072 active duty military personnel, 39,506 of whom were female); Department of Defense, Selected Manpower Statistics 29 (1970) (noting that 1,041,094 military personnel were stationed in foreign countries in 1969); Department of Defense, Selected Manpower Statistics 49, 76 (1999) (reporting that in 1999 there were 1,385,703 active duty military personnel, 200,287 of whom were female); *id.,* at 33 (noting that 252,763 military personnel were stationed in foreign countries in 1999).

When we turn to the conditions which prevail today, we find that the passage of time has produced additional and even more substantial grounds to justify the statutory distinction. The ease of travel and the willingness of Americans to visit foreign countries have resulted in numbers of trips abroad that must be of real concern when we contemplate the prospect of accepting petitioners' argument, which would mandate, contrary to Congress' wishes, citizenship by male parentage subject to no condition save the father's previous length of residence in this country. In 1999 alone, Americans made almost 25 million trips abroad, excluding trips to Canada and Mexico. Visits to Canada and Mexico add to this figure almost 34 million additional visits. And the average American overseas traveler spent 15.1 nights out of the United States in 1999.

Principles of equal protection do not require Congress to ignore this reality. To the contrary, these facts demonstrate the critical importance of the Government's interest in ensuring some opportunity for a tie between citizen father and foreign born child which is a reasonable substitute for the opportunity manifest between mother and child at the time of birth. Indeed, especially in light of the number of Americans who take short sojourns abroad, the prospect that a father might not even know of the conception is a realistic possibility. Even if a father knows of the fact of conception, moreover, it does not follow that he will be present at the birth of the child. Thus, unlike the case of the mother, there is no assurance that the father and his biological child will ever meet. Without an initial point of contact with the child by a father who knows the child is his own, there is no opportunity for father and child to begin a relationship. Section 309 takes the unremarkable step of ensuring that such an opportunity, inherent in the event of birth as to the mother-child relationship, exists between father and child before citizenship is conferred upon the latter.

Justice Kennedy then turned to the question of whether the means chosen by Congress were substantially related to these governmental objectives. He concluded that they met the constitutional standard:

First, it should be unsurprising that Congress decided to require that an opportunity for a parent-child relationship occur during the formative years of the child's minority. In furtherance of the desire to ensure some tie between this country and one who seeks citizenship, various other statutory provisions concerning citizenship and naturalization require some act linking the child to the United States to occur before the child reaches 18 years of age. *See, e.g.,* INA § 320 (child born abroad to one citizen parent and one noncitizen parent shall become a citizen if, *inter alia*, the noncitizen parent is naturalized before the child reaches 18 years of age and the child begins to reside in the United States before he or she turns 18); § 321 (imposing same conditions in the case of a child born abroad to two alien parents who are naturalized).

Second, petitioners argue that § 309(a)(4) is not effective. In particular, petitioners assert that, although a mother will know of her child's birth, "knowledge that one is a parent, no matter how it is acquired, does not guarantee a relationship with one's child." Brief for Petitioners 16. They thus maintain that the imposition of the additional requirements of § 309(a)(4) only on the children of citizen fathers must reflect a stereotype that women are more likely than men to actually establish a relationship with their children. *Id.* at 17.

This line of argument misconceives the nature of both the governmental interest at issue and the manner in which we examine statutes alleged to violate equal protection. As to the former, Congress would of course be entitled to advance the interest of ensuring an actual, meaningful relationship in every case before citizenship is conferred. Or Congress could excuse compliance with the formal requirements when an actual father-child relationship is proved. It did neither here, perhaps because of the subjectivity, intrusiveness, and difficulties of proof that might attend an inquiry into any particular bond or tie. Instead, Congress enacted an easily administered scheme to promote the different but still substantial interest of ensuring at least an opportunity for a parent-child relationship to develop. Petitioners' argument confuses the means and ends of the equal protection inquiry; § 309(a)(4) should not be invalidated because Congress elected to advance an interest that is less demanding to satisfy than some other alternative.

Justice O'Connor, joined by Justices Souter, Ginsburg and Breyer, dissented:

The gravest defect in the Court's [analysis of the first governmental objective] is the insufficiency of the fit between § 309(a)(4)'s discriminatory means and the asserted end. Section 309(c) imposes no particular burden of proof on mothers wishing to convey citizenship to their children. By contrast, § 309(a)(1), which petitioners do not challenge before this Court, requires that "a blood relationship between the person and the father [be] established by clear and convincing evidence." Atop § 309(a)(1), § 309(a)(4) requires legitimation, an acknowledgment of paternity in writing under oath, or an adjudication of paternity before the child reaches the age of 18. It is difficult to see what § 309(a)(4) accomplishes in furtherance of "assuring that a biological parent-child relationship exists," that § 309(a)(1) does not achieve on its own. The virtual certainty of a biological link that modern DNA testing affords reinforces the sufficiency of § 309(a)(1).

* * *

The majority concedes that Congress could achieve the goal of assuring a biological parent-child relationship in a sex-neutral fashion, but then, in a surprising turn, dismisses the availability of sex-neutral alternatives as irrelevant. As the Court suggests, "Congress could have required both mothers and fathers to prove parenthood within 30 days or, for that matter, 18 years, of the child's birth." Indeed, whether one conceives the majority's asserted interest as assuring the existence of a biological parent-child relationship, or as ensuring acceptable documentation of that relationship, a number of sex-neutral arrangements—including the one that the majority offers—would better serve that end. As the majority seems implicitly to acknowledge at one point, a mother will not always have formal legal documentation of birth because a birth certificate may not issue or may subsequently be lost. Conversely, a father's name may well appear on a birth certificate. While it is doubtless true that a mother's blood relation to a child is uniquely "verifiable from the birth itself" to those present at birth, the majority has not shown that a mother's birth relation is uniquely verifiable *by the INS*, much less that any greater verifiability warrants a sex-based, rather than a sex-neutral, statute.

* * *

Assuming, as the majority does, that Congress was actually concerned about ensuring a "demonstrated opportunity" for a relationship, it is questionable whether such an opportunity qualifies as an "important" governmental interest apart from the existence of an actual relationship. By focusing on "opportunity" rather than reality, the majority presumably improves the chances of a sufficient means-end fit. But in doing so, it dilutes significantly the weight of the interest. It is difficult to see how, in this citizenship-conferral context, anyone profits from a "demonstrated opportunity" for a relationship in the absence of the fruition of an actual tie. Children who have an "opportunity" for such a tie with a parent, of course, may never develop an actual relationship with that parent. If a child grows up in a foreign country without any postbirth contact with the citizen parent, then the child's never-realized "opportunity" for a relationship with the citizen seems singularly irrelevant to the appropriateness of granting citizenship to that child. Likewise, where there is an actual relationship, it is the actual relationship that does all the work in rendering appropriate a grant of citizenship, regardless of when and how the opportunity for that relationship arose.

Accepting for the moment the majority's focus on "opportunity," the attempt to justify § 309(a)(4) in these terms is still deficient. Even if it is important "to require that an opportunity for a parent-child relationship occur during the formative years of the child's minority," it is difficult to see how the requirement that *proof* of such opportunity be obtained before the child turns 18 substantially furthers the asserted interest. As the facts of this case demonstrate, it is entirely possible that a father and child will have the opportunity to develop a relationship and in fact will develop a relationship without obtaining the proof of the opportunity during the child's minority.

* * *

Moreover, available sex-neutral alternatives would at least replicate, and could easily exceed, whatever fit there is between § 309(a)(4)'s discriminatory means and the majority's asserted end. According to the Court, § 309(a)(4) is designed to ensure that fathers and children have the same "opportunity which the event of birth itself provides for the mother and child." Even assuming that this is so, Congress could simply substitute for § 309(a)(4) a requirement that the parent be present at birth or have knowledge of birth. Congress could at least allow proof of such presence or knowledge to be one way of demonstrating an opportunity for a relationship. Under the present law, the statute on its face accords different treatment to a mother who is by nature present at birth and a father who is by choice present at birth even though those two individuals are similarly situated with respect to the "opportunity" for a relationship. The mother can transmit her citizenship at birth, but the father cannot do so in the absence of at least one other affirmative act. The different statutory treatment is solely on account of the sex of the similarly situated individuals. This type of treatment is patently inconsistent with the promise of equal protection of the laws.

Indeed, the idea that a mother's presence at birth supplies adequate assurance of an opportunity to develop a relationship while a father's presence at birth does not would appear to rest only on an overbroad sex-based generalization. A mother may not have an opportunity for a relationship if the child is removed from his or her mother on account of alleged abuse or neglect, or if the child and mother are separated by tragedy, such as disaster or war, of the sort apparently present in this case. There is no reason, other than stereotype, to say that fathers who are present at birth lack an opportunity for a relationship on similar terms. The "[p]hysical differences between men and women," *Virginia*, 518 U.S., at 533, therefore do not justify § 309(a)(4)'s discrimination.

* * *

The question that then remains is the sufficiency of the fit between § 309(a)(4)'s discriminatory means and the goal of "establish[ing] . . . a real, practical relationship of considerable substance." If Congress wishes to advance this end, it could easily do so by employing a sex-neutral classification that is a far "more germane bas[i]s of classification" than sex, *Craig* [*v. Boren*, 429 U.S. 190, 198 (1976)]. For example, Congress could require some degree of regular contact between the child and the citizen parent over a period of time.

NOTES AND QUESTIONS ON GENDER DISTINCTIONS AND JUS SANGUINIS

1. In a brief to the Supreme Court in an *Miller v. Albright*, 523 U.S. 420, 118 S.Ct. 1428, 140 L.Ed.2d 575 (1998), the government argued for "deference to congressional decisions concerning immigration and naturalization"—asserting that "policies toward the admission to this country, and most especially to full citizenship therein, of those not born here are uniquely political in character, dealing as they do with the threshold question of who is entitled to any share in the benefits, protections, and responsibilities of the democratic compact that the Constitution represents." Brief for the Respondent, at 22–23. (The Court in *Nguyen* didn't reach this issue because it concluded that the statute met the higher standard generally applied to gender-based distinctions.)

2. Does the fact that a statute regulates the distribution of citizenship call for a lower level of scrutiny? Or, does the importance of citizenship argue in favor of a higher standard?

3. Should usual norms regarding gender discrimination be relaxed in the face of regulations of citizenship and immigration? Is it relevant that prior to *Craig v. Boren*, 429 U.S. 190, 97 S.Ct. 451, 50 L.Ed.2d 397 (1976) the Supreme Court applied rational basis scrutiny to all gender discrimination claims?

EXERCISE

Assume that the President has decided that the gender discrimination should be purged from U.S. citizenship statutes. The Secretary of State has been instructed to draft gender-neutral revisions to the INA. You are an attorney in the Office of Legal Adviser in the State Department, and the Secretary of State has turned to you to eliminate the gender bias in § 309.

Note that simply eliminating § 309 would mean that nonmarital children would be granted equal treatment with marital children under § 301(g) but that U.S. citizen mothers of nonmarital children born overseas would be worse off than they are under § 309 (why?). But to give U.S. citizen fathers of non-marital children equal treatment with U.S. mothers under § 309 would give the parents of non-marital children advantages over U.S. citizen parents of marital children born overseas (under § 301(g)).

> Prepare a draft of a gender-neutral statute, accompanied by an explanatory note that details how and why your proposal changes existing law. Would you make the changes retrospective in operation? If so, could second and third generation descendants claim citizenship?

2. *JUS SOLI*

As noted earlier, the *jus soli* principle is an important part of Anglo–American nationality laws, but the original Constitution of the United States did not define citizenship or the means of transmitting it. And though Congress enacted legislation in 1790 providing for naturalization of noncitizens in the United States and extending citizenship at birth to certain children born abroad, the early Congress did not define citizenship for persons born in the United States. This left the question of the citizenship of Indians, slaves, free blacks, and the children of immigrants to the various answers of the states and the courts. *See* J. Kettner, The Development of American Citizenship, 1608–1870 (1978). The Supreme Court's attempt to solve the problem of the definition of U.S. citizenship— Chief Justice Taney's opinion in the *Dred Scott* case (holding that free blacks born in the U.S. were not citizens of the United States)—had tragic results, and ultimately occasioned legislative and constitutional change.

Congress acted quickly after the end of the Civil War to remove the stain of *Dred Scott*. The 1866 Civil Rights Act provided that "all persons born in the United States and not subject to any foreign power, excluding Indians not taxed, are hereby declared to be citizens of the United States." Act of Apr. 9, 1866, § 1, Ch. 31, 14 Stat. 27. Two years later, it wrote the definition of citizenship into the first sentence of the first section of the Fourteenth Amendment, thereby putting it beyond the power of shifting legislative majorities to alter. It reads: "All persons born or naturalized in the United States, and subject to the jurisdiction thereof, are citizens of the United States and of the State wherein they reside."

Citizenship based on birth in the national territory is now rooted in the Constitution, but the constitutional text includes limiting language: persons must be "subject to the jurisdiction" of the United States. The Supreme Court's first holding on the subject suggested that the court would give a restrictive reading to the phrase, potentially disqualifying significant numbers of persons born within the physical boundaries of the nation. In *Elk v. Wilkins,* 112 U.S. 94, 5 S.Ct. 41, 28 L.Ed. 643 (1884), the Court ruled that native Indians were not U.S. citizens, even if they later severed their ties with their tribes. The words "subject to the jurisdiction thereof," the Court held, mean "not merely subject in some respect or degree to the jurisdiction of the United States, but completely subject to their political jurisdiction, and owing them direct and immediate allegiance." Most Indians could not meet the test. "Indians born within the territorial limits of the United States, members of, and owing immediate allegiance to, one of the Indian tribes, (an alien though dependent power,) although in a geographical sense born in the United States, are no more 'born in the United States and subject to the jurisdiction thereof,' * * * than the children of subjects of any foreign government born within the domain of that government * * *." *Id.* at 102.

Congress eventually passed legislation overcoming the direct effects of this holding. The Allotment Act of 1887 conferred citizenship on many Indians who resided in the United States, and later statutes expanded the scope of the grant. Since at least 1940 (and possibly since 1924—the application of the statute enacted that year to Indians born thereafter was unclear), all Indians born in the United States are U.S. citizens at birth. *See* INA § 301(b); GM & Y § 92.03[3][e].

But in the meantime, the years following *Elk* saw the tightening of federal laws that excluded most Chinese immigrants from the United States. (Chapter Three will consider these Chinese exclusion laws in greater detail.) The question arose whether children born in the United States to Chinese parents would be citizens under *Elk*'s reading of the Fourteenth Amendment. After all, opponents of such citizenship pointed out, Chinese had always been excluded from naturalization.[2] As Section C of this chapter will explain, the original naturalization laws opened citizenship only to "free white persons." In 1870, in the wake of the Civil War, Congress extended naturalization eligibility to "persons of African nativity, or African descent." Western Hemisphere natives were included in 1940. Not until 1943 were Chinese made eligible for naturalization—a somewhat belated token of support extended to a World War II ally.

The Chinese exclusion laws themselves restated this racial bar to naturalization. Did the impossibility of their parents obtaining U.S. citizenship also somehow render such persons not subject to the jurisdiction of the United States, within the meaning of the Fourteenth Amendment, at the time of their birth?

The Supreme Court's answer came in a case involving Wong Kim Ark, who had been born in San Francisco to Chinese parents who had taken up residence in this country under treaties that initially had encouraged such migration. Excluded from entry in 1895 on returning from a brief visit to China, Wong Kim Ark claimed a right to admission as a citizen, based on the locus of his birth.

---

2. Only in 1952 were all racial and national origin bars eliminated from the naturalization laws. INA § 311. *See generally* GM & Y §§ 94.01[2], 94.03[5].

Wong Kim Ark, from the file in his habeas corpus case in the U.S. district court in San Francisco. (Photo: National Archives)

UNITED STATES v. WONG KIM ARK

Supreme Court of the United States, 1898.
169 U.S. 649, 18 S.Ct. 456, 42 L.Ed. 890.

MR. JUSTICE GRAY, after stating the case, delivered the opinion of the court.

The facts of this case, as agreed by the parties, are as follows: Wong Kim Ark was born in 1873 in the city of San Francisco, in the state of

California and United States of America, and was and is a laborer. * * * Wong Kim Ark, ever since his birth, has had but one residence, to wit, in California * * * * * In 1890 (when he must have been about 17 years of age) he departed for China on a temporary visit and with the intention of returning to the United States, and did return thereto by sea in the same year * * *.

* * *

The question presented by the record is whether a child born in the United States, of parents of Chinese descent, who, at the time of his birth are subjects of the Emperor of China, but have a permanent domicil and residence in the United States, and are there carrying on business, and are not employed in any diplomatic or official capacity under the Emperor of China, becomes at the time of his birth a citizen of the United States, by virtue of the first clause of the Fourteenth Amendment of the Constitution: "All persons born or naturalized in the United States, and subject to the jurisdiction thereof, are citizens of the United States and of the state wherein they reside."

* * *

II.   The fundamental principle of the common law with regard to English nationality was birth within the allegiance, also called "ligealty," "obedience," "faith," or "power," of the King. The principle embraced all persons born within the King's allegiance and subject to his protection. Such allegiance and protection were mutual—as expressed in the maxim, "protectio trahit subjectionem, et subjectio protectionem"—and were not restricted to natural-born subjects and naturalized subjects, or to those who had taken an oath of allegiance; but were predicable of aliens in amity, so long as they were within the kingdom. Children, born in England, of such aliens, were therefore natural-born subjects. But the children, born within the realm, of foreign ambassadors, or the children of alien enemies, born during and within their hostile occupation of part of the King's dominions, were not natural-born subjects, because not born within the allegiance, the obedience, or the power, or, as would be said at this day, within the jurisdiction, of the King.

* * *

III.   The same rule was in force in all the English Colonies upon this continent down to the time of the Declaration of Independence, and in the United States afterwards, and continued to prevail under the Constitution as originally established.

* * *

The Supreme Judicial Court of Massachusetts, speaking by Mr. Justice (afterwards Chief Justice) Sewall, early held that the determination of the question whether a man was a citizen or an alien was "to be governed altogether by the principles of the common law," and that it was established, with few exceptions, "that a man, born within the jurisdiction of the common law, is a citizen of the country wherein he is born. By this circumstance of his birth, he is subjected to the duty of allegiance which is claimed and enforced by the sovereign of his native land; and becomes reciprocally entitled to the protection of that sovereign, and to the other rights and advantages which are included in the term 'citizenship.' " *Gardner v. Ward*, (1805) 2 Mass. 244, note. * * *

That all children, born within the dominion of the United States, of foreign parents holding no diplomatic office, became citizens at the time of their birth, does not appear to have been contested or doubted until more than 50 years after the adoption of the Constitution, when the matter was elaborately argued in the Court of Chancery of New York, and decided upon full consideration by Vice Chancellor Sandford in favor of their citizenship. *Lynch v. Clarke*, (1844) 1 Sandf. Ch. 583.

The same doctrine was repeatedly affirmed in the executive departments[.]

* * *

IV.   It was contended by one of the learned counsel for the United States that the rule of the Roman law, by which the citizenship of the child followed that of the parent, was the true rule of international law as now recognized in most civilized countries, and had superseded the rule of the common law, depending on birth within the realm, originally founded on feudal considerations.

But at the time of the adoption of the Constitution of the United States in 1789, and long before, it would seem to have been the rule in Europe generally, as it certainly was in France, that, as said by Pothier, "citizens, true and native-born citizens, are those who are born within the extent of the dominion of France," and "mere birth within the realm gives the rights of a native-born citizen, independently of the origin of the father or mother, and of their domicil[.]" * * *

The later modifications of the rule in Europe rest upon the constitutions, laws or ordinances of the various countries, and have no important bearing upon the interpretation and effect of the Constitution of the United States. * * *

There is, therefore, little ground for the theory that, at the time of the adoption of the Fourteenth Amendment of the Constitution of the United States, there was any settled and definite rule of international law, generally recognized by civilized nations, inconsistent with the ancient rule of citizenship by birth within the dominion.

* * *

V.   In the fore front, both of the Fourteenth Amendment of the Constitution, and of the Civil Rights Act of 1866, the fundamental principle of citizenship by birth within the dominion was reaffirmed in the most explicit and comprehensive terms.

The Civil Rights Act, passed at the first session of the Thirty-ninth Congress, began by enacting that "all persons born in the United States, and not subject to any foreign power, excluding Indians not taxed, are hereby declared to be citizens of the United States; * * *." Act April 9, 1866, c. 31, § 1; 14 Stat. 27.

The same Congress, shortly afterwards, evidently thinking it unwise, and perhaps unsafe, to leave so important a declaration of rights to depend upon an ordinary act of legislation, which might be repealed by any subsequent Congress, framed the Fourteenth Amendment of the Constitution, and on June 16, 1866, by joint resolution, proposed it to the legislatures of the several States; and on July 28, 1868, the Secretary of State issued a proclamation showing it to have been ratified by the legislatures of the requisite number of States. 14 Stat. 358; 15 Stat. 708.

The first section of the Fourteenth Amendment of the Constitution begins with the words, "All persons born or naturalized in the United States, and subject to the jurisdiction thereof, are citizens of the United States and of the State wherein they reside." As appears upon the face of the amendment, as well as from the history of the times, this was not intended to impose any new restrictions upon citizenship, or to prevent any persons from becoming citizens by the fact of birth within the United States, who would thereby have become citizens according to the law existing before its adoption. It is declaratory in form, and enabling and extending in effect. Its main purpose doubtless was, as has been often recognized by this court, to establish the citizenship of free negroes, which had been denied in the opinion delivered by Chief Justice Taney in *Dred Scott v. Sandford*, (1857) 19 How. 393; and to put it beyond doubt that all blacks, as well as whites, born or naturalized within the jurisdiction of the United States, are citizens of the United States. *The Slaughter House Cases*, (1873) 16 Wall. 36, 73. But the opening words, "All persons born," are general, not to say universal, restricted only by place and jurisdiction, and not by color or race—as was clearly recognized in all the opinions delivered in the *The Slaughter House Cases*, above cited.

* * *

The only adjudication that has been made by this court upon the meaning of the clause "and subject to the jurisdiction thereof," in the leading provision of the Fourteenth Amendment, is *Elk v. Wilkins*, 112 U. S. 94, 5 Sup. Ct. 41, in which it was decided that an Indian born a member of one of the Indian tribes within the United States, which still existed and was recognized as an Indian tribe by the United States, who had voluntarily separated himself from his tribe, and taken up his residence among the white citizens of a state, but who did not appear to have been naturalized, or taxed, or in any way recognized or treated as a citizen, either by the United States or by the State, was not a citizen of the United States, as a person born in the United States, "and subject to the jurisdiction thereof," within the meaning of the clause in question.

That decision was placed upon the grounds, that the meaning of those words was "not merely subject in some respect or degree to the jurisdiction of the United States, but completely subject to their political jurisdiction, and owing them direct and immediate allegiance"; that by the Constitution, as originally established, "Indians not taxed" were excluded from the persons according to whose numbers representatives in Congress and direct taxes were apportioned among the several states, and Congress was empowered to regulate commerce, not only "with foreign nations," and among the several States, but "with the Indian tribes"; that the Indian tribes, being within the territorial limits of the United States, were not, strictly speaking, foreign States, but were alien nations, distinct political communities, the members of which owed immediate allegiance to their several tribes, and were not part of the people of the United States; that the alien and dependent condition of the members of one of those tribes could not be put off at their own will, without the action or assent of the United States; and that they were never deemed citizens, except when naturalized, collectively or individually, under explicit provisions of a treaty, or of an act of Congress; and, therefore, that "Indians born within the territorial limits of the United States, members of, and owing immediate allegiance to, one of the Indian tribes (an alien, though dependent, power), although in a geographical sense born in the United States, are no more 'born in the United States, and subject to the jurisdiction thereof,' " within the meaning of the first section of the Fourteenth Amendment, than the children of subjects of any foreign government born within the domain of that government, or the children born within the United States of ambassadors or other public ministers of foreign nations. And it was observed that the language used, in defining citizenship, in the first section of the Civil Rights Act of 1866, by the very Congress which framed the Fourteenth Amendment, was "all persons born in the United States, and not subject to any foreign power, excluding Indians not taxed." 112 U. S. 99–103, 5 Sup. Ct. 44–46.

Mr. Justice Harlan and Mr. Justice Woods, dissenting, were of opinion that the Indian in question, having severed himself from his tribe and become a *bona fide* resident of a State, had thereby become subject to the jurisdiction of the United States, within the meaning of the Fourteenth Amendment; and, in reference to the Civil Rights Act of 1866, said: "Beyond question, by that act, national citizenship was conferred directly upon all persons in this country, of whatever race (excluding only 'Indians not taxed'), who were born within the territorial limits of the United States, and were not subject to any foreign power." And that view was supported by reference to the debates in the Senate upon that act, and to the ineffectual veto thereof by President Johnson, in which he said: "By the first section of the bill, all persons born in the United States, and not subject to any foreign power, excluding Indians not taxed, are declared to be citizens of the United States. This provision comprehends the Chinese of the Pacific States, Indians subject to taxation, the people called Gypsies, as well as the entire race designated as blacks, persons of color, negroes, mulattoes, and persons of African blood. Every individual of those races, born in the United States, is, by the bill, made a citizen of the United States." 112 U. S. 112–114, 5 Sup. Ct. 51, 52.

The decision in *Elk v. Wilkins* concerned only members of the Indian tribes within the United States, and had no tendency to deny citizenship to children born in the United States of foreign parents of Caucasian, African, or Mongolian descent, not in the diplomatic service of a foreign country.

The real object of the Fourteenth Amendment of the Constitution, in qualifying the words "all persons born in the United States" by the addition "and subject to the jurisdiction thereof," would appear to have been to exclude, by the fewest and fittest words (besides children of members of the Indian tribes, standing in a peculiar relation to the national government, unknown to the common law,) the two classes of cases—children born of alien enemies in hostile occupation, and children of diplomatic representatives of a foreign state—both of which, as has already been shown, by the law of England, and by our own law, from the time of the first settlement of the English Colonies in America, had been recognized exceptions to the fundamental rule of citizenship by birth within the country.

* * *

The foregoing considerations and authorities irresistibly lead us to these conclusions: The Fourteenth Amendment affirms the ancient and fundamental rule of citizenship by birth within the territory, in the allegiance and under the protection of the country, including all children here born of resident aliens, with the exceptions or qualifications (as old as the rule itself) of children of foreign sovereigns or their ministers, or born on foreign public ships, or of enemies within and during a hostile occupation of part of our territory, and with the single additional exception of children of members of the Indian tribes owing direct allegiance to their several tribes. The Amendment, in clear words and in manifest intent, includes the children born within the territory of the United States, of all other persons, of whatever race or color, domiciled within the United States. Every citizen or subject of another country, while domiciled here, is within the allegiance and the protection, and consequently subject to the jurisdiction, of the United States. His allegiance to the United States is direct and immediate, and, although but local and temporary, continuing only so long as he remains within our territory, is yet, in the words of Lord Coke in *Calvin's Case*, 7 Rep. 6a, "strong enough to make a natural subject, for, if he hath issue here, that issue is a natural-born subject"; and his child, * * * "If born in the country, is as much a citizen as the natural-born child of a citizen, and by operation of the same principle." It can hardly be denied that an alien is completely subject to the political jurisdiction of the country in which he resides—seeing that, as said by Mr. Webster, when Secretary of State, in his Report to the President on *Thrasher's Case* in 1851, and since repeated by this court,

"Independently of a residence with intention to continue such residence; independently of any domiciliation; independently of the taking of any oath of allegiance or of renouncing any former allegiance, it is well known that, by the public law, an alien, or a stranger born, for so long a time as he continues within the dominions of a foreign government, owes obedience to the laws of that government, and may be punished for treason, or other crimes, as a native-born subject might be, unless his case is varied by some treaty stipulations."

To hold that the Fourteenth Amendment of the Constitution excludes from citizenship the children, born in the United States, of citizens or subjects of other countries, would be to deny citizenship to thousands of persons of English, Scotch, Irish, German or other European parentage, who have always been considered and treated as citizens of the United States.

VI. * * * It is true that Chinese persons born in China cannot be naturalized, like other aliens, by proceedings under the naturalization laws. But this is for want of any statute or treaty authorizing or permitting such naturalization, as will appear by tracing the history of the statutes, treaties, and decisions upon that subject—always bearing in mind that statutes enacted by Congress, as well as treaties made by the President and Senate, must yield to the paramount and supreme law of the Constitution.

* * *

The power of naturalization, vested in Congress by the Constitution, is a power to confer citizenship, not a power to take it away. * * * Congress having no power to abridge the rights conferred by the Constitution upon those who have become naturalized citizens by virtue of acts of Congress, *a fortiori* no act or omission of Congress, as to providing for the naturalization of parents or children of a particular race, can affect citizenship acquired as a birthright, by virtue of the Constitution itself, without any aid of legislation. The Fourteenth Amendment, while it leaves the power, where it was before, in Congress, to regulate naturalization, has conferred no authority upon Congress to restrict the effect of birth, declared by the Constitution to constitute a sufficient and complete right to citizenship.

* * *

The fact, therefore, that acts of Congress or treaties have not permitted Chinese persons born out of this country to become citizens by naturalization, cannot exclude Chinese persons born in this country from the operation of the broad and clear words of the constitution: "All persons born in the United States, and subject to the jurisdiction thereof, are citizens of the United States."

* * *

MR. JUSTICE MCKENNA, not having been a member of the court when this case was argued, took no part in the decision.

MR. CHIEF JUSTICE FULLER, with whom concurred MR. JUSTICE HARLAN, dissenting.

I cannot concur in the opinion and judgment of the court in this case.

* * *

The framers of the Constitution were familiar with the distinctions between the Roman law and the feudal law, between obligations based on territoriality and those based on the personal and invisible character of origin, and there is nothing to show that in the matter of nationality they intended to adhere to principles derived from regal government, which they had just assisted in overthrowing.

Manifestly, when the sovereignty of the Crown was thrown off, and an independent government established, every rule of the common law, and every statute of England obtaining in the Colonies, in derogation of the principles on which the new government was founded, was abrogated.

* * * [C]ongress has persisted from 1795 in rejecting the English rule, and in requiring the alien, who would become a citizen of the United States, in taking on himself the ties binding him to our Government, to affirmatively sever the ties that bound him to any other.

* * *

[I]n *Elk v. Wilkins*, 112 U. S. 94, 5 Sup. Ct. 41, where the subject received great consideration, and it was said:

"By the Thirteenth Amendment of the Constitution, slavery was prohibited. The main object of the opening sentence of the Fourteenth Amendment was to settle the question, upon which there had been a difference of opinion throughout the country and in this court, as to the citizenship of free negroes, *Scott v. Sandford*, 19 How. 393; and to put it beyond doubt that all persons, white or black, and whether formerly slaves or not, born or naturalized in the United States, *and owing no allegiance to any alien power*, should be citizens of the United States, and of the State in which they reside. *Slaughter–House Cases*, 16 Wall. 36, 73.

"This section contemplates two sources of citizenship, and two sources only: birth and naturalization. The persons declared to be citizens are 'all persons born or naturalized in the United States, and subject to the jurisdiction thereof.' The evident meaning of these last words is, not merely subject in some respect or degree to the jurisdiction of the United States, *but completely subject to their political jurisdiction*, and owing them *direct and immediate allegiance*. And the words relate to the time of birth in the one case, as they do to the time of naturalization in the other. *Persons not thus subject to the jurisdiction of the United States at the time of birth* cannot become so afterwards, except by being naturalized, either individually, as by proceedings under the naturalization acts, or collectively, as by the force of a treaty by which foreign territory is acquired."

To be "completely subject" to the political jurisdiction of the United States is to be in no respect or degree subject to the political jurisdiction of any other government.

Now, I take it that the children of aliens, whose parents have not only not renounced their allegiance to their native country, but are forbidden by its system of government, as well as by its positive laws, from doing so, and are not permitted to acquire another citizenship by the laws of the country into which they come, must necessarily remain themselves subject to the same sovereignty as their parents, and cannot, in the nature of things, be, any more than their parents, completely subject to the jurisdiction of such other country.

* * *

These considerations lead to the conclusion that the rule in respect of citizenship of the United States prior to the Fourteenth Amendment differed from the English common law rule in vital particulars, and, among others, in that it did not recognize allegiance as indelible, and in that it did recognize an essential difference between birth during temporary, and birth during permanent, residence. If children born in the United States were deemed presumptively and generally citizens, this was not so when they were born of aliens whose residence was merely temporary, either in fact, or in point of law.

Did the Fourteenth Amendment impose the original English common law rule as a rigid rule on this country?

* * *

"Born in the United States, and subject to the jurisdiction thereof," and "naturalized in the United States, and subject to the jurisdiction thereof," mean born or naturalized under such circumstances as to be completely subject to that jurisdiction, that is, as completely as citizens of the United States who are of course not subject to any foreign power, and can of right claim the exercise of the power of the United States on their behalf wherever they may be. When, then, children are born the United States to the subjects of a foreign power, with which it is agreed by treaty that they shall not be naturalized thereby, and as to whom our own law forbids them to be naturalized, such children are not born so subject to the jurisdiction as to become citizens, and entitled on that ground to the interposition of our Government, if they happen to be found in the country of their parents' origin and allegiance, or any other.

* * *

In other words, the Fourteenth Amendment does not exclude from citizenship by birth children born in the United States of parents permanently located therein, and who might themselves become citizens; nor, on the other hand, does it arbitrarily make citizens of children born in the

United States of parents who, according to the will of their native Government and of this government, are and must remain aliens.

Tested by this rule, Wong Kim Ark never became and is not a citizen of the United States, and the order of the district court should be reversed.

I am authorized to say that MR. JUSTICE HARLAN concurs in this dissent.

———————

NOTES AND QUESTIONS ON WONG KIM ARK

1. Consider *Wong Kim Ark* in its historical context. Two years earlier, the Supreme Court has placed its imprimatur on state-enforced segregation of the races by upholding a Jim Crow law in *Plessy v. Ferguson*, 163 U.S. 537, 16 S.Ct. 1138, 41 L.Ed. 256 (1896). America was on the verge of Empire, annexing Hawaii in 1898, occupying Cuba in the same year, and taking the Philippines and Puerto Rico from Spain under the terms of the 1899 Treaty of Paris. A renewed Anglo–Saxonism in the United States viewed the residents of these new possessions as generally unfit for full American citizenship. In this climate, a number of leading law professors of the day lent a hand in developing legal theories that would deny citizenship to children born to Chinese, and the Justice Department gave full support to that effort. (The full story of this background is set forth in Salyer, Wong Kim Ark: *The Contest Over Birthright Citizenship*, in Immigration Stories 51–85 (D. Martin & P. Schuck eds. 2005).) Against this background, the Court's holding in *Wong Kim Ark* is worthy of note. What accounts for its conclusion? Might the Court's recognition that reaching a contrary result "would be to deny citizenship to thousands of persons of English, Scotch, Irish, German or other European parentage, who have always been considered and treated as citizens of the United States" have something to do with it?

2. Justice John Marshall Harlan, who penned the famous dissent in *Plessy v. Ferguson*, joined Chief Justice Fuller's dissent in *Wong Kim Ark*. How does one reconcile Harlan's attack on Jim Crow as a denial of equal citizenship with the conclusion of the dissent in *Wong Kim Ark* that the government has the power "notwithstanding the Fourteenth Amendment, to prescribe that all persons of a particular race, or their children, cannot become citizens"? *See* Chin, *The* Plessy *Myth: Justice Harlan and the Chinese Cases*, 82 Iowa L.Rev. 151 (1996).

3. Some of the language of the majority opinion in *Wong Kim Ark* seemed to leave open the status of children born within the United States to noncitizen parents only temporarily present within the national borders. What about children born to unauthorized migrants? Does the reasoning in the opinion require lawful presence before *jus soli* applies? Lawful and permanent presence? In fact, the decision has served to establish for the United States a general rule of citizenship by birth: birth in the territorial United States, even to tourists and undocumented migrants, results in U.S. citizenship. The only exceptions to this *jus soli* rule are exceedingly narrow:

birth to foreign sovereigns and accredited diplomatic officials;[3] birth on foreign public vessels—meaning essentially warships, not commercial vessels—even while they are located in U.S. territorial waters (we wonder: does this ever happen?); birth to alien enemies in hostile occupation of a portion of U.S. territory. *See* GM & Y § 92.03[3][d].

4. Special considerations may apply, however, in determining the effect of birth in an outlying territory of the United States. The issue is whether birth there results in full citizenship or only in status as a noncitizen national. Care must be taken to consult the relevant rules in effect for the particular territory at the time of the birth, and, if full citizenship was not granted, to track later developments affecting the status of the territory and its inhabitants. Filipinos, for example, were noncitizen nationals of the United States from 1899 to 1946, but lost their status as U.S. nationals when the Philippines became independent in 1946. In the early 1990s several deportation respondents from the Philippines defended on the basis that they were U.S. citizens, because their parents, born in the Philippines while it was a U.S. territory, were born "in the United States, and subject to the jurisdiction thereof" within the meaning of the Fourteenth Amendment. The Ninth Circuit rejected the claim, over a vigorous dissent. *Rabang v. INS*, 35 F.3d 1449 (9th Cir.1994).

5. Sometimes the governing rules, in light of intervening changes in the political status of the territory, can be exceedingly complex. *See* GM & Y § 92.04. As of today, the regular *jus soli* rules are in effect in all territories except American Samoa and Swains Island—meaning that children now born in any U.S. territorial possessions except those two become full citizens at birth.

Children of Unauthorized Migrants and Temporary Lawful Visitors

Are children born to unauthorized migrants in the United States citizens at birth? Following the reasoning of *Wong Kim Ark*, it has usually been assumed so. But in 1985, Professors Peter Schuck and Rogers Smith authored a book entitled *Citizenship Without Consent: Illegal Aliens in the American Polity*, which argued that *Wong Kim Ark* had not settled the question. They asserted that, properly read, "the Fourteenth Amendment's Citizenship Clause makes birthright citizenship for the children of illegal and temporary visitor aliens a matter of congressional choice rather than of constitutional prescription." *Id*. at 5. Schuck and Smith found room for congressional action in the Fourteenth Amendment's language that only persons "subject to the jurisdiction" of the United States are citizens at birth. According to the authors, this phrase limiting birthright citizenship is grounded in a "consensualist" understanding of citizenship.

A new dimension to the *jus soli* birthright citizenship debate came to the fore after Yaser Hamdi, captured by U.S. forces in Afghanistan in 2001

---

3. Birth on U.S. soil to a diplomat does entitle the child to permanent resident status in the United States, subject to certain administrative requirements. *See Nikoi v. Attorney General*, 939 F.2d 1065 (D.C.Cir.1991) (holding that absences of 11 and 16 years, though begun while the petitioners were minors, resulted in abandonment of resident status).

and held as an enemy combatant at the U.S. Naval Base at Guantánamo Bay, Cuba, disclosed that he had been born in Louisiana to parents from Saudi Arabia who were lawfully present on student visas. At the age of three, Hamdi had left the United States with his parents and had never returned. Based on his birth on U.S. soil, the U.S. government treated him as a U.S. citizen and transferred him to a military prison within the United States, from which he successfully filed a habeas corpus action to challenge his detention, *Hamdi v. Rumsfeld,* 542 U.S. 507, 124 S.Ct. 2633, 159 L.Ed.2d 578 (2004). Ultimately Hamdi was released to Saudi Arabia after he renounced his U.S. citizenship.

Several years after the *Hamdi* case was in the news, reports surfaced that some foreign nationals obtained U.S. tourist visas in order to be in the United States when they gave birth, thus assuring that their children would be U.S. citizens. *See, e.g.*, Richburg, For Many Pregnant Chinese, a U.S. Passport for Baby Remains a Powerful Lure, *Wash. Post,* July 18, 2010. As a consequence, in recent years the *jus soli* birthright citizenship debate has focused on births to lawful temporary visitors to the United States as well as on births to unauthorized migrants.

We begin with a selection from the Schuck and Smith book that, in effect, ignited the current debate. We then explore responses that counter the Schuck and Smith thesis, both as a matter of constitutional interpretation and as a matter of policy. We conclude the section with an excerpt from a recent article that closely reviewed the floor debates and other legislative history of the Fourteenth Amendment's Citizenship Clause.

PETER H. SCHUCK AND ROGERS M. SMITH, CITIZENSHIP WITHOUT CONSENT: ILLEGAL ALIENS IN THE AMERICAN POLITY

Pp. 2–5, 73–74, 76, 82–83, 85–87, 92–96, 99–100, 102, 113 (1985).

Despite the splendor of its constitutional pedigree * * * birthright citizenship is something of a bastard concept in American ideology. For all its appealing simplicity, it remains a puzzling idea. * * * [B]irthright citizenship originated as a distinctively feudal status intimately linked to medieval notions of sovereignty, legal personality, and allegiance. At a conceptual level, then, it was fundamentally opposed to the consensual assumptions that guided the political handiwork of 1776 and 1787. In a polity whose chief organizing principle was the idea of consent, mere birth within a nation's border seems to be an anomalous, inadequate measure or expression of an individual's consent to its rule and a decidedly crude indicator of the nation's consent to the individual's admission to political membership.

* * *

* * * [In] this book we elaborate an important but previously neglected dichotomy between two radically different conceptions of political community, which we call the "ascriptive" and the "consensual." In its

purest form, the principle of *ascription* holds that one's political member-ship is entirely and irrevocably determined by some objective circum-stance—in this case, birth within a particular sovereign's allegiance or jurisdiction. According to this conception, human preferences do not affect political membership; only the natural, immutable circumstances of one's birth are considered relevant.

The principle of *consent* advances radically different premises. It holds that political membership can result only from free individual choices. In the consensualist view, the circumstances of one's origins may of course influence one's preferences for political affiliation, but they need not do so and in any event are not determinative.

* * * [We] propose * * * an essentially consensual ideal of citizen-ship. Such a citizenship * * * would be more legitimate in theory, more flexible in meeting practical policy problems, and more likely to generate a genuine sense of community among all citizens than the existing scheme, while protecting the established human rights of aliens. To those ends, we * * * advocate a combination of measures to render American citizenship law more consensual than it has previously been and to ameliorate what is the greatest contemporary threat to a consensually based political commu-nity—the massive presence of illegal aliens. We * * * propose four related reforms: first, more effective enforcement of existing immigration laws; second, a system of realistic, credible employer sanctions to remove the chief incentive to most illegal immigration; third, more generous legal admission policies, especially within this hemisphere, and fourth, a rein-terpretation of the Fourteenth Amendment's Citizenship Clause to make birthright citizenship for the children of illegal and temporary visitor aliens a matter of congressional choice rather than of constitutional prescription.

THE FOURTEENTH AMENDMENT AND THE 1868 EXPATRIATION ACT

The framers of the [Fourteenth Amendment's citizenship clause] * * * did not write on a blank slate. * * * [T]he clause was adopted against a legal and ideological background in which the common-law view of political membership had found acceptance, a view in which (according to Lord Chief Justice Alexander Cockburn, a critic of the common-law rule writing at the time the clause was considered) "a merely casual birth in the country is to have the effect of conferring the character of a British Subject."[5] That view largely reflected its medieval English origins. But the context in which the clause was adopted was strikingly different. America was a more open, less insular society. Its central political ideas were not ascription and allegiance but consent and individual rights. And the clause was drafted with a very specific purpose in mind. It was designed to elevate to constitutional status the definition of citizenship adopted by statute over President Andrew Johnson's veto only two months earlier and by the very same Congress. A centerpiece of Reconstruction, the Civil

---

5. [Sir A. Cockburn, *Nationality: or the Law relating to Subjects and Aliens considered with a View to Future Legislation*, 194 (1869).]

Rights Act of 1866 had sought to guarantee blacks equal rights, privileges, and immunities under the law. At the same time, it created a new definition of United States citizenship, one that effectively overruled *Dred Scott*: "All, persons born in the United States, and not subject to any foreign power, excluding Indians not taxed, are hereby declared to be citizens of the United States."[7]

* * *

The greatest mystery surrounding the scope of the [Fourteenth Amendment's citizenship] clause * * * concerns the meaning of its phrase "and subject to the jurisdiction [of the United States]." We shall hereafter call this phrase the "jurisdiction requirement." Without that phrase, the clause would appear to demand a universal application, for it speaks of "all" persons, not some, and it employs a geographical referent (birth "in the United States") rather than a legal one. The jurisdiction requirement's conjunctive form, however, clearly suggests that it was meant to narrow the scope of the birthright citizenship principle under the clause. Indeed, we shall argue that the jurisdiction requirement should be understood to impose a consensual qualification on that principle.

[After reviewing the congressional debates, Schuck and Smith conclude that the citizenship clause of the Fourteenth Amendment was clearly intended (1) to extend birthright citizenship to the American-born children of Chinese and other resident aliens, but (2) to deny birthright citizenship to children born to Indians who were living within tribal governmental structures.]

The debates over Indian citizenship did not merely resolve (at least for the time being) a nettlesome question of coverage under the Citizenship Clause, important as that resolution was. They also brought to the surface the central elements around which the 39th Congress organized its more general understanding of the scope and meaning of the jurisdiction requirement under the clause. In the clash between the rival conceptions of its scope that were articulated during the Senate debate, the more demanding formulation—the idea of "full and complete jurisdiction," a jurisdiction precluding "allegiance to anybody else"—was the one advanced by Senators Trumbull and Howard, the chief architects of the clause and indeed of the Fourteenth Amendment as a whole.

The jurisdiction requirement, then, can best be understood as having added to the ineradicably ascriptive birthright citizenship rule a transforming consensual conception of the necessary connection between an individual and his government—a conception that was * * * more profoundly *political* than one emphasizing the individual's mere presence on the soil at birth. The connection must be more than simply the individual's subjection to the government's police power and criminal jurisdiction, more even than the individual's manifest desire for membership in the political community and the absence of any similar allegiance (in Senator

---

7. [Ch. 31, 14 Stat. 27, sec. 1 (April 9, 1866).]

Trumbull's words) "to anyone else." It also demanded a more or less complete, direct power by government over the individual, and a reciprocal relationship between them at the time of birth, in which the government consented to the individual's presence and status and offered him complete protection. In the public-law view, * * * this protection and citizenship extended to the child, but only through the government's consent to the parents, whose consent was in turn taken provisionally to stand for that of the child. In this way, even birthright citizenship's inherently ascriptive nature flowed from consensualist commitments.

This more consensualist reading of the Citizenship Clause is supported by the fact that, although it imposed an obligation of allegiance upon the native-born citizen, Congress could not have conceived of that obligation as perpetual or indissoluble on his part. Only one day before the Fourteenth Amendment was ratified, Congress embraced the consensual conception of citizenship in a more direct and thoroughgoing way, affirming in the Expatriation Act of 1868 the fundamental right of all citizens voluntarily to withdraw their consent and to renounce their citizenship. That act clearly established the principle that membership in the political community must always reflect the individual citizen's consent, a consent that must remain vital and continuing lest the individual withdraw it.

* * *

THE PROBLEM OF ILLEGAL MIGRATION

When the framers of the Citizenship Clause adopted (in a significantly compromised form) the common-law rule of birthright citizenship, immigration to the United States was entirely unregulated. The nation maintained a policy of completely open borders for almost another decade, when the first exclusion law, barring prostitutes and vagabonds, was enacted. Indeed, until well into the first decade of this century, birthright citizenship could plausibly be understood as one ingredient of an integrated national strategy to encourage immigration in order to populate a vast, essentially empty continent with the need for more laborers, mechanics, and farmers than American society itself could produce. An open-border policy was also celebrated as a way to serve liberal, humanitarian values, to make America an "asylum" for the "oppressed and persecuted of all Nations and Religions," as George Washington had urged at the outset.

Today, of course, that strategy of open border is a distant memory, bearing about as much relationship to current immigration policy concerns as the horse-and-buggy does to contemporary modes of transportation. * * *

The number of illegal aliens presently in the United States is a matter of great and continuing controversy. * * * This reality and the fears that it has generated concerning its economic and social effects have transformed political discourse about American immigration policy in ways that * * * the Reconstruction framers of the Citizenship Clause could [not] have anticipated. "Control of our borders," not encouragement of immigration, now dominates contemporary policy discussion. * * *

If mutual consent is the irreducible condition of membership in the American polity, it is difficult to defend a practice that extends birthright citizenship to the native-born children of illegal aliens. The parents of such children are, by definition, individuals whose presence within the jurisdiction of the United States is prohibited by law. They are manifestly individuals, therefore, to whom the society has explicitly and self-consciously decided to deny membership. And if the society has refused to consent to their membership, it can hardly be said to have consented to that of their children who happen to be born while their parents are here in clear violation of American law.

* * * [T]he present guarantee under American law of automatic birthright citizenship to the children of illegal aliens can only operate, at the margin, as one more incentive to illegal migration and violation by nonimmigrant (temporary visitor) aliens already here of their time limited visa restrictions. When this attraction is combined with the powerful lure of the expanded entitlements conferred upon citizen children and their families by the modern welfare state, the total incentive effect of birthright citizenship may well become significant. Certainly, it cannot be ignored. Needless to say, attempts to estimate the precise magnitude of this effect—the number of birthright citizens born to illegal alien parents who would not otherwise have come here—face insuperable data limitations. In addition to anecdotal evidence that many aliens do cross the border illegally to assure United States citizenship for their soon-to-be-born children, a very recent study illuminates two features of this phenomenon. First, the number of births in the United States to illegal alien parents is not trivial; a conservative estimate places the number as in excess of seventy-five thousand each year. Second, these births—and the public costs that they entail—seem to be disproportionately concentrated in a relatively few urban areas.

Congress is not impotent in the face of this challenge to consensualism. Although the Citizenship Clause of the Fourteenth Amendment has been assumed to guarantee birthright citizenship to such children *ex proprio vigore*, the evidence that we [have] reviewed suggests a rather different conclusion. First, the debates that preceded Congress's adoption of the clause establish that the 39th Congress neither considered, nor could have been expected to consider, this question. It legislated in a world in which unrestricted immigration to the United States was actually encouraged. The question of the citizenship status of the native-born children of illegal aliens never arose for the simple reason that no illegal aliens existed at that time, or indeed for some time thereafter.

Second, the debates also establish that the framers of the Citizenship Clause had no intention of establishing a universal rule of birthright citizenship. To be sure, they intended to do more than simply extend citizenship to native born blacks by overruling the reasoning and result in

Dred Scott. But they also intended, through the clause's jurisdiction requirement, to limit the scope of birthright citizenship. The essential limiting principle, discernible from the debates (especially those concerned with the citizenship status of Indians) was consensualist in nature. Citizenship, as qualified by this principle, was not satisfied by mere birth on the soil or by naked governmental power or legal jurisdiction over the individual. Citizenship required in addition the existence of conditions indicating mutual consent to political membership.

* * * [W]hatever the proper reach of the consent principle may be, it cannot logically be applied to include the native-born children of illegal aliens, to whom the nation's consent has expressly been denied.

* * *

* * * If Congress should conclude that the prospective denial of birthright citizenship to the children of illegal aliens would be a valuable adjunct of such national self-definition, the Constitution should not be interpreted in a way that impedes that effort. Illegal aliens, however admirable their initiative in seeking to come here, seem poorly situated, morally speaking, to contest that policy choice. They have migrated here, after all, in knowing defiance of American law, well aware that they may at any moment be obliged to return. If anybody may be said to have taken a calculated risk, they can. Moreover, almost all deported illegal aliens return to their own countries, of which they are still members. Although they would rather not do so—or would prefer to do so at a time of their own choosing—such preferences taken alone are ordinarily not morally compelling. Finally, citizenship status is not necessary to afford illegal aliens and their children at least minimal legal protection and public benefits, for they possess certain procedural and substantive rights under the Constitution merely by reason of their presence within the United States. We do not take any position here concerning what the precise nature and extent of those rights ought to be. It is enough for present purposes to affirm that the Constitution need not and should not be woodenly interpreted either to guarantee their children citizenship or to cast them into outer darkness.

* * *

It should be noted that all of the arguments that we have made against birthright citizenship for the children of illegal aliens apply with equal or greater force to the children of so-called nonimmigrants, aliens who have been allowed to enter under visa restrictions only for a limited period of time and for limited purposes. Unlike the situation with citizens and legal resident aliens, the government has declined to consent to their political membership or permanent presence in the society; indeed, it has admitted them on the express condition that they confine their activities and leave within a specified period. On the view of the Citizenship Clause that we have advanced, their children born here should not be regarded as having been born "subject to the jurisdiction" of the United States. * * *

In the end, the question of birthright citizenship for the children of illegal and nonimmigrant aliens probably should not turn on the conclusions that * * * revenue-cost analyses reach, important as those analyses may be for policy guidance. Instead, we believe, this question should be resolved in the light of broader ideals of constitutional meaning, social morality, and political community. These ideals militate against constitutionally ascribed birthright citizenship in these circumstances. As the earlier discussion suggests, the Citizenship Clause was never intended to guarantee citizenship for such individuals. Beyond the question of textual analysis, moreover, it is simply morally perverse to reward law-breaking by conferring the valued status of citizenship * * *.

STATEMENT OF PROF. GERALD L. NEUMAN

Societal and Legal Issues Surrounding Children Born in the United States to Illegal Alien
Parents, Joint Hearing before the Subcomm. on Immigration and Claims and the
Subcomm. on the Constitution of the House Comm. on the Judiciary,
104th Cong., 1st Sess. 105–09 (Dec. 13, 1995).

The historical purpose of [the Citizenship] Clause is well known: it was intended to overrule the most infamous decision in U.S. constitutional history, the *Dred Scott* decision. *Scott v. Sanford*, 60 U.S. (19 How.) 393 (1857). One of the holdings of that case was that the *jus soli* rule of citizenship applied only to whites: free persons of African descent could not be citizens of the United States, even if they were born in the United States.

The original text of the Constitution had failed to specify any criteria for citizenship in the United States, and the *jus soli* rule had been followed as part of our common law heritage. That omission had made the Dred Scott decision possible. After the Civil War, Congress sought to remedy that tragic error. Senator Howard, the author of the Citizenship Clause, introduced it with the following explanation: "It settles the great question of citizenship and removes all doubt as to what persons are or are not citizens of the United States. This has long been a great desideratum in the jurisprudence and legislation of this country." Cong. Globe, 39th Cong., 1st Sess. 2890 (1866) (remarks of Sen. Howard).

The framers of the Fourteenth Amendment had strong reason for desiring a constitutional settlement of the issue of birthright citizenship. They had just overthrown a system founded on denial of political membership in the country to a hereditary category of inhabitants. The Citizenship Clause was designed to prevent that situation from ever happening again. Both the proponents and the opponents of the Citizenship Clause understood this. For example, Senator Cowan, a vehement opponent of the Fourteenth Amendment, complained that granting citizenship to the children of Chinese alien parents on the Pacific Coast would prevent the states from "dealing with [the Chinese] as in the wisdom they see fit." In response, the supporters of the Citizenship Clause expressly confirmed their intent to protect the children of Chinese parents by recognizing them as citizens. *See* Cong. Globe, 39th Cong., 1st Sess. 2890–92 (colloquy of Sens. Cowan and Conness) (1866); *see also id.* at 498 (colloquy of Sens. Trumbull and Cowan regarding the 1866 Civil Rights Bill). The legislative history of the Fourteenth Amendment provides strong confirmation that birth in the United States would suffice to confer citizenship on children of aliens of any race, as it had earlier done for children of unnaturalized European immigrants.

The legislative history also confirms that the framers of the Fourteenth Amendment intended to deny constitutionally mandated citizenship to a few categories of children, whom they regarded as not "subject to the jurisdiction" of the United States, and therefore not within the protection of the common law *jus soli* rule. * * *

The common law did not consider as subjects or citizens children born to aliens who did not enter the country as individuals, but rather entered under the auspices of their governments with legal or factual immunity from local law. Children born to ambassadors of foreign nations were covered by comity principles of international law that restrain the state's exercise of lawmaking power. Children born to parents accompanying an invading army enter under extraordinary circumstances that temporarily oust the operation of local law. The example repeatedly used in the congressional debates was the children of ambassadors. *See e.g.,* Cong. Globe, 39th Cong, 1st Sess. 2897 (1866) (remarks of Sen. Williams).

The framers of the Fourteenth Amendment also intended to deny constitutionally mandated citizenship to a category of children whose parents were neither citizens nor aliens: American Indians born within their own organized political communities. The tribes were separate, self-governing political communities whose sovereignty predated the Constitution. At the time of the adoption of the Fourteenth Amendment the federal government did not exercise legislative power directly over their members, but negotiated treaties with the tribes as sovereign powers. *See, e.g.,* Cong. Globe, 39th Cong., 1st Sess. 2895 (1866) (remarks of Sen. Howard); *see also Elk v. Wilkins,* 112 U.S. 94 (1884). That is why both the original Constitution and the Fourteenth Amendment excluded "Indians not taxed"—i.e., those living under tribal governance, over whom Congress did not exercise the taxing power—from the basis of apportionment. Indians living in their tribal societies were governed by their own legal systems, like aliens who had remained at home under their own governments and diplomats, and unlike alien immigrants and visitors, who became subject to the laws of the state and federal governments upon entry. The effective legal and military independence of many tribes from state or federal governance made this notion of "domestic dependent nations" more realistic in 1866 than it subsequently became.

This history is consistent with giving the phrase "subject to the jurisdiction [of the United States]" its natural reading as actual subjection to the lawmaking power of the United States; this interpretation fulfills the framers' intentions and echoes the common law notion that children become subjects of the King by being born within his "protection." This is exactly how the Supreme court explained the meaning of the Citizenship Clause in *United States v. Wong Kim Ark.*

Nothing in the language of the Citizenship Clause, its legislative history, or its traditional interpretation, requires that the parents of a child born in the United States must be permanent residents, rather than temporary visitors, for the child to be "subject to the jurisdiction" of the United States. Both the English tradition and the Supreme Court's language in *Wong Kim Ark* treat temporarily present aliens as equivalent to resident aliens for this purpose, because both are subject to the authority of the government. *See Wong Kim Ark*, 169 U.S. at 655, 658, 674, 687, 688, 693; *Calvin's Case*, 7 Co. Rep 1b, 6a ("[F]or [the alien] owed to the King local obedience, that is, so long as he was within the King's protection; which local obedience being but momentary and uncertain is yet strong enough to make a natural subject, for if he hath issue here, that issue is a natural born subject.").

Nor is there anything in the language, legislative history, or traditional interpretation of the Citizenship Clause that would exclude children born in the United States to aliens who are not lawfully present here. Clearly, deportable aliens are subject to the jurisdiction of the United States—that is what makes them deportable, and often subject to criminal punishment as well. Their children born in the United States, though not themselves guilty of violating any law, have no immunity from the lawmaking power of the United States, and are fully subject to its jurisdiction.

The applicability of the constitutional *jus soli* rule to children of nonimmigrant aliens and illegal aliens finds confirmation in the similar interpretation of the rule by the United Kingdom and Canada. The United Kingdom followed this interpretation until 1981, when a different rule was adopted by statute, and Canada still extends citizenship to all children born in the territory except the children of foreign diplomats.

Everything that I have said so far has been well-established for many years. This traditional understanding has been questioned today solely because of a contrary thesis argued in [*Citizenship Without Consent*, by Professors Schuck and Smith.] [T]hat book's argument for a revisionist interpretation of the Fourteenth Amendment is poorly reasoned and historically inaccurate.

* * *

First, the Citizenship Clause sets forth a constitutional rule guaranteeing citizenship to a category of persons. That rule itself expresses the consent of the community, and even on the book's own theory, there should be no need to look further. Nonetheless, the authors of the book assert that the well-established traditional interpretation of the Citizenship Clause would be inappropriate under a consent-based theory, because it confers citizenship on children born to temporary visitors and illegal aliens. The authors attempt to distinguish between permanent resident aliens, on the one hand, and temporary visitors and illegal aliens, on the other, claiming that the community consents to the membership of the children of permanent resident aliens but not to the membership of children temporary visitors or illegal aliens. This argument, however, is circular: the only evidence that the United States has consented to the membership of the children of permanent resident aliens is the same evidence that supports the traditional *jus soli* rule, which is broader.

Second, the revisionist argument requires a new interpretation of the language "subject to the jurisdiction" of the United States, in order to reconcile the theory with the language of the Citizenship Clause. The authors claim that the meaning of "jurisdiction" in the Citizenship Clause is: "a more or less complete, direct power by government over the individual, and a reciprocal relationship between them at the time of birth, in which the government consented to the individual's presence *and status* and offered him complete protection." In other words, a person is not "subject to the jurisdiction of the United States" unless the United States consents to the person's status as a citizen. This is completely circular, and so would really guarantee no one citizenship at birth. And it has no relation to any definition of "jurisdiction" that anyone else has ever proposed. This peculiar definition of "jurisdiction" should be regarded as demonstrating the impossibility of the revisionist project; there is no reasonable interpretation of the constitutional language that will accomplish the revisionists' goals.

Third, the book sometimes states that a person is "subject to the jurisdiction" of the United States only if that person owes no allegiance to any foreign country. But this claim contradicts the book's own thesis that children born to permanent resident aliens are U.S. citizens. It contradicts the legislative history of the Fourteenth Amendment, which emphasized the citizenship of the children of Chinese immigrants, and it directly contradicts the Supreme Court's decision in *United States v. Wong Kim Ark*, which the authors otherwise attempted to preserve.

* * *

Fourth, the authors characterize their interpretation of "subject to the jurisdiction" as adding "a transforming consensual conception" to the traditional *jus soli* rule. But the legislative history makes it very clear that the framers of the Fourteenth Amendment were not trying to adopt a transformative new conception of citizenship by consent. That was what the Supreme Court had done in the infamous *Dred Scott* decision, excluding African–Americans from the *jus soli* rule on the ground that whites did not consider them appropriate partners in the political community. The framers sought to overturn that innovation, and to reaffirm on a racially neutral basis the same principles that had always governed American citizenship for persons of European descent. * * *

Fifth, the book claims that the framers of the Fourteenth Amendment could not have contemplated conferring citizenship on children of illegal aliens "for the simple reason that no illegal aliens existed at the time, or indeed for some time thereafter." This too is a fallacy. The federal government was not actively engaged in regulating immigration from Europe before the Civil War, but many of the states were. And, more importantly, the federal government itself had been attempting to prohibit the international slave trade, a form of involuntary immigration. Under the revisionist theory, children born in the United States to illegally imported slaves would not have been guaranteed citizenship by the Fourteenth Amendment, because the United States government did not consent to their parents' presence in the country. This would contradict the clear purpose of the Civil Rights Act of 1886 and the Fourteenth Amendment to overturn the *Dred Scott* decision and to guarantee U.S. citizenship to all persons of African descent born in the United States.

* * *

If Congress attempts to amend the citizenship statutes without a constitutional amendment, it will be acting unconstitutionally. The courts are certain to invalidate such action and vindicate the children's citizenship just as the Supreme Court did in *Wong Kim Ark*. Unfortunately, however, the court's decision will come only after a period of severe uncertainty for the government and hardship for the children affected by the legislation. It is one thing for academics to propose a speculative new theory and submit it to professional refutation, but quite another thing to experiment with the rights of U.S. citizen children. * * *

DAVID A. MARTIN, MEMBERSHIP AND CONSENT: ABSTRACT OR ORGANIC?

11 Yale J. Int'l L. 278, 282–284, 291–94 (1985).

* * * [C]onsider what happens if the new citizenship rules [proposed by Schuck and Smith] are adopted, but [other measures for controlling illegal immigration] either are not implemented or fail to have an appreciable impact. * * * From the date of the change onward, we would find a growing class of people who were born and raised in the United States but who do not have, and presumably cannot easily obtain, U.S. citizenship. What would be the consequences? What would be the effect on their attitudes toward the country in which they live? What effect would this new and unfortunate status have on the attitudes of citizens, not only toward this new class but toward other "aliens" present?

These are not abstract questions. Many European countries are now struggling with the so-called problems of the second generation. Those countries imported foreign workers during the boom years of the 1950's and 1960's. * * * Over the years, those workers have produced children, born in their parents' European country of residence, but without immediate citizenship rights there, because broadly applicable birthright citizenship rules are not in force.

Those children (many now adults) have known only life in Europe, but in disturbingly large numbers resist identifying with it. Although naturalization is available, relatively few of the guest workers or their children pursue it. * * * Against this background, anti-foreigner political parties have enjoyed increasing success.

In these circumstances, beset with a kind of *"apartheid volontaire"* that resists new governmental programs and augurs continuing and deepening problems for those polities, some European observers look with envy at *"la formidable machine assimilatrice de la société américaine."*[24] Though the fabric of the United States is woven with diverse strands, the country has been notably successful in encouraging newcomers, or at least the children of newcomers, to identify closely with the polity. There are problems, to be sure, but by and large they come to be seen as problems to be solved within the polity, by Americans acting as Americans. That assimilative capacity (which need not entail obliteration of cultural heritage) represents a precious national asset, especially for so large and diverse a country. Its existence and value are sometimes overlooked because its maintenance has so far been relatively effortless. We have no European-style "second generation problem" here, in part because we cannot have second generation aliens. The children may have dual citizenship, of course, and they are free to choose to make the other allegiance their principal one. But if they stay here, a secure citizenship status forms a basic foundation for the shaping of identity and involvement in the polity. They are thereby encouraged to embrace life here as full participants, not as half-hearted, stand-offish "guests." Equally important, other citizens are induced to treat them as coequal members of the polity, not as intruders who stay too long.

* * *

* * * [Schuck and Smith's focus on consent] reflect[s] an incomplete view of the wellsprings of both community and legitimacy. Both may be nurtured by consent, but they do not rest exclusively on consensualism. * * *

Consent *is* basic to certain aspects of democracy, and especially American democracy, but it is not the only principle, and in any event it is more complex and nuanced than the authors acknowledge. * * *

Time and familiarity weave their way into the complex relationship we call citizenship. Their significance fits comfortably with ascriptive citizenship rules, at least as long as ascription is not irrevocable. Most of us were simply born into our most basic affiliations—family, religion, nation. Those ties are not only objects of choice; to a significant extent they are constitutive of one's basic identity, anterior to choice. They help shape the characteristics of mind, preference, and perception that one brings to any particular consensual decision. Later we may exercise a "consensual" power to change some of those affiliations or preferences, but such choices reflect an organic process, not the radical act of a

---

24. Julliard, *Comment on devient un "vrai" Français*, Le Nouvel Observateur, Aug. 30–Sept. 5, 1985, *reprinted in* Actualités Migrations, Sept. 16, 1985, at 13.

sovereign individual able to sweep away all such prior attachments by one magisterial act of consent or non-consent.

Ascriptive citizenship rules, especially generous ones, recognize this reality. They anchor choice—the consensualist political process—in a realistic and protective framework. One does not come into the political world as a naked and lonely individual, wholly dependent for the honoring of one's claims on consensual arrangements that might or might not be worked out with other contracting individuals or associations. Ascription, as the authors occasionally seem ready to recognize, serves to protect fundamental human rights. Indeed, the very notion of basic human rights applicable to all, alien or citizen, is fundamentally ascriptive; it suggests a list of entitlements that one may claim simply by reason of birth as a human being and not by reason of compact. The concept of human rights thus places certain claims beyond the reach of other individuals' refusal to consent.

Certainly after a person's basic affiliative foundation is established, consent plays a significant role. Consent guards the outer boundaries of legitimacy, even if it does not initially give birth to that sentiment, by providing a fundamental check against abuses by the polity of which one finds oneself a member. Consent can be withdrawn either collectively through revolution or individually by renunciation of citizenship and removal from the society. However, it is illusory to think that such a radical withdrawal of consent can be made so rationalistic and apparently cost-free.

Professors Schuck and Smith sometimes disparage the ascriptive principle as "medieval," "feudal," a "bastard concept," or a "vestigial remnant." Ascription without an individual right to withdraw consent may deserve those epithets. But American citizenship rules had worked free of that taint by at least as early as 1868. Modern citizenship rules, through a painful process of trial and error in Congress and the Supreme Court, have now crystallized in a humane mixture of ascription and consent. The ascriptive elements that survive do so for good and protective reasons.

––––––––––

In his examination of the 1866 Senate debates regarding the Citizenship Clause of the Fourteenth Amendment, Garrett Epps argues that the Senators carefully distinguished between the different legal statuses of Indians—some lived in towns and villages, some had settled on reservations, and some had not yet been subdued by U.S. forces—and that the text "subject to the jurisdiction [of the United States]" referred to those in the first group. Epps also highlights the Senate's discussion of whether *jus soli* citizenship should extend to children born in the United States to Chinese laborers and to "Gypsies," a group he analogizes to the "illegal immigrants" of contemporary debate. The excerpt below focuses on these latter points.

GARRETT EPPS, THE CITIZENSHIP CLAUSE:
A "LEGISLATIVE HISTORY"

60 American University L. Rev. 331, 349–361 (2010).

[In the debate on the Fourteenth Amendment, Senator Fessenden of Maine, chair of the Joint Committee on Reconstruction,] suggested the very question that concerns us today: "Suppose a person is born here of parents from abroad temporarily in this country." Wade answered,

> The Senator says a person may be born here and *not* be a citizen. I know that is so in *one* instance, in the case of the children of foreign ministers who reside "near" the United States, in the diplomatic language. By a fiction of law such persons are not supposed to be residing here, and under that fiction of law their children would not be citizens of the United States, although born in Washington. I agree to that, but my answer to the suggestion is that that is a simple matter, for it could hardly be applicable to more than two or three or four persons; and it would be best not to alter the law for that case.

* * *

When the measure returned to the floor on May 30, Senator Jacob Howard of Michigan, a member of the Joint Committee and the Senate sponsor of the draft amendment, proposed new language: "All persons born in the United States, and subject to the jurisdiction thereof, are citizens of the United States and of the States wherein they reside." * * *

> Howard explained the meaning of the new language as

> simply declaratory of what I regard as the law of the land already, that every person born within the limits of the United States, and subject to their jurisdiction, is by virtue of natural law and national law a citizen of the United States. This will not, of course, include persons born in the United States who are foreigners, aliens, who belong to the families of ambassadors or foreign ministers accredited to the Government of the United States, but will include every other class of persons.

Once again, the irrepressible Senator Cowan rose to object that the proponents of the draft amendment could surely not mean that birthright citizenship would extend to children of Chinese immigrants or of "Gypsies":

> Is it proposed that the people of California are to remain quiescent while they are overrun by a flood of immigration of the Mongol race? Are they to be immigrated out of house and home by Chinese? I should think not.

> [My home state of Pennsylvania has to contend with] a certain number of people who invade her borders; who owe to her no allegiance; who pretend to owe none; who recognize no authority in her government; who have a distinct, independent government of

their own—an imperium in imperio; who pay no taxes; who never perform military service; who do nothing, in fact, which becomes the citizen, and perform none of the duties which devolve upon him, but, on the other hand, have no homes, pretend to own no land, live nowhere, settle as trespassers wherever they go.... I mean the Gypsies.... If the mere fact of being born in the country confers that right, then they will have it; and I think it will be mischievous.

* * *

The response on the floor was delivered by Senator John Conness of California, himself a naturalized citizen born in Ireland:

The proposition before us, I will say, Mr. President, relates simply to the children begotten of Chinese parents in California, and it is proposed to declare that they shall be citizens.... I voted for the proposition to declare that the children of all parentage whatever, born in California, should be regarded and treated as citizens of the United States, entitled to equal civil rights with other citizens of the United States.

As for the danger of Gypsy hordes, Conness noted that "I have lived in the United States for now many a year, and really I have heard more about Gypsies within the last two or three months than I have heard before in my life."

NOTES AND QUESTIONS ON UNDOCUMENTED MIGRANTS, TEMPORARY RESIDENTS, AND JUS SOLI

1. Schuck and Smith assert that citizenship for the children of undocumented migrants is not constitutionally compelled. They stop short of expressing a view as to how Congress ought to use the power that they believe it possesses. In testimony before Congress more than a decade after publication of the book, Schuck opposed pending legislation that would have limited birthright citizenship to the children of citizens and permanent resident aliens. He argued:

[The] most important advantage [of a birthright citizenship rule] is that it provides a crude but pragmatic accommodation to a long-standing, apparently intractable policy failure: the substantial ineffectiveness of our border and interior immigration enforcement programs. Our feckless enforcement policies have created a possibility, indeed a certainty, that a large group of illegal aliens are nevertheless long-term or even lifelong residents in the U.S. Without a birthright citizenship rule or other amnesty, these illegals, their children, and their children's children will continue to be outsiders mired in an inferior and illegal status and deprived of the capacities of self-protection and self-advancement. Whatever the disadvantages of birthright citizenship, it has the great virtue of limiting the tragic effects of this problem of inherited outlawry by confining illegal status to a single generation for each family.

Societal and Legal Issues Surrounding Children Born in the United States to Illegal Alien Parents, Joint Hearing before the Subcomm. on Immigration and Claims and Subcomm. on the Constitution, House Comm. on the Judiciary, 104th Cong., 1st Sess. 100 (1995).

Compare Subcommittee Chairman Lamar Smith's comment at the same hearing: "[T]he cost of the children of illegal aliens just in Los Angeles County is over a billion dollars, when you include welfare and education. There's other testimony that 16 percent of the births in all of California now are to the children of illegal aliens. The appearance there, let me say, is that law breakers are being rewarded, taxpayers are being cheated, and citizenship is being cheapened." *Id.* at 84.

2.   Is it relevant to the argument advanced by Schuck and Smith that the constitutional *jus soli* principle does not allow the parents of a child born in the United States to evade deportation based on a claim that it would amount to a de facto deportation of the citizen child? *See, e.g., Acosta v. Gaffney*, 558 F.2d 1153 (3d Cir. 1977). Nor does it permit the U.S. born citizen child to confer any immigration benefits on his or her parents until the child reaches the statutorily prescribed age of 21. INA § 201(b)(2)(A)(i). The lack of immunity from removal proceedings initiated against noncitizen parents of U.S. citizen children, of course, may force families to make difficult personal choices about how—and where—to raise their children, but the immigration laws continue to apply to the parents in full force. The *Acosta* court acknowledged that the parents there could leave the young child in foster care in the United States, though it expected them to take the child with them to Colombia. But the child would retain full rights to return to the United States for residence whenever she chose. Residence abroad does not jeopardize citizenship, as there is no requirement of subsequent presence in order to maintain U.S. nationality.

All countries with expansive *jus soli* rules authorize deportation of noncitizen parents. *See* T. Aleinikoff & D. Klusmeyer, eds., Citizenship Policies for an Age of Migration 11 (2002). Do you think that this is a necessary corollary of a broad *jus soli* rule?

3.   Assume Schuck and Smith are correct on the constitutional question. Should Congress adopt legislation denying birthright citizenship to children of undocumented migrants? To children of tourists and other temporary visitors to the United States? Multiple bills, with broad levels of co-sponsorship, have been introduced in the 112th Congress to eliminate birthright citizenship for children whose parents lack legal status. *See, e.g.,* the proposed Birthright Citizenship Act of 2011, H.R. 140, 112th Cong. (2011).

In addition, legislators in multiple states have introduced bills that would provide special birth certificates for children whose parents lack legal authorization to live in the United States. Preston, *State Lawmakers Outline Plans to End Birthright Citizenship, Drawing Outcry*, N.Y. Times, Jan. 5, 2011. If enacted, would these state laws be constitutional?

4.   How would you evaluate the claims to birthright citizenship for children born to noncitizens who entered without authorization but have resided in the United States for a long time? Do you think their claims are more or less powerful than those of children born to noncitizens, such as

Hamdi, who entered legally for a short time? What about children born to noncitizens who expect to be in the United States for six or possibly more years on an H–1B visa, one of the long-term nonimmigrant visas that will be discussed in Chapter Five?

5. As broad as the U.S. *jus soli* rule is, there are proposals to broaden citizenship acquisition rules even further. For example, foreign-born children who immigrate at an early age—sometimes called the "1.5 generation"—are hard to distinguish from children born and reared in the United States. Granting them citizenship both reflects socialization realities and furthers integration, according to the Comparative Citizenship Project of the Carnegie Endowment for International Peace and the Migration Policy Institute. See T. Aleinikoff & D. Klusmeyer, eds., Citizenship Policies for an Age of Migration (2002). Is such a policy sensible? If integration is the goal, should the proposal apply to all children who have resided and attended school in the United States for a certain number of years? Or should it be limited to children of lawful permanent residents? This, of course, is just another context for the discussion that Schuck and Smith's book engendered.

Towards Convergence?

The traditional line between *jus soli* states and *jus sanguinis* states is blurring. That is, some historically *jus soli* states are cutting back a bit, limiting *jus soli* citizenship to the children of lawfully residing noncitizens. Concomitantly, some historically *jus sanguinis* states have begun to recognize the citizenship of third or long-residing second-generation immigrants. For example, a law that took effect in Germany in 2000 introduced a limited form of *jus soli* citizenship: a child born in Germany acquires *jus soli* citizenship if one parent has lived in Germany for eight years with certain types of residence permits. Furthermore, the child must choose before his or her twenty-third birthday between German and any other citizenship that he or she may hold. *See Gesetz zur Reform des Staatsangehörigkeitsrechts, Bundesgesetzblatt*, I 1618 (1999), amending *Ausländergesetz* § 85.

These developments suggest, perhaps, that a unified theory of birthright citizenship could be developed by focusing on *generations* rather than *descent* or *residence*. Consider the following proposal, developed by the Comparative Citizenship Project of the Carnegie Endowment for International Peace and the Migration Policy Institute (and roughly patterned after current French citizenship rules)[4]:

a. members of the third generation (the grandchildren of immigrants) would be automatically entitled to citizenship at birth;

b. members of the second generation (the children of immigrants) who are lawful residents or whose parents are lawful residents would be entitled to citizenship after having resided in the state for a reasonably determined number of years;

---

4. Aleinikoff & Klusmeyer, *supra*, Citizenship Policies for an Age of Migration.

c. foreign-born children who immigrate at any early age should be considered members of the second generation and should be entitled to citizenship after residing in the state for ten years or completing six years in school.

How do these policies differ from current U.S. citizenship norms (note that they are both more and less generous)? Do they describe a sensible approach to citizenship acquisition norms?

SECTION B. DUAL NATIONALITY AND THE CONCEPT OF CITIZENSHIP

Under *jus soli* and *jus sanguinis* rules, some children at birth are citizens of more than one country, the state where they are born and the state of their parents' nationality. If the parents happen to be from different countries, the child may simultaneously possess citizenship in three states. For many years international law disfavored multiple nationality, allowing states to prevent or reduce instances of dual citizenship in a variety of ways. For example, when dual nationality is created at birth by the overlap of *jus soli* and *jus sanguinis* rules a state may require that a person elect one citizenship or the other at time of majority. For persons attaining citizenship through naturalization, which will be discussed in Section C below, the state of origin may deem such conduct expatriating; and the state granting naturalization may require renunciation of prior citizenship or even documentary proof that the other government recognizes the loss of its citizenship.

Some state-to-state arrangements tolerate dual citizenship but seek to ameliorate the complications it causes. For example, treaties may clarify military obligations of dual citizens. *See, e.g.,* the Articles 5 & 6 of the Council of Europe's Convention on Reduction of Cases of Multiple Nationality and Military Obligations in Cases of Multiple Nationality, 634 U.N.T.S. 221, *entered into force* Mar. 28, 1968. For a thorough discussion, *see* Legomsky, *Dual Nationality and Military Service: Strategy Number Two*, in Rights and Duties of Dual Nationals: Evolution and Prospects 79 (D. Martin and K. Hailbronner, eds., 2003).

For more than 200 years U.S. law has sought to prevent dual nationality. Early in this century, U.S. statutes automatically terminated the citizenship of a U.S. woman who married a foreign national; the presumption was that she would obtain the nationality of her husband. As discussed further on pages 142–145, the Supreme Court upheld the statute on the ground that Congress could take measures to avoid problems of dual nationality. *Mackenzie v. Hare*, 239 U.S. 299, 36 S.Ct. 106, 60 L.Ed. 297 (1915). In addition, to avoid dual nationality occasioned by naturalization, U.S. law requires applicants take an oath that includes a renunciation of prior allegiances, under a provision that dates back to 1795.

Despite the availability of legal means for restricting dual nationality, the trend is decidedly in the other direction—nations around the world are growing more tolerant of plural citizenships. *See* Roth, *Worldwide Liberalization of Dual Citizenship Rules and Potential Side Effects on U.S. Citizenship*, 83 Interp. Rel. 2529 (2006); Jones–Correa, *Dual Nationality in Latin America and its Consequences for Naturalization in the United States*, in Rights and Duties of Dual Nationals: Evolution and Prospects 303 (D. Martin and K. Hailbronner, eds., 2003). The next set of readings surveys different perspectives on citizenship and some of the implications of nationality in more than one state. We begin with a selection about the very concept of citizenship, and then turn to an examination of the norms against dual citizenship. Following that, we look at the debate concerning the growing phenomenon of multiple nationality, and we close this section with an essay that invites thinking about citizenship beyond the nation state.

ROGERS BRUBAKER, CITIZENSHIP AS SOCIAL CLOSURE

Citizenship and Nationhood in France and Germany, Ch. 1 (1992).*

Citizenship is a universal and distinctive feature of the modern political landscape. Every modern state formally defines its citizenry, publically identifying a set of persons as its members and residually designating all others as noncitizens, or aliens. Every state attaches certain rights and obligations to the status of citizenship. These rights and obligations define a region of legal equality—what T. H. Marshall called the "basic human equality associated with ... full membership of a community."[1]

The citizenry of every modern state is internally inclusive. Defined to coincide roughly with the permanent resident population of the state, the modern citizenry excludes only foreigners, that is, persons who belong to other states. Yet citizenship is not a mere reflex of residence; it is an enduring personal status that is not generated by passing or extended residence alone and does not lapse with temporary or prolonged absence. In this respect the modern state is not simply a territorial organization but a membership organization, an association of citizens.

Although citizenship is internally inclusive, it is externally exclusive. There is a conceptually clear, legally consequential, and ideologically charged distinction between citizens and foreigners. The state claims to be the state of, and for, a particular, bounded citizenry; it claims legitimacy by claiming to express the will and further the interests of that citizenry. This bounded citizenry is usually conceived as a nation—as something more cohesive than a mere aggregate of persons who happen legally to belong to the state.

* * * [C]itizenship is not simply a legal formula; it is an increasingly salient social and cultural fact. As a powerful instrument of social closure,

---

1. [T.H.] Marshall, Citizenship and Social Class and Other Essays (1950), p. 8.

citizenship occupies a central place in the administrative structure and political culture of the modern nation-state and state system. The notion of social closure finds its classical exposition in the opening pages of *Economy and Society*, where Max Weber distinguishes between open and closed social relationships.[9] Social interaction may be open to all comers, or it may be closed, in the sense that it excludes or restricts the participation of certain outsiders. A pick-up softball game, for example, may be open, while a game played by teams belonging to an organized league may be restricted to team members, and in this sense closed. Retail commerce is usually open to all buyers, though less often, unconditionally, to all sellers. Worship, conversation, fights, neighborhoods, countries all may be open or more or less closed.

Although closure is most easily visualized in everyday interaction, the notion of closure illuminates large-scale structures and patterns of interaction as well. The nation-state is architect and guarantor of a number of distinctively modern forms of closure. These are embodied in such institutions and practices as the territorial border, universal suffrage, universal military service, and naturalization. Closure pivots in each of these cases on the legal institution of citizenship. Only citizens have an unqualified right to enter (and remain in) the territory of a state. The suffrage and military service are normally restricted to citizens. And naturalization, which governs access to the status of citizen, is itself closed, restricted to the qualified. Citizenship is thus both an instrument and an object of closure.

THE TERRITORIAL STATE AND CLOSURE

In general, closure may occur on the threshold of interaction or "inside" interaction. In the former case initial participation is restricted through barriers to entry or selective admission; in the latter continued participation is controlled through institutions such as probation or performance review. Closure against noncitizens is exercised mainly on the threshold of interaction. This is the case when noncitizens are prevented from entering the territory, or when they are excluded from forms of action reserved for citizens (such as voting or serving in the army). In one important respect, however, closure occurs inside interaction. Citizens alone enjoy an unconditional right to remain and reside in the territory of a state, including the right to reenter should they leave for any reason. The territory of the state is their territory, and they can plan their lives accordingly. Noncitizens' entry and residence rights, in contrast, are never unconditional. Some noncitizens—clandestine entrants, for example, or persons at the end of a legally limited period of residence—have no such rights. But even privileged noncitizens—those formally accepted as immigrants or settlers—remain "probationary" residents, subject to exclusion or deportation in certain circumstances.

---

9. [M.] Weber, *Economy and Society* (1958 ed.), pp. 43–46.

The territorial state * * * has a basic and distinctive interest in being able to control the flow of persons across its borders—in being able to compel, induce, discourage, or forbid the entry or exit of particular categories of persons. The capacity to exclude noncitizens serves this interest, permitting states to compel the exit and forbid the entry of a particular class of persons. * * *

* * * [But w]hy is territorial closure directed against noncitizens alone? It would seem to be in the state's interest to be able to expel or exclude persons regardless of their status. * * *

Unimpeded, the territorial state might seek to externalize the material and ideal costs associated with unruly, unemployed, unfit, unassimilated, or otherwise undesired residents, whatever their status, by excluding or expelling them. But the territorial state is not unimpeded. With the disappearance of "nonstate, semistate or pseudostate areas of the world,"[15] every state is embedded in a system of coordinate territorial states, each with the same vital interest in controlling migration. Jointly, these territorial jurisdictions exhaust the inhabitable surface of the earth. In such a world a person cannot be expelled from one territory without being expelled into another, cannot be denied entry into one territory without having to remain in another. The one exception is that pathetic and characteristically modern form of limbo in which the unwanted may find themselves, shuttled back and forth between states unwilling to admit them. Occasional instances of complementarity aside, exclusion and expulsion become zero-sum games. One state's gain is another's loss: the costs successfully externalized by one must be borne by another. To permit states to exclude or expel persons at will, under these zero-sum background conditions, would multiply occasions for interstate conflict. States into whose territories undesirables had been expelled would threaten or engage in retaliatory "dumping." A state would hesitate to admit any outsider, for fear that it might be stuck with him if his state of origin denied him reentry. Basic conditions for the orderly interstate movement of persons would not exist.

The limitation of states' powers of expulsion and exclusion to noncitizens thus responds to the imperatives of the modern state-system. This limitation, though, presupposes the institution of citizenship, with its internationally recognized rules for allocating persons to states. Yet this allocative institution, this social technique for consistently assigning each individual to one and only one state, had to be invented. The modern system of territorial states engendered not just territorial closure against noncitizens but, more fundamentally, the institution of citizenship as such.

* * *

THE NATION-STATE AND CLOSURE

Territorial closure against noncitizens serves vital and tangible state interests; it is essential to the modern territorial state and state-system.

---

15. [Id.], p. 56.

The same cannot be said for other modes of membership closure. If noncitizens are regularly excluded from the suffrage and from positions in public service, and if they are exempted from military service, this cannot generally be attributed to any overriding tangible state (or group) interest. The interests sustaining domestic closure against noncitizens are often intangible.

The modern state is not only a territorial state, embedded in a system of coordinate territorial states; it is also a nation-state. The concept of the nation-state, to be sure, is much more ambiguous than that of the territorial state, and its appropriateness for the analysis of late twentieth century states is disputed. For some observers the general lack of fit between political and ethnocultural boundaries vitiates the concept of the nation-state. Others, emphasizing states' universal nation-making aspirations and immense nation-making powers, defend its continued analytical usefulness. There is no need, however, to engage these disputes here, for in one uncontested sense almost all modern states are (or claim to be) nation-states. Almost all subscribe to the legitimating doctrine of national or popular sovereignty. Almost all claim to derive state power from and exercise it for (and not simply over) a nation, a people. A state is a nation-state in this minimal sense insofar as it claims (and is understood) to be a nation's state: the state "of" and "for" a particular, distinctive, bounded nation. For present purposes, the manner of distinctiveness is immaterial, the fact of distinctiveness alone essential. *How* the state-bearing and state-justifying nation is culturally and legally bounded is irrelevant; *that* it is bounded is what matters here.

Domestic closure against noncitizens rests on this understanding and self-understanding of modern states as bounded nation-states—states whose telos it is to express the will and further the interests of distinctive and bounded nations, and whose legitimacy depends on their doing so, or at least seeming to do so. The routine exclusion of noncitizens from modern systems of "universal" suffrage is exemplary in this respect. * * *

Domestic closure may serve material interests as well. These may include security interests of state elites in excluding noncitizens, viewed as politically unreliable, from the suffrage, from military service, or from positions in public administration; fiscal interests in limiting noncitizens' participation in costly social programs; or occupational group interests in restricting competition. Where noncitizens comprise a substantial fraction of the population, these material interests might be compelling. Where they are a small minority, though, closure is sustained mainly by the ideal interest, inscribed in the characteristic legitimation claims of modern states, in maintaining a conceptual, legal, and political boundary between members and nonmembers of the nation-state. Domestic closure against noncitizens is essential to the modern state qua nation-state, just as territorial closure against noncitizens is essential to the modern state qua territorial state.

INSIDERS AND OUTSIDERS

All forms of closure presuppose some way of defining and identifying outsiders or ineligibles. Outsiders may be defined and identified residually, as nonmembers, or directly, as bearers of some disqualifying attribute. If insiders are defined positively—as members of a family, clan, association, organization, or state—outsiders are defined negatively and residually. They are excluded not because of what they are but because of what they are not—because they are not recognized or acknowledged as insiders. On the other hand, outsiders may be defined directly, and insiders residually.
* * *

* * *

Closure based on citizenship is regulated by formally articulated norms and enforced by specialized agents employing formal identification routines. Territorial closure, for example, is regulated by immigration law and corresponding administrative regulations. It is enforced by specialized agents such as border patrol officers and officials at points of entry who employ formal identification routines based on specialized instruments such as passports, visas, and computerized files. Closure against noncitizens is necessarily formal, for the legal quality of citizenship is invisible in ordinary interaction and visible only under the special lens of administrative scrutiny. Thus the development of citizenship proceeds *pari passu* with that of an administrative apparatus of classification and surveillance (in the broadest sense) and a corresponding body of administrative knowledge.

* * *

ACCESS TO CITIZENSHIP

Citizenship is not only an instrument of closure, a prerequisite for the enjoyment of certain rights, or for participation in certain types of interaction. It is also an object of closure, a status to which access is restricted. From a global perspective, to be sure, citizenship is virtually universal. In this perspective, citizenship is an international filing system, a mechanism for allocating persons to states. The citizens of a given state comprise the fraction of the world population that "belongs" to that state, rather than to some other state. In a world divided among exhaustive and mutually exclusive jurisdictions of sovereign states, it is axiomatic that every person ought to have a citizenship, that everyone ought to belong to one state or another. And this principle is largely realized in practice. The vast majority of persons possess the citizenship of at least one state. Modern state citizenship differs sharply in this respect from citizenship in the ancient Greek polis or in medieval towns. There it was axiomatic that some persons ought not to be citizens of any city. Persons lacking citizenship were not placeless; their status was not anomalous. Rather, they did not form part of the self-governing or otherwise privileged civic corporation.

Although globally inclusive, citizenship is locally exclusive. Every state limits access to its citizenship. It limits the circle of persons to whom it ascribes its citizenship at birth, and it specifies the terms and conditions on which it will permit others to acquire its citizenship.

Ascription. Every state ascribes its citizenship to certain persons at birth. The vast majority of persons acquire their citizenship in this way. The ascription of citizenship at birth represents a striking exception to the secular trend away from ascribed statuses. And it is difficult to reconcile with a central claim—perhaps the central claim—of liberal political theory: the idea that political membership ought to be founded on individual consent. Why is citizenship typically ascribed at birth?

Administrative convenience is part of the reason. Unlike residence, assimilation, loyalty, and other concepts appearing in naturalization law, birth is an unambiguous event about which states maintain relatively clear administrative records. Attributing citizenship at birth, moreover, makes possible a clear and unambiguous assignment of individuals to states without a period of uncertainty. Some individuals will be assigned incorrectly, in the sense that their formal citizenship does not correspond to their actual ties and attachments. But such mismatches can be corrected later. And in any event they are a small price to pay for the clarity and convenience of assigning persons to states at birth. The alternative—a system of voluntary or contractual citizenship that would leave individuals unassigned until their actual social attachments and individual preferences became clear—would be an administrative nightmare. It would also be politically unacceptable. All states regard their citizens as bound to them by obligations of loyalty and service even when they do not routinely demand service or invoke loyalty. These core obligations of citizenship are too important to the state to permit individuals to opt into or out of them at will. Despite the concern of liberal political theory to found political obligation on the voluntary consent of individuals, the state is not and cannot be a voluntary association. * * *

The ascription of citizenship at birth is based on a presumption of membership. This presumption reflects the fact that at birth certain persons have a high probability of developing the close attachments and loyalties to a particular society and state that are supposed to underlie citizenship. Rules of ascription vary among states, but most use birthplace or parental citizenship or both as indicators of membership. The presumption of membership is strongest in the case of persons born on the territory of the state to a parent or parents possessing the citizenship of the state. * * *

The presumption of membership is ambiguous for persons born abroad to citizen parents and for persons born in the territory to noncitizen parents. It is this ambiguity that allows for variation in states' ascription rules. Variation with respect to the first of these categories is limited and need not concern us. Variation with respect to the second, however, is quite marked, and returns us to the theme of closure.

Traditional countries of immigration—including the United States, Canada, and most Latin American countries—generally ascribe citizenship to all persons born on their territory. * * * At the other extreme, some countries, * * * [such as] Switzerland, make no special provision for conferring citizenship on second- or even third-generation immigrants. Their exclusively descent-based citizenship law takes no cognizance of birth in the territory, not even of birth in the territory over two or more generations. In conjunction with restrictive naturalization policies, the ascription of citizenship on the basis of descent alone effectively excludes second- and third-generation immigrants from citizenship.

Naturalization. Persons to whom the citizenship of a state is not ascribed at birth may be able to acquire it later in life through naturalization. Rules governing the acquisition of citizenship, like those governing its ascription, can be more or less restrictive. At one pole, naturalization is a purely discretionary decision of the state. The candidate must fulfill certain conditions; but even if these are fulfilled, the state must judge whether or not the grant of citizenship is in its own interest. * * * At the other pole, all candidates meeting certain clearly specified conditions are naturalized. In this system naturalization is expected of immigrants; the failure to naturalize is anomalous. Naturalization is actively promoted by the state. The procedure is simple, scrutiny of most applications perfunctory, and the fees low. * * * Yet even in countries of immigration, naturalization remains closed in an important sense. Naturalization may be open to, and expected of, all persons meeting certain conditions, but the opportunity to satisfy these conditions is itself closed. Naturalization may be limited, as in the United States, to persons who have been formally accepted as immigrants; it is almost always limited to persons who have resided legally in the territory for a certain length of time. By restricting immigration, states indirectly restrict access to naturalization.

CONCLUSION

Citizenship is both an instrument and an object of closure. Closure against noncitizens occurs in two stages. Free access to the territory and to certain benefits and activities within it is reserved to citizens; and access to citizenship is reserved to persons meeting certain qualifying conditions. Since the qualifying conditions usually include residence in the territory, there is a circular quality to closure based on citizenship. Only citizens enjoy free access to the territory, yet only residents have access to citizenship. This circularity permits nation-states to remain, albeit in considerably differing degrees, relatively closed and self-perpetuating communities, reproducing their membership in a largely endogenous fashion, open only at the margins to the exogenous recruitment of new members.

NOTES AND QUESTIONS ON THE CONCEPT OF CITIZENSHIP

1. What does Brubaker mean by the assertion that "citizenship is both an instrument and an object of closure"? What does he mean when he says "there is a circular quality to closure based on citizenship"?

2.   Do you agree with Brubaker that nation-states are "open only at the margins to exogenous recruitment of new members"? Is this true of the United States?

3.   Throughout this chapter and this book, we will examine the relationship of the concept of membership to citizenship. Note Brubaker's quotation of T.H. Marshall's famous declaration that citizenship constitutes "full membership of a community." To what extent and in what ways might immigrants be understood as members of the U.S. community? To what extent and in what ways does immigration law—as distinct from citizenship rules—function as an instrument of closure?

T. ALEXANDER ALEINIKOFF, BETWEEN PRINCIPLES AND POLITICS: THE DIRECTION OF U.S. CITIZENSHIP

From Migrants to Citizens: Membership in a Changing World, T. Alexander
Aleinikoff & Douglas Klusmeyer, eds., 137–41 (2000).

International law and practice generally view dual citizenship with disfavor. The preamble to the 1930 Hague Convention Concerning Certain Questions relating to the Conflict of Nationality Laws represents the traditional view. It states that "it is in the interest of the international community to secure that all members should recognize that every person should have a nationality and should have one nationality only." Dual citizenship raises concerns for states regarding diplomatic protection (particularly when a citizen resident in one country travels to another country in which he or she holds citizenship), military service, and voting rights. Beyond these more technical issues are deeper questions of divided loyalty. The German Federal Constitutional Court has stated:

> It is accurate to say that dual or multiple nationality is regarded, both domestically and internationally, as an evil that should be avoided or eliminated in the interest of states as well as in the interests of the affected citizen. * * * States seek to achieve exclusivity of their respective nationalities in order to set clear boundaries for their sovereignty over persons; they want to be secure in the duty of loyalty of their citizens—which extends if necessary as far as risking one's life—and do not want to see it endangered by possible conflicts with a loyalty to a foreign state.[45]

The most serious loyalty issue arises at times of war. But today, in the post-cold war setting, *political* loyalty is a more relevant concern. The fear is that a dual citizen of countries A and B could participate in the political system of country A with the interests of country B in mind, or could exploit dual citizenship status for inappropriate personal gain in carrying on business or collecting government benefits. In such a case, it might be questioned whether the citizen possesses the identification with one state that many states may seek to foster in their citizens.

---

45.   Opinion of German Federal Constitutional Court, May 21, 1974, 37 *BVerGE* 217, 254–55.

In a world nominally dedicated to the idea of assuring that every person is a citizen of at least one but not more than one nation-state, dual citizenship is tolerated to a surprising degree. * * *

In the United States, the incidence of dual citizenship is far more widespread than is generally recognized. Plural citizenship may arise in four situations:

1. *Birth in the United States to immigrant parents.* A citizen of country A moves to the United States and has a child. The child is a dual citizen if country A has *jus sanguinis* rules that recognize the child as a citizen of country A. (Example: a German citizen has a child in Chicago. Note that if a German citizen marries a British citizen and they have a child in the United States, the child may be born with three nationalities.)

2. *Birth outside the United States to one parent who is a U.S. citizen and another who is a foreigner.* A citizen of the United States marries a citizen of country A and has a child in country A. If the U.S. citizen has maintained the ties to the United States necessary for the transmission of citizenship *jure sanguinis*, the child is a citizen of both country A and the United States. (Example: A native-born United States citizen marries a British citizen and has a child in the United Kingdom.)

3. *Naturalization with a renunciation requirement, but renunciation not recognized by country of origin.* A citizen of country A naturalizes in the United States. Even though the naturalization oath demands renunciation of other citizenships, country A does not deem naturalization elsewhere as expatriating the citizen. (Example: A Canadian citizen naturalizes in the United States. The U.S. oath requires renunciation, but Canada does not regard naturalization in the United States as expatriating unless the person specifically notifies Canadian authorities of an intent to renounce citizenship.)

4. *Naturalization, loss of citizenship, and resumption of citizenship.* A citizen of country A naturalizes in the United States. Country A deems the person to have lost citizenship but provides for the resumption of citizenship. (Example: Under Australian law, a citizen who naturalizes in the United States loses Australian citizenship. The person can, however, subsequently apply to resume Australian citizenship—this is not a naturalization process—without losing U.S. citizenship unless he or she expresses the intent to do so.)[46]

The U.S. government does not record and has not estimated the number of U.S. dual citizens, but the total may be quite large. Any U.S.-born child of immigrants in the United States is likely at birth to be a citizen of both the United States and the parents' country of origin. Some of the largest "sending" countries to the United States—including Mexico,

---

46. In the late nineteenth century, the rule was generally that a wife took the citizenship of her husband. This is now almost universally rejected, the result being that individuals preserve their own nationality after marriage, although spouses are frequently given preferential treatment under the immigration quotas. See INA § 201(b). This twentieth-century development is a major contributing factor to increases in dual citizenship, since under *jus sanguinis* rules a child will obtain citizenship from each parent.

the Philippines, the Dominican Republic, Canada and India—recognize children born to their nationals here as citizens of their countries. The Census Bureau's March 1996 Current Population Survey provides data that can supply a rough estimate of the number of children born dual nationals in the United States each year. The study reports that there were 540,000 U.S.-citizen children less than one year of age living with at least one foreign-born parent who was not a naturalized U.S. citizen. It is reasonable to assume that most of these children are dual citizens, although the number is not a precise measure. It *under*counts, for example, the number of dual citizens by not including (1) U.S.-born children whose foreign parents left the United States within a year and (2) children of foreign-born parents who have naturalized in the United States but who are still able to transmit the citizenship under their home countries' *jus sanguinis* rules. The number may *over*count the number of dual nationals by including children of foreign-born parents whose home countries do not permit the transmission of citizenship overseas if the foreign-born child obtains another citizenship at birth (China is the most significant example). Nonetheless, half a million is probably an acceptable order of magnitude for the number of children who obtain dual citizenship at birth each year in the United States. Because most countries do not require dual citizens to elect one citizenship over the other, the status may continue for life, and, indeed, can be passed to generations beyond.

The rising incidence of dual citizenship is also due to the growing number of states that have altered their laws to permit their citizens to retain nationality despite naturalization elsewhere. Canada adopted such a policy in 1977, as have (more recently) Argentina, Colombia, Costa Rica, the Dominican Republic, El Salvador, France, Israel, Ireland, Italy, Panama, Switzerland and the United Kingdom.[48] Even in states that deem naturalization in the United States as constituting expatriation, authorities are likely to be unaware of the U.S. naturalization and therefore may continue to treat naturalized individuals as citizens.

IS DUAL CITIZENSHIP A PROBLEM?

Both theoretically and symbolically, dual citizenship may appear problematic. A regime of nation-states arguably functions more smoothly when persons are assigned citizenship in just one state. Unitary citizenship not only resolves various state administrative problems but also, it might be claimed, provides for an indivisible loyalty that states are likely to seek and value.

But the world is more complicated than this ideal allows, and a desire for tidiness is often in conflict with the practicalities of human life. Migration, marriage, and birth ensure that neither states nor their citizenries are hermetically sealed. Indeed, dual citizenship cannot be attributed simply to the (intentional or unintentional) actions of individuals. The existence of plural citizenships is a function of the unwillingness of

---

48. This list is not all inclusive. [For a more recent list, *see* 83 Interp.Rel. 2551–57 (2006)—eds.]

the international community to establish international norms on the acquisition and maintenance of citizenship; international law leaves such matters to the discretion of states, and the resulting welter of rules is wholly a product of state choices.

Although a post-national world still seems far away, it is clear that the world is increasingly transnational. Modern communications and transportation have brought the world to the United States' door as never before, and many of those coming are less willing to leave their countries of origin behind. This reluctance characterizes business elites who seek to take advantage of commercial opportunities in more than one country as well as lower-skilled workers who seek to improve their condition abroad but remain connected to home communities. And, as already noted, "sending" countries show an increasing interest in maintaining ties with their diaspora populations.

From one perspective, these developments represent a healthy development, making commercial and social ties between nations deeper and stronger, opening up new markets, and fostering appreciation of cultural diversity. Little evidence exists that wide-spread dual citizenship in the United States has been harmful to the national interest. While some dual citizens (and naturalized citizens) have committed espionage against the United States, so have persons of one nationality—either native-born citizens or immigrants. Similarly, while concerns have been voiced that dual nationals may vote the interests of their countries of origin ahead of the interests of the United States, the same would be possible whether or not the person officially retains the citizenship of his or her home country.

From another perspective, there is cause for concern. The growing interest of countries of origin in dual citizenship for their nationals may make it a different phenomenon than it was in the past. Furthermore, with the sovereignty of the nation-state being challenged both from within and without, the idea of citizenship may take on increasing importance. Insistence on unitary citizenship could serve as a brake on transnational developments that undermine the loyalty and commitment needed for the healthy functioning of a polyethnic state.

PETER J. SPIRO, DUAL NATIONALITY AND THE MEANING OF CITIZENSHIP

46 Emory L.J. 1411, 1453, 1457, 1459–61, 1465, 1469–71, 1473, 1477–79 (1997).

* * *

Recent years have witnessed a marked softening in state attitudes towards dual nationality. * * * [I argue here] that dual nationality should not simply be tolerated but embraced.

1.   THE DIMINISHED COSTS OF DUAL NATIONALITY
IN A CHANGED GLOBAL CONTEXT

That the risks of dual nationality have diminished is in large part premised on profound changes in the nature of the international system. As has been explored in the recent political science literature, democracies rarely if ever make war on one another.[219] War is what has distinguished relations among states from relations among other types of social organizations, and it is what has made interstate relations of such preemptive importance relative to the domestic, for survival is at stake. That is ultimately what made dual nationals so problematic in a hostile world. In a malign incarnation, they could undermine from within by doing the command of their other allegiance, threatening the polity at a fundamental level.

That threat is an increasingly implausible one. The prospect of war between any major Northern countries is now as remote as at any time since Westphalia. Moreover, even to the extent that armed engagements remain a possibility for countries such as the United States, the nature of those conflicts are likely to reduce the vulnerabilities otherwise created by large dual national populations. Lightning wars conducted by volunteer armies present few opportunities for shadowy fifth columns. That was the case with the [first] Persian Gulf "war" (and could perhaps also be said of the lengthier theater conflicts in Korea and Vietnam). If for some now unfathomable reason we end up at arms with Mexico, it won't be accompanied by the sorts of vulnerabilities (real or perceived) associated with World War II or the Cold War. Finally, assuming the truth of the democratic peace, those regimes with which we do find ourselves in conflict will be by their nature (that is, anti-democratic) unrepresentative of their citizens, and thus less likely to instill the real loyalties of dual nationals even where they command their formal ones. * * *

Nor does the dual national appear now to pose the other costs historically associated with the status, namely, those implicated by diplomatic protection and state responsibility. Even though these costs implicated an innocent dual national rather than the malign, they could be almost as dramatic (including as well the possibility of causing war). But diplomatic protection is no longer so much a function of nationality, in which states take care of their own, as it is covered by the umbrella of international human rights, in which the international community protects the abused regardless of nationality. The intersection of diplomatic protection and dual nationality was far more uncomfortable in a world in which states could treat their own nationals as they pleased. * * * Now that nation states owe certain obligations *erga omnes* respecting the treatment of individuals—that is, they have an obligation to all other states to respect the human rights of all persons, regardless of their

---

219.   *See, e.g.,* Bruce Russett, Grasping the Democratic Peace (1994); Michael W. Doyle, *Kant, Liberal Legacies, and Foreign Affairs*, 12 Phil. & Pub. Aff. 205 (1986). The notion dates to Immanuel Kant, To Perpetual Peace: A Philosophical Sketch (1795).

nationality—dual nationality no longer adds much risk of interstate conflict. * * *

* * *

2. APPLYING CITIZENSHIP FRAMES

* * *

Perhaps the most serious objection to the acceptance of dual nationality * * * hinges on the question of individual independence. Independence is central to the concept of [republican] civic virtue, on which political participation is conditioned; dependence corrupts the process by vaunting personal interests over the common good. It could be asserted that the individual who retains foreign nationality remains at least potentially beholden to a foreign state that is itself hardly motivated by the common good of the country of naturalization. * * *

This might also be characterized as a "marching orders" phenomenon, in which the other country of allegiance expresses its own preferences on a certain political position in this country, with an expectation that those holding citizenship in the other country will act according to those preferences in this one. Say, for instance, that the government of Mexico starts to endorse candidates in U.S. elections with the purpose of steering the votes of dual Mexican–American citizens. Dual Mexican–American nationals would no doubt in that context be charged with something approaching disloyalty, at least by those who stood opposed to Mexican interests.

But it would be the rare case today in which alternate nationality comprised actual dependence. Governments are now hardly in a position to use their nationals as instruments of policy, at least not consistent with international law; that is, Mexico and other countries would have no concrete means by which to lean on their dual nationals resident in the United States to do their bidding within the American political process. Nor indeed is there any indication that foreign countries will attempt to exploit dual nationals to their national advantage, or that they would be able to should they so desire.

Moreover, to the extent that U.S. citizens are politically motivated to act in the interests of their country of origin, it need not, of course, be by virtue of a continuing formal attachment to that state. Americans have long voted their ethnic affiliation, even where they have not maintained their original nationality. They have in the process sometimes been accused of acting for "unpatriotic" reasons. So long as the interests of the U.S. and the other nation are not unalterably opposed—and at present there are few relationships or issues in which that is the case—it is not clear why those motivations should deform the process.

Indeed, it is becoming increasingly difficult to define "national" interests in the first place, much less regard them as irreconcilable with each other. In the Cold War context, an effective national security clearly qualified as such, and many other interests shared broadly by the citizenry flowed from that priority. "In that earlier age," writes Kenichi Ohmae, the national interest "used to provide a clear and unmistakable dividing line between what was ours and what was someone else's."[264] Today, assertion of the national interest appears increasingly to serve as the cloak of special interests. * * *

* * * In today's world, additional allegiances might also be condemned as representing diminished commitment to the American community, attaching oneself, as it were, with temporary cement, and thus diluting the bond that citizenship is meant to reflect and/or facilitate. * * *

* * * At this juncture it is useful to introduce the fact of other concurrent institutional loyalties that almost all individuals hold in their private capacity. The attachments of civil society—to families, schools, ethnic communities, religions, and other non-state associations of almost infinite variety—involve very real loyalties, sometimes higher than that to the state. For family (as with state), most of us would die; religious affiliation, at least in the abstract, can represent an allegiance stronger than that to nation. Loyalties to state and non-state attachments often conflict, in the sense that the national interest may be defined against the interest of the non-state entity. Loyalty to non-state groupings may also detract from the social cohesion of the greater community, insofar as energy devoted to one may on balance subtract from energy devoted to the other. And yet no one would suggest that these non-state identities are inconsistent with one's status as a citizen, nor that the citizenship oath require the renunciation or even subordination of such attachments. * * *

* * *

In short, there is no longer any danger associated with dual national status, little possibility for forced betrayal or scenarios of entanglement. A dual Mexican–American who advocates policies that benefit Mexico is little different from a Catholic who advocates policies endorsed by the Church or a member of Amnesty International who writes his congressman at the organization's behest. There are no questions here of disloyalty, only of interests and identities and of different modes of social contribution. As for commitment, it may be difficult fully to engage in the civic activity of more than one polity. But as Michael Sandel observes, "[d]eciding which of one's identities is properly engaged—as parent or professional, follower of a faith or partisan of a cause, citizen of one's country or citizen of the world—is a matter of moral reflection and political deliberation that will vary according to the issue at stake."[286] We should not disqualify those who might (though not necessarily) devote their civic energies to our national project, even while they maintain formal ties to others. As one observer notes of Mexicans who may avail themselves of dual nationality,

---

264. Kenichi Ohmae, The End of the Nation State 68 (1995). * * *

286. Michael Sandel, Democracy's Discontents: America in Search of a Public Philosophy 343 (1996).

they "consider themselves true contributors to their adopted homeland [at the same time as] they feel a deep connection to their country of origin in their language, their cultural traditions and a heartfelt *cario* (love) that they are unwilling to leave behind."[287]

The implication of all this may be that national citizenship as an institution is less important than it once was. If the significance of citizenship in another state is now equivalent to membership in a religion or civic organization, then it is likely that citizenship in this state, the United States, has also moved to that level. This is an inescapable facet of the post-national world. As the prospect of hurling oneself out of the trenches for country becomes more remote, the attachment becomes less ultimate; and as the need for physical protection—something at which states have always prospered—diminishes, so does the nature of the loyalty. As the power of nation-states declines, so does the force of membership in them. The state can no longer afford to be a "greedy" institution, one that can command exclusive allegiance.[289]

* * *

Consider the following response to Spiro's claim that changes in international politics have made concerns about dual nationality anachronistic.

While it is true that the Cold War is over and that the Soviet Union has dissolved, some of the resulting smaller nation-states, rather than participating in the establishment of universal peace, highlight the continuing danger of ethnic or sectarian strife with resulting protracted conflicts requiring international mediation. * * *

International intervention on behalf of specific individuals may therefore well be required, and such intervention could include consular protection of dual citizens by one of their countries of citizenship against abuses by the other. In addition, even in the absence of traditional wars involving "formal military campaigns" on either a global or a limited scale, new forms of warfare such as "clandestine acts of terrorism or theft of valuable technologies" continue to exist, and dual citizens arguably have the increased access that allows them to execute such acts more easily than aliens. Thus, even on a purely international basis, some of the problems traditionally associated with dual citizenship that caused the passage and retention of the Oath of Renunciation persist in spite of the dramatically changed global landscape.

---

287. *See* Leticia Quezada, *Mexican, American As A Single Identity*, L.A. Times, Dec. 16, 1996, at B5 (op-ed); *see also* Bob Klapisch, *Duncan Training to Become Citizen*, The Record, Mar. 3, 1997, at S2 (quoting baseball player Mariano Duncan as applying for naturalization because he "loves this country," at the same time as he was "relieved" to be able to maintain his Dominican citizenship). * * *

289. *See* Lewis Coser, Greedy Institutions: Patterns of Undivided Commitment (1974).

This analysis revolving around the perceived dangers of dual citizenship furthermore has an entirely external focus and does not address what such completely open access to (dual) citizenship could mean for the internal, national community. In this context, the fact that naturalized citizens can potentially vote in both their countries of citizenship is particularly relevant.

Supporters of the abolition of the renunciation requirement frequently state that, at least from a U.S. perspective, concern is unwarranted about dual citizens' continued ability to vote in their countries of origin and about the possibility of their votes being influenced, presumably in both countries of citizenship, by their alternate citizenship. However, it is unclear whether individuals really can sustain the continued involvement in the day-to-day affairs of two polities that is required for effective participation in the political process and particularly for making informed electoral choices. Reference to the U.S. practice of voting in elections at several levels (that is, federal, state, and local elections) does not overcome this question because the polities at issue with this type of multiple voting are integrated with each other and form part of an overarching federal nation in which the voter is present. Voting by dual citizens, in contrast, involves polities with potentially different electoral systems that are geographically remote and completely independent. Additionally, the voter permanently resides in only one of the polities involved. Consequently, information relevant to making informed electoral decisions in the country of citizenship of which the dual citizen is not a resident is more difficult to obtain, requiring a much more conscious and determined—and therefore more unlikely—effort on the part of the dual citizen to remain an effective participant in that country's polity.

* * *

[C]oncerns about dual voting in particular and dual citizenship obligations in general are not allayed by the frequent comparison of dual citizens' relationship to their countries of citizenship with mono-citizens' membership in families, churches, clubs, or associations that may also influence the way votes are cast and other political decisions are made. These alternative institutions are fundamentally different from another nation in that they have claims on the individual that are either limited to a particular sphere (that is, religion, environmental protection) or operate on a different level (that is, family). The potential for the interests of the alternative institution to be directly opposed or contrary to those of the country of citizenship is therefore limited. Countries of origin, in contrast, operate directly at a parallel to the United States (that is, they have the same claims on the individual and operate on the same levels) so that the likelihood of their interests being in conflict with those of the United States is considerably greater. Thus, voting in two countries is more akin to membership in two churches of different denominations or to having polygamous marriages, both of which are generally prohibited.

* * *

Scherner–Kim, Note, *The Role of the Oath of Renunciation in Current U.S. Nationality Policy—To Enforce, To Omit, or Maybe to Change?*, 88 Geo. L.J. 329, 350–53 (2000). *See also* Martin, *New Rules on Dual Nationality for a Democratizing Globe: Between Rejection and Embrace*, 14 Geo. Immig. L.J. 1 (1999).

Concerns over dual nationality remain active. In discussing immigration reform, Bruce Fein argued for steps to diminish dual nationality and its impacts:

> Undivided loyalty strengthens. Dual citizenship weakens. * * * Rep. Sam Graves, Missouri Republican, plans to propose an amendment to an immigration bill * * * [to criminally punish] acts that signal disloyalty to the United States, for example, serving in a foreign army or as an official in a foreign state. It should command universal support.

> The United States is defined by common habits, customs, ideas and values—for example, self-initiative, the rule of law, religious freedom and self government. The Founding Fathers recognized divided political or cultural loyalties would endanger the nation's unity and viability.

* * *

These views found expression in the Naturalization Acts of 1795. The statutes required would be citizens to "satisfy a court of admission as to their good moral character and of their attachment to the principles of the Constitution."

Equally important, they required an Oath of Renunciation and Allegiance to protect against citizens whose hearts or minds remained in foreign lands[.] * * *

Single allegiance and devotion to the United States is calculated to encourage a sweeping array of voluntary civic actions essential to national cohesion, community welfare and a flourishing democracy: reporting crime or antisocial activity to proper authorities; testifying at criminal trials and serving as conscientious jurors; voting; joining a political party; writing letters to the editor; peacefully challenging government policies; denouncing hate speech or bigotry; contributing time to the PTA, Little League, public school events or the local fire department; making charitable contributions for municipal, state or national causes; or joining the volunteer armed forces. Unitary allegiance also inclines citizens to believe and act on the idea what is good for the United States is good for them.

A competing citizenship is likely to divert a citizen's energies and ambitions away from the United States and into foreign politics, governments, armies and culture.

The problem is not academic. About 90 percent of contemporary immigrants hail from countries that permit or encourage dual citizenship, including Mexico. It accounts for 30 percent of the immigrant population in the United States.

Mexican officials have candidly acknowledged that offering Americans of Mexican ancestry Mexican citizenship aims to weaken their attachments to the United States. In 1997, a committee chairman of the Mexican Senate elaborated: "[T]he reports [on dual nationality] that we present today ... recognize that Mexicans abroad are equal to those of us who inhabit Mexican national territory. Belonging to Mexico is fixed in bonds of a cultural and spiritual order, in customs, aspirations and convictions that today are the essence of a universally recognized civilization."

Juan Hernandez, 2000–2002 head of the Office for Mexicans Abroad, told ABC's "Nightline," "we are betting" U.S. citizens of Mexican ancestry "will think Mexico first, even to the seventh generation," and to the *Denver Post* that Mexican immigrants "are going to keep one foot in Mexico" and "are not going to assimilate in the sense of dissolving into not being Mexican."

Mexico's success in wooing Americans of Mexican ancestry into its orbit is epitomized by Manuel de la Cruz, a naturalized citizen from Los Angeles who emigrated 34 years ago. On July 4, 2004, Mr. de la Cruz was elected to the legislature of the Mexican state of Zacatecas, where he took an oath of allegiance to the Mexican Republic despite his previous Oath of Renunciation and Allegiance to obtain U.S. citizenship.

Mr. Graves' amendment would seek to deter such blatant evasions [of the renunciation oath] by making criminal voting in a foreign election, seeking electoral office in a foreign state or serving in a foreign government. Its enactment should be but the first step to halt an insidious attenuation of citizen love for the United States.

Learn from the Roman Empire: Its collapse began with the refusal of its citizens to guard the borders.

Fein, *Divided Loyalties*, Wash. Times, Dec. 13, 2005, at A19.*

NOTES AND QUESTIONS ON DUAL CITIZENSHIP

1. Spiro suggests that "it is an inescapable fact of the post-national world" that "the significance of citizenship in another state is now equivalent to membership in a religious or civic organization." Do you agree? In speaking

---

* Copyright © 2005 The Washington Times LLC. This reprint does not constitute or imply any endorsement or sponsorship of any product, service, company or organization.

of these other attachments and loyalties to non-state groups, he states that "no one would suggest that these non-state identities are inconsistent with one's status as a citizen, nor that the citizenship oath require the renunciation or even subordination of such attachments." But another part of the naturalization statute with ancient roots still requires express renunciation of any hereditary title or order of nobility in any foreign state. INA § 337(b). If one accepts Spiro's argument, must that renunciation oath also be eliminated? What does each such renunciation requirement reveal about the underlying concept of American membership?

2. Spiro's article was published several years before the events of September 11, 2001. To what extent might those acts and the war on terrorism alter Spiro's analysis?[5]

Throughout this chapter we have discussed *U.S.* citizenship, with the implicit understanding that citizenship is a status necessarily linked with a nation. Is this assumption valid? In this concluding selection, Linda Bosniak notes that the term is frequently mobilized in other contexts—to connote a system of rights, a form of political activity, or a form of identity and solidarity. She asks whether citizenship is a concept that is necessarily "inextricably bound up with the nation-state."

LINDA BOSNIAK, CITIZENSHIP DENATIONALIZED

7 Ind. J. Global Legal Studies 447, 454–488, 506 (2000).

* * *

A.   CITIZENSHIP AS LEGAL STATUS

In one of its aspects, citizenship is a matter of legal recognition. To be a citizen is to "possess the legal status of a citizen."[24] In this usage, citizenship refers to formal or nominal membership in an organized political community.

* * *

In general terms, treating citizenship as a status exclusively tied to the nation-state is a reasonable premise. As a practical matter, citizenship is almost always conferred by the nation-state, and as a matter of international law, it is nation-state citizenship that is recognized and honored. It is true that people throughout much of the world enjoy formal legal memberships in subnational entities, including provinces, states, and

---

5. For further discussion of a number of aspects of dual nationality, see A. Boll, Multiple Nationality and International Law (2007); S. Renshon, The 50% American: Immigration and National Identity in an Age of Terror (2005); D. Martin & K. Hailbronner, eds., Rights and Duties of Dual Nationals: Evolution and Prospect (2003); R. Hansen & P.Weil, eds., Dual Nationality, Social Rights and Federal Citizenship in the U.S. and Europe: The Reinvention of Citizenship (2002).

24. Carens, *Dimensions of Citizenship and National Identity in Canada*, 28 Phil. F. 111, 112 (1996–97).

municipalities. But these memberships are often subordinated to the demands of national citizenship as a matter of domestic law, and are almost always regarded as subsidiary in the international arena.

Some commentators have pointed to three recent developments, however, which in their view signal an increasing denationalization of citizenship status in the current period. The first and most obvious is the case of the European Union (EU), where efforts have been underway to construct a regionally-framed supranational citizenship—a European citizenship. This development no doubt importantly challenges the conventional correspondence that we ordinarily assume exists between citizenship and national membership, and alerts us to possibilities for nonnation-centered arrangements. A few commentators have seen more dramatic import, however, contending that in light of developments in the EU, the assumption of the territorial nation-state as the "unquestioned terrain of membership has today disintegrated," resulting in a "crisis of citizenship."[28] By "breach[ing] the link between status attached to citizenship and national territory," another suggests, EU citizenship portends "postnational" forms of citizenship the world over.[29]

These characterizations strike me as something of an overstatement. Certainly, citizenship is being dramatically reconstituted in Europe. For EU citizens, Europe's internal borders have been effectively removed with the guarantee of the right to free movement; and EU citizens enjoy economic rights and some political rights at a supranational level. On the other hand, EU citizenship remains subordinate to European national citizenships in important respects. First, the Treaty on European Union specifically defines EU citizens as those persons "holding the nationality of a Member State;" and it is national law that ordinarily determines who will be deemed EU citizens. Furthermore, the entity in which this new citizenship is based is still controlled in important ways by the individual states that comprise it; as one commentator put it, "the real *locus* of political power in the Community remains, as it has since the Community's foundations, with the governments of the Member States."[36]

Finally, it must also be recalled that the case of the European Union is not, as yet, generalizable. Formal citizenship is currently nonexistent in any other supranational body (including at the world level), and its establishment elsewhere is unlikely any time soon. In this respect, while European citizenship represents a real departure from the national model, the departure is limited in both kind and effect.

Somewhat less persuasive are two additional claims made on behalf of the denationalization of citizenship status. One of these, advanced by Soysal, holds that the enjoyment by long-term resident aliens of substantial membership rights in many liberal democratic states signals the

---

28. Vogel & Moran, *Introduction, in* The Frontiers of Citizenship x, xii (U. Vogel & M. Moran eds., 1991).

29. Y. Soysal, Limits of Citizenship: Migrants and Postnational Membership in Europe 147 (1994).

36. S. Hall, Nationality, Migration Rights and Citizenship of the Union 11 (1995).

postnationalization of citizenship.[37] The extension of rights to aliens entails citizenship's postnationalization, Soysal maintains, because the source of many of these rights lies in the international human rights regime, which accords recognition to individuals on the basis of their personhood rather than their national affiliation. As she sees it, the imperatives of national belonging are subordinated to the norms of transnational membership—norms which themselves afford an alternative, denationalized kind of citizenship.

Soysal is not the first to point out that aliens enjoy important rights traditionally associated with citizenship in many host societies. Her innovation is to argue that the source of these rights resides in the international human rights regime. One problem with this claim, however, is that it has limited empirical application. However accurate Soysal's portrait is of the status of aliens in Europe, her model fails to capture the dynamic of alien status in many countries—among them, the United States—where the often-substantial membership rights that aliens enjoy are not grounded in the international human rights regime at all, but in the national system itself. In the United States, the tension between personhood and citizenship as the basis for rights is, in fact, a chronic national preoccupation; and the commitment to personhood over citizenship is often experienced and expressed in the most nationalist of terms. It is the United States Constitution that is invariably invoked to ground the protections aliens have enjoyed here.

There is another more conceptual problem with Soysal's argument as well. The difficulty is that she analytically conflates distinct senses of citizenship in a way that makes for confusion. One may reasonably argue, as she does, that the increasing guarantee of human rights at the level of international law signals that citizenship is becoming denationalized. Here, "citizenship" is treated as a state of enjoying basic rights; it is becoming denationalized, in this argument, in that the enjoyment of rights no longer depends so fundamentally on nationally-based norms. * * *

Notice, however, that this is an argument about citizenship *qua* rights generally; the claim concerns the disarticulation of rights norms from nation-states for *everyone*. It is not a claim about aliens in particular. Aliens can, I believe, be argued to enjoy a modicum of "citizenship" by virtue of the various social and economic rights they have been afforded in national and international law—however paradoxical this may sound. Yet, the fact that aliens enjoy these rights does not mean that their formal or nominal legal status vis-a-vis the political community in which they reside has changed. When citizenship is understood as formal legal membership in the polity, aliens remain outsiders to citizenship: they reside in the host country only at the country's discretion; there are often restrictions imposed on their travel; they are denied the right to participate politically at the national level; and they are often precluded from naturalizing.

---

37. Soysal, Limits of Citizenship, at 2–4.

Furthermore, they symbolically remain outsiders to membership in the polity.

* * *

As a third signal of citizenship's increasing denationalization, some commentators have pointed to the growing incidence around the world of dual, and sometimes multiple, citizenships. Today, more people than ever hold citizenship in more than one nation—the result, in part, of the recent liberalization of different national rules on naturalization, expatriation, and assignment of citizenship at birth, which together make multiple citizenships possible and often routine. Without question, this is a significant development in the history of citizenship; it is significant because historically—and ideally—citizenship has been regarded as an exclusive status, one the individual maintains with a single nation-state. Yet multiple citizenships can hardly be said to represent a "postnational" form of citizenship or membership, as some commentators have suggested. For while it is true that multiple citizenships do entail divided commitments and identities on the part of those who hold them, these commitments and identities remain firmly bound to nation-state entities. In this respect, the "multinationalization" of citizenship would provide a better characterization.

* * *

B.   CITIZENSHIP AS RIGHTS

In twentieth-century social theory, the notion of citizenship has been most closely associated with the enjoyment of certain important rights and entitlements. In this conception of citizenship, the enjoyment of rights is the defining feature of societal membership: citizenship requires the possession of rights, and those who possess the rights are usually presumed thereby to enjoy citizenship.

* * *

Does it make sense to view the growing international human rights regime as a nascent form of citizenship beyond the nation? * * * Assuming that the enjoyment of rights is to remain one aspect of what we understand citizenship to be, it seems fair to conclude that the national grip on citizenship in this particular aspect has been substantially loosened. It is clearly a significant development in the history of claims-making that individuals may today reach beyond state law to press their claims of right against the state itself. On the other hand, there remain serious questions about the extent to which this development signals a transfer in the locus of citizenship given the lack of existing enforcement mechanisms that can give real effect to these claims. In either case, it bears reminding that rights are not the sole measure of citizenship, and that we need to look beyond rights-based conceptions to inquire about the denationalization of citizenship in its other dimensions.

C. CITIZENSHIP AS POLITICAL ACTIVITY

As political theorists use the term, "citizenship" most commonly denotes active engagement in the life of the political community. This political understanding of citizenship derives from the ancient Greeks. According to Aristotle, the citizen is "one who participates in the rights of judging and governing;" he is a man who both rules and is ruled. The tradition was elaborated by later figures, including Machiavelli and Rousseau, and had a critical role in shaping both U.S. and French revolutionary thought.

* * *

* * * [Thus] analysts maintain that citizenship today increasingly traverses national boundaries. There is by now a burgeoning literature on "new transnational forms of political organization, mobilization, and practice"[105] which have emerged in the wake of accelerating processes of globalization. This work addresses the proliferation of transnational political activity in the form of non-governmental organizations (NGOs), grassroots social movements, and other cross-border organizing efforts in the areas, for example, of human rights, the environment, arms control, women's rights, labor rights, and the rights of national minorities.

* * *

Many of [the]e alternative sites of political life have been characterized by scholars as constituting part of the domain of "civil society." Though a contested concept itself, civil society is often described as the sphere of association or sociability—the sphere in which people engage with one another and forge "relational networks" independent of the demands of polity governance. While some theorists presume or posit a contrast between the life people engage in within civil society and their practice of citizenship, others increasingly recognize that politics is not confined to the domain of the state, and that "citizenship shades off into a great diversity of (sometimes divisive) decision-making roles" within civil society.[123] The growth and influence of the "new social movements" are the most salient expression of this trend; they represent the practice of citizenship in the heart of civil society.

* * *

D. CITIZENSHIP AS IDENTITY/SOLIDARITY

Beyond citizenship as a status, as a set of entitlements, or as a mode of political participation and activity, citizenship possesses another dimension, one that concerns people's collective experience of themselves. I refer to citizenship's psychological dimension, that part of citizenship that describes the affective ties of identification and solidarity that we main-

---

105. Smith, *Can You Imagine? Transnational Migration and the Globalization of Grassroots Politics*, 39 Soc. Text 15 (1994).

123. M. Walzer, *The Civil Society Argument*, *in* Dimensions of Radical Democracy 99 (Chantal Mouffe ed., 1992).

tain with groups of other people in the world. The term citizenship here is deployed to evoke the quality of belonging—the felt aspects of community membership.

* * *

* * * Some scholars concerned with citizenship have begun to question the presumption that national identity fundamentally characterizes people's sense of citizenship in liberal democratic nation-states. They point out that people often maintain greater allegiances to and identifications with particular cultural and social groups within the nation than they do with the nation at large. Some further charge that the very notion of a common national identity is a chimera, one dependent upon the suppression and marginalization of social and cultural difference. These and other critics have called for recognition of a "differentiated citizenship,"[142] according to which "members of certain groups would be incorporated into the political community not only as individuals but also through the [cultural] group."[143]

This "cultural pluralist," or multiculturalist position on citizenship, offers a powerful challenge to the default presumption in much political and social theory that people's foremost collective identifications and solidarities are going to be bound up with the state or with their compatriots at large. Yet its departure from the nationalist vision of citizenship is only partial. For despite their critique of a presumed national identity, cultural pluralists continue to posit the nation-state as the discussion's normative frame. * * *

* * *

To argue * * * that national identities and solidarities are not necessarily paramount in many people's experiences is by no means to claim that national affiliations no longer matter; for they clearly do matter to many people in many circumstances. Nor need a critique of liberal nationalism entail the view that all forms of national identity and solidarity should not matter in normative terms. The postnationalist claim is best read, it seems to me, not as a claim advocating the demise of nation-states and nationalism altogether, but on behalf of decentering or "demoting" the nation from its privileged status in political thought. The idea of "postnational citizenship," in other words, should be read to suggest an aspiration toward a multiple, pluralized understanding of citizenship identity and citizen solidarity.

In such a reading, liberal nationalists' apparent openness to plural identities and solidarities would be deepened, and nationality would be regarded as one among many possible sources and sites of identity. We

---

142. Young, *Polity and Group Difference: A Critique of the Ideal of Universal Citizenship*, 99 Ethics 250, 251 (1989).

143. Kymlicka & Norman, *Return of the Citizen: A Survey of Recent Work on Citizenship Theory*, 104 Ethics 352, 370 (1994).

would celebrate not the decline of the nation-state, but the proliferation of a variety of possible sites of identity and solidarity.

QUESTIONS ON DE-COUPLING CITIZENSHIP FROM THE NATION STATE

Do you share Bosniak's "aspiration toward a multiple, pluralized understanding of citizenship identity and citizenship solidarity"? What reasons can you list for maintaining a view of citizenship that is more unitary—one that affirms close and exclusive ties with a community that constitutes a nation-state?

SECTION C. NATURALIZATION

In addition to acquiring citizenship at birth, individuals can seek a new citizenship later in life. Indeed, the Constitution of the United States, a country that envisioned itself as a new land attractive to settlers from other nations, expressly grants Congress the authority to create a "uniform Rule of Naturalization." The following selections first review the history of U.S. naturalization legislation and then turn the focus onto the racial restrictions that characterized those laws until 1952.

New York street corner next to the Federal Building where the U.S. Department of Labor handled naturalization of immigrants (1939) (Photo: National Archives)

CHARLES GORDON, STANLEY MAILMAN, AND STEPHEN YALE–LOEHR, IMMIGRATION LAW AND PROCEDURE

Vol. 4, § 94.01[2] (rev. ed. 2003).*

* * *

In the original statute of March 26, 1790, Congress prescribed that a free white alien who had resided in the United States for two years, including residence of one year in any State, might be naturalized by any common law court of record, provided the person was of good moral character and took an oath to support the Constitution. Five years later the 1790 statute was repealed by the Act of January 29, 1795, which re-enacted most of its provisions, with the following additions: The period of required residence in the United States increased to five years; federal courts were also able to grant naturalization; a formal declaration of intention three years before admission to citizenship was made a prerequisite; applicants were required to renounce their former allegiance and to swear allegiance to the United States; and applicants had to establish to the satisfaction of the court that they were attached to the Constitution of the United States and well disposed to the good order and happiness of the United States.

The statutory requirements for naturalization formulated at this time resembled very closely the substantive requirements now generally prescribed. However, the 1795 law was short-lived. The country entered a period of reaction characterized by outbursts against aliens. One product of this interlude of hysteria was the enactment of the Alien and Sedition acts. Another was the Act of June 18, 1798, which repealed the lenient provisions of the 1795 statute, and announced more restrictive naturalization requirements. The period of required residence was increased to 14 years in the United States and five years in a state; a declaration of intention at least five years before naturalization was prescribed; registration of aliens became mandatory; and residence for the purposes of naturalization could be proved only upon production of a certificate of registry. Naturalization of alien enemies was prohibited.

Fortunately this interval of reaction soon ended. The Act of April 14, 1802 repealed the 1798 statute and restored the reasonable requirements of the 1795 law, which have remained generally in effect through two centuries.

Although the early laws established acceptable substantive requirements, they were silent concerning the procedure to be followed. There were thousands of naturalization courts throughout the country, most of which were local courts in the various states. Each tribunal determined the procedure it would pursue in applications for naturalization. There was no centralized federal agency charged with the responsibility of enforcing the naturalization statutes.

This situation may have been adequate when there were few courts and a moderate quota of applicants for naturalization. With the expansion of immigration and the consequent increase in the number of aliens who sought naturalization, serious shortcomings in the naturalization process became evident. The absence of procedural standards and safeguards bred wide divergences in the practices of different naturalization courts, in the records they maintained, and in the type of evidence of citizenship they issued. The courts had no facilities to investigate the applications presented to them, and many of the court officials were not scrupulous in insisting upon compliance with the requirements fixed by law. As a result of these conditions, widespread frauds developed, which frequently made a mockery of the naturalization process.

On March 1, 1905 President Theodore Roosevelt appointed a commission to investigate abuses in the naturalization process and to recommend appropriate revisions. As the result of the report of this commission, Congress enacted the Naturalization Act of June 29, 1906. Under this statute the courts retained the ultimate authority to grant or deny citizenship, but administrative supervision over naturalization was vested in a federal agency (originally the Bureau of Immigration and Naturalization in the Department of Commerce and Labor).

* * *

Congress [later] enacted the Nationality Act of 1940 as a codification and revision of all existing nationality laws. * * *

The next major milestone in the historical pattern was the Immigration and Nationality Act of 1952, which is now the basic statute for U.S. immigration and nationality law. * * * Among the major changes effected by the 1952 Act were the following:

> The racial qualifications for naturalization were completely eliminated, and the statute specifically prohibited denial of naturalization because of race or sex.

> The statute, incorporating an enactment of 1950, specifically prohibited the naturalization of certain members of subversive groups. * * *

> Naturalization was precluded for aliens against whom a deportation proceeding or order was outstanding. * * *

> The declaration of intention and the certificate of arrival were eliminated as requirements for naturalization.

> The grounds for expatriation and denaturalization were enlarged.

The Immigration Act of 1990 (1990 Act) had a significant effect on naturalization by transferring authority over naturalization from the judiciary to the Attorney General. Consequently, the naturalization process has evolved from a judicial framework to almost entirely an administrative one * * * [—although federal judges are still normally involved in administering the oath as part of the naturalization ceremony. With the abolition of the INS and the transfer of functions to the Department of Homeland Security in 2003, these administrative responsibilities are now lodged in DHS' Bureau of Citizenship and Immigration Services (USCIS).]

* * *

* * * Under administrative naturalization [DHS] now has the exclusive power to make decisions on naturalization applications. [Administrative] officers are no longer making recommendations to the judiciary. In actuality, the new procedures for handling naturalization applications on the administrative level are very similar to past procedures in judicial naturalization. [Administrative officers were] already responsible for most aspects of the naturalization process and established forms, systems, and procedures for handling virtually all phases of the process except the oath. [DHS] continues to evaluate applicants according to virtually the same criteria for eligibility that it used under the judicial system.

IAN F. HANEY LÓPEZ, RACIAL RESTRICTIONS IN THE LAW OF CITIZENSHIP

White By Law: The Legal Construction of Race, 37, 39, 42–46 (1996).

The racial composition of the U.S. citizenry reflects in part the accident of world migration patterns. More than this, however, it reflects the conscious design of U.S. immigration and naturalization laws.

* * *

* * * From this country's inception, the laws regulating who was or could become a citizen were tainted by racial prejudice. * * * Naturalized citizenship, the acquisition of citizenship by any means other than through birth, was conditioned on race until 1952. Like immigration laws, the laws of birthright citizenship and naturalization shaped the racial character of the United States.

Although the Constitution did not originally define the citizenry, it explicitly gave Congress the authority to establish the criteria for granting citizenship after birth. Article I grants Congress the power "To establish a[n] uniform Rule of Naturalization." From the start, Congress exercised this power in a manner that burdened naturalization laws with racial restrictions that tracked those in the law of birthright citizenship. In 1790, only a few months after ratification of the Constitution, Congress limited naturalization to "any alien, being a free white person who shall have resided within the limits and under the jurisdiction of the United States for a term of two years." * * * Though there would be many subsequent changes in the requirements for federal naturalization, racial identity endured as a bedrock requirement for the next 162 years. * * *

The history of racial prerequisites to naturalization can be divided into two periods of approximately eighty years each. The first period extended from 1790 to 1870, when only Whites were able to naturalize. In the wake of the Civil War, the "white person" restriction on naturalization came under serious attack as part of the effort to expunge *Dred Scott*. Some congressmen, Charles Sumner chief among them, argued that racial barriers to naturalization should be struck altogether. However, racial prejudice against Native Americans and Asians forestalled the complete elimination of the racial prerequisites. During congressional debates, one senator argued against conferring "the rank, privileges, and immunities of citizenship upon the cruel savages who destroyed [Minnesota's] peaceful settlements and massacred the people with circumstances of atrocity too horrible to relate." Another senator wondered "whether this door [of citizenship] shall now be thrown open to the Asiatic population," warning that to do so would spell for the Pacific coast "an end to republican government there, because it is very well ascertained that those people have no appreciation of that form of government; it seems to be obnoxious to their very nature; they seem to be incapable either of understanding or carrying it out." Sentiments such as these ensured that even after the Civil War, bars against Native American and Asian naturalization would continue. Congress opted to maintain the "white person" prerequisite, but to extend the right to naturalize to "persons of African nativity, or African descent." After 1870, Blacks as well as Whites could naturalize, but not others.

During the second period, from 1870 until the last of the prerequisite laws were abolished in 1952, the White–Black dichotomy in American race relations dominated naturalization law. During this period, Whites and Blacks were eligible for citizenship, but others, particularly those from Asia, were not. Indeed, increasing antipathy toward Asians on the West Coast resulted in an explicit disqualification of Chinese persons from naturalization in 1882. The prohibition of Chinese naturalization, the only U.S. law ever to exclude by name a particular nationality from citizenship, was coupled with [a] ban on Chinese immigration. * * *

World War II forced a domestic reconsideration of the racism integral to U.S. naturalization law. In 1935, Hitler's Germany limited citizenship to members of the Aryan race, making Germany the only country other than the United States with a racial restriction on naturalization. * * * Furthermore, the United States was open to charges of hypocrisy for banning from naturalization the nationals of many of its Asian allies. During the war, the United States seemed through some of its laws and social practices to embrace the same racism it was fighting. Both fronts of the war exposed profound inconsistencies between U.S. naturalization law and broader social ideals. These considerations, among others, led Congress to begin a process of piecemeal reform in the laws governing citizenship.

In 1940, Congress opened naturalization to "descendants of races indigenous to the Western Hemisphere." Apparently, this "additional limitation was designed 'to more fully cement' the ties of Pan–Americanism" at a time of impending crisis.[40] In 1943, Congress replaced the prohibition on the naturalization of Chinese persons with a provision explicitly granting them this boon. In 1946, it opened up naturalization to persons from the Philippines and India as well. * * * In 1952, Congress moved towards wholesale reform, overhauling the naturalization statute to read simply that "[t]he right of a person to become a naturalized citizen of the United States shall not be denied or abridged because of race or sex or because such person is married."[44] Thus, in 1952, racial bars on naturalization came to an official end.

NOTES AND QUESTIONS ON RACIAL CRITERIA FOR CITIZENSHIP

1. As might be imagined, the statutory requirement that applicants for naturalization be "white" produced difficult questions of interpretation for administrative and judicial authorities. The Supreme Court adopted varying approaches for resolving the question. In *Ozawa v. United States*, 260 U.S. 178, 43 S.Ct. 65, 67 L.Ed. 199 (1922), the Court held that a "person of the Japanese race" is not "white" within the meaning of the statute because, as "sustained by numerous scientific authorities," Japanese are not members of "the Caucasian race." A year later in *United States v. Thind*, 261 U.S. 204, 43 S.Ct. 338, 67 L.Ed. 616 (1923), the Court concluded that "a high-caste Hindu of full Indian blood" was not eligible for naturalization. Whether or not Thind was classified as "Caucasian" by "certain scientific authorities," the word "white" was to be interpreted "in accordance with the understanding of the common man. * * * [W]hatever may be the speculations of the ethnologist, it does not include the body of people to whom [Thind] belongs." The Court noted: "It is very far from our thought to suggest the slightest question of racial superiority or inferiority. What we suggest is merely racial difference, and it is of such character and extent that the great body of our people instinctively recognize it and reject the thought of assimilation." 261 U.S. at 215.

2. The history that Haney López recounts demonstrates that for most of this nation's history, our naturalization laws have excluded persons based solely on their race. The Court's assertion in *Thind* that these exclusions had nothing to do with notions of racial superiority strains credulity. As we shall see, similar notions marked the history of U.S. immigration law. Citizenship and immigration law, as gateways to membership, reflect deep-seated societal views of who belongs. Should we read the history as a progressive vindication of principles of equality and fairness; or is our history more cyclical, with nativist and exclusionary themes regularly coming to the fore? Rogers Smith has suggested that "the very success of liberalizing and democratizing reforms is to unsettle many, creating constituencies for rebuilding ascriptive inequalities in new forms. The overall pattern will be one of fluctuation between consensual and egalitarian and more ascriptive and inegalitarian arrangements, with the long-term trends being products of contingent politics more than inexorable cultural necessities." R. Smith, Civic Ideals: Conflicting

---

40. Note, *The Nationality Act of 1940*, 54 Harv.L.Rev. 860, 865 n.40 (1941).

44. Immigration and Nationality Act of 1952, ch. 2, § 311, 66 Stat. 239 (codified as amended at INA § 311).

Visions of Citizenship in U.S. History 9 (1997). Do the materials in this chapter tend to support or refute this claim?

3.   Note that at the same time that persons were excluded from naturalizing on the basis of their race, their children born in the United States were citizens at birth by force of the Fourteenth Amendment. Is there a coherent theory of citizenship that explains the co-existence of these apparently conflicting rules?

1.   A SNAPSHOT OF NATURALIZATION DEMOGRAPHICS

The number of individuals applying for naturalization in the United States increased significantly in the 1920s, again in the 1940s, and most dramatically in the last three decades. From 1946 to 1984, the number of persons naturalized only once exceeded 200,000 in any single year. Beginning in the late 1980s, the number of both applications and naturalizations increased substantially, with annual naturalizations rising from an

Figure 2.1
Persons Naturalized: Fiscal Years 1907 to 2010

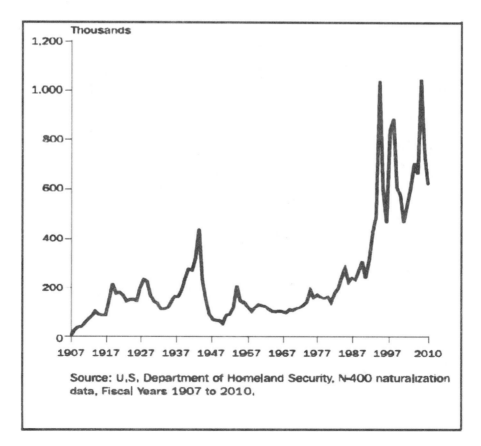

Source: U.S. Department of Homeland Security, N-400 naturalization data, Fiscal Years 1907 to 2010.

average of 248,000 from 1985–1990 to an average of 560,000 from 1991–2000. At least three different factors contributed to this rise. First, the cohort of immigrants legalized under the Immigration Reform and Control Act of 1986 (IRCA), Pub.L. 99–603, 100 Stat. 3359, became eligible for citizenship. (As we will examine below in Chapter Five, naturalization permits the new citizen to sponsor close family members for immigration on far more favorable terms than those that apply to lawful permanent resident (LPR) sponsors.) Second, there can be little doubt that the anti-immigrant rhetoric of the mid–1990s led some immigrants to seek the security of U.S. citizenship. Third, the welfare reform legislation of 1996, which severely limited eligibility of permanent resident aliens for most means-tested benefit programs, sparked a demand for naturalization as immigrants sought to preserve their access (at present or in the future) to the social safety net.

While application numbers fell after hitting a peak of 1,040,991 in 1997, in recent years they have remained at levels that are high by historical standards and have experienced notable one-year jumps. For example, in 2007 naturalization application numbers surged immediately prior to a scheduled application fee increase before returning to levels more in line with previous years.

Table 2.1
Naturalizations, FY 1991–2010

Fiscal year	Applications filed	Persons naturalized	Petitions denied
1991	206,668	307,394	6,268
1992	342,238	239,664	19,293
1993	521,886	313,590	39,931
1994	543,353	429,123	40,561
1995	959,963	485,720	46,067
1996	1,277,403	1,040,991	229,842
1997	1,412,712	596,010	130,676
1998	932,957	461,169	137,395
1999	765,346	837,418	379,993
2000	460,916	886,026	399,670
2001	501,643	606,259	218,326
2002	700,649	572,646	139,779
2003	523,370	462,435	91,599
2004	662,796	537,151	103,339
2005	602,972	604,280	108,247
2006	730,642	702,589	120,722
2007	1,382,993	660,477	89,683
2008	525,786	1,046,539	121,283
2009	570,442	743,715	109,813
2010	710,544	619,913	56,990

Source: DHS, Yearbook of Immigration Statistics: 2010, Table 20; http://www.dhs.gov/xlibrary/assets/statistics/yearbook/2010/table20.xls.

In fiscal year 2010, the leading countries of origin of naturalized citizens were Mexico (10.8 percent of the total), India, the Philippines, China, and Vietnam. This result is not surprising, as these countries have been among the leading source countries of immigrants to the United States for some time.

Over the past two decades, the percentage of foreign born in the United States who have naturalized has risen despite a large increase in the country's total foreign born population. From 1990 to 2009, the percentage of foreign-born persons who are naturalized U.S. citizens rose from 41 percent to 44 percent. During that same period, the total number of foreign born persons living in the United States grew by 95 percent to reach a total of 38,517,234. *See* Table 1. Foreign–Born Population and World Region of Birth (1990, 2000, and 2009) *available at* http://www.migrationinformation.org/datahub/state.cfm?ID=US.

An interesting comparative perspective on the percentage of naturalizations in the United States is offered by Irene Bloemraad:

> In the mid–1900s, almost four of every five foreign-born U.S. and Canadian residents held citizenship in their adopted lands. Fifty years later, citizenship levels had changed little in Canada: about three quarters of the foreign-born had Canadian passports in 2001. In contrast, U.S. citizenship hovered at its lowest level in a century. Only two of every five foreign-born had naturalized in 2000.

Bloemraad, *Becoming a Citizen in the United States and Canada: Structured Mobilization and Immigrant Political Incorporation*, 85 Social Forces 667 (2006).

The large unauthorized immigrant community in the United States accounts for some of the difference in naturalization rates because they cannot become citizens. Further, the 1990s witnessed a very large increase in immigration to the United States, and the naturalization rate in 2000 may not be representative of the overall naturalization process. Nonetheless, Bloemraad theorizes that additional factors may be at work. For example, she asserts that the proximity of the host country to the country of origin will likely have a negative effect, as the ease of return to nearby homelands may be a disincentive to naturalize. In contrast, she suggests that greater government assistance to immigrant groups is likely to increase the rate of naturalization. She notes that Canadian policy more actively fosters integration and citizenship, and that immigrant groups who have received United States government assistance, such as refugees and Cold War-era immigrants from the Soviet bloc, have also naturalized at an unusually high rate. Highlighting the greater political integration in Canada, she points to 45 (of 301) foreign-born members of Parliament in Canada, compared to 8 (of 435) in the U.S. House of Representatiaves in 2000. Bloemraad, *Becoming a Citizen: Incorporating Immigrants and Refugees in the United States and Canada*, 2006, at 60–64; Bloemraad,

Becoming a Citizen in the United States and Canada: Structured Mobilization and Immigrant Political Incorporation, 85 Social Forces at 684.

2. THE BASIC STATUTORY PROVISIONS

Naturalization requirements continue along the general lines set by the 1795 Act. We explore the elements below. But first we take a quick look at the naturalization procedures.

The Immigration Act of 1990 transformed naturalization into almost entirely an administrative procedure under the authority of the Attorney General. Courts are still generally involved in administering the citizenship oath, however, and an especially powerful form of judicial review is available when the administrators deny a naturalization petition. These changes were accomplished primarily in INA § 310 (setting forth the basic administrative procedure and the judicial review provisions), § 335 (examination of application for naturalization), and § 336 (hearing before an immigration officer if application is denied at the examination stage).

Under the system established by the 1990 Act—as altered by the transfer of INS functions to DHS in 2003—an application for naturalization goes to a USCIS officer who examines the applicant and makes a formal determination to grant or deny. INA § 335. That examiner has authority to conduct a wide-ranging investigation and to subpoena witnesses and documents, but in the overwhelming majority of cases the examination consists primarily of an interview of the applicant. If the application is approved, the oath of allegiance can be administered by a court or by DHS, in accordance with INA § 310(b).

If the examiner denies the application, he or she must state the reasons. The applicant may then request a further hearing before an "immigration officer," who must be of equal or higher grade level to the examiner who initially denied the application. INA § 336(a); 8 C.F.R. § 336.2(b). This second officer has the discretion to schedule a full de novo hearing, or to "utilize a less formal review procedure, as he or she deems reasonable and in the interest of justice." *Id.* The latter course is likely if it appears that the problem can be resolved routinely—for example, by administering another test of English language capability or knowledge of U.S. government. If the full-fledged administrative hearing still results in a denial, the applicant can seek judicial review, in accordance with the general provisions of the Administrative Procedure Act, in the federal district court having jurisdiction over the place of his residence. INA § 310(c). The court's review "shall be *de novo,* and the court shall make its own findings of fact and conclusions of law." *Id.* The House committee explained that "citizenship is the most valued governmental benefit of this land and applicants should receive full recourse to the Judiciary when the request for that benefit is denied." H.R.Rep. No. 101–187, *supra,* at 14.

The substantive requirements for naturalization include age, residence and physical presence, good moral character, knowledge of U.S. history and government, English language proficiency, attachment to constitutional principles, and an oath of allegiance to the United States.

a. Age

Applicants for naturalization must generally be at least 18 years old. INA § 334(b)(1). Most children who are naturalized obtain citizenship when one of their parents is naturalized. Known as "derivative citizenship," it occurs by operation of law. The child must have been admitted as a permanent resident and reside with the parent in the United States; there is no waiting period. INA § 320.

Until recently, children adopted overseas by U.S. citizen parents had to go through naturalization proceedings after entering the United States. Because their parents did not need to naturalize, the children did not benefit from derivative naturalization. In 2000, Congress made this process easier by enacting legislation that grants automatic citizenship to all children admitted as lawful permanent residents who are residing in the United States with a citizen parent. Child Citizenship Act of 2000, Pub. L. 106–395, 144 Stat. 1631 (amending INA § 320).

b. Residence and Physical Presence

Naturalization applicants must have been admitted as lawful permanent residents and have resided continuously in the United States for at least five years. During the five years immediately prior to applying for naturalization, the applicant must have been physically present in the United States for at least two and one half years. The applicant must have resided within the State in which the application is filed for at least three months and must reside continuously within the United States between the application and admission to citizenship. INA § 316(a).

Short trips out of the United States do not interrupt the residence requirement; absences between six months and one year are presumed to break the continuous residence requirement, but the presumption can be overcome by evidence that the applicant did not intend to abandon his or her residence. INA § 316(b). Applicants who leave the United States for a continuous period of one year or more will not satisfy the residency requirement; after they return to the United States they must begin anew to complete the residency requirement.

(i) U.S. Employment Abroad

Lawful permanent residents who lived in the United States for at least one year and then go abroad to work for the United States government, certain U.S. research institutions, certain U.S. companies, or certain public international organizations may receive an exception to the continuous residence requirement. INA § 316(b). Exceptions to the residency requirement do not waive the physical presence requirement, except for those employed overseas by the U.S. government, INA § 316(c), or certain religious organizations, INA § 317.

(ii) Spouses of U.S. Citizens

The residence requirement is reduced to three years for spouses of U.S. citizens. They must have been lawfully admitted as permanent residents and since admission have lived in "marital union" with their spouse for the three years immediately before filing their naturalization application. The special provisions applying to spouses and children who have been battered by U.S. citizens also include a three year continuous residence requirement. INA § 319.

(iii) Military Service

Naturalization applicants who have served honorably in the U.S. armed forces for one year do not have to satisfy residency or physical presence requirements. INA § 328. Most striking, noncitizens who serve in active-duty status in the U.S. armed services during recognized periods of military hostilities need not have been permanent resident aliens in order to be naturalized (if they were in the United States lawfully at the time of their enlistment), and no period of residence or physical presence is required. INA § 329(a).

In 2002 President Bush invoked his authority under § 329 to designate "the period beginning on September 11, 2001" as a time in which the United States is engaged in "armed conflict with a hostile force." Executive Order 13269 (July 3, 2002). That period has not been terminated. Accordingly, noncitizens serving in active-duty status—including veterans of the 2003 Iraqi war—are eligible for naturalization under the special provisions of § 329. As of April 2011, 68,974 members of the armed forces had been granted expedited naturalization. There have been 132 grants of posthumous citizenship for noncitizens killed while on active duty during military hostilities. USCIS, Fact Sheet, Naturalization through Military Service, April 11, 2011.

Generally, enlistment is limited to lawful permanent residents or U.S. citizens, but the Department of Defense has initiated a pilot program to enlist noncitizens with special language, medical, or other skills. The Military Accessions Vital to the National Interest (MAVNI) program accepts noncitizens who are legally present, though not lawful permanent residents. For example, asylees, refugees, students, and certain nonimmigrants could seek to join the armed forces through the MAVNI program. See 10 USC § 504(b)(2). For thorough examination of this topic, see Stock, *Recent Developments in Military Enlistment and Naturalization Law*, Imm. Briefings, March 2011.

c. Good Moral Character

Naturalization applicants must establish good moral character for the five years preceding the date of application. INA § 316(a). The INA does not directly define "good moral character"; rather, it provides a (nonexclusive) list of acts that establish a lack of good moral character. INA §§ 101(f), 316(e). Included in that list is a reference to most of the criminal offenses enumerated in § 212(a)(2), including crimes involving moral turpitude and controlled substance offenses. INA § 101(f)(3). Naturalization applicants are asked whether they have ever been arrested or convicted (you may wish to review Form N–400 in the Statutory Supplement); to provide a cross-check of their answers, they must also submit fingerprints, which are then matched against FBI databases.

Section 101(f)(3) applies only to crimes committed during the relevant period (usually five years), but paragraph (f)(8) applies to persons convicted at any time of the offenses it identifies, and it results in a permanent disqualification. Originally § 101(f)(8) listed only the crime of murder, but in 1990 it was amended to apply to any "aggravated felony," as defined in § 101(a)(43). The list of aggravated felonies, rather short in 1990, has expanded greatly over the years. Congress' largest set of additions to the definition, in 1996, was accompanied by a provision stating that the term, as amended, applies to a listed offense "regardless of whether the conviction was entered before, on, or after" the date of enactment. (For highly technical reasons, however, such an aggravated felony conviction before November 29, 1990, is not an automatic bar to good moral character for naturalization purposes. *See General Counsel Speaks on Aggravated Felonies and Good Moral Character*, 74 Interp.Rel. 1515 (1997).)

The effect of these amendments on the naturalization process should be apparent: applicants may be deemed to lack good moral character for crimes committed a number of years before, which were not considered to be aggravated felonies at the time of their commission. As we will see in Chapter Seven, retrospective application of immigration laws is not uncommon and is deemed not to raise a serious constitutional question. Did Congress go needlessly far here, or is the commission of a serious crime properly grounds for denying naturalization whether or not the person knew at the time that it could permanently deny him or her a chance to become a U.S. citizen?

d. Knowledge of Civics and History

Applicants for naturalization must demonstrate "a knowledge and understanding of the fundamentals of the history, and of the principles and form of government, of the United States." INA § 312(a)(2). The civics requirements are waived for persons with physical or developmental disabilities or mental impairments. Furthermore, the statute directs the Attorney General to give "special consideration" regarding compliance with the civics requirement to persons over 65 who have lawfully resided for at least 20 years. INA § 312(b). Regulations instruct naturalization examiners to choose questions and evaluate answers with "due consideration" to an applicant's "education, background, age, length of residence in the United States, opportunities available and efforts made to acquire the requisite knowledge, and any other elements or factors relevant to an appraisal of the adequacy of the applicant's knowledge and understanding." 8 C.F.R. § 312.2(c)(2).

The history and civics requirement is met by an oral test conducted by a DHS examiner during the naturalization interview. For many years, examiners relied upon (although were not limited to) a prepared list of 100 questions that had been informally generated by the INS. It included a range of basic questions about U.S. government ("How many representatives are there in Congress?" "What is the Bill of Rights?" "Who makes the laws in the United States?") and other questions such as "What are the colors of the flag?" and "What Immigration and Naturalization Service form is used to apply for naturalized citizenship?"

In September 2007, after several years of study, the USCIS Office of Citizenship announced a new naturalization test. Prepared in consultation with adult education experts, U.S. history and government scholars and experts on test development, the new test asks questions on American government, American history, and "integrated civics" (geography, symbols, and holidays). It includes questions from the old test (such as the names of one's representatives in Congress and freedoms protected by the First Amendment), as well as more conceptual questions ("What is freedom of religion?" "What is the economic system of the United States?" "What is the rule of law?" "Name one problem that led to the Civil War.") For the complete list, go to the USCIS website at http://www.uscis.gov/files/nativedocuments/100q.pdf.

What kinds of questions ought to be included in the naturalization test? Is knowledge of American history more important than, say, knowledge of American culture? How would one define, and test for, the latter?

e. English Language Proficiency

The INA requires that applicants for naturalization demonstrate "an understanding of the English language, including an ability to read, write, and speak words in ordinary usage in the English language." INA § 312(a)(1). The Act exempts from the English language requirement persons who, at the time of filing their petition, are (a) over the age of fifty and have been lawfully admitted for permanent residence for periods totaling twenty years, (b) over fifty-five and have been living in the United States in LPR status for at least fifteen years. Also exempt are persons who are "unable because of physical or developmental disability or mental impairment" to comply with the requirement. INA § 312(b).

A requirement of knowledge of spoken English first entered U.S. naturalization law in 1906. Act of June 29, 1906, ch. 3592, § 8, 34 Stat. 599. English literacy was added in 1950. Internal Security Act of 1950, § 30, 64 Stat. 1018. *See* Perea, *Demography and Distrust: An Essay on American Languages, Cultural Pluralism, and Official English*, 77 Minn. L.Rev. 269, 337–40 (1992). The wisdom of the English requirement has been hotly debated. We provide a small sample below. First, consider the statement of Cruz Reynoso, a Commissioner on the Select Commission for Immigration and Refugee Policy (SCIRP), commenting on the Commission's 1981 Final Report:

> The Commission report quotes favorably from Webster's notion of language—that it is a unifier of national bonds—and recommends continued use of the English-language requirement for citizenship. The Commission, unknowingly, misinterprets the character of our national union, the reality of our history, and the diversity of our

people. Americans are not now, and never have been, *one* people linguistically or ethnically. American Indians (natives) are not now, and never have been like Europeans. By the treaty which closed the Mexican American war[,] our Country recognized its obligation to protect the property, liberty and religion of the new Americans. In short, America is a *political* union—not a cultural, linguistic, religious or racial union. It is acceptance of our constitutional ideals of democracy, equality and freedom which acts as the unifier for us as Americans.

With respect to language the California Supreme Court said it well in ruling that English may not be a requirement for voting among those who speak Spanish:

> "We cannot refrain from observing that if a contrary conclusion were compelled [that the California Constitution could require knowledge of the English language before a citizen could vote] it would indeed be ironic that petitioners [the Spanish-speaking citizens], who are the heirs of a great and gracious culture, identified with the birth of California and contributing in no small measure to its growth, should be disenfranchised in their ancestral land, despite their capacity to cast an informed vote." (Castro v. State of California [1970] 2 Cal.3d 223, 243.)

* * *

Of course, we as individuals would urge all to learn English for that is the language used by most Americans, as well as the language of the marketplace. *But*, we should no more demand English-language skills for citizenship than we should demand uniformity of religion. That a person wants to become a citizen and will make a good citizen is more than enough.

Every study I have read concludes that language requirements have been used to discriminate. Our early naturalization laws had no language requirement. We should do today as was done before the "nativism" (an early nice word to describe ethnic and racial prejudice) of the 19th Century set in; we should welcome the new arrivals with open arms, to all the obligations *and* the privileges of being full Americans.

SCIRP, *U.S. Immigration Policy and the National Interest* 403–04 (1981).

Now, contrast the following views:

> "I have sympathy for the position that the integrating mechanism of a society is language," Henry Cisneros [former mayor of San Antonio and later Secretary of Housing and Urban Development] says. "The U.S. has been able to impose fewer such integrating mechanisms on its people than other countries, but it needs some tie to hold these diverse people, Irish, Jews, Czechs, together as a nation. Therefore, I favor people learning English and being able to conduct business in the official language of the country."

"The *unum* demands only certain things of the *pluribus,*" Lawrence Fuchs [Executive Director of the Select Commission] says. "It demands very little. It demands that we believe in the political ideals of the republic, which allows people to preserve their ethnic identity. Most immigrants come from repressive regimes; we say, we're asking you to believe that government should *not* oppress you. Then it only asks one other thing: that in the wider marketplace and in the civic culture, you use the official language. No other society asks so little."

"English is not just an instrument of mobility. It is a sign that you really are committed. If you've been here five years, which you must to be a citizen, and if you are reasonably young, you should be able to learn English in that time. The rest of us are entitled to that."

Fallows, *Immigration—How It's Affecting Us*, The Atlantic Monthly 88–89 (Nov. 1983).

Gerald Neuman identifies some additional considerations:

The ability to communicate in *some* language that is in widespread use in political discourse in the United States would be a constitutionally permissible condition on the acquisition of citizenship. The harder question is whether the requirement of ability in English rather than in Spanish is unduly intrusive.

The preference for English is not arbitrary. English is the primary language of the large majority of the current U.S. population and the traditional language of dominant political discourse in the United States. The practical advantages for new citizens of acquiring facility with English are in general greater than would be the practical advantages of acquiring another language. The preference for English in naturalization does not represent the effort of a minority to reserve power for itself. The requirement is not directed hostilely at a particular ethnic group or at the speakers of a particular language. Although speakers of Spanish may be the group most obviously affected by the requirement, that is only because of the large percentage of immigrants and citizens who speak Spanish. English is not harder for native speakers of Spanish to learn than for, say, native speakers of Mandarin.

* * * Whether the English language requirement is instrumentally justified, and in particular whether it is more advantageous than an English-or-Spanish requirement, depend on empirical questions * * *. These include the pace of English language acquisition with and without the requirement, the economic disadvantage suffered by monolingual speakers of Spanish, and the efficacy of political communication across the language divide.

Demographic changes and the changed political forces that accompany them may undermine some of the foregoing reasoning. In particular, the claims of Spanish to equal official status with English may increase * * *.

Neuman, *Justifying U.S. Naturalization Policies*, 35 Va.J.Int'l L. 237, 267–68 (1994).

In light of these and other considerations, do you think the English-language requirement is sound policy? If so, how do you respond to the argument that the United States is a political, not a linguistic, union? If not, would you require the ability to communicate in some language in widespread use in the political domain?

f. Oath of Allegiance

Since 1795, applicants have been required to swear an oath of allegiance to the United States. Here is the current version of the oath, as prescribed by regulation:

> I hereby declare, on oath, that I absolutely and entirely renounce and abjure all allegiance and fidelity to any foreign prince, potentate, state, or sovereignty, of whom or which I have heretofore been a subject or citizen; that I will support and defend the Constitution and laws of the United States of America against all enemies, foreign and domestic; that I will bear true faith and allegiance to the same; that I will bear arms on behalf of the United States when required by the law; that I will perform noncombatant service in the Armed Forces of the United States when required by the law; that I will perform work of national importance under civilian direction when required by the law; and that I take this obligation freely, without any mental reservation or purpose of evasion; so help me God.

8 C.F.R. § 337.1(a).[6] Most of this language comes rather directly from the statute, INA § 337(a). The portions of the statute defining the contents of the oath has changed relatively little since 1795.

The oath is regularly criticized for archaic and abstruse language. Recall that, to meet the statute's requirements, an applicant need only be able to "read or write simple words and phrases."[7] Do you think it should be rewritten? If so, would you simply use more modern language, or would you ask naturalizing citizens to affirm different commitments to their new country? Should native-born citizens be asked to take a similar oath—say at age 21? Should the oath requirement be eliminated, as Spiro and other proponents of multiple citizenship propose? See the earlier discussion of dual nationality in Section B, *supra*.

The Commission on Immigration Reform proposed a new formulation for the oath in its 1997 Final Report. Written to "captur[e] the essence of

---

6. The statute permits conscientious objectors to military service to be exempted from the requirement to bear arms or perform noncombatant service. INA § 337(a).

7. Pub. L. 106–448, 114 Stat. 1939 (2000), amended § 337(a) of the INA to authorize the Attorney General to waive the oath requirement for those applicants whose physical or developmental disability or mental impairment prevents them from understanding the oath. A person for whom the oath is waived is considered "to have met the requirements of section 316(a)(3) with respect to attachment to the principles of the Constitution and well disposition to the good order and happiness of the United States."

naturalization," the Commission's revision would include the following language:

> Solemnly, freely, and without any mental reservation, I, (name) hereby renounce under oath [or upon affirmation] all former political allegiances. My sole political fidelity and allegiance from this day forward is to the United States of America.

U.S. Commission on Immigration Reform, Becoming an American: Immigration and Immigrant Policy 51 (1997). What work does the term "political" do in this proposal? Does it signal a change from the current oath in any material way?

g. Attachment to Constitutional Principles

Applicants for naturalization must establish that they are "attached to the principles of the Constitution of the United States, and well disposed to the good order and happiness of the United States." INA § 316(a). Chief Justice Stone summarized his view of the constitutional tenets to which the statute refers:

> "the principle of constitutional protection of civil rights and of life, liberty and property, the principle of representative government, and the principle that constitutional laws are not to be broken down by planned disobedience. I assume also that all the principles of the Constitution are hostile to dictatorship and minority rule; and that it is a principle of our Constitution that change in the organization of our government is to be effected by the orderly procedures ordained by the Constitution and not by force or fraud."

Schneiderman v. United States, 320 U.S. 118, 181, 63 S.Ct. 1333, 1363, 87 L.Ed. 1796 (1943) (dissenting opinion).

Unquestionably, the Constitution to which an applicant must show "attachment" provides extraordinarily broad protection to political speech and thought—even, as Justice Holmes wrote in a famous dissent in a naturalization case, "for the thought we hate." *United States v. Schwimmer*, 279 U.S. 644, 654, 49 S.Ct. 448, 73 L.Ed. 889 (1929). "Surely," Holmes continued, "it cannot show a lack of attachment to the principles of the Constitution that [one] thinks that it can be improved." *Id.* at 653. But just as surely some calls for constitutional change evidence a rejection of the underlying principles of the Constitution. Imagine, for example, a claim that the United States is a "white person's country" and that the Constitution ought to mandate expulsion of non-whites. Or the view that the United States should be a theocracy, with the laws decreed by a clerical hierarchy. Even if such speech is protected—in the sense that the speaker could not be jailed for uttering it—may it form the basis for a finding that the speaker is not "attached to the Constitution" and therefore ineligible for naturalization?

The Supreme Court addressed this issue during the middle of World War II in *Schneiderman v. United States*, 320 U.S. 118, 63 S.Ct. 1333, 87 L.Ed. 1796 (1943). Schneiderman arrived in the United States from Russia at the age of three, joined the Young Workers League at sixteen, and two years later, in 1924, filed his declaration of intent to naturalize. He joined the Communist Party in 1925, and in 1927 he filed for and was granted naturalization. After his naturalization he attended the Sixth World Congress of the Communist International in Moscow, openly avowed his belief in Marxism as applied by the Communist Party of the United States, was the Communist Party's candidate for governor of Minnesota, and served as secretary of the Party in California.

Twelve years after he had become a citizen, the government filed suit to strip him of citizenship, claiming that he had been ineligible to naturalize at the time of the grant. At the time, membership in the Communist Party was not an express bar to naturalization, although Congress has since enacted statutes precluding naturalization—with minor exceptions—of members of the Communist Party, other totalitarian groups, and those who advocate the overthrow of the United States government by force or violence. *See* INA § 313. Nonetheless, the government argued that a member of the Communist Party could not be "attached to" the principles of the United States Constitution. The Supreme Court summarized the government's main arguments and then rejected them.

The claim that petitioner was not in fact attached to the Constitution and well disposed to the good order and happiness of the United States at the time of his naturalization and for the previous five year period is twofold: First, that he believed in such sweeping changes in the Constitution that he simply could not be attached to it; Second, that he believed in and advocated the overthrow by force and violence of the Government, Constitution and laws of the United States.

In support of its position that petitioner was not in fact attached to the principles of the Constitution because of his membership in the League and the Party, the Government has directed our attention first to petitioner's testimony that he subscribed to the principles of those organizations, and then to certain alleged Party principles and statements by Party Leaders which are said to be fundamentally at variance with the principles of the Constitution. * * * [U]nder our traditions beliefs are personal and not a matter of mere association, and that men in adhering to a political party or other organization notoriously do not subscribe unqualifiedly to all of its platforms or asserted principles. Said to be among those Communist principles in 1927 are: the abolition of private property without compensation; the erection of a new proletarian state upon the ruins of the old bourgeois state; the creation of a dictatorship of the proletariat; denial of political rights to others than members of the Party or of the proletariat; and the creation of a world union of soviet republics. Statements that American democracy "is a fraud" and that the purposes of the Party are "utterly antagonistic to the purposes for which the American democracy, so called, was formed," are stressed.

* * *

The constitutional fathers, fresh from a revolution, did not forge a political strait-jacket for the generations to come. Instead they wrote Article V and the First Amendment, guaranteeing freedom of thought, soon followed. Article V contains procedural provisions for constitutional change by amendment without any present limitation whatsoever except that no State may be deprived of equal representation in the Senate without its consent. This provision and the many important and far-reaching changes made in the Constitution since 1787 refute the idea that attachment to any particular provision or provisions is essential, or that one who advocates radical changes is necessarily not attached to the Constitution. Criticism of, and the sincerity of desires to improve the Constitution should not be judged by conformity to prevailing thought because, "if there is any principle of the Constitution that more imperatively calls for attachment than any other it is the principle of free thought—not free thought for those who agree with us but freedom for the thought that we hate." [*United States v. Schwimmer*, 279 U.S. 644, 654, 49 S.Ct. 448, 73 L.Ed. 889 (1929) (Holmes, J., dissenting).] Whatever attitude we may individually hold toward persons and organizations that believe in or advocate extensive changes in our existing order, it should be our desire and concern at all times to uphold the right of free discussion and free thinking to which we as a people claim primary attachment. To neglect this duty in a proceeding in which we are called upon to judge whether a particular individual has failed to manifest attachment to the Constitution would be ironical indeed.

* * *

With regard to the constitutional changes he desired petitioner testified that he believed in the nationalization of the means of production and exchange with compensation, and the preservation and utilization of our "democratic structure * * * as far as possible for the advantage of the working classes." He stated that the "dictatorship of the proletariat" to him meant "not a government, but a state of things" in which "the majority of the people shall really direct their own destinies and use the instrument of the state for these truly democratic ends." None of this is necessarily incompatible with the "general political philosophy" of the Constitution as outlined above by the Government. It is true that the Fifth Amendment protects private property, even against taking for public use without compensation. But throughout our history many sincere people whose attachment to the general constitutional scheme cannot be doubted have, for various and even divergent reasons, urged differing degrees of governmental ownership and control of natural resources, basic means of production, and banks and the media of exchange, either with or without compensation. And something once regarded as a species of private property was abolished without compensating the owners when the institution of slavery was forbidden. Can it be said that the author of the Emancipation Proclamation and the supporters of the Thirteenth Amendment were not attached to the Constitution? We conclude that lack of attachment to the Constitution is not shown on the basis of the changes which petitioner testified he desired in the Constitution.

* * *

Apart from the question whether the alleged principles of the Party which petitioner assertedly believed were so fundamentally opposed to the Constitution that he was not attached to its principles in 1927, the Government contends that petitioner was not attached because he believed in the use of force and violence instead of peaceful democratic methods to achieve his desires. In support of this phase of its argument the Government asserts that the organizations with which petitioner was actively affiliated advised, advocated and taught the overthrow of the Government, Constitution and laws of the United States by force and violence, and that petitioner therefore believed in that method of governmental change.

* * *

There is a material difference between agitation and exhortation calling for present violent action which creates a clear and present danger of public disorder or other substantive evil, and mere doctrinal justification or prediction of the use of force under hypothetical conditions at some indefinite future time—prediction that is not calculated or intended to be presently acted upon, thus leaving opportunity for general discussion and the calm processes of thought and reason. Cf. Bridges v. California, 314 U.S. 252, 62 S.Ct. 190, 86 L.Ed. 192, and Justice Brandeis' concurring opinion in Whitney v. California, 274 U.S. 357, 372–380, 47 S.Ct. 641, 647–650, 71 L.Ed. 1095. Because of this difference we may assume that Congress intended, by the general test of "attachment" in the 1906 Act, to deny naturalization to persons falling into the first category but not to those in the second. Such a construction of the statute is to be favored because it preserves for novitiates as well as citizens the full benefit of that freedom of thought which is a fundamental feature of our political institutions.

* * *

Schneiderman v. United States, 320 U.S. at 135–36, 137–39, 141–42, 146, 157–59.

Compare this full-throated exposition of freedom of thought under the First Amendment with the next case, which challenges as unconstitutional a question on the naturalization form asking applicants to detail past and present memberships and affiliations.

PRICE v. INS

United States Court of Appeals, Ninth Circuit, 1991.
962 F.2d 836, cert. denied, 510 U.S. 1040, 114 S.Ct. 683, 126 L.Ed.2d 650 (1994).

BEEZER, CIRCUIT JUDGE:

John Eric Price appeals the district court's denial of his petition for naturalization. The district court's order was based on Price's refusal to list all organizations with which he has ever been affiliated. Price argues that the Attorney General does not have statutory authority to require him to supply such a list and that such authority would be unconstitutional. We affirm.

John Price is a native of England and a citizen of the United Kingdom. He was granted lawful resident alien status in the United States in 1960, and has worked and resided in the United States since then.

On April 21, 1984, Price applied to petition for naturalization. Price answered all questions on the application except Question 18, which reads: "List your present and past membership in or affiliation with every organization, association, fund, foundation, party, club, society or similar group in the United States or in any other country or place, and your foreign military service. (If none, write 'None.')." In the space provided for an answer to this question, Price wrote "Please see attached statement." The attached statement is a legal brief contending that Question 18 violates Price's First Amendment right of association.

Price answered negatively all parts of Question 19, which asked whether he was or had ever been a member of or associated with the Communist Party, had ever knowingly aided or supported it, or had ever "advocated, taught, believed in, or knowingly supported or furthered the interests of Communism."

* * *

The Immigration and Naturalization Act [sic] gives the Attorney General the authority to "prescribe the scope and nature of the examination of petitioners for naturalization as to their admissibility to citizenship." INA § 332(a). The examination of petitioners must be limited to

> inquiry concerning the applicant's residence, physical presence in the United States, good moral character, understanding of and attachment to the fundamental principles of the Constitution of the United States, ability to read, write and speak English, and other qualifications to become a naturalized citizen as required by law.

Within these limits, the Attorney General has the authority to require an applicant for naturalization to aver to "*all facts which* in the opinion of the Attorney General *may be material to the applicant's naturalization*," INA § 335(a) (emphasis added), and to designate INS employees to take "testimony concerning *any matter touching or in any way affecting* the admissibility of any petitioner for naturalization." INA § 335(b) (emphasis added). Thus the Attorney General is given very broad authority to make inquiries as long as they are related in some way to the naturalization requirements.

* * *

The INS argues that limiting examination to asking petitioners whether they are members of organizations of the type described in section 313(a) requires the INS to rely on petitioners' own determinations whether particular organizations are of the prohibited type, rather than allowing the Service to make that determination, and does not address the possibility that a petitioner may wrongly believe that an organization with which he is affiliated does not fall within section 313(a).

* * *

The INS also argues that membership in types of organizations not described in section 313(a) may be relevant to other requirements of naturalization such as duration of residence, good moral character or being "well disposed to the good order and happiness of the United States." "The government is entitled to know of any facts that may bear on an applicant's statutory eligibility for citizenship, so it may pursue leads and make further investigation if doubts are raised." *Berenyi v. District Director, INS*, 385 U.S. 630, 638, 87 S.Ct. 666, 671, 17 L.Ed.2d 656 (1967). It is completely reasonable to assume that knowing the organizations with which a petitioner is associated will be relevant to one or more of the requirements for citizenship. * * *

"[A]n alien seeking initial admission to the United States requests a privilege and has no constitutional rights regarding his application, for the power to admit or exclude aliens is a sovereign prerogative." *Landon v. Plasencia*, 459 U.S. 21, 32, 103 S.Ct. 321, 329, 74 L.Ed.2d 21 (1982). However, "once an alien gains admission to our country and begins to develop ties that go with permanent residence, his constitutional status changes accordingly." *Id.* It has long been recognized that resident aliens enjoy the protections of the First Amendment. * * *

However, the protection afforded resident aliens may be limited. The Supreme Court recently stated that the cases establishing constitutional protection for aliens within the territory of the United States "are constitutional decisions of this Court expressly according differing protection to aliens than to citizens, based on our conclusion that the particular provisions in question were not intended to extend to aliens in the same degree as to citizens." *United States v. Verdugo–Urquidez*, 494 U.S. 259, 110 S.Ct. 1056, 1064, 1065, 108 L.Ed.2d 222 (1990) (citations omitted). Additionally, the Court has historically afforded Congress great deference in the area of immigration and naturalization. * * * *Fiallo v. Bell*, 430 U.S. 787, 792, 796, 97 S.Ct. 1473, 1477, 1480, 52 L.Ed.2d 50 (1977) (quotations omitted). "[I]n the exercise of its broad power over immigration and naturalization, 'Congress regularly makes rules that would be unacceptable if applied to citizens.' " *Id.* at 792, 97 S.Ct. at 1478 (quoting *Mathews v. Diaz*, 426 U.S. 67, 80, 96 S.Ct. 1883, 1891, 48 L.Ed.2d 478 (1976)).

The INS relies on *Kleindienst v. Mandel*, 408 U.S. 753, 92 S.Ct. 2576, 33 L.Ed.2d 683 (1972).[a] for the proposition that Price's first amendment rights invoke at most only limited judicial review. * * *

Price argues that because *Kleindienst* involved exclusion rather than naturalization, it does not control his case. However, the determination of who will become a citizen of the United States is at least as "peculiarly concerned with the political conduct of government," *Galvan v. Press*, 347 U.S. 522, 531, 74 S.Ct. 737, 743, 98 L.Ed. 911 (1954), as the decision of who will be allowed to enter, if not more so. While a resident alien may not participate in the process of governing the country, naturalized citizens may. Naturalization decisions, therefore, deserve at least as much judicial deference as do decisions about initial admission.[5] Furthermore, although Price is justified in expecting the greatest degree of constitutional protection afforded a non-citizen, the protection afforded him under the First Amendment certainly is not greater than that of the citizen plaintiffs in *Kleindienst*. For these reasons, the *Kleindienst* standard is appropriate in this case.

Price argues that he is not challenging the political decision underlying the determination of the substantive requirements for naturalization, but that he challenges instead the method of inquiry, which, in the case of Question 18, chills his freedom of association. Because of this posture, he contends, greater judicial scrutiny is appropriate.

A similar claim was rejected in *Kleindienst*. * * * The Court applied only limited judicial scrutiny and held that the requirements of the First Amendment were met because the reasons for refusing to grant the waiver were "facially legitimate and bona fide."

Applying this limited standard of review to the Attorney General's decision to ask Question 18 is also appropriate because "[n]o alien has the slightest right to naturalization unless all statutory requirements are complied with." *See Fedorenko v. United States*, 449 U.S. 490, 506, 101 S.Ct. 737, 747, 66 L.Ed.2d 686 (1981). Additionally, "the burden is on the applicant to show his eligibility in every respect." *See Berenyi*, 385 U.S. at 637, 87 S.Ct. at 671.[7]

* * *

a. In *Kleindienst v. Mandel*, the Attorney General had denied a waiver of excludability for a Belgian scholar deemed inadmissible on the ground that he was a Communist. The Supreme Court announced that although First Amendment rights were implicated by the denial of the waiver, it would sustain the Attorney General's decision if it were based on a "facially legitimate and bona fide reason."—eds.

5. The importance of the naturalization process was the basis for the district court's alternative holding that even under a more demanding First Amendment analysis, the government has a compelling interest in asking questions such as Question 18 that outweighs any First Amendment right a petitioner for naturalization may have.

7. In deportation hearings, the government must prove its case by "clear, unequivocal and convincing evidence." *Berenyi*, 385 U.S. at 636, 87 S.Ct. at 670 (quotation omitted). The fact that

Because a petitioner might be mistaken about whether an organization is of the type prohibited by section 313(a) and because Question 18 could reasonably reveal information relevant to other requirements for naturalization, the Attorney General's decision that Question 18 is relevant to determining qualification for naturalization is facially legitimate and bona fide.

The district court's denial of Price's petition for naturalization is affirmed.

NOONAN, CIRCUIT JUDGE, dissenting:

The Immigration Service propounds a question to persons seeking naturalization that would be intolerable if asked by a government agency of an American citizen. It is an intimidating question. It chills the right of free association guaranteed by the First Amendment.

The Immigration Service's answer is that aliens are different. They are second class people. No doubt for some purposes this characterization is the harsh truth. Since the abolition of slavery aliens are the only adults subject to treatment as second class people in the United States.

* * * [Deference to Congress over the admission of aliens] is defensible when the alien is outside the United States and seeking to enter this country. *Kleindienst*. It is also appropriate to give deference to Congress and the Executive Branch in matters which "may implicate our relations with foreign powers." *Fiallo*.

The case, however, is substantially different when the alien is a resident and a resident of long standing—in the present case 30 years. Realistically such a person has been conducting himself like an American for a very long time. His reactions to an intolerable inquiry are similar to those of a citizen. Rightly so. He has imbibed the air of freedom which permeates our culture. He insists upon a right not to be treated as a second class person where freedom of association is concerned.

* * *

The power of Congress to set standards for naturalization is very large, but like every other power of government it is circumscribed; it is not absolute. In *Girouard v. United States*, 328 U.S. 61, 66 S.Ct. 826, 90 L.Ed. 1084 (1946), the Court refused to construe as mandatory a requirement made by Congress that a petitioner for naturalization swear to

---

the alien carries the burden in naturalization proceedings helps to explain why, despite the sliding-scale theory of alien rights, [derived from *Johnson v. Eisentrager,* 339 U.S. 763, 771, 70 S.Ct. 936, 940, 94 L.Ed. 1255 (1950), which stated that an alien is "accorded a generous and ascending scale of rights as he increases his identity with our society,"] aliens at naturalization are not necessarily entitled to the full protection of the First Amendment arguably afforded in deportation hearings. *See Harisiades v. Shaughnessy,* 342 U.S. 580, 592, 72 S.Ct. 512, 520, 96 L.Ed. 586 (1952) (upholding the deportation of a member of the Communist Party under the then-applicable First Amendment test); *Parcham v. INS,* 769 F.2d 1001, 1005–06 (4th Cir.1985) (First Amendment protection applies in a deportation hearing); *American–Arab Anti–Discrimination Committee v. Meese,* 714 F.Supp. 1060 (C.D.Cal.1989) (same). Further support for this result is found in the fact that admission of an alien to citizenship is at least as fundamental to the identity of the nation as is the initial decision of whom to admit.

support the Constitution by taking up arms in defense of this country. The Court did so because otherwise the statute would have been held as unconstitutional.

In the present case the Immigration Service and this court have construed the statute in such a way that it is unconstitutional. As construed, the statute permits the Immigration Service to undertake an inquiry far broader than any governmental necessity warrants. * * *

A narrowly tailored question could be asked of any petitioner without infringing on First Amendment rights. A petitioner could be asked if he had belonged to any organizations dedicated to the overthrow of the government or advocating or using terrorism or if he belonged to any foreign military, paramilitary or intelligence organization. Such a question would have an obvious relevance to the government's legitimate concerns. A question without bounds as to association has no relation to governmental concerns.

The Immigration Service says that the government is concerned with the petitioner's "character." Beyond excluding persons committed to subversion or terror or under the orders of a foreign government, there is no conceivable way that the government can measure a person's character. Persons of all kinds of character make up the United States. The Immigration Service cannot design some fine test by which only persons of outstanding character will be admitted as citizens. In reality we must take our applicants for citizens, as we take our citizens themselves, as a mix of people. That is the way immigrants have come to the United States and peopled it and that is the way it will always be.

The statute is without rational purpose and, infringing severely on the right of free association, it is unconstitutional. I respectfully dissent.

NOTES AND QUESTIONS ON ATTACHMENT TO THE CONSTITUTION

1. The majority's opinion in *Schneiderman v. United States*, according to Professor Sanford Levinson, "tends to remove any real 'bite' from a decision to affirm one's attachment. The Constitution ends up seeming trivialized by the end of the opinion, even as the cause of civil liberties has probably been vindicated." Levinson raises the hypothetical case of an applicant for naturalization who had been a member of the Nationalist Party in South Africa and a fervent supporter of apartheid. He asks whether the applicant should "be closely examined on his or her political views, and then be excluded if these views prove to oppose the post-*Brown* [*v. Board of Education*] reading of the Constitution as at the very least preventing state-mandated racial separation? To say 'yes' obviously rejects the Holmesian tolerance for thought we hate. A negative answer, though, in effect repeals the 'attachment' statute and brings to the surface the 'meaninglessness' that threatens any serious constitutional faith." S. Levinson, Constitutional Faith 148–49 (1988). *See generally* Fontana, *A Case for the Twenty–First Century Constitutional Canon*: Schneiderman v. United States, 35 Conn. L. Rev. 35 (2002).

2. The *Schneiderman* Court notes that "[t]his is not a naturalization proceeding in which the Government is being asked to confer the privilege of citizenship upon an applicant." 320 U.S. at 122. In a naturalization proceeding, "the burden is on the alien applicant to show his eligibility for citizenship in every respect. The Court has often stated that doubts 'should be resolved in favor of the United States and against the claimant.'" *Berenyi v. District Director*, 385 U.S. 630, 637, 87 S.Ct. 666, 17 L.Ed.2d 656 (1967). *Schneiderman* is actually a landmark decision in equal measure because the Court went on to hold for the first time that the government must prove its case in a denaturalization proceeding by evidence that is "clear, unequivocal and convincing," not "upon a bare preponderance of evidence which leaves the issue in doubt. This is so because rights once conferred should not be lightly revoked. And more especially is this true when the rights are precious and when they are conferred by solemn adjudication, as is the situation when citizenship is granted." 320 U.S. at 125.

Is this difference in burden of proof between naturalization and denaturalization justified? Does this difference, rather than varying levels of devotion to the First Amendment, better account for the diverse judicial outcomes in *Schneiderman* and *Price*? Should *Schneiderman* have been decided differently if it had arisen as an appeal of a denial of naturalization?

3. Is the *Price* majority correct to analogize applications for naturalization to applications for immigrant admissions for the purpose of deciding what level of First Amendment scrutiny to apply? Should the requirement of a complete answer to question 18 be held to satisfy a higher standard in any event?

4. In his dissent to *Price*, Judge Noonan seems to suggest that the government has no business deciding on the character of prospective citizens. Would this mean that the "attachment" and "good moral character" requirements are unconstitutional?

PROBLEMS

Suppose you were representing the following clients in their efforts to become U.S. citizens. In light of the judicial opinions above and the post-September 11, 2001 concern about Al Qaeda threats against the United States, how would you analyze the issues their applications present?

1. Jennifer, an applicant for naturalization, is a Jehovah's Witness who states under oath that she believes in the Constitution and the U.S. form of government but that her religious convictions prevent her from voting, serving on a jury, bearing arms, or participating in civilian service deemed to be of national importance. USCIS denies the naturalization application on the ground that she is not "attached to the principles of the Constitution." Jennifer wants to appeal and has asked you to evaluate her chances of success. What would you tell her?

2. Malcolm, a practicing Muslim, states that while he is willing to take the oath of allegiance, he has reservations about bearing arms on behalf of the United States against persons of the Islamic faith or a predominantly Islamic country. He believes that if he kills, or is killed by, a member of the Islamic faith he would be condemned to hell, and he states that he would bear arms only when allowed under Islamic law. The USCIS examiner denies naturalization on the ground that, while the statute makes special provisions for conscientious objectors, it requires that such objection be to all wars. Here, according to the examiner, Malcolm is in effect seeking to reserve the right to choose which wars he will fight—a position that demonstrates a "mental reservation" about taking the oath as well as a lack of attachment to the Constitution because of the possibility that applicant will refuse to obey the law for certain kinds of conflicts. Malcolm seeks your advice as to the strengths and weaknesses of his claim. How would you assess his arguments and his likelihood of success?

SECTION D. LOSS OF CITIZENSHIP

The Naturalization Act of 1906 established a procedure to take away citizenship if a later judicial proceeding determined that that the naturalization was illegally or fraudulently acquired. For many years, it was also possible for naturalized citizens to lose their citizenship, not for defects in the original grant, but because of certain actions following naturalization—actions which had been declared by Congress to result in such forfeiture. Most of these grounds of expatriation applied equally to naturalized and native-born citizens, but a few imposed more stringent requirements on those who had gained citizenship by naturalization. Occasionally the loss of citizenship in this manner has also been called denaturalization, but we will avoid that terminology here. We will use the term "denaturalization" to mean only the revocation of the citizenship of a naturalized alien based on fraud or illegality in the original naturalization. Any other deprivation of citizenship, whether applied to native-born or naturalized citizens, will be called "expatriation."

1. DENATURALIZATION

Section 340 of the Act provides for denaturalization when naturalization was (a) illegally procured, or (b) procured by concealment of a material fact or by willful misrepresentation. The first appears straightforward: naturalization is illegally procured when the applicant did not in fact meet the statutory requirements at the time of naturalization. For example, an applicant might have illegally procured citizenship if he or she had been convicted of a disqualifying crime, and thus had lacked good moral character at the point of naturalization. See INA § 101(f)(6), (7), (8).

The concealment and willful misrepresentation grounds raise the obvious question of what constitutes a "material" fact. An interpretation that might occur to you—that a material fact is one that, if known, would have produced a denial of naturalization—has not been generally accepted. As discussed in the materials that follow, the Supreme Court has suggested a broader reading of the term.

The Supreme Court's initial standard on materiality was announced in *Chaunt v. United States*, 364 U.S. 350, 81 S.Ct. 147, 5 L.Ed.2d 120 (1960), which held that a misstatement was material if its disclosure would have justified denial of citizenship or might have led to the discovery of other facts that would warrant denial of citizenship. A divided Court struggled with the meaning of *Chaunt* in *Kungys v. United States*, 485 U.S. 759, 108 S.Ct. 1537, 99 L.Ed.2d 839 (1988). The various opinions of the Justices in *Kungys* are examined in the following case, which involves a criminal conviction for unlawful procurement of citizenship.

UNITED STATES v. PUERTA

United States Court of Appeals, Ninth Circuit, 1992.
982 F.2d 1297.

FLETCHER, CIRCUIT JUDGE:

Puerta was born in Almeria, Spain on January 20, 1956. He entered the United States on a student visa in 1981 and was admitted as a permanent resident in 1984. On February 26, 1990, he filed an application for naturalization. Question 5 asked him to list "[a]ny other names you have used (including maiden)." Puerta left this space blank. Questions 27 and 28 asked him to list any absences from the United States (for less or more than six months, respectively) since the time he entered for permanent residence. He wrote "None" in response to both questions.

On June 4, 1990, Puerta was interviewed by Immigration Examiner Robert Johnson. At trial, Johnson testified that he had no recollection of Puerta's interview. However, Johnson explained that his standard practice was to require every applicant to swear that the statements made on the application were true, and to review orally with the applicant the answer to each question. Johnson further explained that the slash marks on Puerta's application were his, undoubtedly made during his interview with Puerta. The slashes, Johnson said, indicated that Puerta orally answered questions 5, 27, and 28 the same way as he had done in writing: he had not used any other names and had never left the United States after entry. Puerta was naturalized shortly after his interview.

[In 1991, Puerta was arrested for attempting to defraud a bank in violation of California law. A search incident to the arrest revealed a number of driver's licenses in different names,] and a Spanish passport in the name Antonio Simon Palmer. The passport contained a United States non-immigrant visa obtained in Madrid, Spain on August 16, 1989, which was used to enter the United States on September 5, 1989. All pieces of identification were dated prior to February 26, 1990, the date Puerta filed his application for naturalization.

* * *

Puerta was convicted of violating 18 U.S.C. § 1425(a), which provides: "Whoever knowingly procures or attempts to procure, contrary to law, the naturalization of any person ... [s]hall be fined not more than $5,000 or imprisoned not more than five years, or both." The statute does not define the phrase "contrary to law." Presumably the "law" referred to is the law governing naturalization, INA title III [§§ 301–62]. Puerta was prosecuted for false statements he made on his naturalization application and to an immigration examiner. No reported cases discuss whether § 1425(a) requires that false statements made to procure naturalization be material in order to be "contrary to law." We note, however, that INA § 340(a) permits denaturalization if citizenship was "procured by concealment of a *material* fact or by willful misrepresentation" (emphasis added). Further, the government agrees with Puerta that § 340(a) implies a materiality requirement similar to the one used in the denaturalization context. This position finds support in *Kungys v. United States*, 485 U.S. 759, 108 S.Ct. 1537, 99 L.Ed.2d 839 (1988), the leading denaturalization case: "While we have before us here a statute revoking citizenship rather than imposing criminal fine or imprisonment, neither the evident objective sought to be achieved by the materiality requirement, nor the gravity of the consequences that follow from its being met, is so different as to justify adoption of a different standard." *Id.* at 770, 108 S.Ct. at 1546. We therefore look to the standards governing materiality in the denaturalization context as a guide to determining what is "contrary to law" under 18 U.S.C. § 1425.

* * *

* * * After *Kungys*, however, it is no simple task to divine the meaning of "material" under the denaturalization statute. The eight Justices who decided *Kungys* (Justice Kennedy did not participate) wrote five separate opinions and offered three distinct tests for determining when a statement is material.[5]

Puerta claims that his false statements were not material because they were not shown to conceal actual ineligibility for naturalization. For support of this position, he cites Justice Stevens' concurrence in *Kungys* (joined by Justices Marshall and Blackmun). *Kungys*, 485 U.S. at 785–95, 108 S.Ct. at 1552–59. Justice Stevens argued for the continued vitality of the test first enunciated in *Chaunt v. United States*, 364 U.S. 350, 355, 81 S.Ct. 147, 150, 5 L.Ed.2d 120 (1960), which suggested that concealments or misrepresentations would not be material if (1) the truth would not have warranted denial of citizenship or (2) the truth would not have been

---

5. Six Justices agreed that under their preferred tests, petitioner Kungys' statements regarding his date and place of birth were not material and did not provide a basis for denaturalization. Justices White and O'Connor dissented.

useful in an investigation possibly leading to the discovery of other facts warranting denial of citizenship.

Unfortunately for Puerta, Justice Stevens' view attracted only three votes. Justice Scalia's opinion for the Court in *Kungys* expressly rejected a "but for" test that would require the Government to "establish that naturalization would not have been granted if the misrepresentations or concealments had not occurred." *Kungys*, 485 U.S. at 776, 108 S.Ct. at 1549.[6] Five members of the Court emphasized that "[i]t has never been the test of materiality that the misrepresentation or concealment would *more likely than not* have produced an erroneous decision, or even that it would *more likely than not* have triggered an investigation." *Id.* at 771, 108 S.Ct. at 1547 (original emphasis). Chief Justice Rehnquist, concurring Justice Brennan, and dissenting Justices White and O'Connor joined this portion (Part II–A) of Justice Scalia's opinion. *Id.* at 783, 801, 803, 108 S.Ct. at 1552, 1562, 1563. A five-member majority of the Court has therefore agreed that *Chaunt* did not establish a minimum burden that the government must meet in order to establish materiality.

While those five agreed on what materiality is *not*, they did not speak with one voice as to what it *is*. Justice Scalia's opinion began from the premise that elsewhere in the criminal law, "materiality" meant "whether the misrepresentation or concealment was predictably capable of affecting, *i.e.*, had a natural tendency to affect, the official decision." *Id.* at 771, 108 S.Ct. at 1547. In his view, the test for materiality in a denaturalization case would be "whether the misrepresentation or concealment had a natural tendency to produce the conclusion that the applicant was qualified" for citizenship. *Id.* at 771–72, 108 S.Ct. at 1547. Under Justice Scalia's test, Puerta's misrepresentations were without a doubt material, because they had a natural tendency to affect the decision by creating the appearance that no further investigation of Puerta's background was necessary.

* * *

Justice Scalia's test, as noted *supra*, was joined in full only by Chief Justice Rehnquist and Justices White and O'Connor (both of whom adopted the test but disagreed with the result of its application to the facts of the case). Justice Brennan, in a concurring opinion, restricted the application of Justice Scalia's test:

> The Court holds that a misrepresentation is material if it has "a natural tendency to produce the conclusion that the applicant was qualified" for citizenship. A misrepresentation or concealment can be said to have such a tendency, the Court explains, if honest representations "would predictably have disclosed other facts relevant to [the applicant's] qualifications." Proof by clear, unequivocal, and convincing evidence that the misrepresentation had this tendency raises a

---

6. Chief Justice Rehnquist and Justice Brennan joined in this part (Part II–B) of Justice Scalia's opinion of the Court.

presumption of ineligibility, which the naturalized citizen is then called upon to rebut.

I agree with this construction of the statute. I wish to emphasize, however, that in my view *a presumption of ineligibility does not arise unless the Government produces evidence sufficient to raise a fair inference that a statutory disqualifying fact actually existed....* Evidence that simply raises the possibility that a disqualifying fact might have existed does not entitle the Government to the benefit of a presumption that the citizen was ineligible. I therefore would not permit invocation of the presumption of disqualification in circumstances where it would not otherwise be fair to infer that the citizen was actually ineligible.

Because nothing in the Court's opinion is inconsistent with this standard, I join it.

Id. at 783–84, 108 S.Ct. at 1552 (Brennan, J., concurring) (emphasis added; citations omitted). This test appears to differ from Justice Stevens' "but for" test only in degree: Justice Stevens would denaturalize where false statements are coupled with a showing of actual ineligibility, whereas, by contrast, Justice Brennan would denaturalize where false statements are coupled with evidence giving rise to a "fair inference" of ineligibility. In any event, four members of the Court (Justices Brennan, Stevens, Marshall, and Blackmun) would require that the government prove more than Justice Scalia's bloc (Justice Scalia, Chief Justice Rehnquist, and Justices White and O'Connor) would require.

Justice Brennan's view of materiality controls here. As a matter of construction, "[w]hen a fragmented Court decides a case and no single rationale explaining the result enjoys the assent of five Justices, 'the holding of the Court may be viewed as that position taken by those Members who concurred in the judgments on the narrowest grounds.' " *Marks v. United States*, 430 U.S. 188, 193, 97 S.Ct. 990, 993, 51 L.Ed.2d 260 (1977) (quoting *Gregg v. Georgia*, 428 U.S. 153, 169 n. 15, 96 S.Ct. 2909, 2923 n. 15, 49 L.Ed.2d 859 (1976) (opinion of Stewart, Powell, and Stevens, JJ.)). Justice Brennan apparently viewed his opinion as a narrowing construction of Justice Scalia's opinion: "Because nothing in the Court's opinion is inconsistent with this standard, I join it." *Kungys*, 485 U.S. at 784, 108 S.Ct. at 1552; *see also id.* at 793, 108 S.Ct. at 1558 (Stevens, J., concurring in judgment) ("Though joining the Court's opinion, Justice Brennan would require more."). Thus, as the fifth vote needed to establish the "controlling" materiality standard, Justice Brennan's construction may be taken as the holding (he requires *less* than the three in the Stevens group that would require in addition to false statements a showing of actual ineligibility, but he requires more than the Scalia group that would require only false statements which discourage further inquiry).

Whether a given quantum of evidence supports a fair inference of ineligibility (the *Kungys* test for the materiality of false statements, as announced by Justice Brennan) will vary with the facts of each case. *This* record contains no evidence from which any finder of fact could fairly infer that Puerta was actually ineligible for naturalization. All we know is that Puerta (1) denied the use of other names, yet carried many conflicting forms of identification, and (2) claimed not to have left the United States, yet carried a Spanish passport indicating at least one trip abroad. These discrepancies are certainly suspicious. But the government has offered no evidence linking them even tangentially to any statutory ground for disqualification. There is no basis for a trier of fact to conclude that Puerta was hiding a criminal record under one of his aliases. The suspicious banking transaction for which he was arrested is useless as proof of ineligibility, because it occurred after his naturalization and had not formed the basis of a state-court criminal conviction at the time of Puerta's federal trial [on the charge of unlawful procurement of citizenship.] Nor does Puerta's single proven absence from the United States fairly support an inference of ineligibility, given that the statute allows up to two and one-half years' absence during the five-year residency period, provided that no single absence exceeds six months (or more under certain circumstances). 8 U.S.C. § 316(a), (b). Under Justice Brennan's approach, "the defendant at least has the benefit of knowing specifically what disqualifying fact must be rebutted." *Kungys*, 485 U.S. at 793, 108 S.Ct. at 1558 (Stevens, J., concurring in judgment). Puerta did not have that opportunity because the existence of any disqualifying fact can only be postulated by indulging in the purest speculation. Under *Kungys*, Puerta's false statements were not material, and therefore may not form the basis of a criminal conviction under § 1425.

We recognize the potential anomaly in Justice Brennan's test in *Kungys*, which contemplates a higher standard of materiality in immigration law than does the criminal law generally. For example, in a prosecution under 18 U.S.C. § 1001 (criminalizing falsification or concealment of material facts in government applications), a false statement is material "if it has the propensity to influence agency action; actual influence on agency action is not an element of the crime." *United States v. Facchini*, 874 F.2d 638, 643 (9th Cir.1989) (en banc) (quoting *United States v. Vaughn*, 797 F.2d 1485, 1490 (9th Cir.1986)); *see also Kungys*, 485 U.S. at 769–70, 108 S.Ct. at 1545–46. Whatever attractions a unitary approach to materiality may have, its application to the immigration laws has failed to win an endorsement from a majority of the Supreme Court.

* * *

Reversed and remanded with instructions to enter a judgment of acquittal.

EXERCISE ON MISREPRESENTATION, "MATERIALITY,"
AND INELIGIBILITY FOR NATURALIZATION

Persons A, B, C, D, and E have recently been naturalized. The fact situations described below all occurred prior to the filing of their naturalization applications, and none was disclosed in the applications. (Take another look at the N–400 to see where such information might have been indicated.)

a. A was arrested 5 years ago and charged with disorderly conduct. The charges were dropped.

b. B was convicted of arson and served 18 months in prison.

c. C was convicted 4 years ago of possession of narcotics with intent to distribute, but was sent to a special community service and drug rehabilitation program instead of being incarcerated. Upon completion of the program, the trial judge entered an "order of expungement." He told C at that time that "your record has been wiped clean" and that C would "never have to worry about this episode again," provided C stay free of criminal activity. C has carefully abided by criminal laws since, not even incurring a traffic ticket.

d. D fathered a child out of wedlock 8 years ago.

e. E was a member of a radical right political group in the 1990s.

Assume that these facts have now become known to the government. Consider each fact situation from these perspectives: (a) You are the government attorney preparing the administrative revocation charges. What do you charge? What are your chances of success? (b) You are the naturalized citizen's attorney. What are your best grounds of defense? What would you like to learn from your client to prepare the case? (c) You are the judge. What results under the applicable case law?

Procedures in Denaturalization Cases

Judicial denaturalization proceedings are initiated by U.S. attorneys, based on an affidavit prepared by DHS. INA § 340(a). The evidence supporting denaturalization must be "clear, unequivocal, and convincing." *Schneiderman v. United States*, 320 U.S. 118, 125, 63 S.Ct. 1333, 87 L.Ed. 1796 (1943). If the government seeks to prosecute the individual for illegally procuring citizenship, 18 U.S.C. § 1425, and obtains a conviction, the court shall cancel the certificate of naturalization. INA § 340(e).

In 1996, the Attorney General promulgated regulations establishing an administrative procedure for denaturalization, basing the rules on the 1990 statute that moved naturalization authority from the courts to the

Attorney General. 61 Fed.Reg. 55550 (1996), adding §§ 340.1–2 to 8 C.F.R. The process was intended to be used only for clear cases warranting denaturalization and had to be initiated within two years of the challenged naturalization. The rules were challenged as beyond the Attorney General's statutory authority, and that claim was sustained by an en banc decision of the Ninth Circuit in *Gorbach v. Reno*, 219 F.3d 1087 (9th Cir.2000). The court rejected the government's argument that the power to denaturalize is inherent in the power to naturalize. "Citizenship in the United States of America is among our most valuable rights. * * * An executive department cannot simply decide, without express statutory authorization, to create an internal executive procedure to deprive people of those rights without even going to court." *Id.* at 1098. Subsequently, the court entered a permanent injunction prohibiting the government from invoking the administrative denaturalization procedures. *See* 78 Interp.Rel. 442 (2001).

2. EXPATRIATION

Denaturalization proceedings constitute one important way in which U.S. citizenship today may be taken away. In such proceedings, the government must establish, under a fairly stringent standard of proof, that the original naturalization was acquired illegally or through fraud. But through the years, Congress also added to the nationality statutes various provisions to deprive individuals of citizenship status based on specified behavior not related to defects in the acquisition process. Whether the citizen subjectively intended to surrender citizenship when the allegedly expatriating behavior occurred was usually irrelevant.

The Supreme Court wrestled for several decades with the constitutionality of these grounds for involuntary expatriation. (We use the term "involuntary expatriation" here to mean a loss of citizenship imposed on persons based on certain chosen behavior, such as lengthy residence abroad or marriage to a foreign national, whether or not they subjectively wished to surrender their citizenship.) The divisions among the Justices were bitter, and for a while, the results in the cases—sometimes sustaining the expatriation provisions, sometimes striking them down—traced an odd pattern. But today the Court has apparently reached unanimity on the basic substantive doctrine, although skirmishing may still be possible regarding some of the procedural details. The materials to follow reveal the historical development of the statute and the constitutional rulings.

DONALD K. DUVALL, EXPATRIATION UNDER UNITED STATES LAW, *PEREZ TO AFROYIM*: THE SEARCH FOR A PHILOSOPHY OF AMERICAN CITIZENSHIP

56 Va.L.Rev. 408, 411–17 (1970).

HISTORICAL DEVELOPMENT OF EXPATRIATION LAW

* * * [B]efore 1907 there was no general statute governing expatriation. As might be expected in an expanding new nation, the United States until the Civil War was primarily concerned with assimilating its millions of immigrants and establishing the legal primacy of national citizenship over state citizenship.

The scope of US citizenship was * * * beclouded in the early days because the judiciary felt bound to apply the adopted English common law of indefeasible perpetual allegiance, which precluded renunciation of citizenship without the consent of the sovereign. Great Britain's adherence to this rule in its impressments on the high seas of naturalized American seamen, formerly of British nationality, contributed to the War of 1812. And events of 1868 further aggravated Anglo–American friction, when the British failed to respect the rights of naturalized US citizens involved in criminal activities with the Fenian movement in Ireland. These incidents led to the passage of the Expatriation Act of 1868, which, *inter alia,* declared "the right of expatriation" to be an "inherent right of all people," thus enabling naturalized Americans to cast off, at least under United States law, the claims to allegiance advanced by their states of origin. The Act further extended to naturalized citizens traveling abroad "the same protection of persons and property that is accorded to native-born citizens in like situations," and declared that whenever a US citizen was unjustly deprived of his liberty by or under the authority of any foreign government, the President had the duty to extend protection in appropriate ways short of war.

While the Act of 1868 clarified the right of expatriation and was construed to include the citizen's right to shed his citizenship, it provided no specific method for exercising that right. Furthermore, even though naturalization under the domestic law of the United States required the citizen to "renounce and abjure" all allegiance to his former sovereign, effective protection of US naturalized citizens abroad still depended upon reciprocal recognition by foreign states of the exclusive nature of voluntarily acquired American citizenship. Accordingly, in 1868 the United States began negotiating bilateral treaties [known as the Bancroft Treaties] with various foreign states to protect the status of its naturalized citizens on a reciprocal basis in an effort to reduce or eliminate the conflicting claims of different sovereignties arising out of dual nationality. Some of these treaties, including the current multilateral Rio Treaty of 1906, provided not only for mutual acceptance of the right to abandon one nationality and acquire another but also that two years continuous residence by a naturalized citizen in his former country gave rise to a rebuttable presumption of intention to remain permanently. Prolonged return to the state of origin was therefore grounds for treating the citizen as having renounced his naturalized citizenship.

Pursuant to the report of a Citizenship Board appointed by the Secretary of State in 1906, Congress enacted the Expatriation Act of 1907, the first general statute providing for loss of US nationality. Section 2 of the Act of 1907 provided for the expatriation of any national who obtained naturalization in a foreign state or took an oath of allegiance to a foreign state. Section 3 of the Act provided for the expatriation of an American woman who married a foreigner. These provisions attempted to prevent dual nationality, which had previously led to conflicting national claims upon the allegiance of the US citizen whenever he returned, even temporarily, to his former country, or voluntarily entered the military or civil service of a third state.

The constitutionality of the 1907 Act was first tested in the landmark decision of *Mackenzie v. Hare,*[40] in which the Supreme Court upheld the power of Congress to expatriate, during the period of coverture, a female US citizen who obtained foreign nationality by marriage to a foreign national, because such action was a "necessary and proper" implementation of the "inherent power of sovereignty" in foreign relations, especially under "conditions of national moment."[b] Conceding that expatriation could not be imposed "without the concurrence of the citizen," the Court inferred assent from the fact that the expatriating act had been "voluntarily entered into, with notice of the consequences." In sum, the concept of voluntary renunciation of citizenship proclaimed in the 1868 Expatriation Act was interpreted in *Mackenzie* to include voluntary performance of an expatriating act without regard to whether the citizen actually intended or desired to lose his US nationality. By extending the meaning of "voluntary," the Court apparently sought to reconcile the intent of Congress to minimize international frictions arising out of dual nationality with the statutory guarantee and tradition of voluntary expatriation.

40. 239 U.S. 299, 36 S.Ct. 106, 60 L.Ed. 297 (1915). Act of Sept. 22, 1922, ch. 411, § 3, 42 Stat. 1022, and Act of March 3, 1931, ch. 442, §§ 4(a), (b), 46 Stat. 1511, eliminated marriage to a foreigner as an expatriating act.

b. Eliminating the gender discrimination in U.S. citizenship law (manifested perhaps most objectionably in that portion of the 1907 Act upheld in *Mackenzie*) was a prominent objective of the women's suffrage movement. An important change was provided just two years after the 19th Amendment became part of the Constitution. The Cable Act of Sept. 22, 1922, 42 Stat. 1021, ended automatic deprivation of citizenship upon marriage to a foreign husband (provided the husband was not ineligible to naturalization; at the time only whites and persons of African descent were eligible). It also allowed most women expatriated under prior law to regain U.S. citizenship through naturalization (again, Asian women, who were ineligible for naturalization, were excluded from this reform). Later statutes through 1930 further eased the requirements for this special procedure. *See Di Iorio v. Nicolls*, 182 F.2d 836, 839–40 (1st Cir.1950). Finally the Act of May 24, 1934, 48 Stat. 797, provided that any child born abroad to one American citizen parent—rather than simply to American fathers—could obtain U.S. citizenship, provided a few other gender-neutral conditions of U.S. residency were met by the parent and (later) by the child. These changes did not have retroactive effect, however. See discussion of *Wauchope v. U.S. Dep't of State*, *supra*, pp. 42–43.—eds.

The 1938 Report of the President's Commission on Revision and Codification of the Nationality Laws led to the Nationality Act of 1940. This Act, the first comprehensive codification of the nationality laws, substantially increased the number of actions which, when performed voluntarily, would automatically result in the loss of US nationality. The increased number of statutory provisions relating to loss of nationality may be explained in several ways. First, most of the provisions were codifications of existing statutory or common law which had evolved from established diplomatic and administrative practice. Second, the 1940 Act was drafted and approved at a time of economic stress and increasing security-consciousness caused by the onset of World War II. Third, World War I and its aftermath had produced a complete reversal of America's traditional "open door" immigration policy, thus leading to stricter requirements for acquisition and retention of US nationality.

Following World War II, the stage was again set for retrenchment and consolidation of the nationality laws. The post-war climate and Cold War hyper-security-consciousness produced the Immigration and Nationality Act of 1952, which Congress approved over President Truman's veto. Essentially a reenactment of the pertinent provisions of the 1940 Act, the 1952 law made few significant changes in loss of nationality. The Act added a section permitting expatriation of persons who acquired dual nationality at birth and "voluntarily sought or claimed benefits" of their foreign nationality and resided in the foreign state for three continuous years after age 22. It also created a non-rebuttable presumption of voluntariness for each of the statute's expatriating acts when performed by a national of a foreign state, who had been physically present in such state for at least ten years.

In 1961 Congress added a statutory standard of proof—preponderance of the evidence—necessary [for the government] to prove performance of an expatriating act or [for the individual] to rebut the usual presumption of voluntariness. This standard was a relaxation of that previously required by the Supreme Court in *Gonzales v. Landon*[53] and *Nishikawa v. Dulles*,[54] where the Court had imposed upon the Government the burden of proving the act and its voluntariness by clear, unequivocal and convincing evidence.

———

For many years, the 1915 *Mackenzie v. Hare* decision seemed to have settled the question of Congress's broad powers over expatriation. But the Supreme Court revisited this issue in multiple instances between 1958 and 1980, with shifting majorities yielding one after another 5–4 decision. Although it was not clear at the time, in retrospect we can see that *Perez v. Brownell*, 356 U.S. 44, 78 S.Ct. 568, 2 L.Ed.2d 603 (1958), was the last gasp of an era in constitutional analysis of expatriation. Perez, a U.S.

---

53. 350 U.S. 920, 76 S.Ct. 210, 100 L.Ed. 806 (1955) (per curiam) (proof of the act).

54. 356 U.S. 129, 78 S.Ct. 612, 2 L.Ed.2d 659 (1958) (proof of voluntariness).

citizen as a result of his birth in Texas, had lived most of his life in Mexico, where he voted in a political election in 1946. The federal statute then in effect provided that U.S. citizens, whether by birth or naturalization, lost their citizenship by voting in a foreign country's political election. For Justice Frankfurter, writing for a majority of five, the foreign relations power was the key.

The first step in our inquiry must be to answer the question: what is the source of power on which Congress must be assumed to have drawn? Although there is in the Constitution no specific grant to Congress of power to enact legislation for the effective regulation of foreign affairs, there can be no doubt of the existence of this power in the law-making organ of the Nation. * * * The Government must be able not only to deal affirmatively with foreign nations, as it does through the maintenance of diplomatic relations with them and the protection of American citizens sojourning within their territories. It must also be able to reduce to a minimum the frictions that are unavoidable in a world of sovereigns sensitive in matters touching their dignity and interests.

The inference is fairly to be drawn from the Congressional history of the Nationality Act of 1940, read in light of the historical background of expatriation in this country, that, in making voting in foreign elections (among other behavior) an act of expatriation, Congress was seeking to effectuate its power to regulate foreign affairs. * * *

* * *

Our starting point is to ascertain whether the power of Congress to deal with foreign relations may reasonably be deemed to include a power to deal generally with the active participation, by way of voting, of American citizens in foreign political elections. Experience amply attests that in this day of extensive international travel, rapid communication and widespread use of propaganda, the activities of the citizens of one nation when in another country can easily cause serious embarrassments to the government of their own country as well as to their fellow citizens.

* * *

Of course, Congress can attach loss of citizenship only as a consequence of conduct engaged in voluntarily. *See Mackenzie v. Hare*, 239 U.S. 299, 311–312, 36 S.Ct. 106, 108, 60 L.Ed. 297. But it would be a mockery of this Court's decisions to suggest that a person, in order to lose his citizenship, must intend or desire to do so. The Court only a few years ago said of the person held to have lost her citizenship in *Mackenzie v. Hare*, supra: "The woman had not intended to give up her American citizenship." *Savorgnan v. United States*, 338 U.S. 491, 501, 70 S.Ct. 292, 298, 94 L.Ed. 287. And the latter case sustained the denationalization of Mrs. Savorgnan although it was not disputed that she "had no intention of endangering her American citizenship or of renouncing her allegiance to the United States." What both women did do voluntarily was to engage in conduct to which Acts of Congress attached the consequence of denationalization irrespective of—and, in those cases, absolutely contrary to—the intentions and desires of the individuals. Those two cases mean nothing—indeed, they are deceptive—if their essential significance is not rejection of the notion that the power of Congress to terminate citizenship depends upon the citizen's assent.

Perez v. Brownell, 356 U.S. at 57–61.

A 1964 decision gave some indication of a change in attitude on the Court. The case involved a provision that decreed loss of U.S. citizenship for a naturalized citizen who returned to reside in his native country for three years (implementing a practice quite common in treaties meant to minimize dual nationality). *Schneider v. Rusk*, 377 U.S. 163, 84 S.Ct. 1187, 12 L.Ed.2d 218 (1964). The majority struck down the section, by a 5–3 vote. Justice Douglas' brief majority opinion restated a belief he had voiced in dissent in *Perez,* that Congress lacked power to expatriate. Acknowledging that this position "has not yet commanded a majority of the entire Court," however, he ultimately rested the invalidation on a different ground. The statute, he wrote, "proceeds on the impermissible assumption that naturalized citizens as a class are less reliable and bear less allegiance to this country than the native born." From that date forward, expatriation provisions would have to apply equally to the naturalized and the native-born (though denaturalization, which is based on fraud or illegality in the initial grant, of course applies only to the former).

Three years later, the Supreme Court returned to the precise ground of expatriation that had been upheld in *Perez* a decade before. In *Afroyim v. Rusk,* 387 U.S. 253, 87 S.Ct. 1660, 18 L.Ed.2d 757 (1967), the petitioner had been born in Poland, immigrated to the United States and become naturalized, and later moved to Israel where he voted in an election for the Knesset, the national parliament. When the U.S. State Department refused to renew his U.S. passport, he filed suit challenging the expatriation statute on constitutional grounds. In another 5–4 decision, the Supreme Court overruled *Perez.* Justice Black wrote the majority opinion:

> First we reject the idea expressed in *Perez* that, aside from the Fourteenth Amendment, Congress has any general power, express or implied, to take away an American citizen's citizenship without his assent. This power cannot, as *Perez* indicated, be sustained as an implied attribute of sovereignty possessed by all nations. Other nations are governed by their own constitutions, if any, and we can draw no support from theirs. In our country the people are sovereign and the Government cannot sever its relationship to the people by taking away their citizenship. Our Constitution * * * limits the Government to those powers specifically granted or those that are necessary and

proper to carry out the specifically granted ones. The Constitution, of course, grants Congress no express power to strip people of their citizenship, whether in the exercise of the implied power to regulate foreign affairs or in the exercise of any specifically granted power. * * *

* * * [T]he unequivocal terms of the [Fourteenth] Amendment * * * [provide their] own constitutional rule in language calculated completely to control the status of citizenship: "All persons born or naturalized in the United States ... are citizens of the United States...." There is no indication in these words of a fleeting citizenship, good at the moment it is acquired but subject to destruction by the Government at any time. Rather the Amendment can most reasonably be read as defining a citizenship which a citizen keeps unless he voluntarily relinquishes it. Once acquired, this Fourteenth Amendment citizenship was not to be shifted, canceled, or diluted at the will of the Federal Government, the States, or any other governmental unit.

* * *

* * * Citizenship is no light trifle to be jeopardized any moment Congress decides to do so under the name of one of its general or implied grants of power. * * * The very nature of our free government makes it completely incongruous to have a rule of law under which a group of citizens temporarily in office can deprive another group of citizens of their citizenship. We hold that the Fourteenth Amendment was designed to, and does, protect every citizen of this Nation against a congressional forcible destruction of his citizenship, whatever his creed, color, or race. Our holding does no more than to give to this citizen that which is his own, a constitutional right to remain a citizen in a free country unless he voluntarily relinquishes that citizenship.

Afroyim v. Rusk, 387 U.S. at 257, 262, 267–268. For a full account of the background to the *Afroyim* case, see Spiro, Afroyim: *Vaunting Citizenship, Presaging Transnationality,* in Immigration Stories 147 (D. Martin & P. Schuck eds. 2005).

———

The durability of *Afroyim* was called into question by a holding, again reached by a 5–4 margin, handed down four years later, after two Justices had retired and been replaced by new appointees. *Rogers v. Bellei*, 401 U.S. 815, 91 S.Ct. 1060, 28 L.Ed.2d 499 (1971). Bellei was born in Italy in 1939 to an Italian father and an American mother. Because the mother had resided in the United States for more than 10 years before his birth, she could transmit U.S. citizenship to him *jure sanguinis*. But the statute then operative also imposed a "condition subsequent" on children obtaining citizenship this way; they had to come to the United States and reside here for a minimum of five years between the ages of 14 and 28. Bellei had not met this condition, but he argued that, under *Afroyim*, Congress lacked the power to deprive him of citizenship. The majority, per Justice Blackmun, ruled for the government:

> The central fact, in our weighing of the plaintiff's claim to continuing and therefore current United States citizenship, is that he was born abroad. He was not born in the United States. He was not naturalized in the United States. And he has not been subject to the jurisdiction of the United States. All this being so, it seems indisputable that the first sentence of the Fourteenth Amendment has no application to plaintiff Bellei. He simply is not a Fourteenth-Amendment-first-sentence citizen. His posture contrasts with that of Mr. Afroyim, who was naturalized in the United States and with that of Mrs. Schneider, whose citizenship was derivative by her presence here and by her mother's naturalization here.

> The plaintiff's claim thus must center in the statutory power of Congress and in the appropriate exercise of that power within the restrictions of any pertinent constitutional provisions other than the Fourteenth Amendment's first sentence.

* * *

> [I]t is conceded here both that Congress may withhold citizenship from persons like plaintiff Bellei and may prescribe a period of residence in the United States as a condition *precedent* without constitutional question.

* * *

> We feel that it does not make good constitutional sense, or comport with logic, to say, on the one hand, that Congress may impose a condition precedent, with no constitutional complication, and yet be powerless to impose precisely the same condition subsequent.

Rogers v. Bellei, 401 U.S. at 827–8, 831, 834.

As noted *supra* p. 40, Congress chose not long after the *Bellei* decision to repeal (but without retroactive effect) all conditions subsequent applicable to persons gaining U.S. citizenship *jure sanguinis*. Under current law, someone born abroad in a situation like Bellei's need never establish residence in the United States in order to preserve his citizenship. He will probably have to do so, however, if he wishes to transmit citizenship to his own children.

Doubt about the vitality of *Afroyim* lingered after *Bellei*, but Justice Black's fears that *Afroyim* had been tacitly overruled proved resoundingly wrong in 1980. The following case seems to have brought relative stability to the constitutional doctrine governing expatriation.

VANCE v. TERRAZAS

Supreme Court of the United States, 1980.
444 U.S. 252, 100 S.Ct. 540, 62 L.Ed.2d 461.

MR. JUSTICE WHITE delivered the opinion of the Court.

Section 349(a)(2) of the Immigration and Nationality Act (Act) provides that "a person who is a national of the United States whether by birth or naturalization, shall lose his nationality by . . . taking an oath or making an affirmation or other formal declaration of allegiance to a foreign state or a political subdivision thereof." The Act also provides that the party claiming that such loss of citizenship occurred must "establish such claim by a preponderance of the evidence" and that the voluntariness of the expatriating conduct is rebuttably presumed. § 349(c), as added, 75 Stat. 656.ᶜ The issues in this case are whether, in establishing loss of citizenship under § 349(a)(2) a party must prove an intent to surrender United States citizenship and whether the United States Constitution permits Congress to legislate with respect to expatriation proceedings by providing the standard of proof and the statutory presumption contained in § 349(c).

I

Appellee, Laurence J. Terrazas, was born in this country, the son of a Mexican citizen. He thus acquired at birth both United States and Mexican citizenship. In the fall of 1970, while a student in Monterrey, Mexico, and at the age of 22, appellee executed an application for a certificate of Mexican nationality, swearing "adherence, obedience, and submission to the laws and authorities of the Mexican Republic" and "expressly renounc[ing] United States citizenship, as well as any submission, obedience, and loyalty to any foreign government, especially to that of the United States of America, . . ." The certificate, which issued upon this application on April 3, 1971, recited that Terrazas had sworn adherence to the United Mexican States and that he "has expressly renounced all rights inherent to any other nationality, as well as all submission, obedience, and loyalty to any foreign government, especially to those which have recognized him as that national." Terrazas read and understood the certificate upon receipt.

A few months later, following a discussion with an officer of the United States Consulate in Monterrey, proceedings were instituted to determine whether appellee had lost his United States citizenship by obtaining the certificate of Mexican nationality. Appellee denied that he had, but in December 1971 the Department of State issued a certificate of loss of nationality. The Board of Appellate Review of the Department of State, after a full hearing, affirmed that appellee had voluntarily renounced his United States citizenship. As permitted by § 360(a) of the

---

c. This presumption now appears in § 349(b).—eds.

Act, appellee then brought this suit against the Secretary of State for a declaration of his United States nationality. Trial was *de novo*.

The District Court recognized that the first sentence of the Fourteenth Amendment, as construed in *Afroyim v. Rusk,* " 'protect[s] every citizen of this Nation against a congressional forcible destruction of his citizenship' " and that every citizen has " 'a constitutional right to remain a citizen ... unless he voluntarily relinquishes that citizenship.' " A person of dual nationality, the District Court said, "will be held to have expatriated himself from the United States when it is shown that he voluntarily committed an act whereby he unequivocally renounced his allegiance to the United States." Specifically, the District Court found that appellee had taken an oath of allegiance to Mexico, that he had "knowingly and understandingly renounced allegiance to the United States in connection with his Application for a Certificate of Mexican Nationality," and that "[t]he taking of an oath of allegiance to Mexico and renunciation of a foreign country [*sic*]citizenship is a condition precedent under Mexican law to the issuance of a Certificate of Mexican Nationality." The District Court concluded that the United States had "proved by a preponderance of the evidence that Laurence J. Terrazas knowingly, understandingly and voluntarily took an oath of allegiance to Mexico, and concurrently renounced allegiance to the United States," and that he had therefore "voluntarily relinquished United States citizenship pursuant to § 349(a)(2) of the ... Act."

In its opinion accompanying its findings and conclusions, the District Court observed that appellee had acted "voluntarily in swearing allegiance to Mexico and renouncing allegiance to the United States," and that appellee "knew he was repudiating allegiance to the United States through his actions." The court also said that "the declaration of allegiance to a foreign state in conjunction with the renunciatory language of United States citizenship 'would leave no room for ambiguity as to the intent of the applicant.' "

The Court of Appeals reversed. As the Court of Appeals understood the law—and there appears to have been no dispute on these basic requirements in the Courts of Appeals—the United States had not only to prove the taking of an oath to a foreign state, but also to demonstrate an intent on appellee's part to renounce his United States citizenship. The District Court had found these basic elements to have been proved by a preponderance of the evidence; and the Court of Appeals observed that, "[a]ssuming that the proper [evidentiary] standards were applied, we are convinced that the record fully supports the court's findings." The Court of Appeals ruled, however, that under *Afroyim v. Rusk,* Congress had no power to legislate the evidentiary standard contained in § 349(c) and that the Constitution required that proof be not merely by a preponderance of the evidence, but by "clear, convincing and unequivocal evidence." The case was remanded to the District Court for further proceedings.

The Secretary took this appeal under 28 U.S.C. § 1252. Because the invalidation of § 349(c) posed a substantial constitutional issue, we noted probable jurisdiction.

II

The Secretary first urges that the Court of Appeals erred in holding that a "specific intent to renounce U.S. citizenship" must be proved "before the mere taking of an oath of allegiance could result in an individual's expatriation." His position is that he need prove only the voluntary commission of an act, such as swearing allegiance to a foreign nation, that "is so inherently inconsistent with the continued retention of American citizenship that Congress may accord to it its natural consequences, *i.e.,* loss of nationality." We disagree.

* * *

The Secretary argues that *Afroyim* does not stand for the proposition that a specific intent to renounce must be shown before citizenship is relinquished. It is enough, he urges, to establish one of the expatriating acts specified in § 349(a) because Congress has declared each of those acts to be inherently inconsistent with the retention of citizenship. But *Afroyim* emphasized that loss of citizenship requires the individual's "assent," in addition to his voluntary commission of the expatriating act. It is difficult to understand that "assent" to loss of citizenship would mean anything less than an intent to relinquish citizenship, whether the intent is expressed in words or is found as a fair inference from proved conduct. *Perez* had sustained congressional power to expatriate without regard to the intent of the citizen to surrender his citizenship. *Afroyim* overturned this proposition. It may be, as the Secretary maintains, that a requirement of intent to relinquish citizenship poses substantial difficulties for the Government in performance of its essential task of determining who is a citizen. Nevertheless, the intent of the Fourteenth Amendment, among other things, was to define citizenship; and as interpreted in *Afroyim,* that definition cannot coexist with a congressional power to specify acts that work a renunciation of citizenship even absent an intent to renounce. In the last analysis, expatriation depends on the will of the citizen rather than on the will of Congress and its assessment of his conduct.

* * *

[W]e are confident that it would be inconsistent with *Afroyim* to treat the expatriating acts specified in § 349(a) as the equivalent of or as conclusive evidence of the indispensable voluntary assent of the citizen. "Of course," any of the specified acts "may be highly persuasive evidence in the particular case of a purpose to abandon citizenship." *Nishikawa v. Dulles,* 356 U.S. 129, 139, 78 S.Ct. 612, 618, 2 L.Ed.2d 659 (1958) (Black, J., concurring). But the trier of fact must in the end conclude that the citizen not only voluntarily committed the expatriating act prescribed in the statute, but also intended to relinquish his citizenship.

* * *

III

With respect to the principal issues before it, the Court of Appeals held that Congress was without constitutional authority to prescribe the standard of proof in expatriation proceedings and that the proof in such cases must be by clear and convincing evidence rather than by the preponderance standard prescribed in § 349(c). We are in fundamental disagreement with these conclusions.

In *Nishikawa v. Dulles,* 356 U.S. 129, 78 S.Ct. 612, 2 L.Ed.2d 659 (1958), an American-born citizen, temporarily in Japan, was drafted into the Japanese Army. The Government later claimed that, under § 401(c) of the Nationality Act of 1940, 54 Stat. 1169, he had expatriated himself by serving in the armed forces of a foreign nation. The Government agreed that expatriation had not occurred if Nishikawa's army service had been involuntary. Nishikawa contended that the Government had to prove that his service was voluntary, while the Government urged that duress was an affirmative defense that Nishikawa had the burden to prove by overcoming the usual presumption of voluntariness. This Court held the presumption unavailable to the Government and required proof of a voluntary expatriating act by clear and convincing evidence.

Section 349(c) soon followed; its evident aim was to supplant the evidentiary standards prescribed by *Nishikawa.* The provision "sets up rules of evidence under which the burden of proof to establish loss of citizenship by preponderance of the evidence would rest upon the Government. The presumption of voluntariness under the proposed rules of evidence, would be rebuttable—similarly—by preponderance of the evidence, . . ." H.R.Rep. No. 1086, 87th Cong., 1st Sess., 41, U.S. Code Cong. & Admin. News, p. 2985 (1961).

We see no basis for invalidating the evidentiary prescriptions contained in § 349(c). *Nishikawa* was not rooted in the Constitution. The Court noted, moreover, that it was acting in the absence of legislative guidance. Nor do we agree with the Court of Appeals that, because under *Afroyim* Congress is constitutionally devoid of power to impose expatriation on a citizen, it is also without power to prescribe the evidentiary standards to govern expatriation proceedings. Although § 349(c) had been law since 1961, *Afroyim* did not address or advert to that section; surely the Court would have said so had it intended to construe the Constitution to exclude expatriation proceedings from the traditional powers of Congress to prescribe rules of evidence and standards of proof in the federal courts. This power, rooted in the authority of Congress conferred by Art. 1, § 8, cl. 9, of the Constitution to create inferior federal courts, is undoubted and has been frequently noted and sustained.

* * * [S]ince Congress has the express power to enforce the Fourteenth Amendment, it is untenable to hold that it has no power whatsoever to address itself to the manner or means by which Fourteenth Amendment citizenship may be relinquished.

We are unable to conclude that the specific evidentiary standard provided by Congress in § 349(c) is invalid under either the Citizenship Clause or the Due Process Clause of the Fifth Amendment. It is true that in criminal and involuntary commitment contexts we have held that the Due Process Clause imposes requirements of proof beyond a preponderance of the evidence. *Mullaney v. Wilbur,* 421 U.S. 684, 95 S.Ct. 1881, 44 L.Ed.2d 508 (1975); *Addington v. Texas,* 441 U.S. 418, 99 S.Ct. 1804, 60 L.Ed.2d 323 (1979). This Court has also stressed the importance of citizenship and evinced a decided preference for requiring clear and convincing evidence to prove expatriation. *Nishikawa v. United States, supra.* But expatriation proceedings are civil in nature and do not threaten a loss of liberty. Moreover, as we have noted, *Nishikawa* did not purport to be a constitutional ruling, and the same is true of similar rulings in related areas. *Woodby v. INS,* 385 U.S. 276, 285, 87 S.Ct. 483, 487, 17 L.Ed.2d 362 (1966) (deportation); *Schneiderman v. United States,* 320 U.S. 118, 125, 63 S.Ct. 1333, 1336, 87 L.Ed. 1796 (1943) (denaturalization). None of these cases involved a congressional judgment, such as that present here, that the preponderance standard of proof provides sufficient protection for the interest of the individual in retaining his citizenship. Contrary to the Secretary's position, we have held that expatriation requires the ultimate finding that the citizen has committed the expatriating act with the intent to renounce his citizenship. This in itself is a heavy burden, and we cannot hold that Congress has exceeded its powers by requiring proof of an intentional expatriating act by a preponderance of evidence.

IV

* * *

It is important at this juncture to note the scope of the statutory presumption. Section 349(c) provides that any of the statutory expatriating acts, if proved, are presumed to have been committed voluntarily. It does not also direct a presumption that the act has been performed with the intent to relinquish United States citizenship. That matter remains the burden of the party claiming expatriation to prove by a preponderance of the evidence. As so understood, we cannot invalidate the provision.[9]

* * * [T]he Court in *Nishikawa,* because it decided that "the consequences of denationalization are so drastic" and because it found nothing indicating a contrary result in the legislative history of the Nationality Act of 1940, held that the Government must carry the burden of proving that the expatriating act was performed voluntarily.

---

9. The Secretary asserts that the § 349(c) presumption cannot survive constitutional scrutiny if we hold that intent to relinquish citizenship is a necessary element in proving expatriation. The predicate for this assertion seems to be that § 349(c) presumes intent to relinquish as well as voluntariness. We do not so read it. Even if we did, and even if we agreed that presuming the necessary intent is inconsistent with *Afroyim,* it would be unnecessary to invalidate the section insofar as it presumes that the expatriating act itself was performed voluntarily.

Section 349(c), which was enacted subsequently, and its legislative history make clear that Congress preferred the ordinary rule that voluntariness is presumed and that duress is an affirmative defense to be proved by the party asserting it. * * * The rationality of the procedural rule with respect to claims of involuntariness in ordinary civil cases cannot be doubted. To invalidate the rule here would be to disagree flatly with Congress on the balance to be struck between the interest in citizenship and the burden the Government must assume in demonstrating expatriating conduct. It would also constitutionalize that disagreement and give the Citizenship Clause of the Fourteenth Amendment far more scope in this context than the relevant circumstances that brought the Amendment into being would suggest appropriate. Thus we conclude that the presumption of voluntariness included in § 349(c) has continuing vitality.

V

In sum, we hold that in proving expatriation, an expatriating act and an intent to relinquish citizenship must be proved by a preponderance of the evidence. We also hold that when one of the statutory expatriating acts is proved, it is constitutional to presume it to have been a voluntary act until and unless proved otherwise by the actor. If he succeeds, there can be no expatriation. If he fails, the question remains whether on all the evidence the Government has satisfied its burden of proof that the expatriating act was performed with the necessary intent to relinquish citizenship.

The judgment of the Court of Appeals is reversed, and the case is remanded for further proceedings consistent with this opinion.

So ordered.

* * *

MR. JUSTICE MARSHALL, concurring in part and dissenting in part.

I agree with the Court's holding that a citizen of the United States may not lose his citizenship in the absence of a finding that he specifically intended to renounce it. I also concur in the adoption of a saving construction of INA § 349(a)(2) to require that the statutorily designated expatriating acts be done with a specific intent to relinquish citizenship.

I cannot, however, accept the majority's conclusion that a person may be found to have relinquished his American citizenship upon a preponderance of the evidence that he intended to do so. The Court's discussion of congressional power to "prescribe rules of evidence and standards of proof in the federal courts," is the beginning, not the end, of the inquiry. It remains the task of this Court to determine when those rules and standards impinge on constitutional rights. As my Brother Stevens indicates, the Court's casual dismissal of the importance of American citizenship cannot withstand scrutiny. * * *

For these reasons I cannot understand, much less accept, the Court's suggestion that "expatriation proceedings ... do not threaten a loss of liberty." Recognizing that a standard of proof ultimately " 'reflects the value society places' " on the interest at stake, *Addington v. Texas*, 441 U.S. 418, 425, 99 S.Ct. 1804, 1809, 60 L.Ed.2d 323 (1979), I would hold that a citizen may not lose his citizenship in the absence of clear and convincing evidence that he intended to do so.

MR. JUSTICE STEVENS, concurring in part and dissenting in part.

The Court today unanimously reiterates the principle set forth in *Afroyim v. Rusk*, that Congress may not deprive an American of his citizenship against his will, but may only effectuate the citizen's own intention to renounce his citizenship. I agree with the Court that Congress may establish certain standards for determining whether such a renunciation has occurred. It may, for example, provide that expatriation can be proved by evidence that a person has performed an act that is normally inconsistent with continued citizenship and that the person thereby specifically intended to relinquish his American citizenship.

I do not agree, however, with the conclusion that Congress has established a permissible standard in § 349(a)(2). Since we accept dual citizenship, taking an oath of allegiance to a foreign government is not necessarily inconsistent with an intent to remain an American citizen. Moreover, as now written, the statute cannot fairly be read to require a finding of specific intent to relinquish citizenship. The statute unambiguously states that

"a national of the United States ... shall lose his nationality by—

* * *

"(2) taking an oath or making an affirmation or other formal declaration of allegiance to a foreign state or a political subdivision thereof."

There is no room in this provision to imply a requirement of a specific intent to relinquish citizenship. The Court does not attempt to do so, nor does it explain how any other part of the statute supports its conclusion that Congress required proof of specific intent.[1]

---

1. It could perhaps be argued that a specific intent requirement can be derived from INA § 349(c). That subsection creates a rebuttable presumption that any expatriating act set forth in subsection (a) was performed "voluntarily." The term "voluntary" could conceivably be stretched to include the concept of a specific intent to renounce one's citizenship. While the person seeking to retain his citizenship would thus have the burden of showing a lack of specific intent, such a construction would at least provide a statutory basis for bringing the issue of intent into the proceeding. The majority apparently would not be willing to accept such a construction in order to salvage the statute, however, inasmuch as it rejects the Secretary's argument that, if there is a requirement of specific intent, it is also subject to the presumption applicable to voluntariness.

The majority's assumption that the statute can be read to require specific intent to relinquish citizenship as an element of proof is also contradicted by the Court's treatment in *Afroyim* of a different subsection of the same statute. Like the subsection at issue here, subsection (a)(5) provided that an American automatically lost his nationality by performing a specific act: in that case, voting in a foreign election. If the majority's analysis in this case was correct, the Court in *Afroyim* should not have invalidated that provision of the statute; rather, it should merely have remanded for a finding as to whether Afroyim had voted in a foreign election with specific intent

I also disagree with the holding that a person may be deprived of his citizenship upon a showing by a mere preponderance of the evidence that he intended to relinquish it. The Court reasons that because the proceedings in question are civil in nature and do not result in any loss of physical liberty, no greater burden of proof is required than in the ordinary civil case. Such reasoning construes the constitutional concept of "liberty" too narrowly.

The House Report accompanying the 1961 amendment to the Immigration and Naturalization Act of 1952 refers to "the dignity and the priceless value of U.S. citizenship." That characterization is consistent with this Court's repeated appraisal of the quality of the interest at stake in this proceeding. In my judgment a person's interest in retaining his American citizenship is surely an aspect of "liberty" of which he cannot be deprived without due process of law. Because the interest at stake is comparable to that involved in *Addington v. Texas,* 441 U.S. 418, 99 S.Ct. 1804, 60 L.Ed.2d 323 [which dealt with involuntary civil commitment], essentially for the reasons stated in the Chief Justice's opinion for a unanimous Court in that case, I believe that due process requires that a clear and convincing standard of proof be met in this case as well before the deprivation may occur.

MR. JUSTICE BRENNAN, with whom MR. JUSTICE STEWART joins as to Part II, dissenting.

The Court holds that one may lose United States citizenship if the Government can prove by a preponderance of the evidence that certain acts, specified by statute, were done with the specific intent of giving up citizenship. Accordingly, the Court, in reversing the judgment of the Court of Appeals, holds that the District Court applied the correct evidentiary standards in determining that appellee was properly stripped of his citizenship. Because I would hold that one who acquires United States citizenship by virtue of being born in the United States, U.S. Const., Amdt. 14, § 1, can lose that citizenship only by formally renouncing it, and because I would hold that the act of which appellee is accused in this case cannot be an expatriating act, I dissent.

I

This case is governed by *Afroyim v. Rusk. Afroyim,* emphasizing the crucial importance of the right of citizenship, held unequivocally that a citizen has "a constitutional right to remain a citizen ... unless he voluntarily relinquishes that citizenship." "[T]he only way the citizenship ... could be lost was by the voluntary renunciation or abandonment by the citizen himself." The Court held that because Congress could not "abridge," "affect," "restrict the effect of," or "take ... away" citizenship, Congress was "without power to rob a citizen of his citizenship" because he voted in a foreign election.

---

to relinquish his American citizenship. That the Court did not do so is strong evidence of its belief that the statute could not be reformed as it is today.

The same clearly must be true of the Government's attempt to strip appellee of citizenship because he swore an oath of allegiance to Mexico. Congress has provided for a procedure by which one may formally renounce citizenship.[2] In this case the appellant concedes that appellee has not renounced his citizenship under that procedure. Because one can lose citizenship only by voluntarily renouncing it and because appellee has not formally renounced his, I would hold that he remains a citizen. Accordingly, I would remand the case with orders that appellee be given a declaration of United States nationality.

II

I reach the same result by another, independent line of reasoning. Appellee was born a dual national. He is a citizen of the United States because he was born here and a citizen of Mexico because his father was Mexican. The only expatriating act of which appellee stands accused is having sworn an oath of allegiance to Mexico. If dual citizenship, *per se,* can be consistent with United States citizenship, *Perkins v. Elg,* 307 U.S. 325, 329, 59 S.Ct. 884, 887, 83 L.Ed. 1320 (1939),[5] then I cannot see why an oath of allegiance to the other country of which one is already a citizen should create inconsistency. One owes allegiance to any country of which one is a citizen, especially when one is living in that country. *Kawakita v. United States,* 343 U.S. 717, 733–735, 72 S.Ct. 950, 960–961, 96 L.Ed. 1249 (1952). The formal oath adds nothing to the existing foreign citizenship and, therefore, cannot affect his United States citizenship.

NOTES AND QUESTIONS ON EXPATRIATION

1. Are the dissenters in *Terrazas* right concerning the procedural issue? Does the Court's approval of the preponderance standard and the presumption of voluntariness represent a significant retreat from its earlier judgments about the preciousness of U.S. citizenship? Why or why not?

2. How do the views of Justice Marshall and Justice Stevens differ? Which is more persuasive on the question of statutory construction? Consider INA § 356 in connection with your answer. Justice Brennan says that citizens may lose that status "only by formally renouncing it." Review the contents of Terrazas' oath of allegiance to Mexico. Why is Brennan in dissent?

3. Suppose Terrazas had been able to show that he executed the renunciation oath—after reading it—only because a Mexican citizenship cer-

---

2. INA § 349(a)(5) provides that "a national of the United States whether by birth or naturalization, shall lose his nationality by . . . making a formal renunciation of nationality before a diplomatic or consular officer of the United States in a foreign state, in such form as may be prescribed by the Secretary of State." The Secretary of State has prescribed such procedures in 22 CFR § 50.50 (1979). *See* Department of State, 8 Foreign Affairs Manual § 225.6 (1972). Congress also provided for renunciation by citizens while in the United States [during time of war. § 349(a)(6).] This last provision is not relevant to our case.

5. *Rogers v. Bellei,* 401 U.S. 815, 91 S.Ct. 1060, 28 L.Ed.2d 499 (1971), is not to the contrary. Bellei's citizenship was not based on the Fourteenth Amendment, and the issue before the Court was whether Bellei could lose his statutory citizenship for failure to satisfy a condition subsequent contained in the same statute that accorded him citizenship.

tificate was required in order to secure a specific job in Mexico. He asserts that, subjectively, his strongest wish throughout the whole process was to retain his dual nationality. Suppose further that he spoke of this wish to many witnesses at the time; hence there is adequate factual support for his assertion. He was not motivated by a desire to surrender his U.S. affiliation, but instead by his desire to get a job. Could he then, consistently with the Constitution, be considered expatriated? What does it mean to find that an individual had a "specific intent to renounce U.S. citizenship"? *See Richards v. Secretary of State*, 752 F.2d 1413, 1421–22 (9th Cir.1985); *Parness v. Shultz*, 669 F.Supp. 7 (D.D.C.1987).

4. In the 1986 INA Amendments, Pub.L. 99–653, 100 Stat. 3655, Congress finally brought the language of § 349 into line with the Supreme Court's expatriation rulings. It changed the operative language of § 349(a), which contains the list of expatriating acts, to provide that U.S. citizens shall lose their nationality only by "voluntarily performing any of the following acts *with the intention of relinquishing United States nationality.*" (Emphasis added.)

5. Meir Kahane, a U.S. citizen by birth and a former activist with the militant Jewish Defense League who moved to Israel, challenged U.S. expatriation law on multiple occasions. Kahane became an Israeli citizen under the Law of Return—a process that does not require express renunciation of other allegiances. Kahane became active in politics, and in 1984 was elected to the Israeli Parliament, the Knesset, as head of the right-wing Kach party. Accepting an office under a foreign government was an expatriating act listed in INA § 349(a)(4). Aware of this, and apparently concerned that a 1971 conviction under U.S. firearms law would prevent even brief visits to the United States if he lost his U.S. citizenship, Kahane told the U.S. State Department that he did not intend to give up his U.S. citizenship. The State Department's Board of Appellate Review nonetheless found that he had committed the expatriating act with intent to relinquish U.S. citizenship. It examined other evidence of his actions, writings, and speeches, and concluded that he had shifted his allegiance to Israel; actions, the Board suggested, speak louder than words.

Kahane challenged this decision in court, which ruled rather readily against the State Department: "Since citizenship is 'beyond the power of any governmental unit to destroy,' [quoting *Afroyim*] it may well be that a declaration of intent to retain citizenship, made simultaneously with commission of the expatriating act, will suffice to preserve the actor's citizenship." *Kahane v. Shultz*, 653 F.Supp. 1486, 1493 (E.D.N.Y.1987). In early 1988, the Knesset passed a law providing that its members could be citizens only of Israel. To hold on to his seat, Kahane executed an express "Oath of Renunciation" of U.S. citizenship before a U.S. consul in Jerusalem. A few weeks later the Israeli Supreme Court barred the Kach party, on other grounds, from running in the November 1988 election. Kahane thereupon sought to revoke his renunciation. Getting nowhere with the State Department, he returned to federal district court, claiming that the Israeli law amounted to compulsion that vitiated the voluntariness of the expatriating act, namely, the oath of renunciation. The court ruled against him. *Kahane v. Secretary of State*, 700 F.Supp. 1162 (D.D.C.1988). Expatriation did not have the expected effect on

Kahane's ability to travel to the United States, however—tragically, as it turned out. He was admitted in 1990 for a speaking tour, but he was assassinated while in New York City. N.Y. Times, Nov. 6, 1990, at A1. For a discussion of the first Kahane case, and further reflections on various theories that might underlie loss-of-citizenship doctrine, see Aleinikoff, *Theories of Loss of Citizenship*, 84 Mich.L.Rev. 1471 (1986).

Should there be room under our Constitution for rules that forbid assumption of an office under a foreign government, on pain of giving up U.S. citizenship? Could Congress constitutionally enforce such rules if it used only criminal or non-expatriating civil sanctions? Could Congress now forbid U.S. citizens from voting in foreign elections, using the same more limited range of sanctions? Should it?

6.   In 1978, several inmates of a state prison in Lucasville, Ohio, wrote to the State Department renouncing their U.S. citizenship and claiming status as citizens of the Soviet Union. Apparently they believed that they might in this way secure the diplomatic interposition of their alleged new country of nationality to protect the human rights they claimed were violated by their incarceration. These letters were clearly meant to be direct expressions of specific intent to terminate U.S. nationality. Relying on the statutory requirement that the formal renunciation of nationality take place outside the United States, INA §§ 349(a)(5), 351(a), the State Department refused to consider the inmates as validly expatriated

What policies are reflected in the provisions just cited, normally requiring that loss of citizenship occur only if the person is outside U.S. territory? Recall the discussion in Brubaker, *Citizenship As Social Closure*, p. 85, *supra*, of citizenship as an "international filing system" and the concerns about preventing statelessness. Do these policies make sense in the conditions of the modern world? Are they workable? However prudent they may be, are they constitutionally valid? That is, in light of the priority *Terrazas* places on the individual's voluntary decisions about his or her own citizenship status, is it permissible to require the commission of specified objective acts (which some persons may have difficulty performing) in addition to an unambiguous expression of intent to renounce? *See generally Davis v. District Director,* 481 F.Supp. 1178 (D.D.C.1979) (native-born citizen who formally renounced citizenship at U.S. consulate in Paris does not retain rights to enter and remain in this country without a proper visa).

The U.S. government has traditionally resisted accepting the surrender of citizenship by persons who are likely to retain residence in the United States. But a recent case, *Kaufman v. Holder,* 686 F.Supp.2d 40 (D.D.C. 2010), may necessitate a change. Kaufman, a registered sex offender imprisoned in Wisconsin, invoked the statutory provision that allows formal renunciation within the United States when the United States is in a state of war. INA §§ 349(a)(6), 351(a). *See* Scarcella, *DOJ Challenges Sex Offender's Effort to Renounce Citizenship*, April 30, 2010, <http://www.law.com/jsp/law/LawArticleFriendly.jsp?id= 1202457435187>. The government argued that this provision was triggered only by a formal declaration of war; the court found the current level of hostilities in Afghanistan and Iraq to be sufficient. The court mentioned only in passing the rather odious history of § 349(a)(6), which was initially adopted in 1944 in the (erroneous) expectation that it would result in widespread surrender of U.S. citizenship by Japanese–Americans interned in relocation camps. The proponents thought that such a change in status would provide a firmer legal footing for the detention, because internment of enemy nationals during wartime was well accepted in international law.

Procedures in Expatriation Cases

Terrazas reflects the usual way in which a controversy over expatriation arises and is resolved. A U.S. consulate, upon learning that a potentially expatriating act has occurred, investigates the facts and files a report with the Department of State. If the Department agrees that expatriation has occurred, a copy of the consulate's Certificate of Loss of Nationality (CLN) is then sent to the individual and to immigration authorities. *See* INA § 358; 22 C.F.R. § 50.40(e). The person may appeal the decision to the Board of Appellate Review (BAR) of the State Department within one year. *Id.* Part 7; § 50.51. It may also happen that the loss-of-nationality issue is adjudicated when a person applies for a U.S. passport. Passport denial may also be appealed to the BAR. *Id.* §§ 7.3. The State Department procedures employed in loss-of-citizenship cases are usefully summarized in James, *The Board of Appellate Review of the Department of State: The Right to Appellate Review of Administrative Determinations of Loss of Nationality,* 23 San Diego L.Rev. 261 (1986), with particular attention to the case law and practice of the BAR. *See also* Endelman, *How to Prevent Loss of Citizenship,* 89–11 & 89–12 Imm.Briefings (1989).

If the finding of expatriation is sustained by the BAR, the person may contest the issue in federal court. Under INA § 360(a), claimants within the United States may obtain a judicial determination of a citizenship claim by means of a declaratory judgment action in accordance with 28 U.S.C.A. § 2201. The action must be initiated within five years after the final administrative denial of a right or privilege of citizenship by any department or agency. Claimants outside the United States are granted by the INA a procedure permitting them to travel to this country in order to apply for admission. Judicial review then is available on habeas corpus. INA § 360(b), (c).[8]

The State Department's Approach

In 1990, the State Department adopted a new statement of evidentiary standards to be applied in expatriation cases. It reflects a wholly new

---

8. A claim of U.S. citizenship may also arise by way of a defense in a removal proceeding, in which case the issue is resolved by the immigration judge and, upon appeal, the BIA, without the direct involvement of the State Department. If the BIA rejects the claim and the alien files a petition for review in the court of appeals, INA § 242(b)(5) makes special provision for transfer, if the claim presents a genuine issue of material fact, to the district court for a new hearing.

attitude far more hospitable to dual citizenship than in earlier years, when the Department often tried to read as narrowly as possible any Supreme Court decisions that restricted expatriation. The standard, as currently posted on the Department's website, provides in part:

> [The actions listed in INA § 349(a)] can cause loss of U.S. citizenship only if performed voluntarily and with the intention of relinquishing U.S. citizenship. **The Department has a uniform administrative standard of evidence based on the premise that U.S. citizens intend to retain United States citizenship when they obtain naturalization in a foreign state, subscribe to routine declarations of allegiance to a foreign state, or accept non-policy level employment with a foreign government.**

* * *

In light of the administrative premise discussed above, a person who:

1. is naturalized in a foreign country;

2. takes a routine oath of allegiance; or

3. serves in the armed forces of a foreign state not engaged in hostilities with the United States, or

4. accepts non-policy level employment with a foreign government,

and in so doing wishes to retain U.S. citizenship need not submit prior to the commission of a potentially expatriating act a statement or evidence of his or her intent to retain U.S. citizenship since such an intent will be presumed.

When, as the result of an individual's inquiry or an individual's application for registration or a passport it comes to the attention of a U.S. consular officer that a U.S. citizen has performed an act made potentially expatriating by Sections 349(a)(1), 349(a)(a)(2), 349(a)(3) or 349(a)(4), the consular officer will simply ask the applicant if there was intent to relinquish U.S. citizenship when performing the act. If the answer is no, the consular officer will certify that it was **not** the person's intent to relinquish U.S. citizenship, and consequently, find that the person has retained U.S. citizenship.

* * *

An individual who has performed **any** of the acts made potentially expatriating by statute who wishes to lose U.S. citizenship may do so by affirming in writing to a U.S. consular officer that the act was performed with an intent to relinquish U.S. citizenship. Of course, a person always has the option of seeking to formally renounce U.S. citizenship in accordance with Section 349(a)(5) INA.

* * *

The premise that a person intends to retain U.S. citizenship is not applicable when the individual:

1. formally renounces U.S. citizenship before a consular officer;

2. serves in the armed forces of a foreign state engaged in hostilities with the United States;

3. takes a policy level position in a foreign state;

4. is convicted of treason; or

5. performs an act made potentially expatriating by statute accompanied by conduct which is so inconsistent with retention of U.S. citizenship that it compels a conclusion that the individual intended to relinquish U.S. citizenship. (Such cases are very rare.)

Cases in categories 2, 3, 4 and 5 will be developed carefully by U.S. consular officers to ascertain the individual's intent toward U.S. citizenship.

* * *

Advice about Possible Loss of U.S. Citizenship and Dual Nationality, http://www.travel.state.gov/law/citizenship/citizenship_778.html.

Are the provisions numbered (2) and (3) in the final quoted paragraph consistent with the Constitution as interpreted in *Afroyim* and *Terrazas?* How would the Department's evidentiary standards apply to someone who takes an oath of allegiance to another nation, including an express renunciation of U.S. citizenship, as part of a naturalization ceremony before an administrative officer of that other nation, but who subjectively wishes to retain U.S. nationality as well?

EXERCISE

Suppose you are consulted by a client who wants to take a particular job overseas that requires the nationality of the host country. She finds that she can naturalize there, but must take a renunciatory oath in order to do so. She wants the job but also wishes to retain her U.S. citizenship and seems happy to know that the State Department apparently won't issue a CLN after the ceremony. How would you advise her? Is perjury a problem? Is the State Department's treatment of such oaths permissible under congressional enactments? Review the language of INA § 349(a)(1) and consider it in connection the wording of the naturalization oath, set forth in INA § 337.

CHAPTER THREE

FOUNDATIONS OF IMMIGRATION LAW

■ ■ ■

SECTION A. THE FEDERAL IMMIGRATION POWER

The historical overview in Chapter One makes clear that the United States, since its founding, has engaged in a national discussion over how many and what kind of immigrants should be permitted to enter and take up residence. What these debates have almost always taken for granted is the power of the Congress to enact laws that regulate which noncitizens may enter the United States and under what conditions those that enter may remain. It is this issue—the source and scope of Congress' immigration power—that we explore in this section.

You may find it curious that the source and scope of Congress' power could be interesting questions. Surely the Framers would have endowed Congress explicitly with a power as important as that of controlling immigration. Yet the Constitution of the United States includes no language that expressly grants Congress such authority. The Supreme Court did not address the question until the second century of this country's existence, primarily because Congress did not enact significant limits on immigration until the 1880s. For most of the nineteenth century, Congress permitted open borders in an attempt to provide the developing nation with labor and capital. What immigration law existed was the creation of the states. Many states had laws that the modern eye may not readily recognize as immigration laws because they often restricted entry by other states' citizens as well as by foreigners, and because they regulated specific concerns, for example public health. In substance, however, these laws had much in common with modern immigration laws. *See* Neuman, *The Lost Century of Immigration Law (1776–1875)*, 93 Colum. L. Rev. 1833 (1993).

This section will first examine the historical setting in which the major federal immigration cases were decided in the late nineteenth century. It will turn then to three landmark Supreme Court opinions, each involving a Chinese immigrant. The following discussion will explore the basic constitutional framework implicated by the government's regulation of immigration.

1. CHINESE IMMIGRATION

The earliest federal statutes limiting immigration, enacted in 1875 and 1882, prohibited the entry of criminals, prostitutes, idiots, lunatics, and persons likely to become a public charge. Act of March 3, 1875, Ch. 141, 18 Stat. 477; Act of August 3, 1882, Ch. 376, 22 Stat. 214. There was a distinct anti-Chinese bias, as the 1875 statute specified that contract laborers from Asia were undesirable, as were Asian women who would engage in prostitution. *Id.* Soon thereafter, in 1882, 1884, 1888 and 1892, Congress enacted the so-called Chinese exclusion laws, and these became the first federal immigration statutes to be subjected to judicial scrutiny. Thus, many of the foundation cases in the immigration law canon involved Chinese litigants. The excerpt below sketches the history of Chinese immigration to the United States; knowing the historical, economic, and political context of this legislation allows a better appreciation for the judicial opinions that interpreted it.[1]

Chinese railroad workers in California, 1880s.
(Photo: Pajaro Valley Historical Association)

---

1. A fuller examination of the background of the two judicial opinions excerpted in this section can be found in Chin, *Chae Chan Ping and Fong Yue Ting: The Origins of Plenary Power*, in Immigration Stories 7–23 (D. Martin & P. Schuck eds. 2005)

HIROSHI MOTOMURA, AMERICANS IN WAITING: THE LOST STORY OF IMMIGRATION AND CITIZENSHIP IN THE UNITED STATES*

15–17, 25–26 (2006).

Chinese immigrants first came to America in large numbers starting with the California Gold Rush in 1849, so drawn by the prospect of riches that among them California came to be called Gold Mountain. Few would find that dream of quick wealth, but the growing economy in the western United States needed cheap labor. At first, most Chinese worked in mines; later they toiled to build the transcontinental railroad. The Central Pacific Railroad's workforce was 90 percent Chinese. Many were enticed by the allure of wages far surpassing what they could earn in China. During the 1860s, a worker could earn $30 per month on the railroad, six times what he could earn in southern China. In 1852, somewhere between 12,000 and 25,000 Chinese were in California. By 1870, this number had grown to about 63,000, and it exceeded 105,000 by 1880, when the U.S. Census reported the total population of California as 865,000. About 250,000 Chinese immigrated to the United States from 1850 until the 1882 Chinese Exclusion Act.

The U.S. government first addressed Chinese immigration when it negotiated and signed the Burlingame Treaty with China in 1868. At the time, the United States was interested in cheap labor and trade with China. By signing the treaty, the U.S. government accepted Chinese immigration, and the Chinese government accepted emigration, which would still remain a crime theoretically punishable by death until 1893. The treaty declared the "inherent and inalienable right of man to change his home and allegiance, and also the mutual advantage of free migration and emigration of [American and Chinese] citizens ... for purposes of curiosity, of trade or as permanent residents."

Even when tens of thousands of Chinese workers were needed to lay the rails, anti-Chinese sentiment was strong throughout the West. "Anti-coolie" clubs depicted Chinese workers as indentured servants not unlike the slaves who had just been freed in the Southern states. There were also boycotts of Chinese-made goods, anti-Chinese newspaper editorials, and licensing requirements for Chinese miners and merchants. In 1852, California enacted a tax on Chinese miners to force them into other employment.

When the completion of the transcontinental railroad in 1869 put some ten thousand Chinese laborers out of work, they spread out into new occupations, depressing wages throughout the western United States. A severe recession from 1873 to 1878 further provoked popular sentiment in California and elsewhere in the American West to blame Chinese workers for American joblessness. During the 1870s, a rising tide of anti-Chinese fervor swept over the western states and gradually influenced national politics.

In 1876, a special joint congressional committee urged renegotiation of the Burlingame Treaty to curb Chinese immigration. In 1879, Congress passed a bill limiting arriving ships to only fifteen Chinese passengers, but President Rutherford Hayes vetoed it on the ground that it conflicted with the Burlingame Treaty. By the 1880 presidential election, however, both the Democratic and Republican Party platforms called for restrictions on Chinese immigration. That year, the two countries entered into a supplemental treaty that allowed the United States to "regulate, limit or suspend" immigration of Chinese laborers whenever their entry or residence in the United States "affects or threatens to affect the interests of that country, or to endanger the good order of [the United States] or of any locality within the territory thereof." But the supplemental treaty allowed those Chinese already in the United States in November 1880 to continue "to go and come of their own free will and accord."

The supplemental treaty did not quiet the crescendo of calls for further limits on Chinese immigration, and some states, impatient and unwilling to wait for federal action, acted on their own. An 1879 California statute required incorporated towns and cities to remove Chinese from their city limits. * * *

* * * [Several] years later, in the spring of 1882, Congress enacted a twenty-year moratorium on immigration of Chinese laborers, but President Chester Arthur vetoed it with a call for a shorter ban. Two months later, wide margins in both houses enacted a ten-year moratorium, which President Arthur signed into law—the first Chinese Exclusion Act. Congress declared that "the coming of Chinese laborers to this country endangers the good order of certain localities." Chinese exclusion was renewed several times and extended indefinitely in 1904, remaining the law of the land until 1943.

The Chinese Exclusion Act was hard to enforce, partly because it was not clear who was exempt as a returning Chinese immigrant who had originally arrived in the United States before the effective date of the ten-year moratorium. The act appeared to require Chinese laborers who were returning from China to show certificates, obtained from the U.S. government when they departed, to prove that they had first come to America before November 17, 1880. Chinese arriving in the United States were also exempt if they were merchants, teachers, students, or travelers. To prove this, they had to show a certificate to that effect, issued by the Chinese government.

At each port, a collector of customs decided whether a Chinese immigrant was barred or exempt. Working before the use of photographs became ordinary in processing, immigration inspectors relied on the certificates, which included "physical marks or peculiarities, and all facts necessary for ... identification." Even after photographs came into widespread use by the end of the nineteenth century, government inspectors measured numerous body parts in great detail.

The collector often denied reentry even if the immigrants had certificates, but federal judges in San Francisco overturned many of these decisions and sometimes even allowed Chinese laborers to prove pre-November 1880 residency without a certificate at all. Federal judges also relaxed the entry requirements for Chinese merchants. In 1884, Congress reacted to these court decisions by making the certificate the "only evidence permissible to establish his right of re-entry." However, federal judges continued to show flexibility in the proof that they demanded, especially of Chinese who claimed to have left the United States before the certificate requirements took effect.

In 1888, Congress responded by changing the law yet again with the Scott Act, which barred a Chinese immigrant's return even with a certificate. This was the law that stranded Chae Chan Ping * * *.

* * *

Chae Chan Ping was a Chinese laborer who [had come] to the United States and settled in San Francisco in 1875, near the end of the first great wave of Chinese immigration. Twelve years later, he took a trip to China to visit his family, who had stayed behind in typical fashion. By the time Chae left on his journey, the Chinese Exclusion Act of 1882 had put a moratorium on the new immigration of laborers from China. Returning Chinese laborers would be readmitted only if they had a U.S. government certificate to prove they had been in America before the ban took effect. Chae left in 1887 with a certificate in hand, issued by the collector of customs in San Francisco.

2. THE FOUNDATION CASES

For decades prior to Chae Chan Ping's odyssey, the Chinese had been the targets of discriminatory legislation in California. They were subjected to entry, license and occupation taxes, originally to raise money for the California treasury and later as a means to deter immigration. Chinese were denied the right to testify in court and prohibited from attending public schools with white children. San Francisco's Chinese community, which had a high degree of social organization and also had experience in dealing with government bureaucracy, filed court challenges to a number of the state laws. Judges declared many of them invalid, either as a violation of the Fourteenth Amendment or as conflicting with federal treaties. *See, e.g., Ho Ah Kow v. Nunan*, 12 F.Cas. 252, 5 Sawyer 552 (C.C.D.Cal.1879) (Mr. Justice Field on circuit) (invalidating San Francisco's "Queue Ordinance" which required that all prisoners have their hair cut to a maximum length of one inch); *People v. Downer*, 7 Cal. 169 (1857) (invalidating $50 tax on Chinese passengers); *Lin Sing v. Washburn*, 20 Cal. 534 (1862) (voiding capitation tax on Chinese). *See generally* L. Salyer, Laws Harsh as Tigers: Chinese Immigrants and the Shaping of Modern Immigration Law (1995).[2]

---

2. Further examination of the impact of U.S. immigration law on Asian migrants can be found in M. Ngai, Impossible Subjects: Illegal Aliens and the Making of Modern America (2004); B.

Against this background, and with the help of the San Francisco Chinese community, Chinese immigrants brought a series of suits alleging that the federal statutes violated international law and the U.S. Constitution. As you read the three major judicial opinions below, it may help to keep in mind several different constitutional concerns. First, what provisions—or other features—of the United States Constitution authorize power to regulate immigration? Second, what roles do the respective branches of the federal government play with regard to immigration measures? Third, what authority do state governments have over immigration?

a. Exclusion at the Border

Chae Chan Ping argued that the U.S. Constitution and international law allowed him to re-enter the United States after his trip to China. When his case reached the Supreme Court, the Court ruled unanimously against his claim.

CHAE CHAN PING v. UNITED STATES
[CHINESE EXCLUSION CASE]

Supreme Court of the United States, 1889.
130 U.S. 581, 9 S.Ct. 623, 32 L.Ed. 1068.

MR. JUSTICE FIELD delivered the opinion of the Court.

* * *

* * * It must be conceded that the act of 1888 is in contravention of express stipulations of the [Burlingame] treaty of 1868 and of the supplemental treaty of 1880, but it is not on that account invalid or to be restricted in its enforcement. The treaties were of no greater legal obligation than the act of Congress. By the Constitution, laws made in pursuance thereof and treaties made under the authority of the United States are both declared to be the supreme law of the land, and no paramount authority is given to one over the other. A treaty, it is true, is in its nature a contract between nations and is often merely promissory in its character, requiring legislation to carry its stipulations into effect. Such legislation will be open to future repeal or amendment. If the treaty operates by its own force, and relates to a subject within the power of Congress, it can be deemed in that particular only the equivalent of a legislative act, to be repealed or modified at the pleasure of Congress. In either case the last expression of the sovereign will must control.

* * *

There being nothing in the treaties between China and the United States to impair the validity of the act of Congress of October 1, 1888, was

Hing, Making and Remaking Asian America Through Immigration Policy, 1850–1990, at 19–26 (1993); R. Takaki, Strangers from a Different Shore: A History of Asian Americans 79–131 (1989); C. McClain, *The Chinese Struggle for Civil Rights in Nineteenth Century America: The First Phase, 1850–1870*, 72 Calif. L. Rev. 529 (1984); M. Coolidge, Chinese Immigration (1909).

it on any other ground beyond the competency of Congress to pass it? If so, it must be because it was not within the power of Congress to prohibit Chinese laborers who had at the time departed from the United States, or should subsequently depart, from returning to the United States. Those laborers are not citizens of the United States; they are aliens. That the government of the United States, through the action of the legislative department, can exclude aliens from its territory is a proposition which we do not think open to controversy. Jurisdiction over its own territory to that extent is an incident of every independent nation. It is a part of its independence. If it could not exclude aliens it would be to that extent subject to the control of another power. As said by this court in the case of *The Exchange*, 7 Cranch 116, 136, speaking by Chief Justice Marshall: "The jurisdiction of the nation within its own territory is necessarily exclusive and absolute. It is susceptible of no limitation not imposed by itself. Any restriction upon it, deriving validity from an external source, would imply a diminution of its sovereignty to the extent of the restriction, and an investment of that sovereignty to the same extent in that power which could impose such restriction. All exceptions, therefore, to the full and complete power of a nation within its own territories, must be traced up to the consent of the nation itself. They can flow from no other legitimate source."

While under our Constitution and form of government the great mass of local matters is controlled by local authorities, the United States, in their relation to foreign countries and their subjects or citizens are one nation, invested with powers which belong to independent nations, the exercise of which can be invoked for the maintenance of its absolute independence and security throughout its entire territory. The powers to declare war, make treaties, suppress insurrection, repel invasion, regulate foreign commerce, secure republican governments to the States, and admit subjects of other nations to citizenship, are all sovereign powers, restricted in their exercise only by the Constitution itself and considerations of public policy and justice which control, more or less, the conduct of all civilized nations. * * *

The control of local matters being left to local authorities, and national matters being entrusted to the government of the Union, the problem of free institutions existing over a widely extended country, having different climates and varied interests, has been happily solved. For local interests the several States of the Union exist, but for national purposes, embracing our relations with foreign nations, we are but one people, one nation, one power.

To preserve its independence, and give security against foreign aggression and encroachment, is the highest duty of every nation, and to attain these ends nearly all other considerations are to be subordinated. It matters not in what form such aggression and encroachment come, whether from the foreign nation acting in its national character or from vast hordes of its people crowding in upon us. The government, possessing the powers which are to be exercised for protection and security, is clothed with authority to determine the occasion on which the powers shall be called forth; and its determination, so far as the subjects affected are concerned, are necessarily conclusive upon all its departments and officers. If, therefore, the government of the United States, through its legislative department, considers the presence of foreigners of a different race in this country, who will not assimilate with us, to be dangerous to its peace and security, their exclusion is not to be stayed because at the time there are no actual hostilities with the nation of which the foreigners are subjects. The existence of war would render the necessity of the proceeding only more obvious and pressing. The same necessity, in a less pressing degree, may arise when war does not exist, and the same authority which adjudges the necessity in one case must also determine it in the other. In both cases its determination is conclusive upon the judiciary. If the government of the country of which the foreigners excluded are subjects is dissatisfied with this action it can make complaint to the executive head of our government, or resort to any other measure which, in its judgment, its interests or dignity may demand; and there lies its only remedy.

* * *

The exclusion of paupers, criminals and persons afflicted with incurable diseases, for which statutes have been passed, is only an application of the same power to particular classes of persons, whose presence is deemed injurious or a source of danger to the country. As applied to them, there has never been any question as to the power to exclude them. The power is constantly exercised; its existence is involved in the right of self-preservation. * * *

The power of exclusion of foreigners being an incident of sovereignty belonging to the government of the United States, as a part of those sovereign powers delegated by the Constitution, the right to its exercise at any time when, in the judgment of the government, the interests of the country require it, cannot be granted away or restrained on behalf of any one. The powers of government are delegated in trust to the United States, and are incapable of transfer to any other parties. They cannot be abandoned or surrendered. Nor can their exercise be hampered, when needed for the public good, by any considerations of private interest. The exercise of these public trusts is not the subject of barter or contract. Whatever license, therefore, Chinese laborers may have obtained, previous to the act of October 1, 1888, to return to the United States after their departure, is held at the will of the government, revocable at any time, at its pleasure. Whether a proper consideration by our government of its previous laws, or a proper respect for the nation whose subjects are affected by its action, ought to have qualified its inhibition and made it applicable only to persons departing from the country after the passage of the act, are not questions for judicial determination. If there be any just ground of complaint on the part of China, it must be made to the political department of our government, which is alone competent to act upon the subject.

* * *

Order affirmed.

b. From Exclusion to Deportation

In 1892, Congress again addressed the issue of Chinese immigration. Act of May 5, 1892, Ch. 60, 27 Stat. 25. The 1892 Act authorized the deportation of any Chinese alien unlawfully in the United States. It further required all Chinese laborers then living in the United States to acquire a "certificate of residence" from the Collector of Internal Revenue within one year after passage of the Act. Under regulations promulgated pursuant to the Act, the government would issue a certificate only on the "affidavit of at least one credible witness," which was construed as a white witness. *See* 149 U.S. at 701 n.1, 703, 731. An alien who failed to obtain the certificate could "be arrested * * * and taken before a United States judge, whose duty it shall be to order that he be deported from the United States." He could escape deportation only upon a demonstration "that by reason of accident, sickness or other unavoidable cause, he has been unable to procure his certificate, * * * and by at least one credible white witness, that he was a resident of the United States at the time of the passage of [the Act]." 27 Stat. 25–26.

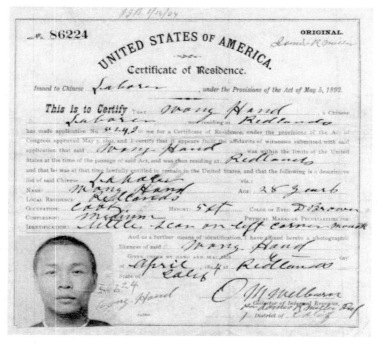

A typical residence certificate issued under the Chinese exclusion laws.
(Photo: Ethnic Studies Library, Asian American Studies
Collections, University of California at Berkeley)

We should note here that "deportation" has two meanings in the immigration laws. As in the 1892 legislation, it may mean the removal of noncitizens already within the United States—in contrast to the "exclusion" of noncitizens at the border who are seeking to enter. "Deportation" may also be used to mean the physical removal to another country of any noncitizen whether inside or at the border of the United States. To minimize confusion, this book will use "exclusion" to refer to a denial of entry and "deportation" or "expulsion" to refer to the removal of a noncitizen who is inside the United States. Since 1996, the INA has used "removal" to refer to both exclusion and deportation, and we will follow that usage here.

The 1892 Act was challenged on numerous constitutional grounds. The Supreme Court's decision follows.

FONG YUE TING v. UNITED STATES

Supreme Court of the United States, 1893.
149 U.S. 698, 13 S.Ct. 1016, 37 L.Ed. 905.

[Three Chinese laborers who were arrested and held by Federal authorities for not having certificates of residence petitioned for writs of habeas corpus. The Circuit Court for the Southern District of New York denied relief, and the Supreme Court consolidated the cases on appeal. The facts of one of the cases are stated.]

* * * On April 11, 1893, the petitioner applied to the collector of internal revenue for a certificate of residence; the collector refused to give him a certificate, on the ground that the witnesses whom he produced to prove that he was entitled to the certificate were persons of the Chinese race and not credible witnesses, and required of him to produce a witness other than a Chinaman to prove that he was entitled to the certificate, which he was unable to do, because there was no person other than one of the Chinese race who knew and could truthfully swear that he was lawfully within the United States on May 5, 1892, and then entitled to remain therein; and because of such unavoidable cause he was unable to produce a certificate of residence, and was now without one. The petitioner was arrested by the marshal, and taken before the judge; and clearly established, to the satisfaction of the judge, that he was unable to procure a certificate of residence, by reason of the unavoidable cause aforesaid; and also established, to the judge's satisfaction, by the testimony of a Chinese resident of New York, that the petitioner was a resident of the United States at the time of the passage of the act; but having failed to establish this fact clearly to the satisfaction of the court by at least one credible white witness, as required by the statute, the judge ordered the petitioner to be remanded to the custody of the marshal, and to be deported from the United States, as provided in the act.

* * *

MR. JUSTICE GRAY, after stating the facts, delivered the opinion of the court.

The general principles of public law which lie at the foundation of these cases are clearly established by previous judgments of this court, and by the authorities therein referred to.

* * *

The right of a nation to expel or deport foreigners, who have not been naturalized or taken any steps towards becoming citizens of the country, rests upon the same grounds, and is as absolute and unqualified as the right to prohibit and prevent their entrance into the country.

* * *

The statements of leading commentators on the law of nations are to the same effect.

Vattel says: "Every nation has the right to refuse to admit a foreigner into the country, when he cannot enter without putting the nation in evident danger, or doing it a manifest injury. What it owes to itself, the care of its own safety, gives it this right; and in virtue of its natural liberty, it belongs to the nation to judge whether its circumstances will or will not justify the admission of the foreigner." "Thus, also, it has a right to send them elsewhere, if it has just cause to fear that they will corrupt the manners of the citizens; that they will create religious disturbances, or occasion any other disorder, contrary to the public safety. In a word, it has a right, and is even obliged, in this respect, to follow the rules which prudence dictates." Vattel's Law of Nations, lib. 1, c. 19, §§ 230, 231.

Ortolan says: "The government of each state has always the right to compel foreigners who are found within its territory to go away, by having them taken to the frontier. This right is based on the fact that, the foreigner not making part of the nation, his individual reception into the territory is matter of pure permission, of simple tolerance, and creates no obligation. The exercise of this right may be subjected, doubtless, to certain forms by the domestic laws of each country; but the right exists none the less, universally recognized and put in force. In France, no special form is now prescribed in this matter; the exercise of this right of expulsion is wholly left to the executive power." Ortolan, Diplomatie de la Mer, lib. 2, c. 14, (4th ed.) p. 297.

* * *

The right to exclude or to expel all aliens, or any class of aliens, absolutely or upon certain conditions, in war or in peace, being an inherent and inalienable right of every sovereign and independent nation, essential to its safety, its independence and its welfare, the question now before the court is whether the manner in which Congress has exercised this right in * * * the act of 1892 is consistent with the Constitution.

The United States are a sovereign and independent nation, and are vested by the Constitution with the entire control of international relations, and with all the powers of government necessary to maintain that control and to make it effective. The only government of this country, which other nations recognize or treat with, is the government of the Union; and the only American flag known throughout the world is the flag of the United States.

The Constitution of the United States speaks with no uncertain sound upon this subject. That instrument, established by the people of the United States as the fundamental law of the land, has conferred upon the President the executive power; has made him the commander-in-chief of the army and navy; has authorized him, by and with the consent of the Senate, to make treaties, and to appoint ambassadors, public ministers and consuls; and has made it his duty to take care that the laws be faithfully executed. The Constitution has granted to Congress the power to regulate commerce with foreign nations, including the entrance of ships, the importation of goods and the bringing of persons into the ports of the United States; to establish a uniform rule of naturalization; to define and punish piracies and felonies committed on the high seas, and offences against the law of nations; to declare war, grant letters of marque and reprisal, and make rules concerning captures on land and water; to raise and support armies, to provide and maintain a navy, and to make rules for the government and regulation of the land and naval forces; and to make all laws necessary and proper for carrying into execution these powers, and all other powers vested by the Constitution in the government of the United States, or in any department or officer thereof. And the several States are expressly forbidden to enter into any treaty, alliance or confederation; to grant letters of marque and reprisal; to enter into any agreement or compact with another State, or with a foreign power; or to engage in war, unless actually invaded, or in such imminent danger as will not admit of delay.

In exercising the great power which the people of the United States, by establishing a written Constitution as the supreme and paramount law, have vested in this court, of determining, whenever the question is properly brought before it, whether the acts of the legislature or of the executive are consistent with the Constitution, it behooves the court to be careful that it does not undertake to pass upon political questions, the final decision of which has been committed by the Constitution to the other departments of the government.

* * *

In Nishimura Ekiu's case, it was adjudged that, although Congress might, if it saw fit, authorize the courts to investigate and ascertain the facts upon which the alien's right to land was made by the statutes to depend, yet Congress might intrust the final determination of those facts to an executive officer; and that, if it did so, his order was due process of law, and no other tribunal, unless expressly authorized by law to do so, was at liberty to re-examine the evidence on which he acted, or to controvert its sufficiency.

The power to exclude aliens and the power to expel them rest upon one foundation, are derived from one source, are supported by the same reasons, and are in truth but parts of one and the same power.

* * *

Chinese laborers * * * like all other aliens residing in the United States for a shorter or longer time, are entitled, so long as they are permitted by the government of the United States to remain in the country, to the safeguards of the Constitution, and to the protection of the laws, in regard to their rights of person and of property, and to their civil and criminal responsibility. But they continue to be aliens, having taken no steps towards becoming citizens, and incapable of becoming such under the naturalization laws; and therefore remain subject to the power of Congress to expel them, or to order them to be removed and deported from the country, whenever in its judgment their removal is necessary or expedient for the public interest.

* * *

* * * Congress, under the power to exclude or expel aliens, might have directed any Chinese laborer, found in the United States without a certificate of residence, to be removed out of the country by executive officers, without judicial trial or examination, just as it might have authorized such officers absolutely to prevent his entrance into the country. But Congress has not undertaken to do this.

The effect of the provisions of * * * the act of 1892 is that, if a Chinese laborer, after the opportunity afforded him to obtain a certificate of residence within a year, at a convenient place, and without cost, is found without such a certificate, he shall be so far presumed to be not entitled to remain within the United States, that an officer of the customs, or a collector of internal revenue, or a marshal, or a deputy of either, may arrest him, not with a view to imprisonment or punishment, or to his immediate deportation without further inquiry, but in order to take him before a judge, for the purpose of a judicial hearing and determination of the only facts which, under the act of Congress, can have a material bearing upon the question whether he shall be sent out of the country, or be permitted to remain.

* * *

If no evidence is offered by the Chinaman, the judge makes the order of deportation, as upon a default. If he produces competent evidence to explain the fact of his not having a certificate, it must be considered by the judge; and if he thereupon appears to be entitled to a certificate, it is to be granted to him. If he proves that the collector of internal revenue has unlawfully refused to give him a certificate, he proves an "unavoidable cause," within the meaning of the act, for not procuring one. If he proves that he had procured a certificate which has been lost or destroyed, he is to be allowed a reasonable time to procure a duplicate thereof.

The provision which puts the burden of proof upon him of rebutting the presumption arising from his having no certificate, as well as the requirement of proof, "by at least one credible white witness, that he was a resident of the United States at the time of the passage of this act," is within the acknowledged power of every legislature to prescribe the evidence which shall be received, and the effect of that evidence, in the courts of its own government. * * * The competency of all witnesses, without regard to their color, to testify in the courts of the United States, rests on acts of Congress, which Congress may at its discretion modify or repeal. The reason for requiring a Chinese alien, claiming the privilege of remaining in the United States, to prove the fact of his residence here, at the time of the passage of the act, "by at least one credible white witness," may have been the experience of Congress, as mentioned by Mr. Justice Field in [the *Chinese Exclusion Case*], that the enforcement of former acts, under which the testimony of Chinese persons was admitted to prove similar facts, "was attended with great embarrassment, from the suspicious nature, in many instances, of the testimony offered to establish the residence of the parties, arising from the loose notions entertained by the witnesses of the obligation of an oath." 130 U.S. 598, 9 S.Ct. 627. And this requirement, not allowing such a fact to be proved solely by the testimony of aliens in a like situation, or of the same race, is quite analogous to the provision, which has existed for seventy-seven years in the naturalization laws, by which aliens applying for naturalization must prove their residence within the limits and under the jurisdiction of the United States, for five years next preceding, "by the oath or affirmation of citizens of the United States." * * *

The proceeding before a United States judge * * * is in no proper sense a trial and sentence for a crime or offence. It is simply the ascertainment, by appropriate and lawful means, of the fact whether the conditions exist upon which Congress has enacted that an alien of this class may remain within the country. The order of deportation is not a punishment for crime. It is not a banishment, in the sense in which that word is often applied to the expulsion of a citizen from his country by way of punishment. It is but a method of enforcing the return to his own country of an alien who has not complied with the conditions upon the performance of which the government of the nation, acting within its constitutional authority and through the proper departments, has determined that his continuing to reside here shall depend. He has not, therefore, been deprived of life, liberty or property, without due process of law; and the provisions of the Constitution, securing the right of trial by jury, and prohibiting unreasonable searches and seizures, and cruel and unusual punishments, have no application.

The question whether, and upon what conditions, these aliens shall be permitted to remain within the United States being one to be determined by the political departments of the government, the judicial department cannot properly express an opinion upon the wisdom, the policy or the justice of the measures enacted by Congress in the exercise of the powers confided to it by the Constitution over this subject.

* * *

In the [case stated above], the petitioner had, within the year, applied to a collector of internal revenue for a certificate of residence, and had been refused it, because he produced and could produce none but Chinese witnesses to prove the residence necessary to entitle him to a certificate. Being found without a certificate of residence, he was arrested by the marshal, and taken before the United States District Judge, and established to the satisfaction of the judge, that, because of the collector's refusal to give him a certificate of residence he was without one by unavoidable cause; and also proved, by a Chinese witness only, that he was a resident of the United States at the time of the passage of the act of 1892. Thereupon the judge ordered him to be remanded to the custody of the marshal, and to be deported from the United States, as provided in that act.

It would seem that the collector of internal revenue, when applied to for a certificate, might properly decline to find the requisite fact of residence upon testimony which, by an express provision of the act, would be insufficient to prove that fact at a hearing before the judge. But if the collector might have received and acted upon such testimony, and did, upon any ground, unjustifiably refuse a certificate of residence, the only remedy of the applicant was to prove by competent and sufficient evidence at the hearing before the judge the facts requisite to entitle him to a certificate. To one of those facts, that of residence, the statute, which, for the reasons already stated, appears to us to be within the constitutional authority of Congress to enact, peremptorily requires at that hearing the testimony of a credible white witness. And it was because no such testimony was produced, that the order of deportation was made.

Upon careful consideration of the subject, the only conclusion which appears to us to be consistent with the principles of international law, with the Constitution and laws of the United States, and with the previous decisions of this court, is that in each of these cases the judgment of the Circuit Court, dismissing the writ of habeas corpus, is right and must be

Affirmed.

MR. JUSTICE BREWER dissenting.

* * *

I rest my dissent on three propositions: First, that the persons against whom the penalties of * * * the act of 1892 are directed are persons lawfully residing within the United States; secondly, that as such they are within the protection of the Constitution, and secured by its guarantees against oppression and wrong; and, third, that [the Act] deprives them of liberty and imposes punishment without due process of law, and in disregard of constitutional guarantees, especially those found in the Fourth, Fifth, Sixth, and Eighth Articles of the Amendments.

And, first, these persons are lawfully residing within the limits of the United States. [Justice Brewer then discusses the Burlingame Treaty and the 1880 Treaty.]

* * *

While subsequently to [these treaties], Congress passed several acts to restrict the entrance into this country of Chinese laborers, and while the validity of this restriction was sustained in the *Chinese Exclusion* case, yet no act has been passed denying the right of those laborers who had once lawfully entered the country to remain, and they are here not as travellers or only temporarily. We must take judicial notice of that which is disclosed by the census, and which is also a matter of common knowledge. There are 100,000 and more of these persons living in this country, making their homes here, and striving by their labor to earn a livelihood. They are not travelers, but resident aliens.

* * * They have lived in this country, respectively, since 1879, 1877, and 1874—almost as long a time as some of those who were members of the Congress that passed this act of punishment and expulsion.

That those who have become domiciled in a country are entitled to a more distinct and larger measure of protection than those who are simply passing through, or temporarily in it, has long been recognized by the law of nations. * * *

* * *

* * * [W]hatever rights a resident alien might have in any other nation, here he is within the express protection of the Constitution, especially in respect to those guarantees which are declared in the original amendments. It has been repeated so often as to become axiomatic, that this government is one of enumerated and delegated powers, and, as declared in Article 10 of the amendments, "the powers not delegated to the United States by the Constitution, nor prohibited by it to the States, are reserved to the States respectively, or to the people."

It is said that the power here asserted is inherent in sovereignty. This doctrine of powers inherent in sovereignty is one both indefinite and dangerous. Where are the limits to such powers to be found, and by whom are they to be pronounced? Is it within legislative capacity to declare the limits? If so, then the mere assertion of an inherent power creates it, and despotism exists. May the courts establish the boundaries? Whence do they obtain the authority for this? Shall they look to the practices of other nations to ascertain the limits? The governments of other nations have elastic powers—ours is fixed and bounded by a written constitution. The expulsion of a race may be within the inherent powers of a despotism. History, before the adoption of this Constitution, was not destitute of examples of the exercise of such a power; and its framers were familiar with history, and wisely, as it seems to me, they gave to this government no general power to banish. Banishment may be resorted to as punishment for crime; but among the powers reserved to the people and not delegated to the government is that of determining whether whole classes in our midst shall, for no crime but that of their race and birthplace, be driven from our territory.

Whatever may be true as to exclusion, * * * I deny that there is any arbitrary and unrestrained power to banish residents, even resident aliens. What, it may be asked, is the reason for any difference? The answer is obvious. The Constitution has no extraterritorial effect, and those who have not come lawfully within our territory cannot claim any protection from its provisions. And it may be that the national government, having full control of all matters relating to other nations, has the power to build, as it were, a Chinese wall around our borders and absolutely forbid aliens to enter. But the Constitution has potency everywhere within the limits of our territory, and the powers which the national government may exercise within such limits are those, and only those, given to it by that instrument. Now, the power to remove resident aliens is, confessedly, not expressed. Even if it be among the powers implied, yet still it can be exercised only in subordination to the limitations and restrictions imposed by the Constitution. * * *

* * *

In the case of *Yick Wo v. Hopkins*, 118 U.S. 356, 369, 6 Sup. Ct. Rep. 1070, it was said: "The Fourteenth Amendment of the Constitution is not confined to the protection of citizens. It says: 'Nor shall any State deprive any person of life, liberty, or property without due process of law; nor deny to any person within its jurisdiction the equal protection of the laws.' These provisions are universal in their application to all persons within the territorial jurisdiction, without regard to any differences of race, of color, or of nationality; and the equal protection of the laws is a pledge of the protection of equal laws." * * *

If the use of the word "person" in the Fourteenth Amendment protects all individuals lawfully within the State, the use of the same word "person" in the Fifth must be equally comprehensive, and secures to all persons lawfully within the territory of the United States the protection named therein; and a like conclusion must follow as to the Sixth.

* * * [The Act] deprives of "life, liberty, and property without due process of law." It imposes punishment without a trial, and punishment cruel and severe. It places the liberty of one individual subject to the unrestrained control of another. Notice its provisions: It first commands all to register. He who does not register violates that law, and may be punished; and so the section goes on to say that one who has not complied with its requirements, and has no certificate of residence, "shall be deemed and adjudged to be unlawfully within the United States," and then it imposes as a penalty his deportation from the country. Deportation is punishment. It involves first an arrest, a deprival of liberty; and,

second, a removal from home, from family, from business, from property. * * *

* * * [I]t needs no citation of authorities to support the proposition that deportation is punishment. Every one knows that to be forcibly taken away from home, and family, and friends, and business, and property, and sent across the ocean to a distant land, is punishment; and that oftentimes most severe and cruel. * * *

But punishment implies a trial: "No person shall be deprived of life, liberty, or property, without due process of law." Due process requires that a man be heard before he is condemned, and both heard and condemned in the due and orderly procedure of a trial as recognized by the common law from time immemorial. * * * And no person who has once come within the protection of the Constitution can be punished without a trial. It may be summary, as for petty offences and in cases of contempt, but still a trial, as known to the common law. * * * But here, the Chinese are * * * arrested and, without a trial, punished by banishment.

Again, it is absolutely within the discretion of the collector to give or refuse a certificate to one who applies therefor. Nowhere is it provided what evidence shall be furnished to the collector, and nowhere is it made mandatory upon him to grant a certificate on the production of such evidence. It cannot be due process of law to impose punishment on any person for failing to have that in his possession, the possession of which he can obtain only at the arbitrary and unregulated discretion of any official. It will not do to say that the presumption is that the official will act reasonably and not arbitrarily. When the right to liberty and residence is involved, some other protection than the mere discretion of any official is required. * * *

* * *

It is true this statute is directed only against the obnoxious Chinese; but if the power exists, who shall say it will not be exercised tomorrow against other classes and other people? If the guarantees of these amendments can be thus ignored in order to get rid of this distasteful class, what security have others that a like disregard of its provisions may not be resorted to? * * *

* * *

In view of this enactment of the highest legislative body of the foremost Christian nation, may not the thoughtful Chinese disciple of Confucius fairly ask, Why do they send missionaries here?

MR. JUSTICE FIELD dissenting.

* * *

I had the honor to be the organ of the court in announcing [the] opinion and judgment [of the Court in the *Chinese Exclusion Case*]. I still adhere to the views there expressed in all particulars; but between legislation for the exclusion of Chinese persons—that is, to prevent them from entering the country—and legislation for the deportation of those who have acquired a residence in the country under a treaty with China, there is a wide and essential difference. The power of the government to exclude foreigners from this country, that is, to prevent them from entering it, whenever the public interests in its judgment require such exclusion, has been repeatedly asserted by the legislative and executive departments of our government and never denied; but its power to deport from the country persons lawfully domiciled therein by its consent, and engaged in the ordinary pursuits of life, has never been asserted by the legislative or executive departments except for crime, or as an act of war in view of existing or anticipated hostilities * * *.

* * *

[Justice Field then discusses the Alien and Sedition Acts of 1798, which among other things, authorized the President to remove aliens adjudged to be dangerous to the peace and safety of the United States.]

The duration of the act was limited to two years, and it has ever since been the subject of universal condemnation. In no other instance, until the law before us was passed, has any public man had the boldness to advocate the deportation of friendly aliens in time of peace. * * * And it will surprise most people to learn that any such dangerous and despotic power lies in our government—a power which will authorize it to expel at pleasure, in time of peace, the whole body of friendly foreigners of any country domiciled herein by its permission * * *. Is it possible that Congress can, at its pleasure, in disregard of the guarantees of the Constitution, expel at any time the Irish, German, French, and English who may have taken up their residence here on the invitation of the government, while we are at peace with the countries from which they came, simply on the ground that they have not been naturalized?

* * *

The purpose of [the 1892 law] was to secure the means of readily identifying the Chinese laborers present in the country and entitled to remain, from those who may have clandestinely entered the country in violation of its laws. * * *

This object being constitutional, the only question for our consideration is the lawfulness of the procedure provided for its accomplishment, and this must be tested by the provisions of the Constitution and laws intended for the protection of all persons against encroachment upon their rights. Aliens from countries at peace with us, domiciled within our country by its consent, are entitled to all the guaranties for the protection of their persons and property which are secured to native-born citizens. The moment any human being from a country at peace with us comes within the jurisdiction of the United States, with their consent—and such consent will always be implied when not expressly withheld, and in the case of the Chinese laborers before us was in terms given by the treaty referred to—he becomes subject to all their laws, is amenable to their punishment and entitled to their protection. Arbitrary and despotic power can no more be exercised over them with reference to their persons and property, than over the persons and property of native-born citizens. They differ only from citizens in that they cannot vote or hold any public office. As men having our common humanity, they are protected by all the guaranties of the Constitution. To hold that they are subject to any different law or are less protected in any particular than other persons, is in my judgment to ignore the teachings of our history, the practice of our government, and the language of our Constitution. Let us test this doctrine by an illustration. If a foreigner who resides in the country by its consent commits a public offence, is he subject to be cut down, maltreated, imprisoned, or put to death by violence, without accusation made, trial had, and judgment of an established tribunal following the regular forms of judicial procedure? If any rule in the administration of justice is to be omitted or discarded in his case, what rule is it to be? If one rule may lawfully be laid aside in his case, another rule may also be laid aside, and all rules may be discarded. In such instances a rule of evidence may be set aside in one case, a rule of pleading in another; the testimony of eye-witnesses may be rejected and hearsay adopted, or no evidence at all may be received, but simply an inspection of the accused, as is often the case in tribunals of Asiatic countries where personal caprice and not settled rules prevail. That would be to establish a pure, simple, undisguised despotism and tyranny with respect to foreigners resident in the country by its consent, and such an exercise of power is not permissible under our Constitution. Arbitrary and tyrannical power has no place in our system. * * *

I utterly dissent from and reject the doctrine expressed in the opinion of the majority, that "Congress, under the power to exclude or expel aliens, might have directed any Chinese laborer found in the United States without a certificate of residence to be removed out of the country by executive officers, without judicial trial or examination, just as it might have authorized such officers absolutely to prevent his entrance into the country." An arrest in that way for that purpose would not be a reasonable seizure of the person within the meaning of the Fourth Article of the amendments to the Constitution. It would be brutal and oppressive. The existence of the power thus stated is only consistent with the admission that the government is one of unlimited and despotic power so far as aliens domiciled in the country are concerned. According to its theory, Congress might have ordered executive officers to take the Chinese laborers to the ocean and put them into a boat and set them adrift; or to take them to the borders of Mexico and turn them loose there; and in both cases without any means of support; indeed, it might have sanctioned towards these laborers the most shocking brutality conceivable. I utterly repudiate all such notions, and reply that brutality, inhumanity, and cruelty cannot be made elements in any procedure for the enforcement of the laws of the United States.

The majority of the court have, in their opinion, made numerous citations from the courts and the utterances of individuals upon the power of the government of an independent nation to exclude foreigners from entering its limits, but none, beyond a few loose observations, as to its power to expel and deport from the country those who are domiciled therein by its consent. * * *

The government of the United States is one of limited and delegated powers. It takes nothing from the usages or the former action of European governments, nor does it take any power by any supposed inherent sovereignty. * * * Sovereignty or supreme power is in this country vested in the people, and only in the people. * * * [T]he Tenth Amendment to the Constitution, passed to avoid any misinterpretation of the powers of the general government * * * declares that "The powers not delegated to the United States by the Constitution, nor prohibited by it to the States, are reserved to the States, respectively, or to the people." When, therefore, power is exercised by Congress, authority for it must be found in express terms in the Constitution, or in the means necessary or proper for the execution of the power expressed. If it cannot be thus found, it does not exist.

* * * [A Chinese laborer's] deportation is thus imposed for neglect to obtain a certificate of residence, from which he can only escape by showing his inability to secure it from one of the causes named. That is the punishment for his neglect, and that being of an infamous character can only be imposed after indictment, trial, and conviction. * * *

The punishment is beyond all reason in its severity. It is out of all proportion to the alleged offence. It is cruel and unusual. As to its cruelty, nothing can exceed a forcible deportation from a country of one's residence, and the breaking up of all the relations of friendship, family, and business there contracted. The laborer may be seized at a distance from his home, his family and his business, and taken before the judge for his condemnation, without permission to visit his home, see his family, or complete any unfinished business. Mr. Madison well pictures its character in his powerful denunciation of the alien law of 1798 in his celebrated report upon the resolutions, from which we have cited, and concludes, as we have seen, that *if a banishment of the sort described be not a punishment, and among the severest of punishments, it will be difficult to imagine a doom to which the name can be applied.*

* * * [H]e is required * * * [to have] *at least one credible white witness.* Here the government undertakes to exact of the party arrested the testimony of a witness of a particular color, though conclusive and incontestible testimony from others may be adduced. The law might as well have said, that unless the laborer should also present a particular person as a witness who could not be produced, from sickness, absence, or other cause, such as the archbishop of the State, to establish the fact of residence, he should be held to be unlawfully within the United States.

* * *

I will not pursue the subject further. The decision of the court and the sanction it would give to legislation depriving resident aliens of the guaranties of the Constitution fills me with apprehensions. Those guaranties are of priceless value to every one resident in the country, whether citizen or alien. I cannot but regard the decision as a blow against constitutional liberty, when it declares that Congress has the right to disregard the guaranties of the Constitution intended for the protection of all men, domiciled in the country with the consent of the government, in their rights of person and property. How far will its legislation go? The unnaturalized resident feels it today, but if Congress can disregard the guaranties with respect to any one domiciled in this country with its consent, it may disregard the guaranties with respect to naturalized citizens. What assurance have we that it may not declare that naturalized citizens of a particular country cannot remain in the United States after a certain day, unless they have in their possession a certificate that they are of good moral character and attached to the principles of our Constitution, which certificate they must obtain from a collector of internal revenue upon the testimony of at least one competent witness of a class or nationality to be designated by the government?

What answer could the naturalized citizen in that case make to his arrest for deportation, which cannot be urged in behalf of the Chinese laborers of to–day?

* * *

MR. CHIEF JUSTICE FULLER dissenting.

I also dissent from the opinion and judgment of the court in these cases.

If the protection of the Constitution extends to Chinese laborers who are lawfully within and entitled to remain in the United States under previous treaties and laws, then the question whether this act of Congress so far as it relates to them is in conflict with that instrument, is a judicial question, and its determination belongs to the judicial department.

However reluctant courts may be to pass upon the constitutionality of legislative acts, it is of the very essence of judicial duty to do so when the discharge of that duty is properly invoked.

* * *

The argument is that friendly aliens, who have lawfully acquired a domicil in this country, are entitled to avail themselves of the safeguards of the Constitution only while permitted to remain, and that the power to expel them and the manner of its exercise are unaffected by that instrument. It is difficult to see how this can be so in view of the operation of the power upon the existing rights of individuals; and to say that the residence of the alien, when invited and secured by treaties and laws, is held in subordination to the exertion against him, as an alien, of the absolute and unqualified power asserted, is to import a condition not recognized by the fundamental law. Conceding that the exercise of the power to exclude is committed to the political department, and that the denial of entrance is not necessarily the subject of judicial cognizance, the exercise of the power to expel, the manner in which the right to remain may be terminated, rest on different ground, since limitations exist or are imposed upon the deprivation of that which has been lawfully acquired. And while the general government is invested, in respect of foreign countries and their subjects or citizens, with the powers necessary to the maintenance of its absolute independence and security throughout its entire territory, it cannot, in virtue of any delegated power, or power implied therefrom, or of a supposed inherent sovereignty, arbitrarily deal with persons lawfully within the peace of its dominion. But the act before us is not an act to abrogate or repeal treaties or laws in respect of Chinese laborers entitled to remain in the United States, or to expel them from the country, and no such intent can be imputed to Congress. As to them, registration for the purpose of identification is required, and the deportation denounced for failure to do so is by way of punishment to coerce compliance with that requisition. No euphuism can disguise the character of the act in this regard. It directs the performance of a judicial function in a particular way, and inflicts punishment without a judicial trial. It is, in effect, a legislative sentence of banishment, and, as such, absolutely void. Moreover, it contains within it the germs of the assertion of an unlimited and arbitrary power, in general, incompatible with the immutable principles of justice, inconsistent with the nature of our government, and in conflict with the written Constitution by which that government was created and those principles secured.

---

c. Deportation and Punishment

The majority opinion in *Fong Yue Ting* held that an "order of deportation is not a punishment for crime"; therefore, "the provisions of the Constitution, securing the right of trial by jury, and prohibiting unreasonable searches and seizures, and cruel and unusual punishments, have no application." Does this mean that Congress could imprison noncitizens unlawfully residing in the United States without providing them the protections mandated by the Constitution in criminal proceedings?

The Supreme Court answered this question in *Wong Wing v. United States*, 163 U.S. 228, 16 S.Ct. 977, 41 L.Ed. 140 (1896), which struck down a section of the 1892 immigration act not considered in *Fong Yue Ting*. The section provided that any Chinese citizen judged to be in the United States illegally "shall be imprisoned at hard labor for a period of not exceeding one year and thereafter removed from the United States." Noncitizens charged under the section were not afforded a trial by jury. Act of May 5, 1892, Ch. 60, 27 Stat. 25. The Court struck down the provision:

> The Chinese exclusion acts operate upon two classes—one consisting of those who came into the country with its consent, the other

of those who have come into the United States without their consent and in disregard of the law. Our previous decisions have settled that it is within the constitutional power of Congress to deport both of these classes, and to commit the enforcement of the law to executive officers.

The question now presented is whether Congress can promote its policy in respect to Chinese persons by adding to its provisions for their exclusion and expulsion punishment by imprisonment at hard labor, to be inflicted by the judgment of any justice, judge or commissioner of the United States, without a trial by jury. * * *

We think it clear that detention, or temporary confinement, as part of the means necessary to give effect to the provisions for the exclusion or expulsion of aliens would be valid. Proceedings to exclude or expel would be vain if those accused could not be held in custody pending the inquiry into their true character and while arrangements were being made for their deportation. Detention is a usual feature of every case of arrest on a criminal charge, even when an innocent person is wrongfully accused; but it is not imprisonment in a legal sense.

So, too, we think it would be plainly competent for Congress to declare the act of an alien in remaining unlawfully within the United States to be an offence, punishable by fine or imprisonment, if such offence were to be established by a judicial trial.

But the evident meaning of the section in question, and no other is claimed for it by the counsel for the Government, is that the detention provided for is an imprisonment at hard labor, which is to be undergone before the sentence of deportation is to be carried into effect, and that such imprisonment is to be adjudged against the accused by a justice, judge or commissioner, upon a summary hearing. * * *

* * *

Our views, upon the question thus specifically pressed upon our attention, may be briefly expressed thus: We regard it as settled by our previous decisions that the United States can, as a matter of public policy, by Congressional enactment, forbid aliens or classes of aliens from coming within their borders, and expel aliens or classes of aliens from their territory, and can, in order to make effectual such decree of exclusion or expulsion, devolve the power and duty of identifying and arresting the persons included in such decree, and causing their deportation, upon executive or subordinate officials.

But when Congress sees fit to further promote such a policy by subjecting the persons of such aliens to infamous punishment at hard labor, or by confiscating their property, we think such legislation, to be valid, must provide for a judicial trial to establish the guilt of the accused.

No limits can be put by the courts upon the power of Congress to protect, by summary methods, the country from the advent of aliens whose race or habits render them undesirable as citizens, or to expel such if they have already found their way into our land and unlawfully remain therein. But to declare unlawful residence within the country to be an infamous crime, punishable by deprivation of liberty and property, would be to pass out of the sphere of constitutional legislation, unless provision were made that the fact of guilt should first be established by a judicial trial. It is not consistent with the theory of our government that the legislature should, after having defined an offence as an infamous crime, find the fact of guilt and adjudge the punishment by one of its own agents.

Id. at 234–37, 16 S.Ct. at 979–81.

NOTES AND QUESTIONS ON EXCLUSION, DEPORTATION, AND PUNISHMENT

1. *The Court's composition.* The Supreme Court decided *Chae Chan Ping*, *Fong Yue Ting*, and *Wong Wing* within a span of seven years. There were no dissents in the first or third, but there were only five votes for the *Fong Yue Ting* opinion. Two of the three *Fong Yue Ting* dissenters, Justice Field and Justice Brewer, had agreed with the *Chae Chan Ping* outcome. The third dissent was filed by Chief Justice Fuller, who joined the Court after *Chae Chan Ping* was decided. (Justice Harlan did not participate, as he was on leave from the Supreme Court to serve as the U.S. representative to the Bering Sea Arbitration, 149 U.S., at iii n.1.)

2. *Are exclusion and deportation two sides of the same coin?* Justice Gray stated that "[t]he right of a nation to expel or deport foreigners, who have not been naturalized or taken any steps towards becoming citizens of the country, rests upon the same ground, and is as absolute and unqualified as the right to prohibit and prevent their entrance into the country." Justice Field, who had written the opinion for the Court in *Chae Chan Ping*, was not convinced that the exclusion case controlled the deportation case. On what grounds did he and the other dissenters rely?

For Justice Brewer the answer was "obvious": "The Constitution has no extraterritorial effect, and those who have not come lawfully within our territory cannot claim any protection from its provisions. * * * But the Constitution has potency elsewhere within the limits of our territory * * *." Does this adequately distinguish *Chae Chan Ping*? The noncitizen in that case was detained upon a steamship within the port of San Francisco. How was he not "within our territory"? Nor does Brewer's second ground (unlawful entry) appear persuasive. Chae Chan Ping was returning to his prior lawful residence in this country.

Chief Justice Fuller seemed to view deportation as different from exclusion because the former entails "deprivation of that which has been lawfully acquired." Does this adequately distinguish *Chae Chan Ping*? Was not Chae Chan Ping being deprived of that which he had lawfully acquired? Does Fuller's analysis suggest that noncitizens who enter without inspection are not entitled to the same constitutional protections against deportation as noncitizens who enter lawfully?

We will see repeated efforts to draw a line between exclusion and deportation based on the *location* (Brewer's ground) or *stake* (Fuller's ground) of the noncitizen. To foreshadow what will be a recurring theme of this book, we do not believe that the location argument makes sense. Furthermore, if one takes the stake argument seriously—which we do—it may require a fundamental rethinking of both *Chae Chan Ping* and *Fong Yue Ting*. We will address these issues more fully after we have considered the later statutory provisions regarding exclusion and deportation.

There is no question that Justices Brewer, Field, and Fuller believed that the Constitution imposes limits on the *exercise* of the deportation power—limits that may not apply to the exclusion power. But did these Justices doubt the *existence* of the power to deport noncitizens? Do the constitutional sources of the exclusion power equally support a power to deport noncitizens who have entered the country?

Under current law, noncitizens may be deported (1) for conduct occurring prior to their entry (e.g., INA § 237(a)(4)(D) (Nazis)); (2) if they were excludable at time of entry (INA § 237(a)(1)(A)); and (3) for conduct occurring after a lawful entry (e.g., INA § 237(a)(2)(A) (conviction of a crime involving moral turpitude)). Does the apparent justification for the first two deportation categories—"delayed exclusion" of those who should not have been allowed to enter—apply to noncitizens in the third category? If not, what is an alternative rationale?

3. *Is all deportation punishment?* The three *Fong Yue Ting* dissenters were still on the Court in *Wong Wing*. They all thought that imprisonment at hard labor constituted punishment, just as they had earlier concluded that deportation of resident noncitizens for failure to procure a certificate of residence constituted punishment. Would they conclude that all deportations constitute punishment? What about the case of someone who entered clandestinely and had been present only a few weeks before the deportation process began?

Consider the following characterization: The statute at issue in *Fong Yue Ting,* unlike that in *Wong Wing,* is an ordinary regulation of immigration. Noncitizens present in this country are asked to demonstrate that they are here lawfully. Those who do so are given a certificate which protects them against deportation; those unable to demonstrate that they are entitled to a certificate are presumed to be here illegally (or deemed to be here illegally), and hence deported. Perhaps the method of determining lawfulness of status is troubling (maybe even a violation of due process), but a defect of procedure does not make the resulting deportation "punishment." In principle it merely compels a person wrongfully present to go back "to his own country," as the majority phrases the point.[3]

---

3. For further readings on deportation, punishment, and the increasing use of criminal sanctions in the immigration sphere, see Kanstroom, Deportation Nation: Outsiders in American History (2007); Legomsky, *The New Path of Immigration Law: Asymmetric Incorporation of Criminal Justice Norms,* 64 Wash & Lee L. Rev. 469 (2007); Stumpf, *The Crimmigration Crisis: Immigrants, Crime, and Sovereign Power,* 56 Am. U. L. Rev. 367 (2006); Miller, *Blurring the*

3. THE CONSTITUTIONAL FRAMEWORK

This trilogy of cases raises profound and complex questions of constitutional law. We will focus on four areas of inquiry. First, what are the sources of federal power to regulate immigration? Second, what roles do the respective branches of the federal government play with regard to immigration measures? Third, what authority do state governments have over immigration? And, fourth, what role does the principle of equal protection play?

a. Sources of Federal Power

(i) Enumerated Powers

A fundamental principle of American constitutional law is that the federal government "is one of enumerated powers"; it can exercise "only the powers granted to it" and powers "necessary and proper" to the execution of delegated powers. *McCulloch v. Maryland*, 17 U.S. (4 Wheat.) 316, 324, 4 L.Ed. 579 (1819).

In *Chae Chan Ping*, what enumerated powers does Justice Field rely upon to support the conclusion that Congress had the authority to pass the Chinese exclusion laws? To what other powers explicit in Article I of the Constitution might he have appealed?

(a) The Commerce Power

Art. I, § 8, cl. 3 of the Constitution authorizes Congress "to regulate Commerce with foreign Nations, and among the several States." In the mid–1800's, the Supreme Court invalidated a number of state statutes that sought to regulate immigration through the imposition of taxes or other regulations on carriers. *See Chy Lung v. Freeman*, 92 U.S. (2 Otto) 275, 23 L.Ed. 550 (1876), discussed *infra*; *Henderson v. New York*, 92 U.S. (2 Otto) 259, 23 L.Ed. 543 (1876) (striking down New York requirement that ship masters pay $1.50 tax per passenger brought to New York or provide $300 bond to indemnify city for relief expenses for four years); *Passenger Cases*, 48 U.S. (7 How.) 283, 12 L.Ed. 702 (1849) (invalidating Massachusetts and New York taxes on immigrants). *Passenger Cases* yielded a 5–4 decision in which eight Justices wrote opinions. While it is difficult to discover a ground for the decision that a majority of the Court agreed upon, the commerce power received prominent attention in the opinions of Justices McLean, Wayne, Catron and Grier.

By 1884, in the *Head Money Cases*, 112 U.S. 580, 5 S.Ct. 247, 28 L.Ed. 798 (1884), the Supreme Court explicitly relied on Congress' Commerce Clause powers to uphold a federal statute, enacted in 1882, that imposed a

Boundaries Between Immigration and Crime Control After September 11, 25 Boston College Third World L. Rev. 81 (2005); Pauw, *A New Look at Deportation As Punishment: Why At Least Some of the Constitution's Criminal Procedure Protections Must Apply*, 52 Admin. L. Rev. 305 (2000); Bleichmar, *Deportation as Punishment: A Historical Analysis of the British Practice of Banishment and Its Impact on Modern Constitutional Law*, 14 Geo. Immig. L.J. 115 (1999).

tax of fifty cents on every noncitizen arriving in the United States. Said the Court: "Congress [has] the power to pass a law regulating immigration as a part of commerce of this country with foreign nations." *Id.* at 600, 5 S.Ct. at 254.

Can the commerce power be relied upon to uphold the regulation of noncitizens who do not come to the United States for commercial purposes? Is the migration of children, refugees, poor people, or spouses of permanent residents "commerce"? The Supreme Court, in at least one case, has concluded that migration is commerce. In *Edwards v. California*, 314 U.S. 160, 62 S.Ct. 164, 86 L.Ed. 119 (1941), a California statute that made it a crime to bring an indigent person into the state was struck down as an unconstitutional interference with Congress' power to regulate interstate commerce. The Court, through Justice Byrnes, stated that "it is settled beyond question that the transportation of persons is 'commerce.'" In a footnote, he added: "It is immaterial whether or not the transportation is commercial in character." *Id.* at 172 n. 1, 62 S.Ct. at 166 n.1.

(b) The Naturalization Power

Art. I, § 8, cl. 4 of the Constitution grants Congress the power to "establish an uniform Rule of Naturalization." This power was expressly delegated to Congress to prevent the confusion and controversy that could arise from separate state laws bestowing citizenship. *See* J. Kettner, The Development of American Citizenship, 1608–1870, at 224–25 (1978).

Does the power to naturalize necessarily imply the power to regulate the admission of immigrants who may eventually be eligible for naturalization? Not obviously. One might well distinguish between regulation of the *physical entry* of noncitizens into the *territory* of the United States and regulation of the entry into the *political community* of the United States through the extension of full political rights to naturalized citizens. Can the Constitution be read as granting Congress only the latter power while reserving the former power to the States?

Interestingly, in the early years of the Republic, Congress viewed the naturalization power as a way to regulate immigration. In most states, noncitizens could not own or inherit land, vote or hold office—disabilities that were removed upon naturalization. Congress could thus encourage or discourage immigration by altering the prerequisites (such as length of residence) for naturalization. *See, e.g.,* 1 Annals of Cong. 1109–1125 (1790) (debate on Naturalization Act of 1790).

(c) The War Power

Art. I, § 8, cl. 11 grants Congress the power "to declare War." It is beyond dispute that the war power gives the federal government the authority to stop the entry of enemy aliens and to expel enemy aliens residing in the United States. This power was first granted to the President by one of the Alien and Sedition Acts and remains on the books today. *See* 50 U.S.C.A. §§ 21–23. The constitutionality of this provision has been consistently upheld. *See, e.g.*, *Ludecke v. Watkins*, 335 U.S. 160, 68 S.Ct. 1429, 92 L.Ed. 1881 (1948). But is it possible to view the war power as authorizing the mass of statutes that presently regulate immigration—or even the statute challenged in *Chae Chan Ping*?

(d) The Migration and Importation Clause

Art. I, § 9, cl. 1 of the Constitution provides:

> The Migration or Importation of such Persons as any of the States now existing shall think proper to admit, shall not be prohibited by the Congress prior to the Year one thousand eight hundred and eight.

The denial of power to Congress *before* 1808 seems to imply the existence of such power *after* that year. Thus, this clause, at first reading, appears to authorize congressional power to *prohibit* immigration after 1808, and probably—by reasonable implication—to regulate it as well.

Unfortunately things are not as clear as they seem. This clause is almost assuredly a veiled reference to an institution that the Founding Fathers could not bring themselves, in a charter of fundamental law, to recognize by name: slavery. *Passenger Cases*, 48 U.S. (7 How.) 283, 512–13, 12 L.Ed. 702 (1849) (opinion of Justice Daniel). Thus this clause has generally been interpreted as prohibiting congressional attempts to stop the slave trade before 1808. In fact, Congress passed a law prohibiting the importation of slaves on March 2, 1807, Ch. 22, 2 Stat. 426, which took effect January 1, 1808. *See generally* D.B. Davis, The Problem of Slavery in the Age of Revolution, 1770–1823, at 119–31 (1975); Berns, *The Constitution and the Migration of Slaves*, 78 Yale L.J. 198 (1968).

(e) The Foreign Affairs Power

In *Chae Chan Ping*, Justice Field sought to associate the power to regulate immigration with the power to conduct foreign affairs: "[T]he United States, in their *relation to foreign countries* and their subjects or citizens, are one nation, invested with powers which belong to independent nations * * *. * * * [F]or national purposes, embracing our *relations with foreign nations*, we are but one people, one nation, one power." 130 U.S. at 604, 606 (emphasis supplied).

In modern constitutional terms, these words would be seen as an appeal to the foreign affairs power of the federal government. But like the immigration power, the foreign affairs power receives no explicit mention in the Constitution. Finding the constitutional basis of the power to conduct foreign relations has proven a vexing task, as Louis Henkin, a leading scholar on foreign affairs and the Constitution, has described:*

> The Constitution does not delegate a "power to conduct foreign relations" to the federal government or confer it upon any of its branches. Congress is given power to regulate commerce with foreign

---

* Reprinted from *Foreign Affairs and the Constitution* by Louis Henkin, copyright © 1972, with permission of Foundation Press.

nations, to define offenses against the law of nations, to declare war, and the President the power to make treaties and send and receive ambassadors, but these hardly add up to the power to conduct foreign relations. Where is the power to recognize other states or governments, to maintain or break diplomatic relations, to open consulates elsewhere and permit them here, to acquire or cede territory, to give or withhold foreign aid, to proclaim a Monroe Doctrine or an Open-Door Policy, indeed to determine all the attitudes and carry out all the details in the myriads of relationships with other nations that are "the foreign policy" and "the foreign relations" of the United States? * * * Congress can regulate foreign commerce but where is the power to make other laws relating to our foreign relations—to regulate immigration, or the status and rights of aliens, or activities of citizens at home or abroad affecting our foreign relations? These "missing" powers, and a host of others, were clearly intended for and have always been exercised by the federal government, but where does the Constitution say that it shall be so?

* * *

The attempt to build all the foreign affairs powers of the federal government with the few bricks provided by the Constitution has not been accepted as successful. It requires considerable stretching of language, much reading between lines, and bold extrapolation from "the Constitution as a whole," and that still does not plausibly add up to all the power which the federal government in fact exercises.

L. Henkin, Foreign Affairs and the Constitution 16–18 (1972).

(ii) Inherent Power

Justice Field writes in *Chae Chan Ping* that "[t]he power of exclusion of foreigners [is] an incident of sovereignty belonging to the government of the United States, as a part of those sovereign powers delegated by the Constitution." Earlier in the opinion he states:

> That the government of the United States * * * can exclude aliens from its territories is a proposition which we do not think open to controversy. Jurisdiction over its own territory to that extent is an incident of every independent nation. It is a part of its independence. If it could not exclude aliens, it would be to that extent subject to the control of another power.

Three years later, the Court's decision in *Nishimura Ekiu v. United States*, 142 U.S. 651, 12 S.Ct. 336, 35 L.Ed. 1146 (1892), upheld the immigration act of 1891, which codified existing exclusion laws and provided for exclusive inspection of arriving aliens by the federal government. Justice Gray, writing for the Court, stated:

> It is an accepted maxim of international law, that every sovereign nation has the power, as inherent in sovereignty, and essential to preservation, to forbid the entrance of foreigners within its domin-

ions, or to admit them only in such cases and upon such conditions as it may see fit to prescribe. In the United States, this power is vested in the national government, to which the Constitution has committed the entire control of international relations, in peace as well as in war.

These powerful and oft-cited passages mask deep and unanswered puzzles. If the federal government is one of enumerated powers, how can it possess "inherent powers" that seem to owe their existence to sources outside the Constitution? Why should "maxims of international law" define the power of Congress? Isn't that what a (or at least our) Constitution is for? Even if we accept the idea that an attribute of sovereignty is the power to regulate immigration, why don't we discover that power in the States, which, under the Tenth Amendment, retain all governmental powers not delegated to the federal government?

In a non-immigration context, the Supreme Court found the foreign affairs power to derive, not from the Constitution, but from the fact of independence itself. *United States v. Curtiss–Wright Export Corp.*, 299 U.S. 304, 57 S.Ct. 216, 81 L.Ed. 255 (1936). *Curtiss–Wright's* theory is particularly troubling in the immigration area. If the power to regulate immigration is extra-constitutional, is it subject to any limits within the Constitution? May noncitizens be excluded without a guarantee of due process? Are noncitizens living in the United States not entitled to the protections of the First, Fourth, Fifth and Sixth Amendments? The Supreme Court has repeatedly stated that they are, at least outside the core immigration law issues of admission and expulsion. But how can these constitutional limits be applied to a power that exists outside the Constitution?

(iii) Constructional and Structural Arguments

Perhaps there is some source of power between enumerated powers and extra-constitutional powers. Let us suggest two.

(a) The Rule of Necessity

Judge Learned Hand has written:

> For centuries it has been an accepted canon in interpretation of documents to interpolate into the text such provisions, though not expressed, as are essential to prevent the defeat of the venture at hand; and this applies with especial force to the interpretation of constitutions, which, since they are designed to cover a great multitude of necessarily unforeseen occasions, must be cast in general language, unless they are constantly amended.

L. Hand, The Bill of Rights 14 (1958).

Is it possible to infer the immigration power using Hand's reasoning—"not [as] a logical deduction from the structure of the Constitution but only as a practical condition upon its successful operation"? *Id.* at 15. Justice Field hints at such a justification when he argues that if the federal government were not able to control immigration, the United

States "would be to that extent subject to the control of another power." Foreign powers could send *agents provocateurs* or suicide bombers to disrupt American institutions; developing nations could send workers to take advantage of American jobs; other countries could seek to solve their problems of overpopulation by exporting people to the United States. Perhaps to lose control of one's borders is to "defeat the venture at hand" by losing our ability to achieve the objects for which the Constitution was established: "to insure domestic Tranquility, provide for the common defense, promote the general Welfare."

(b) Structural Justifications

Charles Black, a leading constitutional scholar, suggested that much of our constitutional law may be seen not as "the explication or exegesis of [a] particular textual passage," but rather as an "inference from the structures and relationships created by the constitution." C. Black, Structure and Relationship in Constitutional Law 7 (1985). The primary purpose of the Constitution is to establish a system of government for a nation, a nation encompassing territory and members ("citizens"). A system of government is the process by which citizens establish rules of conduct for persons within the territory. From these premises, two sorts of structural arguments may follow.

First, to be a sovereign nation, a people must have control over their territory. A nation of open borders runs the risk of not being able to govern itself because its sovereignty, to some extent, is in the hands of the other nations of the world. It seems reasonable to believe that the persons who wrote and ratified the Constitution thought (or hoped) they were creating a nation that would be able to take its place among other nations as an equal; one that would possess the powers of sovereignty generally possessed by all other nations. Second, the relationship of the citizen to the nation is crucial. Citizens, through the process of government, argue about, protect, and further values. Immigration decisions give citizens the ability to regulate who the participants in the discussion will be. By deciding whom we permit to enter the country, we say much about who we are as a nation. As the Chinese exclusion laws demonstrate, the process of self-definition can be ugly, short-sighted, wrong. But perhaps it is one power that every people must possess to be a sovereign people. As Michael Walzer has written:

> [T]he right to choose an admissions policy is * * * not merely a matter of acting in the world, exercising sovereignty, and pursuing national interests. At stake here is the shape of the community that acts in the world, exercises sovereignty, and so on. Admission and exclusion are at the core of communal independence. They suggest the deepest meaning of self-determination.

M. Walzer, Spheres of Justice: A Defense of Pluralism and Equality 61–62 (1983).

Thus we have identified two kinds of structural arguments to justify the immigration power: one based on *self-preservation*, the other on *self-definition*. To what extent are U.S. immigration admission and expulsion rules in fact based on concerns of community self-definition? Consider the following argument:

> "[S]elf-definition" has rarely been a central aspect of immigration regulation. The vast majority of immigration decisions are not club membership rules carefully crafted to preserve a particular group identity. They are much closer to university admission policies than they are to rules regulating religious conversions. We choose how many aliens to admit based on economic, social and moral considerations, attempting to screen out individuals who are likely to threaten the public health, welfare, or security. * * * To be sure, immigration regulations reflect deep social norms and understandings. For example, family reunification policies are based on prevailing American definitions of "nuclear family." But our immigration laws are not primarily concerned with the construction or maintenance of a particular kind of community.

Aleinikoff, *Citizens, Aliens, Membership and the Constitution*, 7 Const. Comm. 9, 33–34 (1990).

b. Plenary Power Doctrine

To generations of law students and lawyers raised on the theory of judicial review articulated in *Marbury v. Madison*, 5 U.S. 137, 2 L.Ed. 60 (1803), the words used by Justice Field in *Chae Chan Ping* are startling: "If * * * [the] legislative department considers the presence of foreigners of a different race * * * to be dangerous to its peace and security, * * * its determination is conclusive upon the judiciary." 130 U.S. 581, 606 (1889). Known as the plenary power doctrine, this exceptional deference to Congress in matters concerning exclusion of noncitizens has been much critiqued in recent decades. As you proceed through the course, you will see that the plenary power doctrine has undergone significant erosion—both directly and indirectly—and courts have become more willing to hear constitutional claims.[4] Nonetheless, in immigration cases the federal judiciary frequently refers to the wide constitutional latitude that Congress enjoys. *E.g., Demore v. Kim*, 583 U.S. 510, 521–22, 123 S.Ct. 1708, 155 L.Ed.2d 724 (2003).

Contrary voices continue to challenge the traditional view of plenary power. One scholar has expressed strong skepticism that there is a plenary

---

4. *See* T. A. Aleinikoff, Semblances of Sovereignty: The Constitution, the State, and American Citizenship 153–65 (2002); S. Legomsky, Immigration and the Judiciary 177–222 (1987); Motomura, *The Curious Evolution of Immigration Law: Procedural Surrogates for Substantive Constitutional Rights*, 92 Colum. L. Rev. 1625 (1992); Motomura, *Immigration Law After a Century of Plenary Power: Phantom Constitutional Norms and Statutory Interpretation*, 100 Yale L.J. 545 (1990); Schuck, *The Transformation of Immigration Law*, 84 Colum. L. Rev. 1 (1984). For a thorough treatment of the constitutional foundations of immigration law and noncitizens' rights in the United States, see G. Neuman, Strangers to the Constitution: Immigrants, Borders, and Fundamental Law (1996).

power doctrine at all, see Chin, *Is There a Plenary Power Doctrine? A Tentative Apology and Prediction for Our Strange But Unexceptional Constitutional Immigration Law*, 14 Geo. Immig. L.J. 257, 258 (1999):

> There is no need for a special plenary power doctrine or other constitutional rule to explain the cases, because the Court has rarely, if ever, tested discrimination against a group in the immigration context at a moment when it had already recognized that the Constitution prohibited discrimination on that ground against citizens. Typically, the Court has upheld discriminatory immigration laws during periods when domestic discrimination against citizens was permitted on the same basis.

Further, it is noteworthy that the concept of plenary power in immigration law developed in the highly racialized context in which the courts decided *Chae Chan Ping*, *Fong Yue Ting*, and other foundation cases. *See* Chin, *Regulating Race: Asian Exclusion and the Administrative State*, 37 Harv. C.–R. C.–L. L. Rev. 1, 50–62 (2002); Chin, *Segregation's Last Stronghold: Race, Discrimination and the Constitutional Law of Immigration*, 46 UCLA L. Rev. 1 (1998); Johnson, *Race, the Immigration Laws, and Domestic Race Relations: A "Magic Mirror" into the Heart of Darkness*, 73 Ind. L.J. (1998).

Professor Louis Henkin has harshly criticized the view that the Constitution imposes no limits on the plenary power of Congress to exclude or deport noncitizens.

> The doctrine that the Constitution neither limits governmental control over the admission of aliens nor secures the right of admitted aliens to reside here emerged in the oppressive shadow of a racist, nativist mood a hundred years ago. It was reaffirmed during our fearful, cold war, McCarthy days. It has no foundation in principle. It is a constitutional fossil, a remnant of a prerights jurisprudence that we have proudly rejected in other respects. Nothing in our Constitution, its theory, or history warrants exempting any exercise of governmental power from constitutional restraint. No such exemption is required or even warranted by the fact that the power to control immigration is unenumerated, inherent in sovereignty, and extra constitutional.
>
> As a blanket exemption of immigration laws from constitutional limitations, *Chinese Exclusion* is a "relic from a different era." That era was one in which constitutional restraints were deemed inapplicable to actions by the United States outside its territory; when orotund generalities about sovereignty and national security were a substitute for significant scrutiny of governmental action impinging on individual rights; when the Bill of Rights had not yet become our national hallmark and the principal justification and preoccupation of judicial review. It was an era before United States commitment to international human rights; before enlightenment in and out of the United States brought an end both to official racial discrimination at home

and to national-origins immigration laws; before important freedoms were recognized as preferred, inviting strict scrutiny if they were invaded and requiring a compelling public interest to uphold their invasion. Since that era, the Supreme Court has held that the Bill of Rights applies to foreign as well as to domestic affairs, in war as well as in peace, to aliens as well as to citizens, abroad as well as at home. The Court has left only immigration and deportation outside the reach of fundamental constitutional protections.

The power of Congress to control immigration and to regulate alienage and naturalization is plenary. But even plenary power is subject to constitutional restraints. I cannot believe that the Court would hold today that the Constitution permits either exclusion on racial or religious grounds or deportation of persons lawfully admitted who have resided peacefully here. * * *

Chinese Exclusion—its very name is an embarrassment—must go.

Henkin, *The Constitution and United States Sovereignty: A Century of Chinese Exclusion and its Progeny*, 100 Harv. L. Rev. 853, 862–63 (1987).

c. State, Local, and Federal Authority

In recent years, as state laws (and state politicians) play a growing role in the national debate about immigration law and policy, it has become increasingly important to consider the exact contours of the federal government's power to control immigration, and the extent to which it displaces any analogous state power. In responding to these questions, consider the following.

Prior to the enactment of the first federal immigration legislation in 1875, states and localities had regulated immigration, sometimes directly, but more often indirectly through quarantine and health laws. *See* Neuman, *The Lost Century of Immigration Law (1776–1875)*, 93 Colum. L. Rev. 1833 (1993). Federal courts, relying on the federal government's power to conduct foreign affairs, invalidated some of these state statutes. The classic statement of this position occurs in *Chy Lung v. Freeman*, 92 U.S. (2 Otto) 275, 23 L.Ed. 550 (1875). The case involved, in the Court's words, "a most extraordinary statute" that authorized the California Commissioner of Immigration to inspect aliens seeking to enter the United States. For any alien determined by the Commissioner to be deaf, dumb, blind, crippled, infirm, or a lunatic, idiot, pauper, convicted criminal or lewd or debauched woman, the master of the vessel was required to give a bond or pay an amount determined by the Commissioner to be sufficient to provide for the alien's care. In litigation filed by a Chinese woman denied entry at the port of San Francisco, the Supreme Court relied in large part on the impact that such a regulation could have on American foreign policy.

Individual foreigners, however distinguished at home for their social, their literary, or their political character, are helpless in the presence of this potent commissioner. Such a person may offer to furnish any amount of surety on his own bond, or deposit any sum of money; but the law of California takes no note of him. It is the master, owner, or consignee of the vessel alone whose bond can be accepted; and so a silly, an obstinate, or a wicked commissioner may bring disgrace upon the whole country, the enmity of a powerful nation, or the loss of an equally powerful friend.

While the occurrence of the hypothetical case just stated may be highly improbable, we venture the assertion, that, if citizens of our own government were treated by any foreign nation as subjects of the Emperor of China have been actually treated under this law, no administration could withstand the call for a demand on such government for redress.

Or, if this plaintiff and her twenty companions had been subjects of the Queen of Great Britain, can anyone doubt that this matter would have been the subject of international inquiry, if not of a direct claim for redress? Upon whom would such a claim be made? Not upon the State of California; for, by our Constitution, she can hold no exterior relations with other nations. It would be made upon the government of the United States. If that government should get into a difficulty which would lead to war, or to suspension of intercourse, would California alone suffer, or all the Union? If we should conclude that a pecuniary indemnity was proper as a satisfaction for the injury, would California pay it, or the Federal government? If that government has forbidden the States to hold negotiations with any foreign nations, or to declare war, and has taken the whole subject of these relations upon herself, has the Constitution, which provides for this, done so foolish a thing as to leave it in the power of the States to pass laws whose enforcement renders the general government liable to just reclamations which it must answer, while it does not prohibit to the States the acts for which it is held responsible?

The Constitution of the United States is no such instrument. The passage of laws which concern the admission of citizens and subjects of foreign nations to our shores belongs to Congress, and not to the States. It has the power to regulate commerce with foreign nations: the responsibility for the character of those regulations, and for the manner of their execution, belongs solely to the national government. If it be otherwise, a single State can, at her pleasure, embroil us in disastrous quarrels with other nations.

Id. at 279–80.

Despite the emphasis on federal power, the view prevailed then that "some actions that might be regulated by Congress under its power over interstate or foreign commerce could also be regulated by a state under its power of police, so long as no actual conflict with federal legislation occurred." Neuman, *The Lost Century*, at 1887 (1993). For example, states might exercise their police power through quarantine and health laws in ways that amounted to immigration control. According to Neuman, several lower court decisions understood the Supreme Court decisions as approving broad state authority over immigration.

Gradually, the federal legislative activity in regulating immigration extinguished state power to control immigration directly. Indirect control by states was still possible, however. This, in turn, has spawned multitudinous litigation examining whether state laws have impermissibly intruded into areas preempted by federal power. In *Hines v. Davidowitz*, 312 U.S. 52, 61 S.Ct. 399, 85 L.Ed. 581 (1941), the Supreme Court invalidated Pennsylvania's statute requiring noncitizens to register with the state and carry a state-issued identity card. The potential impact on foreign relations convinced the Court that preemption applied. But in *DeCanas v. Bica*, 424 U.S. 351, 96 S.Ct. 933, 47 L.Ed.2d 43 (1976), the Court permitted California to penalize employers who knowingly employ unauthorized aliens. States traditionally "possess broad authority under their police power to regulate the employment relationship," *id.* at 356, and Congress had not (as of then) regulated immigration in such a way as to oust state authority. When Congress enacted federal employer sanctions in 1986, it expressly preempted such state authority, with an exception for "licensing and similar laws." In 2011, the Supreme Court upheld an Arizona statute stripping a broad range of licenses from employers who knowingly hire noncitizens unauthorized to work, finding that the explicit exception applied and that this particular Arizona law was generally harmonious with the federal scheme. *Chamber of Commerce v. Whiting*, 563 U.S. ___, 131 S.Ct. 1968, 179 L.Ed.2d 1031 (2011). These and related topics are featured in Chapter Nine.

d. Equal Protection

In its first major examination of the Fourteenth Amendment, the Supreme Court stated that it "doubt[ed] very much whether any action of a state not directed by way of discrimination against the negroes as a class, or on account of their race, will ever be held to come within the purview of [the equal protection clause]." *Slaughter–House Cases*, 83 U.S. (16 Wall.) 36, 21 L.Ed. 394 (1873). Yet in a case of major importance, decided thirteen years later—and three years before *Chae Chan Ping*—the Court held that the equal protection clause protected Chinese nationals against discriminatory enforcement of a San Francisco ordinance regulating laundries. Based on evidence that 200 Chinese laundries had been ordered closed while 80 similar laundries operated by non-Chinese had not, the Court struck down the ordinance as a violation of equal protection, concluding that "no reason for [the discrimination] exists except hostility to the race and nationality to which the petitioners belong." *Yick Wo v. Hopkins*, 118 U.S. 356, 374, 6 S.Ct. 1064, 1073, 30 L.Ed. 220 (1886). First, however, the Court had to address the question whether the plaintiffs could invoke the equal protection clause at all:

> The rights of the petitioners, * * * are not less, because they are aliens and subjects of the Emperor of China. * * *

The Fourteenth Amendment to the Constitution is not confined to the protection of citizens. It says: "Nor shall any state deprive any person of life, liberty, or property without due process of law; nor deny to any person within its jurisdiction the equal protection of the laws." These provisions are universal in their application, to all persons within the territorial jurisdiction, without regard to any differences of race, of color, or of nationality; and the equal protection of the laws is a pledge of the protection of equal laws. * * * The questions we have to consider and decide in these cases, therefore, are to be treated as involving the rights of every citizen of the United States equally with those of the strangers and aliens who now invoke the jurisdiction of the court.

* * *

When we consider the nature and the theory of our institutions of government, the principles upon which they are supposed to rest, and review the history of their development, we are constrained to conclude that they do not mean to leave room for the play and action of purely personal and arbitrary power. Sovereignty itself is, of course, not subject to law, for it is the author and source of law; but in our system, while sovereign powers are delegated to the agencies of government, sovereignty itself remains with the people, by whom and for whom all government exists and acts. And the law is the definition and limitation of power. It is, indeed, quite true that there must always be lodged somewhere, and in some person or body, the authority of final decision; and in many cases of mere administration the responsibility is purely political, no appeal lying except to the ultimate tribunal of the public judgment, exercised either in the pressure of opinion, or by means of the suffrage. But the fundamental rights to life, liberty, and the pursuit of happiness, considered as individual possessions, are secured by those maxims of constitutional law which are the monuments showing the victorious progress of the race in securing to men the blessings of civilization under the reign of just and equal laws, so that, in the famous language of the Massachusetts Bill of Rights, the government of the commonwealth "may be a government of laws and not of men." For, the very idea that one man may be compelled to hold his life, or the means of living, or any material right essential to the enjoyment of life, at the mere will of another, seems to be intolerable in any country where freedom prevails, as being the essence of slavery itself.

* * *

* * * [T]he facts shown establish an administration directed so exclusively against a particular class of persons as to warrant and require the conclusion, that, whatever may have been the intent of the ordinances as adopted, they are applied by the public authorities charged with their administration, and thus representing the State itself, with a mind so unequal and oppressive as to amount to a

practical denial by the State of that equal protection of the laws which is secured to the petitioners, as to all other persons, by the broad and benign provisions of the Fourteenth Amendment to the Constitution of the United States. * * *

118 U.S. at 368–70, 373, 6 S.Ct. at 1070–71, 1073.

If the Fourteenth Amendment protected Chinese citizens operating laundries in San Francisco, why were not the Chinese exclusion laws similarly invalid—evidencing, as they did, hostility based on race and nationality?

The quick answer is that the Fourteenth Amendment applies only to the actions of the States, and not to the federal government. In the late nineteenth century, this formalistic answer probably explains why an equal protection challenge was not made in *Chae Chan Ping*, but that answer cannot suffice today. In *Bolling v. Sharpe*, 347 U.S. 497, 74 S.Ct. 693, 98 L.Ed. 884 (1954), a companion case to *Brown v. Board of Education*, the Court held that segregated schools in the District of Columbia violated the due process clause of the Fifth Amendment. Since *Bolling*, it has usually been understood that "[e]qual protection analysis in the Fifth Amendment area is the same as that under the Fourteenth Amendment." *Buckley v. Valeo*, 424 U.S. 1, 93, 96 S.Ct. 612, 670, 46 L.Ed.2d 659 (1976) (per curiam). Does this mean that the Chinese exclusion laws would be invalid today? Not quite.

A more fundamental difficulty with applying the reasoning of *Yick Wo* to challenge Chae Chan Ping's exclusion would have been that *Chae Chan Ping* involved an immigration question—a noncitizen's right to enter the United States. *Yick Wo* involved an allegation of discrimination against noncitizens in the United States, but not a challenge to a decision to exclude or expel them. This aspect of *Yick Wo* suggests a tension that runs throughout the constitutional materials in this book. On the one hand, *Chae Chan Ping* is a seminal case for the "plenary power doctrine"— which severely limits noncitizens' constitutional rights when it comes to entering and remaining in this country. In contrast, *Yick Wo* suggests that noncitizens and citizens receive similar (but not necessarily identical) constitutional treatment in *nonimmigration* matters. Put differently, our constitutional law relating to *immigration* may differ from our constitutional law relating to noncitizen *immigrants*.

Federal preemption and stronger equal protection scrutiny of state and local laws add other complications to applying *Yick Wo's* reasoning to challenge Chae Chan Ping's exclusion. Besides distinguishing immigration law from discrimination against noncitizens with respect to their rights and conduct as residents, one might also distinguish the federal law in *Chae Chan Ping* from the local law in *Yick Wo*. As we explore in detail in

Chapter Eleven, later Supreme Court decisions recognized broad congressional authority to "make rules [regarding noncitizens] that would be unacceptable if applied to citizens," *Mathews v. Diaz*, 426 U.S. 67, 80, 96 S.Ct. 1883, 1891, 48 L.Ed.2d 478 (1976); but other court decisions vigorously scrutinized most state legislation that discriminates against noncitizens, *see, e.g., Graham v. Richardson*, 403 U.S. 365, 91 S.Ct. 1848, 29 L.Ed.2d 534 (1971).

NOTES AND QUESTIONS ON CONSTITUTIONAL CHALLENGES

1. *Framing the constitutional challenge.* Seven years prior to *Fong Yue Ting*, the Supreme Court had stuck down the discriminatory municipal ordinance in *Yick Wo* and ruled that Chinese nationals in the United States came within the ambit of the equal protection clause. Surprisingly (to a modern observer), despite the vehemence of their opinions, the *Fong Yue Ting* dissenters paid little attention to Congress' decision to single out laborers of Chinese origin. Why do you think this was so? With this question in mind, look again at the opinions to see exactly what the dissenters found objectionable about the statute. Why did they apparently find that objection more persuasive than a nationality or racial discrimination challenge?

2. In both *Wong Wing* and *Yick Wo*, the Supreme Court relied upon generally applicable constitutional norms to invalidate governmental action that involved immigrants. *Wong Wing*, unlike *Yick Wo*, invalidated a *federal* statute—and one that was more closely related to the immigration power. In that respect it may stand more clearly than *Yick Wo* for the proposition that noncitizens are members of the constitutional community, apart from their right to enter and remain in this country.

SECTION B. IMMIGRANTS IN THE UNITED STATES TODAY

The history of immigration to the United States reveals that migration waxed and waned over the centuries. The legal framework developed in the past two hundred and thirty years alternately encouraged and discouraged immigration, and it clearly encouraged and discouraged some immigrant groups more than others. Now that you have begun to see the context in which U.S. immigration policy operates, you may be interested in some basic demographic information about immigrants in the United States now and about those who arrived in the prior century.

1. HISTORICAL COMPARISONS

The first set of graphs reveals dramatic shifts in the numbers of immigrants admitted, their percentage of the U.S. population, and the countries from which they came during the past two centuries. You may wish to consult the immigration history sketched in Chapter One as you consult these data. Figure 3.1 reports the number of legal immigrants who have been admitted to the United States each year since 1820.

Figure 3.1
Legal Immigration to the United States 1820 to 2009

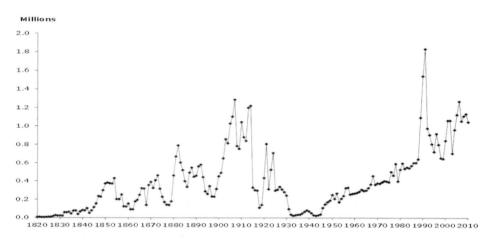

Source: http://www.migrationinformation.org/datahub/charts/historic1.cfm.

In Figure 3.2, the bottom line (at the bottom from 1850 till 2000) indicates the number of foreign-born individuals living in the United States, while the top line reflects their percentage of the population. Thus, it is possible to calculate both the absolute number of immigrants and how much of the population of the United States consists of immigrants. In 1850 the roughly two million foreign-born residents constituted 10 percent of the total population of the country. By 1870, the foreign-born population had doubled to five million, and they made up 15 percent of the U.S. population. One hundred years later, in 1970, ten million foreign-born residents constituted less than 4 percent of the total population. Today, the absolute number—35 million—of immigrants is high, and the percentage of the foreign-born is nearing the peaks experienced at the turn of the 20th century.

Figure 3.2
Foreign–Born Population and Foreign Born as Percentage
of the Total US Population, 1850 to 2009

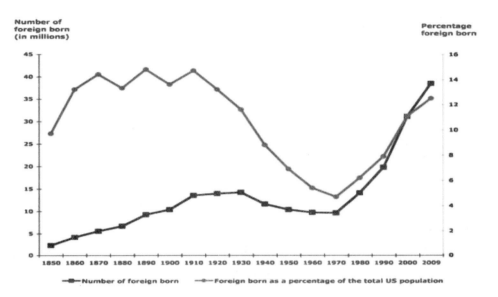

Source: http://www.migrationinformation.org/datahub/charts/final.fb.shtml.

Figure 3.3 reveals, at a glance, several important points. It shows how the countries of origin have varied over the past century. It is a commonplace that during the first part of the twentieth century most of the immigrants to the United States came from Europe. The graph shows, however, that Mexico and Canada were also major source countries throughout this period. Mexico continues to be a top sending country, though it may surprise many to learn that Mexican immigrants account for a smaller percentage of lawful permanent residents (LPRs) in the first decade of the twenty-first century than in prior decades. (LPRs, as described in Chapter Five, have been admitted to the United States pursuant to immigrant visas, and have the right to live permanently in the United States.)

Notice how the diversity of immigrants has changed over time. Prior to 1960, immigrants from three or four countries made up more than half of all LPRs. By 2001–2009 ten source countries account for fifty percent of the immigrants.

Figure 3.3
Top Sending Countries in Selected Periods, 1910 to 2009

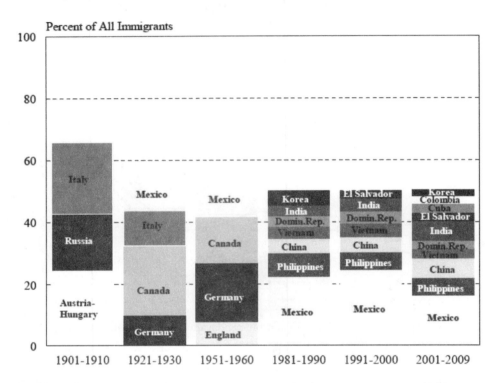

Source: CRS analysis of Table 2, *Statistical Yearbook of Immigration*, U.S. Department of Homeland Security, Office of Immigration Statistics, FY2009.

Figure 3.4, based on U.S. census data, reflects the U.S. population's views of their own immigrant heritage. For example, more than 51 million Americans reported that they had German heritage, more than claimed either Irish or British forebears, while 32 million looked to Mexican roots, and 3.5 million reported Chinese ancestry.

The right-hand columns report the number of current U.S. residents who were born in another country. Mexico leads the way, with more than 11 million, while China accounts for approximately 1.5 million. One of the surprises is that Germany, a major source country a century ago and consequently ranked first in claimed heritage, still accounts for a large number—more than 600,000—of immigrants at the beginning of the twenty-first century.

Figure 3.4
Estimates of the Top Diaspora Groups and Top Foreign–Born Groups, 2009

(the highlighted countries are those on both lists)

Rank	Origin	Diaspora[1] (sorted)	Rank	Countries of Birth	Foreign Born (sorted)
1	Germany	51,263,000	1	Mexico	11,478,000
2	Ireland[2]	42,236,000	2	Philippines	1,726,000
3	United Kingdom[3]	35,500,000	3	India	1,665,000
4	Mexico	32,952,000	4	China[5]	1,642,000
5	Italy	18,130,000	5	Vietnam	1,152,000
6	Poland	10,228,000	6	El Salvador	1,150,000
7	France[4]	9,454,000	7	Korea	1,004,000
8	Netherlands	5,035,000	8	Cuba	991,000
9	Norway	4,655,000	9	Canada[6]	815,000
10	Sweden	4,333,000	10	Guatemala	799,000
11	China[5]	3,526,000	11	Dominican Republic	793,000
12	Canada[6]	3,395,000	12	United Kingdom[3]	695,000
13	Philippines	3,389,000	13	Jamaica	651,000
14	India	3,121,000	14	Germany	623,000
15	El Salvador	2,038,000	15	Colombia	610,000

1. Includes individuals born in the country as well as those who cited that origin as their ancestry, race, and/or ethnicity regardless of where they were born. Ancestry refers to a person's ethnic origin or descent, "roots," or heritage; or the place of birth of the person, the person's parents, or ancestors before their arrival in the United States.

Source: http://www.migrationinformation.org/datahub/charts/diaspora1.cfm.

2. IMMIGRANTS CURRENTLY ARRIVING

Turning now to the flows of contemporary immigration, Figure 3.5 highlights the countries from which the greatest numbers of new lawful permanent residents originate. In 2009 Mexico accounted for the largest number, close to 15 percent of the total, with China, the Philippines, and India each contributing approximately 5 percent.

Figure 3.5

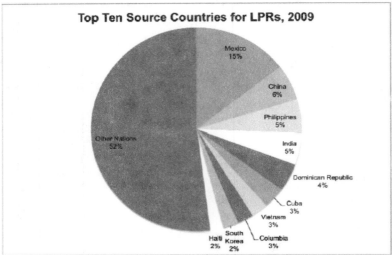

Source: DHS, Office of Immigration Statistics, Yearbook of Immigration Statistics, 2010.

There is a diverse group of source countries, with no country, other than Mexico, contributing more than five or six percent of the annual flow of immigrants. In contrast, a handful of U.S. states attract the majority of new immigrants. Figure 3.6 shows that five states—California, New York, Florida, Texas, and New Jersey—were the destinations of more than 60 percent of the new immigrants in 2008.

Figure 3.6
Percent Admitted LPRs by State or Territory
of Intended Residence, 2008

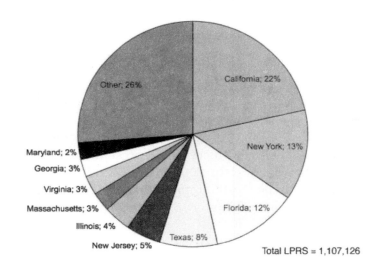

Source: http://www.migrationinformation.org/Feature/print.cfm?ID=730#12.

Although the traditional destination states continue to attract many new noncitizens, their share of the total foreign-born population declined from 75 percent in 1990 to 65 percent in 2009. Figure 3.7 reveals that many recent immigrants have been settling in other states. In 2009 there were 3.5 million immigrants in new-destination states—nearly four times the number in 1990 and more than 12 times the number in 1970. Approximately, one in every eleven immigrants resided in a new-destination state in 2009, compared to one in 25 in 1990.

Figure 3.7
Cumulative Growth in the Foreign–Born Population in New and Traditional Destination States, 1960 to 2009

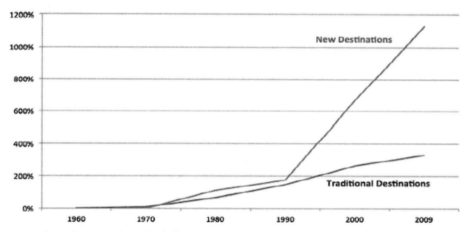

Source: http://www.migrationinformation.org/usfocus/display.cfm?ID=826.

3.   CURRENT FOREIGN–BORN POPULATION

Thus far, the charts and graphs have provided century-long analyses and a look at the lawful permanent residents who arrived in the past year or two. A more complete view of the contemporary immigrant experience in the United States today requires an examination of the information compiled about the total foreign-born population. In rough terms, about a third of the foreign-born have become citizens via the naturalization process. Another third are present in lawful status and the final third are in unauthorized status. A small fraction, born abroad of U.S. citizen parents, have been citizens since birth.

Figure 3.8 illustrates the heritage of the total foreign-born population in the United States as of 2009. Mexico accounts for 30 percent, with the Philippines, India, and China tied at 4 percent each. Vietnam, El Salvador, Korea, and Cuba each constitutes 3 percent. These three Latin American countries and five Asian countries tougher comprise more than 50 percent of the current foreign-born population.

Figure 3.8
Ten Source Countries with the Largest Populations in the United States as Percentages of the Total Foreign–Born Population: 2009

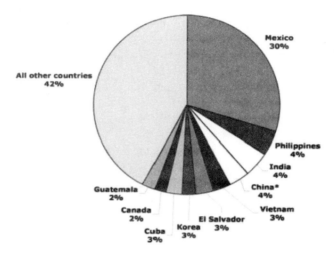

Source: http://www.migrationinformation.org/datahub/charts/10.2009.shtml.

The final set of graphs below displays information about the work-force participation of the foreign-born, their education, and their poverty levels. More than 24 million of the 156 million civilian workers in the United States are foreign born. They constituted more than 15 percent of the labor force in 2008, a substantial increase over the 17 million foreign-born workers who made up 12.4 percent of the U.S. work force in 2000. Congressional Research Service Report, United States and Foreign Born Population: Trends and Selected Characteristics, Jan. 2011, at 21.

Figure 3.9 illustrates the countries in which the foreign-born workers were born. Mexico accounts for almost one-third, followed by Asian workers, who make up roughly one-quarter. Together, Central and South American-born individual workers account for 15 percent, with European and Canadian jointly making up approximately 12 percent of the foreign-born labor force.

Figure 3.9
Foreign–Born Labor Force by Place of Birth, 2009

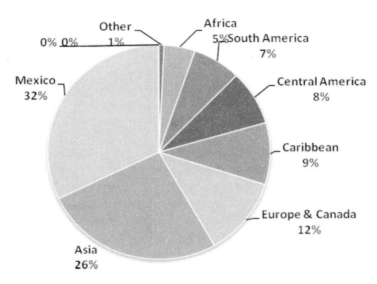

Source: Congressional Budget Office, *The Role of Immigrants in the U.S. Labor Market: An Update*, July 2010, Table 2.

Figure 3.10 depicts the distribution of occupations. Construction work employs the largest percentage, roughly 9 percent. There is a relatively even distribution—7 percent to 8 percent—in seven categories: manufacturing, cleaning and maintenance, sales, management, office support, transportation and moving, and food services. In contrast, almost 14 percent of native-born workers were in office support in 2009, followed by 13 percent in management, and 10% in sales.

Figure 3.10
Top 10 Occupations of Foreign–Born Workers, Age 25–64, 2009

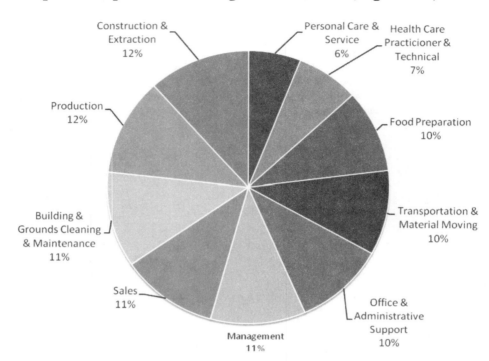

Source: Congressional Budget Office, *The Role of Immigrants in the U.S. Labor Market: An Update*, July 2010, Table 7.

Figure 3.11 shows that roughly 40 percent of the total foreign-born population over the age of 25 have not finished high school, but that number camouflages major differences between those who have naturalized, those present in lawful status, and those whose presence is unauthorized. For example, only 11 percent of naturalized citizens lack high school diplomas.

Similarly, while 13 percent of all foreign-born have college degrees, over 19 percent of naturalized citizens have graduated from college, which is a higher than that of the native-born population.

Figure 3.11
Educational Levels of Foreign–Born and Native–Born, 2009

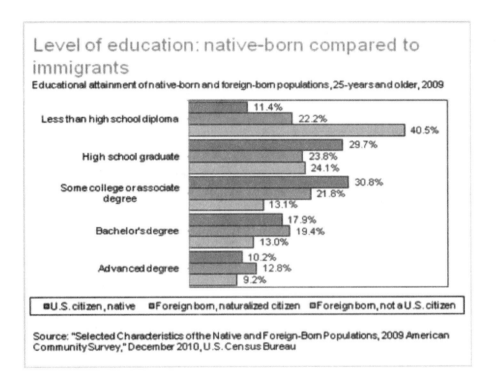

The poverty levels vary less significantly than many imagine. As Figure 3.12 shows, 17 percent of the foreign born live below the poverty level, compared with 14 percent of the native born population. Again, naturalized citizens actually do better economically than the native-born.

Figure 3.12
Poverty Levels of Foreign–Born and Native–Born, 2008

(Based on where individual income falls in relation to the 2008 poverty threshold)

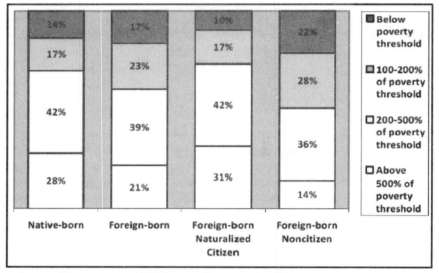

Source: CRS presentation of 2008 American Community Survey data.

Notes: Average poverty levels determined by the Census Bureau in 2008 were $10,400 for individuals (with variation according to whether persons were above or below age 65) and $21,200 for a family with two children under age 18. The federal poverty definition for statistical purposes varies by family size and composition and does not include noncash benefits or account for taxes. Poverty status (in poverty or not in poverty) of a family is assigned to each family member. The Census Bureau does not define poverty status for unrelated individuals under age 15 (e.g., foster children). For a discussion of alternative definitions of poverty, see U.S. Census Bureau, Current Population Reports, P60-227, prepared by Joe Dalaker, 2005.

SECTION C. THEORIES OF MIGRATION

After surveying the history of immigration to the United States and the evolving legal regime that has attempted to respond and regulate the flows of immigrants, it is useful to stand back for a moment and ask a more general question: Why do people migrate? The selections in this section emphasize different perspectives on the migration phenomenon. The first excerpt is from a well-known author, an immigrant himself, whose training as an economist is central to his work.

GEORGE J. BORJAS, HEAVEN'S DOOR: IMMIGRATION POLICY AND THE AMERICAN ECONOMY

47–50 (2001).

Immigrants are not randomly chosen from the populations of the countries of origin. Consider, for instance, the migration of Mexicans to the United States. Even though it is very large (seven million Mexican-born persons lived in the United States in 1997), it is still small when compared to the Mexican population. In 1997, Mexico's population was ninety-eight million, so that fewer than 7 percent of Mexicans had chosen to move to the United States.

It would be hard to blame restrictive immigration policies for Mexico's relatively low emigration rate. The U.S.–Mexico border is notoriously porous, and can be crossed illegally by almost anyone who really wants to. Moreover, per capita income in the United States is more than three times that of Mexico, even after adjusting for differences in purchasing power. In view of the potentially large gains from migrating to the United States, the question is not why so many Mexicans emigrate, but rather, *Why do so few move?*

The answer is simple—although it comes as a shock to most Americans. Not everyone in the world wants to live in the United States. The group of immigrants who end up in the United States is self-selected from the population of the source countries. And because of this self-selection, the typical immigrant who reaches the United States will be different from the typical person who chooses to remain in the source country.

* * *

Why do relatively few persons bother to migrate to the United States? Mainly because it is costly to immigrate. The costs include the expense of transporting the household across thousands of miles and looking for new employment, as well as the psychological burden of leaving family and friends behind and of becoming aliens in a strange land. As a result, the immigrants are typically the persons who have the most to gain from moving—because only those who gain the most would be willing to incur the substantial migration costs.

Does the United States, then, attract the most skilled workers from any given source country, or the least skilled workers?

Suppose that workers make the migration decision by comparing the economic opportunities provided by the source country with those provided by the United States. Consider first a group of workers who live in a country where the payoff to human capital is low, so that highly skilled workers do not earn much more than less-skilled. As long as persons migrate to countries that provide the best economic opportunities, the workers who have the most to gain by moving to the United States are the workers with above-average skills. The United States benefits from a brain drain.

Alternatively, consider workers living in countries where the payoff to human capital is quite high. The rewards to skills are often substantial in many developing countries, such as Mexico and the Philippines. These high rewards to skills partly account for the very unequal distribution of incomes observed in those countries, where the skilled earn substantially more than the less-skilled. Highly skilled workers in these countries often face better economic opportunities than they would face if they migrated to the United States, while less-skilled workers can barely rise above the subsistence level. As long as persons migrate to countries that provide better economic opportunities, the skilled workers in these countries have little incentive to leave. It is the least skilled who want to emigrate, and the immigrant flow will be composed of workers with below-average skills.

As long as economic considerations matter in the migration decision, skills tend to flow to those markets that offer the highest value. The United States is then likely to attract highly skilled workers from some countries (those where the returns to skills are low), and unskilled workers from others (those where the returns to skills are high).

There is, in fact, a negative correlation between measures of the source country's rate of return to skills and the economic performance of immigrants in the United States * * *. In particular, immigrants earn less if they originate in countries where there is a great deal of income dispersion * * *. The income distribution in Mexico, for instance, is much more dispersed than the income distribution in the United Kingdom—and part of this dispersion arises because the rate of return to skills is much higher in Mexico than in the United Kingdom. The [data suggest] that this difference in the return to skills generates a 30 percent wage differential between the two groups. In other words, an important part of the sizable wage gap between Mexican and British immigrants (which was around 125 percent in 1990) arises because different types of person choose to leave those two countries.

In sum, immigrants originating in developing countries will typically have less human capital for a number of reasons. Workers in developing countries tend to have less education than their counterparts in the industrialized economies; the less-skilled in the developing countries sometimes have the greatest incentive to migrate to the United States; and the human capital acquired in developing economies is harder to transfer to an industrialized setting.

The next selection emphasizes the long-term historical processes at work in migration flows. It criticizes the "push-pull" theories of migration, arguing that they ignore powerful political forces and they lack predictive power.

ALEJANDRO PORTES & JÓZSEF BÖRÖCZ, CONTEMPORARY IMMIGRATION: THEORETICAL PERSPECTIVES ON ITS DETERMINANTS AND MODES OF INCORPORATION

23 International Migration Review 606, 607–14 (1989).

ORIGINS

The most widely held approach to the origins of international migration—"push-pull" theories—see labor flows as an outcome of poverty and backwardness in the sending areas. Representatives of this perspective provide lists of "push factors"—economic, social and political hardships in the poorest parts of the world—and "pull factors"—comparative advantages in the more advanced nation-states—as causal variables determining the size and directionality of immigrant flows. These lists are invariably elaborated *post factum*, that is, after particular movements have already been initiated. The compilation of such lists is usually guided by two underlying assumptions: first, the expectation that the most disadvantaged sectors of the poorer societies are most likely to participate in labor migration; and second, the assumption that such flows arise spontaneously out of the sheer existence of inequalities on a global scale.

On the surface, these assumptions appear self-evident: workers migrate from Mexico to the United States and from Turkey to West Germany and not vice versa. However, the tendency of the push-pull model to be applied to those flows which are already taking place conceals its inability to explain why similar movements do not arise out of other equally "poor" nations or why sources of outmigration tend to concentrate in certain regions and not in others within the same sending countries.

Thus, the proclivity of these theories to the post hoc recitation of "obvious" causes makes them incapable of predicting the two principal differences in the origin of migration: 1) differences among collectivities—primarily nation-states—in the size and directionality of migrant flows; 2) differences among individuals within the same country or region in their propensities to migrate. The first question concerns macrostructural determinants of labor displacements while the second concerns their microstructural causes. The difference between these levels of analysis is also absent from most standard push-pull writings.

At the broader level of determination, the onset of labor flows does not arise out of invidious comparisons of economic advantage, but out of a history of prior contact between sending and receiving societies. History is replete with instances in which an absolute wage advantage in economically expanding areas has meant nothing to the population of more isolated regions; when their labor has been required, it has had to be coerced out of them. In general, the emergence of regular labor outflows of stable size and known destination requires the prior penetration by institutions of the stronger nation-state into those of the weaker sending ones. Political and economic conditions in the latter are then gradually molded to the point where migration to the hegemonic center emerges as a plausible option for the subordinate population. The process of external penetration and internal imbalancing of labor-exporting areas has taken very different forms, however, during the history of capitalism[, evolving from conquest and the slave trade, through migrant recruitment using economic inducements, to eventual self-initiated labor flows].

* * *

The various historical forms of penetration * * * form part of a progression guided by the initiatives of states at the center of the international economy and the changing interests of its dominant classes. The outcome of this progression has been to increase consistently the supply of pliable labor while decreasing its costs. The process has reached its culmination today when labor migrants assume the initiative and the full costs of the journey. This outcome is what economists now refer to as "inexhaustible supplies" of labor.

* * *

STABILITY

A second difficulty with standard push-pull theories is their inability to account for individual differences in patterns of migration. Given the same set of expelling forces and external inducements, why is it that some individuals leave while others stay? Why, in particular, given the lopsided "differentials of advantage" in favor of the receiving society, do only a minority of the source populations migrate? Descriptions of Mexican, Dominican or West Indian migration—including those at an exclusively macrostructural level—suggest that "everyone is leaving," which is far from being the case.

A related shortcoming is the inability of conventional theories to explain the resilience of migrant flows once the original economic inducements have disappeared or have been significantly lessened. According to the underlying economic rationale of the push-pull approach, migration should reflect, with some lag, ups and downs in the "differential of advantage" which gives rise to the process in the first place. In reality, migration flows, once established, tend to continue with relative autonomy from such fluctuations.

Contrary to the assertion that international labor migration is basically an outcome of economic decisions governed by the law of supply and demand, * * * the phenomenon is primarily social in nature. Networks constructed by the movement and contact of people across space are at the core of the microstructures which sustain migration over time. More than individualistic calculations of gain, it is the insertion of people into such networks which helps explain differential proclivities to move and the enduring character of migrant flows.

* * *

An important aspect of labor migration is the fact that the social channels which it creates open ways for entry and settlement of individuals who do not directly participate in the labor process. These dependent family members may enter the labor market subsequently. Opportunities may emerge, for example, for wives and for migrant children as they become of age. * * *

More than movement from one place to another in search of higher wages, labor migration should be conceptualized as a process of progressive network building. Networks connect individuals and groups distributed across different places, maximizing their economic opportunities through multiple displacements. Labor migration is thus a device through which individual workers and their households adapt to opportunities distributed unevenly in space. Hence, migration performs a dual function: for capital, it is a source of more abundant and less expensive labor; for the migrants, it is a means of survival and a vehicle for social integration and economic mobility.

———————

Our third excerpt challenges the economic model posited by Borjas and others as incomplete. It argues that multiple factors working simultaneously, and sometimes in tension with each other, account for international migration.

DOUGLAS S. MASSEY, JORGE DURAND, & NOLAN J. MALONE, BEYOND SMOKE AND MIRRORS: MEXICAN IMMIGRATION IN AN ERA OF ECONOMIC INTEGRATION

9–21 (2002)

* * *

WHY PEOPLE MIGRATE

* * *[According to *neoclassical economics*,] international migration stems from geographic differences in the supply of and demand for labor. Countries with large endowments of labor relative to capital have low wages, while those with limited endowments of labor relative to capital have high wages. The resulting international differential causes workers from low-wage countries to move to high-wage countries. As a result of this movement, the supply of labor falls and wages rise in the former while they do the opposite in the latter, leading, at equilibrium, to an international wage differential reflecting the costs of international movement, pecuniary and psychic.

Associated with the macro theory is an accompanying micro-economic model of decisionmaking. Rational actors choose to migrate through a cost-benefit calculation that leads them to expect positive net returns, usually monetary, from international movement. Migration is analogous to investment in human capital, where human capital consists of personal traits and characteristics that increase a worker's productivity. Early in their lives, people invest in education to make themselves more productive and later reap benefits in the form of higher earnings.

Where one lives can be viewed as an individual trait that rational actors change by investing in a move. Migrants seek to go to places where, given their skills, they can be more productive and earn more money. Before they can reap this benefit, however, they must undertake certain investments: the material costs of traveling, the costs of sustenance while moving and looking for work, the effort involved in learning a new language and culture, the difficulty experienced in adapting to a new labor market, and the psychological burden of cutting old ties and forging new ones. According to neoclassical theory, migrants estimate the costs and benefits of moving to various international locations and then go to wherever the expected net returns are greatest.

* * *

A variety of anomalous observations suggest, however, that motivations for migration go beyond such cost-benefit calculations. Under neoclassical theory, migration should not occur in the absence of a wage differential, yet such flows are frequently observed. Moreover, if there are no legal barriers to movement, migration should continue until the wage differential between two areas is eliminated, yet migration streams commonly end well before wage gaps disappear. Widely observed patterns of circular migration are also difficult to explain from a strict neoclassical viewpoint; each year thousands of undocumented migrants and even many legal immigrants decide to return to Mexico. * * *

These anomalies occur because the lifetime maximization of expected income is only one of several potential economic motivations for international migration, and not necessarily the most important. Neoclassical economics *begins* with the assumption that markets for goods and services exist, that they are complete and function well, that information and competition are perfect, and that rational individuals enter the market with exogenous tastes and preferences in order to maximize their utility (that is, they look out for number one). * * *

Yet reality is considerably more complex than the enabling assumptions of neoclassical economics. Markets for goods and services may not exist, they may be imperfect, and sometimes they may fail entirely, especially during the early phases of economic development. In addition, information is usually scarce and constrained by an individual's position on the social structure, and competition is far from perfect. Finally, even if individuals are rational and self-interested, they do not enter markets as atomized individuals but as members of families, households, and sometime larger communities, social groupings that allow for *collective* strategies, which at times may dovetail with those of individuals and at other times be at odds with them.

If we imagine a world where families and households face the prospect of poorly functioning, missing, or failed markets, we come to a very different line of theoretical reasoning known as the *new economics of labor migration*. Unlike the neoclassical model, it does not assume that migration decisions are made by isolated actors, but that they are taken within larger units of interrelated people, typically families or households but sometimes entire communities. Within these units, people not only act individually to maximize expected income but also work collectively to overcome failures in capital, credit, and insurance markets.

In most developed countries the risks to a household's material well-being are managed through private markets and government programs. Crop insurance and futures markets give farmers a means of protecting themselves against natural disasters and price fluctuations, and unemployment insurance and welfare programs protect workers against the vagaries of the business cycle and the dislocations of structural change. Private and government-sponsored pension systems allow citizens to minimize the risk of poverty in old age.

In relatively poor countries like Mexico, markets for futures and insurance are not well developed, and the Mexican government is in no position to fill the gap by offering substitutes. As a result, Mexicans are not only poorer than other North Americans; they are also exposed to substantially greater risk. * * *

Just as investors diversify risk by purchasing stocks across a range of firms, households diversify risks by sending out members to work in different labor markets. While some members (say, the wife and younger children) remain behind to work in the local economy, others (say, older sons and daughters) move to work elsewhere in Mexico, and still others (perhaps the household head and oldest son) migrate to work in the United States. As long as conditions in the various labor markets are negatively or weakly correlated, a household can manage risk through diversification. In the event that conditions at home deteriorate through rising unemployment, falling wages, failing crops, sagging prices, or high inflation, households can rely on migrant remittances as an alternative source of income.

In developing countries such as Mexico, markets for capital and credit are also weak or absent, preventing families from borrowing to smooth consumption or undertake productive activities. In the absence of an efficient banking system, international migration becomes a reasonable strategy that poor families can use to accumulate cash in lieu of formal borrowing for consumption or investment. Households simply send one or more workers abroad to take advantage of higher wages to build up savings over a short time horizon.

CONTEXTS OF DECISIONMAKING

* * *

* * * [A]variety of theorists have linked the origins of international migration not so much to the decisions of individuals or households as to the changing scope and structure of global markets, a line of reasoning that is generally known as *world systems theory*. In this scheme, the expansion of markets into peripheral, nonmarket or pre-market societies creates mobile populations that are prone to migrate.

Driven by a desire for higher profits and greater wealth, owners and managers of large firms in developed nations enter poor countries on the periphery of the world economy in search of land, raw materials, labor, and markets. Migration is a natural outgrowth of the disruptions and dislocations that occur in the process of market expansion and penetration. As land, raw materials, and labor come under the control of markets, flows of migrants are generated. * * * The substitution of cash crops for staples undermines traditional social and economic relations, and the use of modern inputs, by producing high crop yields at low unit prices, drives out peasant farmers. All of these forces contribute to the creation of a mobile labor force: agricultural workers, displaced from the land, experience a weakened attachment to the community and become more prone to migrate internationally.

* * *

Economic globalization also creates cultural links between developed and developing nations. Sometimes the cultural links are long-standing, reflecting prior colonial relationships. Yet even in the absence of colonial history, the cultural consequences of economic penetration can be profound. Although Mexico was colonized by Spain, Mexicans increasingly study at U.S. universities, speak English, and follow U.S. consumer styles, reflecting America's global economic hegemony. These cultural links naturally dispose them to migrate to the United States rather than other places, including Spain.

* * *

THE DEMAND FOR IMMIGRANTS

The bifurcation of labor markets in global cities predicted by world systems theory dovetails with a larger line of theorizing known as *segmented labor market theory,* which grew out of institutional economics. Michael Piore has argued that international migration stems from a relatively permanent demand for unskilled labor that is built into the economic structure of developed nations. In his view, immigration is not caused by push factors in sending countries (such as law wages or high unemployment), but by pull factors in receiving societies (a chronic and unavoidable need for low-wage workers). The intrinsic demand for inexpensive labor stems from four fundamental problems faced by advanced industrial economies.

The first problem is *structural inflation.* Wages not only reflect conditions of supply and demand but confer status and prestige, social qualities inherent to specific jobs. In general, people believe that wages should reflect social status, and they have rather rigid notions about the correlation between occupational status and pay. As a result, wages offered by employers are not free to respond to changes in the supply of workers. A variety of informal social expectations and formal institutional mechanisms (such as union contracts, civil service rules, bureaucratic regulations, and human resource classifications) ensure that wages correspond to the hierarchies of prestige and status that people perceive.

If employers seek to attract workers for unskilled jobs at the bottom of an occupational hierarchy, they cannot simply raise wages for those jobs. Doing so would upset defined relationship between status and remuneration. If wages are increased at the bottom, employers will encounter strong pressure to raise wages at other levels of the job hierarchy. If the wages of busboys are raised in response to a labor shortage, for example, their wages may overlap with those of waitresses, thereby threatening the status of waitresses and prompting them to demand a corresponding wage increase, which threatens the position of cooks, who also pressure employers for a raise, and so on. As a result, the cost of raising wages to attract entry-level workers is typically more than the cost of those workers' wages alone. Thus, the prospect of structural inflation—the need to raise wages proportionately throughout the job hierarchy to maintain consistency with social expectation—provides employers with a strong incentive to seek easier and cheaper solutions, such as the importation of immigrants.

The demand for cheap, flexible labor is also augmented by the *social constraints on motivation* that are inherent to job hierarchies. Most people work not only to generate income but to accumulate social status. Acute motivational problems arise at the bottom of the job hierarchy because there is no status to be maintained and there are few avenues for upward mobility. * * * What employers need are workers who view bottom-level jobs simply as a means to the end of earning money and for whom employment is reduced solely to a matter of income, with no implications for status or prestige.

Immigrants satisfy this need on a variety of counts, at least at the beginning of their migratory careers. Migrants generally begin foreign labor as target earners: they are seeking to make money for a specific goal that will solve a problem or improve their status at home (such as building a new house, buying land, or acquiring consumer goods). Moreover, the disjuncture in living standards between developed and developing societies makes low wages abroad appear generous by the standards of the sending country. Finally, even though a migrant may realize that a foreign job carries low status, he does not view himself as a part of that society but as embedded within the status system of his home community, where hard-currency remittances buy considerable social status.

The demand for immigrant labor also stems from the *duality of labor and capital*. Capital is a fixed factor of production that can be idled by lower demand but not laid off; owners of capital bear the costs of its unemployment. Labor, in contrast, is a variable factor of production that can be released when demand falls, so that workers bear the costs of their own unemployment. Whenever possible, therefore, industrialists seek out the stable, permanent portion of demand and reserve it for the deployment of capital, leaving the variable portion of demand to be met by the addition and subtraction of labor, a dualism that creates distinctions among workers and leads to segmentation of the labor force.

Workers in the capital-intensive primary sector get stable, skilled jobs working with good tools and equipment. Employers are forced to invest in their human capital through training and education. Primary-sector jobs are complicated and require considerable knowledge and experience to perform, leading to the accumulation of firm-and job-specific knowledge. Primary-sector workers also tend to be unionized or highly professionalized, with contracts that require employers to bear a substantial share of the costs of layoffs (in the form of severance pay and unemployment benefits). Because of these costs and continuing obligations, workers in the primary sector become expensive to let go; they become more like capital.

The labor-intensive secondary sector, in contrast, is composed of poorly paid, unstable jobs from which workers may be laid off at any time with little or no cost to the employer. During down cycles an employer's first act is to shed such workers to cut the payroll. The resulting dualism thus yields a segmented labor market structure. Low wages, unstable conditions, and the lack of reasonable mobility prospects make it difficult to attract native workers into the secondary sector. They are instead drawn into the primary, capital-intensive sector, where wages are higher, jobs are more secure, and there is a possibility of occupational advancement. To fill the shortfall in demand within the secondary sector, employers turn to immigrants.

Taken together, motivation problems, structural inflation, and economic dualism create a demand for a particular kind of worker: one who is willing to labor under unpleasant conditions, at low wages, in jobs with great instability and little chance for advancement. In the past this demand was met by women, teenagers, and rural-to-urban migrants. * * *

* * *

In advanced industrial societies, however, these three sources of entry-level workers have drastically shrunk over time because of four fundamental demographic trends: the rise in female labor force participation, which has transformed women's work into a career pursued for social status as well an income; the rise in divorce rates, which has transformed women's employment into a source of primary support; the decline in birthrates and the extension of formal education, which have produced small cohorts of teenagers entering the labor force; and the urbanization of society, which has eliminated farms and rural communities as potential sources for new migrants to the city. The imbalance between the structural demand for entry-level workers and the limited domestic supply of such workers has generated an underlying, long-run demand for immigrants in developed countries.

WHY PEOPLE CONTINUE TO MIGRATE

Immigration may begin for a variety of reasons, but the forces that initiate international movement are quite different from those that perpetuate it. Although wage differentials, market failures, and structural change may motivate people to move in the first place, new conditions arise in the course of migration to make additional movement more likely, leading to the perpetuation of international migration across time and space. * * *

* * * Migrant networks are an important source of social capital for people contemplating a move abroad. They are sets of interpersonal ties that connect migrants, former migrants, and nonmigrants at place of origin and destination through reciprocal ties of kinship, friendship, and shared community origin. They increase the likelihood of international movement because they lower the costs and risks of movement and increase the expected net returns to migration.

* * *

The first migrants who leave for a new destination have no social ties to draw upon, and for them migration is costly, particularly if it involves entering another country without documents. After the first migrants have left, however, the potential costs of migration are substantially lowered for the friends and relatives left behind. * * *

Once international migration has begun, private institutions and voluntary organizations also arise to satisfy the demand created by the growing imbalance between the large number of people seek entry into capital-rich countries and the limited supply of visas they typically offer. This imbalance and the barriers that developed countries erect to keep people out create a lucrative niche for entrepreneurs dedicated to promoting international movement for profit, yielding a black market in migration services. As this underground market creates conditions conducive to exploitation and victimization, humanitarian organizations also arise to enforce the right and improve the treatment of both legal and undocumented migrants. * * *

* * * [The *cumulative causation of migration* occurs as] each act of migration alters the social context within which subsequent migration decisions are made, thus increasing the likelihood of additional movement. Once the number of network connections in a community reaches a critical threshold, migration becomes self-perpetuating because each act of migration creates the social structure needed to sustain it.

In any bounded population, of course, processes of cumulative causation cannot continue ad infinitum. If migration continues long enough, networks eventually reach a point of saturation within any particular community. More and more community members reside in branch settlements overseas, and virtually all of those at home are connected to someone who lives abroad or has substantial foreign experience. When networks reach such a high level of elaboration, the costs of migration do not fall as sharply with each new migrant, and migration loses its dynamic momentum for growth. The prevalence of migration in the community approaches an upper limit, and migratory experience become so diffused that the stock of potential new migrants becomes very small and is increasingly composed of women, children, and the elderly.

If migration continues long enough, labor shortages and rising wages in the home community may further dampen the pressures for emigration, causing the rate of entry into the international migrant workforce to trial off. * * *

Because the theories discussed in this chapter posit causal mechanisms operating at multiple levels of aggregation, the various explanations are not logically contradictory. It is entirely possible for individuals to engage in cost-benefits calculations; for households to seek to minimize risk and overcome barriers to capital and credit; for both individuals and households to draw upon social capital to facilitate international movement; and for the socioeconomic context within which migration decisions are made to be determined by structural forces operating at the national and international levels, often influenced by migration itself. * * *

QUESTIONS ON THEORIES OF MIGRATION

1.   Whose theory of migration do you find most persuasive? Although the authors' emphases differ, can they be viewed as consistent with each other?

2.   What are the implications of their views for the kinds of immigration laws that Congress might consider enacting? For example, how would legislators who agree with Borjas or with Portes & Böröcz adopt different responses to undocumented immigration? How might they adopt different reforms of the immigrant admission categories? What would Massey and his co-authors think about a guest worker program? How would they design a program to control immigration from Mexico to the United States?

SECTION D.   MORAL CONSTRAINTS ON THE EXERCISE OF THE IMMIGRATION POWER

The differing perspectives on why people move do not lead to neat conclusions about what societies should do in response to migration. In the United States, as you know from having read *Chae Chan Ping* and *Fong Yue Ting*, Congress has broad constitutional authority to regulate immigration. How Congress should use this power poses difficult questions, whose disparate answers remain sharply contested. In beginning to formulate answers to those questions we believe that it is important first to explore possible moral bases for, or constraints upon, the exercise of the immigration power. If our presence in the United States is essentially an accident of birth, what gives us the right to keep others from entering? What is the nature of our moral claim to the territory of the United States? What is our responsibility to needy people living in other parts of the world? To needy people in the United States? The following materials are intended to help you focus on these questions.

BRUCE ACKERMAN, SOCIAL JUSTICE IN THE LIBERAL STATE
93–95 (1980).*

* * * Quite unthinkingly, we have come to accept the idea that we have the right to exclude nonresidents from our midst. * * * [But] it is only a very strong empirical claim that can permit the American to justify exclusion of the foreign-born from "his" liberal state.

To simplify the argument, divide the world into two nation-states, the poor East and the rich West. Assume further that Western domestic institutions are organized in a liberalish way while the East is an authoritarian dictatorship in which a small elite explicitly declares its superiority over the masses they exploit. Assume, finally, that as part of its second-best response to this dark reality, the West has adopted a forthcoming immigration policy, admitting a large number, Z, of Easterners on a first-come, first-served basis. Indeed, Z is so large that it strains the capacity of Western institutions to sustain a liberal political conversation. Any more than Z and the West's standing as a liberal society will be endangered; the presence of so many alien newcomers will generate such anxiety in the native population that it will prove impossible to stop a fascist group from seizing political power to assure native control over the immigrant underclass. Nonetheless, the Easterners keep coming at an awesome rate; the scene takes place at the armed Western border:

Easterner: I demand recognition as a citizen of this liberal state.

Western Statesman: We refuse.

Easterner: What gives you the right to refuse me? Do you think I would fail to qualify as a citizen of an ideal liberal state?

Westerner: Not at all.

Easterner: Do you imagine you're better than me simply because you've been born west of this frontier?

Westerner: No. If that were all, I would not hesitate before admitting you.

Easterner: Well, then, what's the trouble?

Westerner: The fact is that we in the West are far from achieving a perfect technology of justice; if we admit more than Z newcomers, our existing institutions will be unable to function in anything but an explicitly authoritarian manner.

Easterner: But why am I being asked to bear the costs of imperfection?

Westerner: Sorry, we're doing everything we can. But Z is the limit on immigrants.

Easterner: But you're not doing everything. Why not expel some of your native-born Westerners and make room for me? Do you think they're better than I am?

Westerner: Z is the limit on our assimilative capacity only on the assumption that there exists a cadre of natives familiar with the operation of liberal institutions. If some of the natives were removed from the population, even Z would be too many.

Easterner: So what am I to do? I'll be dead before I get to the front of the line of immigrants.

Westerner: Go back among your own people and build your own liberal state. We'll try to help you out as best we can.

* * *

The *only* reason for restricting immigration is to protect the ongoing process of liberal conversation itself. Can our present immigration practices be rationalized on this ground?

MICHAEL WALZER, SPHERES OF JUSTICE: A DEFENSE OF PLURALISM AND EQUALITY

31–34, 37–40, 45, 47–49, 61–62 (1983).*

The idea of distributive justice presupposes a bounded world within which distributions [take] place: a group of people committed to dividing, exchanging, and sharing social goods, first of all among themselves. That world * * * is the political community, whose members distribute power to one another and avoid, if they possibly can, sharing it with anyone else. When we think about distributive justice, we think about independent cities or countries capable of arranging their own patterns of division and exchange, justly or unjustly. We assume an established group and a fixed population, and so we miss the first and most important distributive question: How is that group constituted?

I don't mean, How *was* it constituted? I am concerned here not with the historical origins of the different groups, but with the decisions they make in the present about their present and future populations. The primary good that we distribute to one another is membership in some human community. And what we do with regard to membership structures all our other distributive choices: it determines with whom we make those choices, from whom we require obedience and collect taxes, to whom we allocate goods and services.

* * *

* * * Since human beings are highly mobile, large numbers of men and women regularly attempt to change their residence and their membership, moving from unfavored to favored environments. Affluent and free countries are, like élite universities, besieged by applicants. They have to decide on their own size and character. More precisely, as citizens of such a country, we have to decide: Whom should we admit? Ought we to have open admissions? Can we choose among applicants? What are the appropriate criteria for distributing membership?

The plural pronouns that I have used in asking these questions suggest the conventional answer to them: we who are already members do the choosing, in accordance with our own understanding of what membership means in our community and of what sort of a community we want to have. Membership as a social good is constituted by our understanding; its value is fixed by our work and conversation; and then we are in charge (who else could be in charge?) of its distribution. But we don't distribute it among ourselves; it is already ours. We give it out to strangers. Hence the choice is also governed by our relationships with strangers—not only by our understanding of those relationships but also by the actual contacts, connections, alliances we have established and the effects we have had beyond our borders. * * *

* * * In a number of ancient languages, Latin among them, strangers and enemies were named by a single word. We have come only slowly, through a long process of trial and error, to distinguish the two and to acknowledge that, in certain circumstances, strangers (but not enemies) might be entitled to our hospitality, assistance, and good will. This acknowledgment can be formalized as the principle of mutual aid, which suggests the duties that we owe, as John Rawls has written, "not only to definite individuals, say to those cooperating together in some social arrangement, but to persons generally." Mutual aid extends across political (and also cultural, religious, and linguistic) frontiers. The philosophical grounds of the principle are hard to specify (its history provides its practical ground). * * *

It is the absence of any cooperative arrangements that sets the context for mutual aid: two strangers meet at sea or in the desert or, as in the Good Samaritan story, by the side of the road. What precisely they owe one another is by no means clear, but we commonly say of such cases that positive assistance is required if (1) it is needed or urgently needed by one of the parties; and (2) if the risks and costs of giving it are relatively low for the other party. Given these conditions, I ought to stop and help the injured stranger, wherever I meet him, whatever his membership or my own. This is our morality; conceivably his, too. It is, moreover, an obligation that can be read out in roughly the same form at the collective level. Groups of people ought to help necessitous strangers whom they somehow discover in their midst or on their path. But the limit on risks and costs in these cases is sharply drawn. I need not take the injured stranger into my home, except briefly, and I certainly need not care for him or even associate with him for the rest of my life. My life cannot be shaped and determined by such chance encounters. Governor John Winthrop, arguing against free immigration to the new Puritan commonwealth of Massachusetts, insisted that this right of refusal applies also to collective mutual aid: "As for hospitality, that rule does not bind further than for some present occasion, not for continual residence." Whether Winthrop's view can be defended is a question that I shall come to only gradually. Here I only want to point to mutual aid as a (possible) external principle for the distribution of membership, a principle that doesn't depend upon the prevailing view of membership within a particular society. The force of the principle is uncertain, in part because of its own vagueness, in part because it sometimes comes up against the internal force of social meanings. And these meanings can be specified, and are specified, through the decision-making processes of the political community.

* * * [S]o long as members and strangers are, as they are at present, two distinct groups, admissions decisions have to be made, men and women taken in or refused. Given the indeterminate requirements of mutual aid, these decisions are not constrained by any widely accepted standard. That's why the admissions policies of countries are rarely criticized, except in terms suggesting that the only relevant criteria are those of charity, not justice. It is certainly possible that a deeper criticism would lead one to deny the member/stranger distinction. But I shall try, nevertheless, to defend that distinction and then to describe the internal and the external principles that govern the distribution of membership.

* * *

* * * The same writers who defended free trade in the nineteenth century also defended unrestricted immigration. They argued for perfect freedom of contract, without any political restraint. International society, they thought, should take shape as a world of neighborhoods, with individuals moving freely about, seeking private advancement. In their view, as Henry Sidgwick reported it in the 1890s, the only business of state officials is "to maintain order over [a] particular territory ... but not in any way to determine who is to inhabit this territory, or to restrict the enjoyment of its natural advantages to any particular portion of the human race." Natural advantages (like markets) are open to all comers, within the limits of private property rights; and if they are used up or devalued by overcrowding, people presumably will move on, into the jurisdiction of new sets of officials.

Sidgwick thought that this is possibly the "ideal of the future," but he offered three arguments against a world of neighborhoods in the present. First of all, such a world would not allow for patriotic sentiment, and so the "casual aggregates" that would probably result from the free movement of individuals would "lack internal cohesion." Neighbors would be strangers to one another. Second, free movement might interfere with efforts "to raise the standard of living among the poorer classes" of a particular country, since such efforts could not be undertaken with equal energy and success everywhere in the world. And, third, the promotion of moral and intellectual culture and the efficient working of political institutions might be "defeated" by the continual creation of heterogeneous populations. Sidgwick presented these three arguments as a series of utilitarian considerations that weigh against the benefits of labor mobility and contractual freedom. But they seem to me to have a rather different character. The last two arguments draw their force from the first, but only if the first is conceived in non-utilitarian terms. It is only if patriotic sentiment has some moral basis, only if communal cohesion makes for obligations and shared meanings, only if there are members as well as strangers, that state officials would have any reason to worry especially about the welfare of their own people (and of *all* their own people) and the success of their own culture and politics. For it is at least dubious that the average standard of living of the poorer classes throughout the world would decline under conditions of perfect labor mobility. Nor is there firm evidence that culture cannot thrive in cosmopolitan environments, nor that it is impossible to govern casual aggregations of people. As for the last of these, political theorists long ago discovered that certain sorts of regimes—namely, authoritarian regimes—thrive in the absence of communal cohesion. That perfect mobility makes for authoritarianism might suggest a utilitarian argument against mobility; but such an argument would work only if individual men and women, free to come and go, expressed a desire for some other form of government. And that they might not do.

Perfect labor mobility, however, is probably a mirage, for it is almost certain to be resisted at the local level. Human beings, as I have said, move about a great deal, but not because they love to move. They are, most of them, inclined to stay where they are unless their life is very difficult there. They experience a tension between love of place and the discomforts of a particular place. While some of them leave their homes and become foreigners in new lands, others stay where they are and resent the foreigners in their own land. Hence, if states ever become large neighborhoods, it is likely that neighborhoods will become little states. Their members will organize to defend the local politics and culture against strangers. Historically, neighborhoods have turned into closed or parochial communities (leaving aside cases of legal coercion) whenever the state was open: in the cosmopolitan cities of multinational empires, for example, where state officials don't foster any particular identity but permit different groups to build their own institutional structures (as in ancient Alexandria), or in the receiving centers of mass immigration movements (early twentieth century New York) where the country is an open but also an alien world—or, alternatively, a world full of aliens. The case is similar where the state doesn't exist at all or in areas where it doesn't function. Where welfare monies are raised and spent locally, for example, as in a seventeenth-century English parish, the local people will seek to exclude newcomers who are likely welfare recipients. It is only the nationalization of welfare (or the nationalization of culture and politics) that opens the neighborhood communities to whoever chooses to come in.

Neighborhoods can be open only if countries are at least potentially closed. Only if the state makes a selection among would-be members and guarantees the loyalty, security, and welfare of the individuals it selects, can local communities take shape as "indifferent" associations, determined solely by personal preference and market capacity. Since individual choice is most dependent upon local mobility, this would seem to be the preferred arrangement in a society like our own. The politics and the culture of a modern democracy probably require the kind of largeness, and also the kind of boundedness, that states provide. I don't mean to deny the value of sectional cultures and ethnic communities; I mean only to suggest the rigidities that would be forced upon both in the absence of inclusive and protective states. To tear down the walls of the state is not, as Sidgwick worriedly suggested, to create a world without walls, but rather to create a thousand petty fortresses.

The fortresses, too, could be torn down: all that is necessary is a global state sufficiently powerful to overwhelm the local communities. Then the result would be the world of the political economists, as Sidgwick described it—a world of radically deracinated men and women. Neighborhoods might maintain some cohesive culture for a generation or two on a voluntary basis, but people would move in, people would move out; soon the cohesion would be gone. The distinctiveness of cultures and groups depends upon closure and, without it, cannot be conceived as a stable feature of human life. If this distinctiveness is a value, as most people (though some of them are global pluralists, and others only local loyalists) seem to believe, then closure must be permitted somewhere. At some level of political organization, something like the sovereign state must take shape and claim the authority to make its own admissions policy, to control and sometimes restrain the flow of immigrants.

* * *

* * * To say that states have a right to act in certain areas is not to say that anything they do in those areas is right. One can argue about particular admissions standards by appealing, for example, to the condition and character of the host country and to the shared understandings of those who are already members. * * * Decisions of this sort are subject to constraint, but what the constraints are I am not yet ready to say. It is important first to insist that the distribution of membership in American society, and in any ongoing society, is a matter of political decision. The labor market may be given free rein, as it was for many decades in the United States, but that does not happen by an act of nature or of God; it depends upon choices that are ultimately political. What kind of community do the citizens want to create? With what other men and women do they want to share and exchange social goods?

* * *

Can a political community exclude destitute and hungry, persecuted and stateless—in a word, necessitous—men and women simply because they are foreigners? Are citizens bound to take in strangers? Let us assume that the citizens have no formal obligations; they are bound by nothing more stringent than the principle of mutual aid. The principle must be applied, however, not to individuals directly but to the citizens as a group, for immigration is a matter of political decision. Individuals participate in the decision making, if the state is democratic; but they decide not for themselves but for the community generally. And this fact has moral implications. It replaces immediacy with distance and the personal expense of time and energy with impersonal bureaucratic costs. Despite John Winthrop's claim, mutual aid is more coercive for political communities than it is for individuals because a wide range of benevolent actions is open to the community which will only marginally affect its present members * * *. * * * These actions probably include the admission of strangers, for admission to a country does not entail the kinds of intimacy that could hardly be avoided in the case of clubs and families. Might not admission, then, be morally imperative, at least for these strangers, who have no other place to go?

* * *

* * * [Wealth, resources and territory] can be superfluous, far beyond what the inhabitants of a particular state require for a decent life (even as they themselves define the meaning of a decent life). Are those inhabitants morally bound to admit immigrants from poorer countries for as long as superfluous resources exist? Or are they bound even longer than that, beyond the limits of mutual aid, until a policy of open admissions ceases to attract and benefit the poorest people in the world? Sidgwick seems to have opted for the first of these possibilities; he proposed a primitive and parochial version of Rawls's difference principle: immigration can be restricted as soon as failure to do so would "interfere materially ... with the efforts of the government to maintain an adequately high standard of life among the members of the community generally—especially the poorer classes." But the community might well decide to cut off immigration even before that, if it were willing to export (some of) its superfluous wealth. * * * [T]hey could share their wealth with necessitous strangers outside their country or with necessitous strangers inside their country. But just how much of their wealth do they have to share? Once again, there must be some limit, short (and probably considerably short) of simple equality, else communal wealth would be subject to indefinite drainage. The very phrase "communal wealth" would lose its meaning if all resources and all products were globally common. * * *

If we stop short of simple equality, there will continue to be many communities, with different histories, ways of life, climates, political structures, and economies. Some places in the world will still be more desirable than others, either to individual men and women with particular tastes and aspirations, or more generally. Some places will still be uncomfortable for at least some of their inhabitants. Hence immigration will remain an issue even after the claims of distributive justice have been met on a global scale—assuming, still, that global society is and ought to be pluralist in form and that the claims are fixed by some version of collective mutual aid. The different communities will still have to make admissions decisions and will still have a right to make them. If we cannot guarantee the full extent of the territorial or material base on which a group of people build a common life, we can still say that the common life, at least, is their own and that their comrades and associates are theirs to recognize or choose.

There is, however, one group of needy outsiders whose claims cannot be met by yielding territory or exporting wealth; they can be met only by taking people in. This is the group of refugees whose need is for membership itself, a non-exportable good. The liberty that makes certain countries possible homes for men and women whose politics or religion isn't tolerated where they live is also non-exportable: at least we have found no way of exporting it. These goods can be shared only within the protected space of a particular state. At the same time, admitting refugees doesn't necessarily decrease the amount of liberty the members enjoy within that space. The victims of political or religious persecution, then, make the most forceful claim for admission. If you don't take me in, they say, I shall be killed, persecuted, brutally oppressed by the rulers of my own country. What can we reply?

* * *

The distribution of membership is not pervasively subject to the constraints of justice. Across a considerable range of the decisions that are made, states are simply free to take in strangers (or not)—much as they are free, leaving aside the claims of the needy, to share their wealth with foreign friends, to honor the achievements of foreign artists, scholars, and scientists, to choose their trading partners, and to enter into collective security arrangements with foreign states. But the right to choose an admissions policy is more basic than any of these, for it is not merely a matter of acting in the world, exercising sovereignty, and pursuing national interests. At stake here is the shape of the community that acts in the world, exercises sovereignty, and so on. Admission and exclusion are at the core of communal independence. They suggest the deepest meaning of self-determination. Without them, there could not be *communities of character*, historically stable, ongoing associations of men and women with some special commitment to one another and some special sense of their common life.

But self-determination in the sphere of membership is not absolute. It is a right exercised, most often, by national clubs or families, but it is held in principle by territorial states. Hence it is subject both to internal decisions by the members themselves (*all* the members, including those who hold membership simply by right of place) and to the external principle of mutual aid. Immigration, then, is both a matter of political choice and moral constraint. * * *

JOSEPH H. CARENS, ALIENS AND CITIZENS: THE CASE FOR OPEN BORDERS

49 Review of Politics 251, 266–71 (1987).

* * * Walzer compares the idea of open states with our experience of neighborhoods as a form of open association. But in thinking about what open states would be like, we have a better comparison at hand. We can draw upon our experience of cities, provinces, or states in the American sense. These are familiar political communities whose borders are open. Unlike neighborhoods and like countries, they are formally organized communities with boundaries, distinctions between citizens and noncitizens, and elected officials who are expected to pursue policies that benefit the members of the community that elected them. They often have distinctive cultures and ways of life. Think of the differences between New York City and Waycross, Georgia, or between California and Kansas. These sorts of differences are often much greater than the differences among nation-states. Seattle has more in common with Vancouver than it does with many American communities. But cities and provinces and American states cannot restrict immigration (from other parts of the country). So, these cases call into question Walzer's claim that distinctiveness depends on the possibility of formal closure. What makes for distinctiveness and what erodes it is much more complex than political control of admissions.

This does not mean that control over admissions is unimportant. Often local communities would like to restrict immigration. The people of California wanted to keep out poor Oklahomans during the Depression. Now the people of Oregon would like to keep out the Californians. Internal migrations can be substantial. They can transform the character of communities. (Think of the migrations from the rural South to the urban North.) They can place strains on the local economy and make it difficult to maintain locally funded social programs. Despite all this, we do not think these political communities should be able to control their borders. The right to free migration takes priority.

Why should this be so? Is it just a choice that we make as a larger community (*i.e.*, the nation state) to restrict the self-determination of local communities in this way? Could we legitimately permit them to exclude? Not easily. No liberal state restricts internal mobility. Those states that do restrict internal mobility are criticized for denying basic human freedoms. If freedom of movement within the state is so important that it overrides the claims of local political communities, on what grounds can we restrict freedom of movement across states? This requires a stronger case for the *moral* distinctiveness of the nation-state as a form of community than Walzer's discussion of neighborhoods provides.

Walzer also draws an analogy between states and clubs. Clubs may generally admit or exclude whomever they want, although any particular decision may be criticized through an appeal to the character of the club and the shared understandings of its members. So, too, with states. This analogy ignores the familiar distinction between public and private, a distinction that Walzer makes use of elsewhere. There is a deep tension between the right of freedom of association and the right to equal treatment. One way to address this tension is to say that in the private sphere freedom of association prevails and in the public sphere equal treatment does. You can pick your friends on the basis of whatever criteria you wish, but in selecting people for offices you must treat all candidates fairly. Drawing a line between public and private is often problematic, but it is clear that clubs are normally at one end of the scale and states at the other. So, the fact that private clubs may admit or exclude whomever they choose says nothing about the appropriate admission standards for states. When the state acts it must treat individuals equally.

Against this, one may object that the requirement of equal treatment applies fully only to those who are already members of the community. That is accurate as a description of practice but the question is why it should be so. At one time, the requirement of equal treatment did not extend fully to various groups (workers, blacks, women). On the whole, the history of liberalism reflects a tendency to expand both the definition of the public sphere and the requirements of equal treatment. In the United States today, for example, in contrast to earlier times, both public agencies and private corporations may not legally exclude women simply because they are women (although private clubs still may). A white shopkeeper may no longer exclude blacks from his store (although he may exclude them from his home). I think these recent developments, like the earlier extension of the franchise, reflect something fundamental about the inner logic of liberalism. The extension of the right to immigrate reflects the same logic: equal treatment of individuals in the public sphere.

* * *

Any approach like Walzer's that seeks its ground in the tradition and culture of *our* community must confront, as a methodological paradox, the fact that liberalism is a central part of our culture. The enormous intellectual popularity of Rawls and Nozick and the enduring influence of utilitarianism attest to their ability to communicate contemporary understandings and shared meanings in a language that has legitimacy and power in our culture. These theories would not make such sense to a Buddhist monk in medieval Japan. But their individualistic assumptions and their language of universal, ahistorical reason makes sense to us because of *our* tradition, *our* culture, *our* community. For people in a different moral tradition, one that assumed fundamental moral differences between those inside the society and those outside, restrictions on immigration might be easy to justify. Those who are other simply might not count, or at least not count as much. But we cannot dismiss the aliens on the ground that they are other, because we are the products of a liberal culture.

* * *

* * * If my arguments are correct, the general case for open borders is deeply rooted in the fundamental values of our tradition. No moral argument will seem acceptable to *us*, if it directly challenges the assumption of the equal moral worth of all individuals. If restrictions on immigration are to be justified, they have to be based on arguments that respect that principle. Walzer's theory has many virtues that I have not explored here, but it does not supply an adequate argument for the state's right to exclude.

Free migration may not be immediately achievable, but it is a goal toward which we should strive. And we have an obligation to open our borders much more fully than we do now. The current restrictions on immigration in Western democracies—even in the most open ones like Canada and the United States—are not justifiable. Like feudal barriers to mobility, they protect unjust privilege.

Does it follow that there is *no* room for distinctions between aliens and citizens, no theory of citizenship, no boundaries for the community? Not at all. To say that membership is open to all who wish to join is not to say that there is no distinction between members and nonmembers. Those who choose to cooperate together in the state have special rights and obligations not shared by noncitizens. Respecting the particular choices and commitments that individuals make flows naturally from a commitment to the idea of equal moral worth. (Indeed, consent as a justification for political obligation is least problematic in the case of immigrants.) What is *not* readily compatible with the idea of equal moral worth is the exclusion of those who want to join. If people want to sign the social contract, they should be permitted to do so.

Open borders would threaten the distinctive character of different political communities only because we assume that so many people would move if they could. If the migrants were few, it would not matter. A few immigrants could always be absorbed without changing the character of the community. And, as Walzer observes, most human beings do not love to move. They normally feel attached to their native land and to the particular language, culture, and community in which they grew up and in which they feel at home. They seek to move only when life is very difficult where they are. Their concerns are rarely frivolous. So, it is right to weigh the claims of those who want to move against the claims of those who want to preserve the community as it is. And if we don't unfairly tip the scales, the case for exclusion will rarely triumph.

People live in communities with bonds and bounds, but these may be of different kinds. In a liberal society, the bonds and bounds should be compatible with liberal principles. Open immigration would change the character of the community but it would not leave the community without any character. It might destroy old ways of life, highly valued by some, but it would make possible new ways of life, highly valued by others. The whites in Forsythe County who want to keep out blacks are trying to preserve a way of life that is valuable to them. To deny such communities the right to exclude does limit their ability to shape their future character and destiny, but it does not utterly destroy their capacity for self-determination. Many aspects of communal life remain potentially subject to collective control. Moreover, constraining the kinds of choices that people and communities may make is what principles of justice are for. They set limits on what people seeking to abide by these principles may do. To commit ourselves to open borders would not be to abandon the idea of communal character but to reaffirm it. It would be an affirmation of the liberal character of the community and of its commitment to principles of justice.

NOTES AND QUESTIONS ON MORAL PERSPECTIVES ON IMMIGRATION CONTROL

1. To what extent are the positions of Ackerman, Walzer, and Carens reflected in the earlier discussion of the source of congressional authority to restrict immigration? (Recall particularly the structural justifications based on self-preservation and self-determination.)

2. For a comprehensive argument that elimination of U.S. border controls would "end the brutality inherent in enforcement of the current immigration controls," yield "economic benefits from free labor migration in a globalizing world economy," "recognize the economic and social reality of immigration," and lead to foreign policy benefits as well, see Kevin R. Johnson, Opening the Floodgates: Why America Needs to Eliminate its Borders and Rethink Immigration Law (2007).

3. Would a market for visas be an appropriate method fo allocating scarce membership rights? Julian Simon has argued for such a proposal, in order to get beyond the current "narrow range of tired options." Such a system, he contends, would produce better outcomes for our economy and the economies of poorer countries as well. "Individuals with the most to gain economically would offer the highest prices. Inevitably, these people would have the most to contribute economically to all of us." He also addresses one possible objection: "Would an auction mean only the wealthiest would get in? One way to prevent this is to allow 'buyers' to enter now and pay later together with income tax. Failure to pay might result in deportation." Further, "fees from the auction would put additional purchasing power into the hands of native Americans and provide a fund for foreign aid or scholarships in the United States for deserving foreign students." Simon, *Auction the Right to Be an Immigrant*, N.Y.Times, Jan. 28, 1986, at A25. For a similar proposal by Nobel Laureate economist Gary Becker, see *An Open Door for Immigrants—The Auction*, Wall St. J., Oct. 14, 1992, at A14.

4. What is the relationship between admission to, and rights to membership in, a polity? That is, does our thinking about whom we admit to the United States depend in part on the rights and obligations (and opportunity for full membership) entailed by admission? Consider Michael Walzer's view:

> One might insist, as I shall ultimately do, that the same standards apply to naturalization as to immigration, that every immigrant and every resident is a citizen, too—or at least, a potential citizen. That is why territorial admission is so serious a matter. The members must be

prepared to accept, as their own equals in a world of shared obligations, the men and women they admit; the immigrants must be prepared to share the obligations.

Walzer, *supra*, at 52.

In an essay Linda Bosniak expands on Walzer's principle of political inclusiveness for immigrants residing within a country's territory.

> [T]he rights and recognition enjoyed by immigrants are usually understood to derive from either their formal status under law or their territorial presence. According to the status-based conception, a person's rights are determined by the specific legal category she occupies in the country's immigration and nationality regime. The status of citizenship is understood to represent membership's culmination—the moment the individual is entitled to enjoy full rights and entitlements and duties— whereas alienage status of various kinds entails lesser rights.

> * * *

> In contrast to the status-based approach, the territorial conception of rights for immigrants treats a person's geographical presence itself as a sufficient basis for core aspects of membership. * * * This presence is not necessarily tied to, or preceded by, political consent, although it may be. The territorial conception repudiates the notion of differential levels of inclusion, regarding the maintenance of partial membership statuses as illegitimate under liberal and democratic principles. * * *

> * * * It seems to me that ethical territoriality appropriately insists on treating membership as a matter of social fact rather than as a legal formality. And by opposing the imposition of less-than-complete-membership on classes of residents, ethical territoriality honors the egalitarian and anti-caste commitments to which liberal constitutionalism purports to aspire.

> * * *

> * * * [I]t is both anti-democratic and morally wrong in liberal terms to allow for treatment of a class of persons who are living among us as social and political outsiders. Territorialism embodies an ethic of inclusiveness and equality: it is the ground (both literally and figuratively) of national community belonging.

Bosniak, *Being Here: Ethical Territoriality and the Rights of Immigrants*, 8 Theoretical Inquiries in Law 389, 390–392, 394 (2007). For a fuller exposition of these and related ideas, see L. Bosniak, The Citizen and the Alien: Dilemmas of Contemporary Membership (2006).

CHAPTER FOUR

FEDERAL AGENCIES AND COURTS

■ ■ ■

A person who decides she wants to immigrate to the United States may well start the process by visiting the American official most easily accessible: the consular officer posted to her home country. If she looks carefully at the signs around the entrance to the consulate, she may learn that consuls are officers of the Department of State. And, in short order, if she pursues her application, she will come into contact with a rather bewildering variety of other U.S. agencies.

She will probably need an approved visa petition from the Department of Homeland Security (DHS), through a process initiated by a close family member already in the United States, or by a prospective U.S. employer. If an employer is involved, the Department of Labor (DOL) may play an important role. If a family member's petition is denied, an appeal may take the case before the Board of Immigration Appeals (BIA), which is part of the Department of Justice (DOJ). Once a visa petition is approved, the action shifts back to the consulate for thorough screening before a visa issues. A doctor approved by the Public Health Service will probably perform a medical examination. At the port of entry, she will again encounter the DHS (but a different bureau this time) in the person of the immigration inspector, who is entitled to rethink the screening determination of the consular officer. If a dispute arises over eligibility or admission, she might find herself in immigration court, also part of DOJ. Litigation before the federal courts may be possible, but many agency decisions in the immigration arena are insulated from such review. And several other governmental players could become involved as well.

To help understand the key players we will encounter in succeeding chapters as we explore the substantive provisions of the Immigration and Nationality Act, this brief chapter describes the agencies that implement the law and provides a brief introduction to the courts that review some of these agencies' decisions.

SECTION A. FEDERAL AGENCIES

U.S. practice has traditionally divided authority to administer the immigration laws among agencies based on whether the regulatory activity occurs outside the United States, on the one hand, or inside the country or at its borders and ports of entry, on the other. Authority outside the United States, in general, has been given to the Department of State, which has embassies or consulates in virtually all of the 193 other countries of the world. Authority exercised on U.S. soil has been placed in a succession of officers and departments over the past 120 years. Since the creation of the Department of Homeland Security in 2003, it now generally belongs to DHS. The Department of Justice, however, also plays an important role in the domestic sphere. DOJ is the institutional home to the immigration judges (IJs), who preside over removal hearings, and to the Board of Immigration Appeals, which reviews IJ decisions in removal cases as well as a select range of administrative decisions made by DHS officers.

Figure 4.1
Organization of DHS Immigration Functions

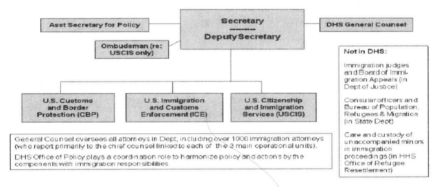

1. THE DEPARTMENT OF HOMELAND SECURITY AND ITS PREDECESSORS

a. History

Early federal regulation of immigration was under the authority of the Secretary of the Treasury, who initially had to act through state officials, usually designated by state governors. In 1891, Congress decided that such divided authority was unworkable. It created the federal post of Superintendent of Immigration within the Treasury Department, and federal officials shortly thereafter took over from the states full responsibility for administering the immigration laws. Federal immigration functions were seen as part of the regulation of labor from 1903 to 1940, and were accordingly housed in the departments holding that general authority. The Border Patrol was chartered in 1924 as part of the Bureau of Immigration in the Department of Labor. A 1940 Executive Order, motivated in part by security concerns as war engulfed Europe, transferred immigration and naturalization functions, which by then had been lodged for several years in a unified Immigration and Naturalization Service

(INS) in DOL, to the Department of Justice. There they remained until 2003, when the Department of Homeland Security came into being. INS was thus the principal unit managing immigration functions for nearly 70 years, and it will still appear as the main governmental agency in some of the cases and other readings presented in this book.

The Immigration and Nationality Act (INA), passed in 1952, also—and confusingly—still reflects this basic twentieth-century institutional structure. By its terms the statute still assigns most immigration authorities to the Attorney General, the cabinet officer who heads DOJ, and specifies a few for "the Service" (INS). But the AG today retains only a fraction of these INA authorities, mostly having to do with matters decided by immigration courts, and INS has been abolished.

After the terrorist attacks of September 11, 2001, Congress passed new legislation, the Homeland Security Act (HSA), Pub.L. 107–296, 116 Stat. 2135 (2002), to create a new cabinet department and consolidate there a host of agencies whose functions relate to homeland security, including the Coast Guard, the Secret Service, the Federal Emergency Management Agency (FEMA), the Transportation Security Administration (responsible for screening airline passengers), and the Customs Service (responsible for regulating the international movement of goods in order to enforce import and export laws and collect taxes on imports). Because the 9/11 attacks were carried out by noncitizens admitted on temporary visas, it is not surprising that most immigration control functions were also moved to the new Department of Homeland Security. The HSA did so through block transfers from DOJ of broadly described authorities, usually without directly amending the INA; hence the confusion. Most of the authorities and powers described in the INA as exercised by the Attorney General—but not all—now actually belong to the Secretary of Homeland Security.

b.   The Components of DHS

Dismay at the failure to block the terrorists' entry or to apprehend them later (after many had violated the terms of their initial admission) combined with other longstanding complaints about INS to win wide support for this reorganization. The HSA, however, did not simply transfer INS intact to the new department. Worried about potentially contradictory missions, Congress also directed a significant restructuring of immigration functions. In general, it divided INS' former authorities between different units, separating enforcement from services. The services function—also called adjudications or benefits—involves the approval or denial of applications filed by would-be migrants seeking to enter the United States or to modify their legal status here, or by their sponsors, as well as petitions for naturalization. Enforcement involves such activities as patrolling the border, investigating violations, arresting violators, and providing for their detention and removal. The HSA contemplated a two-way split between services and enforcement, but before this scheme took effect, the administration of President George W. Bush decided on a

Cars and pedestrians line up for inspection before entering the
United States at the busy port of entry between Tijuana
and San Diego. (Photo: David McNew/Getty Images)

different approach to enforcement, which resulted in three new DHS units inheriting INS functions. In order to present "one face at the border," presidential directives essentially combined immigration enforcement with customs enforcement and then redivided these enforcement functions along geographical lines—in very rough terms, border vs. interior. *See* Martin, *Immigration Policy and the Homeland Security Act Reorganization: An Early Agenda for Practical Improvements,* 80 Interp.Rel. 601 (2003). Obviously the three bureaus of DHS with immigration responsibilities (known as CBP, ICE, and USCIS) still face many common or overlapping issues. In 2005, the Department reorganized further, enhancing the role of the Assistant Secretary for Policy in assuring coordination among the various units with immigration responsibilities. Coordination remains a serious problem, however, and the transfer of immigration functions into DHS certainly has not resolved the longstanding grievances that contributed to Congress' decision to abolish the INS.

(i) Customs and Border Protection (CBP)

The DHS component known as U.S. Customs and Border Protection (CBP) is responsible for the border enforcement mission and is intended to operate as a unified border agency, screening both people and cargo. In fiscal year (FY) 2010, it had over 58,000 employees and a budget of $11.5 billion.

Inspections. CBP inherited the full INS inspector corps—the officers who review passports and visas at the booths in international airports and other ports of entry—as well as customs and agriculture inspectors transferred from the Departments of Treasury and Agriculture. The inspectors' function under the immigration laws is to examine the documents, or other evidence of entitlement to enter, presented by aliens and citizens arriving at more than 330 official ports of entry. CBP also staffs preclearance stations in Canada, Ireland, and the Caribbean, which permit the completion of inspection before passengers board the aircraft bound for the United States.

In recent years, about 400 million persons have been inspected and admitted annually, 50–60 percent of them noncitizens. (The inspections total includes multiple counting of people who make multiple entries.) In a typical year, 98 percent are admitted after what is called primary inspection, the brief encounter with the inspector at the initial booth. The other two percent are referred to secondary inspection for more detailed questioning, but the overwhelming majority of them are found admissible at that point, perhaps after they or their friends present additional information to clear up apparent problems. Of the small number denied entry after inspection (roughly 400,000), only about a fifth are removed pursuant to a formal removal order. Most of the rest are allowed to withdraw their applications for admission (this requires CBP permission), and so head home without the complications that ensue from formal removal. *See* DHS Office of Immigration Statistics, *Immigration Enforcement Actions: 2005* (Nov. 2006); *id.: 2010* (June 2011); TRAC, *Immigration Inspections When Arriving in the U.S.* (2006), available at <http://trac.syr.edu/immigration/reports/142/>.

Border Patrol. The other major component of CBP is the Border Patrol. Its work focuses on the areas between land border ports of entry, in order to prevent or deter unauthorized entries and to apprehend violators. The Border Patrol has its own distinctive geographic and bureaucratic organization pattern, broken down into 20 Sectors that ring the country, each headed by a Chief Patrol Agent. Strengthening border enforcement (as distinct from immigration enforcement in the interior of the United States) has drawn strong support from both Republicans and Democrats over the past decade. Consequently, Congress has greatly increased funding, and the ranks of the Border Patrol have grown from just under 4,000 agents at the end of 1993 to 10,000 in 2004, to over 20,000 in 2010. Congress appears likely to fund continued rapid growth.

The executive branch has also used this enhanced staffing to change strategies and thus make it harder to cross the southwestern border. Since the mid–1990s, the Border Patrol has emphasized "forward deployment," posting agents in visible locations within sight of each other along the border at all significant crossing regions, augmented by better fencing and more lighting. The purpose is to deter any attempt at entry rather than simply, as in the past, chasing and catching an erratic percentage of violators after they move across the line. The new strategy has succeeded in greatly reducing attempted crossings in former high-traffic places like San Diego and El Paso, but smugglers in response turned to guiding persons across more forbidding and remote desert areas. The Border Patrol makes use of technology, including nearly 300 CBP aircraft (some of them remote-operated pilotless planes) and increasingly sophisticated sensors, to locate such clandestine crossers. It has also augmented its search and rescue capacity, because the greater traffic through the deserts resulted in a higher death toll along the border among persons attempting entry. Border Patrol apprehensions have fluctuated between 800,000 and 1.7 million a year from 1983 to 2007. But enhanced deployments, coupled with the declining economy, have reduced attempted crossings thereafter, dropping apprehensions below 800,000 each year, to a new low of 463,000 in FY 2010—a level not seen since the early 1970s.

A Border Patrol agent scouts the boundary fence near Yuma, Arizona.
(Photo: Department of Homeland Security)

(ii) Immigration and Customs Enforcement (ICE)

Overview. Interior enforcement of both customs and immigration laws is the responsibility of U.S. Immigration and Customs Enforcement (ICE). This DHS component is responsible for locating and arresting or charging persons illegally in the country, representing the government in removal proceedings in immigration court, conducting efforts against fraud and smuggling (involving the movement of either human beings or goods), enforcing the laws against unauthorized employment of noncitizens, and also carrying out the former Customs Service's tasks in battling, for example, money laundering and child pornography. In FY 2010,

Congress appropriated $5.7 billion for ICE operations. ICE is the principal investigative arm of DHS and the second largest investigative agency in the federal government, after the Federal Bureau of Investigation (FBI). It has over 7,000 investigative officers in its Office of Homeland Security Investigations (HSI), which focuses primarily on complex criminal investigations, but also has responsibility for investigating violations of the employment verification laws and visa violations in the United States and abroad.

Enforcement and Removal Operations. ICE's civil immigration enforcement duties are handled primarily by its Office of Enforcement and Removal Operations (ERO), with over 8,000 officers and support staff, most based in field offices throughout the country. ERO handles the surprisingly complex logistics of taking custody of noncitizens detained during removal proceedings, assuring their presence every time they have a hearing in immigration court, and securing the ultimate removal of those (detained or not) who receive final removal orders or agree to depart under supervision. ERO also coordinates with state and local law enforcement to identify and detain criminal violators who are removable, and it pursues persons who fail to leave when ordered or who return without permission after being deported, among other duties.

Congress's steadily increased appropriations for immigration enforcement have resulted in ICE operating the largest detention and supervised release system in the country. In FY 2010, ICE detained 363,000 individuals and had over 33,000 detention beds at its disposal, in either its own detention facilities, contract facilities run by private corporations, or local jails that make space available for immigration detention pursuant to intergovernmental agreements. Responding to major controversies over the previous decade regarding conditions of detention, detainee medical care, and access to family and counsel, among other matters, ICE embarked in 2009 on significant reforms to the detention system. The reforms emphasize consolidation of facilities into a smaller network, new facilities located close to major concentrations of noncitizen population, an online detainee locator system opened in 2010, increased use of supervised release during removal proceedings, revamped medical care, revised detention standards, and especially new and better funded mechanisms for monitoring of detention facilities. Full implementation will require many years. *See* ICE, *Immigration Detention Overview and Recommendations* (report mapping reform plans, prepared by Dr. Dora Schriro, Oct. 6, 2009), <http://www.ice.gov/doclib/about/offices/odpp/pdf/ice-detention-rpt.pdf>; DHS Fact Sheet, *ICE Detention Reform: Principles And Next Steps* (Oct. 6, 2009), <http://www.dhs.gov/xlibrary/assets/press_ice_detention_reform_fact_sheet.pdf>.

ICE reported over 380,000 removals and returns in FY 2010. Removals take place under a removal order; returns result from ICE enforcement activity but did not involve a formal order. In effectuating its mission, ICE arranges to transport over 300,000 people to their countries of nationality every year. For these purposes ERO operates its own system of daily or weekly bus routes (with a fleet as large as Greyhound), running, for example, from Minnesota to the southern Texas border, to accomplish the deportation of Mexicans. For other nationalities, deportation officers book air travel on commercial flights (sometimes with officer escorts) or chartered planes, or use DHS planes. A high percentage of non-Mexican removals require ERO to secure travel documents or other permission from the receiving country, in a labor-intensive case-by-case process. Some governments resist or drag their feet in accepting return. A few simply refuse to take back their nationals from the United States.

(iii) Citizenship and Immigration Services (USCIS)

Overview. Consider now the service side of immigration management—adjudicating applications for various benefits. For example, when a grandfather from the old country who has come to visit decides he would like to stay a bit longer with his granddaughter, he must apply for an extension of stay as a tourist or, to use the technical term, a "temporary visitor for pleasure." When a student who has come to this country as a nonimmigrant marries a citizen and decides to settle here (a not infrequent occurrence), she must apply for adjustment of her status to that of a lawful permanent resident. Later, after a specified period of residence, if she decides to become a U.S. citizen, she must petition for naturalization. And when a citizen decides to help her brother come from abroad to resettle here as an immigrant, the process does not start overseas where the brother is located. It begins instead with the citizen filing a visa petition with the immigration authorities in the United States. An examiner will review the petition in order to verify the claimed family relationship and establish prima facie qualification for preference immigration. Before an immigrant visa will issue, several other steps must be completed, many of them by U.S. consular officials in the brother's home country. In each such case (and there are many other examples), the officer who passes on the petition or request must decide whether the application is complete and bona fide, whether it meets the requirements set forth in the statute and the regulations, and in many cases whether the applicant further merits a favorable exercise of the discretion that the INA vests in the agency.

These decisions by examiners amount to adjudication, but in most cases, this is not the kind of "adjudication" that lawyers tend to think of—a formal hearing involving two contestants battling out the issues before a relatively passive decisionmaker. Much of the time the applicant does not even see in person the officer who will make the decision. The case must instead be made in writing on one of dozens of prescribed forms that work their way through the agency by the thousands each day. If personal contact does occur, it usually takes the form of a rather informal interview conducted by an examiner. Quite often, the individual applicant is not represented by counsel. In recent years, over six million applications and petitions for benefits under the INA (including naturalization applications) have been filed annually.

These immigration benefits are adjudicated by U.S. Citizenship and Immigration Services (USCIS), the third component within DHS to inherit a portion of the duties formerly performed by INS. USCIS had a budget of $2.8 billion in FY 2010. Congress has mandated that nearly all of the cost of its operations and capital investments come from fees imposed on applicants for immigration benefits; hence application fees are quite high. USCIS is staffed by over 18,000 employees and contract personnel.

Congress also created an Ombudsman's office in 2003, meant to help deal with customer questions or grievances about immigration services. That office has not been funded at a level that permits detailed investigation of each complaint, but it does draw upon the complaints it receives, plus other inquiry, to issue broader management review reports with suggestions for improvements in specific USCIS functions. The Ombudsman has no jurisdiction over immigration enforcement.

Offices and processes. Nearly all immigration benefit applications are filed today by mail, and sometimes electronically, sent either to one of four Regional Service Centers, to the National Benefits Center, or to a specified centralized intake facility, called a "lockbox." The instructions to the relevant application form indicate precisely how and where it should be filed. (USCIS forms and instructions are available on its website, <http://www.uscis.gov/portal/site/uscis>.) The receipt staff performs initial functions such as checking for completeness of the papers and inclusion of the appropriate fee, logging in the application and generating a receipt to be mailed back to the applicant, creating the administrative file, sending it to the appropriate officer for decision, and scheduling an interview at a field office, if an interview is needed.

USCIS has a variety of different types of field offices, beyond the Service Centers. In addition to dozens of primary offices throughout the country (and in 30 international locations), where interviews are conducted, USCIS has 135 Application Support Centers, designed to take the fingerprints now required for nearly all applications, in a secure and reliable fashion. Also, in recognition that asylum adjudications require unique skills and training, a separate asylum corps considers those applications. USCIS Asylum Offices are located in eight cities around the country, staffed by over 250 asylum officers. USCIS also manages two important computerized immigration status verification systems: Systematic Alien Verification for Entitlements (SAVE), which is checked by federal and state benefit-granting agencies, and E–Verify, which enrolled employers can use to check the employment status of their new hires.

USCIS is in the early stages of a multi-year revamping of all its business processes, in order to move from a paper-based to an electronic-based process. This change will also eventually benefit ICE and CBP as well, because all immigration functions have been dependent on paper files, known as A-files, which are often lost or delayed in transmission, thereby preventing or slowing both adjudications and enforcement actions. The change is known as USCIS Transformation, and it involves redesigning current processes, plus the gradual changeover, benefit by benefit (starting with nonimmigrant benefits) to the new electronic environment. See 88 Interp.Rel. 2065 (2011) (describing the first set of regulation changes to implement Transformation, 76 Fed. Reg. 53764 (Aug. 29, 2011)). In the meantime, USCIS launched in 2009 a new system, accessible at <https://egov.uscis.gov/cris/Dashboard.do>, that allows all of its customers to check the status of their cases online. That same web page provides access to information about average case processing times by specific benefit, so that noncitizens or their lawyers can get an idea of how much longer they may have to wait for a decision.

c. Regulations and Other Forms of Guidance

Immigration regulations are published in Title 8 of the Code of Federal Regulations, usually after notice-and-comment rulemaking in accordance with the Administrative Procedure Act (APA), 5 U.S.C. § 553. For guidance, immigration officers also have relied on "Operations Instructions" (OIs). Although many OIs read like regulations, they were issued without going through the APA rulemaking procedures, and they serve more as an internal operating manual. Unlike regulations, they do not have the force of law. Most such guidance has now been collected into a series of DHS field manuals, which are generally available to the public. (Sections containing classified or law-enforcement-sensitive information are withheld.) Guidance of this type is reprinted in appendix volumes of immigration treatises, such as C. Gordon, S. Mailman, & S. Yale–Loehr, *Immigration Law and Procedure* (1966 & rev. 2011), or A. Gallagher, *Immigration Law Service 2d* (2008 and rev. 2011). Many guidance documents can also be found on the USCIS website, Westlaw, and other online sources. The immigration agencies also communicate guidance to field offices by means of a variety of policy wires, cables, and memoranda. The important ones are carried in weekly reporting services like *Interpreter Releases* (Thomson Reuters/West) and *Bender's Immigration Bulletin* (LexisNexis/ Matthew Bender).

d.   A Glimpse of Front–Line Immigration Services

The following reading provides a feel for what goes on in immigration field offices and for some of the challenges facing DHS officers and the individuals they encounter. In Philadelphia, as you will see, several key USCIS and ICE offices are located together in the same building, but this is not the dominant pattern.

MICHAEL MATZA, HOUSE OF DREAMS

Philadelphia Inquirer, Dec. 19, 2010, at A1.

Bitten by winter wind, baked by summer sun, the impromptu parade of nations inches down 16th Street toward the door to thousands of dearly held dreams, and some bad endings. There are men in turbans, Irish flat caps, and berets, women in rainbow saris and African gele head ties. Their faces are white, black, and every hue between. Many clutch documents, skimming them again and again on the plodding approach to the entryway metal detector.

This is 1600 Callowhill St., Philadelphia—the address that binds a dizzyingly diverse and increasingly populous universe of at least three-quarter million immigrants in Pennsylvania, Delaware, and West Virginia. Here, at the District 5 [field] office of U.S. Citizenship and Immigration Services, the federal government decides who may live legally in America, under what conditions and for how long, and who must go home. * * *

District 5 does not teem with immigrants as do some of the other 25 USCIS districts, the most strained being in the South and West. With satellite centers in Pittsburgh, Dover, and Charleston and an $11.4 million budget, it turned out 17,000 new Americans last year, out of 750,000 nationwide, and issued about 6,000 of the 1.1 million green cards.

Also at 1600 Callowhill, [at the ICE office] on a floor just above the hoopla of twice-a-week swearing-in ceremonies, law enforcement nets are cast for deportation. District 5—home to an estimated 185,000 illegal immigrants—expelled a record-breaking 6,629 last year, up from 2,501 in 2001. * * *

Waiting Their Turn

In a second-floor alcove with neat rows of blue vinyl seats, 16 immigrants wait their turn to take citizenship tests on English usage and American civics. More than 125 will follow. From the walls, George

Washington and the signers of the Declaration of Independence keep watch as Ismaila Adekunle nervously crams, studying a printout of 100 questions and answers from the USCIS website. The examiner will randomly pick 10. If Adekunle gets six right—and about 92 percent of immigrants do—he will be sworn in within a few weeks. If not, he can try again in 60 days.

But time suddenly is of the essence for the 20–year–old Nigerian, dressed for war in desert camouflage and combat boots. Born in Lagos, Adekunle was 3 when his father, Bunyamin, an airline clerk, and his mother, Deborah, immigrated to America for the classic reason: a better life. He was raised near Broad Street and Olney Avenue in North Philadelphia, went to public schools, and last year enrolled at Lincoln University. He also, like older brother Ganiyu, joined the U.S. Army Reserve—"to show my appreciation," he says, "to play my part."

His unit is set to deploy to Afghanistan next year. He wants to go to war as a citizen, he says, to cement the bond with his "battle buddies." But there are other benefits to be reaped. While legal immigrants are welcome in the U.S. military—there are an estimated 45,000 across all branches—only citizens can become officers. Adekunle also would be eligible for federal student loans. * * *

Adekunle must swear to tell the truth, turn over a passel of identification and his Nigerian passport, and answer some pro-forma questions. They range from the quaint "Ever been a member of the Communist party?" to "Are you willing to defend the United States in an emergency?" The young soldier's response to the latter is to look down at his uniform and smile.

Civics proves a tougher challenge. Burroughs [the USCIS officer] fires off the questions: "What does the president's cabinet do?"Adekunle is stumped. "OK, we'll come back to that," she says. "How many judges on the Supreme Court?"

"Nine."

"What did the Declaration of Independence do?"

"Freed the United States from Great Britain."

"How many years does a United States senator serve?" Again, Adekunle draws a blank. He purses his lips. Burroughs moves on. "Who leads the United States if the president and vice president can't serve?"

"The House speaker."

"Name a branch of government."

"Legislative."

"When do we celebrate Independence Day?"

"July Fourth."

"Name the war between the North and the South."

"The Civil War."

It is his sixth correct answer. Finally, Burroughs is smiling. Next comes English usage. Adekunle clearly reads aloud the sentence: "What is the capital of the United States?" [Then, as requested, he] legibly writes: "Mexico is south of the United States."

"Congratulations! You have passed," Burroughs declares. A beaming Adekunle looks like he wants to hug her, but doesn't. * * *

MARRYING: A FAST TRACK

Marrying a U.S. citizen is a fast track to living legally ever after in America. The immigrant spouse can more readily get a green card and then is required to have it for only three years, instead of the standard five, before applying for citizenship. The break can be a reward for love and family values, or an opportunity to game the system. If prosecuted to conviction, phony marriages and other visa frauds are punishable by five years in prison and a $250,000 fine.

It's up to USCIS interviewers such as Lucy Noel to outwit the fakers. An immigration officer for seven years, she handles an average of seven cases a day, not all of them marriages, but all familial. It could be a naturalized citizen's immigrant nephew posing as a son to get benefits. Or a friend claiming to be a blood relative.

On this day, in a third-floor office overlooking the Vine Street Expressway, she [interviews a recently married couple in their fifties—a six-year visa overstayer and her U.S. citizen husband.] * * * The game of gotcha goes on nearly an hour. Were she to catch a whiff of fakery, Noel could separate the two for questioning. She could refer the case to a fraud investigator. But she sees no need. A month after [the wife's] application is approved, her green card should arrive in the mail, Noel tells them. * * *

FERRETING OUT FAKERS

The sixth-floor Fraud Detection and National Security Unit [of US-CIS] is small and quiet, the antithesis of the bustle on lower floors where staff and immigrants intersect. Here, in relative seclusion, Michale Horn leads six investigators in ferreting out those who scam the system—typically for green cards and work permits—and those with far more nefarious deeds in mind.

Most of their cases are the mundane frauds. But there is no denying, 9/11 upped the stakes in the office. * * * It is here, for example, that investigators mine databases for immigrants who are known members of the 47 groups that the State Department defines as "designated terrorist organizations." Whether a case of benefit fraud or a suspected threat against the country, the unit exchanges fingerprints and other data with intelligence agencies to vet immigrants whose applications for legal status have been flagged.

Sometimes, Horn says, tips alleging crimes or terrorist ties come in the mail. Other times, as on this day, cases percolate up from the interview rooms below. Horn parts with details sparingly:

A "man from South America" applied for a green card, and managed to raise an examiner's suspicions. When Horn looks for a fingerprint match in a criminal database, he pops up as a convicted burglar. "Your fingerprints aren't going to lie," Horn says. "He appears to be removable." She sends the case to Immigration and Customs Enforcement—the immigration police unit known as ICE—for his arrest and deportation.

END OF THE JOURNEY

The [ICE/ERO office at the] end of a fifth-floor hallway has been the end of the American journey for legions of immigrants. There, two large cells—one for women, one for men, with a capacity of a dozen people each—await those whose crimes have caught up with them. On this day * * * each cell holds a single prisoner, barely visible through the small windows in the solid steel doors. Exactly why they are there, agents decline to say. * * *

The highest priority for ICE, officials say, is the expulsion of immigrants convicted of felonies. Some are in local jails. Others have served time and are back on the street. To round them up, ICE uses an undisclosed number of officers paired as "fugitive teams."[a]

At a noon meeting around a gray conference table, [ICE] field office director Thomas Decker confers with assistant director Dave O'Neill about one of the day's targets: "a Dominican female" convicted of cocaine possession in 1991. A team is on her trail in North Philadelphia. Sometime after her conviction, * * * [a]pparently thinking she can get away with it, she files for a green card, using either her own name or an alias. Her criminal history is revealed in the green-card interview and subsequent investigation. She is ordered deported in 2005. On this day, the fugitive team does not find her. But knowing her haunts, the agents are confident they will.

ONCE IN A LIFETIME

It happens once in a lifetime, every Wednesday and Friday afternoon.

The large reception room on the fourth floor can comfortably hold the 137 immigrants about to be sworn in as citizens this day—but not the more than 150 relatives and friends who have come along to witness a moment that has been years in the dreaming. Every folding chair is spoken for and the aisles are packed. English mingles with a Rosetta Stone catalogue of languages in a happy buzz.

Twenty-five years ago, the immigrants naturalized in District 5 were predominantly Vietnamese and Filipino. Now, the largest number of them

---

a. ICE counts as "fugitives" persons who have a final order of removal but who neither presented themselves to ICE for expulsion as required nor otherwise departed from the United States. In this usage, fugitives do not necessarily have a criminal charge or conviction.—eds.

are Indian, like Indrani Ray–Mukherji, 37, who was born in Calcutta, came to America in 2004, found work as an Amtrak sales agent, and now lives in Northeast Philadelphia. Of the 17,000 naturalizations last year, more than half were for people between the ages of 25 and 44. Fewer than 300 were unemployed. About 2,100 held management or professional positions. * * *

[T]he group bounds to its feet for the national anthem, followed by the Oath of Allegiance. To a cacophony of cheers, naturalization certificates are handed out. But hold the kisses. Still to come is a short video narrated by President Obama, who intones, "This is now officially your country." * * * In the hall outside the reception room, volunteers help the new citizens register to vote.

Ray–Mukherji is one of the first to sign up. Her husband, Chandra Mukherji, who left India as a child and became a citizen in 1991, teases her for going about it with such solemnity. But she has her reasons, she says. "I feel some responsibility for the country now."

2. THE DEPARTMENT OF JUSTICE

a. Immigration Judges

We have not yet discussed the kind of immigration adjudication that probably generates the most drama and often draws the greatest attention. Certainly it has the highest potential for an immediate impact on the right of a noncitizen physically present in this country to remain. We are speaking, of course, of removal decisions. (Until 1996, these were known as exclusion or deportation decisions.)

Under the statute, a proceeding to remove a noncitizen must generally be conducted by an immigration judge. *See* INA §§ 101(b)(4); § 240(a)(1). (We explore in Chapters Six, Nine, and Ten exceptions permitting DHS officers to conduct less formal removal procedures in specified circumstances, usually involving either arriving aliens or non-LPRs with serious criminal convictions.) Throughout much of our history, the "special inquiry officers" conducting removal proceedings were simply experienced or senior immigration officers, who did not necessarily hold a law degree and, who were designated to hold such hearings as part—but only part—of a range of responsibilities to administer and enforce the immigration laws. Often they would be the only federal official present for the proceedings. In the early decades of federal immigration controls, they might have inspected noncitizens at the border on one day, on another investigated violations, on yet another marshaled the case against a deportable noncitizen, and on still another served as a special inquiry officer to adjudicate the deportation of someone who had been investigated by their colleagues.

This mixture of roles weathered due process challenges, but eventually DOJ's interest in improving the quality and predictability of decisions resulted in the gradual evolution from hearing officers to specialized and professional immigration judges. During this same period, INS steadily expanded the deployment of specialized trial attorneys to represent the government in such proceedings, thus freeing the special inquiry officer for a more passive, judge-like decisionmaking role. *See* Rawitz, *From Wong Yang Sung to Black Robes,* 65 Interp.Rel. 453 (1988).

In 1983, the Department of Justice separated the hearing officers, by then regularly called "immigration judges," from INS, placing them in a new DOJ unit called the Executive Office for Immigration Review (EOIR) that reported directly to the Associate Attorney General. This did not mean that all the immigration judges moved to Washington; most remained physically in their old offices located in or near INS facilities throughout the country. But this different line of accountability provided a better structural assurance of adjudicative neutrality and fostered a strong spirit of professional independence among the judges. Nonetheless critics still sometimes maintained that an enforcement mentality pervaded all immigration-related agencies, including those separate from INS. They have also argued that the structural separation implemented in 1983 was inadequate, because immigration judges and the BIA remained ultimately answerable to the Attorney General, who was until March 2003 the bearer of the chief enforcement responsibilities bestowed by the INA. There have been frequent calls for EOIR to become a wholly independent adjudication agency. *See, e.g.,* Commission on Immigration Reform, Becoming an American: Immigration and Immigrant Policy 54–56 (1997); American Bar Association, Reforming the Immigration System: Proposals to Promote Independence, Fairness, Efficiency, and Professionalism in the Adjudication of Removal Cases (2010), at 6–30, 6–33.

Congress responded, to a limited degree, to this line of criticism when it adopted the Homeland Security Act. Virtually all INS functions were transferred to DHS, but EOIR remained in the Department of Justice. *See* Martin, *supra,* 80 Interp.Rel. at 616; *see generally* Legomsky, *Forum Choices for the Review of Agency Adjudication: A Study of the Immigration Process,* 71 Iowa L.Rev. 1297 (1986).

The major portion of an immigration judge's time is spent presiding over removal proceedings. This includes not only deciding whether the noncitizen is covered by one of the grounds of inadmissibility or deportability, but also passing upon a wide variety of waivers and applications for relief that may be made in such proceedings by those (the vast majority) who concede removability. When considering such matters, the immigration judge often exercises the discretion the statute lodges in the Attorney General. Immigration judges also preside over bond redetermination proceedings for detained noncitizens—essentially an expedited appeal of the terms of release that are set initially by the enforcement agencies.

In fiscal year 1992, there were about 85 immigration judges, who received 110,000 deportation and exclusion cases. By December 2010, following a major hiring surge, there were 272 immigration judges serving in 59 immigration courts (up from 232 at the end of FY 2009). In FY 2010 the judges received over 318,000 removal cases and completed more than 287,000 removal proceedings. Obviously many of these were summary dispositions that did not require full hearings on the merits. They also ruled on nearly 50,000 bond redeterminations and disposed of over 14,000 other motions, primarily motions to reopen to consider new evidence. *See* EOIR, FY 2010 Statistical Year Book, at B7, C3. This translates to roughly 1,200 proceedings per judge per year, and 1,000 decisions. 87 Interp.Rel. 1307, 1308. Plainly, the workload of immigration judges is vast, and their staff support sparse. For example, there are few law clerks for all of EOIR, though EOIR is in the processing of hiring more law clerks and other support staff. And there are no court stenographers; the judge operates the recording machine personally. Caseload pressures require that immigration judges almost always pronounce judgment orally, immediately at the conclusion of the hearing, to be captured on the recording device—and transcribed only if a party appeals the decision.

In recent years, the federal courts have become increasingly vocal in their criticism of those immigration judges whose behavior they see as substandard. But they have also manifested some sympathy, recognizing in print the trying conditions under which immigration judges work and sometimes criticizing Congress and the President for the institutional neglect and minimal funding that produced those conditions. *See, e.g., Apouviepseakoda v. Gonzales,* 475 F.3d 881, 886–87 & n.2 (7th Cir. 2007); *id.* at 898 (Posner, J., dissenting). In 2006, Attorney General Alberto Gonzales heeded these complaints and issued a 22–point reform plan, which included plans for greater resources, better training of IJs and EOIR staff, a formal code of conduct, new monitoring mechanisms to detect and trigger action on substandard or rude actions, and regular performance evaluations of immigration judges. *See Attorney General Outlines Reforms for Immigration Courts,* 83 Interp.Rel. 1725 (2006); American Bar Association, Reforming the Immigration System, *supra,* at 2–27, 2–30. Progress on implementing these reforms has been mixed. Budgetary resources were provided far more slowly than the Gonzales plan contemplated. *See* TRAC, *Immigration Courts: Still a Troubled Institution* (2009), <http://trac.syr.edu/immigration/reports/210/>. As decision times lengthened, Congress finally responded, increasing EOIR's budget (which includes funds for both the IJs and the BIA) by nearly 12 percent in FY 2010 (to $299 million). The judges are still losing ground, however. *See* TRAC, *Immigration Court Decision Times Lengthen* (July 28, 2011), <http://trac.syr.edu/immigration/reports/257/>, and observers from across the political spectrum have expressed concern or alarm. *See, e.g.,* American Bar Association, *supra;* Brennan, *A View from the Immigration Bench,* 78 Fordham L.Rev. 623 (2009); Metcalf, *Built to Fail: Deception and Disorder in America's Immigration Courts* (Center for Imm. Studies Backgrounder, May 2011).

b. The Board of Immigration Appeals, Plus a Sketch of Other Administrative Appeal Procedures

(i) Overview of the BIA

Under 8 C.F.R. § 1003.1(b), noncitizens found removable by immigration judges have a right of appeal to the Board of Immigration Appeals

(BIA), a multi-member review body appointed by the Attorney General. Since 1921, a Board of Review had existed in the Department of Labor, empowered to make recommendations to the Secretary regarding the disposition of appeals in exclusion and deportation cases. In 1940, following the transfer of immigration functions to the Department of Justice, new regulations changed the name to Board of Immigration Appeals and vested in it authority to issue final orders in such matters. The Board has never been recognized by statute; it is entirely a creature of the Attorney General's regulations. Nonetheless, it is important to note that the Board was never a part of INS (a point that has been overlooked in countless court decisions). Instead, the BIA has always been accountable directly to the Attorney General through a separate chain of command. Under the 1983 reorganization, the BIA is one of the constituent units of the Executive Office for Immigration Review in the Department of Justice.

Originally, the BIA had five permanent members, including its chairman. They heard all cases *en banc*, although only a tiny proportion on the basis of oral argument. By 1997, the BIA had grown to 15 permanent members, and regulations later authorized as many as 21. *See* 8 C.F.R. § 3.1(a)(1) (2001). During this period the BIA decided most cases in three-member panels. (Members are assisted in their research and drafting functions by over 100 staff attorneys.) Even these changes did not keep pace, however, with a mushrooming caseload, as shown in Figure 4.2. In FY 1992, the BIA docketed 12,774 cases, up from 3,630 in 1983. *See* 74 Interp.Rel. 534 (1997). By 1997, receipts exceeded 30,000, and they kept climbing to 43,000 in FY 2004. 2001 EOIR Statistical Year Book at E1; 2006 *id.* at S2. Appeals totaled 36,000 for FY 2010. 2010 *id.* at S1.

For most of the 1990s, case completions lagged well behind receipts, and a daunting backlog developed. The Board therefore implemented new streamlining regulations in November 1999. 64 Fed.Reg. 56135 (1999). They allowed a single BIA member to issue an affirmance without opinion (AWO) of certain types of appealed decisions if he or she found "that the result reached in the decision under review was correct [and] that any errors in the decision under review were harmless or nonmaterial." 8 C.F.R. § 3.1(a)(7)(ii) (2001). The immigration judge's opinion then became the final agency determination for purposes of any further appeals. The BIA was able to increase its output by almost 50 percent and to make significant inroads into its backlog under the 1999 streamlining.

Nonetheless, Attorney General John Ashcroft, who took office in 2001, found the progress unsatisfactory and pressed hard for further use of truncated procedures. He promulgated final regulations in August 2002 that made the disposition of appeals by a single member of the Board the norm. 67 Fed. Reg. 54878–905 (2002). A case now goes to a three-member panel only if it falls into one of six categories spelled out in 8 C.F.R. § 1003.1(e)(6), which cover only a minority of appeals. Single members

Figure 4.2
BIA Appeal Receipts and Completions, FY 1996–2010

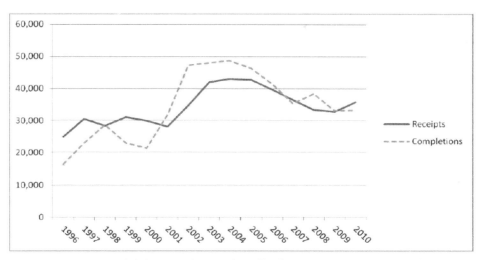

Sources: 2000 Statistical Year Book, Executive Office for Immigration Review (2001) (for 1996-1997); 2002 Statistical Year Book, Executive Office for Immigration Review (2003) (for 1998-2001); 2006 Statistical Year Book, Executive Office for Immigration Review (2007) (for 2002-2005); 2010 Statistical Year Book, Executive Office for Immigration Review (2011) (for 2006-2010).

may affirm with or without opinion, and may also dispose of appeals on procedural grounds. The regulations also imposed presumptive time limits on Board decisions. And they revised the standard of review to require greater deference to the factual findings of the immigration judge. 8 C.F.R. § 1003.1(d)(3). *See* Gallagher, *Practice and Procedure Before the Board of Immigration Appeals: An Update,* 03–2 Imm. Briefings (2003). Most controversially, the Ashcroft regulations decreed a reduction in the size of the BIA to take effect six months after implementation of the new procedures, reducing the size to 11 members. This counterintuitive shrinkage in the face of a growing caseload drew sharp criticism as a device that the administration used to remove the more liberal members from the Board. *See generally* Legomsky, *Deportation and the War on Independence,* 91 Cornell L.Rev. 369 (2006). Others charged that the pressure for completions, coupled with the high-volume clearance rate and wide use of affirmances without opinion, prevented a proper consideration of appeals by noncitizens and undermined what had been an admirable record of Board professionalism and independence.

Implementation of the August 2002 streamlining regulations largely eliminated a massive BIA case backlog, enabling more timely completion of new administrative appeals. But one byproduct was a surge in immigration appeals to the federal courts. Not only did the BIA issue a great many more decisions during this period, but the rate of appeal to the courts rose from approximately 10 percent to 25 percent. *See* Palmer, Yale–Loehr, & Cronin, *Why are So Many People Challenging BIA Decisions in Federal Court? An Empirical Analysis of the Surge in Petitions for Review,* 20 Geo. Immigr. L.J. 1, 52–53 (2005). Some critics attributed the higher appeal rate to unhappiness with the new BIA procedures, including the greater use of affirmances without opinion, which accounted for one-third of BIA decisions in the initial period of operation under the Ashcroft reforms. Many federal judges expressed deep concern about the burgeoning immigration caseload, and often remanded AWOs to the Board because they deemed an issue of such importance that the BIA itself needed to address the merits.

Some elements of the reforms adopted in 2006 by Attorney General Gonzales to improve IJ adjudications (discussed above) addressed problems at the BIA. The reforms included an increase in the size of the permanent BIA to 15, and the use of temporary members (immigration judges or senior EOIR attorneys assigned to the Board for up to one year) to augment the appeals capacity and permit the issuance of fewer AWOs. In May 2011 the Director of EOIR reported that AWOs had declined to two percent of decisions and that the BIA is now publishing more precedent decisions than at any time since the 1990s. Reversals in the federal courts dropped from 17.5 percent in 2006 to 11.5 percent in 2010. *EOIR Director Juan Osuna Discusses the Immigration Court System with the Senate Committee on the Judiciary,* 88 Interp.Rel. 1370–71 (2011).

In short, the partial walkback from the 2002 Ashcroft changes has had beneficial effects. But the recent progress has not quieted calls for restructuring the Board (and usually the framework for the immigration courts as well). The critics' proposals range from an article I court, *see, e.g.,* Metcalf, *Built to Fail, supra,* at 13; Marks, *An Urgent Priority: Why Congress Should Establish an Article I Immigration Court,* 13 Bender's Immigr. Bull. 3 (Jan. 1, 2008); Ramji–Nogales, Schoenholtz, Schrag, *Refugee Roulette: Disparities in Asylum Adjudication,* 60 Stan. L. Rev. 295, 386 (2007); to a new article III Court of Immigration Appeals that would replace both the BIA and the federal courts of appeals in immigration cases, see Legomsky, *Restructuring Immigration Adjudication,* 59 Duke L.J. 1635 (2010).

The overwhelming majority of cases before the Board consists of appeals from immigration judge decisions in removal proceedings, including related rulings on bonds and motions. 8 C.F.R. § 1003.1(b)(3). (In FY 2010, such appeals totaled 27,200 of 35,700 total BIA receipts. 2010 EOIR Statistical Year Book at T2). But the Board also hears appeals from specified DHS decisions, such as those imposing administrative fines and penalties on aircraft and vessels, refusing a limited class of waivers of inadmissibility, or denying certain kinds of visa petitions for intending immigrants. 8 C.F.R. § 1003.1(b)(4)–(7). The BIA's jurisdiction over visa petition denials reaches only those petitions based on a family relationship (other than adoptions); petitions based on occupational preferences follow a different avenue of appeal entirely within the DHS, to be discussed below.

Figure 4.3
Review of Immigration Judge Decisions: Primary Patterns

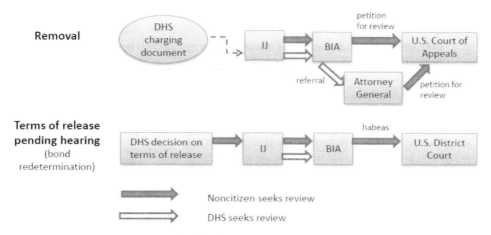

Note: AG may also take referral *sua sponte* or on BIA request. Referrals are quite infrequent.

Cases before the BIA are subject to further review by the Attorney General personally, although such review is infrequently invoked (rarely more than five per year; in some years, none). BIA cases may be "referred" to the Attorney General for a final authoritative decision, either before or after an initial ruling by the Board, in three circumstances (none at the noncitizen's behest): when the Attorney General so directs; when the Chair or a majority of the BIA decides that the case should be referred; or when the Secretary of Homeland Security requests referral. 8 C.F.R. § 1003.1(h). In practice, referrals almost always take place after the BIA rules.

What about all the other adjudications not directly reviewable by the BIA? A few are simply not appealable administratively—for instance, if a USCIS examiner denies an application to extend an admission period for a temporary visitor or to change from one nonimmigrant status to another (say, from student to tourist, or vice versa). 8 C.F.R. §§ 214.1(c)(5), 248.3(g). A few other types of decisions are not subject to administrative appeal as such, but USCIS does not really have the final administrative word, for the noncitizen may renew the application once removal proceedings have begun. The immigration judge then considers the application *de novo,* followed by possible appeal to the BIA. The primary forms of benefit that follow this pattern are asylum, 8 C.F.R. §§ 208.14(c)(1), 1208.14(c)(1), and adjustment of status to lawful permanent resident *id.* §§ 245.2(a)(5)(ii), 1245.2(a)(5)(ii).

(ii) Review Within DHS: The Administrative Appeals Office (AAO)

One other important appeal pattern exists, involving review within DHS. For example, if an examiner denies a visa petition based on occupational grounds—for permanent workers under the employment-based preference categories or for nonimmigrant temporary workers or trainees—such decisions are reviewable within USCIS and not by immigration judges or the Board. Such appeals (there are 40 specific types) are heard by USCIS's Administrative Appeals Office (AAO, also sometimes called the Administrative Appeals Unit), staffed by appellate examiners and their support staff, a total of 88 employees as of 2011, divided into nine branches that specialize by type of appeal. *See* 8 C.F.R. § 103.3; USCIS, *Administrative Appeals Office*, available via the USCIS website, <http://www.uscis.gov/>. The regulations also provide a possibility for "certification" of a case to higher officials for a definitive decision, at the initiative of the reviewing official or of the initial decisionmaker, when the case involves an unusually complex or novel issue of law or fact. 8 C.F.R. § 103.4. Certification is quite infrequent.

Thus two main administrative appellate tribunals or decisionmakers now exist for immigration decisions issued within the United States: the BIA and the AAO. No easy rule of thumb differentiates between the two zones of appellate jurisdiction, except that removal orders issued by an immigration judge are almost always appealed to the BIA. Beyond this, in order to appeal an adverse determination, consult the regulations to determine the forum. Title 8 C.F.R. §§ 1003.1(b) and 103.3 are the most important such regulations. More significantly, the document that communicates an agency's decision usually informs of any appeal rights, the forum that would hear the appeal, and time limits or other specifications governing review.

(iii) Precedent Decisions—And a Word of Warning About Relying on the Statute

A large volume of appellate decisions are handed down each month. Only a tiny fraction are designated as precedent decisions for inclusion in the official reports. *See* 8 C.F.R. §§ 103.3(c), 1003.1(i). These precedents are published in the multi-volume set known as "Administrative Decisions Under Immigration and Nationality Laws of the United States" (I & N Dec.). 8 C.F.R. § 103.9(a). In these volumes you will find reported decisions by the BIA and the AAO, and also some by the INS Commissioner, the Deputy Commissioner, Regional Commissioners, and occasionally the Attorney General. The overwhelming majority, however, are BIA decisions. Today BIA precedent decisions are also made available almost immediately via the "Virtual Law Library" on the EOIR website, <http://www.usdoj.gov/eoir>, with the final volume and page numbers already affixed. (The EOIR website also provides other useful information, including statistical reports and practice manuals, as well as easy access to local immigration court rules.) Under 8 C.F.R. § 1003.1(g), the interpretations of statute and regulations included in published BIA precedent decisions are binding on all other agencies, under the proviso in INA § 103(a)(1), which states that "determination and ruling by the Attorney General with respect to all questions of law shall be controlling."

This reference to the statutory language prompts one further caveat. Most of the INA, adopted in 1952 and frequently amended thereafter, by its express terms bestows enforcement, benefit-granting, and adjudication powers on the Attorney General. He then delegated these authorities, usually either to INS or to EOIR. When Congress created the Department of Homeland Security, it transferred virtually all of the power formerly exercised by INS to DHS or to specific DHS components, leaving the EOIR-related authorities to the Attorney General. But Congress did this via generic references in the Homeland Security Act, and generally did not amend the INA itself to reflect the new allocation of powers. Later statutes have made some further specific amendments to the INA language, referring directly to the Secretary of Homeland Security when an authority now belongs to DHS. But those corrections remain spotty. Hence consulting the INA alone can give a highly misleading picture of institutional responsibilities as they currently exist. Most of the AG's stated INA powers, unless they relate to the formal adjudication handled by EOIR, are now wielded by the Secretary of Homeland Security and his or her delegates. Similarly confusing is the fact that relatively few regulations in 8 C.F.R. have been amended since 2003 to clarify the new allocation of responsibility to DHS.

c. Other DOJ Units

Three other units in the Department of Justice should be mentioned. The first two were created because of the passage of the Immigration Reform and Control Act of 1986 (IRCA), Pub.L. No. 99–603, 100 Stat. 3359. As Chapter One indicated, IRCA enacted a system of employer sanctions to penalize those who knowingly hire undocumented noncitizens or fail to perform certain documentary verification at the time of hiring. INA § 274A. In an attempt to assure that this system did not increase discrimination against ethnic minorities, IRCA also added new provisions barring discrimination based on national origin or citizenship status. INA § 274B. Under the statute, allegations of employer violations of either of these provisions are heard by administrative law judges (who are not immigration judges) in the Department of Justice. Accordingly, the Department added a new unit to EOIR, the Office of Chief Administrative Hearing Officer (OCAHO), who supervises ALJs to carry out this function. *See* 28 C.F.R. Part 68. Several years later Congress also bestowed authority on the ALJs to impose civil penalties for document fraud under INA § 274C. OCAHO's caseload remains small, however, in part because the enforcement units have been fairly successful in negotiating settlements of complaints or charges. Receipts reached 91 cases in FY 2010, up from 23 in 2006. 2010 EOIR Statistical Year Book at Z1.

The principal investigating and charging responsibility under the employer sanctions and civil document fraud provisions rests with ICE. But the 1986 statute created a new office in the Department of Justice, the Office of Special Counsel for Immigration–Related Unfair Employment Practices, to fulfill agency responsibilities under IRCA's antidiscrimination provisions. The Special Counsel is appointed by the President, subject to the advice and consent of the Senate. *See* INA § 274B(c); 28 C.F.R. Part 44. After the creation of DHS, the Special Counsel's office remained in DOJ, where it is part of the Civil Rights Division.

Finally, the well-known Federal Bureau of Investigation (FBI) plays an increasingly important, but focused, role in immigration decisions. Statutes and regulations over the last 20 years—and particularly since the 9/11 attacks—have imposed ever more stringent requirements for checking names and fingerprints against watchlists and various criminal and terrorist databases before immigration benefits can be issued. *See generally USCIS Issues Fact Sheet on Security Checks,* 83 Interp.Rel. 827 (2006). The FBI plays a crucial role in this process, drawing on information available from other agencies and the intelligence community. The system now produces clearances in most cases fairly quickly, but for those not promptly cleared, the security check process can cause delays lasting months or years.

3. THE DEPARTMENT OF STATE

a. The Bureau of Consular Affairs

For over 85 years, most persons wishing to travel to the United States, even for a short visit, have been required to secure preliminary documents known as visas from a U.S. official overseas. (Chapter Six will discuss this process and also describe the exceptions to the visa requirement.) State Department officials, called consular officers, are stationed at over 200 offices throughout the world to decide on applications for visas. *See* INA §§ 221, 222. From FY 2006 to 2010, they issued roughly six million nonimmigrant visas annually, down from over seven million in the years preceding the September 11, 2001, attacks, but up from about five million in the preceding half-decade. In each of those years the Department also issued 400–500,000 immigrant visas. *See* Dep't of State, Immigrant and Nonimmigrant Visas Issued at Foreign Service Posts: Fiscal Years 1992–2010, available at <http://travel.state.gov/pdf/MultiYearTable I.pdf>.

Securing a visa, as arduous a process as it may be for some, does not guarantee admission—and many of the relevant documents bear a warning to this effect. Visas do not constitute permission to enter the United States. They are more in the nature of permission to travel to the United States and apply for admission at the border. The immigration inspector at the port of entry is entitled to disagree with the consular officer and thus to detain for a formal removal hearing a noncitizen with a duly issued visa (or under many circumstances to order the person's removal after further interviewing and supervisory review, but without an immigration court hearing). Fortunately, such disagreement is infrequent. Indeed, the system would break down if visas did not usually function to secure admission. But because airlines and other carriers are subject to substantial fines and other penalties if they bring noncitizens here without proper documents, INA § 273, a traveler cannot board unless the papers presented at the foreign ticket counter are all in order. A visa is therefore indispensable for noncitizens wishing to come here from most countries around the globe.

Although INA § 104 places these documentation responsibilities in officials of the Department of State, the formal authority of the Secretary of State is circumscribed. Note the curious language of § 104(a)(1), giving the Secretary broad authority, but excepting from that control "those powers, duties, and functions conferred upon the consular officers relating to the granting or refusal of visas." Can it really be intended to give consular officers autocratic power, immune from the supervision of their nominal superiors, to decide whether to issue documents indispensable to noncitizens who wish to come to this country? Critics have often charged that the system operates this way. *See, e.g.,* Whom We Shall Welcome: Report of the President's Commission on Immigration and Naturalization 147 (1953). Their complaints are the more vehement because federal courts routinely deny review of visa denials. But there is a different theory that underlies this provision: that such separation insulates what are meant to be routine bureaucratic decisions on admissibility from the high politics that are the stock-in-trade of the Secretary of State and her subordinates on the diplomatic side of the Department. *See, e.g.,* Simpson, *Policy Implications of U.S. Consular Operations*, in The Consular Dimension of Diplomacy 11 (M. Herz ed. 1983). Whether that purpose is truly advanced—and whether, even so, it justifies vesting so much power in the front-line consular officer—has often been questioned.

In any event, this putative insulating measure does serve to complicate the normal bureaucratic or managerial business of review and supervision to assure timeliness, consistency of outcomes, and legal validity. Nevertheless, these reasonable imperatives have still found expression through informal review mechanisms, crafted with close attention to

§ 104(a)(1). The regulations direct supervisors to review a random selection of visa decisions by consular officers. *See* 22 C.F.R. §§ 41.113(i), 41.121(c); 9 FAM 41.113 PN 18.1–2, *id.* 41.121 PN 1.2–8 (2008). Officially this review is done as "a significant management and instructional tool useful in maintaining the highest professional standards of adjudication and ensuring uniform and correct application of the law and regulations." 71 Fed.Reg. 37494 (2006) (explanatory statement accompanying new regulations). In some circumstances a second consular officer, upon disagreeing with the first, can issue a visa on his or her own authority despite an initial denial. Cases can also be referred to Washington for what are carefully labeled advisory opinions, but which in fact are ordinarily given effect. Legal rulings in advisory opinions are binding on the consular officer. 22 C.F.R. § 41.121(d).

Visa issuance falls under the general responsibility of the Bureau of Consular Affairs, headed by an Assistant Secretary of State. In 2002, congressional concerns stemming from the receipt of visas by the September 11 hijackers prompted calls to remove the visa function from the State Department. The Homeland Security Act did not go quite that far. Visas are still issued by consular officers, who remain part of the Department of State, but authority over visa *policy*, including the issuance of regulations governing visas, was transferred to the Department of Homeland Security. DHS was also given significant authority to monitor the issuance of visas in foreign posts, and may even veto the issuance of an individual visa. DHS may not, however, direct the granting of a visa when the consular officer has refused it. HSA § 428. The two departments agreed upon a lengthy Memorandum of Understanding in September 2003 that carefully allocates their respective powers over visas and related matters. 80 Interp. Rel. 1365 (2003). In practice, State retains the lion's share of operational authority over the issuance of visas.

In 1994, the Department of State created a National Visa Center (NVC), based at a decommissioned military base in New Hampshire, to take over from consuls the more routine functions involved in visa issuance. The Center checks visa requests for accuracy and completeness, creates immigrant visa files and computer records, and communicates necessary notices and requests for information to applicants or their attorneys, even when the actual visa will be issued at a consular post abroad. Over the last decade, the Department has progressively implemented new procedures allowing (and later requiring) the completion and submission of electronic visa applications, completed through an interactive online process. Today most nonimmigrant visa applications must be done electronically. *See* 73 Fed.Reg. 23067–01 (2008).

In addition to Visa Services, the Bureau of Consular Affairs contains two other major divisions, Overseas Citizens Services and Passport Services. The former supervises consular protection and assistance provided to Americans in foreign countries (for example, in connection with foreign arrests, business transactions, or U.S. citizen deaths abroad). With regard to passports, through more than 20 domestic passport agencies and centers in the United States, and through State Department posts abroad, the Bureau has issued between 13 and 18 million passports per year from 2007 to 2010. Demand for passports has surged since 2004, largely because Congress acted that year on a recommendation of the 9/11 Commission and required that U.S. citizens must have passports or comparably secure U.S. travel documents, including new "passport cards," even for travel to Canada, Mexico, or the Caribbean. *See DHS and DOS Announce Issuance of Final Rule for Land and Sea Portion of WHTI,* 85 Interp.Rel. 1004 (2008); *Final Rules Issued Regarding Passport Requirements for WHTI Air Travel,* 83 Interp.Rel. 2573 (2006).

b. Other Bureaus

Another State Department bureau, the Bureau of Population, Refugees and Migration (PRM), plays the key role for the Department of State in connection with overseas refugee programs. PRM deals with both assistance to refugees in camps in first asylum countries (or occasionally displaced persons still within their countries of nationality) and admissions to the United States through the organized refugee resettlement program. It is also the principal point of contact with the Office of the UN High Commissioner for Refugees (UNHCR).

The Bureau of Educational and Cultural Affairs (ECA) manages a host of programs meant to enhance mutual understanding between Americans and the citizens of other countries. For immigration-law purposes, ECA's most important functions involve exchange arrangements, like the Fulbright program, that send Americans to other countries and bring several thousand foreign nationals here each year. Many such programs involve governmental or university exchanges, but others involve the private sector, including a program for *au pairs*. A specific nonimmigrant status (known as J–1) exists for "exchange visitors." *See* INA § 101(a)(15)(J). Although the participating programs take the lead in administering the exchange visitor arrangements, ECA oversees their functioning. The visa office in the Bureau of Consular Affairs also plays a role in deciding whether some of the restrictions on exchange visitors can be waived. *See* INA § 212(e).

c. Regulations and Other Guidance

The State Department publishes a Foreign Affairs Manual (FAM), certain chapters of which are devoted to interpretations and instructions relating to immigration and nationality questions, amplifying the regulations appearing in 22 C.F.R. Parts 40–53. *See* Merrell, *Everything You Always Wanted to Know About the FAM, But Were Too Discouraged to Dig for Yourself,* 4 Bender's Imm.Bull. 540 (1999). Portions of the Manual have been released to the public, and are available in various immigration treatises, as well as online at <http://www.state.gov/m/a/dir/regs/>. Most of the documents and records involved in individual visa processing, however, are confidential under specific statutory direction. INA § 222(f). Immigration-related information is available from the Department of

State's Visa Services website, <http://travel.state.gov/visa/visa_1750.html>. Highly useful monthly charts on immigrant visa processing (showing visa allocation priority dates currently being processed—an indication of how far down the waiting list the Department is reaching) may be found at the Visa Bulletin site, <http://travel.state.gov/visa/bulletin/bulletin_1360.html>.

4. OTHER FEDERAL AGENCIES

a. The Department of Labor

The INA requires USCIS to cooperate with the Department of Labor (DOL) in the process that leads to the granting of visas to persons who are subject to the labor certification requirement. If this requirement applies, the Department of Labor, through its Employment and Training Administration, must certify that American workers in the applicant's field are unavailable in the locality of the applicant's destination and that the applicant's employment will not adversely affect wages and working conditions of American workers. Labor certification is required for many immigrants who enter under the employment-based preference categories of INA § 203(b). If certification is denied, the employer may appeal to the Board of Alien Labor Certification Appeals (BALCA), which usually sits in panels of three administrative law judges, and has authority to affirm, reverse, or remand. We will examine the complicated and specialized process of labor certification in some detail in Chapter Five. The Department of Labor also has similar regulatory responsibilities in connection with several of the business-related categories for nonimmigrants, notably including those for temporary workers. DOL's Wage and Hour Division, which enforces the minimum wage, overtime, and child labor laws, also plays a limited role in monitoring employer compliance with the laws against the hiring of undocumented noncitizens.

b. The Public Health Service

The Public Health Service (PHS), headed by the Surgeon General, is an agency in the Department of Health and Human Services. Because several grounds of inadmissibility relate to medical conditions, PHS physicians and other authorized medical officials play a role under the Immigration and Nationality Act, both at ports of entry and overseas. PHS-designated doctors conduct medical examinations of intending immigrants, and some of their determinations are unreviewable by INS or any other body, save a special medical review panel established pursuant to statute. *See* INA §§ 232, 240(c)(1)(B).

c. The Office of Refugee Resettlement

The INA and other statutes provide certain forms of assistance to refugees who are resettled within the United States. *See* INA § 412. Most of these programs are administered by the Office of Refugee Resettlement, another unit within the Department of Health and Human Services. INA

§ 411. The Homeland Security Act also gave that Office an important set of new authorities. As of early 2003, ORR took over from INS the responsibility for the care and custody of unaccompanied minors involved in immigration proceedings. HSA § 462. These authorities were expanded and refined in subsequent statutes, notably the William Wilberforce Trafficking Victims Protection Reauthorization Act, Pub.L. 110–457, 122 Stat. 5044 (2008).

d. The Social Security Administration

The Social Security Administration (SSA) manages the nation's systems for monetary support to the elderly and disabled, including the crediting of payroll taxes to the individual account of the proper employee. Anyone employed in the United States must have a Social Security card. For this reason, Social Security records play a role in the databases used to verify work authorization or eligibility for public benefits. In addition, SSA sends "no-match" letters to employers when the combination of a particular name and social security number for which they report earnings does not match with information contained in agency records, which, under some circumstances, may put an employer on notice that the employee is a noncitizen unauthorized to work in the United States— though SSA sends the letters to assure correct crediting of payments and not for immigration control purposes. More directly, SSA is closely involved with USCIS in the operation of the web-based employment verification system known as E–Verify, because a high percentage of new hires present a driver's license and social security card as their primary evidence of work authorization. We will consider verification procedures and employer obligations under the immigration laws in Chapter Nine.

SECTION B.   COURTS

No overview of the government bodies involved with immigration and citizenship would be complete without a brief treatment of the role of the courts. We offer here a basic sketch, intended to supply a bit of background that may help understand how the cases in this book reached the courts. We defer full consideration of court review until Chapter Ten.

Before 1961, no immigration statute expressly permitted judicial review of exclusion and deportation orders or of other government decisions in immigration cases. The courts found a basis for jurisdiction, however, because exclusion and deportation require the government to take the noncitizen into physical custody at some point. A longstanding provision of the Judicial Code, 28 U.S.C. § 2241, gives federal district courts jurisdiction to issue writs of habeas corpus for persons "in custody in violation of the Constitution or laws ... of the United States." The Great Writ is guaranteed in the Constitution by the Suspension Clause, Article I, section 9, clause 2, which states: "The privilege of the writ of habeas corpus shall not be suspended, unless when in Cases of Rebellion or Invasion the public Safety may require it."

In 1961 Congress restructured judicial review by specifying habeas corpus in federal district courts as the exclusive means for court review of exclusion orders, that is, orders issued to persons applying for admission at a port of entry (today called "arriving aliens"). If unsuccessful there, the noncitizen could seek further review, first in the federal court of appeals, and then by certiorari in the Supreme Court. For deportation orders, the noncitizen was ordinarily expected to proceed, after exhausting administrative remedies, directly to the federal court of appeals, under a procedure called a petition for review. If unsuccessful there, she could seek a writ of certiorari in the Supreme Court.

The Illegal Immigration Reform and Immigrant Responsibility Act of 1996 (IIRIRA) substantially restructured court review. INA § 242. Initially, it consolidated exclusion and deportation hearings into a single form of removal proceeding at the administrative level, and then essentially provided that all judicial review of removal should proceed to the courts of appeals on petition for review. INA § 242(b) sets out the procedural requirements with regard to deadlines for filing, venue, and service.

Section 242 as enacted in 1996, however, purported to eliminate judicial review in several specific categories of cases, including most cases involving persons removable under the crime-related grounds of deportability, and most cases involving discretionary waivers and discretionary relief from removal. INA § 242(a)(2)(B), (C). These 1996 restrictions on review came under constitutional challenge, but the Supreme Court avoided direct pronouncement on the major constitutional questions by reading the preclusions narrowly. It construed the 1996 amendments to leave open habeas review in the district courts, at least to consider "pure questions of law" that could not be heard in the courts of appeals. *INS v. St. Cyr*, 533 U.S. 289, 121 S.Ct. 2271, 150 L.Ed.2d 347 (2001). Congress responded with legislation that reasserts in more precise language the exclusivity of the petition for review process in the courts of appeals, for noncitizens who want to get judicial review of a removal order. REAL ID Act of 2005, Pub. L. 109–13, Div. B, § 106, 119 Stat. 231, 302–05 (2005). But Congress also relented in some of its previous court-stripping ardor, in apparent recognition of the constitutional warnings in the Supreme Court's *St. Cyr* decision. A new INA § 242(a)(2)(D) specifically preserves review in the courts of appeals of "constitutional claims or questions of law," notwithstanding virtually any other INA provision "which limits or eliminates judicial review." Today judicial review of removal-related matters flows directly to the courts of appeals (with the primary exception of challenges to detention unrelated to the merits of the removal case). *See* Figure 4.3 *supra*. District courts may also hear APA-based challenges to USCIS decisions, at least in those circumstances where the issue is not open to consideration in a pending removal proceeding (which would raise an exhaustion-of-remedies barrier).

In the last decade the federal courts experienced a dramatic rise in immigration cases. From calendar year 2001 to 2006, appeals from the BIA rose by 555 percent. In 2001 such appeals constituted three percent of the appellate judicial caseload; in 2006, 17 percent. *BIA Appeals Still Significant Part of Federal Appellate Caseload,* The Third Branch, May 2007 (newsletter of the federal courts). Most of the caseload growth followed the changes in BIA operations described in Section A2b above, which both cleared a massive BIA backlog (leaving more cases eligible for court review) and implemented controversial decision procedures, such as wider use of affirmance without opinion. These changes apparently prompted many more litigants to challenge in court an adverse BIA outcome. Some of the increase, however, may also have derived from the pendency during those years of prominent presidential and congressional proposals to legalize the undocumented population—but only those noncitizens who were still in the country whenever enactment was secured. Such legislation failed in mid–2007 and has not been successfully revived. Whether for that reason or because of progress in implementing EOIR reforms, including greatly reduced use of summary dispositions without opinion, federal court appeals have dropped noticeably, as shown in Figure 4.4. Nonetheless, they remain well above the levels that were common before the 2002 Ashcroft streamlining reforms at the BIA.

Figure 4.4
Appeals to Federal Courts of Appeals of BIA Decisions, 1993–2010

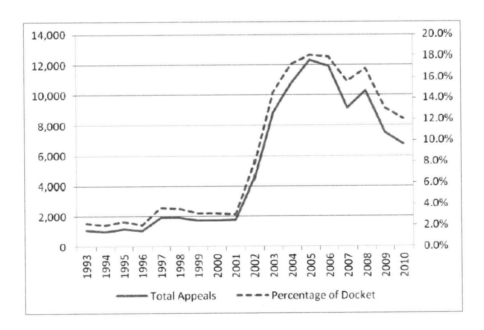

Source: Judicial Business of the U.S. Courts (1997-2010), http://uscourts.gov/ Statistics/JudicialBusiness.aspx.

SECTION C.   A LOOK AT IMMIGRATION PRACTICE

The following article by an experienced Miami practitioner provides an idea of the ways in which an immigration lawyer may interact with clients and the federal government. Though some of the agencies and procedures have changed since this was written, it still reflects accurately many features of today's immigration practice.

ELAINE WEISS, A DAY IN THE LIFE OF AN IMMIGRATION PRACTITIONER

The Florida Bar Journal, May 1992, at 74–75.

4:00 a.m.: I'm on the telephone to the U.S. Consulate in Copenhagen. It's taken jurisdiction of the immigration case of a Polish client currently in the U.S. By statute, he must pick up his green card at a U.S. Consulate abroad. The Consulate in Warsaw has mandatory jurisdiction, but my client refuses to return there. The Consulate in Copenhagen is the only U.S. consular office among the 40 that I surveyed that agreed to take discretionary jurisdiction. My client's wife and children—whom he hasn't seen since coming to the U.S. 10 years ago—will be meeting him in Copenhagen, hopefully for a successful permanent residence interview at the Consulate there. Organizing a reunion for the family in a third country is nerve-wracking; they could be stuck there if any of the documents I am readying is faulty or goes astray. Yet the case is exciting, too. * * *

With rare exception, there are people—not companies, not property— at the heart of immigration cases, and the life stories of these people— particularly the pro bono clients—are often compelling.[a]

* * *

7:15 a.m.: I'm on the road to the [INS district office] to attend a so-called "adjustment interview" for a Haitian man. If all goes right, he'll leave INS a permanent resident of the U.S.

9:30 a.m.: We're finally called for our 7:30 a.m. interview. The hearing will likely take only 10 minutes. Overworked and understaffed, the Miami INS office often runs an hour or two behind. * * * Case approved.

Noon: I attend an executive board meeting of the local chapter of the American Immigration Lawyers Association. * * *

[We] discuss our association's efforts to get the local U.S. Attorney's office to prosecute [a certain kind of fraud under one of the 1986 legalization programs.] * * * The problem is that many aliens—frequently assisted by unscrupulous lawyers—are making fraudulent skeleton appli-

---

a.   Relocated paragraph.—eds.

cations [as allowed by a court decision]. While these have the immediate effect of providing aliens with much sought after work authorizations, this "benefit" derives of material misstatement. When these same people come to reputable practitioners to make their immigration status right and permanent, we can promise nothing, since the statute takes a very dim view of fraud in obtaining immigration benefits. One way to discourage aliens from such fraud is by prosecuting the lawyers and others who promote it. Unfortunately, the already overburdened U.S. Attorney's office in Miami has not made [such] fraud a priority. Our board members grimly joke about limousines picking up aliens at Miami International Airport and driving them directly to INS to apply for [these] work authorizations—and, at best, immigration limbo.

2:00 p.m.: I meet with a prospective client. From the facts she presents, I tell her there is an excellent chance of fulfilling her goal of permanent residence based on a recent job offer. However, I tell her, the process will take no less than one to two years from start to finish. And, during this time, the process will accord her no interim work authorization. * * * I am singing a familiar refrain: I can likely get what you want, but not within your preferred timeframe.

* * *

3:00 p.m.: I am called by a senior partner in a Cleveland law firm. His son's girlfriend—an Italian national—has had difficulties with INS airport personnel in Detroit. The immigration inspectors accuse her of lying: they say she really intends to enter the U.S. to live permanently rather than merely visit as permitted by her visa. They have put her into exclusion proceedings. As an alleged "excludable alien," the girlfriend must now prove to an immigration judge that she is seeking to enter the U.S. for purposes consistent with the terms of her visitor's visa.

Many experienced lawyers unfamiliar with immigration law err in this situation, thinking that approaching INS with courtly manners and a reasonable story—or, perhaps, advising the alien to just get on an airplane and depart—will have the desired result of getting the alien unstuck at INS. They are in for a rude awakening: a false move and the alien may find it nearly impossible to visit the U.S. again.

* * *

CHAPTER FIVE

IMMIGRANTS AND NONIMMIGRANTS: QUALIFYING CATEGORIES AND A LOOK AT THE UNDOCUMENTED

■ ■ ■

The American immigration system allows for the lawful admission of two broad groups of noncitizens: immigrants and nonimmigrants. Immigrants, as the label suggests, come to take up permanent residence, whereas nonimmigrants enter for a specific purpose to be accomplished during a temporary stay—which might nonetheless last for many years. A noncitizen in either group must show initially that he or she qualifies for admission by meeting one of several *categorical qualifying requirements*, and must also demonstrate that none of the multiple *grounds for inadmissibility* appearing in § 212(a) of the INA renders him or her ineligible. This chapter examines the most commonly used qualifying admission categories, for both immigrants and nonimmigrants, and also takes a look at undocumented migration and the 10–11 million persons now living in the United States in unauthorized status. Chapter Seven will consider the inadmissibility grounds (along with the related but somewhat less expansive set of deportability grounds), and Chapter Eight will touch briefly on the admission of refugees. Chapters Six and Seven will describe specialized discretionary procedures, such as parole and deferred action, that may permit a noncitizen to be physically present with a form of legal blessing, despite certain disqualifications.

A brief discussion of terminology may be helpful at the outset. We will use the term *immigrant* here as the statute does, to mean a noncitizen authorized to take up permanent residence in the United States. This is a subset of the group that common or journalistic usage often labels immigrants, meaning noncitizens who have been present for a while and wish to stay indefinitely, legally or illegally. After admission, immigrants, as distinguished from *nonimmigrants* here for a temporary stay, are also often referred to as *lawful permanent residents* (LPRs), until they obtain citizenship through naturalization. Informal lingo may refer to LPRs as *green card holders,* after the vernacular name for the chief document they receive. Permanent resident status means that they may stay as long as they wish, provided only they do not commit crimes or a limited list of other post-entry acts that may render them deportable. Most immigrants who choose to apply for naturalization after meeting the residence requirement—ordinarily five years—qualify rather routinely, but there is no obligation to apply for citizenship. A person may remain in LPR status indefinitely.

SECTION A. IMMIGRANTS

1. OVERVIEW

a. Categories

Summary. The story of the American immigrant admission system is largely a story of numbers, along with the intricate substantive distinctions used to define the categories to which those numbers are assigned. Since 1921, the law has imposed annual numerical limitations—known in the immigration world as "quotas"—on most immigrant categories. The character of those limitations, as we have seen in Chapter One, changed considerably in 1965, when Congress abandoned the former national origins quota system in favor of a more neutral preference system. A variety of modest refinements occurred in succeeding years, before the Immigration Act of 1990, Pub.L. 101–649, 104 Stat. 4978, thoroughly rewrote the key immigrant admission provisions of the INA.

The current system essentially provides for four grand categories of immigrants, each governed by its own detailed rules and ceilings. They are: (1) family-sponsored immigrants; (2) employment-based immigrants; (3) diversity immigrants; and (4) humanitarian admissions. Refugee admissions constitute the largest component of humanitarian admissions, counting both overseas resettlement programs and persons who obtain status through the filing of an asylum application on U.S. soil.[1] The law governing overseas refugee admissions provides for the fixing of an admission ceiling at the beginning of each fiscal year (subject to adjustment for emergencies), based on a judgment about likely refugee needs and feasible U.S. responses. Over the past decade, overseas refugee admissions have run between 26,000 and 75,000 annually, and asylum grants have run between 20,000 and 40,000. Because these humanitarian category totals are subject to wide variation and are independent of the developments in the other three categories, the refugee provisions will be considered separately in Chapter Eight. The balance of this section focuses on the other three grand categories.

The basic framework for today's permanent immigration categories was established in the Immigration Act of 1990. The 1990 Act set an annual baseline for employment-based admissions at 140,000 (subject to

---

1. Beneficiaries of nonimmigrant visa categories T and U, which cover certain victims of human trafficking or of other specified forms of criminal abuse, also can become eligible for LPR status through that route. These relatively recent additions to the admissions alphabet could also be considered types of humanitarian admissions. They will receive attention in Part B of this chapter, relating to nonimmigrants.

certain complex adjustments in some years). Because accompanying family members of the selected worker also count against these ceilings, only about half the available numbers are used for the workers themselves. The 140,000 spaces are parceled out among five primary employment-based preference categories. INA § 203(b). The highest numbers of annual immigrant admissions go for family based-migration. The system allows for numerically unlimited admission of "immediate relatives" of U.S. citizens (recently running about a half-million per year), plus about 226,000 admissions (again subject to limited annual adjustment under formulas set in the statute). These capped family slots are allotted among four family-sponsored preference categories, which are defined on the basis of specified relationships to citizens or LPRs. INA §§ 201(b)(2)(A), 203(a). The diversity admission provision is meant, in part, to reflect a treasured national self-image—an image of a pluralistic America open to all comers with the pluck and good fortune to make a go of it in a new land. It establishes a lottery to select 50,000 noncitizens each year from among people who meet the threshold requirements, a lottery that has recently attracted over 12 million applicants. Nationals of 15–20 countries that already send us a high volume of immigration are not eligible.

Table 5.1
Immigrant Admission Category Overview
(with approximate number of annual admissions*)

- **Family-sponsored**
  - ○ Immediate relatives of US citizens (500,000 – no statutory ceiling)
    - ▪ Spouses, children, and (if petitioner is 21 or older) parents
  - ○ Preference categories (226,000)
    - ▪ 1: Unmarried sons and daughters of US citizens
    - ▪ 2A: Spouses and children of LPRs
    - ▪ 2B: Unmarried sons and daughters of LPRs
    - ▪ 3: Married sons and daughters of US citizens
    - ▪ 4: Brothers and sisters of US citizens (if petitioner is 21 or older)
- **Employment-based**
  - ○ Preference categories (140,000)
    - ▪ 1A: aliens with extraordinary ability
    - ▪ 1B: outstanding professors and researchers
    - ▪ 1C: multinational executives and managers
    - ▪ 2: aliens with advanced degrees or exceptional ability
    - ▪ 3: aliens with bachelor's degrees or workers in shortage occupations (unskilled workers limited to 5,000/year)
    - ▪ 4: special immigrants
    - ▪ 5: investors
- **Humanitarian**
    - ▪ Overseas refugee admissions (70,000 – no statutory ceiling)
    - ▪ Asylum (25,000 – no statutory ceiling)
- **Diversity lottery** (50,000)

---

* Rough indicators, based on normal statutory ceilings, where applicable, or average of admissions in recent years, where no fixed ceiling applies. Annual numbers can fluctuate significantly.

The U.S. immigrant selection scheme is quite complex, sometimes bewilderingly so. At times only subtle and easily missed differences distinguish one category from another. The following pages provide an introduction into these complexities, broadly describing the system for the family, employment, and diversity categories. Later parts of this Chapter then look far more closely at selected provisions and issues. Before we embark on this initial overview, however, a brief sketch of immigration procedures will be useful, to foster understanding of how the substantive categories are actually implemented. (Such procedures will be considered in detail in Chapter Six.)

Procedural overview. Most American immigration today formally begins not with the action of the noncitizen overseas who wishes to immigrate, but with a document called a *visa petition* filed by a person already in the United States—usually a family member or prospective employer—whose relation to the noncitizen will become the basis for the noncitizen's proof that he fits within a qualifying category. The family member or employer is known as the *petitioner;* the noncitizen who wishes to immigrate is the *beneficiary.* For family categories, the family member typically files a visa petition with U.S. Citizenship and Immigration Services (USCIS), a part of the Department of Homeland Security, accompanied by proof, such as birth or marriage certificates, of the necessary relationship. For occupational categories, the process typically begins one stage earlier. The prospective employer first files documents with the Department of Labor in order to obtain *labor certification*, i.e., certification from the Department that the noncitizen will not be taking a job for which qualified U.S. workers (citizens or authorized aliens) are available. After the labor certification is issued, the employer files a visa petition with USCIS, which verifies other qualifications, such as the prospective immigrant's identity and the employer's ability to pay the stated salary or wage. Once USCIS is satisfied that the relationship (either family or employment) is genuine and meets the legal requirements, it approves the visa petition and transmits a copy to the consulate in the country the petitioner has designated as the place where the noncitizen beneficiary will actually apply for the immigrant visa, normally the closest U.S. consular facility in the country of nationality. The consular officer usually takes as a given the basic qualifying category; his or her main function is to apply the inadmissibility grounds of INA § 212(a) (based on characteristics of the intending immigrant, such as prior crimes, contagious disease, or prior immigration violations), which are treated in Chapter Seven. The statutory provisions governing the petition procedures are set forth in INA §§ 204–206.

U.S. consulates are located exclusively in foreign countries. What if the beneficiary of the visa petition is already in the United States? This is an increasingly frequent scenario, particularly for business-related immigration, and the law has made allowance for such persons without requiring them to go abroad to get a visa and reenter as an immigrant. Under specified conditions (usually but not always requiring lawful status as a nonimmigrant), the beneficiary may apply to a USCIS office in the United States for *adjustment of status*, once the visa petition has been approved. INA § 245. The phrase signifies that his immigration status will be changed—adjusted—usually from nonimmigrant to immigrant, if his application is approved. A USCIS examiner then typically interviews the applicant and applies the scrutiny of the applicant's qualifications that would have been performed by the consular officer if that part of the process were occurring in a foreign country. One other important variation also deserves mention. Since 1994, under the provisions of the Violence Against Women Act (VAWA), certain noncitizens who are the victims of domestic violence at the hands of a citizen or LPR spouse are eligible to file a visa petition on their own behalf, to establish that they have the qualifying relationship even if the abuser will not initiate the process. Congress adopted this self-petition procedure in order to minimize the chance that the abuser can threaten the withholding of immigration benefits in order to continue his or her dominance.

The materials in the next few parts of this chapter provide a detailed introduction to the workings of the preference categories and other admission provisions. The following problems may provide a useful focus for your study of these complex sections and for understanding who may petition and who may benefit from a visa petition. Keep them in mind as you work your way through the statute and the descriptions that follow.

PROBLEMS

For each problem below, assume you are an attorney approached for advice. What do you recommend? What additional information must you develop, if any? (As to some, you should remember that a lawful permanent resident qualifies for naturalization, in most cases, after five years' residence in this country.) There may be many ways to accomplish the client's aims; try to find the most expeditious one, paying attention to any backlogs in the preference categories for which your client may qualify. In this respect, the latest monthly visa admission allocation charts (a sample appears as Table 5.5 below, p. 289) are indispensable.

1. Your client has been a lawful permanent resident of the United States for 10 years. Last month in Nairobi he married a national of Kenya who has a six-year-old child by a previous marriage (which was properly terminated by a valid divorce action), and naturally he wants to bring his wife and her child to this country as soon as possible.

2. Your client is a lawful permanent resident who entered this country in that status 15 years ago. He wants to bring his brother here from Greece.

3. Your client, a citizen of the Philippines, entered as a lawful permanent resident two years ago under the third family-sponsored preference, for married sons and daughters of U.S. citizens. At the time he brought with him his wife and three of his four children, leaving behind his eldest, a daughter who was then 19. This daughter had already entered college and believed at the time that she did not want to emigrate. Now she has changed her mind, and would like to come to the United States and take up studies in this country as soon as possible.

4. You have been contacted by a 20–year–old Swiss national who wishes to immigrate to the United States. He has heard that family ties are the key to immigration, and he reports that he has an uncle in Chicago who is a U.S. citizen and would be willing to do any necessary paperwork. He also reports that he has worked as a researcher for an engineering professor at his university, where he is completing his baccalaureate degree in biomedical engineering.

5. Your client, a high school dropout, is the principal sharehold-er and chief executive officer of a Brazilian software firm with annual gross receipts equivalent to several million dollars. For many years, he has been thinking of establishing sales outlets in a variety of other countries, possibly including the United States. In any event, whatev-er happens with the business, he wishes to take up permanent residence here. What do you advise? If he had finished high school, would this make a difference in his chances? If he had finished college? If he had a Ph.D. in mathematics?

b. Family–Sponsored Immigration

To obtain permanent residence in the United States based on a family relationship, noncitizens must qualify either under one of the four prefer-ence categories assigned to family reunification, INA § 203(a), or as *immediate relatives* of U.S. citizens. INA § 201(b)(2)(A). You may find it useful to consult those sections of the INA at this point and refer back to them as you make your way through the following material.

Immediate relatives. "Immediate relative" is defined to include spouses and children, and, if the petitioning citizen is over 21, parents as well. This limitation on petitioning for parents was adopted in view of America's uniquely strong *jus soli* citizenship rules. As we discussed in Chapter Two, virtually any child born on U.S. soil, even to parents illegally present, is a U.S. citizen. If not for the age 21 requirement, the newborns could immediately petition for permanent resident status for their parents. (Moreover, under current law, as we shall see in Chapter Six, a 21–year–old citizen may face serious obstacles to obtaining admis-sion for noncitizen parents if the parents have past immigration viola-tions.)

The statutory definition of "child," INA § 101(b)(1), is lengthy and precise. The subtle differences among the various family categories derive primarily from the specific terms of this definition, and the related definition of "parent" in § 101(b)(2). Those definitions merit very close attention. Note that a "child" must be under 21 and unmarried. The definition includes stepchildren and legitimated children, if the qualifying relationship was established before the child reached age 18, and it includes adopted children if the adoption occurred before age 16. With certain qualifications, it also includes children born out of wedlock. Status as a "parent" depends upon relationship to a "child" as defined in § 101(b)(1). The parent may be eligible if the son or daughter is now over 21 or married, provided that the relationship was established while the offspring still satisfied the statutory definition of "child."

No numerical ceilings apply to immediate relatives. All who meet the qualitative requirements by showing the requisite family relationship qualify, making this perhaps the most favored of all immigration categories.[2] As shown in Table 5.2, the number of such admissions has increased markedly over the last 40 years.

Table 5.2
Immediate Relatives Admitted

Fiscal Year	Number Admitted
1970	79,213
1975	85,871
1980	145,992
1985	204,368
1995	220,360
2000	347,870
2005	436,115
2006	580,348
2007	494,920
2008	488,483
2009	535,554
2010	476,414

Sources: 1980 Statistical Abstract of the United States, Table 133 (for 1970–1975); 1980 INS Statistical Yearbook, Table 4 (for 1980); 1992 INS Statistical Yearbook, Table 4 (for 1985); 1996 INS Statistical Yearbook, Table 4 (for 1990); 2004 Yearbook of Immigration Statistics, Table 4 (for 1995, 2000); 2010 Yearbook of Immigration Statistics, Table 6 (for 2005–2010).

Family-sponsored preference categories. In contrast to immediate relatives, the family-sponsored (FS) preference categories of INA

---

2. INA § 201(b) lists other categories that are not subject to the "worldwide" numerical limitations of § 201(a), but only a few are truly exempt from all ceilings, and most are not numerically significant in any event. For example, special immigrants under § 101(a)(27)(A) are lawful permanent residents "returning from a temporary visit abroad." These are all readmissions of persons who went through the full immigrant screening in the past. Without this escape hatch, they would be double-counted against relevant quotas. Further, section 201(b) exempts from the worldwide ceilings refugees and asylees, but persons brought in through overseas refugee resettlement programs are subject to their own separate quotas established annually under § 207, and asylees must satisfy a fairly rigorous statutory test, INA § 208, to obtain this status. Section 208 is covered in detail in Chapter Eight. Finally, § 201(b)(2)(B) exempts from numerical limitation those children "born to an alien lawfully admitted for permanent residence during a temporary visit abroad." These admissions typically run between 2,000 and 3,000 per year.

§ 203(a) are subject to annual numerical ceilings. When there are more applicants than admission spaces, which has been uniformly the case since the 1990s, backlogs develop. Admissions are processed within each family preference in chronological order, based on the time when the visa petition or other document initiating the process was filed with the immigration authorities. The family-based preferences are as follows:

- The first preference provides 23,400 admissions annually for *unmarried sons and daughters of U.S. citizens*. Unmarried children of citizens, you will recall, can come in as immediate relatives, without quota limits. (Ask yourself: why then is this preference category necessary?)

- The second preference allows for a minimum of 114,200 admissions annually, of the *spouses and unmarried sons and daughters of lawful permanent resident aliens*. Congress subdivided this preference into categories (A) and (B), to help assure that a higher percentage of admissions would go to spouses and minor children (category 2A)—those for whom lengthy separation is especially harsh—as opposed to offspring who had already reached age 21. These older offspring (category 2B) may not claim more than 23 percent of the admissions available under the second preference. Furthermore, any additional numbers over the baseline family preference ceiling of 226,000 that happen to become available for family-sponsored immigration in a given year, owing to the annual adjustments to the ceilings discussed below, are all given to category 2A. A glance at Table 5.5, p. 289, reveals that the waiting time is indeed many years shorter for 2A than 2B, but it still stretched to almost 4 years as of June 2011.

- The third preference provides 23,400 admissions for *married sons and daughters of U.S. citizens*—those who cannot qualify, because of marital status, for the immediate relative category or for first preference.

- The fourth preference provides 65,000 admissions each year for *brothers and sisters of U.S. citizens*. The statutory definition of "child" is consulted to decide whether the requisite sibling relationship is satisfied.

c. Employment–Based Immigration

As revised by the 1990 Act, 140,000 admissions are normally available for the five employment-based (EB) categories (INA § 203(b)):

- The first preference provides roughly 40,000 numbers[3] for "priority workers," a category that is further subdivided to include (1) aliens

---

3. INA § 203(b) states the employment-based preference category totals in terms of percentages of the worldwide ceiling on employment-based admissions (the baseline allocation is 140,000): 28.6 percent each for the first three categories, and 7.1 percent each for the fourth and fifth. In years when the 140,000 total is augmented for the reasons discussed in Section 1f below, each employment-based category's quota rises proportionally. In contrast, all extra numbers for

with "extraordinary ability" (the statute says that qualification requires "sustained national or international acclaim"), (2) outstanding professors and researchers, and (3) certain multinational executives and managers (these two terms are defined in INA § 101(a)(44)).

• The second preference provides roughly 40,000 admissions for professionals holding advanced degrees "or their equivalent" or who, "because of their exceptional ability in the sciences, arts, or business, will substantially benefit prospectively the national economy, cultural or educational interests, or welfare of the United States." Their services must be sought by an employer, unless this requirement is waived by the Attorney General "in the national interest."

• The third preference is for professionals having only baccalaureate degrees, and for skilled and unskilled workers who would fill positions for which there is a shortage of American workers. Roughly 40,000 admissions are available for this preference each year. In the debates on the 1990 Act, some lawmakers proposed eliminating admission of unskilled workers altogether, arguing that employers with a need for unskilled labor should be forced to train or otherwise attract unemployed Americans. As a compromise, Congress allowed only a small portion of third preference numbers to be used for unskilled workers each year (currently capped at 5,000).[4]

• The fourth preference, with about 10,000 annual admissions, is for certain "special immigrants" as defined in INA § 101(a)(27)(C) through (M). These categories include religious workers, former long-time employees of the U.S. government or of international organizations, and a host of other miscellaneous provisions.

• The fifth preference provides roughly 10,000 numbers for investors whose investments will create a minimum of 10 jobs in the U.S. economy. The baseline minimum investment is $1,000,000, but the required amount is lowered if the investment is in a rural area or high unemployment area, or if the money is invested through a "regional center" designated by USCIS based on a submitted economic growth plan. Concerned about possible fraud in this category, Congress provided that fifth-preference immigrants initially receive only conditional permanent residence status, with a review of the bona fides of the investment after two years. INA § 216A.

the family-sponsored preference categories are assigned to the second preference, destined for the nuclear family members of lawful permanent residents (category FS–2A).

4. The INA prescribes 10,000 spaces for "other workers," but for many years to come, only 5,000 admissions will be available because of an offset to cover admissions of the special beneficiaries of the Nicaraguan Adjustment and Central American Relief Act (NACARA), Pub.L. 105–100, 111 Stat. 2160 (1997). NACARA also mandated a similar reduction of 5,000 for diversity immigrants (leaving that category with 50,000 annual admissions).

Under the 1990 Act, labor certification is required only for the second and third employment-based preferences, *see* INA §§ 204(b), 212(a)(5)(A). Also, noncitizens in the first, second and third preferences generally cannot initiate the petitioning process themselves; an employer interested in using their services usually must petition. INA § 204(a)(1)(F). By way of exception, however, aliens with extraordinary ability (part A of the first preference), and second-preference aliens given a national-interest waiver can petition for themselves. Most fourth-and fifth-preference aliens may also self-petition. INA § 204(a)(1)(E), (G), (H).

d. Diversity Immigration

When Congress ended national origins quotas in 1965, it anticipated that, under the new system, preference immigrants would not use all the numbers potentially available. The excess would be open for "nonpreference" immigration, on a first-come first-served basis, to those who met certain minimal requirements. Such immigration did not require a petition by a family member here already; hence it could cover a more diverse population. But by 1978, demand in the preference categories exceeded the supply of numbers available under the overall preference ceiling, and nonpreference immigration therefore disappeared. By 1986, Congress was searching for ways to recapture some of the openness that nonpreference immigration signaled. Congress also sought to ameliorate the steep reduction in European migration that—according to the prevailing view—had been an unexpected byproduct of the 1965 amendments.[5] Supporters of the new provisions most often voiced concern about reduced immigration opportunities from Ireland.

After trying several different formulas for annual lotteries open to nationals of countries deemed underrepresented in U.S. admissions, Congress settled in 1990 on the permanent diversity system, set forth in INA § 203(c). The statute employs an extraordinarily intricate formula, based on the immigration statistics from the immediately preceding five-year period, to decide which countries can share in the diversity (DV) admissions each year. People from "high admission countries" are not eligible to participate in the diversity lottery. For fiscal year 2012, this provision will disqualify nationals from 19 countries: Brazil, Canada, China (mainland-born), Colombia, Dominican Republic, Ecuador, El Salvador, Guatemala,

---

5. Later scholarship has cast doubt on whether Congress was truly surprised by the demographic impact of the 1965 amendments. *See* Chin, *The Civil Rights Revolution Comes to Immigration Law: A New Look at the Immigration and Nationality Act of 1965*, 75 N.C.L.Rev. 273 (1996) (citing evidence that Congress understood that the 1965 Act would increase Asian immigration). For a thorough account of the lengthy history and peculiar politics that produced the diversity provisions, see Law, *The Diversity Visa Lottery—A Cycle of Unintended Consequences in United States Immigration Policy*, 21 J. Am. Ethnic Hist. 3 (2002). Diversity visas remain controversial. Critics argue, for example, that the 50,000 admissions could be better used to reduce the massive backlogs in the family categories. *See* Wasem, Diversity Immigrant Visa Lottery Issues (Congressional Research Service, Apr. 1, 2011).

Haiti, India, Jamaica, Mexico, Pakistan, Peru, Philippines, Poland, South Korea, United Kingdom (except Northern Ireland), and Vietnam. Natives of all other countries qualify, but their relative share of the total depends on whether their country of origin is in a high-admission or a low-admission region. The 1990 Act provided for 55,000 diversity admissions annually, but a later offset provision has reduced that level to 50,000 for many years to come. See footnote 4 *supra*.

The number of diversity admissions by region for fiscal year 2010 appears in Table 5.3.

Table 5.3
Allocation of Diversity Admissions for FY 2010

Area	Number Admitted
Africa	23,148
Asia	14,575
Europe	9,938
North America	694
South America	561
Oceania	647
Unknown or not reported	200
Total	49,763

Source: 2010 Yearbook of Immigration Statistics, Table 11.

Individuals must meet certain threshold requirements to qualify for these diversity visas. INA § 203(c)(2). They must (1) have a high school education or its equivalent, or (2) within five years preceding the application, have had at least two years of experience in an occupation that requires at least two years of training or experience. Aspirants for diversity immigration may file only one application per year—typically during a one-month window about a year before the fiscal year in which the admissions will be available. Applications now must be filed online, accompanied by digital photographs. Instructions appear on the State Department's web page at <http://travel.state.gov/visa/immigrants/types/types_1318.html>. A random lottery then selects the actual beneficiaries. INA § 203(e)(2). Winners can bring their immediate families, but family members count against the total diversity ceiling. There is a separate registration and a separate lottery each year.

Registration for diversity admissions to occur during FY 2011 was held from October 2 to November 30, 2009. Over 12.1 million qualified applications were received. From these, the Department selected approximately 106,000 who were notified that they may be eligible to apply and so should gather the needed information. This figure is far above the annual limit of 50,000 diversity admissions, but takes into account a drop-off rate for persons who choose not to pursue their cases or ultimately prove not to qualify. The Department provides each notified individual a rank-order number, and it then allows only those above a certain cut-off number to apply in the early months. As the actual response and qualification rate becomes clear (including the number of derivative family members who will be admitted with the principals), the Department then makes monthly adjustments in the cut-off number to allow persons further down the list to apply for a visa or for adjustment. This process therefore brings some agonizing uncertainty to the process, particularly for those whose rank-order number is reached only late in the fiscal year. If a notified person is tardy in completing an application or the processing office is slow, an ostensible lottery winner can become a loser at midnight September 30, when the fiscal year expires, or earlier, if the 50,000 ceiling is reached. The top recipient countries for FY 2011, based on notifications rather than admissions, were: Ghana, Bangladesh, Nigeria, Ukraine, Uzbekistan, Ethiopia, Kenya, and Egypt, in that order. Department of State, *Diversity Visa Lottery 2011 (DV–2011) Results,* <http://travel.state.gov/visa/immigrants/types/types_5073.html>.

e. Derivatives: Family Members Who Accompany or Follow to Join

Consider the case of a noncitizen who enters under the third family preference, as a married daughter of a U.S. citizen. What about her husband and children, who do not personally meet the statutory requirements for third preference and have no other way of directly qualifying for admission to the United States? Must they wait until she is admitted as an LPR and then wait still further until she successfully petitions for them under the second family preference?

The answer is no. The statute takes an important step toward avoiding such separation of nuclear families. Section 203(d) (which also applies to employment-based and diversity immigration) provides that the spouse or child may be admitted in the same preference category and in the "same order of consideration" (i.e., at the same spot on the waiting list, when there is a backlog) as the principal alien. These are known as *derivative beneficiaries.* Their admissions are then charged against the ceiling for the principal's preference category. (This feature has sometimes prompted criticism from observers who believe that the United States should admit more immigrants based on their skills; they note that over half the 140,000 admission spaces nominally available for employment-based immigration actually get used by derivatives.)

Section 203(d) applies to accompanying family members and also those "following to join." Administrative practice governing the preference categories treats noncitizens as "following to join" at any time after the migration of the principal, so long as the family member remains a spouse or child at the time of his or her admission. The benefits of § 203(d) are available, however, only when the specified family relationship existed at the time when the principal was *admitted*. "After-acquired" spouses and children of lawful permanent residents must use the second preference. *See Matter of Naulu*, 19 I & N Dec. 351, 352 n.1 (BIA 1986); R. Divine & B. Chisam, Immigration Practice § 8–4(a)(1) (2010–11 ed.); 22 C.F.R. §§ 40.1(a)(1), 42.53(c); 9 FAM 40.1 N7.

Note also that because § 203(d) refers only to admission under § 203(a), (b), or (c), it does not apply to a spouse or child of those who are admitted as immediate relatives of U.S. citizens, a category governed by § 201(b)(2)(A)(i). Take a look at that last provision, and the definition of child in § 101(b)(1), to see why children of persons who can enter as immediate relatives will nonetheless still qualify, most of the time, to accompany their immigrant parent, as immediate relatives in their own right—but identify a few scenarios where they will not.

f. Ceilings and Floors

Fluctuating ceilings and admission shortfalls. At first glance, INA § 201(c) appears to set a ceiling on all family-sponsored immigration, including immediate relatives, at the level of 480,000. A firm cap of this sort was in fact the intent of some early versions of the legislation that became the 1990 Act. Because those bills would still have assured unhindered admission of all immediate relatives of U.S. citizens (provided those numbers did not exceed the overall family cap), critics objected to the likely steady shrinkage of admissions for the family preference categories as immediate relative admissions increased. The critics ultimately prevailed in the final version of the 1990 Act. But instead of taking the most logical step and simply eliminating a family ceiling, Congress adopted the complex formula of INA § 201(c). It guarantees a floor for the family-sponsored preference categories—a minimum of 226,000 available admission spaces every year—even though this will mean that the overall family cap is "pierced" when immediate relative admissions exceed 254,000 (as they now regularly do, by large margins). INA § 201(c)(1)(B)(ii). The net result is unlimited admission of immediate relatives, plus what will normally work out, given the high demand for immediate relative admissions, to about 226,000 available admission spaces for the family-sponsored preference categories.

Table 5.4 shows admission totals, broken down by the major categories, for selected years since 1995. You can see that admissions by category can fluctuate rather substantially, however, and for some years appear higher or lower, sometimes much lower, than the apparent statutory allotment for particular preference categories, even though there are millions of individuals on the waiting lists, ready and eager to use those admissions spaces.

Table 5.4
Immigrants Admitted by Major Category of Admission, Selected Years FY 1995–2010

Category	1995	2000	2006	2007	2008	2009	2010
All Immigrants	720,461	841,002	1,266,129	1,052,415	1,107,126	1,130,818	1,042,625
Immediate relatives of US citizens	220,360	346,350	580,348	494,920	488,483	535,554	476,414
Family-sponsored preferences	238,122	235,092	222,229	194,900	227,761	211,859	214,589
1st preference	15,182	27,003	25,432	22,858	26,173	23,965	26,998
2nd preference	144,535	112,015	112,051	86,151	103,456	98,567	92,088
3rd preference	20,876	24,830	21,491	20,611	29,273	25,930	32,817
4th preference	57,529	67,851	63,255	65,280	68,859	63,397	62,686
Employment-based preferences	85.336	106,642	159,075	161,733	164,741	140,903	148,343
1st preference	17,339	27,566	36,960	26,697	36,678	40,924	41,055
2nd preference	10,475	20,255	21,911	44,162	70,046	45,552	53,946
3rd preference	50,245	49,589	89,922	85,030	48,903	40,398	39,762
4th preference	6,737	9,014	9,533	5,038	7,754	10,341	11,100
5th preference	540	218	749	806	1,360	3,688	2,480
Diversity Programs	40,301	50,920	44,471	42,127	41,761	47,879	49,763
Refugees and Asylees*	114,664	62,928	216,454	136,125	166,392	177,368	136,291
Other	17,411	39,070	43,552	22,610	17,988	17,255	17,225

* Refugees and asylees are counted in the year in which they gain full LPR status through adjustment of status (at least one year, and often multiple years, after initial admission). A 2005 relaxation in the rules governing asylee adjustments (repealing a low annual ceiling) accounts for most of the large increase in refugee and asylee admissions thereafter, while the system catches up with a large asylee adjustment backlog.

Sources: 2004 Yearbook of Immigration Statistics, Table 4 (for 1995); 2009 Yearbook of Immigration Statistics, Table 6 (for 2000); 2010 Yearbook of Immigration Statistics, Table 6 (for 2006–2010).

Figures 5.1 and 5.2 provide additional ways of visualizing the composition of immigrant admissions and adjustments in the United States to the United States, focusing on fiscal year 2009. The first graph shows LPR admissions by category. Family admissions constitute nearly two-thirds of the total, and immediate relatives constituted over 70 percent of the family admissions. Figure 5.2 then breaks down by admission category the immigration from each of the top ten sending countries (which together accounted for 48 percent of overall permanent migration). You will notice strikingly divergent patterns among these populations—for example, a vast predominance of family admissions for Mexico, heavy refugee-type admissions for Cuba, and the major concentrations of employment-based admissions from India and South Korea, followed by China and the Philippines.

Figure 5.1
Legal Permanent Residents by Major Category, FY 2009

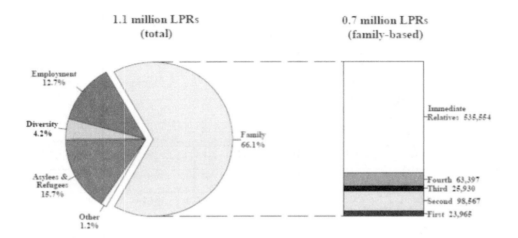

Source: CRS presentation of FY2009 data from the DHS Office of Immigration Statistics.

Most of the fluctuation apparent in Table 5.4 has resulted from processing bottlenecks that trace largely to resource allocations within DOL and DHS (and earlier, INS). Immigration demand is not so fickle as to account for a change from under 195,000 family preference admissions in FY 2007, for example, to over 227,000 the following year. Instead, USCIS processing resources were squeezed in 2007, before a major fee increase enabled the hiring of hundreds of new adjudicators. Other processing bottlenecks, such as far more intense security-related background checks mandated in the wake of the September 11 attacks, or complications or inefficiency in DOL's process for issuing labor certification, have also contributed at various times to lengthy delays in adjudication. These problems have sometimes pushed average processing times for adjustment of status to as long as 36 months, and meant that the system simply did not manage to use the available admission spaces. DOL and USCIS have made major strides over the last few years, however, in matching resources to demand and also redesigning business practices, automating routine parts of the process, and streamlining others. Processing times are now far more reliably matching target times (under six months for adjustment or naturalization applications, for example), and the new resources and processes should help reduce fluctuations and shortfalls in the future. Attorneys and applicants can check current processing times for specific types of applications on the USCIS website, <https://egov. uscis.gov/cris/processTimesDisplayInit.do>.

Admission spaces that go unused in the preference categories are not lost, however. The statute essentially assures that unused numbers in one year are added to totals for the following year, though these added numbers are distributed in a highly complex fashion and often are usable

Figure 5.2
Top Ten LPR–Sending Countries, FY 2009

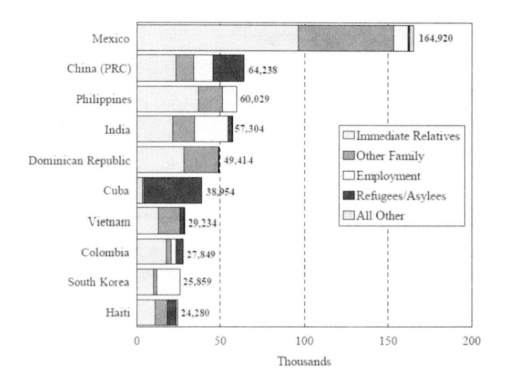

Source: CRS presentation of FY2009 data from the DHS Office of Immigration Statistics.

in a different category than the one that fell short the year before. The provisions governing ceiling adjustments, including spill-downs and cross-category carryovers, are described in the footnote for those who hunger for such detail.[6] (Others can skip these technical descriptions.) It should be noted that any added numbers for the family preferences in a given year

---

6. The preference categories, both family-sponsored and employment-based, allow for "spill-down." That is, if there are not enough qualified applicants to use all 23,400 family first-preference numbers, for example, the balance spills down and becomes available for second preference *that same year*, and so on. Numbers also recycle back up to the top of the respective set of preferences if the lowest preference has unused numbers. Because demand exceeds supply in the family-sponsored preferences, little spill-down occurs there, but the process has been important in the employment categories. Few admissions occur in the 5th employment-based preference, leaving a total that recycles back up to the first employment-based preference, and often then spills down to the highest-demand employment categories, the second and third preferences.

Under separate cross-category carryover provisions, if not all employment-based numbers are used in a given year, the unused balance can be applied to family-sponsored immigration *the following year* (and vice versa—from family to employment categories). INA § 201(c)(3), (d)(2). This has frequently caused a given year's ceiling in either family-sponsored or employment-based categories to wind up many thousands higher than what the basic statutory provisions would seem to call for. (See, for example, the employment-based admissions for FY 2008: more than 164,000, as against a normal EB ceiling of 140,000.) Even in high-demand years, some such cross-category carryover to the following fiscal year occurs simply because of the logistical complexity of

are all assigned to category 2A, for spouses and children of LPRs. Added numbers for the employment-based preferences are distributed pro rata among among all five categories.

Per-country ceilings. The calculation of annual category ceilings is complicated enough, but one other set of ceilings adds further complexity: per-country ceilings under INA § 202. Congress added such ceilings in 1965 when it repealed the national origins quotas. They were, in their own way, a kind of diversity provision, assuring that no one country received over 20,000 of the preference admissions in any one year. The ceilings had particularly harsh effects on Mexico and the Philippines, where, owing to geography or historical ties, demand for U.S. immigration is particularly strong. In the 1990 Act, Congress changed the formula, but retained the idea of per-country ceilings. You need not bother with the complexity of § 202, but you should know that the ceiling will now be at least 25,620, and it will be somewhat higher whenever categorical ceilings are above the normal levels. Under specific and limited circumstances set forth in statute, some particular preference admissions are exempted from the per-country ceiling. *See, e.g.,* INA § 202(a)(5).

This per-country provision is sometimes misunderstood. It does not mean that each nation is entitled to send 25,000 preference immigrants each year. Instead it is an override provision that kicks in only if the normal operation of the worldwide preference system would happen to send more than the per-country ceiling in a given year, based on demand from qualifying applicants from that particular state.[7] Chargeability to a foreign state is based on location of birth, not nationality (although these usually coincide), with a few exceptions designed primarily to keep immigrating families together. INA § 202(b).

The per-country ceilings of INA § 202 apply only to preference immigration in the employment-based and family-sponsored categories. Importantly, immediate relatives are not affected by per-country ceilings, and even a massive use of immediate relative admissions by a particular state will not reduce the per-country ceiling available for preference immigrants from that country. Diversity immigrants are subject to their own separate per-country ceiling provision (currently 3,500). INA § 203(c)(1)(E)(v).

g. Implementing the Ceilings: Visa Charts, Conversion, and Aging Out

Visa allocation priority date charts. Fortunately, practicing immigration lawyers never have to attempt the ceiling calculations required under §§ 201, 202, and 203. That complex task falls to officials of the Visa Office of the Department of State, who prepare charts showing how far

---

the system, which involves visa issuance and adjustment of status carried out in hundreds of offices throughout the globe. It is impossible to make the numbers come out exactly even on September 30, when the fiscal year ends. *See generally* Stapleton, *Immigrant Visa Availability under the Immigration Act of 1990: Initial Observations from the Visa Office,* 68 Interp.Rel. 373 (1991); Devoren & Hernandez, *Priority Dates: More Important Than Ever,* 11–20 Bender's Immig. Bull. 2 (2006).

7. Also, the statute provides special allocation rules for countries that are at the per-country ceiling, to assure that not all of that country's numbers are used up by the higher preferences. INA § 202(e). Those special allocation rules account for why the visa allocation chart in Table 5.5 shows separate cut-off dates for China, India, Mexico, and the Philippines, the four countries then affected by § 202(e).

down the waiting list consular officers will reach in processing preference immigrant visas for a particular month. Those charts—rather than the statutory sections—are frequently consulted by the immigration bar, particularly in order to advise clients about approximately when they can expect to immigrate in any category for which they might qualify. The charts are published monthly in the State Department's *Visa Bulletin* and on its website, <http://travel.state.gov/visa/bulletin/bulletin_1360.html>, as well as in various periodical reporting services like *Interpreter Releases.*

Table 5.5 reprints one of these charts, showing visa allocation priority dates for June 2011. Use this table to familiarize yourself with this basic

Table 5.5
Visa Preference Admissions for June 2011

	All chargeability areas except those listed	CHINA-mainland born	INDIA	MEXICO	PHILLIPINES
Priority Dates for Family–Sponsored Categories					
1st Preference	May 1, 2004	May 1, 2004	May 1, 2004	Mar. 1, 1993	Feb. 22, 1996
2nd Preference (A)	Aug. 22, 2007	Aug. 22, 2007	Aug. 22, 2007	July 22, 2007	Aug. 22, 2007
2nd Preference (B)	Apr. 15, 2003	Apr. 15, 2003	Apr. 15, 2003	Aug. 22, 1992	June 8, 2000
3rd Preference	June 1, 2001	June 1, 2001	June 1, 2001	Nov. 15, 1992	Mar. 8, 1992
4th Preference	Mar. 8, 2000	Mar. 8, 2000	Mar. 8, 2000	Feb. 15, 1996	May 1, 1988
Priority Dates for Employment–Based Categories					
1st Preference	Current	Current	Current	Current	Current
2nd Preference	Current	Oct. 15, 2006	Oct. 15, 2006	Current	Current
3rd Preference	Sept. 15, 2005	May 15, 2004	Apr. 22, 2002	Dec. 22, 2004	Sept. 15, 2005
Other Workers	Nov. 8, 2003	Apr. 22, 2003	Apr. 22, 2002	Nov. 8, 2003	Nov. 8, 2003
4th Preference	Current	Current	Current	Current	Current
Certain Religious Workers	Current	Current	Current	Current	Current
5th Preference	Current	Current	Current	Current	Current

Source: Department of State, Visa Bulletin No. 33, Volume IX (June 2011).

tool of immigration practice, and also compare it with the chart that is current at the time of your reading. The chart also gives a useful indication of the lengthy quota-induced backlogs that have developed under several of the categories, especially for the high-demand countries that are affected by the per-country ceilings.

How the charts and the allocation system operate. The dates in the columns in Table 5.5 set forth visa allocation priority dates, which, roughly speaking, show an applicant's position on the waiting list. Preference visas are distributed, within each relevant classification, in chronological order of application. No immigrant subject to the quotas may receive a visa (or become a permanent resident by means of adjustment of status) until his or her priority date is current. The immigrant's priority date is the date when the first relevant document was properly filed with the appropriate administrative agency (visa petition for the family categories and some employment categories; application for labor certification for those employment preferences subject to this requirement). Note that this is a date many months in advance of any determination by those agencies that the individual is in fact eligible. Naturally, no visa will issue until all the eligibility determinations are concluded, even when the admission category is current.

To take an example of how priority dates are assigned, assume that an employer applies for labor certification for a stated position on April 1, 2010, and that the certification is issued by the U.S. Department of Labor on August 4. The employer then promptly files with USCIS a visa petition for the appropriate employment-based preference category. It is approved on May 15, 2011, and information about the approved visa petition is sent to the consulate in the country where the alien is expected to apply for the actual visa, or to the USCIS office that will handle the adjustment application. In these circumstances, the alien's visa allocation priority date is April 1, 2010. As of June 2011, was his priority date current so that he could then pursue the last stages of processing? Using the chart shown in Table 5.5, you can see that the answer depends on which of the two employment categories covered by the labor certification requirement he fits—which will be indicated on his approved visa petition. The second employment-based preference is current (unless the intending immigrant is from China or India); he may go ahead and file his adjustment application or, if overseas, be scheduled for his final consular interview. But if he is filing in the third preference, he must wait. Only applicants with a priority date before September 15, 2005, could be processed in that category in June 2011.

As of June 2011, most employment-based categories were current, but all third-preference applicants were subject to quota-caused backlogs. ("Other workers"—meaning the unskilled, whose numbers are limited to a fraction of the EB–3 category by INA § 203(b)(3)(B)—were subject to even more extensive delays.) The family preference categories, in sharp contrast, are all chronically backlogged because of high qualifying demand.

As an example of the workings of the priority date system in a family-sponsored preference category, assume that a U.S. citizen father petitions for his 26–year–old daughter, a Brazilian national, under the first preference, filing his visa petition with USCIS on February 7, 2009. Because of a controversy over the foreign birth certificate he submits, necessitating the filing of additional evidence, the petition is not approved until April 20, 2011, and approval is communicated to the U.S. consulate in Rio de Janeiro in May. The daughter's visa allocation priority date is February 7, 2009. She fits the first preference in the family-sponsored categories, and thus still faces a lengthy wait. As of June 2011, only those FS–1 cases with a priority date before May 1, *2004,* were current. You can check the most recent Visa Bulletin chart online to see how much this category has advanced since June 2011.

Conversion. If the Brazilian daughter in the hypothetical marries before admission to the United States, she becomes ineligible for the first preference, but she can still retain the same priority date for the category that now pertains: the third family-sponsored preference. That is, the visa petition automatically *converts* to a petition in the family category that is now relevant, retaining the original priority date. Consider closely what effects both the marriage and the rule allowing her to retain the same priority date will have on the actual timing of her admission. Conversion also applies in other circumstances based on changes in the status of petitioner or beneficiary. 8 C.F.R. § 204.2(i). Most important may be the situation when a petitioner seeking status for his spouse and offspring in the second preference category naturalizes. The visa petition then converts automatically to an immediate relative petition for the spouse and minor children (formerly in category FS–2A). For unmarried offspring over 21 (formerly in category FS–2B), the petition converts to the first preference (subject to a limited exception described below).

Aging out. In many settings, children under 21 are treated more favorably for immigration purposes than are sons and daughters who have passed their 21st birthday. But what is the date that counts for calculating the child's age? Several candidates are possible: the date when the petitioner files the visa petition, the date of its approval, the date when the beneficiary files for the visa or adjustment of status, the issuance of the visa, the date of adjustment or actual admission to the United States. Until 2002, the pertinent date was the latest, the actual date of admission or adjustment, which maximized the chances for "aging out." If the child had turned 21 before then, he or she would either fall into a less favorable category or lose any immediate avenue of eligibility. INS had procedures for expediting consideration if a child had a current visa priority allocation date but was close to aging out. Nonetheless, expedited treatment was not always successful in securing admission before the 21st birthday.

As backlogs in family preference categories have grown (because of higher demand confronting fixed annual admission ceilings), aging out became a more pressing issue. But it gained particular attention because of the other potential source of delay in admission—agency processing times. These times expanded to unprecedented lengths in the late 1990s, particularly for adjustment applications, but also for approval of visa petitions. In August 2002, Congress responded by changing the rules on aging out. Once again its handiwork is not neat or straightforward, but instead imposes different rules for different categories of offspring. Child Status Protection Act, Pub. L. No. 107–208, 116 Stat. 927 (2002) (principally codified in INA §§ 201(f), 203(h), 204(k)).

For immediate relative petitions, the child's age is now deemed to be the age at the time when the parent files the visa petition. *See Matter of Avila–Perez,* 24 I & N Dec. 78 (BIA 2007). If the petition began as a second preference petition but converts to immediate relative because the parent naturalizes, the child's age on the date of the parent's naturalization is what counts. INA § 201(f). In some circumstances, the parent's naturalization will move the son or daughter only from preference FS–2B to the first preference. Normally that is advantageous, but in the limited circumstances where it might slow down the admission, INA § 204(k) allows the son or daughter to elect still to be treated in category FS–2B.

For the FS–2A preference category and for derivative beneficiaries (remember: § 203(d) applies only to children, not older or married offspring), the rules grow more complicated. The child's age is determined as of the date when the relevant category becomes current, which at present could still be as many as 11 years (for the fourth preference) after the petitioning process began—or even 22 years for the Philippines fourth preference. *See* Table 5.5. But Congress provided that the age calculated in that fashion shall be reduced by the period of time consumed while the visa petition was pending (*only* the visa petition—not delays in processing a visa or adjustment of status). Furthermore, the beneficiary must apply for the visa or adjustment within one year of the date when the category becomes current or else lose the benefit of these anti-age-out rules. INA § 203(h).

An example from the preference categories may be useful. Assume that a U.S. citizen petitioned many years ago for the admission of his noncitizen brother. When that visa petition was filed, the intending immigrant brother had a daughter who was then 10. When, 13 years later (let us assume), his fourth preference priority date becomes current, the daughter's actual age is 23—too old by itself to take advantage of derivative status under § 203(d). But she might still qualify based on the reduction for visa petition processing times. If the immigration authorities took three years to approve the visa petition for the parent, that period is now deducted from her age. She is deemed to be 20, and she qualifies for derivative status—provided her father moves ahead with the immigration process for the family within a year from the date a visa number became available. On the other hand, if the authorities had approved her uncle's visa petition with greater alacrity, within one year of the filing, she is considered 22 and is ineligible. For more information on how these rules work, see 79 Interp.Rel. 1433, 1503, 1520 (2002); 80 *id.* 243 (2003).

You may want to return to item 3 in the Problems on pp. 276–77 and reconsider your answer, in order to check your understanding of the Child Status Protection Act. One possible question presented in that problem, if the daughter has in fact aged out despite CSPA, has to do with the application of the savings clause for aged-out children set forth in INA § 203(h)(3). (Look closely at that provision to see what that clause entails and what would be the most favorable interpretation for your hypothetical client.) The BIA eventually decided that the savings clause does not apply to the intending immigrant in cases of this type, with regard to the applicable priority date. *Matter of Wang,* 25 I & N Dec. 28 (BIA 2009); *see also Li v. Renaud,* 654 F.3d 376 (2d Cir. 2011) (approving BIA approach).

2. CONSTITUTIONAL STANDARDS FOR EVALUATING ADMISSION CATEGORIES

The preference categories and the other provisions of the INA governing immigrant admissions inevitably draw a host of fine distinctions among categories of noncitizens who might wish to immigrate to the United States. Much room is left to dispute the fairness and desirability of such distinctions. Is it fair, for example, to burden citizens of Mexico or the Philippines with inordinately long waiting lists, solely because the country ceiling provisions fail to take account of the lengthy historical ties between the United States and those nations? Is it fair to hold India or the People's Republic of China, with over a billion people, to the same country ceiling as Belize? Why should marriage disqualify the offspring of permanent residents?

Questions like these are the stuff of wide-ranging debates over legislative reform of the U.S. immigration system. But to what extent are they constitutional questions, subject to the policing of the federal courts? The Supreme Court considered these matters in the following case. The litigation presented a challenge to the definition of "child" in INA § 101(b)(1)(D) as it read before an amendment in 1986. At the time of the decision, the statute recognized only the relationship between illegitimate children and their natural mothers, excluding such relationships with the natural fathers.

FIALLO v. BELL

Supreme Court of the United States, 1977.
430 U.S. 787, 97 S.Ct. 1473, 52 L.Ed.2d 50.

MR. JUSTICE POWELL delivered the opinion of the Court.

This case brings before us a constitutional challenge to §§ 101(b)(1)(D) and 101(b)(2) of the Immigration and Nationality Act of 1952 (Act).

I

The Act grants special preference immigration status to aliens who qualify as the "children" or "parents" of United States citizens or lawful permanent residents. Under § 101(b)(1), a "child" is defined as an unmarried person under 21 years of age who is a legitimate or legitimated child, a stepchild, an adopted child, or an illegitimate child seeking preference by virtue of his relationship with his natural mother. The definition does not extend to an illegitimate child seeking preference by virtue of his relationship with his natural father. Moreover, under § 101(b)(2), a person qualifies as a "parent" for purposes of the Act solely on the basis of the person's relationship with a "child." As a result, the natural father of an illegitimate child who is either a United States citizen or permanent resident alien is not entitled to preferential treatment as a "parent."

The special preference immigration status provided for those who satisfy the statutory "parent-child" relationship depends on whether the immigrant's relative is a United States citizen or permanent resident alien.[a] A United States citizen is allowed the entry of his "parent" or "child" without regard to *either* an applicable numerical quota *or* the labor certification requirement. On the other hand, a United States permanent resident alien is allowed the entry of the "parent" or "child" subject to numerical limitations but without regard to the labor certification requirement.

Appellants are three sets of unwed natural fathers and their illegitimate offspring who sought, either as an alien father or an alien child, a special immigration preference by virtue of a relationship to a citizen or resident alien child or parent. In each instance the applicant was informed that he was ineligible for an immigrant visa unless he qualified for admission under the general numerical limitations and, in the case of the alien parents, received the requisite labor certification.

* * * At the outset, it is important to underscore the limited scope of judicial inquiry into immigration legislation. This Court has repeatedly emphasized that "over no conceivable subject is the legislative power of Congress more complete than it is over" the admission of aliens. *Oceanic Navigation Co. v. Stranahan*, 214 U.S. 320, at 339, 29 S.Ct. 671, at 676 (1909). Our cases "have long recognized the power to expel or exclude aliens as a fundamental sovereign attribute exercised by the Government's political departments largely immune from judicial control." *Shaughnessy v. Mezei*, 345 U.S. 206, at 210, 73 S.Ct. 625, at 628 (1953). Our recent decisions have not departed from this long-established rule. Just last Term, for example, the Court had occasion to note that "the power over aliens is of a political character and therefore subject only to

---

a. Before the 1976 amendments to the INA, most Western Hemisphere immigration was subject to an annual ceiling of 120,000, but the preference system did not apply. Noncitizens who were not excludable simply queued up for available numbers. All were subject to the labor certification requirement, however, unless it was waived because of specified family relationships. The Court treats the *Fiallo* case under pre–1976 law, but you should keep in mind that parents of lawful permanent residents—unlike parents of American citizens—no longer receive any special immigration benefits.—eds.

narrow judicial review." *Hampton v. Mow Sun Wong*, 426 U.S. 88, at 101 n. 21, 96 S.Ct. 1895, at 1904–1905, (1976), *citing Fong Yue Ting v. United States*, 149 U.S. 698, at 703, 13 S.Ct. 1016, at 1022 (1893). And we observed recently that in the exercise of its broad power over immigration and naturalization, "Congress regularly makes rules that would be unacceptable if applied to citizens." *Id.*, at 80, 96 S.Ct., at 1891.

Appellants apparently do not challenge the need for special judicial deference to congressional policy choices in the immigration context,[5] but instead suggest that a "unique coalescing of factors" makes the instant case sufficiently unlike prior immigration cases to warrant more searching judicial scrutiny.

Appellants first observe that since the statutory provisions were designed to reunite families wherever possible, the purpose of the statute was to afford rights not to aliens but to United States citizens and legal permanent residents. Appellants then rely on our border-search decisions * * * for the proposition that the courts must scrutinize congressional legislation in the immigration area to protect against violations of the rights of citizens. At issue in the border-search cases, however, was the nature of the protections mandated by the Fourth Amendment with respect to Government procedures designed to stem the illegal entry of aliens. Nothing in the opinions in those cases suggests that Congress has anything but exceptionally broad power to determine which classes of aliens may lawfully enter the country.

Appellants suggest a second distinguishing factor. They argue that none of the prior immigration cases of this Court involved "double-barreled" discrimination based on sex and illegitimacy, infringed upon the due process rights of citizens and legal permanent residents, or implicated "the fundamental constitutional interests of United States citizens and permanent residents in a familial relationship." But this Court has resolved similar challenges to immigration legislation based on other constitutional rights of citizens, and has rejected the suggestion that more searching judicial scrutiny is required. In *Kleindienst v. Mandel* [408 U.S. 753, 92 S.Ct. 2576 (1972), considered in Chapter Seven, p. 615 below], for example, United States citizens challenged the power of the Attorney General to deny a visa to a noncitizen who, as a proponent of "the economic, international, and governmental doctrines of World communism", was ineligible to receive a visa * * * absent a waiver by the Attorney General. The citizen-appellees in that case conceded that Congress could prohibit entry of all noncitizens falling into the class defined by [that section]. They contended, however, that the Attorney General's statutory discretion to approve a waiver was limited by the Constitution

---

5. The appellees argue that the challenged sections of the Act, embodying as they do "a substantive policy regulating the admission of aliens into the United States, [are] not an appropriate subject for judicial review." Our cases reflect acceptance of a limited judicial responsibility under the Constitution even with respect to the power of Congress to regulate the admission and exclusion of aliens, and there is no occasion to consider in this case whether there may be actions of the Congress with respect to aliens that are so essentially political in character as to be nonjusticiable.

and that their First Amendment rights were abridged by the denial of Mandel's request for a visa. The Court held that "when the Executive exercises this [delegated] power negatively on the basis of a facially legitimate and bona fide reason, the courts will neither look behind the exercise of that discretion, nor test it by balancing its justification against the First Amendment interests of those who seek personal communication with the applicant." We can see no reason to review the broad congressional policy choice at issue here under a more exacting standard than was applied in *Kleindienst v. Mandel,* a First Amendment case.[6]

Finally, appellants characterize our prior immigration cases as involving foreign policy matters and congressional choices to exclude or expel groups of aliens that were "specifically and clearly perceived to pose a grave threat to the national security," * * * "or to the general welfare of this country." * * * We find no indication in our prior cases that the scope of judicial review is a function of the nature of the policy choice at issue. To the contrary, "[s]ince decisions in these matters may implicate our relations with foreign powers, and since a wide variety of classifications must be defined in the light of changing political and economic circumstances, such decisions are frequently of a character more appropriate to either the Legislature or the Executive than to the Judiciary," and "[t]he reasons that preclude judicial review of political questions also dictate a narrow standard of review of decisions made by the Congress or the President in the area of immigration and naturalization." * * *

III

As originally enacted in 1952, § 101(b)(1) of the Act defined a "child" as an unmarried legitimate or legitimated child or stepchild under 21

---

6. The thoughtful dissenting opinion of our Brother Marshall would be persuasive if its basic premise were accepted. The dissent is grounded on the assumption that the relevant portions of the Act grant a "fundamental right" to American citizens, a right "given only to the citizen" and not to the putative immigrant. The assumption is facially plausible in that the families of putative immigrants certainly have an interest in their admission. But the fallacy of the assumption is rooted deeply in fundamental principles of sovereignty.

We are dealing here with an exercise of the Nation's sovereign power to admit or exclude foreigners in accordance with perceived national interests. Although few, if any, countries have been as generous as the United States in extending the privilege to immigrate, or in providing sanctuary to the oppressed, limits and classifications as to who shall be admitted are traditional and necessary elements of legislation in this area. It is true that the legislative history of the provision at issue here establishes that congressional concern was directed at "the problem of keeping families of United States citizens and immigrants united." * * * To accommodate this goal, Congress has accorded a special "preference status" to certain aliens who share relationships with citizens or permanent resident aliens. But there are widely varying relationships and degrees of kinship, and it is appropriate for Congress to consider not only the nature of these relationships but also problems of identification, administration, and the potential for fraud. In the inevitable process of "line drawing," Congress has determined that certain classes of aliens are more likely than others to satisfy national objectives without undue cost, and it has granted preferential status only to those classes.

As Mr. Justice Frankfurter wrote years ago, the formulation of these "[p]olicies pertaining to the entry of aliens . . . is entrusted exclusively to Congress". *Galvan v. Press,* 347 U.S., at 531, 74 S.Ct., at 743. This is not to say, as we make clear in n. 5, *supra,* that the Government's power in this area is never subject to judicial review. But our cases do make clear that despite the impact of these classifications on the interests of those already within our borders, congressional determinations such as this one are subject only to limited judicial review.

years of age. The Board of Immigration Appeals and the Attorney General subsequently concluded that the failure of this definition to refer to illegitimate children rendered ineligible for preferential nonquota status both the illegitimate alien child of a citizen mother, and the alien mother of a citizen born out of wedlock. The Attorney General recommended that the matter be brought to the attention of Congress, and the Act was amended in 1957 to include what is now § 101(b)(1)(D). Congress was specifically concerned with the relationship between a child born out of wedlock and his or her natural mother, and the legislative history of the 1957 amendment reflects an intentional choice not to provide preferential immigration status by virtue of the relationship between an illegitimate child and his or her natural father.

This distinction is just one of many drawn by Congress pursuant to its determination to provide some—but not all—families with relief from various immigration restrictions that would otherwise hinder reunification of the family in this country. In addition to the distinction at issue here, Congress has decided that children, whether legitimate or not, cannot qualify for preferential status if they are married or are over 21 years of age. Legitimated children are ineligible for preferential status unless their legitimation occurred prior to their 18th birthday and at a time when they were in the legal custody of the legitimating parent or parents. Adopted children are not entitled to preferential status unless they were adopted before the age of 14 and have thereafter lived in the custody of their adopting or adopted parents for at least two years.[b] And stepchildren cannot qualify unless they were under 18 at the time of the marriage creating the stepchild relationship.

With respect to each of these legislative policy distinctions, it could be argued that the line should have been drawn at a different point and that the statutory definitions deny preferential status to parents and children who share strong family ties. But it is clear from our cases that these are policy questions entrusted exclusively to the political branches of our Government, and we have no judicial authority to substitute our political judgment for that of the Congress.

Appellants suggest that the distinction drawn in § 101(b)(1)(D) is unconstitutional under any standard of review since it infringes upon the constitutional rights of citizens and legal permanent residents without furthering legitimate governmental interests. Appellants note in this regard that the statute makes it more difficult for illegitimate children and their natural fathers to be reunited in this country than for legitimate or legitimated children and their parents, or for illegitimate children and their natural mothers. And appellants also note that the statute fails to establish a procedure under which illegitimate children and their natural fathers could prove the existence and strength of their family relationship. Those are admittedly the consequences of the congressional decision not

---

b. Later amendments raised the age limit for adoption to 16 and deleted "thereafter" from the definition, thus recognizing two years' custody whether it occurred before or after formal adoption. See current INA § 101(b)(1)(E).—eds.

to accord preferential status to this particular class of aliens, but the decision nonetheless remains one "solely for the responsibility of the Congress and wholly outside the power of this Court to control." Congress obviously has determined that preferential status is not warranted for illegitimate children and their natural fathers, perhaps because of a perceived absence in most cases of close family ties as well as a concern with the serious problems of proof that usually lurk in paternity determinations.[8] In any event, it is not the judicial role in cases of this sort to probe and test the justifications for the legislative decision.[9] *Kleindienst v. Mandel,* 408 U.S., at 770, 92 S.Ct., at 2585.

IV

We hold that §§ 101(b)(1)(D) and 101(b)(2) of the Immigration and Nationality Act of 1952 are not unconstitutional by virtue of the exclusion of the relationship between an illegitimate child and his natural father from the preferences accorded by the Act to the "child" or "parent" of a United States citizen or lawful permanent resident.

Affirmed.

MR. JUSTICE MARSHALL, with whom MR. JUSTICE BRENNAN joins, dissenting.

Until today I thought it clear that when Congress grants benefits to some citizens, but not to others, it is our duty to insure that the decision comports with Fifth Amendment principles of due process and equal protection. Today, however, the Court appears to hold that discrimination among citizens, however invidious and irrational, must be tolerated if it occurs in the context of the immigration laws. Since I cannot agree that Congress has license to deny fundamental rights to citizens according to the most disfavored criteria simply because the Immigration and Nationality Act is involved, I dissent.

* * *

* * * The definitions [in § 101(b)] cover virtually all parent-child relationships except that of biological father-illegitimate child. Thus while all American citizens are entitled to bring in their alien children without regard to either the numerical quota or the labor certification require-

---

8. The inherent difficulty of determining the paternity of an illegitimate child is compounded when it depends upon events that may have occurred in foreign countries many years earlier. Congress may well have given substantial weight, in adopting the classification here challenged, to these problems of proof and the potential for fraudulent visa applications that would have resulted from a more generous drawing of the line. Moreover, our cases clearly indicate that legislative distinctions in the immigration area need not be as " 'carefully tuned to alternative considerations,' " * * * as those in the domestic area.

9. Appellants insist that the statutory distinction is based on an overbroad and outdated stereotype concerning the relationship of unwed fathers and their illegitimate children, and that existing administrative procedures, which had been developed to deal with the problems of proving paternity, maternity, and legitimation with respect to statutorily recognized "parents" and "children," could easily handle the problems of proof involved in determining the paternity of an illegitimate child. We simply note that this argument should be addressed to the Congress rather than the courts. Indeed, in that regard it is worth noting that a bill introduced in the 94th Congress would have eliminated the challenged distinction.

ment, fathers are denied this privilege with respect to their illegitimate children. Similarly, all citizens are allowed to have their parents enter without regard to the labor certification requirement, and, if the citizen is over 21, also without regard to the quota. Illegitimate children, however, are denied such preferences for their fathers.

The unfortunate consequences of these omissions are graphically illustrated by the case of appellant Cleophus Warner. Mr. Warner is a naturalized citizen of the United States who * * * petitioned the Attorney General for an immigrant visa for his illegitimate son Serge, a citizen of the French West Indies. Despite the fact that Mr. Warner acknowledged his paternity and registered as Serge's father shortly after his birth, has his name on Serge's birth certificate, and has supported and maintained Serge since birth, the special dispensation from the quota and labor certification requirements was denied because Serge was not a "child" under the statute. It matters not that, as the Government concedes, Serge's mother has abandoned Serge to his father and has, by marrying another man, apparently rendered impossible, under French West Indies law, Mr. Warner's ever legitimating Serge. Mr. Warner is simply not Serge's "parent."

* * * This case, unlike most immigration cases that come before the Court, directly involves the rights of citizens, not aliens. "[C]oncerned with the problem of keeping families of United States citizens and immigrants united", Congress extended to American citizens the right to choose to be reunited in the United States with their immediate families. The focus was on citizens and their need for relief from the hardships occasioned by the immigration laws. The right to seek such relief was given only to the citizen, not the alien. INA § 204. If the citizen does not petition the Attorney General for the special "immediate relative" status for his parent or child, the alien, despite his relationship, can receive no preference. It is irrelevant that aliens have no constitutional right to immigrate and that Americans have no constitutional right to compel the admission of their families. The essential fact here is that Congress did choose to extend such privileges to American citizens but then denied them to a small class of citizens. When Congress draws such lines among citizens, the Constitution requires that the decision comport with Fifth Amendment principles of equal protection and due process. The simple fact that the discrimination is set in immigration legislation cannot insulate from scrutiny the invidious abridgment of citizens' fundamental interests.

* * * Once it is established that this discrimination among citizens cannot escape traditional constitutional scrutiny simply because it occurs in the context of immigration legislation, the result is virtually foreordained. One can hardly imagine a more vulnerable statute.

The class of citizens denied the special privilege of reunification in this country is defined on the basis of two traditionally disfavored classifications—gender and legitimacy. Fathers cannot obtain preferred status for their illegitimate children; mothers can. Conversely, every child except the illegitimate—legitimate, legitimated, step-, adopted—can obtain preferred status for his or her alien father. The Court has little tolerance for either form of discrimination.

* * * In view of the legislation's denial of this right to these classes, it is clear that, whatever the verbal formula, the Government bears a substantial burden to justify the statute. * * *

The legislative history, however, gives no indication of why these privileges were absolutely denied illegitimate children and their fathers. The Government suggests that Congress may have believed that "such persons are unlikely to have maintained a close personal relationship with their offspring." If so, Congress' chosen shorthand for "closeness" is obviously overinclusive. No one can dispute that there are legitimate, legitimated, step-, and adoptive parent-child relationships and mother-illegitimate child relationships that are not close and yet are accorded the preferential status. Indeed, the most dramatic illustration of the overinclusiveness is the fact that while Mr. Warner can never be deemed a "parent" of Serge, nevertheless, if he should marry, his wife could qualify as a stepparent, entitled to obtain for Serge the preferential status that Mr. Warner cannot obtain. *Andrade v. Esperdy,* 270 F.Supp. 516 (S.D.N.Y. 1967); *Nation v. Esperdy,* 239 F.Supp. 531 (S.D.N.Y.1965). Similarly, a man who, in an adulterous affair, fathers a child outside his marriage cannot be the "parent" of that child, but his wife may petition as stepparent. *Matter of Stultz,* 15 I & N Dec. 362 (1975).

That the statute is underinclusive is also undisputed. Indeed, the Government could not dispute it in view of the close relationships exhibited in appellants' cases, recognized in our previous cases, and established in numerous studies.

The Government suggests that Congress may have decided to accept the inaccurate classifications of this statute because they considered a case-by-case assessment of closeness and paternity not worth the administrative costs. This attempted justification is plainly inadequate. In *Stanley v. Illinois,* [405 U.S. 645, 92 S.Ct. 1208, 31 L.Ed.2d 551 (1972) (which found unconstitutional a state statute that automatically treated children born out of wedlock as wards of the state upon the death of the mother, without any hearing on the father's fitness)], we expressed our low regard for the use of "administrative convenience" as the rationale for interfering with a father's right to care for his illegitimate child.

> "Procedure by presumption is always cheaper and easier than individualized determination. But when, as here, the procedure forecloses the determinative issues of competence and care, when it explicitly disdains present realities in deference to past formalities, it needlessly risks running roughshod over the important interests of both parent and child. It therefore cannot stand." 405 U.S., at 656–657, 92 S.Ct., at 1215.

This Court has been equally intolerant of the rationale when it is used to deny rights to the illegitimate child. While we are sensitive to " 'the lurking problems with respect to proof of paternity,' " we are careful not to allow them to be " 'made into an impenetrable barrier that works to shield otherwise invidious discrimination.' " We require, at a minimum, that the statute [be] " 'carefully tuned to alternative considerations' ", and not exclude all illegitimates simply because some situations involve difficulties of proof.

Given such hostility to the administrative-convenience argument when invidious classifications and fundamental rights are involved, it is apparent that the rationale is inadequate in the present case. As I observed earlier, since Congress gave no indication that administrative costs were its concern we should scrutinize the hypothesis closely. The likelihood of such a rationale is diminished considerably by the comprehensive and elaborate administrative procedures already established and employed by the INS in passing on claims of the existence of a parent-child relationship. All petitions are handled on a case-by-case basis with the petitioner bearing the burden of proof. Moreover, the INS is no stranger to cases requiring proof of paternity. When, for example, a citizen stepmother petitions for the entrance of her husband's illegitimate child, she must necessarily prove that her husband is the child's father. Indeed, it is ironic that if Mr. Warner marries and his wife petitions for Serge, her proof will, in fact, be one step more complex than his would be—not only must she prove his paternity, but she must also prove their marriage. Nevertheless, she would be entitled to an opportunity to prove those facts; he is not.

Nor is a fear of involvement with foreign laws and records a persuasive explanation of the omission. In administering the Act with respect to legitimated children, for example, the critical issue is whether the steps undertaken are adequate under local law to render the child legitimate, and the INS has become expert in such matters. I note, in this connection, that where a child was born in a country in which all children are legitimate, proof of paternity is the critical issue and the proof problems are identical to those involved with an illegitimate child.

Given the existence of these procedures and expertise, it is difficult indeed to give much weight to the hypothesized administrative-convenience rationale. Moreover, as noted previously, this Court will not allow concerns with proof to justify "an impenetrable barrier that works to shield otherwise invidious discrimination." As the facts of this case conclusively demonstrate, Congress has "failed to consider the possibility of a middle ground between the extremes of complete exclusion and case-by-case determination of paternity." Mr. Warner is a classic example of someone who can readily prove both paternity and closeness. Appellees concede this. The fact that he is denied the opportunity demonstrates beyond peradventure that Congress has failed to " 'carefully tun[e] [the statute] to alternative considerations.' " That failure is fatal to the statute.

When Congress grants a fundamental right to all but an invidiously selected class of citizens, and it is abundantly clear that such discrimination would be intolerable in any context but immigration, it is our duty to strike the legislation down. Because the Court condones the invidious discrimination in this case simply because it is embedded in the immigration laws, I must dissent.

MR. JUSTICE WHITE also dissents, substantially for the reasons stated by MR. JUSTICE MARSHALL in his dissenting opinion.

NOTES AND QUESTIONS

1.   Justice Marshall's dissent seems to suggest that the Court can apply more rigorous constitutional review to the classifications in *Fiallo* without necessarily having to apply such scrutiny in most other immigration cases. "This case," he writes, "unlike most immigration cases that come before the Court, directly involves the rights of citizens." But does this factor really distinguish most immigration cases? The vast majority of permanent immigration today, except for refugees, begins with a petition filed with USCIS by a U.S. citizen. (For the family-sponsored second preference, the petitioner could be an LPR, but the category of beneficiaries is more limited: spouse or unmarried son or daughter.) Even the employment-based preferences and many nonimmigrant admissions usually begin in this way, with a petition filed by the prospective American employer. *See generally* Motomura, *Whose Immigration Law?: Citizens, Aliens, and the Constitution*, 97 Colum.L.Rev. 1567 (1997) (suggesting more serious consideration of how immigration regulation affects the constitutional rights of citizens); Motomura, *Whose Alien Nation?: Two Models of Constitutional Immigration Law*, 94 Mich.L.Rev. 1927 (1996) (same).

2.   After *Fiallo,* could Congress amend the INA to make all but members of the Caucasian race ineligible for immigration? What standard should a court use in considering an equal protection challenge to such a statute? *Cf. Dunn v. INS,* 499 F.2d 856 (9th Cir.1974), *cert. denied,* 419 U.S. 1106, 95 S.Ct. 776, 42 L.Ed.2d 801 (1975) (using the "rational basis" test in denying an equal protection challenge to a provision rendering only Mexican nationals ineligible to adjust status from nonimmigrant to immigrant while within the United States; the INA was later amended to remove this preclusion). Before the 1965 INA amendments abolished the national-origins quota system, courts rather easily disposed of constitutional challenges to the lines Congress had drawn. *See, e.g., Hitai v. INS,* 343 F.2d 466 (2d Cir.1965). *Hitai* even presented an aggravated example of purely racial theories as manifested in the INA at that time. Hitai was born in Brazil to naturalized Brazilian citizens. But because his parents had been born Japanese citizens, he came within the small Japanese quota under the INA as then written, rather than being treated like other citizens of Brazil. Even in this setting, the court sustained the constitutionality of the statute.

Against the background of cases like *Hitai,* it is somewhat surprising that the Supreme Court in *Fiallo* goes so far as to state (in footnote 5) that "[o]ur cases reflect acceptance of a limited judicial responsibility" to review Congress' line-drawing, rather than no responsibility at all. Perhaps the Court speaks of a "limited responsibility" precisely to preserve the possibility that it might strike down any modern immigration legislation that established preference categories based explicitly on racial distinctions.

It is virtually inconceivable today that a statute drawing explicit racial lines that disadvantage nonwhite groups would issue forth from Congress. But as a judge, how would you evaluate a special security screening regulation that explicitly applies only to nationals of countries in the Middle East, if it were challenged as discriminatory against Arabs as a racial group? Is a distinction based on nationality (a durable but not wholly immutable trait) equivalent to one based on national origin? If strict scrutiny applies in this sort of case, would it be possible for the United States to have specially favorable procedures or substantive provisions for certain nationalities—for example, for the admission of nationals of Canada (as has been the case along the northern border for decades)? Could U.S. treaties provide for special reciprocal immigration benefits limited to the nationals of the treaty countries?

On the other hand, should statutes drawing nationality distinctions be upheld if they rest on a "rational basis" or—perhaps even less demanding—a "facially legitimate and bona fide reason"? Are there other tests that could help determine when an explicit nationality distinction should be seen as a pretext for racial discrimination? If the government claims that foreign policy concerns justify the use of these immigration restrictions, how should a court evaluate the genuineness and strength of such factors? Are courts institutionally capable of handling such review? We will return to consider many of these questions at several points in this book when we address immigration control measures based on national security and foreign policy concerns.

3.   Justice Marshall states that if Cleophus Warner were now to marry, his wife could petition to bring in Serge Warner as her stepchild, citing *Andrade v. Esperdy,* 270 F.Supp. 516 (S.D.N.Y.1967). Some judicial decisions had indeed held that the statutory definition of stepchild, INA § 101(b)(1)(B), is to be applied in this literal (if anomalous) fashion. But the Board of Immigration Appeals resisted such an interpretation, arguing that the statutory purpose could be fulfilled by granting petitions for stepchildren only where there is evidence of a pre-existing family unit or equivalent ties. *Matter of Moreira,* 17 I & N Dec. 41, 46–47 (BIA 1979).

In *Palmer v. Reddy,* 622 F.2d 463 (9th Cir.1980), however, the court explicitly rejected the *Moreira* standards and directed that the "stepchild" provision be construed literally, i.e., to require only marriage to the natural parent, whether or not there was a showing of "active parental interest." Which approach is more consistent with the congressional plan? Which better honors Justice Marshall's principle of "closeness"? Which makes more sense to you? The Board eventually decided, reluctantly, to apply the *Palmer* result nationwide. *Matter of McMillan,* 17 I & N Dec. 605 (BIA 1981).

4.   If the purpose of the family reunification provisions in the immigration laws is to permit persons in the U.S. to live with close family members, why doesn't the law simply test for the actual "closeness" of ties among family members, as Justice Marshall's dissent suggests? Why shouldn't aunts,

uncles, or cousins be given family reunification immigration benefits if the petitioner shows that in his ethnic group—or perhaps only in his particular family—such ties are as close as the average ties among members of the usual suburban American nuclear family? *See* SCIRP, Staff Report, at 371 (quoting the testimony of Father Joseph A. Cogo, urging immigration benefits for grandparents and "fireside relatives like an aunt who's not married * * * and living with the family. * * * [T]hey should not be subjected to a definition by other ethnic groups just because other ethnic groups have different definitions in their tradition.") Indeed, why require biological relationships at all? Why not adopt a system allowing family reunification-type immigration benefits based on proof of functional family ties, whatever the biological relationship?

Once we work our way through to these possible alternative schemes, however, we should pause to take stock of the administrative implications. How would a scheme allowing preferential treatment whenever the petitioner shows family-like "closeness" be implemented? What kinds of evidence would be relevant in proving closeness? Do we want DHS agents or consular officers asking about the intimate details of life around the family fireside in order to decide whether the relationship to an aunt is close enough to merit immigration benefits? What more precise criteria could be provided to help assure uniform standards and practices in determining whether a relationship is sufficiently close? On a different plane, is it inappropriate for a receiving country to apply its own predominant cultural conceptions of family in deciding who should receive immigration benefits? Why or why not?

These administrative challenges may help account for decisions by the INS and the BIA (and now DHS) to use bright-line tests, despite occasional outcomes that may seem arbitrary, rather than employ vague criteria expanding the inquiry into other areas. Case-by-case judgments of "closeness" or other elusive concepts (like the likelihood of fraud in the use of a particular legitimation procedure) would give rise to a related concern. They are much harder for supervisors—ultimately running all the way up to the Secretary of Homeland Security—to monitor, in order to assure that like cases are treated alike, and even to detect whether an officer has issued a decision in a given case because of corruption or other improper favoritism.

In *Nguyen v. INS*, 533 U.S. 53, 121 S.Ct. 2053, 150 L.Ed.2d 115 (2001), discussed in Chapter Two, p. 43, *supra*, the Supreme Court spoke to some of the reasons why a bright-line rule might be preferable to a type of "closeness" determination. (*Nguyen* rejected a gender discrimination challenge to a statutory distinction quite similar to that in *Fiallo,* providing easier rules for mothers to transmit U.S. citizenship at birth to out-of-wedlock children born overseas, as compared to fathers of such children.) The plaintiffs there had argued that Congress should have pursued its objectives through a statute that confers citizenship on any out-of-wedlock child of a U.S. citizen father born overseas whenever "an actual father-child relationship is proved," rather than specifying concrete acts that the father would have to perform in order to transmit citizenship. The Court observed with approval that Congress rejected this approach, "perhaps because of the subjectivity, intrusiveness, and difficulties of proof that might attend an inquiry into any particular bond or tie," opting instead for "an easily administered scheme." 533 U.S. at 69, 121 S.Ct. at 2064.

Of course, an important policy question remains: whether these benefits to sound administration from the use of bright-line tests are outweighed by the inevitability of arbitrary outcomes and their impact in the particular setting. Judging that balance can be a difficult task, and administrators may have incentives for erring in favor of fixed rules. But judges may similarly be too quick to dismiss as "administrative convenience" certain concerns that are far more complex than simply adding to the annual agency appropriation. A useful discussion of these issues appears in Diver, *The Optimal Precision of Administrative Rules*, 93 Yale L.J. 65 (1983). *See also Fook Hong Mak v. INS*, 435 F.2d 728, 730 (2d Cir.1970) (Friendly, J.) ("an administrator, vested with discretionary power, [may] determine by appropriate rulemaking that he will not use it in favor of a particular class on a case-by-case basis, if his determination is founded on considerations rationally related to the statute he is administering. * * * This may be an even 'juster justice' than to accord different treatment because of trivial differences of fact"); *American Hospital Ass'n v. NLRB*, 899 F.2d 651, 660 (7th Cir.1990) (Posner, J.) ("The decision how much discretion to eliminate from the decisional process is itself a discretionary judgment, entitled to broad judicial deference").

5.   In 1986 Congress amended the definition of "child" to cover certain relationships like those at issue in *Fiallo*. INA § 101(b)(1)(D) now includes:

> a child born out of wedlock, by, through whom, or on whose behalf a status, privilege, or benefit is sought by virtue of the relationship of the child to its natural mother or to its natural father if the father has or had a bona fide parent-child relationship with the person.

Should this amendment be considered a vindication of the majority's 1977 position in *Fiallo:* namely, that changes in arguably objectionable immigration provisions may satisfactorily be left to the political branches?

The subsection of the 1986 legislation containing the amendment to § 101(b)(1)(D) was titled "Equal Treatment of Fathers," but this caption is not quite accurate. What does the final clause, beginning with "if the father," mean? Why would Congress have added it? How should the immigration authorities apply it? See 54 Fed.Reg. 36753 (1989) (implementing regulations, amending 8 C.F.R. § 204.2(c)); *Matter of Pineda,* 20 I & N Dec. 70 (BIA 1989). The implementing regulations referred to sophisticated blood tests that had been developed between 1977 and 1986 allowing for far more reliable objective determinations of paternity. If the *Fiallo* case had arisen after those tests became available, should the Court have approached the issue differently? Should it do so today with even more precise DNA testing available? Are courts or Congress better positioned to act on the basis of such scientific developments?

3.   FAMILY REUNIFICATION CATEGORIES: KEY ISSUES AND AN INTRODUCTION TO THE *CHEVRON* DOCTRINE

The dominant feature of current arrangements for permanent immigration to the United States is family reunification. Immediate relatives of U.S. citizens, as we have seen, can immigrate without numerical limitation, and well over half of the numerically limited immigration spaces are reserved for family members who qualify under the family-sponsored preferences of INA § 203(a). Take a look at these provisions. Which family members are covered by the statute? Which are not? Should other relationships be recognized for purposes of conferring immigration benefits? What values do the statute's categories reflect?

The materials that follow touch upon these issues. They examine some of the technical questions that can arise in implementing these provisions, and they also consider the extent of the authority of the administrative agencies to define "family" for immigration purposes, in the course of implementing the general definitions that Congress has supplied. We will consider proposals to restructure the family admissions provisions in Chapter Nine below. The materials in Section 3b below also deserve close attention, because they introduce and explore a highly significant administrative law doctrine that generally calls for deference to administrative agencies in the interpretation of statutes they administer. It is known as the *Chevron* doctrine, after the Supreme Court case that crystallized it. Such deference, along with the rules determining when deference does not apply, factors into judicial review—as well as agency adjudication—in a wide variety of immigration cases.

a. Immigration Based on Marriage

Well over a third of the immigrants who enter the United States each year do so on the basis of a marriage to a U.S. citizen or lawful permanent resident. We will consider here how the statute and case law have defined marriage for the purposes of immigration benefits and how administrative practice has dealt with the tension between the highly valued objective of family unification and the objective of avoiding fraud or abuse.

(i) What Marriages Are Recognized by the INA?

Marriage is a legal concept, wholly established and regulated by law. But whose law applies? Suppose a foreign country permits marriages between first cousins or between uncles and nieces or aunts and nephews, or allows persons to marry at age 12. Should USCIS recognize such marriages for purposes of the INA?

The general rule is that "the validity of a marriage ordinarily is judged by the law of the place where it is celebrated." C. Gordon, S. Mailman & S. Yale–Loehr, *Immigration Law and Procedure* § 36.02[2][a]. This rule applies for marriages in foreign countries or in a state or territory of the United States. There are exceptions, however. As we explore below, otherwise valid marriages entered into solely for the purpose of obtaining immigration benefits are not recognized for immigration purposes. Furthermore, the INA expressly excludes so-called proxy marriages—defined as marriages "where the contracting parties thereto are not physically present in the presence of each other, unless the marriage shall have been consummated." INA § 101(a)(35). And marriages that may be valid in the country of origin may not be recognized for immigration purposes if they are deemed to conflict with public policy, which is generally understood to mean that the marriage must be lawful in the intended place of residence in the United States. *See Matter of Darwish*, 14 I & N Dec. 307 (BIA 1973) (polygamous marriage not recognized for immigration purposes even though valid under Jordanian law; plural marriages violate U.S. public policy); *Matter of Zappia*, 12 I & N Dec. 439 (BIA 1967) (marriage between first cousins resident in Wisconsin but entered into in South Carolina, where such marriages are legal, during a brief visit there, is invalid for immigration purposes because void in Wisconsin).

Suppose a foreign country or a U.S. state recognizes the lawfulness of same-sex marriages. May a same-sex spouse of a U.S. citizen qualify for immigrant status? We explore a case that reflects the long-standing answer to this question, and then consider recent developments that have called this outcome into question.

ADAMS v. HOWERTON

United States Court of Appeals, Ninth Circuit, 1982.
673 F.2d 1036, cert. denied, 458 U.S. 1111, 102 S.Ct. 3494, 73 L.Ed.2d 1373.

WALLACE, CIRCUIT JUDGE:

Adams, a male American citizen, and Sullivan, a male alien, appeal from the district court's entry of summary judgment for Howerton, Acting District Director of the Immigration and Naturalization Service (INS). The district court held that their homosexual marriage did not qualify Sullivan as Adams's spouse pursuant to section 201(b) of the Immigration and Nationality Act of 1952, as amended (the Act). We affirm.

I

Following the expiration of Sullivan's visitor's visa, Adams and Sullivan obtained a marriage license from the county clerk in Boulder, Colorado, and were "married" by a minister. Adams then petitioned the INS for classification of Sullivan as an immediate relative of an American citizen, based upon Sullivan's alleged status as Adams's spouse. The petition was denied, and the denial was affirmed on appeal by the Board of Immigration Appeals. * * *

II

* * * Cases interpreting the Act indicate that a two-step analysis is necessary to determine whether a marriage will be recognized for immigration purposes. The first is whether the marriage is valid under state law. The second is whether that state-approved marriage qualifies under the Act. * * * Test

It is not clear * * * whether Colorado would recognize a homosexual marriage. There are no reported Colorado cases on the subject. The Colorado Attorney General in an informal, unpublished opinion addressed to a member of the Colorado legislature three days after the alleged marriage in question occurred, stated that purported marriages between persons of the same sex are of no legal effect in Colorado. Colorado statutory law, however, neither expressly permits nor prohibits homosexual marriages. Some statutes appear to contemplate marriage only as a relationship between a male and a female.

While we might well make an educated guess as to how the Colorado courts would decide this issue, it is unnecessary for us to do so. We decide this case solely upon construction of section 201(b), the second step in our two-step analysis.

III

* * * So long as Congress acts within constitutional constraints, it may determine the conditions under which immigration visas are issued. Therefore, the intent of Congress governs the conferral of spouse status under section 201(b), and a valid marriage is determinative only if Congress so intends.

It is clear to us that Congress did not intend the mere validity of a marriage under state law to be controlling. Although the 1965 amendments do not define the term "spouse," the Act itself limits the persons who may be deemed spouses. Section 101(a)(35) of the Act specifically provides that the term "spouse" does not include

> a spouse, wife, or husband by reason of any marriage ceremony where the contracting parties thereto are not physically present in the presence of each other, unless the marriage shall have been consummated.

Furthermore, valid marriages entered into by parties not intending to live together as husband and wife are not recognized for immigration purposes. Therefore, even though two persons contract a marriage valid under state law and are recognized as spouses by that state, they are not necessarily spouses for purposes of section 201(b).

* * * Where a statute has been interpreted by the agency charged with its enforcement, we are ordinarily required to accord substantial deference to that construction, and should follow it "unless there are compelling indications that it is wrong." *New York Dept. of Social Services v. Dublino*, 413 U.S. 405, 421, 93 S.Ct. 2507, 2517, 37 L.Ed.2d 688 (1973). Thus, we must be mindful that the INS, in carrying out its broad responsibilities, has interpreted the term "spouse" to exclude a person entering a homosexual marriage.

While we do accord this construction proper weight, we base our decision primarily on the Act itself. Nothing in the Act, the 1965 amendments or the legislative history suggests that the reference to "spouse" in section 201(b) was intended to include a person of the same sex as the citizen in question. It is "a fundamental canon of statutory construction" that, "unless otherwise defined, words will be interpreted as taking their ordinary, contemporary, common meaning." The term "marriage" ordinarily contemplates a relationship between a man and a woman. *See*

Webster's Third New International Dictionary 1384 (1971); Black's Law Dictionary 876 (5th ed. 1979). The term "spouse" commonly refers to one of the parties in a marital relationship so defined. Congress has not indicated an intent to enlarge the ordinary meaning of those words. In the absence of such a congressional directive, it would be inappropriate for us to expand the meaning of the term "spouse" for immigration purposes. Our role is only to ascertain and apply the intent of Congress.

Our conclusion is supported by a further review of the 1965 amendments to the Act. These amendments not only added section 201(b) in its present form, but also amended the mandatory exclusion provisions of section 212(a) of the Act. Yet, both * * * the amendments and the accompanying Senate Report clearly express an intent to exclude homosexuals. *See Boutilier v. INS,* 387 U.S. 118, 121, 87 S.Ct. 1563, 1565, 18 L.Ed.2d 661 (1967). As our duty is to ascertain and apply the intent of Congress, we strive to interpret language in one section of a statute consistently with the language of other sections and with the purposes of the entire statute considered as a whole. We think it unlikely that Congress intended to give homosexual spouses preferential admission treatment under section 201(b) of the Act when, in the very same amendments adding that section, it mandated their exclusion. * * *

Affirmed.

NOTES AND QUESTIONS: LAWRENCE V. TEXAS AND THE DEFENSE OF MARRIAGE ACT

1. What evidence does the court cite of congressional intent not to include same-sex marriages in the definition of spouse? In a general overhaul of the INA's exclusion grounds in 1990, Congress repealed the provision in the law under which homosexuals were deemed excludable. Pub.L. 101–649, § 601(a), 104 Stat. 4978 (1990). Congress did not amend the definition of spouse. Should *Adams* be decided differently following repeal of the exclusion ground? Following the 2010 congressional repeal of the "don't ask, don't tell" policy that restricted the opportunities for gays and lesbians to serve in the U.S. military? *See* Hulse, *Senate Ends Military Ban on Gays Serving Openly,* New York Times, Dec. 19, 2010, at A1.

2. In 1996, Congress enacted the Defense of Marriage Act (DOMA), Pub.L. 104–199, 110 Stat. 2419 (1996). Section 3 of the statute provides:

> In determining the meaning of any Act of Congress, or of any ruling, regulation, or interpretation of administrative bureaus and agencies of the United States, the word "marriage" means only a legal union between one man and one woman as husband and wife, and the word "spouse" refers only to a person of the opposite sex who is a husband or wife.

Does this provision affect your answer to the questions in the preceding note?

3. In October 1997, the British Home Office Immigration Minister announced that the United Kingdom would recognize same-sex relationships for immigration purposes where the partners have been living together for

four years "in a relationship akin to marriage" and "intend to live together permanently." Minister Mike O'Brien stated that the prior rules were "unsustainable and may have breached human rights law." Watt, *Immigration law changed for gay partners*, The Times [of London], Oct. 11, 1997. By 2011, at least 28 nations worldwide extended benefits in some form to the same-sex partners of citizens or permanent residents. They are Andorra, Australia, Belgium, Brazil, Canada, Colombia, Croatia, the Czech Republic, Denmark, Finland, France, Germany, Greenland, Iceland, Ireland, Israel, Luxembourg, the Netherlands, New Zealand, Norway, Portugal, Slovenia, South Africa, Spain, Sweden, Switzerland, the United Kingdom, and Uruguay. *See generally* Ayoub & Wong, *Separated and Unequal*, 32 Wm. Mitchell L. Rev. 559, at 560 fn. 1; *Same-Sex Marriage Around the World: Overview and Status of Debate*, 13 N.Y.L.School Int'l Rev. 11, 17 (2011). If you were redrafting the U.S. immigration laws to provide benefits to same-sex couples, what specific criteria would you adopt?

4. In a portion of the *Adams* case not reprinted above, the court rejected a constitutional challenge to the statute. Applying a deferential standard of review, it concluded:

> Congress has determined that preferential status is not warranted for the spouses of homosexual marriages. Perhaps this is because homosexual marriages never produce offspring, because they are not recognized in most, if in any, of the states, or because they violate traditional and often prevailing societal mores. In any event, having found that Congress rationally intended to deny preferential status to the spouses of such marriages, we need not further "probe and test the justifications for the legislative decision." [*Fiallo v. Bell*, 430 U.S.] at 799, 97 S.Ct. at 1481.

Using societal mores as a justification for this type of distinction gained support in the Supreme Court's decision in *Bowers v. Hardwick*, 478 U.S. 186, 106 S.Ct. 2841, 92 L.Ed.2d 140 (1986), which upheld a Georgia statute criminalizing homosexual sodomy. The Court found the "belief of a majority of the electorate in Georgia that homosexual sodomy is immoral and unacceptable" a sufficient rational basis for the statute. But in *Lawrence v. Texas*, 539 U.S. 558, 123 S.Ct. 2472, 156 L.Ed.2d 508 (2003), the Court overruled *Bowers* and found a state law punishing homosexual conduct unconstitutional to be a violation of substantive due process. Justice Kennedy's majority opinion explained the Court's reasoning:

> Freedom extends beyond spatial bounds. Liberty presumes an autonomy of self that includes freedom of thought, belief, expression, and certain intimate conduct. The instant case involves liberty of the person both in its spatial and more transcendent dimensions. * * *

> [The *Bowers* Court failed] to appreciate the extent of the liberty at stake. To say that the issue in *Bowers* was simply the right to engage in certain sexual conduct demeans the claim the individual put forward, just as it would demean a married couple were it to be said marriage is simply about the right to have sexual intercourse. The laws involved in *Bowers* and here are, to be sure, statutes that purport to do no more than prohibit a particular sexual act. Their penalties and purposes, though, have more far-reaching consequences, touching upon the most private

human conduct, sexual behavior, and in the most private of places, the home. The statutes do seek to control a personal relationship that, whether or not entitled to formal recognition in the law, is within the liberty of persons to choose without being punished as criminals.

This, as a general rule, should counsel against attempts by the State, or a court, to define the meaning of the relationship or to set its boundaries absent injury to a person or abuse of an institution the law protects. It suffices for us to acknowledge that adults may choose to enter upon this relationship in the confines of their homes and their own private lives and still retain their dignity as free persons. When sexuality finds overt expression in intimate conduct with another person, the conduct can be but one element in a personal bond that is more enduring. The liberty protected by the Constitution allows homosexual persons the right to make this choice. * * *

The issue is whether the majority may use the power of the State to enforce these views [that homosexual conduct is immoral] on the whole society through operation of the criminal law. "Our obligation is to define the liberty of all, not to mandate our own moral code." *Planned Parenthood of Southeastern Pa. v. Casey,* 505 U.S. 833, 850, 112 S.Ct. 2791, 120 L.Ed.2d 674 (1992). * * *

The petitioners are entitled to respect for their private lives. The State cannot demean their existence or control their destiny by making their private sexual conduct a crime. Their right to liberty under the Due Process Clause gives them the full right to engage in their conduct without intervention of the government. "It is a promise of the Constitution that there is a realm of personal liberty which the government may not enter." *Casey, supra,* at 847, 112 S.Ct. 2791. The Texas statute furthers no legitimate state interest which can justify its intrusion into the personal and private life of the individual.

539 U.S. at 562, 566, 571, 578, 123 S.Ct. at 2475, 2478, 2480, 2484. A few months later, informed by *Lawrence,* but relying solely on liberty and equality guarantees of the state constitution, the Massachusetts Supreme Judicial Court barred the state from rejecting same-sex marriages while recognizing heterosexual marriages. *Goodridge v. Department of Public Health*, 440 Mass. 309, 798 N.E.2d 941 (2003). *Goodridge* and similar legal challenges, plus the actions of some local governments to issue marriage licenses to same-sex couples, triggered a reaction. Both before and after 2003, many states have adopted, via legislation or referendum, provisions reaffirming that marriage consists of a union between one man and one woman.

After *Lawrence,* must a case like *Adams* be decided differently? Must Congress recognize homosexual marriages? Can Congress and the courts refuse to grant family-type immigration rights in cases involving other long-standing intimate relationships? If applied to immigration laws, how far would *Lawrence* reach? Must all the spouses in a polygamous or plural marriage be given equal immigration rights? *See generally* Note, *When Love, Comity, and Justice Conquer Borders: INS Recognition of Same–Sex Marriages,* 28 Colum.Hum.Rights L.Rev. 97 (1996); Hawley, *Gays, Lesbians, and Immigration,* 99–08 Immigration Briefings (1999). For more on these general issues, see Medina, *Of Constitutional Amendments, Human Rights, and Same–Sex Marriages*, 64 La. L. Rev. 459 (2004); Hernandez–Truyol, *Querying Lawrence*, 65 Ohio St. L.J. 1151 (2004); Abrams, *Polygamy, Prostitution, and the Federalization of Immigration Law*, 105 Colum. L. Rev. 641 (2005).

5. As of 2011, six states within the United States (Connecticut, Iowa, Massachusetts, New Hampshire, New York, Vermont) and the District of Columbia now recognize same-sex marriages, either through legislative changes or as a result of judicial decisions. The issue is pending in several other jurisdictions. Hawley, *First Gay Marriages Held in New York*, Wash. Post, July 24, 2011, <http://www.washingtonpost.com/politics/2011/07/24/g IQALSaQXL_story.html>. These changes in state law have focused new attention on the wisdom and constitutional validity of the 1996 federal Defense of Marriage Act, *supra*.

On February 23, 2011, Attorney General Holder announced a new DOJ policy regarding litigation over DOMA. The federal government would no longer defend the constitutionality of DOMA in those federal circuits where precedent had not already determined that rational-basis review, instead of heightened scrutiny, applies. Holder explained:

> [T]he President and I have concluded that classifications based on sexual orientation warrant heightened scrutiny and that, as applied to same-sex couples legally married under state law, Section 3 of DOMA is unconstitutional. * * *

> As you know, the Department has a longstanding practice of defending the constitutionality of duly-enacted statutes if reasonable arguments can be made in their defense, a practice that accords the respect appropriately due to a coequal branch of government. However, the Department in the past has declined to defend statutes despite the availability of professionally responsible arguments, in part because the Department does not consider every plausible argument to be a "reasonable" one. * * * This is the rare case where the proper course is to forgo the defense of this statute. * * *

> In light of the foregoing, I will instruct the Department's lawyers to immediately inform the district courts in [two pending cases in the Second Circuit] of the Executive Branch's view that heightened scrutiny is the appropriate standard of review and that, consistent with that standard, Section 3 of DOMA may not be constitutionally applied to same-sex couples whose marriages are legally recognized under state law. If asked by the district courts in the Second Circuit for the position of the United States in the event those courts determine that the applicable standard is rational basis, the Department will state that, consistent with the position it has taken in prior cases, a reasonable argument for Section 3's constitutionality may be proffered under that permissive standard. Our attorneys will also notify the courts of our interest in providing Congress a full and fair opportunity to participate in the litigation in those cases. * * *

Letter from the Attorney General to Congress on Litigation Involving the Defense of Marriage Act, Feb. 23, 2011, available at <http://www.justice.gov/opa/pr/2011/February/11–ag–223.html>. Congress did then proceed to make arrangements to defend DOMA in court, hiring former Solicitor General Paul Clement. Shear & Schwartz, *Law Firm Won't Defend Marriage Act,* N.Y.Times, Apr. 25, 2011, <http://www.nytimes.com/2011/04/26/us/politics/26 marriage.html>.

In the meantime, however, consistent with longstanding DOJ practice, the letter stated that federal agencies would continue to enforce DOMA:

> [T]he President has instructed Executive agencies to continue to comply with Section 3 of DOMA, consistent with the Executive's obligation to take care that the laws be faithfully executed, unless and until Congress repeals Section 3 or the judicial branch renders a definitive verdict against the law's constitutionality. This course of action respects the actions of the prior Congress that enacted DOMA, and it recognizes the judiciary as the final arbiter of the constitutional claims raised.

USCIS announced that it would continue to apply DOMA to benefit applications, consistent with the President's instructions. But there are signs that DHS may exercise prosecutorial discretion so as not to remove noncitizens who have a solid claim to status if DOMA is ruled unconstitutional. Further, Attorney General Holder accepted review of a BIA decision that had applied DOMA to deny immigration benefits, and he vacated and remanded the decision in April 2011 with a brief opinion. *Matter of Dorman,* 25 I & N Dec. 485 (AG 2011). He directed that the Board on remand "make such findings as may be necessary to determine whether and how the constitutionality of DOMA is presented in this case, including, but not limited to: 1) whether the respondent's same-sex partnership or civil union qualifies him to be considered a 'spouse' under New Jersey law; 2) whether absent the requirements of DOMA, respondent's same-sex partnership or civil union would qualify him to be considered a 'spouse' under the Immigration and Nationality Act." Administrative bodies like the BIA do not have the authority to declare statutes unconstitutional. Holder is evidently directing the creation of a more complete record that would present the constitutional issue squarely to any reviewing federal court considering it in the immigration setting.

6. Adams and Sullivan left the United States in 1985, after the last round in their unsuccessful litigation, and after holding a painful "deportation sale" of many of their prized possessions. According to a 2004 article on the two men, "their first port of call was England. From there, they began traveling across Europe looking for a country that would accept them as a couple. Eventually, they alighted in Ireland, where they stayed six months." The article reported that they are still a couple—still married, in their view, since the 1975 marriage has never been declared invalid and remains of record in the Colorado archives. By 2004 they had been back in the United States for several years, a place they consider home (though the article said nothing about how they returned, what status Sullivan now holds, or the precise location where they now live). They have watched with interest as U.S. jurisdictions wrestle with the issue of same-sex marriage, and they are treated as pioneers by many of their friends and colleagues. Meadows, *A Marriage Made in Boulder,* Rocky Mountain News, April 3, 2004.

(ii) Sham Marriages

Because a high percentage of immigrant admissions are based on marriage, policing against sham marriages has been an ongoing issue for legislators, administrators, and courts. But what exactly is a sham marriage? The case law, statute, regulations, and administrative practice require something more than simple validity under the law of the jurisdiction where the marriage was performed for a marriage to be considered valid for immigration purposes, but they have used many different formulations to describe just what that extra requirement might be. As it happens, to specify conceptually just what constitutes a sham marriage is more complex than might initially appear. Moreover, all three branches have wrestled with a related administrative question: how can we fashion procedures that maintain respect for human dignity and privacy while still providing efficient means for effective detection and enforcement against bogus marriages?

We introduce these issues with a case that reflects the early efforts of courts and administrators to develop standards for judging the validity of a marriage for immigration purposes, followed by a brief article that illustrates what can happen in an adjustment interview when the benefit sought is based on marriage. These materials set the stage for considering the more comprehensive framework Congress adopted in the Immigration Marriage Fraud Amendments of 1986 (IMFA), Pub.L. 99–639, 100 Stat. 3537. Finally we will consider further legislative amendments, adopted starting in 1991, which permit self-petitioning by certain noncitizen spouses. These changes are part of an ongoing effort by Congress, largely under the Violence Against Women Act (VAWA) and its successors, to minimize the risk that the immigration laws will contribute to domestic violence.

DABAGHIAN v. CIVILETTI

United States Court of Appeals, Ninth Circuit, 1979.
607 F.2d 868.

CHOY, CIRCUIT JUDGE:

Dabaghian appeals from the district court's judgment upholding a decision of the Immigration and Naturalization Service which stripped him of permanent-resident status. We reverse and remand with instruction to enter judgment for Dabaghian.

Dabaghian is a native and citizen of Iran. He entered the United States as a visitor in 1967 and obtained student status in 1968. In September 1971 he married a United States citizen. In October 1971 he applied for adjustment of status to "alien lawfully admitted for permanent residence" under § 245 of the Immigration and Nationality Act. The adjustment of status was granted on January 13, 1972, a date on which there is contested evidence to show that he was separated from his wife. On January 28, 1972, Dabaghian filed for divorce, which was granted seven months later. In September 1973 he married an Iranian citizen.

In August 1974 the Attorney General moved under § 246 of the Act, to rescind the adjustment of status on the ground that Dabaghian had not in fact been eligible for it at the time it was granted. The Immigration Judge revoked Dabaghian's status as a permanent resident; a split Board of Immigration Appeals dismissed Dabaghian's appeal. His action for review and relief in the district court was then dismissed on summary judgment.

The INS, it is important to note, never has claimed or proved that Dabaghian's first marriage was a sham or fraud when entered. Instead, the INS moved to rescind on the ground that on January 13, 1972, when the adjustment of status was granted, his marriage was dead in fact even though it was still legally alive. Thus, says the INS, he was not the "spouse" of a United States citizen and was ineligible for the adjustment of status.

We reject the INS' legal position. If a marriage is not sham or fraudulent from its inception, it is valid for the purposes of determining eligibility for adjustment of status under § 245 of the Act until it is legally dissolved.

The INS contention has no support in any statute or federal decision. Indeed, it has been rejected time and again in recent immigration cases.

In *Bark v. INS*, 511 F.2d 1200 (9th Cir. 1975), the applicant married a woman who was a resident alien. She filed a petition on his behalf under § 204 of the Act to qualify him for preference as the spouse of a resident alien under § 203(a)(2). He then applied for adjustment of status to that of a permanent resident under § 245 of the Act. The INS denied the adjustment on the ground that the marriage was a sham, primarily on evidence of separation. This court held that the key issue in a sham marriage case is "Did the petitioner and his wife intend to establish a life together at the time of their marriage?" Since the later separation was alone insufficient to answer this question, the case was reversed and remanded.

The court stated,

> Aliens cannot be required to have more conventional or more success-ful marriages than citizens.... Evidence that the parties separated after their wedding is relevant in ascertaining whether they intended to establish a life together when they exchanged marriage vows. But evidence of separation, standing alone, cannot support a finding that a marriage was not bona fide when it was entered. The inference that the parties never intended a bona fide marriage from proof of separa-tion is arbitrary unless we are reasonably assured that it is more probable than not that couples who separate after marriage never intended to live together.... Common experience is directly to the contrary. Couples separate, temporarily and permanently, for all kinds of reasons that have nothing to do with any preconceived intent not to share their lives, such as calls to military service, educational

needs, employment opportunities, illness, poverty, and domestic difficulties.

Id. at 1201–02.

* * * The court in *Chan* [*v. Bell,* 464 F.Supp. 125, 130 (D.D.C.1978),] stated that the INS "has no expertise in the field of predicting the stability and growth potential of marriages—if indeed anyone has—and it surely has no business operating in that field." Moreover, the very effort to apply the "factually-dead" test would trench on constitutional values; it "would inevitably lead the INS into invasions of privacy which even the boldest of government agencies have heretofore been hesitant to enter." * * *

Dabaghian's purported ineligibility turns upon whether he was the "spouse" of an American citizen at the time of adjustment of status. If he was, he was eligible then to receive permanent-resident status, not subject to any quota. The word "spouses" in § 201(b) includes the parties to all marriages that are legally valid and not sham. There is no exception for marriages that the INS thinks are "factually dead" at the time of adjustment. For the INS to give such an interpretation to "spouses" and for the Attorney General to be satisfied that Dabaghian was not a "spouse" are abuses of discretion. Since no other reason for ineligibility under § 245 of the Act has been alleged or proven, there can be no rescission of Dabaghian's permanent-resident status.

Reversed and Remanded to the district court with instruction to enter a judgment directing the INS to reinstate Dabaghian as a permanent resident.

MELISSA NANN BURKE, TO HAVE AND HOLD A GREEN CARD

Legal Affairs, January/February, 2006, at 10.

* * * When Lavinia, 24 years old, a waitress, and a nonresident alien [from Romania], married Cristian [Popoiu], a 27–year–old truck driver and a United States citizen, she instantly became eligible for a green card—the coveted documentation granting her the right to live and work in the U.S. It had been nine months since she applied for her green card when the two came to [Andrew] Garcia's interview room to clear one of the last hurdles in the application process: to convince him, as an official of the U.S. Citizenship and Immigration Services, that their marriage was the genuine article and not a union designed to win Lavinia U.S. residency.

The most common way for immigrants to settle legally in the United States is to marry a U.S. citizen. It's a process that last year made legal residents of 252,193 spouses of U.S. citizens—each one of them interviewed by a CIS officer. But not surprisingly, this path to legal residency has been littered with fraud and more than a few sham marriages. Sniffing out the illegitimacy of these unions falls to immigration officers like Garcia. He's one of 12 officers in Philadelphia who each interview between 10 and 18 green card applicants a day—many of them married couples—in an effort to root out the pretenders.

Though sham marriages that lead to green cards have been used as comedic Hollywood tropes (see, for instance, the Gérard Depardieu romp, *Green Card*), CIS officials say the job of sizing up immigrants is always serious business. * * *

In the last year, the federal government has scored big wins in the fight against fraudulent marriages, breaking up nuptial scam rings in South Florida, Chicago, Des Moines, and Seattle. In those cases, ring leaders are said to have paid U.S. citizens to marry aliens so that the aliens could earn permanent residency. The implicated U.S. citizens who went along with the scheme earned several thousand dollars each. * * *

Officer Garcia didn't waste time with pleasantries when he met the Popoius. He * * * launched into questions that got very personal, very fast. He asked the two about their tax filings and about the day they first met. Perhaps curious about whether she had demonstrated any proclivity to mix money with affection, he also asked Lavinia if she had ever worked as a prostitute.

Lavinia, her palms laid in her lap, took deep, calming breaths as she worked through Garcia's questions. In a voice that was commanding but soft, Garcia asked to see the couple's passports, which Lavinia removed from a fat file folder she had placed on Garcia's desk. It held birth certificates, bank statements, copies of an apartment lease, tax returns, even photos from their vacations to Key West, Fla., and Washington, D.C.—evidence of a life together.

The law doesn't detail what makes a marriage valid for immigration purposes, and immigration officers like Garcia aren't long on specifics about what exactly they're looking for when testing a marriage's validity. But they say that they keep their eyes peeled for inconsistencies that creep into stories or tax documents or green card application forms. Husbands and wives who haven't known each other for very long or who don't live together tend to raise eyebrows. Couples whose nuptials weren't attended by family often have some explaining to do. Even more suspicious are weddings that families aren't aware of. * * *

Meeting with couples gives immigration officers a chance to see how the husband and wife treat each other. Donald J. Monica, who heads the Philadelphia CIS office, explained that the interviewers ask themselves, "Does it look like the people interact with each other normally?" When the answer isn't yes, or when things seem not to add up, the immigration officer will take one of the pair across the hall into a separate room where the questions get more specific. Is there a washer-dryer in the house? Who does the grocery shopping? What did you give your wife for her birthday?

Fishy stories sometimes encourage an interviewer to call for a deeper look into a couple's life, through a visit to their home or interviews with their bosses. But that's not always necessary to smoke out a fraud. One husband and wife recently exposed during a visit to the Philadelphia office couldn't agree on the color of their bedroom walls or carpet. Or the number of siblings each other had, or where they met. An even more brazen pair saw its faux marriage come apart when officials found that the husband and wife couldn't speak the same language.

For Lavinia and Cristian, there were no snags. They'd hired an immigration lawyer to give them a sense of what they should expect at their meeting with Garcia, and the lawyer told them not to be shy if they were asked questions about lingerie—or even more intimate details. What they encountered in their 25–minute session was tame compared with what they were ready for. * * *

After [several detailed questions and] a few clicks of his mouse, Garcia looked at them both. "Lavinia, it's my pleasure to grant you lawful permanent residence today," he said. "You should get your green card in the mail in 10 days."

NOTES AND QUESTIONS

1. INS and the Board traditionally sought to deny visa petitions for alleged spouses in two distinct situations: (1) when the underlying marriage was sham or fraudulent—that is, when the parties "did not intend to establish a life together at the time they were married," *Bark v. INS, supra;* and (2) when the underlying marriage was nonviable or "factually dead" at the time when the immigration benefit was sought. The agencies persisted in using both grounds for denial for many years after the first court decisions holding the use of the second test invalid. In 1980, the Board finally capitulated and ruled that, in the future, visa petitions would not be denied based solely on a finding that the underlying marriage is not viable. *Matter of McKee,* 17 I & N Dec. 332 (BIA 1980).

The *McKee* decision emphasized, however, that adjudicators still will scrutinize evidence of current separation in order to determine whether the initial marriage was sham or fraudulent. This position is consistent with *Bark,* as is apparent from the long quoted passage in *Dabaghian.* The *Bark* court went on to say that "[o]f course, the time and extent of separation, combined with other facts and circumstances, can and have adequately supported the conclusion that a marriage was not bona fide." 511 F.2d, at 1202.

In 1986, as will be considered below, Congress amended the relevant statutes and provided a statutory standard addressing the sham marriage issue. The parties must show that the marriage "was not entered into for the purpose of procuring an alien's admission as an immigrant." INA § 216(d)(1)(A)(i)(III). *See also* id. § 204(a)(2)(A)(ii) ("was not entered into for the purpose of evading any provision of the immigration laws"). This standard will usually—but not always—overlap with the *Bark* test. Despite this and related statutory provisions, courts continue to use the *Bark* standard in judging the validity of marriages for immigration purposes. *See, e.g., Aran v. Napolitano,* 2010 WL 4906549 (D.Ariz.2010).

2. Could the government have defended the rescission of LPR status more effectively in *Dabaghian* if it had already fully accepted the *Bark* test but then recast the dispute simply as a matter of timing? That is, instead of applying the *Bark* test only to the parties' intentions at the time they married, the government might have argued that an examiner should also consider the parties' intent to sustain a life together at the time the noncitizen is poised to receive the immigration benefit. This approach, the government might have said, would be more consistent with what many cases have held is the "foremost policy" of our permanent immigration provisions—family unification. *See, e.g., Lau v. Kiley,* 563 F.2d 543, 547 (2d Cir.1977). All of 15 days elapsed between Dabaghian's adjustment of status and his filing for divorce from the U.S. citizen wife who had petitioned for his adjustment. Why should Dabaghian benefit when his family—at the time when the benefit took effect—manifestly had no interest in unifying? Why not reserve admission spaces (a politically scarce resource) for family members who really do want to live together? In this light, INS might have argued, the "factually dead" standard, recast simply as *Bark* applied in a different time frame, is most consistent with Congress' overriding purpose.

3. One reason for the court's rejection of the "factually dead" test in *Bark* was the court's concern about the potential intrusiveness of the questioning that examiners might conduct to see if the marriage were still alive. Yet, is not a similarly intrusive inquiry necessary to determine whether a marriage is a sham? Consider the questioning process as described in the Burke article above. *See also* Note, *The Constitutionality of the INS Sham Marriage Investigation Policy*, 99 Harv.L.Rev. 1238 (1986).

4. The Board has held that applications may not be granted on the basis of marriages *legally* terminated as of the date that the immigration benefit is to be conferred. *Matter of Boromand,* 17 I & N Dec. 450, 453 (BIA 1980). Nor may immigration benefits be granted when the spouses have legally separated under a formal, written separation agreement. *Matter of Lenning,* 17 I & N Dec. 476 (BIA 1980).

5. The BIA has also encountered sham divorces—formal dissolution of marriage bonds for the sole purpose of claiming benefits that are available only to unmarried persons, such as family-sponsored second preference visas for sons and daughters. In *Matter of Aldecoaotalora,* 18 I & N Dec. 430 (BIA 1983), the Board ruled that such a divorce would not be recognized for immigration purposes, where the former spouses continued to live together and to hold property jointly. It based this conclusion on its view that "the intent of Congress in providing for preference status for unmarried sons and daughters of lawful permanent residents was to reunite with their parents unmarried children who, although not minors, were still part of a family unit. * * * By her own admissions, the beneficiary has established that, although divorced from her husband, she has neither severed her relationship with him nor returned to the family unit of her parents." Is this an accurate reading of congressional intent? Could DHS deny second preference benefits to otherwise eligible persons who have never been married on the grounds that they have long lived apart from the parents' family unit?

(iii) IMFA and VAWA: The Immigration Marriage Fraud Amendments and the Violence Against Women Act

Today immigration based on marriage is governed primarily by provisions added to the INA in the Immigration Marriage Fraud Amendments of 1986 (IMFA), Pub.L. 99–639, 100 Stat. 3537. Under the most important provision added by IMFA, INA § 216, all persons who obtain lawful permanent resident status based on a marriage that is less than two years old at the time (whether under the second preference or as an immediate relative) receive such status "on a conditional basis." They thus receive papers valid only for that period, and must provide additional information to USCIS just before the two-year mark in order to obtain unconditional LPR status.

Beginning shortly after IMFA's enactment, however, Congress was persuaded that some of the provisions could be used to enhance the power of abusive spouses. To help guard against that possibility, Congress made additional changes to the overall provisions for immigration based on marriage, initially by expanding the waiver provisions in § 216 that would permit graduation to full LPR status despite the lack of cooperation by the citizen or LPR who initially filed the visa petition (whom we will call the anchor spouse). Later, in the Violence Against Women Act of 1994 (and in successor VAWA enactments) and in related legislation, Congress adopted broader provisions permitting self-petitioning by noncitizen spouses in certain circumstances.

The materials below explain more fully these provisions governing immigration based on marriage and also discuss certain issues the provisions raise. Use the problems immediately below to familiarize yourself with the procedures and standards established by § 216, which is awkwardly drafted and requires careful attention. Some of the problems will require attention as well to INA § 204(a)(2), (c), (g) and § 245(d), (e), all of which were added by IMFA, and to the self-petitioning provisions initially added by VAWA, INA § 204(a)(1)(A)(iii), (A)(iv), (A)(v), (B)(ii), (B)(iii), (B)(iv). For useful commentary and practice guides, see Wheeler, *Until INS Do Us Part: A Guide to IMFA*, 90–3 Imm. Briefings (1990); Stickney, *Conditional and Permanent Residency Through Marriage, Parts I and II*, 99–10 and 99–11 Imm. Briefings (1999); Poole, *The Quickest Way to a Green Card is Harder than You Think*, Orange County Lawyer, July, 2007, at 18.

PROBLEMS

1. Noncitizens A and B (both living in Venezuela) were married one year ago. A has just been granted a visa under the employment-based third preference and plans to move with B to the United States. B therefore also received a visa in the third-preference category as a derivative beneficiary (INA § 203(d)). Will B's permanent resident status be granted on a conditional basis?

2. (a) Noncitizen C marries U.S. citizen D and is admitted as an immediate relative under INA § 201(b). Eighteen months later, C separates from D. Six months pass, and the couple has not reconciled. What happens? *conditional. If still legally married, gets PR.*

(b) Suppose instead that C and D are legally divorced after twenty months. What result? *was conditional - ends.*

(c) What if D instead had died after twenty months?

3. (a) Noncitizen E marries U.S. citizen F and is admitted as an immediate relative. One year later, a daughter is born. Six months after that, F walks out and refuses to help E in any further immigration proceedings. What result?

(b) Suppose instead that the daughter had been born outside the United States after the marriage but before E's admission. Would this make any difference?

(c) Now consider additional variations on this basic set of facts. Suppose that it is noncitizen E who leaves with the child after 18 months of marriage, because F had become angry and moody after losing his job. He frequently spent the evenings berating her, finding fault with her decisions, and occasionally threatening to strike her. Would this make any difference in outcome or opportunities for E? What if F actually beat E? What if instead he threatened the child, but not E, in his angry rages?

4. (a) Noncitizen G is admitted as a nonimmigrant and does not leave the United States at the end of her authorized stay. She is thus present illegally. DHS locates her one month after the admission period expires and begins removal proceedings. G then marries U.S. citizen H, and H files a visa petition on her behalf so that she may adjust her status under INA § 245. What result?

(b) Now suppose instead that after the marriage she obtains agreement from DHS to depart voluntarily, the removal proceedings are dropped, and she leaves the country in the fifth month after expiration of her admission period. Her plan is to return with an immigrant visa based on her marriage to H. How soon can she immigrate on the basis of the marriage under these circumstances?

5. Noncitizen I marries U.S. citizen J and is admitted as a conditional permanent resident. The conditional basis is removed two years later, but six months after that they are divorced. One year later, I marries K, a noncitizen not admitted to the United States, and files a second preference petition on K's behalf. What result?

IMFA. Under § 216, the conditional period lasts for two years, unless DHS acts before that time to terminate the noncitizen's resident status. The conditional period counts fully toward the necessary residence period to qualify for naturalization. INA § 216(e). Within the last 90 days of the two-year period, both spouses are to take the initiative to petition DHS, by filing Form I–751, to have the conditional basis "removed," although under certain circumstances the noncitizen may secure a "hardship waiver" of the requirement of a joint filing. INA § 216(c)(4). DHS has clear statutory authority to call both spouses for an interview at this point, although the interview is often waived, thus reserving examiners' time for those cases where the papers raise a question meriting further inquiry. 8 C.F.R. §§ 216.4, 216.5.

The terminology used in INA § 216 is potentially confusing. DHS *terminates* the permanent resident *status* if it finds during the two-year period that the underlying marriage was improper (as defined in the Act) or has been judicially annulled or terminated. INA § 216(b)(1). *See also* § 216(c)(2) (termination for failure to file timely removal petition). After a termination, the person is deportable under INA § 237(a)(1)(D). But DHS *removes* the *conditional basis* at the end of the two years, if it finds that the underlying marriage was valid and has not ended. *Id.* § 216(c), (d)(1). Removal signifies that the conditional period is over and the noncitizen has graduated to full permanent resident status. Noncitizens will want removal (in this specific sense); they will hope to avoid termination.

If removal of the conditional basis is denied at the end of the two-year period (or if no petition for removal is filed), the noncitizen becomes deportable, but the relevant determinations are open for reconsideration in the removal proceedings before the immigration judge. Moreover, DHS bears the burden of proof, under a "preponderance of the evidence" standard, on most such issues, if contested—for example, to show that the marriage has been annulled or that a fee was paid for the filing of the visa petition. *See* INA § 216(b)(2), (c)(2), (c)(3). If the noncitizen seeks a waiver of some of the provisions requiring a joint petition for removal of the conditional basis, under § 216(c)(4), the noncitizen bears the burden of proof. Waiver requests must be presented to USCIS, specifying exactly which waiver ground is invoked; they may not be first introduced upon appearance before the immigration judge. (The BIA has been fairly generous in ordering continuances of immigration court proceedings in order to allow the presentation of waiver claims first to an immigration examiner.) Extreme-hardship waivers under INA § 216(c)(4)(A) impose a fairly demanding standard. The good faith/not at fault waiver, § 216(c)(4)(B), and the battered spouse waiver, INA § 216(c)(4)(C), may be somewhat easier to obtain, but only if the noncitizen meets the basic threshold requirements. The (c)(4)(B) waiver requires actual termination of the marriage, not just separation, and the (c)(4)(C) waiver requires domestic violence or extreme cruelty.

Congress also used IMFA as the occasion to stiffen a few other provisions meant to prevent or punish marriage fraud. For example, it tightened the requirements for the nonimmigrant category for fiancées and fiancés (the K category), INA §§ 214(d), 245(d); strengthened the restrictions on future immigration of persons who have ever been involved in marriage fraud, INA § 204(c); established criminal sanctions for involvement in marriage fraud, with penalties up to five years imprisonment and a fine of $250,000, INA § 275(c); made it more difficult for a person who immigrated on the basis of a first marriage to bring in a second spouse thereafter (following divorce from the first), INA § 204(a)(2) (either five years must have passed since the initial grant of LPR status to the current petitioner or the petitioner must show by clear and convincing evidence that the initial marriage was valid); and rendered it considerably more difficult for noncitizens in removal proceedings in immigration court to cure their problems by means of "eleventh hour" marriages, entered into while those proceedings were pending. INA §§ 204(g), 245(e). Under the last-mentioned provisions, such a marriage cannot be the basis for adjustment of status, unless the noncitizen proves the genuineness of the marriage by clear and convincing evidence—a more demanding burden of proof than the usual preponderance of the evidence standard.

NOTES AND QUESTIONS

1. Suppose, as in Problem 3a above, that the resident or citizen spouse who initially petitioned for the noncitizen's admission based on the marriage refuses to join in the joint petition ordinarily required for removal of the conditional basis at the end of the two-year period. It remains possible for the noncitizen spouse to obtain a waiver under INA § 216(c)(4) and still have the conditional basis removed. Consider this statutory provision closely.

For purposes of § 216(c)(4)(A), what is "extreme hardship"? Suppose a child was born to the marriage. Should the child's birth lead to a finding of extreme hardship (a) if the anchor spouse has been awarded custody or joint custody; (b) if the noncitizen spouse has been awarded custody?

INA § 216(c)(4)(B), provides for a "good faith/not at fault" waiver. *See generally Matter of Balsillie*, 20 I & N Dec. 486 (BIA 1992) (holding that, to invoke this waiver, the applicant does not also have to show extreme hardship despite the caption on § 216(c)(4)). What should the couple do if they are in the process of obtaining a divorce, but final judicial proceedings will not occur until well after the two-year mark and the anchor spouse (at least for now) appears willing to cooperate in the process for removal of the conditional basis? For a discussion of the options and dilemmas in this scenario, see R. Divine & B. Chisam, Immigration Practice § 14–7(a)(5)(i) (2010).

2. Section 216(c)(4) may not lead to waiver in all situations where the marriage was initially genuine and was valid under the *Bark* test but later fell apart. Whether waiver is available in such a situation depends on what tests are used by examiners in applying the good faith requirement in subparagraph (B) or the extreme hardship requirement in subparagraph (A) (particularly where divorce is not final but the anchor spouse refuses to join in filing the I–751 petition). It will also depend on the examiner's or immigration judge's exercise of the discretion explicitly granted by § 216(c)(4). Should the possibility of losing permanent residence in this fashion be considered a defect in the statute? Overly harsh? Consider the response of Senator Alan Simpson, who chaired the key Senate subcommittee when IMFA was considered (quoted in 65 Interp.Rel. 1339 (1988)):

With regard to the marriage fraud amendments, we realize that there could be cases in which the alien spouse was not primarily responsible for the failure of the marriage, and during debate, some pointed out that this would give rise to an opportunity for "unfairness." However, if we all understand that the only real purpose in giving the substantial immigration benefit our laws provide to an alien spouse is to keep the family together, then we would wish that all will further understand that if the marriage just simply doesn't work—for whatever reason—even when the alien spouse is not at fault, there is no longer a family to "keep together."

3. It is not only spouses who may obtain conditional permanent residence. Sometimes children from a prior marriage of the noncitizen spouse will also fall into this category. Look closely at the language of § 216 to see why this is so. Issues concerning such children are examined in Stickney, *supra*, 99–10 and 99–11 Imm. Briefings.

4. INA § 204(a)(2)(A), added by IMFA, prevents a noncitizen petitioner who gained lawful permanent resident status on the basis of an earlier marriage from successfully petitioning for a new spouse under the second preference (as in Problem 5 above) unless (1) five years have passed since the petitioner attained resident status or (2) the noncitizen "establishes to the satisfaction of [DHS] by clear and convincing evidence that the prior marriage * * * was not entered into for the purpose of evading any provision of the immigration laws." What policy underlies the imposition of this more stringent burden of proof? What kinds of evidence might be offered to satisfy it? *See Matter of Patel*, 19 I & N Dec. 774 (BIA 1988); *cf. Matter of Pazandeh*, 19 I & N Dec. 884 (BIA 1989).

How does the test for sham marriages here (which is quite similar, but not identical, to the basic test IMFA created for § 216; *see, e.g.,* § 216(b)(1)(A)(i)) differ from the sham marriage standard set forth in *Bark* and *Dabaghian*? Why is there a different test? Which is better?

5. Does IMFA exacerbate or alleviate the problems that concerned the *Bark* and *Dabaghian* courts? Compare the kinds of investigation and questioning required before IMFA (as allowed by those two cases) to the kinds of inquiry required or facilitated by IMFA. *See generally* Wheeler, *supra*, 90–3 Imm.Briefings, at 11–12.

Benefits for widows, widowers, and certain other relatives of deceased citizens or LPRs. In 1991 Congress added a provision allowing widows and widowers of U.S. citizens to self-petition for immediate relative status, if they had been married to the citizen for two years, have not remarried, and file within two years after the citizen spouse's death. Pub. L. 102–232, 105 Stat. 1733 (1991). In October 2009, after litigation and publicity regarding poignant cases of widows who had been married for less than two years by the time of the citizen's death, Congress amended the INA to expand explicitly the category of spouses eligible for immediate relative status, essentially by eliminating the requirement for two years of marriage before the death of the citizen. The amendment opened the self-petitioning process to such shorter-duration widows and widowers, and also provided that a noncitizen spouse for whom an immediate relative petition was already filed remains a "spouse" for that purpose even after the petitioner's death. *See* Pub. L. No. 111–83, § 568, 123 Stat. 2142 (2009). The key language appears in the second and third sentences of INA § 201(b)(2)(A)(i) and in § 204(a)(1)(A)(ii).

That statute also provided a similar possibility to continue the adjudication of the applications for other categories of relatives despite the death of the petitioner or, for derivatives, of the principal beneficiary. This provision, however, applies only to beneficiaries already residing in the United States and seeking adjustment of status (not admission on an immigrant visa), and only if the relevant visa petition had already been filed at the time of the sponsor's or principal's death. INA § 204(*l*).

QUESTIONS

1. The 2009 amendments suggest a different set of underlying purposes for the family-based immigration provisions than the ones indicated in Senator Simpson's statement quoted in Note 2 immediately above. How would you describe those different purposes? (Pay attention to the precise bounds on the class of persons who can benefit from § 204(*l*).) How weighty are those goals in comparison to the family togetherness purposes of which Simpson speaks (purposes often highlighted in congressional speeches and judicial decisions such as *Fiallo*)?

2. Section 204(*l*) gives the Secretary of Homeland Security unreviewable discretion to bar approvals under that subsection. How should the Secretary use that authority?

Domestic violence and the expansion of IMFA waivers. Congress enacted IMFA to deal with the perceived problem of visa fraud. The thinking behind the statute's two-year waiting period was that sham marriages were unlikely to be sustainable for that period of time. Congress later recognized that the statute might have the unintended consequence of contributing to the problem of domestic violence by giving the anchor spouse significant power over the noncitizen spouse. Victims of such violence may be deterred from going to authorities for fear that the abuser will retaliate by preventing removal of the victim spouse's conditional status—for example, by refusing to join in a petition to remove the conditional basis or by claiming that the marriage was a sham. Abusers could also control (and misrepresent to the other spouse) information about the immigration process. Together these factors could put immigrant spouses at particular risk, and make them feel they are being compelled to accept an abusive relationship in order to attain lawful status in the United States. For an early summary and analysis of these issues, see Anderson, *A License to Abuse: The Impact of Conditional Status on Female Immigrants,* 102 Yale L.J. 1401 (1993).

In 1990, Congress adopted amendments to IMFA in an attempt to deal with these problems. Most significant was the addition of a third waiver ground to make it easier for battered spouses to obtain removal of the conditional status. INA § 216(c)(4)(C). The provision has occasionally been amended since then in an effort to provide additional protection for victims of domestic abuse, as further problems have come to light. The section now provides a waiver to the joint petition requirement (that is, it allows the abuse victim to file a petition to remove the conditional basis without the anchor spouse's involvement) when:

> the qualifying marriage was entered into in good faith by the alien spouse and during the marriage the alien spouse or child was battered by or was the subject of extreme cruelty perpetrated by his or her spouse or citizen or permanent resident parent and the alien was not at fault in failing to meet the requirements of paragraph (1).

The section goes on to provide that the "Attorney General shall, by regulation, establish measures to protect the confidentiality of information concerning any abused alien spouse or child, including information regarding the whereabouts of such spouse or child." INA § 216(c)(4).

Self-petitions under VAWA. Although the early amendments to IMFA provided relief to spouses in abusive marriages who had already been granted conditional status, they did not provide assistance in another frequent situation—where an abusive spouse refuses to file a visa petition for immigrant status on behalf of a spouse or threatens to withdraw a pending petition. This problem was addressed in 1994 amendments to the INA, enacted as part of the Violence Against Women Act of 1994 (VAWA), Pub.L. 103–322, 108 Stat. 1902–1955. Those amendments permit a battered spouse who is eligible for immigration based on marriage to file a petition on his or her own behalf for lawful permanent residence status, without the involvement of the abusive partner. This provision initially required specific findings that the marriage was bona fide and that the self-petitioner was a person whose removal would result in extreme hardship to her or her children.

Although opening a self-petition option was welcomed, critics identified further shortcomings in the 1994 amendments. *See, e.g.,* Espenoza, *No Relief for the Weary: VAWA Relief Denied for Battered Immigrants Lost in the Intersections*, 83 Marquette L. Rev. 163 (1999). Congress responded in the Battered Immigrant Women Protection Act of 2000 (often called VAWA 2000), which was enacted as §§ 1501–1513 of the Victims of Trafficking and Violence Protection Act of 2000, Pub.L.106–386, 114 Stat.1464, 1518. VAWA 2000 expands the class of battered spouses and children who can self-petition, particularly through elimination of the requirement that extreme hardship be shown and by allowing relief for abused spouses who entered the marriage in good faith but later find that it is invalid because of bigamy by the anchor spouse. INA § 204(a)(1)(A)(iii), (A)(iv), (A)(v), (B)(ii), (B)(iii), (B)(iv). The amendments also provide discretion to examiners to find that the self-petitioner possesses good moral character despite certain criminal convictions, if the criminal act was "connected to the alien's having been battered or subjected to extreme cruelty." INA § 204(a)(1)(C).

Early in the implementation process, INS centralized all handling of VAWA self-petitions in the Vermont Service Center, in order to help assure that they would be handled with appropriate sensitivity and confidentiality—an arrangement continued by USCIS. Successful self-petitioners in the second preference (who, unlike "immediate relatives," may have to wait several years before their priority date becomes current) now are routinely provided with deferred action status and work authorization, benefits that go far toward assuring that they can remain in the United States until they can adjust to LPR status. A useful and detailed summary of the self-petitioning process appears in Dinnerstein, *Violence Against Women Act (VAWA) Self–Petitions,* Immigration and Nationality Law Handbook 331 (American Immigration Lawyers Association, 2006–07 ed.).

Related Protective Provisions

Over the past two decades, Congress has passed other measures meant to reduce immigration-law obstacles to the protection of domestic violence victims as well as certain other threatened noncitizens.

Inadmissibility, deportability, and relief from removal. Certain grounds of inadmissibility and deportability can be waived or overcome if the petitioner shows that the violation had "a connection" to the battery or cruelty. *See, e.g.,* INA §§ 212(a)(6)(A)(ii), 212(a)(9)(B)(iii)(IV), 212(a)(9)(C)(ii), 237(a)(7). Provisions of this type permitting waivers or other special treatment for such victims now appear at many points in the INA, but they are couched in cryptic language and are sometimes overlooked or misunderstood (thought to provide waivers for a wider class of intending immigrants). Be alert as you read the statute, especially the inadmissibility and deportability grounds and their associated waiver provisions, for cross-references that apply solely to the designated class of abused spouses and children. Often the only such indication is a highly technical cross-reference, without any express mention of battery or abuse, to INA §§ 204(a)(1)(A)(iii), (A)(iv), (A)(v), (B)(ii), (B)(iii), (B)(iv), which are the principal abuse-related self-petitioning provisions. Amendments enacted in 2006 did help alleviate this problem somewhat, by replacing some of these cross-references in the INA with the general and more easily understood term "VAWA self-petitioners."

Beyond this, VAWA also expanded the special avenue of relief from removal known as cancellation of removal as it applies to the victims of battery by U.S. citizen or LPR family members. INA § 240A(b)(2). We will explore this form of relief from removal when we treat cancellation in more detail in Chapter Seven. And in 1996 Congress bolstered the INA's provisions against domestic violence by adding a new and strict deportation ground for noncitizens convicted of a crime of domestic violence or found in violation of protection orders. INA § 237(a)(2)(E).

T and U visas. The above provisions mostly cover persons related to abusers who are U.S. citizens or LPRs. Until 2000, the INA provided little express relief for persons victimized by nonrelatives or by persons who themselves lacked enduring immigration status. (We leave aside for now the evolving treatment of domestic violence-based asylum claims, which will be considered in Chapter Eight.) In VAWA 2000, Congress expanded the possibilities for such relief, through provisions that begin by providing temporary status but then permit most recipients to adjust status after a few years by satisfying modest additional requirements. The amendments added two new nonimmigrant visa categories, T and U, which significantly expand the possibilities to help protect victims of gender-related abuse, though neither is, strictly speaking, limited to that type of victim. T visas are for victims of "a severe form of human trafficking" who show that removal would result in extreme hardship, and U visas are for persons who "have suffered substantial physical or mental abuse" as victims of certain kinds of crimes—a broad and varied statutory list. INA §§ 101(a)(15)(T), (U); 214(*o*), (p). We consider these two types of visas in more detail in Section B below.

The International Marriage Brokers Regulation Act. Congress acted in 2005 to address one other potential source of domestic violence, based on evidence that "mail-order brides" from other countries are vulnerable to abuse by the men who select them and then file the visa petition that becomes the basis for the bride's immigration The International Marriage Brokers Regulation Act (IMBRA) was enacted as part of the VAWA reauthorization of 2005, and is codified at 8 U.S.C. § 1375a. It requires covered international marriage brokers to do extensive background checks on their U.S. clients, including checking sex offender public registries, and to provide broad disclosures to the noncitizen before immigration processing begins. The Act spells out which matchmaking organizations are covered; religious organizations and certain services (including most internet dating sites) that do not specialize in international matches are exempt. A helpful discussion of IMBRA may be found in Abrams, *Immigration Law and the Regulation of Marriage*, 91 Minn. L. Rev. 1625, 1653–64 (2007).

(iv) Sham Marriages and the Ethical Responsibilities of an Attorney

As the Burke article above indicates, the immigration agencies and federal prosecutors regard marriage fraud as a serious problem. The benefits resulting from successful fraud are high and, they believe, the risk of detection is relatively low, even though prosecution of organizers has received a higher priority in recent years. *See, e.g.,* Markon, *Task Force on Immigration Fraud Becomes a Model: U.S., Local Agencies Attacking Visa Scams,* Wash. Post, Sept. 21, 2006, at VA03; Sheridan, *D.C. Vendor Arrested in Marriage Fraud Network,* Wash. Post, Jan. 20, 2005, at

B3; Bernstein, *Do You Take This Immigrant?*, N.Y. Times, June 13, 2010, at MB1.

Attorneys representing persons seeking immigration benefits on the basis of marriage may well encounter situations where something about the relationship appears questionable. Does an attorney have an ethical obligation to determine the *bona fides* of the client's marriage? As you consider the following material on ethical issues in this field, consider how you would answer these questions:

1. What would you do if you suspected a sham marriage on the part of a couple seeking either the initial immigration benefit or removal of conditional status?

2. What would you do if you suspected that the noncitizen was using the citizen (sometimes called a "gigolo marriage")?

3. What if the citizen spouse wanted you to withdraw the visa petition after the couple had a fight?

4. What if the noncitizen spouse told you that the citizen spouse was beating her?

Rule 1.6 of the Model Rules of Professional Conduct (as adopted by the American Bar Association in 1983) states: "A lawyer shall not reveal information relating to representation of a client unless the client consents after consultation"—with certain narrow exceptions. The Comment to this rule makes clear that it "applies not merely to matters communicated in confidence by the client but also to all information relating to the representation, whatever its source." An earlier draft of the Model Rules would have permitted a lawyer to reveal information "to rectify the consequences of a client's criminal or fraudulent act in the commission of which the lawyer's services had been used." Model Rules of Professional Conduct, Rule 1.6(b)(3) ("final" draft, 1981). This language was deleted, however, from the version adopted by the ABA in 1983. The 1981 draft of Rule 1.2(d) of the Model Rules prohibited a lawyer from assisting a client "in conduct that the lawyer knows or reasonably should know is criminal or fraudulent." The final approved version, however, deletes the words "or reasonably should know" from the rule. Model Rules of Professional Conduct, Rule 1.2(d) (1983).

Despite the obvious effort of the ABA in 1983 to strengthen client confidentiality and reduce attorney obligations unilaterally to reveal or rectify questionable practices, some state bars enforce a conception of ethical responsibility more in line with the 1981 draft. The following appeared in the Texas Bar Journal, and is reprinted from 61 Interp.Rel. 442 (1984):

The District 10 Grievance Committee issued a private reprimand to an attorney of San Antonio on Dec. 22, 1983. The committee found that the attorney failed to undertake an adequate investigation into the marital status of his client before assisting him in an application for temporary status with the Immigration and Naturalization Service. The attorney knew, or should have known, that his client's marital status was questionable. Also, the attorney failed to timely advise the Immigration and Naturalization Service as to false information given to it at the time of the application for temporary status. Shortly thereafter, the attorney knew that false information had been given.

The current version of Rule 1.6 of the ABA Model Rules (2006) provides:

> (b) A lawyer may reveal information relating to the representation of a client to the extent the lawyer reasonably believes necessary: * * * to prevent, mitigate or rectify substantial injury to the financial interests or property of another that is reasonably certain to result or has resulted from the client's commission of a crime or fraud in furtherance of which the client has used the lawyer's services.

How would this rule apply in the context of a lawyer's discovery of his client's apparent falsehood in applying for an immigration benefit?

The current immigration regulations are more specific and demanding. They call for the Department of Justice to impose disciplinary sanctions on any attorney who "[k]nowingly or with reckless disregard makes a false statement of material fact or law, or willfully misleads, misinforms, threatens, or deceives any person (including a party to a case or an officer or employee of the Department of Justice), concerning any material and relevant matter relating to a case, including knowingly or with reckless disregard offering false evidence. If a practitioner has offered material evidence and comes to know of its falsity, the practitioner shall take appropriate remedial measures." 8 C.F.R. § 1003.102(c) (2007), applied in *Matter of Shah*, 24 I & N Dec. 282 (BIA 2007). *See also United States v. Zalman*, 870 F.2d 1047 (6th Cir.), cert. denied sub nom. *Sharifinassab v. United States*, 492 U.S. 921, 109 S.Ct. 3248, 106 L.Ed.2d 594 (1989) (sustaining attorney's conviction for fraud and failing to disclose sham marriages when clients applied for adjustment of status); Joyce, *Ethical Issues for Immigration Lawyers*, 98–10 Imm. Briefings (1998); Joe, *Ethics in Immigration Law: Immigration Benefit Fraud and the Peril of Conscious Avoidance*, 02–06 Imm. Briefings (2002); Rubin, *Filing Immigration Applications and Petitions: Ethical Responsibilities and Criminal Penalties*, N.J. Lawyer, April 2004, at 39; Gilbert, *Facing Justice: Ethical Choices in Representing Immigrant Clients*, 20 Geo.J. Legal Ethics 219 (2007).

(v) A Perspective on Immigration and Family Law

In *Immigration Law and the Regulation of Marriage*, 91 Minn. L. Rev. 1625, 1653–64 (2007), Kerry Abrams describes the surprisingly extensive ways in which today's immigration law winds up intruding into the traditional state family-law domain—a phenomenon insufficiently perceived by either immigration lawyers or family lawyers. Abrams considers the provisions discussed in this section, as well as many other parts of the INA, including the requirement, to be addressed in Chapter Seven below, that the sponsoring spouse must execute an affidavit of support potentially enforceable for life by the immigrant spouse, even if the marriage dissolves. She analyzes the impact of immigration law at four separate stages of the marital relationship: regulating courtship, entry into marriage, the intact marriage, and exit from marriage. The article concludes with these observations:

> In each of the four stages, immigration law regulates marriage very differently than family law does. In the first and third—courtship and the intact marriage—it regulates even where state family law has an explicitly hands-off attitude toward regulation. In the second and fourth stages—entry and exit—it regulates more intrusively and extensively than does state family law.

> Sometimes this regulation of marriage, as with IMFA, appears to be an unintentional side effect of implementing immigration policy. In the case of IMFA, Congress was attempting to police the fraud that was the inevitable by-product of an immigration system that privileges spouses of citizens over other potential immigrants. Congress's goal of fraud prevention necessarily required it to spell out what kinds of marriages would qualify as legitimate. In other cases, Congress is engaged in a kind of backpedaling, attempting to intervene in marriage because of problems caused by immigration law itself. The provisions of VAWA that exempt battered spouses from the joint petition requirement, for example, make sense as an attempt to mitigate the harshness of the usual immigration rules. Finally, a third type of regulation intervenes in marriage because of congressional disapproval of certain relationships. IMBRA makes exceptions for "cultural" or "religious" matchmaking organizations not because matchmaking through these organizations has been proven to result in a better, smarter, or wealthier immigrant population, but rather because it believes the marriages emerging from these entities are exempt from the unacceptable power dynamics it believes most "mail-order bride" marriages possess. In each case, regardless of Congress's intent, immigration law is functioning as a form of family law for those who are regulated by it.

> * * * The plenary power doctrine has been chipped away at, modified, criticized, and debated by courts, scholars, and lawyers for over a hundred years, but its tension with state control over family law has never before been explored. Lawmakers might decide that principles of federalism mandate that laws be drafted in a way that will least intrude on state family law's policy objectives while still fulfilling the goals of federal immigration policy. Courts interpreting these laws might construe them narrowly, so that minimal damage would be done to state law understandings of marriage.

> Even in cases where Congress is clearly regulating immigration, and the impact on marriage is an incidental or unintended by-product

of its immigration goals, Congress might do well to acknowledge the effect that immigration law has on marriage and consider the wealth of experience and information that state family law might provide. Family law offers organizing principles and theoretical models that would help us to understand the effects immigration law has on families. Immigration scholars and lawmakers should examine state family law to see how and why various doctrines have developed. They would then be in a better position to calibrate the effects of immigration law on the family. * * *

Abrams, *supra,* at 1707–08.

b.   Siblings, Adoptions, and an Introduction to the *Chevron* Doctrine of Statutory Interpretation

The following case addresses a precise legal issue that affects relatively few potential immigrants. The case is important, however, because it illuminates application of the Supreme Court's *Chevron* doctrine in the administration and application of the immigration laws. It also gives insight into immigration based on adoption and it clarifies the interplay between the definitions of "child" and "parent."

YOUNG v. RENO

United States Court of Appeals, Ninth Circuit, 1997.
114 F.3d 879.

TROTT, CIRCUIT JUDGE.

* * *

BACKGROUND

Karen Yuen Fong Young was adopted as a child by a paternal aunt in Hong Kong and was permitted to immigrate to the United States because of this adoptive parent-child relationship. In 1984, she filed petitions seeking to confer preferential immigration status on her four biological siblings, pursuant to § 203(a)(4) of the INA. The INS approved the petitions and forwarded them to the U.S. State Department consulate in Hong Kong for processing as visas became available. Young's siblings applied for immigration visas in 1994, when visas first became available to fourth-preference individuals with 1984 priority dates. However, the consulate returned Young's petitions to the INS for visa-revocation proceedings, explaining that the petitions should not have been approved because Young's adoption had severed her legal relationship to her natural siblings. Young filed this action for a declaratory judgment in district court, before the INS revoked the petitions. The INS subsequently revoked three of the four petitions. Young challenged the revocation of these three petitions in the district court, and the district court granted summary judgment in favor of the INS. * * *

STANDARD OF REVIEW

The Attorney General may revoke an approved visa petition at any time for "good and sufficient cause." INA § 205; *see* 8 C.F.R. § 205.2. "A court may review the denial of the INS of a preferential visa petition to determine if the denial was an abuse of discretion." *Kaliski v. District Director of INS*, 620 F.2d 214, 216 n. 1 (9th Cir.1980). The INS abuses its discretion if it bases its decision upon an improper understanding of the law. *Id.*

In *Chevron, U.S.A., Inc. v. Natural Resources Defense Council, Inc.*, the Supreme Court set forth the two-step process for reviewing an agency's construction of a statute that it administers:

> First, always, is the question whether Congress has directly spoken to the precise question at issue. If the intent of Congress is clear, that is the end of the matter; for the court, as well as the agency, must give effect to the unambiguously expressed intent of Congress. If, however, the court determines Congress has not directly addressed the precise question at issue, the court does not simply impose its own construction of the statute, as would be necessary in the absence of an administrative interpretation. Rather, if the statute is silent or ambiguous, the question for the court is whether the agency's answer is based on a permissible construction of the statute.

467 U.S. 837, 842–43, 104 S.Ct. 2778, 2781–82, 81 L.Ed.2d 694 (1984) (footnotes omitted).

"An agency interpretation of a relevant provision which conflicts with the agency's earlier interpretation is 'entitled to considerably less deference' than a consistently held agency view." *INS v. Cardoza–Fonseca*, 480 U.S. 421, 447 n. 30, 107 S.Ct. 1207, 1221 n. 30, 94 L.Ed.2d 434 (1987).

DISCUSSION

I

At issue in this case is whether a child who was given up for adoption can seek to confer preferential immigration status on her natural siblings. The INA prevents a natural parent from receiving any immigration privilege through that adopted child. Adoption severs the legal relationship, for immigration purposes, between an adopted child and her natural parents. The INA, however, is silent as to the effect of adoption on the legal relationship between an adopted child and her natural siblings.

Section 203(a)(4) of the INA establishes a fourth-level preference for "[q]ualified immigrants who are the brothers and sisters of citizens of the United States." Although the Act does not define "brother" or "sister," it does define "child" and "parent." The term "child" includes:

> a child adopted while under the age of sixteen years if the child has been in the legal custody of, and has resided with, the adopting parent or parents for at least two years: Provided, That no natural parent of

any such adopted child shall thereafter, by virtue of such parentage, be accorded any right, privilege, or status under this chapter.

INA § 101(b)(1)(E). The Act then defines "parent" by reference to the definition of "child":

> The terms "parent", "father", or "mother" mean a parent, father, or mother only where the relationship exists by reason of any of the circumstances set forth in subdivision (1) of this subsection....

Id. at § 101(b)(2). In the absence of explicit provisions defining "brother" or "sister," the INS defines siblings by their relationship to a common parent. Young, on the other hand, argues that their ordinary, biological meaning must prevail.

A. *The INS's Interpretation*

The BIA's most recent decision in *Matter of Li* [, 20 I. & N. Dec. 700 (BIA 1993),] followed two prior cases which also addressed the impact of adoption on the sibling relationship.

In *Matter of Fujii*, 12 I. & N. Dec. 495 (Dist.Dir.1967), the INS District Director held that a U.S. citizen could petition for visa preference on behalf of her natural brother, who had been given up for adoption as a child. Recognizing that the Act did not define the terms "brother" or "sister," the Director noted that the "normal definition is a person having the same parent or parents as another." * * * The Director also observed that, although § 101(b)(1)(E) of the INA prevented the natural parent of an adopted child from obtaining an immigration right, privilege, or status via that child, there was no similar proscription regarding the natural siblings of an adopted child.

In *Matter of Kong*, 17 I. & N. Dec. 151 (BIA 1979), the petitioner had been adopted as a child by the natural parents of the beneficiary. However, that adoption was terminated after the petitioner's natural mother immigrated to the United States so that the natural mother could seek a familial visa preference on the petitioner's behalf. The petitioner subsequently immigrated to the United States and became a U.S. citizen. The petitioner then applied for preferential visa status pursuant to § 203(a)(4) on behalf of the natural son of her adoptive parents (and thus her adoptive brother).

The BIA held that a sibling relationship created by an adoption does not survive the termination of that adoption for immigration purposes. Clarifying a prior BIA statement suggesting that the status of "parent," once established, cannot be terminated, the BIA explained that to qualify as siblings under [§ 203(a)(4)] of the INA, a petitioner must establish: (1) that both she and the beneficiary "once qualified as children of a common parent," and (2) that the parent is still a parent of each of them. *Id.* at 153. Although the petitioner and the beneficiary once qualified as children of a common parent, they no longer shared a common parent because the petitioner's adoption had been terminated. Her adoptive parents were no longer her parents for immigration purposes.

Finally, in *Matter of Li*, the BIA considered "whether a petitioner, who qualifies as an adopted child within the provisions of § 101(b)(1)(E) of the Act, can successfully petition for a natural sibling on the basis of their relationship to a common natural parent?" Relying on its decision in *Matter of Kong*, the Board stated that "to qualify as siblings under § [203(a)(4)] of the Act, a petitioner must establish both that he and the beneficiary once qualified as children of a common parent and that the parental relationship has not been severed."

Focusing on the § 101(b)(1)(E) proviso which provides that, upon an adoption that meets the requirements of the section, no natural parent can thereafter be accorded any "right, privilege, or status" under the Act, the Board held that such an adoption (which meets the statutory requirements) severs the relationship between natural parent and adopted child. Because the natural parent no longer has the status of parent under the Act, the legal relationship between adopted child and natural sibling also ceases. They no longer have a common parent for immigration purposes.

The Board rejected the District Director's analysis in *Matter of Fujii*, which depended on the absence of a prohibition of benefits for natural siblings similar to that of the § 101(b)(1)(E) proviso. Recognizing that § 101(b) of the Act defined only the parent-child relationship, the Board concluded that "[a]ll other familial relationships are dependent on these [parent-child] definitions." Because "[a] sibling relationship can only be recognized through the fact of having a common parent within the definition of the Act," no sibling relationship can be recognized through a natural parent who loses his or her "status" as a "parent" under the Act as a result of the proviso to section 101(b)(1)(E). "To the extent that a relationship between the petitioner and his natural parents was terminated by virtue of his adoption, he cannot now establish that he and the beneficiary are children of a common parent as is required by the Act for the purpose of establishing a sibling relationship." With this understanding of the statutory provisions and the INS's construction, we proceed with our *Chevron* analysis.

B. Congress has not spoken on this issue

In reviewing the INS's construction of these statutory provisions, *Chevron* dictates that we first consider whether Congress has directly spoken to the precise question at issue. Young urges that Congress has so spoken, through its use of the words "brothers and sisters." Young contends that the *Li* definition of "brothers and sisters" is contrary to the plain meaning of those terms. Additionally, Young faults the BIA's conclusion that the sibling relationship is terminated with the severance of the natural-parent/adopted-child relationship, because the statute does not explicitly preclude natural siblings from gaining an immigration benefit through the adopted child.

Young relies primarily on *Gee v. INS*, 875 F.Supp. 666 (N.D.Cal.1994), in which the district court faced the same question of the effect of adoption on natural-sibling relationships. The district court in *Gee* recognized that the first step of the *Chevron* inquiry was "to determine congressional intent, using 'traditional tools of statutory construction.' " *Id.* at 670. The court determined that it need not proceed beyond this step, because it concluded that Congress intended to grant a natural sibling of an adopted child a "brother and sister" immigration preference, regardless of any intervening adoption. It based its conclusion on the plain meaning rule and the doctrine of *"expressio unius est exclusio alterius."*[5]

First, because the statute does not define "brothers" and "sisters" as used in § 203(a)(4), the *Gee* court looked to Webster's Dictionary for the settled meaning of the terms. The court concluded that the dictionary definition of "brother"—"a male human being considered in his relation to another person having the same parents or having one parent in common"—is not affected by adoption "because a natural sibling shares the same parents as an adopted sibling." *Id.* However, the court fails to recognize that under the statute's definitions of "parent" and "child," adoption terminates the legal relationship between a natural parent and an adopted child. *See* § 101(b)(1)(E) (proviso). An adopted child's only "parents" under the statute are her adoptive parents. The natural sibling therefore does not share the same legal parents. * * *

The *Gee* court next relied on the *"expressio unius est exclusio alterius"* statutory tool of construction, which provides that when a statute names the parties that come within its provisions, other unnamed parties are excluded. Because Congress expressly precluded natural parents from gaining advantage through an adopted child but did not mention natural siblings, the *Gee* district court reasoned, it would be unreasonable to interpret the statute as impliedly excluding natural siblings from qualifying for family-based preferences. Although the District Director relied on this construction in *Matter of Fujii*, the BIA explicitly rejected it in *Matter of Li*, pointing out that the sibling relationship is dependent upon the parent-child relationship, which is the only familial relationship defined.

In rejecting the *Fujii* analysis, the BIA in *Li* also noted that "the restrictive proviso of § 101(b)(1)(E) could be rendered meaningless over time." As the district court in this case cogently explained:

> Like the BIA in *Li*, this court recognizes that Plaintiff's interpretation of "brothers" and "sisters" may increase the potential for fraud and eviscerate the prohibition contained in [INA § 101(b)(1)(E)], as ultimately, Plaintiff would be permitted to petition for preferential immigration status on behalf of her natural siblings, who in turn, would be able to petition on behalf of their (including the Plaintiff's) natural parents. In light of Congress's express language that "no natural parent of any [ ] adopted child shall, by virtue of such parentage," benefit from his or her status under the Act, and absent any indication to the contrary, the court cannot agree that Congress intended the result suggested by Plaintiff.

---

5. Meaning that "the expression of one thing is the exclusion of another." Black's Law Dictionary 521 (5th ed. 1979).

931 F.Supp. at 1503–04. The *Gee* court, however, thought this scenario "unrealistic" and concluded that Congress did not share this concern either, as evidenced by its failure to close this supposed loophole by including language regarding siblings in the statute. Since *Li*, however, Congress twice amended the INA but did not interfere with the Board's interpretation of § 203(a)(4).

We once again agree with the district court in the instant matter and reject the *Gee* court's analysis. Although Congress did not expressly address preferences for natural siblings, we must give full meaning to its clear intention to prevent natural parents from gaining benefits—regardless of whether the *Gee* court finds this possibility realistic. Thus, neither the plain language rule nor the failure by Congress to exclude preferences for natural siblings after adoption indicates that Congress clearly intended that the natural sibling relationship survive adoption for immigration purposes.

The legislative history of § 101(b)(1)(E) further indicates that, when Congress adopted these provisions, it was not concerned with, and did not contemplate, whether the legal relationship between natural siblings would survive adoption. Prior to the enactment of § 101(b)(1)(E) in 1957, United States citizens were unable to bring adopted children into the U.S. because the definition of "child" did not include adopted children. Although Congress's general purpose in enacting this provision was to keep families intact, their concern was focused on the adoptive, not the natural, family. Indeed, many of the adopted children were orphans. However, Congress did contemplate the effect of adoption on the natural-parent/adopted-child relationship, specifically providing that adoption severs that relationship. While Young is correct that congressional intent in adopting this provision was to preserve the family unit, there is no indication that this intention extended to natural siblings of adopted children.

We therefore conclude that Congress has not spoken on this precise issue, and we disapprove of the *Gee* court's contrary conclusion.

C.　*The INS's construction is permissible*

The second step of the *Chevron* analysis is to consider whether the INS's interpretation is a permissible construction of the statute. The district court considered the BIA's analysis in both *Matter of Kong* and *Matter of Li* and found permissible the INS's requirement that to qualify as legal siblings under the Act, a petitioner must show that she and the beneficiary once qualified as children of a common parent and that the parental relationship has not been severed.

We agree with the district court's analysis and conclusion. The INS's two-part test reasonably ties the sibling relationship to the primary familial relationship defined in the Act—the parent-child relationship. By so doing, the INS's construction: 1) stays within four corners of the INA and does not rely on external definitions; 2) gives full meaning to the express language of the § 101(b)(1)(E) proviso prohibiting natural parents from benefitting from adoption; 3) prevents a scenario specifically prohibited by Congress whereby adopted children obtain preferences for natural siblings who then obtain preferences for natural parents; and 4) is consistent with the overall structure of Act, which emphasizes the primacy of the parent-child relationship and confers more benefits on parents than other relatives.

We therefore hold that the INS's [*sic*] interpretation of the INA, as set forth in *Matter of Kong* and *Matter of Li*, is a reasonable and permissible construction of the statute. * * *

Affirmed.

NOTES AND QUESTIONS

1. In answering the question in the case, the court devotes most of its analysis to the plain meaning of the words used in the statute, the structure of the statute and related statutory provisions, and canons of statutory construction. All of these are common tools of statutory interpretation. But it is also important to examine the underlying purpose of the statutory provision at issue. Why might Congress have created the sibling category? Is that purpose advanced or defeated by recognizing the plaintiff's relationship with her biological siblings under the facts of the case? As the court reports, the INA prevents a biological parent from claiming immigration benefits based on a child who has entered the U.S. as an adopted child. INA § 101(b)(1)(E). Is that provision based on a purpose that is relevant in the instant case? Why or why not?

2. In 1999 Congress responded, but in a very limited way, to the situation of siblings like those involved in the *Young* case, by extending the time during which the adoptive parents of the first child may later adopt the siblings and confer an immigration status upon them. This is done by allowing such later adoptions up to age 18, rather than the usual age 16. INA §§ 101(b)(1)(E)(ii), (F)(ii). *See* 77 Interp.Rel. 476 (2000); 78 *id.* 336 (2001). In 2000, Congress adopted the Intercountry Adoption Act, Pub.L. 106–279, 114 Stat. 825 (2000), to implement the Hague Convention on Protection of Children and Cooperation in Respect of Intercountry Adoption. The Act designates the State Department as the U.S. Central Authority to monitor intercountry adoptions, a measure required by the Convention. The Act also added subparagraph (G) to INA § 101(b)(1) directly counting as a "child" a young person adopted in accordance with the Hague Convention.

The *Chevron* Doctrine, *Mead,* and *Brand X*

The reasons underlying *Chevron*. *Young* relies heavily on *Chevron, U.S.A., Inc. v. Natural Resources Defense Council*, 467 U.S. 837, 104 S.Ct. 2778, 81 L.Ed.2d 694 (1984), a landmark of administrative law. *Chevron* and successor cases amplifying its doctrine have had a major impact in defining the respective roles of agencies and courts in implementing regulatory statutes. *See generally* Schuck & Elliott, *To the*

Chevron Station: An Empirical Study of Federal Administrative Law, 1990 Duke L.J. 984; Schuck & Wang, *Continuity and Change: Patterns of Immigration Litigation in the Courts, 1979–1990*, 45 Stan.L.Rev. 115, 169–72 (1992). The passage quoted by the *Young* court has been frequently deployed in hundreds of administrative law cases. Review that passage, *supra* p. 333, and then consider the Supreme Court's following paragraph, which explains some of the functional reasons for that doctrine (467 U.S. at 842–44, 104 S.Ct. at 2781–83):

> "The power of an administrative agency to administer a congression-ally created . . . program necessarily requires the formulation of policy and the making of rules to fill any gap left, implicitly or explicitly, by Congress." *Morton v. Ruiz*, 415 U.S. 199, 231, 94 S.Ct. 1055, 1072, 39 L.Ed.2d 270 (1974). If Congress has explicitly left a gap for the agency to fill, there is an express delegation of authority to the agency to elucidate a specific provision of the statute by regulation. Such legislative regulations are given controlling weight unless they are arbitrary, capricious, or manifestly contrary to the statute. Sometimes the legislative delegation to an agency on a particular question is implicit rather than explicit. In such a case, a court may not substi-tute its own construction of a statutory provision for a reasonable interpretation made by the administrator of an agency.

Such deference may also be defended on additional grounds. First, the agency works with the statute on a daily basis and is likely to have a better understanding of the operational implications of a narrow or broad construction of a statute. The agency's experts will also better understand how the various possible alternative constructions would fit with or affect other provisions whose connection to the provision at issue may not be obvious to a generalist court (this factor could be especially relevant for a statute as complex as the INA). Second, the agency may have aided in the drafting of the statute and therefore may have greater insight than the courts into the intent of the language chosen and the purposes of the statutory provision. Finally, deference to agency interpretation may create greater uniformity in application of the statute than would be achieved under different opinions among courts of appeals. What counterarguments against agency deference on matters of statutory interpretation should be considered, particularly in the immigration context? Does the *Chevron* approach give too much authority to the administrators?

Mead. The application of the *Chevron* doctrine was limited in *United States v. Mead Corp.*, 533 U.S. 218, 121 S.Ct. 2164, 150 L.Ed.2d 292 (2001). The Court ruled that "administrative implementation of a particu-lar statutory provision qualifies for *Chevron* deference when it appears that Congress delegated authority to the agency generally to make rules carrying the force of law, and that the agency interpretation claiming deference was promulgated in the exercise of that authority." 533 U.S. at 227, 121 S.Ct. at 2171. The opinion suggests that interpretations embod-ied in notice-and-comment rulemaking and adjudications in a "relatively formal administrative procedure" would ordinarily meet this test. Less formal statements of the agency's interpretation, like the Customs Service "letter ruling" at issue in that case, are entitled only to a lower level of deference under *Skidmore v. Swift & Co.*, 323 U.S. 134, 139–40, 65 S.Ct. 161, 89 L.Ed. 124 (1944). Under *Skidmore*, the "fair measure of deference" varies with the circumstances, and courts should look "to the degree of the agency's care, its consistency, formality, and relative expertness, and to the persuasiveness of the agency's position." 533 U.S. at 228. Most immigration cases will probably still call for *Chevron* rather than *Skidmore* deference to the agency interpretations, because most such interpretations under the immigration laws are embodied either in regulations issued after notice and comment or in BIA precedent decisions, which are plainly the product of a highly formal adjudicative procedure.

Brand X. The BIA, like other administrative agencies, generally yields to a court interpretation in any circuit where the legal question has been settled. Sometimes this means that it applies one interpretation in, say, the Eleventh Circuit and the contrary interpretation in the Ninth Circuit—a practice known as "intra-circuit acquiescence." When the BIA is confronted with the same question in a case arising in another circuit that has not yet ruled on the issue, it will decide for itself, thus signaling which interpretation it regards as superior, to be followed by immigration judges and DHS officers in any circuit that has not adopted a conflicting interpretation. In such circumstances, uniform national application would appear to require waiting for a decision by the Supreme Court—and of course one important ground for a grant of certiorari is the need to resolve a split among the circuits. But a 2005 Supreme Court decision applied *Chevron* in a manner that sometimes opens another avenue for establishing uniform national application.

In *National Cable & Telecommunications Assn. v. Brand X Internet Services*, 545 U.S. 967, 125 S.Ct. 2688, 162 L.Ed.2d 820 (2005), the circuit court had overruled an interpretation by the Federal Communications Commission because the court of appeals had already construed the statute, reaching a different result, before the administrative agency had occasion to decide the issue. The agency, it ruled, was bound by the earlier judicial precedent. The Supreme Court disagreed:

> A court's prior judicial construction of a statute trumps an agency construction otherwise entitled to *Chevron* deference only if the prior court decision holds that its construction follows from the unambiguous terms of the statute and thus leaves no room for agency discretion. This principle follows from *Chevron* itself. *Chevron* established a "presumption that Congress, when it left ambiguity in a statute meant for implementation by an agency, understood that the ambiguity would be resolved, first and foremost, by the agency, and desired the agency (rather than the courts) to possess whatever degree of discretion the ambiguity allows." *Smiley [v. Citibank (South Dakota), N. A.,* 517 U.S. 735, 740–41 (1996)]. Yet allowing a judicial precedent to foreclose an agency from interpreting an ambiguous statute, as the Court of Appeals assumed it could, would allow a court's interpreta-

tion to override an agency's. *Chevron*'s premise is that it is for agencies, not courts, to fill statutory gaps. The better rule is to hold judicial interpretations contained in precedents to the same demanding *Chevron* step one standard that applies if the court is reviewing the agency's construction on a blank slate: Only a judicial precedent holding that the statute unambiguously forecloses the agency's interpretation, and therefore contains no gap for the agency to fill, displaces a conflicting agency construction.

A contrary rule would produce anomalous results. It would mean that whether an agency's interpretation of an ambiguous statute is entitled to *Chevron* deference would turn on the order in which the interpretations issue: If the court's construction came first, its construction would prevail, whereas if the agency's came first, the agency's construction would command *Chevron* deference. Yet whether Congress has delegated to an agency the authority to interpret a statute does not depend on the order in which the judicial and administrative constructions occur. The Court of Appeals' rule, moreover, would "lead to the ossification of large portions of our statutory law," *Mead, supra,* at 247 (Scalia, J., dissenting), by precluding agencies from revising unwise judicial constructions of ambiguous statutes. Neither *Chevron* nor the doctrine of *stare decisis* requires these haphazard results.

The dissent answers that allowing an agency to override what a court believes to be the best interpretation of a statute makes "judicial decisions subject to reversal by Executive officers." ([O]pinion of Scalia, J.). It does not. Since *Chevron* teaches that a court's opinion as to the best reading of an ambiguous statute an agency is charged with administering is not authoritative, the agency's decision to construe that statute differently from a court does not say that the court's holding was legally wrong. Instead, the agency may, consistent with the court's holding, choose a different construction, since the agency remains the authoritative interpreter (within the limits of reason) of such statutes. In all other respects, the court's prior ruling remains binding law (for example, as to agency interpretations to which *Chevron* is inapplicable). The precedent has not been "reversed" by the agency, any more than a federal court's interpretation of a State's law can be said to have been "reversed" by a state court that adopts a conflicting (yet authoritative) interpretation of state law.

545 U.S., at 982–85. For examples of the BIA's exercise of the authority recognized in *Brand X,* see *Matter of Castaneda,* 25 I & N Dec. 188 (BIA 2010); *Matter of Guevara Alfaro,* 25 I & N Dec. 417 (BIA 2011).

Inconsistent agency interpretations. *Brand X* also appears to limit the dictum from *INS v. Cardoza–Fonseca,* quoted by the *Young* court, calling for reduced deference when an agency changes its initial interpretation:

> Agency inconsistency is not a basis for declining to analyze the agency's interpretation under the *Chevron* framework. Unexplained inconsistency is, at most, a reason for holding an interpretation to be

an arbitrary and capricious change from agency practice under the Administrative Procedure Act. For if the agency adequately explains the reasons for a reversal of policy, "change is not invalidating, since the whole point of *Chevron* is to leave the discretion provided by the ambiguities of a statute with the implementing agency." *Smiley* v. *Citibank (South Dakota), N. A.,* 517 U.S. 735, 742 (1996). "An initial agency interpretation is not instantly carved in stone. On the contrary, the agency ... must consider varying interpretations and the wisdom of its policy on a continuing basis," *Chevron, supra,* at 863–864, for example, in response to changed factual circumstances, or a change in administrations.

545 U.S. at 981.

4. INVESTORS AS IMMIGRANTS

Until the 1990 Act, U.S. law contained no specific provisions favoring the immigration of prospective investors in the American economy, although investors and their lawyers sometimes found ways to use an investment as the basis for admission in another category. Proponents urging adoption of such an admission category often used arguments along these lines: we provide preferences for those who come to *fill* jobs for which American workers are unavailable; why not provide a preference for noncitizens who would *create* jobs for American workers? The Select Commission on Immigration and Refugee Policy, which issued its report in 1981, was persuaded that we should do so. SCIRP, Final Report 131–32. Father Theodore M. Hesburgh, the Commission's chair, dissented, arguing that "the rich should not be able to buy their way into this country." *Id.* at 336.

Congress finally agreed to the addition of an investor provision in 1990. INA § 203(b)(5) establishes a fifth employment-based preference (EB–5) and gives it 10,000 admission spaces. It requires an investment that will create no fewer than 10 jobs for U.S. workers, not counting the investor and his or her family. The baseline investment is $1 million, but this can be reduced to $500,000 for "targeted employment areas"—rural communities or designated high-unemployment regions. As a safeguard against misuse or manipulation, all EB–5 immigrants and their families receive permanent residence on a conditional basis for two years under INA § 216A, which is closely modeled on the procedures of INA § 216, the conditional residence provision for noncitizen spouses. Consider the criteria that must be satisfied when the noncitizen petitions to have the conditional status removed at the end of the two-year period. INA § 216A(d)(1). *See also* 8 C.F.R. § 216.6; Yanni, *Business Investors: E–2 Nonimmigrants and EB–5 Immigrants,* 92–8 Imm.Briefings (1992).

Figure 5.3
Admissions of Immigrant Investors (EB–5), FY 1992–2010

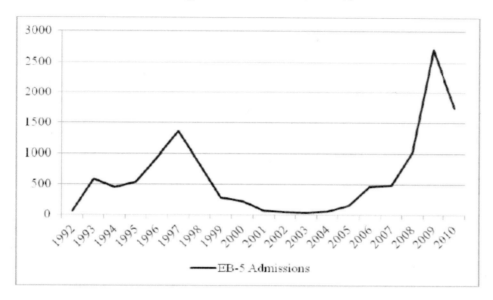

Source: 1999 INS Statistical Yearbook (2002) (for years 1992–1994); 2004 Year-book of Immigration Statistics, table 4 (for years 1995–2000); 2010 Yearbook of Immigration Statistics, table 6 (for years 2001–2010).

As Figure 5.3 depicts, usage of the investor visa category has been quite modest, running to only a few hundred admissions per year through most of the life of this provision. The growth in EB–5 admissions in the mid–1990s, it turned out, reflected the inventiveness of promoters who marketed complex financing schemes that minimized the real investment exposure and up-front cash requirements of the participating investors who were looking to obtain a green card. INS was slow to react, but in 1998 its Administrative Appeals Office issued a series of rulings that significantly tightened the requirements, in order to help assure that the underlying investments are genuine, draw from the applicant's own law-fully acquired funds, and place the full statutory amount at risk in the business.

The promoters' borderline EB–5 filings, coupled with INS's delayed but vigorous reaction, provoked what one article called a "near-death experience" for the entire EB–5 program, as potential investors then shied away for many years. Meyer & Caco, *Spreading Like Wildfire!: What Explains the Explosive Growth of EB–5 Regional Centers?*, 10–02 Imm. Briefings 5 (Feb. 2010). Starting in 2007, however, interest rebounded considerably, based in part on a more stable, centralized, and welcoming regulatory process at USCIS for EB–5 applications (*id.* at 6–7), but also on the greatly expanded use of a provision allowing investments in a business entity known as a "regional center" located in a targeted employment area. Investing in an approved regional center permits the investor to count indirect job creation resulting from his investment (not just the construction worker building the building, for example, but a portion of the jobs at the restaurants where he eats, at the gas station where he buys fuel, etc.). EB–5 admissions reached 3,688 in FY 2009 and 2,480 in FY 2010.

The regional center option was adopted by Congress in 1992. It did not become fully workable and attractive until amendments in 2000–2003 opened up a much wider array of possible investments that would qualify for a regional center's operations. USCIS has also taken steps meant to improve the agency's capacity to handle regional center applications and to monitor the viability and implementation of the center's plans. In 2010 it adopted a formal immigration form to be used by interested localities or business entities in applying for approval of a center, the I–924 (which requires a filing fee of nearly $7000). As of July 2011 there are 151 approved regional centers. Immigrant Investor Regional Centers, USCIS (Jul. 28, 2011), <http://www.uscis.gov>.

USCIS describes regional centers this way:

> Regional Centers submit I–924 applications in one of two varieties. First, "actual" applications present "shovel-ready" business projects that are sufficiently developed to support the immediate filing of actual I–526 petitions from participating investors. "Actual" applications are supported by specific business plans and economic analysis [documenting the judgment of sufficient indirect job creation], the actual capital-investment structures and documentation for the investment offering, the anticipated regional economic impacts, and the Regional Center's operating plan and structure. * * * Second, "exemplar" applications present feasible business projects that are not yet "shovel ready," together with an exemplar I–526 petition, for a preliminary determination of EB–5 compliance. The "exemplar" process allows Regional Centers to seek approval of new, job-creating projects in principle before the business projects are fully developed to the point where participating investors can submit their I–526 petitions.

USCIS, *Proposed Changes to USCIS's Processing of EB–5 Cases,* discussed and reprinted in 88 Interp.Rel. 1303, 1333 (2011).

More concretely, consider one investment opportunity heavily advertised to potential EB–5 investors in recent years—a long-established ski and golf resort called Jay Peak in northern Vermont. The resort is in a targeted employment area, and the Vermont Agency of Commerce and Community Development operates a regional center there designed to invest in a multi-phase expansion and renovation of the lodging and conference facilities at the resort. It reports 300 successful EB–5 investors in its first years of operation. The Jay Peak website for investors explains the advantages of this type of EB–5 investment (http://www.eb5 jaypeakresort.com/eb5–visa/):

> This involves a passive investment of $500,000 made in a Targeted Employment Area (TEA) within a Designated Regional Center.

The EB–5 policy management requirement is minimal in that the investor can be a limited partner and still qualify as long as the limited partners have a policy-making role. * * *

The investor is not required to live in the place of investment; rather, he or she can live wherever he/she wishes in the United States. * * *

The EB–5 Regional Center Program Benefits

● A direct route to a *Green Card* * * *

● *Permanent residency* in the United States for you, your partner and any children under 21

● Live, work and retire anywhere in the United States

The website also describes plans for an "exit strategy" after a minimum of two years: "Upon removal of temporary green card conditions for all eligible limited partners in the project, there is an exit strategy available whereby the limited partners will own individual fractional residential units within the deeded real property of the partnership. Jay Peak will manage the sale or rental of those units on behalf of the limited partners with all sales or rental proceeds being paid to the limited partner less any closing cost, realtor commission or management fee." Finally, there is this additional enticement: "Become a part of the excitement[.] EB–5 Visa Investors benefit from *2 weeks complimentary vacation* at Jay Peak Resort each year."

Meyer and Caco, *supra*, at 3, explain the attractions of the regional center option to potential investors (particularly as backlogs have lengthened for EB–3 and certain EB–2 immigrants):

> Rewind to 2003. Options for immigrant investors were scarce, unattractive, non-existent, or exceptionally difficult to manage within the confines of the Immigration and Nationality Act (INA). Investors who would have previously considered the $1 million EB–5 option are now assessing whether this option makes any sense. Potential immigrant investors are questioning whether they should invest a minimum of $1 million in a "new" enterprise and then be burdened with the stress of needing to create 10 new "full-time" jobs within a two-year period for qualifying employees, when the same result (obtaining permanent residence and developing a successful business) can be achieved concurrently by passively investing $500,000 in a Regional Center project (which effectively outsources the job creation stress to the Regional Center operators), while engaging in either full-time employment or developing a separate business entity. An effective Regional Center program allows such investors to decouple their efforts in obtaining permanent residence from their efforts to continue their ongoing employment or develop their business interests as they see fit.

The EB–5 program, both in its basic form and through regional centers, has been a challenge for agency implementation, requiring detailed examination of complex business plans and transactions that are not typically part of its regulatory domain. The EB–5 program also presents many snares and pitfalls for immigration law practitioners. *See* Meyer & Caco, *Now for the Hard Part: Attracting Investors to EB–5 Regional Centers,* 10–03 Imm. Briefings (March 2010). Critics have also questioned whether the investments result in a significant level of enduring job creation, noting that USCIS does not track these cases in a manner that readily provides information about the business's longevity or the number of jobs actually created. *See generally* North, *Charging More for Immigration: Closing Financial Loopholes in the U.S. Migration Process* (Center for Immigration Studies Backgrounder, May 2010); General Accounting Office, *Immigrant Investors: Small Number of Participants Attributed to Pending Regulations and Other Factors* (GAO–05–256, Apr. 1, 2005). Moreover, the minimum investment level is fixed in the statute and has not been adjusted for inflation–or other changes in the American economy—since enactment in 1990. (It would require nearly $900,000 today to make an investment equivalent to $500,000 in 1990 dollars.)

Does the EB–5 admission provision represent good policy? Does it make good sense to provide the highly sought-after green card based on what may amount to little more than a partial investment in a ski resort condo? Would it be more effective, given the enormous simplification in administration that would result, simply to require investors to send the requisite sum to the U.S. Treasury for deficit reduction? Or perhaps to auction the 10,000 spaces now available under EB–5 to the highest bidder?

5. EMPLOYMENT–BASED IMMIGRATION

The INA provides distinctive standards and procedures governing employment-based admissions, and an elaborate, multi-agency process has developed to apply them. We start our consideration with a snapshot of that process, drawn from a *New Yorker* article written in 1984 after Calvin Trillin spent several weeks examining the practice of immigration law in Houston. Though many details of the labor certification procedure he describes have changed since then, the key elements remain the same, and the article provides a lively depiction of many of the dynamics, tensions, and even contradictions inherent in the process. After that, we will examine the EB immigration categories and the labor certification process in more detail, and finally consider alternative avenues for employment-based immigration that do not involve the expensive and time-consuming process of labor certification.

CALVIN TRILLIN, MAKING ADJUSTMENTS

The New Yorker, May 28, 1984, at 61–62, 65–66.

The process of getting labor certification amounts to staging a sort of sham employment offer. The lawyer writes a job description that complies with the Department of Labor's standards, and the potential employer of the alien actually advertises such a job through the state employment commission. If someone shows up who is a citizen and has the qualifications outlined in the ad and is willing to work for the stated wage, the labor certification is not granted—although the employer has no obligation to give the citizen a job. If the lawyer who wrote the job description has been skillful, there is a good chance that no qualified citizen will show up. Writing job descriptions that pass the Department of Labor but attract no other potential employees is what Ed Prud'homme calls "one of the few art forms in the business," and Beaumont Martin is considered one of the artists. One of the Chinese students had managed to get a job in the accounting department of a small oil company, and, since the job required some computer expertise, Martin decided to write a job description that nudged her over a bit from accounting to computer analysis. ("There are a lot of people running around with accounting degrees.") When he had typed it up, he handed it to her:

SYSTEMS ANALYST 020.067–018

Conduct analyses of accounting, management, and operational problems and formulate mathematical models for solution by IBM computer system, using FORTRAN, COBOL, and PASCAL. Analyze problems in terms of management information. Write computer programs and devise and install accounting system and related procedures. Masters or equal in management information systems. $1667/month.

She read it over. "It's beautiful," she said. * * *

Along with the forms and folders on the floor next to Beaumont Martin's lounge chair was a worn copy of a fourteen-hundred-page government book called Dictionary of Occupational Titles—known to immigration lawyers as the D.O.T. For anyone who wants to make labor certification into an art form, the D.O.T. is an essential piece of equipment. It contains one-paragraph descriptions of virtually every occupation practiced by anybody in the United States. It describes the task of a neurosurgeon and it describes the task of a fibre-glass-container-winding operator. In a consistently direct style, it says what a leak hunter does ("Inspects barrels filled with beer or whisky to detect and repair leaking barrels") and what a sponge buffer does ("Tends machine that buffs edges of household sponges to impart rounded finish") and what an airline pilot does ("Pilots airplane"). Using the D.O.T. as a guide, an immigration lawyer tries to give the client an occupational title in the least crowded field available and then describe the job in a paragraph that sounds pretty much like a paragraph in the D.O.T. but happens to describe almost nobody but the client in question. "Immigration law is taking a short-order cook and making him into an executive chef," Pete Williamson told me. "What we're talking about here is a matter of focus."

When I was discussing labor certification with Pete Williamson one afternoon, he mentioned a young woman he had seen that day who wanted to stay in the country but did not fall into any of the categories of family reunification. She obviously did not qualify for any of the non-immigrant visas available to businessmen or investors. She was already married—to someone who, as it happened, had more or less the same visa problems that she did. Her only hope for a green card was labor certification. Her only occupation was looking after the children of a neighbor.

I said that it didn't sound promising. A few days with immigration lawyers had greatly broadened my view of how the employment sections of the immigration law were actually used. I was no longer under the delusion that the law worked to bring to this country people who had rare skills or worked in fields where there were serious shortages of American workers. "It's a matter of nudging the client's situation over a bit one way or another in order to make it fit into a category that's eligible," one lawyer had told me. "And sometimes, if you want to stay in the United States, you have to shape your career to fit the immigration law." Williamson had explained that it was possible for, say, a South American shirt manufacturer who wanted to resettle here to come in on a visitor's visa or a business visa, establish a corporation, have the personnel department of the corporation file an application to have him labor-certified as the president of a shirt firm doing business with Latin America ("Must know Spanish. Must be familiar with South American cottons . . ."), apply for a green card through the labor certification, and settle in for life. Still, it seemed unlikely that being a mother's helper in Texas was a job "for which a shortage of employable and willing persons exists."

There were two other important elements in the case, Williamson said. The young woman in question was a college graduate. Also, both she and the children she looked after were Muslims—all from Pakistan. Williamson intended to nudge her over from a nanny to a tutor—a tutor qualified to instruct the children in their own culture and religion. He thought it unlikely that any citizen with similar qualifications would respond to the ad. Williamson takes some satisfaction in such focusing—enough, he says, to offset the repetitiousness of certain aspects of the practice and the frustrations of dealing with the Immigration and Naturalization Service. "It's a competent, involved, technical job in which, if you're successful, you can see the consequences of your actions," he told me when I asked what appealed to him about practicing immigration law. "Also, I don't like the government."

---

a. Introduction

In fiscal year 2010, 148,343 immigrants were admitted to the United States under the employment-based categories. (Recall that these numbers include spouses and children of the principal aliens.) Our usual historical narrative of immigration depicts largely unskilled workers coming to the United States to toil on farms, to work in factories and mines, to build railroads—and eventually perhaps to raise themselves or their families to higher rungs of the socio-economic ladder. To be sure, thousands of persons continue to enter this country each year to take up unskilled or low-skilled employment. Many of them are beneficiaries of family-based visas, or they may enter the United States illegally. But the vast majority of noncitizens explicitly admitted on the basis of employment-based visas are skilled workers, usually members of a profession.

The United States has a population of more than 300,000,000 people. Why does it have special admission categories for workers who fill relatively high-paying and prestigious jobs? Is the country unable to educate and train its own population for such jobs? Or does the United States seek to take advantage of the costs that other countries have incurred in producing skilled workers and professionals? What about the 5,000 visas the INA now makes available each year for persons "performing unskilled labor"? INA § 203(b)(3)(A)(iii). Are there no U.S workers able and willing to take these jobs?

The formal employment-based immigration system is at least nominally structured with the domestic labor market very much in mind. Employers seeking the services of most immigrants who enter under the employment-based categories must demonstrate that there are no domestic workers available to perform such work and that the entry of the noncitizen will not adversely affect the wages and working conditions of similarly employed U.S. workers. INA § 212(a)(5)(A)(i). The usual process for meeting these requirements is labor certification. Some entrants, however, are not subject to a market test. The first preference category (EB–1), offering approximately a quarter of total employment-based admissions, is comprised of noncitizens who have "extraordinary ability in the sciences, arts, education, business, or athletics," are professors or researchers "recognized internationally as outstanding in a specific academic area," or are managers or executives in multinational corporations. The employers of these noncitizens need not show that domestic workers are unavailable to perform the services that they will undertake in the United States. The apparent reasoning is that either such immigrants have talents beyond compare, or that their contributions are so manifest that their admission is desirable whether or not they compete with domestic talent. And there are a few other limited circumstances in which parties seeking employment-based immigration can avoid the rigors of labor certification—explored in Section A5f below.

As we examine the details of labor certification and the employment categories, ask yourself how Congress has sought to balance the interests of employers in accessing a labor supply at low cost versus the interests of U.S. workers in protecting wages and working conditions. It may also be helpful to focus on the specific situation set forth in the Exercise immediately below as you gain understanding of the various legal requirements. As with many other exercises in this book, the significance of many elements of the factual situation will become apparent only gradually, as you work your way through the statutory provisions, the regulations, and the case law set forth in the remainder of this section. You may also have to ask further questions of the client or develop additional information from other sources. Note what additional information you will need and think about where you would turn to obtain it.

EXERCISE: LABOR CERTIFICATION

A local sociology professor comes to your law office for help. "I met the finest young student at a recent conference in Switzerland," he tells you. "His thoughtful comments at a seminar where I was a guest speaker attracted my attention. He's about to complete his bachelor's degree in sociology, and he wants to move to the United States. I told him I'd help him, and he said gratefully he'd be happy to serve as my research assistant. I could pay him minimum wage, and he'd drive me to work and mow my lawn as well. Surely it's easy to get a visa for an educated and upstanding young man like this." In your subsequent conversation with the professor, you learn that the young man is 23 years old and is fluent in English, German, French and Turkish.

What do you advise? How could you best construct a situation that might lead to the student's admission as an immigrant? What additional information do you need? What parts of the professor's and the student's plans would need to be altered to qualify the latter for an immigrant visa? What exactly are the procedural steps that must be followed, all the way from the initial job description to the student's admission at a port of entry (if that can be accomplished)?

---

b. Labor Certification: Background and Basic Procedures

The impulse to protect American workers against competition from immigrant laborers has long played a role in the shaping of our immigration laws. As we have seen, the first sustained federal immigration controls were imposed in 1875. Just ten years later Congress adopted the first labor-related immigration measure, the Contract Labor Law of 1885. Act of February 26, 1885, Ch. 164, 23 Stat. 332. Its enforcement provisions were strengthened two years later. Act of Feb. 23, 1887, Ch. 220, 24 Stat. 414. As described by a later congressional committee, this law

> was aimed at the practice of certain employers importing cheap labor from abroad. This importation practice began in 1869. Advertisements were printed offering inducements to immigrants to proceed to this country, particularly to the coal fields, for employment. Many advertisements asserted that several hundred men were needed in places where there were actually no vacancies. The object was to oversupply the demand for labor so that the domestic laborers would be forced to work at reduced wages. * * *

The alien contract labor law made it unlawful to import aliens or assist in importation or migration of aliens into the United States, its Territories, or the District of Columbia under contract, made previous to the importation or migration, for the performance of labor or service of any kind in the United States.

H.R.Rep. No. 1365, 82d Cong., 2d Sess. 12–13 (1952).

These provisions remained on the books until the major restructuring and codification of our immigration laws that took place with passage of the Immigration and Nationality Act in 1952. By then, opinion concerning foreign labor recruitment had changed considerably. In the view of many, the country needed at least selective efforts to fill gaps in the U.S. personnel pool with immigrant workers. And it was thought that other measures, such as the National Labor Relations Act and the Fair Labor Standards Act, afforded adequate protection against the earlier employer abuses. *See generally* Rodino, *The Impact of Immigration on the American Labor Market,* 27 Rutgers L.Rev. 245 (1974). The 1952 Act therefore repealed the 1885 law and adopted in its place the first labor certification provision of our immigration laws. In its initial form, operative until 1965, this section permitted the Secretary of Labor to block the entry of persons seeking to enter for the purpose of skilled or unskilled labor upon a finding that such entry would displace U.S. workers or "adversely affect" the wages and working conditions of U.S. workers similarly employed. The initiative rested with the Secretary of Labor to declare an occupation oversupplied, and Secretaries rarely bestirred themselves to invoke the provision.

In 1965, responding to effective lobbying led by the AFL–CIO, Congress reversed the operation of the labor certification process. Since that date the law has essentially presumed that foreign workers are not needed; the noncitizen and her intending employer must take the initiative to secure affirmative certification. The current version of the labor certification provision appears in INA § 212(a)(5).

(i) Overview and Background

Take a close look at the language of INA § 212(a)(5). How far must an employer search for U.S. workers? What if qualified workers are available in the state's largest city but they don't want to work at the employer's place of business 200 miles away? What if one U.S. worker would do so, provided he received a 20 percent boost in salary over the employer's initial offer? In what circumstances may the employer reject a U.S. applicant because he is not equally qualified with the noncitizen, even though he is minimally qualified for the job? To what preference categories under INA § 203(b) do the "equally qualified" provisions correlate?

The basic labor certification provision appears in § 212, as part of the lengthy list of grounds of inadmissibility, which we will consider at greater length in Chapter Seven. Labor certification is more usefully conceptualized, however, as one of the key elements in the initial categorical qualifications that most intending immigrants in the employment-based preferences must fulfill. Section 204(b) makes this conceptual linkage more explicit. As that provision indicates, the labor certification requirement is a prerequisite that must be satisfied by entering immigrants in the employment-based second and third preferences, which provide for roughly 80,000 admissions each year (plus any spill-down numbers). *Cf.* INA § 212(a)(5)(D). (Importantly, a second-preference immigrant can avoid labor certification if he or she receives a "national interest" waiver—to be discussed below.) Before a noncitizen in these categories can become the beneficiary of an approved visa petition, then, labor certification must be secured from the Department of Labor (DOL). Certification establishes that a shortage of available and qualified workers exists in the noncitizen's field at the place of intended employment, and that her hiring on the offered terms would not adversely affect the wages or working conditions of similarly employed U.S. workers. In sharp contrast, immigrants entering by virtue of a family relationship are not hindered by the labor certification requirement, even if they intend to compete with American workers in fields already well supplied.

For most of the history of labor certification, DOL structured the process in a way that channeled most employer interest into a time-consuming individualized procedure, under which an employer, having a particular noncitizen in mind, would take steps to secure the necessary Labor Department approval. Under that procedure, operative until 2005, an employer would ordinarily file initial papers with a state workforce agency (SWA), and would await preliminary approval of the papers before starting recruitment of U.S. workers. Recruitment would include advertising (local, regional or national, depending on the type of job) and normally use of the SWA's job bank. After the recruitment period, the employer would collect detailed information on the recruitment (e.g., what publicity was used, how many U.S. workers applied and were interviewed, what valid job-related reasons led to the rejection of such applicants) and file it with the SWA, which would then transmit the package to DOL. A DOL regional certifying officer (CO) would review the file, perhaps seek additional information, and then either grant the certification or issue a Notice of Findings setting forth the reasons supporting denial.

Demand for labor certification increased considerably in the 1990s, a reflection of the booming economy. But this was also a time when the resources of the DOL and the SWAs were shrinking. An enormous backlog developed in labor certifications, often requiring employers to wait two or three years after filing before receiving a decision. (And they then still had to file a visa petition with INS or DHS; that petition's approval would be followed by further delays while the individual applied for adjustment of status or an immigrant visa.) DOL began to look for ways to make the process more efficient.

(ii) PERM

In 2005, DOL implemented a considerably revamped process known as Program Electronic Review Management, or PERM. 69 Fed. Reg. 77326 (2004) (amending 20 C.F.R. Parts 655 and 656). PERM is designed to rely primarily on attestations by employers (subject to audit) that they had complied with regulatory requirements, rather than having certifying officers comb through voluminous files to determine whether the application was appropriate. By spelling out clearer requirements for all portions of the process, the regulations are supposed to reduce the discretion of certifying officers, produce more uniform and predictable results, and thus enable employers to take more complete responsibility for the adequacy of their own recruitment process. The changes also reduce the labor-intensive role of SWAs, limit the amount of information filed with DOL (while requiring that relevant information be kept available in the employer's files to be checked in case of audit), encourage electronic filing and thus permit computer-aided review of the applications.

PERM generally results in decisions by certifying officers in a much shorter time period. For FY 2006, the Labor Department reported that it had resolved 86 percent of new PERM applications within six months of filing—a considerable improvement over the earlier system. DOL Annual Report, Fiscal Year 2006 Performance and Accountability Report. (Meantime, specially created Backlog Centers processed a massive accumulation of pre-PERM cases, finally eliminating the backlog in 2007.) In the spring of 2011, the Department of Labor was reporting processing times of one to two months for initial PERM application filings, a significant improvement following processing times that had increased to nine to ten months in 2010. DOL updates its processing times for PERM labor certification applications each month on the DOL's iCERT Visa Portal System website, <http://icert.doleta.gov/>.

The fundamental conceptual structure of labor certification is unchanged by PERM. Employers are supposed to make a good-faith recruitment effort to find qualified U.S. workers able and willing to work at the place of intended employment, and they will be denied certification if such workers are available or if the labor market testing was inadequate. Employers must show that they offered the "prevailing wage" as defined in the regulations, that the job requirements (as set forth in the job descriptions used as the basis for U.S. recruitment) are not unduly restrictive, and that they interviewed interested U.S. workers and rejected any such applicants for lawful, job-related reasons.

Recruitment phase. Under PERM, the employer must obtain a prevailing wage determination from the SWA before filing, but in practice most obtain it before beginning recruitment, to make sure they are offering the proper terms of employment. SWAs draw on standard wage surveys to make the determination, but employers can offer their own alternative surveys and try to persuade the SWA of the latter survey's superiority for the particular job or locality. The employer must set forth job requirements (such as years and type of education or training) that are normal for the occupation. Employers formerly looked to the Dictionary of Occupational Titles for this information; now they are guided by a computerized database system called O*NET (Occupational Information Network), that can be accessed online. *See* <http://www.onetcenter.org>.

The regulations set forth detailed requirements for advertising and posting the job opening. Employers manage their own recruitment without the oversight of the SWA, but they normally must post the position with the SWA's job bank. Under the regulations, the recruitment requirements are more extensive if the position is considered a professional one—i.e., in a field where a bachelor's degree is normally considered an educational requirement.

After recruitment, the employer (or more likely, its immigration attorney) prepares a recruitment report. This "must include a description of the recruitment steps and the results achieved, including the number of hires and the number of U.S. workers who were rejected, categorized by the lawful job-related reasons for such rejection." Shore, *Labor Certification in the 21st Century: PERM, the Wave of the Future: Ironing out the Kinks: Combating Fraud and Streamlining the Process,* 05–03 Immigration Briefings 9 (2005). The report is not filed with the application, but the employer must retain it in readily retrievable form for five years, so that DOL can look more closely if the employer is selected for audit.

The application. Labor certification applications are filed directly with DOL on Form ETA 9089. (The form is reprinted in the Statutory Supplement; you may wish to consult it now as a way of helping to understand the application process described here.) The form must be submitted no less than 30 and no more than 180 days after the recruitment period. Electronic filing is strongly encouraged, in order to facilitate data entry and automated processing. The form includes an expansive set of employer attestations, sworn to under penalty of perjury—attesting, inter alia, that the position has been and is open to any U.S. worker without discrimination, that the job opportunity did not become available as a result of a strike or lockout, and that the employer has the financial ability to pay the stated compensation.

In addition to the information about the employer, the job, and the recruitment process, Form ETA 9089 requires detailed information about the noncitizen whom the employer wishes to hire. In reality, the majority of employees for whom employers file labor certifications are already working for the employer, for example, in a nonimmigrant status like H–1B that permits such work (discussed in Section B of this chapter). Some of this required information about the prospective employee helps the certifying officer (CO) determine whether the noncitizen obtained a portion of the work experience required for the job described in the application by means of training with this employer. If so, this fact may raise doubts about the job requirements, on the theory that the employer could equally well hire a U.S. worker with lower skills than advertised and then provide equivalent on-the-job training. The PERM regulations place emphasis on counting U.S. workers as qualified if they can obtain the needed job skills through a reasonable period of on-the-job training with the applicant employer. 20 C.F.R. § 656.17(g)(2). The noncitizen must also sign the form under penalty of perjury and further declare that she intends to take the job if labor certification is approved.

Employers are to maintain at their places of business the remaining documentation, including the recruitment report and the resumés or applications received from job applicants. They must submit the full file to DOL if the application is selected for audit. Audits can be demanded based on information in the completed Form ETA–9089 (some of the triggers for an audit will be identified by an automated system), or on a random basis. The CO will either approve the application, require additional information, notify the employer that the application has been selected for audit, or deny the application if clearly deficient. Denials may be appealed to the Board of Alien Labor Certification Appeals (BALCA). In his or her discretion, the CO may require a new round of federally supervised recruitment in connection with an audit. Employers who misuse the system or violate the regulations can find their right to file future certifications suspended, be required to use supervised recruitment for future applications, or suffer criminal sanctions for willful falsehoods. In promulgating the PERM regulations, DOL stated its expectation that selective audits, coupled with the risk of sanctions, would provide adequate deterrence against abuse, without the ongoing need for detailed individual review of each application—the centerpiece of the former system. Judicial review of a labor certification denial is normally available in federal district court under the Administrative Procedure Act, after the employer has exhausted the administrative remedies. *See, e.g., Reddy, Inc. v. Department of Labor*, 492 F.2d 538, 542–44 (5th Cir.1974).

Visa petition. Once the labor certification is approved, the employer is then responsible for filing that document with USCIS, accompanied by the employer's actual visa petition on Form I–140. The Department of Labor's certification is conclusive regarding labor market conditions, but USCIS is entitled to question the noncitizen's qualifications for the certified job or the employer's ability to pay the stated wage or salary, or otherwise to investigate fraud or misrepresentation by the individual or the employer, and to deny a visa petition on such grounds despite labor certification. If no such defects are found, approval of the visa petition is then communicated to a consular officer in the noncitizen's country for the ultimate processing of the immigrant visa or, far more commonly, to the USCIS office that will consider the noncitizen's adjustment of status.

Schedule A. If the occupational category at issue appears on DOL's Schedule A, 20 C.F.R. § 656.5, the employer can skip the DOL application process and go directly to USCIS with his I–140 visa petition. *Id.* § 656.15(a). Schedule A lists occupations judged chronically short of qualified U.S. workers. It amounts to a blanket determination that anyone seeking that kind of work in the United States will not displace U.S. workers or adversely affect wages and working conditions. The Schedule has been reduced over the years, because Congress has moved some of its former categories into the first or fourth employment-based preferences, which do not require labor certification. As of May 2011, Schedule A includes only licensed nurses, physical therapists, and certain noncitizens "of exceptional ability" in the sciences, arts, or performing arts. The employer must prove as part of the I–140 petitioning process that the prospective employee has the qualifications to fit Schedule A.

Rules restricting the time and scope of labor certification approvals. Regulations that took effect in July 2007 greatly tightened a few other specific requirements in order to deter abuses that had come to light in prosecutions for large-scale fraud in the employment-based immigration system. *See* 72 Fed. Reg. 27904 (2007). The regulations prohibit payments by or on behalf of the employee to reimburse the employer's costs for obtaining certification. Approved certifications no longer have indefinite validity. They must be filed with USCIS along with the I–140 visa petition within 180 days; otherwise they expire. Importantly, the regulations now forbid substitution of a different noncitizen as beneficiary after the filing. This limitation could impose difficulties, particularly as categories become backlogged, but DOL persisted with this change based on its judgment that the possibility of substitution had led to considerable abuse. Some employers or attorneys would obtain certification, DOL reported, then essentially auction or sell the approved position to another employee. Barter or sale of applications and approved certifications is also expressly prohibited by the 2007 regulations. *See DOL Issues Final Rule Enacting Major Changes to Permanent Labor Certification Process,* 84 Interp.Rel. 1119 (2007).

c. Labor Certification: Defining the Job and Setting Its Requirements

How can the Labor Department guard against the obvious incentives, evident in the Trillin article, *supra,* for employers and attorneys to write job descriptions that are tailored so precisely to the background of the noncitizen intended as a beneficiary that it would be nearly impossible that qualified American workers will be found? Consider, for instance, the creative lawyering at work in *Oriental Rug Importers v. E.T.A.*, 696 F.2d 47 (6th Cir.1982), where the employer, a rug importer and vendor, sought the services of an experienced buyer. The required qualifications, drawn neatly to fit the intended beneficiary, included 30 years experience and training, proficiency in French and German, and possession of tools for reweaving rugs. The certifying officer found the qualifications unduly restrictive and denied the application for labor certification.

Controversies over an employer's job requirements are a significant part of practice in this field. The next case is BALCA's leading precedent interpreting the controlling Labor Department regulation on this issue. This is a pre-PERM case, and the regulations have since been reorganized, but the basic requirements remain the same.

IN THE MATTER OF INFORMATION INDUSTRIES, INC.

Board of Alien Labor Certification Appeals, 1989.
1989 WL 103627, 88–INA–82.

* * *

STATEMENT OF THE CASE

The Employer, Information Industries, Inc., is a nationwide computer consulting business headquartered in Aurora, Colorado. Employer's business consists of hiring technical and professional computer specialists and contracting out their services to other companies. The job in question in this case was entitled a "Systems Engineer" by Employer. The employee hired for this position was to be contracted out to AT & T in Denver. The application for certification filed on December 15, 1986 listed the duties of the job as follows:

> Use UNIX and IBM operating systems to develop, implement and service scientific based operating systems for engineering firms and other clients. Includes converting symbolic statements of administrative data or business problems to detailed logical flow charts of coding into computer language. Analyzing business problems by applying knowledge of computer capabilities, subject matter, algebra, and symbolic logic to develop sequence of program steps. Analyzing, reviewing, and rewriting programs to increase operating efficiency or adapt to new requirements. Compiling documentation of program development and subsequent revisions.

The only requirements for the job listed by Employer were a B.S. in Engineering and an M.S. in Computer Science.

In a Notice of Findings ("NOF") issued on August 10, 1987, the Certifying Officer ("CO") found that Employer's application had not met the requirements of the regulations. Employer filed a lengthy rebuttal on October 13, 1987. Certification was denied by a Final Determination issued on October 19, 1987, on the ground that the requirement of two degrees, a B.S. in Engineering and an M.S. in Computer Science, is unduly restrictive in violation of [20 C.F.R.] § 656.21(b)(2). * * *

DISCUSSION

* * *

b. *Business Necessity*

In 20 C.F.R. Part 656, DOL has set out procedures through which an employer, on behalf of an alien, can establish the factors required for certification. The regulations contain detailed requirements for the employer to advertise the job, recruit through the local job service office and otherwise, and offer terms and conditions of employment that match those prevailing in the relevant job market. If, after complying with these regulations, the employer can establish that there are no U.S. workers both qualified for the job and available to perform it, certification will be granted.

In advertising and recruiting for the job, § 656.21(b)(2)[c] requires that:

The employer shall document that the job opportunity has been and is being described without unduly restrictive job requirements:

(i) The job opportunity's requirements, unless adequately documented as arising from business necessity:

(A) Shall be those normally required for the job in the United States;

(B) Shall be those defined for the job in the Dictionary of Occupational Titles (D.O.T.) including those for subclasses of jobs;

(C) Shall not include requirements for a language other than English.

What constitutes business necessity in the context of alien labor certification cases has produced some of the most controversial and diverse decisions in this area of the law. Since this is the first case in which the Board is attempting to address this issue in a definitive manner, it will be analyzed in great detail below.

[handwritten: How judges have interpreted] — In labor certification cases, judges have viewed business necessity from different perspectives. These different focuses have led to the development of inconsistent business necessity standards. The case law shows that those judges who have upheld the denial of labor certifications have often disregarded the employer's need to effectively operate its business, by focusing exclusively on the stated legislative purpose of protecting the U.S. workers. Courts following this rationale have adopted stringent business necessity standards. For instance, in *Pesikoff v. Secretary of Labor*, 501 F.2d 757 (D.C.Cir.1974), *cert. denied*, 419 U.S. 1038 (1974), the court stressed in its decision denying certification that the 1965 legislative shift in [the INA] was intended to protect the U.S. labor market from an influx of aliens. The court reasoned, therefore, that the Secretary has discretion "... to ignore employer specifications which he [the Secretary] deems in accordance with his labor market expertise, to be irrelevant to the basic job which the employer desires performed." *Id.* at 762. In a subsequent decision upholding a denial of certification in which it followed *Pesikoff*, the D.C. Circuit rejected a District Court's holding that "[e]very employer is entitled to hire persons who have qualifications that can be utilized in a manner that will contribute to the efficiency and quality of the business." *Acupuncture Center of Washington v. Dunlop*, 543 F.2d 852, 858 (D.C.Cir.1976).

[handwritten: 2) strict standard would undermine the essence of the business operation] — Additionally, some judges have focused on how the term "business necessity" has been interpreted under Title VII of the Civil Rights Act of 1964 (42 U.S.C. § 2000e), adopting the strict business necessity standard set out in an early Title VII case, *Diaz v. Pan Am. World Airways, Inc.*, 442 F.2d 385 (5th Cir.1971). In the preamble to the Notice of Proposed

[handwritten left margin: 1) Focusing on legislative purpose of protecting US workers.]

---

c. The equivalent PERM regulation appears at 20 C.F.R. § 656.17(h) (2011), but it is substantially similar to the language that BALCA applies here.—eds.

Rulemaking for the current labor certification regulations, DOL defined "business necessity" as something the absence of which would undermine the essence of the business operation.

45 F.R. 4920 (Jan. 22, 1980). This definition was substantively identical to the definition set out in *Diaz*. However, DOL and the Certifying Officer no longer contend that this definition should be adopted, conceding that it is not necessary that an entire business be undermined before certification can be granted. Rather, they agree that business necessity must be measured "in the context of the employment opportunity for which certification is being sought." In any event, the inappropriateness to alien labor certification cases of *Diaz* or similar standards holding business necessity to have been established "only when the essence of the business operation is undermined" (*Diaz, supra*, at 388) is readily apparent. For under this standard, business necessity could rarely, if ever, be established by any sizeable business entity. As an example, it is doubtful that a company such as AT & T could ever establish that the inability to fill a single job would undermine the essence of its business. Having created a procedure by which alien labor certification can be obtained, and allotting [a specific number of] visas yearly for this purpose, it is illogical to believe that Congress intended it would be virtually impossible for employers to obtain such certification. Therefore, since none of the parties advocate the *Diaz* test, and we believe it is inherently inappropriate to apply this standard in labor certification cases, that test will not be adopted by the Board.

In contrast, judges who have refused to substitute their own business judgments for those of the employer have often accepted any offered business justification for hiring an alien. As a result, courts which have focused on the needs of employers have adopted a more lenient business necessity standard. The court, in granting labor certification in *Silva v. Secretary of Labor*, 518 F.2d 301 (1st Cir.1975), concluded that the legislative intent after 1965 was not to confer on the Secretary a right to treat as irrelevant the employer's job preferences. *Id.* at 310. Similarly, the court in *Ratnayake v. Mack*, 499 F.2d 1207 (8th Cir.1974), in its grant of certification, reasoned that some deference must be accorded to employers in setting forth the needed employment qualifications, because an employer is in the best position to judge what is needed for its business. The court held that "the job requirements of an employer are not to be set aside if they are shown to be reasonable and tend to contribute to or enhance the efficiency and quality of the business." *Id.* at 1212. In that same vein, the court in *Jadeszko v. Brennan*, 418 F.Supp. 92, 95 (E.D.Pa. 1976), stated that "Congress has not given [the Secretary] the authority to say that one who wants to employ a baker in the morning must be content with a candle stick maker who is willing to work in the afternoon."

c. Business Necessity Standard

Having analyzed the legislative history of the Act, the applicable regulations, and the relevant case law, it is the Board's opinion that in adopting a business necessity standard, consideration must be given both to the preference system which recognizes that the United States can benefit from alien labor, and to the purpose of labor certification, i.e., the protection of the American worker. Since the statutory burden is on the employer to justify certification, emphasis should be placed on protecting the American worker; but Congress's recognition that alien labor can benefit the United States should not be ignored.

Our task is somewhat easier following oral argument, since the more extreme positions have been rejected by the parties. Not only has the Certifying Officer disaffirmed a strict "essence of the business operation" test, but conversely both Employer and amicus agree that more can be required in establishing business necessity then merely "tend[ing] to contribute to or enhance the efficiency and quality of the business." *See* Statement of American Immigration Lawyer's Association's Alternative Business Necessity Test, at 3, quoting *Ratnayake, supra,* at 1212. * * *

Holding /
Rule

We hold that, to establish business necessity under § 656.21(b)(2)(i), an employer must demonstrate that the job requirements bear a reasonable relationship to the occupation in the context of the employer's business and are essential to perform, in a reasonable manner, the job duties as described by the employer. This standard, in assuring both that the job's requirements bear a reasonable relationship to the occupation and are essential to perform the job duties, gives appropriate emphasis to the Act's presumption that qualified U.S. workers are available. An employer cannot obtain alien labor certification by showing that the job requirements merely "tend to contribute to or enhance the efficiency and quality of the business."[9] On the other hand, this standard is not impossible to meet. An employer has the discretion, within reason, to obtain certification for any job whose requirements are directly related to its business, and does not have to establish dire financial consequences if the job is not filled or is filled by a U.S. worker who is not fully qualified.

Turning to the facts of this case, the Certifying Officer denied certification because she found that Employer's job requirements were unduly restrictive, in violation of § 656.21(b)(2). It is Employer's position that its requirements are normal for this job in the United States, and conform to the D.O.T. If Employer is correct, then it is not required to establish that the job requirements arise from business necessity.

In addressing Employer's contention, first, the specific title of the job must be determined. The CO contends that the position is that of "Programmer, Engineering and Scientific;" D.O.T. Code 020.167–022; Employer states that the position is that of "Systems Engineer," D.O.T. Code 003.167–062. Until the correct job title is determined, it cannot be decided whether the job requirements are normal for the job in the United

---

9. For example, for a position as a lawyer, a job requirement of the ability to play golf usually cannot be justified as a business necessity even if the employer listed playing golf as a job duty on the Form 750–A. Although it may "tend to contribute to or enhance the efficiency and quality of the business" socially and perhaps even economically, playing golf generally does not bear a reasonable relationship to the occupation of practicing law.

States. That the requirements conform to the D.O.T. is clear, for the only job requirement for either job title in the D.O.T. is a Specific Vocational Preparation rating ("SVP") of 8. An SVP of 8 means that it is permissible for the Employer to require up to 10 years of education and experience; thus, the two-degree requirement in this case does not conflict with the D.O.T. Moreover, the position does not require fluency in a foreign language.

In regard to whether the job requirements are normal for this job in the U.S., neither party's position is established by the record. Although the duties of the job are set out in the Form ETA 750–A, they are expressed in technical jargon which cannot be precisely understood by laymen. Neither party attempted to explain these job duties in lay terms. That a so-called expert body offered an opinion which was relied upon by the CO is insufficient, since that evidence contains little more than the conclusions of that body, without explanation or reasoning. Nor did either party attempt to analyze the job's requirements in terms of the job duties, as required under our business necessity test. Thus Employer has not explained which job duties require its systems engineers to have a B.S. in Engineering, and the CO has not explained why this degree, or a Masters in Computer Science, are not bona fide requirements for the position regardless of which title best suits it.

Moreover, as counsel for the CO apparently admitted at the oral argument, it cannot be determined exactly which job requirement the CO alleged to be unduly restrictive—the requirement that the applicant have a B.S. specifically in engineering, or the requirement of having both a Bachelor's and a Master's degree.

Under these circumstances, this case must be remanded to the Certifying Officer. On remand, the CO shall determine which job title best describes this job, and further determine whether the job requirements are normal for that job title in the U.S. If the CO finds that the job requirements are not normal, and are unduly restrictive, a Notice of Findings clearly setting out her findings and the reasoning behind them shall be issued. Employer shall than have the opportunity to file an appropriate rebuttal addressing, inter alia, the business necessity standard set out in this decision.

ORDER

The Certifying Officer's denial of certification is vacated, and the case is remanded to the CO for further proceedings consistent with this decision.

[Concurring opinions of JUDGES LITT and BRENNER omitted.]

NOTES AND QUESTIONS

1. On remand, the certifying officer again denied labor certification, still unconvinced that the two-degree requirement was justifiable. The CO's opinion noted:

The two-degree requirement is found to be unduly restrictive as it exceeds those defined for the occupation in the DOT and is not normally required for similar jobs in the U.S.

This finding is based on a comparison with other labor certification applications processed by the Certifying Officer, including those previously filed and currently pending by the employer. * * *

It appears employer has structured the requirements around the alien's qualifications, thus they do not represent the actual minimum requirements for the job * * *.

Notice of Findings, Nov. 6, 1989. The noncitizen subsequently moved to Michigan, where his employer obtained labor certification and ultimately permanent residence for him. (This outcome reflects the kind of regional variation that DOL sought to remedy through the greater centralization and standardization of the PERM system.)

2. Has BALCA succeeded, with the *Information Industries* decision, in providing workable and effective guidelines that are consistent with the basic policies underlying the statute? BALCA cases since *Information Industries* have tended to show that the first prong of the test, requiring a "reasonable relationship" between job requirements and the occupation is relatively easy to satisfy. Of greater importance in most cases is the second prong, requiring a showing that the job requirements "are *essential* to perform, in a reasonable manner, the job duties." (Emphasis added.) *See Business Necessity: A Year After* Information Industries, 67 Interp.Rel. 253, 256 (1990).

3. Consider the following facts: Employer has applied for a labor certification for a "cleaning manager" to manage the company's "home cleaning division which cleans and maintains residences occupied by handicapped and aged customers unable to attend to their own needs." The ability to speak Spanish is included as a requirement for the job. Employer defends the requirement on the ground that it is virtually impossible to find Americans willing to take janitorial jobs and therefore it is essential that the supervisor of the employees, most of whom are new immigrants, be Spanish-speaking. Is the requirement permissible? *See Matter of Home Assistance, Inc.,* 1997 WL 580520, No. 95–INA–391 (BALCA 1997). The PERM regulations set forth in Note 6 below also address in more detail the question of foreign-language requirements.

4. The Dictionary of Occupational Titles, a standard part of labor certification practice for decades, has been replaced by a new computerized database system called O*NET, "the system developed by the Department of Labor, Employment and Training Administration, to provide to the general public information on skills, abilities, knowledge, work activities, interests and specific vocational preparation levels associated with occupations. O*NET is based on the Standard Occupational Classification system." 20 C.F.R. § 656.3. It can be accessed online through <http://www.onetcenter.org>. Occupational category descriptions in O*NET list such things as the tasks typically performed, the knowledge, skills and abilities engaged, and—significantly for labor certification—the specific vocational preparation (SVP) normally required (sometimes also referred to in terms of "job zones"). The regulations, *id.,* define SVP as:

the amount of lapsed time required by a typical worker to learn the techniques, acquire the information, and develop the facility needed for average performance in a specific job-worker situation. * * * The various levels of specific vocational preparation are provided below.

1. Short demonstration.

2. Anything beyond short demonstration up to and including 30 days.

3. Over 30 days up to and including 3 months.

4. Over 3 months up to and including 6 months.

5. Over 6 months up to and including 1 year.

6. Over 1 year up to and including 2 years.

7. Over 2 years up to and including 4 years.

8. Over 4 years up to and including 10 years.

9. Over 10 years.

5. As proposed in May 2002, the PERM regulations would have made significant changes in the business necessity test. The explanatory material accompanying the notice of proposed rulemaking explained why:

> The business necessity standard, currently at 20 CFR 656.21(b), often works to the disadvantage of U.S. workers. This regulation has been difficult to administer and has generated a greater amount of litigation than any other regulatory provision in the current regulations. Since the position for which certification is sought is usually held by an alien worker who is the beneficiary of the application, job requirements tend to be manipulated to favor the selection of the alien. The existing business necessity standard requires the CO to evaluate the unique standards of an employer's business. In highly technical areas this is an extremely difficult undertaking and may be subject to employer manipulation since we are in no position to second guess the employer in such circumstances.

> We have concluded that any business necessity standard that may be adopted would present similar problems. Therefore, the proposed rule would not retain a business necessity standard as a justification for employer's job requirements that exceed requirements that are normal to jobs in the United States.

67 Fed.Reg. 30466, 30472 (2002). Under the proposed rules, employers could deviate from normal requirements only in limited circumstances that, the Department suggested, would more readily lend themselves to objective determination. Foreign language requirements could be justified if clearly required for the job (for example, a translator) or if the employer documented that a large majority of its customers or contractors cannot communicate in English and that the employee would have significant contact with them. For other nonstandard requirements, the employer would have to show either that it had employed a U.S. worker for the position on those terms within the two years preceding the filing, or that the requirements are ''normal to the occupation'' and routinely required by other employers in the industry. What are the advantages and disadvantages of these proposed changes?

6. The final PERM rules dropped the major proposed changes to the business necessity standard discussed immediately above, but they did provide more specific criteria to be met if the employer wants to require foreign language skills. They also address another issue that we have seen in the *Information Industries* case, the employer's desire to combine occupations. The pertinent regulations now read (20 C.F.R. § 656.17):

(h) Job duties and requirements.

(1) The job opportunity's requirements, unless adequately documented as arising from business necessity, must be those normally required for the occupation and must not exceed the Specific Vocational Preparation level assigned to the occupation as shown in the O*NET Job Zones. To establish a business necessity, an employer must demonstrate the job duties and requirements bear a reasonable relationship to the occupation in the context of the employer's business and are essential to perform the job in a reasonable manner.

(2) A foreign language requirement can not be included, unless it is justified by business necessity. Demonstrating business necessity for a foreign language requirement may be based upon the following:

(i) The nature of the occupation, e.g., translator; or

(ii) The need to communicate with a large majority of the employer's customers, contractors, or employees who can not communicate effectively in English, as documented by:

(A) The employer furnishing the number and proportion of its clients, contractors, or employees who can not communicate in English, and/or a detailed plan to market products or services in a foreign country; and

(B) A detailed explanation of why the duties of the position for which certification is sought requires frequent contact and communication with customers, employees or contractors who can not communicate in English and why it is reasonable to believe the allegedly foreign-language-speaking customers, employees, and contractors can not communicate in English.

(3) If the job opportunity involves a combination of occupations, the employer must document that it has normally employed persons for that combination of occupations, and/or workers customarily perform the combination of occupations in the area of intended employment, and/or the combination job opportunity is based on a business necessity. Combination occupations can be documented by position descriptions and relevant payroll records, and/or letters from other employers stating their workers normally perform the combination of occupations in the area of intended employment, and/or documentation that the combination occupation arises from a business necessity.

(4) (i) Alternative experience requirements must be substantially equivalent to the primary requirements of the job opportunity for which certification is sought; and

(ii) If the alien beneficiary already is employed by the employer, and the alien does not meet the primary job requirements and only potentially qualifies for the job by virtue of the employer's alternative requirements, certification will be denied unless the application states that any suitable combination of education, training, or experience is acceptable.

d. Labor Certification and an Attorney's Professional Responsibility

The Trillin article that opened our consideration of employment-based immigration uses language in describing the certification process, such as "sham employment offer," that obviously departs from the way practicing attorneys would think of their role—or would want others to think of that role. (Those characterizations were Trillin's, not those of the attorneys he had observed, and the article was sharply criticized by the immigration bar.) Around the time that article appeared, INS and the Departments of Labor and State began an extensive investigation of possible fraud in labor certification and marriage cases. Several lawyers were indicted, but some of the government's investigative tactics, particularly interrogation of employer clients without notice to the attorneys, drew vigorous denunciation. A few of the highly publicized indictments were dropped, but others led to convictions of attorneys. Eventually some of the more questionable investigative techniques were abandoned. *See* 62 Interp.Rel. 416 (1985); 63 *id.* 392 (1986); 64 *id.* 1291 (1987); New York Times, Oct. 21, 1985, at A1; *id.,* May 1, 1986, at A25.

These experiences prompted more explicit attention to ethical issues involved in the labor certification process. The following excerpts from a useful and wide-ranging article both warn of the pitfalls and provide revealing glimpses of the substantial practical problems confronting an attorney handling a labor certification case.[8]

ETHICAL CONSIDERATIONS IN IMMIGRATION CASES

4 Immigration Law Report 169 (Dec. 1985).

* * * One source of the significant ethical problems faced by immigration practitioners is the ambiguity and inconsistency in interpretation of the Immigration and Nationality Act, the statute governing the standards and procedures for obtaining immigration benefits for aliens. Another source is the aliens themselves, since obtaining an immigration benefit, particularly U.S. permanent residence, can be perceived by some aliens as virtually a matter of life and death for which they would not hesitate to fabricate facts or commit fraud.

Between the complexity of the law and the fervor with which the client desires to achieve his or her goal, unwary or simply incautious

---

8. The article was written by attorneys from the experienced immigration firm of Fragomen, Del Rey & Bernsen (now Fragomen, Del Rey, Bernsen and Loewy), which produced the *Immigration Law Report* periodical. It refers to the American Bar Association's Model Code of Professional Responsibility, which has now been superseded in nearly all states by the ABA's Model Rules of Professional Conduct (of particular relevance to the discussion here are Rules 1.2(d), 1.7, 3.1, 3.3). The basic points in the article are not affected by that change.

immigration practitioners can become enmeshed in a situation which may not only threaten their adherence to professional standards, but possibly lead to prosecution for perpetrating or abetting an immigration fraud.

* * *

The most pertinent canon under the Code with regard to fraudulent conduct is Canon 7: "A lawyer should represent a client zealously within the bounds of the law." * * *

[Ethical Consideration (E.C.) 7–6] states: "Whether the proposed action of a lawyer is within the bounds of the law may be a perplexing question when his client is contemplating a course of conduct having legal consequences that vary according to the client's intent, motive, or desires at the time of the action. Often a lawyer is asked to assist his client at a particular time. He may properly assist his client in the development and preservation of evidence of existing motive, intent or desire; obviously, he may not do anything furthering the creation or preservation of false evidence. In many cases a lawyer may not be certain as to the state of mind of his client, and in those situations he should resolve reasonable doubts in favor of his client."[d] * * *

While the largest employers often have "canned" job descriptions and statements of minimum requirements for most positions in their corporate hierarchy, most employers do not have such sophisticated personnel operations. Even after an employer has filled the position in question by hiring the alien after an extensive recruitment and interview process, the employer's hiring agent may still have a difficult time verbalizing its minimum requirements in filling a position. It would not be unusual for an employer to have no minimum requirements, but rather a set of preferences which, however, could be replaced by the correct subjective elements, such as the "right" personality for the job or a desirable aggressiveness or flair. The practitioner in this situation is confronted with the daunting task of somehow translating the employer's criteria for the position into the quantifiable criteria demanded by the [Department of Labor (DOL)]. While the employer might not initially think of its criteria in terms of minimum requirements, it is obvious that not every person would be considered qualified by the employer.

It therefore becomes the role of the attorney, who is aware of the vocabulary and standards of the DOL, to aid the employer in verbalizing in acceptable form the "minimum requirements" which must be provided for labor certification purposes. The attorney who must engage in this process with the employer enters upon dangerous terrain, since the employer may be convinced that its actual requirements are nothing like the final result of the process and who therefore believes that the

---

d. Compare today's Model Rule 1.2(d), which provides: "A lawyer shall not counsel a client to engage, or assist a client, in conduct that the lawyer knows is criminal or fraudulent, but a lawyer may discuss the legal consequences of any proposed course of conduct with a client and may counsel or assist a client to make a good faith effort to determine the validity, scope, meaning or application of the law."—eds.

requirements have been manufactured by the attorney. The attorney, on the other hand, may be convinced that he or she has successfully translated those factors important to the employer in hiring the alien into a statement of the minimum requirements sufficient to satisfy the DOL. Given the disparity between the employer's and the attorney's perceptions, it is not surprising that attorneys who may be investigated for engaging in the perpetration of a fraud in framing the minimum requirements would consider the suggestion of fraud to be unfair. The reality of these investigations, however, requires the conscientious attorney to follow certain procedures, as much for self-preservation as for ethical considerations, which he or she may believe have not been transgressed.

The attorney must be certain that the employer is aware and understands that the labor certification application is the employer's application, not the alien's. The employer is responsible for the statements made in the certification and must be comfortable with all of the affirmations contained in it. If, after the attorney works with the employer to verbalize the employer's minimum requirements, the employer is not convinced that those requirements really underlie its hiring decision, the attorney should not file an application containing those requirements. The attorney has an obligation under the Code to inform the employer of the prospects of success in filing the labor certification application, and should inform the employer of the impact of failing to include certain requirements, but the attorney must be satisfied that the employer is not accepting a given statement of requirements simply because of the attorney's assessment of the likelihood of success without those requirements.

The difficulty of this situation is compounded when the attorney is retained to represent the alien. It may happen in this situation that the employer agrees to the attorney's representation of it but does not make its personnel representative sufficiently available to the attorney, apparently in the belief that the attorney is fundamentally representing the alien. Proceeding on this basis is a tremendous mistake, since the DOL expects the employer to take responsibility for the application and conduct the recruitment of U.S. workers without the involvement of the alien. The danger of the employer repudiating the certification application or recruitment results in this type of case should serve as sufficient deterrent to the practitioner faced with this arrangement.

NOTES AND QUESTIONS

1. There is a considerable literature on the ethical questions discussed in this article. *See, e.g.,*Hake, *Dual Representation in Immigration Practice: The Simple Solution is the Wrong Solution*, 5 Geo.Immig.L.J. 581 (1991); Hake, *Dual Representation In Immigration Practice*, in Ethics In A Brave New World 28 (AILA ed. 2004); Mehta, *Finding the Golden Mean in Dual Representation—Updated*, 06–08 Immigration Briefings (Aug. 2006).

2. Ethical lapses—and crimes—committed by immigration attorneys handling labor certification contributed significantly to the 2007 regulations

flatly forbidding substitution of beneficiaries. The preambular material accompanying those regulations pointed out that the DOL had been seeking to ban this practice since 1991:

> The 1991 Interim Final Rule included a provision prohibiting substitution. That provision was overturned by the U.S. Court of Appeals for the D.C. Circuit on Administrative Procedure Act procedural grounds. *Kooritzky v. Reich*, 17 F.3d 1509 (D.C. Cir. 1994). DOL addressed the court's concern through [a new notice-and-comment rulemaking procedure.] * * * It is of no small significance that the plaintiff in that suit, an attorney, was later convicted for the criminal sale of fraudulent labor certifications used for substitution.

> The Department's review of recent prosecutions by DOJ, in particular, revealed that the ability to substitute alien beneficiaries has turned labor certifications into commodities which can be sold by unscrupulous employers, attorneys, or agents to those seeking a "green card." Similarly, the ability to sell labor certifications has been greatly enhanced by their current open-ended validity, providing a lengthy period during which a certification may be marketed. In many of these applications, the job offer was fictitious. In others, the job in question existed but was never truly open to U.S. workers. Rather, the job was steered to a specific alien in return for a substantial fee or "kickback." * * * One attorney filed approximately 2,700 fraudulent applications with DOL for fees of up to $20,000 per application. Many of these applications were filed for the sole purpose of later being sold to aliens who would be substituted for named beneficiaries on the approved labor certifications. * * *

72 Fed. Reg. 27904, 27905 (2007).

3. In 2008, DOL issued new guidance regarding attorney involvement in the actual recruitment and hiring process required in connection with PERM. It indicates the difficult balancing act an attorney must perform in advising on legal requirements while not improperly distorting the labor market test that the recruitment is supposed to accomplish:

> The Department has long held the view that good faith recruitment requires that an employer's process for considering U.S. workers who respond to certification-related recruitment closely resemble the employer's normal consideration process. In most situations, that normal hiring process does not involve a role for an attorney or agent * * * in assessing the qualifications of applicants to fill the employer's position. It also does not involve any role for the foreign worker or foreign national in any aspect of the consideration process. However, given that the permanent labor certification program imposes recruitment standards on the employer that may deviate from the employer's normal standards of evaluation, the Department understands and appreciates the legitimate role attorneys and agents play in the permanent labor certification process. Additionally, the Department respects the right of employers to consult with their attorney(s) or agent(s) during that process to ensure that they are complying with all applicable legal requirements. * * *

> Attorneys and agents may receive resumes and applications of U.S. workers who respond to the employer's recruitment efforts; however,

they may not conduct any preliminary screening of applications before the employer does so, other than routine clerical or ministerial organizing of resumes which does not include any assessment of, or comments on, the qualifications of any applicants, unless the attorney or agent is the representative of the employer who routinely performs this function for positions for which labor certifications are not filed. The attorney or agent may not withhold from the employer any resumes or applications that it receives from U.S. workers.

Attorneys and agents may not participate in the interviewing of U.S. worker applicants, unless the attorney or agent is the representative of the employer who routinely performs this function for positions for which labor certifications are not filed. Such involvement has resulted in an impermissible "chilling effect" on the interests of U.S. worker-applicants in the position.

DOL, Restatement of PERM Program Guidance Bulletin on the Clarification of Scope of Consideration Rule in 20 CFR § 656.10(b)(2), <http://www.foreign laborcert.doleta.gov/pdf/PERM_Guidance_Final_082908.pdf>.

e. Labor Certification: The Prevailing Wage Requirement

The Labor Department's regulations, *see* 20 C.F.R. § 656.40, require employers to pay the certified noncitizen at least the prevailing wage, even if she would be willing to work for less. Under PERM, the employer must obtain a prevailing wage determination from the state workforce agency before filing the ETA–9089 with the DOL. The regulations impose this requirement, in major part, to implement the statutory directive that employment of the noncitizen not "adversely affect the wages and working conditions of the workers in the United States similarly employed." But what wage level is "prevailing"? What is the relevant group for comparison, and how much discretion should the Secretary have in making such decisions?

In *Matter of Tuskegee University*, 5 Imm.L. & Proc.Rep. B3–172 (BALCA, Feb. 23, 1988), the DOL certifying officer initially denied certification for a position as associate professor of physics. He found that Tuskegee was not offering the prevailing wage as measured by the pay scales used at other nearby colleges. Tuskegee argued that the relevant standard for comparison was instead the 43 schools that were part of the United Negro College Fund; by this standard its proposed pay scale was well above the prevailing rate. A divided Board of Alien Labor Certification Appeals agreed with the university: "It is clear that it is not only the job titles, but the nature of the business or institution where the jobs are located—for example, public or private, secular or religious, profit or nonprofit, multi-national corporation or individual proprietorship—which must be evaluated in determining whether the jobs are 'substantially comparable.' "

In 1994, however, BALCA revisited the issue and unanimously overruled *Tuskegee*, in a case involving a nonprofit treatment center for handicapped children that wanted to hire a "maintenance repairer."

Matter of Hathaway Children's Services, 1994 WL 29778, 91–INA–388 (BALCA, 1994), summarized in 71 Interp.Rel. 357 (1994). The center argued that the relevant standard for comparison was wages paid at other United Way nonprofit agencies, but the Board took a different view:

> [N]either the record in *Tuskegee*, nor the record before us today, suggests that the skills and knowledge required to perform the duties of the job opportunity being offered are any different depending on the employer's financial ability to pay the going rate. Specifically, there is no evidence to suggest that the duties of the job offered [in either case] differed as between charitable non-profit institutions and businesses operated for a profit.

The Board ruled that it could not allow Hathaway to pay substandard wages to its maintenance staff while telling "the Mom-and-Pop shop next door or around the corner" that the INA and the regulations allow no waivers of the prevailing wage requirement on the basis of the employer's hardship.

Should *Tuskegee* have been overruled? What policy is served if the job goes unfilled because Tuskegee or Hathaway cannot pay the DOL-determined prevailing wage?

In 1998 Congress overruled the *Hathaway* decision as it applies to employees of institutions of higher education and of affiliated nonprofit entities, and to employees of all nonprofit and governmental research organizations. The prevailing wage for such a position is therefore to be determined by reference to comparable nonprofit institutions, and not by comparison to researchers employed by private, for-profit employers. INA § 212(p). DOL has provided additional guidance on prevailing wage determinations in General Administration Letter (GAL) 2–98 and GAL 1–00. *See* 77 Interp.Rel. 694 (2000), 74 *id.* 1712 (1997). The PERM regulations also maintain this approach. An employer like Hathaway is still covered by the wider economy's prevailing wage. Should it be?

The Department's "prevailing wage" approach raises deeper issues as well. Insisting on such wages prevents a *deterioration* of pay scales as currently provided in the relevant industry. But deterioration is not the only possible adverse effect that wages might suffer. Should the Department be equally concerned about retarding increases in wages that might otherwise occur in times of labor shortage?

Consider a concrete example. Professional nurses are in such short supply that licensed nurses are exempt from individual labor certification, under the provisions of Schedule A. In fact, however, there are large numbers of trained U.S. workers in the field who simply do not practice that profession. Wages have traditionally been low, and many trained nurses find better opportunities for higher pay in other fields. Indeed, some claim that wages have remained low in the nursing field because it has traditionally been regarded as "women's work." If hospitals were unable to hire noncitizen nurses at current wage scales, what would be likely to happen? If you conclude that employers would bid up wages, drawing many qualified workers back into the labor pool, and inducing more people to develop the necessary skills and training, consider what other conditions must hold for this conclusion to be sound. Would the same results occur in the restaurant or hotel business, in factories, in marginal small businesses, in agriculture?

The availability of foreign nurses under Schedule A may well interfere with improvements in wages. Should this result be considered an adverse effect? In other words, is the Department of Labor's time horizon too short or vision too restricted in light of the fundamental workings of a free-market system? On the other hand, should the Department's approach be seen instead as a valid measure to keep down hospital costs or to keep marginally profitable hospitals open and functioning? Is the Labor Department the appropriate agency or branch to make such a policy decision?

f. Easing the Task of Labor Certification—Or Avoiding It Altogether

As is evident from the earlier cases and discussion, individual labor certification is a time-consuming, highly technical, and expensive process, even after the PERM reforms. For these reasons, good immigration lawyers seek to avoid labor certification whenever that is possible. Use the following exercise as a way of gaining greater familiarity with the statutory provisions governing the occupational preferences and the implementing regulations (the key regulations are referred to in the exercise and reprinted in the Statutory Supplement). The following materials then explore in somewhat closer detail two of the procedures that permit the avoidance of individual labor certification.

EXERCISE

An American university seeks to hire a promising young scientist from India for the physics department, with the rank of assistant professor. Even though he obtained his Ph.D. degree just three years ago, the university's interest was attracted by a "brilliant" article he published in an international journal. University officials have not decided just how much teaching they would want him to perform, because they are primarily interested in his joining a high-powered research team that they hope will win large foundation and government grants for the university. The employment-based second preference would seem to fit, but that category ordinarily requires labor certification, and the university is concerned that the process will take years.

The university has engaged you as its lawyer to speed the approval of his immigration papers. What do you advise? Consider at least the following:

- the "equally qualified" provisions of INA § 212(a)(5)(A)(ii) (*see* 20 C.F.R. § 656.18)

- Schedule A (*see* 20 C.F.R. §§ 656.5(b)(1), 656.15)
- the national interest waiver of the employer petition requirement, authorized by § 203(b)(2)(B)(i)
- the "priority worker" categories of INA § 203(b)(1) (the EB–1 preference)

What would each of these procedures accomplish for your client? Which would permit you to avoid the labor certification process?

(i) National Interest Waivers

INA § 203(b)(2)(B) allows the Attorney General to waive the requirement that a second-preference immigrant's services be sought by an employer in the United States, when waiver is deemed "in the national interest." The regulations, without further elaboration of the "national interest" standard, provide that such a waiver also exempts the individual from labor certification. 8 C.F.R. § 204.5(k)(4)(ii).

Decisions by the INS' Administrative Appeals Office (AAO) initially adopted a generous stance in construing the national interest in this setting. They allowed broad consideration of whether the noncitizen's admission: (1) will improve the U.S. economy; (2) will improve wages and working conditions of U.S. workers; (3) will improve educational and training programs for U.S. children and underqualified workers; (4) will improve health care; (5) will provide more affordable housing for young, aged, or poor U.S. residents; (6) will improve the U.S. environment and lead to more productive use of national resources; or (7) is requested by an interested U.S. government agency. *See National Interest Waivers in the EB–2 Category*, 13 Imm.L.Rep. 69–70 (1994) (summarizing initial AAO standards and illustrative case law, particularly the *Mississippi Phosphate* case). Are these standards consistent with the statute? Do they reflect wise policy?

After gaining a few years' experience with this waiver, INS became concerned that the initial approach was too lenient. The AAO then changed course, in the precedent decision of *Matter of New York State Dept. of Transportation (NYSDOT)*, 22 I & N Dec. 215 (Assoc. Comm'r 1998), discussed in 75 Interp.Rel. 1289–99 (1998). *NYSDOT* sets out a three-pronged test. It requires the employer to show that the noncitizen will be employed "in an area of substantial intrinsic merit" and that "the proposed benefit will be national in scope." The AAO then described the third prong as follows (22 I & N Dec. at 217–18):

> The final threshold is * * * specific to the alien. The petitioner seeking the waiver must persuasively demonstrate that the national interest would be adversely affected if a labor certification were required for the alien. The petitioner must demonstrate that it would be contrary to the national interest to potentially deprive the prospective employer of the services of the alien by making available to U.S. workers the position sought by the alien. The labor certification

process exists because protecting the jobs and job opportunities of U.S. workers having the same objective minimum qualifications as an alien seeking employment is in the national interest. An alien seeking an exemption from this process must present a national benefit so great as to outweigh the national interest inherent in the labor certification process.

Stated another way, the petitioner, whether the U.S. employer or the alien, must establish that the alien will serve the national interest to a substantially greater degree than would an available U.S. worker having the same minimum qualifications.

In 1999, Congress enacted additional specifications stating when a national interest waiver should be granted for physicians who agree to serve for a specified number of years in a medically underserved area. INA § 203(b)(2)(B)(ii). For a critical review of the *NYSDOT* standards and a summary of later AAO cases implementing them, see Gafner & Yale–Loehr, *Attracting the Best and Brightest: A Critique of the Current U.S. Immigration System*, 38 Fordham Urb. L.J. 183, 203–208 (2010); Waxman & Craig, *Seeking the Inscrutable National Interest Waiver: They've All Come to Look for America,* 02–09 Imm.Briefings (2002). A 2006 revision to the USCIS Adjudicators' Field Manual emphasizes that *NYSDOT* establishes only minimum requirements and that the adjudicator is not compelled to grant the waiver just because the minimum requirements are satisfied. See *USCIS Update to AFM Chapter 22: Employment–Based Petitions (Continued)*, 83 Interp. Rel. 2374, 2379 (2006).

(ii) Aliens of Extraordinary Ability (The EB–1A Category)

The first subcategory of priority workers, individuals with "extraordinary ability in the sciences, arts, education, business, or athletics" (who also meet certain other stipulations) occupies a highly favored position. Not only are such workers exempt from labor certification, but they may self-petition and need not persuade an employer to file on their behalf. They may file a visa petition on Form I–140 directly with the USCIS. But picture yourself as the USCIS examiner considering the petition. How do you decide whether the petitioner's abilities are extraordinary? And exactly what is the difference between extraordinary ability and merely exceptional ability (the stuff of the second employment-based preference)?

The agencies have sought to translate these broad statutory phrases into administrable form in the regulations: *See* 8 C.F.R. § 204.5(g)–(*l*) (in the Statutory Supplement) (giving operational content to some of the vague terms used for various EB–1 and EB–2 categories, e.g., "outstanding," "extraordinary ability," "exceptional ability"). The regulations tend to use a menu approach, suggesting that a petition will be granted if the petitioner presents evidence that falls within a specified number of listed items in the regulation. One writer observed that many practitioners have "developed a warm and welcoming relationship with the extensive and detailed lists of qualifying criteria set out in [these] regulations. [They] provide a cogent and well-directed road map which, if closely followed, should lead to eventual [petition] approval." Van Deusen, *National Interest Waivers,* 13 Imm.L.Rep. 73, 75–76 (1994). But even with the additional level of detail provided in the regulations, significant controversies can arise, as the following case illustrates.

MUNI v. INS

United States District Court for the Northern District of Illinois, 1995.
891 F.Supp. 440.

MORAN, CHIEF JUDGE.

Plaintiff Craig Muni brings this action * * * challenging the Service's denial of his visa petition. In June or July 1993 Muni, a player in the National Hockey League (NHL), petitioned the INS for an immigrant visa, claiming that he was a worker with extraordinary ability and therefore deserved priority treatment under § 203(b)(1)(A) of the Immigration and Naturalization Act. The director of the INS' Northern Service Center denied his petition, and the Administrative Appeals Unit (AAU) affirmed. Muni now appeals that decision to this court. Both parties have moved for summary judgment. For the reasons set forth below, Muni's motion is granted and the INS' motion is denied.

FACTS

Muni was born in Canada on July 19, 1962 and is a Canadian citizen. In 1980, he was drafted by the Toronto Maple Leafs, an NHL team, and he began his career as a defenseman for that team in the 1981–82 season. In October 1986 he was traded to the Edmonton Oilers, where he stayed for seven years. In the 1986–87, 1987–88, and 1989–90 seasons, the Oilers won the Stanley Cup, the NHL's championship trophy. At that time Muni was a regular player and had one of the best plus-minus ratios[5] on the team. In the 1988–89 season he had the fourth best plus-minus ratio in the entire NHL. A poll taken by Goal magazine (an NHL publication) rated him the "most underrated defenseman" in the League in 1990, and in 1991 Hockey Digest named him one of the top ten hitting defensemen.

In March 1993 Muni was traded to the Chicago Blackhawks. He now plays for the Buffalo Sabres, whom he joined in October 1993. Muni presently earns $550,000 per year; in the 1992–93 season, when his petition was filed, his annual salary was $400,000. The average salary for an NHL defenseman in 1992–93 was $387,914.

In addition to salary information, Muni submitted to the INS numerous magazine and newspaper articles purporting to establish his stature in the hockey world. He also submitted affidavits from eight veteran NHL players stating that he is highly regarded by other players and is one of the best defensemen in hockey. Finally, Muni alleged that other NHL

---

5. The plus-minus ratio is not really a ratio; it is the number of goals scored by a player's team while he is on the ice minus the number of goals scored against the team when the player is on the ice. The plus-minus ratio is a standard measure of a defensive player's ability: the higher the number, the better the player.

players of comparable ability—Steve Smith, Rob Brown, and Brent Sutter—have received immigrant visas under § 203(b)(1)(A).

The director of the INS's Northern Service Center denied Muni's petition. She found that there was no evidence that Muni's salary is high compared with what other NHL players receive; that he failed to explain the reputation, significance, or selection criteria of the awards from Hockey Digest and Goal; that the newspaper articles established only his improvement as a player after joining the Oilers, his contributions to the Oilers' Stanley Cup victories, and the fact that he is remembered for playing while sutures on his face were leaking; and that the affidavits showed that Muni was an excellent, hard-hitting defenseman. The director concluded that [w]hile [Muni] appears to enjoy a noteworthy career as a professional hockey player, there is no evidence that [he] has been selected to all-star teams or received official recognitions as an extraordinary hockey player. The evidence submitted does not establish that [he] is one of the few who have risen to the very top of his field of endeavor.

The AAU affirmed. In addition to reiterating the arguments made by the regional director in her initial decision, the AAU found that Muni had not established his role in the Oilers' Stanley Cup victories; that his extended membership in the NHL was not sufficient in itself to establish extraordinary ability; and that he had not presented enough evidence comparing the experience, abilities, and salaries of players who have already received immigrant visas with his own qualifications. The AAU rejected Muni's argument that anyone who plays in the NHL for an extended period of time has extraordinary ability. Instead, because Muni was not "within the small percentage at the very top of the players in the NHL," the AAU concluded that he was not an alien of extraordinary ability and affirmed the director's decision to deny his petition.

DISCUSSION

* * * The INS does not contend that Muni has failed to meet the [first two requirements of INA § 203(b)(1)—that he intends to continue work in his area of alleged extraordinary ability and that his entry will bring substantial prospective benefit to the United States]. Therefore, the only issue before this court is whether the INS properly concluded that Muni is not an alien of extraordinary ability under subsection (b)(1)(A)(i).

A. Definition of Extraordinary Ability

* * * The INS regulations interpreting § 203(b)(1)(A) define extraordinary ability as "a level of expertise indicating that the individual is one of that small percentage who have risen to the very top of the field of endeavor." 8 C.F.R. § 204.5(h)(2). As further clarification, the regulations explain as follows [the court then sets forth 8 C.F.R. § 204.5(h)(3), (4), reprinted in the Statutory Supplement].

Under the INS' view, membership on a major league team does not by itself qualify an athlete as one having extraordinary ability, though it may help to establish that the athlete meets several of the criteria listed. In the INS' words, "Not all athletes, particularly those new to major league competition, would be able to meet [the sustained national or international acclaim] standard. A blanket rule for all major league athletes would contravene Congress' intent to reserve this category to 'that small percentage of individuals who have risen to the very top of their field of endeavor.'" 56 Fed.Reg. 60897, 60899 (Nov. 29, 1991).

We agree with prior decisions in this district holding that the INS' definition of extraordinary ability is a permissible interpretation of § 203(b)(1)(A) and therefore is controlling here. But our conclusion that the INS' definition is binding does not mean that the Service correctly applied the definition to the facts of Muni's case, and that is the central question posed by the motions for summary judgment.

B. Application of the Definition to the Facts

In reviewing the denial of a visa petition we must defer to the decision of the INS unless it constituted an abuse of discretion. The Seventh Circuit has held that the INS abuses its discretion when its decision (a) is made without rational explanation, (b) inexplicably departs from established policies, or (c) rests on an impermissible basis such as race discrimination. Muni does not contend that the INS' decision rested on an impermissible basis, but he does argue that it was against the weight of the evidence and deviated from its own policies and precedents. We need consider only his first contention because we find it dispositive of the motions before us.

The INS acts without rational explanation (and therefore abuses its discretion) "when it fails to weigh important factors and to state its reasons for denying relief." We find that the INS abused its discretion here because it failed to consider several facts that supported Muni's petition and failed to explain why the facts it did consider were insufficient to establish Muni's extraordinary ability.

1. Individual Facts

First, the INS found that Muni's role in the Oilers' three Stanley Cup victories had not been established. This conclusion overlooks some rather obvious facts. As Muni points out, there is a direct correlation between a team's performance and its players' performances, and the correlation is even stronger where key players are concerned. The facts that Muni was a starting defenseman for the Oilers and had one of the team's top plus-minus ratios strongly suggest that he was a key player.[8] Thus the team's performance reflects his individual ability. The INS seems to believe that being a good player on a great team does not establish one's ability, but it offers no explanation why we should accept such a counterintuitive belief.

---

8. We take judicial notice of the fact that a team's best players are usually those in its starting lineup. Even if this was not the case here, other evidence establishes that Muni was one of the team's leaders in plus-minus ratios, which indicates that he was indeed one of the team's best defensemen.

Second, the INS discounted the awards Muni received, saying that he had not shown what was necessary to qualify for the awards or what significance they have. We disagree. We think the awards—best hitting defenseman, most underrated defenseman—are rather self-explanatory, and the publications—the official NHL magazine and the largest hockey magazine—are certainly significant and reputable. The INS had no legitimate basis for refusing to consider the awards as evidence of Muni's ability.

Third, the INS did not adequately address evidence that Muni commands a high salary. The evidence showed that he made more than the average NHL defenseman in 1992–93 and that his pay increased by $150,000 for the 1993–94 and 1994–95 seasons. Thus his salary is well above average. Moreover, since a few very highly paid players can skew the average salary upward, it is reasonable to assume that a player making even the average salary is making more than most other players.[9] Yet the INS stated that because Muni's salary "is well below the top salaries earned in the NHL ... it has not been established that [his] salary is high in relation to that of other professional hockey players." This statement contains two errors: ignorance of the simple math explained above and an assumption (which we reject below) that a player must be one of the League's superstars to be considered to have extraordinary ability.

Fourth, the INS gave short shrift to the articles Muni submitted to support his petition. These articles do not establish that Muni is one of the stars of the NHL, but that is not the applicable standard. Under the INS' own regulations, all Muni need show is that there is "[p]ublished material about [him] in professional or major trade publications or other major media, relating to [his] work in the field for which classification is sought." 8 C.F.R. § 204.5(h)(3)(iii). The articles Muni submitted, which appeared in various newspapers and hockey magazines, clearly fit this requirement; even the INS admits that some of the articles "discuss [Muni's] hitting ability and his record as a defenseman." Yet the INS did not explain why the articles did not qualify as proof of Muni's ability.

Finally, the INS completely ignored the eight affidavits Muni submitted. Those affidavits, sworn to by veteran NHL players of considerable renown, describe Muni as "an excellent defenseman," "one of the best defenseman in professional hockey," "a prominent hockey player in the NHL with great skating and defensive abilities," "one of the better defenders in the game," and "one of the premier defensemen in the NHL" The INS' failure even to consider these affidavits is clear evidence that it did not adequately evaluate the facts before it. The affidavits establish that Muni is, at minimum, an above-average player whose peers—the world's best hockey players—respect his athletic abilities. Better evidence

---

9. In other words, the median salary would probably be a more useful figure for the INS to consider.

of an alien's extraordinary ability would be difficult to find, yet the INS did not even mention it in its decision.

2. *Totality of the Evidence*

In sum, Muni presented evidence that he is an NHL veteran who was a starting player on the League's best team for several years, has a reputation among his peers as an excellent defenseman, earns a salary well above average for a defenseman, and has been recognized in major media publications. As previously noted, 8 C.F.R. § 204.5(h)(3) requires an alien to show that he has sustained national or international acclaim and recognition in his field. Such evidence must include "evidence of a one-time achievement (that is, a major, international[ly] recognized award)" or evidence that falls into at least three of the ten categories set forth in subsections (h)(3)(i)–(x) of the regulations.[12] The Oilers' Stanley Cup victories while Muni was a key player arguably are evidence of a major, internationally recognized award that establishes Muni's international acclaim and recognition in his field. But even if sustained membership on the championship team is not enough, Muni's evidence still fits into five of the ten categories. While the satisfaction of the three-category production requirement does not mandate a finding that the petitioner has sustained national or international acclaim and recognition in his field, it is certainly a start, and the INS made no attempt to explain why Muni's evidence did not meet the acclaim and recognition standard. Thus, it has not only failed to explain why it does not accept some of the individual facts Muni presents, it has also failed to explain why the sum of those facts and others is insufficient to warrant granting his petition. We deem such arbitrary decisionmaking an abuse of discretion.

We think there is a deeper problem here than the INS' failure to give fair consideration to all the evidence Muni presented in support of his petition. The Service also misapplied its own definition of extraordinary ability. It apparently was under the impression that only all-stars or the League's highest-paid players have extraordinary ability. That is an overly grudging interpretation of its own regulation, which defines an athlete of extraordinary ability as "one of that small percentage who have risen to the very top of the field of endeavor." 8 C.F.R. § 204.5(h)(2). There was considerable evidence before the INS that Muni is a very good professional hockey player—and therefore one of those at the top of his field—yet the INS disregarded that evidence.

CONCLUSION

We conclude that the INS' denial of Muni's petition was an abuse of discretion. Muni's motion for summary judgment is granted and the INS' motion is denied. The case is remanded for further proceedings consistent with this opinion.

---

12. The evidence seems to satisfy categories (i), (ii), (iii), (viii), and (ix).

NOTE AND QUESTIONS

1. Would Muni have been admissible in the first preference if he had not played for a Stanley Cup champion hockey team? What categories would be available for major league sports figures who fall short of the priority worker standards?

2. Muni was traded by the Sabres during the season following this decision (1995–96) and then twice more before retiring from the NHL in 1998. As of 2006 he was working as a scout for the Tampa Bay Lightning. *See* Lukow, *Ice in His Veins: Former NHL Defenseman Never Far from the Rink,* available at <http://www.bestofwny.com/sports/lukow/muni.htm>.

3. Even after *Muni,* the agencies deciding on EB–1A applications often continue with a narrow and demanding approach. For example, an internal memo of the California Service Center, which handles initial adjudication of many such cases, emphasizes that "it takes more than just submitting three documents" from this list to meet the category's evidentiary standard. "The quality of the submitted documentation will show if the alien is of [this] caliber, not the quantity." The memo goes on to emphasize the requirement that the individual represent a "small percentage who has risen to the very top" of the field of endeavor. The total size of the field should be considered. The "very top" of the field may be a larger or smaller percentage, depending on the size of that total population. The memo also calls for a careful definition of the actual field of endeavor. 78 Interp.Rel. 885 (2001).

4. Examiners have also taken a narrow view of the second requirement imposed by the statute: that "the alien seeks to enter the United States to continue work in the area of extraordinary ability." Top-ranking athletes who petition for EB–1A immigration only when they are past their prime have sometimes sought to meet this requirement by stating that they intend to coach. Such petitions are usually denied, unless the petitioners show that they have earned national or international acclaim as a coach. *See Lee v. Ziglar,* 237 F.Supp.2d 914 (N.D.Ill.2002) (sustaining the restrictive approach.)

5. The other categories of the first employment-based preference, for outstanding professors and researchers and for multinational executives and managers, share with the EB–1A category the important feature of avoiding labor certification. But those categories do require that the noncitizen seeking to immigrate has a job offer from a U.S. employer.

g. The Premises of Labor Certification: Reflections on Portability and Whether the System Serves Its Stated Goals

The labor certification process appears to be based on a straightforward model: when an employer who is looking to fill an existing job cannot find a qualified U.S. worker to take it, he or she should be able to tap into the foreign labor market to fill a job important to the conduct of the business. As you now know, however, this is not how the process works in practice. Because of the rule barring substitution of beneficiaries, the employer already must know the noncitizen he or she would like to employ. Indeed, usually the noncitizen is already working for the employer—legally (in an appropriate nonimmigrant category) or illegally. The employer then describes the job in a manner tailored, to the extent legally possible, to the specific qualifications of the would-be immigrant and attempts to demonstrate to the Department of Labor that no U.S. worker is available with those particular qualifications to perform the carefully defined job duties.

In 1996 the Labor Department's Office of Inspector General (OIG) performed an audit on the operation of the labor certification process, which bore out the observations above and also provided a more complete picture of the problems with the current system. U.S. Department of Labor, Office of the Inspector General, The Department of Labor's Foreign Labor Certification Programs: The System is Broken and Needs To Be Fixed, Rep. No. 06–96–002–03–321 (1996). The audit found that for the 24,150 noncitizens for whom labor certification applications were approved during the audit period, 99 percent were in the United States at the time the application was filed; 74 percent were working for the U.S. employer at the time of application (16 percent of whom were working illegally); 11 percent never worked for the petitioning employer after adjustment to LPR status; and 17 percent left the employer within six months after attaining LPR status. In examining in detail 600 randomly selected cases, the OIG also found that in almost a quarter of the cases, the employers received no resumes in response to their advertising of the job; for the three-quarters of the cases that did generate applications from U.S. workers, only 0.08 percent of such workers were hired—and then to fill other jobs with the employer, not to take the job for which the noncitizen's services were sought. The Audit thus concluded that the labor certification process was "perfunctory at best and a sham at worst," a "time-consuming paper shuffle that employers endure to give the appearance of complying with the law." It is "ineffective in ensuring that qualified, willing, and available U.S. workers are given a fair opportunity to compete for the jobs for which aliens are hired." *Id.* at 2, 7, 12. For a strong critique of the audit's methodology and conclusions, see Bell, *Analysis of the Inspector General's Audit of the Department of Labor's Foreign Labor Certification Programs* (NAFSA Working Paper No. 63, 1999), summarized at 76 Interp.Rel. 1494 (1999).

Developments in the late 1990s revealed more about these problems. As we will explore more fully in Section B, employers' use of the H–1B nonimmigrant category, which is essentially for professional employees, grew explosively during this period, particularly in the information technology (IT) industry. Persons admitted in this nonimmigrant category, which does not require labor certification, have traditionally been allowed to hold that status for as long as six years. Estimates placed the total of such nonimmigrants as high as 500,000 by 2001, of whom one-half to two-thirds intended to stay permanently. Martin, Lowell, & Martin, *U.S. Immigration Policy: Admission of High–Skilled Workers*, 16 Geo. Immig. L.J. 619, 633 (2002). Most employers share that expectation (assuming that the employee proves to be a satisfactory worker), and employers regularly initiate the process for second- or third-preference status—which of course usually does require labor certification—before the H–1B admission period ends. As H–1B admissions rose in the late 1990s, however, DOL and INS resources devoted to the employment-based immigration process declined, owing either to funding cuts or other more pressing priorities. Labor certification came to take well over two years, and adjustment of status was subject to processing backlogs of as much as three years in some INS districts.

Congress responded to the business outcry (during these boom years) by both raising the ceiling on H–1B admissions (later reduced) and easing the situation of H–1B workers awaiting permanent residence status. The American Competitiveness in the Twenty-first Century Act (AC21), Pub.L. 106–313, 114 Stat. 1251 (2000), allowed H–1B workers to switch jobs more readily while waiting, and also provided for extensions of H–1B status beyond six years if needed because of delays in processing. It then went so far as to adopt the following "portability" provision, a new INA § 204(j), which—it turns out—calls into question many of the labor protections once thought (at least formally) to be hallmarks of the traditional labor certification system. The section provides:

> *Job flexibility for long delayed applicants for adjustment of status to permanent residence.*—A petition under subsection (a)(1)(D)[e] for an individual whose application for adjustment of status pursuant to section 245 has been filed and remained unadjudicated for 180 days or more shall remain valid with respect to a new job if the individual changes jobs or employers if the new job is in the same or a similar occupational classification as the job for which the petition was filed.

In essence, § 204(j) provides that certain employment-based adjustment applicants remain eligible for adjustment of status despite a change in job or employer if the adjustment of status application, Form I–485, has been pending for 180 days or more and the new job is in "the same or similar" field as the job for which the originating visa petition (Form I–140) was filed. Where these factors are met, the adjustment applicant can "port" or carry the adjustment application to the new job or employer. Under a concurrent amendment to INA § 212(a)(5)(A)(iv), the labor certification likewise remains valid under these circumstances. Note that this benefit is triggered only by delays in adjustment of status, not in labor certification. But 180 days is not usually considered a long delay in this context; this period is approximately USCIS's target processing time for adjustment of status.

Consider what happens if the 180–day processing time is exceeded. The alien can switch to another job or employer in the same occupational classification—or actually into a different job classification, as long as the job is "similar." The employee's taking of a new job in a different region will render irrelevant any protection to U.S. workers ostensibly provided

---

e. The cross reference to subsection (a)(1)(D) was almost surely intended to refer instead to INA § 204(a)(1)(F).—eds.

by the labor certification, which was premised on a finding that there were no U.S. workers available *at the place* mentioned in the original application. INA § 212(a)(5)(A)(i)(I). Prevailing wages are also determined, in most instances, according to a specific geographic market. Should the new employer in a high-wage region now be allowed to pay the lower wage? Further, in adjudicating the related I–140 petitions, INS has traditionally paid close attention to whether the petitioning employer is capable of paying the wage or salary stated in the labor certification process. Will this requirement apply to the new employer? Suppose that the original employer, around the time the employee is switching jobs, withdraws the I–140 visa petition—an unsurprising reaction in such circumstances. Should that prevent the noncitizen from gaining LPR status? Why—if Congress already contemplated that he might not work for that employer anyway? *See* Klasko, *American Competitiveness in the 21st Century: H–1Bs and Much More,* 77 Interp.Rel. 1689, 1695 (2000).

Implementing regulations for § 204(j) have not yet been issued as of late 2011, and initial administrative guidance has addressed few of these questions. USCIS has explained a bit further its "totality of the circumstances" approach to determining whether the new job is in "the same or similar job classification." <http://www.uscis.gov/portal/site/uscis/menuitem.5af9bb95919f35e66f614176543f6d1a/?vgnextoid=1efbac8ec3d2f 210VgnVCM100000082ca60aRCRD & vgnextchannel=6abe6d26d17df110 VgnVCM1000004718190aRCRD>. The AAO's principal precedent decision on § 204(j) analyzes some of the background to the statute, but resolves only a limited issue. *Matter of Al Wazzan,* 25 I & N Dec. 359 (AAO 2010) (visa petitions are not automatically made valid under § 204(j) once the adjustment application remains pending for 180 days; USCIS must still judge the visa petition's initial validity).

It would appear that § 204(j) subtly but fundamentally challenges many underlying protection premises of labor certification altogether—to the point that one commentator has suggested that this section "may sound the death knell for labor certification." Weiss, *Employment-based (EB) Immigration at the Millennium: An Examination of the Immigration Act of 1990, Its Aftermath, and The American Competitiveness in the Twenty First Century Act,* 00–12 Imm.Briefings 15 (2000). That obituary was premature, but we will consider in Chapter 9D various proposed reforms for the admissions system, including some that are built on a recognition of the ways in which the provisions for employment-based immigration have changed gradually but significantly over the years.

SECTION B. NONIMMIGRANTS

1. INTRODUCTION

A nonimmigrant, generally speaking, is a noncitizen who seeks entry to the United States for a specific purpose to be accomplished during a temporary stay. The qualifying categories for nonimmigrants are set forth, rather surprisingly, as part of the statutory definition of "immigrant" in INA § 101(a)(15). But an examination of § 214, which is captioned "Admission of nonimmigrants," will reveal the reason for this placement.

Section 214(b) establishes a presumption that is fundamental to the workings of the admission process. Under that section, almost every noncitizen who wishes to come to the United States is presumed to be an immigrant—and therefore subject to the more restrictive requirements applicable to the latter category. The noncitizen applicant therefore must shoulder the burden of demonstrating that he or she is entitled to nonimmigrant status. Section 101(a)(15) simply mirrors this basic presumption in definitional form. It defines "immigrant," without further embellishment, as "every alien except" those who happen to fall within one of the carefully defined categories of nonimmigrants which § 101(a)(15) then proceeds to list. Other detailed requirements for specific categories appear in § 214.

The nonimmigrant categories range from tourists, who are now generally granted an admission period of six months (even if they intend a shorter visit); through students and various business-related categories, which may allow entry for longer periods; to diplomats and employees of foreign governments or affiliated with international organizations, whose stay may be extended indefinitely and who are exempted from several other requirements because of their official status. *See, e.g.,* INA § 102. The Visa Office of the Department of State has developed a set of visa symbols for the various nonimmigrant categories, generally tracking the alphabetical subparagraphs in § 101(a)(15), and sometimes subdividing the categories even further than is suggested by the statutory language. For example, a tourist enters as a "temporary visitor for pleasure" on a B–2 visa. A noncitizen here temporarily on business, perhaps to negotiate a contract with an American supplier, will enter on a B–1 visa, as a "temporary visitor for business." A student headed for an academic institution receives an F–1 visa; the student's spouse and children receive F–2 visas. DHS employs the same symbols for nonimmigrant admission categories.

You can gain a sense of the wide array of the nonimmigrant categories and relative demand for them by examining Table 5.6, which shows total admissions for selected admission categories in FY 2009.[9] The table counts admissions, not individuals who made an entry. A single individual can be admitted multiple times in a year. Visitors for business or pleasure constituted almost 90 percent of the 36 million nonimmigrant admissions

---

9. The table, like the DHS data on which it is based, counts only persons admitted using a Form I–94, the arrival-departure record. It therefore does not include most short-term admissions along our land borders. Specifically, neither Canadian nationals coming for a short stay nor Mexican nationals holding a Border Crossing Card issued by U.S. authorities are included in this count. Those uncounted nonimmigrant admissions, which are technically B1/B2 admissions, totaled over 126 million in FY 2009, or 87 percent of the 163 million total nonimmigrant admissions; a very high proportion of the 126 million represent multiple crossings by eligible individuals. (These various documents and procedures are discussed in more detail in Chapter Six.)

DHS counted that year. Just under half of these were admissions under the visa waiver program (described below and in more detail in Chapter Six). For this reason, and because most visas permit multiple entries, the annual number of admissions greatly exceeds the number of nonimmigrant visas issued each year by the State Department.

Table 5.6
Nonimmigrant Admissions (Selected Categories), Fiscal Year 2009

Visitors for business	B1	4,390,888
Visitors for pleasure	B2	27,800,027
Transit aliens	C	346,695
Treaty traders and investors, spouses and children	E	229,301
Students, exchange visitors, spouses and children	F, M, J	1,411,372
Diplomats and other representatives	A, G, N, NATO	323,183
Temporary workers and trainees, spouses and children	H, O, P, Q, R, TN	936,272
Foreign media representatives	I	44,132
Spouses of U.S. citizens with visa pending or fiancé(e)s of U.S. citizens, and their children	K	47,524
Intra-company transfers, spouses and children	L	493,992

Source: 2009 DHS Yearbook of Immigration Statistics, Table 25.

The statute places no fixed numerical limits on nonimmigrant admissions, with limited exceptions—most prominently in the H–1B, H–2B, T, and U categories, as discussed below. Control over nonimmigrant admissions is maintained by applying the qualitative requirements for each category and the inadmissibility grounds in INA § 212(a).

For the vast majority of noncitizens, there are three basic procedural paths to a given nonimmigrant status in the United States. (Chapter Six will treat admission procedures more fully.) First, a noncitizen who plans to enter the United States as a nonimmigrant applies for a visa at a consulate overseas. The visa serves to authorize travel to the United States in order to apply for admission at the port of entry, but it does not guarantee admission if the immigration officer at the border finds that the noncitizen is not entitled to enter. After admission, the category and expiration date shown in the admission documents (Form I–94) issued at the border, or later modified or extended at a DHS office in the United States, determine the rights and limitations attached to the nonimmigrant entry, regardless of what might have been shown on the visa. Second, citizens of 36 countries (predominantly European countries, along with a few other developed states) can enter the United States without a visa as a business visitor or tourist for up to 90 days. More than 16 million persons entered the United States under the visa waiver program in FY 2009. The third procedural path is for a noncitizen who has been lawfully admitted as a nonimmigrant, and who is maintaining that status, to change to a different nonimmigrant status under INA § 248.

Whichever procedure is used, some nonimmigrant visas require supporting documentation generated through prior application procedures before the noncitizen can apply for the visa overseas or a change of nonimmigrant status in the United States. For some employment-related categories, the employer must gain approval of a preliminary petition filed with USCIS. Prospective students and scholars must present documents from the school or exchange program, most typically a Form I–20, which is reproduced in the Statutory Supplement. These supporting requirements are discussed more fully later in this section.

Short-term visitors (the B category) and students garner the lion's share of the nonimmigrant admissions each year. As noted in Chapter 9A, *infra*, the government responded to security concerns after the September 11 attacks by instituting an array of new procedures for students and tourists who enter outside the visa waiver program. Nonetheless, admissions under these categories are fairly straightforward substantively and do not usually demand the attention of an attorney. The procedures for business categories, also a high percentage of nonimmigrant admissions, however, are more complex and frequently necessitate legal counsel for their successful navigation.

Accordingly, after a brief examination of the general issue of nonimmigrant intent and study-related statuses, we concentrate primarily on issues relating to selected business and employment-based nonimmigrant categories. Much of the practice of immigration lawyers involves guiding their clients in selecting and applying for the proper nonimmigrant visa for themselves or their employees. The factors to be examined in counseling such a choice include:

- Basic requirements (e.g., diplomas, degrees, or licensure, period of past work for the company or its affiliates, admission to an accredited institution)

- Type of labor market test or attestation required

- Duration of stay allowed, including renewal possibilities

- Scope of work authorization, if any

- Possibility of later gaining LPR status

- Treatment of family members, including their work authorization

- Procedural steps and fees required

Our goal is to convey a basic understanding of the most important categories, and of how they differ from each other and from immigrant categories as a matter of both practice and policy. We leave the intricacies of the voluminous and detailed regulations to the many excellent practitioner texts available. The Exercise immediately below should provide a concrete focus for your study of the materials that follow, keeping in mind the factors just listed. (The Exercise poses issues whose answers draw upon materials presented throughout this Section.)

EXERCISE

Shoshi Productions, Inc. (SPI), a Japanese corporation based in Tokyo, manufactures computer microchips. Its subsidiary, Shoshi Foreign Distributions (SFD), is responsible for selling and distributing the parent's products outside of Japan. SPI owns fifty percent of SFD. SPI has recently purchased a small American computer company, New World Chips.

For each of the individuals mentioned below, what nonimmigrant categories are available? Among the options, which is best for each? What further information would you seek from your clients in order to be able to respond sensibly?

Then assume that each individual wants to stay permanently in the United States. How does this alter your assessment of the available nonimmigrant categories? What *immigrant* categories may available to each individual?

Engineer: To enable New World to manufacture the microchips currently being produced in Japan, SPI would like its top engineer (who holds a degree from a first-rate Japanese engineering school) to come to the United States to supervise the retooling of New World's factory.

Vice President: SPI also seeks to have its Vice President for Personnel come to the United States to run New World temporarily while he trains New World supervisors and employees in Japanese-style management techniques. The Vice President, who began working for SPI ten years ago in the sales department, has no college degree.

Vice President's wife: The Vice President's spouse would like to accompany him to the United States. She is a concert violinist who has a national reputation within Japan, but whose work is not widely known outside her home country.

Vice President's children: The Vice President has two children (ages 13 and 17) who would like to accompany him to the United States. The older child, who is about to graduate from high school in Japan, would like to enroll in a U.S. college, but feels she needs to visit a number of campuses before deciding where to apply. She also hopes to work for her father at New World while attending school.

Canadian architects: SPI would like to redesign the New World workspace, and has hired a Canadian industrial architecture firm to do the job. That firm has informed SPI that its architects will have to spend at least six months on site, drawing up blueprints and later returning to supervise the reconstruction.

Start-up staff for SFD's U.S. office: SFD wants to open a U.S. office from which it could sell and distribute SPI's microchips. SFD would like to send to the United States a three-person delegation that could scout out an appropriate location for the office. SFD hopes to assign some of its sales staff from its Japanese operations to work in the office on a temporary basis until U.S. workers can be found. SFD also would like to send salespeople to the United States to drum up new customers for SPI and New World and to locate talented American computer engineers who might like to work in the SPI design laboratories in Tokyo.

2. THE ISSUE OF "IMMIGRANT INTENT"— WITH A BRIEF LOOK AT THE CATEGORIES FOR STUDENTS AND EXCHANGE VISITORS

For many of the nonimmigrant categories, the most important requirement is that the noncitizen "has a residence in a foreign country which he has no intention of abandoning." *See, e.g.,* INA § 101(a)(15)(B), (F), (J), (M), (O), (P). In deciding whether to issue nonimmigrant visas, State Department consular officers tend to be especially careful in this regard, particularly in countries known for a high incidence of visa abuse. This care reflects the fear that the noncitizen is not a bona fide nonimmigrant, but in fact intends to remain in the United States indefinitely. It is estimated that nonimmigrant overstayers constitute at least 25% and perhaps as much as 40% of the unauthorized population. *See* Martin, *Eight Myths About Immigration Enforcement*, 10 N.Y.U. J. Legis. & Pub. Pol'y 525, 544 (2007).

A noncitizen is not a bona fide nonimmigrant if his or her intent from the beginning is to remain in the United States permanently by any means possible, legal or otherwise. But many cases have held that "a desire to remain in this country permanently in accordance with the law, should the opportunity to do so present itself, is not necessarily inconsistent with lawful nonimmigrant status." *Matter of Hosseinpour*, 15 I & N Dec. 191, 192 (BIA 1975). *See also Lauvik v. INS*, 910 F.2d 658, 660–61 (9th Cir.1990); *Brownell v. Carija*, 254 F.2d 78, 80 (D.C. Cir.1957). This is the "dual intent" doctrine, which potentially makes the permanent foreign residence requirement less rigid than it might be otherwise. As stated, the doctrine applies in principle to any nonimmigrant, and courts have shown themselves likely (as in the cited cases) to frown on efforts to deport nonimmigrants that are initiated when they allegedly reveal their earlier improper intent by applying for adjustment of status based on a new job or a new marriage. *See, e.g, Garavito v. INS*, 901 F.2d 173, 177 (1st Cir. 1990) (filing of immigrant visa petition naming respondent as beneficiary does not negate nonimmigrant intent). At the front end, nonetheless, when a visa applicant in the student or tourist categories appears before a consular officer overseas, the expression of a strong desire to seek and obtain permanent residence even through legal means is likely to result in denial of the nonimmigrant visa.

In practice, therefore, the dual intent doctrine is more likely to be of use to other categories where the INA and the regulations are more hospitable to changes of status. For example, Congress expressly protected the possibility of dual intent for the H–1B and L categories—categories prominently used by businesses, as we will explore below—in a 1990 amendment adding INA § 214(h). Immigration Act of 1990, Pub.L. No. 101–649, § 205(b)(2), 104 Stat. 4978, 5020 (1990). In the categories for which dual intent is not clearly recognized in statute, difficult problems remain when consular officers and other government personnel try to decide if any given would-be nonimmigrant should be denied a visa or admission because of her immigrant intent.

To consider how this rule works in practice, assume that you are a consular officer whose job includes granting or denying applications for student visas. How do you go about deciding whether to issue a student visa to the applicants who come before you? The first reading below lays out the basics of the nonimmigrant categories that may be available to a noncitizen who wants to study in the United States, and the second provides recent State Department guidelines on applying the nonimmigrant intent requirement to students.

CHAD C. HADDAL, FOREIGN STUDENTS IN THE UNITED STATES: POLICIES AND LEGISLATION

Congressional Research Service Report for Congress 1–4 (2007).

There are three main avenues for students from other countries to temporarily come to the United States to study, and each involves admission as a nonimmigrant. * * * The three visa categories used by foreign students are F visas for academic study; M visas for vocational study; and J visas for cultural exchange.

F Visa

The most common visa for foreign students is the F–1 visa. It is tailored for international students pursuing a full-time academic education. The F–1 student is generally admitted as a nonimmigrant for the period of the program of study, referred to as the duration of status. The law requires that the student have a foreign residence that they have no intention of abandoning. Their spouses and children may accompany them as F–2 nonimmigrants.

To obtain an F–1 visa, prospective students also must demonstrate that they have met several criteria:

- They must be accepted by a school that has been approved by the Attorney General.

- They must document that they have sufficient funds or have made other arrangements to cover all of their expenses for 12 months.

- They must demonstrate that they have the scholastic preparation to pursue a full course of study for the academic level to which they wish to be admitted and must have a sufficient knowledge of English (or have made arrangements with the school for special tutoring, or study in a language the student knows).

Once in the United States on an F visa, nonimmigrants are generally barred from off-campus employment. Exceptions are for extreme financial hardship that arises after arriving in the United States and for employment with an international organization. F students are permitted to engage in on-campus employment if the employment does not displace a U.S. resident. In addition, F students are permitted to work in practical training that relates to their degree program, such as paid research and teaching assistantships. An alien on an F visa who otherwise accepts employment violates the terms of the visa and is subject to removal and other penalties * * *.

J Visa

Foreign students are just one of many types of aliens who may enter the United States on a J–1 visa, sometimes referred to as the Fulbright program. Others admitted under this cultural exchange visa include scholars, professors, teachers, trainees, specialists, foreign medical graduates, international visitors, au pairs, and participants in student travel/work programs. Those seeking admission as a J–1 nonimmigrant must be participating in a cultural exchange program that the U.S. Department of State's Bureau of Educational and Cultural Affairs (BECA) has designated. They are admitted for the period of the program. Their spouses and children may accompany them as J–2 nonimmigrants.

* * * The programs that wish to sponsor J visas also must satisfy the following criteria:

- be a bona fide educational and cultural exchange program, with clearly defined purposes and objectives;
- have at least five exchange visitors annually;
- provide cross-cultural activities;
- be reciprocal whenever possible;
- if not sponsored by the government, have a minimum stay for participants of at least three weeks (except for those designated as "short term" scholars);
- provide information verifying the sponsoring program's legal status, citizenship, accreditation, and licensing;
- show that they are financially stable, able to meet the financial commitments of the program, and have funds for the J nonimmigrant's return airfare;
- ensure that the program is not to fill staff vacancies or adversely affect U.S. workers;

- assure that participants have accident insurance, including insurance for medical evacuations; and

- provide full details of the selection process, placement, evaluation, and supervision of participants.

As with F visas, those seeking J visas must have a foreign residence they have no intention of abandoning. However, many of those with J visas have an additional foreign residency requirement in that they must return abroad for two years if they wish to adjust to any other nonimmigrant status or to become a legal permanent resident in the United States. This foreign residency requirement applies to J nonimmigrants who meet any of the three following conditions:

- An agency of the U.S. government or their home government financed in whole or in part—directly or indirectly—their participation in the program.

- The BECA designates their home country as clearly requiring the services or skills in the field they are pursuing.

- They are coming to the United States to receive graduate medical training.

There are very few exceptions to the foreign residency requirement for J visa holders who meet any of these criteria—even J visa holders who marry U.S. citizens are required to return home for two years. Although many aliens with J–1 visas are permitted to work in the programs in which they are participating, the work restrictions for foreign students with a J–1 visa are similar to those for the F visa.

M Visa

Foreign students who wish to pursue a non-academic (e.g., vocational) course of study apply for an M visa. This visa is the least used of the foreign student visas. Much as the F students, those seeking an M visa must show that they have been accepted by an approved school, have the financial means to pay for tuition and expenses and otherwise support themselves for one year, and have the scholastic preparation and language skills appropriate for the course of study. Their spouses and children may accompany them as M–2 nonimmigrants. As with all of the student visa categories, they must have a foreign residence they have no intention of abandoning. Those with M visas are also barred from working in the United States, including in on-campus employment.

NOTES ON STUDENT STATUS

1. F–1 visas issuances fell below 216,000 in FY 2003, down from 293,000 in FY 2001, largely because of new screening procedures adopted in the wake of the 9/11 attacks. But that number rebounded to 385,000 in FY 2010. J–1 visa issuances (which include a variety of programs, not simply students) were 321,000 in FY 2010, while M–1 issuances (for vocational programs) totaled 9,436. Table XVI(A): Classes of Nonimmigrants Issued Visas, Department of State (2010), <http://www.travel.state.gov/pdf/MultiYearTableXVI.pdf>.

2. Since 2002, schools have been required to use an automated web-based system known as SEVIS (Student and Exchange Visitor Information System) to share timely information about foreign students and scholars. The system records and makes this information available to consular officers, inspectors at the border, and other immigration officers. The required information includes issuance of the key initial form for F–1 students, the I–20, by the school at the time it approves admission, ongoing reports about the student's address and satisfaction of requirements (such as arriving for the term, maintaining a full load of courses, changing degree programs, on-campus employment, off-campus employment during or after completion of studies—known as "practical training," or transferring to another school), and withdrawal or completion of studies. The SEVIS system, which is managed by ICE, affords better tracking of students and monitoring of whether they are maintaining status than was possible before 2002.

3. Though the statute does not provide for this, under long-standing administrative practice, F–1 students can engage in "practical training"—work for an off-campus employer in a field related to their studies—during term breaks or for a period after finishing the course of study. (This training has often served as a stepping stone to longer-term employment in the United States with that employer, perhaps under the H–1B category followed by eventual petitioning for employment-based permanent immigration.) For many years the practical training opportunity was limited to a maximum of 12 months, but regulations adopted by the George W. Bush administration opened an option for up to 29 months, under specific conditions, for persons working in the so-called STEM fields: science, technology, engineering, or mathematics. Fragomen, *The New OPT Rule: New Options, Lingering Uncertainties for Foreign Students*, 85 Interp. Rel. 2173, 2173–76 (2008).

STUDENTS AND IMMIGRANT INTENT
U.S. Department of State cable (No. 2005 State 274068),
reprinted in 82 Interp. Rel. 1762 (2005).

1. Summary: This cable provides some guidance for consular officers in how to interpret the immigrant intent provisions when adjudicating student visa applications. Consular officers adjudicating student visa applications should evaluate the applicant's requirement to maintain a residence abroad in the context of the student's present circumstances; they should focus on the student applicant's immediate and near-term intent. * * *

2. Residence abroad requirement in general terms: * * * [T]he immigrant intent requirement applies in only certain nonimmigrant visa classifications. Most of these visa classifications require the visa applicant to satisfactorily demonstrate that s/he possesses a residence abroad that s/he has no intention of abandoning. This residence abroad requirement is found in the B, F, J, M, O–2, P, and Q visa classifications.

3. The purpose of travel is always the controlling criterion for determining a proper visa classification. Each classification differs fundamentally in terms of activities permitted and time period contemplated in the United States. Student visa adjudication is made more complex by the fact that students typically stay in the U.S. longer than do many other non-immigrant visitors. In these circumstances, it is important to keep in mind that the applicant's intent is to be adjudicated based on present intent—not on contingencies of what might happen in the future, during a lengthy period of study in the United States.

4. *Context of residence abroad for students*: While the concept of "ties" is very useful in evaluating many nonimmigrant visa applicants, it is relatively less useful in assessing the present intent of a student. The typical student is young, without employment, without family dependents, and without substantial personal assets. Students may have only general rather than specific plans for the future. These personal circumstances differ greatly from those of persons usually qualifying for B–1's or P visas for example. The residence abroad requirement for a student should therefore be considered in a broader light, focusing on the student applicants' immediate intent. While students may not be able to demonstrate strong "ties", their typical youth often conveys a countervailing major advantage in establishing their bona fides: they don't necessarily have a long-range plan, and hence are relatively less likely to have formed an intent to abandon their homes.

5. *Intended course of study*: The fact that the alien plans on studying a subject for which there is no or little employment opportunity in his country of residence is not a basis for denying the visa; because circumstances may change, this fact should not be deemed a negative factor in adjudicating the case. Nor, on the other hand, is the fact that the country of residence can provide the equivalent quality courses in the same subject matter. The student has the right to choose where s/he will obtain an education if accepted by the school.

6. *Visa renewal during course of study*: Some students have to apply for new visas if they go home or travel during their period of study. Returning student applications should generally be reissued in the normal course of business, unless circumstances have changed significantly from the time of previous issuance. Students should be encouraged to travel home during their studies in order to maintain ties to their country of origin. If students feel that they will encounter difficulties in seeking a new student visa or that a visa will not be issued to them so they can continue their studies, they may be less inclined to leave the United States during their studies and hence may distance themselves culturally from their homeland. Posts should facilitate the reissuance of student visas so that these students can travel freely back and forth between the homeland and the United States.

7. *Student Visa Reminders*:

A. *Educational qualifications*: The I–20 is evidence that the school has accepted the applicant as a student. The choice of the subject matter is not determinative of the applicant's scholastic aptitude. Consular officers should not go behind the I–20 to adjudicate the alien's qualifications as a student for that institution. If the consular officer has reason to believe that the applicant engaged in fraud or mis[re]presentation to garner acceptance into the school as laid out in 9 FAM 41.61 Note 8, then that information is an important factor to consider in determining if the applicant has a bona fide intent to engage in study in the United States. * * *

B. Community colleges or lesser-known schools: All legitimate schools must be accorded the same weight under the law. The INA does not distinguish among schools qualifying for I–20 authorization based on size or recognition. There is no legal difference between community colleges, English language schools and four-year institutions. Applicants should be adjudicated on their bona fides as students regardless of institution of program of study. * * *

NOTES AND QUESTIONS ON NONIMMIGRANT INTENT

1. The State Department issued this cable at a time when it was trying to reverse a decline in student admissions that had occurred after the implementation of strict issuance policies in light of the terrorist attacks of September 11, 2001. Does this cable provide you with enough guidance to determine if any given applicant for a student visa is a bona fide nonimmigrant? If not, what more would you, as a consular officer, want by way of guidance?

2. For contrasting criticism of the application of nonimmigrant intent requirement, see Walfish, *Student Visas and the Illogic of the Intent Requirement*, 17 Geo. Immigr. L.J. 473 (2003); Vaughan, *Shortcuts to Immigration: The 'Temporary' Visa Program Is Broken* (Center for Imm. Studies Backgrounder, Jan. 2003).

3. Perhaps problems with the doctrine and its application derive primarily from the formulation in the statute, "having a residence in a foreign country which he has no intention of abandoning," which was adopted in an era where foreign travel was an infrequent and expensive occurrence. Today, for example, a foreign national may be engaged to a U.S. citizen and have firm plans to settle here in three years after finishing an advanced degree in her home country—but wish first to make several short-term lawful visits. Would it be more realistic in the modern era of frequent and multi-layered international contacts to delete the quoted language and replace it with something like "possessing the intent to leave the United States at the end of his or her period of authorized stay"? If so, is there any reason not to apply this requirement to all nonimmigrant categories, rather than simply to those categories in § 101(a)(15) where the "no intention of abandoning" provision is now found? Would application of this standard be any more difficult for consular officers than the current provision?

3. BUSINESS AND ENTREPRENEURIAL NONIMMIGRANTS

The United States economic system—the largest of any nation in the world—attracts literally millions of noncitizens a year interested in pursuing business opportunities here. Some come as temporary laborers, picking apples and lettuce, harvesting tobacco, even herding sheep. Others come to drum up business for foreign corporations. Multinational corporations send employees to receive training and manage American subsidiaries. Foreign investors may enter to investigate opportunities for purchasing U.S. businesses and property or opening businesses of their own. Professional athletes enter for the length of a sports season. Performers and entertainers may plan an American tour.

An increasingly interdependent world combined with significant waits for some employment-based immigrant visas has guaranteed an exceptionally high demand for nonimmigrant work visas. Naturally, this demand comes in large part from the nonimmigrants themselves, but it also comes at least as much from the many employers in the United States who believe that they have an inadequate domestic labor force at their disposal.

Much of modern immigration practice concerns the entry of these nonimmigrants seeking work or business opportunities and meeting the needs of U.S. employers. The job of the immigration practitioner is to understand the needs of the client (the noncitizen, the sponsoring organization or both) and to assess the availability and implications of the various possible avenues of entry. As you consider the following materials, try to resist the temptation to believe that categories are fixed, that they describe a set of natural relations (employer/employee; professional; investor), or that an immigration attorney merely matches a client with the appropriate nonimmigrant category. Quite to the contrary, the INA leaves important concepts and terms undefined; and administrative agencies and courts sometimes disagree about the definition and boundaries of the categories. Furthermore, it is not as if noncitizens walk into an attorney's office with "H–1" or "E–2" stamped on their heads. Commercial relations are extraordinarily complex and varied, and the general business and migration objectives the client has in mind can possibly be served under a variety of categories—each bearing its own advantages and disadvantages. The sophisticated immigration lawyer may need to spend a considerable amount of time understanding and then shaping or describing the nature and terms of the work intended for the noncitizen in a way that both meets the needs of the client and the requisites of the INA. Throughout the discussion, of course, you should be digging for the underlying justifications for the categories (and testing those justifications against alternative policy considerations and other possible constructions of categories).

One fundamental policy tension runs through these materials on business and entrepreneurial nonimmigrants. American employers often seek to hire foreign employees. It may well be sensible national policy to permit the entry of noncitizens who are needed by domestic industry, as well as those who as entrepreneurs will create opportunities in the domestic economy. Since the earliest immigration laws, however, immigration policy has sought to protect American labor from competition from foreign workers—and an employer's claimed need may simply reflect a desire for more workers at a lower wage or salary.

For noncitizens seeking entry as immigrants, the labor certification process mediates these two goals—although its actual success in doing so remains controversial. But the immigrant categories are sometimes unsuitable for business and entrepreneurial nonimmigrants. First, the employer may need workers only temporarily, and the relatively complicated labor certification process can be expensive. Second, the employer may need workers immediately, whereas it takes time to process labor certification and immigrant visa applications, and immigrant visa categories may be backlogged. Or the needed stay may be only for a limited duration—such as would be the case for truly seasonal workers such as ski lift operators in Vermont or farm labor in Minnesota. Thus the INA includes a number of nonimmigrant classifications that allow, by comparison, relatively quick entry for particular purposes and limited time periods. (We consider in Chapter Nine, Section D, certain immigration reform proposals sparked by this increasing reliance of employers on nominally temporary admissions to meet long-term business needs.) To ensure that employers and workers do not use nonimmigrant visas as a way around restrictions on immigrant admissions or other intended protections for U.S. workers, DHS, DOL, and the Department of State seek to patrol the categories carefully.

a. B–1 Nonimmigrant Visas

Noncitizens who are "visiting the United States temporarily for business"—the B–1 category—constitute the largest category of business-related nonimmigrants. In FY 2009, DHS recorded nearly 4.4 million B–1 admissions, nearly 2 million of which were under the visa waiver program.

From the noncitizen's perspective, B–1 classification offers advantages over other business-related nonimmigrant categories. A noncitizen initiates the process overseas; no petition on his or her behalf need be filed with USCIS in the United States. And no labor certification is required. This stands in sharp contrast to the H–2B category, the other classification (along with H–1 categories) that would seem primarily available to fit persons coming to engage in short-term nonagricultural temporary work. H–2 has historically been the only nonimmigrant category that requires a petition for labor certification.

One can easily imagine a wide range of business activities that would qualify for B–1 status. Individual entrepreneurs and representatives of foreign corporations might seek to enter the United States to find U.S. customers, investigate potential investments, engage in a sports competition, attend an industry conference, look for locations to establish a U.S. subsidiary, arrange international deals, or negotiate contracts. Indeed, it has become a catch-all provision, used by the government to admit nonimmigrants for business purposes when other nonimmigrant classifications are not applicable. There is one important proviso: the noncitizen must receive no remuneration from a U.S. source other than reimbursement for expenses incident to the temporary stay. *See* 22 C.F.R. § 41.31; 9 FAM § 41.31.

Importantly, the statute excludes from the B–1 category noncitizens "coming for the purpose * * * of performing skilled or unskilled labor." INA § 101(a)(15)(B). Similarly, State Department regulations provide: "The term 'business,' as used in INA 101(a)(15)(B), refers to conventions, conferences, consultations and other legitimate activities of a commercial or professional nature. It does not include local employment or labor for hire." 22 C.F.R. § 41.31(b)(1). Yet this conceptual distinction between B–1s and the H visa categories is sometimes hard to apply in the real world. Consider, for example, a foreign corporation that intends to send its employees to the United States to help perform a contract in the United States. For the reasons mentioned above, the firm is likely to prefer B–1 classification to H–1B or H–2B. How should USCIS decide which nonimmigrant category is appropriate in such a case? Should it view the noncitizens as employees of the foreign corporation whose labor in the United States enables the overseas firm to enter into such contracts (in which case B–1 might be a sensible classification), or should it see them as undertaking labor in the United States that domestic workers might be able to perform (in which case utilizing H–2B and its labor certification requirement might be advisable)? The next case explores these difficult questions of definition and the sometimes conflicting goals behind nonimmigrant classifications.

INTERNATIONAL UNION OF BRICKLAYERS AND ALLIED CRAFTSMEN v. MEESE

United States District Court for the Northern District of California, 1985.
616 F.Supp. 1387.

LEGGE, DISTRICT JUDGE.

* * * Homestake [Mining Company] began construction in early 1984 on its McLaughlin Gold Project in order to open a new gold mine. Due to metallurgical problems in the Lake County region, Homestake concluded that it was necessary to employ technology not used previously in the gold mining industry. * * *

[It later] agreed to purchase a newly-designed gold ore processing system from Didier–Werke ("Didier"), a West German manufacturing company. Although the purchase agreement required Didier to supply an integrated processing system, it was not possible to premanufacture the entire system in West Germany. The purchase agreement was therefore made contingent upon Didier's West German employees completing the work on the system at the project site in Lake County.

In September 1984, Didier submitted B–1 "temporary visitor for business" visa petitions on behalf of ten of its West German employees to United States consular officers in Bonn, West Germany. Relying upon INS Operations Instruction 214.2(b)(5), consular officers approved the petitions and issued B–1 visas to the West Germans. In January 1985, the West Germans entered the United States to work on the processing system. The work involves the installation of the interior linings of the system's autoclaves, and requires certain technical bricklaying skills. * * *

Plaintiffs allege that the federal defendants' practice of issuing B–1 "temporary visitor for business" visas under the authority of INS Operations Instruction 214.2(b)(5) violates two provisions of the Act. First, plaintiffs allege that the practice violates section 101(a)(15)(B) of the Act, because the issuance of B–1 visas to aliens coming to the United States to perform skilled or unskilled labor is expressly prohibited by section 101(a)(15)(B). Second, plaintiffs allege that the practice violates section 101(a)(15)(H)(ii) of the Act, because aliens have been permitted to bypass the labor certification requirements contained in the regulations under section 101(a)(15)(H)(ii). * * *

THE VALIDITY OF THE OPERATIONS INSTRUCTION UNDER THE ACT

* * *

The Language of the Act and the Operations Instruction

* * * [The] Operations Instruction * * * provides that an alien may be classified as a "temporary visitor for business" nonimmigrant if:

> *he/she is* to receive no salary or other remuneration from a United States source (other than an expense allowance or other reimbursement for expenses incidental to the temporary stay) ... [and is] *coming to install, service, or repair commercial or industrial equipment or machinery purchased from a company outside the U.S.* or to train U.S. workers to perform such service....

INS Operations Instruction 214.2(b)(5) (emphasis added).

* * * Section 101(a)(15)(B) [of the INA] unequivocally excludes from the B–1 "temporary visitor for business" classification an alien who is "coming for the purpose of ... performing skilled or unskilled labor." * * * INS Operations Instruction 214.2(b)(5), however, does not contain an exclusion for an alien seeking to enter the United States to perform skilled or unskilled labor. The Operations Instruction provides that an alien may be classified as a "temporary visitor for business" if the alien is "coming to install, service, or repair commercial or industrial equipment or machinery." The effect of this language is to authorize the issuance of a B–1 visa to an alien coming to this country to perform skilled or unskilled labor. In the present case, for example, the West Germans undeniably are performing labor—whether it be deemed skilled or unskilled—in connec-

tion with the installation of the gold ore processing system at the McLaughlin Gold Project.

Similarly, a comparison of the language of section 101(a)(15)(H)(ii) of the Act with the language of INS Operations Instruction 214.2(b)(5) shows that the Operations Instruction also contravenes that section of the Act. Section 101(a)(15)(H)(ii) classifies an H–2 "temporary worker" as an alien "coming ... to perform temporary services or labor, if unemployed persons capable of performing such service or labor cannot be found in this country." Because the Act requires the Attorney General to consult other agencies of the government concerning "temporary worker" visas, *see* INA § 214(c), the Attorney General has established H–2 labor certification procedures. Thus, an H–2 visa petition cannot be approved unless the alien's employer obtains either *"[a] certification from the Secretary of Labor* ... stating *that qualified persons in the United States are not available and that the employment* of the beneficiary *will not adversely affect wages and working conditions of workers in the United States* similarly employed ... [*or*] notice that such certification *cannot* be made." 8 C.F.R. § 214.2(h)(3) (1985) (emphasis added).

In contrast, * * * the Operations Instruction authorizes the issuance of a nonimmigrant visa to an alien performing skilled or unskilled labor, though qualified Americans may be available to perform the work involved. The Operations Instruction therefore lacks the safeguards contained in section 101(a)(15)(H)(ii) of the Act and the regulation promulgated under that section. Again, the present case illustrates this point, because the parties have stipulated that neither the West Germans nor their employer was required to seek labor certification from the Secretary of Labor prior to the issuance of the visas to the West Germans. * * *

The Intent of Congress

* * * [The court summarizes the history of labor-protective immigration provisions since the Contract Labor Act of 1885.] In taking these actions, Congress evidenced a continuing concern for the protection of American workers from unnecessary foreign competition. The House Report accompanying the 1952 Act explained that the purpose of section 101(a)(15)(H)(ii) was to:

grant the Attorney General sufficient authority to admit *temporarily certain alien workers,* industrial, agricultural, or otherwise, *for the purpose of alleviating labor shortages as they exist or may develop* in certain areas or certain branches of American productive enterprises. . . .

H.R. Rep. No. 1365, 82d Cong., 2d Sess., *reprinted in* 1952 U.S. Code Cong. & Ad. News 1653, 1698 (emphasis added). * * *

The foregoing legislative history demonstrates that one of Congress' central purposes in the Act was the protection of American labor. The legislative history also demonstrates that sections 101(a)(15)(B) and 101(a)(15)(H)(ii) of the Act were intended to restrict the influx of aliens seeking to perform skilled or unskilled labor in the United States. Thus, to the extent that INS Operations Instruction 214.2(b)(5) permits aliens to circumvent the restrictions enacted by Congress in those sections, the Operations Instruction is inconsistent with both the language and the legislative intent of the Act. * * *

Defendants' Arguments

Defendants contend that INS Operations Instruction 214.2(b)(5) should be upheld because it embodies a reasonable administrative interpretation of the Act.

Defendants' argument centers on the purposes Congress sought to achieve in sections 101(a)(15)(B) and 101(a)(15)(H)(ii) of the Act. Defendants contend that those sections evidence Congress' intent to foster multiple purposes. Although defendants acknowledge that one such purpose was the protection of American labor, they argue that another was the promotion of international commerce. Further, defendants assert that the language in sections 101(a)(15)(B) and 101(a)(15)(H)(ii) reveals a tension between American labor interests and international commerce interests; that the Operations Instruction seeks to minimize the tension; and that the Operations Instruction is therefore consistent with the multiple purposes in the Act.

Defendants rely primarily upon the decision of the Board of Immigration Appeals in *Matter of Hira,* 11 I. & N. Dec. 824 (BIA 1966). In *Hira,* an alien employed by a Hong Kong custom-made clothing manufacturer had entered the United States under the authority of a B–1 "temporary visitor for business" visa. While in this country, the alien took orders on behalf of his employer from prospective customers, and took the measurements of those customers. Prior to the expiration of the alien's visa, the INS commenced deportation proceedings against him. The INS concluded that the alien's activities involved the performance of skilled labor, and ordered that the alien be deported for failure to maintain his B–1 "temporary visitor for business" status. On appeal, the Board of Immigration Appeals focused its analysis on the term "business" within section 101(a)(15)(B) of the Act. Adopting the Supreme Court's definition from an earlier version of the Act, the Board held that "business," for purposes of section 101(a)(15)(B) of the Act, "contemplate[s] only 'intercourse of a commercial character.'" *Id.* at 827 (quoting *Karnuth v. United States ex rel. Albro,* 279 U.S. 231, 49 S.Ct. 274, 73 L.Ed. 677 (1929)). In support of that definition, the Board alluded to prior administrative cases in which aliens were found eligible for "temporary visitor for business" status because "there was involved international trade or commerce and the employment was a necessary incident thereto." *Id.* at 830 (citations omitted). The Board also elaborated upon the underlying requirements for eligibility as a "temporary visitor for business" nonimmigrant:

> The significant considerations to be stressed are that there is a clear intent on the part of the alien to continue the foreign residence and not to abandon the existing domicile; the principal place of business

and the actual place of eventual accrual of profits, at least predominantly, remains in the foreign country; the business activity itself need not be temporary, and indeed may long continue; the various entries into the United States made in the course thereof must be individually or separately of a plainly temporary nature in keeping with the existence of the two preceding considerations.

Id. at 827 (footnote omitted).

Applying those principles the Board in *Hira* concluded that the alien's business was intercourse of a commercial character, even though he took prospective customers' measurements in connection with the business. Thus, the Board held that the alien was entitled to B–1 "temporary visitor for business" status. The Attorney General subsequently affirmed the Board's decision, and certified it as controlling.

* * * Defendants argue that here the West Germans came to this country only as a necessary incident to the purchase and sale of the gold-ore processing system, rather than as individuals hired expressly as laborers. * * *

Defendants' arguments are answered primarily by the language of the Act. * * * [T]he language of section 101(a)(15)(B) of the Act, which *excludes* an alien "coming for the purpose of ... performing skilled or unskilled labor," precludes defendants' purported distinction between business and labor in this case; so does the expressed congressional intent of protecting American labor. * * *

The interpretation of a federal statute by the officials responsible for its administration is entitled to deference. A court, however, must reject an administrative interpretation "that [is] inconsistent with the statutory mandate or that frustrate[s] the policy that Congress sought to implement." *Securities Industry Ass'n v. Board of Governors,* 468 U.S. 137, 143, 104 S.Ct. 2979, 2983, 82 L.Ed.2d 107 (1984).

The court concludes from both the language and legislative intent of the Act that the federal defendants' interpretation embodied in the Operations Instruction contravenes the Act. The court therefore decides that INS Operations Instruction 214.2(b)(5) violates sections 101(a)(15)(B) and 101(a)(15)(H)(ii) of the Act. * * *

ORDER

* * * INS Operations Instruction 214.2(b)(5) is declared unlawful and in violation of sections 101(a)(15)(B) and 101(a)(15)(H)(ii) of the Immigration and Nationality Act. * * * [Defendants] are permanently enjoined from issuing B–1 "temporary visitor for business" visas under the authority of INS Operations Instruction 214.2(b)(5).

NOTES AND QUESTIONS

1. An appeal in the *Bricklayers* litigation was dropped when the parties reached agreement on a new regulation regarding the entry of building and

construction workers. In its announcement of the amended rule, INS reported the reaction of foreign countries and corporations to the court's opinion:

> Following the District Court's order, which precluded the admission of even the most highly specialized technicians, the Service and the Department of State received communications from U.S. industries and foreign governments which indicated a problem of crisis proportions. Industry predicted that equipment under warranty would not be repaired or serviced, with resultant losses of investment and lay-offs of American workers, and that access to state-of-the-art foreign technology would be limited with resultant losses of competitive position. Foreign governments generally viewed this new restriction as a constraint on trade and hinted at reciprocal actions.

51 Fed.Reg. 44266 (1986).

The post-litigation regulation, still in effect, provides:

> Aliens seeking to enter the country to perform building or construction work, whether on-site or in-plant, are not eligible for classification or admission as B–1 nonimmigrants * * *. However, alien nonimmigrants otherwise qualified as B–1 nonimmigrants may be issued visas and may enter for the purpose of supervision or training of others engaged in building or construction work, but not for the purpose of actually performing any such building or construction work themselves.

8 C.F.R. § 214.2(b)(5). The State Department adopted a regulation to the same effect. 22 C.F.R. § 41.31(b)(1).

The new rule is apparently premised on a narrow reading of *Bricklayers*—that is, that the decision extends no further than the situation of building or construction workers. But doesn't the court's reasoning cast doubt on the validity of several other categories for which B–1 admissions are allowed?

2. The BIA's *Hira* precedent permits certain actions that might appear to be the performance of skilled or unskilled labor if "the employment was a necessary incident" to intercourse of a commercial character, and the labor is minimal and tied to a business principally based elsewhere. Does *Bricklayers* distinguish or overrule *Matter of Hira*? How should any remaining dividing line be drawn? Which is the more realistic test in dealing with short-term migration for business reasons in the conditions of the 21st century? The Exercise below provides one context in which to consider the applicable tests.

EXERCISE ON B–1 VISA RULES

Gordon Rogers, a clerk employed by a Canadian railroad, seeks to enter the United States on a daily basis. On a typical workday, he reports to work in Niagara Falls, Ontario, where he obtains documents related to the train shipment bound for Canada he is to monitor. He then drives to Niagara Falls, New York, where he checks the train for safety and for compliance with documentation requirements. He fills out customs paperwork and enters information about the shipment into the railroad's computer system. He then leaves the documentation for the train crew and returns to Canada.

Rogers spends about one-third of his work day in the United States. He uses the rest on additional paperwork for these shipments, and on checking the train when it arrives from the United States. If U.S. Customs and Border Protection wants to inspect the train leaving the United States, he returns from Canada to the border to open the cars.

Rogers is the only employee regularly assigned to this duty. Customary railroad practices, both in the United States and Canada, prohibit these functions from being performed by the train's operating crew.

Is Rogers eligible for a B–1 visa?

b. H–1B and L–1 Visas

(i) H–1B

The H–1B classification covers noncitizens coming temporarily to the United States to provide services in a "specialty occupation," loosely meaning professional positions. More precisely, § 214(i) of the INA defines "specialty occupation" as an occupation that requires "theoretical and practical application of a body of highly specialized knowledge," as well as attainment of a bachelor's or higher degree as a minimum for entry into the occupation. In principle, the H–1B program is meant to complement and not displace U.S. workers, but controversy exists over whether, in structure and especially in application, the regulatory regime effectively accomplishes this aim.

Employers, not employees, initiate the H–1B petitioning process. Before filing the visa petition (Form I–129) with USCIS, the employer must first file a Labor Condition Application (LCA), also known as an "attestation," with the Department of Labor. A prospective H–1B employer need only show that it has filed an attestation and DOL accepted it (after a review merely for "completeness and obvious inaccuracies"). DOL approval of the LCA is not required. Attestations are subject to potential review later, under a set of procedures that circumscribe DOL's investigatory authority. *See* INA §§ 101(a)(15)(H), 212(n), (t). In the LCA, the employer must attest, among other things, that it has notified the appropriate bargaining representative of its employees of the filing, with job details including salary. Alternatively, if there is no union, it must post notice of the filing "in conspicuous locations at the place of employment." The employer must also attest to DOL that the job is being offered at the prevailing wage or actual wage paid to similar individuals (whichever is greater), and that it will provide working conditions for the noncitizen that will not adversely affect the working conditions of similarly employed workers.

Additional obligations apply to "H–1B dependent" employers—meaning firms of more than 50 employees for which H–1B workers constitute at least 15 percent of the workforce, or specified higher percentages for smaller firms. Such employers generally pay higher fees, and must provide additional assurances in their labor condition applications. They must attest that they have taken good-faith steps to recruit U.S. workers, such as advertising or participating in industry job fairs, and have made an offer to any U.S. worker with equal or better qualifications. *See* INA § 212(n)(1). H–1B dependent firms must also attest that the H–1Bs do not displace U.S. workers—meaning that no one in an equivalent job was or will be laid off. But the non-displacement period covers only the time between 90 days before and 90 days after the date of filing of a visa petition. Note that non-dependent employers are not required to attest to either recruitment or non-displacement.

Once USCIS has approved the visa petition, a noncitizen applying for H–1B classification must demonstrate that she is qualified to work in the specialty occupation. She usually does this by having the required bachelor's or advanced degree. Qualification may also be established by professional licensure, when that is required for the field, or by experience in the specialty equivalent to the completion of such a degree and "recognition of expertise in the specialty through progressively responsible positions relating to the specialty." 8 C.F.R. § 214.2(h)(4)(iii)(C)(4).

H–1B nonimmigrants can be admitted for up to three years initially, extendable to a maximum authorized stay of six years. *See* INA § 214(g)(4), 8 C.F.R. § 214.2(h)(9)(iii)(A), 8 C.F.R. § 214.2(h)(15)(ii)(B). Under the "H–1B portability" provision, an individual previously granted H–1B status may start working for a new employer once that employer files a new "non-frivolous" H–1B petition, rather than having to wait for USCIS approval of the new petition. *See* INA § 214(n). Moreover, H–1B status may be extended beyond six years in certain circumstances, primarily when a request for labor certification and adjustment of status (to obtain permanent resident status in one of the EB categories) has been pending for more than 365 days. *See* American Competitiveness in the Twenty-first Century Act, § 106, Pub. L. 106–313, 114 Stat. 1251 (2000). Spouses and children can be admitted as H–4 nonimmigrants, but this status does not allow them to work.

The 1990 Act eliminated the requirement that an H–1B nonimmigrant have "a foreign residence which he has no intention of abandoning," and under the regulations a noncitizen may legitimately come to the United States as an H–1B nonimmigrant and, "at the same time, lawfully seek to become a permanent resident." 8 C.F.R. § 214.2(h)(16)(i). What is the effect of eliminating the foreign residence requirement for H–1Bs? Why might Congress have done so?

Initially, H–1B temporary workers were limited to 65,000 per fiscal year. That cap was reached for the first time in FY 1997, reflecting primarily the dramatic increase in demand for high-tech workers in the

United States during the 1990s boom. Powerful information technology industry interests lobbied for a congressional remedy. They won temporary increases for many years, ultimately enjoying a ceiling of 195,000 for FY 2001 through 2003. In October 2003, the limit reverted to 65,000, where it remains as of 2011. *See* INA § 214(g)(1)(A), (g)(2), 8 C.F.R. § 214.2(h)(8). From FY 2004 through 2009, however, demand for H–1B admissions ran far above that limit. In fact, USCIS received twice the number of petitions needed to fill the quota for FY 2008 on the very first day of the filing period, April 2, 2007—a date six months before the fiscal year began. The Great Recession that started in late 2008 led to reduced demand for FY 2010 and 2011, but in each case, filings still eventually reached the limit—9–10 months after the filing period opened. 88 Interp.Rel. 401 (2011); 87 *id.* 1 (2010).

During the past decade, Congress has resisted cap increases. Opponents regard the cap as the one effective method that minimizes negative impact on U.S. workers and their wage scales from H–1B admissions. But Congress has adopted and refined a series of significant exemptions from the cap. Employees of institutions of higher education or affiliated nonprofit entities, or nonprofit or governmental research organizations do not count toward the H–1B cap at all. Up to 20,000 H–1B workers with at least a master's degree from a U.S. institution of higher education are also exempt. H–1B extensions and petitions for a current H–1B worker to change to a different employer also do not count against the ceiling. With all these exemptions, usage of the H–1B is far higher than the caps suggest. Actual H–1B admissions in FY 2009 reached 339,243 (down from 461,730 in 2007), with India taking the largest share, at 36 percent of the total, and Canada second at 6.5 percent. *See* 2009 Yearbook of Immigration Statistics, Table 32.[10]

Besides the cap, other measures that address the concerns of critics of the H–1B program include a statutorily imposed extra fee of $1500 to file an initial petition or an extension of stay, or to hire an H–1B worker from another U.S. employer. (It is $750 for employers with 25 or fewer workers in the United States.) *See* INA § 214(c)(9). The funds are channeled to the National Science Foundation and the Department of Labor, to be used primarily for job training programs for U.S. workers, college scholarships for low-income students in engineering, math, and computer science, and certain other science enrichment courses. *See* INA § 286(s). Colleges, universities, and nonprofit research institutions are exempt from this fee.

Also, since 2004 a fraud prevention and detection fee of $500 has been imposed on petitioners for H–1B and L (intracompany transferee) nonimmigrants (discussed below). *See* INA §§ 214(c)(12), 286(v). This responded to a series of government studies and reports, dating back at least as far as 1996, that documented problems with employer compliance—and with the government's ability to detect violations—of the various requirements

---

10. Admissions provide only a rough indicator of usage of the category, because an H–1B worker who travels internationally could be admitted more than once in a year.

for H–1B workers. And in 2010, Congress imposed an additional fee of at least $2,000 per new worker in the H–1B or L category if the petitioning firm has more than 50 percent of its workforce in those categories (combined). *See* 87 Interp.Rel. 1641 (2010).

The O and P Nonimmigrant Categories

Until 1990, noncitizens who had attained prominence in their field of endeavor could be admitted as H–1 nonimmigrants of "distinguished merit and ability." The primary beneficiaries were entertainers and athletes. The 1990 Act revised the categories and limited H–1B to members of specialty occupations, keyed to the requirement of a bachelor's or higher degree. Although this change eliminated many previously eligible performing artists and athletes from the H–1B category, Congress created two new nonimmigrant classifications to accommodate them.[11]

Take a close look at INA § 101(a)(15)(O) and (P). What other occupations qualify for the O and P classifications? The O provision requires of noncitizens in its main subcategory "extraordinary ability * * * which has been demonstrated by sustained national or international acclaim." Congress has defined "extraordinary ability" for purposes of admission in the O category simply as "distinction," but the definition applies, curiously, only "in the case of the arts"—therefore not to those eligible for admission based on extraordinary ability in the fields of science, education, business, or athletics. INA § 101(a)(46). In practice, the standards for O visas are generally less demanding than the EB–1A category that is also designated by statute for people with "extraordinary ability." INA § 203(b)(1)(A). Does the O or P classification impose any kind of labor certification or attestation requirement? *See* INA § 214(c)(3), (4). For what periods of time may Os and Ps be admitted? *See* INA § 214(a)(2). Do the categories favor famous, established performers over cutting edge artists who are well-respected by the cognoscenti but have not yet received wide public attention? Under the regulations, a person may legitimately come to the United States as an O or P nonimmigrant and, "at the same time, lawfully seek to become a permanent resident." 8 C.F.R. § 214.2(*o*)(13), (p)(15). In contrast to H–1B visas, there is no numerical limit on O or P nonimmigrants.

(ii) L–1

In 1970, Congress acknowledged the growing importance of multinational corporations to the U.S. economy by creating L nonimmigrant visas for noncitizens seeking transfer from an office overseas to the firm's operations in the United States. Persons granted L visas are generally

---

11. Interestingly, Congress kept fashion models in the H–1B category even while separating the other performance categories into O and P. We do not treat here the specialized rules for fashion models.

referred to as "intra-company transferees." The category was originally designed to help domestic corporations with foreign operations bring employees to the United States for management training. But with the increasingly global economy of the 21st century, the L classification is extensively used today by foreign corporations to transfer employees of a certain rank or with certain qualifications to this country to work in its U.S. branch or subsidiary. The number of L nonimmigrant visas (including spouses and children) has increased steadily over the past 30 years— from 26,535 in FY 1980 to 143,952 in 2010. India accounted for nearly half the L visas issued, with 65,956, followed by the United Kingdom (10,610), Japan (9,391), and Mexico (4,724). *See* Department of State, Report of the Visa Office 2010, Tables XIV(A), XVII(Part II); Wasem, Immigration Policy for Intracompany Transfers (L Visa): Issues and Legislation (Congressional Research Service, Oct. 24, 2005). These are visa counts, not admissions; admissions can include multiple counts of single individuals who travel abroad. For FY 2009, L–1 admissions (the principal workers) for FY 2009 totaled 333,386, very close to that year's total of H–1B admissions. Spouses and children of L–1 nonimmigrants accounted for another 160,606 admissions that year.

Crucial to the L classification is the requirement that the person "render his services * * * in a capacity that is managerial, executive, or involves specialized knowledge." The definitions of "managerial" and "executive" capacity appear in INA § 101(a)(44). "Specialized knowledge" is defined as "special knowledge of the company product and its application in international markets or * * * an advanced level of knowledge of processes and procedures of the company." INA § 214(c)(2)(B). The statute stipulates that a noncitizen seeking L classification must have been employed by the sponsoring firm for at least one year within the three years preceding the date of his application for entry. No such requirement applies to the H categories.

The administering agencies have taken steps to minimize possible misuse of the category by entrepreneurs who owned a small business overseas and then bought or started up a small U.S. firm solely to allow the business to petition for the transfer of its president or sole stockholder. The regulations impose special requirements if the noncitizen is being transferred to the United States to open or work in a new office. *See* 8 C.F.R. § 214.2(*l*)(3)(v), (vi). They also require that the foreign entity continue doing business during the noncitizen's stay in the United States. *See* 8 C.F.R. § 214.2(*l*)(1)(ii)(G). This prevents the entrepreneur from liquidating the business to which he supposedly would have returned.

L nonimmigrant visas require that the employer file a preliminary petition with DHS. Large corporations meeting certain requirements relating to size and prior L–1 usage may file blanket L–1 petitions, rather than petitions for individual noncitizens. *See* 8 C.F.R. § 214.2(*l*)(4). L–1 nonimmigrants may be granted an initial authorized stay of up to one or three years (depending on certain factors), extendable to a maximum of seven years for managers and executives and five years for those with "specialized knowledge." *See* INA § 214(c)(2)(D), 8 C.F.R. § 214.2(*l*)(7), 8 C.F.R. § 214.2(*l*)(15)(ii). Their spouses are classified as L–2 nonimmigrants, and L–2s are allowed to work, unlike the spouses of H–1Bs. *See* INA § 214(c)(2)(E). An L–1 nonimmigrant is expressly permitted to have dual intent; she may legitimately come to the United States as an L–1 nonimmigrant and, "at the same time, lawfully seek to become a permanent resident." 8 C.F.R. § 214.2(*l*)(16). Because the definitions of "managerial" and "executive" for L–1 purposes also apply to managers and executives who qualify under the first employment-based preference for immigrant visas (EB–1C), managerial and executive L–1 nonimmigrants can readily qualify for an immigrant visa as well. *See* INA § 203(b)(1)(C). L–1s with "specialized knowledge" lack such a direct route to LPR status but can often qualify, if they and the employer choose to pursue the process, for EB–2 or EB–3 admission.

In recent years there have been concerns that the L–1 category is increasingly used by businesses to get around the statutory cap on H–1B admissions and perhaps to evade the (rather modest) worker protections that come from the H–1B attestation requirements. Over the last decade, numerous journalistic accounts told of corporations requiring existing professional employees of a multinational firm to train a new cadre of L–1 workers, only to be laid off thereafter. *See, e.g.,* Armour, *Workers Asked to Train Foreign Replacements,* USA Today, April 6, 2004; Grow, *A Mainframe-size Visa Loophole: More Companies are Using L–1 Visas to Bring in Low-wage Foreign Info–Tech Workers—and Replace Americans,* Business Week, March 6, 2003.

Much of this concern focuses on use of the "specialized knowledge" component of L–1 admissions. The DHS Inspector General warned in a 2006 report that the term "specialized knowledge" has no meaningful limits that adjudicators can apply to deny petitions. *See* Office of Inspector General, Department of Homeland Security, Review of Vulnerabilities and Potential Abuses of the L–1 Visa Program 4–9 (2006). Look again at the definition of "specialized knowledge" reprinted above. As an adjudicating officer, how would you decide whether a person who has already worked in a foreign office of the firm for at least a year has the required knowledge? Perhaps in response to these concerns, USCIS's Administrative Appeals Office has issued a series of recent decisions imposing more demanding standards. As summarized by a knowledgeable author, the AAO holds that specialized knowledge: "is narrowly held within the company; is possessed by an elevated class of workers who are key personnel; requires unusual duties, skills, and knowledge beyond that of a skilled worker; requires more than a short period of experience; and is determined by a comparison of the petition beneficiary with the general market and with the petitioner's workforce." Fragomen, *Specialized Knowledge Revisited,* 86 Interp.Rel 3057, 3061–63 (2009) (criticizing the AAO decisions as inconsistent with the statute).

(iii) Controversy and Possible Reforms

The contending camps in the ongoing policy debate over H–1B and L–1 visas often strike diametrically opposing positions. Proponents see the restrictions on high-level business immigration, particularly the cap on H–1Bs (but also constraints on the L category and on permanent employment-based immigration), as limiting the nation's ability to compete globally and actually inducing companies to move offshore. Their opponents see these visas as reducing salaries in high-tech fields, making such vocations less attractive to young U.S. workers choosing a field, and even actually facilitating the offshoring of high-level U.S. jobs. The readings below reflect the major contentions. (For a thorough overview, see Fulmer, Note, *A Critical Look at the H–1B Visa Program and Its Effects on U.S and Foreign Workers—A Controversial Program Unhinged from Its Original Intent,* 13 Lewis & Clark L. Rev. 823 (2009).) We will return to some of these issues in our broader survey of immigration reform proposals in Chapter 9D.

BILL GATES, HOW TO KEEP AMERICA COMPETITIVE
Washington Post, February 25, 2007**f**

For centuries people assumed that economic growth resulted from the interplay between capital and labor. Today we know that these elements are outweighed by a single critical factor: innovation. Innovation is the source of U.S. economic leadership and the foundation for our competitiveness in the global economy. Government investment in research, strong intellectual property laws and efficient capital markets are among the reasons that America has for decades been best at transforming new ideas into successful businesses.

The most important factor is our workforce. Scientists and engineers trained in U.S. universities—the world's best—have pioneered key technologies such as the microprocessor, creating industries and generating millions of high-paying jobs. But our status as the world's center for new ideas cannot be taken for granted. Other governments are waking up to the vital role innovation plays in competitiveness. This is not to say that the growing economic importance of countries such as China and India is bad. On the contrary, the world benefits as more people acquire the skills needed to foster innovation. But if we are to remain competitive, we need a workforce that consists of the world's brightest minds.

Two steps are critical. First, we must demand strong schools so that young Americans enter the workforce with the math, science and problem-solving skills they need to succeed in the knowledge economy. We must also make it easier for foreign-born scientists and engineers to work for U.S. companies.

Education has always been the gateway to a better life in this country, and our primary and secondary schools were long considered the world's best. But * * * [t]o remain competitive in the global economy, we must * * * commit to an ambitious national agenda for education. Gov-

---

f. Paragraphing altered—eds.

ernment and businesses can both play a role. Companies must advocate for strong education policies and work with schools to foster interest in science and mathematics and to provide an education that is relevant to the needs of business. Government must work with educators to reform schools and improve educational excellence.

American competitiveness also requires immigration reforms that reflect the importance of highly skilled foreign-born employees. Demand for specialized technical skills has long exceeded the supply of native-born workers with advanced degrees, and scientists and engineers from other countries fill this gap. This issue has reached a crisis point. Computer science employment is growing by nearly 100,000 jobs annually. But at the same time studies show that there is a dramatic decline in the number of students graduating with computer science degrees.

The United States provides 65,000 temporary H–1B visas each year to make up this shortfall—not nearly enough to fill open technical positions. Permanent residency regulations compound this problem. Temporary employees wait five years or longer for a green card. During that time they can't change jobs, which limits their opportunities to contribute to their employer's success and overall economic growth.

Last year, reform on this issue stalled as Congress struggled to address border security and undocumented immigration. As lawmakers grapple with those important issues once again, I urge them to support changes to the H–1B visa program that allow American businesses to hire foreign-born scientists and engineers when they can't find the homegrown talent they need. This program has strong wage protections for U.S. workers: Like other companies, Microsoft pays H–1B and U.S. employees the same high levels—levels that exceed the government's prevailing wage.

Reforming the green card program to make it easier to retain highly skilled professionals is also necessary. These employees are vital to U.S. competitiveness, and we should welcome their contribution to U.S. economic growth.

We should also encourage foreign students to stay here after they graduate. Half of this country's doctoral candidates in computer science come from abroad. It's not in our national interest to educate them here but send them home when they've completed their studies. * * *

EDWARD ALDEN, AMERICA'S 'NATIONAL SUICIDE'
Newsweek, April 10, 2011*

* * * While there has been much debate about how to secure the southern border against illegal immigration, the deterioration of the system for attracting and retaining skilled immigrants has received scant notice, though the consequences for the U.S. economy are far more

significant. Since much manufacturing and back-office work has been sent overseas, what the United States has left is its brains and still-unmatched ability to design and market the next big thing. In a country where economic success depends largely on innovation, it is worth noting that foreign-born researchers account for a quarter of all patents earned by American companies, and that nearly half the Ph.D. scientists and engineers working in the U.S. were born abroad. Furthermore, between 1995 and 2005 more than a quarter of the technology companies launched in the United States had a key founder who was foreign-born; in Silicon Valley that number was more than half. At General Electric, 64 percent of researchers weren't born in America; at Qualcomm, the figure is close to 72 percent.

Technology executives including Microsoft's Bill Gates and Intel's Paul Otellini have warned for years that restrictions on skilled immigration are forcing companies to expand in other countries where laws make it easier to hire a global workforce. Rather than enlarge its campus in Washington state, Microsoft opened a big software-development facility in Vancouver in 2007. The Canadian facility, Microsoft said in a statement, would "allow the company to continue to recruit and retain highly-skilled people affected by immigration issues in the U.S."

Not surprisingly, many young would-be immigrants are turning their backs on the U.S. Vivek Wadhwa, a Duke University professor, and AnnaLee Saxenian, from the University of California, Berkeley, interviewed more than 1,000 foreign students at American universities in 2008. The results were alarming. Only 6 percent of the Indians and 10 percent of the Chinese said they planned to remain in the U.S. Three quarters of those surveyed said they feared they could not obtain a visa. "The United States," Wadhwa concluded, "is experiencing a brain drain for the first time in its history, yet its leaders do not appear to be aware of this."

Ganti [an electrical engineer from India who obtained an M.B.A. at Purdue University as an F–1 student] was hired by Sharpridge [Capital Management] in December 2006 [shortly after completing his U.S. studies] to help build the proprietary mathematical models at the core of the company's business. He was able to start under a program known as Optional Practical Training, which allows foreign students to work in the U.S. for a short time following graduation. "It was really tough to find the skills that we needed," says Grant, the CEO. "This is the world of financial rocket science. We needed somebody who understood that stuff. It's hard to find people, even out of graduate schools, who really have the skills." Importantly, Grant says, Ganti "had that fire in his belly. He really wanted to be with a small startup."

To remain at Sharpridge after his [one year] training period was over, Ganti needed a work visa known as an H–1B. Created by Congress in 1990, the H–1B is the primary visa for skilled foreign workers who lack family ties in America. Securing an H–1B, which is valid only for three years, requires a job offer, with wages and benefits comparable to what skilled Americans would get. Ganti's application was submitted on April 1, 2007, the day the quota opened. On that day alone, American companies filed more than 150,000 applications for 85,000 slots, and a lottery was drawn. Ganti was in luck, and in July 2007 the government awarded him an H–1B.

While that would allow him to live and work in America, coming back would still require a stamp in his passport and an interview with a State Department official at an embassy or consulate overseas. With his new work visa in hand, however, Ganti assumed it was safe to return home for the first time in three years. After visiting his family in December 2007, he went to the American Consulate in Chennai for permission to return to the U.S. The visa officer reviewed his application and told Ganti that he had no problem issuing a visa, Ganti later told Sharpridge's lawyers. There was just one hitch. The officer handed him a pink sheet of paper, telling him that final approval required additional scrutiny. For some reason, despite Ganti's years as a student in the United States and his employment with a reputable firm in Boston, his application had raised a red flag. [Ganti was apparently flagged for additional security screening. A multi-year delay, with him stalled in India, resulted in loss of his job. He is now pursuing from New Delhi another visa opportunity based on a job offer from a software consulting firm in Washington, D.C.] * * *

RON HIRA, THE H–1B AND L–1 VISA PROGRAMS: OUT OF CONTROL

Economic Policy Institute, Briefing Paper #280 (2010).

* * * Both of these visa programs need immediate reform. The goals of the H–1B and L visa programs have been to bring in foreign workers who complement the U.S. workforce. Instead, the loopholes in both programs have made it too easy to bring in cheaper foreign workers who directly substitute for, rather than complement, workers already in the country. They are clearly displacing and denying opportunities to U.S. workers.

Furthermore, the programs have conferred competitive advantages to the offshore outsourcing business model—speeding up the process of shipping *high-wage, high-tech* jobs overseas. It has disadvantaged companies that primarily hire American workers and forced those firms to accelerate their own offshoring, threatening America's future capacity to innovate and ability to create sufficient high-wage, high-technology jobs. * * *

The programs are now populated with significant shares, and perhaps even majorities, of foreign workers with ordinary skills, who are paid below-market wages and placed in poor working conditions.

* * *

For at least the past five years most of the top employers of H–1B and L–1 visas have been offshore outsourcing firms, whose business model is to shift as many American jobs as possible offshore. * * *

Large shares of American IT workers rightly believe that [the H–1B and L visa] programs undermine their economic interests and working conditions. * * * Incumbent workers in any profession serve as the most important ambassadors for their profession to the next generation. Their views of their labor market and future opportunities in their profession have a major impact on whether they recommend the profession to young people.

One outrageous employer practice is particularly demoralizing and demeaning: employers like Pfizer, Siemens, Nielsen, Wachovia, and Bank of America have reportedly forced their U.S. workers to train foreign replacements on H–1B or L–1 visas. * * * This practice, unfortunately enough, appears to be perfectly legal under the current sets of regulations and laws. We do not know how widespread it is because employers have threatened workers with lawsuits and conditioned their unemployment insurance and severance packages to guaranteed silence. Each new report, however, further reduces the attractiveness of IT to students of American universities. * * *

The programs also stifle American businesses trying to offer U.S.-based alternatives to offshoring. American technology companies that hire American workers are competing directly with firms that can legally bring in foreign workers at lower wages. This unlevel and unfair playing field is especially problematic when the competitor is a multi-national company that can make use of the L–1 visa, since the L–1 has no wage standard at all. * * *

The programs should be overhauled rather than eliminated. They can, and do, serve as an important way for many highly skilled foreign workers and students to stay here permanently, but that pathway must be improved and expedited. * * *

FOUR FUNDAMENTAL DESIGN FLAWS

What causes the gap between the promise and reality of these programs? The H–1B and L–1 programs do not live up to the promises of their supporters because of four reinforcing design flaws. * * *

Flaw 1—No Labor Market Test

The most significant and glaring design flaw is the absence of a labor market test. This flaw strikes right at the heart of the rationale for the program—the supposed shortage of American workers with specialized skills, particularly in science and engineering. * * * [C]ompanies are not required to demonstrate that a shortage of U.S. workers exists, and they can even force a U.S. worker to train his or her own foreign replacement. * * *

The U.S. Department of Labor (DOL) has expressed the practical implications of this fact regarding H–1Bs in a straightforward manner: "H–1B workers may be hired even when a qualified U.S. worker wants the job, and a U.S. worker can be displaced from the job in favor of the foreign worker." The L–1 visa program similarly can be used to displace U.S. workers even when a qualified U.S. worker is available and willing to take the job. * * *

The belief that the H–1B program is a last resort, available only if no qualified U.S. worker can be found, is widespread. For example, while Congress was debating comprehensive immigration reform legislation in 2007, news stories from major newspapers such as the *Los Angeles Times*, *San Diego Union Tribune*, and *The Wall Street Journal* all mistakenly claimed that the program has a labor market test. * * *

In early 2009, Microsoft announced it would lay off 5,000 workers. After meeting that target by late 2009 it announced another round of 800 layoffs. Yet it continued to import H–1B workers, ranking fifth in FY08 and moving up to second in FY09 on the top H–1B employers list. It received 2,355 H–1Bs in those two years alone. Microsoft also extensively contracts with leading offshore outsourcing firms like Infosys and Satyam (now Mahindra Satyam), which provide on-site personnel on guest worker visas. In addition, it recently signed a major three-year contract with Infosys to "handle all the technology services and support for Microsoft itself." Given Infosys' statements in its SEC filings, the vast majority of the workers servicing the Microsoft contract will almost surely be guest workers on H–1B and L–1 visas. * * *

When confronted with these facts, firms sometimes explain that the workers being laid off have "cold" skills that cannot be utilized for new business and that guest workers have the right sets of skills. But given the fact that there is no labor market test and guest workers can be paid more cheaply, it is possible that the reality is that guest workers are simply less expensive than the American workers being laid off, creating larger profit margins for the company. * * *

Flaw 2—Wage Requirements Are Too Low or Non–Existent

The description of the L–1 visa program's wage requirement is simple. It has none. This means that firms can, and many do, continue to pay workers' wages at their home country levels while they work in the United States. To get some sense of the potential wage advantages, a typical information technology worker gets paid $7,000 per year in India and senior project managers are paid about $20,000. Given that India is the largest source of L–1 workers and that the top six L–1 employers are India-based offshore outsourcing firms, it is highly likely that a significant share of L–1 visa use is for very cheap labor. * * *

* * * Many journalists believe H–1B visas are awarded only to the best and the brightest workers from overseas, who are paid high wages for their talent. For example, in 2006, *Washington Post* columnist David Broder wrote a column about Microsoft CEO Bill Gates' campaign to convince Washington policy makers to expand the H–1B visa program. Broder reported that, "Salaries for these jobs at Microsoft start at about $100,000 a year." Yet Broder never verified this claim by checking the

publicly available data on what Microsoft actually paid. The U.S. Department of Labor LCA data indicated that the median wage for a Microsoft H–1B was $80,172—meaning half were paid less—and only 12.5% of the 2,156 positions were paid more than $100,000. And USCIS data indicated that the national median wage for a new H–1B visa was $52,000, and even the 75th percentile wage was only $61,000. * * *

[A]pproximately half of the 58,074 H–1B computing professionals admitted in FY2008 earned less than entry-level wages for computer scientists, * * * a far cry from Bill Gates' portrayal. * * *

While many H–1B workers are underpaid, not all of them are. Some are in fact highly compensated, as publicly available data from both the Departments of Labor and Homeland Security indicate. The policy recommendations contained in this brief would permit the continued admission of these highly skilled workers. * * *

Flaw 3—Work Permits Are Held by the Employer

* * * H–1B and L–1 visa workers can only switch jobs in very limited circumstances, and their employer could revoke the visa at any time by terminating their employment, forcing the worker out of status with immigration authorities. If employment is terminated, the worker must leave the country immediately. In contrast to the employment rights of citizens and permanent residents, H–1B and L–1 rules place most of the power in the hands of the employer at the expense of the guest worker, creating sizeable opportunities for the exploitation of these temporary workers. * * *

The limited portability granted to H–1B workers, allowing them to switch employers only if the new employer sponsors an H–1B visa for them, does not come close to providing them the same level of bargaining power in the workplace as an American worker or permanent resident.

Flaw 4—Deficient Oversight and Enforcement

* * * A 2008 USCIS investigation found that 21% of H–1Bs are granted under false pretenses—either outright fraud or serious technical violations. The most common violations found were instances where employers did not pay H–1B workers what they were legally required, or placed them in a different geographic location. USCIS is reportedly conducting 25,000 site visits to employers to ferret out fraud in the program. The agency has not yet reported its findings, but the effort, if real, should be applauded. * * *

Also problematic are [the extra attestations required of] "H–1B-dependent" firms. * * * [T]hese additional attestations are irrelevant if firms are never investigated or audited, and no investigations of compliance with H–1B-dependent rules have ever been reported. Further, many of the top H–1B employers, including Cognizant and Satyam, are H–1B dependent, but year after year they continue to receive thousands of H–1Bs and file tens of thousands LCAs. And there is little evidence that these firms make a serious effort to recruit American workers. Searches of the "job opening" sections of their Web sites yield few, if any, openings in the United States, in spite of their rapid H–1B workforce growth.

Firms applying for an H–1B must attest that they are not "adversely affecting the American workforce." Given that the U.S. IT industry shed 250,000 jobs in 2009, it is remarkable that the U.S. Department of Labor has not applied closer scrutiny to a program that brought 85,000 new foreign workers to the United States to compete with them for work.

ARGUMENTS AGAINST REFORM FALL SHORT

Remarkably, many in the business and university community have lobbied not only against common sense reform but have gone so far as to argue for expansion of these programs. * * *

This coalition [supporting expansion] typically makes three claims against reform. First, they claim that there is a systemic shortage of U.S. scientists and engineers, and the only way to fill the gap between domestic demand and supply of high-skill workers is by importing guest workers through the H–1B program. They argue that, without a large increase in the H–1B program, they will be forced to outsource the jobs by hiring foreign scientists and engineers in their home countries. Second, they claim that the H–1B program serves as the gateway to immigration for the "best and brightest" foreigners. Third, they claim that *most* H–1B workers are advanced degree (MS and Ph.D.) STEM holders [science, technology, engineering, and mathematics] from U.S. universities, and the visa cap is keeping out workers the nation needs.

But none of these claims is supported by an analysis of actual program operation. Rather than preventing the outsourcing of jobs, the H–1B and L–1 visa programs function in just the opposite way, by accelerating the outsourcing of high-wage, high-skill jobs to low-cost countries. * * *

As for the second claim, I have shown in another paper that most of the top H–1B and L–1 employers sponsor very few, and for some employers like IBM India, sponsor *none* of their guest workers for permanent residence. In fact, the top 20 H–1B employers applied for permanent residence on behalf of just 13% of their H–1B workers.

The claim that most of the H–1B workers hold science or engineering master's or Ph.D. degrees from U.S. universities is factually incorrect. The vast majority of H–1B workers do not come from this group. According to the National Science Foundation (NSF) in 2007, 35,213 temporary residents earned either a master's or Ph.D. degree in a science, technology, engineering and mathematics field. In that same year 120,031 new H–1Bs were issued. Even if, implausibly, all of these graduates were granted H–1Bs, they would only account for 29% of the H–1Bs visas issued that year. * * *

We have no data on wages, occupation, or education level for L–1 visa holders. There is no wage or educational requirement for L–1 workers, and the government does not collect this critical information. Most L–1 workers are not likely to have been recently educated in the United States since L–1 recipients must have worked in a non-U.S. facility for at least one year.

NOTES AND QUESTIONS ON THE *H–1B* AND *L–1* VISA SYSTEM

1. The attestation requirement, added to the H–1B provision in 1990, is clearly a compromise. It is ostensibly intended to protect (somewhat) U.S. workers, but its stops well short of a full labor certification process and thus is meant to maintain the flexibility and speed of H–1B hiring. How effective is today's H–1B provision at accomplishing either goal—worker protection or speedy and flexible use by employers?

How would you design changes to improve H–1B? Should the cap be raised or even eliminated? That is, perhaps a somewhat overinclusive category, in reality permitting a bit of worker displacement, is untroubling for a nonimmigrant classification established for temporary employment, especially in fields that can change rapidly? How temporary is H–1B employment? Alternatively, should labor certification be required? Or should the basic H–1B qualifications be tightened in other ways, to focus admissions on those who are truly the best and the brightest? How would such a test be framed?

Should the same requirements, either labor certification or a higher skills threshold, be adopted for L–1s? On the other hand, if employees have specialized knowledge, foreign financial backing, and the required prior employment by the frim (which is not required for H–1B workers), why shouldn't that allow them to avoid the labor market test and any numerical cap?

2. Should special rules be provided to facilitate the H–1B hiring of graduates (top graduates?) of U.S. science and engineering schools? Should they cover all degrees or only degrees at the masters or doctoral level? (Australia had a similar provision but abandoned it before 2011, based on a judgment that it had mainly served to stimulate the creation of questionable educational programs for persons whose aim was simply to immigrate. *See House Subcommittee Addresses H–1B Visas*, 86 Interp. Rel. 1139 (2011).)

3. Should L–1 admissions be capped? All of them or only the specialized knowledge category? Should the statute impose wage requirements? In what form?

c. E Nonimmigrant Visas

The discussion of H visas started from the assumption that an employer in the United States seeks the labor of foreign workers. L visas suggest, however, that much of the demand for nonimmigrant visas comes from foreign enterprises that seek to create or exploit business and investment opportunities here. As international trade and investment opportunities in the United States have grown, E status has also become a prominent vehicle for nonimmigrant admissions.

Examine the language of INA § 101(a)(15)(E), which establishes two distinct E classifications. The crucial requirement for both categories is that the United States and the noncitizen's country of nationality have an international agreement under whose terms an E nonimmigrant seeks to carry on activities in this country. The E–1 category is for a "treaty trader"; the E–2 category is for a "treaty investor." As the next reading explains, both categories can include employees of the investor or trader. In FY 2010, 36,318 E visas were issued, including those for spouses and children. *See* Department of State, Report of the Visa Office 2006, Table XVII (Part I).

An E nonimmigrant may be admitted for up to two years initially, with two-year extensions, *see* 8 C.F.R. § 214.2(e)(19), and may remain in the United States as long as he or she continues to undertake the activities for which entry was initially granted. Thus, E status offers a distinct advantage over H–1B and L classifications, which are subject to a five, six, or seven-year cap. Another advantage over the H and L categories is that an E visa does not require a preliminary petition by a sponsoring entity in the United States. The noncitizen initiates the process by applying for an E visa at a consular office overseas, or by applying for a change of nonimmigrant status in the United States. Like H–1B and L nonimmigrants, however, E nonimmigrants need not show that they intend to retain their foreign residence. *See* 8 C.F.R. § 214.2(e)(5). Spouses of E nonimmigrants may work. *See* 8 C.F.R. § 214.2(e)(6).

The following excerpt explains the basics of the E category.

CHARLES GORDON, STANLEY MAILMAN & STEPHEN YALE–LOEHR, IMMIGRATION LAW AND PROCEDURE

§§ 17.01, 17.03, 17.05, 17.06 (2007).*

A nonimmigrant classification which most closely approximates the status of an immigrant is that of treaty trader (E–1) or treaty investor (E–2). * * * So long as eligibility continues, "E" status not only permits the alien to engage in the qualifying trade or investment, but permits incidental activities, as well, and a stay of indefinite duration. It also allows the spouse and children to join the principal alien in the same status, and the accompanying spouse to have work authorization* * *. An indispensable requirement, however, is that the principal alien be a national of a country with which the United States has a treaty of commerce and navigation, providing for the trade or investor activity. The nationality of the accompanying spouse or children is immaterial to their "E" status.

The treaty trader must carry on trade of a substantial nature that is international in scope and principally between the United States and the treaty country. The treaty investor must have invested or be in the process of investing a substantial amount of capital in an enterprise which he or she will develop and direct and which will not be a marginal enterprise entered into solely to earn a living.

Employees of qualified treaty persons or business organizations may be classified as treaty traders or investors if they have the treaty nationality. They must be engaged, however, in an executive or supervisory capacity, or have special qualifications essential to the enterprise. An agent of a qualified foreign person or organization, may also qualify for E–1. * * *

The statute specifies that the agreement, under which the nonimmigrant may enter for the specified trade or investor purposes, is to be "a treaty of commerce and navigation." The agreements recognized by the State Department as treaties of "friendship, commerce, and navigation" (FCN) and listed in the Visa Office, Foreign Affairs Manual are by and large so entitled or similarly named.[1] Not all such agreements, however, are strictly FCNs. * * *Authorization for treaty status (E–1 and E–2) was accomplished, in the case of the Philippines, Mexico and Canada by diplomatic agreements that are not formally treaties, after specific statutory authorization.

Bilateral investment treaties (BITs) negotiated by the United States with other countries are also recognized as FCNs, but only for purposes of conferring E–2 authorization. * * *

Prototypical of FCN language authorizing both treaty trader and treaty investor classification is the text of the 1953 treaty with Japan, at Article I, paragraph 1:

Nationals of either Party shall be permitted to enter the territories of the other Party and to remain therein: (a) for the purpose of carrying on trade between the territories of the two Parties and engaging in related commercial activities; (b) for the purpose of developing and directing the operations of an enterprise in which they have invested, or in which they are actively in the process of investing, a substantial amount of capital; and (c) for other purposes subject to the laws relating to the entry and sojourn of aliens.[8]

* * * [The United States has entered in treaties with about 80 countries authorizing treaty trader (E–1) and treaty investor (E–2) classifications to their nationals.] For citations, effective dates, geographic coverage and other useful details relating to the treaties, generally, consult the [State Department's] Foreign Affairs Manual (FAM).

* * *

Although the treaty trader (E–1) and treaty investor (E–2) classifications are identical in most of their characteristics, inherent in their definition are marked differences. Distinguishing the treaty trader, in terms of the required commercial activity, is the operative phrase "solely to carry on substantial trade, including trade in services or trade in technology, principally between the United States and the foreign state of which he is a national. . . . "Under a rule that is both old and questiona-

---

1. *See* 9 FAM § 41.51 n.2, Exhibit I * * *.

8. 4 U.S.T. 2063, 2066 (1953).

ble, the trade must already exist at the time classification is sought; this means binding contracts, that "call for the immediate exchange of qualifying items of trade," not merely negotiations.

The concept of "trade," which had been largely restricted in the past to transactions involving goods and certain few quasi-services, has * * * been expanded by regulation to include services more generally and by statute to include services and technology. The Immigration Act of 1990 further solidified this expansion by specifically including "trade in services or trade in technology" within the definition of a treaty trader at INA § 101(a)(15)(E)(i). What is meant by "substantial trade" has never been defined by regulation, but interpretations have emphasized a regularity of transactions in amounts sufficient to support the trader and his or her family. * * * More than half of the trade must be between the United States and the treaty country. The trade must constitute an exchange; it must be international in scope; and it must involve qualifying activities. * * *

The statutory language which speaks directly to the E–2 investor is: "solely to develop and direct the operations of an enterprise in which he has invested, or of an enterprise in which he is actively in the process of investing, a substantial amount of capital. . . ." Issues suggested by this language relate to the extent the investment must be committed before status is granted, the nature of the capital investment permitted, the meaning of "substantial" in this context and the special significance, if any, of the phrase "solely to develop and direct the operations. . . ." * * *

In the State Department's view, a hallmark of the investment intended by the statute is the placing of funds or other capital assets at risk to generate a profit. The nature of the asset invested ordinarily does not matter so long as it is subject to loss. According to the 1952 House report, Congress contemplated investments in "commercial enterprises," and that the new status would be for "aliens who will be engaged in ... a real operating enterprise and not a fictitious paper operation." E–2 classification was not designed for retirees, for philanthropists as such, or for the employees of non-profit organizations.

Being "actively in the process of investment" involves something more than a mere intention to invest. How much more, can be hard to assess. According to the State Department, "the alien must be close to the start of actual business operations, not merely in the stage of signing contracts (which may be broken) or scouting for suitable locations and property. Mere intent to invest, or possession of uncommitted funds in a bank account, or even prospective investment arrangements entailing no present commitment, will not suffice."

d. Nonimmigrant Categories and Free Trade Agreements

Other international agreements besides treaties of commerce and navigation can have a direct bearing on nonimmigrant admissions. Free trade agreements are the primary example. Though the United States is not a party to any free trade treaty as ambitious as those that created the European Union, which led to a broad regime of free movement of labor and capital among the contracting states, some of its free trade compacts do contain specific provisions facilitating the migration of designated categories of workers.

Most prominently, the North American Free Trade Agreement (NAF-TA), which took effect January 1, 1994, brought Mexico into the free trade zone that had existed since 1988 by virtue of the U.S.–Canadian Free Trade Agreement (FTA), 27 I.L.M. 293 (1988). NAFTA makes no provision for permanent immigration, but it allows four categories of Canadian and Mexican citizens to enter the United States as nonimmigrants if they are "businesspersons"—defined as those "engaged in trade in goods, the provision of services or the conduct of investment activities." NAFTA, ch.16, Annex 1603. These categories are labeled business visitors, traders and investors, intra-company transferees, and professionals. The first three categories roughly correspond to the B–1, E–1 and E–2, and L–1 categories, respectively. The professionals category appears to correspond to the H–1B category, but consists of a carefully negotiated list of specifically eligible occupations.

For business visitors and intra-company transferees, entry under NAFTA is accommodated under the existing INA sections. For E visas, the implementing legislation allows access by Canadians and Mexicans. *See* Pub.L. 103–182, § 341(a), 107 Stat. 2057 (1993); INA § 214(e). NAFTA also led to the creation of a new TN category for professionals. The procedure for TN noncitizens parallels that for H–1Bs, except that employers of Canadian citizens need not file a labor attestation nor a preliminary petition with DHS. Also, TN professionals are not subject to the 65,000 cap on H–1B visas. For assessments of the TN category in the context of Mexican immigration to the United States, see Oliver, *In the Twelve Years of NAFTA, the Treaty Gave to Me ... What Exactly?: An Assessment of Economic, Social, and Political Developments in Mexico Since 1994 and Their Impact on Mexican Immigration Into the United States*, 10 Harv. Latino L. Rev. 53, 125–30 (2007); Hollifield & Osang, *Trade and Migration in North America: The Role of NAFTA*, 11 Law & Business Rev. of the Americas 327 (2005).

Similar country-specific arrangements have become part of the INA as a result of free trade agreements with Chile and Singapore, which not only provide for E visas but also created a new H–1B1 "fast track" category, which dispenses with some of the substantive and procedural requirements for H–1B visas. *See* INA §§ 101(a)(15)(H)(i)(b1), 214(g)(8).

To the extent that Congress considers reforms to the business nonimmigrant provisions in the INA, it becomes highly relevant that free trade agreements incorporate formal promises by the United States to refrain from certain types of changes to such categories, as applied to nationals of the treaty partner. For example, the U.S.–Singapore Free Trade Agreement states that the United States shall not require labor certification or other similar procedures as a condition of entry and shall not impose any numerical limits on intracompany transfers from Singapore. *See* Chapter 11, § 3 of the U.S.–Singapore Free Trade Agreement, Annex 11A, signed May 6, 2003. *See also* Chapter 14, § 3 of the U.S.–Chile Free Trade Agreement, Annex 14.3, signed June 6, 2003. Similarly, no party to NAFTA may impose numerical limits or labor market tests as a condition of entry for intracompany transferees. *See* Chapter 16, of the North American Free Trade Agreement, Annex 1603 § C, signed Dec. 17, 1992. *See generally* Wasem, Immigration Policy for Intracompany Transfers (L Visa), *supra*, at 7–9.

4. LAW ENFORCEMENT–RELATED OR VICTIM VISAS (T AND U)

In order to encourage victims to come forward and assist law enforcement, the Victims of Trafficking and Violence Protection Act of 2000 (VTVPA), Pub. L. 106–386, 114 Stat. 1464, created two new nonimmigrant visa categories for certain victims of abuse-or trafficking-related crimes if they are being helpful in prosecution or investigation of the perpetrators. Advocates and lawmakers had in mind a variety of stories, among which this one was typical:

Various setbacks led the workers * * * to leave their homes and families in Mexico in 2004 and, ultimately, arrive in rural Hudson, Colorado. * * * Yet none of the group ever imagined—much less consented to—debt bondage in a farm labor camp.

Moises Rodriguez, a labor contractor or crew boss, had purchased a farm labor camp (the Highway 52 compound) in Hudson in 2001. The Highway 52 Compound contained two two-story, barrack-style buildings with detached bathroom facilities. As the growing season began in March 2004, Rodriguez began recruiting workers in Mexico to come to Colorado to work in agriculture. * * * [D]uring the spring of 2004, Rodriguez made arrangements via various agents and *polleros* (smuggling guides) to bring groups of workers to the U.S.–Mexico border where the workers would cross the border without inspection by U.S. authorities and travel to Phoenix, Arizona where he had arranged temporary housing.

* * * Once the workers arrived in Phoenix, Rodriguez and family members then personally traveled from Hudson to Phoenix on several occasions to pay off the smugglers and pick up the groups of workers. From Phoenix, Rodriguez transported workers to the Highway 52 compound. Rodriguez failed to make any of the disclosures about the terms and conditions of employment that are required under federal laws protecting migrant farm workers. For example, such laws require that migrant farm workers receive, at recruitment, written disclosures of the place of employment, the wage rates to be paid, the crops and kinds of activities in which the worker may be employed, the period of employment, the transportation, housing, and any other

employee benefit to be provided, and any costs to be charged for each of them, among other details. These laws also require the payment of wages and prohibit employers from violating the terms of the working arrangement entered into with a worker.

While traveling from Phoenix to the Highway 52 compound, Rodriguez forced the workers to lie down in the back of his vehicle without seatbelts so that they could not be viewed from outside of the vehicle. * * *

Approximately forty workers lived in the compound, with four to six workers in each unit. Some people had to sleep on the floor. The water in the camp was not drinkable and had made people sick in the past. The compound contained a bathhouse with only two showers for all of the men. Usually only one toilet out of four in the bathhouse was functional. Inside the units, the beds and kitchens were infested with insects. Each night the workers were bitten by insects as they slept.

When each worker arrived at the Highway 52 compound, Rodriguez imposed a system of debt bondage that is prohibited under the TVPA and [the Trafficking Victims Protection Reauthorization Act of 2003]. Rodriguez informed the workers that they each owed him $1300 in smuggling fees. He further stated they would not be permitted to leave his employment until they paid the debt and indicated that he would track them down if they attempted to escape. The workers also understood that they would be forced to pay the debt of any coworker who fled. Rodriguez instructed the workers to behave so that the camp would not come to the attention of police.

Rodriguez served as landlord, supervisor, and coyote, and thus exercised enormous power and control over the workers. Six or seven days a week, a foreman transported the workers sixty to ninety minutes each way in a yellow school bus to work in fields in and around Wellington, Colorado. * * *

[Rodriguez] sat daily [in his vehicle] and watched the workers in the fields through binoculars to ensure they did not stray too far from the rest of the group. Because the Highway 52 compound was so far from the farm, the workers generally were away from the compound from 4:30 a.m. until 8 p.m. Thus, they had little contact with the outside world. * * *

Rodriguez further imposed a complex system of debts and other illegal deductions so that the workers were unable to earn more than a pittance and were unable to pay off their debt. For example, pay statements provided to the workers included the following deductions: rent charges of $50 twice per month, charges for rides to work of $48 twice per month, bathroom cleaning charges for filthy bathrooms, a deposit for clippers, rain gear, knives for work, illegal Social Security, and the ongoing total of smuggling fees owed. The deductions for Social Security appeared to be completely fabricated[.] * * *

* * * [T]he exploitation constituted involuntary servitude under the TVPA. On some weeks the workers were paid as little as $2.90 per hour for more than sixty hours of work. * * *

By late in the season, the Hudson workers determined that they would take a stand against this abuse. * * * However, they had no idea that to seek justice, they would undergo numerous law enforcement interviews, fingerprinting, photographing by three federal agencies, and interactions with several other federal and social service agencies between September 2004 and October 2005.

Medige, *The Labyrinth: Pursuing A Human Trafficking Case in Middle America*, 10 J. Gender, Race & Just. 269, 273–78 (2007). Medige recounts the workers' interaction with the law enforcement agencies that successfully prosecuted Rodriguez for immigration violations (but not trafficking).

The workers in the above excerpt all eventually received T visas. This is a nonimmigrant category for victims of a "severe form of trafficking in persons," which includes the legal categories of forced commercial sex and forced labor. (The definition generally requires the use of "force, fraud, or coercion" by the trafficker. *See* 8 C.F.R. § 214.11(a).) The statute also requires a finding that the individual "would suffer extreme hardship involving unusual and severe harm upon removal," and that the individual (unless under 18 years of age) "has complied with any reasonable request for assistance in the Federal, State, or local investigation or prosecution of acts of trafficking or the investigation of crime where acts of trafficking are at least one central reason for the commission of that crime." *See* INA §§ 101(a)(15)(T), 214(*o*).

The U category, also created by statute in 2000, is for persons who "have suffered substantial physical or mental abuse" as victims of certain kinds of crimes—a broad and varied statutory list. *See* INA §§ 101(a)(15)(U), 214(p). Eligibility requires that the individual possesses information concerning that criminal activity, and "has been helpful, is being helpful, or is likely to be helpful" to law enforcement officials, prosecutors, judges, or other Federal, state, or local authorities. Up to 10,000 U visas may be granted each year.

Visas are capped at 5,000 per year for T visas and 10,000 for U. The statute imposes subtly different requirements in each category for judging the adequacy of assistance the applicant provides in the investigation and prosecution of the offender, as well as slightly variant procedures and presumptions. In U cases, for example, a law enforcement agency, prosecutor, or judge must submit a certification of assistance. For T visas, law enforcement letters or endorsements are useful evidence, but not indispensable. T and U status both result in work authorization, but only T status qualifies the individual for public benefits. VTVPA, Pub. L. 106–386, 114 Stat. 1464, § 107(b)(1)(A) (2000).

T and U visa holders can adjust to LPR status after three years' physical presence in the United States, with certain modest qualifications such as continued willingness to assist in the investigation or prosecution. INA § 245(*l*), (m). T and U nonimmigrants have real incentives to make timely application for adjustment, because T or U status is normally limited to four years' duration unless adjustment is pending. Spouses and children, and in some circumstances parents or siblings, can qualify for the initial status and also for adjustment as derivatives. Derivatives do not count against the annual ceilings on grants of the status.

We reprint as Tables 5.7 and 5.8 two tables from a DHS report that helpfully summarize and compare the requirements for the two types of visa and the two procedures, initial grant and adjustment to LPR status. Citizenship and Immigration Services Ombudsman, *Improving the Process for Victims of Human Trafficking and Certain Criminal Activity: The T and U Visa* 16–18 (Jan. 29, 2009) [hereafter *Improving the Process for Victims*].

Table 5.7
Comparison of T and U Non–Immigrant Eligibility Requirements

Eligibility	T Non–Immigrant Visa	U Non–Immigrant Visa
Type of Abuse	Victim of severe trafficking	Suffered substantial physical or mental abuse from certain criminal activity.
Where	Applicant must have been physically present in the United States or at a U.S. port of entry on account of such trafficking	Crime occurred in the United States or otherwise violated U.S. law
Helpfulness with Investigation or Prosecution	Comply with reasonable request for assistance with the investigation of trafficking act	Provide law enforcement certificate that victim has been, is likely to be or is being helpful to an investigation or prosecution of criminal activity.
Other	Applicant would suffer extreme hardship involving unusual and severe harm if removed	Victim possesses information about the criminal activity.

Table 5.8
Comparison of T and U Visa Adjustment of Status
Eligibility Requirements

Eligibility	T Visa Adjustment of Status	U Visa Adjustment of Status
Lawful Admission	As T non-immigrant	As U non-immigrant
Physical Presence	Continuous period of 3 years since T non-immigrant status was granted OR a continuous period during the investigation, provided that it has been certified [before 3 years] that the investigation is complete	Continuous period of 3 years since U non-immigrant status was granted
Character	Good moral character since being admitted as T non-immigrant	N/A
Helpfulness with Investigation or Prosecution	Continued compliance with reasonable requests for assistance in the investigation or prosecution OR extreme hardship involving unusual and severe harm upon removal	No unreasonable refusal to provide assistance in the criminal investigation or prosecution
Admissible	Admissible at the time of adjustment or otherwise have been granted a waiver for any ground of inadmissibility.	The only [sic] inadmissibility issue that is not waivable includes: Nazi persecution, genocide, or act of torture or extrajudicial killing. Not required to establish that they are admissible. USCIS uses discretion.

The agencies adopted T visa regulations in 2002, 8 C.F.R. §§ 212.16, 214.11, and 245.23, but U visa regulations were not finalized until 2007, *id.* §§ 212.17, 214.14, and 245.24, resulting in a significant backlog of U cases held for adjudication. (Applicants judged prima facie eligible generally did receive interim work authorization and an administrative form of permission to stay known as deferred action.) T visa grants have run between 100 and 350 per year since 2005, not counting derivatives. Because of the delayed regulations, virtually no U visas were granted before FY 2009, but over 5800 were approved that year, and grants then reached the 10,000 ceiling in FY 2010, resulting in the carryover of remaining cases into FY 2011. *USCIS Reaches U Visa Cap for First Time,*

87 Interp. Rel. 1430 (2010). It is too early to know whether this high grant level reflects a catch-up on demand that arose while regulations languished, or whether chronic backlogs are likely. There has also been very limited experience to date with adjustments to LPR status for T visa holders, and none for U visas.

USCIS has reported informally that at least three-fourths of the U visa applicants have based their claims on domestic violence. Ellison, *A Special Visa Program Benefits Abused Illegal Immigrants,* N.Y. Times, Jan. 8, 2010, at A19. Perhaps this is not surprising; the caption on the U visa adjustment provision, INA § 245(m), reads "adjustment of status for victims of crimes against women," though the substance of the adjustment provision is not so limited. This odd caption also reflects the primary concerns that animated enactment of the U provision, as well as the rather limited and hasty legislative deliberation that preceded adoption.

NOTES AND QUESTIONS ON T AND U VISAS

1. One of the fundamental questions raised by both the T and U nonimmigrant categories is implied by the title of this subsection: are these statuses intended to provide assistance to law enforcement, or are they statuses intended to provide relief to survivors and victims of criminal activity? *See generally* Chacon, *Tensions and Trade-offs: Protecting Trafficking Victims in the Era of Immigration Enforcement,* 158 U. Pa. L. Rev. 1609 (2010); Haynes, *(Not) Found Chained to a Bed in a Brothel: Conceptual, Legal, and Procedural Failures to Fulfill the Promise of the Trafficking Victims Protection Act,* 21 Geo. Immigr. L.J. 337 (2007). What balance should be struck when assisting survivors and victims amounts to overcoming their prior unauthorized presence in the United States? Note the strong form of assistance the statute makes available: a nonimmigrant status that is designed to lead fairly routinely to a green card. How vulnerable is this system to manipulation or collusion by smugglers? What checks, if any, exist against such possible misuse?

2. The USCIS Ombudsman report that is cited above described one important way in which the tension between statutory objectives works its way into practice. The report said the following, in discussing the certification required from a law enforcement agency for U visa applicants:

> The certificate must be signed by a "certifying official," which is explicitly defined in the regulations as "[t]he head of the certifying agency or any person(s) in a supervisory role who has been specifically designated by the head of the certifying agency to issue U non-immigrant status certifications on behalf of that agency; or a Federal, State, or local judge."

> Stakeholders have reported to the Ombudsman that the requirement that the certification be signed by a supervisor or agency head is a significant administrative obstacle for applicants because the supervisor or agency head is often unavailable or not as familiar with the case as another officer who worked on the case. Also, stakeholders have indicated that some officials are not always cooperative and are unaware of the protections afforded to victims in the [statute]. Others claim that officers are more responsive to certain types of crimes, such as sexual assault, but not other crimes, such as domestic violence.

USCIS Ombudsman, *Improving the Process for Victims, supra,* at 10. Some advocates have been urging that Congress delete the certification requirement altogether, permitting USCIS to assess helpfulness to investigation and prosecution based on the individual's own account plus any papers he or she chooses to submit. Do you agree?

3.   What differentiates trafficking from smuggling? What would be the "extreme hardship involving unusual and severe harm upon removal" that the victims of Moises Rodriguez's trafficking could have asserted upon return to Mexico? How strict should these standards be?

Blurring the Immigrant–Nonimmigrant Line?

T and U visas may signal a growing trend in the law: the blurring of the line between immigrant and nonimmigrant status. Traditionally, U.S. immigration law has sharply distinguished between persons admitted as permanent resident aliens—admitted for an indefinite stay and entitled to most of the opportunities available to citizens—and nonimmigrants, admitted for a specific time and a specific purpose. Nonimmigrants were permitted to adjust (under INA § 245) to LPR status if they qualified under one of the appropriate categories, but nonimmigrants were generally not admitted with the expectation that they would become LPRs. (An obvious but rather minor exception is the long-standing K nonimmigrant category for fiancé(e)s.)

T and U visas, in contrast, are designed to permit their beneficiaries to reside and work in the United States in a nonimmigrant status for three years, at which time virtually all can apply for LPR status. The only significant qualification is that they provide—or stand ready to provide—an appropriate level of cooperation with law enforcement throughout that period. That proviso is not meant to impose a significant obstacle to LPR status. Changes in the H–1B requirements, described in Section B3b above, reflect a similar evolution. Although it was long understood that many H–1B visa-holders would seek to qualify for an employment-based green card in the United States, that link was made explicit by legislation adopted in 2000 permitting extensions of H–1B status beyond the former ceiling of six years in cases where a request for labor certification and adjustment of status (to obtain permanent resident status in one of the EB categories) has been pending for more than a year. *See* American Competitiveness in the Twenty-first Century Act, § 106, Pub.L. 106–313, 114 Stat. 1251 (2000). (Chapter 9D contains readings that discuss a new concept of provisional admission categories, meant to reflect more forthrightly some of this evolution in U.S. practices.)

Although most admission categories still meet the traditional U.S. model, the developments just described move U.S. immigration law in the direction of European-style policies. Many European states admit noncitizens generally, and then permit permanent settled status to be acquired over time. The scope of rights, opportunities, and responsibilities might also grow as a noncitizen's ties to the country of residence mature. Generalization of this approach, of course, would work a major change in U.S. law: establishing perhaps new immigrant categories (based on time spent in the United States rather than family ties or a specific employment opportunity) and getting rid of the rule applied to many nonimmigrant categories that prohibits dual intent. What are the benefits and costs in this shift in conceptualization of immigration categories? *See generally* H. Motomura, Americans in Waiting: The Lost Story of Immigration and Citizenship in the United States 139–42 (2006).

5. TRULY TEMPORARY VISAS?—H–2A, H–2B AND THE CONTROVERSY OVER GUEST WORKERS

The employment-related nonimmigrant visas so far discussed permit admission for limited periods, though they are not usually tied to work or other economic activity that itself is of limited duration. But visas of the latter sort do exist, linked—at least in concept—to work that is seasonal or intermittent in nature. Classic examples would be ski instructors or ski lift operators, as well as a host of jobs within agriculture, tied to the planting and harvesting cycle. We explore here the primary nonimmigrant categories that focus on truly temporary work, H–2A and H–2B—categories that are most likely to be associated with the shorthand description, "guest workers." We conclude with selections from an ongoing debate, one that was particularly intense in 2006–2007, over whether to expand or contract the use of guest workers. It is a political debate with economic, social, and moral or philosophical dimensions.

a. H–2A

Agriculture provides what many assert is the paradigmatic case of a need for short-term labor. Crops ripen and must be picked quickly; following the harvest, labor is not needed again until the next growing season begins. Not surprisingly, then, temporary worker programs have operated for decades in the agricultural industry. Historically the most important example may be the Mexican Bracero program, operative from 1942 to 1964. "Bracero" literally means one who works with his arms; the closest English equivalent is probably "field hand." Beginning in 1942 the United States entered into a series of agreements with Mexico for the employment of temporary agricultural workers, under a variety of statutes authorizing the practice. Between four and five million Mexican workers were employed under this program before the special statutory authority was allowed to lapse in 1964. Many observers believe that the Bracero program contributed significantly to the illegal immigration of later decades because the migration patterns established under the Bracero program simply continued even after the legal authority ended.

In 1986, when Congress attempted to staunch the flow of undocumented labor with the imposition of employer sanctions, growers argued that without a large-scale temporary worker program crops would rot in the field. Some early versions of the legislation included a massive temporary worker program, but the statute as enacted rejected such approaches. What Congress did do was divide the former H–2 category in two: H–2A for temporary workers in agriculture, and H–2B for temporary workers in other fields. The 1986 Act tried to assure growers of an adequate supply of workers through several provisions, including a streamlined set of labor certification procedures for the entry of H–2A temporary agricultural workers. See INA §§ 101(a)(15)(H)(ii), 218.

There is no statutory ceiling on the issuance of H–2A visas. Their use has grown considerably since the early 1990s, with a large surge from 2005 to 2008, when the total exceeded 60,000 before declining somewhat in the following years. See Figure 5.4. To put these figures in broader context, the Congressional Research Service comments that the H–2A program "remains quite small relative to total hired farm employment, which stood at about 1 million in 2008." Bruno, Immigration: Policy Considerations Related to Guest Worker Programs 3 (Congressional Research Service 2010). In contrast, at the Bracero program's highest levels in the late 1950s, it was the legal vehicle for more than 400,000 Braceros coming to work in the United States each year.

Figure 5.4
H–2A Visas Issued, FY 1992–FY 2009

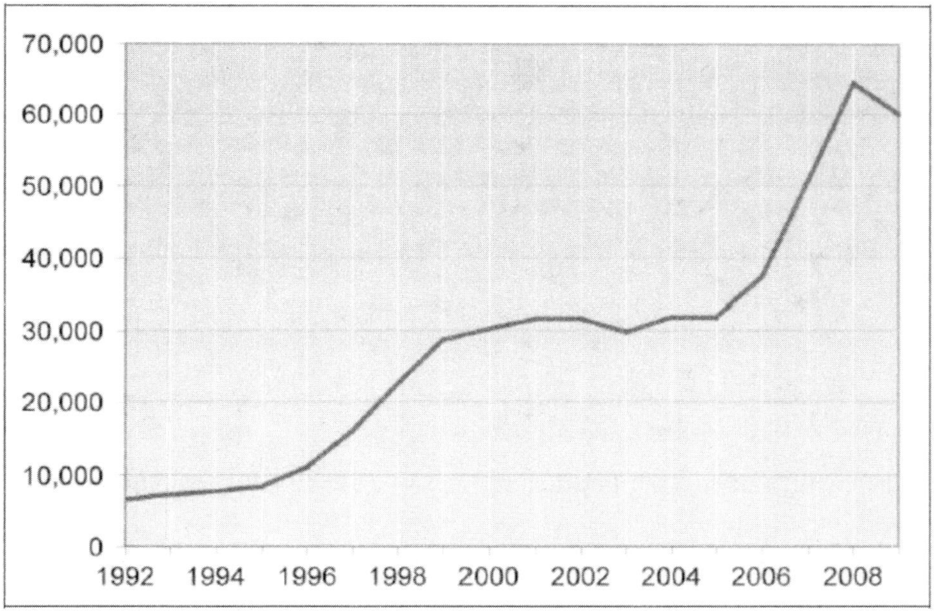

Source: Bruno, Congressional Research Service, Immigration: Policy Considerations Related to Guest Worker Programs (Mar. 16, 2010), figure 1.

Usage of the H–2A program was once heavily concentrated in the southeastern quadrant of the country, reflecting the fact that agriculture in the southwest and California relied much more on undocumented labor. Although southeastern states still lead in certifications requested and granted, H–2A usage is now more common throughout the nation. In FY 2009, the Department of Labor certified more than 5,000 jobs to be filled with H–2A workers in each of five southeastern states, North Carolina, Louisiana, Georgia, Florida, and Kentucky. But New York was next, with 4,300, while California and Arizona had over 3,400 farm jobs certified. *See* Office of Foreign Labor Certification, Department of Labor, The Foreign Labor Certification Report: 2009 Data, Trends and Highlights Across Programs and States, <http://www.foreignlaborcert.doleta.gov/pdf/2009_Annual_Report.pdf>.

To bring in H–2A agricultural workers, an employer must first file a labor certification application with the Department of Labor, to show that "(A) there are not sufficient workers who are able, willing and qualified, and who will be available at the time and place needed, to perform the [agricultural] labor or services involved in the petition, and (B) the employment of the alien in such labor or services will not adversely affect the wages and working conditions of workers in the United States similarly employed." INA § 218(a)(1). If the labor certification is granted, next the employer must have a petition approved by USCIS before the individual workers can obtain visas for entry.

As with labor certification for employment-based immigrant preferences, the employer must undertake recruitment efforts directed at U.S. workers that are governed in some detail by the statute and regulations. *See* INA § 218(b)(4), 20 C.F.R. §§ 655.150–655.158. The governing regulations, however, have recently changed dramatically—twice. The Bush administration firmly supported significant expansion of temporary worker programs. When broad legislation to this end failed in Congress, it turned to promoting this objective through rulemaking. The resulting new H–2A regulations were published in late 2008 (along with a new set for H–2B), and took effect three days before the inauguration of President Obama in 2009. 73 Fed. Reg. 77,110 (Dec. 18, 2008). They streamlined the labor certification process by reducing the prior submission of documentation to be reviewed by DOL officers, in favor of a system that would rely heavily on attestations by employers. Such attestations would be subject to later audit, and the Bush rules ratcheted up the consequences of a violation. The regulations also changed the long-standing formula for computing the "adverse effect wage rate" (AEWR) that farm employers must pay in the particular agricultural area where the work will take place—the primary mechanism used to implement INA § 218(a)(1)(B), quoted above.

The Obama Labor Department began within its first year to replace those rules. It concluded that the reliance on attestation had caused significant erosion in worker protections. Meantime, because H–2A applications fell in 2009, the streamlining was not successful in fostering use of H–2A. A return to greater oversight by DOL of labor certification resulted, in final rules that took effect in March 2010. DOL also determined that the methodology shift governing AEWRs had cost workers an average of one dollar per hour. The 2010 rules therefore restored the earlier approach. *See* 74 Fed. Reg. 45,906, 45,908, 45,911 (Sept. 4, 2009) (proposed rules) 75 Fed. Reg. 6,884 (Feb. 12, 2010) (final rules).

The Obama regulations, most of them codified in 20 C.F.R. Part 655, Subpart B, became the occasion as well to enhance other protections for workers, including through greater pre-employment disclosures, assured transportation reimbursement, better standards and monitoring for employer-provided housing, the provision of meals or convenient cooking facilities, workers compensation insurance, and a guarantee that the H–2A workers' employment will continue for at least three-quarters of the contract period. 20 C.F.R. § 655.122. There is no requirement to provide health insurance. DOL retained from the Bush rules a provision meant to provide incentives for source countries to cooperate in implementation of the program and more generally in accepting return of its nationals who are ordered removed: only the nationals of countries on a designated list would be eligible for H–2A visas. The list is updated annually—adding and subtracting based on prior cooperative experience. (The same list applies to H–2B workers as well. For FY 2011, 53 countries were on the list. *Identification of Foreign Countries Whose Nationals Are Eligible to Participate in the H–2A and H–2B Nonimmigrant Worker Programs*, 76 Fed. Reg. 2,915 (2011).)

DOL also used the 2010 rules to act on long-standing complaints from farmworker advocacy groups that the agency would insist on good terms and conditions of employment for imported foreign workers, but without vigilance to see that H–2A employers provide the same to domestic workers seeking a farm job. Some charged that this failure was a reason (or even a deliberate strategy by growers) for the low recruitment and retention of agricultural workers among the domestic workforce. The 2010 regulations impose far more detailed requirements for domestic recruitment than had the 2009 version, with most of the recruitment to occur before the employer files the labor certification application. *See* 20 C.F.R. §§ 655.150–655.158. DOL has also created a new electronic job registry to facilitate the job hunt by available workers. The regs basically require parity among comparable workers, foreign or domestic, on the terms and conditions of employment, generally including housing arrangements and transportation, plus pay at a rate at least equal to the AEWR rate. *See, e.g., id.* § 655.122(a), (d)(1). Employers must remain open to hiring U.S. workers until 50 percent of the contract period has passed. *Id.* § 655.150(b).

Rural Migration News reported reactions to the 2010 rules that followed predictable lines. Agricultural employers objected, while farmworker advocates were generally pleased. For example, "Sonoma County's Jeff Carlton, who hires foreign workers under the H–2A program, said 'by adding more layers of bureaucracy to the process, it will be tougher for us to find workers, because no one around here wants to do this work.' " But there were a few less predictable responses as the rules were under consideration: "Several Colorado growers reported that they were switching from H–2A to local workers. Bob Sakata of Sakata Farms said 'we decided in June [2009] to hire local people who were filling out job applications. We realized it would take more tender love and care, but we did it' for 200 workers. The Colorado Farm Bureau said that peach growers on the Western Slope 'seem to be hiring a lot of local people' in 2009 and 2010." *H–2A: Old Rules, Reactions, Cases,* Rural Migration News, April 2010, <http://migration.ucdavis.edu/rmn/more.php?id=1531_0_4_0>.

Although the 2010 rules generally provide greater worker protections than the earlier version, a wide range of farmworker organizations continue their support for a proposed bill, known as AgJOBS, which reflects a broad compromise between grower and worker organizations reached several years earlier. AgJOBS would move instead to a streamlined attestation-based system (clearly favored by agribusiness), particularly for jobs covered by collective bargaining agreements. *See* Bruno, *supra,* at 11–12. The bill gained support from the farmworker side not only because of the boost it could give to unionization, but also because it would open an avenue to LPR status for farmworkers. Under most versions of the bill that have appeared since 2007, those who work approximately 150 days in agriculture over a period of two years would gain an interim ("blue card") status. If they then perform specified amounts of agricultural labor over the next three to five years, they qualify for a green card. AgJOBS has been a fairly stable component in most versions of comprehensive immigration reform since 2007.

Why treat agriculture separately? Are the workforce needs for agricultural labor more pressing or different in some other way from needs that arise in other sectors of the U.S. economy? What else might explain the persistence of agricultural temporary worker programs as distinct from programs of more general application? And how would a large-scale temporary agricultural worker program affect U.S. farms and U.S. farmworkers? According to U.S. census data, 55% of those employed in farming (including forestry and fishing) are native-born, and because this percentage does not include naturalized citizens or lawful permanent residents, it understates the involvement of authorized workers in agriculture. *See* Martin, *Eight Myths About Immigration Enforcement,* 10 N.Y.U. J. Legis. & Pub. Pol'y 525, 539 (2007).

b. H–2B

The H–2B category is for temporary nonagricultural workers, and it is currently capped at 66,000 admissions per year. The governing definition has a double requirement of temporariness, as well as a requirement for a labor market test: H–2B is open to a noncitizen "who is coming *temporarily* to the United States to perform [nonagricultural] *temporary* service or labor if unemployed persons capable of performing such service or labor cannot be found in this country." INA § 101(a)(15)(B)(ii)(b) (emphasis added).

What makes service or labor temporary? In *Matter of Artee Corp.*, 18 I & N Dec. 366 (Comm'r 1982), the INS Commissioner ruled that "[i]t is not the nature or the duties of the position which must be examined to determine the temporary need. It is the nature of the need for the duties to be performed which determines the temporariness of the position." The regulation restates this requirement as a job "in which the petitioner's need for the duties to be performed by the employee(s) is temporary, whether or not the underlying job can be described as permanent or temporary." 8 C.F.R. § 214.2(h)(6)(ii).

Consider this case. A company had been providing highly skilled personnel to the nuclear power industry. For each of the past five years, it had successfully petitioned for nuclear start-up technicians to perform temporary services for nuclear power plants around the United States. The agency then denied a petition for thirty more technicians, citing the five-year history and the lack of evidence that the demand for the start-up technicians would be "non-recurring or infrequent." Upholding this denial in *Volt Technical Services Corp. v. INS*, 648 F.Supp. 578, 581 (S.D.N.Y. 1986), a federal district court rejected as "nonsensical" the idea that positions "are temporary merely because a single task or assignment is temporary."

How temporary must a temporary job be? New DHS regulations promulgated in 2008 (which, like the H–2A rules, took effect just before Inauguration Day in 2009) rephrased the traditional test somewhat. The new regs state that the "employer must establish that the need for the employee will end in the near, definable future." Generally that period "will be limited to one year or less, but in the case of a one-time event could last up to 3 years." 8 C.F.R. § 214.2(h)(6)(ii)(B). Also, the need must be "a one-time occurrence, a seasonal need, a peak load need, or an intermittent need." *Id.* These rules make it very difficult to use the H–2B category for certain types of workers—nannies, for example. More generally, note the tension between the statutory demands that the job be temporary and that there be no U.S. workers available to perform it: "By demonstrating this unavailability, * * * the employer has also demonstrated some very good reasons why the need for such workers might persist and why the real intentions of the employer are permanent employment of alien workers." A. Fragomen, Jr., A. Del Rey, Jr., & S. Bernsen, Immigration Law and Business, § 2:65 (2007).

Processing of H–2B applications follows what should now be a familiar three-step pattern applicable to admissions in categories that require a labor market test. The employer must first secure labor certification from DOL and then win approval of a visa petition filed with USCIS. Thereafter the worker obtains the visa at a U.S. consulate (though in some circumstances, the worker can gain the status while already in the United States).

The rules adopted in late 2008 changed the DOL framework that had prevailed for many years to a streamlined labor certification process that primarily relies on employer attestations. 73 Fed. Reg. 78,020 (Dec. 19, 2008). The 2008 rules, in keeping with the Bush administration's support for wider use of guest workers, expanded the possible period of work. H–2B nonimmigrants are generally admitted for up to one year at first, but they can continue working, for the same or a different employer, for up to three years in the United States. Those rules also reduced the length of time that a worker who had reached the limit would have to spend outside the United States in order to resume qualification (90 days for someone who had three years' work, lower requirements for shorter work records). See 8 C.F.R. § 214.2(h)(9)(iii)(B), 214.2(h)(15)(ii)(C). In March 2011, DOL formally proposed new rules that would undo many of the Bush administration's H–2B changes. Primarily, they would reduce the role of attestation and require greater advance submission of documentation regarding recruiting on the part of petitioning employers. As proposed, the rules would also move the date of the employer's labor market tests closer to the date of need, and would extend H–2B program protections and benefits to U.S. workers of the employer engaged in the same field. 76 Fed. Reg. 15,130 (Mar. 18, 2011). At press time, no final rule had been published, and the Bush administration's H–2B regulations remained in place.

In FY 2009, the occupations for which DOL approved the most H–2B labor certifications were landscaping laborers (which alone accounted for 31 percent of positions certified), forestry workers, cleaners, amusement park workers, housekeepers, and construction workers. See Office of Foreign Labor Certification, 2009 Report, supra, at 32–35. DOL certifications slipped by 38 percent in 2009, a reflection of the recession, but still totaled over 154,000. Still, only a minority of certified positions gets filled with H–2B workers, because the program is limited by statute to 66,000 per fiscal year, with this cap split into equal shares for each half of the fiscal year. See INA §§ 214(g)(1)(B), (g)(2), (g)(10). (A limited range of H–2B admissions do not count against the cap.) Moreover, USCIS visa petition filings typically run well below the total of DOL H–2B certifications, because employers can understandably change their plans as they near the start time for employing the temporary worker—especially in difficult economic times.

Figure 5.5 shows H–2B admissions over the past two decades. The surge in admissions for 2005–2007 reflected special provisions in the Save Our Small and Seasonal Business Act (SOSSBA) of 2005, Pub. L. No. 109–13, 119 Stat. 318 (2005), that exempted returning H–2B workers from the cap. Congress chose not to renew that provision beyond 2007.

Figure 5.5
H–2B Visas Issued, FY1992–FY2009

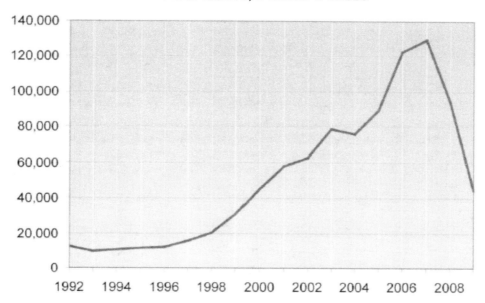

Source: Bruno, Congressional Research Service, Immigration: Policy Considerations Related to Guest Worker Programs (Mar. 16, 2010), figure 2.

c. The Guest Worker Debate

The desirability and the contours of any temporary worker program—in agriculture or in other sectors of the U.S. economy—have been hotly debated in this generation as they have been in earlier times. Several themes are perennially at the core of the legislative and public discussion. First, is there truly a shortage of U.S. workers in any given sector of the economy? Second, even assuming that the economic need exists, a further question is whether a temporary worker program is preferable to the alternatives, which include generating a pool of U.S. workers (through various means including allowing wages to rise), restructuring the relevant economic sector of to be less reliant on labor, and relocating some or all of that sector's activities outside the United States where a labor force may be more readily available.

Speaking directly to farm labor, the Commission on Immigration Reform chaired by former Congresswoman Barbara Jordan addressed both of these issues when it "unanimously and strongly agree[d]" that a guest worker program "would be a grievous mistake." U.S. Commission on Immigration Reform, Legal Immigration: Setting Priorities 172 (1995). First, the Commission expressed skepticism that farm labor is in short supply, and then it made a more fundamental point:

> Even if labor shortages develop, the Commission would be cautious about recommendations for a guestworker program to address them. Guestworker programs effectively expand rural poverty. Moreover, guestworker programs are predicated on limitations on the freedom of

those who are invited to enter and work. Experience has shown that such limitations are incompatible with the values of democratic societies worldwide. For that very reason, "temporary" guestworkers tend to become permanent residents, *de facto* or even *de jure*. We cannot ignore the inconsistency between the stated intent of guestworker programs and their actual consequences.

Id. at 173.

In the years after the Jordan Commission report, however, high-level interest in new measures for agricultural workers—and for other temporary workers—steadily increased, until provisions to that end became a standard part of most comprehensive immigration reform proposals during the first decade of the 21st century. In January 2004, President George W. Bush proposed, as the centerpiece of his initial immigration reform plans, a very broad guest worker program, apparently usable in any employment field, but only after a labor market test involving domestic recruitment conducted by the employer. His initial plans would have permitted employees to bring their families, and to receive stays that could be extended up to six years. The Senate passed a bill in 2006 that followed this basic framework (but the House did not agree). S. 2611, 109th Cong., 2d Sess. (2006). After another year of difficult and controversy-laden congressional deliberation, the leading proposal became the Kennedy–McCain bill of 2007, which narrowly failed in the Senate that year. S. 1639, 110th Cong., 1st Sess. (2007). That bill embodied far more stringent provisions, reflecting lawmakers' concerns that guest workers would not remain truly temporary workers under the terms President Bush had envisioned. S. 1639 allowed shorter stays extendable only up to two years before a required period of one year outside the United States. And it greatly tightened the conditions under which spouses and children could join the principal worker—even then, for only a part of the maximum permitted stay.

The following readings provide additional insight into the economic, social, and philosophical dimensions of this debate for and against guest worker programs. The clash of views on these issues to some extent underlies the pendulum swing on the H–2A and H–2B regulations from 2008 to 2011, and it will also revive in earnest whenever Congress re-engages on immigration reform. We begin with readings largely supportive of temporary worker programs, then look at arguments on the other side.

JORGE DURAND AND DOUGLAS S. MASSEY, BORDERLINE SANITY

The American Prospect, Sept. 24, 2001, at 28.

* * * [I]mmigration from Mexico * * * is going to continue. We are talking, after all, about two countries with more than just a 2,000–mile border in common. * * * [B]ilateral trade has grown to $200 billion per year, and the border is now marked by a string of rapidly growing twin cities and a booming manufacturing sector. The two nations also share a

60–year history of uninterrupted migration. The Mexican-born population of the United States now stands at eight million. * * *.

But if the international flow of workers is inevitable, other empirical data suggest how it might be better managed. Our own research, for instance, which involved interviews with close to 5,000 immigrants over the last 15 years, shows that when migrants first enter a developed country, most are not motivated, as Americans tend to imagine, by a desire to live where they can maximize earnings. In reality, most migrants move in an attempt to solve economic problems at home. They are leaving countries with inadequate capital, credit, and mortgage markets—countries also without unemployment insurance, crop insurance, futures markets, and other protections against sudden losses of family income. Initially, most migrants seek to work abroad only temporarily, and mainly in order to diversify family-income risks, to accumulate cash unavailable at home (most often so they can build a house), or to finance a small business or a consumer purchase (such as a car).

In other words, international migration is often less influenced by conditions in labor markets than conditions in other kinds of markets. So U.S. policies, which to date have chiefly aimed to make the American labor market less attractive to Mexican migrants, have been of little use. Programs designed to improve the performance and accessibility of a sending country's credit and insurance markets are far more likely to affect migration decisions. * * *

Our first proposal is to [increase substantially] * * * the U.S. immigration quota for Mexico. * * * But our research shows that not all immigrants do want to move here permanently. To a great extent, Mexicans seek permanent-resident visas because that is the only door open to them. If another option were available—such as a temporary-worker program—more people would opt for it. Indeed, an enlightened policy, rather than making it difficult for migrants to come and go, would support their evident desire to return home by granting them temporary-work visas that allow them to enter, leave, live, and work in the United States without restriction for a period of, say, two years. We propose such visas as the mainstay of U.S.–Mexican immigration management. They would be renewable once in the lifetime of the migrant, but only after the worker returned home for at least a year. A binational agency managed by the U.S. and Mexican governments, to which aspiring migrants would apply directly, would distribute the temporary-worker visas, thus getting employers out of the corruption-prone business of labor recruitment. And if these visas were generously available, they would go a long way toward reducing undocumented migration and the ills that accompany it.

In order to guarantee labor rights, these visas would not be tied to specific employers or jobs but issued directly to the migrants themselves. Whenever a work visa is tied to a particular job, as in the current guest-worker program, the migrant is left vulnerable to exploitation, unable to exercise the most fundamental right a worker can have: the right to withhold his or her labor. Granting migrants the right to change jobs would free them to participate in unions and to report violations of their labor rights. It would also make it more difficult for unscrupulous employers to use immigrants to lower the wages of native workers or cut corners on ensuring their health and safety.

If something on the order of 300,000 two-year visas were issued annually, the temporary migrants working in the United States at any time would constitute only a small share of the U.S. workforce but a large fraction of those who presently migrate with permanent visas they don't really want or with no papers at all. What's more, we have historical evidence of the efficacy of such programs. In the 1950s, the United States issued 450,000 temporary visas annually to Mexicans [as part of the Bracero program]—and reduced undocumented migration to near zero.

* * * [A substantial portion of the funds raised through special fees for these visas] should be used to facilitate the improvement of markets and the social infrastructure in Mexico. The integration of Spain and Portugal into the European Union offers a successful model. During the 1960s and 1970s, hundreds of thousands of emigrants left those two nations for work in the wealthier countries of northern Europe (particularly Germany), and northern officials worried that admitting Spain and Portugal into the European labor market would unleash even larger waves of emigration. But in preparation for their integration into the union, EU members invested substantial funds in Spain and Portugal. Transportation, communication, banking, and social-welfare networks were all upgraded. As a result, when unification finally occurred, in 1986, there was no rise in emigration. On the contrary, Spain and Portugal immediately began to experience large net return migrations, despite the fact that per capita income in both countries was (and still is) well below that in Germany.

* * * Immigrant flows do not last forever. Historical data indicate that most European nations in the course of economic development underwent an "emigration transition" from low-to high-to low-emigration rates. In Europe this process took eight or nine decades, but recent experience suggests that the transition time is now considerably shorter. Take South Korea. In 1965 it ranked among the world's poorest nations; by 1998 it was one of the wealthy industrialized nations. In the interim, some 780,000 Koreans emigrated to the United States. Yet by the end of South Korea's transition, gross emigration was only 13,000 a year and net migration was near zero. The goal of U.S. policy should be to help Mexico move as quickly as possible through its own emigration transition and assume its place as a full and equal partner in the North American market. * * *

DANIEL T. GRISWOLD, WILLING WORKERS: FIXING THE PROBLEM OF ILLEGAL MEXICAN MIGRATION TO THE UNITED STATES

Cato Institute, Center for Trade Policy Studies, Trade Policy
Analysis No. 19 (Oct. 15, 2002), at 2, 19–22.

America's immigration laws are colliding with reality, and reality is winning. Today an estimated eight million or more people live in the United States without legal documents, and each year the number grows by an estimated 250,000 as more enter illegally or overstay their visas. More than half of the illegal immigrants entering and already here come from Mexico. * * *

The realities of the North American labor market demand a system of legal, regulated migration to and from Mexico that conforms to how millions of people on both sides of the border "actually arrange their lives." A reformed immigration system must create a legal channel through which Mexican nationals can enter and remain in the United States for a definite time to work.

A reformed system must accomplish three broad goals: creating a legal channel for future workers to enter the United States, granting legal status for workers already here, and sharply reducing illegal immigration.

Temporary Worker Visas

A temporary work visa (TWV) should be created that would allow Mexican nationals to remain in the United States to work for a limited period. The visa could authorize work for a definite period, perhaps three years, and would be renewable for an additional limited period; would allow unlimited multiple entries for as long as the visa was valid; would allow complete mobility between employers and sectors of the U.S. economy; and would entitle the holder to "national treatment."

Mobility is essential so that workers can exercise full freedom to change jobs to realize maximum pay and working conditions, under the theory that a worker's best protection against below-market pay and working conditions is the ability to leave for a better offer. On an economy-wide scale, full mobility would allow the supply of labor to shift between sectors to meet changing demand. The visa must also confer on the immigrant worker national treatment, that is, the same legal protections extended by law to native workers. That would ensure that temporary workers do not enjoy any unfair legal advantage or suffer any legal disadvantage compared to other workers.

Mobility and national treatment will protect immigrant workers from the real and perceived abuses of past "guest worker" programs that tied workers to specified employers. The fatal flaw of the *Bracero* program and other proposed "guest-worker" programs is that they tie workers to specific employers and industries, making visa holders overly dependent on the good will of their employers. The best model for the TWV is not the current H2–A or H2–B visas, which tie workers to certain employers, but the standard employment authorization document[, which] * * * allows full mobility among employers and sectors. * * *

The number of visas issued should be sufficient to meet demand in the U.S. labor market. Using the current estimated net inflow of undocumented workers, 300,000 visas per year would be a reasonable starting point. Distribution of visas could be rationed through a one-time application fee. The fee should be set high enough to offset costs and regulate demand, but low enough to undercut smugglers, perhaps in the range of $1,000. If a black market in smuggling reappeared or persisted, that would signal that the number of legal visas should be increased or the fee lowered. * * *

"Earned Adjustment" for Honest Work

A program should be created to allow undocumented workers already in the United States to earn legal status based on years of work and other productive behavior. Undocumented workers already in the United States should be issued TWVs immediately provided they register with the government and do not pose a threat to our internal or national security. Those who have lived and worked in the United States for more than a certain period should be eligible to apply for permanent residence status and, ultimately, citizenship. * * *

Work and (Nuclear) Family

As a compromise for those concerned about future migration, the ability of temporary workers to sponsor relatives could be curtailed. Workers with TWVs should be able to sponsor their spouses and minor children to enter the country temporarily while the TWV is still valid. Keeping families together is not only just and humane; it also encourages more responsible social behavior. But those objectives would not require that temporary workers be allowed to sponsor relatives outside their nuclear family, such as siblings, parents, and adult children. With modern communications and transportation available, it is easier for immigrants to keep in touch and visit their extended families in the home country. The multiple-entry nature of the TWV would allow immigrants to easily visit their extended families back in their home country.

Start with Mexico

For practical reasons, any legalization program should start with Mexican migrants. By virtue of its location and the number of its workers already in the United States, Mexico is far and away the most important source country for immigration. * * * Our long land border with Mexico and the increasing cross-border commercial traffic stimulated by the NAFTA argue for a comprehensive agreement to legalize what is already a largely integrated North American labor market.

* * *A legalized system of Mexican migration would, in one stroke, bring a huge underground market into the open. It would allow American

producers in important sectors of our economy to hire the workers they need to grow. It would raise wages and working conditions for millions of low-skilled workers and spur investment in human capital. * * *

NOTES AND QUESTIONS ON ARGUMENTS SUPPORTING GUEST WORKER PROGRAMS

1. Howard Chang also supports guest-worker programs, as a second-best policy in light of political constraints. (Best, in his view, would be elimination or drastic reduction of barriers to free movement of labor.) He comments: "Through guest-worker programs, natives enjoy the benefits of unskilled alien workers in the labor market but do not bear the fiscal burden of providing the full set of public benefits that these workers would receive if they had ready access to permanent residence and ultimately citizenship." Chang, *Liberal Ideals and Political Feasibility: Guest–Worker Programs as Second–Best Policies*, 27 N.C.J. Int'l L. & Commercial Reg. 465, 466 (2002).

2. Eleanor Brown argues that guest worker programs could be far better managed, in ways that would greatly improve the workers' compliance with the temporary terms of their visas, if we would move away from "the dominant uninational conceptualization of immigration law" toward a greater use of binational cooperation treaties. Based on field research, she describes in detail a binational program for importing temporary workers from Jamaica to Canada, explaining why that program enjoys a far higher compliance rate than do comparable (and largely unilateral) programs bringing temporary workers from Jamaica to the United States. She summarizes the reasons, pointing to an information screening component, a legal compliance component, and a collective sanctions component:

> The information screening component argues that persons who are proximate to visa applicants may be incentivized to share with officials inside information as to which persons are likely to be law-abiding short-term guests. The legal compliance component contends that, among the subjects of this study, visa compliance is dominant even when they leave their home countries because their communal norms prioritize visa compliance, and they lose status in their communities if they deviate from these norms. The collective sanctions component contends that astute officials utilize group accountability rules to send signals to community members about the costs associated with breaking immigration laws, which incentivize them to enforce these norms.
>
> * * * [A] central role[is] played by the community screener [in the community of origin of the workers]. She functions as an "intermediary in trust" who stands to lose her primary currency, namely, the credibility of her advice, if those who she recommends abscond. Building on Richard McAdams's esteem-based model and Eric Posner's signaling model of norms promulgation, * * * there is a persuasive case that governmental policy can amplify visa-compliance norms in the communities from which guest workers originate [through the stigmatization of visa violators].

Brown, *Outsourcing Immigration Compliance*, 77 Fordham L.Rev. 2475, 2482 (2009).

Brown describes further advantages of the binational model:

> [S]ource-labor countries are also well-placed to aid in sanctioning noncompliant aliens, even when those aliens are already on American soil, through their influence on communities from which aliens originate. Thus, the United States also stands to benefit from partially outsourcing the sanctioning function. Can the United States expect other countries to reliably meet their screening and sanctioning commitments? This Article argues that the answer is yes. In a competitive globalized context in which developing countries prize the access that their nationals have to the American labor market, the repeated game-like nature of their interactions with the United States increases the likelihood that source-labor countries will actually meet their commitments and will incentivize their nationals to do the same.

Id. at 2481.

3. The apparent acceptance of a guest worker plan in the 2006–2007 debates by certain labor and Latino interest groups came as something of a surprise. They had historically opposed such plans, in part because of the problematic history of the most prominent of earlier large-scale guest worker programs, the bracero program, in effect from 1942 to 1964. One explanation of the changed position was offered by Janet Murguia, president of the National Council of La Raza, in 2007:

> Many Latinos still have searing memories of the infamous bracero program, which more than 50 years ago became synonymous with worker abuse. * * * [Such guest-worker programs risk creating] a permanent, sizable subclass of workers who endure harsh treatment while simultaneously undercutting their American co-workers.

> Despite these concerns, * * * my organization and many Latino leaders find ourselves in the interesting position of being principal advocates for a significant new worker visa program as part of comprehensive immigration reform. * * * [We believe that this proposal will] do what previous reforms did not: Acknowledge that there will continue to be a flow across the border and that we will do everything we can to control and regulate it. * * *

> The immigration reform bill the Senate passed last year contains a much different model of a worker visa program than the unjust model we have lived with for decades. Workers would not be at the mercy of abusive employers in that they could change jobs and alert the authorities to mistreatment. Rather than becoming a permanent second-class workforce, they would have the opportunity to earn a path to permanent status—and ultimately citizenship—as one of the only classes of migrants able to petition for themselves rather than relying on an employer or relative to petition for them. There are important labor protections for immigrant workers as well as for their American co-workers, including a requirement that immigrant workers be paid the prevailing wage in an industry to avoid undercutting the wages of American workers employed there. * * *

Murguia, *A Change of Heart on Guest Workers*, Wash. Post, Feb. 11, 2007, at B7.

4. How effective are the labor protections Murguia and some of the other authors highlight? What enforcement measures do they require? More broadly, how much does her support and that provided by the other authors above depend on the assumption that enforcement of immigration limits is impossible? If that assumption is true, why would the contemplated labor-law enforcement be expected to work in the face of the same economic pressures for low-wage labor? Conversely, if labor-law enforcement could work (presumably with greater resources and better institutional design), why couldn't a more amply resourced enforcement regime against future illegal migration or against the hiring of future unauthorized migrants be expected to work, so that there would not necessarily continue to be a significant flow across the border?

The readings that follow offer diverse critical perspectives on guest worker programs.

PHILIP L. MARTIN AND MICHAEL S. TEITELBAUM, THE MIRAGE OF MEXICAN GUEST WORKERS
80 Foreign Affairs 117–21 (2001).

* * * The theoretical benefits of temporary labor programs have seduced politicians in many countries, just as they are now enticing the Fox and Bush administrations. Many U.S. and Mexican proponents seem surprisingly unaware, however, of the long and checkered history of such policies, and quite innocent of the unwanted effects they have produced in both origin and destination countries. The negotiators are advancing the discussions and making decisions with a dangerously myopic perspective on their consequences.

U.S. and Mexican advocates promote temporary worker programs as a "win-win" game. According to their arguments, U.S. employers would benefit from a guest worker program because they would obtain legal access to workers who would accept low wages and be unlikely to unionize. At the same time, the temporary Mexican workers would win jobs at wages far higher than those available at home. * * * [Many] assume they could design a guest worker program to make the Mexican workers "temporary" and "returnable," ineligible for social services, and unable to gain citizenship. For their part, Mexico's politicians hope to gain votes by providing a new source of jobs to the country's underemployed work force. In addition, the government hopes to gain economic benefits from the extra dollars their workers send back home, and to increase its political leverage in the United States.

The only problem with this "win-win" scenario is that it will not work. Bush's proposal ignores the fact that virtually no low-wage "temporary worker'' program in a high-wage liberal democracy has ever turned out to be genuinely temporary. On the contrary, most initially small (and often "emergency") temporary worker programs have grown much larger, and lasted far longer, than originally promised.

This tendency toward permanence is easily explained—guest worker programs are virtual recipes for mutual dependence between employers and the migrants who work for them. Employers naturally grow to depend on the supply of low-wage and compliant labor, relaxing their domestic recruitment efforts and adjusting their production methods to take advantage of the cheap labor. History has shown that in agriculture (where many Mexican guest workers would be employed), a pool of cheap workers gives farm owners strong incentives to expand the planting of labor-intensive crops rather than invest in mechanized labor-saving equipment and the crops suitable for it. Thus, although the labor supply is supposed to be available only temporarily, farmers adapt in ways that ensure their continued need for workers willing to accept such low wages. On the other side of the coin, those bargain wages for employers are a boon for the "temporary" workers, who earn much more than they could at home. For instance, laborers in U.S. fruit and vegetable agriculture make between $5 and $7 an hour, as opposed to 50 cents an hour in Mexico. Past guest worker programs have shown that the participants and their families grow accustomed to the increased income; they therefore have no incentive to return home unless rapid economic and job growth there creates commensurate opportunities. As the workers' "temporary" sojourns extend over time, the odds of their ever returning to their homeland diminish, and young people in the home country come to regard employment abroad as normal.

Meanwhile, the promised "win-win" outcomes for politicians have often turned out to be as illusory as the temporary nature of the work. For the countries that send their surplus labor abroad, the eagerly awaited worker remittances bring decidedly mixed economic blessings: the country receives needed capital, some of which is productively invested, but the influx of cash drives up real estate prices, stimulates conspicuous consumption of imported goods, and is unevenly distributed. The remittances also tend to decline over time, unless the number of new emigrants continues to grow. So the source country earns capital temporarily but loses many emigrant workers permanently. To make matters worse, the anticipated enhancement of political influence in the destination country has proved disappointing and often double-edged. * * *

For the host country, the permanent settlement of guest workers also tends to require greater spending on social services than the government initially anticipated. Many workers find ways to bring their families to join them, creating a large pool of poorly paid and often undereducated people. They, along with any children born in the host country, require government-financed services such as public education and health care. In the United States specifically, the settlement of millions of Mexicans would increase the numbers of U.S. residents who lack health insurance and rely on publicly financed clinics and other safety nets. Finally, political leaders have often belatedly discovered that admitting temporary low-wage workers unnaturally sustains industries with low productivity and wages, such as garment manufacturing, labor-intensive agriculture, and domestic services. In consequence, the economy's overall productivity and growth suffer. * * *

CRISTINA M. RODRÍGUEZ, GUEST WORKERS AND INTEGRATION: TOWARD A THEORY OF WHAT IMMIGRANTS AND AMERICANS OWE ONE ANOTHER

2007 U.Chi.Legal Forum 219, 219–24.

The presence of over eleven million unauthorized immigrants in the United States has generated a wide-ranging and charged debate in recent years over the need to overhaul our immigration laws. Among the suggested reforms, the most novel (for the United States) and controversial has been the proposal that we adopt a large-scale temporary worker program to address current labor needs and channel future flows of unskilled migrants, who come primarily from Mexico and Latin America. * * * A guest worker program has become the measure favored by those who eschew enforcement-only strategies in favor of reform that accommodates the market realities that have generated the unauthorized population. * * *

This need to devise a solution to the problem of unauthorized migration, that recognizes the limitations of enforcement-only strategies in an integrated hemisphere, is urgent. Unsurprisingly, powerful interest groups and public officials in both the United States and Mexico support a temporary worker program. Such a program seemingly would suit the labor market needs of the U.S., satisfying domestic employers and consumers, and the development needs of Mexico, which depends heavily on remittances from abroad. In addition, the regularization of cross-border traffic appeals to our humanitarian impulses by providing a legal avenue of migration for those who otherwise are willing to risk their lives by crossing the Arizona or Texas deserts illegally. * * * [I]t is easy to see why diverse parties on both sides of the U.S.–Mexico border support a policy that facilitates temporary or cyclical migration.

Despite the idea's appeal, however, * * * we should resist the temptation to adopt a large-scale guest worker program, because such a program is likely to fail on two interrelated counts: It will fail to achieve the short-term objectives supporters claim for it, and it will thwart what should be the long-term goals of our immigration policy. On the first count, the implicit promise of the guest worker program is that it will satisfy the United States' labor needs while reducing illegal immigration, thus restoring the rule of law to the system and enabling the government to better track immigrants to the U.S. As studies of guest worker programs consistently reveal, however, though a guest worker program may address labor market demands, it will do so at the risk of compounding the illegal immigration problem and perpetuating the poor treatment of migrant workers.

But second, and more importantly, though a guest worker program may satisfy many short-term interests, in the long term it will compromise our ability to integrate immigrants effectively into the American body politic, in large part precisely because it will fail to prevent the emergence of a new undocumented population. This insight has not been clearly articulated in the debate over the guest worker idea, but it should be central to the discussion. Important participants in the current immigration debate have emphasized that the United States can no longer do without a meaningful integration policy to complement our immigration control measures. But whether the U.S. should adopt a separate integration policy or not, it is critical that the system of immigrant admissions and controls itself reflects integrationist aspirations. Proposed reforms should be judged in part by whether they will facilitate the incorporation of immigrants and their descendants into American social and civic life. * * *

Temporary worker programs ultimately thwart this incorporation objective, because they erect undesirable and otherwise avoidable obstacles to the integration process by constraining the two key mechanisms of immigrant integration: mobility and reciprocity. Incorporation depends on immigrants having mobility—the ability to move freely among society's various sectors as well as in and out of ethnic communities. Receiving societies logically and rightly expect immigrants to adapt to their new surroundings, but immigrants cannot make good on that obligation without mobility. This mobility depends on immigrants' ability to emerge from immigrant sectors of the economy and to develop the social and cultural capital necessary for interacting with people and institutions at large—both of which depend on the security of what I call the right to remain, or the security of a continued presence in the U.S. that guest worker programs do not provide.

Incorporation also depends on extant members of the receiving society displaying a reciprocal willingness to adapt to the presence of immigrant communities. A society's failure to adapt blocks immigrant assimilation by preventing immigrants from becoming part of important social institutions and community relations. The failure to treat immigrants as potential members also reflects an absence of the spirit of social cooperation that should characterize a democratic society. * * *

Guest worker programs ultimately fail to encourage either mobility or reciprocity. They impose bureaucratic requirements that constrain immigrant mobility in the economy and therefore in society at large. Indeed, guest worker programs historically have compounded immigrant isolation and resulted in serious exploitation, both in the U.S. and in other societies. These restraints are exacerbated by the uncertainty guest workers experience regarding their long-term prospects in the United States. What is more, by treating the immigrant as a temporary fix for the domestic economy's current labor needs, guest worker programs encourage the receiving society to treat immigrants as mere means to an end rather than as potentially permanent members of their communities. The treatment of the immigrant as a temporary guest contributes to a climate of inflexibility and intolerance *vis-à-vis* the cultural pluralism immigrants inevitably generate—a belief that immigrants should be temporary and should not change the "character" of our communities. Temporary worker programs thus give the receiving society no incentive to adapt to demographic changes or to incorporate immigrants into mainstream institutions. The United States' relative success at assimilating large groups of immigrants over time has depended on our willingness to treat immigrants as potentially permanent members of our society, but current guest worker proposals attempt to address a large demographic phenomenon without calling upon that willingness.* * *

* * * The United States' adoption of a large-scale guest worker program in response to the current crisis of undocumented immigration would signal an important and risky shift in our conceptualization of immigration—from an immigration policy designed to create permanent members to a policy dependent on temporary and ad hoc solutions to inescapable problems. This paradigm shift may be satisfying in the short-term to immigrants and employers, but it represents a troubling turn for a democratic society based on principles of social cooperation. * * *

MICHAEL WALZER, SPHERES OF JUSTICE: A DEFENSE OF PLURALISM AND EQUALITY

Pp. 52–53, 56–61 (1983).*

* * * One might insist, as I shall ultimately do, that the same standards apply to naturalization as to immigration, that every immigrant and every resident is a citizen, too—or, at least, a potential citizen. That is why territorial admission is so serious a matter. The members must be prepared to accept, as their own equals in a world of shared obligations, the men and women they admit; the immigrants must be prepared to share the obligations. But things can be differently arranged. Often the state controls naturalization strictly, immigration only loosely. Immigrants become resident aliens and, except by special dispensation, nothing more. Why are they admitted? To free the citizens from hard and unpleasant work. Then the state is like a family with live-in servants.

That is not an attractive image, for a family with live-in servants is—inevitably, I think—a little tyranny. * * *

Live-in servants have not disappeared from the modern world. As "guest workers" they play an important role in its most advanced economies.

---

* Copyright © 1984 Michael Walzer. Reprinted by permission of Basic Books, a member of the Perseus Books Group.

* * * Consider, then, a country like Switzerland or Sweden or West Germany, a capitalist democracy and welfare state, with strong trade unions and a fairly affluent population. The managers of the economy find it increasingly difficult to attract workers to a set of jobs that have come to be regarded as exhausting, dangerous, and degrading. But these jobs are also socially necessary; someone must be found to do them. Domestically, there are only two alternatives, neither of them palatable. The constraints imposed on the labor market by the unions and the welfare state might be broken, and then the most vulnerable segment of the local working class driven to accept jobs hitherto thought undesirable. But this would require a difficult and dangerous political campaign. Or, the wages and working conditions of the undesirable jobs might be dramatically improved so as to attract workers even within the constraints of the local market. But this would raise costs throughout the economy and, what is probably more important, challenge the existing social hierarchy. Rather than adopt either of these drastic measures, the economic managers, with the help of their government, shift the jobs from the domestic to the international labor market, making them available to workers in poorer countries who find them less undesirable. The government opens recruiting offices in a number of economically backward countries and draws up regulations to govern the admission of guest workers.

It is crucial that the workers who are admitted should be "guests," not immigrants seeking a new home and a new citizenship. For if the workers came as future citizens, they would join the domestic labor force, temporarily occupying its lower ranks, but benefiting from its unions and welfare programs and in time reproducing the original dilemma. Moreover, as they advanced, they would come into direct competition with local workers, some of whom they would outdo. Hence the regulations that govern their admission are designed to bar them from the protection of citizenship. They are brought in for a fixed time period, on contract to a particular employer; if they lose their jobs, they have to leave; they have to leave in any case when their visas expire. They are either prevented or discouraged from bringing dependents along with them, and they are housed in barracks, segregated by sex, on the outskirts of the cities where they work. Mostly they are young men or women in their twenties or thirties; finished with education, not yet infirm, they are a minor drain on local welfare services (unemployment insurance is not available to them since they are not permitted to be unemployed in the countries to which they have come). Neither citizens nor potential citizens, they have no political rights. The civil liberties of speech, assembly, association—otherwise strongly defended—are commonly denied to them, sometimes explicitly by state officials, sometimes implicitly by the threat of dismissal and deportation. * * *

Their existence is harsh and their wages low by European standards, less so by their own standards. What is most difficult is their homelessness: they work long and hard in a foreign country where they are not encouraged to settle down, where they are always strangers. For those workers who come alone, life in the great European cities is like a self-imposed prison term. They are deprived of normal social, sexual, and cultural activities (of political activity, too, if that is possible in their home country) for a fixed period of time. During that time, they live narrowly, saving money and sending it home. Money is the only return that the host countries make to their guests; and though much of it is exported rather than spent locally, the workers are still very cheaply had. The costs of raising and educating them where they work, and of paying them what the domestic labor market requires, would be much higher than the amounts remitted to their home countries. So the relation of guests and hosts seems to be a bargain all around: for the harshness of the working days and years is temporary, and the money sent home counts there in a way it could never count in a European city.

But what are we to make of the host country as a political community? Defenders of the guest-worker system claim that the country is now a neighborhood economically, but politically still a club or a family. As a place to live, it is open to anyone who can find work; as a forum or assembly, as a nation or a people, it is closed except to those who meet the requirements set by the present members. The system is a perfect synthesis of labor mobility and patriotic solidarity. But this account somehow misses what is actually going on. The state-as-neighborhood, an "indifferent" association governed only by the laws of the market, and the state-as-club-or-family, with authority relations and police, do not simply coexist, like two distinct moments in historical or abstract time. The market for guest workers, while free from the particular political constraints of the domestic labor market, is not free from all political constraints. State power plays a crucial role in its creation and then in the enforcement of its rules. Without the denial of political rights and civil liberties and the ever present threat of deportation, the system would not work. Hence guest workers can't be described merely in terms of their mobility, as men and women free to come and go. While they are guests, they are also subjects. They are ruled, like the Athenian metics, by a band of citizen-tyrants.

But don't they agree to be ruled? Isn't the contractualist argument effective here, with men and women who actually come in on contracts and stay only for so many months or years? Certainly they come knowing roughly what to expect, and they often come back knowing exactly what to expect. But this kind of consent, given at a single moment in time, while it is sufficient to legitimize market transactions, is not sufficient for democratic politics. Political power is precisely the ability to make decisions over periods of time, to change the rules, to cope with emergencies; it can't be exercised democratically without the ongoing consent of its subjects. And its subjects include every man and woman who lives within the territory over which those decisions are enforced. * * *

These guests experience the state as a pervasive and frightening power that shapes their lives and regulates their every move—and never asks for their opinion. Departure is only a formal option; deportation, a continuous practical threat. As a group, they constitute a disenfranchised class. They are typically an exploited or oppressed class as well, and they are exploited or oppressed at least in part because they are disenfranchised, incapable of organizing effectively for self-defense. Their material condition is unlikely to be improved except by altering their political status. Indeed, the purpose of their status is to prevent them from improving their condition; for if they could do that, they would soon be like domestic workers, unwilling to take on hard and degrading work or accept low rates of pay. * * *

The relevant principle here is not mutual aid but political justice. The guests don't need citizenship—at least not in the same sense in which they might be said to need their jobs. Nor are they injured, helpless, destitute; they are able-bodied and earning money. Nor are they standing, even figuratively, by the side of the road; they are living among the citizens. They do socially necessary work, and they are deeply enmeshed in the legal system of the country to which they have come. Participants in economy and law, they ought to be able to regard themselves as potential or future participants in politics as well. And they must be possessed of those basic civil liberties whose exercise is so much preparation for voting and office holding. They must be set on the road to citizenship. They may choose not to become citizens, to return home or stay on as resident aliens. Many—perhaps most—will choose to return because of their emotional ties to their national family and their native land. But unless they have that choice, their other choices cannot be taken as so many signs of their acquiescence to the economy and law of the countries where they work. And if they do have that choice, the local economy and law are likely to look different: a firmer recognition of the guests' civil liberties and some enhancement of their opportunities for collective bargaining would be difficult to avoid once they were seen as potential citizens. * * *

[T]he principle of political justice is this: that the processes of self-determination through which a democratic state shapes its internal life, must be open, and equally open, to all those men and women who live within its territory, work in the local economy, and are subject to local law. Hence, second admissions (naturalization) depend on first admissions (immigration) and are subject only to certain constraints of time and qualification, never to the ultimate constraint of closure. When second admissions are closed, the political community collapses into a world of members and strangers, with no political boundaries between the two, where the strangers are subjects of the members. Among themselves, perhaps, the members are equal; but it is not their equality but their tyranny that determines the character of the state. Political justice is a bar to permanent alienage—either for particular individuals or for a class of changing individuals. At least, this is true in a democracy. * * * No democratic state can tolerate the establishment of a fixed status between citizen and foreigner (though there can be stages in the transition from one of these political identities to the other). Men and women are either subject to the state's authority, or they are not; and if they are subject, they must be given a say, and ultimately an equal say, in what that authority does. Democratic citizens, then, have a choice: if they want to bring in new workers, they must be prepared to enlarge their own membership; if they are unwilling to accept new members, they must find ways within the limits of the domestic labor market to get socially necessary work done. And those are their only choices. Their right to choose derives from the existence in this particular territory of a community of citizens; and it is not compatible with the destruction of the community or its transformation into yet another local tyranny.

NOTES AND QUESTIONS ON THE VIEWS OF THE CRITICS

1.   How would you design a guest worker program to avoid the problems that have plagued earlier such schemes, in both the United States and Mexico, as described by Philip Martin and Michael Teitelbaum? What enforcement assumptions would go into such a design—regarding both labor law enforcement and future immigration law enforcement?

2.   What responses might the supporters of guest worker programs offer to the critiques of Rodriguez and Walzer?

SECTION C.   UNAUTHORIZED MIGRANTS IN THE UNITED STATES

1.   INTRODUCTION

Unauthorized migrants obviously do not constitute an admission category, but unauthorized migration has been a significant feature of the immigration landscape for several decades, with a major impact on both the substance and tone of public discourse over immigration. By 2007, the best available estimates placed this population at 12 million, representing a major increase from an estimated 2.5 million in1988, when the legalization program enacted in the 1986 Immigration Reform and Control Act came to an end. Since 2007, however, the number has declined to about 11 million and apparently stabilized. See Figure 5.6. Because facts and perceptions (including misperceptions) about the undocumented population feature prominently in policy debates, institutional design decisions, and the allocation of resources to the various parts of the immigration management business, we devote a few introductory pages here to the underlying history and current facts. We revisit some of the key issues later, especially in the discussion of immigration law enforcement in Chapter Nine, Section A.

Figure 5.6
Unauthorized Migrants Living in the United States: 1980–2010

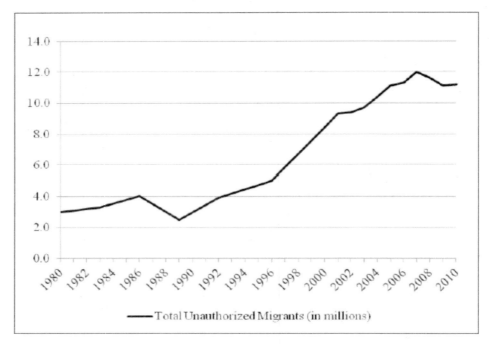

Source: Graph derived from Passel, Pew Hispanic Center, The Size and Character-istics of the Unauthorized Migrant Population in the U.S.: Estimates Based on the March 2006 Current Population Survey (Mar. 7, 2006) (for years 1980–2000); Pew Hispanic Center, Unauthorized Immigrant Population: National and State Trends, 2010 (Feb. 1, 2011) (for years 2001–2010).

This Section begins with two narrative snapshots of unauthorized migration. One is from the late1990s, depicting the impact on one commu-nity and its new arrivals during a period of rapid increase in its unautho-rized population. The other, far more recent, focuses on Mexico, the source of 58% of the current undocumented population, and it contains suggestive indications about the recent decline in unauthorized migration and possible paths for the future. We then turn to readings that illumi-nate, first, the history of the conflicted governmental response to illegal migration, and second, the social processes that mark the various stages of such movements. Against that background, we conclude with readings that offer a more detailed description of the current unauthorized popula-tion and the trends that led us to the present situation.

A Note on Terminology

The terms "illegal aliens," "undocumented aliens," and "unauthorized migrants" are all in common usage. Some object to "illegal aliens," noting that many persons unlawfully in the United States may ultimately qualify for legal status or obtain discretionary relief from deportation; it is also argued that the United States has tolerated and even encouraged the presence of persons deemed "illegal." But others counter that "undocumented" is a euphemism for entry or continuing presence that violates federal law; moreover, many aliens not authorized to be in the United States possess documents (although they may be fraudulent). A Supreme Court majority consistently used "undocumented alien" in *McNary v. Haitian Refugee Center*, 498 U.S. 479, 111 S.Ct. 888, 112 L.Ed.2d 1005 (1991) (upholding district court jurisdiction to hear challenges to INS policies). The dissent consistently used "illegal alien." We generally adopt here the term "unauthorized" (used by the Mexico/United States Binational Study on Migration) or "undocumented" to describe a person whose presence in the United States is in violation of law.

MARCUS STERN, JOBS MAGNET

San Diego Union–Tribune, Nov. 2, 1997.**g**

MORGANTON, N.C.—Luis Alberto Gonzalez's job hunt led him from his hometown in the rugged highlands of Guatemala to the pastoral Blue Ridge Mountains of North Carolina. Most of the 500 people who cut up chickens alongside him at the Case Farms poultry plant are Guatemalan. Many entered the country as he did—illegally.

After the Guatemalan workers started arriving in 1990, the plant's traditional work force of low-skilled African–Americans faded quietly into the community. "They brought in all these Guatemalan and Mexican workers because they figured they'd work for nothing," recalled Katherine Harbison, 33, a black worker whose first job after high school was at the plant. "The supervisors treated the American workers real bad to give them a reason to quit. Most of them did."

What has happened at Case Farms and in the once-sleepy town of Morganton is happening in other small towns across America. Undocumented foreign workers, feeding eagerly on the economic crumbs of America's vast and lightly regulated low-skill labor markets, have pushed far beyond their traditional destinations in California, Texas and Florida. In Storm Lake, Iowa, and Garden City, Kan., legal and illegal immigrants attracted to meat-packing plants have transformed the ethnic makeup of quintessential Midwestern communities. On the Eastern Shore of the Chesapeake Bay, the availability of jobs at poultry plants has turned Georgetown, Del., into a Guatemalan outpost. And in Dalton, Ga., the carpet plants have drawn thousands of workers from Mexico.

Even though the nation's border enforcement laws have been overhauled twice in 11 years and the immigration service budget doubled in five, the nation's undocumented population continues rising each year by 275,000, according to the Immigration and Naturalization Service. The newcomers are hired as parking lot attendants, janitors, housekeepers, dishwashers, construction workers and factory workers. Those jobs that have historically offered low-skilled Americans and legal immigrants a first step into the middle class now also are being held by undocumented workers.

---

g. We have altered the paragraphing.—eds.

The flow continues partly because of the nation's mixed attitude toward these people. The U.S. government builds barriers at the border and hires guards to keep them out, but once they're here U.S. businesses offer them jobs. * * *

In Morganton, Alberto is part of an exploding population of new legal and illegal foreign-born residents who have settled in this Appalachian town of 18,000. The recent influx of thousands of Hispanics—mostly Guatemalans—has transformed the ethnic composition of [Morganton.] * * * [In] 1990, the U.S. Census Bureau found 344 Hispanics living in Morganton and surrounding Burke County. Seven years later unofficial estimates run as high as 10,000.

There is still disagreement and confusion here over how Case Farms switched so quickly from employing poor African–American workers to poor Guatemalans. John Vail, former executive director of Catawba Valley Legal Services, remembered getting a call in about 1991 from a nun in Immokalee, Fla., a rural town where migrant workers from Mexico, the Caribbean and Central America gather looking for work. A man had arrived in a van. He wanted to take Guatemalans back to work at Case Farms, the nun told Vail. Company officials deny sending the man or recruiting workers directly. But they do acknowledge paying a finder's fee for each new worker delivered to the plant.

Phyllis Palmieri also became aware of the shift about the same time. She was working as a legal services attorney in Morganton when several black workers came to her office and said they had been fired and replaced by Hispanics. They called it discrimination.

In a brief interview, Ken Wilson, human relations manager at Case Farms, said the company regularly checks the work permits of its foreign workers to ensure they're still valid. But workers said the company checked the documents earlier this year for the first time since mid–1995. The company does it to intimidate them, not to keep them off the payroll, several undocumented workers said. * * * Some Hispanics earn extra money by driving to Florida and bringing back workers for Case Farms, said Daniel Gutierrez, who is active in Morganton's immigrant community. For each recruit, they collect $100 from the worker and $50 from the company, he said.

"If you give an employer a choice between illegal immigrants and low-skill, native-born workers, they're going to choose illegal aliens every time because many of them don't see the wages as being low," said Cornell University immigration expert Vernon Briggs. "They don't understand labor law in the United States so they don't think they're being exploited. Or if they do know they are, there's not much they can do about it, given their illegal status."

Alberto, like many Case Farms workers, is from the rural Guatemalan town of Huehuetenango * * *. Today, children living in the thatched-roof huts of Huehuetenango eat better because of the paychecks distributed on the factory floor at Case Farms. Like the other Guatemalan workers,

Alberto earns about $54 a day, far more than the $3 he said he'd earn in Guatemala. But the illegal workers pay dearly for this opportunity. Entering the United States through its "back door" is undignified, inhumane and fraught with danger. Once here, they remain vulnerable to exploitation.

Alberto initially slipped into Mexico hoping to make a living. But things didn't work out. Three years ago, he sneaked across the U.S. border at Nogales, Ariz., and rode in a smuggler's van to the sweltering citrus fields of south Florida. He boarded yet another van to get to Morganton. He arrived safely. But others sneaking into the country have drowned in the rain-flooded Tijuana River, frozen in the mountains of San Diego's East County or died of dehydration in the Arizona desert. Some are dropped nameless into paupers' graves in Texas border towns like Brownsville.

As many as 3,200 undocumented immigrants died along the Texas–Mexico border between 1985 and 1994, according to a study last year by the University of Houston. Most of them drown in the Rio Grande. More recent research found that at least 1,185 crossers died along the entire U.S.–Mexico border between 1993 and 1996. * * * Those who survive the journey work hard and scared. Benefits such as health care, overtime, holidays and vacations are sporadic. They may face a mandatory 70–hour workweek, unjustified firing, petty indignities and other forms of harassment.

At Case Farms, workers get $6.85 an hour. Health benefits begin after three months. They get a week of vacation and five paid holidays a year. What they don't get, they say, are safe and dignified working conditions. That's why Case Farms' employees voted in 1995 to form a union. The company so far hasn't entered into negotiations and many of the workers' complaints persist. * * * The company has made some improvements, workers say, but turnover rates remain extremely high. Case Farms, like most other poultry plants, needs a constant supply of new workers.

At 21, Jose Luis Hernandez still has the delicate features of a boy. The Guatemalan slipped across the border into Nogales, Ariz., traveled to Morganton and went right to work cutting chicken shoulders, the toughest job on the line, he said. Chickens passed in front of him at the rate of 28 per minute. Each time, he made the same slicing motion with his right hand. Within months, his wrist became sore. But the company doctor told him it was a problem from birth and he was ordered back on the line, he said. "I asked for a different job but they wouldn't move me," he said.

* * * Why do he and the others put up with such treatment? Many of them aren't legally authorized to work, so if they make a fuss, they can be fired with impunity, he said. The legal status of others is hazy. The company checked their documents, the workers said. But they freely admit many of these documents are forgeries and some valid work permits have expired. Even those who are in the country legally tend to feel they have little recourse in a strange land. * * *

In Morganton, local officials are wrestling with their community's sudden need for interpreters in the courts and police department and for bilingual teachers for the schools. The problem is compounded because many of the workers and their children speak Mayan dialects instead of Spanish—and quite a few are illiterate even in those. The community has scrambled to find housing and provide medical care for the newcomers. Many are packed into trailers and public housing units.

Still, Morganton's longtime residents see the newcomers as a boon rather than a burden. Unemployment is relatively low in their town, and these newcomers work hard. They also buy potato chips and used Pontiacs and their purchases help the economy grow.

Tensions can flare over little things like loud music at night. Newcomers sometimes drive without valid permits and fail to follow traffic laws. But even low-income African–Americans who are unemployed express little resentment. Some say the jobs aren't worth fighting for. Working conditions at the plant are just too bleak.

Jimmy Jacumin, head of the county commission, has a reputation for speaking his mind about the newcomers. He argues against hiring interpreters for the court because he believes the immigrants need to learn to speak English. But he, too, sees economic opportunity in these people who have traveled so far to improve their lives. "They'll lift everybody else, too," he said.

The diaspora of undocumented workers across America has made the task of stopping the flow more daunting today than it was a generation ago, before modern transportation shrunk the world and mass media raised expectations in less prosperous lands. Today, immigrant networks reach deep into the American heartland and sophisticated smuggling operations crisscross the country with the help of the Internet, 1–800– numbers, fleets of vans, CB radios and cellular phones. * * *

The INS office nearest Morganton is 90 minutes away. But during the past seven years, as the town has gone through its bewildering ethnic transformation, no INS agent has visited Case Farms.

If ignoring the flow of undocumented workers hurts anyone, it hurts those at the bottom of the economy, according to a recent National Academy of Sciences study. Illegal workers compete with legal workers living in the same area, it concluded. These findings reflect the situation in Morganton. "If an American goes in and applies for a job and a Guatemalan goes in after him, they're going to hire the Guatemalan before they hire the American," said Harbison, the former Case worker.

For those African–Americans living in poverty who once worked at the plant, the new welfare law could be yet another turn of the screw. If the law cuts their benefits in an effort to push them into the job market, they needn't bother to apply at Case Farms. Those jobs are taken.

DAMIEN CAVE, BETTER LIVES FOR MEXICANS CUT ALLURE OF GOING NORTH[h]

New York Times, July 6, 2011.[*]

The extraordinary Mexican migration that delivered millions of illegal immigrants to the United States over the past 30 years has sputtered to a trickle, and research points to a surprising cause: unheralded changes in Mexico that have made staying home more attractive. A growing body of evidence suggests that a mix of developments—expanding economic and educational opportunities, rising border crime and shrinking families—are suppressing illegal traffic as much as economic slowdowns or immigrant crackdowns in the United States.

Here in the red-earth highlands of Jalisco, one of Mexico's top three states for emigration over the past century, a new dynamic has emerged. For a typical rural family like the Orozcos, heading to El Norte without papers is no longer an inevitable rite of passage. Instead, their homes are filling up with returning relatives; older brothers who once crossed illegally are awaiting visas; and the youngest Orozcos are staying put.

"I'm not going to go to the States because I'm more concerned with my studies," said Angel Orozco, 18. Indeed, at the new technological institute where he is earning a degree in industrial engineering, all the students in a recent class said they were better educated than their parents—and that they planned to stay in Mexico rather than go to the United States.

Douglas S. Massey [of Princeton] * * * said his research showed that interest in heading to the United States for the first time had fallen to its lowest level since at least the 1950s. "No one wants to hear it, but the flow has already stopped," Mr. Massey said, referring to illegal traffic. "For the first time in 60 years, the net traffic has gone to zero and is probably a little bit negative." * * *

The question is why. Experts and American politicians from both parties have generally looked inward, arguing about the success or failure of the buildup of border enforcement and tougher laws limiting illegal immigrants' rights—like those recently passed in Alabama and Arizona. Deportations have reached record highs as total border apprehensions and apprehensions of Mexicans have fallen by more than 70 percent since 2000.

But Mexican immigration has always been defined by both the push (from Mexico) and the pull (of the United States). * * * In simple terms, Mexican families are smaller than they had once been. The pool of likely migrants is shrinking. * * * [B]irth control efforts have pushed down the

---

h. We have altered the paragraphing.—eds.

fertility rate to about 2 children per woman from 6.8 in 1970, according to government figures. So while Mexico added about one million new potential job seekers annually in the 1990s, since 2007 that figure has fallen to an average of 800,000, according to government birth records. By 2030, it is expected to drop to 300,000. * * * At the same time, educational and employment opportunities have greatly expanded in Mexico. Per capita gross domestic product and family income have each jumped more than 45 percent since 2000, according to one prominent economist, Roberto Newell. Despite all the depictions of Mexico as "nearly a failed state," he argued, "the conventional wisdom is wrong."

A significant expansion of legal immigration—aided by American consular officials—is also under way. * * * State Department figures show that Mexicans who have become American citizens have legally brought in 64 percent more immediate relatives, 220,500 from 2006 through 2010, compared with the figures for the previous five years. Tourist visas are also being granted at higher rates of around 89 percent, up from 67 percent, while American farmers have legally hired 75 percent more temporary workers since 2006. * * *

HARD YEARS IN JALISCO

When Angel Orozco's grandfather considered leaving Mexico in the 1920s, his family said, he wrestled with one elemental question: Will it be worth it? At that point and for decades to come, yes was the obvious answer. * * * [T]he wages paid by the railroads, where most early migrants found legal work, were five times what could be earned on farms in Arandas, the municipality that includes Agua Negra.

* * * When Angel's father, Antonio, went north to pick cotton in the 1950s and '60s with the Bracero temporary worker program, which accepted more than 400,000 laborers a year at its peak, working in the United States made even more sense. The difference in wages had reached 10 to 1. Arandas was still dirt poor. * * *

Legal status then meant little. After the Bracero program ended in 1964, Antonio said, he crossed back and forth several times without documentation. Passage was cheap. Work lasting for a few months or a year was always plentiful. So when his seven sons started to become adults in the 1990s, he encouraged them to go north as well. Around 2001, he and two of his sons were all in the United States working—part of what is now recognized as one of the largest immigration waves in American history.

But even then, illegal immigration was becoming less attractive. In the mid–1990s, the Clinton administration added fences and federal agents to what were then the main crossing corridors beyond Tijuana and Ciudad Juárez. The enforcement push, continued by President George W. Bush and President Obama, helped drive up smuggling prices from around $700 in the late 1980s to nearly $2,000 a decade later, and the costs continued to climb * * *. It also shifted traffic to more dangerous desert areas near Arizona.

Antonio said the risks hit home when his nephew Alejandro disappeared in the Sonoran Desert around 2002. A father of one and with a pregnant wife, Alejandro had been promised work by a friend. It took years for the authorities to find his body in the arid brush south of Tucson. Even now, no one knows how he died. * * *

A PERIOD OF PROGRESS

Another important factor is Mexico itself. Over the past 15 years, this country once defined by poverty and beaches has progressed politically and economically in ways rarely acknowledged by Americans debating immigration. Even far from the coasts or the manufacturing sector at the border, democracy is better established, incomes have generally risen and poverty has declined.

* * * [By 2003, research showed that the wage disparity between Arandas and] the United States had narrowed: migrants in the north were collecting 3.7 times what they could earn at home.

That gap has recently shrunk again. The recession cut into immigrant earnings in the United States, * * * even as wages have risen in Mexico * * *. Jalisco's quality of life has improved in other ways, too. About a decade ago, the cluster of the Orozco ranches on Agua Negra's outskirts received electricity and running water. New census data shows a broad expansion of such services: water and trash collection, once unheard of outside cities, are now available to more than 90 percent of Jalisco's homes. * * *

Still, education represents the most meaningful change. The census shows that throughout Jalisco, the number of senior high schools or preparatory schools for students aged 15 to 18 increased to 724 in 2009, from 360 in 2000, far outpacing population growth. The Technological Institute of Arandas, where Angel studies engineering, is now one of 13 science campuses created in Jalisco since 2000—a major reason professionals in the state, with a bachelor's degree or higher, also more than doubled to 821,983 in 2010, up from 405,415 in 2000.

* * * If these trends—particularly Mexican economic growth—continue over the next decade, [Jeffrey] Passel [of the Pew Hispanic Center] said, changes in the migration dynamic may become even clearer. "At the point where the U.S. needs the workers again," he said, "there will be fewer of them." * * *

How did this happen? Partly, emigrants say, illegal life in the United States became harder. Laws restricting illegal immigrants' rights or making it tougher for employers to hire them have passed in more than a dozen states since 2006. The same word-of-mouth networks that used to draw people north are now advising against the journey. "Without papers all you're thinking about is, when are the police going to stop you or what other risks are you going to face," said Andrés Orozco. Andrés, a horse lover who drives a teal pickup from Texas, is one of many Orozcos now pinning their hopes on a visa. And for the first time in years, the chances have improved.

Mexican government estimates based on survey data show not just a decrease in migration overall, but also an increase in border crossings with documents. In 2009, the most recent year for which data is available, 38 percent of the total attempted crossings, legal and illegal, were made with documents. In 2007, only 20 percent involved such paperwork.

* * * Advocates of limited immigration worry that the issuing of more visas creates a loophole that can be abused. Between 40 and 50 percent of the illegal immigrants in the United States entered legally with visas they overstayed, as of 2005, according to the Pew Hispanic Center. More recent American population data, however, shows no overall increase in the illegal Mexican population. That suggests that most of the temporary visas issued to Mexicans—1.1 million in 2010—are being used legitimately even as American statistics show clearly that visa opportunities have increased.

Easing a Chaotic Process

One man, [Edward] McKeon, the minister counselor who oversees all consular affairs in Mexico, has played a significant role in that expansion. * * * Working within administrative rules, State Department officials say, he re-engineered the visa program to de-emphasize the affordability standard that held that visas were to be denied to those who could not prove an income large enough to support travel to the United States. * * * This led to an almost immediate decrease in the rejection rate for tourist visas. Before he arrived, around 32 percent were turned down. Since 2008, the rate has been around 11 percent.

Mr. McKeon—praised by some immigration lawyers for bringing consistency to a chaotic process—was also instrumental in expanding the temporary visa program for agricultural workers. * * * For H–2As, Mexican workers can now receive their documents the same day that they apply.

Mr. McKeon also pushed to make the program more attractive to Mexicans who might otherwise cross the border illegally. * * * Specifically, consulate workers dealing with H–2A applicants who were once illegal—making them subject to 3–or 10–year bans depending on the length of their illegal stay—now regularly file electronic waiver applications to the United States Customs and Border Patrol. About 85 percent of these are now approved, Mr. McKeon said, so that in 2010 most of the 52,317 Mexican workers with H–2A visas had previously been in the United States illegally. * * *

A Divisive Topic

* * * On the other side, Steven A. Camarota, a demographer at the Center for Immigration Studies in Washington, which favors reduced immigration, said that increasing the proportion of legal entries did little good. "If you believe there is significant job competition at the bottom end of the labor market, as I do, you're not fixing the problem," Mr. Camarota

said. "If you are concerned about the fiscal cost of unskilled immigration and everyone comes in on temporary visas and overstays, or even if they don't, the same problems are likely to apply." By his calculations, unskilled immigrants like the Orozcos have, over the years, helped push down hourly wages, especially for young, unskilled American workers. Immigrants are also more likely to rely on welfare, he said, adding to public costs.

The Orozco clan, however, may point to a different future. * * * After graduating, [Angel Orozco] hopes to work for a manufacturing company in Arandas, which seems likely because the director of his school says that nearly 90 percent of graduates find jobs in their field. Then, Angel said, he will be able to buy what he really wants: a shiny, new red Camaro.

NOTES AND QUESTIONS

1. The years between the writing of these two articles saw both a major economic recession, beginning in 2007, and a massive increase in the federal resources devoted to border policing and, to a somewhat lesser extent, interior enforcement. (We will explore the enforcement changes more thoroughly in Chapter Nine, Section A.) If the changed trends in migration from Mexico described in the Cave article continue, what are the implications for future policy, both medium term and long term?

2. The articles generally portray Latin American migrants who entered the United States by evading inspection at the border. As the next reading indicates, about three-quarters of the unauthorized population in the United States comes from Latin America. And while most unauthorized workers entered the United States unlawfully over the southwest border, at least 25% and perhaps as many as 40% of the unauthorized population entered on visas and overstayed their authorized time. *See* Martin, *Eight Myths About Immigration Enforcement*, 10 N.Y.U. J. Legis. & Pub. Pol'y 525, 544 (2007).

3. For a detailed study of the Guatemalan migrant community in Morganton and the lengthy labor conflicts between Case Farms and the immigrant union, see L. Fink, The Maya of Morganton: Work and Community in the Nuevo New South (2003). For an insightful and influential history of U.S. treatment of undocumented migrants in the first half of the 20th century, see M. Ngai, Impossible Subjects: Illegal Aliens and the Making of Modern America, ch. 2 (2004).

2. UNAUTHORIZED MIGRATION AS AN HISTORICAL AND SOCIAL PROCESS

Persons enter the United States unlawfully for varied reasons. Some come to join family members, some to flee persecution in their homeland, some to go to school. Virtually all scholars agree, however, that economic factors—jobs—provide the most important incentive for illegal entry and residence. America offers jobs to unemployed or underemployed laborers from less developed nations at wages that are generally substantially above prevailing wages in the aliens' countries of origin (even if the wages the migrants receive here are below wages normally paid to U.S. citizens or legal immigrants). But as noted in the readings in Chapter Three, Section C, *supra,* simple economic disparity does not account for actual migration patterns. Past private efforts at the promotion of work-based migration to the major receiving states, often augmented by explicit government policy (whether or not that role was officially acknowledged), plus the eventual creation of social networks linking particular source communities and receiving communities, have played a major role. The following readings provide additional insight into these dynamics and the lingering effects of government policies.

KITTY CALAVITA, THE IMMIGRATION POLICY DEBATE: CRITICAL ANALYSIS AND FUTURE OPTIONS

Mexican Migration to the United States: Origins, Consequences, and Policy Options 151, 155–59 (W. Cornelius & J. Bustamante, eds., 1989).

MEXICAN MIGRATION AS A BACKDOOR LABOR SOURCE

Mexican immigration to the United States gained momentum in the pre-World War I period, as policymakers and even some employers reassessed the costs versus the benefits of European immigration. The European immigrant was a reputed troublemaker who frequently became a permanent member of American society and was increasingly the backbone of labor strikes. In 1911, the Dillingham Commission, responding to these concerns, noted the special advantages of Mexican migration:

Because of their strong attachment to their native land ... and the possibility of their residence here being discontinued, few become citizens of the United States. The Mexican migrants are providing a fairly adequate supply of labor.... While they are not easily assimilated, this is of no very great importance as long as most of them return to their native land. In the case of the Mexican, he is less desirable as a citizen than as a laborer.

The most significant restrictions of the early twentieth century exempted Mexicans from their orbit. A response to warnings from Southwestern growers that successful harvests depended on abundant Mexican labor excluded Mexicans from the literacy test requirement of 1917 for the duration of the war. As World War I came to a close, the labor secretary and immigration commissioner extended the exemptions. As a result of these policies and employers' recruitment efforts, legal immigration from Mexico soared from eleven thousand in 1915 to fifty-one thousand in 1920. Industries as far north as Chicago drew labor from this back door. By 1926, 35 percent of Chicago Inland Steel's labor force was Mexican.

The passage of the quotas in the 1920s again exempted Mexicans. The argument against restricting Mexican immigration was strong:

The Mexican, they pointed out, was a vulnerable alien living just a short distance from his homeland. . . . He, unlike Puerto Ricans or Filipinos . . . could easily be deported. No safer or more economical unskilled labor force was imaginable.

The shift from European to Mexican migration as a source of labor did enhance flexibility, as evidenced by the repatriation of thousands of Mexican workers and their families during the depression of the 1930s. As World War II refueled the U.S. economy, the United States again needed and used Mexican contract laborers imported through the Bracero Program, whose formal and informal policies contributed to the rise of the undocumented nature of Mexican migration that characterizes the contemporary period. The program attempted to institutionalize the primary virtue of this labor supply, its flexibility.

The Bracero Agreement of 1949 provided that "illegal workers, when they are located in the United States, shall be given preference under outstanding U.S. Employment Service Certification." Illegals, or "wetbacks," were "dried out" by the U.S. Border Patrol which escorted them to the Mexican border, had them step to the Mexican side, and brought them back as braceros. Employers often accompanied their undocumented workers back to the border and contracted them there as legal workers. In some cases, the border patrol "paroled" illegals directly to employers. In 1951 the President's Commission on Migratory Labor estimated that between 1947 and 1949 the United States legalized more than 142,000 undocumented Mexicans in this way, while recruiting only 74,600 new braceros from Mexico.

In addition to these more or less official policies of encouraging illegal migration, Immigration and Naturalization Service (INS) district chiefs enhanced, at their discretion, the supply of undocumented workers for seasonal employment. The chief inspector at Tucson, for example, reported to the President's Commission on Migratory Labor that he "received orders from the District Director at El Paso each harvest to stop deporting illegal Mexican labor." In other cases, Border Patrol officials told agents to stay away from designated ranches and farms in their district. The implicit message from Congress to the Border Patrol was consistent with this laissez-faire approach. Congress was "splendidly indifferent" to the rising number of illegals during the bracero period, reducing the budget of the Border Patrol just as undocumented migration increased.

By the time the United States terminated the Bracero Program in 1964, the symbiosis between Mexican migrants and employers in the Southwest was well entrenched, the product of over fifty years of formal and informal policy-making. Almost five million Mexican workers had been brought to the United States as braceros; more than five million illegal aliens were apprehended during the same period.

While policies associated with the Bracero Program were instrumental in enhancing the appeal of illegal migration from the migrants' point of view, a key congressional decision immunized employers from any risk involved in their employment. In 1952, the McCarran–Walter Act made it illegal to "harbor, transport, or conceal illegal entrants." An amendment to the provision, referred to as the Texas Proviso after the Texas growers to whom it was a concession, excluded employment per se from the category of "harboring." Whether or not "knowing" employment of undocumented workers would constitute harboring remained ambiguous despite congressional discussion. Nonetheless, the amendment was interpreted by the INS as carte blanche to employ undocumented workers.

Of course, the U.S. attitude toward Mexican migrants has not been unequivocal. Mass expulsions and roundups of Mexican workers and their families during Operation Wetback in 1954 and 1955 were reminiscent of the depression policies of the 1930s. In part, these mass deportations reflected the militaristic approach of the new INS commissioner, Joseph Swing, a former U.S. Army general known within the INS bureaucracy as "The General," in apparent reference both to his former military career and to his leadership style. More generally, however, they represented the long-held view of Mexican labor as eminently flexible—welcomed during periods of high demand and deported when the demand had waned. In any case, such periodic deportations neither significantly interrupted the now-institutionalized patterns of migration nor reflected any fundamental change in the perception of Mexico as a backdoor source of labor.

Given the historical pattern, the following excerpt provides a model for understanding how, as one leading scholar put it, "Mexican migration to the United States represents a deeply institutionalized, multigenerational social process." W. Cornelius, Mexican Migration to the United States: The Limits of Government Intervention 2–4 (Working Papers in U.S.–Mexican Studies, 5; 1981).

DOUGLAS S. MASSEY, LUIN GOLDRING, AND JORGE DURAND, CONTINUITIES IN TRANSNATIONAL MIGRATION: AN ANALYSIS OF NINETEEN MEXICAN COMMUNITIES

99 American Journal of Sociology 1492, 1496–1502 (1994).*

Transnational labor migration may originate for a variety of complementary reasons. Migrants may observe wage differentials between origin and destination areas and respond to expected positive returns to foreign labor. Households may seek to diversify risks to their economic well-being by sending family members to work in different regional labor markets, one of which is foreign. Migrants may be recruited by foreign employers seeking to import workers for specific tasks. People may be impelled to move because structural transformations in the local economy eliminate traditional sources of sustenance or because political upheavals cause people to fear for their physical safety.

No matter how international migration begins, the first migrants from a community are likely to experience it as a very costly and risky enterprise, both in monetary and psychological terms. They have little or no knowledge of conditions in the host country and are ignorant of its culture, language, and ways of life. In most cases, they incur the expenses of the trip and absorb the opportunity costs of income forgone while moving and looking for work. They arrive having to pay off these overhead expenses and are thus relatively dependent on their first employer. Given their lack of knowledge about prevailing wage rates, work habits, legal conventions, and social expectations, they are vulnerable to exploitation and mistreatment, especially if they are undocumented and do not speak the language of the host country.

Given these costs and risks, the first transnational labor migrants usually come not from the bottom of the socioeconomic hierarchy but from the lower middle ranges. Such people have enough resources to absorb the costs and risks of the trip but are not so affluent that foreign labor is unattractive. * * *

[T]he earliest migrants leave their families and friends behind and strike out for solitary work in an alien land. Most transnational migrants begin as target earners, seeking to earn as much money as possible as quickly as possible in order to recoup their initial investment, attain a predetermined income goal, and return home to family and friends. They have little interest in permanent settlement abroad.

Once one or more people have come and gone in this fashion, however, the situation in the sending community does not return to the status quo ante. Each act of migration generates a set of irreversible changes in individual motivations, social structures, and cultural values that alter the context within which future migration decisions are made. These changes accumulate across time to create conditions that make additional migration more likely. * * *

At the individual level, participation in a high-wage economy induces changes in tastes and motivations that turn people away from target earning and toward persistent migration. Satisfaction of the wants that originally led to migration creates new wants. Access to high wages and the goods they buy creates new standards of material well-being, and first-hand experiences in an affluent society raise expectations and create new ambitions for upward mobility. As migrants earn high wages and alter their consumption patterns, they adopt new lifestyles and local economic pursuits become less attractive.

The first-hand experience gained from migration makes the satisfaction of these new wants increasingly feasible. Once someone has migrated and returned, that person has direct knowledge of employment opportunities, labor-market conditions, and ways of life in the destination country; they use these understandings to migrate again with fewer risks and costs than before. Once it has been experienced, therefore, migration becomes a familiar and reliable socioeconomic resource that can be employed again and again as new needs arise and motivations change.

Empirical research in Mexico shows conclusively that once a man has migrated to the United States, the odds are extremely high that he will migrate again. Indeed, the probability of taking an additional trip rises monotonically as the number of trips increases. The more a man migrates, the more he is likely to continue migrating, a pattern that has proved to be remarkably persistent in the face of restrictive immigration policies.

Given their status as target earners, during the first few trips and in the early history of migration from a community, migrants tend to live under rather spartan conditions, sleeping in barracks or sharing apartments with other men and sleeping in shifts to save money. They work long hours and have little social life. In some cases they work two eight-hour shifts in the same day. Most of their earnings are repatriated in the form of savings or remittances. Migrants see themselves as members of their home communities and not as participants in the host society.

As migrants spend increasing time abroad, however, this form of social life becomes more and more problematic. As stays abroad lengthen and the number of trips rises, pressure from family members wanting to migrate grows. The first relatives to accompany a married migrant are typically unmarried sons of working age, since they have the greatest earnings potential after the father and their migration is consistent with prevailing gender roles. Over time, however, unmarried working-age daughters, wives, and younger children are likely to accompany him as well. Other relatives, such as nephews, nieces, and cousins, eventually join experienced migrants. As increasing numbers of young men acquire migrant experience, they also begin to travel north in groups based on friendship as well as kinship. As a result, the demographic base of migration steadily widens and the mean age of migration drops.

The act of migration not only induces changes within individual migrants that make further movement more likely, it also initiates changes in social structures that spread migration through the community. Each migrant is inevitably linked to a set of nonmigrants through a variety of social ties that carry reciprocal obligations for assistance based on shared understandings of kinship, friendship, and common community origin. Given the expectations and practices associated with kinship and friendship, each act of migration creates a set of people with social ties to the receiving country. Nonmigrants draw upon these ties to gain access to employment and assistance abroad, substantially reducing the costs and risks of movement compared to earlier migrants.

Every new migrant thus reduces the costs and risks and increases the attractiveness and feasibility of migration for a set of friends and relatives. With these lowered costs and risks, additional people are induced to migrate for the first time, which further expands the set of people with ties abroad. This additional migration reduces costs and risks for a new set of people, causing some of them to migrate, and so on. Once the number of network connections reaches a critical threshold, migration becomes self-perpetuating because each act of movement creates the social structure necessary to sustain it. Empirical studies in Mexico clearly show that having network connections greatly increases the likelihood of international movement.

As migrants make successive trips, they accumulate foreign experience and knowledge that render ties to them increasingly valuable. As information about the destination country and its socioeconomic resources accumulates in the population, the costs of migration steadily drop to make the cost-benefit calculation positive for an increasingly large set of people, while the risks of movement steadily fall to render migration a feasible risk-diversification strategy for a growing number of households. Over time, therefore, migration becomes progressively less selective and more representative of the community as a whole.

Migration also changes the cultural context within which decisions are made, and international movement becomes increasingly attractive for reasons that are not purely economic. Migrants evince a widely-admired lifestyle that others are drawn to emulate. Although some of its attractiveness is material—based on the ability to consume goods and purchase property—the lifestyle also acquires a strong normative component. In communities where foreign wage labor has become fully integrated into local values and expectations, people contemplating entry into the labor force literally do not consider other options: they expect to migrate frequently in the course of their lives and assume they can go whenever they wish.

As migration assumes a greater role in the community, it becomes increasingly important as a rite of passage for young men, providing an accepted means of demonstrating their worthiness, ambition, and manhood to others. Moreover, as women become more integrated within postindustrial society, they begin to push for more egalitarian gender roles and encourage activities that lead to longer stays abroad, such as investing in household goods and buying property in the destination country.

Over time and with extensive movement back and forth, communities of origin and destination increasingly come to comprise transnational circuits—social and geographic spaces that arise through the constant circulation of people, money, goods, and information. As these circuits develop, practices and values that once demarcated distinct societies begin to have a transformative influence on each other. Over time, migrant communities become culturally "transnationalized," incorporating ideologies, practices, expectations, and political claims from both societies to create a "culture of migration" that is distinct from the culture of both the sending and receiving nation.

As migration is increasingly taken for granted, the demographic composition and socioeconomic role of the place of origin undergo a dramatic transformation. In many places, women, children, and older people dominate a reduced population except during the few weeks or months when migrants return for holidays and celebrations. In economically marginal agricultural areas, farming and other traditional activities lose importance. As the place of origin becomes a site of rest and recreation, in sharp contrast to the routine of work abroad, its social meaning undergoes changes. Migrants spend money collectively on infrastructure and other community projects aimed at transforming the landscape into a place of leisure, a place where migrants and their families can display their status and exercise political claims and power.

The first migrants from a community typically go to a specific niche in the destination country's political economy, yielding little diversity with respect to destination, occupation, or strategies of movement. Early migrants follow the path of the first migrant because that is where the costs and risks of migration are lowest and the chances of success greatest. Once they have identified a promising migrant worker, moreover, labor recruiters and contractors tend to use them as vehicles to recruit additional workers from their circle of friends and relatives. As experience in the host country accumulates, however, and as more people are drawn into the process, some migrants inevitably seek out better opportunities in new places and occupations. In this way the diversity of foreign destinations, jobs, and strategies increases.

As the migration process proceeds, however, typically someone from the sending community achieves a position of responsibility that enables him or her to channel employment, housing, and other resources to fellow townspeople. The position may be a crew boss in a railroad, a foreman in a factory, a union representative in a company, a majordomo in a restaurant, a labor contractor for a grower, or perhaps even a business owner. Although it is impossible to predict where or how it will occur, sooner or later someone attains such a position and begins to recruit fellow townspeople for work. * * *

As migrants make repeated trips and accumulate more time abroad, as wives and children join the migrant workforce, as more people become involved in the migration process, and as stronger links are formed with specific employers in particular locations, a growing number of migrants and families settle in the host society. They acquire informal ties to its inhabitants and establish formal links with institutions such as banks, government, and schools. They learn the host-country language and become permanent legal residents. Empirical studies show that the probability of settlement rises steadily as migrant experience increases.

As families settle around specific places of employment, branch communities of long-term and permanent out-migrants begin to form. These communities anchor the networks and further reduce the costs and risks of movement by providing a secure and familiar environment within which new migrants can arrive, find housing and employment, and learn the ropes in the receiving country. Increasingly, migration is channeled to these communities and the diversity of destinations associated with a place of origin is further reduced.

As migrants become part of established communities in the host country, they adapt themselves to the local setting. Whether or not they have legal documents, they send their children to school, learn a minimum of the host country's language, and use financial institutions and social services. Over time the local landscape of the receiving community is transformed. Whether or not they are immigrant entrepreneurs, the migrants contribute to the creation and growth of a market for specialized foods, entertainment, and cultural products. The formation of ethnic neighborhoods represents a process of socioeconomic adaptation and transformation that permits many "foreign" practices to be maintained in the new setting.

3. CHARACTERISTICS OF THE UNAUTHORIZED POPULATION IN THE UNITED STATES

Not surprisingly, it is difficult to gauge the number of unauthorized migrants in the United States. Demographer Jeffrey Passel has been a pioneer in developing a widely respected method for estimating this population and identifying a host of further detailed information. We reprint here his latest available report, based on 2010 data. Consider as you read how the processes described by Calavita and by Massey, Goldring and Durand in the preceding Section have actually played out in shaping the unauthorized population now resident in the United States.

JEFFREY S. PASSEL & D'VERA COHN, UNAUTHORIZED IMMIGRANT POPULATION: NATIONAL AND STATE TRENDS, 2010

Pew Hispanic Center, Feb. 1, 2011,
<http://pewhispanic.org/reports/report.php?ReportID=133>i

CURRENT ESTIMATES AND TRENDS

The shrinkage of the unauthorized immigrant population from its 2007 peak apparently has halted, at least temporarily. According to Pew Hispanic Center estimates, there were 11.2 million unauthorized immigrants living in the United States in March 2010, statistically unchanged from the March 2009 estimate of 11.1 million.

The * * * March 2009 estimate had represented the first reversal in the size of the unauthorized-immigrant population in two decades. There were 3.5 million unauthorized immigrants living in the United States in 1990, a number that grew to 8.4 million in 2000. The population leveled off for two years and grew steadily from 2003 to 2007, when it peaked at 12 million. From 2007 to 2009, it shrank by 8%. [See Figure 5.6 above.]

---

i. Figures and tables are all drawn (selectively) from this report, but have been renumbered for the casebook.—eds.

Unauthorized immigrants represented 28% of the nation's foreign-born population of 40.2 million in March 2010 * * *. The share is the same as it was in 2009 but a decline from 2007's 31%.

The other components of the foreign-born population are its 29 million legal immigrants: 14.9 million naturalized citizens, 12.4 million permanent residents and 1.7 million legal temporary migrants. The number of naturalized citizens grew significantly from 13.7 million in 2007; this increase is part of a longer-term trend in which more immigrants are choosing to naturalize. The number of legal permanent residents or legal temporary migrants showed no significant change.

Table 5.9
Foreign–Born Population by Legal Status, 2010

(population in millions)

	Population	Share of Foreign Born
Total foreign born	40.2	100%
Legal immigrants	29.0	72%
Naturalized citizens	14.9	37%
Legal permanent resident aliens	12.4	31%
Legal temporary migrants	1.7	4%
Unauthorized immigrants	11.2	28%

Notes: Numbers may not sum to total due to rounding.

The decline in the size of the unauthorized immigrant population from its peak in 2007 appears to be driven mainly by a decrease in the number of such immigrants from Mexico. In 2007, there were an estimated 7 million unauthorized immigrants from Mexico. In 2010, the number of Mexican unauthorized immigrants had declined to 6.5 million.

The unauthorized population from Mexico had grown steadily from 2001, when it was 4.8 million, to its peak level in 2007. After that, there were no statistically significant changes in the Mexican-born unauthorized population until 2010, when the number showed a decline from three years earlier.

In a report last year, the Pew Hispanic Center concluded that inflows of unauthorized immigrants from Mexico had fallen off sharply, presaging the decline found in the 2010 estimates. According to the center's estimates, an average of 150,000 unauthorized immigrants from Mexico arrived annually during the period from March 2007 to March 2009, which was 70% below the annual average of 500,000 during the first half of the decade.

In addition to reduced inflows, the other ways in which an unauthorized population could decline are via an increase in the number of migrants voluntarily leaving the country, deportations, deaths or conversion to legal status. * * * [A]lthough many Mexican migrants voluntarily return home each year, there is no evidence that this number has grown in recent years.

Removals (deportations) have more than doubled over the past decade, reaching almost 400,000 in fiscal 2009. Mexicans have constituted the majority of deportations for at least the past decade. In 2009, more than 70% of deportees were Mexican, according to the Department of Homeland Security.

Because this population is relatively young, mortality is not likely to be an important factor. As for conversion to legal status, that is more difficult now than in the 1990s or earlier; the number of all status adjustments in the last three years is unchanged from average levels for 2001–2006, according to figures from the Department of Homeland Security's Yearbook of Immigration Statistics. * * *

Mexicans make up the majority of the unauthorized immigrant population, 58%, or 6.5 million. Other nations in Latin America account for 23% of unauthorized immigrants, or 2.6 million. Asia accounts for 11%, or about 1.3 million, and Europe and Canada account for 4%, or 500,000. African countries and other nations represent about 3%, or 400,000.

Births and Children

Among births from March 2009 to March 2010, 350,000 newborns had at least one unauthorized parent, a number that statistically is no different from the estimate of 340,000 published by the Pew Hispanic Center for 2008–2009.

These newborns represented 8% of all births during this period, the same share as for the previous year. Unauthorized immigrants represent about 4% of the U.S. population but are relatively young and have high birthrates, which is why their newborns make up a higher share of all births.

Among all births in the U.S. in 2009–2010, 74% were to U.S.-born parents and 17% to legal immigrants. The Pew Hispanic Center analysis also examined year-of-arrival patterns for unauthorized immigrant parents of babies born from March 2009 to March 2010, to see how long the parents had been in the United States before their children were born. If year of arrival was available for both parents, the analysis used the most recently arrived parent.

According to the analysis, 9% of these unauthorized immigrants who had babies in 2009–2010 had arrived in the U.S. in 2008 or later. An additional 30% arrived from 2004 to 2007, and the remaining 61% arrived in the United States before 2004.

Figure 5.7
Children with at Least One Unauthorized Immigrant Parent,
by Status, 2000–2010

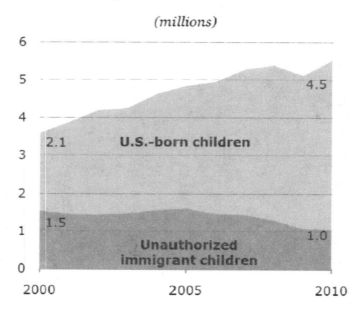

(millions)

Note: Children are persons under age 18 who are not married.

As with previous analyses, the Pew Hispanic Center finds that among all children of unauthorized immigrants—an estimated 5.5 million in 2010—a growing share was born in the United States and therefore they are U.S. citizens by birthright.

Among children of unauthorized immigrants, an estimated 4.5 million are U.S.-born; 1 million are foreign-born and therefore unauthorized. The number of unauthorized children has declined from a peak of 1.6 million in 2005. The number of U.S.-born children has more than doubled from 2.1 million in 2000.

The 14th Amendment to the U.S. Constitution, adopted in 1868, grants an automatic right to citizenship to anyone born in the United States. In recent months, some prominent national and state elected officials have urged that this right be repealed at the national or state level, on the grounds that it attracts unauthorized immigrants to the United States. A nationwide survey by the Pew Research Center in October found that registered voters are split (46% to 46%) about whether to amend the Constitution to end birthright citizenship. A majority of Republican respondents (67%) favor amending the Constitution, compared with about half of independents (48%) and a minority of Democrats (30%).

* * *

STATE SETTLEMENT PATTERNS

Analysis of state trends from 2007 to 2010 indicates that four states had a statistically significant decline in their populations of unauthorized immigrants, and the combined population of three other contiguous states in the Mountain West decreased. There was a statistically significant increase in the combined population of three contiguous West South Central states. No other states had statistically significant change over this period.

The four individual states where the number of unauthorized immigrants declined from March 2007 to March 2010 were New York, Florida, Virginia and Colorado. Additionally, the combined unauthorized immigrant population in Arizona, Nevada and Utah also decreased during that period, although the change was not statistically significant for any of those states individually. * * *

Counter to the national trend, the combined unauthorized immigrant population grew in some West South Central states. In 2007, Louisiana, Oklahoma and Texas had a combined 1.55 million unauthorized immigrants living within their borders. In 2010, that number had grown to 1.8 million. Texas, with an unauthorized immigrant population of 1.65 million, ranks second only to California in the size of this group.

California has by far the largest unauthorized-immigrant population (2.55 million). It also is among the states where unauthorized immigrants constitute the largest shares of the overall populations. In addition to California (6.8%), other top states are Nevada (7.2%) and Texas (6.7%).

Unauthorized immigrants are concentrated in a relatively small number of states. The dozen states with the largest unauthorized numbers account for more than three-quarters (77%) of this population. Nearly a quarter (23%) lives in California. Nonetheless, unauthorized immigrants live in every state, and several of their top destinations, including Georgia and North Carolina, housed relatively few unauthorized immigrants two decades ago.

Mexicans account for half or more of the unauthorized population in all but 22 states and Washington, D.C. In seven states, they make up 80% or more of the unauthorized immigrant population. At the national level, 58% of unauthorized immigrants are Mexicans. Among the five states with the largest unauthorized populations, Mexicans constitute less than half the stock in three of them—New York, New Jersey and Florida. * * *

Figure 5.8
Unauthorized Immigrant Share of Population by State, 2010

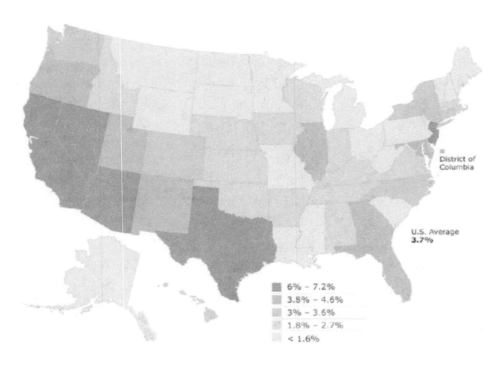

District of
Columbia

U.S. Average
3.7%

- 6% – 7.2%
- 3.8% – 4.6%
- 3% – 3.6%
- 1.8% – 2.7%
- < 1.6%

WORKERS

There were 8 million unauthorized immigrants in the workforce in March 2010, down slightly from 2007, when there were 8.4 million. They represent 5.2% of the workforce, similar to their proportion for the past half-decade, when they represented 5% to 5.5% of workers.

State patterns differ widely, but generally states with large numbers or shares of unauthorized immigrants also have relatively large numbers or shares in the workforce.

States with the largest share of unauthorized immigrants in the workforce include Nevada (10%), California (9.7%), Texas (9%) and New Jersey (8.6%). Because unauthorized immigrants are more likely than the overall population to be of working age, their share in a state's workforce is substantially higher than their share of a state's population.

Table 5.10
**Unauthorized Immigrants in the U.S. Civilian
Labor Force, 2000–2010**

(millions)

Year	Estimated Labor Force	Share of Labor Force
2010	8.0	5.2%
2009	7.8	5.1%
2008	8.2	5.3%
2007	8.4	5.5%
2006	7.8	5.2%
2005	7.4	5.0%
2004	6.8	4.6%
2003	6.5	4.4%
2002	6.4	4.4%
2001	6.3	4.3%
2000	5.5	3.8%

Note: Includes employed and unemployed workers.

California also has the largest number of people in the labor force who are unauthorized immigrants (1.85 million), followed by Texas (1.1 million), Florida (600,000) and New York (450,000.).

[METHOD AND TERMINOLOGY[j]]

* * * The estimates [in this report] are produced using a multistage method that subtracts the legal foreign-born population from the total adjusted foreign-born population, with the residual then used as the source of information about unauthorized immigrants. The source of these data is the U.S. Census Bureau's March Current Population Surveys.

Because these estimates are derived from sample surveys, they are subject to uncertainty from sampling error, as well as other types of error. Each annual estimate of the unauthorized population is actually the middle point of a range of possible values that could be the true number. Additionally, the change from one year to the next has its own margin of error.

---

j. Relocated section.—eds.

Figure 5.9
Unauthorized Immigrants as Share of Labor Force by State, 2010

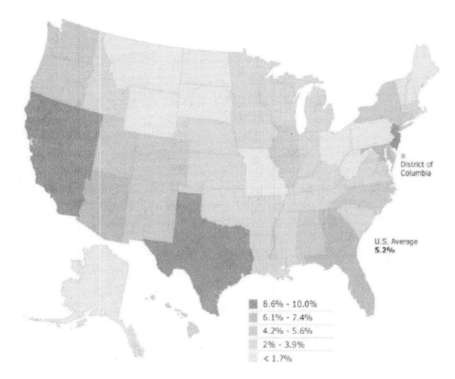

Because of the margin of error in these estimates, two numbers may look different but cannot be said definitively to be different. For example, there is no statistically significant difference between the estimate of the unauthorized population for 2009 (11.1 million) and the estimate for 2010 (11.2 million). Similarly, some state estimates for single years are based on small samples; especially in less populous states, two single years should not be compared. * * *

The "legal immigrant" population is defined as people granted legal permanent residence; those granted asylum; people admitted as refugees; and people admitted under a set of specific authorized temporary statuses for longer-term residence and work. This group includes "naturalized citizens," legal immigrants who have become U.S. citizens through naturalization; "legal permanent resident aliens," who have been granted permission to stay indefinitely in the U.S. as permanent residents, asylees or refugees; and "legal temporary migrants," who are allowed to live and, in some cases, work in the U.S. for specific periods of time (usually longer than one year).

"Unauthorized immigrants" are all foreign-born non-citizens residing in the country who are not "legal immigrants." These definitions reflect standard and customary usage by the Department of Homeland Security and academic researchers. The vast majority of unauthorized immigrants entered the country without valid documents or arrived with valid visas but stayed past their visa expiration date or otherwise violated the terms of their admission. Some who entered as unauthorized immigrants or violated terms of admission have obtained work authorization by applying for adjustment to legal permanent status or by obtaining Temporary Protected Status (TPS). Data are very limited, but this "quasi-legal" group could account for as much as 10% of the unauthorized population. Many could also revert to unauthorized status. * * *

Although the estimates presented here indicate trends in the size and composition of the unauthorized-immigrant population, they are not designed to answer the question of why these changes occurred. There are many possible factors. The deep recession that began in the U.S. economy in late 2007 officially ended in 2009, but recovery has been slow to take hold and unemployment remains high. Immigration flows have tended to decrease in previous periods of economic distress.

The period covered by this analysis also has been accompanied by changes in the level of immigration enforcement and in enforcement strategies, not only by the federal government but also at state and local levels. Immigration also is subject to pressure by demographic and economic conditions in sending countries. This analysis does not attempt to quantify the relative impact of these forces on levels of unauthorized immigration. * * *

NOTES AND QUESTIONS ON DEMOGRAPHIC TRENDS AND FAMILY PATTERNS

1. The increase in the unauthorized population during the past two decades has been accompanied by another changing demographic—major growth of the unauthorized population in new areas of residence. (See also Figure 3.7, p. 207 *supra*.) According to Passel, the share of the unauthorized population outside of the six states that have traditionally received the largest number of unauthorized migrants—California, Florida, Illinois, New Jersey, New York, and Texas—tripled in the 1990s and kept growing until the recession that began in 2007. The total number of unauthorized migrants in the other 44 states increased from 900,000 to 3.9 million from 1990 to 2005. The "new settlement" states stretched "from the northwest through the mountain states to the southeast," and in these states "the unauthorized make up 40% or more of the total foreign-born population." Passel, *Unauthorized Migrants: Numbers and Characteristics*, Background Briefing Prepared

for Task Force on Immigration and America's Future 11–15 (Pew Hispanic Center, June 14, 2005). By 2010, 25 states had unauthorized populations exceeding 100,000 people. Many of the recent state-level enforcement initiatives, discussed in Chapter Nine *infra*, have been adopted in the states that experienced rapid growth in the unauthorized population over the preceding 20 years, such as Georgia, Arizona, Alabama, and Indiana.

2. The Passel and Cohn article reports that over three-quarters of the children in families with an unauthorized migrant parent are U.S. citizens. What policy implications for removal priorities, relief from removal, and legalization proposals follow from the large number of mixed families—i.e., families that include both unauthorized migrants and some combination of authorized noncitizens and U.S. citizens?

The Fiscal Impact of Unauthorized Migration

Significant debate over the fiscal impact of unauthorized migration has existed for decades. Unauthorized migrants are not eligible for most means-tested benefit programs, including Temporary Assistance for Needy Families, food stamps (now known as SNAP, Supplemental Nutrition Assistance Program), Supplemental Security Income, non-emergency Medicaid, public housing, and legal services. *See, e.g.,* 7 U.S.C.A. § 2015(f) (SNAP); 42 U.S.C.A. § 1382c (SSI). Nor are they eligible for unemployment compensation, postsecondary financial aid, or job training. These bars were reaffirmed in the 1996 welfare legislation. Personal Responsibility and Work Opportunity Reconciliation Act of 1996 (PRWORA), Pub.L. 104–193, 110 Stat. 2105, §§ 402(b), 431(b).

But unauthorized migrants are eligible for some public benefits, including emergency Medicaid, school meal programs, and immunization for and treatment of communicable diseases. PRWORA §§ 562, 742. Most importantly, the 1982 Supreme Court decision in *Plyler v. Doe*, 457 U.S. 202, 102 S.Ct. 2382, 72 L.Ed.2d 786 (1982), considered in detail in Chapter Nine *infra*, held that Texas could not deny undocumented children access to public elementary and secondary education, under the equal protection clause of the Fourteenth Amendment.

A 2007 study by the Congressional Budget Office on this subject provided the following summary of its findings:

> In preparing its analysis, the Congressional Budget Office (CBO) reviewed 29 reports published over the past 15 years that attempted to evaluate the impact of unauthorized immigrants on the budgets of state and local governments. * * * The estimates—whether from formal studies, analyses of data on particular topics, or less-formal inquiry—show considerable consensus regarding the overall impact of unauthorized immigrants on state and local budgets. However, the scope and analytical methods of the studies vary, and the reports do not provide detailed or consistent enough data to allow for a reliable

assessment of the aggregate national effect of unauthorized immigrants on state and local budgets. * * * After reviewing the estimates, CBO drew the following conclusions:

• *State and local governments incur costs for providing services to unauthorized immigrants and have limited options for avoiding or minimizing those costs.* * * * Rules governing many federal programs, as well as decisions handed down by various courts, limit the authority of state and local governments to avoid or constrain the costs of providing services to unauthorized immigrants. * * *

• *The amount that state and local governments spend on services for unauthorized immigrants represents a small percentage of the total amount spent by those governments to provide such services to residents in their jurisdictions.* * * * Costs were concentrated in programs that make up a large percentage of total state spending—specifically, those associated with education, health care, and law enforcement. In most of the estimates that CBO examined, however, spending for unauthorized immigrants accounted for less than 5 percent of total state and local spending for those services.

• *The tax revenues that unauthorized immigrants generate for state and local governments do not offset the total cost of services provided to those immigrants.* Most of the estimates found that even though unauthorized immigrants pay taxes and other fees to state and local jurisdictions, the resulting revenues offset only a portion of the costs incurred by those jurisdictions for providing services related to education, health care, and law enforcement. Although it is difficult to obtain precise estimates of the net impact of the unauthorized population on state and local budgets * * *, that impact is most likely modest.

• *Federal aid programs offer resources to state and local governments that provide services to unauthorized immigrants, but those funds do not fully cover the costs incurred by those governments.*

Congressional Budget Office, The Impact of Unauthorized Immigrants on the Budgets of State and Local Governments 2–3 (Dec. 2007).

One of the studies used by the CBO examined in close detail the fiscal impact on the seven states that then hosted over 80 percent of the unauthorized population. It estimated that education of that population cost those states $3.1 billion in the study year, emergency Medicaid $200–300 million, and incarceration of undocumented persons convicted of crime another $500 million. Against these outlays, the study counted an estimated $1.9 billion in taxes collected from unauthorized migrants by those states in that year. The authors commented: "The share of tax revenues paid by undocumented aliens is far less than their share of the population in each state, largely because of the lower-than-average incomes of undocumented aliens." But they cautioned that their study focused only on present tax revenues from the current generation, and did not take account of possible economic growth and a wider tax base after the children of the undocumented have entered the work force. R. Clark, J. Passel, W. Zimmerman & M. Fix, Fiscal Impacts of Undocumented Aliens: Selected Estimates for Seven States, i–iv, 3 (1994).

A 2004 study by Steven Camarota examined the impact of unauthorized migration on the federal budget. It concluded that federal costs attributable to households headed by unauthorized migrants exceed the taxes such households pay by about $10.4 billion per year.

> [T]he primary reason households [headed by unauthorized migrants] create a fiscal deficit is that their much lower levels of education result in low incomes and tax payments that are only 28 percent that of other households. Thus, even though the costs they impose are estimated to be only 46 percent those of other households on average, there remains a significant net deficit. * * * Although many Americans are upset about [the] use of public services [by unauthorized migrants], there is little evidence that they come to America to take advantage of public benefits. Most * * * come for jobs, and the vast majority are in fact employed. But low levels of education mean that they unavoidably create large costs for taxpayers.

Camarota, *The High Cost of Cheap Labor: Illegal Immigration and the Federal Budget* 37 (Center for Immigration Studies 2004). Other studies suggest that the federal treasury derives a net benefit from unauthorized migrants, particularly with regard to Social Security receipts and outlays. *See, e.g.*, Porter, *Illegal Immigrants Are Bolstering Social Security With Billions*, N.Y. Times, Apr. 5, 2005; The New Americans: Economic, Demographic, and Fiscal Effects of Immigration 353 (National Research Council; J. Smith & B. Edmonston eds. 1997).

FURTHER ECONOMIC CHARACTERISTICS OF THE UNDOCUMENTED: NOTES AND QUESTIONS

1. A more extensive report by the Pew Hispanic Center in 2009, Jeffrey S. Passel & D'Vera Cohn, A Portrait of Unauthorized Immigrants in the United States (Pew Hispanic Center, Apr. 14, 2009), <http://pewhispanic.org/reports/report.php?ReportID=107>, included these additional findings (*id.* at iv–v):

- Adult unauthorized immigrants are disproportionately likely to be poorly educated. Among unauthorized immigrants ages 25–64, 47% have less than a high school education. By contrast, only 8% of U.S.-born residents ages 25–64 have not graduated from high school.

- An analysis of college attendance finds that among unauthorized immigrants ages 18 to 24 who have graduated from high school, half (49%) are in college or have attended college. The comparable figure for U.S.-born residents is 71%.

- The 2007 median household income of unauthorized immigrants was $36,000, well below the $50,000 median household income for U.S.-born residents. In contrast to other immigrants, undocumented immigrants do not attain markedly higher incomes the longer they live in the United States.

- A third of the children of unauthorized immigrants and a fifth of adult unauthorized immigrants lives in poverty. This is nearly double the poverty rate for children of U.S.-born parents (18%) or for U.S.-born adults (10%).

- More than half of adult unauthorized immigrants (59%) had no health insurance during all of 2007. Among their children, nearly half of those who are unauthorized immigrants (45%) were uninsured and 25% of those who were born in the U.S. were uninsured.

The unauthorized migrant share of the workforce in the specific occupations where they are prominent, appears in Table 5.11, drawn from Table B3 in that same 2009 Pew report. Note that no occupation, including agricultural work, has a majority of workers who are unauthorized, despite frequently voiced assertions that there are jobs that Americans won't do.

2. "It is popularly believed," writes Wayne Cornelius, "that undocumented immigrant workers toil in the informal or 'underground' economy, where employers pay sub-minimum wages and escape government regulation of labor standards. But field research in California and Illinois has found that most *indocumentados* work in relatively small or medium-sized 'formal sector' firms that are very much part of the mainstream economy. They tend to concentrate in firms and industries that are under intense foreign and/or domestic competitive pressures and that suffer from sharp fluctuations in demand for the goods or services they produce." He continues:

> For such firms, the principal advantage of undocumented immigrant labor is not its cheapness but its *flexibility* (or *disposability*, in the more critical view of many academics and labor-union leaders). The immigrant work force is more willing than U.S.-born workers to accept high variability in working hours, working days per week, and months per year, and low job security. * * * Immigrant workers are ideal "shock absorbers," enabling businesses to adapt more quickly and easily to rapidly changing market conditions and consumer preferences. * * * Thus, the U.S. labor markets in which Mexican undocumented workers typically participate are not so much *illegal* as they are *fluid* and *volatile*.

Table 5.11
Detailed Occupations with High Shares of
Unauthorized Immigrants, 2008 (thousands)

Detailed Occupation	Total Workers	Unauthorized Immigrants		U.S.-born Share	Legal Immigrant Share
		Workers	Share		
Total, Civilian Labor Force (with an occupation)	154,135	8,258	5%	84%	11%
Brickmasons, blockmasons and stonemasons (6220)	325	131	40%	45%	15%
Drywall installers, ceiling tile installers and tapers (6330)	255	94	37%	43%	20%
Roofers (6510)	246	76	31%	52%	17%
Miscellaneous agricultural workers (6050)	910	269	30%	50%	20%
Helpers, construction trades (6600)	184	52	28%	64%	8%
Dishwashers (4140)	364	101	28%	62%	10%
Construction laborers (6260)	2,055	556	27%	54%	19%
Maids and housekeeping cleaners (4230)	1,555	417	27%	49%	24%
Cement masons, concrete finishers and terrazzo workers (6250)	109	29	27%	53%	20%
Packaging and filling machine operators and tenders (8800)	369	96	26%	55%	19%
Grounds maintenance workers (4250)	1,413	356	25%	60%	15%
Packers and packagers, hand (9640)	504	119	24%	59%	18%
Butchers and other meat, poultry and fish processing workers (7810)	305	71	23%	57%	20%
Carpet, floor, and tile installers and finishers (6240)	306	68	22%	63%	14%
Painters, construction and maintenance (6420)	791	173	22%	60%	18%
Parking lot attendants (9350)	100	21	21%	60%	18%
Chefs and head cooks (4000)	377	75	20%	63%	17%
Sewing machine operators (8320)	248	49	20%	55%	26%
Refuse and recyclable material collectors (9720)	112	22	19%	71%	10%
Cooks (4020)	2,219	427	19%	69%	12%
Other "unauthorized" occupations**	34,979	3,130	9%	78%	13%
All other occupations	106,407	1,928	2%	89%	9%

Note: Occupations included in this table have at least 100,000 workers nationally and more than three times the national share of unauthorized immigrant workers. Four-digit occupation codes in parentheses.

** "Unauthorized" occupations have a higher percentage of workers who are unauthorized immigrants than the national average but do not qualify for a separate listing.

Cornelius, *Mexican Migration to the United States: Introduction*, in Mexican Migration to the United States: Origins, Consequences, and Policy Options 1, 4–8 (W. Cornelius & J. Bustamante eds., 1989). Later survey work by Cornelius and his colleagues, focused on unauthorized migrants who did receive some form of public benefit (such as medical care or children in school), found a minimum 74 percent compliance rate with tax obligations. López, Oliphant, and Tejeda, *U.S. Settlement Behavior and Labor Market Participation,* in Impacts of Border Enforcement on Mexican Migration: The View from Sending Communities 75, 88 (W. Cornelius & J. Lewis eds. 2007).

3. Consider the following summary of a study, based on Census Bureau data, comparing immigration—both legal and illegal—and job market performance during the past two decades, which saw the highest levels of immigration in U.S. history (about 13 million each decade). The studied showed only limited or delayed responsiveness of migration levels to economic conditions, especially the unemployment rate. The study also provides a rough annual picture of out-migration, which rose significantly in 2008–10.

New Census Bureau data collected in March [2010] show that 13.1 million immigrants (legal and illegal) arrived in the previous 10 years, even though there was a net decline of a million jobs during the decade. In contrast, during the 1990s there was a net growth of 21 million jobs and 12.1 million new immigrants arrived. Despite fundamentally different economic conditions, the level of immigration was remarkably similar for both 10–year periods.

- The March 2010 data show that 13.1 million immigrants (legal and illegal) have arrived in the United States since January 2000. This is the case despite two significant recessions during the decade and a net loss of a million jobs.

- Data collected in March 2000 show one million fewer immigrants arrived from January 1990 to March 2000 (12.1 million), while 21 million jobs were created during the decade.

- In 2008 and 2009, 2.4 million new immigrants (legal and illegal) settled in the United States, even though 8.2 million jobs were lost over the same period.

- The new data indicate that in the absence of a change in U.S. immigration policy, the level of new immigration can remain high even in the face of massive job losses.

- Immigration is a complex process. It is not simply a function of U.S. labor market conditions. Factors such as the desire to be with relatives or to access public services in the United States also significantly impact migration.

- Although new immigration remains high, the 2.4 million new arrivals represent a decline from earlier in this decade. In the two years prior to 2006, for example, there were 2.9 million arrivals, according to Census Bureau data.

- There was no significant change in legal immigration during the past decade. Although the number of jobs declined in the decade just completed, 10.3 million green cards were issued from 2000 to 2009, more than in any decade in American history.

- Illegal immigrants also continue to arrive, though prior research indicates that the number coming dropped significantly at the end of the decade.

- The new data not only indicate that there was a slowdown in immigration in 2008 and 2009, it also indicates there was a substantial increase in the number of immigrants who returned to their home counties, particularly in 2008.

S. Camarota, *Immigration and Economic Stagnation: An Examination of Trends 2000 to 2010* (Center for Immigration Studies Backgrounder, Nov. 2010).

4. For decades many observers have regarded unauthorized migration as essentially a win-win situation, supported by an underlying economic logic. Gordon Hanson writes of "the underlying economic reality that despite its faults, illegal immigration has been hugely beneficial to many US employers, often providing benefits that the current legal immigration system does not." He explains:

> Unauthorized immigrants provide a ready source of manpower in agriculture, construction, food processing, building cleaning and maintenance, and other low-end jobs, at a time when the share of low-skilled native-born individuals in the US labor force has fallen dramatically.

> Not only do unauthorized immigrants provide an important source of low-skilled labor, they also respond to market conditions in ways that legal immigration presently cannot, making them particularly appealing to US employers. Illegal inflows broadly track economic performance, rising during periods of expansion and stalling during downturns (including the present one). By contrast, legal flows for low-skilled workers are both very small and relatively unresponsive to economic conditions.

> Despite all this, illegal immigration's overall impact on the US economy is small. Low-skilled native workers who compete with unauthorized immigrants are the clearest losers. US employers, on the other hand, gain from lower labor costs and the ability to use their land, capital, and technology more productively. * * * [T]he small net gain that remains after subtracting US workers' losses from US employers' gains is tiny. And if we account for the small fiscal burden that unauthorized immigrants impose, the overall economic benefit is close enough to zero to be essentially a wash.

> * * * Because the net impact of illegal immigration on the US economy does not appear to be very large, one would be hard pressed to justify a substantial increase in spending on border and interior enforcement, at least in terms of its aggregate economic return.

Gordon H. Hanson, The Economics and Policy of Illegal Immigration in the United States 1–2 (MPI Dec. 2009). *See also* Cox & Posner, *The Second–Order Structure of Immigration Law*, 59 Stan. L. Rev. 809 (2007) (suggesting that unauthorized immigration functions, in effect, as an ex post screening mechanism—supplying low-skilled workers, seeking to remove those who commit criminal offenses after entry, and eventually regularizing the status of unauthorized migrants who prove to be productive workers).

Are these assessments correct? If so, is unauthorized migration a problem at all? What are the major counterarguments? How weighty are they? Consider these possible responses:

- Undocumented migrants work for lower wages and tolerate worse working conditions than native workers (or at least find themselves unable to complain effectively owing to their status), thereby undermining labor standards in the United States, particularly in times of high unemployment.

- Businesses may win from illegal migration, but significant segments of the labor force lose. It is not a coincidence that average worker wages have stagnated over the last decade, a period of massive illegal migration, while the business executives in top brackets have claimed a much larger share of overall income.

- The presence of large numbers of undocumented migrants creates disrespect for the law and in effect penalizes noncitizens who wait many years for lawful entrance.

- Undocumented migrants cost states and localities money due to their use of hospitals and their children's enrollment in public schools. Higher overall tax revenues benefit mainly the federal government.

- Because they live in the shadow of the law, undocumented migrants are less likely to assimilate. They are also less likely to report crimes or cooperate with criminal investigations.

Drawing on the earlier readings in this Section, how would you evaluate these competing claims? If you find them persuasive, what follows? Tougher border enforcement? Better interior enforcement? Legalization for unauthorized migrants in the United States? An increase in legal immigration? All of the above? We return to some of these questions in Chapter Nine.

CHAPTER SIX

ADMISSION PROCEDURES

■ ■ ■

The efforts of Congress, agencies, and courts to implement the complex substantive provisions outlined in Chapter Five have resulted in an elaborate set of admission procedures and a distinctive due process jurisprudence. We begin with a short overview of immigration processing in the early twentieth century and the legislation that resulted in the primary admission screening occurring overseas rather than stateside. We then look at the current procedures that apply to noncitizens seeking admission to the United States, examining consular processing of immigrants and nonimmigrants, followed by a look at the adjustment of status provisions that allow individuals to complete the immigration process while remaining in the United States. After surveying new expedited processing and screening systems, we turn to the constitutional framework that has developed regarding admission procedures. We close the chapter by examining the expedited procedures that are applied in some circumstances at or near the border.

SECTION A. ADMISSION PROCEDURES

1. HISTORICAL OVERVIEW

Ellis Island, for many years the principal port of entry for immigrants to the United States, has become a fixture in American folklore as the site of immigrant processing. More than 12 million immigrants passed through Ellis Island from its opening in 1892 to its closing in 1954. The first selection paints a composite picture of immigrant processing at Ellis Island in 1907, the year that still holds the record for the highest number of immigrants processed at U.S. ports-of-entry. Keep in mind that this was before the national-origins quotas were adopted. Indeed, no numerical ceilings applied at all, but each immigrant had to satisfy various qualitative exclusion criteria.

The second excerpt describes the immigration processing center on Angel Island, the largest island in San Francisco Bay. From 1910 to 1940 Angel Island screened immigrants on the West Coast. As you know from Chapter Three, Congress passed a wave of anti-Chinese legislation in the late nineteenth and early twentieth centuries. As a consequence, the majority of the immigrants who came to Angel Island were Chinese, but many other Asian and European nationalities also passed through.

ANN NOVOTNY, STRANGERS AT THE DOOR: ELLIS ISLAND, CASTLE GARDEN, AND THE GREAT MIGRATION TO AMERICA

10–23 (1971).

Heads on deck turned as a small cutter came alongside. A ladder was raised against the ship's rail, and two men and a woman in uniforms climbed aboard and pushed their way quickly through the crowd of immigrants toward the second cabin-class area. * * * In the saloon, the immigration inspector asked two or three brief questions of each waiting second-cabin passenger, while the other man, a doctor from the U.S. Public Health Service, looked quickly at their eyes as they filed past. Full information about these travelers was listed, as required by law, on the ship's official passenger list or "manifest." Because the shipping companies had made a great fuss when regular inspections in this class had begun about five years earlier, the inspector did his job as quickly as possible. * * * If the [passengers] could afford to travel in [cabin class, they] would obviously never become a public charge. When the last second-cabin passenger had been passed, the inspector ran his eyes down the first-cabin list of Americans and wealthy foreign visitors who were coming to tour or settle in this country (no one ever called *them* "immigrants"), and simply muttered, "Okay, that'll do." The Public Health Service officer was chatting with the ship's doctor, making sure that there had been no cases of epidemic diseases such as cholera, yellow fever or typhoid. If any serious contagious illnesses had been reported, the patients would have been taken at once on the quarantine boat, the *James W. Wadsworth*, to hospital wards on Hoffman Island, while other passengers would have been held in strict isolation on nearby Swinburn Island until the danger of their developing symptoms had passed. * * *

The liner had been moving slowly north into the Upper Bay while this inspection was taking place. As the enormous harbor came into view, expressions of wonder and awe could be heard on the steerage deck, and people in the center pushed and craned to get a better look at the spectacular sight * * * [of] the towering Statue of Liberty, lifting her torch of freedom to the sky. * * * [J]ust beyond * * * were the red brick buildings of Ellis Island where the immigrants would be taken. They had all heard of the Island and knew its name. That was the famous Island of Tears—*Tränen Insel* to the Germans, *Isola delle Lacrime* to the Italians— where those whom the inspectors judged too weak, old or poor to support themselves would be detained, then deported back to Europe to rebuild a broken life there.

Immigrants arrive at Ellis Island, 1902. The newly constructed hospital appears in the background. (Photo: Library of Congress)

* * *

[The steamer discharged its passengers at a pier in Manhattan. Cabin-class passengers were allowed to proceed to their destination, but the other immigrants were ushered onto a tightly packed ferry-boat or barge for the trip to Ellis Island. They might spend several hours aboard, waiting just off the crowded docks at the island before landing space became available. After disembarking, there was more waiting, in groups clustered according to big numbers on the tags tied to their coats.]

* * * Then the shouting began once more and, one by one, groups of thirty people at a time moved slowly forward, through the big door into dark tiled corridors, then—jostling two or three abreast—up a steep flight of stairs.

Their eyes blinking in the sudden bright light, they paused for a moment at the top. Sunshine streamed through the arched windows of the largest room they had ever seen. An unbelievable crowd of men, women and children was on all sides—enough to populate ten villages back home—and the hall was so huge that it might have contained their farm animals as well.

* * *

The immigrants at the top of the stairs were not given any more time to stand and stare. "This way! Hurry up!" an interpreter shouted in several languages, and they were pushed along one of the dozens of metal railings which divided the whole floor into a maze of open passageways. Although they did not realize it, they were already passing their first test as they hastened down the row in single file. Twenty-five feet away a doctor, in the smart blue uniform of the U.S. Public Health Service, was watching them carefully as they approached him. All children who looked over two years old were taken from their mothers' arms and made to walk.

It took only a few moments for the immigrants to reach the doctor, but that was time enough for his sharp eyes to notice one man who was breathing too heavily, a woman who was trying to hide her limp behind a big bundle, and a young girl whose shuffle and bewildered gaze might have been symptoms of a feeble mind. As each immigrant paused in front of him, the doctor looked hard at his face, hair, neck and hands; at the same time, with an interpreter at his side to help, he asked short questions about the immigrant's age or work to test his alertness. When a mother came up with children, each child in turn, starting with the oldest, was asked his name to make sure that he was not deaf or dumb.

In the doctor's hand was a piece of chalk; on the coats of about two out of every ten or eleven immigrants who passed him he scrawled a large white letter—"H" for possible heart trouble, "L" for lameness, a circled "X" for suspected mental defects, or "F" for a bad rash on the face. Then the immigrants filed on to a second doctor who was looking for diseases specifically mentioned in the law as reasons for deportation: signs of tuberculosis, leprosy, or a contagious skin disease of the scalp called *favus*.

* * *

At the end of the aisle interpreters waved immigrants whose coats were unmarked back toward the main part of the Registry Hall. But those whose coats bore chalk letters were pushed aside into a "pen," an area enclosed by a wire screen, to wait for more detailed medical examinations by other doctors. If they had any of the diseases proscribed by the immigration laws, or seemed too ill or feeble-minded to earn their living, they would be deported. One sobbing mother was pushed into the enclosure to wait with her little girl of eight or nine. The law said a parent had to accompany any very young child who was deported; but children of ten or older were sent back to Europe alone and simply released in the port from which they had sailed. Several weeping families in the hall were trying to make a terrible decision—"Shall we all go back together? Who will stay?"

Those immigrants waiting on benches for their final test talked anxiously and rehearsed for the last time their answers to probable questions about jobs, cash and relatives. Some said it was best to answer questions as fully as possible. Others said that inspectors were just like lawyers, always trying to trip you up, and it was best to keep your mouth shut and just say "Yes" and "No" so they couldn't muddle you.

* * *

* * * Before this long day was over, the interpreter would have helped the inspector question between four and five hundred immigrants, so that between them the two officials had only about two minutes in which to decide whether each immigrant was "clearly and beyond a doubt entitled to land," as the law specified. Every doubtful case was detained for further questioning.

The rapid queries, designed to verify the most important of the twenty-nine bits of information about each immigrant on the manifest, began: "What work do you do?" "Do you have a job waiting for you?" "Who paid for your passage here?" "Is anyone meeting you?" "Where are you going?" "Can you read and write?" "Have you ever been in prison?" "How much money do you have?" "Show it to me now." "Where did you get it?"

Nearly all of the immigrants quickly got curt nods from the inspector, who handed them landing cards, and sudden friendly smiles from the interpreter. * * * For most of the group, the ordeal was over. After only three or four hours on Ellis Island, they were free to go.

* * *

But the beginning was delayed, perhaps forever, for the unfortunate immigrants who were kept behind at Ellis Island. As one manifest group passed, for example, the inspector singled out a pretty Swedish girl who said she was going to Chicago alone to get married; he ordered her detained until her fiancé or a representative from the Lutheran Pilgrim House came to get her. Immigration officials refused to send single women alone into the streets of strange cities. If the Swedish girl's boy friend came East to meet her, an interpreter would probably escort the young couple to City Hall to be married on the spot to prevent any deception (in earlier days hundreds of marriages were performed on Ellis Island itself to combat "white slavery"). * * *

[A]bout two out of every ten * * * were held at the Island for more than a few hours. More than half of them * * * were detained for two or three days for their own protection. [The rest] faced more questioning before a Board of Special Inquiry * * *. Immigrants were brought before the board for many different reasons, including violations of the Contract Labor Law. A telegram from Europe might have brought word that an immigrant was a criminal wanted by the police in his own country; perhaps a man's wife had reported that he was deserting her. Sometimes inspectors felt that an immigrant was really a pauper who had been given a steamship ticket and a suit of clothes by a foreign government eager to get him off its charity rolls. Unfortunate people physically or mentally handicapped in earning a living would be deported if they seemed "likely to become public charges." The law ordered deportation for anyone who was a criminal, a prostitute, or suffering from insanity or a contagious disease. A few immigrants were sent back because of their political or religious beliefs: they were usually anarchists who wanted to overthrow organized government, or polygamists who believed that a man should have several wives.

A detained immigrant went into a small side office to face the Board of Special Inquiry, made up of three inspectors and an interpreter sitting behind a long desk. He swore on the Bible or a crucifix to tell the truth, then answered questions about his right to land, as a stenographer recorded his words. No lawyers were present, but an immigrant's friends and relatives were often brought to the Island to testify in his behalf. The votes of two out of the three inspectors decided a case, but if the third inspector or the immigrant himself felt that a sentence of deportation was unfair, he could appeal the decision to the Secretary of Commerce and Labor in Washington. At this stage, the immigrant was allowed to hire a lawyer to help him. In fact, the secretary often sustained an immigrant's appeal, or ordered a new hearing to be held if fresh evidence was presented. Sometimes the immigrant would be admitted after a bond was posted guaranteeing that he would not become dependent on public charity.

* * *

The shipping companies, who were supposed to screen out all "undesirables" in Europe, had to transport the immigrants home without charge and to pay for the cost of keeping them on the Island until their next ships arrived.

ROGER DANIELS, NO LAMPS WERE LIT FOR THEM: ANGEL ISLAND AND THE HISTORIOGRAPHY OF ASIAN AMERICAN IMMIGRATION*

Journal of American Ethnic History 3, 3–10 (Fall 1997).

* * *

The need for an immigration facility in San Francisco—and for a national immigration bureaucracy—was a direct result of anti-Chinese legislation, the Page Act of 1875 and the Chinese Exclusion Act of 1882. These were the first effective pieces of American restrictive immigration legislation; the latter was the hinge on which the legal history of immigration turned. With the passage of the exclusion act, the immigration of Chinese laborers was outlawed for ten years; this was renewed for another ten years in 1892, and the law was made "permanent" early in Theodore Roosevelt's administration. Beginning in the 1870s Chinese immigrants in difficulty with the immigration regulations were held in a ramshackle wooden two-story warehouse leased from the Pacific Mail Steamship Company and located at the end of a wharf on the San Francisco waterfront. It was commonly called "the shed." The building, about 100 feet square, held up to 200 people at a time, with men on the first floor and women on the second. Dorene Askin, a historian for the California Department of Parks and Recreation, described it as "crowded and unsanitary," while a contemporary inspector for the Department of Commerce and Labor reported that it was a "death trap."

* * *

By 1910 the [Angel Island] facility was opened. It was located on the island's north shore at China Cove and consisted of a number of wooden buildings—the detention barracks, administration building, hospital, and powerhouse—and a wharf. Soon after twelve cottages, a laundry, a stable, a carpenter shop, and water tanks were added and the station acquired a ferry boat. The architect supposedly used Ellis Island as a model, so that the analogy between Ellis Island and Angel Island existed even before the immigration station was built. It is not clear what, if anything, the architect learned by visiting Ellis: he chose to build in wood and Ellis Island was largely brick. The location was pleasant and scenic, although quite damp. The ferry trip from San Francisco took forty-five minutes.

* * *

In the very year that the station opened local immigration officials began to complain about the inadequacy of the facility. The buildings were, the man in charge of the San Francisco immigration district wrote on 19 December 1910, dangerous firetraps, unsanitary, and vermin infested. * * * These complaints were buttressed by a report from the Public Health Service Surgeon, who also noted the contaminated water supply and fly and cockroach infested kitchen facilities. He calculated the gross overcrowding: one dormitory room with enough air space for ten persons was equipped with fifty-four bunks, all of which were sometimes used. * * * Despite these and subsequent protests nothing was done about either moving the facility or improving it significantly until a disastrous but happily nonfatal fire destroyed the administration building and many of the records on 12 August 1940. On 5 November 1940 the last Angel Island detainees—125 Chinese men and 19 Chinese women, a few Filipinos and 35 Central European refugees—were ferried to the mainland and the history of the Angel Island Immigration Station was ended. One wonders whether the intolerable conditions would have been allowed to go on for so long if the facility had held mostly Europeans.

It is not possible, at this time, to be precise about the number of people who passed through Angel Island. Some workers connected with the state park have estimated it at 500,000 persons, but this figure is much too high. My own current guess is that perhaps 100,000 persons, mostly Asians, spent some time on the island. I assume that most of the nearly 60,000 Chinese who are recorded as entering the United States

Young Chinese immigrants undergo medical examination
on Angel Island, c. 1920. (Photo: National Archives)

between 1910 and 1940 passed through Angel Island, as did most of the
nearly 10,000 Chinese who were deported in those years. Although one
sometimes gets the impression from the literature that most Chinese who
attempted to enter were denied admission, this was not the case, but the
rate of rejection was very high. Some 50,000 came in, while perhaps 9,000
were barred, a rejection rate of about one in six, many times larger than
the rate for Ellis Island. To put these numbers into perspective, during
the Angel Island years, Chinese who never constituted as much as 1
percent of the nation's foreign born, were more than 4 percent of those
deported.

* * *

The Chinese [held on Angel Island] were of four categories. Apart
from diplomatic personnel—who were never held on the island—the only
Chinese who were admissible to the United States in the Angel Island era
were merchants and their families, students, legitimate travelers, and
persons who could claim American citizenship. Would-be Chinese immigrants to the United States in the exclusion era, like oppressed groups
everywhere, developed a wide array of resistance strategies to combat
what one of them called "laws harsh as tigers." From the mid–1870s on,
as both Charles McClain and Lucy Salyer have shown us, Chinese immigrants, with the help of their attorneys, demonstrated an ability to adapt

successfully to American institutions by utilizing the courts to an extraordinary degree.[10] As McClain and Laurene Wu McClain have written:

> Contrary to the popular image of the Chinese in the United States as passive victims ... the court cases ... demonstrate that while the Chinese were indeed victims, they were not passive. Angered by the discriminatory laws enacted to humiliate and exclude them, the Chinese decided to take their grievances to the American courts. While such litigants were probably more interested in getting results than in establishing legal principles, their cases did profoundly affect the course of American jurisprudence, contributing in a significant way to the molding of due-process and equal-protection jurisprudence under the Fourteenth Amendment.

> The willingness of Chinese litigants to confront the government in a succession of cases gave rise to sharper delineations of limits on governmental authority and the rights of citizens and noncitizens. In defining these limits and rights, they contributed far more to the ideals of democracy and republicanism upon which their adopted country was based than did their antagonists.[11]

Another form of resistance was invented after the San Francisco earthquake and fire of 18–19 April 1906, destroyed most of the city's vital statistics records. A significant number of Chinese successfully represented themselves as native-born American citizens. The advantage of making such a claim was that a citizen could not only travel to China and return, but any children he might father there were also American citizens and admissible, although their mothers were not. Many of those travelers brought in, not only their own offspring but other male relatives, while some sold the "slots" to the highest bidder. Other immigrants managed to pass themselves off as close relatives of Chinese American merchants. The persons thus admitted, under false names, were known in the Chinese American community as paper sons, although there were also, as Judy Yung has noted, some paper daughters.[12] Immigration officials were convinced that some 90 percent of the Chinese claims of citizenship were fraudulent, and, given the number of Chinese women of child-bearing age in the United States before 1906, they may well have been correct. * * *

All Chinese seeking admission through San Francisco were subjected to detailed scrutiny and delay, and almost all of them were detained on

---

10. Charles McClain, In Search of Equality: The Chinese Struggle against Discrimination in Nineteenth–Century America (Berkeley, Calif., 1994); Lucy E. Salyer, Laws Harsh as Tigers: Chinese Immigrants and the Shaping of Modern Immigration Law (Chapel Hill, N.C. 1995).

11. Charles J. McClain & Laurene Wu McClain, "The Chinese Contribution to the Development of American Law," in Entry Denied: Exclusion and the Chinese Community in America, ed. Sucheng Chan (Philadelphia, 1991), pp.21–22. * * *

12. Judy Yung, Unbound Feet: A Social History of Chinese Women in San Francisco (Berkeley, 1995), pp.3, 106.

Angel Island. Even elite Chinese arriving with student visas, whose right to enter was guaranteed by both statute law and Sino–American treaties, endured long delays. For example, a few years before Angel Island opened, one of the now-famous Soong sisters, Ai-ling, was subjected to two weeks confinement when she came to attend Wesleyan College in Georgia, even though she was traveling with two white American missionaries.

The immigration service developed a number of interrogative techniques to deal with Chinese immigrants. For those claiming derivative American citizenship, both "father" and "son" would be grilled intensively about even minute details of their biographies and of the putative village of their origin. These interrogations and investigations could go on for weeks and months—the longest individual confinement is said to have been two years—and, in some instances investigators working out of the Hong Kong consulate would actually visit a Guangdong village in an attempt to break down a cover story. Many of the paper sons came with crib sheets—in some cases books of more than a hundred pages—which were supposed to be disposed of before landing. The INS tried to isolate the prospective entrant from any support system on the mainland. Oral tradition describes how the isolation was breached: sometimes messages were enclosed in capsules hidden in the food by the Chinese cooks. And, of course, the bribery that has plagued the immigration service from its inception also existed—and was sometimes discovered—at Angel Island. To fail the immigration hearing meant sure exclusion and return to China or wherever the unsuccessful entrant had come from. * * *

* * *

In 1970, thirty years after Angel Island had been abandoned by the INS, a California park ranger, Alexander Weiss, noticed a large number of Chinese characters carved into the walls of what had been the detention barracks * * * *.

The calligraphy on the walls * * * were the now famous Angel Island poems. Their rediscovery * * * sparked a flurry of interest and publication. The most important work to emerge was a book called Island, first published in 1980 by the doyen of the historians of Chinese America, Him Mark Lai, and two younger scholars, Genny Lim and Judy Yung.[20] In addition to the English and Chinese texts of the 135 extant poems, with English annotations, the volume contains excerpts from a number of oral histories and a wonderful collection of pictures. These poems are all by men. There were apparently some by women, but if so, they were destroyed in the 1940 fire. All of the poems are sad, and some are also angry. An angry poem reads:

> . . . I hastened to cross the American ocean.

---

20. Him Mark Lai, Genny Lim & Judy Yung, Island: Poetry and History of Chinese Immigrants on Angel Island, 1910–1940 (1980: reprint ed., Seattle, 1991). * * *

How was I to know that the western barbarians had lost their hearts, and reason?

With a hundred kinds of oppressive laws, they mistreat us Chinese.

It is still not enough after being interrogated and investigated several times;

We also have to have our chests examined while naked.

Our countrymen suffer this treatment

All because our country's power cannot yet expand.

If there comes a day when China will be united,

I will surely cut out the heart and bowels of the western barbarian.[21]

The foregoing should explode any notion that Angel Island was, as is often stated, the Ellis Island of the West. * * *

The Evolution of the Visa Requirement

Although Congress forbade permanent immigration of Chinese laborers in 1882, immigrants from other countries faced qualitative restrictions, but no numerical limits. This changed when Congress enacted national-origins quotas in the 1920s. The following excerpt describes the chaos that occurred in 1921 when the quotas were first applied. The 1924 quota legislation responded to the problem by shifting from reliance on state-side immigration processing to a visa system that relies primarily on the screening of would-be immigrants overseas.

The First Quota Law, or Johnson Act, which went into effect on June 3, 1921, specified that no more than twenty per cent of a nation's quota could be filled in any one month. Officials of the shipping companies were close to panic; during the last few days of grace they organized a mad dash to land thousands of immigrants in American ports before the deadline. Any ship that could make the transatlantic passage was crammed with passengers and some vessels racing through the Narrows actually collided in their haste. During June, once the new system was in effect, steamships still raced to land their passengers on Ellis Island as soon as possible, and within the first few days of the month the specified twenty per cent of all national quotas had been filled. Then the first scenes of a human tragedy began. Some ten thousand aliens arrived at Ellis Island to be told that their quotas had been filled for June—there was no room for them in America. It was an impossible situation that no one, apparently, had foreseen. Puzzled officials held the surplus immigrants on their ships and asked Washington for instructions; the answer came

---

21. Lai et al., Island, Poem #46, p.162.

back that the immigrants were to be admitted on bond, and their numbers subtracted from July's quotas.

But in July, and during the first days of every succeeding month, the same thing happened, as the steamships continued their race to grab as large a share as possible of the quotas for their own passengers. Whole shiploads of immigrants were now turned back to Europe in scenes of terrible anguish described by one Public Health Service doctor as "one of my most painful reminiscences of service at the Island." She recalled one particular group of five hundred southeastern Europeans who had sold their homes and possessions and traveled four thousand miles to start a new life, only to hear after they had passed the Statue of Liberty that they were inadmissible. "They screamed and bawled and beat about like wild animals, breaking the waiting-room furniture and attacking the attendants, several of whom were severely hurt. It was a pitiful spectacle...." * * * Commissioner Wallis complained bitterly to Washington in October, 1921, that "our nation is committing a gross injustice." He urged that immigrants be examined by American consuls in European ports, to save all this "indescribable" suffering "that would melt a heart of granite."

* * *

* * * The restrictive law and the sad tales of rejection which were taken back to Europe reduced the volume of arrivals; physical improvements were made; and the staff was better organized. The First Quota Law, never intended to be more than a temporary measure, was replaced in July, 1924, by a second, more restrictive, act * * *. [T]he overall ceiling was slashed from 358,000 to 164,000 people a year. Italy's quota, under this arrangement, was cut from 42,057 under the First Quota Law to a mere 3,845 per year. The second law's most important provision, as far as Ellis Island's history is concerned, was a rule that all immigrants were to be inspected at the American consular offices in Europe, where visas would be issued to those found acceptable. Consuls would slowly fill the national quotas, issuing no more than ten per cent of the available visas in one month, in an attempt to end the first-come-first-served system used by the steamships and the inevitable disappointments in American ports.

As soon as the second law went into effect, the Secretary of Labor visited Ellis Island and boasted that the place looked "like a 'deserted village.'" Immigrants were still examined there, but they arrived in an evenly-spaced flow over the months, and very few of those who had been judged acceptable by the consuls had to be detained. * * * By 1926, much of Ellis Island's staff had been disbanded. Dust began to settle in the empty rooms.

Novotny, Strangers at the Door, 127–30.

2. IMMIGRANT ADMISSIONS

Today, at the beginning of the twenty-first century, the process of securing status as a lawful permanent resident in the United States is elaborate and time-consuming. First, a visa petition is generally required. After approval of the petition, there are two different paths toward permanent residence status: (1) obtaining an immigrant visa at a U.S. consulate and then traveling to the United States; or (2) becoming a permanent resident through adjustment of status while remaining in the United States. (Concurrent requests for consular processing and adjustment of status are treated as withdrawal of the adjustment application.) We will defer discussion of adjustment of status until later in this section and focus here on immigrant visa processing at a consulate outside the United States. The relevant regulations are in 22 C.F.R. Part 42.

First, though, a word about terminology. Although we generally use the term noncitizen, our discussion of admission procedures will sometimes include references to an "arriving alien." Under the regulations an arriving alien is "an applicant for admission coming or attempting to come into the United States at a port-of-entry." 8 C.F.R. 1.1(q). Would-be immigrants, as well as nonimmigrants, who present themselves at a U.S. port of entry are deemed arriving aliens. In contrast, noncitizens who enter the United States surreptitiously are not viewed as arriving aliens. And immigrants already admitted as lawful permanent residents who are returning to the United States from a subsequent short trip abroad are generally not regarded as arriving aliens. INA § 101(a)(13)(C).

a. Filing a Visa Petition

Obtaining an immigrant visa typically involves two steps: (1) filing a visa petition with the Department of Homeland Security in the United States, and (2) completing the visa process at a U.S. consulate abroad. As you recall from Chapter Five, generally a family member or an employer in the United States begins the process by filing a visa petition on behalf of the noncitizen beneficiary. The petition, Form I–130 for family reunification and Form I–140 for employment, serves to verify the underlying relationship and to demonstrate that the beneficiary satisfies all the requirements of the appropriate immigrant category. (Remember that many of the employment-based visas require the employer to secure labor certification from the Department of Labor before filing the I–140.) Some noncitizens, such as most special immigrants (fourth preference), investors (fifth), and individuals of extraordinary ability (first), do not need an employer and can petition directly on their own. *See* INA § 204(a)(1).

Petitioners usually file visa petitions by mail with the U.S. Citizenship and Immigration Services (USCIS), accompanied by the appropriate fee. The petitioner usually remains in command of the process at this stage and can withdraw the petition at any time without the beneficiary's consent. Certain events, such as the petitioner's death, may mean automatic revocation. 8 C.F.R. § 205.1. If the petition has been approved, but the beneficiary has not yet traveled to the United States under the immigrant visa, or has not yet been accorded adjustment of status, the revocation may block or void the beneficiary's admission as an immigrant. An exception on humanitarian grounds to automatic revocation based on the petitioner's death may be possible. 8 C.F.R. § 205.1(a)(3). Also, the spouse of a U.S. citizen can self-petition for two years as an immediate relative after the death of the citizen spouse, as described in Chapter Five, Section A. *See* INA § 201(b)(2)(A)(i). Battered spouses and children may sometimes also self-petition. *See* INA § 204(a)(1)(A)(iii), (A)(iv), (B)(ii), (B)(iii), (B)(iv); Mehta & Benach, *Keeping Battered Noncitizens in the United States Until Permanent Residency*, 77 Interp.Rel. 225 (2000).

If USCIS denies a visa petition, the petitioner can usually seek administrative review—by the Board of Immigration Appeals in family-sponsored cases and by the Administrative Appeals Office of USCIS in the employment-based categories. Many courts have held that the administrative decision on a visa petition is subject to judicial review, applying standard doctrine under the Administrative Procedure Act. *See, e.g., Bangura v. Hansen*, 434 F.3d 487 (6th Cir. 2006) (spousal visa petition); *Soltane v. USDOJ*, 381 F.3d 143, 148 (3d Cir. 2004) (denial of a visa petition for a religious worker special immigrant); *but see Jilin Pharmaceutical USA, Inc. v. Chertoff*, 447 F.3d 196 (3d Cir. 2006) (no jurisdiction to review revocation of visa petition). We will discuss judicial review in more detail in Chapter Ten.

b. After a Visa Petition Is Approved

Once a visa petition is approved, USCIS forwards the endorsed visa petition to the State Department's National Visa Center (NVC) in Portsmouth, New Hampshire (unless the petitioner has indicated that the beneficiary will adjust status within the United States). The NVC creates a case file, provides instructions to petitioners and beneficiaries, and receives fees and many required documents. The NVC sends to the applicant or his agent the "Instruction Package for Immigrant Visa Applicants," with instructions, a summary biographical form, and detailed information about the rest of the necessary documentation and how to obtain it. Certified copies of any birth records, prison records, military records, and sometimes certificates reflecting local police records, are required, in addition to "all other records or documents which the consular officer considers necessary." 22 C.F.R. § 42.65(b). A certified translation must accompany any documents not in English.

The applicant is told to return the completed biographical data sheet to the NVC immediately. The NVC also obtains from sponsors the executed Affidavit of Support forms (I–864) (For categories to which that requirement applies, *see* INA §§ 212(a)(4), 213A.) As described in Chapter Seven, these affidavits are legally binding documents meant to ensure that recent immigrants will not pose a financial burden to the taxpayers.

Once the NVC has received any required affidavits of support, checked for completeness of all the information submitted, and completed the administrative processing, it determines whether the visa priority date is current. (A visa is available only when the processing in the particular immigrant's preference category has reached the priority date, the date marking the noncitizen's place on the waiting list.) If a visa is not immediately available, the officer notifies the noncitizen that the petition has been received and will be held until one is.

c. Overseas Processing

When the priority date is current and the visa file is complete, the NVC sends the visa file to the consulate where the beneficiary will complete the application process in person. Noncitizens (other than those using the adjustment process, discussed below) are ordinarily expected to complete the visa process at a U.S. consulate in their home countries. In limited circumstances, they may persuade a consulate elsewhere to process the case and issue the visa, especially if they can demonstrate that returning to their homeland would be a hardship due to factors such as physical infirmity, advanced age, the presence of war or widespread civil disturbance, or the unavailability of U.S. visa services there. Such cases are sometimes known as "orphan visa" or "homeless visa" cases.

The NVC sends the applicant the "Appointment Package for Immigrant Visa Applicants," containing the date of the visa appointment, the visa application form, instructions regarding the required medical examination by an approved physician, and instructions for fee payments. Usually the consulate directly schedules the medical appointment shortly before the interview.

The prior USCIS approval of the visa petition does not mean that the applicant has been found admissible; that issue, based on application of the § 212(a) inadmissibility grounds discussed in Chapter Seven, must be decided by the consul—or by the examiner considering an adjustment application. If the consular officer finds the applicant admissible, she issues an immigrant visa, valid for six months. *See* INA § 221(c). The State Department issued 482,052 immigrant visas in FY 2010. *See* Bureau of Consular Affairs, Visa Statistics, Report of the Visa Office 2010, table 1. Unlike a nonimmigrant visa, an immigrant visa is not affixed to the applicant's passport. It consists instead of a set of documents to be presented in a special envelope to the admitting immigration officer at the port of entry.

d. At the Port of Entry

When the intending immigrant arrives in the United States, the responsibility switches from the State Department's consular staff back to Customs and Border Protection (CBP), which is part of DHS. The immigration officer at the port of entry inspects the set of visa documents prepared at the consulate and may question the visa holder. If that officer finds no disqualifications, he will keep the immigrant visa, make a notation of admission as a lawful permanent resident in the immigrant's passport, and forward the necessary papers for issuance of the Permanent Resident Card, Form I–551.

The I–551 is the celebrated "green card." I–551 cards issued today are valid for ten years and contain counterfeit-resistant optical patterns. The system also allows government computers to store and transmit images of the photo, fingerprint, and signature on the card, to thwart impostors claiming to have lost an earlier card. The green card was introduced initially to serve as evidence of compliance with the INA's fingerprinting and registration requirements, *see* INA § 264(d), and for many years was formally known as the "Alien Registration Receipt Card."

If a permanent resident plans to leave this country temporarily, she may do so and upon return is counted as a "special immigrant" under INA §§ 101(a)(27)(A), 211(b). (Otherwise she might be double-counted against any relevant quotas or caps.) For purposes of return, it is important that she take along proof that she is a returning permanent resident. If she will be gone from the country no longer than 12 months, the green card may be used as the needed re-entry permit. *See* INA § 223; 8 C.F.R. § 211.1(a)(2). But a returning permanent resident may sometimes be regarded as "seeking admission" to the United States, making all the inadmissibility grounds of § 212(a) apply afresh, as Chapter Seven will explain more fully. *See* INA § 101(a)(13)(C). Possession of a green card thus will not assure readmission; it merely dispenses with certain documentary requirements.

3. NONIMMIGRANT ADMISSIONS

a. Nonimmigrant Visas

Most individuals who wish to come to the United States for a temporary stay must first secure a nonimmigrant visa from a U.S. consular officer in a foreign country. The Department of State received 7.6 million nonimmigrant visa applications in FY 2010, and of these it approved 6.4 million, or 84 percent. *See* Department of State, Report of the Visa Office 2010, Visa Statistics, tables 1 and 20. The number of nonimmigrant visas issued is well short of the total number of visits to the United States annually. For example, 46.5 million nonimmigrants (excluding Canadians and Mexicans, discussed below) were admitted to the United States in FY 2010. *See* DHS Office of Immigration Statistics, Annual Flow Report: Nonimmigrant Admissions to the United States: 2010 (2011). Many visitors make multiple visits on the same visa. Consular officers, relying on their individualized judgment, can issue visas valid for a single admission or multiple entries; they can also issue visas for a short duration or a multi-year period. In addition, as described below, many visitors require no visa at all for admission.

The Homeland Security Act transferred some responsibility for visa policy and monitoring from the Department of State to the Department of

Homeland Security, to ensure that security concerns are fully reflected in the visa process. Under a carefully negotiated Memorandum of Understanding between the departments, 80 Interp.Rel. 1365 (2003), DHS has authority to issue regulations regarding visa issuance, reviews most field guidance before it is issued, and assigns its own officers to selected consular posts to advise, review, and conduct investigations. The Department of State retains the principal operational and management responsibilities.

The noncitizen bears the burden of proving that he qualifies for the visa, and the most important issue in the high-demand categories (especially B–1 and B–2 visitors, F and M students, and J exchange visitors) will often be whether he truly has a home in a foreign country to which he intends to return. (As discussed in Chapter Five, however, the dual intent doctrine may relax this requirement, at least for certain nonimmigrant categories.) The consular officer has discretion to require any kind of documentary support she deems necessary. *See* INA §§ 221(g), 222(c)–(d).

The fee for processing a nonimmigrant visa application, as of late 2011, is $140. Since 2004, as a security measure, Congress has required an in-person interview before the issuance of a visa for all applicants aged 14 to 79, subject only to highly limited waivers. INA § 222(h). At the interview, the consular officer makes sure that all the information has been correctly supplied on the application form and then proceeds to question the applicant, especially on any matters that raise doubts about admissibility. The State Department leaves to the discretion of the U.S. consul whether an attorney will be allowed to attend the interview; many posts forbid such attendance. DHS staff can veto the issuance of a visa they believe should not be granted, but they cannot grant a visa to someone denied by a consular officer. *See generally* Martin, *Immigration Policy and the Homeland Security Act Reorganization: An Early Agenda for Practical Improvements*, 80 Interp.Rel. 601, 603–04 (2003).

If the consular officer finds that any of the inadmissibility grounds apply, she may deny the visa. Or if a waiver of the applicable ground is available, the officer usually assists with that application, to be forwarded for adjudication, along with the officer's report of any pertinent information bearing on the waiver and developed during the interview. Waivers are usually in the discretion of the Department of Homeland Security, not the Secretary of State.

If the visa application is approved, the consular officer affixes a nonimmigrant visa into the applicant's passport. The sticker, which contains security features to guard against counterfeiting and photo substitution, shows a visa number, date and place of issue, expiration date, and visa classification. (Take a look now at the sample nonimmigrant visa in the Statutory Supplement.) Unless otherwise specified, the visa is good for multiple entries before its expiration. The basic regulations governing the nonimmigrant visa process are in 22 C.F.R. Parts 40, 41.

b. Exceptions to the Visa Requirement

(i) Mexico and Canada

There are two major exceptions to the visa requirement: border crossing cards (BCCs) and the visa waiver program. For years the United States has issued BCCs to accommodate Mexican nationals living in the border area. The BCC serves as an identity document, obviating the need for a Mexican passport, and also as a B–1/B–2 visa. A BCC is sufficient immigration documentation for Mexican nationals entering the United States at a southern land border port of entry who will remain within 25 miles of the Mexican border (or a wider area in Arizona) for 72 hours or less.

Issuance and quality requirements have been progressively tightened since 2001. The card now must contain prescribed biometric identifiers (such as fingerprint scans and photos), and in that form is often known as a "laser visa." Mexican nationals qualifying in the B–1 or B–2 admission category usually receive this form of document, whether traveling to the border region or beyond. Since 2006, applicants for a laser visa must present a Mexican passport to qualify for issuance of the card.

Canadian nationals have benefited from a long-time exception. They may enter to study or visit temporarily without a visa or a BCC, *see* 8 C.F.R. §§ 212.1(a), 212.6(b)(1), by presenting their passports. Together, Mexicans entering with BCCs and Canadians accounted for more than 110 million nonimmigrant admissions in 2010. *See* DHS Office of Immigration Statistics, Annual Flow Report: Nonimmigrant Admissions to the United States: 2010 (2011).

(ii) Visa Waiver Program

Until 1986, the United States required citizens of all countries other than Canada or Mexico to obtain visas from U.S. consulates overseas. This policy continued long after most other countries allowed Americans to visit temporarily without a visa. Congress authorized a visa waiver pilot program in 1986, and made it permanent in 2000. The Visa Waiver Program applies only to temporary visitors in the B–1 or B–2 nonimmigrant categories who seek admission for up to 90 days from selected countries that meet specified statutory criteria, such as reciprocal rights for U.S. citizens, issuance of machine readable passports, and low visa refusal rates. INA § 217. Since 2009, those who want to travel on a visa waiver have been required to obtain advance clearance through an automated web-based system known as the Electronic System for Travel Authorization (ESTA). The traveler provides biographic information that allows DHS to check him or her against databases to identify security- or crime-based concerns. Upon clearance the noncitizen receives a code number, meant to be checked by the airline before boarding, indicating eligibility to travel without a visa. *See* <https://esta.cbp.dhs.gov/esta/>.

As of late 2011, the nationals of 36 countries are eligible for the program: Andorra, Australia, Austria, Belgium, Brunei, Czech Republic,

Denmark, Estonia, Finland, France, Germany, Greece, Hungary, Iceland, Ireland, Italy, Japan, Latvia, Liechtenstein, Lithuania, Luxembourg, Malta, Monaco, the Netherlands, New Zealand, Norway, Portugal, San Marino, Singapore, Slovakia, Slovenia, South Korea, Spain, Sweden, Switzerland, and the United Kingdom. *See* 8 C.F.R. § 217.2; Temporary Visitors to the U.S., <http://travel.state.gov>. In FY 2010, the program admitted 17 million visitors, nearly half of the reported total of nonimmigrant admissions. *See* 2010 Yearbook of Immigration Statistics, table 25. The visa waiver program led to a considerable drop in the consular workload, from the record high of 8.7 million nonimmigrant visas issued in FY 1988 to a low of 5.8 million in FY 2006 and to 6.4 million in FY 2010. *See* Report of the Visa Office 1999, table 1; Report of the Visa Office 2006, table 1; Report of the Visa Office 2010, Visa Statistics, tables 1 and 20.

The visitor who enters under the visa waiver program waives significant rights. She cannot extend her stay, change nonimmigrant status under § 248, or adjust to permanent resident status under § 245(a) once she is in the United States (except as an immediate relative of a U.S. citizen). *See* INA §§ 245(c); 248. She also waives her right to a removal hearing, except that she may apply for and have a hearing on asylum. INA § 217(b). These waivers have been sustained against constitutional challenges. *See, e.g., Bingham v. Holder,* 637 F.3d 1040 (9th Cir.2011). (Efforts, including ESTA, to reduce the vulnerability of the visa waiver program to terrorists or others seeking to evade entry restrictions are discussed in Chapter Nine, Section A.)

c. At the Port of Entry

Without a visa (or a proper showing that she is visa-exempt), a noncitizen probably will not be able to board a plane or other vessel for the United States. Carrier enforcement of the visa requirement has been a feature of U.S. practice since the 1920s. Carriers are subject to fines and other expenses for bringing passengers without adequate documentation. *See* INA §§ 241(c), (e), 273.

At the port of entry, a CBP officer inspects the noncitizens. The consul's prior decisions on admissibility do not bind the immigration officers at the border checkpoint or port of entry. The statute emphasizes that the immigration inspectors may refuse to admit a noncitizen even with a visa. INA § 221(h). Nonetheless, most arrivals are admitted after a few quick and routine questions. If any questions about admissibility cannot be readily cleared up, the person is referred to what is known as secondary inspection for more extensive questioning, usually conducted in offices or cubicles nearby at the port of entry but away from the primary inspection booths.

Each year, between 400 and 500 million admissions occur at U.S. ports of entry. *See* DHS Customs & Border Protection Summary of Performance and Financial Information, Fiscal Year 2010, 3 (Jan. 2011). (These totals include multiple counting of individuals who enter more than once.) Of those noncitizens who are not admitted, the vast majority are turned back without ever seeing an immigration judge, in part because noncitizens believed inadmissible are usually given a chance to withdraw their applications for admission. (Withdrawal is not an automatic right; both the inspector and the applicant must consent.) *See* INA § 235(a)(4).

Noncitizens are typically asked to fill out a Form I–94 card, the Arrival–Departure Record, before arriving in the United States, and to carry it with them through inspection. (A blank Form I–94 is included in the Statutory Supplement.) The I–94 asks for basic personal information and has spaces for the inspector at the port of entry to record key information reflecting the processing, such as a routine admission stamp, or data regarding the reasons for a referral to secondary inspection and the disposition of such inspection.

Upon admission, the inspector keeps the upper portion of the I–94 card and gives the nonimmigrant the bottom portion—with both portions stamped and endorsed to show the classification in which the noncitizen is admitted (usually, but not always, the same as the visa classification), the time allowed for her to remain in the United States, and any other specific conditions of entry. This card is usually stapled into the passport, and is meant to be surrendered upon departure from the United States. It is a highly important document, usually the first item that should be checked if a nonimmigrant poses questions about her status. Formerly, if a nonimmigrant had permission to work (most do not), she received a stamp or endorsement to this effect on the I–94. But because these notations were easily counterfeited, most work-authorized noncitizens now receive a uniform, counterfeit-resistant card, known as the Employment Authorization Document (EAD), Form I–766, with a photograph and embedded fingerprint.

Although people often speak of a noncitizen being here "on a tourist visa" or "on a student visa," this usage is technically incorrect—and potentially misleading. The visa only helps move the noncitizen to the port of entry. The type and length of her actual admission will be determined by what is written on the I–94.

Say, for example, a noncitizen has a B–2 visa that expires on September 1, 2012. She is admitted to the United States on January 1, 2012. If her I–94 indicates admission in B–2 status until March 1, 2012, she must leave by that date. If she does nothing to extend her authorized stay, it will do her no good on March 2 to point out that her visa is valid until September 1. In fact, a nonimmigrant visa holder generally voids her visa if she overstays her authorized admission period. *See* INA § 222(g).

Suppose she does not extend or change her status but instead leaves in late February before the end of her authorized stay. She can then use the visa to return to the United States at any time before it expires on September 1 (unless it was a single-entry visa). If she returns on August 1 and the admitting officer determines that the new visit is bona fide, she would receive a new I–94 that is valid, for example, for three months, until

November 1, 2012. She may stay for that full period, even though her visa expires one month after admission.

Alternatively, while she still is in lawful status based on the January 1 admission, she can apply to DHS to have her admission period extended, or to have her nonimmigrant classification changed under INA § 248 (*e.g.,* from B–2 tourist to F–1 student). If permission is granted, she need not have the visa amended, as long as she plans no further travel outside the United States before the new admission period expires. The change will be reflected on the I–94 or a tear-off slip attached to the notice of action (Form I–797B) and meant then to be carried with the I–94 and passport.

PROBLEMS

1. Beatrice, a British national, is interested in traveling to the East Coast of the United States to visit several college campuses. She has been accepted at three U.S. universities, but she is not sure if she would like to enroll. What kind of visa should she seek and where should she apply for it? (You may wish to consult Chapter Five, Section B again. Do not consider inadmissibility grounds, which will be discussed in Chapter Seven.) Is she eligible for the visa waiver program? If she has a choice between seeking a visa or traveling under the visa waiver program, what factors should she consider in deciding how to proceed?

2. Beatrice's cousins, Clark, a Canadian citizen, and Mariana, a Mexican citizen, would like to meet her in the United States and visit the colleges together. Assuming they are not prospective students and that no inadmissibility grounds apply to them, can they rely on the visa waiver program for entry into the United States? What other options do they have?

3. Suppose that Mariana, a Mexican citizen, has been accepted at a college in Dallas, Texas. Will Mariana's border crossing card allow her entry to the United States to attend classes for the fall semester?

---

4. CONSULAR PROCESSING IN ACTION

Though the basic patterns of consular processing are standardized, each consulate has its own unique procedures and folkways, often shaped by the primary types of issues its officers face daily (e.g., is visa fraud seen as a major problem in that location?). This reading describes practices at the U.S. consulate in Mumbai, India. For similar portraits of the day-to-day workings of consular processing, see 83 Interp. Rel. 1553 (2006) (Madrid); 82 Interp.Rel. 105 (2005) (Taiwan); 77 Interp.Rel. 1153 (2000) (Tokyo & Osaka–Kobe); 75 Interp.Rel. 1469 (1998) (Tel Aviv); 75 Interp.Rel. 1009 (1998) (Ciudad Juarez); 75 Interp.Rel. 37 (1998) (London).

POORVI CHOTHANI, CERTAIN U.S. IMMIGRANT AND NONIMMIGRANT VISA PROCESSES AND OTHER SERVICES AVAILABLE AT THE U.S. CONSULATE GENERAL IN MUMBAI

83 Interp. Rel. 1597 (2006).

INTRODUCTION

In the last fiscal year, U.S. Consulates in India issued more than 350,000 nonimmigrant visas. About one-third of a total of 122,981 intra-company transfer visas (L visas) issued by the U.S. were issued in India for the same fiscal year. Of the total student visas issued this year, 18,600 were issued to Indian students, and there are about 81,000 Indian students presently studying in the U.S.

The U.S. Embassy in India, which has a visa section, is located in New Delhi. There are three additional consular posts: Mumbai (Bombay), Kolkata (Calcutta) and Chennai (Madras). The U.S. Department of State (DOS) recently announced that it would open a new post at Hyderabad, which is an important center of several Information Technology (IT) and IT Enabled Services (ITES) companies.

* * * The Mumbai Post is one of the busiest consulates and is reported to receive a large number of fraudulent cases and also sees a high incidence of forged documents. Forged documents are often presented by NIV applicants[, thus] reducing the value of documentary proof of assets.

* * *

Due to space constraints and security reasons, only the visa applicant is allowed at any interview; attorneys, relatives or other "interested parties" are not allowed into the Mumbai Post. Since 9/11, the security measures in and around the Mumbai Post have increased. In exceptional cases, a relative who is a U.S. citizen may be permitted to accompany an IV applicant.

Most applicants prefer to conduct their visa interview in English. However, the Mumbai Post does provide interpreters for regional languages including Hindi, Gujarati and Marathi.

NONIMMIGRANT VISA PROCESSING

Persons applying for nonimmigrant visas at the Mumbai Post include visitors, students, participants in exchange programs, religious workers, temporary workers, persons with extraordinary abilities, performing artists, professional journalists, and representatives of foreign governments. Applicants are required to apply at the consular office responsible for the consular district in which they live. * * *

Subsequent to the U.S. Visitor and Immigrant Status Indicator Technology (US–VISIT) program that requires applicants to provide biometric information, all posts in India have discontinued the "drop box" facility for submitting U.S. visa applications. All posts in India collect fingerprint impressions and photographs from all visa applicants, except those traveling on official government business or those who are under age 14 or over age 79.

At the time of the visa interview, applicants are asked to electronically scan the index (second) finger of each hand. Applicants who are required to be fingerprinted, who have a cut or blister or other temporary skin injury on their index fingers may not be issued a visa until their finger heals and they can be fingerprinted. The scanned fingerprint data collected at the time of the visa application will be compared with fingerprint scans at the U.S. port of entry to prevent the use of U.S. visas by imposters and by those wanted for more serious offenses.

Persons already in possession of valid U.S. visas acquired before the implementation of US–VISIT may travel to the U.S. on their current visas and are not required to reapply for new visas until their current ones expire. They will be fingerprinted at the border or port of arrival.

BOOKING AN APPOINTMENT FOR THE VISA INTERVIEW

All nonimmigrant visa applicants are required to schedule an appointment with the Visa Facilitation Services (VFS), which is an organization retained by the U.S. Consulate as the off-site interview scheduler. There are significant delays in obtaining visa interview appointments. However, all consular posts in India are working towards reducing appointment wait times.

Applicants can schedule appointments online on the VFS website or by visiting the VFS Center closest to the applicant. * * *

It is advisable to apply very early for an appointment for the visa interview. The U.S. Consulate at Mumbai's website provides typical waiting periods for NIV visa appointments (as of June 28, 2006): [visitors: 157 days; students and exchange visitors: 18 days; others: 21 days].

* * *

* * * Prior to booking an appointment online or in person at any VFS Application Center, it is necessary to pay the fees and obtain a visa fee receipt [at a designated bank]. The fee receipt is issued with a unique barcode number, which is required when booking an online interview. The bank requires each applicant to present a photocopy of the first page of the passport when paying the fees.

* * * After booking an appointment the applicant should submit copies of the passport, one photograph, the appointment letter (generated online), original fee receipt (which contains two barcode stickers) obtained from the HDFC Bank, duly completed visa application forms and a signed copy of the checklist that is generated online, to the VFS Center. The photograph has to conform to the requirements stipulated by the U.S. government. It is important that these documents be submitted five working days before the appointment date. The applicant should then

report to the Mumbai Post as per the details in the appointment letter. The applicant should carry copies of the documents presented to the VFS Center and all supporting documents to help him or her prove ability to finance the visit to the U.S., nonimmigrant intent and purpose of visit. Students should also submit the SEVIS fee receipt with the documents. * * * Applicants should be forthcoming about their purpose and plans in visiting the U.S.; applicants should prepare for the interview by being able to clearly and concisely describe their intentions.

At the time of granting an appointment for visa interview the VFS Center checks the documents, retains the visa application forms and returns the passport along with a photocopy of the applicant's passport page with the VFS' stamp.

* * *

All consular posts in India, including the Mumbai Post[,] have set aside some appointment slots for emergency applications involving humanitarian or medical emergencies; students with valid Form I–20s; returning H or L visa applicants; and certain unforeseen business related needs. Weddings, graduation ceremonies and other foreseeable events are not considered emergencies. * * *

VISA INTERVIEW

Visa applicants should be at the U.S. Consulate 15 minutes before the scheduled appointment. The interviewing officer retains the passport for stamping after he or she has determined that a visa will be issued. The passport is then couriered to the applicant and usually reaches the applicant within the next two working days.

Some applications, however, may require additional processing that could delay visa issuance for an extended period of time. The applicant will be notified if there is any delay in his or her case and if the applicant requires any security or additional checks or tests. * * * The Mumbai Post usually conducts additional checks within 30 days of the interview. However, some applicants face longer delays.

* * *

FAMILY BASED IMMIGRANT VISA PROCESSING

The Mumbai Post ranks among the busiest posts for immigrant visa [IV] issuance including family-based and employment-based visas. Persons born in India are ineligible to participate in the Diversity Visa Program.

* * *

Family-based cases require that a petition be filed with and approved by USCIS before any U.S. Consulate can take action. Petitions approved by USCIS are generally forwarded to the National Visa Center (NVC) in Portsmouth, New Hampshire for processing and are then sent to the U.S. Embassy or Consulate where the applicant lives. Most of the immigrant visa petitions for Indian nationals are subject to numerical limitations and are assigned a priority date. Cases with priority dates are kept at the National Visa Center until the priority date is nearly current and only then are sent to the Embassy or Consulate.

* * *

IV Visa Appointment

After an Embassy or Consulate has received an approved petition from the National Visa Center or the U.S. Embassy in New Delhi, an appointment is scheduled and the applicant is notified. The applicant is requested to fill out form DS 230 Part II and submit it with other documents, before the interview date, to a VFS Center * * *.

* * *

Fees must be paid for each intending immigrant regardless of age and are not refundable. Fees should be sent to the consular office only if they have not been paid to the National Visa Center or if the petition was approved by the U.S. Embassy at New Delhi. It is necessary to carry proof of payment of fees to the interview. It is necessary to pay the VFS courier fees when submitting the documents at a VFS Center.

* * *

Every IV applicant, regardless of age, must undergo a medical examination before he or she goes for the visa interview. The Mumbai Post has designated certain doctors and institutes to conduct the examination. Costs for such examinations must be borne by the applicant in addition to the visa fees.

* * *

Police Clearance

All IV visa applicants, over the age of 16 years, are required to produce police clearance certificates from the passport office and from the local police station where the applicant resides. Police certificates must cover the entire period of the applicant's residence in any area. The term "police certificate" means a certification by appropriate police authorities stating what their records show concerning each applicant, including all arrests, the reasons for the arrests, and the disposition of each case of which there is a record. Police certificates are not required for periods spent in the U.S. Police certificates from certain countries are considered unobtainable. All police certificates are considered to be valid for one year from the date of issuance and must be valid on the day the immigrant visa is issued.

* * * It sometimes takes a long time to process [police certificates], and the procedure should be initiated well in advance.

* * *

IV applicant interviews are sometimes scheduled as early as 7:30 a.m. Attorneys can help the visa applicant prepare for the interview by explaining the nature of information required from the applicants. The posts in India do not permit attorneys to accompany the applicants. However, an attorney may represent the client via e-mail or letters. It is sometimes possible to make e-mail inquiries with members in the office. In our experience we have found that the Mumbai Post responds promptly to e-mails.

Fraud

Officers at the Mumbai Post have indicated that they very often have to determine whether the visa applications are based on genuine relationships or not. They have also found on many occasions that documents presented as proof of a relationship may be forged or may not reflect the true nature of the relationship. On occasion, the Mumbai Post sends its officers to conduct field visits where they personally interview the applicant's family members and/or neighbors to determine the genuineness of the relationship claimed.

---

5. ADJUSTMENT OF STATUS

a. Historical Background

In 1924, federal immigration controls began clearly to distinguish nonimmigrants from immigrants, as a logical corollary to the new system that placed numerical ceilings on immigrants. For the first few decades under such a system, the only avenue for gaining lawful permanent residence required the issuance of an immigrant visa, and visas were not—and still are not—issued in the United States. The government thus found itself faced increasingly with noncitizens in this country in nonimmigrant status who could show that they qualified for permanent immigration and who wished to avoid a costly trip overseas. Some have grumbled over the years that such persons deserve no special favors, as their new immigration plans reveal that they were not legitimate nonimmigrants from the start. Suspicion about such concealed intentions lingers, but the administrators eventually concluded that many who sought an easier way to change status had honestly undergone a change of heart after arrival here—perhaps associated with marriage to a U.S. citizen or permanent resident or the acquisition of permanent employment in a field marked by shortages.

In 1935, the agency developed a "pre-examination" process that simplified the acquisition of immigrant status for some of these nonimmigrants. Clearly qualified noncitizens could complete most of the necessary paperwork in this country, and then travel briefly (and less expensively) to a U.S. consulate in Canada to secure the actual immigrant visa, bolstered by a letter from U.S. authorities assuring Canada that the person would be allowed to travel back into the United States in any event. Except for a brief period, this pre-examination process was unavailable to Mexican and Caribbean migrants, first by practice, then by regulation. Mae Ngai has cited this administrative willingness to facilitate the adjustment of certain out-of-status noncitizens—primarily Europeans—but not others, as evidence for racialization of the notion of the "illegal alien." *See* M. Ngai, Impossible Subjects: Illegal Aliens and the Making of Modern America 84– 87, 90 (2004).

The administrative innovation of pre-examination eventually built pressure for Congress to amend the statute and authorize a simpler procedure. In 1952, with the new Immigration and Nationality Act, Congress adopted § 245, which authorizes "adjustment of status" from nonimmigrant to immigrant for noncitizens who meet certain requirements. This whole process can be carried out in the United States.

b. Overview of § 245

In its purest form, the adjustment of status process simply provides a replacement for traveling overseas to obtain an immigrant visa from a consular officer. The statute gives DHS discretion to grant adjustment of status to noncitizens who fulfill the requirements for an immigrant visa, who are not inadmissible, and for whom an immigrant visa is immediately available. Adjustment does not eliminate the need for a visa petition in those immigrant categories where it is required. Generally, the visa petition must first be submitted to USCIS, and the adjustment application can be filed only after that visa petition is approved. (In some circumstances the petition can be submitted at the same time as the application for adjustment. *See* 8 C.F.R. § 245.2(a)(2)(C).)

Once the visa petition is approved, the applicant files an application for adjustment of status on Form I–485, and mails it to a USCIS office within the United States. The USCIS examiner makes all the same determinations as a consular officer would in considering an immigrant visa applicant—that is, whether any of the inadmissibility grounds apply. For this process, the applicant for adjustment, although physically present in the United States, is considered as though he were at the border applying for initial admission. The examiner also must apply additional criteria for adjustment, some of which are specified by §§ 245(a) and (c), which will be considered below. Adjustment applicants may be scheduled for an interview, conducted by a USCIS examiner, but the interview is often waived, especially for those in the employment-based categories. Adjustment applicants are routinely given work authorization while the application is pending. *See* 8 C.F.R. § 274a.12(c)(9).

The adjustment process may take several months. Leaving the United States is treated as abandonment of the adjustment application, *see* 8 C.F.R. § 245.2(a)(4)(ii), and in any event could lead to difficulty gaining readmission on the earlier visa, owing to the nonimmigrant intent doctrine. Acknowledging this dilemma, the agencies allow applicants to apply for a grant of "advance parole," which provides solid assurance (though not a guarantee) that they can depart and return to the United States without jeopardizing their adjustment application or their eligibility for work authorization. DHS now expects that adjustment applicants will need advance parole. As of late 2011, USCIS charges a single fee ($985) for adjustment of status, as well as all applications for advance parole and work authorization, for however long the application is pending.

As mentioned earlier, the deciding officer has discretion to allow applicants to adjust to immigrant status without going overseas. Factors relevant to the exercise of discretion have included family ties in the United States, hardship in traveling abroad, length of residence in the United States, preconceived intent to remain, and any repeated violations of immigration law. *See, e.g., Mamoka v. INS*, 43 F.3d 184, 187–89 (5th Cir.1995). If adjustment of status is granted to an applicant who qualifies in one of the preference categories, the applicant counts toward the quota allowed in that preference for the current fiscal year. *See* INA § 245(b).

Although discretionary, and occasionally characterized as extraordinary, adjustment of status has become an increasingly popular, frequently used avenue toward permanent residence. In FY 1987, adjustments accounted for 21.5 percent of all immigrant admissions. For FY 2010, this figure was 54 percent of the combined total of immigrants in the immediate relative category, the family-based preferences, the employment-based preferences, and the diversity lottery. The percentage of adjustments varies greatly by type of immigrant. It is 92 percent for the employment-based preferences, 53 percent for immediate relatives, 12 percent for family-based preferences, and only 3 percent for diversity immigrants. *See* DHS 2010 Yearbook of Immigration Statistics, table 6.

In addition to allowing would-be immigrants to avoid the expense and disruption entailed in traveling overseas for visa processing, adjustment of status has become significant in a much more substantive way. As Chapter Seven will detail, the 1996 immigration law amendments added new inadmissibility grounds for unlawful presence in the United States, triggered only if the noncitizen *leaves* the United States. A noncitizen who has been unlawfully present for a period longer than 180 days is barred for three years. A period of unlawful presence of one year or more can mean a ten-year bar. INA § 212(a)(9)(B)(i). If noncitizens have been unlawfully present for at least 180 days, they cannot just leave and go through consular processing, as they could have under prior law. Once they leave, they are barred for three or ten years. As a consequence of these penalties for unlawful presence, adjustment of status has become for many people the only route to permanent residence without a delay of many years. (Although waivers of the three- and ten-year bars are available, the standards are quite strict.)

For noncitizens placed in removal proceedings in the United States, adjustment of status can also work as a form of relief from removal. In the removal proceeding, the noncitizen can request the immigration judge to grant adjustment to lawful permanent resident status. *See* 8 C.F.R.

§ 1245.2(a)(1). The noncitizen must then introduce evidence at the removal hearing to demonstrate that she has the basis for becoming an immigrant, for example as an immediate relative of a U.S. citizen, and satisfies the statutory requirements for adjustment of status. If the judge determines the applicant is eligible to adjust her status, the judge will exercise discretion as to whether to grant this relief. Noncitizens who have unsuccessfully applied to USCIS for adjustment of status prior to a removal hearing may renew their adjustment application at the hearing, and the immigration judge is not bound by the earlier USCIS denial.

c. Adjustment Under § 245(a) and (c)

You should now read INA § 245(a) and (c). The first subsection sets forth the requirements for adjustment of status, and the second sets forth significant disqualifications. These complex subsections are the core provisions governing the ordinary form of adjustment of status. In addition to proving eligibility for an immigrant visa and the absence of any grounds of inadmissibility, noncitizens seeking adjustment of status must have been inspected and admitted or paroled. (Note that noncitizens allowed to enter the United States after presenting themselves for admission and inspection are deemed admitted, even if the immigration law did not authorize their admission. See Chapter Seven, p. 583.) In contrast, persons who entered without inspection do not qualify for adjustment under § 245(a).

Moreover, even for those previously inspected and admitted, § 245(c) forbids adjustment of status in multiple circumstances. For example, noncitizens initially admitted under the visa waiver program are ineligible for adjustment of status unless they are now immediate relatives of U.S. citizens. Similarly, persons admitted as alien crewmen and those in the United States under "transit without visa" arrangements are ineligible to adjust status.

Paragraph (c)(2) provides that adjustment is unavailable to noncitizens who worked without authorization before filing, unless they are immediate relatives of U.S. citizens. The same prohibition applies to noncitizens who are "in unlawful immigration status on the date of filing the application for adjustment of status or who [have] failed (other than through no fault of [their] own or for technical reasons) to maintain continuously a lawful status since entry into the United States." Suppose a nonimmigrant went out of status while waiting for action on a request to extend his nonimmigrant status. Is he now ineligible to adjust? The answer is no, according to the regulations. *See* 8 C.F.R. § 245.1(d)(2)(ii). Such failure to maintain status is considered to have happened for a technical reason. Similarly, expiration of nonimmigrant status while an adjustment application is pending does not run afoul of (c)(2).

Paragraph (c)(7) expands the ineligible group beyond § 245(c)(2), by prohibiting adjustment for parolees and others allowed to be present in the United States without nonimmigrant status. (Note that this paragraph does not affect adjustments in the family categories.) Paragraph (c)(8) bars from adjustment noncitizens who have worked without authorization or "otherwise violated the terms of a nonimmigrant visa." There is no express exception in (c)(8) for immediate relatives, but the government position has been that (c)(8) does not supersede the more specific language of (c)(2) exempting immediate relatives (and a few specified groups of "special immigrants") from the bar to adjustment because of unauthorized work or a status violation. *See* Memorandum From Associate Commissioner Crocetti, Dec.20, 1996, *reprinted in* 74 Interp.Rel. 123 (1997).

Another subsection, § 245(k), provides a safe haven that overcomes disqualification under (c)(2), (7), or (8) in limited circumstances. It protects only persons applying in the employment-based categories, and only if their defaults lasted no longer than 180 days in the aggregate.

Now that you have seen the outlines of the adjustment of status process, test your understanding by applying the statutory framework to the situations presented in the next set of problems. For these problems, you must consult the adjustment of status provisions, INA § 245. You also will need to glance ahead at the inadmissibility ground regarding entry without inspection, INA § 212(a)(6)(A)(i), and the unlawful presence ground with its three- and ten-year bar that is triggered when a noncitizen leaves the United States, INA § 212(a)(9)(B)(i). (Chapter Seven will provide in-depth discussion of the statutory inadmissibility grounds contained in INA § 212.)

PROBLEMS

4. Gary has obtained labor certification for a child tutor, Nora, a British national, who has actually been working for the family for the past few years after entering on a B–2 tourist visa. Gary filed the labor certification application several years ago. Nora's priority date has just been reached. Nora has never been authorized to work in the United States. Is Nora eligible to adjust status to assume lawful permanent residence in the United States?

5. Nora has two siblings in the United States. One is her brother, Dennis, who has worked without authorization as a cook in a restaurant since being admitted as a B–1 business visitor four months ago. His authorized stay expired 30 days ago. Dennis has just married Vera, a U.S. citizen, who wants to help him get a green card. Can Dennis adjust status? If not, what are his prospects for becoming a permanent resident of the United States by returning to the United Kingdom in order to obtain an immigrant visa from the U.S. consulate there?

6. Nora also has a sister, Zelda, who was admitted in F–1 status several years ago to study at Duke University, where she graduated with a masters degree a few months ago. Zelda was then authorized by DHS to undertake 12 months of "practical training" with a firm in Durham, (an authorized complement to her schooling, which is often granted to F–1 students). After a few weeks, however, she quit

> following a dispute with her boss. She then took a job with a local restaurant and has been working without authorization ever since. Before graduation, Zelda accepted a permanent job offer from a U.S. biomedical engineering firm, contingent upon proper immigration approvals. The firm filed for a labor certification for Zelda a few months ago, and that application has just been approved. Can Zelda adjust status now? If not, can she receive an immigrant visa at a U.S. consulate in the United Kingdom?

d. Adjustment Under § 245(i)

In August 1994, Congress introduced a three-year trial program that significantly liberalized the adjustment of status process. Many people eligible for an immigrant visa who did not fall within any of the inadmissibility grounds were able to overcome their entry without inspection or the disqualifications in § 245(c) by paying a penalty fee ($1000 on top of the normal I–485 filing fee). INA § 245(i). One commentator called the measure "the most sweeping change in the checkered history of adjustment." Mailman, *The New Adjustment of Status Law: Background and Analysis*, 71 Interp.Rel. 1505, 1506 (1994).

When § 245(i) was enacted, opening adjustment to many more noncitizens, it was primarily intended as a convenience. In 1994, ineligibility for adjustment through § 245(a) or § 245(i) did not keep a noncitizen from becoming a permanent resident. He simply had to leave the United States to obtain a visa. In this light, the 1994 change could be seen as a procedural mechanism that diverted funds from airlines to the U.S. Treasury. As § 245(i) took effect, the workload decreased noticeably at many U.S. consulates and increased at INS offices. In 1995 and 1996, about 345,000 persons adjusted under § 245(i) each year.

Adjustment carried additional advantages for the noncitizen. In contrast to the visa process at many consulates overseas, the adjustment of status process in the United States included the right to be accompanied by counsel during the procedure, plus more ample appeal rights. Furthermore, after 1996, when Congress added new inadmissibility grounds for unlawful presence in the United States, along with the three- and ten-year bars to reentry (which apply only to a person who has *departed* the United States after accruing either 180 days or one year of unlawful presence), adjustment of status became the sole avenue for many who were otherwise eligible for an immigrant visa.[1]

---

1. The 1996 amendments also seemed to interpose another legal barrier for entrants without inspection. Section 245(i) is expressly available to EWIs (paragraph (1)(A)(i)), but the subsection also requires that the person be "admissible to the United States for permanent residence" (paragraph (2)(A)). After 1996, entrance without inspection became a ground of inadmissibility instead of deportability. INA § 212(a)(6)(A)(i). INS ruled that EWIs nonetheless remained eligible for § 245(i) adjustment, to avoid rendering superfluous the specific language to this effect in paragraph (1)(A)(i). *See INS General Counsel Issues Important Opinion on EWI Eligibility for Adjustment,* 74 Interp.Rel. 499 (1997).

As the initial § 245(i) provision neared its expiration in 1997, proponents of making § 245(i) permanent argued that it was a sensible way (with significant financial advantages for the federal government) to regularize the status of noncitizens who had qualified and waited in line for their immigrant visas under the quota system. Opponents charged, however, that § 245(i) amounted to an amnesty for illegal aliens, because it allowed them to avoid the three- and ten-year bars. Congress ultimately adopted a compromise, allowing § 245(i) to lapse but with a broad grandfather clause, benefiting people on whose behalf a visa petition or labor certification application was filed on or before January 14, 1998.

Congress later extended the grandfather provision to cover persons who were in the United States on December 21, 2000, and who had a visa petition or labor certification application filed for them by April 30, 2001. As the April deadline neared, tens of thousands of applicants stood in long lines at INS offices to file the initial papers so that they—or more often a family member—could be included in the grandfathered group. For many of them, actual adjustment would be years away, owing to backlogs in admission categories, as well as processing delays. That spectacle brought new pressure for a further extension. Both the House and the Senate, under White House urging, passed an extension bill, but before they could reconcile the two versions, the September 11 terrorist attacks occurred and the legislative effort lost momentum. *See* 78 Interp.Rel. 1429 (2001). Although § 245(i) remains on the books, it now provides relief for a finite and diminishing class of beneficiaries for whom initial papers were filed before May 2001.

PROBLEMS

7. Suppose that Nora, the British national in Problem 4, had entered without inspection from Canada in November 2000. She has never left the United States since that time. In March 2001 she began working as a nanny for Gary's family. Gary applied for labor certification for Nora as a child tutor the next month, and the application was denied. Gary appealed to the Board of Alien Labor Certification Appeals (BALCA), and ultimately prevailed. Gary then applied for an immigrant visa for Nora, and the visa application was denied. Again, Gary appealed, this time to the USCIS Administrative Appeals Office. After several remands, reversals, and submission of additional information, the immigrant visa was approved. Finally, Nora's priority date has been reached. During her years in the United States, Nora has never been authorized to work. Is Nora eligible to adjust her status to assume lawful permanent residence in the United States?

8. Suppose that Gary's wife died while the immigrant visa petition was pending, and that Gary then married Nora. If Gary petitions for her as his spouse, would this affect Nora's eligibility to adjust her status?

e. Appealing an Adverse Adjustment Decision

An applicant denied adjustment of status by USCIS has no administrative appeal. Instead, in most instances she may renew her adjustment application before the immigration judge conducting her removal proceedings (assuming such proceedings occur). 8 C.F.R. §§ 245.2(a)(5)(ii), 1245.2(a)(1), (a)(5)(ii). As discussed above, the earlier USCIS denial does not bind the immigration judge, who instead applies the statutory grounds and exercises discretion anew, based on any information in the appropriate forms or developed at the removal hearing. Adjustment may also be sought from the immigration judge during proceedings even if the noncitizen had not applied for it earlier before USCIS.

The immigration judge's decision—unlike USCIS's—is appealable to the Board of Immigration Appeals. Whatever the BIA's decision turns out to be, however, judicial review is now quite limited. INA § 242(a)(2)(B), which is captioned "Denials of discretionary relief," expressly limits judicial jurisdiction over adjustment of status decisions, although the statute does leave jurisdiction intact to decide "constitutional claims or questions of law" upon review of a final order of removal. INA § 242(a)(2)(D). In Chapter Ten we will explore the reach of the review-stripping provision and the review-preserving exception.

f. Rescission of Adjustment

INA § 246(a) provides for rescission of adjustment of status acquired under § 245 if, at any time within five years after adjustment, "it shall appear to the satisfaction of the Attorney General that the person was not in fact eligible for such adjustment of status." What happens after five years have passed since adjustment? Is the adjusted permanent resident then immune from removal based on initial ineligibility discovered later? The BIA's answer is no. See *Matter of Belenzo*, 17 I & N Dec. 374 (BIA 1980; AG 1981). Moreover, a removal order suffices to rescind lawful permanent resident status, whenever issued, without a separate, prior rescission proceeding. See INA § 246(a). The Third Circuit has reached a contrary conclusion, *Garcia v. Attorney General*, 553 F.3d 724 (3d Cir. 2009), but no other Circuit agrees, and the BIA has reaffirmed *Belenzo* for application elsewhere. *Matter of D–R–*, 25 I & N Dec. 445, 462–63 (2011).

6. PAROLE

Suppose a noncitizen is detained at the border and ultimately ruled inadmissible under § 212 on a nonwaivable ground. What happens if she becomes gravely ill before the government can remove her? Can officials send her to the hospital without admitting her and thus violating the Act? Must the government instead condemn a portion of the hospital and make it technically a part of the detention facility?

Immigration authorities developed the concept of parole, under which an excludable noncitizen was allowed to travel away from the border and the detention facilities, in order to cope with such emergencies. Originally parole was a purely administrative invention, but in 1952 it was given statutory sanction. Parole is now permissible "for urgent humanitarian reasons or significant public benefit." Once the purposes of the parole have been served, or upon a revocation of parole, the person "shall forthwith return or be returned to the custody from which he was paroled," and continues to be treated as an applicant for admission. INA § 212(d)(5)(A).

Under pre–1996 practice, paroled noncitizens remained subject to exclusion proceedings when it came time to test their right to remain, rather than being covered by the somewhat more protective deportation procedures and substantive law, as those distinctions were drawn under the pre–1996 dual procedural framework. That is, parolees were physically present in the United States, but they had not technically "entered," and entry marked the dividing line between exclusion and deportation. Under an important legal fiction, a noncitizen paroled into the country near San Diego remained constructively at the border, even if she was authorized to travel all the way to Omaha and actually remained there for several years.

Some parolees in this latter situation argued that their lengthy presence should entitle them to consideration for some benefits denied to excludable aliens but available to deportable aliens. The Supreme Court disagreed:

> The parole of aliens seeking admission is simply a device through which needless confinement is avoided while administrative proceedings are conducted. It was never intended to affect an alien's status, and to hold that petitioner's parole placed her legally "within the United States" is inconsistent with the congressional mandate, the administrative concept of parole, and the decisions of this Court.

Leng May Ma v. Barber, 357 U.S. 185, 190, 78 S.Ct. 1072, 1075, 2 L.Ed.2d 1246 (1958).

The 1996 Act, as Chapter Seven will explain more fully, changed the law to make admission rather than entry the key dividing line. Primarily, those who have been admitted are subject only to the deportability grounds in INA § 237(a). Those who have not been admitted (either because they are seeking admission at a port of entry or because they entered without inspection), are subject to the inadmissibility grounds in § 212(a). Nonetheless, it is clear that parolees remain on the less favored side of the line; the statute states explicitly that parole is not admission into the United States. Under the old system, entrants without inspection could not qualify for parole, because they had already entered. After admission replaced entry as the primary distinction, the INS General Counsel's office ruled that EWIs can qualify for parole, at least in limited circumstances. *See* 76 Interp.Rel. 1050, 1067 (1999). By the summer of 2010 USCIS was also selectively using parole for EWIs on a slightly wider scale, most prominently for the unauthorized immigrant family members of U.S. citizens in the U.S. armed forces who had entered without inspection. *See* Preston, *Immigration Policy Aims to Help Military Families*, N.Y. Times, Aug. 1, 2010. This step, sometimes known as "parole in place," not only gives the beneficiaries a form of legal permission to remain, but it also allows them to adjust status without leaving the United States (and thus without triggering the three- or ten-year bar of INA § 212(a)(9)(B)). Recall that EWIs are usually ineligible for adjustment under the precise terms of INA § 245(a), but persons who have been paroled are eligible.

Although the INA gives the parole authority to the Attorney General, the statutes creating the Department of Homeland Security in 2003 essentially transferred the parole-granting authority to DHS. It is now exercised by specified officials in USCIS, ICE, and CBP. Immigration judges have no general authority to grant parole. For a discussion of parole, see Gafner & Yale–Loehr, *Immigration Parole: Recent Developments*, 15–3 Bender's Immig. Bulletin 1 (Feb. 2010).

As the *Leng May Ma* decision hints, one major use of parole has been to release from detention persons applying for admission while they await a final decision on their cases. But parole also proved to be an outstandingly flexible tool in the hands of the executive branch, permitting the physical presence of selected noncitizens despite other disqualifications— whether those were the application of the exclusion grounds of § 212(a) or the lack of an admission number under the national-origins quotas, or later, under the preference system. Presidents eventually began to take vigorous—and controversial—advantage of this flexibility to bring in large groups of refugees in compelling circumstances. The practice began when the Soviet Union sent tanks into Hungary to put down a revolution there in 1956. Hungarian quotas were full, but the Eisenhower administration came under increasing pressure to admit large numbers of Hungarian refugees. The President ultimately decided to make innovative use of the parole power to bring some 30,000 refugees to this country.

Thus began a long and controversial practice of paroling in refugees when ordinary statutory provisions proved inadequate. Hundreds of thousands of people fleeing Cuba and Indochina, along with a few from other countries, were later beneficiaries. Many in Congress protested. Parole, they insisted, was supposed to be temporary, whereas the refugees were clearly coming for an indefinite stay, and it was supposed to be used in individual cases, not for large groups. When Congress enacted the Refugee Act of 1980, it added a provision forbidding the paroling of refugees except in individual cases for individually compelling reasons, INA § 212(d)(5)(B).

Nonetheless, the executive branch again invoked the parole authority to respond to mass exoduses from Cuba in 1980 and again in 1994. Parole may have been technically consistent with § 212(d)(5)(B) because the Cubans had not been determined to be refugees when they were paroled in 1980, and they were not being paroled as part of an official refugee program. In 1994 the United States responded to a sudden and dangerous increase in the use of small boats or homemade rafts to escape by negotiating an agreement with Cuba to curtail the outflow in return for a U.S. commitment to accept at least 20,000 Cubans annually through regular channels. This program, still in existence, involves parole of several thousand Cubans selected through an annual lottery. *See* Cuban Family Reunification Parole Program, 72 Fed. Reg. 65,588 (Nov. 21, 2007); Hughes & Alum, *Rethinking the Cuban Adjustment Act and the U.S. National Interest*, 23. St. Thomas L. Rev. 197 (2011).

Parole can thus be used for a wide variety of purposes, either before or after an administrative finding of inadmissibility. These include the following objectives: to permit medical treatment, to allow appearance in litigation or a criminal prosecution, to respond to foreign policy dilemmas, to prevent inhumane separation of families or permit physical presence for other humanitarian reasons, to allow a noncitizen to leave and return to the United States while an application for lawful status is pending, or to permit release from detention pending adjudication of an inadmissibility charge.

SECTION B. EXPEDITED PROCESSING AND SCREENING SYSTEMS

One of the many consequences of the September 11 terrorist attacks has been much closer scrutiny of both nonimmigrant and immigrant visa applications. This scrutiny has taken various forms that have heightened the inherent tension between national security and the expeditious processing of immigration-related applications. Moreover, the sheer magnitude of the many security-related tasks facing the government necessarily requires choices about law-enforcement priorities, and such selective enforcement can raise discrimination issues.

1. EXPEDITED PROCESSING

Greater scrutiny of individuals arriving in the United States has resulted in greater delay. In response, government funding has increased to expedite admission at ports of entry, primarily through an array of "trusted traveler" programs. The basic idea is that frequent travelers can apply for inclusion in these systems, pay a fee, undergo a thorough background and fingerprint check, and then receive documentation, cards, or devices that permit use of kiosks or dedicated lanes to speed passage through a port of entry. More than 800,000 individuals have enrolled in these programs, *see* 88 Interp. Rel. 601 (2011), several of which are outlined below.

a. Global Entry

The Global Entry program allows travelers to use special kiosks at participating international airports to speed their way through the immigration inspection process. Those who want to participate in Global Entry file an application prior to travel, undergo background screening, and have a personal interview. Upon approval, individuals traveling through participating airports can go straight to the Global Entry kiosks, insert their machine-readable passport or U.S. permanent resident card, make a customs declaration, and have their fingertips scanned. The machine issues a receipt and directs the traveler to the baggage claim area. *See* DHS, Customs and Border Protection, Global Entry, <http://www.global entry.gov/about.html>.

The Global Entry program is available for citizens and lawful permanent residents of the United States, Mexico, Canada, and the Netherlands. *See* 88 Interp.Rel. 2 (2011). By the close of 2010, more than 100,000 people had enrolled in the program. *See id.* at 601 (2011). As of late 2011, the application fee is $100, which includes the charge for a special card that allows Global Entry participants to use the expedited commuter lanes developed as part of the SENTRI and NEXUS programs described below. *See* DHS, Customs and Border Protection, Global Entry, <http://www. globalentry.gov.html>; 88 Interp. Rel. at 1927 (2011).

b. SENTRI

The Secure Electronic Network for Travelers Rapid Inspection (SENTRI) program allows prescreened travelers to use dedicated commuter lanes at the southern land borders. SENTRI is similar to the E–Z PASS system that speeds the payment of tolls on many highways within the United States. A radio frequency identification device on the vehicle and in the individual's SENTRI card triggers the provision of information, including photographs, to the inspector's computer screen, thus speeding visual confirmation of identity and the inspector's decision on admissibility. As of late 2011, the fee for a five-year SENTRI card is $122.25. DHS, Customs and Border Protection, SENTRI Program Description, <http:// www.cbp.gov/xp/cgov/travel/trusted_traveler/sentri/sentri.xml>.

c. NEXUS

The United States and Canada both use the NEXUS system to coordinate and speed cross-border travel. Citizens and lawful permanent residents of Canada and the United States are eligible to apply for travel cards that allow them to use expedited travel lanes at airports, on land, and in waterways. More than 400,000 individuals had enrolled in the program, as of May 2010. The application fee is $50 in late 2011. DHS Customs and Border Protection, Nexus Fact Sheet, FY 2010 <http://www. cbp.gov/linkhandler/cgov/newsroom/fact_sheets/travel/nexus_fact.ctt/ nexus_fact.pdf>.

2. NATIONAL SECURITY

The September 11 attacks brought a host of new statutory and regulatory initiatives meant to enhance the government's capacity to use the immigration system to keep out dangerous individuals or to locate dangerous persons already in the United States. Most of these initiatives built on systems already in place, but the initiatives gave a new urgency to expanding the systems, improving their accuracy and interconnection, and otherwise refining them. Some triggered sharp controversy.

a. Entry–Exit Controls: US–VISIT

Congress first called for the development of a comprehensive entry-exit control system in the 1996 Act. Early plans for this system sparked strong opposition from border communities on both sides of the frontiers (particularly in Canada), which feared a damaging impact on cross-border trade and tourism, and opponents won modifications of the mandate and a stretch-out of the timetable. *See President Signs Entry/Exit Control Legislation*, 77 Interp.Rel. 828 (2000). But the September 11 attacks renewed interest and led to several pieces of new legislation imposing new requirements and stronger deadlines. DHS deployed the first major components of the permanent system, now known as US–VISIT (Visitor and Immigrant Status Indicator Technology), in international airports in 2003. Its originally stated objective was "to create an integrated, automated entry and exit system * * * that records the arrival and departure of aliens; verifies the identities of aliens; and authenticates travel documents presented by such aliens through the comparison of biometric identifiers." 69 Fed.Reg. 53318 (2004) (also describing the statutory provisions governing the system).

The early focus of US–VISIT has been on entry processing, to capture biometric information (photo and fingerprints) on noncitizens who are admitted, so as to facilitate checking that information against coordinated databases, and, for persons entering on visas, to use the biometrics to verify that the person presenting the visa is the same individual to whom it was issued. Noncitizens at the primary inspection booth are photographed, and they also place their fingers on an electronic reader which both makes a permanent record of the prints and also compares identity against information contained in the visa. Since October 2004 the Department of State has issued only machine-readable visas with encoded biometric information that can be readily compared in this fashion.

Certain categories, including individuals traveling on diplomatic visas, children under 14, and travelers over 79, are also exempt from the US–VISIT screening. *See* DHS, US–VISIT Enrollment Requirements, <http://www.dhs.gov/files/programs/editorial_0527.shtm>. Furthermore, universal use of US–VISIT's entry fingerprinting process would present logistical complications at land borders. Partially in response, most Canadian nationals are not required to be fingerprinted in US–VISIT, and Mexican nationals using "laser visas" as a Border Crossing Card (BCC), discussed earlier in this chapter, are also exempt. Mexicans using a BCC to travel beyond the border zone, however, are supposed to be processed through the US–VISIT system. And most persons referred to secondary inspection at the land borders are likewise fingerprinted and photographed.

DHS completed deployment of this entry system in international airports in 2004, and in all fixed port-of-entry facilities by the end of 2005. It has done limited pilot-testing of biometric exit systems at airports, but the logistical and financial challenges are immense, and DHS is questioning whether a full exit system is cost effective. We return to that question in Chapter Nine *infra*.

b. Student Monitoring: SEVIS

Another initiative finalized since 2001 is the Student and Exchange Visitor Information System (SEVIS), meant to monitor students and exchange visitors in the F, J, and M categories from the time they receive their documentation to study until they graduate or leave school. It is an internet-based system overseen by ICE that allows for quick transmission of relevant information to and from schools where the student is registered (such as the student's arrival and enrollment, graduation or other departure, or signing up for an insufficient number of courses). The SEVIS rules impose extensive reporting requirements on schools and also require the use of SEVIS communications in connection with visa issuance. *See* 70 Fed. Reg. 7853 (2005) (State Department SEVIS regulations, codified at 22 C.F.R. §§ 41.61 and 41.62); 67 Fed. Reg. 76256 (2002) (DHS regulations, codified at 8 C.F.R. §§ 214.2(f) and (j)). The SEVIS fee for students is $200, as of late 2011; the fee for most exchange visitors is $180.

The 1996 Act had required a student tracking system, partly in response to the discovery that one of the 1993 bombers at the World Trade Center had been admitted as an F–1 student. *See* Pub. L. 104–208, § 641, 110 Stat. 3009. Resistance from universities and colleges staved off implementation, but that resistance dissolved after the September 11 attacks. *See House Subcommittees Mull Need for Closer Monitoring of Student Visas*, 78 Interp.Rel. 1710 (2001). Congress responded by requiring full implementation of SEVIS, as well as an interim version in the meantime. *See* Enhanced Border Security and Visa Entry Reform Act, §§ 501, 502, Pub. L. 107–173, 116 Stat. 434 (2002); USA PATRIOT Act § 416, Pub. L. 107–56, 115 Stat. 354–55 (2001); 67 Fed.Reg. 76256 (2002) (final regulation). For more information about implementation and improvements to the SEVIS system, see, e.g., *ICE Addresses Designated School Officials' "Anxieties, Concerns, and Misconceptions" Regarding SEVIS II*, 88 Interp. Rel. 1376 (2011).

c. Databases and Screening Systems

For several decades the immigration agencies have relied on lookout systems meant to flag cases of potentially dangerous or otherwise ineligible individuals, but different agencies maintained their own separate systems and tended to share information only on a limited basis. After the 9/11 attacks, Congress enacted several statutes calling for greatly improved sharing of information among U.S. agencies, the development of interoperable systems to facilitate such sharing, and the consolidation of databases in many circumstances. Meanwhile, it mandated completion of specified checks before most types of immigration benefits could be granted. In part to fulfill these requirements, USCIS operates a system of Application Support Centers throughout the country. Their primary function is to provide a venue for accurate taking of digital fingerprints and photographs, after a reliable identity check, of persons who are applying or have been preliminarily approved for immigration benefits. The ASCs replaced an earlier system that relied largely on manual fingerprint cards prepared by local law enforcement agencies. Those arrangements frequently resulted in the federal screener's receipt of inadequate images, and it was vulnerable to identity fraud.

The post 9/11 screening requirements initially outstripped the capacities of the implementing agencies, particularly the FBI, and immigration checks often fell to a low priority for completion. Thousands of cases languished for a year, and hundreds for multiple years. The delays often triggered lawsuits seeking a court order simply requiring the agency to make a decision on the benefit.

Those systems that were fingerprint-based were better able to adjust to the new demands because biometrics can connect the subject with high accuracy to any derogatory information. But most of the lookout systems have been name check systems (which usually use both name and date of birth), and they are far less exact. Because names written in foreign alphabets or scripts can be transliterated in different ways, because many people might have the same name and date of birth, and because other inaccuracies can exist, such systems check for name variations and often also use a range of dates near the stated birth date. An apparent match—a "hit"—thus does not necessarily mean that the noncitizen is disqualified. Further manual investigation is required to establish whether this applicant is the same person as the one in the database, and perhaps also to decide whether the negative information makes the person legally inadmissible.

By 2011, real progress had been made in staffing the screening systems, improving the technological systems, and assuring better sharing of information, though additional resources and further improvements are needed. Lengthy screening delays are now infrequent. For useful summaries, see DHS Office of Inspector General, Information Sharing on Foreign Nationals: Overseas Screening (OIG–11–68, April 2011) [hereafter "Overseas Screening"]; Department of Justice, Office of the Inspector General, Follow–Up Audit of the Terrorist Screening Center i, v (Audit Report 07–41, Sept. 2007).

d. Regular and Special Registration

The INA requires all noncitizens in the United States for more than 30 days to be registered and fingerprinted, but permits waiver of some of the requirements. INA §§ 261–266. A comprehensive federal alien registration system of this sort was first adopted in 1940, spurred by concerns about security risks as World War II broke out in Europe. *See Hines v.*

Davidowitz, 312 U.S. 52, 61 S.Ct. 399, 85 L.Ed. 581 (1941) (striking down a state alien registration scheme because pre-empted by the federal law). Because of workload concerns, by the 1980s INS had adopted regulations and notices waiving most nonimmigrant fingerprinting requirements and counting the normal processing documents, particularly the I–94 form and the alien registration receipt card (green card) carried by permanent residents, as sufficient to comply with the registration mandate.

The INA also required an annual report of address by all noncitizens until 1982, but then replaced that provision with a requirement for them simply to report when they changed addresses. INA § 265. That requirement was widely ignored, but failures rarely triggered any follow up enforcement—until the new enforcement push generated by the September 11 attacks spurred sporadic use of such a charge against certain suspects. Possible penalties for noncompliance with the registration requirements can be severe. They include removal from the United States, a fine, and imprisonment. *See* INA §§ 237(a)(3)(A), 266.

In addition to the "regular registration" requirements, INA § 263 permits the Attorney General (now DHS) to require specified classes of noncitizens to submit to special registration and fingerprinting. In response to the September 11 attacks, Attorney General John Ashcroft deployed this authority with respect to both arriving aliens and persons already in the United States, by adopting a controversial program known as the National Security Entry–Exit Registration System, or NSEERS. Starting on September 11, 2002, the INS began requiring certain nonimmigrants from listed countries (and some nonimmigrants from other countries as well, identified by individual characteristics deemed to signal risk) who arrive at U.S. ports of entry to undergo "special registration" under NSEERS. They were photographed, fingerprinted, and subjected to a more intensive interview under oath about their background and the purpose and itinerary of their visit to the United States. They were then obligated to report to INS after 30 days and thereafter annually, and to report changes of address, employment, or educational institution (as applicable) within ten days of a change. When departing the United States, they were required to appear personally before an immigration officer at designated ports of entry. *See* 67 Fed.Reg. 52584 (2002); 79 Interp.Rel. 899 (2002).

Over the next several months the list of designated countries grew to 25, all predominantly Muslim except for North Korea. Furthermore, a significant number of arriving aliens from *other* countries were also subject to special registration, according to individualized criteria set out in an INS memorandum. *See* 79 Interp.Rel. 1481 (2002). These criteria include, among other things, whether the noncitizen has made unexplained trips to any of several listed countries, whether he had previously overstayed an authorized period of admission, or whether "the nonimmigrant alien's behavior, demeanor, or answers indicate that alien should be monitored in the interest of national security." *Id.*

In November 2002, the INS expanded its NSEERS special registration program to reach individuals inside the United States through what is sometimes termed "call-in registration." Male nationals of the designated 25 countries, who were at least 16 years of age and were admitted to the United States as nonimmigrants before special registration took effect at ports of entry, had a six-week window (later extended in some cases) to report to a designated government office to be photographed, fingerprinted, and interviewed under oath. Failure to comply was deemed a failure to maintain nonimmigrant status and thus a deportability ground under INA § 237(a)(1)(C)(i), as well as a criminal violation under § 266. This program raised issues regarding the use of nationality, ethnicity, religion, and race in immigration enforcement, which we consider from constitutional and policy perspectives in Chapter Nine.

In December 2003, DHS announced a major scaling back of the special registration, while retaining authority to impose new programs as needed. The call-in portion ended, and persons in the program no longer had to report after 30 days or annually. Instead they would be notified individually whenever additional reporting was required. *See Special Registration to End, be Replaced by Upcoming 'U.S. VISIT' Monitoring Program for All Visitors,* 80 Interp. Rel. 690 (2003).

In April 2011, DHS formally terminated the NSEERS registration requirements. The Department explained that US–VISIT and other automated screening systems developed since 2002 (discussed more fully in Chapter Nine) now provide sufficient information to meet security objectives without the need to impose burdensome requirements on whole categories of nonimmigrant travelers. 76 Fed. Reg. 23830 (2011).

NOTES AND QUESTIONS ON SCREENING SYSTEMS

1. Top-level officials quickly became aware of the negative effects of inefficient processing or security procedures that are seen as inhospitable. Worried that such situations create diplomatic ill will or damage the competitiveness of U.S. businesses or universities, Secretary of State Condoleeza Rice and Secretary of Homeland Security Michael Chertoff announced broad new steps in 2006 to facilitate travel while honoring security needs. *See Rice–Chertoff Joint Conference on Secure Borders and "Open Doors,"* 83 Interp.Rel. 161 (2006). The number of student visas has continued to increase steadily, with 295,000 new F student visas issued in 2006; 320,000 in 2007; 365,000 in 2008; 353,000 in 2009; and 411,000 in 2010. *See* DOS Visa Office Report 2010, table XVI(A). The number of student visa admissions at ports of entry has also expanded significantly each year. (Recall from Chapter Five that many visas are valid for multiple entries and for multiple years.) DHS reported that 740,000 individuals were admitted on F visas in 2006; 840,000 in 2007; 940,000 in 2008; 950,000 in 2009; and 1,595,000—an increase of 600,000 over the prior year—in 2010. *See* DHS Yearbook 2010, table 25.

2. The NSEERS special registration program generated controversy, with some critics particularly troubled that all of the designated countries,

with the sole exception of North Korea, had predominantly Muslim populations. Others protested that many nonimmigrants within the United States were arrested for immigration status violations after appearing promptly for the "call-in registration." Supporters noted that the September 11 attacks by individuals with nonimmigrant visas highlighted the importance of keeping track of noncitizens. They emphasized that special registration procedures at the border also applied to individuals from many non-Muslim countries. How would you weigh the various arguments concerning NSEERS registration? What additional facts would be important to know in order to evaluate the program? We will revisit the NSEERS program and examine challenges to the use of race and ethnicity in enforcement in Chapter Nine, Section B.

3. RESPONSES TO PROCESSING DELAYS

Increased scrutiny of noncitizens who wished to travel to the United States meant that the admission and adjustment procedures became backlogged and resulted in major delays. A substantial increase in the application fees for most immigration benefits, implemented in July 2007, permitted USCIS to reduce backlogs and processing times through the wider use of electronic processing and other modernization. *See* 84 Interp.Rel. 285 (2007). Processing time for visa petition approvals from DHS now generally take less than six months, although a few difficult cases may take years. If the applicable preference category is backlogged, a delay may be of no practical consequence, because the visa priority date is established by the date of the *filing*, and the approval can be expected well before the time when the person could immigrate in any case. But for preference categories that are current and for immediate relatives (particularly newlyweds), such delays are a real imposition.

DHS has introduced initiatives to reduce processing backlogs. For example, in 2003, it began to accept the electronic filing of certain forms, and it has gradually expanded the list of applications for which this process is available. *See* 68 Fed.Reg. 23010 (2003). In addition to DHS initiatives, Congress has adopted several major innovations to alleviate processing delays, including the following:

a. K–3 Visa

In late 2000 Congress adopted a new nonimmigrant category for spouses of U.S. citizens, now known as K–3. The longstanding K–1 visa, for fiancés and fiancées of citizens, allowed admission to marry in this country within 90 days. Historically, no special provision had been made for U.S. citizens who marry overseas, on the assumption that their spouses could enter promptly as immediate relatives, for which there is no quota. But delayed visa petition processing often meant a lengthy separation between the time of the wedding abroad and the foreign spouse's admission. With a K–3 visa, the spouse may be admitted and work while awaiting approval of the visa petition and eventual adjustment of status. Only a consular officer in the country where the marriage occurred may issue the K–3 visa, and the U.S. citizen must have filed the I–130 visa petition and a special K–3 petition. INA §§ 101(a)(15)(K)(ii), 214(p); 66 Fed.Reg. 42587 (2001); 8 C.F.R. § 214.2(k)(7)–(11).

b. Aging Out

The Child Status Protection Act, Pub. L. 107–208, 116 Stat. 927 (2002), discussed in Chapter Five, protects offspring of U.S. citizens and permanent residents from "aging out" of immigrant categories while waiting for processing and for their priority dates to become current. For example, the determination of whether a U.S. citizen's unmarried son or daughter is under 21—and therefore a "child" who qualifies as an immediate relative—is now made as of when the immigrant petition (Form I–130) is filed on the child's behalf, not as of the child's admission. More complex rules apply to minimize aging out in the preference categories.

c. Premium Processing

The statute now authorizes "premium processing" for covered employment-based petitions and applications handled by DHS (not visa issuance by the Department of State). INA § 286(u). Businesses may pay a premium fee, in addition to the usual processing fee, to obtain guaranteed priority processing within 15 calendar days of receipt for specified applications. In addition, they receive special phone access to the service center handling the application. As of late 2011, the premium processing fee is $1225. *See* USCIS, How Do I Use the Premium Processing Service? <http://www.uscis.gov/portal/site/uscis/menuitem>.

d. Employment Flexibility

In other efforts to respond to processing delays in employment-based visas, Congress enacted the H–1B extension and portability provisions in 2000, discussed in Chapter Five, pp. 381–82. The first provides for the extension of the H–1B status beyond the previous six-year limit for certain nonimmigrants who applied for labor certification at least a year earlier and are awaiting final processing. *See* 8 U.S.C. § 1184 Note. The portability provision in INA § 204(j) allows an applicant for an employment-based preference to change jobs or employers in the same or similar field if an adjustment application has been pending for 180 days.

Delays in processing have prompted lawsuits seeking court orders requiring prompt adjudication. Several have led to judgments, in the nature of mandamus, against the government. *See, e.g., Al–Rifahe v. Mayorkas,* 776 F.Supp.2d 927 (D.Minn. 2011) (jurisdiction to review thirteen year delay in adjustment of status processing); *Al Shamsawi v. Holder,* 2011 WL 1870284 (D.Utah 2011) (mandamus warranted by six year delay on adjustment of status application). Other courts have ruled for the government, on the basis that they lacked jurisdiction to consider such a suit, that the pacing of decision was within the discretion of the agency, that to grant such an order would enable those who sue to cut in line ahead of others, or that other barriers to relief existed. *See, e.g., Bian v. Clinton,* 605 F.3d 249 (5th Cir. 2010), vacated as moot, 2010 WL 3633770 (5th Cir. 2010) (no jurisdiction to compel action on adjustment of status application); *Qiu v. Chertoff,* 486 F.Supp.2d 412 (D.N.J. 2007) (no jurisdiction to issue mandamus despite three year delay in completing adjustment of status process). For an overview of the issues, see Seipp, *Federal Court Jurisdiction to Review Immigration Decisions: A Tug of War Between the Three Branches,* 07–04 Immigr. Briefings 1 (2007); Wettstein, *Wasted Days and Wasted Nights: INS Visa Processing Delays and How to Combat Them,* 76 Interp.Rel. 1441 (1999).

What is the broader significance of delays for the immigration system as a whole? Consider this comment:

> Congress, by enacting substantive immigration law, defines our selective admission system. These laws erect legal borders that reflect the policy choices Congress has made about who may enter to work or to join family in the United States. But beyond this initial border, the agencies that implement the immigration laws have erected powerful process borders. These process borders, fostered by congressional neglect and strengthened by a lack of coordination among the agencies, distort substantive immigration policy. Far too often, the bureaucratic process borders control who immigrates.

Benson, *Breaking Bureaucratic Borders: A Necessary Step Toward Immigration Law Reform,* 54 Admin. L. Rev. 203, 205 (2002).

NOTES AND QUESTIONS ON RESPONSES TO PROCESSING DELAYS

1. Do you think these changes to the INA are good policy? Will they prove counterproductive, as the government diverts resources to adjudicate the additional applications, such as the additional K–3 petitions? If DHS efficiency initiatives (boosted by the significantly higher fees implemented in 2007) succeed in bringing most processing within the six-month target time, should the visa changes described above be eliminated?

2. In many ways it makes sense to charge an extra fee for premium processing, and this is common in many industries and systems. Is it an appropriate part of American immigration policy? If so, should it be limited to business-related applications, as the statute now provides?

SECTION C. THE CONSTITUTIONAL REQUIREMENT OF DUE PROCESS

Thus far we have examined the admission procedures established by statutes and regulations. We turn now to the constitutional framework. The Due Process Clause of the Fifth Amendment to the United States

Constitution imposes a duty on the government to use fair procedures when a person may be "deprived of life, liberty or property." When government officials inspect noncitizens at the borders to the United States, what procedures does the Due Process Clause mandate? Would refusal of admission to a foreign national be a deprivation of life, liberty, or property?

Since 1950, the due process rights of aliens at the border might well be summarized in one famous (and rather chilling) sentence written by Justice Minton: "Whatever the procedure authorized by Congress is, it is due process as far as an alien denied entry is concerned." *United States ex rel. Knauff v. Shaughnessy*, 338 U.S. 537, 544, 70 S.Ct. 309, 313, 94 L.Ed. 317 (1950). *Knauff* was a case involving immigration under the War Brides Act of 1945, Pub. L. 79–271, 59 Stat. 659. This statute gave preferential immigration status (and in turn, naturalization eligibility) to the foreign spouses and children of American World War II veterans. Nonetheless the Court found no reason to soften its general due process rule even for a war bride.

Knauff has never been overruled; hence you might expect this discussion of due process for arriving aliens to be exceedingly short. Instead we will spend several pages examining the doctrine derived from *Knauff* and the 1903 case with which it is often contrasted, *Yamataya v. Fisher*, which stands for at least some measure of independent judicial scrutiny of procedures, in the case of an alien who has already entered the country. We will also examine two 1953 cases, *Kwong Hai Chew* and *Mezei*. *Chew* seemed to ameliorate the apparent harshness of *Knauff*, but *Mezei*, decided just one month after *Chew*, accomplished the improbable feat of rendering the *Knauff* outcome even more severe.

We examine these cases precisely because we view the *Knauff–Mezei* doctrine as extreme. It has provoked a steady stream of critical academic commentary, and some post–1950s decisions suggest that modification of the doctrine may be possible. Prominent among these is the U.S. Supreme Court's *Plasencia* decision, set out later in this Section, which drew on some of the moderating aspects of *Chew*.

Part of the criticism of the *Knauff–Mezei* doctrine has rested on the way the Supreme Court assigned noncitizens arriving at the border or a port of entry to constitutional limbo. Criticism has also focused on the odd way the 1950s Court seemed to draw the lines between the noncitizens who fell into this disfavored class (traditionally, those who were in exclusion proceedings) and those who managed to get more complete due process protection (traditionally, those in deportation proceedings).

UNITED STATES EX REL. KNAUFF v. SHAUGHNESSY

Supreme Court of the United States, 1950.
338 U.S. 537, 70 S.Ct. 309, 94 L.Ed. 317.

MR. JUSTICE MINTON delivered the opinion of the Court.

May the United States exclude without hearing, solely upon a finding by the Attorney General that her admission would be prejudicial to the interests of the United States, the alien wife of a citizen who had served honorably in the armed forces of the United States during World War II? The District Court for the Southern District of New York held that it could, and the Court of Appeals for the Second Circuit affirmed. We granted certiorari to examine the question especially in the light of the War Brides Act of December 28, 1945.

Petitioner was born in Germany in 1915. She left Germany and went to Czechoslovakia during the Hitler regime. There she was married and divorced. She went to England in 1939 as a refugee. Thereafter she served with the Royal Air Force efficiently and honorably from January 1, 1943, until May 30, 1946. She then secured civilian employment with the War Department of the United States in Germany. Her work was rated "very good" and "excellent." On February 28, 1948, with the permission of the Commanding General at Frankfurt, Germany, she married Kurt W. Knauff, a naturalized citizen of the United States. He is an honorably discharged United States Army veteran of World War II. He is, as he was at the time of his marriage, a civilian employee of the United States Army at Frankfurt, Germany.

On August 14, 1948, petitioner sought to enter the United States to be naturalized. On that day she was temporarily excluded from the United States and detained at Ellis Island. On October 6, 1948, the Assistant Commissioner of Immigration and Naturalization recommended that she be permanently excluded without a hearing on the ground that her admission would be prejudicial to the interests of the United States. On the same day the Attorney General adopted this recommendation and entered a final order of exclusion. To test the right of the Attorney General to exclude her without a hearing for security reasons, *habeas corpus* proceedings were instituted in the Southern District of New York, based primarily on provisions of the War Brides Act. The District Court dismissed the writ, and the Court of Appeals affirmed.

The authority of the Attorney General to order the exclusion of aliens without a hearing flows from the Act of June 21, 1941, amending § 1 of the Act of May 22, 1918 (55 Stat. 252, 22 U.S.C. § 223). By the 1941 amendment it was provided that the President might, upon finding that the interests of the United States required it, impose additional restrictions and prohibitions on the entry into and departure of persons from the United States during the national emergency proclaimed May 27, 1941. Pursuant to this Act of Congress the President on November 14, 1941, issued Proclamation 2523. This proclamation recited that the interests of the United States required the imposition of additional restrictions upon the entry into and departure of persons from the country and authorized the promulgation of regulations jointly by the Secretary of State and the Attorney General. It was also provided that no alien should be permitted to enter the United States if it were found that such entry would be prejudicial to the interests of the United States.

Pursuant to the authority of this proclamation the Secretary of State and the Attorney General issued regulations governing the entry into and departure of persons from the United States during the national emergency. Subparagraphs (a) to (k) of § 175.53 of these regulations specified the classes of aliens whose entry into the United States was deemed prejudicial to the public interest. Subparagraph (b) of § 175.57 provided that the Attorney General might deny an alien a hearing before a board of inquiry in special cases where he determined that the alien was excludable under the regulations on the basis of information of a confidential nature, the disclosure of which would be prejudicial to the public interest.

It was under this regulation § 175.57(b) that petitioner was excluded by the Attorney General and denied a hearing. We are asked to pass upon the validity of this action.

At the outset we wish to point out that an alien who seeks admission to this country may not do so under any claim of right. Admission of aliens to the United States is a privilege granted by the sovereign United States Government. Such privilege is granted to an alien only upon such terms as the United States shall prescribe. It must be exercised in accordance with the procedure which the United States provides. *Nishimura Ekiu v. United States*, 142 U.S. 651, 659, 12 S.Ct. 336, 338, 35 L.Ed. 1146; *Fong Yue Ting v. United States*, 149 U.S. 698, 711, 13 S.Ct. 1016, 1021, 37 L.Ed. 905.

Petitioner contends that the 1941 Act and the regulations thereunder are void to the extent that they contain unconstitutional delegations of legislative power. But there is no question of inappropriate delegation of legislative power involved here. The exclusion of aliens is a fundamental act of sovereignty. The right to do so stems not alone from legislative power but is inherent in the executive power to control the foreign affairs of the nation. When Congress prescribes a procedure concerning the admissibility of aliens, it is not dealing alone with a legislative power. It is implementing an inherent executive power.

Thus the decision to admit or to exclude an alien may be lawfully placed with the President, who may in turn delegate the carrying out of this function to a responsible executive officer of the sovereign, such as the Attorney General. The action of the executive officer under such authority is final and conclusive. Whatever the rule may be concerning deportation of persons who have gained entry into the United States, it is not within the province of any court, unless expressly authorized by law, to review the determination of the political branch of the Government to exclude a given alien. *Nishimura Ekiu v. United States*, 142 U.S. 651, 659–660, 12 S.Ct. 336, 338, 35 L.Ed. 1146; *Fong Yue Ting v. United States*, 149 U.S. 698, 713–714, 13 S.Ct. 1016, 1022, 37 L.Ed. 905; *Ludecke v. Watkins*, 335 U.S. 160, 68 S.Ct. 1429, 92 L.Ed. 1881. *Cf. Yamataya v. Fisher*, 189 U.S. 86, 101, 23 S.Ct. 611, 614, 47 L.Ed. 721. Normally Congress supplies the conditions of the privilege of entry into the United States. But because the power of exclusion of aliens is also inherent in the executive department of the sovereign, Congress may in broad terms authorize the executive to exercise the power, e.g., as was done here, for the best interests of the country during a time of national emergency. Executive officers may be entrusted with the duty of specifying the procedures for carrying out the congressional intent. What was said in *Lichter v. United States*, 334 U.S. 742, 785, 68 S.Ct. 1294, 1316, 92 L.Ed. 1694, is equally appropriate here:

> It is not necessary that Congress supply administrative officials with a specific formula for their guidance in a field where flexibility and the adaptation of the congressional policy to infinitely variable conditions constitute the essence of the program.... Standards prescribed by Congress are to be read in the light of the conditions to which they are to be applied. "They derive much meaningful content from the purpose of the Act, its factual background and the statutory context in which they appear."

Whatever the procedure authorized by Congress is, it is due process as far as an alien denied entry is concerned. *Nishimura Ekiu v. United States*, *supra*; *Ludecke v. Watkins*, *supra*.

In the particular circumstances of the instant case the Attorney General, exercising the discretion entrusted to him by Congress and the President, concluded upon the basis of confidential information that the public interest required that petitioner be denied the privilege of entry into the United States. He denied her a hearing on the matter because, in his judgment, the disclosure of the information on which he based that opinion would itself endanger the public security.

We find no substantial merit to petitioner's contention that the regulations were not "reasonable" as they were required to be by the 1941 Act. We think them reasonable in the circumstances of the period for which they were authorized, namely, the national emergency of World War II. * * * We reiterate that we are dealing here with a matter of *privilege*. Petitioner had no vested *right* of entry which could be the subject of a prohibition against retroactive operation of regulations affecting her status.

Affirmed.

Mr. Justice Jackson, whom Mr. Justice Black and Mr. Justice Frankfurter join, dissenting.

I do not question the constitutional power of Congress to authorize immigration authorities to turn back from our gates any alien or class of aliens. But I do not find that Congress has authorized an abrupt and brutal exclusion of the wife of an American citizen without a hearing.

* * *

Congress held out a promise of liberalized admission to alien brides, taken unto themselves by men serving in or honorably discharged from our armed services abroad * * *. The petitioning husband is honorably discharged and remained in Germany as a civilian employee. Our military authorities abroad required their permission before marriage. The Army in Germany is not without a vigilant and security-conscious intelligence service. This woman was employed by our European Command and her record is not only without blemish, but is highly praised by her superiors.

* * *

Congress will have to use more explicit language than any yet cited before I will agree that it has authorized an administrative officer to break up the family of an American citizen or force him to keep his wife by becoming an exile. Likewise, it will have to be much more explicit before I can agree that it authorized a finding of serious misconduct against the wife of an American citizen without notice of charges, evidence of guilt and a chance to meet it.

I should direct the Attorney General either to produce his evidence justifying exclusion [in this habeas corpus proceeding] or to admit Mrs. Knauff to the country.

[JUSTICE FRANKFURTER'S dissenting opinion is omitted. JUSTICE DOUGLAS and JUSTICE CLARK took no part in deciding the case.]

Justice Minton's majority opinion in *Knauff* contains an unelaborated "cf." cite to *Yamataya v. Fisher*, with no real acknowledgment of the sharply contrasting vision of a person's due process rights in immigration proceedings that *Yamataya* potentially embodies. Here is what the Court had to say in that case, decided in the early decades of federal immigration laws, not quite 50 years before *Knauff*.

YAMATAYA v. FISHER (THE JAPANESE IMMIGRANT CASE)

Supreme Court of the United States, 1903.
189 U.S. 86, 23 S.Ct. 611, 47 L.Ed. 721.

[Kaoru Yamataya, a citizen of Japan, landed at Seattle on July 11, 1901. Four days later an immigration inspector, after investigation, decided that she was deportable because she had been excludable at time of entry as a pauper and a person likely to become a public charge. Yamataya asserted that the procedure had been inadequate because she did not understand English, did not realize that the investigation involved her deportability, was not assisted by counsel, and had not been given an opportunity to show she was not deportable.]

MR. JUSTICE HARLAN delivered the opinion of the Court.

* * *

The constitutionality of the legislation in question, in its general aspects, is no longer open to discussion in this court. That Congress may exclude aliens of a particular race from the United States; prescribe the terms and conditions upon which certain classes of aliens may come to this country; establish regulations for sending out of the country such aliens as come here in violation of law; and commit the enforcement of such provisions, conditions and regulations exclusively to executive officers, without judicial intervention, are principles firmly established by the decisions of this court. *Nishimura Ekiu v. United States*, 142 U.S. 651, 35 L.Ed. 1146, 12 Sup. Ct. Rep. 336; *Fong Yue Ting v. United States*, 149 U.S. 698, 37 L.Ed. 905, 13 Sup. Ct. Rep. 1016.

* * *

[The statute authorized the Secretary of the Treasury to remove noncitizens later found to have been within an "excluded class" at the time of entry.] The immigrant must be taken to have entered subject to the condition that he might be sent out of the country by order of the proper executive officer if within a year he was found to have been wrongfully admitted into or had illegally entered the United States. * * *

It is contended, however, that in respect of an alien who has already landed it is consistent with the acts of Congress that he may be deported without previous notice of any purpose to deport him, and without any opportunity on his part to show by competent evidence before the executive officers charged with the execution of the acts of Congress, that he is not here in violation of law; that the deportation of an alien without provision for such a notice and for an opportunity to be heard was inconsistent with the due process of law required by the Fifth Amendment of the Constitution.

Leaving on one side the question whether an alien can rightfully invoke the due process clause of the Constitution who has entered the country clandestinely, and who has been here for too brief a period to have become, in any real sense, a part of our population, before his right to remain is disputed, we have to say that the rigid construction of the acts of Congress suggested by the [government] are not justified. Those acts do not necessarily exclude opportunity to the immigrant to be heard, when such opportunity is of right. It was held in *Murray's Lessee v. Hoboken Land & Improvement Co.*, 18 How. 272, 280, 281, 283, 15 L.Ed. 372, 376, 377, that * * * "though, generally, both public and private wrong are redressed through judicial action, there are more summary extra-judicial remedies for both." Hence, it was decided in that case to be consistent with due process of law for Congress to provide summary means to compel revenue officers—and in case of default, their sureties—to pay such balances of the public money as might be in their hands. Now, it has been settled that the power to exclude or expel aliens belonged to the political department of the Government, and that the order of an executive officer, invested with the power to determine finally the facts upon which an alien's right to enter this country, or remain in it, depended, was "due process of law, and no other tribunal, unless expressly authorized by law to do so, was at liberty to reexamine the evidence on which he acted, or to controvert its sufficiency." *Fong Yue Ting v. United States*, 149 U.S. 698, 713, 37 L.Ed. 905, 913, 13 Sup. Ct. Rep. 1016. But this court has never held, nor must we now be understood as holding, that administrative officers, when executing the provisions of a statute involving the liberty of persons, may disregard the fundamental principles that inhere in "due process of law" as understood at the time of the adoption of the Constitution. One of these principles is that no person shall be deprived of his liberty without opportunity, at some time, to be heard, before such officers, in respect of the matters upon which that liberty depends—not necessarily an opportunity upon a regular, set occasion, and according to the forms of judicial procedure, but one that will secure the prompt, vigorous action contemplated by Congress, and at the same time be appropriate to the nature of the case upon which such officers are required to act. Therefore, it is not competent for the Secretary of the Treasury or any executive officer, at any time within the year limited by the statute, arbitrarily to cause an alien, who has entered the country, and has become subject in all respects to its jurisdiction, and a part of its population, although alleged to be illegally here, to be taken into custody and deported without giving him all opportunity to be heard upon the questions involving his right to be and remain in the United States. No such arbitrary power can exist where the principles involved in due process of law are recognized.

This is the reasonable construction of the acts of Congress here in question, and they need not be otherwise interpreted. * * * Besides, the record now before us shows that the appellant had notice, although not a formal one, of the investigation instituted for the purpose of ascertaining whether she was illegally in this country. The traverse to the return made by the Immigration Inspector shows upon its face that she was before that officer pending the investigation of her right to be in the United States, and made answers to questions propounded to her. It is true that she pleads a want of knowledge of our language; that she did not understand the nature and import of the questions propounded to her; that the investigation made was a "pretended" one; and that she did not, at the time, know that the investigation had reference to her being deported from the country. These considerations cannot justify the intervention of the courts. They could have been presented to the officer having primary control of such a case, as well as upon an appeal to the Secretary of the Treasury, who had power to order another investigation if that course was demanded by law or by the ends of justice. It is not to be assumed that either would have refused a second or fuller investigation, if a proper application and showing for one had been made by or for the appellant. Whether further investigation should have been ordered was for the officers, charged with the execution of the statutes, to determine. Their action in that regard is not subject to judicial review. Suffice it to say, it does not appear that appellant was denied an opportunity to be heard. And as no appeal was taken to the Secretary from the decision of the Immigration Inspector, that decision was final and conclusive. If the appellant's want of knowledge of the English language put her at some disadvantage in the investigation conducted by that officer, that was her misfortune, and constitutes no reason, under the acts of Congress, or under any rule of law, for the intervention of the court by *habeas corpus.* We perceive no ground for such intervention—none for the contention that due process of law was denied to appellant.

The judgment is affirmed.

MR. JUSTICE BREWER and MR. JUSTICE PECKHAM dissented [without opinion].

NOTES AND QUESTIONS ON DUE PROCESS AND IMMIGRANT ADMISSION PROCEDURES

1.   Make a list of the factors that distinguish Knauff's case from Yamataya's. Which make Knauff the more attractive candidate for expanded procedures to enhance the assurance of an accurate and fair outcome? Which would point toward Yamataya? The *Yamataya* opinion suggests several factors that might possibly set the boundary line between those who are entitled to independent court scrutiny of the adequacy of the procedures from those who don't, but it does not fully resolve the question. Assuming that we keep a multi-tiered structure for deciding when (or with what intensity) judges are to perform constitutional audits of the procedures, which factors *should* we use to distinguish the tiers? How would your preferred system answer the question reserved by Justice Harlan in *Yamataya*—whether a noncitizen who has recently entered without inspection can invoke the due process clause of the Constitution in challenging removal procedures?

2.   The *Yamataya* Court applies constitutional standards to evaluate procedures, but it suggests that no such scrutiny applies to the substantive provisions of the deportation law itself, relying on cases like *Fong Yue Ting,* considered in detail in Chapter Three. This distinction (often described as the difference between substantive and procedural due process review) is generally followed in immigration cases today. Why might a court distinguish procedural from substantive constitutional challenges and apply closer scrutiny to the former? Should such a distinction be drawn?

3.   Procedural due process cases generally pose two distinct questions. First, does the due process clause apply, so that the individual is entitled to constitutional review of the sufficiency of the procedures? Second, if so, what process was due (or fair) for the particular type of decisionmaking at issue? *See generally Cleveland Board of Education v. Loudermill,* 470 U.S. 532, 538–42, 105 S.Ct. 1487, 84 L.Ed.2d 494 (1985).

Yamataya stands for the proposition that deportation procedures—at least for lawfully admitted noncitizens—must conform to the due process clause. But note that Yamataya's deportation was then upheld, even though she had had no formal hearing, alleged that she could neither speak nor understand English, and claimed that she was unaware of the nature of the proceedings. In so concluding, the Court stated that Yamataya had not raised these objections before the immigration officer or the administrative agency.

As the Court put it: "It is not to be assumed that either would have refused a second or fuller investigation...." It is clear that the Court was applying rather undemanding standards to decide what process is due. Such standards, however, have evolved considerably in the century since that decision. The current tests will receive greater attention later in this section, especially in connection with *Landon v. Plasencia*.

The next two cases were decided in 1953, half a century after *Yamataya* and three years after *Knauff*. In both cases lawful permanent residents of the United States ran afoul of a federal regulation that denied admission to noncitizens whose entry was deemed prejudicial to the public interest. Further, acting under the regulation, the government rejected their admission without providing any hearing at all. The noncitizens were detained at Ellis Island while they challenged the constitutionality of the government's actions.

KWONG HAI CHEW v. COLDING

Supreme Court of the United States, 1953.
344 U.S. 590, 73 S.Ct. 472, 97 L.Ed. 576.

MR. JUSTICE BURTON delivered the opinion of the Court.

* * *

Petitioner, Kwong Hai Chew, is a Chinese seaman last admitted to the United States in 1945. Thereafter, he married a native American and bought the home in which they reside in New York. Having proved his good moral character for the preceding five years, petitioner secured suspension of his deportation. In 1949, he was admitted to permanent residence in the United States as of January 10, 1945. In World War II, he served with credit in the United States Merchant Marine. He never has had any difficulty with governmental authorities. In April, 1950, he filed a petition for naturalization which is still pending. In November, 1950, he was screened and passed by the Coast Guard for employment as a seaman on a merchant vessel.[3] In the same month he signed articles of employment as chief steward on the S.S. Sir John Franklin, a vessel of American registry with its home port in New York City. The voyage was to include calls at several foreign ports in the Far East. He remained aboard the vessel on this voyage but, at San Francisco, in March, 1951, the immigration inspector ordered him "temporarily excluded," under 8 C.F.R.

---

3. * * * Section 6.10–1 [of Executive Order No. 10173, of October 18, 1950], as it existed at the date of petitioner's clearance, provided:

> Issuance of documents and employment of persons aboard vessels. No person shall be issued a document required for employment on a merchant vessel of the United States nor shall any licensed officer or certificated man be employed on a merchant vessel of the United States if the Commandant is satisfied that the character and habits of life of such person are such as to authorize the belief that the presence of the individual on board would be inimical to the security of the United States * * *.

§ 175.57, as an alien whose entry was deemed prejudicial to the public interest.

On the vessel's arrival in New York, March 29, petitioner's "temporary exclusion" was continued and he was not permitted to land. March 30, he sought a writ of habeas corpus from the United States District Court for the Eastern District of New York, charging that his detention was arbitrary and capricious and a denial of due process of law in violation of the Fifth Amendment to the Constitution of the United States. Purporting to act under 8 C.F.R. § 175.57(b), the Attorney General directed that petitioner be denied a hearing before a Board of Special Inquiry and that his "temporary exclusion be made permanent." The Attorney General continues to deny petitioner all information as to the nature and cause of any accusations against him and all opportunity to be heard in opposition to the order for his "exclusion." He is detained at Ellis Island "for safekeeping on behalf of the master of the S.S. Sir John Franklin."

* * *

The issue is petitioner's detention, without notice of any charge against him and without opportunity to be heard in opposition thereto. Petitioner contends that such detention is not authorized by 8 C.F.R. § 175.57(b). He contends also that, if that regulation does purport to authorize such detention, the regulation is invalid as an attempt to deprive him of his liberty without due process of law in violation of the Fifth Amendment. Agreement with petitioner's first contention makes it unnecessary to reach his second.

The case of *Knauff v. Shaughnessy*, relied upon below, is not in point. It relates to the rights of an alien entrant and does not deal with the question of a resident alien's right to be heard. For purposes of his constitutional right to due process, we assimilate petitioner's status to that of an alien continuously residing and physically present in the United States. To simplify the issue, we consider first what would have been his constitutional right to a hearing had he not undertaken his voyage to foreign ports but had remained continuously within the territorial boundaries of the United States.

1. It is well established that if an alien is a lawful permanent resident of the United States and remains physically present there, he is a person within the protection of the Fifth Amendment. He may not be deprived of his life, liberty or property without due process of law. Although it later may be established, as respondents contend, that petitioner can be expelled and deported, yet before his expulsion, he is entitled to notice of the nature of the charge and a hearing at least before an executive or administrative tribunal.[6] Although Congress may prescribe conditions for his expulsion and deportation, not even Congress may expel him without allowing him a fair opportunity to be heard.[7] For example, he

---

6. * * * *Yamataya v. Fisher*, 189 U.S. 86, 100–101, 23 S.Ct. 611, 614, 47 L.Ed. 721.

7. *See Fong Yue Ting v. United States*, 149 U.S. 698, 13 S.Ct. 1016, 37 L.Ed. 905 * * *.

is entitled to a fair chance to prove mistaken identity. At the present stage of the instant case, the issue is not one of exclusion, expulsion or deportation. It is one of legislative construction and of procedural due process.

[The Court analyzes the language and intent of the regulation.] Accordingly, we find no language in the regulation that would have required its application to petitioner had he remained continuously and physically within the United States. It thus seems clear that the Attorney General would not have had the authority to deny to petitioner a hearing in opposition to such an order as was here made, provided petitioner had remained within the United States.

* * *

2. Petitioner's final contention is that if an alien is a lawful permanent resident of the United States and also is a seaman who has gone outside of the United States on a vessel of American registry, with its home port in the United States, and, upon completion of such voyage, has returned on such vessel to the United States and is still on board, he is still, from a constitutional point of view, a person entitled to procedural due process under the Fifth Amendment. We do not regard the constitutional status which petitioner indisputably enjoyed prior to his voyage as terminated by that voyage. From a constitutional point of view, he is entitled to due process without regard to whether or not, for immigration purposes, he is to be treated as an entrant alien, and we do not now reach the question whether he is to be so treated.

Section 175.57(b)'s authorization of the denial of hearings raises no constitutional conflict if limited to 'excludable' aliens who are not within the protection of the Fifth Amendment. The assimilation of petitioner, for constitutional purposes, to the status of a continuous resident physically present in the United States also accords with the Nation's immigration and naturalization program. [The Court noted that "[c]ontinuous service by a seaman on a vessel or vessels whose home port is in the United States and which are of American registry or American owned" would satisfy the residency requirement for naturalization.]

* * *

This preservation of petitioner's right to due process does not leave an unprotected spot in the Nation's armor. Before petitioner's admission to permanent residence, he was required to satisfy the Attorney General and Congress of his suitability for that status. Before receiving clearance for his foreign cruise, he was screened and approved by the Coast Guard. Before acceptance of his petition for naturalization, as well as before final action thereon, assurance is necessary that he is not a security risk.

We do not reach the issue as to what would be the constitutional status of 8 C.F.R. § 175.57(b) if it were interpreted as denying to petitioner all opportunity for a hearing. Also, we do not reach the issue as to what will be the authority of the Attorney General to order the deportation of petitioner after giving him reasonable notice of the charges against him and allowing him a hearing sufficient to meet the requirements of procedural due process.

For the reasons stated, we conclude that the detention of petitioner, without notice of the charges against him and without opportunity to be heard in opposition to them, is not authorized by 8 C.F.R. § 175.57(b). Accordingly, the judgment of the Court of Appeals is reversed and the cause remanded to the District Court.

Judgment reversed and cause remanded to the District Court.

MR. JUSTICE MINTON dissents.

SHAUGHNESSY v. UNITED STATES EX REL. MEZEI

Supreme Court of the United States, 1953.
345 U.S. 206, 73 S.Ct. 625, 97 L.Ed. 956.

MR. JUSTICE CLARK delivered the opinion of the Court.

This case concerns an alien immigrant permanently excluded from the United States on security grounds but stranded in his temporary haven on Ellis Island because other countries will not take him back. [The trial court had concluded that the government's continued exclusion of Mezei without a hearing amounted to an unlawful detention, and allowed him to enter the United States temporarily after posting a bond.]

Respondent's present dilemma springs from these circumstances: Though, as the District Court observed, "[t]here is a certain vagueness about [his] history," respondent seemingly was born in Gibraltar of Hungarian or Rumanian parents and lived in the United States from 1923 to 1948. In May of that year he sailed for Europe, apparently to visit his dying mother in Rumania. Denied entry there, he remained in Hungary for some 19 months, due to "difficulty in securing an exit permit." Finally, armed with a quota immigration visa issued by the American Consul in Budapest, he proceeded to France and boarded the *Ile de France* in Le Havre bound for New York. Upon arrival on February 9, 1950, he was temporarily excluded from the United States by an immigration inspector acting pursuant to the Passport Act as amended and regulations thereunder [the same statute and regulations applied in the *Knauff* and *Chew* cases].

Pending disposition of his case he was received at Ellis Island. After reviewing the evidence, the Attorney General on May 10, 1950, ordered the temporary exclusion to be made permanent without a hearing before a board of special inquiry, on the "basis of information of a confidential nature, the disclosure of which would be prejudicial to the public interest." That determination rested on a finding that respondent's entry would be prejudicial to the public interest for security reasons. But thus far all attempts to effect respondent's departure have failed: Twice he shipped out to return whence he came; France and Great Britain refused him permission to land. The State Department has unsuccessfully negotiated with Hungary for his readmission. Respondent personally applied for entry to about a dozen Latin American countries but all turned him down. So in June 1951 respondent advised the Immigration and Naturalization Service that he would exert no further efforts to depart. In short, respondent sat on Ellis Island because this country shut him out and others were unwilling to take him in.

Asserting unlawful confinement on Ellis Island, he sought relief through a series of habeas corpus proceedings. After four unsuccessful efforts on respondent's part, the United States District Court for the Southern District of New York on November 9, 1951, sustained the writ. The District Judge, vexed by the problem of "an alien who has no place to go," did not question the validity of the exclusion order but deemed further "detention" after 21 months excessive and justifiable only by affirmative proof of respondent's danger to the public safety. When the Government declined to divulge such evidence, even *in camera*, the District Court directed respondent's conditional parole on bond. By a divided vote, the Court of Appeals affirmed. Postulating that the power to hold could never be broader than the power to remove or shut out and that to "continue an alien's confinement beyond that moment when deportation becomes patently impossible is to deprive him of his liberty," the court found respondent's "confinement" no longer justifiable as a means of removal elsewhere, thus not authorized by statute, and in violation of due process. Judge Learned Hand, dissenting, took a different view: The Attorney General's order was one of "exclusion" and not "deportation"; respondent's transfer from ship to shore on Ellis Island conferred no additional rights; in fact, no alien so situated "can force us to admit him at all."

* * *

It is true that aliens who have once passed through our gates, even illegally, may be expelled only after proceedings conforming to traditional standards of fairness encompased in due process of law. *The Japanese Immigrant Case (Kaoru Yamataya v. Fisher)*, 1903, 189 U.S. 86, 100–101, 23 S.Ct. 611, 614, 47 L.Ed. 721; *Wong Yang Sung v. McGrath*, 1950, 339 U.S. 33, 49–50, 70 S.Ct. 445, 453–454, 94 L.Ed. 616; *Kwong Hai Chew v. Colding*, 1953, 344 U.S. 590, 598, 73 S.Ct. 472, 478. But an alien on the threshold of initial entry stands on a different footing: "Whatever the procedure authorized by Congress is, it is due process as far as an alien denied entry is concerned." *United States ex rel. Knauff v. Shaughnessy*, *supra*. And because the action of the executive officer under such authority is final and conclusive, the Attorney General cannot be compelled to disclose the evidence underlying his determinations in an exclusion case; "it is not within the province of any court, unless expressly authorized by law, to review the determination of the political branch of the Government." *United States ex rel. Knauff v. Shaughnessy*. In a case such as this, courts cannot retry the determination of the Attorney General.

Neither respondent's harborage on Ellis Island nor his prior residence here transforms this into something other than an exclusion proceeding. Concededly, his movements are restrained by authority of the United States, and he may by habeas corpus test the validity of his exclusion. But that is true whether he enjoys temporary refuge on land, or remains continuously aboard ship. In sum, harborage at Ellis Island is not an entry into the United States. For purposes of the immigration laws, moreover, the legal incidents of an alien's entry remain unaltered whether he has been here once before or not. He is an entering alien just the same, and may be excluded if unqualified for admission under existing immigration laws.

To be sure, a lawful resident alien may not captiously be deprived of his constitutional rights to procedural due process. *Kwong Hai Chew v. Colding,* 1953, 344 U.S. 590, 601, 73 S.Ct. 472, 479; *cf. Delgadillo v. Carmichael,* 1947, 332 U.S. 388, 68 S.Ct. 10, 92 L.Ed. 17. Only the other day we held that under some circumstances temporary absence from our shores cannot constitutionally deprive a returning lawfully resident alien of his right to be heard. *Kwong Hai Chew v. Colding, supra.* Chew, an alien seaman admitted by an Act of Congress to permanent residence in the United States, signed articles of maritime employment as chief steward on a vessel of American registry with home port in New York City. Though cleared by the Coast Guard for his voyage, on his return from four months at sea he was "excluded" without a hearing on security grounds. On the facts of that case, including reference to § 307(d)(2) of the Nationality Act of 1940, we felt justified in "assimilating" his status for constitutional purposes to that of continuously present alien residents entitled to hearings at least before an executive or administrative tribunal. Accordingly, to escape constitutional conflict we held the administrative regulations authorizing exclusion without hearing in certain security cases inapplicable to aliens so protected by the Fifth Amendment.

But respondent's history here drastically differs from that disclosed in Chew's case. Unlike Chew who with full security clearance and documentation pursued his vocation for four months aboard an American ship, respondent, apparently without authorization or reentry papers,[9] simply left the United States and remained behind the Iron Curtain for 19 months. Moreover, while § 307 of the 1940 Nationality Act regards maritime service such as Chew's to be continuous residence for naturalization purposes, that section deems protracted absence such as respondent's a clear break in an alien's continuous residence here. In such circumstances, we have no difficulty in holding respondent an entrant alien or "assimilated to [that] status" for constitutional purposes. That being so, the Attorney General may lawfully exclude respondent without a hearing as authorized by the emergency regulations promulgated pursuant to the

---

9. * * * Of course, neither a reentry permit, issuable upon proof of prior lawful admission to the United States, nor an immigration visa entitles an otherwise inadmissible alien to entry. An immigrant is not unaware of this; [the statute] directs those facts to be "printed conspicuously upon every immigration visa." * * *

Passport Act. Nor need he disclose the evidence upon which that determination rests. *United States ex rel. Knauff v. Shaughnessy*, 1950, 338 U.S. 537, 70 S.Ct. 309, 94 L.Ed. 317.

There remains the issue of respondent's continued exclusion on Ellis Island. Aliens seeking entry from contiguous lands obviously can be turned back at the border without more. While the Government might keep entrants by sea aboard the vessel pending determination of their admissibility, resulting hardships to the alien and inconvenience to the carrier persuaded Congress to adopt a more generous course. By statute it authorized, in cases such as this, aliens' temporary removal from ship to shore. But such temporary harborage, an act of legislative grace, bestows no additional rights. Congress meticulously specified that such shelter ashore "shall not be considered a landing" nor relieve the vessel of the duty to transport back the alien if ultimately excluded. And this Court has long considered such temporary arrangements as not affecting an alien's status; he is treated as if stopped at the border.

Thus we do not think that respondent's continued exclusion deprives him of any statutory or constitutional right. It is true that resident aliens temporarily detained pending expeditious consummation of deportation proceedings may be released on bond by the Attorney General whose discretion is subject to judicial review. *Carlson v. Landon*, 1952, 342 U.S. 524, 72 S.Ct. 525, 96 L.Ed. 547. By that procedure aliens uprooted from our midst may rejoin the community until the Government effects their leave. An exclusion proceeding grounded on danger to the national security, however, presents different considerations; neither the rationale nor the statutory authority for such release exists. Ordinarily to admit an alien barred from entry on security grounds nullifies the very purpose of the exclusion proceeding; Congress in 1950 declined to include such authority in the statute. That exclusion by the United States plus other nations' inhospitality results in present hardship cannot be ignored. But, the times being what they are, Congress may well have felt that other countries ought not shift the onus to us; that an alien in respondent's position is no more ours than theirs. Whatever our individual estimate of that policy and the fears on which it rests, respondent's right to enter the United States depends on the congressional will, and courts cannot substitute their judgment for the legislative mandate.

Reversed.

MR. JUSTICE BLACK, with whom MR. JUSTICE DOUGLAS concurs, dissenting.

Mezei came to this country in 1923 and lived as a resident alien in Buffalo, New York, for twenty-five years. He made a trip to Europe in 1948 and was stopped at our shore on his return in 1950. Without charge of or conviction for any crime, he was for two years held a prisoner on Ellis Island by order of the Attorney General. Mezei sought habeas corpus in the District Court. He wanted to go to his wife and home in Buffalo. The Attorney General defended the imprisonment by alleging that it would be dangerous to the Nation's security to let Mezei go home even temporarily on bail. Asked for proof of this, the Attorney General answered the judge that all his information was "of a confidential nature" so much so that telling any of it or even telling the names of any of his secret informers would jeopardize the safety of the Nation. Finding that Mezei's life as a resident alien in Buffalo had been "unexceptional" and that no facts had been proven to justify his continued imprisonment, the District Court granted bail. The Court of Appeals approved. Now this Court orders Mezei to leave his home and go back to his island prison to stay indefinitely, maybe for life.

Mr. Justice Jackson forcefully points out the danger in the Court's holding that Mezei's liberty is completely at the mercy of the unreviewable discretion of the Attorney General. I join Mr. Justice Jackson in the belief that Mezei's continued imprisonment without a hearing violates due process of law.

* * *

MR. JUSTICE JACKSON, whom MR. JUSTICE FRANKFURTER joins, dissenting.

Fortunately it still is startling, in this country, to find a person held indefinitely in executive custody without accusation of crime or judicial trial. Executive imprisonment has been considered oppressive and lawless since John, at Runnymede, pledged that no free man should be imprisoned, dispossessed, outlawed, or exiled save by the judgment of his peers or by the law of the land. The judges of England developed the writ of habeas corpus largely to preserve these immunities from executive restraint.

Under the best tradition of Anglo–American law, courts will not deny hearing to an unconvicted prisoner just because he is an alien whose keep, in legal theory, is just outside our gates. Lord Mansfield, in the celebrated case holding that slavery was unknown to the common law of England, ran his writ of habeas corpus in favor of an alien, an African Negro slave, and against the master of a ship at anchor in the Thames.

I.

What is our case?[2] In contemplation of law, I agree, it is that of an alien who asks admission to the country. Concretely, however, it is that of a lawful and law-abiding inhabitant of our country for a quarter of a century, long ago admitted for permanent residence, who seeks to return home. After a foreign visit to his aged and ailing mother that was prolonged by disturbed conditions of Eastern Europe, he obtained a visa for admission issued by our consul and returned to New York. There the Attorney General refused to honor his documents and turned him back as a menace to this Nation's security. This man, who seems to have led a life

---

2. I recite facts alleged in the petition for the writ. Since the Government declined to try the case on the merits, I think we must consider the question on well-pleaded allegations of the petition. Petitioner might fail to make good on a hearing; the question is, must he fail without one?

of unrelieved insignificance, must have been astonished to find himself suddenly putting the Government of the United States in such fear that it was afraid to tell him why it was afraid of him. He was shipped and reshipped to France, which twice refused him landing. Great Britain declined, and no other European country has been found willing to open its doors to him. Twelve countries of the American Hemisphere refused his applications. Since we proclaimed him a Samson who might pull down the pillars of our temple, we should not be surprised if peoples less prosperous, less strongly established and less stable feared to take him off our timorous hands. With something of a record as an unwanted man, neither his efforts nor those of the United States Government any longer promise to find him an abiding place. For nearly two years he was held in custody of the immigration authorities of the United States at Ellis Island, and if the Government has its way he seems likely to be detained indefinitely, perhaps for life, for a cause known only to the Attorney General.

Is respondent deprived of liberty? The Government answers that he was "transferred to Ellis Island on August 1, 1950 for safekeeping," and "is not being detained in the usual sense, but is in custody solely to prevent him from gaining entry into the United States in violation of law. He is free to depart from the United States to any country of his choice." Government counsel ingeniously argued that Ellis Island is his "refuge" whence he is free to take leave in any direction except west. That might mean freedom, if only he were an amphibian! Realistically, this man is incarcerated by a combination of forces which keeps him as effectually as a prison, the dominant and proximate of these forces being the United States immigration authority. It overworks legal fiction to say that one is free in law when by the commonest of common sense he is bound. Despite the impeccable legal logic of the Government's argument on this point, it leads to an artificial and unreal conclusion. We must regard this alien as deprived of liberty, and the question is whether the deprivation is a denial of due process of law.

The Government on this point argues that "no alien has any constitutional right to entry into the United States"; that "the alien has only such rights as Congress sees fit to grant in exclusion proceedings"; that "the so-called detention is still merely a continuation of the exclusion which is specifically authorized by Congress"; that since "the restraint is not incidental to an order [of exclusion] but is itself the effectuation of the exclusion order, there is no limit to its continuance" other than statutory, which means no limit at all. The Government all but adopts the words of one of the officials responsible for the administration of this Act who testified before a congressional committee as to an alien applicant, that "He has no rights."

The interpretations of the Fifth Amendment's command that no person shall be deprived of life, liberty or property without due process of law, come about to this: reasonable general legislation reasonably applied to the individual. The question is whether the Government's detention of respondent is compatible with these tests of substance and procedure.

II. SUBSTANTIVE DUE PROCESS.

Substantively, due process of law renders what is due to a strong state as well as to a free individual. It tolerates all reasonable measures to insure the national safety, and it leaves a large, at times a potentially dangerous, latitude for executive judgment as to policies and means.[5]

After all, the pillars which support our liberties are the three branches of government, and the burden could not be carried by our own power alone. Substantive due process will always pay a high degree of deference to congressional and executive judgment, especially when they concur, as to what is reasonable policy under conditions of particular times and circumstances. Close to the maximum of respect is due from the judiciary to the political departments in policies affecting security and alien exclusion. *Harisiades v. Shaughnessy*, 342 U.S. 580, 72 S.Ct. 512, 96 L.Ed. 586.

Due process does not invest any alien with a right to enter the United States, nor confer on those admitted the right to remain against the national will. Nothing in the Constitution requires admission or sufferance of aliens hostile to our scheme of government.

Nor do I doubt that due process of law will tolerate some impounding of an alien where it is deemed essential to the safety of the state. Even the resident, friendly alien may be subject to executive detention without bail, for a reasonable period, pending consummation of deportation arrangements. *Carlson v. Landon*, 342 U.S. 524, 72 S.Ct. 525, 96 L.Ed. 547. The alien enemy may be confined or his property seized and administered because hostility is assumed from his continued allegiance to a hostile state.

If due process will permit confinement of resident aliens friendly in fact because of imputed hostility, I should suppose one personally at war with our institutions might be confined, even though his state is not at war with us. In both cases, the underlying consideration is the power of our system of government to defend itself, and changing strategy of attack by infiltration may be met with changed tactics of defense.

* * *

I conclude that detention of an alien would not be inconsistent with substantive due process, provided—and this is where my dissent begins—he is accorded procedural due process of law.

III. PROCEDURAL DUE PROCESS.

Procedural fairness, if not all that originally was meant by due process of law, is at least what it most uncompromisingly requires. Procedural due process is more elemental and less flexible than substantive due process. It yields less to the times, varies less with conditions, and

---

5.   *Korematsu v. United States*, 323 U.S. 214, 65 S.Ct. 193, 89 L.Ed. 194.

defers much less to legislative judgment. Insofar as it is technical law, it must be a specialized responsibility within the competence of the judiciary on which they do not bend before political branches of the Government, as they should on matters of policy which compromise substantive law.

If it be conceded that in some way this alien could be confined, does it matter what the procedure is? Only the untaught layman or the charlatan lawyer can answer that procedures matter not. Procedural fairness and regularity are of the indispensable essence of liberty. Severe substantive laws can be endured if they are fairly and impartially applied. Indeed, if put to the choice, one might well prefer to live under Soviet substantive law applied in good faith by our common-law procedures than under our substantive law enforced by Soviet procedural practices. Let it not be overlooked that due process of law is not for the sole benefit of an accused. It is the best insurance for the Government itself against those blunders which leave lasting stains on a system of justice but which are bound to occur on ex parte consideration. *Cf. United States ex rel. Knauff v. Shaughnessy*, 338 U.S. 537, 70 S.Ct. 309, 94 L.Ed. 317, which was a near miss, saved by further administrative and congressional hearings from perpetrating an injustice. *See* Knauff, *The Ellen Knauff Story* (New York) 1952.

Our law may, and rightly does, place more restrictions on the alien than on the citizen. But basic fairness in hearing procedures does not vary with the status of the accused. If the procedures used to judge this alien are fair and just, no good reason can be given why they should not be extended to simplify the condemnation of citizens. If they would be unfair to citizens, we cannot defend the fairness of them when applied to the more helpless and handicapped alien. This is at the root of our holdings that the resident alien must be given a fair hearing to test an official claim that he is one of a deportable class. *Wong Yang Sung v. McGrath*, 339 U.S. 33, 70 S.Ct. 445, 94 L.Ed. 616.

The most scrupulous observance of due process, including the right to know a charge, to be confronted with the accuser, to cross-examine informers and to produce evidence in one's behalf, is especially necessary where the occasion of detention is fear of future misconduct, rather than crimes committed.

* * *

Because the respondent has no right of entry, does it follow that he has no rights at all? Does the power to exclude mean that exclusion may be continued or effectuated by any means which happen to seem appropriate to the authorities? It would effectuate his exclusion to eject him bodily into the sea or to set him adrift in a rowboat. Would not such measures be condemned judicially as a deprivation of life without due process of law? Suppose the authorities decide to disable an alien from entry by confiscating his valuables and money. Would we not hold this a taking of property without due process of law? Here we have a case that lies between the taking of life and the taking of property; it is the taking of liberty. It seems to me that this, occurring within the United States or its territorial waters, may be done only by proceedings which meet the test of due process of law.

Exclusion of an alien without judicial hearing, of course, does not deny due process when it can be accomplished merely by turning him back on land or returning him by sea. But when indefinite confinement becomes the means of enforcing exclusion, it seems to me that due process requires that the alien be informed of its grounds and have a fair chance to overcome them. This is the more due him when he is entrapped into leaving the other shore by reliance on a visa which the Attorney General refuses to honor.

It is evident that confinement of respondent no longer can be justified as a step in the process of turning him back to the country whence he came. Confinement is no longer ancillary to exclusion; it can now be justified only as the alternative to normal exclusion. It is an end in itself.

The Communist conspiratorial technique of infiltration poses a problem which sorely tempts the Government to resort to confinement of suspects on secret information secretly judged. I have not been one to discount the Communist evil. But my apprehensions about the security of our form of government are about equally aroused by those who refuse to recognize the dangers of Communism and those who will not see danger in anything else.

Congress has ample power to determine whom we will admit to our shores and by what means it will effectuate its exclusion policy. The only limitation is that it may not do so by authorizing United States officers to take without due process of law the life, the liberty or the property of an alien who has come within our jurisdiction; and that means he must meet a fair hearing with fair notice of the charges.[9]

It is inconceivable to me that this measure of simple justice and fair dealing would menace the security of this country. No one can make me believe that we are that far gone.

NOTES AND QUESTIONS ON MEZEI

1. The rest of the story

Congressional and public pressure eventually secured the release of both Knauff and Mezei. Ellen Knauff was ultimately granted a full hearing at which the adverse information was revealed. Although the special inquiry officer ruled against her, the BIA reversed that result on appeal and admitted

---

9. The trial court sought to reconcile due process for the individual with claims of security by suggesting that the Attorney General disclose *in camera* enough to enable a judicial determination of the legality of the confinement. The Attorney General refused. I do not know just how an *in camera* proceeding would be handled in this kind of case. If respondent, with or without counsel, were present, disclosures to them might well result in disclosures by them. If they are not allowed to be present, it is hard to see how it would answer the purpose of testing the Government's case by cross-examination or counter-evidence, which is what a hearing is for. The questions raised by the proposal need not be discussed since they do not call for decision here.

her to the United States, in a lengthy opinion setting forth in detail the slender evidence that had formed the basis for the Justice Department's initial judgment that she was dangerous. The BIA opinion is reprinted as an appendix to the book she wrote about her experience. E. Knauff, *The Ellen Knauff Story* (1952).

Ignatz Mezei also received a hearing, at which the government sought to exclude him not only for communist associations, but also for giving false information to consular officers to obtain an immigrant visa, and for a petty larceny conviction in 1935 for receipt of seven bags of stolen flour. With the conviction alone enough to exclude him, Mezei sought discretionary relief by presenting character witnesses and evidence that he had never been a Communist Party member. He was initially unsuccessful, but Mezei later secured his release under a special clemency measure after he had spent nearly four years in detention on Ellis Island. Unlike Knauff, he was not formally admitted, but rather paroled into the United States. For rich accounts of the lives and cases, see Weisselberg, *The Exclusion and Detention of Aliens: Lessons from the Lives of Ellen Knauff and Ignatz Mezei*, 143 U. Pa. L. Rev. 933, 954–85 (1995).

2. The rule in *Mezei*

a.   The same year that the U.S. Supreme Court decided *Chew* and *Mezei*, Henry Hart published his famous dialogue on the power of Congress to control the jurisdiction of the federal courts. The dialogue, long the center-piece of many law school courses on Federal Courts, had this to say about the *Knauff–Mezei* doctrine:

Q.   Do you mean to say that you don't think there are any material differences between the case of an alien trying to get into the country and the case of one whom the Government is trying to put out?

A.   No. Of course there are differences in these alien cases—not only those simple ones but many others.[92] But such differences are material only in determining the content of due process in the particular situation. What process is due always depends upon the circumstances, and the Due Process Clause is always flexible enough to take the circumstances into account.

The distinctions the Court has been drawing recently, however, are of a different order. They are distinctions between when the Constitution applies and when it does not apply at all. Any such distinction as that produces a conflict of basic principle, and is inadmissible.

Q.   What basic principle?

---

92. For example, if the alien is applying for admission, the force of his claim may vary according to whether he is coming for the first time or seeking to resume a permanent residence previously authorized. If he is coming for the first time, it may make a difference whether he is a stowaway or in possession of a duly authorized visa. If he has a visa, it may make a difference whether it is one for permanent residence or only for a temporary visit. If he is seeking to resume a previously authorized residence, it may make a difference whether he carries a reentry permit, border crossing card, or other document purporting to facilitate reentry.

Similarly, if the alien is resisting expulsion, the force of his claim may vary according to whether he entered legally or illegally. If he entered legally, it may make a difference whether he was duly admitted for permanent residence or came in only as a seaman, student, or other temporary visitor for business or pleasure.

A. The great and generating principle of this whole body of law— that the Constitution always applies when a court is sitting with jurisdiction in habeas corpus. For then the court has always to inquire, not only whether the statutes have been observed, but whether the petitioner before it has been "deprived of life, liberty, or property, without due process of law," or injured in any other way in violation of the fundamental law.

* * *

Q. Would it have made any difference in *Knauff* and *Mezei* if the Court had said that the aliens were entitled to due process and had got it, instead of saying that they weren't entitled to it at all?

A. At least the opinions in that case might have been intellectually respectable. Whether the results would have been different depends upon subtler considerations. Usually, however, it *does* make a difference whether a judge treats a question as not properly before him at all, or as involving a matter for decision.

Take *Knauff*, for example. Remember that the War Brides Act was highly ambiguous on the point in issue of whether exclusion without a hearing was authorized. If one approaches such a question on the assumption that it is constitutionally neutral, as Justice Minton declared it to be, it is at least possible to resolve the doubt as he resolved it. But if one sees constitutional overtones, the most elementary principles of interpretation call for the opposite conclusion. Note how crucially important constitutional assumptions have been in the interpretation of statutes throughout this whole area.

Again, take the facts of *Mezei*, in comparison with its *dicta*. The *dicta* say, in effect, that a Mexican wetback who sneaks successfully across the Rio Grande is entitled to the full panoply of due process in his deportation. But the holding says that a duly admitted immigrant of twenty-five years' standing who has married an American wife and sired American children, who goes abroad as the law allows to visit a dying parent, and who then returns with passport and visa duly issued by an American consul, is entitled to nothing—and, indeed, may be detained on an island in New York harbor for the rest of his life if no other country can be found to take him.

I cannot believe that judges adequately aware of the foundations of principle in this field would permit themselves to trivialize the great guarantees of due process and the freedom writ by such distinctions. And I cannot believe that judges taking responsibility for an affirmative declaration that due process has been accorded would permit themselves to arrive at such brutal conclusions.

Q. But that is what the Court has held. And so I guess that's that.

A. No, it isn't.

The deepest assumptions of the legal order require that the decisions of the highest court in the land be accepted as settling the rights and wrongs of the particular matter immediately in controversy. But the judges who sit for the time being on the court have no authority to remake by fiat alone the fabric of principle by which future cases are to be decided. They are only the custodians of the law and not the owners of it. The law belongs to the people of the country, and to the hundreds of thousands of lawyers and judges who through the years have struggled, in their behalf, to make it coherent and intelligible and responsive to the people's sense of justice.

And so, when justices of the Supreme Court sit down and write opinions in behalf of the Court which ignore the painful forward steps of a whole half century of adjudication, making no effort to relate what then is being done to what the Court has done before, they write without authority for the future. The appeal to principle is still open and, so long as courts of the United States sit with general jurisdiction in habeas corpus, that means an appeal to them and their successors.

Hart, *The Power of Congress to Limit the Jurisdiction of the Federal Courts: An Exercise in Dialectic*, 66 Harv. L. Rev. 1362, 1392–96 (1953).

b. Hart reads *Mezei* as stating, in dicta, that clandestine entrants receive the full panoply of due process rights in deportation proceedings (that is, that they fall under *Yamataya v. Fisher*). If so, *Mezei* creates an obvious inducement to enter without inspection, for the noncitizen then winds up in a better constitutional position than the unfortunate soul who does as he should and presents himself for inspection at the port of entry. Such a result is at best ironic, but it is the traditional understanding of *Mezei*: that a noncitizen's entitlement to constitutional due process depends on whether he stands at the border trying to get in (even if he has been here before), or instead has already made an entry and must be removed. In other words, due process depends on the traditional statutory category in which the noncitizen finds himself—exclusion or deportation—thus largely (but not entirely) on location, rather than on the stakes involved for him.

But does *Mezei* have to be read that way? The Court describes the constitutionally preferred class as "aliens who have once passed through our gates, even illegally." Aliens who enter without inspection would seem to have jumped the fence, rather than passing through the gates. Maybe the Court meant to protect only those who were inspected at entry and who are later brought into deportation proceedings because of some defect—some illegality—that comes to light thereafter, revealing that the original entry was illegal, despite compliance with the formalities of inspection. Should such a distinction be made? Hart actually suggests, in his footnote 92, the possibility of a much more nuanced range of distinctions, for purposes of deciding what process is due. For an extended discussion of the way in which various sorts of distinctions might properly play a role in deciding on due process rights in immigration proceedings, see Martin, *Due Process and Membership in the National Community: Political Asylum and Beyond*, 44 U. Pitt. L. Rev. 165 (1983); Aleinikoff, *Aliens, Due Process and "Community Ties": A Response to Martin*, 44 U. Pitt. L. Rev. 237 (1983). Aleinikoff highlights the ways in which full judicial review fosters a healthy evolution of procedures, to the benefit of both the government and applicants. *Id.* at 258–59.

3. Drawing the line

a. This brings us to a related, fundamental question. The constitutional doctrine relating to admission developed for over a century within the traditional exclusion-deportation framework that was fundamental to the INA until 1996. As Chapter Seven explains more fully, before the 1996 Act noncitizens who had entered the United States—even surreptitiously—were subject to deportation grounds. Noncitizens who had not entered were subject to exclusion grounds. The 1996 Act shifted the structure so that the most important statutory line is now admission (that is, inspection by an officer and authorization to establish presence in the United States) rather than entry. The inadmissibility grounds in § 212 apply to noncitizens who have not been admitted. The deportability grounds in § 237 apply only after admission.

The main effect is to alter the treatment of clandestine border crossers. Before 1996, they would have been deportable; hence their constitutional rights were determined under the rubric of rights of deportable noncitizens. Now, they are considered inadmissible. Does this mean that their due process rights will be decided by applying *Mezei*, and not the more generous due process analysis of *Yamataya*? Would such a result make sense in light of the considerations outlined in Note 2 above? Fifteen years after the 1996 Act, courts have yet to answer this question with any clarity. What should the answer be? Now that the statutory line has shifted, should we reconsider the traditional reading of *Mezei* and adopt a new constitutional due process doctrine as well?

b. With regard to people at the border, how should the constitutional dividing line be drawn between protected permanent residents like *Chew* and unprotected noncitizens like *Mezei*—length of absence, nature of activities while outside the United States, types of preclearance before departure? Justice Clark's opinion in *Mezei* mentions several factors but does not reveal which was decisive. The BIA ultimately decided that, at least for purposes of allocating the burden of proof in removal proceedings of any kind, a noncitizen would be treated like Chew whenever he presented "a colorable claim to returning lawful resident alien status." *Matter of Kane*, 15 I & N Dec. 258, 264 (BIA 1975), relying on *Kwong Hai Chew v. Rogers*, 257 F.2d 606 (D.C.Cir.1958) (upon remand after the Supreme Court's decision). Is this a reasonable reading? Can it account for what happened to Mezei?

Thirty years after *Chew* and *Mezei*, a lawful permanent resident, refused admission to the United States after a brief stay in Mexico, again filed a constitutional challenge to the procedures that led to her rejection. How much of the *Mezei* doctrine survives the Supreme Court's 1982 analysis of the Due Process Clause?

LANDON v. PLASENCIA

Supreme Court of the United States, 1982.
459 U.S. 21, 103 S.Ct. 321, 74 L.Ed.2d 21.

JUSTICE O'CONNOR delivered the opinion of the Court.

* * *

I

Respondent Maria Antonieta Plasencia, a citizen of El Salvador, entered the United States as a permanent resident alien in March, 1970. She established a home in Los Angeles with her husband, a United States citizen, and their minor children. On June 27, 1975, she and her husband travelled to Tijuana, Mexico. During their brief stay in Mexico, they met with several Mexican and Salvadoran nationals and made arrangements to assist their illegal entry into the United States. She agreed to transport the aliens to Los Angeles and furnished some of the aliens with alien registration receipt cards that belonged to her children. When she and her husband attempted to cross the international border at 9:27 on the evening of June 29, 1975, an INS officer at the port of entry found six nonresident aliens in the Plasencias' car. The INS detained the respondent for further inquiry pursuant to § 235(b) of the Immigration and Nationality Act of 1952. In a notice dated June 30, 1975, the INS charged her under § 212(a)(31) of the Act, which provides for the exclusion of any alien seeking admission "who at any time shall have, knowingly and for gain, encouraged, induced, assisted, abetted, or aided any other alien to enter or to try to enter the United States in violation of law,"[a] and gave notice that it would hold an exclusion hearing at 11:00 a.m. on June 30, 1975.

An immigration law judge conducted the scheduled exclusion hearing. After hearing testimony from the respondent, her husband, and three of the aliens found in the Plasencias' car, the judge found "clear, convincing and unequivocal" evidence that the respondent did "knowingly and for gain encourage, induce, assist, abet, or aid nonresident aliens" to enter or try to enter the United States in violation of law.

* * *

[Plasencia first argued that, as a returning resident absent only briefly, she should have been placed in deportation proceedings rather than exclusion proceedings under the statute. The Court rejected this contention.]

IV

* * * Plasencia [also] argued * * * that she was denied due process in her exclusion hearing. We agree with Plasencia that under the circumstances of this case, she can invoke the Due Process Clause on returning to this country, although we do not decide the contours of the process that is due or whether the process accorded Plasencia was insufficient.

This Court has long held that an alien seeking initial admission to the United States requests a privilege and has no constitutional rights regarding his application, for the power to admit or exclude aliens is a sovereign prerogative. *See, e.g., United States ex rel. Knauff v. Shaughnessy,* 338

---

a. In 1990, Congress eliminated the "for gain" requirement in this exclusion ground, which now appears as INA § 212(a)(6)(E). Section 212(d)(11) allows a discretionary waiver if only close family members were smuggled in.—eds.

U.S. 537, 542, 70 S.Ct. 309, 312, 94 L.Ed. 317 (1950); *Nishimura Ekiu v. United States*, 142 U.S. 651, 659–660, 12 S.Ct. 336, 338, 35 L.Ed. 1146 (1892). Our recent decisions confirm that view. *See, e.g., Fiallo v. Bell*, 430 U.S. 787, 792, 97 S.Ct. 1473, 1477, 52 L.Ed.2d 50 (1977); *Kleindienst v. Mandel*, 408 U.S. 753, 92 S.Ct. 2576, 33 L.Ed.2d 683 (1972). As we explained in *Johnson v. Eisentrager*, 339 U.S. 763, 770, 70 S.Ct. 936, 939, 94 L.Ed. 1255 (1950), however, once an alien gains admission to our country and begins to develop the ties that go with permanent residence his constitutional status changes accordingly. Our cases have frequently suggested that a continuously present resident alien is entitled to a fair hearing when threatened with deportation, and, although we have only rarely held that the procedures provided by the executive were inadequate, we developed the rule that a continuously present permanent resident alien has a right to due process in such a situation.

The question of the procedures due a returning resident alien arose in *Kwong Hai Chew v. Colding*. There, the regulations permitted the exclusion of an arriving alien without a hearing. We interpreted those regulations not to apply to Chew, a permanent resident alien who was returning from a five-month voyage abroad as a crewman on an American merchant ship. We reasoned that, "For purposes of his constitutional right to due process, we assimilate petitioner's status to that of an alien continuously residing and physically present in the United States." Then, to avoid constitutional problems, we construed the regulation as inapplicable. Although the holding was one of regulatory interpretation, the rationale was one of constitutional law. Any doubts that *Chew* recognized constitutional rights in the resident alien returning from a brief trip abroad were dispelled by *Rosenberg v. Fleuti*, [374 U.S. 449, 83 S.Ct. 1804, 10 L.Ed.2d 1000 (1963),] where we described *Chew* as holding "that the returning resident alien is entitled as a matter of due process to a hearing on the charges underlying any attempt to exclude him."

If the permanent resident alien's absence is extended, of course, he may lose his entitlement to "assimilat[ion of his] status," *Kwong Hai Chew v. Colding, supra,* 344 U.S., at 596, 73 S.Ct., at 477, to that of an alien continuously residing and physically present in the United States. In *Shaughnessy v. United States ex rel. Mezei*, 345 U.S. 206, 73 S.Ct. 625, 97 L.Ed. 956 (1953), this Court rejected the argument of an alien who had left the country for some twenty months that he was entitled to due process in assessing his right to admission on his return. We did not suggest that no returning resident alien has a right to due process, for we explicitly reaffirmed *Chew*. We need not now decide the scope of *Mezei*; it does not govern this case, for Plasencia was absent from the country only a few days, and the United States has conceded that she has a right to due process.

The constitutional sufficiency of procedures provided in any situation, of course, varies with the circumstances. * * * In evaluating the procedures in any case, the courts must consider the interest at stake for the individual, the risk of an erroneous deprivation of the interest through the procedures used as well as the probable value of additional or different procedural safeguards, and the interest of the government in using the current procedures rather than additional or different procedures. *Mathews v. Eldridge*, 424 U.S. 319, 334–335, 96 S.Ct. 893, 902–903, 47 L.Ed.2d 18 (1976). Plasencia's interest here is, without question, a weighty one. She stands to lose the right "to stay and live and work in this land of freedom." Further, she may lose the right to rejoin her immediate family, a right that ranks high among the interests of the individual. The government's interest in efficient administration of the immigration laws at the border also is weighty. Further, it must weigh heavily in the balance that control over matters of immigration is a sovereign prerogative, largely within the control of the executive and the legislature. The role of the judiciary is limited to determining whether the procedures meet the essential standard of fairness under the Due Process Clause and does not extend to imposing procedures that merely displace congressional choices of policy. Our previous discussion has shown that Congress did not intend to require the use of deportation procedures in cases such as this one. Thus, it would be improper simply to impose deportation procedures here because the reviewing court may find them preferable. Instead, the courts must evaluate the particular circumstances and determine what procedures would satisfy the minimum requirements of due process on the re-entry of a permanent resident alien.

Plasencia questions three aspects of the procedures that the government employed in depriving her of these interests. First, she contends that the immigration law judge placed the burden of proof upon her. [The BIA had generally placed the burden on the government when the noncitizen was a lawful permanent resident. The regulations were silent on the issue and the opinions below had not directly addressed the question.]

Second, Plasencia contends that the notice provided her was inadequate. She apparently had less than eleven hours' notice of the charges and the hearing. The regulations do not require any advance notice of the charges against the alien in an exclusion hearing, and the BIA has held that it is sufficient that the alien have notice of the charges at the hearing. The United States has argued to us that Plasencia could have sought a continuance. It concedes, however, that there is no explicit statutory or regulatory authorization for a continuance.

Finally, Plasencia contends that she was allowed to waive her right to representation,[8] without a full understanding of the right or of the consequences of waiving it. Through an interpreter, the immigration law judge informed her at the outset of the hearing, as required by the regulations, of her right to be represented. He did not tell her of the availability of free legal counsel, but at the time of the hearing, there was no administrative requirement that he do so. The Attorney General has since revised the regulations to require that, when qualified free legal

---

8. The statute provides a right to representation without expense to the government. Section 292. Plasencia has not suggested that she is entitled to free counsel.

services are available, the immigration law judge must inform the alien of their existence and ask whether representation is desired. As the United States concedes, the hearing would not comply with the current regulations.

If the exclusion hearing is to ensure fairness, it must provide Plasencia an opportunity to present her case effectively, though at the same time it cannot impose an undue burden on the government. It would not, however, be appropriate for us to decide now whether the new regulation on the right to notice of free legal services is of constitutional magnitude or whether the remaining procedures provided comport with the Due Process Clause. Before this Court, the parties have devoted their attention to the entitlement to a deportation hearing rather than to the sufficiency of the procedures in the exclusion hearing.[9] Whether the several hours' notice gave Plasencia a realistic opportunity to prepare her case for effective presentation in the circumstances of an exclusion hearing without counsel is a question we are not now in a position to answer. Nor has the government explained the burdens that it might face in providing more elaborate procedures. Thus, although we recognize the gravity of Plasencia's interest, the other factors relevant to due process analysis— the risk of erroneous deprivation, the efficacy of additional procedural safeguards, and the government's interest in providing no further procedures—have not been adequately presented to permit us to assess the sufficiency of the hearing. We remand to the Court of Appeals to allow the parties to explore whether Plasencia was accorded due process under all of the circumstances.

Accordingly, the judgment of the Court of Appeals is

Reversed and remanded.

Justice Marshall, concurring in part and dissenting in part.

I agree that the Immigration and Nationality Act permitted the INS to proceed against respondent in an exclusion proceeding. The question then remains whether the exclusion proceeding held in this case satisfied the minimum requirements of the Due Process Clause. While I agree that the Court need not decide the precise contours of the process that would be constitutionally sufficient, I would not hesitate to decide that the process accorded Plasencia was insufficient.

The Court has already set out the standards to be applied in resolving the question. Therefore, rather than just remand, I would first hold that

---

9. Thus, the question of Plasencia's entitlement to due process has been briefed and argued, is properly before us, and is sufficiently developed that we are prepared to decide it. Precisely what procedures are due, on the other hand, has not been adequately developed by the briefs or argument. The dissent undertakes to decide these questions, but, to do so, must rely heavily on an argument not raised by Plasencia: to wit, that she was not informed at the hearing that the alleged agreement to receive compensation and the meaningfulness of her departure were critical issues. Also, the dissent fails to discuss the interests that the government may have in employing the procedures that it did. The omission of arguments raised by the parties is quite understandable, for neither Plasencia nor the government has yet discussed what procedures are due. Unlike the dissent, we would allow the parties to explore their respective interests and arguments in the Court of Appeals.

respondent was denied due process because she was not given adequate and timely notice of the charges against her and of her right to retain counsel and to present a defense.[2]

While the type of hearing required by due process depends upon a balancing of the competing interests at stake, due process requires "at a minimum ... that deprivation of life, liberty or property by adjudication be preceded by notice and opportunity for hearing." *Mullane v. Central Hanover Bank & Trust Co.*, 339 U.S. 306, 313, 70 S.Ct. 652, 656, 94 L.Ed. 865 (1950). Permanent resident aliens who are detained upon reentry into this country clearly are entitled to adequate notice in advance of an exclusion proceeding.

To satisfy due process, notice must "clarify what the charges are" in a manner adequate to apprise the individual of the basis for the government's proposed action. Notice must be provided sufficiently in advance of the hearing to "give the charged party a chance to marshal the facts in his defense." * * *

[Plasencia received less than 24 hours notice of the hearing, and only received notice in Spanish at the beginning of the hearing of the charges against her, her right to retain counsel, and her right to present evidence.]

The charges against Plasencia were also inadequately explained at the hearing itself. The immigration judge did not explain to her that she would be entitled to remain in the country if she could demonstrate that she had not agreed to receive compensation from the aliens whom she had driven across the border. Nor did the judge inform respondent that the meaningfulness of her departure was an issue at the hearing.

These procedures deprived Plasencia of a fair opportunity to show that she was not excludable under the standards set forth in the Immigration and Nationality Act. Because Plasencia was not given adequate notice of the standards for exclusion or of her right to retain counsel and present a defense, she had neither time nor opportunity to prepare a response to the government's case. The procedures employed here virtually assured that the Government attorney would present his case without factual or legal opposition.

When a permanent resident alien's substantial interest in remaining in this country is at stake, the Due Process Clause forbids the Government to stack the deck in this fashion. Only a compelling need for truly summary action could justify this one-sided proceeding. In fact, the Government's haste in proceeding against Plasencia could be explained only by its desire to avoid the minimal administrative and financial burden of providing her adequate notice and an opportunity to prepare for the hearing. Although the various other government interests identified by the Court may be served by the exclusion of those who fail to meet the eligibility requirements set out in the Immigration and Nationality Act, they are not served by procedures that deny a permanent resident alien a

---

2. Because Plasencia did not receive constitutionally sufficient notice, I find it unnecessary to address the other constitutional deficiencies she asserts.

fair opportunity to demonstrate that she meets those eligibility requirements.

I would therefore hold that respondent was denied due process.

NOTES AND QUESTIONS ON DUE PROCESS FOR RETURNING PERMANENT RESIDENTS

1. The rest of the story

For a detailed history of the Plasencias' trip to Mexico, Maria Plasencia's heartfelt (though legally naive) *pro se* defense in the exclusion proceedings, including the candid testimony offered by her and her husband, and the aftermath of the ruling, see Johnson, *Maria and Joseph Plasencia's Lost Weekend: The Case of* Landon v. Plasencia, *in* Immigration Stories 221 (D. Martin & P. Schuck eds. 2005). Johnson reports that Mrs. Plasencia was paroled into the United States for the duration of the court proceedings, and that the government did not pursue the case after the remand to the district court. "The government presumably decided not to proceed against Maria because of the pro-immigrant due process law that the courts might have created if they had addressed her due process claims." *Id.* at 239. Her attorneys lost touch with her after the Supreme Court's decision, but speculated that she might still be living in the United States as a lawful permanent resident. *Id.* at 238–39.

2. *Plasencia*, *Mezei*, and *Fleuti*

Plasencia distinguishes *Mezei* but does not purport to overrule it. Nonetheless, the Court has now alleviated much of the threat that *Mezei* seemed to pose to permanent residents who travel (though *Mezei* continue to cast a large shadow for all other inadmissible noncitizens). Henceforth, full due process entitlement seems to be the norm for nearly all returning permanent residents, even those seeking admission, and *Mezei* marks out an ill-defined exception.

But how should we draw the line that distinguishes these exceptional cases? The Court says only that a permanent resident may lose his protected status if his "absence is extended." Presumably this provides more protection than the standard that the U.S. Supreme Court announced in *Rosenberg v. Fleuti*, 374 U.S. 449, 83 S.Ct. 1804, 10 L.Ed.2d 1000 (1963), a decision which Justice O'Connor notes in *Plasencia*.

In *Fleuti*, the issue was whether George Fleuti, a native and citizen of Switzerland and a permanent resident since 1952, was reentering the United States upon his return from a short trip of "about a couple hours" to Ensenada, Mexico in 1956. This mattered because in 1959 the INS tried to deport him as an alien "excludable by the law existing at the time of ... entry." The exclusion ground in question (based on Fleuti's homosexuality) had not been on the books when Fleuti initially entered the United States in 1952, but it had become law by 1956.

In *Fleuti*, the Supreme Court found that a noncitizen was not making an entry when returning from a temporary absence that was not "meaningfully interruptive" of permanent residence. The Court read into the statute an exception for "innocent, casual, and brief" trips. Congress later modified the *Fleuti* exception in 1996, but it was the law when the Court decided *Plasencia* in 1982. The Court held that even if Maria Plasencia's trip to Mexico fell outside the *Fleuti* exception, she was still entitled to procedural due process protection as a returning permanent resident.

In deciding when an absence is extended for constitutional purposes, should courts apply the one-year rule that governs for some purposes under the immigration laws? For example, a returning resident who has been absent for more than one year may not rely on his green card as a reentry permit. 8 C.F.R. § 211.1(a)(2). Or, rather than relying mechanically on length of absence, should courts try to determine whether the permanent resident intended to abandon his status? *See, e.g., Ahmed v. Ashcroft*, 286 F.3d 611, 612–13 (2d Cir.2002); *Aleem v. Perryman*, 114 F.3d 672, 676–79 (7th Cir.1997). The BIA uses a multiple factor test to decide if a permanent resident intended to abandon that status. *See Matter of Huang*, 19 I & N Dec. 749, 752–54 (BIA 1988).

If any subjective intent test is ultimately employed, the Court probably could not avoid *de facto* overruling *Mezei*. According to the facts as Mezei pleaded them, he had no intention of making a lengthy journey, much less of abandoning his U.S. home. And the fact that his family remained behind in Buffalo while he traveled lends a strong measure of plausibility to these facts.

As amended by the 1996 Act, INA § 101(a)(13) says that a returning permanent resident is not seeking admission unless certain facts are present: for example, a continuous absence in excess of 180 days, abandonment or relinquishment of the permanent resident status, or the commission of a crime that would make a noncitizen inadmissible. Are these guidelines a sensible way of defining those returning permanent residents who receive heightened due process protection based on prior attachments to the United States (and notwithstanding their physical departure)? If so, should *Plasencia* come out the same way today, under the current INA? The larger question here is whether Congress, even if it cannot define constitutional rights by statute, might nonetheless create categories that influence how the Court draws constitutional lines.

3. Who gets due process, and what process is due?

So far, we have considered whether due process applies to a given case, but we have not examined closely what specific procedures due process might require. This is the point of contention in *Plasencia* between the majority's decision to remand for decision on whether Maria Plasencia received due process, and Justice Marshall, who "would not hesitate to decide that the process accorded Plasencia was insufficient."

To decide what process is due and to understand how the Court approaches this question in *Plasencia*, it is important to note that in the 1970s the Supreme Court initiated a major reconceptualization of due process analysis in civil cases:

> This fundamental transformation occurred in the "due process revolution" that began with the Supreme Court's 1970 decision in *Goldberg v. Kelly* [397 U.S. 254, 90 S.Ct. 1011, 25 L.Ed.2d 287 (1970)]. In that line of

cases, the Court moved beyond the restrictive due process doctrines that guaranteed procedural safeguards only for traditional forms of property. * * * The Court rejected wooden reliance on the right-privilege distinction in the context of a procedural due process claim. Instead, it interpreted procedural due process much more broadly to include statutory "entitlements" or other forms of "new property," such as welfare benefits.

Goldberg and its progeny established a two-step analysis for procedural due process claims, in which the Court first asks whether a claimant possesses a "liberty" or "property" interest under the Fifth Amendment's Due Process Clause. Given [such] an "entitlement," the second analytical step is to decide on a case-by-case basis exactly what procedural protections due process requires.

Motomura, *The Curious Evolution of Immigration Law: Procedural Surrogates for Substantive Constitutional Rights*, 92 Colum. L. Rev. 1625, 1651–52 (1992).

a. In *Board of Regents v. Roth*, 408 U.S. 564, 571, 92 S.Ct. 2701, 2706, 33 L.Ed.2d 548 (1972), the Court placed new emphasis on a careful threshold assessment of the nature of the individual interest at stake. The Due Process Clause protects only against deprivations of "life, liberty, or property," the Court stressed, and not all government actions negatively affecting individuals deprive them of such interests.

To have a property interest in a benefit, a person clearly must have more than an abstract need or desire for it. He must have more than a unilateral expectation of it. He must, instead, have a legitimate claim of entitlement to it. * * *

Property interests, of course, are not created by the Constitution. Rather, they are created and their dimensions are defined by existing rules or understandings that stem from an independent source like state law * * *.

408 U.S. at 577, 92 S.Ct. at 2709.

Liberty, according to *Roth*, enjoys a more expansive conception: "In a Constitution for a free people, there can be no doubt that the meaning of 'liberty' must be broad indeed." 408 U.S. at 572, 92 S.Ct. at 2707. *Roth* also quotes from *Meyer v. Nebraska*, 262 U.S. 390, 399, 43 S.Ct. 625, 626, 67 L.Ed. 1042 (1923):

Without doubt [liberty] denotes not merely freedom from bodily restraint but also the right of the individual to contract, to engage in any of the common occupations of life, to acquire useful knowledge, to marry, establish a home and bring up children, to worship God according to the dictates of his own conscience, and generally to enjoy those privileges long recognized ... as essential to the orderly pursuit of happiness by free men.

Later cases have cut back on *Roth*'s definition of liberty, *see, e.g., Sandin v. Conner*, 515 U.S. 472, 483–84, 115 S.Ct. 2293, 2300, 132 L.Ed.2d 418 (1995) (holding that prisoners have no liberty interest in not being placed in disciplinary segregation for thirty days).

A long-time lawful permanent resident with a family in the United States, like Plasencia or Mezei, can argue that prohibition of reentry implicates their liberty to carry on their established life, but can a first-time applicant for admission like Ellen Knauff be brought within the *Roth* framework? What is the liberty interest noncitizens have as they seek to enter the United States for the first time? To be sure, exclusion imposes bodily restraints on their freedom of movement, but do all non-U.S. citizens in the world who might happen to present themselves at our borders have a legitimate claim of entitlement to free movement in this very potent sense?

If we think of their claims under the property rubric, do they have more than a unilateral expectation or hope that they would be permitted to enter the United States? Does the U.S. immigration law provide the independent source for a "legitimate claim of entitlement"? If so, do all first-time applicants for admission who have a visa have a property interest? What if they do not have a visa? When someone who has never been in the United States is denied admission, has there been a *deprivation* of liberty or property? Or to put the questions in functional terms, can the United States afford to provide due process to everyone in the world who simply presents himself or herself at a port of entry? If so, how much process? If not, how should we decide when due process rights attach?

b.   If a noncitizen has a liberty or property interest, the next question is what process is due. In his footnote 9 in *Mezei*, Justice Jackson suggests that *in camera* disclosure of the evidence would not solve the underlying problem. His resistance to *in camera* procedures may stem from his uniquely inflexible view of procedural due process requirements. As part III of his *Mezei* dissent reveals, Justice Jackson seems to regard due process requirements as a rather fixed set, apparently defined by the usual elements of the traditional adversarial model familiar to us from, for example, criminal trials.

Whatever the merits of Justice Jackson's view, the Supreme Court has not accepted it. Modern cases stress the flexibility of the concept of due process; procedures acceptable in some settings may be wholly unacceptable in others. The prevailing mode of inquiry is a three-part balancing test set forth in the landmark case of *Mathews v. Eldridge*, 424 U.S. 319, 96 S.Ct. 893, 47 L.Ed.2d 18 (1976). The test requires courts to consider (1) the interests at stake for the individual, (2) the interest of the government, and (3) the gain to accurate decisionmaking that can be expected from the procedural protection sought. *Id.* at 335, 96 S.Ct. at 903.

4. National security and admission procedures after *Mezei*

In 1952, Congress provided explicit statutory authority for the kinds of secret procedures that had been employed against Knauff and Mezei on the authority of regulations alone. INA § 235(c) permits the government to order removal of an arriving alien on most of the national security inadmissibility grounds without a further hearing if it acts on the basis of "confidential information," the disclosure of which "would be prejudicial to the public interest, safety, or security." The section 235(c) procedure was invoked less frequently as the Cold War thawed than it was in the 1950s, but it was still employed, and not only against suspected Soviet bloc sympathizers. *See, e.g., Azzouka v. Sava*, 777 F.2d 68, 76 (2d Cir. 1985), *cert. denied*, 479 U.S. 830,

107 S.Ct. 115, 93 L.Ed.2d 62 (1986) (sustaining government's power to exclude summarily based on national security grounds PLO dissident seeking asylum in U.S.); *Avila v. Rivkind*, 724 F.Supp. 945 (S.D.Fla.1989) (sustaining summary exclusion of Orlando Bosch, who had often been involved in violent anti-Castro activity); *El–Werfalli v. Smith*, 547 F.Supp. 152 (S.D.N.Y.1982) (sustaining exclusion, based on confidential information, of a Libyan student coming to attend classes in aircraft training, under an exclusion ground making excludable those aliens believed likely to "engage in activities which would be prejudicial to the public interest, or endanger the welfare, safety, or security of the United States").

Since the terrorist attacks of September 11, 2001, the government has increasingly invoked various enforcement measures based on national security. Several of them pose significant questions about the fairness of using secret information not shared with the alien in removal proceedings. We will consider in greater detail in Chapters Nine and Ten the due process and policy issues such measures pose, and also look at alternative procedures that might provide a better balance between security needs and individual rights.

As a final way of pulling together the many strands in *Knauff*, *Yamataya*, *Chew*, *Mezei*, and *Plasencia*, consider the following scenario.

EXERCISE: DUE PROCESS AT THE BORDER

Mohammed Adawallah was born in Yemen in 1982. He has been a lawful permanent resident of the United States since 2001. He currently lives near Cincinnati, Ohio, with his wife and child, both of whom are U.S. citizens, and has 34 other relatives in the United States. Adawallah is a graduate of Ohio State University. He has been politically active while living in this country, being particularly outspoken in his opposition to U.S. policies in the Middle East. Eleven months ago, Adawallah filed a naturalization application, which is still pending.

Eight months ago, Adawallah applied for and obtained a reentry permit from the government, as is the standard procedure when a permanent resident plans an extended trip abroad. He stated on his application for the permit that he wished to go to Cyprus to be with his mother while she underwent and recuperated from "major heart surgery."

Approximately 26 weeks after departing, Adawallah arrived at Kennedy Airport in New York on a flight from Heathrow Airport in London. His itinerary showed that he had flown to London from Beirut, Lebanon. When questioned by inspectors, Adawallah said that he had not gone to Cyprus because his mother's surgery had been cancelled as not medically necessary. The government asserted during the questioning that Adawallah went instead to Egypt with two other men, with whom he attended a gathering of Hamas, which the U.S. government has officially designated as a terrorist organization. Adawallah categorically denied that he has ever been affiliated with

Hamas or any other terrorist group, or that he has ever engaged in any terrorist activity. After the questioning, he was detained for removal proceedings. To what sort of procedures is he entitled under the statute? Is he an arriving alien?

Shortly thereafter, DHS charged Adawallah with being inadmissible to the United States on national security grounds, citing INA § 212(a)(3)(B), on the basis of confidential information. DHS also instituted summary exclusion proceedings under § 235(c), but gave Adawallah no indication of the details of the confidential information that supported their conclusion that he is affiliated with a terrorist organization.

Is a constitutional due process challenge to the government's use of this confidential information likely to be successful?

SECTION D.   REVIEW OF ADMISSIONS DECISIONS

It has been three decades since the Supreme Court ruled that the Due Process Clause required immigration inspectors to give Maria Plasencia a fair hearing, and remanded the case for the lower courts to assess the adequacy of the procedures provided. As the earlier section of this chapter emphasizes, seeking lawful admission to the United States is a multi-step process, and a noncitizen may receive a negative decision at different points in the proceedings. What procedures apply to these decisions, both as to the initial decisions and for review or appeal? Answering this question implicates statutory and regulatory provisions, as well as the Constitution.

Visa petition denials in the United States are reviewable in court under the Administrative Procedure Act, after exhaustion of administrative remedies. But what about visa denials by consular officers overseas? What happens today when immigration officers at the border refuse admission to a noncitizen who has arrived at the border for the first time bearing a visa issued by a U.S. consulate overseas? Are there circumstances in which noncitizens can be rejected without any hearing at all? We will consider these issues one at a time.

1.   REJECTION AT THE CONSULATE

You may recall from Chapter Four that an unusual provision in INA § 104(a) exempts individual visa determinations from the supervision and control of the Secretary of State. Nonetheless the State Department long ago developed a *de facto* internal review mechanism, which provided that denials would be considered by another officer within the consulate, who could not, strictly speaking, reverse the initial decision, but instead could issue the visa in his or her own name upon a judgment that the person was eligible. This was an internal control measure rather than an appeal the applicant could seek, and in some busy posts it apparently was applied only on a spot-check basis. *See* Nafziger, *Review of Visa Denials by Consular Officers*, 66 Wash.L.Rev. 1, 19–25 (1991); 54 Fed.Reg. 53496 (1989) (report and recommendations of the Administrative Conference of the U.S. regarding review of consular visa decisions).

In 2006, the State Department revised the regulations and the Foreign Affairs Manual to make explicit the selective nature of this review and also to direct more supervisory attention to visa issuances and not just denials—a byproduct of enhanced security concerns. The regulations now direct supervisors to review a random selection of both positive and negative visa decisions by consular officers—a process the Department describes as "a significant management and instructional tool * * * [to ensure] uniform and correct application of the law and regulations." 9 FAM § 41.113 PN 17.1 (2010); *see also* 22 C.F.R. §§ 41.113(i), 41.121(c); 9 FAM § 41.121 PN 18.1–2, *id.* 41.121 PN 1.2–8 (2011). In addition to these internal processes, applicants may also submit additional information to overcome a visa refusal, and in many circumstances are entitled to reconsideration upon doing so. *See, e.g.*, 22 C.F.R. § 41.121(c), 42.81(e). Also, under a practice in place for many decades, the Department's headquarters Visa Office may request a report on a specific case or class of cases, and sometimes issues an advisory opinion "to the consular officer for assistance in considering the case further." Suggestions in such opinions regarding factual determinations are advisory, in keeping with INA § 104, but rulings on matters of law are binding on the consular officer. 22 C.F.R. §§ 41.121(d), 42.81(d).

There is no procedure, however, that permits the applicant to appeal a consular visa denial to some higher administrative authority. Nor is there an explicit statutory provision regarding judicial review. In cases construing and applying the Administrative Procedure Act (APA), 5 U.S.C.A. §§ 701–706, the Supreme Court has held that agency action today is presumptively reviewable in the courts, absent clear signals from the Congress making court review inapplicable, *see Lincoln v. Vigil*, 508 U.S. 182, 190, 113 S.Ct. 2024, 2030, 124 L.Ed.2d 101 (1993). Nonetheless, since the early twentieth century, consular decisions made overseas have generally been held to be beyond the jurisdiction of the courts. This rule has been applied not only to a person seeking a visa for a short vacation or business trip to the United States, but also to a person seeking an immigrant visa based on his or her relation to a U.S. citizen or permanent resident—and equally to a suit filed by the citizen or LPR sponsor seeking to challenge the family member's immigrant visa denial. *See, e.g., Pena v. Kissinger,* 409 F.Supp. 1182 (S.D.N.Y. 1976).

Several circuits have explicitly reaffirmed this doctrine over the last few decades. *See, e.g., Onuchukwu v. Clinton*, 408 Fed. Appx. 558 (3d Cir. 2010) (consular nonreviewability precludes jurisdiction over challenge to diversity visa denial); *Saavedra Bruno v. Albright*, 197 F.3d 1153, 1158–64 (D.C.Cir.1999) (no judicial review of challenge filed by Bolivian national temporarily residing in U.S. to denial of visa by consular official overseas). Some courts have found jurisdiction, however, to consider underlying questions regarding the constitutionality of the statute under which the consul acted, despite the consular nonreviewability doctrine. *See, e.g., Martinez v. Bell*, 468 F.Supp. 719 (S.D.N.Y.1979) (sustaining the government on the merits). Others have found jurisdiction when the key decisions were actually made not by the consular officer overseas but by officials in the United States. *See, e.g., American Academy of Religion v. Napolitano*, 573 F.3d 115, 123–25 (2d Cir. 2009) (sustaining judicial review of failure to issue visa to Ramadan, a Swiss citizen and Islamic scholar). *See generally* Dobkin, *Challenging the Doctrine of Consular Nonreviewability in Immigration Cases*, 24 Geo. Immigr. L. J. 113 (2010).

Visa revocations have also traditionally been considered immune to judicial review, and Congress expressly barred judicial review in an amendment to INA § 221(i) adopted in 2004. But in the past such a revocation made a difference only for noncitizens who had not yet traveled to the United States. When such persons arrived at the border, they would be inadmissible for failure to have a valid visa. INA § 212(a)(7). After admission, the expiration or revocation of the visa had no direct impact, until the person chose to travel again. In 2004, however, Congress made revocation of the underlying visa by the Department of State a ground for deportability of a nonimmigrant as well. Intelligence Reform and Terrorism Prevention Act, § 5304, Pub. L. 108–458, 118 Stat. 3638, 3735 (2004) (amending INA § 237(a)(1)(B)). This change in the grounds of deportability could have a drastic impact, particularly if visa revocation is unreviewable. Perhaps for that reason, the 2004 legislation provided that judicial review of the visa revocation, normally barred, is permitted as part of the review of a removal order, when revocation is the sole ground of deportability. *See* INA § 221(i).

NOTES AND QUESTIONS ON REVIEW OF CONSULAR DECISIONS

1. Does the *Landon v. Plasencia* ruling hold any relevance to decisions made by U.S. State Department officials overseas? Does the Due Process Clause apply, even if the overseas setting means that minimal procedures are sufficient? Does the interview with the consular official constitute a hearing? Would it matter to the constitutional analysis if the consular official denied an immigrant visa to the son or daughter of a U.S. citizen, as opposed to a nonimmigrant visa to a prospective tourist?

2. The U.S. Commission on Immigration Reform, a blue-ribbon commission chartered by Congress to consider reforms to the immigration system, issued wide-ranging recommendations in the late 1990s on our overall immigration system, after a multi-year study and nationwide hearings. The Commission proposed in its September 1997 report a system for review of certain visa denials and revocations by consular officers. The Commission explained:

> When a visa is denied, important interests are at stake. To be sure, the visa applicant is adversely affected—but more importantly at stake

are the interests of the United States citizens, lawful permanent residents, employers, and businesses who have petitioned the admission of the applicant or who otherwise have an interest in having the applicant present in the United States. Given the lack of formal administrative and judicial review of consular decisions, these individuals are left with little or no recourse.

The Commission believes that consular decisions denying or revoking visas in specified visa categories, including all immigrant visas and those [nonimmigrant] categories where there is a petitioner in the United States who is seeking the admission of the visa applicant, should be subject to formal administrative review. The visa applicant would have no right to appeal an adverse determination. Instead, standing to appeal a visa denial or revocation would lie only with United States petitioners, whether U.S. citizens, lawful permanent residents, or employers.

U.S. Commission on Immigration Reform, Becoming an American: Immigration and Immigrant Policy 181–82 (1997). Neither Congress nor the executive branch has acted on this recommendation.

3.   Turning to statutory analysis, if the APA presumptively makes administrative decisions reviewable in the courts on the suit of anyone "aggrieved" by the agency action, why shield consular officers? Are there functional reasons to support the doctrine of consular nonreviewability? Foreign affairs implications? The sheer number of disappointed visa applicants? Other factors?

4.   The *American Academy of Religion* case distinguishes between decisions made by consular officers and by DHS officials. If a decision is not reviewable when reached by a consular officer, why should the same decision be reviewable once an officer from a different department (or indeed the Secretary of State personally) becomes involved? Do you think the location of the officer making the decision—overseas versus within the United States—is a more critical distinction than the category of decisionmaker?

The *American Academy of Religion* litigation continued for several more years. After ruling that the consular nonreviewability doctrine did not prevent the federal courts from considering the visa denial, the Second Circuit considered the merits and concluded that the case must be remanded to afford Tariq Ramadan an opportunity to respond to the charge that he had knowingly contributed to a terrorist organization. 573 F.3d at 128–34 (2d Cir. 2009). Subsequently, Ramadan obtained an exemption from the terrorist grounds of inadmissibility and successfully applied for a ten-year multiple entry visa. *American Academy of Religion v. Napolitano*, 2011 WL 1157698 (S.D.N.Y.) Litigation continued over attorney fees, which the court denied in March 2011. *Id.* For further discussion of this case, see Chapter Seven, pp. 637–38.

5.   Assume that you are a staffer to the Senate Judiciary Committee, assigned to rethink the overall system for review of visa denials. What would you propose? If it is appropriate to subject only a subset of visa decisions to judicial review, how would you select the subset? Or better, what mix of more formalized administrative review plus judicial review would be optimal for our complex admissions system? What objectives do you take into account in making that choice?

2. REJECTION AT THE BORDER

Noncitizens who arrive in the United States generally must present visas at the border or show that they are exempt from the visa requirement. The immigration officer at the port of entry ordinarily assesses admissibility through a quick inspection of the entry documents and the screening databases described earlier in this chapter. If the officer has doubts that the noncitizen should be admitted, another immigration officer asks more extensive questions, known as secondary inspection. Noncitizens may, at the discretion of the immigration officer, withdraw their application for admission during primary or secondary inspection and return to the country they left. INA § 235(a)(4).

Noncitizens refused entry to the United States who do not withdraw their applications have the right to a removal hearing before an immigration judge. The noncitizen bears the burden of proving admissibility, INA § 291, and the statute requires applicants for admission to prove "clearly and beyond doubt" that they are entitled to be admitted. INA § 240 (c)(2)(A).

Removal proceedings in immigration court are discussed at greater length in Chapter Ten. Such proceedings are adversarial, and both the noncitizen and the government have the right to present evidence and to examine and cross-examine witnesses. INA § 240. Immigration judges preside; noncitizens have the right to be represented by counsel at their own expense. *Id.* Obtaining counsel can be difficult, especially for respondents with limited means, and the statute requires that the noncitizen shall have at least 10 days before the hearing date in order to attempt to secure legal representation. INA § 239(b)(1). An unsuccessful challenge to a border official's refusal of entry has serious consequences, as removal pursuant to the formal order of an immigration judge results in a five year bar to readmission to the United States. INA § 212(a)(9)(A)(i), discussed in Chapter Seven. Noncitizens can appeal the immigration judge's order to the Board of Immigration Appeals and, in multiple instances noted in Chapter Ten, to the federal courts.

3. EXPEDITED REMOVAL

In 1996 Congress enacted an expedited removal procedure that generally applies to arriving aliens who seek admission to the United States but (1) have no documents, (2) have fraudulent or invalid documents, or (3) have committed immigration fraud in the past. *See* INA § 235(b)(1). Mandatory detention during the initial portion of the procedure, often followed by detention as a matter of discretion during later stages, constitutes an important component of the process. The House Judiciary Committee explained the reasons why this measure was adopted:

> One urgent problem in recent years has been the arrival at U.S. airports of smuggled aliens who possess fraudulent or otherwise

invalid travel documents, or who have destroyed their documents en route, and who make claim to asylum in order to be able to remain in the U.S. Because of delays in the asylum system, hearings were often scheduled for months later. If not detained, the aliens would most often disappear and become long-term illegal residents.

H.R.Rep. No. 104–879, 104th Cong., 2d Sess. 107 (1997).

Because Congress recognized that asylum seekers sometimes use fraudulent documents to escape persecution, it built into the expedited removal system special provisions to allow those with a credible fear of asylum, as determined in an interview with a specialist asylum officer, to have access to a full immigration court hearing. We will outline here the basic expedited removal provisions and procedures, first noting the geographical locations where expedited removal may occur, and then detailing the provisions related to asylum. You may find it useful to read through INA § 235(b)(1) before proceeding further.

a.   At Ports of Entry

The law applies expedited removal at all times to arriving aliens, if they are judged inadmissible under INA § 212(a)(6)(C) (relating to attempts to obtain admission or other immigration benefits through fraud or misrepresentation), or § 212(a)(7) (lack of a valid passport, visa, or other required document).[2] The expedited removal statute authorizes an immigration officer who finds an arriving alien inadmissible on the specified grounds to order him removed "*without further hearing or review* unless the alien indicates either an intention to apply for asylum under section 208 or a fear of persecution." INA § 235(b)(1)(A)(i) (emphasis added). Under the regulations and operating manuals, such an order may be issued only after an extended interview in secondary inspection, followed by supervisory review of the officer's conclusion that the person meets the criteria for expedited removal. *See* 8 C.F.R. § 235.3.

Departure under an expedited removal order carries the same consequences as that based on an order issued by an immigration judge. In particular, when issued to an arriving alien, the order makes the person inadmissible for five years, subject to a limited waiver. *See* INA § 212(a)(9)(A)(i). But immigration officers interviewing persons who initially seem subject to expedited removal have discretion to allow them to withdraw their applications for admission. *See* INA § 235(a)(4), 8 C.F.R. § 235.4(a). The individual has no absolute right to withdraw the application; withdrawal must be approved by the officer. The stakes are high in this decision, because withdrawal, though it ordinarily entails immediate return to the country of departure, is not considered removal under a formal order. Thus the person incurs no bar to reapplying for admission later—for example, after returning home and correcting any technical problem with the visa he or she initially presented.

---

2. An obscurely worded exception exempts Cubans arriving by air from the coverage of expedited removal. INA § 235(b)(1)(F).

b. Expansion Beyond Ports of Entry

In addition to applying expedited removal automatically to all arriving noncitizens, the statute gives the Secretary of Homeland Security (former-ly the Attorney General) the "sole and unreviewable discretion" to apply expedited removal to noncitizens who have not been admitted or paroled into the United States, if they do not "affirmatively show[], to the satisfaction of an immigration officer," that they have been continuously present in the United States for the preceding two years. INA § 235(b)(1)(A)(iii), 8 C.F.R. § 235.3(b)(1). This means that expedited removal can, but need not, be applied to all noncitizens who entered the United States without inspection and have been present less than two years. In the interior, as well as at the border, expedited removal is applicable only to noncitizens deemed inadmissible who lack valid entry documents or are using false or invalid entry documents.

The first use of this authority was precipitated by the landing of a boat full of Haitian asylum seekers on the beach at Key Biscayne, Florida, in October 2002, apparently after evading the normal Coast Guard inter-diction. In order to be sure that such cases could be handled in summary fashion in the future, Attorney General John Ashcroft designated for expedited removal "aliens who arrive in the United States by sea, either by boat or other means, who are not admitted or paroled, and who have not been physically present in the United States continuously for the two-year period prior to the determination of inadmissibility." Cuban nation-als are excluded from the designation. 67 Fed. Reg. 68924 (2002).

In 2004 the Department of Homeland Security announced another major expansion of the expedited removal program. It applies to nonciti-zens who entered without inspection and who are stopped within 100 miles of the U.S.–Mexico border or the U.S.–Canada border, unless they can show that they have been continuously present in the United States for more than 14 days. 69 Fed. Reg. 48877 (2004). In 2006, DHS an-nounced that it would also apply expedited removal on these terms within 100 miles of the maritime borders. *See DHS Announces Expedited Remov-al Along Northern Border and All Coastal Areas*, 83 Interp. Rel. 253 (2006). The 2004 official notice explained:

> DHS has a pressing need to improve the security and safety of the nation's land borders, and expanding expedited removal between ports of entry will provide DHS officers with a valuable tool to meet that objective. Presently DHS officers cannot apply expedited removal procedures to the nearly 1 million aliens who are apprehended each year in close proximity to the borders after illegal entry. It is not logistically possible for DHS to initiate formal removal proceedings against all such aliens. * * *

> Without limiting its ability to exercise its discretion in the event of a national emergency, other unforeseen events, or change in circumstances, DHS plans under this designation as a matter of prosecutorial discretion to apply expedited removal only to (1) third

country nationals and (2) to Mexican and Canadian nationals with histories of criminal or immigration violations, such as smugglers or aliens who have made numerous illegal entries. * * *

It is anticipated under this designation that expedited removal will be employed against those aliens who are apprehended immediately proximate to the land border and have negligible ties or equities in the U.S. Nevertheless, this designation extends to a 100–mile operational range because many aliens will arrive in vehicles that speedily depart the border area, and because other recent arrivals will find their way to near-border locales seeking transportation to other locations within the interior of the U.S.

Id. at 48878–79. The notice made it clear that such individuals would be subject to the same procedures for asylum claims and credible fear screening that apply to arriving aliens in expedited removal.

In 1997, the first year of the new procedure, there were roughly 23,000 expedited removals of the total 114,000 removals. Since then the number of removals has grown steadily each year; the number of expedited removals increased until 2000, dipped substantially between 2001 and 2004, and then began to grow again. There have been more than 100,000 expedited removals each year since 2006, when expedited removals accounted for 39 percent of the total removals. Expedited removals averaged 31 percent of all removals between 2006 and 2010.

In 2010, there were 111,000 expedited removals out of 387,000 removals. Ninety-four percent of the expedited removals involved citizens of four countries: Mexico, Honduras, Guatemala, and El Salvador. Mexican citizens alone constituted 77 percent of the expedited removals. See DHS Office of Immigration Statistics, Immigration Enforcement Actions: 2010, at 4 (June 2011). Table 6.1 shows the growth in the numbers.

c. Judicial Review

Judicial review of expedited removal orders is available, through habeas corpus, only in extremely limited circumstances. A person subject to an expedited removal order may go to court with an identity challenge—i.e., the petitioner alleges that she is not the person named in the expedited removal order, a highly unlikely eventuality. Status claimants (persons who claim under oath that they are U.S. citizens, lawful permanent residents, or previously admitted asylees or refugees) may also secure court review of that particular allegation after exhausting administrative review. *See* INA §§ 235(b)(1)(C), 242(e)(2).

Table 6.1
Total and Expedited Removals: 1997–2010

Fiscal year	Total removals*	Expedited removals
2010	387,242	111,116
2009	395,165	106,025
2008	359,795	112,716
2007	319,382	106,196
2006	280,974	110,663
2005	246,431	87,888
2004	240,665	51,014
2003	211,098	43,920
2002	165,168	34,624
2001	189,026	69,923
2000	186,391	85,939
1999	181,194	89,172
1998	173,146	76,078
1997	114,432	23,242

* Counts only departures under formal orders of removal.

Source: DHS Office of Immigration Statistics, Immigration Enforcement Actions: 2010, table 2 (June 2011); Immigration Enforcement Actions: 2005, table 2 (Nov. 2006).

The statute also provides for expedited hearing of challenges to "the validity of the system." INA § 242(e)(3). Such a case, however, must be filed within 60 days of the implementation of the challenged regulation, procedure, or policy, and venue lies only in the district court for the District of Columbia. It is evident from the disposition of the primary case so far considered under this provision—a broad challenge to the overall system filed shortly after its effective date—that standing and other jurisdictional obstacles are considerable. *See American Immigration Lawyers Assn. v. Reno,* 18 F.Supp.2d 38 (D.D.C. 1998), *aff'd,* 199 F.3d 1352 (D.C.Cir.2000). The plaintiffs in that case argued that Congress did not intend expedited removal to apply to arriving aliens with facially valid visas and challenged the regulations governing secondary inspection. After rejecting the statute- and regulation-based claims, the court reviewed the plaintiffs' constitutional challenges to the expedited removal procedure. Relying on long-standing Supreme Court and circuit precedent, the court concluded that "[w]hatever the procedure authorized by Congress is, it is due process as far as an alien denied entry is concerned." *United States ex rel. Knauff v. Shaughnessy,* 338 U.S. 537, 544, 70 S.Ct. 309, 94 L.Ed. 317 (1950). Accordingly, aliens have "no constitutional right[s] with respect to their applications for admission," citing *Landon v. Plasencia,* 459 U.S. 21, 32, 103 S.Ct. 321, 74 L.Ed.2d 21 (1982). *Id.* at 58–59 (internal quotation marks omitted).

NOTES AND QUESTIONS ON EXPEDITED REMOVAL

1. Does *Landon v. Plasencia*, which held that Maria Plasencia was entitled to due process when she was stopped at the border, suggest that the expedited removal procedure might be constitutionally infirm? Can arriving aliens who are turned away by an immigration officer without a hearing in immigration court mount a successful constitutional challenge? Recall that the two-step due process analysis, pp. 561–563, *supra*, requires us to ask first if the individual has a liberty or property interest. If the answer is affirmative, we then examine whether the procedures afforded were sufficient.

In *Plasencia*, the Supreme Court concluded that a "returning resident alien" has a right to due process and remanded the case to allow the lower court to evaluate the adequacy of the procedures. In contrast, the expedited removal law generally applies to "arriving aliens." Refusal of admission to the United States may constitute a serious harm to them, but do they have a property interest, a "legitimate claim of entitlement" to enter? Does possession of an entry document issued by a U.S. consulate create such a claim? What if the document has been altered? What about those subject to expedited removal because they have no entry document? If they lack a property interest, can they nonetheless identify a liberty interest? Would it be relevant if the noncitizen subject to expedited removal claimed to be the son or daughter of a U.S. citizen? Does it affect the liberty or property interest analysis when expedited removal is applied in the interior of the United States to a noncitizen who arrived 18 months earlier?

Turning to the second step of the analysis, if a liberty or property interest is implicated, what process is due? The statute authorizes the immigration inspector to order the noncitizen removed "without further hearing or review" unless the individual seeks asylum. Does the initial inspection constitute a hearing? Is it sufficient under the *Mathews v. Eldridge* approach adopted in *Plasencia*? What are the competing interests of the arriving alien and the government? The benefits and costs of more extensive proceedings? Does the Constitution require more than the statute—say, an extended interview by a second immigration inspector, as the regulations currently mandate? More than the concurrence of two executive branch officials?

2. Whether or not constitutionally mandated, should there be judicial review of expedited removal orders? Could the procedure remain truly expedited if judicial review were involved?

3. What is your assessment of the expansions of expedited removal beyond ports of entry? Is there a stronger case for applying summary procedures to persons who attempt to enter clandestinely than to arriving aliens who are, after all, presenting themselves for inspection in the regular setting at the border? What are the advantages and disadvantages in each setting?

What additional risks of misapplication arise when expedited removal is expanded beyond ports of entry? Beyond the immediate vicinity of the border? Consider, in this regard, news reports that Border Patrol agents routinely board trains between New York and Chicago and ask passengers to produce immigration papers and identification. See Bernstein, *Border Sweeps In North Reach Miles Into the U.S.,* N.Y.Times, Aug. 29, 2010.

4.   The Commission on Immigration Reform concluded in the late 1990s that expedited removal should apply only during migration emergencies, as had been proposed in some earlier versions of the 1996 legislation, and urged Congress to amend the law accordingly. Concerns about screening asylum seekers, discussed in the following section, led the Commission to conclude that expedited removal should only be relied on in the rare emergency situations when an overloaded system might need some way to do preliminary sorting.

d.   Asylum Seekers

As noted earlier, the expedited removal statute directs the removal of the noncitizen "without further hearing or review," but includes an express exception for noncitizens who indicate "an intention to apply for asylum * * * or a fear of persecution." INA § 235(b)(1)(A)(i). Therefore, if the person claims asylum or asserts a fear of return, the immigration inspector may not issue a removal order. Instead, after completing the interview and making a summary record of the results, she arranges for the noncitizen to be sent to a detention facility where he will be interviewed by a specially trained asylum officer.

(i) Identifying Asylum Seekers

One major concern has been that persons wishing to claim asylum would not be able to do so effectively. They might be too intimidated in the expedited removal setting, and so might not even voice a fear of return before being hurried back across the border or onto a return flight. Or expressions of such fear might be ignored or overridden. Or the noncitizens might not realize that the words exchanged with the immigration inspectors would be their only opportunity to request protection.

The regulation addresses this concern by requiring a fairly extensive initial interview by the inspector in every expedited removal case (whether or not asylum was requested), usually taking an hour or more and always resulting in a sworn statement. 8 C.F.R. § 235.3. The individual is to initial each page of the statement and to sign the document at the end. That statement, written out by the inspector (in English) as the interview proceeds, summarizes the person's story but is not a verbatim transcript. The regulations require an extended interview in order both to gain full information that will foster an accurate decision by the officer on whether the stated inadmissibility grounds apply and to provide an opportunity for the person to request asylum. The regulations also mandate review of the file by a high-ranking supervisor before an expedited removal order is issued. *See* Martin, *Two Cheers for Expedited Removal in the New Immigration Laws,* 40 Va.J. Int'l L. 673 (2000).

Further, as you can see by consulting Form I–867A/B, Record of Sworn Statement in Proceedings under Section 235(b)(1) of the Act (reprinted in the Statutory Supplement), the form structures the inspector's interview so as to assure the conveyance of certain key information and the posing of specific questions about fears of return. In an expedited removal case, the examining officer in secondary inspection must read the following, early in the interview, in a language that the noncitizen can understand:

> U.S. law provides protection to certain persons who face persecution, harm or torture upon return to their home country. If you fear or have a concern about being removed from the United States or about being sent home, you should tell me so during the interview because you will not have another chance. You will have the opportunity to speak privately and confidentially to another officer about your fear and concern. That officer will determine if you should remain in the United States and not be removed because of that fear.

Toward the end of the interview, the officer must pose the following questions, spelled out on the Form I 867A/B, and record the individual's answers:

> Q. Why did you leave your home country or country of last residence?
>
> Q. Do you have any fear or concern about being returned to your home country or being removed from the United States?
>
> Q. Would you be harmed if you are returned to your home country or country of last residence?
>
> Q. Do you have any questions or is there anything you would like to add?

Inclusion of these required advisories and questions alleviated some of the initial concerns, but a 2005 report by the U.S. Commission on International Religious Freedom (CIRF), a bipartisan independent government body, identified several ongoing problems. CIRF, Report on Asylum Seekers in Expedited Removal (2005). The Commission did a detailed analysis of data from 2001 and 2003, examined closely the files involved in a random sample of 855 cases, and also sent observers to a total of 79 proceedings. Although it generally accepted that policies and procedures governing the interview were sound, it identified significant deficiencies in implementation. In 50 percent of the cases observed, the officer did not read the full set of questions required on the I–867A/B form, though in 95 percent they did read at least one of the key queries. Further, 15% of noncitizens who expressed fear of return in the observed proceedings were removed without access to asylum officers for credible fear interviews, based on the inspector's judgment that the expression of fear did not qualify. "The 12 cases that were not referred included expressions of economic fear, but also fear related to political, religious, or ethnic persecution, as well as unspecified fear, fear of spouse abuse, and fear of smugglers. Under DHS regulations, all of these aliens should have been referred for a credible fear interview." I CIRF Report 54. The Commission recommended the development of clearer guidance to govern this part of the process, structural changes to accomplish better coordination among the governmental agencies involved, and enhanced quality assurance measures, including expanded use of videotapes of the secondary inspection interviews. *Id.* at 8–9.

The progress report issued by the Commission in 2007 found that CBP had done nothing in the intervening two years to implement the Commission's recommendations to address these problems. CIRF, Expedited Removal Study Report Card: 2 Years Later 3–4 (Feb. 2007), <http:// www.uscirf.gov/reports/scorecard_FINAL.pdf>. One court decision was also highly critical of CBP's practices, as discussed in the CIRF report, and largely on that basis declined to lift a 20–year old injunction that had imposed special procedures for the processing of Salvadorans apprehended by DHS. *Orantes–Hernandez v. Gonzales,* 504 F.Supp.2d 825 (C.D.Cal. 2007).

(ii) The Credible Fear Interview

All noncitizens who ask for asylum or express a fear of return are supposed to be scheduled for an interview with an asylum officer. The asylum officer's duty is to determine whether the individuals has a "credible fear of persecution," which the statute defines as follows:

> a significant possibility, taking into account the credibility of the statements made by the alien in support of the alien's claim and such other facts as are known to the officer, that the alien could establish eligibility for asylum under section 208.

INA § 235(b)(1)(B)(v).

Concerns that asylum seekers would not have a fair opportunity to tell their stories during the credible fear process, owing to fatigue after a long journey or predictable reticence deriving from the fact of detention or from interrogation by officials in a wholly unfamiliar setting, led to guidelines that the credible fear interview should not take place earlier than 48 hours after the person's arrival in a detention center following referral from secondary inspection. *See* 62 Fed. Reg.10,312, 10,320 (1997). Most interviews are held two to fourteen days after arrival. 1 CIRF Report 29.

By statute, the noncitizen may consult with anyone of his choosing after secondary inspection and before the credible fear interview, so long as it is at no expense to the government and does not cause "unreasonable delay." The delay built in to the schedule allows the possibility of consultation with counsel or with accredited NGO representatives prior to the interview. In some detention facilities arrangements have been made with NGOs to facilitate meetings with attorneys or representatives, but many of the detention facilities housing persons involved in expedited removal lack such arrangements. 2 CIRF Report 234, 240–41.

If the asylum officer finds that a credible fear exists, the noncitizen is scheduled for a full merits hearing in immigration court in which to develop the asylum claim. The noncitizen may be released on parole while the merits hearing is pending. If the asylum officer does not find a credible fear, she issues an expedited removal order. The noncitizen may request review of the credible fear issue by an immigration judge in a special procedure that must be completed within seven days. If unsuccessful, the noncitizen is subject to immediate removal on the basis of the order previously issued. If the immigration judge finds a credible fear, the noncitizen is scheduled for a full merits hearing, and may be released on bond pending the hearing.

Since the beginning of expedited removal, the credible fear process has resulted in a high approval rate. For example, in fiscal year 2004 approximately 8,000 of the 55,000 placed in expedited removal proceedings expressed a fear of return and were referred to an asylum officer. Roughly 94 percent of the group were found to have a credible fear and were scheduled for a full hearing before an immigration judge. DHS Office of Immigration Statistics, Immigration Enforcement Actions: 2004, at 6 (Nov. 2005).

The 2005 CIRF Report determined that asylum officers found credible fear in over 90 percent of cases in which they conducted an interview. Only one percent resulted in a negative credible fear determination. 1 CIRF Report 4. (In the rest, apparently the request was abandoned or the person's status was otherwise resolved.) This high referral rate has muted some of the early criticism of procedural difficulties, including concerns about the adequacy of translation in these interviews. But the Commission, somewhat surprisingly, hinted that the approval rate may be too high. It added the following to its recommendations (I CIRF Report 76):

> The credible fear determination by an asylum officer, which—by law—is reviewable by an immigration judge, has proven successful at ensuring that bona fide asylum seekers referred from the port of entry will not be removed without a full asylum hearing. The credible fear process fails, however, at making asylum more efficient by failing to screen out invalid claims and thus putting more strain on detention and immigration court resources. With a screen-in rate consistently exceeding 90 percent, and a negative determination rate of approximately 1 percent, some view the credible fear process itself as somewhat lacking in credibility. The Asylum Division subjects negative determinations to a much more intensive quality assurance process than positive determinations. * * * We would suggest that this bias

in favor of positive credible fear determinations be addressed by subjecting them to similar quality assurance procedures * * *.

The Commission's 2007 report card found that USCIS had adopted and implemented this recommendation. CIRF, Report Card, *supra,* at 6–7.

From 2006 through 2009, approximately 5,000 were referred for credible fear interviews each year; this constituted roughly five percent of those in expedited removal. Larger numbers—9,000 and 11,000 respectively—were referred for credible fear screening in 2010 and 2011. Between 2006 and 2011, asylum officers found credible fear, on average, in 80 percent of the individuals they interviewed. DHS, USCIS, Asylum Division, Briefing Paper on Expedited Removal and Credible Fear Process, Oct. 19, 2011.

(iii) Detention

The expedited removal statute and regulations require detention, with very limited exceptions (for medical emergency or "legitimate law enforcement reasons"), throughout the initial stages of consideration by the inspector and the asylum officer. 8 C.F.R. § 235.3(b)(2)(iii). Release on parole is permitted, however, for those who pass the credible fear test, in the discretion of the director of the appropriate DHS field office. *See* 62 Fed.Reg. 10312, 10320 (1997) (supplemental information accompanying the main 1996 Act rulemaking). That decision is supposed to be guided by the usual release criteria, focusing on whether the person is likely to abscond or would be a danger to the community.

Actual practice, however, has varied widely. I CIRF Report 2, 60–62. The Commission found that as of 2005 some districts regularly released those who have passed credible fear, while a few rarely did. The Commission recommended more detailed codification of the release criteria in regulations, accompanied by the development of DHS forms and procedures to monitor this process and assure consistency. It also criticized the conditions in most ICE detention facilities holding asylum seekers in expedited removal and urged the development of alternatives to prison-like detention. *Id.* at 67–68.

In 2009 DHS announced major reforms in the detention of noncitizens, creating an Office of Detention Policy and Planning (ODPP), and charging it with centralizing and improving the detention system and developing community supervision programs and other alternatives to detention. ICE Fact Sheet, 2009 Immigration Detention Reforms (2009), <http://www.ice.gov/news/library/factsheets/reform–2009reform.htm>. Throughout 2009, DHS also worked with nongovernmental organizations and the Office of the UN High Commissioner for Refugees, among others, to develop better release standards and procedures for persons who pass credible fear screening. As a result, ICE Director John Morton issued a policy directive, effective January 2010, concerning parole for individuals judged to have a credible fear of persecution or torture. All such persons are to receive an advice form indicating the possibility of release and the applicable process, and within seven days of a credible fear finding, an ICE officer must interview the asylum seeker and assess her eligibility for parole using a standardized worksheet. The guidance provides that the interviewing officer should recommend for parole those persons whose identity is established, who do not pose a flight risk or a danger to the community, and who have no other risk factors weighing against release. Officials who do not recommend parole must explain their denial in writing, and the guidance sets out a detailed quality assurance monitoring system. ICE Directive 11002.1, Parole of Arriving Aliens Found to Have a Credible Fear of Persecution or Torture (Dec. 8, 2009), <http://www.ice. gov/doclib/dro/pdf/11002.1–hd-parole_of_arriving_aliens_found_credible_ fear.pdf>.

(iv) *Administrative and Judicial Review*

As described earlier, inspectors' orders that do not refer a noncitizen for a credible fear interview are not appealable. Noncitizens whose interviews with an asylum officer result in negative credible fear determinations may challenge the determination before an immigration judge in an oral procedure generally completed within 24 hours, and in all cases in no longer than seven days. INA § 235(b)(1)(B)(iii)(III). Those who pass the credible fear screening, either based on the asylum officer's interview or on review before the immigration judge, are referred for full hearing of their asylum claims in immigration court; they have access to the BIA and federal court for review if asylum is denied.

NOTES AND QUESTIONS ON ASYLUM SCREENING

1. Are there sufficient safeguards for asylum seekers in the expedited removal system? There are four levels of screening: primary inspection, secondary inspection, asylum officer, immigration judge. Precisely what additional procedures would you recommend? In what ways would those additional safeguards reduce errors and how much would they cost, both in terms of efficiency and in financial terms?

2. As described above, the 2005 CIRF Report found significant implementation deficiencies by DHS field offices (such as failures to provide all required advisories or to refer cases to an asylum officer when the person mentioned a fear of return), prompting calls for the abolition of expedited removal. CIRF offered several recommendations intended to assure more consistent implementation of existing regulations and guidance and to facilitate monitoring by managers, so as to detect and correct departures from policy. Would sufficient safeguards exist under the design of the current expedited removal system if these CIRF recommendations were adopted?

3. The CIRF Report also noted that only about one percent of arriving noncitizens who are referred to asylum officers are found to lack a credible fear, and it was mildly critical of that outcome. Do you think that statistic is troublesome? Does it suggest that those who mention fear to an inspector at the border should go straight to a full removal hearing in immigration court, bypassing the credible fear screening? That the expedited removal legislation

should be amended to delete the credible fear screening and instead require a removal hearing for all who say they fear persecution? Or does the very presence of credible fear screening, even with a low formal screen-out rate, provide a deterrent to ill-founded or fraudulent claims—the original concern that led Congress to adopt expedited removal in the first place.

4. In the 1990s the Commission on Immigration Reform concluded that credible fear screening is not an appropriate standard for deciding who will have access to the full procedure, except in migration emergencies. U.S. Commission on Immigration Reform, U.S. Refugee Policy: Taking Leadership 30–32 (1998). Do you think this screening mechanism would be workable in a migration emergency? Should the credible fear standard, at least in a migration emergency, be tightened? How would you do so?

5. The Commission on Immigration Reform also concluded, however, that the current credible fear procedure could appropriately function to decide which asylum seekers should be released during the pendency of full-fledged immigration court proceedings. Continued confinement of those who could not make such a showing would provide a justifiable deterrent against future abuse of the asylum system. U.S. Commission on Immigration Reform, U.S. Refugee Policy: Taking Leadership 30–32 (1998). Do you agree with this assessment?

EXERCISE: EXPEDITED REMOVAL

Chen was apprehended by Border Patrol officers while hiding in a remote area on the beach at the eastern end of Long Island. He admits that he is a Chinese national. He has no identification or travel documents. Chen has refused to talk about how he arrived in the United States, but he was discovered two weeks after a freighter ran aground on a sandbar around 1:45 AM several hundred yards offshore, about a half-mile from where Chen was found. About 300 Chinese nationals tried to swim ashore. Most made it, but a few drowned in the choppy waters. Of those who reached shore, almost all were apprehended within several hours, but a few remain unaccounted for. Chen has only a small satchel of clothes and a bedroll with him. He seems to have been surviving by scavenging food from dumpsters behind nearby restaurants.

You are a DHS attorney and have been asked by your supervisor to analyze whether it is lawful to put Chen into expedited removal pursuant to the Federal Register notices using the power given by INA § 235(b)(1)(A)(iii).

Chapter Seven

Inadmissibility, Deportability, and Relief From Removal

■ ■ ■

Chapter Five explained the categories for admission to the United States, and Chapter Six addressed the procedures for administering them. But there is more to the story. Noncitizens who fit into an admission category will be barred if they are inadmissible under INA § 212(a). For example, someone who qualifies for an immigrant visa as an immediate relative may be inadmissible if she is a member of a terrorist organization. And even after admission, an admitted noncitizen might become deportable under INA § 237(a). For example, a criminal conviction might mean that a lawful permanent resident is deportable.

Inadmissible and deportable noncitizens are the two subcategories of removable noncitizens. Because the basic issue is being able to come to or stay in the United States lawfully, inadmissibility and deportability are often hotly contested. To explore this key area of immigration law, this chapter covers the inadmissibility grounds in INA § 212, the deportability grounds in INA § 237, as well as discretionary waivers and various forms of relief from removal. Inadmissibility and deportability grounds are often parallel. They share the fundamental idea that some noncitizens should not be admitted or allowed to stay in the United States, even if they meet the most basic underlying criteria for doing so. But inadmissibility and deportability grounds are rarely identical, with inadmissibility generally broader in coverage. This makes intuitive sense, since taking away something a person already enjoys—lawful presence in the United States—generally has greater impact than withholding initial admission.

Removal under a formal order carries several negative consequences for the noncitizen beyond expulsion itself. Noncitizens previously removed are generally inadmissible for five or ten years unless the federal government permits an earlier application for admission, but the bar can be longer or even permanent. *See* INA § 212(a)(9)(A). Once ordered removed, a noncitizen who later reenters without permission is subject to summary removal through reinstatement of the earlier order and to criminal punishment. *See* INA §§ 241(a)(5); 276. Removal also may end a noncitizen's eligibility for social security benefits. *See* 42 U.S.C.A § 402(n). And noncitizens who fail to depart are subject in theory to fines up to $500 per day under INA § 274D, though no such fines have yet been imposed.

The Line Between Inadmissibility and Deportability

When do inadmissibility grounds apply, and when do deportability grounds apply? The key is whether the noncitizen has been *admitted* to the United States or instead is seeking "admission," which INA § 101(a)(13)(A) defines as lawful entry "after inspection and authorization by an immigration officer." What matters is whether the noncitizen complied with procedures for admission by presenting herself for inspection and admission—not whether she should have been admitted under the governing immigration law. For the purpose of drawing the line between inadmissibility and deportability, then, an erroneous admission is still an admission. *See Matter of Quilantan*, 25 I & N Dec. 285 (BIA 2010).

Inadmissibility grounds apply to any noncitizen who has not been admitted. Deportability grounds apply only after a noncitizen has been admitted. For example, a noncitizen who crosses the border without inspection at a port of entry is inadmissible, not deportable. A noncitizen who is in the United States unlawfully after overstaying a period of admission is deportable, not inadmissible. But a noncitizen who entered without inspection is subject to the inadmissibility grounds, even if she has lived in the United States for many years.

What about a permanent resident who travels outside the United States? When she returns, is she seeking admission and thus subject to the inadmissibility grounds? Under the general rule in INA § 101(a)(13)(C)—which the BIA has held is a presumption—a permanent resident "shall not be regarded as seeking an admission into the United States." This provision sets out significant exceptions, but the government must show that at least one applies, if it asserts that a returning permanent resident is seeking admission. *See* 78 Interp.Rel. 523 (2001) (nonprecedent decision).[1]

In case you see the terms "exclusion" and "deportation" in immigration cases, a glance at history may help avoid confusion. Until 1996, noncitizens who had made an "entry" were subject to deportation grounds, and those who had not made an entry were subject to exclusion. Of course, inspection and admission was an entry, but so was a surreptitious border crossing. Entrants without inspection (EWIs) escaped the more demanding exclusion grounds and enjoyed modestly greater procedural protections. The 1996 Act abandoned this entry-based line between exclusion and deportation. Exclusion grounds are now called inadmissibili-

---

1. Section 101(a)(13)(C) supersedes pre–1996 cases, especially *Rosenberg v. Fleuti*, 374 U.S. 449, 462, 83 S.Ct. 1804, 1812, 10 L.Ed.2d 1000 (1963), holding that permanent residents were not seeking "entry" when returning from an "innocent, casual, and brief excursion" outside the United States. *See, e.g., Camins v. Gonzales*, 500 F.3d 872, 878 (9th Cir. 2007) (holding that § 101(a)(13)(C) supersedes *Fleuti*, at least for prospective application).

ty grounds, deportation grounds are now deportability grounds, and the new line is based on admission.

SECTION A. INADMISSIBILITY GROUNDS

Section 212(a) lists groups of "aliens who are ineligible to receive visas and ineligible to be admitted to the United States." This language is a practical reminder that a noncitizen who seeks admission may be screened on several occasions. Suppose, for example, that she applies for an immigrant visa at a U.S. consulate in her home country. The inadmissibility grounds will be first applied to her by the consular officer—an employee of the Department of State—who decides whether to issue any visa that may be required for admission. But when the immigrant next arrives at a port of entry bearing a duly issued visa, the inspector at the port of entry—an officer of the Bureau of Customs and Border Protection (CBP) of the Department of Homeland Security—has full authority to consider anew whether any inadmissibility ground applies to her. *See* INA § 221(h). Or consider another noncitizen who was admitted several years ago as a student in F–1 status. If he applies to become a permanent resident through adjustment of status under INA § 245(a), USCIS within the Department of Homeland Security will apply the inadmissibility grounds to him before considering him eligible to adjust.

1. OVERVIEW

INA § 212(a) contains the inadmissibility grounds themselves. In addition, INA § 237(a)(1)(A) makes any noncitizen deportable if he was inadmissible at the time of entry or adjustment of status. Simply put, any inadmissibility ground can become a deportability ground later, if the inadmissibility goes undetected at the port of entry. The rest of § 212 consists primarily of waiver provisions that cut back in intricate ways on the inadmissibility grounds in subsection (a). These waiver provisions set out statutory prerequisites (which can be quite daunting) but also require a favorable exercise of discretion from a federal government official. Though the application of statutory requirements is subject to judicial review, discretionary decisions generally are not. *See* INA § 242(a)(2)(B).

For noncitizens who intend to enter the United States as nonimmigrants, INA § 212(d)(3) provides DHS with discretionary power to waive nearly all the inadmissibility grounds. New immigrants have far fewer waiver opportunities, but those with a spouse, child, or parent who is a U.S. citizen or lawful permanent resident are most likely to be eligible. Each waiver has its own precise requirements.

Sprinkled through the rest of § 212 are additional requirements that must be met to avoid inadmissibility in certain defined circumstances. For example, § 212(n) describes in detail the labor condition attestation process required for H–1B nonimmigrants. Section 212(f) gives the President extensive authority to issue a proclamation suspending the entry of specific classes of noncitizens or all noncitizens, when he or she finds that entry "would be detrimental to the interests of the United States."

Of course, you are not expected to memorize the inadmissibility grounds, but you should become familiar with the general structure of § 212, and know where to find the answers to specific questions that a client might pose. The problems in this Section will help establish that familiarity with both the inadmissibility grounds and the waivers. As you work through them, carefully read §§ 212(a) and 221(g), as well as the key waivers, which are: § 212(d)(3), (d)(5), (d)(11), (e), (g), (h), and (i). If the facts provided do not allow you to answer some of the problems completely, identify what else you would need to learn by interviewing the client or otherwise investigating.

2. CRIMES

The next three problems introduce you to the basic rules on crime-related inadmissibility under § 212(a)(2) and possible waivers under § 212(h). The application of these provisions depends on how certain terms are defined, such as "crime involving moral turpitude," "aggravated felony," and "conviction." The INA does not define "crime involving moral turpitude"—a key concept for both inadmissibility and deportability. The statute defines "aggravated felony," *see* INA § 101(a)(43), which is principally a deportability ground. An aggravated felony does not make a noncitizen inadmissible under § 212, but a crime that is an aggravated felony can disqualify a person from an inadmissibility waiver, and it may also be a crime involving moral turpitude. Section 101(a)(48) defines conviction and the length of sentence for immigration purposes.

Most of the cases defining these terms have arisen in the deportability context, so we will defer a closer look at their meaning until the materials on deportability in Section B of this chapter. For now, in working through these problems, you should assume a valid conviction and identify what difference it would make if an offense is a crime involving moral turpitude or an aggravated felony.

PROBLEMS

1. Your client, A, qualifies for the family-sponsored first preference, but was convicted of petty larceny seven years ago and sent to prison for a total of three months. Is A inadmissible? What if she had been convicted of two counts of petty larceny? What if the conviction was for grand theft? What if it was for possession of 150 grams of marijuana? If an inadmissibility ground applies, what waivers might be available?

2. A German national employed in the U.S. consulate in Frankfurt recognizes an individual, B, who comes in to apply for a B–2 visa.

She takes the consular officer aside and says that B is well known on the streets for running an illegal gambling operation in the region; she wouldn't be surprised if B means to set up a similar operation in Minneapolis, where he says he will visit friends. Is B inadmissible? Should he be?

3.   C, a native and citizen of the Dominican Republic, has been a lawful permanent resident of the United States for 25 years. Nineteen years ago, when he was 19, he pled guilty to statutory rape after his underage girlfriend's mother discovered their relationship, but he received a suspended sentence as part of the plea agreement and served no jail time. This conviction was not a ground of deportation at the time. He has a spotless criminal record thereafter, operates a successful business with 20 employees, and is now married to a U.S. citizen and has three U.S. citizen children. Last month he took a two-week trip to his native country. Upon his return from this trip, is he inadmissible? Are any waivers available?

3. IMMIGRATION CONTROL

The immigration control grounds appear principally in paragraphs (6), (7), and (9) of § 212(a). Their evolution reflects Congress' attempts to attach more serious consequences to a wider range of immigration-related violations. To start developing an understanding of these grounds, consider the following problem.

PROBLEM

4. Two Border Patrol officers come across D, a national of Costa Rica, on a Florida beach at night, tugging a small vessel up away from the waterline. One officer thinks he saw other figures rushing away into nearby brush as their car approached, but a later search discovers nothing. Undaunted, D tells the officers that he is glad to see them and wishes to apply for admission as a tourist. He presents his passport. Is D inadmissible? On what ground? Are any waivers available?

a. Fraud and Willful Misrepresentation of Material Facts

The substance of INA § 212(a)(6)(C)(i), pertaining to fraud and willful misrepresentation, is a long-standing feature of the INA. In 1996, Congress added clause (ii) for false claims of U.S. citizenship (and a related inadmissibility ground for unlawful voting in § 212(a)(10)(D)). INA § 212(i) provides a waiver, but it is limited to inadmissibility under § 212(a)(6)(C)(i). Along with this substantive expansion, § 212(a)(6)(C) became procedurally pivotal in 1996, in that inadmissibility for fraud or willful misrepresentation—or inadmissibility under § 212(a)(7) for lack of proper documents—can trigger expedited removal under INA § 235(b)(1), as Chapter Six discussed, pp. 569–81.

The next readings are, first, relevant sections of the Foreign Affairs Manual, a Department of State document that gives consular officers more precise guidance for carrying out their functions under the INA, followed by a BIA decision that applies the inadmissibility ground and decides on a waiver.[2] Then try assessing the fact patterns in the problems that follow.

U.S. DEPARTMENT OF STATE, FOREIGN AFFAIRS MANUAL

Section 40.63, Notes, as amended through September 2010.[3]

* * *

APPLICATION OF SECTION 212(A)(6)(C)(I)

Intent of Congress. INA 212(a)(6)(C)(i) constitutes a ground of inadmissibility which was not included in legislation prior to 1952. The adoption of this provision expresses the concern with which Congress viewed cases of aliens resorting to fraud or willful misrepresentations for the purpose of obtaining visas or otherwise effecting an unauthorized entry into the United States. The section is intended to prevent aliens from attempting to secure entry into this country by fraudulent means and then, when the falsity is discovered, proceeding with an application as if nothing had happened. * * *

* * *

Nature of Penalty. In applying the provisions of INA 212(a)(6)(C)(i), keep in mind the severe nature of the penalty the alien incurs: lifetime inadmissibility, unless a waiver is *obtained*. (See 9 FAM 40.63 N9.) When considering whether to impose such a dire penalty, keep in mind the words quoted by the Attorney General in his landmark opinion on this matter. (The *Matter of S– and B–C–,* 9 I & N Dec. 436, at [446 (A.G. 1961)]): "Shutting off the opportunity to come to the United States actually is a crushing deprivation to many prospective immigrants. Very often it destroys the hopes and aspirations of a lifetime, and it frequently operates not only against the individual immediately but also bears heavily upon his family in and out of the United States."

* * *

INTERPRETATION OF THE TERM "MISREPRESENTATION"

Misrepresentation Defined. As used in INA 212(a)(6)(C)(i), a misrepresentation is an assertion or manifestation not in accordance with the facts.

---

2. The Supreme Court has also struggled with the issue of deciding what misrepresentations and concealments are "material." *See* Chapter Two, pp. 134–38, discussing *Kungys v. United States,* 485 U.S. 759, 108 S.Ct. 1537, 99 L.Ed.2d 839 (1988).

3. Internal numbering for headings and subheadings is omitted here.—eds.

Misrepresentation requires an affirmative act taken by the alien. A misrepresentation can be made in various ways, including in an oral interview or in written applications, or by submitting evidence containing false information.

Differentiation Between Misrepresentation and Failure to Volunteer Information. In determining whether a misrepresentation has been made, it is necessary to distinguish between misrepresentation of information and information that was merely concealed by the alien's silence. Silence or the failure to volunteer information does not in itself constitute a misrepresentation for the purposes of INA 212(a)(6)(C)(i).

Misrepresentation Must Have Been Before U.S. Official. For a misrepresentation to fall within the purview of INA 212(a)(6)(C)(i), it must have been practiced on an official of the U.S. Government, generally speaking, a consular officer or a Department of Homeland Security (DHS) officer.

Misrepresentation Must Be Made in Alien's Own Application. The misrepresentation must have been made by the alien with respect to the alien's own visa application. Misrepresentations made in connection with some other person's visa application do not fall within the purview of INA 212(a)(6)(C)(i). Any such misrepresentations may be considered with regard to the possible application of INA 212(a)(6)(E).

Misrepresentation Made by Applicant's Attorney or Agent. The fact that an alien pursues a visa application through an attorney or travel agent does not serve to insulate the alien from liability for misrepresentations made by such agents, if it is established that the alien was aware of the action being taken in furtherance of the application. This standard would apply, for example, where a travel agent executed a visa application on an alien's behalf. Similarly, an oral misrepresentation made on behalf of an alien at the port of entry by an aider or abettor of the alien's illegal entry will not shield the alien in question from inadmissibility under INA 212(a)(6)(C)(i), irrespective of what penalties the aider or abettor might incur, if it can be established that the alien was aware at the time of the misrepresentation made on his or her behalf.

* * *

INTERPRETATION OF THE TERM "WILLFULLY"

"Willfully" Defined. The term "willfully" as used in INA 212(a)(6)(C)(i) is interpreted to mean knowingly and intentionally, as distinguished from accidentally, inadvertently, or in an honest belief that the facts are otherwise. In order to find the element of willfulness, it must be determined that the alien was fully aware of the nature of the information sought and knowingly, intentionally, and deliberately made an untrue statement.

Misrepresentation Is Alien's Responsibility. An alien who acts on the advice of another is considered to be exercising the faculty of conscious and deliberate will in accepting or rejecting such advice. It is no defense for an alien to say that the misrepresentation was made because someone else advised the action unless it is found that the alien lacked the capacity to exercise judgment.

* * *

MATTER OF CERVANTES–GONZALEZ

Board of Immigration Appeals, 1999.
22 I & N Dec. 560.

GRANT, BOARD MEMBER:

In an oral decision dated January 21, 1997, an Immigration Judge denied the respondent's requests for a waiver of inadmissibility and adjustment of status pursuant to sections 212(i) and 245 of the Immigration and Nationality Act. * * *

* * *

In determining whether to grant the application for a section 212(i) waiver, the Immigration Judge found that the respondent had failed to establish extreme hardship to his spouse in the event he is deported. Additionally, the Immigration Judge denied the respondent's application for adjustment of status as a matter of discretion.

On appeal, the respondent argues that the Immigration Judge erred in finding no extreme hardship and that he also gave improper weight to the negative factors in this case.

* * *

WHETHER A WAIVER IS REQUIRED UNDER SECTION 212(I) OF THE ACT

The respondent first argues that he does not require a waiver of inadmissibility under section 212(i) of the Act because he is not inadmissible under section 212(a)(6)(C)(i) of the Act. Specifically, he states that his sole conviction for possession of a false identification document (namely, a counterfeit Texas birth certificate) with the intent to defraud the United States (by obtaining a United States passport) does not fall within the definition of fraud in the Act. As he was convicted only of possession, he asserts that it is error to find him guilty of seeking to procure a fraudulent document. We disagree. Section 212(a)(6)(C)(i) of the Act states:

> [A]ny alien who, by fraud or willfully misrepresenting a material fact, seeks to procure (or has sought to procure or has procured) a visa, other documentation, or admission into the United States or other benefit provided under this Act is inadmissible.

Obviously, the respondent admits to *procuring* one document in the form of a fraudulent birth certificate. The respondent testified that he purchased the birth certificate in Los Angeles, California, for approximately $400 or $500 so that he could obtain employment. He then used the birth certificate to procure by fraud a social security number, and he used both documents to *seek to procure* a passport. The latter document was necessary in order for the respondent to be able to travel into and out of the United States and to aid him in obtaining employment.

We note also that in finding the respondent's conviction fell within section 212(a)(6)(C) of the Act, the Immigration Judge and the Immigration and Naturalization Service did not improperly "go behind" the conviction record as contended by the respondent. Rather, they were merely establishing the facts regarding the respondent's fraud, which would have constituted grounds for inadmissibility whether or not the respondent had been convicted. *See* section 212(a)(6)(C) of the Act (no conviction is required in order to establish inadmissibility).

In sum, we agree with the Immigration Judge that the respondent's activities clearly fall within the purview of section 212(a)(6)(C)(i) of the Act. By fraud and by willful misrepresentation of a material fact, he sought to procure both "documentation" and "other benefits" under the Act. * * *

* * *

EXTREME HARDSHIP

* * *

1. Factors To Be Considered

The factors deemed relevant in determining extreme hardship to a qualifying relative include, but are not limited to, the following: the presence of lawful permanent resident or United States citizen family ties to this country; the qualifying relative's family ties outside the United States; the conditions in the country or countries to which the qualifying relative would relocate and the extent of the qualifying relative's ties to such countries; the financial impact of departure from this country; and, finally, significant conditions of health, particularly when tied to an unavailability of suitable medical care in the country to which the qualifying relative would relocate.

While not all of the foregoing factors need be analyzed in any given case, we will now apply those factors to the present case to the extent they are relevant in determining extreme hardship to the respondent's spouse. We emphasize again, however, that the list of factors noted above is not exclusive and also that the Attorney General and her delegates have the authority to construe extreme hardship narrowly. *INS v. Jong Ha Wang*, [450 U.S. 139, 144 (1981)]. In addition, we note that establishing extreme hardship does not create any entitlement to relief. Although extreme hardship is a requirement for section 212(i) relief, once established, it is but one favorable discretionary factor to be considered.

2. Analysis

The respondent is a 24–year–old native and citizen of Mexico. He has resided in the United States since 1989 and was recently married in 1995. At the time of the marriage, the respondent's wife was a lawful permanent resident; she became a naturalized United States citizen in 1996. Both the respondent and his wife reside with her family and provide them some financial support in return for room and board. Most of the respondent's family, however, resides in Mexico.

The respondent testified that he and his wife have very little money. Therefore, if forced to accompany the respondent to Mexico, the respondent's wife would be unable to travel back and forth to visit her family in the United States. In addition, the respondent's wife testified that she would have difficulty in obtaining employment in Mexico.

Having fully weighed the factors mentioned above, we find that the respondent has failed to establish extreme hardship to his spouse.[4] As noted in the Immigration Judge's decision, the respondent's wife knew that the respondent was in deportation proceedings at the time they were married. In contrast to the respondent's assertions on appeal, this factor is not irrelevant. Rather, it goes to the respondent's wife's expectations at the time they were wed. Indeed, she was aware that she may have to face the decision of parting from her husband or following him to Mexico in the event he was ordered deported. In the latter scenario, the respondent's wife was also aware that a move to Mexico would separate her from her family in California. We find this to undermine the respondent's argument that his wife will suffer extreme hardship if he is deported. *See Perez v. INS*, 96 F.3d 390, 392 (9th Cir.1996) (stating that " '[e]xtreme hardship' is hardship that is 'unusual or beyond that which would normally be expected' upon deportation. 'The common results of deportation are insufficient to prove extreme hardship.' "); *Shooshtary v. INS*, [39 F.3d 1049, 1051 (9th Cir.1994)] (holding that the uprooting of family and separation from friends does not necessarily amount to extreme hardship but rather represents the type of inconvenience and hardship experienced by the families of most aliens being deported); *Silverman v. Rogers*, 437 F.2d 102, 107 (1st Cir.1970) (stating that "[e]ven assuming that the federal government had no right either to prevent a marriage or destroy it, we believe that here it has done nothing more than to say that the residence of one of the marriage partners may not be in the United States"), *cert. denied*, 402 U.S. 983 (1971).

Additionally, at no time during the hearing did the respondent's wife suggest that she would suffer any particular hardship, let alone extreme hardship, by moving to Mexico. Furthermore, although the respondent's spouse would lose the physical proximity to her family, she speaks Spanish

---

4. IIRIRA § 349 amended section 212(i) of the Act to require a showing of extreme hardship to an alien's United States citizen or permanent resident alien spouse or parent. This section of the IIRIRA also limited the availability of section 212(i), which had previously allowed aliens to establish eligibility if they were parents of United States citizens or lawful permanent resident aliens. [footnote relocated—eds.]

and the majority of her family is originally from Mexico. Therefore, she should have less difficulty adjusting to life in a foreign country.

In addition, neither the respondent nor his wife have any real financial ties to the United States. The respondent's wife is currently unemployed. Although the respondent is a musician in a band, he provided no evidence to prove that it had experienced success such that deportation would cause him to relinquish a lucrative career and, therefore, plunge his wife into unaccustomed poverty. Even if this were the case, we have generally not found financial hardship alone to amount to extreme hardship.

In sum, the respondent has failed to show that his spouse would suffer extreme hardship over and above the normal economic and social disruptions involved in the deportation of a family member. Therefore, we agree with the Immigration Judge's decision denying the respondent a waiver of inadmissibility under section 212(i) of the Act.

Having found the respondent statutorily ineligible for relief, we decline to discuss whether or not he merits a waiver as a matter of discretion. * * *

* * *

Based on the foregoing, we conclude that the respondent has failed to establish statutory eligibility for a waiver of inadmissibility under section 212(i) of the Act. Therefore, he is also ineligible for adjustment of status. * * * Accordingly, his appeal will be dismissed.

VILLAGELIU, BOARD MEMBER, concurring:

* * *

While I generally concur with both the result and reasoning of the majority opinion, I write separately to address briefly [certain] minor points in the majority's precedent opinion that may be misinterpreted.

* * *

* * * [T]he majority's opinion may be read to imply that the time the respondent and his spouse wed is determinative as to whether to discount the spouse's hardship because of diminished expectations when marrying an alien in deportation proceedings. I disagree with that implication. Such diminished expectations clearly must relate to the actual circumstances, both of the marriage, and of the pending deportation proceedings, and the totality of the circumstances is paramount. Moreover, we only "discount" equities acquired after a final order of deportation. *See Matter of Correa*, 19 I & N Dec. 130 (BIA 1984). In this case no final order was entered since an appeal was pending. *See Matter of Lok*, 18 I & N Dec. 101 (BIA 1981) (stating that an order is final when the Board renders its decision on appeal).

Here, such a discount was appropriate, as the majority properly pointed out that the respondent's spouse at no time suggested that she would suffer any particular hardship if she moved to Mexico with the respondent. A different situation would arise, for instance, where the marriage takes place after proceedings are initiated, but was preceded by a long-term cohabitative relationship; where the alien was in protected status and deportation was neither imminent nor likely in the foreseeable future; or where eligibility for adjustment of status without the need for a discretionary waiver of inadmissibility has been established. A respondent's relationship to his spouse's offspring may also be an appropriate consideration in the extreme hardship determination. Any hardship to a qualifying spouse must always be considered. In short, as we have often stated, extreme hardship is not a definable term of fixed and inflexible meaning, and the elements to establish extreme hardship are dependent upon the facts and circumstances of each case. Under the specific facts of this case extreme hardship was not established, and this case should not be misinterpreted as requiring a discount of the hardships present in all cases where the wedding ceremony takes place after proceedings are initiated.

* * * [T]he majority's opinion correctly notes that in purchasing the fraudulent birth certificate, using it to procure a fraudulent social security card, and subsequently using these documents to seek to procure a United States passport in order to travel into and out of the United States and seek employment, the respondent sought to procure both "documentation" and "other benefits" under the Act. The majority's finding is consistent with the close scrutiny of such a finding required by *Matter of Healy and Goodchild*, 17 I & N Dec. 22 (BIA 1979), because of its harsh consequences. However, a small clarification is needed. The other benefits under the Act the respondent sought to procure are the right to travel with a United States passport pursuant to section 215(b) of the Act. The majority's language may be misinterpreted as suggesting that using the fraudulent passport to obtain employment is obtaining a benefit under the Act.

Although the use or possession of such document is punishable under section 274C of the Act, working in the United States is not "a benefit provided under this Act," and we have specifically held that a violation of section 274C and fraud or misrepresentation under section 212(a)(6)(C)(i) of the Act are not equivalent. *See Matter of Lazarte*, [21 I & N Dec. 214] (BIA 1996). It is long settled that inadmissibility for immigration fraud does not ensue from the mere purchase of fraudulent documents, absent an attempt to fraudulently use the document for immigration purposes.

Finally, the majority points out that the Supreme Court has indicated that we may permissibly construe the element of extreme hardship narrowly. However, such permissibility does not require a narrow construction of extreme hardship, and we have recently declined to do so, choosing instead to rely on our precedents for guidance in our case-by-case determinations. * * *

[The opinion of ROSENBERG, BOARD MEMBER, concurring and dissenting, is omitted.]

PROBLEMS

5.   Noncitizen E, a high-school teacher from Istanbul, presents a fraudulent Turkish passport, bearing his picture and what appears to be a legitimate B–2 visa affixed thereto (nonimmigrant visitor for pleasure), at the Turkish Airlines check-in counter at the Istanbul airport. E states that he obtained it for a fee from someone who held himself out as a travel agent, that he never appeared before a U.S. consular officer, that he believed this procedure to be the proper way to obtain a passport and visa, and that he thought his documents were perfectly valid. The airline refused to let him board, and E did not come to the United States on that occasion. Later, E applies in proper fashion for a visa to come to the United States. Is E inadmissible under INA § 212(a)(6)(C)(i)? If he is inadmissible, is a waiver available? Would it make a difference if E were instead a farmer from rural Turkey who had only a fourth-grade education?

6.   Noncitizen F used a bogus green card to secure entry into the United States, successfully, one time eight years ago. Now he has developed a substantial international import-export business and seeks to enter the United States lawfully as a nonimmigrant E–1 treaty trader. Is F inadmissible? F's widowed mother already lives in the United States and recently became a U.S. citizen. They have been estranged and he is not sure whether she would petition for his permanent residence. If she will, would that make any difference in F's possible admissibility? Are any waivers available? Would it make a difference if he and his mother were on better terms? If the mother were afflicted with a chronic illness? If he were?

---

b.   Bars Based on Other Immigration Violations

(i) Entrants Without Inspection (EWIs)

The central inadmissibility ground based on immigration violations is INA § 212(a)(6)(A)(i), which makes inadmissible "an alien present in the United States without being admitted or paroled, or who arrives in the United States at any time or place other than as designated by the Attorney General." Simply put, this provision covers EWIs (entrants without inspection).

(ii) Prior Removal

Also important is INA § 212(a)(9)(A), which bars readmission for any noncitizen who has been ordered removed. The current bar is ten years for a person removed from inside the United States, or five years for removal at the border or a port of entry. The government may consent in advance to the admission of a noncitizen who was removed previously—essentially a discretionary waiver, with virtually no other statutory prerequisites. Consent has been granted sparingly but is possible, given the right showing, in a balancing process that loosely resembles the reasoning in *Cervantes–Gonzalez*.

(iii) Unlawful Presence

Before 1996, a noncitizen's prior unlawful stay generally did not bar her lawful admission later, not even as a permanent resident—so long as no formal exclusion or deportation order was issued against her. Today, three provisions adopted in 1996 impose more serious consequences for prior unlawful presence, even if she has never been ordered removed. Of these, INA § 212(a)(9)(B) has drawn the most attention. As interpreted and applied, this subsection provides that a noncitizen who has been unlawfully present for a single period of more than 180 days but less than one year, and then voluntarily departs, is inadmissible for three years. If she has been unlawfully present for a single period of one year or more, a ten-year bar applies, triggered once she departs or is removed.

Section 212(a)(9)(B)(ii) defines "unlawful presence" to cover noncitizens who entered without inspection or stayed beyond the expiration date of a nonimmigrant admission. But suppose a temporary worker, who is still within her admission period, violates the terms of her nonimmigrant status by working for a different employer? She is certainly unlawfully present in the sense that DHS could initiate a removal proceeding. But is she unlawfully present for purpose of the three- or ten-year bar? Generally not, as explained in guidance issued by USCIS, summarized and reprinted at 86 Interp.Rel. 1393, 1420 (2009). The rationale is that though overstays are easy to determine and accrue unlawful presence, violations of other conditions of admission are sometimes quite technical and do not necessarily notify noncitizens that they are running "bad time." Other than overstayers, nonimmigrants accrue unlawful presence only after the government gives them notice that they have violated the conditions of their admission, as might appear in a ruling denying an extension or change of status. A noncitizen in removal proceedings generally accrues unlawful presence.

Section 212(a)(9)(B) does not apply to noncitizens in the United States, if they have not *departed* the United States after accumulating 180 days or one year of unlawful presence. The policy behind this limitation is obscure at best, but this feature makes it highly desirable for any noncitizen who qualifies for permanent residence to adjust status without leaving the United States, as Chapter Six discussed.

Another inadmissibility ground, INA § 212(a)(9)(C), penalizes unlawful presence, by making any noncitizen inadmissible who has been unlawfully present for an *aggregate* period of more than one year or has been ordered removed, and thereafter enters or attempts to enter without being admitted—that is, crosses or tries to cross the border clandestinely. This bar is permanent, but after ten years outside the United States, an advance consent procedure is available like the one in § 212(a)(9)(A).

The third provision added in 1996 that attaches tougher consequences to immigration violations is INA § 222(g). It says that if a noncitizen is admitted on a nonimmigrant visa and stays longer than the authorized time period, that visa is void at the conclusion of his authorized period of stay. He is not necessarily barred from a later nonimmigrant admission, but for the rest of his life such admissions must be on the basis of a new visa issued in his home country, with an exception for "extraordinary circumstances." The State Department has explained that this requirement is meant to assure knowledgeable special scrutiny of his qualifications before any new visa issues. 75 Interp.Rel. 45 (1998).

The following problems will acquaint you with the statutory basics of these inadmissibility grounds relating to immigration control.

PROBLEMS

7.   G, a Honduran national, recently married an American citizen in Tegucigalpa, but she had been removed from the United States three years ago for overstaying her admission as a B–2 visitor for pleasure. Is G inadmissible? If so, how long before she becomes admissible again? Can you speed up her access? Are any waivers available?

8.   H, who seeks to come as an F–1 nonimmigrant student, admits that he entered the United States from Mexico, his home country, without inspection three times over the last five years. Each time, H stayed for about five months and left of his own accord. Is he inadmissible? What if he came a fourth time for another five month stay? What if he came only once but stayed eight months? What if H traveled with his brother at the time of his second entry, with H serving as a kind of guide because he already knew the route? Are any waivers or exceptions available?

9.   J, a citizen of Korea, was admitted on a business visitor (B–1) visa, with an authorized period of stay that expired on May 1 of last year. J did not return to Korea at the time. Instead, he stayed in the United States until January 1 of the current year, working without authorization for much of that time. J is now back in Korea. An immigrant visa has finally become available to him based on a family fourth preference petition that his U.S. citizen sister filed for him many years ago. Is J inadmissible? Are any waivers or exceptions available? Would it be different if he had never left the United States?

Self–Enforcement and Immigration Control

Is an inadmissibility ground for prior unlawful presence (with waivers) a good or bad idea? Both the three-year and ten-year bars and the voiding of visas for nonimmigrant overstays can be seen as attempts to build a measure of self-enforcement into the immigration laws. Their drafters evidently meant to give noncitizens a real incentive to leave the United States voluntarily when their admission period is over, rather than stay unlawfully. But consider these comments on the bars, written by one of the co-authors of this book who was initially inclined to favor the provision:

> [E]xperience has shown that the bars are ill-designed to promote self-enforcement. Those who have no prospects for immigration benefits when Day 180 rolls around are totally untouched. If they leave then, they can be virtually certain they'll never qualify for U.S. residence. If they stay, there's just a chance they might get lucky. Maybe they'll find a U.S. spouse or qualifying employer. And [maybe they'll find a loophole or Congress will change the rules, as has already happened twice, but only for limited groups of beneficiaries.]

> But there's a deeper reason why the bars aren't a credible part of enforcement * * *. The bars carry real consequences only when individual aliens are finally poised for immigration benefits. At that point, they invariably have U.S. citizens or permanent residents deeply invested in their staying. It is exactly the moment when enforcement will seem maximally cruel and controversial. However attractive the bars may seem in the abstract, they have to be implemented one individual or family at a time. * * *

> * * * We need to repeal the three- and 10–year bars.

Martin, *Waiting for Solutions*, Legal Times, May 29, 2001, at 66.

Waivers of the Unlawful Presence Bar

Noncitizens who qualify for permanent resident status but who are ineligible to adjust status must leave the United States to obtain an immigrant visa through consular processing. They thus trigger a three- or ten-year bar if they have been unlawfully present for the specified length of time. The key decision will be the grant or denial of a waiver, as set out, along with exceptions and tolling provisions, in § 212(a)(9)(B)(iii)–(v).

A crucial practical consideration under current regulations is that the noncitizen cannot apply for a waiver of inadmissibility (which is decided by USCIS) until she leaves the United States to undergo consular processing. The procedural context forces the noncitizen to decide on what is often an agonizing, high-risk gamble. She might choose to remain in the United States without lawful immigration status. If she leaves the United States and applies for a waiver, she may face a long wait for a decision. If her application is approved, she can return to the United States as a lawful permanent resident. But if her application is denied, she faces an even longer separation due to the three- or ten-year bar.

DHS waiver decisions under § 212(a)(9)(B) have often drawn by analogy on the § 212(i) standards in *Cervantes–Gonzalez* and similar cases. Compare these two excerpts from two decisions separated by just one day, both involving appeals from denials of a waiver to the Mexican spouse of a U.S. citizen:

> On appeal, the applicant indicates that since the denial of the waiver application his wife is experiencing the hardship of raising their two-year-old daughter without him. He states that his wife is a bank teller and is trying to financially support her parents and his mother and needs financial assistance from him. The applicant conveys that his wife is taking care of her mother, who has high blood pressure. He states that his wife has had to give up her educational goals to support the family and his daughter is without a father. The applicant indicates that moving to Mexico would halt his wife's career, cause them to lose their house, and separate his wife from her parents. He indicates that his child would live in poverty in Mexico and would not have educational opportunities.

> * * *

> The applicant indicates that his spouse will experience financial hardship if he remains in Mexico. The applicant's spouse states in a letter dated October 28, 2005, that if her husband stays in Mexico she will not be able to afford her monthly expenses, which now include a babysitter. She indicates that her husband has a job offer in the United States. This is reflected in a letter by Central Air Conditioning, Inc. in the record. Contained in the record are wage statements reflecting the applicant's wife's gross bi-weekly earnings ranged from $938—1,169, with the higher figure reflecting overtime. * * * The after-tax income of the applicant's spouse is not adequate to meet her monthly financial expenses. As a consequence of this, the AAO [Administrative Appeals Office] finds that the applicant's spouse would experience extreme financial hardship if she were to remain in the United States without her husband.

> * * *

> Difficulty in finding employment and inability to find employment in one's trade or profession and loss of a family business and home were not sufficient to justify relief in *Matter of Pilch*, 21 I & N Dec. 627 (BIA 1996). Furthermore, courts have routinely held that a lower standard of living in an alien's homeland is not sufficient to constitute extreme hardship. Regarding separation from family members in the United States, in *Sullivan v. INS*, 772 F.2d 609, 611 (9th Cir. 1985), the Ninth Circuit stated that deportation is not without personal distress and emotional hurt; and that courts have upheld orders of the BIA that resulted in the separation of aliens from

members of their families. There is no evidence in the record demonstrating that the applicant's spouse provides financial support to her parents or to the applicant's mother, nor is there any documentation of the medical condition of the applicant's mother-in-law or that there are no other relatives who could provide assistance. The record presented here, considered collectively, fails to establish extreme hardship to the applicant's spouse if she were to join him to live in Mexico.

In Re ___, AAU CDJ 20 047 29817, 2009 WL 3555507 (Admin. App. Office 2009).

The applicant's spouse, [redacted] indicates that she will experience hardship if her husband remains in Mexico. In her letter dated October 29, 2005, she indicates that her salary is not enough to pay rent and bills and babysitting expenses so she must get financial assistance from the government such as food stamps. She states in a letter dated July 24, 2006, she and her daughter live with her parents and depend upon them financially; that she has no energy to find a job and is nervous all the time, and bites her hands until they bleed and pulls out her hair. She states that she feels out of control and is nothing without her husband and sometimes feels that she does not want to live. [redacted] states that relatives took her to a doctor and he recommended counseling, but she cannot afford to visit a therapist. The letter by [redacted] with Sana Medical Group, Inc. conveys that [redacted] was seen in his office on July 14, 2006, and was treated for anxiety and depression was referred to counseling, and that [redacted] is undergoing difficult stressful situations with her family in Mexico and social stress in the United States. He prescribed Ativan for [redacted]. In addition, [redacted], an obstetrics and gynecologist, prescribed Ambien for [redacted]. Ms. [redacted] pastor indicates that she has visited him on account of her depression. [redacted] mother states that her daughter is depressed and has changed since separation from the applicant. She indicates that her daughter cannot sleep, cries and is awake early. She conveys that [redacted] son is living with his father in Mexico. She states that her daughter needs money and is not working and that she cannot give her money because she is supporting three of her own children. [redacted] mother indicates that the applicant took care of the children while her daughter worked. The letters by family members convey that Ms. [redacted] is very depressed and some of the letters describe her as having no money to support herself and her daughter.

The psychological evaluation dated June 30 and July 1, 2006, conveys the applicant is depressed due to separation from his wife and children, and it reflects that he is unemployed. The record contains money remittances sent to the applicant since February 2006. The letter by [redacted] dated July 6, 2006, states that the applicant's income is low and his living conditions are poor and it would be hard on his children to adapt to this. The letter by [redacted] dated July 4,

2006, conveys that the applicant is depressed and unable to find work in Mexico. She conveys that her family members collect and send money to the applicant so that he can support his son and himself.

* * *

The hardship presented in this case is both financial and emotional in nature. The applicant's wife is described as having depression and as being in financial straits. In light of the evidence in the record, the AAO finds that the cumulative general emotional effect that family separation has had on the applicant's wife, combined with the increased familial burdens that she has faced since her husband's departure from the United States, render the hardship in this case beyond that which is normally experienced in most cases of removal. Accordingly, the AAO finds that the applicant has established that his wife would suffer extreme hardship if she remained in the United States without him.

Furthermore, given the evidence of hardship, considered in the aggregate and in light of the *Cervantes–Gonzalez* factors cited above, the AAO finds that the hardship to the applicant's spouse, in view of her husband's poor living conditions in Mexico and his reliance upon financial support from family members in the United States to survive in Mexico, rises to the level of "extreme" hardship if she joins the applicant to live in Mexico.

* * * Once extreme hardship is established, the Secretary then determines whether an exercise of discretion is warranted.

The favorable factors in this matter are the extreme hardship to the applicant's spouse and his U.S. citizen children, their close ties to their church, the letters commending the applicant's character, and the passage of approximately nine years since the applicant's immigration violation. The unfavorable factors in this matter are the applicant's entry into the United States without inspection, his periods of unauthorized presence, and unauthorized employment. The AAO notes that the applicant does not appear to have a criminal record.

While the AAO cannot emphasize enough the seriousness with which it regards the applicant's breach of the immigration laws of the United States, the severity of the applicant's immigration violation is at least partially diminished by the fact that nine years have elapsed since the applicant's immigration violation. The AAO finds that the hardship imposed on the applicant's spouse as a result of his inadmissibility outweighs the unfavorable factors in the application. Therefore, a favorable exercise of the Secretary's discretion is warranted in this matter.

In Re ___, AAU CDJ 20 047 67148, 2009 WL 3555586 (Admin. App. Office 2009).

What explains the difference in outcomes between the denial in the July 7 case and the approval in the July 8 case, both decided by the Administrative Appeals Office?

4. PUBLIC CHARGE

Concern about an influx of paupers underlay many of the earliest attempts—then by the state governments—to restrict immigration. *See generally* Neuman, *The Lost Century of American Immigration Law (1776–1875)*, 93 Colum.L.Rev. 1833, 1846–59 (1993). In 1882, Congress enacted the first federal provision barring from entry "any person unable to take care of himself or herself without becoming a public charge." Act of Aug. 3, 1882, ch. 376, § 2, 22 Stat. 214. There has been a public charge excludability or inadmissibility ground ever since.

INA § 237(a)(5) also makes deportable any "alien who, within five years from the date of entry, has become a public charge from causes not affirmatively shown to have arisen since entry." But case law has limited this deportability ground to the rare cases where (1) the public assistance program imposed on the noncitizen or other persons an obligation to repay the agency; and (2) the agency's demand for reimbursement has not been satisfied. *See Matter of B–*, 3 I & N Dec. 323 (BIA 1948). Only eight public charge deportations occurred from 1961 through 1970, and only 31 from 1971 through 1980, when the government stopped publishing the figures.

In contrast, the public charge *inadmissibility* ground—now in INA § 212(a)(4)—is highly significant for the number of visa applicants that it disqualifies. The administering officer has broad discretion, since any alien is inadmissible who *"in the opinion of the consular officer ... or in the opinion of the Attorney General ... is likely at any time to become a public charge"* (emphasis added).

Much of the recent history of this inadmissibility concerns the sponsor's affidavit of financial support, which became a standard method of overcoming the public charge exclusion ground. *See, e.g., Matter of Kohama*, 17 I & N Dec. 257 (Assoc. Comm'r 1978). Concerned by numerous state court cases holding that affidavits of support were not legally binding on the sponsor as a matter of state law, some in Congress tried unsuccessfully in the 1980s to make them legally enforceable under federal law. Congress then took a different path. It began to modify federally funded assistance programs such as food stamps, Assistance to Families with Dependent Children (AFDC), and Supplemental Security Income (SSI) by adding new "deeming provisions." For purposes of determining public assistance eligibility, a sponsor's income and assets were deemed to be available to the sponsored noncitizen, with exemptions for refugees and certain other groups.

The 1996 Immigration Act and the Personal Responsibility and Work Opportunity Reconciliation Act, Pub.L. 104–193, 110 Stat. 2105 (1996)

(1996 Welfare Act), took the next step by requiring affidavits of support for most immigrants and making the affidavits enforceable, while also leaving the deeming mechanism in place. One of the legislative reports on an early version of the 1996 Act, noting the increasing use of public assistance by recent immigrants, explained: "In effect, immigrants make a promise to the American people that they will not become a financial burden." S.Rep. No. 249, 104th Cong., 2d Sess. 6 (1996).

An enforceable affidavit of support is now required for all immigrants qualifying as immediate relatives of citizens or under the family-based preferences—regardless of the immigrant's own assets or earning potential, with exceptions for surviving spouses of citizens, battered spouses and children, and certain others. *See* INA § 212(a)(4), 213A. Around 700,000 immigrants in each of the years 2008 through 2010 had to satisfy this requirement. The affidavit requirement also applies to employment-based immigrants where the employer is a relative or an entity in which the relative has a five-percent ownership interest. (For admission categories not requiring an affidavit, the assessment of public charge inadmissibility is discretionary.)

The sponsor must show the ability to support all sponsored immigrants *plus his or her own household* at a minimum of 125 percent of the federal poverty line. *See* INA § 213A(a)(1)(A). In 2011, this minimum for four persons was $27,937, which amounts to one wage-earner working full-time at $13.43 per hour. (Higher levels apply to Hawaii and Alaska, but active duty U.S. military personnel must show only 100 percent of the federal poverty line.)

In addition to the sponsor's income, assets may also be counted if they can be converted to cash within one year. If so, one-fifth of their value is added to annual income, or one-third if only a spouse and minor children are sponsored. The sponsor generally must be the petitioner, but another person who meets the minimum may accept joint and several liability with a petitioner whose income and assets are insufficient. The intending immigrant's past or prospective income is counted only if he or she (a) has income at the time of filing, (b) will continue to receive income from the same source upon approval of the petition, and (c) will live with the sponsor.

The sponsor must be eighteen years of age and domiciled in the United States. Each sponsor must file an affidavit of support on Form I–864. If the sponsor needs to count the income of other household members to meet the minimum, the other members have to execute similar pledges on Form I–864A. (All these forms appear in the Statutory Supplement.)

The affidavit is quite durable—enforceable until the sponsored immigrant is credited with work for 40 Social Security quarters (*i.e.*, usually ten years), naturalizes, leaves the United States and relinquishes permanent resident status, or dies. If a citizen or permanent resident sponsors a spouse and they later divorce, the support obligation survives.

To put the affidavit requirement in context, first consider that the 1996 Welfare Act's limits on noncitizen eligibility for public benefits provide that new lawful immigrants are ineligible for five years for any "federal means-tested public benefits"—food stamps, SSI, and nonemergency Medicaid. *See* Welfare Act § 403, 8 U.S.C.A. § 1613. (Chapter Eleven will discuss these restrictions.) Even after five years, the deeming provisions carried over from prior law will bar most sponsored immigrants until they naturalize or work 40 quarters without receiving federal means-tested public benefits. *See* Welfare Act § 421, 8 U.S.C.A. § 1631.

Suppose that, despite the initial five-year ineligibility period and the deeming provisions, a new immigrant receives means-tested benefits, for example from a state or local government. The government entity that pays out those benefits may rely on the affidavit to sue the immigrant's sponsor for reimbursement. Moreover, sponsored immigrants themselves may enforce the support obligation against their sponsors. INA § 213A(b), (e).

EXERCISE ON AFFIDAVITS OF SUPPORT

Advise the sponsor and others who might potentially assume financial responsibility on the following facts. Most of these questions can be addressed by consulting INA §§ 212(a)(4) and 213A, but you should also examine Forms I–864 and I–864A in the Statutory Supplement, as well as the latest federal poverty level guidelines in Form I–864P.

Juan gained permanent resident status in the United States and then naturalized 12 years ago. Soon after becoming a citizen, he filed an immigrant visa petition for his brother Antonio, a Mexican citizen. His brother's priority date has just become current, and Juan has been informed that he must complete an affidavit of support. Juan earns $33,000 a year, and his wife, who works part-time and was recently laid off, earned $6,000 last year. They have three children, the oldest of whom is in high school. Although their means are modest, they live comfortably in a small community in south Texas where the cost of living is among the lowest in the United States. They have $1,000 in savings and own their own house. Their equity interest in the home is $30,000.

Antonio has been a successful small farmer in Mexico and has $5,000 in savings. Juan works for a landscaping service, and his boss is interested in hiring Antonio after he arrives. Antonio would initially be paid $10.00 an hour ($20,000 annually), but the boss says he can advance quickly to $12.00 per hour ($24,000 annually) if he proves to be a hard worker. Antonio is married and has one son, four years old. He speaks little English. He told Juan in a recent phone call that he suffered a back injury, but he is sure it is nothing serious.

What advice can you give Juan about how he might help Antonio and Antonio's family immigrate to the United States?

QUESTIONS ON PUBLIC CHARGE INADMISSIBILITY

1. Might the 125 percent requirement bar too many immigrants who could achieve economic self-sufficiency, if not real prosperity?

2. Was it necessary *both* to require support affidavits and to restrict immigrant eligibility for public benefits? If new immigrants are barred from the major federal welfare programs for their first five years (and longer in most cases due to the deeming provisions), why also require an affidavit of support? Or if an affidavit is required, why is it necessary to restrict immigrant eligibility? Or should Congress take a different approach and make the public-charge *deportability* ground easier to enforce? Which approach most closely reflects the idea that immigrants likely to become a public charge should not be admitted?

5. PUBLIC HEALTH

From early on, U.S. immigration law has had an exclusion ground for persons with dangerous contagious diseases. *See* INA § 212(a)(1)(A)(i). The spread of AIDS (acquired immune deficiency syndrome) in the 1980s prompted regulations and statutes addressing whether noncitizens with AIDS or the associated human immunodeficiency virus (HIV) would be barred from the United States. In the late 1980s, regulations contained such a bar. The 1990 Immigration Act then made excludable only noncitizens with communicable diseases "of public health significance." The Department of Health and Human Services proposed new regulations to remove AIDS and several other diseases from the exclusion list because they cannot be spread by casual contact. But Congress intervened in early 1993, amending this exclusion ground to specify "infection with the etiologic agent for acquired immune deficiency syndrome" as a "communicable disease of public health significance."

In 2008, Congress deleted the specific enumeration of HIV infection from INA § 212(a)(1)(A)(i). But the governing regulation did not change until January 2010, when the Department of Health and Human Services removed HIV from the list of communicable diseases of public health significance. 74 Fed. Reg. 56547 (2009). As of mid–2011, nine diseases are on the list. Active tuberculosis is the most important, especially with the appearance of treatment-resistant strains, but the list also includes infectious leprosy and several sexually transmitted diseases. In addition, two other categories of diseases could lead to inadmissibility: (1) quarantinable diseases designated by Presidential Executive Order and (2) diseases constituting a public health emergency of international concern. *See* 42 C.F.R. § 34.2(b).

Three related inadmissibility grounds deserve mention. One requires immigrants to document vaccination against certain vaccine-preventable diseases. *See* § 212(a)(1)(A)(ii). Another makes noncitizens inadmissible if they have a mental or physical disorder with accompanying threatening behavior. *See* § 212(a)(1)(A)(iii). And INA § 212(a)(1)(A)(iv) makes drug abusers or addicts inadmissible.

Waivers of these public health-related inadmissibility grounds may be available under INA § 212(g) or, for nonimmigrants, 212(d)(3)(A). A final practical note: even if § 212(a)(1)(A) does not bar noncitizens with medical issues, § 212(a)(4), the public charge ground, may pose a problem if they face significant future medical expenses.

6. NATIONAL SECURITY, FOREIGN POLICY, AND THE CONSTITUTION

The terrorist attacks of September 11, 2001, were carried out by foreigners, mostly nationals of Saudi Arabia, all of whom had been admitted to the United States as nonimmigrants. At least two had violated their student status but had not been the subjects of any enforcement action.

After the attacks, the connection between immigration controls and national security drew a great deal of attention. The Department of Justice made unprecedented use of immigration powers as a major part of its immediate response. Citing immigration law violations, it detained without bond over 700 noncitizens deemed to be "of interest" on security grounds. It delayed the filing of charges or slowed hearings or final removal in many cases to allow further FBI investigation into the person's possible terrorist connections. DOJ closed many removal hearings to the public, sometimes relying on classified evidence not shared with the noncitizen respondent. The Department of State tightened consular screening of visa issuance. Far more thorough and time-consuming background checks against security databases came to be required.

Congress also got into the act. The USA PATRIOT Act, passed about seven weeks after September 11, made significant changes to immigration-related statutes. *See* Pub. L. 107–56, 115 Stat. 349 (2001). And in 2002, the Enhanced Border Security and Visa Entry Reform Act further amended immigration processes to assure better databases and better database integration, with the goal of generating timely lookout information for those suspected of terrorist or criminal connections. *See* Pub.L. 107–173, 116 Stat. 543 (2002). Congress also set a tight timetable for the completion of a comprehensive entry-exit monitoring system that could quickly identify nonimmigrant overstays, though it never provided significant funding for the infrastructure needed to complete a comprehensive system. The new laws also required a variety of documents and records to include biometric identifiers such as fingerprints.

The Homeland Security Act abolished the INS as of March 2003 and moved most of its functions into separate units of the new Department of Homeland Security. *See* Pub.L. 107–296, 116 Stat. 2135 (2002). And in 2005, the REAL ID Act, to combat fraud of a type used by several 9/11 hijackers to obtain driver's licenses, essentially required states to standardize and restrict the issuance of state identity documents. (Because Congress cannot directly command states to implement such changes, the REAL ID Act sets conditions that must be met if states want their IDs to remain valid for use in federal or federally-regulated activities, including air travel.) *See* Pub. L. 109–13, Div. B, §§ 201–202, 119 Stat. 231, 302–05.

As this brief account indicates, national security concerns have strongly influenced immigration law in both procedure and substance. This subsection focuses on inadmissibility grounds related to national security and foreign policy. We start by surveying the history of measures that target noncitizens believed to be subversives or terrorists. The survey also introduces the constitutional issues that national-security measures can pose in immigration law. Though our detailed consideration of national security and foreign policy will start with inadmissibility and defer deportability until later in this chapter, this introductory subsection provides background that is common to both.

a. Background and Constitutional Framework

BRIAN N. FRY, RESPONDING TO IMMIGRATION: PERCEPTIONS OF PROMISE AND THREAT

Chapter 3: American Nativism in Historical Perspective Pp. 64–74 (2001).

* * *

Anti–Catholicism was the most prevalent form of nativism in the colonial period. Distilled from "No–Popery" laws and a series of real and imagined Catholic conspiracies in seventeenth century England, English settlers tried to limit the immigration and rights of Catholics. Religious intolerance varied from one colony to the next, but Catholics were routinely barred from entering certain colonies, holding public office and voting. Even though it is impossible to chronicle and characterize every instance of anti-Catholicism, colonial nativists generally viewed Roman Catholicism as an "authoritarian" religion endangering the political stability of their settlements. To guard against this presumed danger, colonists strove to minimize their numbers and participation in civic affairs.

Catholics were prohibited from naturalizing throughout much of the colonial era, and until 1806, did not assume public office in most states, largely because of objectionable oaths. England's Glorious Revolution of 1689 (where Parliament overthrew the Catholic King, James II) exacerbated anti-Catholic nativism in the colonies, precipitating rumors that Catholics were conspiring with Indians to massacre the Protestants. In 1690, during the French and Spanish Wars, Catholics were viewed as potential saboteurs, a fifth column.[1] "Every Catholic within the colonies was looked upon as a potential enemy who might let his papal allegiance supersede his loyalty to the crown by co-operating with the armies of French Canada and the Spanish Florida against the settlers."[2] As a result, Catholics were—in some of the colonies—burdened with additional taxes, forbidden to settle in large groups, and disarmed. Later, in 1755, Britain deported more than six thousand Acadians (French-speaking Catholic peasants from Nova Scotia) to the southern colonies. Their reception was a hostile one, and some even became indentured servants.

* * *

Jews, French Huguenots, Protestant Irish and Germans also faced native hostility. Like the Catholics, Jews were often barred from voting and holding office. The Protestant French Huguenots seemed more French than Protestant to the colonists, particularly during the Anglo–French wars in 1689. One of their settlements in Rhode Island was attacked by a mob, some were [compelled] to leave their homes in New York, and others were unjustly imprisoned in Pennsylvania. German loyalty was questioned during the French and Indian Wars. Their large numbers and "clannishness" were especially resented in Pennsylvania. Benjamin Franklin worried that they might "Germanize" Pennsylvanians rather than assimilate—a fear clearly shared by the Pennsylvania, Delaware, and New Jersey legislatures. * * * Lastly, the poverty and [large] numbers of the Protestant Irish drew nativist accusations and violence. In Boston, they were blamed for the increase in wheat prices, and in 1734, had their new Presbyterian church in Worcester destroyed.

Support for the new government replaced religion as the litmus test for loyalty as Catholics joined the revolutionary army and Catholic France became the colony's ally against the British. Not until the mid–1830s would a strident anti-Catholicism reemerge. In the interim, two short ruptures of nativism occurred in the 1790s—one against foreign ideas, the other against foreigners. In the late 1790s, secret societies of Illuminati (composed mainly of Freemasons and other anti-Catholics) were accused of trying to abolish the republic's political and religious institutions. Their zeal to bring all people under the rules of reason, and secretive manner, allegedly violated—among other things—property rights, organized religion, and the innocence of women. But by 1799 the thesis of an "Illuminism conspiracy" could not endure public scrutiny and the movement fell into disrepute. The second rupture, the passage of the Alien and Sedition Acts in 1798, was primarily directed against the foreign-born and was

---

1. The origin of the fifth column metaphor stems from the "column of supporters which General Mola declared himself to have in Madrid, when he was besieging it in the Spanish Civil War, in addition to the four columns of his army outside the city" (Oxford English Dictionary 1989: 890).

2. [Ray Allen Billington, The Protestant Crusade 1800–1860: A Study of the Origins of American Nativism 9 (1963).]

propelled in part by the Federalists' resentment and distrust of the many foreigners who sided with the Jeffersonians.

* * *

The destruction of churches and convents, Catholic scare literature, and violent clashes between Protestants and Catholics were standard fare in the 1830s. In New York, St. Mary's was set afire in 1831—the first in a series of church burnings and desecrations that would continue up until the Civil War. The 1834 burning of the Ursuline Convent School in Charlestown, Massachusetts on August 10 was perhaps the most notorious example of Protestant violence. Drawing from Samuel F.B. Morse's book warning of an international Catholic conspiracy, the Reverend Beecher delivered three anti-Catholic speeches in Boston during the day and incited forty to fifty Bostonians to cross the river and torch the school. Other anti-Catholic publications followed, often excusing these acts of violence and encouraging new ones. *The Awful Disclosures of Maria Monk* (1836) falsely alleged that priests were raping young women and killing their offspring after baptizing them. The book sold 300,000 copies by the Civil War, and until surpassed by *Uncle Tom's Cabin*, was the best selling book in American history.

* * *

The nativist societies born in the 1840s, such as the Order of the United Americans (OUA) and Order of United American Mechanics (OUAM), carried the nativist "seed" into the fifties, facilitating the development of what later became known as the Know Nothing movement. In 1850, the Order of the Star Spangled Banner was founded in New York, and their ranks quickly swelled, often with OUA members. Instructed to say they "know nothing" when outsiders asked about their society, Horace Greeley of the New York Tribune contemptuously labeled them as such in 1853. At one time, the Know Nothings had over 1.25 million members and ten thousand councils. Most effective as a local movement, their council system doubled as a political system for the American Party (the official name of Know Nothings) to elect seven governors, eight U.S. senators, and 104 U.S. Representatives by 1856. So effective and popular was the American Party in 1855 that the *New York Herald* unhappily predicted a presidential victory in 1856. But the very issue which helped unite the American Party in the early 1850s—slavery—proved too divisive just a few years later.

Unable to ignore the slavery crisis in their own national meetings between 1854 and 1856, and accentuated by regional differences in group membership and objectives, consensus in the American Party began to wane. * * *

In 1856, the party's candidate for President, Millard Fillmore, came in a distant third, bringing the party's activities to a close in most states. Except in a few border states, the Know Nothings were little more than a shell by 1860. It would take a Civil War, one fought by Catholics and immigrants alike, to expunge the anti-immigrant and anti-Catholic sentiment of the sixties. * * *

The Civil War may have brought organized nativism to a transitory halt, but it was the expanding economy and frontier that allowed immigrants to retain their wartime laurels for the next two decades. Suspicions of disloyalty did however emerge during the war. General Grant expelled Jews from his military jurisdiction in 1862, but revoked the order three weeks later at Lincoln's request. In 1863, an effort to revive the Know Nothing movement failed in New York as discontents from the Irish working class participated in the four-day "draft riots" which were "widely interpreted as a disloyal Irish conspiracy inspired by Confederate agents."[3] During the 1860s and 1870s, European immigrants seemed to be a national blessing, but on the West Coast, the Chinese were attacked by mobs and saddled with discriminatory laws.

* * *

In May 1886, "the Haymarket Affair was to go down as the most important single incident in late nineteenth century nativism."[4] In the midst of a national strike for an eight-hour day, a meeting was called by Chicago anarchists in the Haymarket Square. A bomb exploded as the police closed in on the peaceful group. "Instantly, a torrent of nationalist hysteria coursed through the cities of the Northeast and Midwest."[5] Even though the police were unable to determine the bomber's identity, six immigrants and one native-born American were sentenced to death. The aftershock of the Haymarket Affair revived some of the old fraternal organizations of the 1840s and 1850s, especially the Junior Order United American Mechanics, whose membership list quadrupled in just four years. The fraternal orders were anti-radical first, and anti-Catholic second, but local anti-Catholic societies sprang up in the eighties to carry on the crusade. In 1887, the American Protective Association (APA) was established in Iowa, and by 1890 "its local councils were flourishing in communities from Detroit to Omaha."[6] But nativism never garnered a national following as it had in the 1850s. It seemingly lacked the kind of nationalist formula that equated specific immigrant groups with subversive activity or inherently "un-American" ideas.

Following the economic downturns of the mid–1870s and mid–1880s, the depression in the 1890s contributed to a resurgence of nativist activities. European aliens found themselves ineligible for certain jobs and Catholics increasingly became the targets of the American Protective Association. The APA, over a half-million strong in 1894, was particularly active in the Midwest. They accused Catholics of intentionally disrupting the economy for the purpose of facilitating a Roman takeover, boycotted their businesses, and were involved in two Protestant–Catholic riots. They

---

3. [John Higham, Strangers in the Land 13 (1992).]

4. [Id. at 54.]

5. [Id.]

6. [Id. at 63.]

helped re-elect William McKinley as governor of Ohio and aided sympa-thizers in their bids for Congress. But by the latter part of 1894, internal dissension racked the organization, and the religious fervor of the organization carried less weight with a changing middle-class. * * *

Anti-radical nativism also surfaced in the nineties, but in a much more violent show of force. In 1897, deputies opened fire on a group of unarmed Hungarian and Polish strikers in Pennsylvania, injuring forty immigrants and killing twenty-one. In 1891, eleven Italians were lynched in New Orleans. However, an improving economy and the swift defeat of Spain in the 1898 Spanish–American War seemed to dam the current of restriction for a short while, but another crisis would shortly reappear.

The twentieth century began on the restrictionist foot with the Immigration Acts of 1903 and 1907. In response to the assassination of President McKinley in 1901 by Leo Czolgosz, a native-born anarchist of obvious foreign extraction, Congress pushed for the exclusion and deporta-tion of alien anarchists. This objective was incorporated into the more general 1903 bill, which expanded the criteria for excluding and deporting aliens, and for the first time since the Aliens Act of 1798, penalized immigrants for their political beliefs. * * *

* * *

* * * [In 1917] the war with Germany [directed] the public's atten-tion to another "fifth column"—German–Americans. The German–Ameri-can Alliance's bold support for Germany, the virtually unanimous pro-Germany stance of the German–American press, and a few blundered attempts at sabotage by a group of Germans, was intolerable to a country drunk on "100 per cent Americanism." Federal agents used the 1798 Alien Enemies Act to arrest 6,300 Germans ("enemy aliens"), of whom 2,300 were interned. Congress also enacted the 1917 Espionage Act and 1918 Sedition Act to prosecute U.S. citizens of German origin who [criticized the war effort or obstructed the draft.] * * * During the war, German–Americans not only "swatted" the hyphen, but also American-ized names—for example, Schmidt became Smith, East Germantown, Indiana was renamed Pershing, and sauerkraut became "liberty cabbage." Nonetheless, these last minute demonstrations of loyalty did little to pacify official or public sentiment. Volunteer "spy-hunting" organizations, such as the American Protective League, continued to harass German Americans, and by early 1915, fifteen states passed laws requiring that English be the language of instruction in all public and private schools.

* * *

The Alien and Sedition Acts of 1798

Fry mentions the Alien and Sedition Acts of 1798, passed at a time of wide public concern about subversion stemming from revolutionary

France. Those laws constitute a highly important chapter in the history of U.S. legal responses to perceived national security threats posed by immigration.

The Alien Act (often called the Alien Friends Act), ch. 58, 1 Stat. 570 (1798), gave the President the power "at any time during the continuance of this act, to order all such aliens as he shall judge dangerous to the peace and safety of the United States, or shall have reasonable grounds to suspect are concerned in any treasonable or secret machinations against the government thereof, to depart out of the territory of the United States, within such time as shall be expressed in such order." The Act was never directly applied to any alien, but some foreigners departed to avoid its application, and President Adams signed a small number of arrest warrants, whose targets either went into hiding or left before being caught. J. Smith, Freedom's Fetters: The Alien and Sedition Laws and American Civil Liberties 159–76 (1956).[4]

The Alien Act law stimulated one of the nation's first extended debates about the constitutional rights of noncitizens. Against the claim that aliens enjoyed no such rights because not parties to the compact, Madison and Jefferson contended that because aliens owed a temporary allegiance during their stay, they were entitled to certain protections as a matter of mutuality. *See* G. Neuman, Strangers to the Constitution: Immigrants, Borders, and Fundamental Law 52–63 (1996). The Aliens Act was allowed to expire in 1800, and the Jeffersonian view of its invidiousness has generally carried the day in the court of history.

A second law—the Alien Enemies Act—passed in 1798 in response to public fears about foreign machinations, was accepted by the Jeffersonians and survives with little change today. *See* ch. 66, 1 Stat. 577 (1798), now codified at 50 U.S.C. §§ 21–23. It authorizes the internment and removal of nationals of states with which the United States is at war, after a congressional declaration of war or in certain other circumstances involving threatened hostilities, upon the public proclamation of the President. As the Fry excerpt indicates, it has been used during many conflicts, including World War II, although always selectively. Presidents have stopped short of rounding up all citizens of the foreign state present in the United States. During World War II, German and Japanese nationals were only selectively detained. The notorious internment of Japanese–Americans removed from the West Coast—over 60 percent of whom were U.S. citizens—was ordered on the basis of general military powers, not the Alien Enemies Act, which applies only to foreign nationals.

---

4. Smith recounts several Federalist judges' efforts to collect derogatory information on foreigners—including what newspapers they subscribed to and the fact that one was "very inquisitive" about his neighbors. Smith at 168. A Federalist newspaper wrote: "Would to God the immigrants could be collected and retransported to the climes from which they came." *Id.* at 159. One reputed target, who came to this country originally to flee the Reign of Terror in France in 1794, wrote in his diary in 1798 that "everybody was suspicious of everybody else; everywhere one saw murderous glances." When President Adams was asked what was the charge against this man, he replied: "Nothing in particular, but he's too French." *Id.* at 170.

We now pick up the historical thread where the Fry account leaves off. The 1903 Act had provided for the exclusion of specified subversives but authorized deportation only for those who should have been excluded on this ground when they entered. In 1917, Congress extended the deportation grounds to include *post-entry* subversive conduct. Any "alien who at any time after entry shall be found advocating or teaching [subversion]" could be deported. Immigration Act of 1917, ch. 29, § 19, 39 Stat. 889. As World War I continued, this deportation ground expanded further to cover aliens who were "members of or affiliated with any organization that entertains a belief in" violent overthrow of the government or anarchism. Anarchist Act of 1918, ch. 186, § 1, 40 Stat. 1012. Aliens who wrote, published, circulated or possessed subversive literature also became deportable. Act of June 5, 1920, ch. 251, § 1, 41 Stat. 1008.

The aftermath of World War I and the rise of the Bolshevik regime in Russia soon brought the Palmer Raids, a repressive campaign to deport noncitizens affiliated with allegedly subversive organizations. Thousands were imprisoned, and over five hundred were eventually deported. What follows is a portion of historian John Higham's account of the Raids.

A new [U.S.] Attorney General, A. Mitchell Palmer, took over * * * in March 1919. Palmer's bulldog jaw belied his simple, placid face. Once the implacable opponent of the political bosses and liquor interests in Pennsylvania, he approached the war against Germany with the same crusading belligerence. * * * He was an ambitious man as well: his eye rested lovingly on the White House. The failure of Palmer's agents to find the perpetrators of several bombing episodes in April must have exasperated him considerably, and when another infernal machine battered the front of his own home in June, Palmer was ready to go with the current. He appealed to Congress for a special appropriation, telling the frightened legislators that he knew exactly when the Reds were planning "to rise up and destroy the Government at one fell swoop." The appropriation became available during the summer, and with it Palmer created a new division of the Bureau of Investigation for the war against radicalism. In anticipation of a peacetime sedition law, the division proceeded to assemble data on all revolutionary activities * * *. * * * [T]he Union of Russian Workers * * * was chosen as the first target.

On November 7, 1919, the second anniversary of the Bolshevik régime in Russia, Palmer's men descended on Russian meeting places in eleven cities and seized hundreds of members of the organization. Screening for once was swift. Little more than a month later 249 aliens, most of them netted in the November raids, were on a specially chartered transport en route to Finland. From there they traveled overland to Russia through snows and military lines. Some had to leave behind in America their wives and children, at once destitute and ostracized.

* * *

Basking in the popularity of his anti-Russian raid, Palmer now prepared a mightier blow. On January 2 the Department of Justice, aided by local police forces in thirty-three cities, carried out a vast roundup of alien members of the two communist parties. Officers burst into homes, meeting places and pool rooms, as often as not seizing everyone in sight. The victims were loaded into trucks, or sometimes marched through the streets handcuffed and chained to one another, and massed by the hundreds at concentration points, usually police stations. There officials tried to separate out the alien members of radical organizations, releasing the rest or turning them over to the local police. Many remained in federal custody for a few hours only; some lay in crowded cells for several weeks without a preliminary hearing. For several days in Detroit eight hundred men were held incommunicado in a windowless corridor, sleeping on the bare stone floor, subsisting on food which their families brought in, and limited to the use of a single drinking fountain and a single toilet. Altogether, about three thousand aliens were held for deportation, almost all of them eastern Europeans.

J. Higham, Strangers in the Land: Patterns of American Nativism 1860–1925, at 229–31 (1955).

The January 1920 raids in Boston and other New England towns netted about 1000 persons. Twenty who had been arrested and ordered deported brought suit challenging the proceedings' legality. Judge George Weston Anderson, in setting aside most of the deportations on due process grounds, described the raids and their aftermath:

Pains were taken to give spectacular publicity to the raid, and to make it appear that there was great and imminent public danger, against which these activities of the Department of Justice were directed. The arrested aliens, in most instances perfectly quiet and harmless working people, many of them not long ago Russian peasants, were handcuffed in pairs, and then, for the purposes of transfer on trains and through the streets of Boston, chained together. The Northern New Hampshire contingent were first concentrated in jail at Concord and then brought to Boston in a special car, thus handcuffed and chained together. On detraining at the North Station, the handcuffed and chained aliens were exposed to newspaper photographers and again thus exposed at the wharf where they took the boat for Deer Island. The Department of Justice agents in charge of the arrested aliens appear to have taken pains to have them thus exposed to public photographing.

Private rooms were searched in omnibus fashion; trunks, bureaus, suit cases, and boxes broken open; books and papers seized. I doubt whether a single search warrant was obtained or applied for.
* * *

* * *

At Deer Island the conditions were unfit and chaotic. No adequate preparations had been made to receive and care for so large a number of people. Some of the steam pipes were burst or disconnected. The place was cold; the weather was severe. The cells were not properly equipped with sanitary appliances. There was no adequate number of guards or officials to take a census of and properly care for so many. For several days the arrested aliens were held practically incommunicado. There was dire confusion of authority as between the immigration forces and the Department of Justice forces, and the city officials who had charge of the prison. Most of this confusion and the resultant hardship to the arrested aliens was probably unintentional * * *. Undoubtedly it did have some additional terrorizing effect upon the aliens. Inevitably the atmosphere of lawless disregard of the rights and feelings of these aliens as human beings affected, consciously or unconsciously, the inspectors who shortly began at Deer Island the hearings, the basis of the records involving the determination of their right to remain in this country.

In the early days at Deer Island one alien committed suicide by throwing himself from the fifth floor and dashing his brains out in the corridor below in the presence of other horrified aliens. One was committed as insane; others were driven nearly, if not quite, to the verge of insanity.

After many days of confusion, the aliens themselves, under the leadership of one or two of the most intelligent and most conversant with English, constituted a committee, and represented to Assistant Commissioner Sullivan that, if given an opportunity, they would themselves clean up the quarters and arrange for the orderly service of food and the distribution of mail. This offer was wisely accepted, and thereupon the prisoners created a government of their own, called, ironically, I suppose, "The Soviet Republic of Deer Island." Through the assistance of this so-called Soviet government, conditions orderly, tolerable, not inhumane, were created after perhaps 10 days or 2 weeks of filth, confusion, and unnecessary suffering. It is not without significance that these aliens, thus arrested under charges of conspiracy to overthrow our government by force and violence, were, while under arrest, many of them illegally, found to be capable of organizing amongst themselves, with the consent of and in amicable co-operation with their keepers, an effective and democratic form of local government.

Colyer v. Skeffington, 265 Fed. 17, 44–45 (D.Mass.1920), *reversed in part sub nom. Skeffington v. Katzeff*, 277 Fed. 129 (1st Cir.1922).

b. Constitutional Limits on National Security Inadmissibility

The leading modern precedent on the constitutionality of inadmissibility grounds is the 1972 U.S. Supreme Court decision in *Kleindienst v. Mandel*. In reading *Mandel*, you may find it useful to know that the Supreme Court has long struggled—in many contexts not involving immigration and citizenship—to define First Amendment limits on government restrictions or punishments for subversive activities or for advocacy of unlawful action. An early twentieth century milestone was Justice Holmes' "clear and present danger" test in *Schenck v. United States,* 249 U.S. 47, 39 S.Ct. 247, 63 L.Ed. 470 (1919).

Several years before *Mandel,* the Court seemed to have reached an important landmark by providing the tightest limits yet on government action. In *Brandenburg v. Ohio,* 395 U.S. 444, 89 S.Ct. 1827, 23 L.Ed.2d 430 (1969) (per curiam), the Court ruled that the First Amendment forbids government action proscribing unlawful advocacy "except where such advocacy is directed to inciting or producing imminent lawless action and is likely to incite or produce such action." *Brandenburg* led some to think that the Court might substantially limit exclusion based on writings or speech when *Mandel* appeared on its docket.

KLEINDIENST v. MANDEL

Supreme Court of the United States, 1972.
408 U.S. 753, 92 S.Ct. 2576, 33 L.Ed.2d 683.

MR. JUSTICE BLACKMUN delivered the opinion of the Court.

[Ernest Mandel was a well-known Belgian author who described himself as "a revolutionary Marxist" but not a member of the Communist party. His writings and activities rendered him excludable under the pre–1990 version of INA § 212(a)(28), which set forth a long list of excludable aliens, including "anarchists," "those who advocate or teach ... opposition to all organized government," and members of any branch of the Communist Party. Mandel had visited the United States twice before filing the unsuccessful visa application that led to this litigation. Both times, apparently unbeknownst to him, he had been adjudged excludable under § 212(a)(28) as one who advocates or teaches or publishes material advocating or teaching "the economic, international, and governmental doctrines of world communism." Both times he had been the beneficiary of a waiver under INA § 212(d)(3). Then in 1969 he applied for a nonimmigrant visa to attend conferences in the United States. He was informed of his excludability, and after several rounds of correspondence, he was told that the Attorney General would not grant a waiver this time, because, in the Attorney General's view, he had violated the terms of his earlier admissions by deviating from the stated purposes of those trips. Mandel and several of those who had invited him to this country filed suit. The District Court ruled for the plaintiffs.]

II

Until 1875 alien migration to the United States was unrestricted. The Act of March 3, 1875, 18 Stat. 477, barred convicts and prostitutes. Seven years later Congress passed the first general immigration statute. * * * Section 2 of [a 1903] Act made ineligible for admission "anarchists, or persons who believe in or advocate the overthrow by force or violence of the Government of the United States or of all government or of all forms of law." * * * [In 1918,] Congress expanded the provisions for the exclusion of subversive aliens. Title II of the Alien Registration Act of 1940, 54 Stat. 671, amended the 1918 Act to bar aliens who, at any time, had advocated or were members of or affiliated with organizations that advocated violent overthrow of the United States Government.

In the years that followed, after extensive investigation and numerous reports by congressional committees, Congress passed the Internal Security Act of 1950, 64 Stat. 987. This Act dispensed with the requirement of the 1940 Act of a finding in each case, with respect to members of the Communist Party, that the party did in fact advocate violent overthrow of the Government. These provisions were carried forward into the Immigration and Nationality Act of 1952.

We thus have almost continuous attention on the part of Congress since 1875 to the problems of immigration and of excludability of certain defined classes of aliens. The pattern generally has been one of increasing control with particular attention, for almost 70 years now, first to anarchists and then to those with communist affiliation or views.

III

It is clear that Mandel personally, as an unadmitted and nonresident alien, had no constitutional right of entry to this country as a nonimmigrant or otherwise. *United States ex rel. Turner v. Williams,* 194 U.S. 279, 292, 24 S.Ct. 719, 723, 48 L.Ed. 979 (1904); *United States ex rel. Knauff v. Shaughnessy,* 338 U.S. 537, 542, 70 S.Ct. 309, 312, 94 L.Ed. 317 (1950); *Galvan v. Press,* 347 U.S. 522, 530–532, 74 S.Ct. 737, 742–743, 98 L.Ed. 911 (1954); *see Harisiades v. Shaughnessy,* 342 U.S. 580, 592, 72 S.Ct. 512, 520, 96 L.Ed. 586 (1952).

The appellees concede this. Indeed, the American appellees assert that "they sue to enforce their rights, individually and as members of the American public, and assert none on the part of the invited alien." "Dr. Mandel is in a sense made a plaintiff because he is symbolic of the problem."

The case, therefore, comes down to the narrow issue whether the First Amendment confers upon the appellee professors, because they wish to hear, speak, and debate with Mandel in person, the ability to determine that Mandel should be permitted to enter the country or, in other words, to compel the Attorney General to allow Mandel's admission.

IV

In a variety of contexts this Court has referred to a First Amendment right to "receive information and ideas":

> It is now well established that the Constitution protects the right to receive information and ideas. "This freedom [of speech and press] ... necessarily protects the right to receive...."

Stanley v. Georgia, 394 U.S. 557, 564, 89 S.Ct. 1243, 1247, 22 L.Ed.2d 542 (1969).

* * *

In the present case, the District Court majority held:

The concern of the First Amendment is not with a non-resident alien's individual and personal interest in entering and being heard, but with the rights of the citizens of the country to have the alien enter and to hear him explain and seek to defend his views * * *.

The Government disputes this conclusion on two grounds. First, it argues that exclusion of Mandel involves no restriction on First Amendment rights at all since what is restricted is "only action—the action of the alien in coming into this country." Principal reliance is placed on *Zemel v. Rusk*, 381 U.S. 1, 85 S.Ct. 1271, 14 L.Ed.2d 179 (1965), where the Government's refusal to validate an American passport for travel to Cuba was upheld. The rights asserted there were those of the passport applicant himself. The Court held that his right to travel and his asserted ancillary right to inform himself about Cuba did not outweigh substantial "foreign policy considerations affecting all citizens" that, with the backdrop of the Cuban missile crisis, were characterized as the "weightiest considerations of national security." *Id.*, at 13, 16, 85 S.Ct., at 1279. The rights asserted here, in some contrast, are those of American academics who have invited Mandel to participate with them in colloquia debates, and discussion in the United States. In light of the Court's previous decisions concerning the "right to receive information," we cannot realistically say that the problem facing us disappears entirely or is nonexistent because the mode of regulation bears directly on physical movement. * * *

The Government also suggests that the First Amendment is inapplicable because appellees have free access to Mandel's ideas through his books and speeches, and because "technological developments," such as tapes or telephone hook-ups, readily supplant his physical presence. This argument overlooks what may be particular qualities inherent in sustained, face-to-face debate, discussion and questioning. While alternative means of access to Mandel's ideas might be a relevant factor were we called upon to balance First Amendment rights against governmental regulatory interests—a balance we find unnecessary here in light of the discussion that follows in Part V—we are loath to hold on this record that existence of other alternatives extinguishes altogether any constitutional interest on the part of the appellees in this particular form of access.

V

Recognition that First Amendment rights are implicated, however, is not dispositive of our inquiry here. In accord with ancient principles of the international law of nation-states, the Court in *The Chinese Exclusion Case,* 130 U.S. 581, 609, 9 S.Ct. 623, 631, 32 L.Ed. 1068 (1889), and in *Fong Yue Ting v. United States,* 149 U.S. 698, 13 S.Ct. 1016, 37 L.Ed. 905 (1893), held broadly, as the Government describes it, that the power to exclude aliens is "inherent in sovereignty, necessary for maintaining normal international relations and defending the country against foreign encroachments and dangers—a power to be exercised exclusively by the political branches of government...." Since that time, the Court's general reaffirmations of this principle have been legion. The Court without exception has sustained Congress' "plenary power to make rules for the admission of aliens and to exclude those who possess those characteristics which Congress has forbidden." *Boutilier v. Immigration and Naturalization Service,* 387 U.S. 118, 123, 87 S.Ct. 1563, 1567, 18 L.Ed.2d 661 (1967). "[O]ver no conceivable subject is the legislative power of Congress more complete than it is over" the admission of aliens. *Oceanic Navigation Co. v. Stranahan,* 214 U.S. 320, 339, 29 S.Ct. 671, 676, 53 L.Ed. 1013 (1909). * * *

We are not inclined in the present context to reconsider this line of cases. Indeed, the appellees, in contrast to the *amicus,* do not ask that we do so. The appellees recognize the force of these many precedents. In seeking to sustain the decision below, they concede that Congress could enact a blanket prohibition against entry of all aliens falling into the class defined by §§ 212(a)(28)(D) and (G)(v), and that First Amendment rights could not override that decision. But they contend that by providing a waiver procedure, Congress clearly intended that persons ineligible under the broad provision of the section would be temporarily admitted when appropriate "for humane reasons and for reasons of public interest." S.Rep.No. 1137, 82d Cong., 2d Sess. 12 (1952). They argue that the Executive's implementation of this congressional mandate through decision whether to grant a waiver in each individual case must be limited by the First Amendment rights of persons like appellees. Specifically, their position is that the First Amendment rights must prevail, at least where the Government advances no justification for failing to grant a waiver. They point to the fact that waivers have been granted in the vast majority of cases.

Appellees' First Amendment argument would prove too much. In almost every instance of an alien excludable under § 212(a)(28), there are probably those who would wish to meet and speak with him. The ideas of most such aliens might not be so influential as those of Mandel, nor his American audience so numerous, nor the planned discussion forums so impressive. But the First Amendment does not protect only the articulate, the well known, and the popular. Were we to endorse the proposition that governmental power to withhold a waiver must yield whenever a bona fide claim is made that American citizens wish to meet and talk with an alien excludable under § 212(a)(28), one of two unsatisfactory results would necessarily ensue. Either every claim would prevail, in which case the plenary discretionary authority Congress granted the Executive becomes a nullity, or courts in each case would be required to weigh the strength of the audience's interest against that of the Government in refusing a waiver to the particular alien applicant, according to some as yet undetermined standard. The dangers and the undesirability of making that determination on the basis of factors such as the size of the audience or the probity of the speaker's ideas are obvious. Indeed, it is for precisely this reason that the waiver decision has, properly, been placed in the hands of the Executive.

Appellees seek to soften the impact of this analysis by arguing, as has been noted, that the First Amendment claim should prevail, at least where no justification is advanced for denial of a waiver. The Government would have us reach this question, urging a broad decision that Congress has delegated the waiver decision to the Executive in its sole and unfettered discretion, and any reason or no reason may be given. This record, however, does not require that we do so, for the Attorney General did inform Mandel's counsel of the reason for refusing him a waiver. And that reason was facially legitimate and bona fide.

* * *

In summary, plenary congressional power to make policies and rules for exclusion of aliens has long been firmly established. In the case of an alien excludable under § 212(a)(28), Congress has delegated conditional exercise of this power to the Executive. We hold that when the Executive exercises this power negatively on the basis of a facially legitimate and bona fide reason, the courts will neither look behind the exercise of that discretion, nor test it by balancing its justification against the First Amendment interests of those who seek personal communication with the applicant. What First Amendment or other grounds may be available for attacking exercise of discretion for which no justification whatsoever is advanced is a question we neither address or decide in this case.

Reversed.

MR. JUSTICE DOUGLAS, dissenting.

Under *The Chinese Exclusion Case*, 130 U.S. 581, 9 S.Ct. 623, 32 L.Ed. 1068, rendered in 1889, there could be no doubt but that Congress would have the power to exclude any class of aliens from these shores. The accent at the time was on race. Mr. Justice Field, writing for the Court, said: "If, therefore, the government of the United States, through its legislative department, considers the presence of foreigners of a different race in this country, who will not assimilate with us, to be dangerous to its peace and security, their exclusion is not to be stayed because at the time there are no actual hostilities with the nation of which the foreigners are subjects." *Id.*, at 606, 9 S.Ct., at 630.

An ideological test, not a racial one, is used here. But neither, in my view, is permissible, as I have indicated on other occasions. Yet a narrower question is raised here. * * *

* * *

As a matter of statutory construction, I conclude that Congress never undertook to entrust the Attorney General with the discretion to pick and choose among the ideological offerings which alien lecturers tender from our platforms, allowing those palatable to him and disallowing others. The discretion entrusted to him concerns matters commonly within the competence of the Department of Justice—national security, importation of drugs, and the like.

I would affirm the judgment of the three-judge District Court.

MR. JUSTICE MARSHALL, with whom MR. JUSTICE BRENNAN joins, dissenting.

* * *

I, too, am stunned to learn that a country with our proud heritage has refused Dr. Mandel temporary admission. I am convinced that Americans cannot be denied the opportunity to hear Dr. Mandel's views in person because their Government disapproves of his ideas. Therefore, I dissent from today's decision and would affirm the judgment of the court below.

* * *

Today's majority apparently holds that Mandel may be excluded and Americans' First Amendment rights restricted because the Attorney General has given a "facially legitimate and bona fide reason" for refusing to waive Mandel's visa ineligibility. I do not understand the source of this unusual standard. Merely "legitimate" governmental interests cannot override constitutional rights. Moreover, the majority demands only "facial" legitimacy and good faith, by which it means that this Court will never "look behind" any reason the Attorney General gives. No citation is given for this kind of unprecedented deference to the Executive, nor can I imagine (nor am I told) the slightest justification for such a rule.

Even the briefest peek behind the Attorney General's reason for refusing a waiver in this case would reveal that it is a sham. The Attorney General informed appellees' counsel that the waiver was refused because Mandel's activities on a previous American visit "went far beyond the stated purposes of his trip . . . and represented a flagrant abuse of the opportunities afforded him to express his views in this country." But, as the Department of State had already conceded to appellees' counsel, Dr. Mandel "was apparently not informed that [his previous] visa was issued only after obtaining a waiver of ineligibility and therefore [Mandel] may not have been aware of the conditions and limitations attached to the [previous] visa issuance." There is *no* basis in the present record for concluding that Mandel's behavior on his previous visit was a "flagrant abuse"—or even willful or knowing departure—from visa restrictions. For good reason, the Government in this litigation has *never* relied on the Attorney General's reason to justify Mandel's exclusion. In these circumstances, the Attorney General's reason cannot possibly support a decision for the Government in this case. But without even remanding for a factual hearing to see if there is *any* support for the Attorney General's determination, the majority declares that his reason is sufficient to override appellees' First Amendment interests.

Even if the Attorney General had given a compelling reason for declining to grant a waiver under § 212(d)(3)(A), this would not, for me, end the case. As I understand the statutory scheme, Mandel is "ineligible" for a visa, and therefore inadmissible, solely because, within the terms of § 212(a)(28), he has advocated communist doctrine and has published writings advocating that doctrine. The waiver question under § 212(d)(3)(A) is totally secondary and dependent, since it is triggered here only by a determination of (a)(28) ineligibility. * * *

Accordingly, I turn to consider the constitutionality of the sole justification given by the Government here and below for excluding Mandel—that he "advocates" and "publish[es] ... printed matter ... advocating ... doctrines of world communism" within the terms of § 212(a)(28).

Still adhering to standard First Amendment doctrine, I do not see how (a)(28) can possibly represent a compelling governmental interest that overrides appellees' interests in hearing Mandel. Unlike (a)(27) or (a)(29), (a)(28) does not claim to exclude aliens who are likely to engage in subversive activity or who represent an active and present threat to the "welfare, safety, or security of the United States." Rather, (a)(28) excludes aliens solely because they have advocated communist doctrine. Our cases make clear, however, that government has no legitimate interest in stopping the flow of ideas. It has no power to restrict the mere advocacy of communist doctrine, divorced from incitement to imminent lawless action. For those who are not sure that they have attained the final and absolute truth, all ideas, even those forcefully urged, are a contribution to the ongoing political dialogue. The First Amendment represents the view of the Framers that "the path of safety lies in the opportunity to discuss freely supposed grievances and proposed remedies; and that the fitting remedy for evil counsels is good ones"—"more speech." *Whitney v. California*, 274 U.S., at 375, 377, 47 S.Ct., at 648, 649, 71 L.Ed. 1095 (Brandeis, J., concurring). * * *

* * *

The heart of Appellants' position in this case * * * is that the Government's power is distinctively broad and unreviewable because "[t]he regulation in question is directed at the admission of aliens." Thus, in the appellants' view, this case is no different from a long line of cases holding that the power to exclude aliens is left exclusively to the "political" branches of Government, Congress, and the Executive.

These cases are not the strongest precedents in the United States Reports, and the majority's baroque approach reveals its reluctance to rely on them completely. They include such milestones as *The Chinese Exclusion Case*, 130 U.S. 581, 9 S.Ct. 623, 32 L.Ed. 1068 (1889), and *Fong Yue Ting v. United States*, 149 U.S. 698, 13 S.Ct. 1016, 37 L.Ed. 905 (1893), in which this Court upheld the Government's power to exclude and expel Chinese aliens from our midst.

But none of these old cases must be "reconsidered" or overruled to strike down Dr. Mandel's exclusion, for none of them was concerned with the rights of American citizens. All of them involved only rights of the excluded aliens themselves. At least when the rights of Americans are involved, there is no basis for concluding that the power to exclude aliens is absolute. "When Congress' exercise of one of its enumerated powers clashes with those individual liberties protected by the Bill of Rights, it is our 'delicate and difficult task' to determine whether the resulting restriction on freedom can be tolerated." *United States v. Robel*, 389 U.S. 258, 264, 88 S.Ct. 419, 424, 19 L.Ed.2d 508 (1967). * * *

* * *

I do not mean to suggest that simply because some Americans wish to hear an alien speak, they can automatically compel even his temporary admission to our country. Government may prohibit aliens from even temporary admission if exclusion is necessary to protect a compelling governmental interest.[6] Actual threats to the national security, public health needs, and genuine requirements of law enforcement are the most apparent interests that would surely be compelling. But in Dr. Mandel's case, the Government has, and claims, no such compelling interest. Mandel's visit was to be temporary. His "ineligibility" for a visa was based solely on § 212(a)(28). The only governmental interest embodied in that section is the Government's desire to keep certain ideas out of circulation in this country. This is hardly a compelling governmental interest. Section (a)(28) may not be the basis for excluding an alien when Americans wish to hear him. Without any claim that Mandel "live" is an actual threat to this country, there is no difference between excluding Mandel because of his ideas and keeping his books out because of their ideas. Neither is permitted.

* * *

NOTES AND QUESTIONS: THE IMPLICATIONS OF MANDEL

1. The *Mandel* majority takes an unusual approach. It works hard to find that a First Amendment issue exists, because of the interests of prospective U.S. citizen listeners, even though the circulation of Mandel's books and ideas was not hindered, but then adopts a novel standard for resolving First Amendment questions in some immigration settings.

If the First Amendment is implicated, why not apply strict scrutiny, as the First Amendment rights of citizens normally require? Recall that in *Fiallo v. Bell,* 430 U.S. 787, 97 S.Ct. 1473, 52 L.Ed.2d 50 (1977), in Chapter Five, p. 293 *supra*, the Court rejected a citizens' rights argument, but in a setting that did not involve the First Amendment. Consider these comments on approach-

---

6. I agree with the majority that courts should not inquire into such things as the "probity of the speaker's ideas." Neither should the Executive, however. Where Americans wish to hear an alien, and their claim is not a demonstrated sham, the crucial question is whether the Government's interest in excluding the alien is compelling.

ing the constitutional aspects of immigration law by asking how immigration decisions affect citizens:

> Looking at constitutional immigration law by focusing on citizens' rights might seem to banish aliens from the constitutional fold. In fact, however, a citizens' rights focus leaves considerable room for treating aliens fairly within our constitutional traditions. Poor treatment of aliens often means poor treatment of citizens. For example, if we discriminate on the basis of race in selecting immigrants, we may be hurting citizens in several ways. We may deprive them of reunification with family members, and we may cast a stigma upon members of particular groups as being less worthy of inclusion in our immigrant stream. We may also hurt citizens by adopting discriminatory principles that can be applied detrimentally to citizens in other contexts.

Motomura, *Whose Immigration Law?: Citizens, Aliens, and the Constitution*, 97 Colum.L.Rev. 1567, 1572 (1997).

On the other hand, would a focus on the rights of citizens who wish to meet and talk with the noncitizen really distinguish the "old cases" that Justice Marshall says "involved only rights of the excluded aliens themselves"? Many of those noncitizens could have found citizen co-plaintiffs, had that been seen as crucial.

2. What does it mean that the Court asks the government for a "facially legitimate and bona fide reason" for its action? Perhaps it makes little difference to unsuccessful plaintiffs whether they lose on the merits because the court defers so much to the government or because no real First Amendment issue exists when the government merely refuses admission, or they lose because the court lacks jurisdiction. But the differences among these rationales may matter for the ultimate development of a sound body of law. *Mandel* may be significant not for its deference to the government, but rather for suggesting that the courts might have any role at all in reviewing immigration decisions of this type.

This view received a boost in 1977, when the Court stated in *Fiallo* that past cases "reflect acceptance of a limited judicial responsibility under the Constitution even with respect to the power of Congress to regulate the admission and exclusion of aliens." Several federal appeals courts have treated the "facially legitimate and bona fide reason" test as the same as rational basis review. *See, e.g., Johnson v. Whitehead*, 647 F.3d 120, at 127 (4th Cir. 2011); *Ablang v. Reno*, 52 F.3d 801, 804 (9th Cir. 1995); *Azizi v. Thornburgh*, 908 F.2d 1130, 1133 n.2 (2d Cir. 1990). There is some support for viewing the standard as even more deferential to the political branches than rational basis review. *See Bangura v. Hansen*, 434 F.3d 487, 495 (6th Cir. 2006) (citing *Fiallo v. Bell*, 430 U.S. 787, 798–99, 97 S.Ct. 1473, 52 L.Ed.2d 50 (1977)).

Though courts applied *Mandel* to reject many challenges to occasional heavy-handed visa denials during the 1980s, a few decisions gave modest teeth to the "facially legitimate and bona fide reason" standard. One court struck down certain State Department travel restrictions on representatives of the Palestine Liberation Organization (PLO). According to the court, the government's reasons were not facially legitimate under the First Amendment, because they were based on the content of the proposed discussions and were "directly related to the suppression of a political debate with American citizens." *Harvard Law School Forum v. Shultz*, 633 F.Supp. 525, 531 (D.Mass.1986), *vacated without published opinion*, 852 F.2d 563 (1st Cir. 1986). A thorough account of how *Mandel* led to curtailing ideological exclusion, through both litigation and the decisions of the political branches—and of the lawyers' battle in *Mandel* itself—appears in Schuck, *Kleindienst v. Mandel: Plenary Power v. the Professors*, in Immigration Stories 169 (D. Martin & P. Schuck eds. 2005).

If courts are at least considering these constitutional arguments, can they refine the substantive test without intruding unduly on national security concerns or upsetting U.S. foreign relations? Could courts fashion standards that would defer less to the government than the "facially legitimate and bona fide reason," and better serve First Amendment values while still attending to the needs of an efficient immigration system? Or is more deference to the executive branch necessary to be very certain that terrorists and other truly dangerous foreigners may not enter the country?

3. Alternatively, imagine a different way that *Mandel* might have been litigated. Consider the array of potential plaintiffs. Might any of them have been more successful if they had framed the case not as a first amendment issue at all, but as a denial of procedural due process? Would it have made a difference, for example, if they had challenged the lack of an opportunity to present evidence to overcome the waiver denial?

4. Chapter Six, pp. 565–68, explained that consular decisions made overseas are generally not reviewable in court. What is the relevance of *Mandel* for this consular nonreviewability? Does *Mandel* endorse consular nonreviewability, or does asking the government for a "facially legitimate and bona fide reason" cast doubt on complete insulation of consular decisions? Alternatively, is consular nonreviewability most vulnerable if viewed as a denial of procedural due process?

5. Justice Douglas would overturn the visa denial based solely on his reading of the statute and the underlying congressional intent. Apparently he would find that the Attorney General, under the statute, *must* waive excludability unless he finds that the alien's presence would raise concerns "commonly within the competence of the Department of Justice—national security, importation of drugs, and the like." Can this possibly have been the intent of Congress in enacting paragraph (28) and making it waivable under subsection (d)(3)? Why would Congress have added paragraph (28) when other subsections addressed security and criminal concerns directly?

6. Objections to exclusions under former INA § 212(a)(28) emphasized not only the provision's substantive reach, but also the very process of administering it. One commentator quotes a letter from an official of a British association of teachers declining an invitation to a U.S. conference in the United States. The official wrote:

> The record of actual refusals [of visas under these sections] is small, not because of the liberal attitude of the United States Government, but because many of our members, as a matter of principle, consider it anathema to have to attest to their political views and affiliations; thus,

many academics will not apply because they do not wish to place themselves in the position of signing declarations to that effect.

Scanlan, *Aliens in the Marketplace of Ideas: The Government, the Academy, and the McCarran–Walter Act,* 66 Tex.L.Rev. 1481, 1499 (1988). How much weight should these concerns about process carry in the post–9/11 world?

c. Terrorism-related Inadmissibility Grounds

After the fall of the Berlin Wall, Congress used the Immigration Act of 1990, Pub.L. 101–649, 104 Stat. 4978, to completely recast the national security-related exclusion grounds, now in INA § 212(a)(3). (INA § 237(a)(4) reflects similar reworking of the analogous deportation grounds.) Congress repealed or greatly curtailed exclusion or deportation grounds for anarchists, members of the Communist Party and other totalitarian parties, as such—replacing those grounds with removal based on terrorism and foreign policy findings.

(i) Defining Terrorism

Terrorism is notoriously hard to define. Gerald Neuman, writing before September 11, 2001, summarized the difficulties:

> One [difficulty] is identifying the forms of violent action that are sufficiently extreme, whether because of the methods employed or because of the victims targeted, that they deserve condemnation as terrorism. Another is the problem of distinguishing terroristic acts performed by governments—"state terrorism"—from other acts of governmental force. A third is the justifiability of acts otherwise characterized as terrorism when they are performed by "national liberation" movements vindicating the right of a people to self-determination. International cooperation against terrorism has attempted to finesse this difficulty of definition by focusing piecemeal on particular forms of violence employed by terrorists, and agreeing upon measures addressed to those forms of violence as objectively defined, regardless of any characterization as "terrorist" and regardless of the political motivations of the actors. Thus, conventions concern themselves with unlawful acts against the safety of aircraft, and unlawful acts against the safety of ships, as well as violence against international protected persons (such as heads of states and representatives of states). The International Convention Against the Taking of Hostages includes the intention of compelling a third party to perform an action as an element of its definition of hostage-taking, but does not require that the purpose be political rather than economic or personal.

Neuman, *Terrorism, Selective Deportation and the First Amendment after Reno v. AADC,* 14 Geo. Imm.L.J. 313, 322–23 (2000). For a comprehensive survey, see Perry, *The Breadth and Impact of the Terrorism–Related Grounds of Inadmissibility of the INA,* 06–10 Imm. Briefings (2006).

Current INA § 212(a)(3)(B) reflects significant post–9/11 expansion by the USA PATRIOT Act, Pub.L. 107–56, 115 Stat. 272 (2001), and the REAL ID Act of 2005, Pub.L. 109–13, Div. B., §§ 103–105, 119 Stat. 231, 306–10. Noncitizens are inadmissible if, among other things, they have engaged in terrorist activity, or if a consular officer has reasonable ground to believe they are likely to engage in such activity after entry. Also inadmissible are a wide group of noncitizens who publicly endorse or espouse terrorist activities, and representatives of organizations that do so.

Terrorist activity. "Terrorist activity" is defined in terms of violent acts committed or planned, regardless of motivation. Spouses and children of persons barred under this ground may also be inadmissible. INA § 212(a)(3)(B)(i), (ii). "Engage in terrorist activity" is defined broadly in § 212(a)(3)(B)(iv) to include providing "material support" for terrorist activity or organizations. INA § 212(a)(3)(F) bars persons determined by the Attorney General and the Secretary of State to have been *associated* with a terrorist organization and who intend to engage, even incidentally, in activities that could endanger the welfare, safety, or security of the United States.

Terrorist organizations. Key to these inadmissibility grounds is the definition of "terrorist organization" in § 212(a)(3)(B)(vi). INA § 219 sets out a procedure for the Secretary of State to designate terrorist organizations; these are now known as "Tier I" organizations. Designation under § 219 has major ramifications beyond immigration. Any person—citizen or noncitizen—who provides material support to a § 219 organization is subject to severe criminal penalties, and the Secretary of the Treasury may freeze the organization's assets. 18 U.S.C. § 2339B; INA § 219(a)(2)(C). In May 2011, there were over 40 Tier I terrorist organizations. Several lawsuits by organizations challenging these designations have established that the procedures must conform to due process. *See National Council of Resistance of Iran v. Department of State*, 251 F.3d 192 (D.C.Cir. 2001). Courts also review the findings that an organization is a foreign organization and that it engages in terrorist activity. But the third requirement for § 219 designation—that an organization's terrorist activity threatens U.S. security—is a nonjusticiable political question. *See People's Mojahedin Organization of Iran v. Department of State*, 327 F.3d 1238 (D.C.Cir. 2003).

A second, more streamlined procedure allows the Secretary of State to designate additional organizations, though this "Tier II" designation has only immigration consequences and does not trigger criminal sanctions or asset forfeiture. A third part of the terrorist organization definition, known as Tier III, expansively includes any "group of two or more individuals, whether organized or not," which engages in committing a terrorist activity or (with certain limitations) inciting it, preparing or planning a terrorist activity, and gathering information on potential targets.

Even before their post–9/11 expansion, Neuman commented: "the statutory definitions of 'terrorist activity' and 'engag[ing] in terrorist activity' are extraordinarily broad, so broad that Congress surely never intended that they be enforced against all aliens who come within them. Congress has cast a very broad net in order to facilitate the effective enforcement of restrictions against a narrower class of terrorists on a discretionary basis." Neuman, 14 Geo. Imm.L.J. at 321–22. For example, in 1997 the Department of State issued a visitor's visa to Gerry Adams, the leader of Sinn Fein, the political wing of the Irish Republican Army. Adams was classified as a "terrorist" in view of his association with the IRA, but he was granted a waiver—as on past occasions—in view of the prevailing cease-fire in Northern Ireland. *See* Associated Press, *Sinn Fein leader granted U.S. visa*, Aug. 15, 1997. Adams was later a key figure accepting a comprehensive April 1998 agreement that ultimately led to the restoration of the Northern Ireland Assembly, the creation of a broad government structure involving both Catholics and Protestants, and the decommissioning of armed militias in the country. Is there anything wrong with making visa decisions in these ways, giving broad discretion to the executive branch?

To better understand these provisions, try applying INA § 212(a)(3) to the following problems. Then assess, based on the constitutional decisions that you have considered thus far, whether a finding of inadmissibility under the statute would withstand a constitutional challenge.

PROBLEMS

10. W was convicted in the United Kingdom 23 years ago for his involvement, as a 19–year–old, with an attack on a British military base in Northern Ireland. Three soldiers were injured, but no one was killed. W was later caught and convicted, serving a seven-year sentence in a British prison. After his release he found work as a skilled mechanic, severed ties with the Irish Republican Army, and later became a local leader with an ecumenical peace group seeking to build channels of communication and friendship between Catholics and Protestants. Two years ago he married an woman, a U.S. citizen, whom he had met at an NGO conference. Her visa petition for his admission as an immediate relative has been approved. Is W inadmissible? If so, are any waivers available?

11. You are a consular officer considering the issuance of a student visa to graduate student Y under § 101(a)(15)(F). A check of government lookout databases reveals intelligence information about Y, which the analyst says is well-corroborated. It states that Y has attended six meetings of a front organization for a clandestine group believed to be responsible for recent bombings in Y's home country. A check with local police authorities there, however, reveals no convictions or even arrests for any offenses. They believe him to be a legitimate student. During his interview with you, Y presents a

thorough and complete story about his bachelor's and master's degree programs, where he had a strong record. Recommendation letters from his professors and employers vouch for the seriousness of his academic pursuits, and the prominent U.S. university in which he has enrolled has sent messages to you, bolstered by letters from that state's congressional delegation, about how eager they are to receive him. Nothing in the interview suggests any affiliation with the organization, despite several lines of questions meant to probe for weaknesses in his account. What should you do? If you are uncertain about whether he is a risk, should you approve or disapprove the visa? Is Y inadmissible? On what ground or grounds? Are there other steps that you or the State Department must pursue before applying the ground?

12.   You are an immigration attorney recently contacted by Z, admitted to the United States in H–1B status five years ago from Ruritania. Shortly after his departure, a violent civil war broke out in Ruritania, and Z's ethnic group, the Rodolfians, has suffered greatly from damage to structures and the economy of the region and from government crackdowns, because the group is identified with the insurgents. Three years ago Z sent a $1,000 contribution in response to an appeal from the Rodolfian Liberation League (RLL), which has always billed itself as a political party and mutual aid society. It had invited successful Rodolfians living abroad to contribute to a special fund meant to support families that had suffered during the conflict and to rebuild communities damaged in the fighting. Z also persuaded other U.S. citizen and immigrant friends to send similar contributions. He sent a smaller donation the following year, but then ceased support, because he read that the RLL had become directly involved in the violent struggle. Z's employer has now obtained approval of an employment-based visa petition for him, and his priority date is current. He is ready to apply for adjustment of status, but he is deeply worried that these gifts may disqualify him. What is his risk? What grounds of inadmissibility might apply to him?

Policy Aspects of Terrorism–Based Inadmissibility

1.   The preceding problems highlight the discretion of immigration authorities to act against noncitizens on the basis of speech or association. Is such discretion a necessary tool in protecting the nation against terrorism and other threats? Or is it instead a worrisome grant of power to the executive branch? Could the statute be drawn more narrowly and still afford adequate diplomatic tools and protection against terrorist entry?

2.   In 1987, without amending the INA itself, Congress responded to objections to "ideological exclusion" with a temporary measure prohibiting exclusion or deportation "because of any past, current, or expected beliefs, statements, or associations which, if engaged in by a United States

citizen in the United States, would be protected under the Constitution of the United States." Foreign Relations Authorization Act, Fiscal Years 1988 and 1989, Pub.L. 100–204, § 901(a), 101 Stat. 1331 (1987).

Would this approach better serve First Amendment values? Or could consular officers no longer act on the basis of reasonable but imperfect information suggesting that a visa applicant has engaged or is likely to engage in terrorism? Short of a past conviction or an unlikely confession during an interview to violent activities or plans, what can a consular officer or intelligence officer rely on in determining whether a person is involved in terrorism *besides* past associations or statements? Given that such judgments will almost always be uncertain, how should we allocate the risk of error—in favor of admission or in favor of exclusion?

3. Membership in a Communist or "other totalitarian party" remains an inadmissibility ground, but only for noncitizens coming as immigrants. INA § 212(a)(3)(D). What views of free speech and membership in the national community—or any other rationales—underlie this distinction between immigrants and nonimmigrants? More generally, can a society based on tolerance validly bar prospective members based solely on a disapproved ideology, or on affiliation with a disapproved organization? Or may democratic societies legitimately be intolerant of Communists, fascists, white supremacists, believers in theocracy, or others who do not accept the basic principle of tolerance itself? Does the answer vary depending on how serious a threat the alternative ideology happens to pose at the time?

(ii) Material Support to Terrorism

It plainly makes sense to bar admission to persons who knowingly provide funds or other support to violent terrorist activity. But achieving that goal raises several separate questions. First, since most financial supporters of violence seek to mask their involvement, what quantum of evidence must the government produce—or at least gather for internal review—to justify exclusion? Second, must the person intend that the funds support violence, or is it enough that person intends to support political or charitable activities carried out by organizations with terrorist wings? And third, what degree of intent is required—mere negligence or some other level of knowledge, awareness, or intent?

If the law requires proof of intent to support violent activities, the government's task in marshaling the necessary information is obviously more daunting. It can be hard enough to follow the money as it passes to largely clandestine organizations, to show that the person's contributions actually went to a questionable recipient. It can be quite difficult to prove the donor's intent, especially as to organizations with both violent and nonviolent purposes. Inadmissibility grounds that are sweeping, with a low *mens rea* threshold and a broad definition of terrorist organizations or activities, may bar entry based on utterly innocent acts—a classic case of overbreadth. But narrowly tailored inadmissibility grounds may let some truly dangerous terrorism supporters into the country—where they might go beyond fundraising to help perpetrate violent acts.

The BIA's primary decision on the material support bar follows. The issue was whether the noncitizen, a national of Burma, qualified for asylum or withholding of removal. (As Chapter Eight will explain, these are forms of protection against return to a country where persecution is threatened.) Because persons inadmissible under many of the terrorism-related grounds are ineligible for asylum or withholding of removal, the BIA had to decide if the noncitizen's admitted donation of $685 to the Chin National Front amounted to material support for a terrorist organization.

MATTER OF S–K–

Board of Immigration Appeals, 2006.
23 I & N Dec. 936.

PAULEY, BOARD MEMBER:

* * *

The respondent, a native and citizen of Burma, is a Christian and an ethnic Chin. According to the respondent, she faces persecution and/or torture if returned to Burma because the Government, currently a military dictatorship ruled by the majority Burman ethnic group, regularly commits human rights abuses against ethnic and religious minorities and, in fact, arrested and detained both the respondent's brother and fiancé, the latter ultimately being killed by the military.

In 2001, the respondent became acquainted with an undercover agent for the Chin National Front ("CNF") who was a friend of her deceased fiancé, became sympathetic to the CNF's goal of securing freedom for ethnic Chin people and donated money to the organization for approximately 11 months. In addition, she attempted to donate some other goods, such as a camera and binoculars, to the CNF, but they were confiscated after she had given them to the undercover agent. The agent informed the respondent that she should flee Burma because the Burmese military, known to torture anyone affiliated with the CNF, had seen a letter written by the respondent to the CNF; the military knew that the respondent was the person who had attempted to provide the material goods. The respondent was actually residing in Singapore at the time, but since her temporary work visa was about to expire and she could not return to Burma, she fled to the United States in order to request asylum.

Although the Immigration Judge found that the respondent had established a well-founded fear of persecution in order to qualify for asylum, he denied her application for relief because, by providing money and other support to the CNF, an organization which uses land mines and engages in armed conflict with the Burmese Government, the respondent provided material support to an organization or group of individuals who she knew, or had reason to know, uses firearms and explosives to endanger the safety of others or to cause substantial property damage. Therefore, she was statutorily barred from asylum and from withholding of removal * * *.

* * * We granted the respondent's request for oral argument in order for the parties to address what we viewed as the major questions arising in the case: (1) what standards or definition should be used to assess whether the term "material support" should be defined narrowly or more broadly; whether it should take into consideration the mens rea of the provider, as proposed by the respondent; and whether it includes the type of support provided by the respondent to the CNF; and (2) to what extent, in light of our precedent, we should factor in an organization's purpose and goals in order to assess whether an organization, like the CNF, is engaged in terrorist activity. In other words, we asked the parties to address whether the use of justifiable force against an illegitimate regime and the right of people to self-determination, which the respondent argues is the CNF's purpose, is a valid purpose, which would not fall within the definition of terrorist activity under the Act. We will address these issues in reverse order.

II. ANALYSIS

A. *Terrorist Organization*

During oral argument and on appeal, the respondent argued that the Burmese Government is not legitimate because the military junta rules the country under martial law and crushes any attempts at democratic reform. According to the respondent, the United States does not recognize the Burmese Government's legislative acts, and therefore the CNF's actions are not unlawful under Burmese law. Rather, she asserts, the organization's actions are similar to those of forces fighting the Taliban in Afghanistan or forces rebelling against Saddam Hussein in Iraq, which are supported by the United States. Its goals are democracy and it uses force only in self-defense. Moreover, the CNF is allied with the National League of Democracy, which the United States has recognized as a legitimate representative of the Burmese people and is recognized by the United Nations. Therefore, the respondent contends that the Immigration Judge erred in concluding that the CNF is a terrorist organization.

Whether the CNF's actions are lawful in Burma is a question of foreign law and is a factual issue on which the respondent bears the burden of proof, inasmuch as the "evidence indicates" that the terrorism bar to asylum may apply. * * *

During oral argument, the respondent pointed to testimony from the Assistant Secretary of State describing the Burmese military as a "group of thugs," as well as to the fact that the United States Government has passed the Burmese Freedom and Democracy Act of 2003, acknowledging that the National League of Democracy is the legitimate representative of the Burmese people. * * *

* * * [T]he respondent acknowledged, upon questioning, that the United States does maintain a diplomatic relationship with the Burmese Government and maintains an embassy there. Therefore, in some sense or degree, the United States recognizes as legitimate the Burmese Government, which appears to consider the activities of the CNF unlawful.

Although the respondent urges us to determine that the Burmese Government is illegitimate and argues that we have such authority, we are unable to agree with the respondent's argument. While there may have been cases in which we determined that certain acts by foreign governments were unlawful in terms of harming individuals who sought asylum here, we have not gone so far as to determine that a foreign sovereignty would not be recognized by the United States Government. Such a determination is beyond our delegated authority and is a matter left to elected and other high-level officials in this country.

Furthermore, the respondent cites to past case law interpreting asylum applicants' claims and granting relief where aliens have attempted to overthrow governments that do not allow citizens to change the political structure and therefore exercise illegitimate power when prosecuting such individuals. In other words, she asserts that the motivation of the group seeking to effect change in a country must be analyzed in order to determine whether the harm produced is persecution or, as claimed in this case, terrorist activity. *See Matter of Izatula*, 20 I & N Dec. 149 (BIA 1990) (holding, in a case involving an alien who actively assisted the mujahedin in Afghanistan, that the general rule that prosecution for an attempt to overthrow a lawfully constituted government does not constitute persecution is inapplicable in countries where a coup is the only means of effectuating political change). During oral argument, counsel for the respondent acknowledged that by utilizing such factors to determine whether an organization falls within section 212(a)(3) of the Act, he was advocating that we apply a "totality of the circumstances" test.

We are unable to find any support for the respondent's assertion that such a test should be utilized. Our past case law is not inconsistent with some of the respondent's arguments. However, that case law does not address the bar to relief in section 212(a)(3)(B)(i)(I) of the Act. In this case, we are dealing with specific statutory language, which we read as applying to the respondent.

* * * [H]aving reviewed the statutory sections, we find that Congress intentionally drafted the terrorist bars to relief very broadly, to include even those people described as "freedom fighters," and it did not intend to give us discretion to create exceptions for members of organizations to which our Government might be sympathetic. Rather, Congress attempted to balance the harsh provisions set forth in the Act with a waiver [in INA § 212(d)(3)(B)], but it only granted the power to make exemptions to the Attorney General and the Secretaries of State and Homeland Security, who have not delegated such power to the Immigration Judges or the Board of Immigration Appeals.

* * * [T]here is no exception in the Act to the bar to relief in cases involving the use of justifiable force to repel attacks by forces of an illegitimate regime. As noted by the Immigration Judge, there was sufficient evidence in the record to conclude that the CNF uses firearms and/or explosives to engage in combat with the Burmese military, and the respondent has not provided evidence that would rebut this conclusion or lead us to interpret the Act differently. Moreover, the record shows that the respondent knew or should have known of the CNF's use of arms. Thus, assuming the respondent provided material support to the CNF, her sole remedy to extricate herself from the statutory bar appears to lie in the waiver afforded by Congress for this purpose, for which the DHS stated at oral argument she is eligible to apply. However, the Immigration Judges and the Board have no role in the adjudication of such a waiver.

B. *Materiality of Support Provided*

The respondent also argues that the type and amount of support which she provided to the CNF was not material. She asserts that the Immigration Judge failed to take into consideration whether the funds and goods she provided were relevant to the planning or implementation of a terrorist act, as allegedly required by the United States Court of Appeals for the Third Circuit in *Singh–Kaur v. Ashcroft*, [385 F.3d 293 (3d Cir. 2004)]. Since no evidence was submitted to support a conclusion that the respondent's contributions were relevant to a specific terrorist goal, the respondent asserts that finding that her contributions were material goes against the congressional intent to tie materiality to terrorist activity. * * *7

* * *

We are unaware of any legislative history which indicates a limitation on the definition of the term "material support." * * * Rather, the statute is clearly drafted in this respect to require only that the provider afford material support to a terrorist organization, with the sole exception being a showing by clear and convincing evidence that the actor did not know, and should not reasonably have known, that the organization was of that character. Section 212(a)(3)(B)(iv)(VI)(dd) of the Act. We thus reject the respondent's assertion that there must be a link between the provision of material support to a terrorist organization and the intended use by that

---

7. * * * While it is clear that our government leaders have taken a strict approach to dealing with suspected terrorists and have attempted to make it more difficult for those involved in terrorism to gain relief of any kind, they also have expressly provided a waiver that may be exercised in cases where the result reached under the terrorist bars to relief would not be consistent with our international treaty obligations or where, as a matter of discretion, the Secretary of State or the Secretary of Homeland Security determines that the facts of a specific case warrant such relief. Accordingly, while the Immigration Judges and the Board do not have the authority to grant the respondent or similarly situated aliens a discretionary waiver, other officials, including the Secretary of State, prior to the instigation of removal proceedings, or the Secretary of Homeland Security, at any time upon consultation with other agency officials, have been granted this power. [INA § 212(d)(3)(B).] We find no reason to assume they will not act consistently with our international treaty obligations [under the UN Convention and Protocol relating to the Status of Refugees] in exercising their power to grant such a waiver. [relocated footnote—eds.]

recipient organization of the assistance to further a terrorist activity. Especially where assistance as fungible as money is concerned, such a link would not be in keeping with the purpose of the material support provision, as it would enable a terrorist organization to solicit funds for an ostensibly benign purpose, and then transfer other equivalent funds in its possession to promote its terrorist activities.

We turn then to the respondent's claim that the statute's requirement of material support means that trivial or unsubstantial amounts of assistance, such as she allegedly provided, are not within the statutory bar. In *Singh–Kaur v. Ashcroft, supra,* the Third Circuit found that the provision of very modest amounts of food and shelter to individuals who the alien reasonably should have known had committed or planned to commit terrorist activity did constitute material support. The court also found that the listed examples in section 212(a)(3)(B)(iv)(VI) of the Act were not exhaustive but were "intended to illustrate a broad concept rather than narrowly circumscribe a term with exclusive categories." *Id.* at 298.

* * *

As the DHS contends, it is certainly plausible in light of the decision in *Singh–Kaur v. Ashcroft,* and recent amendments to the Act, that the list in section 212(a)(3)(B) was intended to have an expanded reach and cover virtually all forms of assistance, even small monetary contributions. Congress has not expressly indicated its intent to provide an exception for contributions which are de minimis. Thus the DHS asserts that the term "material support" is effectively a term of art and that all of the listed types of assistance are covered, irrespective of any showing that they are independently "material."

On the other hand, the respondent's contrary argument that "material" should be given independent content is by no means frivolous. However, we find it unnecessary to resolve this issue now, inasmuch as we agree with the DHS that based on the amount of money the respondent provided, her donations of S$1100 (Singapore dollars) constituted material support.[13] Specifically, the respondent testified that she contributed approximately S$100 per month over an 11–month period, representing approximately one-eighth of her monthly income. This was sufficiently substantial by itself to have some effect on the ability of the CNF to accomplish its goals, whether in the form of purchasing weaponry or providing routine supplies to its forces, for example. We therefore agree with the Immigration Judge that the respondent provided material support to the CNF.

III. CONCLUSION

Based on the foregoing, we agree with the Immigration Judge's decision that the respondent is statutorily ineligible for asylum and withholding of removal for having provided material support to a terrorist

---

13. We take administrative notice that this corresponded at the time to approximately US$685. By contrast, the average annual per capita income in Burma was approximately US$225.

organization. [The case is remanded because she was nonetheless still eligible for protection under the Convention Against Torture.] * * *

OSUNA, ACTING VICE CHAIRMAN, concurring:

* * *

We are finding that a Christian member of the ethnic Chin minority in Burma, who clearly has a well-founded fear of being persecuted by one of the more repressive governments in the world, one that the United States Government views as illegitimate, is ineligible to avail herself of asylum in the United States despite posing no threat to the security of this country. It may be, as the majority states, that Congress intended the material support bar to apply very broadly. However, when the bar is applied to cases such as this, it is difficult to conclude that this is what Congress intended.

* * *

In enacting the material support bar, Congress was rightly concerned with preventing terrorists and their supporters from exploiting this country's asylum laws. It is unclear, however, how barring this respondent from asylum furthers those goals. The respondent provided funds and some equipment to a member of the CNF, an organization that has *not* been designated by the Department of State as a terrorist organization under section 212(a)(3)(B)(vi) of the Act. The available information in the record indicates that the CNF engages in violence primarily as a means of self-defense against the Burmese Government, a known human rights abuser that has engaged in systematic persecution of Burmese ethnic minorities, including the Chin Christians. * * *

The CNF, however, is a group that has resorted to violence in self-defense, including the use of explosives. The Immigration Judge was thus correct to find that the assistance that the respondent provided to the CNF constituted material support to any individual who the respondent knew, or should have known, "has committed or plans to commit a terrorist activity." Section 212(a)(3)(B)(iv)(VI)(bb) of the Act. The fact that this language goes beyond common notions of "terrorism" is immaterial in the context of this case.

Yet, the statutory language is breathtaking in its scope. * * * [T]he DHS conceded at oral argument that an individual who assisted the Northern Alliance in Afghanistan against the Taliban in the 1990s would be considered to have provided "material assistance" to a terrorist organization under this statute and thus would be barred from asylum. This despite the fact that the Northern Alliance was an organization supported by the United States in its struggle against a regime that the United States and the vast majority of governments around the world viewed as illegitimate.

It also includes groups and organizations that are not normally thought of as "terrorists" per se. Read literally, the definition includes, for example, a group of individuals discharging a weapon in an abandoned house, thus causing "substantial damage to property." Section 212(a)(3)(B)(iii)(V) of the Act. This may constitute inappropriate or even criminal behavior, but it is not what we normally think of as "terrorist" activity.

The broad reach of the material support bar becomes even starker when viewed in light of the nature of the Burmese regime, and how it is regarded by the United States Government. In 2003, Congress passed the Burmese Freedom and Democracy Act of 2003, Pub. L. No. 108–61, 117 Stat. 864, which, among other things, imposes sanctions on the Burmese Government as a result of its deplorable human rights record. The Secretary of State has designated Burma as one of a handful of "countries of particular concern" in light of this record, including its treatment of ethnic and religious minorities. Bureau of Democracy, Human Rights and Labor, U.S. Dep't of State, Burma—International Religious Freedom Report 2003 (Dec. 18, 2003) available at http://www.state.gov/g/drl/rls/irf/ 2003/23823.htm. In particular, the Burmese Government has engaged in arrests of Christian clergy, destruction of churches, prohibition of religious services and proselytizing by Christians, and forced conversions of Christians. These efforts are part of a larger effort to "Burmanize" the Chin ethnic minority.

* * *

In sum, what we have in this case is an individual who provided a relatively small amount of support to an organization that opposes one of the most repressive governments in the world, a government that is not recognized by the United States as legitimate and that has engaged in a brutal campaign against ethnic minorities. It is clear that the respondent poses no danger whatsoever to the national security of the United States. Indeed, by supporting the CNF in its resistance to the Burmese junta, it is arguable that the respondent actually acted in a manner consistent with United States foreign policy. And yet we cannot ignore the clear language that Congress chose in the material support provisions; the statute that we are required to apply mandates that we find the respondent ineligible for asylum for having provided material support to a terrorist organization.

* * *

NOTES AND QUESTIONS ON MATERIAL SUPPORT

1. Why doesn't the Board have enough information, particularly in the form of U.S. legislative or executive branch condemnations of the Burmese regime, to decide that the CNF should be considered freedom fighters rather than terrorists? Should judgments about the legitimacy of the goals of an organization that uses violence be made by judicial or quasi-judicial officers, or instead by the executive branch?

In the 1980s and 1990s, the executive branch fairly consistently regarded as terrorists the members of the Irish Republican Army who had been involved in violence in Northern Ireland. But many judges explicitly or implicitly regarded IRA actions as justifiable support of Irish independence, and so ruled against British government extradition requests or found IRA members eligible for asylum despite analogous bars for terrorist activity. What are the advantages and disadvantages to assigning such judgments about legitimacy of goals to judges? To the executive branch?

2. Exactly why does the text of § 212(a)(3)(B) cover a situation like S–K–'s? Which part of clause (i), the primary list of disqualifying criteria, makes her inadmissible? Focusing on the definitions in § 212(a)(3)(B), is she barred for giving to a terrorist organization? For supporting terrorist activity? In what terrorist activity did the CNF engage? What actions were "unlawful" in the sense required? Whose laws apply?

3. **Knowledge?** How reasonable is the current version of the knowledge standards and allocation of the burden of proof regarding the nature of a terrorist organization? Consider this critique from Tariq Ramadan, a Swiss citizen and Muslim scholar, denied a visa in 2004 as he was preparing to assume a position at the University of Notre Dame as a professor of religion.

> For more than two years now, the U.S. government has barred me from entering the United States to pursue an academic career. The reasons have changed over time, and have evolved from defamatory to absurd, but the effect has remained the same: I've been kept out.
>
> First, I was told I couldn't enter because I had endorsed terrorism and violated the USA Patriot Act. It took a lawsuit for the government eventually to abandon this baseless accusation. * * * [This latest time] U.S. authorities offered a new rationale for turning me away: Between 1998 and 2002, I had contributed small sums of money to a French charity supporting humanitarian work in the Palestinian territories. * * *
>
> I should note that the investigation did not reveal these contributions. As the department acknowledges, I brought this information to its attention myself two years earlier, when I reapplied for a visa.
>
> In its letter, the U.S. Embassy claims that I "reasonably should have known" that the charities in question provided money to Hamas. But my donations were made between December 1998 and July 2002, and the United States did not blacklist the charities until 2003. How should I reasonably have known of their activities before the U.S. government itself knew? I donated to these organizations for the same reason that countless Europeans—and Americans, for that matter—donate to Palestinian causes: not to help fund terrorism, but to provide humanitarian aid to people who desperately need it.

Ramadan, *Why I'm Banned in the USA*, Wash. Post, Oct. 1, 2006, at B1. A federal appeals court later ruled that the government had to provide Ramadan with an opportunity to show that he lacked actual or constructive knowledge that his contributions went to a terrorist organization. The court added: "The need to confront Ramadan with a claim that he knew ASP [Association de Secours Palestinien] funded Hamas is especially important in this case because of the timing of Ramadan's contributions." *American Academy of*

Religion v. Napolitano, 573 F.3d 115, 133 (2d Cir. 2009). In January 2010, Secretary of State Hillary Clinton, after the required interagency consultation, signed an exemption under INA § 212(d)(3)(B) that allowed a visa to be issued to Ramadan. In April 2010, he visited the United States for five days of meetings and public appearances. *See* Semple, *At Last Allowed, Muslim Scholar Visits*, N.Y. Times, April 8, 2010, at A29.

4. **De minimis?** Besides arguing the legitimacy of the CNF's actions, S–K–also contended that small amounts of aid should not be considered *material* support. Because the BIA judged her donation large enough to cross any such threshold, it did not resolve this question. DHS and the Department of Justice have regularly argued against such a reading. Does this government position correctly interpret the statute? Is it sensible policy? Does it reflect the realities of detecting and proving support for terrorism?

Does the government work on a tip-of-the-iceberg theory: small contributions may be all we can prove, out of what could be much more extensive support in the past. Or someone who has given small-scale help may be willing to foster more lethal activities in the future, should a better opportunity arise (such as through admission to U.S. territory). Which side should get the benefit of the doubt? Should the rules be more generous toward persons who have proven a genuine risk of persecution in their country of origin, as compared with ordinary applicants for admission?

NOTES AND QUESTIONS ON DISCRETIONARY EXEMPTIONS

1. What if support is given at the point of a gun or due to other sorts of coercion? In a society riven by civil war, people might be forced to provide food, supplies, or the payment of "revolutionary taxes" to guerrillas coming through the village. In fact, the violence or threats used to coerce such support may be precisely the reason that unwilling donors flee and seek asylum. Even more graphically, children are kidnapped to join an armed band, then forced (and often drugged) to commit atrocities or lead armed attacks as child soldiers. Are such actions "terrorist activity" that should disqualify the coerced person from admission or refugee status? Does the text of the statute give answers to these questions?

Duress is an established defense in the criminal law, but with fairly demanding proof requirements. *See, e.g., United States v. Bravo*, 489 F.3d 1, 10 (1st Cir. 2007) ("In order to establish a claim of duress, the defendant must show that: (1) he acted under an immediate threat of serious bodily injury; (2) he had a well-grounded belief that the threat would be carried out; and (3) he had no reasonable opportunity to escape or otherwise frustrate the threat."). At the time of this writing, we are unaware of a case that has definitively ruled on the legal availability of a duress defense under the "material support" inadmissibility ground. The government has maintained, however, that no such defense exists. This stance drew sustained criticism for its impact on refugees. *See, e.g.,* Laufer, Note, *Admission Denied: In Support of a Duress Exception to the Immigration and Nationality Act's "Material Support for Terrorism" Provision*, 20 Geo. Imm. L.J. 437 (2006). *See also* Simon, Comment, *Change is Coming: Rethinking the Material Support Bar*

Following the Supreme Court's Holding in Negusie v. Holder,[5] 40 Hous. L. Rev. 707, 737–38 (2010) (commenting on "the Supreme Court's recognition that Congress need not have provided an explicit duress exemption for one to exist").

2. The sheer breadth of the terrorism-related inadmissibility grounds almost inevitably requires some mechanism to decide on cases that should not be barred even though within the broad wording. Congress has provided and has gradually expanded one such mechanism, a purely discretionary authority to exempt certain persons or groups from most, but not all, of the parts of § 212(a)(3)(B). This provision appears in INA § 212(d)(3)(B), which is only slightly less complicated than the provisions for which it can provide a waiver. In February 2007, for example, DHS issued a discretionary determination making the material support bar inapplicable, with certain qualifications, to support given to eight specific named groups, including the CNF. 72 Fed.Reg. 9954 (2007). Other exercises of that authority in 2007 were conduct-based rather than group-based. *Id.* at 9954, 26138. They allowed for individual determinations by USCIS officers to exempt "material support provided under duress" to terrorist organizations.

Later, the Consolidated Appropriations Act (CAA) of 2008 provided legislatively that certain specified groups, including the CNF, would not be considered a terrorist organization on the basis of any act or event before enactment of the legislation. The same enactment expanded the power of the Secretary of State and the Secretary of Homeland Security to waive the application of § 212(a)(3)(B), though not in several enumerated situations, and it also limited court review of any such decision. *See* Pub.L. No. 110–161, 121 Stat. 1844, Div. J, § 691. After these developments, the BIA issued a decision indicating that S–K–would be granted asylum, but that the 2006 decision in her case would retain its precedential effect as to the application and interpretation of the material support provisions. *See Matter of S–K–*, 24 I & N Dec. 475 (BIA 2008).

The executive branch continues to work on and issue exemptions under INA § 212(d)(3)(B). Some have been group-based and some conduct-based. *See generally* Nezer, Recent Developments: Terrorism–Related Inadmissibility Grounds (Lexis/Nexis 2011); Guilfoyle, Update on Terrorism–Related Inadmissibility Grounds: Most Recent Exemptions (CLINIC 2011), available at <http://ip–173–201–111–59.ip.secureserver.net/may2011newsletter/ terrorism>. For example, two recent exemptions essentially expand the 2007 material support duress exemption to reach noncitizens who, under duress, received military-type training from a terrorist organization, or solicited funds or members for a terrorist organization. (Such actions could not be the subject of a waiver before the CAA of 2008.) Two memoranda issued by USCIS in February 2011 set out the current framework for these exemptions, and reflect the basic standards and procedures that apply to any of the duress-based waivers. The memo on solicitation provides:

---

5. In *Negusie v. Holder*, 555 U.S. 511, 129 S.Ct. 1159, 173 L.Ed.2d 20 (2009), in Chapter Eight, p. 891, the U.S. Supreme Court addressed the availability of a duress exception to the bars in INA §§ 208(b)(2)(A)(i) and 241(b)(3)(B)(i) to eligibility for asylum and withholding of removal (a related form of protection from persecution) for those who themselves participated in persecution.

Duress only

USCIS may consider a discretionary exemption only for those cases in which the solicitation activities occurred under duress. Voluntary solicitation of funds or members is not covered by this exemption. Duress is established if the solicitation activities occurred in response to a *reasonably-perceived threat of serious harm.* To determine whether duress exists, adjudicators must consider the following, non-exhaustive list of factors: whether the applicant reasonably could have avoided, or took steps to avoid, soliciting; the severity and type of harm inflicted or threatened and to whom the harm was directed; and the perceived imminence of the harm threatened and the perceived likelihood that the harm would be inflicted. A threat of serious harm need not be expressly communicated or demonstrated; an alien may reasonably perceive a threat from the context and circumstances of his or her encounter with a terrorist organization.

Conduct Exempted

The Secretary's Exercise of Authority provides that "subsections 212(a)(3)(B)(iv)(IV) and 212(a)(3)(B)(iv)(V) of the INA, shall not apply, with respect to an alien, for solicitation of funds or other things of value *for a terrorist organization* . . . or for solicitation of any individual *for membership in a terrorist organization.* . . ." (emphasis added). As such, the Exercise of Authority does not include the activities described in INA subsections 212(a)(3)(B)(iv)(IV)**(aa)** (solicitation for "a terrorist activity") and 212(a)(3)(B)(iv)(V)**(aa)** (solicitation "to engage in [terrorism-related] conduct"). The exemption applies to subsections (bb) and (cc) of each form of solicitation. This exemption is not limited to undesignated terrorist organizations as defined at INA section 212(a)(3)(B)(vi)(III) (Tier III organization) but also includes Tier I and II terrorist organizations as defined at INA sections 212(a)(3)(B)(vi)(I) and (II).

Threshold Eligibility

To be considered for an exemption, an applicant must satisfy the following threshold requirements:

- Establish that he or she is otherwise eligible for the immigration benefit or protection being sought;

- Undergo and pass all required background and security checks;

- Fully disclose, to the best of his or her knowledge, in all relevant applications and interviews with U.S. Government representatives and agents, the nature and circumstances of each instance of solicitation and any other TRIG [terrorism-related inadmissibility grounds] activity or association; and

- Establish that he or she poses no danger to the safety and security of the United States.

Discretion

For those applicants who have met all threshold requirements, adjudicators will consider whether the applicant warrants a discretionary exemption in the totality of the circumstances. When considering the totality of the circumstances, factors to be considered, in addition to the duress-related factors stated above, may include, among others: the amount, type, and frequency of solicitation provided; the nature of the activities committed by the terrorist organization; the alien's awareness of those activities; whether the applicant participated in any violent activities; the length of time since the solicitation was provided; the alien's conduct since the last instance of solicitation; and any other relevant factors.

U.S. Citizenship and Immigration Services, *Policy Memorandum on Implementation of New Discretionary Exemption Under INA Section 212(d)(3)(B)(i) For the Solicitation of Funds or Members under Duress*, Feb. 23, 2011. Parallel requirements apply to the receipt of military-type training under duress. *See generally* 88 Interp.Rel. 584 (2011).

3. Some members of Congress have proposed amending the INA to reduce the impact of the "material support" provision on refugees, but without undermining its use (and that of a related criminal provision, 18 U.S.C. § 2339A) to deal with real supporters of dangerous terrorist organizations or activities. What are the key issues that such legislation should address, both as to substantive criteria and the procedures for deciding what is a terrorist organization? How would you change the statute to provide a more targeted inadmissibility provision? Or do the DHS memoranda on exemptions overcome objections to the current statute?

(iii) Designated Terrorist Groups—Guilt by Association?

Advocates and noncitizens in removal cases have contended for many years that provisions like § 212(a)(3)(B) impose "guilt by association," and that the wide discretion applied to their enforcement violates the First Amendment. The First Amendment doctrine on which these critics rely is captured in the following passage from *NAACP v. Claiborne Hardware Co.*, 458 U.S. 886, 918–20, 102 S.Ct. 3409, 3428–29, 73 L.Ed.2d 1215 (1982):

> The First Amendment * * * restricts the ability of the State to impose liability on an individual solely because of his association with another. In *Scales v. United States*, 367 U.S. 203, 229, 81 S.Ct. 1469, 1486, 6 L.Ed.2d 782, the Court noted that a "blanket prohibition of association with a group having both legal and illegal aims" would present "a real danger that legitimate political expression or association would be impaired." The Court suggested that to punish association with such a group, there must be "clear proof that a defendant 'specifically intend[s] to accomplish [the aims of the organization] by resort to violence.' " * * *

> * * * "The government has the burden of establishing a knowing affiliation with an organization possessing unlawful aims and goals, and a specific intent to further those illegal aims." [Citing *Healy v. James*, 408 U.S. 169, 186, 92 S.Ct. 2338, 2348, 33 L.Ed.2d 266,]

The plaintiffs in *Holder v. Humanitarian Law Project*, 561 U.S. ___, 130 S.Ct. 2705, 177 L.Ed.2d 355 (2010), were organizations and individuals who wished to donate to two Tier I organizations designated under INA § 219: the Kurdistan Workers Party (PKK) and the Liberation Tigers of Tamil Eelam. The plaintiffs argued that their donations would aid only nonviolent humanitarian and political activities, and that the broad ban on support was impermissibly vague and violated their freedoms of speech and association under the First Amendment. The precise issue was the constitutionality of the criminal penalties in 18 U.S.C. § 2339B for contributing material support to organizations designated as foreign terrorist organizations under § 219—a setting where the constitutional restrictions are arguably more stringent than in the immigration context.

The U.S. Supreme Court first declined to interpret the statute narrowly to not cover the plaintiffs' intended activities, and then rejected the argument that the statute was unconstitutionally vague. The Court then reached and rejected the First Amendment argument:

> The First Amendment issue before us is more refined than either plaintiffs or the Government would have it. It is not whether the Government may prohibit pure political speech, or may prohibit material support in the form of conduct. It is instead whether the Government may prohibit what plaintiffs want to do—provide material support to the PKK and LTTE in the form of speech.

* * *

> * * * Congress considered and rejected the view that ostensibly peaceful aid would have no harmful effects.

> We are convinced that Congress was justified in rejecting that view. * * *

> Material support meant to "promot[e] peaceable, lawful conduct," can further terrorism by foreign groups in multiple ways. "Material support" is a valuable resource by definition. Such support frees up other resources within the organization that may be put to violent ends. It also importantly helps lend legitimacy to foreign terrorist groups—legitimacy that makes it easier for those groups to persist, to recruit members, and to raise funds—all of which facilitate more terrorist attacks. * * *

* * *

> In analyzing whether it is possible in practice to distinguish material support for a foreign terrorist group's violent activities and its nonviolent activities, we do not rely exclusively on our own inferences drawn from the record evidence. We have before us an affidavit stating the Executive Branch's conclusion on that question. The State Department informs us that "[t]he experience and analysis of the U.S. government agencies charged with combating terrorism strongly suppor[t]" Congress's finding that all contributions to foreign terrorist organizations further their terrorism. McKune Affidavit, App. 133, ¶ 8. In the Executive's view: "Given the purposes,

organizational structure, and clandestine nature of foreign terrorist organizations, it is highly likely that any material support to these organizations will ultimately inure to the benefit of their criminal, terrorist functions—regardless of whether such support was ostensibly intended to support non-violent, non-terrorist activities." McKune Affidavit, App. 133, ¶ 8.

That evaluation of the facts by the Executive, like Congress's assessment, is entitled to deference. This litigation implicates sensitive and weighty interests of national security and foreign affairs. The PKK and the LTTE have committed terrorist acts against American citizens abroad, and the material-support statute addresses acute foreign policy concerns involving relationships with our Nation's allies. We have noted that "neither the Members of this Court nor most federal judges begin the day with briefings that may describe new and serious threats to our Nation and its people." *Boumediene v. Bush,* 553 U.S. 723, 797, 128 S.Ct. 2229, 171 L.Ed.2d 41 (2008). It is vital in this context "not to substitute ... our own evaluation of evidence for a reasonable evaluation by the Legislative Branch." *Rostker v. Goldberg,* 453 U.S. 57, 68, 101 S.Ct. 2646, 69 L.Ed.2d 478 (1981).

Our precedents, old and new, make clear that concerns of national security and foreign relations do not warrant abdication of the judicial role. We do not defer to the Government's reading of the First Amendment, even when such interests are at stake. We are one with the dissent that the Government's "authority and expertise in these matters do not automatically trump the Court's own obligation to secure the protection that the Constitution grants to individuals." But when it comes to collecting evidence and drawing factual inferences in this area, "the lack of competence on the part of the courts is marked," *Rostker,* 453 U.S. at 65, 101 S.Ct. 2646, and respect for the Government's conclusions is appropriate.

One reason for that respect is that national security and foreign policy concerns arise in connection with efforts to confront evolving threats in an area where information can be difficult to obtain and the impact of certain conduct difficult to assess. The dissent slights these real constraints in demanding hard proof-with "detail," "specific facts," and "specific evidence"—that plaintiffs' proposed activities will support terrorist attacks. That would be a dangerous requirement. In this context, conclusions must often be based on informed judgment rather than concrete evidence, and that reality affects what we may reasonably insist on from the Government. The material-support statute is, on its face, a preventive measure—it criminalizes not terrorist attacks themselves, but aid that makes the attacks more likely to occur. The Government, when seeking to prevent imminent harms in the context of international affairs and national security, is not required to conclusively link all the pieces in the puzzle before we grant weight to its empirical conclusions.

* * *

At bottom, plaintiffs simply disagree with the considered judgment of Congress and the Executive that providing material support to a designated foreign terrorist organization—even seemingly benign support—bolsters the terrorist activities of that organization. * * *

130 S.Ct. at 2724–28.

On freedom of association, the Court responded similarly:

The Court of Appeals correctly rejected this claim because the statute does not penalize mere association with a foreign terrorist organization. * * *

Plaintiffs also argue that the material-support statute burdens their freedom of association because it prevents them from providing support to designated foreign terrorist organizations, but not to other groups. Any burden on plaintiffs' freedom of association in this regard is justified for the same reasons that we have denied plaintiffs' free speech challenge. * * *

130 S.Ct. at 2730–31.

Justice Breyer, joined by Justices Ginsburg and Sotomayor, dissented, urging a narrow interpretation of the statute to avoid the constitutional issues, but then addressing them:

* * * I cannot agree with the Court's conclusion that the Constitution permits the Government to prosecute the plaintiffs criminally for engaging in coordinated teaching and advocacy furthering the designated organizations' lawful political objectives. In my view, the Government has not met its burden of showing that an interpretation of the statute that would prohibit this speech- and association-related activity serves the Government's compelling interest in combating terrorism.

130 S.Ct. at 2731.

d. Inadmissibility Grounds Based on Foreign Policy

Closely related to the terrorism-related inadmissibility grounds are the foreign policy grounds in INA § 212(a)(3)(C). The conference committee report accompanying the 1990 Act explained this provision as follows. A closely comparable ground of deportability is in INA § 237(a)(4)(C).

Under current law there is some ambiguity as to the authority of the Executive Branch to exclude aliens on foreign policy grounds * * *. The foreign policy provision in this title would establish a single clear standard for foreign policy exclusions (which is designated as 212(a)(3)(C) of the INA). The conferees believe that granting an alien admission to the United States is not a sign of approval or agreement and the conferees therefore expect that, with the enactment of this provision, aliens will be excluded not merely because of the potential signal that might be sent because of their admission, but when there would be a clear negative foreign policy impact associated with their admission.

This provision would authorize the executive branch to exclude aliens for foreign policy reasons in certain circumstances. Specifically, under this provision, an alien could be excluded only if the Secretary of State has reasonable ground to believe an alien's entry or proposed activities within the United States would have potentially serious adverse foreign policy consequences. However, there are two exceptions to this general standard.

First, an alien who is an official of a foreign government or a purported government, or who is a candidate for election to a foreign government office (and who is seeking entry into the United States during the period immediately prior to the election) would not be excludable under this provision solely because of any past, current or expected beliefs, statements or associations which would be lawful in the United States. The word "solely" is used in this provision to indicate that, in cases involving government officials, the committee intends that exclusions not be based merely on, for example, the possible content of an alien's speech in this country, but that there be some clear foreign policy impact beyond the mere fact of the speech or its content, that would permit exclusion.

In particular, the conferees expect that the authority to exclude aliens with a government connection would apply primarily to senior government officials (or candidates for senior government posts). While, as a general matter, admitting foreign government officials is not necessarily a signal of approval, the conferees recognize that in cases involving senior officials it may be difficult to avoid conveying that impression.

The second exception, which applies to all other aliens, would prevent exclusion on the basis of an alien's past, current or expected beliefs, statements or associations which would be lawful within the United States unless the Secretary of State personally determines that the alien's admission to the United States would compromise a compelling United States foreign policy interest, and so certifies to the relevant Congressional Committees. It is the intent of the conference committee that this authority would be used sparingly and not merely because there is a likelihood that an alien will make critical remarks about the United States or its policies.

Furthermore, the conferees intend that the "compelling foreign policy interest" standard be interpreted as a significantly higher standard than the general "potentially serious adverse foreign policy consequences standard." In particular, the conferees note that the general exclusion standard in this provision refers only to the "potential" for serious adverse foreign policy consequences, whereas exclusion under the second exception (under which an alien can be excluded because of his beliefs, statements or associations) must be linked to a "compelling" foreign policy interest. The fact that the Secretary of State personally must inform the relevant Congressional Committees when a determination of excludability is made under this provision is a further indication that the conferees intend that this provision be used only in unusual circumstances.

With regard to the second exception, the following include some of the circumstances in which exclusion might be appropriate: when an alien's mere entry into the United States could result in imminent harm to the lives or property of United States persons abroad or to property of the United States government abroad (as occurred with the former Shah of Iran), or when an alien's entry would violate a treaty or international agreement to which the United States is party.

H.R.Rep. 101–955, 101st Cong., 2d Sess. 128–131 (1990).

The major BIA precedent applying INA § 237(a)(4)(C) is *Matter of Ruiz–Massieu*, 22 I & N Dec. 833 (1999). The case grew out of the U.S. government's effort to deport Mario Ruiz–Massieu, a former Deputy Attorney General of Mexico, to his native country. One major issue throughout the litigation was just who has authority under § 237(a)(4)(C)(i) to decide which version of events to credit—the Secretary of State, the immigration judge, or perhaps the federal courts. Here is the BIA's answer:

> [T]he Secretary of State's reasonable determination in this case should be treated as conclusive evidence of the respondent's deportability. The Immigration Judge thus erred in holding that the [INS] is obliged to present clear, unequivocal, and convincing evidence in support of the Secretary of State's belief. [This evidentiary] requirement * * * is met by the Secretary's facially reasonable and bona fide determination that the respondent's presence here would cause potentially serious adverse foreign policy consequences for the United States.

22 I & N Dec. at 842.

PROBLEMS

13. X, head of a right-wing, anti-foreigner party in the Netherlands that has been gaining strength recently, is planning a two-week trip to the United States to make speeches and raise funds for an upcoming election campaign. Because the Netherlands is a visa waiver program country, he will not need a visa. You are an Under Secretary of State and are concerned that X's admission will give the impression that the U.S. government supports him. At the very least you do not want to do anything that helps his fundraising. Can you block his admission? Should you? What grounds might apply, and what would you have to establish to invoke them?

14. Could the State Department:

(a) prevent the French deputy foreign minister (and his extended family members?) from vacationing at Lake Winnipesaukee in New Hampshire, because of U.S. anger at France's position at the United Nations regarding an uprising in the Middle East?

(b) bar specific members of the Turkish parliament who have publicly criticized or insulted prominent members of the U.S. Congress who supported a congressional resolution condemning the Armenian genocide that occurred in the Ottoman Empire in 1915–17?

(c) block the admission of anti-globalization protesters coming to Washington, D.C., to participate in demonstrations during an annual meeting of the World Bank? Past demonstrations of this sort have often turned violent.

(d) bar any official, at any level, of the government of Burma (Myanmar), as well as selected businessmen who have supported the regime, in retaliation for another government crackdown on the Burmese democracy movement?

In September 1995 the United States used the foreign policy exclusion provisions to revoke the visa of General Hector Gramajo, then a candidate for the Guatemalan Presidency, based on allegations of atrocities committed while he had served as Guatemalan defense minister. The revocation followed a $47.5 million federal court judgment against Gramajo in a suit brought by an American nun who had been tortured and eight Guatemalans who had been terrorized by the Guatemalan military while Gramajo served as defense minister. *See* 73 Interp.Rel. 293 (1996).

Compare the refusal of a visa for Markus Wolf, who had been deputy minister of state security and head of the foreign espionage branch of former East Germany. Wolf wanted to travel to New York to meet with his editors at Random House, the publisher of his autobiography. A State Department official explained that Wolf's agency "actively abetted and fostered state-supported terrorism." *See* Fisher, *Ex–East German Spymaster Is Barred From U.S.*, Washington Post, March 12, 1997.

The Conference report suggests that the Shah of Iran could have been excluded from the United States. The Shah's entry into the United States in 1979 after his government fell triggered the seizure and 14–month detention of 63 U.S. diplomats as hostages in Tehran by militants who supported the new regime of the Ayatollah Khomeini. Would such an exclusion be consistent with the actual language of § 212(a)(3)(C)? Wouldn't any concern about the repercussions of his admission have been based on associations—associations that would have been lawful in the United States as protected by the First Amendment?

SECTION B. DEPORTABILITY GROUNDS

Deportation statutes are nearly as old as the Republic. As mentioned in Section A of this chapter, the Alien and Sedition Acts of 1798 authorized the President to deport (1) resident aliens who were citizens of nations at war with the United States and (2) aliens whom the President judged "dangerous to the peace and safety of the United States." Act of June 25, 1798, ch. 58, 1 Stat. 570; Act of July 6, 1798, ch. 66, 1 Stat. 577.

For most of the nineteenth century, federal law had no general deportation statute. Noncitizens who entered the country were allowed to remain as long as they wished. But in the late 1800s, as the federal government began to restrict who could enter, it recognized the need to remove those whose entry had violated those restrictions. At first, then, deportation statutes were meant primarily to supplement exclusion laws.

For example, contract labor laws enacted in 1885 and 1887 prohibited the "importation or migration" of persons who had pre-existing contracts to perform most kinds of labor or services in the United States. Act of February 26, 1885, ch. 164, 23 Stat. 332; Act of February 23, 1887, ch. 220, 24 Stat. 414. (The statutes did not apply to skilled jobs for which American workers could not be found, domestic servants, professional actors, artists, singers or lecturers.) These laws were amended in 1888 to authorize the *deportation* of an immigrant who had been "allowed to land contrary to the prohibition" in the earlier laws. Act of Oct. 19, 1888, ch. 1210, 25 Stat. 566. Similarly, the 1892 statute at issue in *Fong Yue Ting,* p. 171, *supra,* which authorized the deportation of Chinese laborers who failed to obtain certificates of residence, was enacted to help enforce the earlier Chinese exclusion laws. Then, sweeping more broadly, the 1891 amendments to the immigration laws, while adding new exclusion grounds, broadened the deportation provision of the 1888 Act to encompass "any alien who shall come into the United States in violation of law." Act of March 3, 1891, ch. 551, § 11, 24 Stat. 1086.

In 1907, Congress amended the immigration laws to authorize deportation of a noncitizen who was a prostitute "at any time within three years after she shall have entered the United States." Act of February 20, 1907, ch. 1134, § 3, 34 Stat. 899–900. For the first time since the Alien and Sedition Acts, this statute authorized the deportation of a noncitizen based on conduct in the United States *after* a lawful entry.

In the century since then, Congress has added considerably to the list of post-entry acts by a lawfully admitted noncitizen that can render her deportable. This chapter devotes attention to a number of these provisions, but it is helpful to step back and look at key concepts reflected in the deportability grounds. Daniel Kanstroom's history of deportation in the United States suggests two different models:

> [Th]ere are two basic types of deportation laws: *extended border control* and *post-entry social control.* The extended border control

model implements basic features of sovereign power: the control of territory by the state and the legal distinction between citizens and noncitizens. Extended border control deportation laws have two variants, each of which has been a part of U.S. law for many years. First, there are laws that mandate the deportation of persons who have evaded border controls, either by surreptitious entry or by fraud or misrepresentation. These laws most directly support the border control regime, and their legitimacy, such as it is, is most closely linked to that of sovereignty itself.

There are also laws that permit the deportation of persons who violate an explicit condition on which they were permitted to enter the country. For example, a person who enters the United States as a student must maintain a full course load, and a person with a work visa must work for a particular employer. The legitimacy of such laws, also derived from border control and sovereignty, is enhanced by the contractual aspect of the deal that permitted entry.

* * *

[Other] deportation laws * * * combine extended border control with a rather different goal: post-entry social control. Deportation laws routinely govern conduct for a specific period following the time of admission. The purest post-entry social control laws, however, proscribe criminal or political conduct within the United States, often without time limit. They are often not directly connected to visa issuance, admission, or immigration processes at all. There is no requirement that a noncitizen be informed of them at entry. Indeed, they may be changed retroactively: a noncitizen may be deported for conduct that was not a deportable offense when it occurred.

Such post-entry social control deportation laws derive from what might be termed an "eternal probation" or an "eternal guest" model. The strongest version of this model would suggest that the millions of noncitizens among us, including long-term lawful permanent residents, are harbored subject to the whim of the government and may be deported for any reason. The earliest federal post-entry social control law, the 1798 Aliens Act, authorized highly discretionary executive deportation power to be used against noncitizen dissidents. A fierce debate arose not only over the politics of the law, but also over its basic legal legitimacy. As James Madison put it, "it can not be a true inference, that because the admission of an alien is a favor, the favor may be revoked at pleasure."[29]

D. Kanstroom, Deportation Nation: Outsiders in American History 5–6 (2007). For additional thought-provoking perspectives on the evolution of grounds of deportability amid the maelstrom of American political, economic, and social changes, see A. Zolberg, A Nation by Design: Immigration Policy in the Fashioning of America (2006).

---

29. Report to the General Assembly of Virginia (Jan. 7, 1800), 4 *Elliot's Debates on the Federal Constitution* 541, 546 (Lippincott, 2d ed. 1097).

Section 237 of the INA lists deportability grounds. A single individual might be deportable under more than one. The numerically significant broad categories are noncitizens who: (1) were inadmissible at time of entry or later violated their immigration status; or (2) were convicted of criminal offenses. Also noteworthy but much less numerous are noncitizens who: (3) falsified documents or failed to register; (4) engaged in activity raising national security or foreign policy concerns; (5) became a public charge; or (6) voted unlawfully. But of course, many deportable noncitizens are not removed, because they are eligible for relief from removal, as explained later in this chapter, or because they are not identified or located by immigration authorities, a pattern influenced by enforcement priorities, as addressed in Chapter Nine.

As you read the statutory provisions, ask yourself: If you were a member of Congress, would you vote to maintain, modify, or delete any of the deportability grounds in § 237(a)? Would you add grounds that subject those who violate civil rights laws to removal? Those who decide not to naturalize within a certain number of years? What principles and values should guide your choices? Would you remove a noncitizen for conduct (or a trait) that is not unlawful for a U.S. citizen—e.g., poverty or drug addiction? Should we insist that those who want to immigrate to the United States and join the American community have fewer faults or be less of a burden on society than persons born here? Is Congress using immigration laws to protect its image of ideal members of our community—an ideal that citizens sometimes fail to fulfill?

More generally, consider whether these deportability grounds function as an extension of the border, or post-entry social control, or some blend of the two models. Do you detect a trend toward one or the other of these approaches? If so, does it matter? If the statutes reflect one model or the other, does it affect their constitutionality? Should the distinction affect whether relief from removal is available?

1. IMMIGRATION CONTROL

Immigration control deportability grounds embody what Kanstroom calls extended border control. In analyzing these grounds, recall that inadmissibility grounds apply to noncitizens who arrive at a port of entry, or who are in the United States but have not been admitted—that is, because they entered without inspection or were paroled into the country. Deportability grounds apply to noncitizens who have been admitted.

a. Inadmissible at Time of Entry or Adjustment of Status

Under INA § 237(a)(1)(A), a noncitizen is deportable if she was inadmissible when she entered the United States or when she adjusted her status to permanent resident. This provision turns *all* the inadmissibility grounds in § 212(a) into deportability grounds even after noncitizens have been inspected and admitted. Section 237(a)(1)(A) applies, for example, if she presented herself for inspection and was admitted, but she did not actually meet all the admission requirements because she made some misrepresentations to obtain an immigrant visa. Being admitted refers to procedural regularity—whether she presented herself for inspection and admission. If erroneous admission did not count as an admission at all, § 237(a)(1)(A) would serve no purpose.

Because § 237(a)(1)(A) has no statute of limitations, acts long ago can come back to haunt someone after decades living in the United States, if he had no lawful basis for admission. Moreover, this provision applies not just to a permanent resident's initial admission to the United States, but to later admissions as well. *See* INA § 101(a)(13)(C), discussed in Section A of this chapter.

Recognizing the potential harshness of § 237(a)(1)(A), Congress provided a waiver for noncitizens who are deportable because they were inadmissible for fraud or misrepresentation in obtaining an immigrant visa or admission. INA § 237(a)(1)(H). A spouse, parent, son, or daughter of a U.S. citizen or permanent resident may apply for this waiver of deportability. In contrast, a parent of a citizen or permanent resident is ineligible to apply for the analogous inadmissibility waiver in § 212(i).

b. Presence in the United States in Violation of Law

If a noncitizen is admitted after inspection, but then overstays his authorized period of admission, he is deportable under INA § 237(a)(1)(B) for being unlawfully present in the United States. (He is also deportable under § 237(a)(1)(C), as explained immediately below.) This ground does not apply to EWIs, who face inadmissibility grounds.

c. Failure to Maintain Nonimmigrant Status

If a noncitizen fails to maintain his status or violates the conditions of his admission, he is deportable under INA § 237(a)(1)(C)(i). This ground is primarily applied to nonimmigrants who stay beyond their authorized admission period. But it also covers nonimmigrants who work without authorization, students who leave school, and temporary workers who abandon their authorized employment.

d. Failure to Register and Document Fraud

Noncitizens who stay in the United States for more than 30 days must register, be fingerprinted, and provide their U.S. address and written notice of any address changes, *see* INA §§ 262, 265(a). In addition, the INA authorizes requirements for special registration of groups of non-permanent residents, and for additional information from noncitizens (or a subgroup) from particular countries, *see* INA §§ 263 § 265(b). These provisions have been part of federal immigration statutes since 1940. Failure to register or provide notice of a change of address is both a deportability ground and a criminal offense, *see* INA §§ 237(a)(3), 266.

A noncitizen who commits fraud or misrepresentation to gain admission, documentation, or some other immigration benefit is typically deportable under INA § 237(a)(1)(A) for have being inadmissible under § 212(a)(6)(C). The use of fraudulent immigration documents can also make a noncitizen deportable under § 237(a)(3)(C), but only after an extra procedural step. INA § 274C imposes civil and criminal penalties on persons and entities that engage knowingly in certain types of immigration-related document fraud. The § 274C adjudication does not occur in the removal proceeding, but rather through a process supervised by an administrative law judge who is part of the office of the Chief Administrative Hearing Officer in EOIR. A final order under § 274C makes a noncitizen deportable under § 237(a)(3)(C).

PROBLEMS

With the foregoing overview in mind, apply the text of the immigration control deportability grounds to the problems below.

1. A is a permanent resident living in Detroit. She crossed the border to Canada and picked up B in Toronto. When A drove B back across the border to Detroit, B showed the immigration inspector someone else's green card. (B looks enough like the other person to escape detection.) The government later discovers that B entered the United States in this way. Both A and B are put in removal proceedings. What immigration charges may be lodged against A? Against B?

2. C was admitted to the United States to attend UCLA. After successfully completing his first year, he took a reduced sophomore course load to devote considerable time to surfing. The next year, he dropped out and now works full-time at a souvenir shop in Santa Monica, believing that he has no immigration law worries because he has been in the United States for less than the four years it usually takes to get a college degree. DHS has begun removal proceedings. Is C deportable?

---

2. IDEOLOGY, NATIONAL SECURITY, AND THE CONSTITUTION

The plenary power doctrine enunciated in the *Chinese Exclusion Case* and *Fong Yue Ting* arose in an era of rampant anti-Chinese sentiment in the United States in the late nineteenth century. Are the constitutional perspectives articulated in those opinions a relic of a bygone age, or have they retained their influence over several generations? To answer this question, we look at twentieth-century constitutional challenges to deportability based on noncitizen speech and association.

Recall the historical overview in the inadmissibility materials in Section A of this chapter; it also provides essential background on deportability up through the 1920s. In the period between the World Wars, U.S. citizens who joined the Communist Party did not violate the law. Indeed, the Communist Party ran candidates for public office throughout the United States. But noncitizen members could be accused of belonging to an organization that advocated the violent overthrow of the U.S. government, thus exposing them to deportation.

A 1918 deportation law made aliens deportable who were "members of or affiliated with any organization that entertains a belief in" violent overthrow of the government or anarchism. Anarchist Act of 1918, ch. 186, § 1, 40 Stat. 1012. In 1938, the government invoked this statute to put Harry Bridges, a well-known radical labor organizer, into deportation proceedings, asserting that he was a member of, or had been affiliated with, the Communist Party of the United States. The U.S. Supreme Court quashed the deportation order in *Bridges v. Wixon,* 326 U.S. 135, 65 S.Ct. 1443, 89 L.Ed. 2103 (1945). Writing for the majority, Justice Douglas concluded on statutory grounds that the evidence against Bridges did not sustain a deportability finding. In a widely quoted concurrence, Justice Murphy wrote:

> The Bill of Rights is a futile authority for the alien seeking admission for the first time to these shores. But once an alien lawfully enters and resides in this country he becomes invested with the rights guaranteed by the Constitution to all people within our borders. Such rights include those protected by the First and the Fifth Amendments and by the due process clause of the Fourteenth Amendment. None of these provisions acknowledges any distinction between citizens and resident aliens. They extend their inalienable privileges to all "persons" and guard against any encroachment on those rights by federal or state authority. * * *

> Since resident aliens have constitutional rights, it follows that Congress may not ignore them in the exercise of its "plenary" power of deportation. * * * [T]he First Amendment and other portions of the Bill of Rights make no exception in favor of deportation laws or laws enacted pursuant to a "plenary" power of the Government. Hence the very provisions of the Constitution negative the proposition that Congress, in the exercise of a "plenary" power, may override the rights of those who are numbered among the beneficiaries of the Bill of Rights.

> Any other conclusion would make our constitutional safeguards transitory and discriminatory in nature. Thus the Government would be precluded from enjoining or imprisoning an alien for exercising his freedom of speech. But the Government at the same time would be free, from a constitutional standpoint, to deport him for exercising that very same freedom. The alien would be fully clothed with his constitutional rights when defending himself in a court of law, but he would be stripped of those rights when deportation officials encircle

him. I cannot agree that the framers of the Constitution meant to make such an empty mockery of human freedom.

Id. at 161–62, 65 S.Ct. 1443, 1455–56, 89 L.Ed. 2103 (1945).

In 1939, while Bridges' case was pending, the U.S. Supreme Court dropped a bombshell on Congress. In *Kessler v. Strecker*, 307 U.S. 22, 59 S.Ct. 694, 83 L.Ed. 1082 (1939) the Court ruled that a noncitizen who had joined the Communist Party after entering the United States, but was no longer a member when arrested, was not deportable based on subversive connections. After *Kessler*, radical organizations expelled noncitizen members to protect them from deportation.

Congress, reacting to *Kessler* and the radical organizations' response, overrode *Kessler* by enacting the Alien Registration Act of 1940, ch. 439, § 23(b), 54 Stat. 673. It made deportable any alien who had been a member of a subversive group "at any time" after entering the United States. The statute applied to noncitizens "irrespective of the time of their entry into the United States," and according to the Senate Report, it was intended to apply to all aliens who were associated with subversive organizations "for no matter how short a time or how far in the past." S.Rep. No. 1796, 76th Cong., 3d Sess. (1940).[6]

With the onset of the Cold War in the late 1940s, the deportation grounds broadened substantially. *See, e.g.,* Act of May 25, 1948, ch. 338, § 1, 62 Stat. 268. In contrast to earlier statutes that had based deportation on required proof of membership in an organization that advocated the violent overthrow of the government, Congress sought to overcome this obstacle in 1950 by identifying the Communist Party by name and basing deportation on mere membership in, or affiliation with, the Party. Subversive Activities Control Act, Title I of the Internal Security Act of 1950, ch. 1024, § 22, 64 Stat. 1006 (1950).

The McCarran–Walter Act of 1952 codified federal immigration statutes into the Immigration and Nationality Act (INA), incorporating the numerous deportation grounds for subversive activities that Congress had enacted. The INA became law over a veto by President Truman, who objected, among other things, to the breadth and vagueness of the subversion-related deportation grounds. *See* Veto Statement of President Truman, June 25, 1952, *reprinted in* President's Commission on Immigration and Naturalization, Whom We Shall Welcome 281–82 (1953).

All of this supplied the political setting for the next case. Deportation orders had been issued against Peter Harisiades, a labor organizer and active member of the Communist Party until expelled by the party, Luigi Mascitti, and Dora Coleman. These permanent residents gave new mean-

---

6. For further historical background, see Neuborne, *Harisiades v. Shaughnessy: A Case Study in the Vulnerability of Resident Aliens,* in Immigration Stories (D. Martin & P. Schuck eds., 2005), D. Kanstroom, Deportation Nation: Outsiders in American History 46–63, 136–155, 186–206 (2007); Johnson, *The Antiterrorism Act, the Immigration Reform Act and Ideological Regulation in the Immigration Laws: Important Lessons for Citizens and Noncitizens,* 28 St. Mary's L.J. 833, 834–60 (1997).

ing to the word "long-term." They had lived in the United States for a combined total of 106 years.

HARISIADES v. SHAUGHNESSY

Supreme Court of the United States, 1952.
342 U.S. 580, 72 S.Ct. 512, 96 L.Ed. 586.

MR. JUSTICE JACKSON delivered the opinion of the Court.

The ultimate question in these three cases is whether the United States constitutionally may deport a legally resident alien because of membership in the Communist Party which terminated before enactment of the Alien Registration Act, 1940.

Harisiades, a Greek national, accompanied his father to the United States in 1916, when thirteen years of age, and has resided here since. He has taken a wife and sired two children, all citizens. He joined the Communist Party in 1925, when it was known as the Workers Party, and served as an organizer, Branch Executive Committeeman, secretary of its Greek Bureau, and editor of its paper "Empros." The party discontinued his membership, along with that of other aliens, in 1939, but he has continued association with members. He was familiar with the principles and philosophy of the Communist Party and says he still believes in them. He disclaims personal belief in use of force and violence and asserts that the party favored their use only in defense. A warrant for his deportation because of his membership was issued in 1930 but was not served until 1946. The delay was due to inability to locate him because of his use of a number of aliases. After hearings, he was ordered deported on the grounds that after entry he had been a member of an organization which advocates overthrow of the Government by force and violence and distributes printed matter so advocating. * * *

Mascitti, a citizen of Italy, came to this country in 1920, at the age of sixteen. He married a resident alien and has one American-born child. He was a member of the Young Workers Party, the Workers Party and the Communist Party between 1923 and 1929. His testimony was that he knew the party advocated a proletarian dictatorship, to be established by force and violence if the capitalist class resisted. He heard some speakers advocate violence, in which he says he did not personally believe, and he was not clear as to the party policy. He resigned in 1929, apparently because he lost sympathy with or interest in the party. A warrant for his deportation issued and was served in 1946. After the usual administrative hearings he was ordered deported on the same grounds as Harisiades. * * *

Mrs. Coleman, a native of Russia, was admitted to the United States in 1914, when thirteen years of age. She married an American citizen and has three children, citizens by birth. She admits being a member of the Communist Party for about a year, beginning in 1919, and again from 1928 to 1930, and again from 1936 to 1937 or 1938. She held no office and her activities were not significant. She disavowed much knowledge of party principles and program, claiming she joined each time because of some injustice the party was then fighting. The reasons she gives for leaving the party are her health and the party's discontinuance of alien memberships. She has been ordered deported because after entry she became a member of an organization advocating overthrow of the Government by force and violence. * * *

* * *

I.

These aliens ask us to forbid their expulsion by a departure from the long-accepted application to such cases of the Fifth Amendment provision that no person shall be deprived of life, liberty or property without due process of law. Their basic contention is that admission for permanent residence confers a "vested right" on the alien, equal to that of the citizen, to remain within the country, and that the alien is entitled to constitutional protection in that matter to the same extent as the citizen. Their second line of defense is that if any power to deport domiciled aliens exists it is so dispersed that the judiciary must concur in the grounds for its exercise to the extent of finding them reasonable. The argument goes on to the contention that the grounds prescribed by the Act of 1940 bear no reasonable relation to protection of legitimate interests of the United States and concludes that the Act should be declared invalid. Admittedly these propositions are not founded in precedents of this Court.

For over thirty years each of these aliens has enjoyed such advantages as accrue from residence here without renouncing his foreign allegiance or formally acknowledging adherence to the Constitution he now invokes. Each was admitted to the United States, upon passing formidable exclusionary hurdles, in the hope that, after what may be called a probationary period, he would desire and be found desirable for citizenship. Each has been offered naturalization, with all of the rights and privileges of citizenship, conditioned only upon open and honest assumption of undivided allegiance to our Government. But acceptance was and is not compulsory. Each has been permitted to prolong his original nationality indefinitely.

So long as one thus perpetuates a dual status as an American inhabitant but foreign citizen, he may derive advantages from two sources of law—American and international. He may claim protection against our Government unavailable to the citizen. As an alien he retains a claim upon the state of his citizenship to diplomatic intervention on his behalf, a patronage often of considerable value. The state of origin of each of these aliens could presently enter diplomatic remonstrance against these deportations if they were inconsistent with international law, the prevailing custom among nations or their own practices.

The alien retains immunities from burdens which the citizen must shoulder. By withholding his allegiance from the United States, he leaves outstanding a foreign call on his loyalties which international law not only permits our Government to recognize but commands it to respect. * * *

Under our law, the alien in several respects stands on an equal footing with citizens,[9] but in others has never been conceded legal parity with the citizen.[10] Most importantly, to protract this ambiguous status within the country is not his right but is a matter of permission and tolerance. The Government's power to terminate its hospitality has been asserted and sustained by this Court since the question first arose.[11]

* * *

That aliens remain vulnerable to expulsion after long residence is a practice that bristles with severities. But it is a weapon of defense and reprisal confirmed by international law as a power inherent in every sovereign state. Such is the traditional power of the Nation over the alien and we leave the law on the subject as we find it.

This brings us to the alternative defense under the Due Process Clause—that, granting the power, it is so unreasonably and harshly exercised by this enactment that it should be held unconstitutional.

In historical context the Act before us stands out as an extreme application of the expulsion power. There is no denying that as world convulsions have driven us toward a closed society the expulsion power has been exercised with increasing severity, manifest in multiplication of grounds for deportation, in expanding the subject classes from illegal entrants to legal residents, and in greatly lengthening the period of residence after which one may be expelled. This is said to have reached a point where it is the duty of this Court to call a halt upon the political branches of the Government.

It is pertinent to observe that any policy toward aliens is vitally and intricately interwoven with contemporaneous policies in regard to the conduct of foreign relations, the war power, and the maintenance of a republican form of government. Such matters are so exclusively entrusted to the political branches of government as to be largely immune from judicial inquiry or interference.[16]

These restraints upon the judiciary, occasioned by different events, do not control today's decision but they are pertinent. It is not necessary and

---

9. This Court has held that the Constitution assures him a large measure of equal economic opportunity. *Yick Wo v. Hopkins,* 118 U.S. 356, 6 S.Ct. 1064, 30 L.Ed. 220; *Truax v. Raich,* 239 U.S. 33, 36 S.Ct. 7, 60 L.Ed. 131; he may invoke the writ of habeas corpus to protect his personal liberty, *Nishimura Ekiu v. United States,* 142 U.S. 651, 660, 12 S.Ct. 336, 338, 35 L.Ed. 1146; in criminal proceedings against him he must be accorded the protections of the Fifth and Sixth Amendments, *Wong Wing v. United States,* 163 U.S. 228, 16 S.Ct. 977, 41 L.Ed. 140; and, unless he is an enemy alien, his property cannot be taken without just compensation. *Russian Volunteer Fleet v. United States,* 282 U.S. 481, 51 S.Ct. 229, 75 L.Ed. 473.

10. He cannot stand for election to many public offices. For instance, Art. I, § 2, cl. 2, § 3, cl. 3, of the Constitution respectively require that candidates for election to the House of Representatives and Senate be citizens. See Borchard, Diplomatic Protection of Citizens Abroad, 63. The states, to whom is entrusted the authority to set qualifications of voters, for most purposes require citizenship as a condition precedent to the voting franchise.

11. *Fong Yue Ting v. United States,* 149 U.S. 698, 707, 711–714, 730, 13 S.Ct. 1016, 1019, 1021–1022, 1028, 37 L.Ed. 905.

16. *United States v. Curtiss–Wright Export Corp.,* 299 U.S. 304, 319–322, 57 S.Ct. 216, 220–222, 81 L.Ed. 255.

probably not possible to delineate a fixed and precise line of separation in these matters between political and judicial power under the Constitution. Certainly, however, nothing in the structure of our Government or the text of our Constitution would warrant judicial review by standards which would require us to equate our political judgment with that of Congress.

Under the conditions which produced this Act, can we declare that congressional alarm about a coalition of Communist power without and Communist conspiracy within the United States is either a fantasy or a pretense? This Act was approved by President Roosevelt June 28, 1940, when a world war was threatening to involve us, as soon it did. Communists in the United States were exerting every effort to defeat and delay our preparations. Certainly no responsible American would say that there were then or are now no possible grounds on which Congress might believe that Communists in our midst are inimical to our security.

Congress received evidence that the Communist movement here has been heavily laden with aliens and that Soviet control of the American Communist Party has been largely through alien Communists. It would be easy for those of us who do not have security responsibility to say that those who do are taking Communism too seriously and overestimating its danger. But we have an Act of one Congress which, for a decade, subsequent Congresses have never repealed but have strengthened and extended. We, in our private opinions, need not concur in Congress' policies to hold its enactments constitutional. Judicially we must tolerate what personally we may regard as a legislative mistake.

We are urged, because the policy inflicts severe and undoubted hardship on affected individuals, to find a restraint in the Due Process Clause. But the Due Process Clause does not shield the citizen from conscription and the consequent calamity of being separated from family, friends, home and business while he is transported to foreign lands to stem the tide of Communism. If Communist aggression creates such hardships for loyal citizens, it is hard to find justification for holding that the Constitution requires that its hardships must be spared the Communist alien. When citizens raised the Constitution as a shield against expulsion from their homes and places of business, the Court refused to find hardship a cause for judicial intervention.[17]

We think that, in the present state of the world, it would be rash and irresponsible to reinterpret our fundamental law to deny or qualify the Government's power of deportation. However desirable world-wide amelioration of the lot of aliens, we think it is peculiarly a subject for international diplomacy. It should not be initiated by judicial decision which can only deprive our own Government of a power of defense and reprisal without obtaining for American citizens abroad any reciprocal privileges or immunities. Reform in this field must be entrusted to the branches of

---

17. *Hirabayashi v. United States*, 320 U.S. 81, 63 S.Ct. 1375, 87 L.Ed. 1774 (1943); *Korematsu v. United States*, 323 U.S. 214, 65 S.Ct. 193, 89 L.Ed. 194 (1944). [These cases upheld discriminatory wartime measures, including internment, taken against U.S. citizens of Japanese descent on the West Coast.—eds.]

the Government in control of our international relations and treaty-making powers.

We hold that the Act is not invalid under the Due Process Clause. These aliens are not entitled to judicial relief unless some other constitutional limitation has been transgressed, to which inquiry we turn.

II.

The First Amendment is invoked as a barrier against this enactment. The claim is that in joining an organization advocating overthrow of government by force and violence the alien has merely exercised freedoms of speech, press and assembly which that Amendment guarantees to him.

The assumption is that the First Amendment allows Congress to make no distinction between advocating change in the existing order by lawful elective processes and advocating change by force and violence, that freedom for the one includes freedom for the other, and that when teaching of violence is denied so is freedom of speech.

Our Constitution sought to leave no excuse for violent attack on the status quo by providing a legal alternative—attack by ballot. To arm all men for orderly change, the Constitution put in their hands a right to influence the electorate by press, speech and assembly. This means freedom to advocate or promote Communism by means of the ballot box, but it does not include the practice or incitement of violence.[18]

True, it often is difficult to determine whether ambiguous speech is advocacy of political methods or subtly shades into a methodical but prudent incitement to violence. Communist governments avoid the inquiry by suppressing everything distasteful. Some would have us avoid the difficulty by going to the opposite extreme of permitting incitement to violent overthrow at least unless it seems certain to succeed immediately. We apprehend that the Constitution enjoins upon us the duty, however difficult, of distinguishing between the two. Different formulae have been applied in different situations and the test applicable to the Communist Party has been stated too recently to make further discussion at this time profitable.[19] We think the First Amendment does not prevent the deportation of these aliens.

III.

The remaining claim is that this Act conflicts with Art. I, § 9, of the Constitution forbidding *ex post facto* enactments. An impression of retroactivity results from reading as a new and isolated enactment what is actually a continuation of prior legislation.

During all the years since 1920 Congress has maintained a standing admonition to aliens, on pain of deportation, not to become members of any organization that advocates overthrow of the United States Govern-

18. *Dennis v. United States*, 341 U.S. 494, 71 S.Ct. 857, 95 L.Ed. 1137.

19. *Ibid.*

ment by force and violence, a category repeatedly held to include the Communist Party. These aliens violated that prohibition and incurred liability to deportation. They were not caught unawares by a change of law. There can be no contention that they were not adequately forewarned both that their conduct was prohibited and of its consequences.

In 1939, this Court decided *Kessler v. Strecker,* 307 U.S. 22, 59 S.Ct. 694, 83 L.Ed. 1082, in which it was held that Congress, in the statute as it then stood, had not clearly expressed an intent that Communist Party membership remained cause for deportation after it ceased. The Court concluded that in the absence of such expression only contemporaneous membership would authorize deportation.

The reaction of the Communist Party was to drop aliens from membership, at least in form, in order to immunize them from the consequences of their party membership.

The reaction of Congress was that the Court had misunderstood its legislation. In the Act here before us it supplied unmistakable language that past violators of its prohibitions continued to be deportable in spite of resignation or expulsion from the party. It regarded the fact that an alien defied our laws to join the Communist Party as an indication that he had developed little comprehension of the principles or practice of representative government or else was unwilling to abide by them.

However, even if the Act were found to be retroactive, to strike it down would require us to overrule the construction of the *ex post facto* provision which has been followed by this Court from earliest times. It always has been considered that that which it forbids is penal legislation which imposes or increases criminal punishment for conduct lawful previous to its enactment. Deportation, however severe its consequences, has been consistently classified as a civil rather than a criminal procedure. Both of these doctrines as original proposals might be debatable, but both have been considered closed for many years and a body of statute and decisional law has been built upon them.

* * *

It is contended that this policy allows no escape by reformation. We are urged to apply some doctrine of atonement and redemption. Congress might well have done so, but it is not for the judiciary to usurp the function of granting absolution or pardon. We cannot do so for deportable ex-convicts, even though they have served a term of imprisonment calculated to bring about their reformation.

When the Communist Party as a matter of party strategy formally expelled alien members en masse, it destroyed any significance that discontinued membership might otherwise have as indication of change of heart by the individual. Congress may have believed that the party tactics threw upon the Government an almost impossible burden if it attempted to separate those who sincerely renounced Communist principles of force and violence from those who left the party the better to serve it. Congress, exercising the wide discretion that it alone has in these matters, declined to accept that as the Government's burden.

We find none of the constitutional objections to the Act well founded. * * *

MR. JUSTICE CLARK took no part in the consideration or decision of these cases.

MR. JUSTICE FRANKFURTER, concurring.

It is not for this Court to reshape a world order based on politically sovereign States. In such an international ordering of the world a national State implies a special relationship of one body of people, *i.e.,* citizens of that State, whereby the citizens of each State are aliens in relation to every other State. Ever since national States have come into being, the right of people to enjoy the hospitality of a State of which they are not citizens has been a matter of political determination by each State. (I put to one side the oddities of dual citizenship.) Though as a matter of political outlook and economic need this country has traditionally welcomed aliens to come to its shores, it has done so exclusively as a matter of political outlook and national self-interest. This policy has been a political policy, belonging to the political branch of the Government wholly outside the concern and the competence of the Judiciary.

* * *

The Court's acknowledgment of the sole responsibility of Congress for these matters has been made possible by Justices whose cultural outlook, whose breadth of view and robust tolerance were not exceeded by those of Jefferson. In their personal views, libertarians like Mr. Justice Holmes and Mr. Justice Brandeis doubtless disapproved of some of these policies, departures as they were from the best traditions of this country and based as they have been in part on discredited racial theories or manipulation of figures in formulating what is known as the quota system. But whether immigration laws have been crude and cruel, whether they may have reflected xenophobia in general or anti-Semitism or anti-Catholicism, the responsibility belongs to Congress. Courts do enforce the requirements imposed by Congress upon officials in administering immigration laws * * *. But the underlying policies of what classes of aliens shall be allowed to enter and what classes of aliens shall be allowed to stay, are for Congress exclusively to determine even though such determination may be deemed to offend American traditions and may, as has been the case, jeopardize peace.

In recognizing this power and this responsibility of Congress, one does not in the remotest degree align oneself with fears unworthy of the American spirit or with hostility to the bracing air of the free spirit. One merely recognizes that the place to resist unwise or cruel legislation touching aliens is the Congress, not this Court.

I, therefore, join in the Court's opinion in these cases.

MR. JUSTICE DOUGLAS, with whom MR. JUSTICE BLACK concurs, dissenting.

There are two possible bases for sustaining this Act:

(1) A person who was once a Communist is tainted for all time and forever dangerous to our society; or

(2) Punishment through banishment from the country may be placed upon an alien not for what he did, but for what his political views once were.

Each of these is foreign to our philosophy. We repudiate our traditions of tolerance and our articles of faith based upon the Bill of Rights when we bow to them by sustaining an Act of Congress which has them as a foundation.

The view that the power of Congress to deport aliens is absolute and may be exercised for any reason which Congress deems appropriate rests on *Fong Yue Ting v. United States,* 149 U.S. 698, 13 S.Ct. 1016, 37 L.Ed. 905, decided in 1893 by a six-to-three vote. That decision seems to me to be inconsistent with the philosophy of constitutional law which we have developed for the protection of resident aliens. We have long held that a resident alien is a "person" within the meaning of the Fifth and the Fourteenth Amendments. * * * He is entitled to habeas corpus to test the legality of his restraint, to the protection of the Fifth and Sixth Amendments in criminal trials, and to the right of free speech as guaranteed by the First Amendment.

An alien, who is assimilated in our society, is treated as a citizen so far as his property and his liberty are concerned. He can live and work here and raise a family, secure in the personal guarantees every resident has and safe from discriminations that might be leveled against him because he was born abroad. Those guarantees of liberty and livelihood are the essence of the freedom which this country from the beginning has offered the people of all lands. If those rights, great as they are, have constitutional protection, I think the more important one—the right to remain here—has a like dignity.

The power of Congress to exclude, admit, or deport aliens flows from sovereignty itself and from the power "To establish an uniform Rule of Naturalization." U.S. Const., Art. I, § 8, cl. 4. The power of deportation is therefore an *implied* one. The right to life and liberty is an *express* one. Why this *implied* power should be given priority over the *express* guarantee of the Fifth Amendment has never been satisfactorily answered. * * *

The right to be immune from arbitrary decrees of banishment certainly may be more important to "liberty" than the civil rights which all aliens enjoy when they reside here. Unless they are free from arbitrary banishment, the "liberty" they enjoy while they live here is indeed illusory. Banishment is punishment in the practical sense. It may deprive a man and his family of all that makes life worth while. Those who have their roots here have an important stake in this country. Their plans for themselves and their hopes for their children all depend on their right to stay. If they are uprooted and sent to lands no longer known to them, no longer hospitable, they become displaced, homeless people condemned to bitterness and despair.

This drastic step may at times be necessary in order to protect the national interest. There may be occasions when the continued presence of an alien, no matter how long he may have been here, would be hostile to the safety or welfare of the Nation due to the nature of his conduct. But unless such condition is shown, I would stay the hand of the Government and let those to whom we have extended our hospitality and who have become members of our communities remain here and enjoy the life and liberty which the Constitution guarantees.

Congress has not proceeded by that standard. It has ordered these aliens deported not for what they are but for what they once were. Perhaps a hearing would show that they continue to be people dangerous and hostile to us. But the principle of forgiveness and the doctrine of redemption are too deep in our philosophy to admit that there is no return for those who have once erred.

NOTES AND QUESTIONS: THE IMPLICATIONS OF HARISIADES

1. Despite the broad wording of the deportation grounds for subversion, they were used infrequently. In the 1950s, 230 noncitizens were deported on these grounds. The number declined to 15 in the 1960s, and to 18 in the 1970s. The federal government then stopped publishing separate statistics for this ground. 2001 INS Statistical Yearbook, table 67.

2. *Harisiades* was sorely disappointing to those who thought the Supreme Court rulings in *Kessler* and *Bridges* foretold more robust constitutional protections for lawful permanent residents. But both decisions had relied on statutory grounds, allowing the Court to avoid constitutional issues. *Harisiades*, facing the constitutional challenges head on, was different in tone and result. The times had changed. In the seven years between *Bridges* and *Harisiades*, World War II had ended, the U.S.–U.S.S.R. alliance had dissolved, and the Cold War had begun. Moreover, the Communist Party's effort to take advantage of *Kessler* by expelling noncitizen members had provoked a widespread negative reaction.

3. Justice Jackson wrote for the *Harisiades* majority more than fifty years ago. The Cold War has since ended, and the Soviet Union dissolved in 1992. Yet, the references to perilous global politics and world-wide hostile movements may sound eerily familiar in the United States post-September 11. But do the fundamental changes in international law, which now acknowledges the rights of individuals as well as the rights of states, undermine the *Harisiades* rationale? What about the substantial rise in the number of states, including the United States, that authorize dual nationality? What is the impact of later Supreme Court decisions that have distinguished between procedural due process guarantees at the border and in the interior? Does the analysis in *Harisiades* allow room for analogous distinctions suggesting closer

constitutional scrutiny of deportability, not inadmissibility, is at issue? What view of permanent residence does *Harisiades* reflect, and is that view persuasive today?

These questions may become less daunting as we work through the next subsection, which addresses several themes that they raise, including how removal is related to (a) punishment, (b) retroactivity, (c) statutory interpretation, (d) the meaning of permanent residence, (e) the passage of time, and (f) constitutional liberties.

3. THE CONCEPT OF DEPORTABILITY

a. Removal and Punishment

Justice Jackson summarily dismissed the idea that expulsion is punishment for constitutional purposes. But it is doubtful that he really meant that deportation is not punishment in the sense of harm or sanctions for misconduct or violation of law. James Madison forcefully made this argument long ago against the Alien and Sedition Acts:

> If the banishment of an alien from a country into which he has been invited as the asylum most auspicious to his happiness,—a country where he may have formed the most tender connections; where he may have invested his entire property, and acquired property of the real and permanent, as well as the movable and temporary kind; where he enjoys, under the laws, a greater share of the blessings of personal security, and personal liberty, than he can elsewhere hope for; * * *—if a banishment of this sort be not a punishment, and among the severest of punishments, it will be difficult to imagine a doom to which the name can be applied.

4 Elliot's Debates 555 (Philadelphia, J.B. Lippincott & Co., 1881 ed.). Rather, it seems clear that Jackson was distinguishing civil from criminal punishments to protect immigration statutes from the substantive and procedural limits the Constitution places on criminal proceedings.

The Court's distinction between deportation and punishment is most evident in contrasting the landmark cases of *Fong Yue Ting v. United States*, 149 U.S. 698, 13 S.Ct. 1016, 37 L.Ed. 905 (1893), and *Wong Wing v. United States*, 163 U.S. 228, 16 S.Ct. 977, 41 L.Ed. 140 (1896), pp. 171, 184, *supra*. Recall that *Fong Yue Ting* upheld the deportation of Chinese noncitizens under the 1892 immigration statute for lack of a residence certificate that could be obtained only on the basis of testimony from a white witness. The decision also held that the constitutional protection against cruel and unusual punishment does not apply to deportation. In contrast, the Court in *Wong Wing* struck down, in the same statute, a section that authorized imprisonment, without a judicial trial, of noncitizens found deportable. *Wong Wing* sharply distinguished deportation from punishment:

> No limits can be put by the courts upon the power of Congress to protect, by summary methods, the country from the advent of aliens

whose race or habits render them undesirable as citizens, or to expel such if they have already found their way into our land and unlawfully remain therein. But to declare unlawful residence within the country to be an infamous crime, punishable by deprivation of liberty and property, would be to pass out of the sphere of constitutional legislation, unless provision were made that the fact of guilt should first be established by a judicial trial.

Id. at 237.

Though the doctrine persists that removal from the United States is not punishment for constitutional purposes, we will see later in this chapter that the Supreme Court has been more receptive to arguments for greater constitutional protection in some settings based on the sheer severity of removal. *See Padilla v. Kentucky*, 559 U.S. ___, 130 S.Ct. 1473, 176 L.Ed.2d 284 (2010), p. 683, *infra*.

b. Retroactivity

The ex post facto clause. By reaffirming that removal is not punishment for constitutional purposes, *Harisiades* was able to invoke the well-established corollary that the Constitution's prohibition against ex post facto laws does not apply to deportation statutes. A noncitizen may be deported for past conduct that did not render the noncitizen deportable at the time the act was committed. Part III of Justice Jackson's opinion addressed the ex post facto challenge briefly, noting that Congress had given notice, via anti-subversive speech statutes, that membership in certain organizations could lead to deportation, and that in any event the ex post facto clause is implicated only in criminal proceedings.

Two years later, the Supreme Court rejected an ex post facto challenge to the deportation of Juan Galvan, who had lived in the United States since arriving from Mexico in 1918. Applying the Subversive Activities Control Act of 1950, an INS hearing officer ordered Galvan deported after finding that he had belonged to the Communist Party from 1944 to 1946. Writing for the Court, Justice Frankfurter explained:

> In light of the expansion of the concept of substantive due process as a limitation upon all powers of Congress, * * * much could be said for the view, were we writing on a clean slate, that the Due Process Clause qualifies the scope of political discretion heretofore recognized as belonging to Congress in regulating the entry and deportation of aliens. And since the intrinsic consequences of deportation are so close to punishment for crime, it might fairly be said also that the *ex post facto* Clause, even though applicable only to punitive legislation, should be applied to deportation.

> But the slate is not clean. As to the extent of the power of Congress under review, there is not merely "a page of history," *New York Trust Co. v. Eisner*, 256 U.S. 345, 349, 41 S.Ct. 506, 507, 65 L.Ed. 963, but a whole volume. Policies pertaining to the entry of aliens and their right to remain here are peculiarly concerned with

the political conduct of government. * * * [T]hat the formulation of these policies is entrusted exclusively to Congress has become about as firmly imbedded in the legislative and judicial tissues of our body politic as any aspect of our government. And whatever might have been said at an earlier date for applying the *ex post facto* Clause, it has been the unbroken rule of this Court that it has no application to deportation.

Galvan v. Press, 347 U.S. 522, 530–31, 74 S.Ct. 737, 742, 98 L.Ed. 911 (1954).

Justice Black dissented, joined by Justice Douglas:

* * * [D]uring the period of his membership * * * [Communist] Party candidates appeared on California election ballots, and no federal law then frowned on Communist Party political activities. * * *

For joining a lawful political group years ago—an act which he had no possible reason to believe would subject him to the slightest penalty—[Galvan] now loses his job, his friends, his home, and maybe even his children, who must choose between their father and their native country.

Id. at 532–33, 74 S.Ct. at 743–44 (Black, J., dissenting).

The Supreme Court has consistently rejected ex post facto challenges to other deportability grounds. *See, e.g., Mahler v. Eby,* 264 U.S. 32, 44 S.Ct. 283, 68 L.Ed. 549 (1924) (upholding the retroactive application of a 1920 statute to a 1918 conviction under the Selective Draft and the Espionage Acts of 1917); *Marcello v. Bonds,* 349 U.S. 302, 75 S.Ct. 757, 99 L.Ed. 1107 (1955) (upholding the retroactive application of a 1952 deportation statute to a 1938 marijuana-related conviction). Similarly futile have been ex post facto challenges to a deportability ground, added in 1978 and now in INA § 237(a)(4)(D), for former Nazis who had "ordered, incited, assisted, or otherwise participated" in the persecution of others between 1933 and 1945. *See Artukovic v. INS,* 693 F.2d 894 (9th Cir. 1982); *Matter of Kulle,* 19 I & N Dec. 318 (BIA 1985). The section has also withstood arguments that it is an unconstitutional bill of attainder. *See Linnas v. INS,* 790 F.2d 1024 (2d Cir.1986).

Similar retroactivity issues arose from Congress' efforts in the 1990s to add new criminal deportability grounds and expand existing ones. Legislation in 1996 significantly expanded criminal deportability grounds, sometimes retroactively. Under § 321(b) of the 1996 Act, the expanded definition of aggravated felony in INA § 101(a)(43) applies "regardless of whether the conviction was entered before, on, or after the date of enactment." *See also* AEDPA § 435(b) (expanded deportability ground for crimes of moral turpitude applies in all proceedings begun after the date of enactment, but irrespective of when the crime was committed). Ex post facto challenges to retroactive applications of this sort have consistently failed. *See, e.g., Kuhali v. Reno,* 266 F.3d 93, 111–12 (2d Cir. 2001) (expanded definition of aggravated felony); *United States v. Yacoubian*, 24 F.3d 1, 9–10 (9th Cir.1994) (deportation ground for firearms offenses); *Campos v. INS*, 16 F.3d 118, 122 (6th Cir.1994) (bar to waiver of deportation for aggravated felons).

The due process clause. The Supreme Court has applied the due process clause to scrutinize legislation that imposes new civil duties or liabilities based on past acts, but it has demanded no more than a rational basis for the retroactive application. In one decision, the Court added:

> Our decisions, however, have left open the possibility that legislation might be unconstitutional if it imposes severe retroactive liability on a limited class of parties that could not have anticipated the liability, and the extent of that liability is substantially disproportionate to the parties' experience.

Eastern Enterprises v. Apfel, 524 U.S. 498, 524–28, 118 S.Ct. 2131, 2146–49, 141 L.Ed.2d 451 (1998). The Court's recent receptivity to greater constitutional protection based on the severity of removal—*see Padilla v. Kentucky*, 559 U.S. ___, 130 S.Ct. 1473, 176 L.Ed.2d 284 (2010), p. 683, *infra*—may signal an opening for a due process argument against retroactive deportability grounds.

Policy considerations. Though courts have swallowed the fiction that deportation is not punishment, they have rarely addressed what interests are served by banishing a long-term resident of the United States for something that could not have led to her deportation at the time. Retroactive deportability prompts at least two policy objections, that it is unjust (1) to impose harsh sanctions for conduct that was lawful when undertaken; and (2) to deport someone who made a mistake long ago but since has lived a peaceful and productive life in the United States. For Justice Douglas, this second problem amounted to "the absence of a rational connection between the imposition of the penalty of deportation and the *present* desirability of the alien as a resident in this country." *Marcello v. Bonds,* 349 U.S. 302, 321, 75 S.Ct. 757, 767, 99 L.Ed. 1107 (1955) (Douglas, J., dissenting).

c. Statutory Interpretation and the Rule of Lenity

Though retroactive deportability grounds have been sustained, concerns about retroactivity can play a significant role in statutory interpretation. For example, when *Galvan* rejected the ex post facto challenge, the Court seemed to read any *scienter* requirement out of the deportation ground. Communist Party membership could lead to deportation, regardless of the member's attitude toward violent change or his understanding of the Party's mission or tactics. Yet, applying that deportability ground retroactively may have led to second thoughts. Three years later, Justice Frankfurter construed the deportation statute to require a "meaningful association" with the Party. *See Rowoldt v. Perfetto,* 355 U.S. 115, 120, 78 S.Ct. 180, 183, 2 L.Ed.2d 140 (1957).

Much more recently, and more directly on the retroactivity issue, the Supreme Court addressed legislation in 1996 that tightened eligibility for discretionary relief from removal. The Court held that the changes were not retroactive, because there is a presumption against retroactivity that only a clear congressional statement could overcome. *See INS v. St. Cyr*, 533 U.S. 289, 121 S.Ct. 2271, 150 L.Ed.2d 347 (2001). But so long as Congress has explicitly provided for retroactivity, courts have deferred.

Reaching beyond retroactivity to the interpretation of deportation statutes generally, a classic approach has been to read such statutes narrowly. Justice Douglas penned the classic statement of this canon of interpretation, sometimes called the "rule of lenity":

> We resolve the doubts in favor of that construction [urged by the noncitizen] because deportation is a drastic measure and at times the equivalent of banishment or exile * * *. It is the forfeiture for misconduct of a residence in this country. Such a forfeiture is a penalty. To construe this statutory provision less generously to the alien might find support in logic. But since the stakes are considerable for the individual, we will not assume that Congress meant to trench on his freedom beyond that which is required by the narrowest of several possible meanings of the words used.

Fong Haw Tan v. Phelan, 333 U.S. 6, 10, 68 S.Ct. 374, 376, 92 L.Ed. 433 (1948). In *Fong Haw Tan*, the government sought to deport a permanent resident alien on the basis of a criminal record; the Supreme Court ultimately interpreted the statute not to establish deportability.

Does this canon of statutory interpretation surprise you, in light of the plenary power doctrine as a substantial obstacle to challenges to the government's immigration decisions? Or does the canon make sense in light of the plenary power doctrine? That is, the Court recognizes broad congressional authority, but because of deportation's harsh consequences, will insist that Congress state clearly when noncitizens are deportable. This "clear statement" rule of statutory construction imposes a duty on Congress to consider carefully the scope of deportation grounds—an indirect means for the Court to help make sure the political check is fully operative, because the legislators and the public are explicit about what is at issue. It also helps clarify for noncitizens what specific acts may carry harsh consequences.

Paralleling *Fong Haw Tan*'s rule of lenity, courts have sometimes construed immigration-related statutes in the noncitizen's favor because the statute might otherwise tread close to—or possibly transgress—constitutional limits. This is an application of the doctrine of constitutional avoidance—the principle that statutes should be read to avoid interpretations that raise serious constitutional questions. As noted in Chapter Six's discussion of procedural due process, courts sometimes read a statute in the noncitizen's favor even when the plenary power doctrine could preclude constitutional challenge. *See* Motomura, *Immigration Law After a Century of Plenary Power: Phantom Constitutional Norms and Statutory*

Interpretation, 100 Yale L.J. 545 (1990). This idea of phantom norms is one way to explain why statutes relating to deportability are not retroactive unless Congress clearly states that they are.

d. The Significance of Permanent Residence

Justice Murphy's concurrence in *Bridges v. Wixon*, *supra*, p. 653, reflects a view of permanent resident status that contrasts sharply with Justice Jackson's emphasis in *Harisiades* that Harisiades, Coleman, and Mascitti lived in the United States for decades without embracing the Constitution, becoming citizens, and renouncing their foreign allegiances. To assess this contrast, consider the framework proposed by Hiroshi Motomura in Americans in Waiting: The Lost Story of Immigration and Citizenship in the United States (2006).*

> * * * [F]or much of its history, America treated lawful immigrants as future citizens, and immigration as a transition to citizenship. Lawful immigrants—or as I will outline later, *some* lawful immigrants—could become "intending citizens." For more than a century and a half—from 1795 to 1952—every applicant for naturalization had to file a declaration of intent several years in advance. This declaration gave any noncitizen who was eligible to naturalize a precitizenship status that elevated him, even from his first day in America, well above those who had not filed declarations and therefore were not seen as on the citizenship track. Many statutes throughout this period expressly preferred intending citizens. The Homestead Act of 1862, the key to settling the western frontier, made noncitizens eligible for grants of land once they filed declarations. The U.S. government sometimes extended diplomatic protection to intending citizens who got into trouble overseas. And until the early twentieth century, many intending citizens could vote.

> * * *

> To capture this way of viewing immigration, I have coined the term *immigration as transition*. It treats lawful immigrants as Americans in waiting, as if they would eventually become citizens of the United States, and thus confers on immigrants a *presumed equality*. * * *

> * * *

> * * * [Another view] of immigration is what I call *immigration as contract*. [L]awful immigrants [may] have "promised" to stay out of trouble with the law, on pain of deportation. Or even if they do not commit any crimes, their admission to this country may be just a temporary grant of permission that the government can revoke at any time. Or perhaps [they] promised to support themselves financially. On the other hand, the U.S. government may have promised not to

change the rules governing their vulnerability to deportation, or the rules governing their access to public benefits. These similar ideas appear frequently in the making of law and policy, past and present.

* * *

[B]y contract I mean a certain way of making immigration decisions. The offer that immigrants accept by coming to America may be a take-it-or-leave-it proposition. Their bargaining power is very weak, and there is no real negotiation. And yet, immigration as contract is accurate to describe this view of immigration because it adopts ideas of fairness and justice often associated with contracts. The core idea is thinking about coming to America as a set of expectations and understandings that newcomers have of their new country, and their new country has of newcomers.

Underlying this way of talking about fairness and justice in our treatment of lawful immigrants is a certain way of thinking about equality in immigration and citizenship. Immigration as contract is based on the sense that fairness and justice for lawful immigrants does not require us to treat them as the equals of citizens. Though immigration as contract is a model of justice, it is a model of *unequal justice* that turns not on conferring equality itself, but on giving notice and protecting expectations.

* * *

[A] third view of immigration alongside transition and contract * * * I call *immigration as affiliation*. This is the view that the treatment of lawful immigrants and other noncitizens should depend on the ties that they have formed in this country. Newcomers put down roots. Immigration as affiliation is the foundation for the argument that lawful immigrants * * * should be treated just like citizens, now that they have paid taxes, have children who are U.S. citizens, and have shown themselves to be reliable and productive workers.

As a way of thinking and talking about fairness and justice in immigration, affiliation drives arguments that lawful immigrants—though convicted of crimes that make them deportable—should be allowed to stay in the United States, if they have been here for a long time and have strong family and community ties. The longer they are here, and the more they become enmeshed in the fabric of American life, the more these lawful immigrants and citizens should be treated equally. This view of immigration is not based on the justice without equality of immigration as contract, nor on the presumed equality of immigration as transition, but rather on an *earned equality*.

Id. at 9–11.

For Justice Jackson, any presumed equality would have vanished when the noncitizens had lived in the United States long enough to naturalize and had failed to become citizens. In contrast, Justice Murphy implied that their affiliation was key: their lawful residence, time during which they paid taxes, raised U.S. citizen children, and were members of the U.S. community. In your view, what is the difference between being a permanent resident and being a U.S. citizen? What is the difference between being a permanent resident and another type of noncitizen in the United States—for example, a lawfully present nonimmigrant, or a long-term resident who lacks lawful immigration status?

e. Deportability Grounds and the Passage of Time

Suppose a noncitizen was convicted of a crime many years after being admitted to the United States. Suppose she was admitted as an infant and committed the offense as an adult. Or suppose she committed a crime twenty years ago that could have led to her deportation, but she has led an exemplary life since then, and only now is the government taking steps to enforce the law against her. Or suppose a new deportability ground applies retroactively to something that she did long ago. Should the passage of time affect removal? If so, how?

(i) Time Before the Initiation of Removal Proceedings

In criminal law, a statute of limitations normally begins running when a crime has been committed. The rationales include: (1) the desirability that prosecutions be based on fresh evidence; (2) the likelihood that a person who has refrained from further criminal activity for a period of time has reformed; (3) the decline of the retributive impulse over time; (4) the desirability of lessening the possibility of blackmail based on a threat to prosecute or disclose evidence to law enforcement officials; and (5) the promotion of repose. American Law Institute, Model Penal Code and Commentaries, Comment Part I § 1.06 (1985). A similar rule in immigration law could require removal proceedings to be initiated a certain number of years after the act that is the basis for deportability.

The "excludable at entry" deportation ground once had a statute of limitations. The 1903 Act provided: "any alien who shall come into the United States in violation of law * * * shall be deported * * * at any time within two years after arrival." Act of March 3, 1903, ch. 1012, § 20, 32 Stat. 1218. This period later became three years, Act of February 20, 1907, ch. 1134, § 20, 34 Stat. 904, and then five years, Immigration Act of 1917, ch. 29, § 19, 39 Stat. 889. When Congress repealed the limitation in 1952, the Senate Judiciary Committee explained: "If the cause for exclusion existed at the time of entry, it is believed that such aliens are just as undesirable at any subsequent time as they are within the five years after entry." S.Rep. No. 1515, 81st Cong., 2d Sess. 389 (1950).

Mae Ngai argues that some of the criminal law rationales apply to the initiation of removal proceedings against noncitizens who are in the United States unlawfully. (As a technical matter, some of them would be inadmissible, and some deportable.) Referring to the statutes of limitations in some early federal immigration statutes, she explains:

* * * This policy recognized an important reality about illegal immigrants: They settle, raise families and acquire property—in other words, they become part of the nation's economic and social fabric. * * *

* * *

A statute of limitations on unlawful entry is * * * consistent with basic legal and moral principles. It does not condone or reward illegal immigration: Unauthorized presence would remain a violation of the law and continue to carry the risk of apprehension and removal, at least for some period of time. But it would allow us to recognize that the undocumented become, for better or worse, members of the community, and to accept them as such.

Restoring the statute of limitations would not solve our immigration problems. But it would go a long way toward stemming the accretion of a caste population that is easily exploitable and lives forever outside the polity.

Ngai, *We Need A Deportation Deadline*, Wash. Post, June 14, 2005, at A21. *See also* Aleinikoff, *Illegal Employers*, American Prospect, Dec. 4, 2000 (proposing a ten-year statute of limitations for unauthorized migrants).

But consider the rebuttal that the concept of a statute of limitations does not apply as Ngai urges. Even if the unlawful entry was long ago, the noncitizen is unlawfully present today. Faced with a related issue, the U.S. Supreme Court held in 2006 that it was not retroactive to apply a newly enacted removal procedure to a noncitizen someone who had unlawfully entered many years before. Justice David Souter's majority opinion explained that the relevant time was not the original entry, but unlawful presence today:

> While the law [INA § 241(a)(5)] looks back to a past act in its application to "an alien [who] has reentered ... illegally," the provision does not penalize an alien for the reentry (criminal and civil penalties do that) * * *. Thus, it is the conduct of remaining in the country after entry that is the predicate action; the statute applies to stop an indefinitely continuing violation that the alien himself could end at any time by voluntarily leaving the country. It is therefore the alien's choice to continue his illegal presence, after illegal reentry and after the effective date of the new law, that subjects him to the new and less generous legal regime, not a past act that he is helpless to undo up to the moment the Government finds him out.

Fernandez–Vargas v. Gonzales, 548 U.S. 30, 44, 126 S.Ct. 2422, 165 L.Ed.2d 323 (2006). By this reasoning, how can any statute of limitations even *start* to run while the noncitizen is in the United States unlawfully?

One current INA section operates roughly like a statute of limitations as Ngai uses the term. Noncitizens who entered the United States before January 1, 1972, may become permanent residents—as a matter of government discretion—via registry under § 249. Continuous residence in the

United States and good moral character are required, and some inadmissibility and deportability grounds apply. With the cutoff date so far in the past, it is unsurprising that only 163 noncitizens became permanent resident through registry in fiscal year 2009. DHS, 2009 Yearbook of Immigration Statistics 27, table 7.

As a member of Congress, would you support advancing the registry cutoff date? Would you support a five-year (or ten-year?) statute of limitations for all deportability grounds? Some grounds and not others?

(ii) Time Between Admission and the Commission of a Deportable Act

A related but distinct concern asks if it is appropriate to expel a long-term resident. It often seems unusually harsh to remove some who has spent most of her life in the United States, even if removal proceedings start promptly after the deportability ground arises. These considerations are even more powerful for children who came to the United States at an early age and have been socialized here. This group—sometimes called the 1.5 generation or Generation 1.5—is most likely to have deep social and cultural ties in the United States, and unlikely to have many ties to rely on if they are forced to return to their country of origin. In these situations, the "immigration as affiliation" perspective identified by Hiroshi Motomura, p. 670, *supra*, would support the view that these long-term residents, like citizens, should not be banished from their homes.

The deportability ground of a crime involving moral turpitude applies to a noncitizen "convicted of a crime involving moral turpitude committed within five years * * * after admission." INA § 237(a)(2)(A)(i). Should the same idea—that acts should no longer make a noncitizen deportable after certain period of residence in the United States—be applied to other deportability grounds? For some grounds but not others, or different time periods for different grounds, such as a longer period for deportability based on a violent crime as compared to a nonviolent one?

One response might be that long-term residents can avoid removal by becoming citizens. This echoes *Harisiades v. Shaughnessy*, p. 655, *supra*, where Justice Jackson emphasized that the three longtime residents had failed to pursue their opportunity to naturalize. This may reflect an "immigration as transition" perspective that would confer on lawful permanent residents a presumed equality with citizens that would not continue if they failed to apply for citizenship once eligible. Alternatively, one might apply a version of "immigration as contract" to argue that permanent residence is granted with the understanding that it remains revocable, and that the law clearly signaled at the time of contracting (admission) that criminal misconduct could jeopardize residence or in any event that no noncitizen in the United States enjoys complete security of residence.

f.   The First Amendment and Other Constitutional Liberties

The final theme raised by *Harisiades* is the relationship between deportability and constitutional liberties. Are deportability statutes limited by general constitutional guarantees—such as due process and equal protection under the Fifth Amendment, or freedom of speech and association under the First Amendment?

Under *Yamataya v. Fisher,* 189 U.S. 86, 23 S.Ct. 611, 47 L.Ed. 721 (1903), discussed in Chapter Six, the Fifth Amendment's guarantee of procedural due process applies to a deportation hearing, but *Yamataya* did not address substantive deportability grounds. In contrast, *Harisiades* did not involve a challenge to deportation procedures. Instead the Court's decision rejected a First Amendment constitutional challenge, among others, to a statutory deportation ground based on Communist Party membership. Does this mean that Congress could pass a law ordering the removal of any noncitizen who marches in a parade supporting legalization of marijuana, or who joins the Ku Klux Klan? Perhaps you could read Justice Jackson's opinion that way, but the constitutional reasoning deserves a closer look.

Justice Jackson seemed to say that the speech in question was not protected and thus deportation based on such speech could not offend the First Amendment. He cited *Dennis v. United States,* 341 U.S. 494, 71 S.Ct. 857, 95 L.Ed. 1137 (1951), decided the year before *Harisiades. Dennis* sustained the criminal convictions of Communist organizers under the Smith Act, a 1940 statute (passed as a rider to the statute in *Harisiades*) that prohibited knowingly or willfully advocating the overthrow of the United States government. *Dennis* held that speech is not protected by the First Amendment "where there is a 'clear and present danger' of the substantive evil which the legislature had the right to prevent." 341 U.S. 494, 515, 71 S.Ct. 857, 870, 95 L.Ed. 1137 (1951).

In 1969, *Brandenburg v. Ohio,* 395 U.S. 444, 89 S.Ct. 1827, 23 L.Ed.2d 430 (1969) (per curiam), cast substantial doubt on the continuing vitality of *Dennis* by striking down a statute similar to the Smith Act. Applying a standard less deferential to the government, the Court effectively expanded First Amendment protections. *Brandenburg* held that the government may not "forbid or proscribe advocacy of the use of force or of law violation except where such advocacy is directed to *inciting or producing imminent lawless action* and is likely to incite or produce such action." 395 U.S. at 447, 89 S.Ct. at 1829 (emphasis added).

Did *Brandenburg* change what *Harisiades* says about First Amendment protections for lawful permanent residents? How would you respond to the following argument?

> The First Amendment as construed in *Dennis* did not protect what Harisiades, Mascitti, and Coleman did, and this conclusion did not depend on whether they were citizens or noncitizens. Thus, *Harisiades* stands for the proposition that the First Amendment protects citizens and noncitizens equally. Now that *Brandenburg* has

expanded the scope of the First Amendment beyond what it was in *Dennis*, noncitizens should enjoy the same expanded coverage as citizens. Thus, *Brandenburg*, by superseding *Dennis*, in effect overrules *Harisiades*.

See generally Aleinikoff, *Federal Regulation of Aliens and the Constitution*, 83 Am. J. Int'l L. 862, 868–69 (1989).

The meaning of *Harisiades* became central to convoluted litigation that fought efforts to deport eight noncitizens for their associations with the Popular Front for the Liberation of Palestine. The government first charged the noncitizens with membership in an organization that advocated world communism. Against the six who were not permanent residents, the government then dropped these charges, substituting deportation grounds based on overstaying or otherwise violating their terms of admission. The government persisted with the communism-related grounds against the two permanent residents. The federal district court held that the charged provisions relating to subversive speech were unconstitutional. *American–Arab Anti–Discrimination Committee v. Meese*, 714 F.Supp. 1060 (C.D.Cal.1989).

The Immigration Act of 1990 then repealed the communism-related deportation grounds. The government turned to the new antiterrorist deportability provisions in INA § 237(a)(4)(B) that makes deportable any alien covered by under the terrorism-related inadmissibility grounds in §§ 212(a)(3)(B) or (F), discussed earlier in this chapter.

The district court preliminarily enjoined the proceedings against the six nonimmigrants, holding that the government was engaged in unlawful selective prosecution based on their political associations. On appeal, the Ninth Circuit rejected the government's claim that "aliens are not entitled to the same First Amendment protections that citizens enjoy":

> The Supreme Court has consistently distinguished between aliens in the United States and those seeking to enter from outside the country, and has accorded to aliens living in the United States those protections of the Bill of Rights that are not, by the text of the Constitution, restricted to citizens. *Kwong Hai Chew v. Colding*, 344 U.S. 590, 596 n. 5, 73 S.Ct. 472, 477 n. 5, 97 L.Ed. 576 (1953). Accordingly, the Court has explicitly stated that "[f]reedom of speech and of press is accorded aliens residing in this country." *Bridges v. Wixon*, 326 U.S. 135, 148, 65 S.Ct. 1443, 1449, 89 L.Ed. 2103 (1945).

* * *

Because we are a nation founded by immigrants, this underlying principle is especially relevant to our attitude toward current immigrants who are a part of our community. Aliens, who often have different cultures and languages, have been subjected to intolerant and harassing conduct in our past, particularly in times of crises. It is thus especially appropriate that the First Amendment principle of tolerance for different voices restrain our decisions to expel a participant in that community from our midst. *See Bridges*, 326 U.S. at 149, 65 S.Ct. at 1450 ("[W]here the fate of a human being is at stake the presence of the evil purpose may not be left to conjecture.").

American–Arab Anti–Discrimination Committee v. Reno, 70 F.3d 1045, 1063–64 (9th Cir.1995).

The Ninth Circuit rejected the government's argument that "First Amendment constitutional protections are unnecessary because deportation is not a criminal proceeding":

> It is true that some constitutional protections, available to citizens and aliens alike in the criminal setting, do not apply in civil proceedings and thus do not apply to the non-criminal deportation proceedings. However, because the First Amendment's protections apply equally to non-criminal and criminal proceedings, constitutionally protected activities that the Government cannot punish by means of a criminal statute are likewise beyond its reach in a deportation proceeding.

Id. at 1065.

The government invoked plenary power—"the broad authority of the political branches over immigration matters justifies limited First Amendment protection for aliens at deportation"—but the court replied:

> First, although Congress and the President may regulate aliens' admission and residence in the country, that regulation must be "consistent with the Constitution." *Fong Yue Ting v. United States*, 149 U.S. 698, 712, 13 S.Ct. 1016, 1021, 37 L.Ed. 905 (1893). "Since resident aliens have constitutional rights, it follows that Congress may not ignore them in the exercise of its 'plenary' power of deportation." *Bridges*, 326 U.S. at 161, 65 S.Ct. at 1455 (Murphy, J., concurring). Thus, Congress' less restrained power to decide which aliens to exclude from entry, using processes and procedures that would be constitutionally suspect for citizens, is not dispositive regarding the constitutional constraints that operate at deportation. *Cf. Fiallo v. Bell*, 430 U.S. 787, 97 S.Ct. 1473, 52 L.Ed.2d 50 (1977) (upholding immigration preference categories for aliens at entry); *Shaughnessy v. United States ex rel. Mezei*, 345 U.S. 206, 73 S.Ct. 625, 97 L.Ed. 956 (1953) (upholding summary processes for exclusion of aliens at entry).
>
> Second, our First Amendment jurisprudence rests on the fundamental principle that limitations on First Amendment rights are themselves damaging to the values underlying First Amendment protections. If aliens do not have First Amendment rights at deportation, then their First Amendment rights in other contexts are a nullity, because the omnipresent threat of deportation would permanently chill their expressive and associational activities.

Id. at 1065–66.

On review, the U.S. Supreme Court ruled for the government on jurisdictional grounds, finding that the limits on judicial review in INA § 242 did not allow the noncitizens to raise their claims in court, at least not before there was a final removal order. *Reno v. American–Arab Anti–Discrimination Committee*, 525 U.S. 471, 119 S.Ct. 936, 142 L.Ed.2d 940 (1999). Writing for the Court, Justice Scalia rejected the noncitizens' argument that jurisdiction was necessary because delaying review of their selective prosecution claim would chill their First Amendment rights. Scalia wrote: "an alien unlawfully in this country has no constitutional right to assert selective enforcement as a defense against his deportation." Justice Ginsburg, concurring, agreed that the First Amendment did not require immediate judicial review of the selective enforcement claim. But she wrote, citing *Bridges v. Wixon*, that she was "not persuaded" that the selective enforcement of deportation laws would survive a properly presented First Amendment challenge. *See* 525 U.S. at 497–98, 119 S.Ct. at 950 (Ginsburg, J., concurring in part and concurring in the judgment).

Though the Court ruled against the noncitizens on both jurisdiction and selective prosecution, it did not rule on the constitutionality of the terrorism-related deportability ground invoked against the two permanent residents. In 2007, eight years after the Court's ruling and 21 years after the case began, immigration judge Bruce Einhorn dismissed the immigration charges, holding that the government's failure to disclose potentially exculpatory evidence as to the noncitizens' alleged PFLP activities violated the two permanent residents' due process rights. In the meantime, Aiad Barakat, one of the six nonimmigrants when the story started, prevailed on the revised status violation charge, became a lawful permanent resident, and became a U.S. citizen in 2006. *See* Weinstein, *20–Year Bid to Deport 2 Is Dismissed*, L.A. Times, Jan. 31, 2007.

NOTES AND QUESTIONS ON DEPORTABILITY AND THE CONSTITUTION

1. To consolidate your understanding of any First Amendment limits on the government's power to define deportability, how would the U.S. Supreme Court decide a First Amendment challenge to removing permanent residents based on membership in a terrorist organization? In answering this question, consider the significance of the following paragraph, which is part of a longer passage quoted earlier in this chapter, *supra* p. 641, from *Holder v. Humanitarian Law Project*, 561 U.S. ___, 130 S.Ct. 2705, 177 L.Ed.2d 355 (2010).

> Our precedents, old and new, make clear that concerns of national security and foreign relations do not warrant abdication of the judicial role. We do not defer to the Government's reading of the First Amendment, even when such interests are at stake. We are one with the dissent that the Government's "authority and expertise in these matters do not automatically trump the Court's own obligation to secure the protection that the Constitution grants to individuals." But when it comes to collecting evidence and drawing factual inferences in this area, "the lack of competence on the part of the courts is marked," *Rostker*, 453 U.S. at

65, 101 S.Ct. 2646, and respect for the Government's conclusions is appropriate.

130 S.Ct. at 2727.

Does it make a difference that *Humanitarian Law Project* was a criminal prosecution and involved the constitutionality of the criminal penalties in 18 U.S.C. § 2339B for contributing material support to organizations designated as foreign terrorist organizations under § 219?

2 The Ninth Circuit's First Amendment holding in *AADC*—that the six nonimmigrants and the two permanent residents are equally protected— referred to "current immigrants who are a part of our community," 70 F.3d at 1064, reflecting a view of immigration as affiliation. Compare Justice Murphy's reasoning in *Bridges v. Wixon*, p. 653, *supra*: "once an alien *lawfully enters and resides* in this country he becomes invested with the rights guaranteed by the Constitution to all people within our borders." (Emphasis supplied.) Do lawfully present nonimmigrants have the same First Amendment protections as permanent residents? Or is it the length of residence that matters more than lawful presence? What about long-term residents who are unlawfully present? Does Justice Murphy's dictum apply to the six nonimmigrants involved in AADC, who were admitted as B, F, and H–1 nonimmigrants and so were not lawful permanent residents of the United States? If the dictum did apply initially, would it continue to apply once they overstayed their admission period? (Recall that the issue for them was not whether they could be prosecuted for giving a speech, which the First Amendment would almost surely forbid. It was whether the government had to carry the burden of negating a selective prosecution claim before it could apply the law to uncontested violations.)

3. Justice Murphy also wrote that if the First Amendment prohibits the government from imprisoning a noncitizen for protected speech, it also must prohibit the government from deporting the noncitizen. Do you agree? Would recognizing that immigration decisions are intimately tied to national self-definition suggest that the nation may deport noncitizens on political grounds, even if it is unable to control the conduct of citizens? Is it persuasive to distinguish imprisonment from deportation because the latter is simply the withdrawal of a privilege to remain in the United States? What about a deportability ground for noncitizens who advocate changing the United States into a theocracy? What about a deportability ground for noncitizens who advocate, but do not imminently incite, suicide bombing to achieve that goal?

4. Another related deportability ground is potentially very broad, though it has been invoked quite sparingly. Section 237(a)(4)(C) makes removable noncitizens whom the Secretary of State has reasonable grounds to believe would, by their presence or activities, have potentially serious adverse foreign policy consequences for the United States. This ground is parallel to the inadmissibility ground discussed in Section A of this chapter, and is subject to the same limits and exceptions.

5. The number of cases filed in immigration court in which the government relies on terrorism-related deportability is very small. Only 12 such cases were filed in fiscal years 2004–2006, and 114 cases relied on national security deportability grounds, out of a total 814,073 cases in that period.

Transactional Records Access Clearinghouse (TRAC), *Immigration Enforcement: The Rhetoric, The Reality*, May 28, 2007, <trac.syr.edu/immigration/reports/178/>. (TRAC reports deportability under § 237(a)(4)(A) as national security-related and under § 237(a)(4)(B) as terrorism-related.) But do the charged deportability grounds accurately measure the impact of DHS enforcement? If you were an ICE investigator and had substantial evidence of a noncitizen's terrorist involvement, when would you seek removal on a terrorism charge? Would it matter that the individual was admitted as a nonimmigrant? Entered without inspection? Think about the evidence you are likely to have and what you would present in immigration court.

6. Now consider other constitutional protections, such as equal protection. Could Congress order the removal of all noncitizen males of Arab descent? All Jewish noncitizens? All noncitizens from North Korea? Recall the *Chinese Exclusion Case*, p. 167, *supra, Fiallo v. Bell*, p. 293, *supra*, and this from Justice Frankfurter's *Harisiades* concurrence: "the underlying policies of what classes of aliens shall be allowed to enter and what classes of aliens shall be allowed to stay, are for Congress exclusively to determine even though such determination may be deemed to offend American traditions and may, as has been the case, jeopardize peace."

Exercise: Rethinking Deportability

Before we examine the crime-related grounds of deportability, consider all of the deportability grounds in § 237(a) that are not crime-related.

Which of these grounds would you keep? Which would you delete? What grounds would you add? Would you add a ground for violations of civil rights laws?

Would you reword deportability grounds to differ more from any analogous inadmissibility grounds? Would you distinguish more sharply between permanent residents and other noncitizens? Would it matter that a permanent resident has not naturalized after a certain number of years??

Would you deport a noncitizen for conduct (or a trait) which is not unlawful for a U.S. citizen—e.g., drug addiction or poverty? What principles and values guide your choices?

---

4. CRIMES

In fiscal year 2010, 168,532 noncitizens with criminal convictions and 218,710 without criminal convictions were formally removed, about 43 percent of all removals based on formal removal orders. The following table shows the recent trend:

Figure 7.1

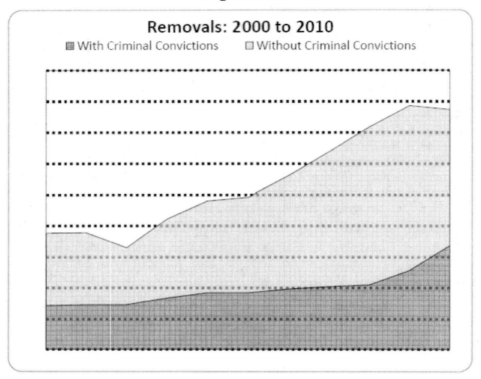

Source: DHS, 2010 Yearbook of Immigration Statistics 96–103, table 38.[7]

These 168,532 removals in 2010 of noncitizens with criminal convictions include removals based on both inadmissibility and deportability grounds. Of this total, about 31,000 had convictions for immigration-related crimes (including entry, reentry, false claims to citizenship, and alien smuggling). DHS Office of Immigration Statistics, Immigration Enforcement Actions: 2010, at 4, table 4 (2011).

DHS reports as a criminal removal any noncitizen with a criminal conviction, even if it was not the legal basis for removal. Through 2005, DHS reported the number of removals for which a criminal violation was the legal basis, as well as the number of removals of noncitizens with criminal convictions. In 2005, a criminal violation was the formal legal

---

7. The DHS Yearbook of Immigration Statistics understates the number of removals of noncitizens with criminal convictions, because information regarding criminal convictions is not collected for all noncitizens who are removed. In particular, a new data system in use since 2008 does not capture the criminal history on persons removed by CBP. *See* DHS, 2010 Yearbook of Immigration Statistics 103, table 38, note. For 2010, the number of such removals reported in the DHS Yearbook is 168,532 or 43 percent of all removals, but the number reported by ICE (based on removals in which it participated) is 195,772 removals or virtually half of removals conducted by ICE. For the years 2008 through 2010, ICE Enforcement and Removal Operations has reported a higher number of removals of noncitizens with criminal convictions than those reported in the DHS Yearbook. *See* <http://www.ice.gov/doclib/about/offices/ero/pdf/ero-removals.pdf>.

ground charged for 40,018 removals, or fewer than half of the year's removals of noncitizens with criminal convictions. DHS, 2005 Yearbook of Immigration Statistics 96, table 40.

The government only infrequently relies on a criminal ground of deportability for noncitizens who have deportable convictions but are not lawful permanent residents. Citing the conviction to prove deportability would be an unnecessary complication for DHS. If the noncitizen is an EWI or an overstay and also involved in crime, DHS typically charges the more accessible immigration control ground, which usually can be readily proven based solely on DHS records. Even if the noncitizen committed the crime while in lawful nonimmigrant status, that status will often have expired or been violated by the end of the criminal proceedings. Though the conviction is relevant to DHS's charging priorities and to eligibility for possible relief (treated in Section C), it need not be made the basis of the deportability charge. Keep in mind as you read the cases in this Section that most of the doctrine is developed in, and has relevance for, cases involving lawful permanent residents.

Daniel Kanstroom argues that the "war on crime" in the 1890s and early 1900s, and the assertions of greater criminality in the foreign born, gave birth to modern post-entry social control deportation laws. D. Kanstroom, Deportation Nation: Outsiders in American History 125 (2007). But are immigrants more likely than citizens to commit crimes? Empirical research suggests not. For example, a study based on 2000 Census data reported that foreign-born males between 18–39 years of ages are incarcerated at a significantly lower rate than their native-born counterparts. *See* Rumbaut et al., *Debunking the Myth of Immigrant Criminality: Imprisonment Among First– and Second–Generation Young Men*, Migration Information Source (June 2006), <www.migration information.org/ Feature /display.cfm?id=403>. The study's author, Rubén Rumbaut, offered related observations in a later co-authored paper:

> Nationally, rates of incarceration among immigrant men are lower than among their U.S. born counterparts—a pattern that seems to apply for every ethnic group. That was true during the last era of mass migration in the early twentieth century, and it remains so today. In fact, instead of being responsible for increasing crime in the United States, immigrants may be a factor in reducing it. Since the early 1990s, when the immigrant population (and especially the undocumented population) was increasing sharply to historic highs, the overall rates of property and violent crimes in the United States decreased significantly, in many instances to historic lows, and those decreases have been especially noticeable in cities and areas of immigrant concentration. Additionally, survey data from the Los Angeles metropolitan area showed lower rates of arrest and incarceration among the foreign born (including the groups with the highest proportion of undocumented immigrants) than among native born young men. The problem of crime in the United States is not caused by

immigration, and never has been. That is largely a bogus claim, albeit a persistent one—an enduring stereotype.

Dingeman & Rumbaut, *The Immigration–Crime Nexus and Post–Deportation Experiences: En/Countering Stereotypes in Southern California and El Salvador*, 31 U. La Verne L. Rev. 363, 400 (2010).

In light of the facts that Dingeman and Rumbaut describe, the increasing number of criminal removals over the past decade reflects not increased crime by immigrants, but rather greater government resources and better technical means devoted to identifying those noncitizens (most of them already lacking a legal status) who commit crimes.

———

Juliet Stumpf offers an observation that further helps to frame the issues:

> While criminal law is animated by the idea that the punishment must be proportionate to the crime, proportionality is scarce in immigration law. Criminal law embodies proportionality in punishment schemes that impose milder sanctions such as short or suspended sentences for lesser crimes, and harsher sanctions for graver crimes. In contrast, the statutory sanction for every immigration violation is removal from the country.

Stumpf, *Fitting Punishment*, 66 Wash. & Lee L. Rev. 1683, 1687–88 (2009). Are you troubled by the largely binary nature of immigration punishment? What would a better, more proportional approach look like? How would it apply, if at all, to non-LPRs who have a criminal conviction and are then placed in removal proceedings, since their removability normally is not dependent on the criminal conduct? *Cf.* Chin, *Illegal Entry as Crime, Deportation as Punishment: Immigration Status and the Criminal Process*, 58 UCLA L.Rev. 1417 (2011) (proposing that immigration status play a more substantial role in the criminal prosecution and sentencing of noncitizens for nonimmigration crimes).

Ask yourself, as you read about the types of criminal convictions that can make a noncitizen deportable: what interests are served by removing noncitizens who have completed the sentence the judge imposed? Should lawful permanent residents receive the same treatment as citizens, who cannot be banished? Or do they have a greater duty to comply with society's rule that justifies removal as an added penalty for violations? Should it matter how long they have lived in the United States? Should there be comparable protections for long-term unauthorized residents? On what terms? What about those who arrived in the United States as infants and have never lived elsewhere?

a. Criminal Prosecution/Defense and Immigration Law

In 2010, the U.S. Supreme Court issued *Padilla v. Kentucky*, a decision with potential implications for the characterization of deportation as a matter of constitutional law, and for the relationship between criminal and immigration law, especially the immigration consequences of convictions. It also has prompted lawyers in the criminal justice system to seek more training on immigration law and consider immigration consequences in plea bargaining. *Padilla* shows how immigration law and criminal law are impossible to separate when the defendant in a criminal case is not a U.S. citizen, at least when the defendant is a lawful permanent resident.

Consider also the immediate implications of *Padilla*. How should an immigration lawyer advise a defense attorney or prosecutor about the immigration consequences of various possible plea agreements? What options are available to a noncitizen to undo a prior conviction that makes her deportable? Crucial to answering this second question is that one of the main constitutional challenges to a prior conviction is ineffective assistance of counsel. A successful challenge will invalidate the conviction.

PADILLA v. KENTUCKY

Supreme Court of the United States, 2010
559 U.S. ____, 130 S.Ct. 1473, 176 L.Ed.2d 284

JUSTICE STEVENS delivered the opinion of the Court.

Petitioner Jose Padilla, a native of Honduras, has been a lawful permanent resident of the United States for more than 40 years. Padilla served this Nation with honor as a member of the U.S. Armed Forces during the Vietnam War. He now faces deportation after pleading guilty to the transportation of a large amount of marijuana in his tractor-trailer in the Commonwealth of Kentucky.[1]

In this postconviction proceeding, Padilla claims that his counsel not only failed to advise him of this consequence prior to his entering the plea, but also told him that he " 'did not have to worry about immigration status since he had been in the country so long.' " Padilla relied on his counsel's erroneous advice when he pleaded guilty to the drug charges that made his deportation virtually mandatory. He alleges that he would have insisted on going to trial if he had not received incorrect advice from his attorney.

* * *

While the 1917 [Immigration and Nationality] Act was "radical" because it authorized deportation as a consequence of certain convictions, the Act also included a critically important procedural protection to minimize the risk of unjust deportation: At the time of sentencing or within 30 days thereafter, the sentencing judge in both state and federal prosecutions had the power to make a recommendation "that such alien shall not be deported." [39 Stat.] at 890. This procedure, known as a judicial recommendation against deportation, or JRAD, had the effect of

---

1. Padilla's crime, like virtually every drug offense except for only the most insignificant marijuana offenses, is a deportable offense under INA § 237(a)(2)(B)(i).

binding the Executive to prevent deportation; the statute was "consistent-ly . . . interpreted as giving the sentencing judge conclusive authority to decide whether a particular conviction should be disregarded as a basis for deportation," *Janvier v. United States,* 793 F.2d 449, 452 (C.A.2 1986). Thus, from 1917 forward, there was no such creature as an automatically deportable offense. Even as the class of deportable offenses expanded, judges retained discretion to ameliorate unjust results on a case-by-case basis.

* * *

However, the JRAD procedure is no longer part of our law. Congress first circumscribed the JRAD provision in the 1952 Immigration and Nationality Act (INA), and in 1990 Congress entirely eliminated it. In 1996, Congress also eliminated the Attorney General's authority to grant discretionary relief from deportation, an authority that had been exercised to prevent the deportation of over 10,000 noncitizens during the 5–year period prior to 1996. Under contemporary law, if a noncitizen has commit-ted a removable offense after the 1996 effective date of these amendments, his removal is practically inevitable but for the possible exercise of limited remnants of equitable discretion vested in the Attorney General to cancel removal for noncitizens convicted of particular classes of offenses. Subject to limited exceptions, this discretionary relief is not available for an offense related to trafficking in a controlled substance.

These changes to our immigration law have dramatically raised the stakes of a noncitizen's criminal conviction. The importance of accurate legal advice for noncitizens accused of crimes has never been more important. These changes confirm our view that, as a matter of federal law, deportation is an integral part—indeed, sometimes the most impor-tant part—of the penalty that may be imposed on noncitizen defendants who plead guilty to specified crimes.

Before deciding whether to plead guilty, a defendant is entitled to "the effective assistance of competent counsel." *McMann v. Richardson,* 397 U.S. 759, 771, 90 S.Ct. 1441, 25 L.Ed.2d 763 (1970); *Strickland [v. Washington,* 466 U.S. 668, 686, 104 S.Ct. 2052, 80 L.Ed.2d 674 (1984)]. The Supreme Court of Kentucky rejected Padilla's ineffectiveness claim on the ground that the advice he sought about the risk of deportation concerned only collateral matters, *i.e.,* those matters not within the sentencing authority of the state trial court. In its view, "collateral consequences are outside the scope of representation required by the Sixth Amendment," and, therefore, the "failure of defense counsel to advise the defendant of possible deportation consequences is not cognizable as a claim for ineffective assistance of counsel." 253 S.W.3d, at 483. The Kentucky high court is far from alone in this view.

We, however, have never applied a distinction between direct and collateral consequences to define the scope of constitutionally "reasonable professional assistance" required under *Strickland,* 466 U.S., at 689, 104

S.Ct. 2052. Whether that distinction is appropriate is a question we need not consider in this case because of the unique nature of deportation.

We have long recognized that deportation is a particularly severe "penalty," *Fong Yue Ting v. United States,* 149 U.S. 698, 740, 13 S.Ct. 1016, 37 L.Ed. 905 (1893); but it is not, in a strict sense, a criminal sanction. Although removal proceedings are civil in nature, deportation is nevertheless intimately related to the criminal process. Our law has enmeshed criminal convictions and the penalty of deportation for nearly a century. And, importantly, recent changes in our immigration law have made removal nearly an automatic result for a broad class of noncitizen offenders. Thus, we find it "most difficult" to divorce the penalty from the conviction in the deportation context. *United States v. Russell,* 686 F.2d 35, 38 (C.A.D.C.1982). Moreover, we are quite confident that noncitizen defendants facing a risk of deportation for a particular offense find it even more difficult.

Deportation as a consequence of a criminal conviction is, because of its close connection to the criminal process, uniquely difficult to classify as either a direct or a collateral consequence. The collateral versus direct distinction is thus ill-suited to evaluating a *Strickland* claim concerning the specific risk of deportation. We conclude that advice regarding deportation is not categorically removed from the ambit of the Sixth Amendment right to counsel. *Strickland* applies to Padilla's claim.

III

Under *Strickland,* we first determine whether counsel's representation "fell below an objective standard of reasonableness." 466 U.S., at 688, 104 S.Ct. 2052. Then we ask whether "there is a reasonable probability that, but for counsel's unprofessional errors, the result of the proceeding would have been different." *Id.,* at 694, 104 S.Ct. 2052. The first prong—constitutional deficiency—is necessarily linked to the practice and expectations of the legal community * * *.

The weight of prevailing professional norms supports the view that counsel must advise her client regarding the risk of deportation. * * *

We too have previously recognized that " '[p]reserving the client's right to remain in the United States may be more important to the client than any potential jail sentence.' " *St. Cyr,* 533 U.S., at 323, 121 S.Ct. 2271 (quoting 3 Criminal Defense Techniques §§ 60A.01, 60A.02[2] (1999)). * * *

In the instant case, the terms of the relevant immigration statute are succinct, clear, and explicit in defining the removal consequence for Padilla's conviction. See INA § 237(a)(2)(B)(i). Padilla's counsel could have easily determined that his plea would make him eligible for deportation simply from reading the text of the statute, which addresses not some broad classification of crimes but specifically commands removal for all controlled substances convictions except for the most trivial of marijuana possession offenses. Instead, Padilla's counsel provided him false assurance that his conviction would not result in his removal from this country. This is not a hard case in which to find deficiency: The consequences of Padilla's plea could easily be determined from reading the removal statute, his deportation was presumptively mandatory, and his counsel's advice was incorrect.

Immigration law can be complex, and it is a legal specialty of its own. Some members of the bar who represent clients facing criminal charges, in either state or federal court or both, may not be well versed in it. There will, therefore, undoubtedly be numerous situations in which the deportation consequences of a particular plea are unclear or uncertain. The duty of the private practitioner in such cases is more limited. When the law is not succinct and straightforward (as it is in many of the scenarios posited by Justice Alito), a criminal defense attorney need do no more than advise a noncitizen client that pending criminal charges may carry a risk of adverse immigration consequences. But when the deportation consequence is truly clear, as it was in this case, the duty to give correct advice is equally clear.

* * *

The Solicitor General has urged us to conclude that *Strickland* applies to Padilla's claim only to the extent that he has alleged affirmative misadvice. In the United States' view, "counsel is not constitutionally required to provide advice on matters that will not be decided in the criminal case . . .," though counsel is required to provide accurate advice if she chooses to discusses these matters.

* * *

A holding limited to affirmative misadvice would invite two absurd results. First, it would give counsel an incentive to remain silent on matters of great importance, even when answers are readily available. Silence under these circumstances would be fundamentally at odds with the critical obligation of counsel to advise the client of "the advantages and disadvantages of a plea agreement." *Libretti v. United States,* 516 U.S. 29, 50–51, 116 S.Ct. 356, 133 L.Ed.2d 271 (1995). When attorneys know that their clients face possible exile from this country and separation from their families, they should not be encouraged to say nothing at all. Second, it would deny a class of clients least able to represent themselves the most rudimentary advice on deportation even when it is readily available. It is quintessentially the duty of counsel to provide her client with available advice about an issue like deportation and the failure to do so "clearly satisfies the first prong of the *Strickland* analysis." *Hill v. Lockhart,* 474 U.S. 52, 62, 106 S.Ct. 366, 88 L.Ed.2d 203 (1985) (White, J., concurring in judgment).

* * *

It seems unlikely that our decision today will have a significant effect on those convictions already obtained as the result of plea bargains. For at least the past 15 years, professional norms have generally imposed an obligation on counsel to provide advice on the deportation consequences of a client's plea. We should, therefore, presume that counsel satisfied their obligation to render competent advice at the time their clients considered pleading guilty.

Likewise, although we must be especially careful about recognizing new grounds for attacking the validity of guilty pleas, in the 25 years since we first applied *Strickland* to claims of ineffective assistance at the plea stage, practice has shown that pleas are less frequently the subject of collateral challenges than convictions obtained after a trial. Pleas account for nearly 95% of all criminal convictions. But they account for only approximately 30% of the habeas petitions filed. The nature of relief secured by a successful collateral challenge to a guilty plea—an opportunity to withdraw the plea and proceed to trial—imposes its own significant limiting principle: Those who collaterally attack their guilty pleas lose the benefit of the bargain obtained as a result of the plea. Thus, a different calculus informs whether it is wise to challenge a guilty plea in a habeas proceeding because, ultimately, the challenge may result in a *less favorable* outcome for the defendant, whereas a collateral challenge to a conviction obtained after a jury trial has no similar downside potential.

Finally, informed consideration of possible deportation can only benefit both the State and noncitizen defendants during the plea-bargaining process. By bringing deportation consequences into this process, the defense and prosecution may well be able to reach agreements that better satisfy the interests of both parties. As in this case, a criminal episode may provide the basis for multiple charges, of which only a subset mandate deportation following conviction. Counsel who possess the most rudimentary understanding of the deportation consequences of a particular criminal offense may be able to plea bargain creatively with the prosecutor in order to craft a conviction and sentence that reduce the likelihood of deportation, as by avoiding a conviction for an offense that automatically triggers the removal consequence. At the same time, the threat of deportation may provide the defendant with a powerful incentive to plead guilty to an offense that does not mandate that penalty in exchange for a dismissal of a charge that does.

In sum, we have long recognized that the negotiation of a plea bargain is a critical phase of litigation for purposes of the Sixth Amendment right to effective assistance of counsel. The severity of deportation—"the equivalent of banishment or exile," *Delgadillo v. Carmichael,* 332 U.S. 388, 390–391, 68 S.Ct. 10, 92 L.Ed. 17 (1947)—only underscores how critical it is for counsel to inform her noncitizen client that he faces a risk of deportation.[15]

---

15. To this end, we find it significant that the plea form currently used in Kentucky courts provides notice of possible immigration consequences. Further, many States require trial courts to advise defendants of possible immigration consequences. [The Court cited 22 such state statutes.]

It is our responsibility under the Constitution to ensure that no criminal defendant—whether a citizen or not—is left to the "mercies of incompetent counsel." *Richardson,* 397 U.S., at 771, 90 S.Ct. 1441. To satisfy this responsibility, we now hold that counsel must inform her client whether his plea carries a risk of deportation. Our longstanding Sixth Amendment precedents, the seriousness of deportation as a consequence of a criminal plea, and the concomitant impact of deportation on families living lawfully in this country demand no less.

Taking as true the basis for his motion for postconviction relief, we have little difficulty concluding that Padilla has sufficiently alleged that his counsel was constitutionally deficient. Whether Padilla is entitled to relief will depend on whether he can demonstrate prejudice as a result thereof, a question we do not reach because it was not passed on below.

* * *

JUSTICE ALITO, with whom THE CHIEF JUSTICE joins, concurring in the judgment.

I concur in the judgment because a criminal defense attorney fails to provide effective assistance within the meaning of *Strickland v. Washington,* 466 U.S. 668, 104 S.Ct. 2052, 80 L.Ed.2d 674 (1984), if the attorney misleads a noncitizen client regarding the removal consequences of a conviction. In my view, such an attorney must (1) refrain from unreasonably providing incorrect advice and (2) advise the defendant that a criminal conviction may have adverse immigration consequences and that, if the alien wants advice on this issue, the alien should consult an immigration attorney. I do not agree with the Court that the attorney must attempt to explain what those consequences may be. * * *

I

* * *

The Court tries to downplay the severity of the burden it imposes on defense counsel by suggesting that the scope of counsel's duty to offer advice concerning deportation consequences may turn on how hard it is to determine those consequences. Where "the terms of the relevant immigration statute are succinct, clear, and explicit in defining the removal consequence[s]" of a conviction, the Court says, counsel has an affirmative duty to advise the client that he will be subject to deportation as a result of the plea. But "[w]hen the law is not succinct and straightforward . . ., a criminal defense attorney need do no more than advise a noncitizen client that pending criminal charges may carry a risk of adverse immigration consequences." This approach is problematic * * *.

First, it will not always be easy to tell whether a particular statutory provision is "succinct, clear, and explicit." How can an attorney who lacks general immigration law expertise be sure that a seemingly clear statutory provision actually means what it seems to say when read in isolation? What if the application of the provision to a particular case is not clear but a cursory examination of case law or administrative decisions would provide a definitive answer?

Second, if defense counsel must provide advice regarding only one of the many collateral consequences of a criminal conviction, many defendants are likely to be misled. To take just one example, a conviction for a particular offense may render an alien excludable but not removable. If an alien charged with such an offense is advised only that pleading guilty to such an offense will not result in removal, the alien may be induced to enter a guilty plea without realizing that a consequence of the plea is that the alien will be unable to reenter the United States if the alien returns to his or her home country for any reason, such as to visit an elderly parent or to attend a funeral. Incomplete legal advice may be worse than no advice at all because it may mislead and may dissuade the client from seeking advice from a more knowledgeable source.

Third, the Court's rigid constitutional rule could inadvertently head off more promising ways of addressing the underlying problem—such as statutory or administrative reforms requiring trial judges to inform a defendant on the record that a guilty plea may carry adverse immigration consequences. As *amici* point out, "28 states and the District of Columbia have *already* adopted rules, plea forms, or statutes requiring courts to advise criminal defendants of the possible immigration consequences of their pleas." Brief for State of Louisiana et al. 25. A nonconstitutional rule requiring trial judges to inform defendants on the record of the risk of adverse immigration consequences can ensure that a defendant receives needed information without putting a large number of criminal convictions at risk; and because such a warning would be given on the record, courts would not later have to determine whether the defendant was misrepresenting the advice of counsel. Likewise, flexible statutory procedures for withdrawing guilty pleas might give courts appropriate discretion to determine whether the interests of justice would be served by allowing a particular defendant to withdraw a plea entered into on the basis of incomplete information.

* * *

* * * [S]everal considerations support the conclusion that affirmative misadvice regarding the removal consequences of a conviction may constitute ineffective assistance.

First, a rule prohibiting affirmative misadvice regarding a matter as crucial to the defendant's plea decision as deportation appears faithful to the scope and nature of the Sixth Amendment duty this Court has recognized in its past cases. * * * [T]horough understanding of the intricacies of immigration law is not "within the range of competence demanded of attorneys *in criminal cases*." By contrast, reasonably competent attorneys should know that it is not appropriate or responsible to hold themselves out as authorities on a difficult and complicated subject matter with which they are not familiar. * * *

Second, incompetent advice distorts the defendant's decisionmaking process and seems to call the fairness and integrity of the criminal proceeding itself into question. When a defendant opts to plead guilty without definitive information concerning the likely effects of the plea, the defendant can fairly be said to assume the risk that the conviction may carry indirect consequences of which he or she is not aware. That is not the case when a defendant bases the decision to plead guilty on counsel's express misrepresentation that the defendant will not be removable. * * *

Third, a rule prohibiting unreasonable misadvice regarding exceptionally important collateral matters would not deter or interfere with ongoing political and administrative efforts to devise fair and reasonable solutions to the difficult problem posed by defendants who plead guilty without knowing of certain important collateral consequences.

Finally, the conclusion that affirmative misadvice regarding the removal consequences of a conviction can give rise to ineffective assistance would, unlike the Court's approach, not require any upheaval in the law. As the Solicitor General points out, "[t]he vast majority of the lower courts considering claims of ineffective assistance in the plea context have [distinguished] between defense counsel who remain silent and defense counsel who give affirmative misadvice." * * *

In concluding that affirmative misadvice regarding the removal consequences of a criminal conviction may constitute ineffective assistance, I do not mean to suggest that the Sixth Amendment does no more than require defense counsel to avoid misinformation. When a criminal defense attorney is aware that a client is an alien, the attorney should advise the client that a criminal conviction may have adverse consequences under the immigration laws and that the client should consult an immigration specialist if the client wants advice on that subject. By putting the client on notice of the danger of removal, such advice would significantly reduce the chance that the client would plead guilty under a mistaken premise.

* * *

JUSTICE SCALIA, with whom JUSTICE THOMAS joins, dissenting.

In the best of all possible worlds, criminal defendants contemplating a guilty plea ought to be advised of all serious collateral consequences of conviction, and surely ought not to be misadvised. The Constitution, however, is not an all-purpose tool for judicial construction of a perfect world; and when we ignore its text in order to make it that, we often find ourselves swinging a sledge where a tack hammer is needed.

The Sixth Amendment guarantees the accused a lawyer "for his defense" against a "criminal prosecutio[n]"—not for sound advice about the collateral consequences of conviction. For that reason, and for the practical reasons set forth in Part I of Justice Alito's concurrence, I dissent from the Court's conclusion that the Sixth Amendment requires counsel to provide accurate advice concerning the potential removal consequences of a guilty plea. For the same reasons, but unlike the concurrence,

I do not believe that affirmative misadvice about those consequences renders an attorney's assistance in defending against the prosecution constitutionally inadequate; or that the Sixth Amendment requires counsel to warn immigrant defendants that a conviction may render them removable. * * *

* * *

The Sixth Amendment as originally understood and ratified meant only that a defendant had a right to employ counsel, or to use volunteered services of counsel. We have held, however, that the Sixth Amendment requires the provision of counsel to indigent defendants at government expense, *Gideon v. Wainwright,* 372 U.S. 335, 344–345, 83 S.Ct. 792, 9 L.Ed.2d 799 (1963), and that the right to "the assistance of counsel" includes the right to *effective* assistance, *Strickland v. Washington,* 466 U.S. 668, 686, 104 S.Ct. 2052, 80 L.Ed.2d 674 (1984). Even assuming the validity of these holdings, I reject the significant further extension that the Court, and to a lesser extent the concurrence, would create. * * *

There is no basis in text or in principle to extend the constitutionally required advice regarding guilty pleas beyond those matters germane to the criminal prosecution at hand—to wit, the sentence that the plea will produce, the higher sentence that conviction after trial might entail, and the chances of such a conviction. * * * Because the subject of the misadvice here was not the prosecution for which Jose Padilla was entitled to effective assistance of counsel, the Sixth Amendment has no application.

* * *

The Court's holding prevents legislation that could solve the problems addressed by today's opinions in a more precise and targeted fashion. If the subject had not been constitutionalized, legislation could specify which categories of misadvice about matters ancillary to the prosecution invalidate plea agreements, what collateral consequences counsel must bring to a defendant's attention, and what warnings must be given. Moreover, legislation could provide consequences for the misadvice, nonadvice, or failure to warn, other than nullification of a criminal conviction after the witnesses and evidence needed for retrial have disappeared. Federal immigration law might provide, for example, that the near-automatic removal which follows from certain criminal convictions will not apply where the conviction rested upon a guilty plea induced by counsel's misadvice regarding removal consequences. Or legislation might put the government to a choice in such circumstances: Either retry the defendant or forgo the removal. But all that has been precluded in favor of today's sledge hammer.

* * *

NOTES AND QUESTIONS ON PADILLA

1. How will defense counsel or a court know when, as Justice Stevens puts it for the majority, "deportation consequence is truly clear"? If the deportation consequence is not clear, what is defense counsel's duty?

2. Is *Padilla* retroactive, that is, does it apply to convictions entered before the U.S. Supreme Court issued the decision on March 31, 2010? Yes, held the first federal appellate case to speak to the issue, explaining first the background requirements for retroactive application:

> In *Teague v. Lane,* 489 U.S. 288, 109 S.Ct. 1060, 103 L.Ed.2d 334 (1989), the Supreme Court set forth two regimes governing the retroactive application of constitutional principles to criminal cases. *Teague* divided the world into two categories, "old rules" and "new rules." A rule is a "new rule" for *Teague* purposes "if the result was not dictated by precedent existing at the time the defendant's conviction became final." *Id.* at 301. *Teague* held that a "new rule" is retroactively applicable to cases on collateral review if and only if one of two exceptions apply: (1) the new rule places certain kinds of criminal conduct beyond the power of the criminal law-making authority to proscribe; or (2) the new rule is a "watershed rule [ ] of criminal procedure" that "alter[s] our understanding of the *bedrock procedural elements* that must be found to vitiate the fairness of a particular conviction." *Teague,* 489 U.S. at 311 (emphasis in original) (internal quotation marks omitted). By contrast, an "old rule," applies on both direct and collateral review.

United States v. Orocio, 645 F.3d 630, 637 (3d Cir. June 29, 2011). The court found that "because *Padilla* followed directly from *Strickland* and long-established professional norms, it is an 'old rule' for *Teague* purposes and is retroactively applicable on collateral review." *Id.* at 641. Two later federal appellate cases reached the opposite conclusion. In *United States v. Chang Hong,* ___ F.3d ___, 2011 WL 3805763, at *6 (10th Cir. 2011), the court found: "While grounded in *Strickland,* we still conclude *Padilla* is a new rule of constitutional law. Before *Padilla,* most state and federal courts had considered the failure to advise a client of potential collateral consequences of a conviction to be outside the requirements of the Sixth Amendment." *Accord, Chaidez v. United States,* 655 F.3d 684 (7th Cir. 2011). The question is far from settled.

3. Failure to advise amounting to ineffective assistance of counsel is not enough to establish relief after *Padilla.* The defendant must also show actual prejudice. In this regard, it may be relevant that, as both the *Padilla* majority and Justice Alito's concurrence point out, a number of states—including California, Florida, New York, and Texas, and the District of Columbia—already had statutes requiring a trial judge, before accepting a plea of guilty (or nolo contendere in most states), to inform defendants that if they are not United States citizens a criminal conviction may lead to their removal from the United States.

What is the relationship between advisals under such state statutes and the duties recognized by the U.S. Supreme Court in *Padilla*? If a trial judge gives such an advisal to a defendant, how if at all are the defense attorney's obligations under *Padilla* affected? Does such a judicial warning cure the failure of defense counsel to advise about immigration consequences? To what extent can a defense attorney fulfill her obligations under *Padilla* by reading such an advisal to her client? Do the answers to these questions depend on whether the consequence of deportability is truly clear, as opposed to just a possibility?

4. Jenny Roberts argues that the traditional inquiry into prejudice—whether the defendant would have rejected the plea and proceeded to trial—is too narrow in the *Padilla* context because it fails to account for how ineffective assistance of counsel affects plea negotiations. She urges courts to broaden the traditional understanding of ineffective counsel and recognize that, for example, failure to negotiate an attainable plea can deprive noncitizen defendants of other options:

> First, counsel might re-negotiate, leading to a likely second plea structured to avoid imposition of the consequence (even if it means a higher penal sentence). Second, counsel might secure a sentence that is significantly discounted to account for the harshness of the collateral consequence. Third, a defendant might make a different risk calculation in deciding whether to plead guilty or go to trial.

Roberts, *Proving Prejudice, Post–*Padilla, 54 How. L.J. 693, 698 (2011).

5. As a practical matter, the defendant needs a procedural vehicle for post-conviction relief, see p. 697 *infra*, that will allow him to show that the conviction is invalid based on ineffective assistance and prejudice.

6. How does *Padilla* modify the traditional rule (or its practical consequences) that deportation or removal is not "punishment" for constitutional purposes? Even if *Padilla* proves to be a very important decision, will its impact be confined to the precise questions presented by the case?

b. The Basics of Crime–Related Deportability

Padilla underscores what is at stake and shows that accurate assessment of the immigration consequences of criminal convictions is essential over a long period of time—from plea negotiations in the criminal case all the way through determinations about deportability in a later removal proceeding in immigration court as well as post-conviction relief in the criminal justice system. With issues so framed, we now consider the immigration consequences of criminal convictions.

The major categories of crime-based deportability grounds in INA § 237(a)(2) are: crimes involving moral turpitude, aggravated felonies, drug crimes, firearms offenses, crimes of domestic violence, and several miscellaneous offenses. These categories often overlap in the sense that a particular conviction may trigger multiple grounds. Moreover, the same conviction can be the basis of both deportability and inadmissibility. After the following overview of the grounds that arise most frequently, we present several problems that allow you to check your understanding of the statutory basics.

(i) Crimes Involving Moral Turpitude

For most of the past century, conviction of a "crime involving moral turpitude" was the chief deportability ground based on crimes. Though the aggravated felony ground has prompted more litigation recently, the archaic-sounding moral turpitude ground remains in the statute.

One conviction of a crime involving moral turpitude makes a noncitizen deportable if he committed it within five years after the date of admission and a sentence of one year or longer may be imposed. INA § 237(a)(2)(A)(i). What counts as the date of admission? The BIA has held this provision refers to the admission by virtue of which a noncitizen is present in the United States. If, for example, a noncitizen is admitted as a nonimmigrant and later adjusts status to permanent resident without ever leaving the United States, the adjustment does not restart the five years. *See Matter of Alyazji*, 25 I & N Dec. 397 (BIA 2011). Convictions of two or more crimes involving moral turpitude (arising out of more than a single criminal scheme) make a noncitizen deportable regardless of the date of commission or length of sentence. INA § 237(a)(2)(A)(ii).

But what exactly is a crime involving moral turpitude? This term is maddeningly vague and the case law just as maddeningly intricate. The leading immigration practice treatise observes, "[a]ttempts to arrive at a workable definition of moral turpitude never have yielded entire satisfaction. * * * [T]his term defies precise definition, since its limits are charted by human experience." GM & Y § 71.05[1][d][i]. The administrative and judicial case law has adopted various formulations, such as the definition borrowed from Black's Law Dictionary: "an act of baseness, vileness, or depravity in the private and social duties which a man owes to his fellow men, or to society in general, contrary to the accepted and customary rule of right and duty between man and man."[1]

Moral turpitude provides a standard of conduct in other areas of law, such disbarment of attorneys, revocation of licenses, and impeachment of witnesses. In immigration law, there is broad agreement as to whether the generic versions—phrased in commonplace terms like "theft," "fraud," or "assault"—of many crimes involve moral turpitude. Thus serious crimes against persons (e.g., murder, voluntary manslaughter, rape, aggravated assault, kidnapping) and property (e.g., arson, burglary, embezzlement) are deemed to involve moral turpitude. Crimes with an element of fraud make up another general category of generic crimes involving moral turpitude. Leading authorities publish long lists that report whether convictions under particular statutes have been have been held to involve or not involve moral turpitude. *See, e.g.,* GM & Y § 71.05[1][d][iii]; M.E. Kramer, Immigration Consequences of Criminal Activity: A Guide to Representing Foreign–Born Defendants 204–16 (4th ed. 2009).

(ii) Aggravated Felonies

Section 237(a)(2)(A)(iii) makes deportable any noncitizen who has been convicted of an aggravated felony at any time after admission. INA

---

1. *See, e.g., United States v. Smith*, 420 F.2d 428, 431 (5th Cir.1970).

§ 101(a)(43) defines aggravated felony in broad terms that ensures that a wide range of state criminal offenses fall within the definition—imagine the difficulty of listing in a statute all relevant offenses from the 50 states.

The Anti–Drug Abuse Act of 1988 added "aggravated felony" to the INA in an effort to target crimes committed by participants in the drug trade, defining it at that time to include only murder, drug trafficking and trafficking in firearms. Legislative amendments in 1990, 1994, 1996, and 2001 greatly expanded the term in two dimensions. The statutory definition of aggravated felony is now much broader, with over 20 separate categories, many including multiple offenses. Under INA § 101(a)(43)(M), for example, an offense that involves fraud or deceit is an aggravated felony if the loss to the victim(s) exceeds $10,000. Until the 1996 amendments, this part of the aggravated felony definition required a loss exceeding $200,000. (Are all the crimes described in § 101(a)(43) appropriately labeled *aggravated* felonies?) Moreover, the definition is retroactive, though not all consequences of an aggravated felony conviction reach back into the indefinite past.

An aggravated felony conviction has severe consequences beyond deportability. Aggravated felons are ineligible for most forms of relief from removal (discussed in section C of this chapter). They may not obtain asylum, INA §§ 208(b)(2)(B)(i), cancellation of removal, § 240A(a)(3), or voluntary departure, § 240B(a)(1), (b)(1)(C). They are barred for life from re-entering the United States, unless they obtain consent to apply for readmission, § 212(a)(9)(A)(iii). Under INA § 238(b), aggravated felons who are not lawful permanent residents are subject to administrative removal without an immigration judge hearing. See p. 1210 *infra*. Aggravated felony convictions can also have major non-immigration law consequences, such as substantially enhancing the severity of a sentence. *See* U.S. Sentencing Commission, Guidelines Manual § 2L1.2 (2010). This is why many judicial decisions interpreting the aggravated felony statute are criminal cases with no immigration law implications.

Note that an aggravated felony conviction is not an explicit basis for inadmissibility, but it may also be a conviction for a crime involving moral turpitude or make a noncitizen inadmissible on some other ground. Whether the offense is an aggravated felony may also still be relevant because of the effect this may have on eligibility for waivers or relief from removal.

(iii) Drug Offenses

For more than half a century, the INA has made persons deportable if convicted of most drug offenses. The Anti–Drug Abuse Act of 1988 expanded the provision to cover any conviction "relating to a controlled substance." Pub.L. 100–690, § 1751(b), 102 Stat. 4181. (Of course, such crimes may also constitute crimes involving moral turpitude or aggravated felonies.) In 1990, Congress amended the deportation ground for any "narcotic drug addict" to include any alien who is a "drug abuser or addict," whether or not there has been a criminal conviction. INA § 237(a)(2)(B)(ii).

The current version of this deportability ground, INA § 237(a)(2)(B), applies to a conviction for violating *any* law, including that of a foreign country, relating to a controlled substance. The sole exception is narrow—for a single offense of possession of 30 grams or less of marijuana for personal use.

(iv) Crimes of Domestic Violence

In 1996, Congress added crimes involving domestic violence as a deportability ground. Noncitizens are deportable for convictions that occur at any time after admission on a list of specific crimes: domestic violence, stalking, child abuse, child neglect, or child abandonment, INA § 237(a)(2)(E)(i). It also includes those who have violated protection orders by making threats of violence, causing bodily injury, or engaging in repeated harassment, § 237(a)(2)(E)(ii).

The statutory definition of domestic violence includes two aspects: (1) the crime must be a crime of violence within the meaning of 18 U.S.C. § 16; and (2) the crime must be committed against a person who is a current or former spouse, or someone in a relationship similar to that of a spouse, § 237(a)(2)(E)(i). The statute also covers attacks against persons protected under federal or local domestic or family violence laws.

The Violence Against Women Act of 2000 (VAWA), Violence of Trafficking and Violence Protection Act of 2000, Pub. L. No. 106–386, 114 Stat. 1464, added a waiver for victims of domestic violence. The Attorney General may waive the domestic violence deportability ground for a noncitizen who has been the victim of battering or extreme cruelty if the noncitizen was acting in self defense or if other extenuating circumstances exist, § 237(a)(7).

As a practical matter, noncitizens who have been convicted of domestic violence might be charged as removable under three grounds of deportability: crime of domestic violence, § 237(a)(2)(E), crime involving moral turpitude, § 237(a)(2)(A)(i), and, if it was a crime of violence and the prison term was more than one year, aggravated felony, § 237(a)(2)(A)(iii).

PROBLEMS

3. E was admitted as a permanent resident seven years ago. Three years ago, he committed and was convicted of embezzlement and sentenced to six months to two years in prison, with all but six months of the sentence suspended.

4. F was admitted as a permanent resident seven years ago. Five years ago, he committed and was convicted of cocaine trafficking and sentenced to five years in prison.

5. G was admitted as a permanent resident ten years ago. Five years ago, he was convicted of tax fraud committed a year prior to the conviction. Two years ago, he committed and was convicted of money-laundering.

6. H, admitted as a permanent resident eight years ago, committed and was convicted of alien smuggling last year.

c. What Is a "Conviction"?

Most of the deportability grounds in INA § 237(a)(2) require a conviction. Under the definition in INA § 101(a)(48)(A), a conviction can occur without the entry of an adjudication of guilt, if defendant pleads nolo contendere or admits to facts sufficient to warrant a finding of guilt. The BIA has held that immigration consequences attach in deferred adjudications, if the defendant pled guilty but later had the charge dismissed upon successful completion of community service or probation. *Matter of Punu*, 22 I & N Dec. 224 (BIA 1998). Courts have agreed. *See, e.g, Madriz–Alvarado v. Ashcroft*, 383 F.3d 321 (5th Cir. 2004). But a similar procedure in Virginia does not lead to a conviction where the defendant pled not guilty, and the judge found facts justifying a finding of guilt, but did not actually reach a finding of guilt. *Crespo v. Holder*, 631 F.3d 130, 133–36 (4th Cir. 2011).

INA § 101(a)(48)(A) does not address probation, but the BIA has ruled that probation constitutes punishment for purposes of applying the definition of conviction. *See Matter of Punu*, 22 I & N Dec. 224 (BIA 1998). As for the length of a sentence, § 101(a)(48)(B) provides that a suspended sentence counts as a term of imprisonment.

If a conviction is reversed on appeal for procedural or substantive defects, the underlying crime cannot be the basis for removal. *Matter of Adamiak*, 23 I & N Dec. 878 (BIA 2006); *Alim v. Gonzales*, 446 F.3d 1239 (11th Cir. 2006). But it remains effective for removal purposes if it was vacated to avoid immigration consequences. *Matter of Pickering*, 23 I & N Dec. 621 (BIA 2003). The BIA has held that the noncitizen has the burden to prove that a conviction was vacated on substantive or procedural grounds. *Matter of Chavez–Martinez*, 24 I & N Dec. 272 (BIA 2007). However, the federal courts are split on this issue. *Compare Nath v. Gonzales*, 467 F.3d 1185, 1188–89 (9th Cir. 2006) (DHS has the burden of proving that the conviction remains valid for removal purposes); *with Rumierz v. Gonzales*, 456 F.3d 31, 40–41 (1st Cir. 2006) (noncitizen bears the burden of proving that the conviction was vacated for substantive or procedural error).

(i) Expungements

State and federal laws permit courts to expunge criminal records in certain circumstances. Under many statutes, courts may set aside or expunge a conviction and seal the criminal record after a certain amount of time has passed, the sentence has been served, and the defendant has satisfied other obligations.

An expungement differs in effect from the reversal of a conviction on appeal for legal error. A conviction reversed on appeal for substantive or procedural error cannot be the basis for removal because it was not lawful, but expungement merely limits a lawful conviction's subsequent effect. The BIA has applied § 101(a)(48)(A) to hold that expungement pursuant to a state rehabilitative statute has no impact on a conviction's immigration consequences. *Matter of Roldan–Santoyo*, 22 I & N Dec. 512 (BIA 1999). The courts that have addressed the issue have generally agreed. *See, e.g., Nath v. Gonzales*, 467 F.3d 1185, 1188–89 (9th Cir. 2006); *Pickering v. Gonzales*, 465 F.3d 263 (6th Cir. 2006). The BIA has made one exception: an expungement under a state statute that is analogous to federal juvenile delinquency laws will eliminate immigration consequences. *Matter of Devison–Charles*, 22 I & N Dec. 1362 (BIA 2000).

(ii) Sentence Reductions

Suppose a noncitizen successfully petitioned a court to vacate his one-year sentence and impose a 360 day sentence instead. The BIA has ruled that the new sentence replaces the old one for determining any immigration law consequences. *Matter of Song*, 23 I & N Dec. 173 (BIA 2001). The new sentence determines the immigration consequences even if the noncitizen seeks to vacate the sentence for the express purpose of avoiding removal and asserts no substantive or procedural defect in the original sentence. *Matter of Cota–Vargas*, 23 I & N Dec. 849 (BIA 2005).

(iii) Pardons

A pardon is more effective than judicial expungement of a criminal conviction, at least for some crime-related deportability grounds. A "full and unconditional pardon" by a state governor or the President of the United States eliminates the immigration consequences of convictions for crimes involving moral turpitude, aggravated felonies, and high speed flight from an immigration checkpoint. *See* INA § 237(a)(2)(A)(vi).

What about pardons for convictions of crimes of domestic violence or controlled substance crimes? *See Matter of Suh*, 23 I & N Dec. 626, 627 (BIA 2003) (pardon does not eliminate deportability for domestic violence or controlled substance crime). At least two federal circuits have held the pardon provision applies only to grounds of deportability, not inadmissibility. *Aguilera–Montero v. Mukasey*, 548 F.3d 1248, 1251–52 (9th Cir. 2008); *Balogun v. U.S. Attorney General*, 425 F.3d 1356, 1362–63 (11th Cir. 2005).

(iv) Other Post–Conviction Relief

A variety of procedural vehicles are potentially available to a noncitizen who seeks to vacate a prior conviction that is the basis of deportability. The appropriate court filing might be a writ of habeas corpus, or one of several possible common law writs, especially *coram nobis*. These procedural vehicles and their availability to raise ineffective assistance claims in general and *Padilla* claims in particular vary from state to state. Some states have restrictions that may make it impossible for some noncitizens facing removal to file *Padilla* claims because they missed a filing deadline, or because they has served out the criminal sentence and therefore are no longer in custody. *See, e.g., People v. Carrera*, 239 Ill.2d 241, 245–59, 940 N.E.2d 1111, 346 Ill.Dec. 507 (2010) (relief is unavailable under Illinois Post–Conviction Hearing Act to an individual who has served his criminal sentence). The constitutionality of such limitations, if they eliminate or severely restrict the practical possibility of relief based on *Padilla* in certain cases, is an open question.

(v) Waivers

Recall from Section A of this chapter on deportability that INA § 212(h) authorizes a waiver of inadmissibility based on criminal convictions if certain requirements are met. Though the statute refers only to inadmissibility, the BIA has extended its application to some deportability situations. If a permanent resident departed from and has been readmitted to the United States after committing a deportable offense, § 212(h) is available. *Matter of Sanchez*, 17 I & N Dec. 218 (BIA 1980). What if she has stayed in the United States since committing the offense? If she qualifies for an immigrant visa, for example as an immediate relative, she can file for adjustment of status as a form of relief from removal and seek a § 212(h) waiver in that context. *Matter of Parodi*, 17 I & N Dec. 608 (BIA 1980). What if she stayed in the United States and has no basis for adjustment, but wants to use § 212(h)? The circuits have split on this issue. *Compare Malagon de Fuentes v. Gonzales*, 462 F.3d 498 (5th Cir. 2006) (§ 212(h) not available); *Klementanovsky v. Gonzales*, 501 F.3d 788 (7th Cir. 2007) (same); *with Yeung v. INS*, 76 F.3d 337 (11th Cir. 1995) (§ 212(h) available).

In 1996, Congress made aggravated felons not only deportable but also ineligible for a form of relief from removal called cancellation of removal, discussed in Section C of this chapter. Congress also apparently anticipated that lawful permanent residents convicted of aggravated felonies might circumvent these new restrictions by obtaining § 212(h) waivers of crime-based inadmissibility and then adjusting their status to permanent resident as a form of relief from removal. To block this option, Congress limited waiver eligibility by adding the following proviso to the end of § 212(h):

> No waiver shall be granted under this subsection in the case of an alien who has previously been admitted to the United States as an alien lawfully admitted for permanent residence if either since the date of such admission the alien has been convicted of an aggravated felony or the alien has not lawfully resided continuously in the United States for a period of not less than 7 years immediately preceding the date of initiation of proceedings to remove the alien from the United States.

The BIA has ruled that the proviso bars a permanent resident no matter how he became one—whether through adjustment or an immigrant visa admission—but at least two circuits have held the proviso inapplicable to permanent residents by adjustment. *Compare Lanier v. U.S. Atty. Gen.,* 631 F.3d 1363 (11th Cir. 2011); *Martinez v. Mukasey,* 519 F.3d 532, 546 (5th Cir.2008); *with Matter of Koljenovic,* 25 I & N Dec. 219 (BIA 2010).

To the extent that the proviso treats a noncitizen who is not a permanent resident better than one who is, courts have found no equal protection violation. The Seventh Circuit explained:

> We find that a rational basis exists for Congress' decision to declare only those aggravated felons who have previously been admitted as LPRs ineligible for § 212(h) relief. One of Congress' purposes in enacting reforms to the INA through IIRIRA was to expedite the removal of criminal aliens from the United States. Eliminating the availability of § 212(h) relief for LPR aggravated felons would eradicate one source of delay that might thwart this effort. * * * LPRs enjoy rights and privileges by virtue of their status which are not shared by non-LPRs, and they typically have closer and long-standing ties to the United States through employment and family relationships. Therefore, Congress may rationally have concluded that LPRs who commit serious crimes despite these factors are uniquely poor candidates for relief from removal through the "backdoor" of waiver of inadmissibility. * * * Congress might have reasoned that LPR aggravated felons were a higher risk of recidivism, and were generally less deserving of a second chance than were non-LPR aggravated felons.

Lara–Ruiz v. INS, 241 F.3d 934, 947–48 (7th Cir.2001).

As an alternative to a waiver, noncitizens who are deportable due to a criminal conviction may also be able to obtain a form of relief from removal that is more general in scope and not specifically tailored to crime-based removability. Section C of this chapter explores those provisions for relief.

Section § 212(h) also poses a general question about agency discretion in deciding on waivers of inadmissibility and deportability. A regulation, 8 C.F.R § 212.7(d), addresses discretion in § 212(h) waivers:

> The Attorney General, in general, will not favorably exercise discretion under section 212(h)(2) of the Act to consent to an application or reapplication for a visa, or admission to the United States, or adjustment of status, with respect to immigrant aliens who are inadmissible under section 212(a)(2) of the Act in cases involving violent or dangerous crimes, except in extraordinary circumstances, such as those involving national security or foreign policy considerations, or cases in which an alien clearly demonstrates that the denial of the application for adjustment of status or an immigrant visa or admission as an immigrant would result in exceptional and extremely unusual hardship. Moreover, depending on the gravity of the alien's

underlying criminal offense, a showing of extraordinary circumstances might still be insufficient to warrant a favorable exercise of discretion under section 212(h)(2) of the Act.

Former BIA Member Lory Rosenberg criticized this regulation for "limit[ing] access to a waiver where Congress expressly provided that a waiver would be available." She reasoned that the regulation "violates the principle that every discretionary determination requires a weighing and balancing of the relevant factors." Rosenberg, *Where Have All the Waivers Gone: An Examination of Extremely and Exceptionally Unusual Discretionary Standards*, 8 Bender's Imm. Bull. 185 (Feb. 2003).

Are you persuaded? Compare *Fook Hong Mak v. INS*, 435 F.2d 728 (2d Cir. 1970), which upheld a regulation precluding discretionary relief for noncitizens who failed to leave after being allowed to transit the United States without a visa. Judge Friendly explained:

> We are unable to understand why there should be any general principle forbidding an administrator, vested with discretionary power, to determine by appropriate rulemaking that he will not use it in favor of a particular class on a case-by-case basis, if his determination is founded on considerations rationally related to the statute he is administering. The legislature's grant of discretion to accord a privilege does not imply a mandate that this must inevitably be done by examining each case rather than by identifying groups.

Id. at 730. The circuits addressing the validity of 8 C.F.R § 212.7(d) have upheld it. *See, e.g., Samuels v. Chertoff*, 550 F.3d 252, 257 (2d Cir. 2008).

d. Classifying Convictions: The Categorical and Modified Categorical Approaches

Much intricate case law has emerged from deciding if particular convictions make a noncitizen deportable under various subparts of INA § 237(a)(2). But more important for our purposes than the details of that body of doctrine is an understanding of the approaches that the BIA and the courts have adopted to classify a particular conviction as one that makes a noncitizen deportable.

In practice, it is not enough to decide simply if a generic crime such as "assault" is a crime involving moral turpitude. Ascertaining crime-related deportability under § 237(a)(2) requires examining a particular conviction under a particular statute. Or suppose the assault victim was married to the perpetrator. Does this fact turn the conviction into a "crime of domestic violence" that makes a noncitizen deportable under INA § 237(a)(2)(E), even if the conviction is for "assault"? In practice, answering this question requires immigration judges and other decisionmakers to decide whether and how to use the information that might be available about a particular conviction to determine a noncitizen's deportability.

As a doctrinal starting point, the traditional "categorical approach" to classifying a conviction regards as immaterial the noncitizen's particular conduct in committing the crime. Instead, the focus is on the range of conduct criminalized by the statute. If the statute of conviction is broad enough to support a conviction for a criminal act that does not involve moral turpitude, then the noncitizen has not been convicted of a crime involving moral turpitude. *See, e.g., Goldeshtein v. INS*, 8 F.3d 645 (9th Cir. 1993). But as these decisions show, the categorical approach has sometimes become just one stage of analysis.

We now consider five decisions—involving drug offenses, crimes involving moral turpitude, aggravated felonies, and domestic violence—that trace the contours of evolving doctrine on this fundamental question of approach. Though these five decisions illustrate general approaches to classifying crimes, they arise out of efforts to define the specific boundaries of these categories. These decisions show not only how each category poses its own unique issues, but also how they collectively draw on a common, fundamental set of practical and conceptual challenges. The first case shows this expanded approach in deciding whether certain money laundering convictions are convictions "relating to a controlled substance."

LARA–CHACON v. ASHCROFT

United States Court of Appeals, Ninth Circuit, 2003.
345 F.3d 1148.

TASHIMA, CIRCUIT JUDGE.

Rafael Lara–Chacon ("Petitioner" or "Lara–Chacon"), a native and citizen of Mexico, * * * was admitted to the United States in 1970 as an immigrant. In 1999, he was convicted, based on a guilty plea, of five counts of conspiracy to commit money laundering in violation of Ariz. Rev. Stat. §§ 13–1003, 13–2317(A)(1) and (C), and was sentenced to three and one-half years' imprisonment. As a result of these convictions, the Immigration and Naturalization Service ("INS") charged Petitioner with being subject to removal for being an alien convicted of an aggravated felony under the Immigration and Nationality Act ("INA"), § 237(a)(2)(A)(iii). The INS initially charged Lara–Chacon with removability based on money laundering in excess of $10,000, which is defined as an aggravated felony in INA § 101(a)(43)(D). In two subsequent amendments to the charging document, the INS added charges of removability based on illicit trafficking in a controlled substance, INA § 101(a)(43)(B), an aggravated felony, and controlled substance violation, INA § 237(A)(2)(B)(i). * * *

The INS attached a copy of Petitioner's Presentence Report ("PSR") to its brief. After receiving the briefs and without holding any hearing on the issue, the IJ issued an order finding Petitioner removable for having been convicted of the aggravated felony of trafficking in controlled substances and for violating a law related to a controlled substance. Based solely on information in the PSR, he concluded that Petitioner's money laundering convictions were predicated upon trafficking in marijuana, a controlled substance. The IJ cited the PSR as follows:

[T]he Presentence Report states that the respondent was identified as a "drug broker, who put drug deals together." Consequently, other criminal cohorts would "call Lara [the petitioner] when they needed marijuana." On the basis of the foregoing, it is evident to this Court that the respondent's state felony conviction for racketeering/money laundering involved marijuana.

. . .

Again the Presentence Report indicates that "Rafael Lara was identified as a drug broker, who put drug deals together ... Defendants Carlos Taylor and David Garcia called Lara when they needed marijuana. [sic]

The IJ found that marijuana is a controlled substance under the Controlled Substance Act, and therefore that the conviction was for trafficking in an illicit controlled substance. Additionally, the IJ found Lara–Chacon removable because the conviction constituted a "violation[ ] of a law of a State *relating to* a controlled substance with the meaning of § 237(a)(2)(B)(i) of the Act." (emphasis in original). The IJ found that the exception from removability in the INA for aliens convicted only of a "single offense involving possession for one's own use of thirty grams or less of marijuana" under § 237(a)(2)(B)(i) did not apply because "respondent was a drug dealer, who dealt in large quantities of marijuana." The IJ based this conclusion on an exhibit to the PSR "indicating that respondent's cohorts were found transporting *15 pounds* of marijuana." (emphasis in the original).

The IJ dismissed the charge for the aggravated felony of money laundering because there was no showing of the amount of funds that was laundered.

Petitioner appealed to the BIA, which dismissed his appeal. The BIA rejected Petitioner's challenge to the use of the PSR, finding it admissible under 8 C.F.R. § 3.41(a)(6) and § 3.41(d). The BIA noted the parts of the PSR that referred to Lara–Chacon as a " 'drug dealer, who put drug deals together' " and to the fact that his "criminal cohorts would' call Lara [the petitioner] when they needed marijuana.' " Additionally, the BIA noted that the PSR indicated that the conviction involved the transportation of 15 pounds of marijuana. The BIA found that because marijuana is a controlled substance, the conviction constituted trafficking in a controlled substance, an aggravated felony under INA § 101(a)(43)(B), Additionally, the BIA agreed with the IJ's reasoning for the second charge of removability under INA § 237(a)(2)(B)(i) (conviction relating to a controlled substance). The BIA also agreed with the IJ's dismissal of the money laundering charge.

* * *

II. REMOVABILITY

Because the initial basis charged for removing Lara–Chacon (money laundering) was insufficient, the INS attempted to stretch two provisions to Lara–Chacon's conviction in order to establish it as a removable offense by adding charges of removability based on the aggravated felonies of drug trafficking and a controlled substance violation. The record, however, does not establish that Lara–Chacon was convicted of these offenses.

To determine whether an offense qualifies as an aggravated felony, we first make a categorical comparison of the elements of the statute of conviction to the generic definition, and decide whether the conduct proscribed by the statute of conviction is broader than, and so does not categorically fall within, this generic definition. For this purpose we " 'look only to the fact of conviction and the statutory definition of the prior offense.' " *United States v. Corona–Sanchez,* 291 F.3d 1201, 1203 (9th Cir. 2002) (en banc) (quoting *Taylor v. United States,* 495 U.S. 575, 602, 110 S.Ct. 2143, 109 L.Ed.2d 607 (1990)). *Taylor* also permits us "to go beyond the mere fact of conviction in a narrow range of cases." In cases where a state statute criminalizes both conduct that does and does not qualify as an aggravated felony, we review the conviction using a modified categorical approach. "Under the modified categorical approach, we conduct a limited examination of documents in the record to determine if there is sufficient evidence to conclude that a defendant was convicted of the elements of the generically defined crime even though his or her statute was facially overinclusive." *Chang,* 307 F.3d at 1189. In *Corona–Sanchez,* we explained what documents are adequate to provide evidence of the elements of the conviction:

> [I]n the case of a jury trial, the charging document and jury instructions from the prior offense may demonstrate that the "jury was actually required to find all the elements" of the generic crime. Similarly, if a defendant enters a guilty plea, the sentencing court may consider the charging documents in conjunction with the plea agreement, the transcript of a plea proceeding, or the judgment to determine whether the defendant pled guilty to the elements of the generic crime. Charging papers alone are never sufficient. However, charging papers may be considered in combination with a signed plea agreement.

291 F.3d at 1211 (internal citations omitted).

A. Drug Trafficking

[The court first analyzed the Arizona money laundering statute under which Lara–Chacon had been convicted, and concluded that it encompassed conduct, such as laundering proceeds from counterfeiting, false claims, obscenity, and prostitution, that is not punishable under the federal Controlled Substances Act, which is an element of drug trafficking as defined in the INA. The court then examined the record to ascertain if Lara–Chacon's conviction was actually based on laundering money gained from trafficking in controlled substances. Concluding that the Pre Sentence Report, which provided the only information linking Lara–Chacon's money laundering to a controlled substance, was insufficient on its own to establish such a connection, the court ruled that Lara–Chacon's conviction did not satisfy the drug trafficking ground of deportability.]

B. Controlled Substance Violation

The BIA also affirmed the IJ's finding that Lara–Chacon was also removable for being convicted of violating a law "relating to a controlled substance" under INA § 237(a)(2)(B)(i). Lara–Chacon was convicted of violating a statute that punishes activities relating to "racketeering proceeds." Ariz. Rev. Stat. § 13–2317. This statute does not mention controlled substances, but does refer to the definition of racketeering proceeds contained in Ariz. Rev. Stat. § 13–2301(D)(4), which, as discussed above, refers to proceeds derived from many sources, including "prohibited drugs."

Although the "relating to" language in INA § 237(a)(2)(B)(i) is construed broadly, we have recognized that there are limits. For example, in *Coronado–Durazo* [*v. INS*, 123 F.3d 1322 (9th Cir. 1997)], we refused to find that "solicitation to possess cocaine" was "a violation of . . . [a] law . . . relating to a controlled substance" because to do so would render meaningless statutory language limiting convictions for generic crimes that may result in deportation to conspiracy and attempt. We also indicated that "Arizona courts have explicitly held that solicitation, a preparatory offense, is a separate and distinct offense from the underlying crime because it requires a different mental state and different acts." * * *

The BIA has also recognized limits on the "relating to" language when the statute of conviction does not explicitly concern controlled substances. *See Matter of Carrillo*, 16 I. & N. Dec. 625, 626 (BIA 1978) ("[W]hen a criminal statute 'does not by its language indicate [that] it was contemplated to be a "narcotic law",' and historically has constituted a 'criminal offense separate and distinct from the [underlying] felony,' such a statute is not a 'law relating to . . . narcotic drugs. . . .' " (emendations in [*Carrillo*])).

* * *

The facts of this case exceed the limits of the "relating to" language. Arizona's money laundering offense is a distinct crime from the underlying crime and does not require proof of the underlying crime. In addition, because of the breadth of the Arizona statute, Lara–Chacon's money-laundering conviction could have concerned proceeds from a number of illegal activities unrelated to controlled substances. Thus, nothing about the fact of Lara–Chacon's conviction demonstrates violation of a law related to a controlled substance.

Respondent's reliance on *Johnson v. INS*, 971 F.2d 340 (9th Cir. 1992), is misplaced. In that case, we found that a conviction under the Travel Act, 18 U.S.C. § 1952, which prohibits transacting in interstate commerce with the proceeds of any "unlawful activity," was a conviction under a law "relating to" a controlled substance. Like the Arizona statute, the Travel Act refers the reader to another section to learn that the definition of "unlawful activity" includes, among many other things, "any business enterprise involving . . . narcotics or controlled substances." The key to our ruling in that case, however, was that by its very terms the conviction incorporated the illegal drug activity. * * * *Johnson* applies where an immigrant explicitly pleads guilty to (or the jury finds) a violation of the specific statutory provision that obviously relates to drugs. This is not the case here, where Lara–Chacon's plea concerned the money laundering charge only.

The government has not cited a case in which we have looked at the underlying conduct, rather than the terms of the conviction itself to determine whether the conviction constituted a controlled substance violation. Even were we to do so, it would not be based on something as unreliable as a PSR. Lara–Chacon was not convicted of violating a law related to a controlled substance.

The fact that Lara–Chacon's conviction was not for violation of a statute related to controlled substances is also supported by the difference between the purpose of the INA's provision for removing aliens convicted of crimes relating to controlled substances and the nature of the statute of conviction. The broad language of INA § 237(a)(2)(B)(i) indicates that it is directed at deporting "aliens who abuse the hospitality of the United States by committing drug related crimes." *Coronado–Durazo*, 123 F.3d at 1326. The intent here is to ensure that "aliens who have been convicted of violating laws specifically aimed at the regulation or prohibition of controlled substances are deportable." Arizona's racketeering statute is not specifically aimed at regulating controlled substances.

* * *

Based on the foregoing, we conclude that Petitioner's conviction did not constitute an aggravated felony under INA § 101(a)(43)(B), or a violation of a statute relating to controlled substances under § 237(a)(2)(B)(i). The petition for review is therefore granted. * * *

NOTES AND QUESTIONS ON CLASSIFYING CRIMES, AND ON CONTROLLED SUBSTANCE CONVICTIONS

1. *In Matter of R–*, 6 I & N Dec. 444, 447–48 (BIA 1954), the BIA advanced the following rationale for the traditional categorical approach:

> The rule set forth exists because a standard must be supplied to administrative agencies; it eliminates the burden of going into the evidence in a case; it eliminates the situation where a nonjudicial agency retries a judicial matter; and it prevents the situation occurring where two people convicted under the same specific law are given different treatment because one indictment may contain a fuller or different description of the same act than the other indictment; and makes for uniform administration of law.

Matter of R–, supra, 6 I & N Dec. at 448 n.2.

Are you persuaded? Should a noncitizen who commits a serious crime with "evil" intent escape deportation simply because some conduct condemned by the statute would not constitute a crime involving moral turpitude? Or, conversely, should the need for administrative efficiency, convenience, and uniformity condemn to deportation a noncitizen whose moral blameworthiness is greatly reduced in light of the particular circumstances of the offense?

2. On the basic issue of how to classify a conviction, consider how, in practice, the information that becomes available about any given criminal case is generated. The fundamental question here is whether it is accurate or fair to rely on facts that appear in the criminal file but were not necessary to convict. *Cf.* Restatement of Judgments (Second) § 27 & comment j (issue preclusion is limited to matters that were actually litigated and determined in the prior case and essential to the judgment). Put in practical terms, a defense attorney who heeds the call in *Padilla* to anticipate possible immigration consequences will try to keep out of the criminal file any facts that might establish deportability later, even if those facts are irrelevant to the outcome in the criminal case.

Rebecca Sharpless provides this helpful overview:

> The charging document in a criminal case must allege the elements, the "essential facts constituting the offense charged." A conviction is subject to reversal if the prosecutor has failed to charge all of the elements of the crime. But not all facts that appear in a charging document are essential facts. While alleging the essential elements of a crime is the most important function of the charging document, it is not its sole function. A second function of a charging document is to give the defendant sufficient notice in ordinary language of the crime being alleged. The charging document must "provide the accused with a sufficient description of the acts he is alleged to have committed to enable him to defend himself adequately." [5 W.R. LaFave et al., Criminal Procedure § 19.3(a), at 249 (3d ed. 2007).] This requirement has been described as mandating that the charging document describe the "who ..., what, where, and how" of the crime. For example, in an assault case, a charging document typically identifies the alleged victim. In a crime against property, the charging document typically describes the type of property that was involved. Courts have found a federal constitutional violation when pleadings in state cases lack specificity.

> Nonessential facts also typically appear in the factual basis for a plea. The federal criminal rules of procedure and many states require a factual basis as a condition of pleas to guard against defendants pleading guilty to crimes they could not have committed. There are typically no, or virtually no, standards governing them. A statement of factual basis, even more so than a charging document, contains a broad range of facts, typically using everyday language to describe the manner in which the crime was allegedly carried out.

> To prevail at trial, the prosecution does not have to prove every fact in the charging document. Nor would the prosecution have needed to prove every fact that later appears in a statement of factual basis. In a

Florida battery case, for example, guilt would not turn on whether the victim was the defendant's spouse or whether the battery was carried out by a blow to the victim's head or by a de minimis unwanted touching. In a Florida theft case, guilt would not depend on showing that the property at issue was gum or a shopping cart.

A conviction does not exist apart from its elements. To say that a person has been found guilty of a crime is simply to say that he or she has been found guilty of each element of the crime. Another way of expressing this point is to say that a conviction consists of only facts that are necessarily decided by the criminal justice system. All other alleged facts concerning the defendant's conduct are extraneous and, for both the prosecutor and the defendant, irrelevant to the proceedings. From the prosecutor's perspective, only facts that are elements need be proven. From the defendant's perspective, only element facts can result in the deprivation of the defendant's liberty. Extraneous facts need not be proven at all and therefore certainly are not proven beyond a reasonable doubt. A defendant therefore has no reason to dispute (or to exclude from the record) nonelement facts.

Sharpless, *Toward a True Elements Test:* Taylor *and the Categorical Analysis of Crimes in Immigration Law,* 62 U. Miami L.Rev. 979, 983–85 (2008).

3. Turning to the merits, can the Ninth Circuit seriously believe that Congress did not intend the drug offense deportability ground to apply to an individual involved in transporting 15 pounds of marijuana? On the other hand, how does the immigration judge know that it was 15 pounds or marijuana? As *Lara–Chacon* indicated, the Ninth Circuit had earlier reached another surprising conclusion when it had ruled that a conviction for solicitation to possess cocaine is not a violation of a law relating to a controlled substance. *Coronado–Durazo v. INS,* 123 F.3d 1322 (9th Cir.1997). On this issue, the Ninth Circuit disagreed with the BIA's conclusion in *Matter of Beltran,* 20 I & N Dec. 521 (BIA 1992) (solicitation is a deportable offense when the underlying solicited conduct is a drug violation).

4. In some cases, courts have taken a more expansive view of crimes "relating to a controlled substance." *E.g., Al–Najar v. Mukasey,* 515 F.3d 708, 715 (6th Cir. 2008) (guilty plea to possession of controlled substance under Michigan state law is a violation of a state law relating to a controlled substance even though the substance, khat, is not on the federal controlled substances list); *Urena–Ramirez v. Ashcroft,* 341 F.3d 51 (1st Cir. 2003) (conviction of Travel Act triggers drug offense deportation ground when defendant was traveling to distribute drug proceeds); *Luu–Le v. INS,* 224 F.3d 911 (9th Cir. 2000) (possession of drug paraphernalia is a crime relating to a controlled substance); *Flores–Arellano v. INS,* 5 F.3d 360 (9th Cir. 1993) (misdemeanor state conviction of being under the influence of amphetamine/methamphetamine is a crime related to a controlled substance).

Decisions that reflect a narrower reading include *Medina v. Ashcroft,* 393 F.3d 1063, 1065–66(9th Cir. 2005) (under modified categorical approach, this conviction under state law involving use rather than possession falls within the "personal use" exception because nothing in the statute or limited documents negates the likelihood that the conviction was for less than 30 grams of marijuana for personal use); and *Leyva–Licea v. INS,* 187 F.3d 1147 (9th Cir. 1999) (under categorical approach this conviction of solicitation to possess marijuana for sale is neither a crime relating to a controlled substance nor an aggravated felony).

5. Section 237(a)(2)(B)(i) refers to other provisions of federal law to define "controlled substance." *See* 21 U.S.C. §§ 802, 811–812. Under 21 U.S.C. § 811, the Attorney General can add or remove drugs or substances from the "controlled substance" lists. If the Attorney General adds another item, how will an individual have notice that the deportability ground has expanded?

Section 237(a)(2)(B)(ii) raises a similar issue by rendering deportable any noncitizen drug abuser and addict. The provision applies to those who currently fall into these categories or who did at any time after admission, even if they no longer do. The statute does not define "drug abuser" or "addict." How can immigration authorities decide what constitutes drug abuse? Is an abuser of alcohol a drug abuser? Would this scheme survive a challenge that it fails to provide adequate notice, or that it is void for vagueness?

The next case addresses what it means to apply the traditional categorical approach. This time, the deportability at issue is INA 237(a)(2)(A)(iii), for aggravated felony convictions.

GONZALES v. DUENAS–ALVAREZ

Supreme Court of the United States, 2007.
549 U.S. 183, 127 S.Ct. 815, 166 L.Ed.2d 683.

JUSTICE BREYER delivered the opinion of the Court.

Immigration law provides for removal from the United States of an alien convicted of "a *theft offense* (including receipt of stolen property) . . . for which the term of imprisonment [is] at least one year." INA § 101(a)(43)(G) (emphasis added); § 237(a)(2)(A). The question here is whether the term "theft offense" in this federal statute includes the crime of "*aiding and abetting*" a theft offense. We hold that it does. * * *

I

* * * In determining whether a conviction (say, a conviction for violating a state criminal law that forbids the taking of property without permission) falls within the scope of a listed offense (*e.g.,* "theft offense"), the lower courts uniformly have applied the approach this Court set forth in *Taylor v. United States,* 495 U.S. 575, 110 S.Ct. 2143, 109 L.Ed.2d 607 (1990).

Taylor concerned offenses listed in the federal Armed Career Criminal Act, 18 U.S.C. § 924(e). That Act mandates a lengthy prison sentence for offenders with previous convictions for, *e.g.,* a "violent felony"; and the

Act sets forth certain specific crimes, *e.g.,* "burglary," included in this category. The Court, in *Taylor,* considered whether a conviction for violating a state statute criminalizing certain burglary-like behavior fell within the listed federal term "burglary." 495 U.S., at 589, 598, 110 S.Ct. 2143.

The Court held that Congress meant its listed term "burglary" to refer to a specific crime, *i.e.,* " 'burglary' " in *"the generic sense in which the term is now used in the criminal codes of most States." Id.,* at 598, 110 S.Ct. 2143 (emphasis added). The Court also held that a state conviction qualifies as a burglary conviction, "regardless of" the "exact [state] definition or label" as long as it has the "basic elements" of "generic" burglary, namely, "unlawful or unprivileged entry into, or remaining in, a building or structure, with intent to commit a crime." *Id.,* at 599, 110 S.Ct. 2143. The Court added that, when a sentencing court seeks to determine whether a particular prior conviction was for a generic burglary offense, it should normally look not to the facts of the particular prior case, but rather to the state statute defining the crime of conviction.

The Court further noted that a "few States' burglary statutes" "define burglary more broadly" to include both a (generically defined) listed crime and also one or more nonlisted crimes. *Id.,* at 599, 110 S.Ct. 2143. For example, Massachusetts defines "burglary" as including not only breaking into " 'a building' " but also breaking into a "vehicle" (which falls outside the generic definition of "burglary," for a car is not a " 'building or structure' "). See *Shepard v. United States,* 544 U.S. 13, 16, 17, 125 S.Ct. 1254, 161 L.Ed.2d 205 (2005). In such cases the Court's "categorical approach" permits the sentencing court "to go beyond the mere fact of conviction" in order to determine whether the earlier "jury was actually required to find all the elements of generic burglary." *Id.,* at 602, 110 S.Ct. 2143 "For example," the sentencing court might examine "the indictment or information and jury instructions" in the earlier case. 495 U.S., at 602, 110 S.Ct. 2143. In *Shepard,* we added that, in a nonjury case, the sentencing court might examine not only the "charging document" but also "the terms of a plea agreement," the "transcript of colloquy between judge and defendant," or "some comparable judicial record" of information about the "factual basis for the plea." 544 U.S., at 26, 125 S.Ct. 1254.

II

The case before us concerns the application of the framework just set forth to Luis Duenas–Alvarez, the respondent here, a permanent resident alien of the United States. In 2002, Duenas–Alvarez was convicted of violating Cal. Veh. Code Ann. § 10851(a) (West 2000). That section states:

"Any person who drives or takes a vehicle not his or her own, without the consent of the owner thereof, and with intent either to permanently or temporarily deprive the owner thereof of his or her title to or possession of the vehicle, whether with or without intent to steal the vehicle, or *any person who is a party or an accessory to or an accomplice in* the driving or unauthorized taking or stealing, *is guilty* of a public offense." (Emphasis added.)

After Duenas–Alvarez was convicted, the Federal Government, claiming that the conviction was for a generic theft offense, began removal proceedings. A Federal Immigration Judge, agreeing with the Government that the California offense is "a theft offense . . . for which the term of imprisonment [is] at least one year," found Duenas–Alvarez removable. § 101(a)(43)(G); § 237(a)(2)(A). The Board of Immigration Appeals (BIA) affirmed. Duenas–Alvarez sought review of the BIA's decision in the Court of Appeals for the Ninth Circuit.

While respondent's petition for court review was pending, the Ninth Circuit, in *Penuliar v. Ashcroft*, 395 F.3d 1037 (2005), held that the relevant California Vehicle Code provision, § 10851(a), sweeps more broadly than generic theft. In particular, the court said that generic theft has as an element the taking or control of others' property. But, the court added, the California statutory phrase " '[who] is a party or an accessory . . . or an accomplice' " would permit conviction "for aiding and abetting a theft." *Id.,* at 1044 (emphasis deleted). And the court believed that one might "aid" or "abet" a theft without taking or controlling property. Hence, in the Court of Appeals' view, the provision must cover some generically defined "theft" crimes and also some other crimes (aiding and abetting crimes) that, because they are not generically defined "theft" crimes, fall outside the scope of the term "theft" in the immigration statute.

* * *

III

The Ninth Circuit, like other Circuits and the BIA, accepted as a generic definition of theft, the "taking of property or an exercise of control over property without consent with the criminal intent to deprive the owner of rights and benefits of ownership, even if such deprivation is less than total or permanent." *Penuliar v. Gonzales*, 435 F.3d 961, 969 (2006) (internal quotation marks omitted). The question before us is whether one who aids or abets a theft falls, like a principal, within the scope of this generic definition. We conclude that he does.

* * *

* * * "[T]he generic sense in which" the term "theft" "is now used in the criminal codes of most States," *Taylor*, 495 U.S., at 598, 110 S.Ct. 2143, covers such "aiders and abettors" as well as principals. And the criminal activities of these aiders and abettors of a generic theft must themselves fall within the scope of the term "theft" in the federal statute.

A

Duenas–Alvarez does not defend the Ninth Circuit's position. He agrees with the Government that generically speaking the law treats aiders and abettors during and before the crime the same way it treats principals; and that the immigration statute must then treat them similarly as well. Instead, Duenas–Alvarez argues that the California Vehicle Code provision in other ways reaches beyond generic theft to cover certain nongeneric crimes.

* * * To succeed, Duenas–Alvarez must show something *special* about California's version of the doctrine—for example, that California in applying it criminalizes conduct that most other States would not consider "theft."

Duenas–Alvarez attempts to make just such a showing. In particular, he says that California's doctrine, unlike that of most other States, makes a defendant criminally liable for conduct that the defendant did not intend, not even as a known or almost certain byproduct of the defendant's intentional acts. * * *

We have reviewed those cases, however, and we cannot agree that they show that California's law is somehow special. * * *

Moreover, in our view, to find that a state statute creates a crime outside the generic definition of a listed crime in a federal statute requires more than the application of legal imagination to a state statute's language. It requires a realistic probability, not a theoretical possibility, that the State would apply its statute to conduct that falls outside the generic definition of a crime. To show that realistic probability, an offender, of course, may show that the statute was so applied in his own case. But he must at least point to his own case or other cases in which the state courts in fact did apply the statute in the special (nongeneric) manner for which he argues.

Because Duenas–Alvarez makes no such showing here, we cannot find that California's statute * * *, through the California courts' application of a "natural and probable consequences" doctrine, creates a subspecies of the Vehicle Code section crime that falls outside the generic definition of "theft."

* * *

[The opinion of JUSTICE STEVENS, concurring in part and dissenting in part, is omitted.]

QUESTIONS ON GONZALES v. DUENAS–ALVAREZ

1. Why didn't the Court delve into the facts of the criminal case to decide whether the noncitizen had been convicted of an aggravated felony?

2. How did the Court decide whether the statute was generic or special?

The following decision relies on *Duenas–Alvarez* to broaden the traditional categorical approach as applied to § 237(a)(2)(A)(i) for convictions of crimes involving moral turpitude, but it then goes much further in allowing immigration judges to undertake an inquiry into the facts of the criminal case.

MATTER OF SILVA–TREVINO

Attorney General of the United States, 2008.
24 I & N Dec. 687.

Attorney General Mukasey:

* * * Attorney General Gonzales directed the Board of Immigration Appeals to refer to him for review its decision in this matter. * * * I vacate the Board's decision and remand this matter for further proceedings in accordance with the opinion.

* * *

The issue in this case is whether respondent's conviction under a Texas statute that criminalizes acts of "indecency with a child" should be deemed a conviction for a "crime involving moral turpitude" that renders respondent inadmissible, and therefore ineligible for discretionary relief from deportation, under the Immigration and Nationality Act. * * *

There are a few basics on which the Board and the Federal courts have generally agreed. To begin with, they generally agree that in deciding whether an alien's prior criminal conviction constitutes a conviction for a crime involving moral turpitude—that is, whether moral turpitude "necessarily inheres" in a violation of a particular State or Federal criminal statute—immigration judges and the Board should engage in a "categorical" inquiry and look first to the statute of conviction rather than to the specific facts of the alien's crime. Where this categorical inquiry does not establish that an alien's prior crime necessarily involved moral turpitude, the Board and most Federal courts permit some inquiry into the particular facts of the alien's prior offense. This secondary inquiry is sometimes referred to as a "modified" categorical analysis.

Although each of the Federal courts of appeals has endorsed some form of this two-step categorical inquiry (and the Board typically employs the form endorsed by the circuit in which a case arises), the courts have not uniformly applied it. Instead, courts have applied a wide range of approaches with respect to both prongs of the test, resulting in a patchwork of conflicting legal and evidentiary standards. Moreover, many of these approaches do not adequately perform the function they are supposed to serve: distinguishing aliens who have committed crimes involving moral turpitude from those who have not. These shortcomings point to the need for a new, standardized approach—one that accords with the statutory text, is administratively workable, and furthers the policy goals underlying the Act.

The Act delegates to the Department of Justice—the agency charged with interpreting and implementing many of its provisions—the authority to craft such an approach. *See* INA 103(a)(1) (providing that the "determination and ruling by the Attorney General with respect to all questions of law shall be controlling"); *National Cable & Telecomms. Ass'n v. Brand X Internet Servs.*, 545 U.S. 967, 982 (2005) ("*Chevron*'s premise is that it is for the agencies, not courts, to fill statutory gaps."). Accordingly, this opinion establishes an administrative framework for determining whether an alien has been convicted of a crime involving moral turpitude. First, in evaluating whether an alien's prior offense is one that categorically involves moral turpitude, immigration judges must determine whether there is a "realistic probability, not a theoretical possibility," that the State or Federal criminal statute pursuant to which the alien was convicted would be applied to reach conduct that does not involve moral turpitude.

Second, where this categorical analysis does not resolve the moral turpitude inquiry in a particular case, an adjudicator should proceed with a "modified categorical" inquiry. In so doing, immigration judges should first examine whether the alien's record of conviction—including documents such as the indictment, the judgment of conviction, jury instructions, a signed guilty plea and the plea transcript—evidences a crime that in fact involved moral turpitude. When the record of conviction is inconclusive, judges may, to the extent they deem it necessary and appropriate, consider evidence beyond the formal record of conviction. The goal of this inquiry is to discern the nature of the underlying conviction where a mere examination of the statute itself does not yield the necessary information; it is not an occasion to relitigate facts or determinations made in the earlier criminal proceeding.

* * *

I

Respondent is a native and citizen of Mexico who was admitted to the United States as a lawful permanent resident in 1962. On October 6, 2004, respondent entered a plea of no contest to the criminal offense of "indecency with a child" under Title 5, Section 21.11(a)(1) of the Texas Penal Code, a second-degree felony punishable by a 2– to 20–year prison term. Section 21.11(a)(1) makes it illegal for a person to engage in "sexual contact" with a child younger than 17 years old who is not the person's spouse, unless the person is "not more than three years older than the victim and of the opposite sex." Texas Penal Code § 21.11(a)(1), (b)(1) (2003). The statute defines "sexual contact" to mean "any touching by a person, including touching through clothing, of the anus, breast, or any part of the genitals of a child" or "any touching of any part of the body of a child, including touching through clothing, with the anus, breast, or any part of the genitals of a person," if "committed with the intent to arouse or gratify the sexual desire of any person." The State court [accepted the plea, fined respondent $250, placed him under community supervision for a period of 5 years, and ordered him to attend sex offender counseling sessions.]

DHS initiated removal proceedings against respondent on the ground that he had been convicted of an "aggravated felony." The Immigration Judge held, inter alia, that respondent's State conviction constituted a conviction for "sexual abuse of a minor"—an "aggravated felony" that renders an alien removable.

Respondent then requested discretionary relief from removal through adjustment of status to lawful permanent resident under section 245(a) of the Act. Respondent contended that his "aggravated felony" conviction did not bar adjustment of status because the conviction did not fall within one of the specific grounds for inadmissibility listed in section 212(a)(2) of the Act, one of which is conviction of a crime involving moral turpitude. Respondent argued that his State conviction should not be considered a conviction for a crime involving moral turpitude because (1) both the Board and the United States Court of Appeals for the Fifth Circuit focus on whether the entire category of offenses covered by a State criminal statute involves moral turpitude; and (2) the Texas statute under which he was convicted does not require "that a person have knowledge that the individual with whom the perpetrator has sexual contact is a child" and thus permits convictions in cases that do not involve moral turpitude where the defendant honestly and reasonably believed his sexual contact was with a consenting adult.

The Immigration Judge * * * concluded [that this crime was] "analogous to a statutory rape offense," an offense that many courts and the Board have categorically "held to be a crime involving moral turpitude" whether or not the conviction required that a defendant knew or should have known his victim's age. [This crime made him ineligible for adjustment of status.]

On appeal to the Board, respondent conceded removability and challenged only the Immigration Judge's determination that he was ineligible for the discretionary relief of adjustment of status. * * * Believing it was "constrained" by Fifth Circuit law to "consider the minimum circumstances possible for a conviction," [t]he Board noted that Texas Penal Code § 21.11(a)(1) "presents a wide range of scenarios which could support a conviction," some of which "clearly involve reprehensible conduct which is contrary to the accepted rules of morality." But * * * the Board held that respondent's conviction, whatever its actual facts, should *not* be considered a conviction for a crime involving moral turpitude because section 21.11(a)(1) of the Texas Penal Code criminalizes at least some conduct that does not involve moral turpitude. Thus, having reversed the Immigration Judge's moral turpitude determination, the Board remanded for consideration of respondent's claim for discretionary adjustment of status.

II

A

This opinion begins, as it must, with the statutory text. The Act refers to "moral turpitude" in two separate provisions. Section 212(a)(2)(A)(i)(I) provides that "any alien convicted of, or who admits having committed, or who admits committing acts which constitute the essential elements of . . . a crime involving moral turpitude (other than a purely political offense) or an attempt or conspiracy to commit such a crime" is inadmissible. Section 245(a), in turn, provides that an inadmissible alien is ineligible for discretionary adjustment of status. Section 237(a)(2)(A)(i) of the Act separately provides that "[a]ny alien who . . . is convicted of a crime involving moral turpitude committed within five years . . . after the date of admission, and . . . for which a sentence of one year or longer may be imposed" is deportable.

* * *

The Department and the Federal courts agree that, to determine whether a crime involves moral turpitude, immigration judges should first engage in a "categorical" inquiry and look to the statute of conviction rather than to the specific facts of an alien's crime. As noted, the courts of appeals have to date adopted three basic approaches: (1) the "minimum conduct" approach, which looks to whether moral turpitude inheres in the most minimal conduct that could hypothetically permit a conviction; (2) the "common case" approach, which looks to whether moral turpitude inheres in the "usual" case or in the general nature of a crime; and (3) the "realistic probability" approach, which asks whether moral turpitude necessarily inheres in all cases that have a realistic probability of being prosecuted.

As also noted, the "minimum conduct" and "common case" approaches, especially when combined with evidentiary limitations, can result in under- or over-inclusive application of the Act's moral turpitude provisions. The "realistic probability" method mitigates these problems by taking a more refined approach to immigration inquiries. Specifically, it focuses the adjudicator on a criminal statute's actual scope and application and tailors the categorical moral turpitude inquiry by asking whether, at the time of an alien's removal proceeding, any actual (as opposed to hypothetical) case exists in which the relevant criminal statute was applied to conduct that did not involve moral turpitude. If the statute has not been so applied in any case (including the alien's own case), the adjudicator can reasonably conclude that all convictions under the statute may categorically be treated as ones involving moral turpitude. In such circumstances, the history of adjudication generally establishes no realistic probability that the statute, whatever its language may hypothetically allow, would actually be applied to acts that do not involve moral turpitude. By contrast, if the language of the criminal statute could encompass both conduct that involves moral turpitude and conduct that does not, *and* there is a case in which the relevant criminal statute has been applied to the latter category of conduct, the adjudicator cannot categorically treat all convictions under that statute as convictions for crimes that involve moral turpitude.

The Supreme Court recently adopted the "realistic probability" approach in *Duenas–Alvarez*, where the question was whether a conviction under a California theft statute constituted a "theft offense" within the meaning of section 101(a)(43)(G) of the Act, rendering the alien removable under section 237(a). * * *

Duenas–Alvarez was not a moral turpitude case, and in any event its approach to categorical inquiries would not bind the Department here because moral turpitude determinations turn on the Department's application of ambiguous statutory text. *See National Cable & Telecommunications Ass'n v. Brand X Internet Services*, 545 U.S. 967, 982 (2005). That said, the *Duenas–Alvarez* Court's adoption of the "realistic probability" approach is grounded in the realization that immigration penalties ought to be based on criminal laws as they are actually applied. And the question in *Duenas–Alvarez*—whether a conviction under a particular State statute was within the scope of a general category of offenses for immigration purposes—is similar to the question presented here. I thus find the analysis in *Duenas–Alvarez* persuasive and conclude that, in evaluating whether an alien's prior offense is categorically one that involved moral turpitude, immigration judges should determine whether there is a "realistic probability, not a theoretical possibility," that a State or Federal criminal statute would be applied to reach conduct that does not involve moral turpitude.

Like any categorical approach, however, the realistic probability approach cannot assure proper resolution of all moral turpitude inquiries: It provides no answer where a statute encompasses both conduct that involves moral turpitude *and* conduct that does not (as evidenced by its application to the latter category in an actual case). Recognizing this weakness of a pure categorical approach, the Department and many courts have proceeded to a second stage, or "modified categorical," inquiry pursuant to which adjudicators consider whether the alien's record of conviction evidences a crime that in fact involved moral turpitude.

I agree that adjudicators should engage in such a second-stage inquiry when necessary and conclude (as have many courts) that they should do so in every case where (because the criminal statute in issue has at some point been applied to conduct that did not involve moral turpitude) the categorical analysis does not end the moral turpitude inquiry. Most courts, however, have limited this second-stage inquiry to the alien's record of conviction, including documents such as the indictment, the judgment of conviction, jury instructions, a signed guilty plea, or the plea transcript. In my view, when the record of conviction fails to show whether the alien was convicted of a crime involving moral turpitude, immigration judges should be permitted to consider evidence beyond that record if doing so is necessary and appropriate to ensure proper application of the Act's moral turpitude provisions. I reach these conclusions for several reasons.

First, the documents generally considered part of the formal record of conviction typically focus only on the charging elements of a specific criminal offense. But moral turpitude is not an element of an offense. And although in many, if not most, cases (for example, cases in which proof of fraudulent intent is required for conviction), examination of the alien's record of conviction may establish that the alien was in fact convicted of a crime involving moral turpitude, there are other cases (such as the instant one) in which an examination of the formal record by itself does not yield an answer to the question.

This restriction is hard to square with the text of the Act. The relevant provisions contemplate a finding that the particular alien did or did not commit a crime involving moral turpitude before immigration penalties are or are not applied. Section 212(a)(2)(A)(i)(I), the inadmissibility provision at issue in this case, refers to "any alien convicted of, or who admits having committed, or who admits committing acts which constitute the essential elements of a crime involving moral turpitude." (Emphasis added.) Section 237's removability provisions similarly pertain only to "[a]ny alien who is convicted of a crime involving moral turpitude" under certain enumerated circumstances, one of which relates to the alien's date of admission—a fact that would not typically be reflected in a criminal record of conviction. Sections 237(a)(2)(A)(i)–(ii) of the Act. To impose evidentiary limitations with the result that immigration penalties under section 212(a) or section 237 apply to aliens whose crimes did *not* involve moral turpitude, or with the result that aliens whose crimes *did* involve moral turpitude escape those penalties, is in tension with the text of those sections.

Related provisions of the Act further support the conclusion that an individualized moral turpitude inquiry is warranted where a categorical analysis is not conclusive. The Act's evidentiary provisions, for example, call for analysis of whether "the alien" in a particular proceeding is or is not subject to the Act's moral turpitude provisions. By their terms, these provisions indicate that the statute should be applied only to aliens who have themselves committed acts that trigger the provisions and their associated immigration consequences.

Because restricting administrative moral turpitude inquiries to an alien's formal record of conviction is not compelled by the Act—and indeed, appears to be in some tension with it—[I reject this approach.] * * *

* * *

In short, to determine whether an alien's prior conviction triggers application of the Act's moral turpitude provisions, adjudicators should: (1) look first to the statute of conviction under the categorical inquiry set forth in this opinion and recently applied by the Supreme Court in *Duenas–Alvarez*; (2) if the categorical inquiry does not resolve the question, look to the alien's record of conviction, including documents such as the indictment, the judgment of conviction, jury instructions, a signed guilty plea, and the plea transcript; and (3) if the record of conviction does not resolve the inquiry, consider any additional evidence the adjudicator determines is necessary or appropriate to resolve accurately the moral turpitude question. * * *

III

Applying the foregoing framework to the facts of this case, I vacate the Board's decision and remand for reconsideration consistent with this opinion. * * * The Board concluded that moral turpitude does not necessarily inhere in a conviction under Texas Penal Code § 21.11(a)(1) because the statute criminalizes sexual contact with minors that falls short of rape. * * *

In my view, so long as the perpetrator knew or should have known that the victim was a minor, *any* intentional sexual contact by an adult with a child involves moral turpitude. Such contact is "inherently base, vile, or depraved, and contrary to the accepted rules of morality and the duties owed between persons or to society in general," when measured "in terms either of the magnitude of the loss that [it] cause[s] or the indignation that [it] arouse[s] in the law-abiding public," The sexual abuse of children destroys, in a way that cannot be described as anything other than "base" and "vile," the trust and innocence of society's most vulnerable members. * * *

That said, whether the perpetrator knew or should have known the victim's age is a critical factor in determining whether his or her crime involved moral turpitude for immigration purposes. A finding of moral turpitude under the Act requires that a perpetrator have committed the reprehensible act with some form of scienter. * * *

Accordingly, convictions obtained under statutes that limit convictions to defendants who knew, or reasonably should have known, that their intentional sexual acts were directed at children categorically should be treated as convictions for crimes involving moral turpitude. The inclusion of a mistake-of-age defense—that is, an affirmative defense that the defendant reasonably believed that his or her victim was not a child at the time of the offense—ensures that individuals will be convicted only if they willfully or knowingly directed sexual conduct towards someone they knew, or reasonably should have known, was a child. * * *

The Texas statute at issue in this case applies only to intentional sexual contact. But it does not, on its face, provide for a mistake-of-age defense. It is therefore possible to imagine, as the Board did, a case in which a defendant could be convicted even though his conduct did not involve moral turpitude. * * * Imagination is not, however, the appropriate standard under the framework set forth in this opinion. Instead, the question is whether there is a "realistic probability, not a theoretical possibility," that the Texas statute would be applied to reach conduct that does not involve moral turpitude.

In this case, the answer to that question is yes. In *Johnson v. State*, 967 S.W.2d 848, 849 (Tex. Crim. App. 1998) (en banc), the Texas Court of Criminal Appeals rejected a 19–year–old defendant's contention that he should not be convicted of criminal sexual contact with a child under section 21.11(a)(1) because his victim and her friend both told him that the victim was 17, and because the victim in fact appeared older than her age. Because Texas Penal Code § 21.11(a)(1) has been applied to conduct that does not involve moral turpitude (the defendant in *Johnson* was convicted despite his contention that he had no reason to know that his sexual conduct was directed at a child), respondent's conviction cannot categorically be treated as one that did involve moral turpitude. I therefore agree with the Board that an analysis of Texas Penal Code § 21.11(a)(1) fails to establish that respondent's conviction qualifies categorically as a crime involving moral turpitude * * *.

This categorical determination, however, does not end the moral turpitude inquiry. [The adjudicator must now] engage in a modified categorical inquiry, considering whether the facts of the alien's prior conviction in fact involved moral turpitude. In so doing, the adjudicator should look first to the alien's record of conviction—including the indictment, the judgment of conviction, jury instructions, a signed guilty plea, or the plea transcript—and if the record of conviction does not resolve the inquiry, consider any additional evidence or factfinding the adjudicator determines is necessary or appropriate to resolve accurately the moral turpitude question.

In this case, the Board * * * declined to engage in any further inquiry because it believed that a beyond-the-record-of-conviction analysis was prohibited,. * * * I remand this case for further consideration by the Board. If the Board deems further inquiry appropriate, it may in turn remand the case to the Immigration Judge for additional proceedings consistent with this opinion.

* * *

NOTE ON THE MODIFIED CATEGORICAL APPROACH

Rebecca Sharpless describes the difference between two versions of the modified categorical approach. What she calls the majority version authorizes a relatively limited inquiry into the facts of the criminal case, whereas the minority version allows a broader inquiry:

> Under the majority rule, if a statute is divisible and only some offenses trigger removal, an adjudicator is permitted to look at the record of conviction, but only to determine whether the noncitizen was convicted of the statutory elements that trigger removal. * * *

* * *

* * * [T]he BIA and many federal courts have generally adopted the majority, elements test approach. In a minority of cases, however, the BIA and federal courts appear to sanction recourse to the record of conviction even when a statute is nondivisible. These cases permit a judge or adjudicator to look at all facts contained in the record of conviction,

even to extraneous facts that describe the manner in which the crime was carried out.

* * *

* * * While the term "modified categorical approach" is used to describe both the minority and majority approaches, the approaches are radically different. In the first, the record of conviction serves only to clarify which of multiple possible crimes in a statute was the actual crime of conviction. The majority rule is an elements test because it permits recourse to the record of conviction only to clarify what facts were established to prove elements of the crime. In the second, the minority rule, any fact in the record of conviction can be used to establish the nature of the conviction, even if the fact was not necessary to an element.

Sharpless, *supra*, 62 U. Miami L.Rev. at 997–1000.

In the second step of his analysis in *Silva–Trevino*, Attorney General Mukasey adopted the broad-ranging version of the modified categorical approach. The third step of *Silva–Trevino* goes further in allowing the removal proceeding to probe the facts of the prior criminal case. The next case, which also addressed whether a conviction is for a crime involving moral turpitude, undertakes a much more restrained inquiry into the facts of the criminal case. Usually considered to have overruled *Silva–Trevino* in the Third Circuit, it adopts the more limited version of the modified categorical approach, and it completely eschews the inquiry in the third step of *Silva–Trevino*.

JEAN–LOUIS v. ATTORNEY GENERAL

United States Court of Appeals for the Third Circuit, 2009.
582 F.3d 462.

RENDELL, CIRCUIT JUDGE.

We are called upon to decide whether simple assault under Pennsylvania law, where the victim is under 12 years of age and the assailant is over 20 years of age, is a crime involving moral turpitude for purposes of cancellation of removal. In doing so we must address a recent opinion of the Attorney General that adopts a novel framework for determining whether a petitioner has been convicted of a crime involving moral turpitude ("CIMT"). We conclude that the petitioner was not convicted of a CIMT, and that we will apply our established methodology for analyzing CIMT, rather than the approach recently adopted by the Attorney General.

I. BACKGROUND AND PROCEDURAL HISTORY

Appellant Lyonel Jean–Louis, a native and citizen of Haiti, was admitted to the United States in 1994 as a refugee, and became a lawful permanent resident in 1996. In 2001, Jean–Louis pled guilty to committing simple assault against a child under twelve years of age, in violation of 18 Pa. Cons. Stat. §§ 2701(b)(2). The Department of Homeland Security ("DHS") subsequently filed a Notice to Appear ("NTA"), charging Jean–Louis as removable under the Immigration and Nationality Act

("INA") § 237(a)(2)(E)(I). Jean–Louis conceded removability but sought to cancel his removal under INA § 240(A)(a).

Under the INA, discretionary cancellation of removal is available to an alien who has resided continuously in the United States for seven years. INA § 240A(a)(2). An alien's period of continuous residency terminates, however, if he "commits an offense referred to in section 212(a)(2) of this title that renders the alien inadmissible to the United States under section 212(a)(2) of this Act or removable from the United States under section 237(a)(2)." INA § 240A(d)(1). Crimes involving moral turpitude are among the offenses listed in § 212(a)(2)(A)(i)(I). Prior to his seventh year of residency in the U.S., Jean–Louis struck his wife's daughter, who was under the age of 12, to discipline her and was subsequently convicted of the Pennsylvania crime of simple assault, 18 Pa.C.S. § 2701(b)(2). The Immigration Judge ("IJ") concluded, and the Board of Immigration Appeals ("BIA") affirmed, that Jean–Louis's conviction for simple assault of a child under 12 years of age under subpart 2701(b)(2) constituted a CIMT, rendering Jean–Louis ineligible for cancellation of removal.

The Pennsylvania simple assault statute to which Jean–Louis pled guilty provides in pertinent part:

> (a) *Offense defined.*—A person is guilty of assault if he:
>
>> (1) attempts to cause or *intentionally, knowingly or recklessly* causes bodily injury to another;
>>
>> (2) negligently causes bodily injury to another with a deadly weapon; or
>>
>> (3) attempts by physical menace to put another in fear of imminent serious bodily injury.
>
> (b) *Grading.*—Simple assault is a misdemeanor of the second degree unless committed:
>
>> . . .
>>
>> (2) against a child under 12 years of age by an adult 21 years of age or older, in which case it is a misdemeanor of the first degree.

18 Pa.C.S. § 2701 (emphasis added). Noting that, "[I]t is unclear from the record of conviction whether the assault Respondent committed was intentional, knowing, or reckless," the IJ assumed that Jean–Louis "recklessly" inflicted bodily injury on another-the least culpable mental state specified in § 2701(a)(1). Confining her analysis to that subpart of the statute, the IJ did not address whether there was a culpability requirement under subpart 2701(b)(2). Accordingly, the IJ did not consider whether subpart 2701(b)(2) required the defendant to have known of the underage status of the victim, or would apply in a situation in which the defendant was not aware, and had no reason to believe, that the victim was a minor. * * *

II. DISCUSSION

On appeal, Jean–Louis contends that he is eligible for discretionary cancellation of removal because his conviction of simple assault does not qualify as a CIMT. Crimes involving moral turpitude have been held to require conduct that is "inherently base, vile, or depraved." *Knapik v. Ashcroft*, 384 F.3d 84, 89 (3d Cir.2004). In determining whether a state law conviction constitutes a CIMT, the agency, and we, have historically applied a "categorical" approach, "focusing on the underlying criminal statute 'rather than the alien's specific act.' " *Id.* at 88 (quoting *DeLeon–Reynoso v. Ashcroft*, 293 F.3d 633, 635 (3d Cir.2002)). We thus "look to the elements of the statutory state offense, not to the specific facts," reading the applicable statute to ascertain the least culpable conduct necessary to sustain conviction under the statute. *Id.* (quoting *Wilson v. Ashcroft*, 350 F.3d 377, 381 (3d Cir.2003)).

Where a statute of conviction contains disjunctive elements, some of which are sufficient for conviction of the federal offense and others of which are not, we have departed from a strict categorical approach. In such a case, we have conducted a limited factual inquiry, examining the record of conviction for the narrow purpose of determining the specific subpart under which the defendant was convicted. We have applied this "modified" categorical approach, even when clear sectional divisions do not delineate the statutory variations, in order to determine the least culpable conduct sufficient for conviction, and, where a CIMT is asserted, measure that conduct for depravity.

* * *

* * * [W]e independently conclude that no culpability requirement attaches, explicitly or implicitly, to subpart 2701(b)(2). Unlike subpart 2701(a)(1), which expressly requires that the defendant intentionally, knowingly, or recklessly inflict bodily injury, subpart 2701(b)(2) does not specify the minimum culpability required to trigger enhanced penalties. * * *

* * *

Thus, we conclude that the Pennsylvania assault statute as written permits a conviction under subpart 2701(b)(2) where the defendant did not know that the victim was under 12 years old. * * *

Based upon the foregoing analysis, we conclude that the least culpable conduct necessary for conviction under subpart 2701(b)(2) would be a reckless assault by a person over 20 years of age, where the victim, unbeknownst to the defendant, is under 12 years of age. * * *

We normally defer to the agency as to what conduct constitutes a CIMT. Our view that reckless assault of a minor, without more, does not constitute a CIMT is bolstered by a recent decision of the Attorney General, *Matter of Silva–Trevino*, 24 I & N Dec. 687, 706–708 (2008). There, the Attorney General considered whether a statute criminalizing intentional sexual acts directed at a child constituted a CIMT. The statute did not include a mistake-of-age defense. Hence, a defendant who did not know, and had no reason to believe, that the complainant was a minor could face conviction. The Attorney General concluded, therefore, that the statute lacked the "hallmark of moral turpitude"—a "reprehensible act committed with an appreciable level of consciousness or deliberation." * * *

The foregoing analysis tracks the modified categorical approach that we have historically applied. Under that approach, our inquiry concludes when we determine whether the least culpable conduct sufficient to sustain conviction under the statute "fits" within the requirements of a CIMT. However, in the recent opinion we cited above, *Matter of Silva–Trevino,* the Attorney General suggested that more is required. * * *

In *Silva–Trevino,* * * * [t]he Attorney General urged that because conflicting methodologies had been adopted by courts of appeals in conducting the CIMT inquiry, producing a veritable "patchwork of different approaches across the nation," he would use the case as "an opportunity to establish a uniform framework" for adjudicating CIMT cases under the INA.[11] The Attorney General's novel methodology departs from our precedents in two significant respects.

First, *Silva–Trevino* alters the focus of the categorical analysis. Under the categorical approach * * * we look to the elements of the statutory offense to ascertain the least culpable conduct hypothetically necessary to sustain a conviction under the statute. Under our precedents, the possibility of conviction for non-turpitudinous conduct, however remote, is sufficient to avoid removal; proof of actual application of the statute of conviction to the conduct asserted is unnecessary. * * *

Silva–Trevino eschews our approach of analyzing the least culpable conduct hypothetically sufficient to sustain conviction, in favor of a "realistic probability" test. Under this approach, "in evaluating whether an alien's prior offense is categorically one that involved moral turpitude, immigration judges should determine whether there is a 'realistic probability, not a theoretical possibility,' that a State or Federal criminal statute would be applied to reach conduct that does not involve moral turpitude." * * *

---

11. The unusual circumstances of *Silva–Trevino*'s referral to, and adjudication by, the Attorney General bear mention. After the IJ determined that Silva–Trevino's conviction under section 2.11(a)(1) of the Texas Penal Code constituted a CIMT, rendering him removable, the BIA, applying the categorical approach, concluded that his conviction did not meet the criteria for a CIMT and, accordingly, vacated the decision of the IJ and remanded the case. Subsequently, while the case was pending before the IJ, the Attorney General certified the case to himself *sua sponte*. Despite requests by Silva–Trevino's counsel, the Attorney General refused to identify the issues to be considered, to define the scope of his review, to provide a briefing schedule, or to apprise counsel of the applicable briefing procedure. In fact, neither the IJ decision nor the Attorney General's certification order were made publicly available, thus denying stakeholders, including immigrant and refugee advocacy organizations, the opportunity to register their views. As a result, the first opportunity of *amici curiae* to file comment was *after* entry of the Attorney General's opinion. * * *

Second, *Silva–Trevino* renders the strict *"categorical"* approach not "categorical." Prior to *Silva–Trevino,* we departed from a strict categorical analysis only where the statute of conviction featured disjunctive variations, some of which were sufficient for conviction of the federal offense and others of which were not. * * * In such a case, we modified the approach, but our inquiry remained a limited one, focused on the crime of conviction: we reviewed only the record of the conviction to ascertain the particular variation of the statute under which the defendant was convicted. Accordingly, the focus under the categorical approach has always been the conviction, aimed at determining exactly what the defendant was convicted of.

Silva–Trevino, by contrast, directs adjudicators to depart from a categorical approach, and to conduct an "individualized moral turpitude inquiry," in every instance in which a "categorical analysis is not conclusive" as to whether the alien was convicted of a CIMT. The aim of this "individualized" inquiry is to ascertain the alien's particular acts—to determine "whether the facts of the alien's prior conviction in fact involved moral turpitude"—not merely to determine the elements of the statutory offense of which the alien was convicted.

Rather than limiting the CIMT inquiry to an examination of the formal record of conviction, which could include the charging document, the terms of the plea agreement or transcript of the colloquy between judge and defendant in which the factual basis for the plea is confirmed by the defendant, or some comparable judicial record of this information, *Silva–Trevino* abandons these restrictions * * *. Hence, an adjudicator may, in his or her discretion, consider not only evidence from the prior criminal proceedings but also *"any* additional evidence or factfinding the adjudicator determines is necessary or appropriate to resolve accurately the moral turpitude question." (emphasis added). *Silva–Trevino* sets no limitations on the kinds of evidence adjudicators may consider.

The Attorney General asserts that two aspects of the INA support his authority to direct courts to employ his novel approach and compel our deference. First, he contends that the CIMT provisions in the immigration statute are ambiguous. He urges that Congress employed conflicting terminology, alternately using "convicted of" and "committed" throughout the statute. In the Attorney General's view, these terms, which cut in "different directions," do not endorse a single methodology for adjudicating CIMT cases, but rather confer discretion on the Attorney General to define a reasonable approach. Second, the Attorney General urges that the phrase "crime *involving* moral turpitude" invites, if not requires, a fact-intensive inquiry as to whether the underlying conduct was turpitudinous. The Attorney General urges that deference is owed to his interpretation of these provisions, and that the methodology that he espouses is obligatory, notwithstanding our contrary precedents.[12]

---

12. As a general rule, an agency's construction of an ambiguous statute under its purview, and in which it has special expertise, is entitled to deference. *Nat'l Cable & Telecomms. Ass'n v.*

We conclude that we are not bound by the Attorney General's view because it is bottomed on an impermissible reading of the statute, which, we believe, speaks with the requisite clarity. The ambiguity that the Attorney General perceives in the INA is an ambiguity of his own making, not grounded in the text of the statute, and certainly not grounded in the BIA's own rulings or the jurisprudence of courts of appeals going back for over a century. The specific ambiguity is as to the use of the words "convicted" and "committed." The inclusion of "committed," the Attorney General urges, permits inquiry into any and all acts—whether or not admitted by the alien, and whether or not established by the record of conviction—to determine whether the petitioner was convicted of a CIMT. To say that this reading has been rejected is an understatement: the BIA, prior attorneys general, and numerous courts of appeals have repeatedly held that the term "convicted" forecloses individualized inquiry in an alien's specific conduct and does not permit examination of extra-record evidence. It could not be clearer from the text of the statute—which defines "conviction" as a "formal judgment of guilt," and which explicitly limits the inquiry to the record of conviction or comparable judicial record evidence [the court quoted INA § 240(c)(3)(B)]—that the CIMT determination focuses on the *crime* of which the alien was *convicted*—not the specific *acts* that the alien may have *committed*. INA § 101(a)(48)(A). The statute presents no ambiguity.

* * *

We also take issue with the Attorney General's view that the phrase "crime *involving* moral turpitude" invites inquiry into an alien's specific acts. The Attorney General's argument is premised on a fundamental misreading of the relevant language. The Attorney General views "crime" and "involving moral turpitude" as distinct grammatical units and, accordingly, reasons that the clause "involving moral turpitude" modifies "crime." He thus concludes that Congress intended to authorize inquiry into whether an alien committed the offense in a manner reflecting depravity—that is whether the alien's particular acts "involv[ed] moral turpitude." The Attorney General's view, however, overlooks a crucial fact: crime involving moral turpitude is a term of art, predating even the immigration statute itself. As such, its division into a noun and subordinate clause, as the Attorney General seeks to do, distorts its intended meaning. It refers to a specific class of offenses, not to all conduct that happens to "involve" moral depravity, because of an alien's specific acts in a particular case. Because the Attorney General's position is premised on a clearly erroneous interpretation of "crime involving moral turpitude," no deference is owed to his view.

Brand X Internet Servs., 545 U.S. 967, 982, 125 S.Ct. 2688, 162 L.Ed.2d 820 (2005) ("*Chevron's* premise is that it is for agencies, not courts, to fill statutory gaps."). The INA delegates to the Department of Justice authority to interpret and implement its provisions.

However, where Congress has spoken clearly on the precise issue, no deference is owed to the agency's interpretation of a statute. *See Chevron*, 467 U.S. at 843 n. 9, 104 S.Ct. 2778. Further, where an agency interpretation reflects an impermissible construction of the statute, we will not defer to the agency's view. *See Chevron*, 467 U.S. at 843, 104 S.Ct. 2778.

Moreover, although the Attorney General observes—correctly—that "moral turpitude" is rarely an element of the underlying crime triggering removal, it is the offense that must be scrutinized for the requisite degree of depravity. Because the INA requires the conviction of a *crime*—not the commission of an *act*—involving moral turpitude, the central inquiry is whether moral depravity inheres in the crime or its elements—not the alien's underlying conduct. In this way, the concept of a crime involving moral turpitude does not lend itself to an examination of acts, rather than elements of the crime, any more than does the concept of "crime of violence" under section 101(a)(43)(F) of the INA. Violence, like moral turpitude, is not an element of the underlying offense; rather, we must look at the elements of the crime and measure them against the requirement of "violence." The use of the term "involves" in "crime involving moral turpitude" is no more expansive than the word "of" in "crime of violence."

* * *

Based on the foregoing analysis, we will not defer to the methodology adopted by the Attorney General, which we conclude is predicated on an impermissible reading of the INA, is contrary to Congress's intent, and would overturn nearly a century of jurisprudence. Accordingly, we will follow our established methodology for adjudicating crimes involving moral turpitude, as set forth in *Partyka,* and conclude that Jean–Louis was not convicted of a CIMT.

* * *

NOTES AND QUESTIONS ON THE CATEGORICAL AND MODIFIED CATEGORICAL APPROACHES

1. Do the crime-based deportability grounds adequately warn noncitizens of what may make them deportable, or is it unconstitutionally void for vagueness? Addressing vagueness doctrine outside of immigration law, the U.S. Supreme Court has explained: "The more important aspect of vagueness doctrine 'is not actual notice, but the other principal element of the doctrine—the requirement that a legislature establish minimal guidelines to govern law enforcement.' " *Kolender v. Lawson,* 461 U.S. 352, 358, 103 S.Ct. 1855, 1858, 75 L.Ed.2d 903 (1983), *quoting Smith v. Goguen,* 415 U.S. 566, 574, 94 S.Ct. 1242, 1247, 39 L.Ed.2d 605 (1974). From this perspective, and given the decades of case law under the categorical approach that had placed specific offenses in or out of the CIMT characterization, it is unsurprising that the Court has rejected a "void for vagueness" challenge to the statutory phrase "crime involving moral turpitude." *Jordan v. DeGeorge,* 341 U.S. 223, 71 S.Ct. 703, 95 L.Ed. 886 (1951).

But do deviations from the categorical approach resurrect concerns about arbitrariness (or unpredictability) in enforcement, or raise due process concerns more generally, especially if the facts that may emerge to establish deportability in an immigration removal proceeding were not essential—and thus perhaps not seriously contested—in the prior criminal prosecution?

2. How if at all does *Padilla v. Kentucky* affect your answer to the preceding question? Does the possible reliance in an immigration proceeding on the various aspects of the file in a prior criminal case affect the meaning of "effective assistance of counsel"?

In the following Supreme Court decision involving the deportability ground for an aggravated felony conviction, a new wrinkle—the circumstance-specific approach—may alter the analysis in yet another way.

NIJHAWAN v. HOLDER

Supreme Court of the United States, 2009.
557 U.S. 29, 129 S.Ct. 2294, 174 L.Ed.2d 22.

BREYER, J., delivered the opinion for a unanimous Court.

Federal immigration law provides that any "alien who is convicted of an *aggravated felony* at any time after admission is deportable." INA § 237(a)(2)(A)(iii) (emphasis added). A related statute defines "aggravated felony" in terms of a set of listed offenses that includes "an offense that . . . involves fraud or deceit *in which the loss to the victim or victims exceeds $10,000*." § 101(a)(43)(M)(i) (emphasis added). The question before us is whether the italicized language refers to an element of the fraud or deceit "offense" as set forth in the particular fraud or deceit statute defining the offense of which the alien was previously convicted. If so, then in order to determine whether a prior conviction is for the kind of offense described, the immigration judge must look to the criminal fraud or deceit statute to see whether it contains a monetary threshold of $10,000 or more. We conclude, however, that the italicized language does not refer to an element of the fraud or deceit crime. Rather it refers to the particular circumstances in which an offender committed a (more broadly defined) fraud or deceit crime on a particular occasion.

I

Petitioner, an alien, immigrated to the United States in 1985. In 2002 he was indicted for conspiring to commit mail fraud, wire fraud, bank fraud, and money laundering. 18 U.S.C. §§ 371, 1341, 1343, 1344, 1956(h). A jury found him guilty. But because none of these statutes requires a finding of any particular amount of victim loss, the jury made no finding about the amount of the loss. At sentencing petitioner stipulated that the loss exceeded $100 million. The court then imposed a sentence of 41 months in prison and required restitution of $683 million.

In 2005 the Government, claiming that petitioner had been convicted of an "aggravated felony," sought to remove him from the United States. The Immigration Judge found that petitioner's conviction was for crimes of fraud and deceit; that the sentencing stipulation and restitution order showed that the victims' loss exceeded $10,000; and that petitioner's conviction consequently fell within the immigration statute's "aggravated felony" definition. See §§ 101(a)(43)(M)(i), (U). The Board of Immigration Appeals agreed. So did the Third Circuit. 523 F.3d 387 (2008). The Third Circuit noted that the statutes of conviction were silent as to amounts, but, in its view, the determination of loss amounts for "aggravated felony" purposes "requires an inquiry into the underlying facts of the case." *Id.,* at 396.

The Courts of Appeals have come to different conclusions as to whether the $10,000 threshold in subparagraph (M)(i) refers to an element of a fraud statute or to the factual circumstances surrounding commission of the crime on a specific occasion.* * *

II

The interpretive difficulty before us reflects the linguistic fact that in ordinary speech words such as "crime," "felony," "offense," and the like sometimes refer to a generic crime, say, the crime of fraud or theft in general, and sometimes refer to the specific acts in which an offender engaged on a specific occasion, say, *the* fraud that the defendant planned and executed last month. The question here, as we have said, is whether the italicized statutory words "offense that involves fraud or deceit *in which the loss to the . . . victims exceeds $10,000*" should be interpreted in the first sense (which we shall call "categorical"), *i.e.,* as referring to a generic crime, or in the second sense (which we shall call "circumstance-specific"), as referring to the specific way in which an offender committed the crime on a specific occasion. If the first, we must look to the statute defining the offense to determine whether it has an appropriate monetary threshold; if the second, we must look to the facts and circumstances underlying an offender's conviction.

A

* * *

* * * [S]ometimes a separately numbered subsection of a criminal statute will refer to several different crimes, each described separately. And it can happen that some of these crimes involve violence while others do not. A single Massachusetts statute section entitled "Breaking and Entering at Night," for example, criminalizes breaking into a "building, ship, vessel or vehicle." Mass. Gen. Laws, ch. 266, § 16 (West 2006). In such an instance, we have said, a court must determine whether an offender's prior conviction was for the violent, rather than the nonviolent, break-ins that this single five-word phrase describes (*e.g.,* breaking into a building rather than into a vessel), by examining "the indictment or information and jury instructions," *Taylor [v. United States,* 495 U.S. 575, 602, 110 S.Ct. 2143, 109 L.Ed.2d 607 (1990)] or, if a guilty plea is at issue, by examining the plea agreement, plea colloquy or "some comparable judicial record" of the factual basis for the plea. *Shepard v. United States,* 544 U.S. 13, 26, 125 S.Ct. 1254, 161 L.Ed.2d 205 (2005).

Petitioner argues that we should interpret the subsection of the "aggravated felony" statute before us as requiring use of this same "categorical" approach. He says that the statute's language, read naturally as in *Taylor,* refers to a generic kind of crime, not a crime as committed on a particular occasion. He adds that here, as in *Taylor,* such a reading avoids the practical difficulty of determining the nature of prior conduct from what may be a brief paper record, perhaps noting only a statutory section number and a guilty plea; or, if there is a more extensive record, combing through that record for evidence of underlying conduct. Also, the categorical approach, since it covers only criminal statutes with a relevant monetary threshold, not only provides assurance of a finding on the point, but also assures that the defendant had an opportunity to present evidence about the amount of loss.

B

Despite petitioner's arguments, we conclude that the "fraud and deceit" provision before us calls for a "circumstance-specific," not a "categorical," interpretation. The "aggravated felony" statute of which it is a part differs in general from ACCA, the statute at issue in *Taylor.* And the "fraud and deceit" provision differs specifically from ACCA's provisions.

1

* * *

Now compare the "aggravated felony" statute before us. INA § 101(a)(43). We concede that it resembles ACCA in certain respects. The "aggravated felony" statute lists several of its "offenses" in language that must refer to generic crimes. Subparagraph (A), for example, lists "murder, rape, or sexual abuse of a minor." * * *

More importantly, however, the "aggravated felony" statute differs from ACCA in that it lists certain other "offenses" using language that almost certainly does not refer to generic crimes but refers to specific circumstances. For example, subparagraph (P), after referring to "an offense" that amounts to "falsely making, forging, counterfeiting, mutilating, or altering a passport," adds, *"except in the case of a first offense for which the alien . . . committed the offense for the purpose of assisting . . . the alien's spouse, child, or parent . . . to violate a provision of this chapter"* (emphasis added). The language about (for example) "forging . . . passport[s]" may well refer to a generic crime, but the italicized exception cannot possibly refer to a generic crime. That is because there is no such generic crime; there is no criminal statute that contains any such exception. Thus if the provision is to have any meaning at all, the exception must refer to the particular circumstances in which an offender committed the crime on a particular occasion.

The statute has other provisions that contain qualifying language that certainly seems to call for circumstance-specific application. Subparagraph

(K)(ii), for example, lists "offense[s] . . . described in section 2421, 2422, or 2423 of title 18 (relating to transportation for the purpose of prostitution) *if committed for commercial advantage*" (emphasis added). Of the three specifically listed criminal statutory sections only one subsection (namely, § 2423(d)) says anything about *commercial advantage*. Thus, unless the "commercial advantage" language calls for circumstance-specific application, the statute's explicit references to §§ 2421 and 2422 would be pointless.

Subparagraph (M)(ii) provides yet another example. It refers to an offense "described in section 7201 of title 26 (relating to tax evasion) *in which the revenue loss to the Government exceeds $10,000*" (emphasis added). There is no offense "described in section 7201 of title 26" that has a specific loss amount as an element. Again, unless the "revenue loss" language calls for circumstance-specific application, the tax-evasion provision would be pointless.

The upshot is that the "aggravated felony" statute, unlike ACCA, contains some language that refers to generic crimes and some language that almost certainly refers to the specific circumstances in which a crime was committed. The question before us then is to which category subparagraph (M)(i) belongs.

2

Subparagraph (M)(i) refers to "an offense that . . . involves fraud or deceit *in which the loss to the victim or victims exceeds $10,000*" (emphasis added). The language of the provision is consistent with a circumstance-specific approach. The words "in which" (which modify "offense") can refer to the conduct involved *"in"* the commission of the offense of conviction, rather than to the elements *of* the offense. Moreover, subparagraph (M)(i) appears just prior to subparagraph (M)(ii), the internal revenue provision we have just discussed, and it is identical in structure to that provision. Where, as here, Congress uses similar statutory language and similar statutory structure in two adjoining provisions, it normally intends similar interpretations.

Moreover, to apply a categorical approach here would leave subparagraph (M)(i) with little, if any, meaningful application. We have found no widely applicable federal fraud statute that contains a relevant monetary loss threshold. * * *

We recognize, as petitioner argues, that Congress might have intended subparagraph (M)(i) to apply almost exclusively to those who violate certain state fraud and deceit statutes. So we have examined state law. We have found, however, that in 1996, when Congress added the $10,000 threshold in subparagraph (M)(i), 29 States had no major fraud or deceit statute with any relevant monetary threshold. * * *

* * *

We conclude that Congress did not intend subparagraph (M)(i)'s monetary threshold to be applied categorically, *i.e.,* to only those fraud and deceit crimes generically defined to include that threshold. Rather, the monetary threshold applies to the specific circumstances surrounding an offender's commission of a fraud and deceit crime on a specific occasion.

III

Petitioner, as an alternative argument, says that we should nonetheless borrow from *Taylor* what that case called a "modified categorical approach." He says that, for reasons of fairness, we should insist that a jury verdict, or a judge-approved equivalent, embody a determination that the loss involved in a prior fraud or deceit conviction amounted to at least $10,000. To determine whether that is so, petitioner says, the subsequent immigration court applying subparagraph (M)(i) should examine only charging documents, jury instructions, and any special jury finding (if one has been requested). If there was a trial but no jury, the subsequent court should examine the equivalent judge-made findings. If there was a guilty plea (and no trial), the subsequent court should examine the written plea documents or the plea colloquy. To authorize any broader examination of the prior proceedings, petitioner says, would impose an unreasonable administrative burden on immigration judges and would unfairly permit him to be deported on the basis of circumstances that were not before *judicially determined* to have been present and which he may not have had an opportunity, prior to conviction, to dispute.

We agree with petitioner that the statute foresees the use of fundamentally fair procedures, including procedures that give an alien a fair opportunity to dispute a Government claim that a prior conviction involved a fraud with the relevant loss to victims. But we do not agree that fairness requires the evidentiary limitations he proposes.

* * *

[P]etitioner and those in similar circumstances have at least one and possibly two opportunities to contest the amount of loss, the first at the earlier sentencing and the second at the deportation hearing itself. They also mean that, since the Government must show the amount of loss by clear and convincing evidence, uncertainties caused by the passage of time are likely to count in the alien's favor.

We can find nothing unfair about the immigration judge's having here relied upon earlier sentencing-related material. The defendant's own stipulation, produced for sentencing purposes, shows that the conviction involved losses considerably greater than $10,000. The court's restitution order shows the same. In the absence of any conflicting evidence (and petitioner mentions none), this evidence is clear and convincing.

The Court of Appeals concluded that petitioner's prior federal conviction consequently falls within the scope of subparagraph (M)(i). And we affirm its judgment.

NOTES AND QUESTIONS ON NIJHAWAN

1. How far does the circumstance–specific analysis in *Nijhawan* go toward an open–ended inquiry into the facts in the criminal prosecution?

2. Does the third step of *Silva–Trevino* (which addressed crimes involving moral turpitude) function like the circumstance–specific analysis set forth in *Nijhawan*?

3. Even if the third step of *Silva–Trevino* functions like the *Nijhawan* circumstance-specific analysis for certain aggravated felonies, does *Nijhawan* effectively mean that for all other classifications of crimes, courts may not look at facts set forth in the criminal case to supply an element that is missing from the statute of conviction? If *Nijhawan* says that courts generally may not do so, how much, if any, of *Silva–Trevino* is inconsistent with *Nijhawan*?

Further illustrating the evolution of approaches to classifying a criminal conviction, our fifth and final case applies *Nijhawan*. The issue in this case is whether a conviction is for a crime of domestic violence, which is a deportability ground, set out in INA § 237(a)(2)(E)(i).

BIANCO v. HOLDER

United States Court of Appeals for the Fifth Circuit, 2010.
624 F.3d 265.

SOUTHWICK, CIRCUIT JUDGE.

* * *

Bianco is a citizen of Venezuela who was first admitted to the United States as a nonimmigrant in 2001. She became a lawful permanent resident on January 10, 2005.

On November 21, 2007, the Department of Homeland Security ("Department") filed a Notice to Appear for Bianco. It alleged that * * * on October 27, 2006, she was convicted in Pennsylvania of aggravated assault and possessing an instrument of crime, *i.e.,* something made or adapted for criminal use, with intent to employ it criminally. *See* 18 Pa. Cons. Stat. §§ 907 & 2702(a)(4).

* * *

[The court explained that Bianco was not deportable for a conviction of a crime involving moral turpitude because it was committed more than five years after admission.]

The IJ * * * held that the Department met its burden to prove Bianco was convicted of aggravated assault, a crime that satisfied the definition of a "crime of violence" under 18 U.S.C. § 16(a). The record was found to contain sufficient evidence that Bianco's crime was committed against her spouse, even though the victim being her husband was not an element of the offense. The IJ held that evidence from outside the record of the criminal proceeding could be used to determine the relationship between Bianco and her victim. Consequently, the IJ ordered Bianco removed for having committed a crime of domestic violence.

* * *

Bianco * * * contends the BIA erred in concluding that her conviction for aggravated assault constituted a crime of *domestic* violence pursuant to Section 237(a)(2)(E)(i). She complains the BIA either should have limited its review to the statutory elements of her prior conviction or, at most, to a small category of evidence that would not include the affidavit of probable cause and the criminal complaint. To be clear, Bianco does not deny that her husband was the victim of the assault. The issue is whether proof of the domestic relationship must appear in certain limited records of the conviction.

* * *

Bianco argues that the evidence used to prove her marriage to the victim of her assault was inadmissible. She urges us to apply to this fact issue the principle that evidence supporting the details of a prior conviction must in some circumstances come solely from the statute of conviction or, if the statute contains multiple offenses, from certain other documents contained in the record of the conviction. The "categorical approach" of examining only the statute of conviction, and the "modified categorical approach" of looking at a limited set of documents apart from the conviction itself, apply in several contexts when a prior conviction has relevance to a current order against the individual.

We have applied the modified categorical approach to determine whether a prior offense committed by an alien was a crime involving moral turpitude. *Amouzadeh v. Winfrey,* 467 F.3d 451, 455 (5th Cir.2006). We wrote that our search is for the "inherent nature of the crime, as defined in the statute ... rather than the circumstances surrounding the particular transgression." *Id.* (quoting *Okabe v. INS,* 671 F.2d 863, 865 (5th Cir.1982)). When the statute of conviction has discrete subsections, some involving crimes of moral turpitude and others not, we look at the record of conviction to determine which subsection applied. Appropriate documents to examine include the charging document such as an indictment, a written plea agreement, a plea colloquy transcript, and any factual finding explicitly made by the trial judge and assented to by the defendant. [In *Shepard v. United States,* 544 U.S. 13, 15–16, 125 S.Ct. 1254, 161 L.Ed.2d 205 (2005),] the Court permitted introduction only of the "records of the convicting court approaching the certainty of the record of conviction," as such documents avoid mini-trials on the issues and satisfy concerns that the relevant facts have been found by a jury or were confirmed by the defendant. *Id.* at 23–26, 125 S.Ct. 1254.

Bianco argues the same limited evidence must be the source of any proof that her conviction was for domestic violence. The immigration statute in question provides that an "alien who at any time after admission is convicted of a crime of domestic violence ... is deportable." INA

§ 237(a)(2)(E)(i). The statute also defines "crime of domestic violence" to be:

> any crime of violence (as defined in section 16 of Title 18) against a person committed by a current or former spouse of the person, by an individual with whom the person shares a child in common, by an individual who is cohabitating with or has cohabitated with the person as a spouse, by an individual similarly situated to a spouse of the person under the domestic or family violence laws of the jurisdiction where the offense occurs. . . .

Bianco does not challenge that her aggravated assault conviction is a crime of violence. She does argue, though, that because nothing in the record of conviction identifies the victim as her husband, the offense cannot qualify for these purposes as one of domestic violence.

The Pennsylvania statute under which Bianco was convicted provided seven alternative methods by which the offense could be committed. Bianco was charged under subsection (4), which provides that a person who "attempts to cause or intentionally or knowingly causes bodily injury to another with a deadly weapon" is guilty of aggravated assault. Pa. Cons. Stat. § 2702(a)(4). This subsection was cited in the charging instrument, and the charge itself tracked the statutory language. Focusing on the specific relevant elements of this Pennsylvania statute does not bring into view any required domestic relationship between perpetrator and victim. Thus, neither the categorical nor the modified categorical approach give the answer to whether Bianco committed a crime of domestic violence.

Our answer is not found in any precedent in this circuit. The Ninth Circuit has dealt with the same issue of categorizing a prior state criminal conviction under the Section 237(a)(2)(E) definition of a crime of domestic violence. *See Tokatly v. Ashcroft,* 371 F.3d 613 (9th Cir. 2004). It determined that a categorical or modified categorical approach must be applied strictly to the entire definition of a crime of domestic violence. The court held that where the domestic relationship is not apparent from the statutory definition itself or from a limited record of conviction, the court is "compelled to hold that the government has not met its burden of proving that the conduct of which the defendant was convicted constitutes a predicate offense, and the conviction may not be used as a basis for removal." *Id.*

The Ninth Circuit's resolution of this issue is entitled to respectful consideration. We must, though, view that court's analysis in light of two subsequent Supreme Court decisions that arguably opened the door to a new "circumstance-specific" approach. *See United States v. Hayes,* 129 S.Ct. 1079, 172 L.Ed.2d 816 (2009); *Nijhawan v. Holder,* 129 S.Ct. 2294, 174 L.Ed.2d 22 (2009). In *Nijhawan,* the Supreme Court examined a statute declaring that an "alien who is convicted of an aggravated felony at any time after admission is deportable." INA § 237(a)(2)(A)(iii). The relevant definition of "aggravated felony" was "an offense that . . .

involves fraud or deceit in which the loss to the victim or victims exceeds $10,000." *Nijhawan,* 129 S.Ct. at 2297. At issue was whether the amount-of-loss language referred to an element that could be proved by information extrinsic to the statute of conviction. The Court concluded that it referred not to a necessary element but to the particular circumstances in which the offense occurred on a particular occasion. Thus, instead of confining itself only to the statute to determine whether the prior conviction qualified as a predicate offense, the Court "look[ed] to the facts and circumstances underlying an offender's conviction." *Id.* at 2299.

* * *

The other recent Supreme Court decision relevant here examined a statute that prohibited those convicted of a misdemeanor crime of domestic violence from possessing firearms or ammunition. *Hayes,* 129 S.Ct. at 1082 (analyzing 18 U.S.C. § 922(g)(9)). The Court held that the criminal statute under which the defendant was earlier convicted need not have as a specific element that the accused and victim be in a domestic relationship.

* * *

We now examine the statute relevant to this appeal. It begins by allowing the Attorney General to order the removal of an alien who "is within one or more of the following classes" of individuals. INA § 237(a). * * *

We elide and combine the statutory language to provide the following language to interpret: "Any alien . . . in and admitted to the United States shall, upon the order of the Attorney General, be removed if the alien . . . at any time after admission is convicted of a crime of domestic violence. . . ."

Applying *Hayes,* we seek an understanding of whether the relevant crime must have as an "element" that the victim have been in a domestic relation with the defendant. From the statutory language quoted, we know the alien must have been "convicted" of a crime of domestic violence. A " 'crime of domestic violence' means any crime of violence (as defined in section 16 of Title 18) against a person committed by a current or former spouse of the person. . . ." INA § 237(a)(2)(E)(i). The parenthetically-cited statute provides that a "crime of violence" includes "an offense that has as an element the use, attempted use, or threatened use of physical force against the person or property of another. . . ." 18 U.S.C. § 16(a).

The only use of the word "element" in the entire statutory array is in requiring an element of violence. Bianco makes no argument that the Pennsylvania crime failed to include an appropriate element of violence. The definition of a "crime of domestic violence" speaks of a crime of violence *committed by* someone in a domestic relationship.

A plain reading of the statute reveals a requirement that the offense of conviction have elements of the use, attempted use, or threat of force, which must be proved, as appropriate, by the categorical or modified categorical approach. The crime also must have been committed by a person in the correct domestic status, though the prior crime need not have the domestic relationship as an element.

Besides statutory interpretation, the Court in *Hayes* articulated certain practical considerations. Congress was identifying a factor in a crime—*domestic* violence—that may not often be an element in state criminal statutes. Applying the categorical or modified categorical approach would frustrate Congress's purpose. That reasoning applies here, too.

Of particular importance to us is that statutes specifically describing crimes of domestic violence are relatively scarce. Most perpetrators are prosecuted in state court under general assault and battery laws. A categorical approach would render the crime of domestic violence as a basis for removal under Section 237(a)(2)(E)(i) inapplicable in about one-half of the States. By making the operation of the provision "so limited and so haphazard" as to undermine its purpose, such an interpretation is unreasonable. *Nijhawan,* 129 S.Ct. at 2302.

Based on these precedents, we conclude that under Section 237(a), a crime of domestic violence need not have as an element the domestic relation of the victim to the defendant. We also conclude that the government has the burden to prove the domestic relationship by clear and convincing evidence, using the kind of evidence generally admissible before an immigration judge. The alien may present contrary evidence.

* * *

To be clear, the categorical and modified categorical approaches remain the analysis in the areas of their traditional application, including a court's application of those approaches to identifying the elements of offenses for which aliens may be removed under Section 237(a)(2).

We have determined that the domestic relationship that must exist for application of Section 237(a)(2)(E)(i) can be proven by evidence generally admissible for proof of facts in administrative proceedings. Bianco specifically complains about the use of the affidavit of probable cause and criminal complaint to establish the domestic relationship. Those documents identified the victim as Bianco's husband. Both the probable cause affidavit and the criminal complaint credibly established the spousal relationship.

Importantly, Bianco admitted repeatedly in her pleadings that the victim of her aggravated assault was her husband. The sentencing sheet shows that she was sentenced to make restitution to her husband and was ordered to participate in a domestic violence program. There was sufficient, admissible proof that Bianco had been convicted of a crime of domestic violence.

* * *

QUESTIONS ON THE "CIRCUMSTANCE-SPECIFIC" APPROACH

1. Recall that in *Nijhawan*, the U.S. Supreme Court distinguished, within the aggravated felony definition, between two types of crimes, observing that it "contains some language that refers to generic crimes and some language that almost certainly refers to the specific circumstances in which a crime was committed." It went on to identify "murder, rape, or sexual abuse of a minor" as offenses listed in that definition in "language that must refer to generic crimes." Into which of these two categories does a "crime of domestic violence" fall?

2. Regarding what evidence may be used in a immigration court hearing to decide deportability based on a prior conviction, *Nijhawan* concluded: "We can find nothing unfair about the immigration judge's having here relied upon earlier sentencing-related material." Did the Fifth Circuit go further in *Bianco*? Does *Bianco* allow DHS, in any removal proceeding charging deportability under *any* provision of § 237(a)(2), to introduce any evidence on the facts in the criminal case and require the immigration judge to decide if those facts have been established by clear and convincing evidence? If so, is this handling of evidence faithful to *Nijhawan*?

3. Has *Bianco* in effect used *Nijhawan* to abandon the categorical and modified categorical approaches completely? What if anything is wrong with such a doctrinal development? Or does *Bianco* make a persuasive argument that *Nijhawan* applies to INA § 237(a)(2)(E)(i) in ways that do not have such a far-reaching effect?

EXERCISE: CRIMINAL DEPORTABILITY GROUNDS

As a matter of general approach, how should Congress define the criminal conduct that would justify the removal of a noncitizen from the United States? This question has both substantive and procedural aspects. As to both, try drafting provisions that would implement your recommendations.

(A) On substance:

Should all of the crimes now in § 237(a)(2) make a noncitizen deportable? Is there other criminal activity you would add?

More generally, how much should Congress rely on a broad phrase like "crime involving moral turpitude," and how much on the kind of detailed specification found in INA § 101(a)(43)?

How might a statutory provision effectively delineate what information in the prior criminal proceeding may be used to decide deportability under § 237(a)(2)?

(B) On procedure:

Should Congress restore the judicial recommendation against deportation (JRAD) discussed in *Padilla*, p. 683 *supra*?

Should Congress go further and make sentencing in the criminal case the exclusive venue for deciding the immigration law consequences of a conviction?[8]

e. Defining "Aggravated Felony"

Our emphasis up to this point has been the fundamental issue of how to classify convictions. We now take a closer look at the definition of aggravated felony, which has been the question presented in several recent U.S. Supreme Court decisions. As explained earlier in this Section B, an aggravated felony conviction makes a noncitizen not only deportable, but also ineligible for asylum, cancellation of removal, and voluntary departure. Noncitizens with an aggravated felony conviction are also barred for life from re-entering the United States, unless they obtain consent to apply for readmission.

(i) Crimes of Violence

The part of the aggravated felony definition that includes "crime of violence," was the focus of the first case. Does a state DUI offense qualify as a crime of violence, if it requires only a showing of negligence in operating a motor vehicle or completely lacks a *mens rea* component?

LEOCAL v. ASHCROFT

Supreme Court of the United States, 2004.
543 U.S. 1, 125 S.Ct. 377, 160 L.Ed.2d 271.

CHIEF JUSTICE REHNQUIST delivered the opinion of the Court.

* * *

Petitioner immigrated to the United States in 1980 and became a lawful permanent resident in 1987. In January 2000, he was charged with two counts of DUI causing serious bodily injury under Fla. Stat. § 316.193(3)(c)(2), after he caused an accident resulting in injury to two people. He pleaded guilty to both counts and was sentenced to two and a half years in prison.

* * * Section 101(a)(43) of the INA defines "aggravated felony" to include, *inter alia*, "a crime of violence (as defined in section 16 of title 18, but not including a purely political offense) for which the term of imprisonment [is] at least one year." Title 18 U.S.C. § 16, in turn, defines the term "crime of violence" to mean:

> (a) an offense that has as an element the use, attempted use, or threatened use of physical force against the person or property of another, or

---

8. *See* Taylor & Wright, *The Sentencing Judge as Immigration Judge*, 51 Emory L.J. 1131 (2002).

(b) any other offense that is a felony and that, by its nature, involves a substantial risk that physical force against the person or property of another may be used in the course of committing the offense.

* * *

Florida Stat. § 316.193(3)(c)(2) makes it a third-degree felony for a person to operate a vehicle while under the influence and, "by reason of such operation, caus[e] ... [s]erious bodily injury to another." The Florida statute, while it requires proof of causation of injury, does not require proof of any particular mental state. * * * The question here is whether § 16 can be interpreted to include such offenses.

* * * The plain text of § 16(a) states that an offense, to qualify as a crime of violence, must have "as an element the use, attempted use, or threatened use of physical force against the person or property of another." We do not deal here with an *attempted* or *threatened* use of force. Petitioner contends that his conviction did not require the "use" of force against another person because the most common employment of the word "use" connotes the *intentional* availment of force, which is not required under the Florida DUI statute. The Government counters that the "use" of force does not incorporate any *mens rea* component, and that petitioner's DUI conviction necessarily includes the use of force. To support its position, the Government dissects the meaning of the word "use," employing dictionaries, legislation, and our own case law in contending that a use of force may be negligent or even inadvertent.

Whether or not the word "use" alone supplies a *mens rea* element, the parties' primary focus on that word is too narrow. Particularly when interpreting a statute that features as elastic a word as "use," we construe language in its context and in light of the terms surrounding it. The critical aspect of § 16(a) is that a crime of violence is one involving the "use ... of physical force *against the person or property of another*." (Emphasis added.) * * * The key phrase in § 16(a)—the "use ... of physical force against the person or property of another"—most naturally suggests a higher degree of intent than negligent or merely accidental conduct. Petitioner's DUI offense therefore is not a crime of violence under § 16(a).

Neither is petitioner's DUI conviction a crime of violence under § 16(b). Section 16(b) sweeps more broadly than § 16(a), defining a crime of violence as including "any other offense that is a felony and that, by its nature, involves a substantial risk that physical force against the person or property of another may be used in the course of committing the offense." But § 16(b) does not thereby encompass all negligent misconduct, such as the negligent operation of a vehicle. It simply covers offenses that naturally involve a person acting in disregard of the risk that physical force might be used against another in committing an offense. The reckless disregard in § 16 relates *not* to the general conduct or to the possibility that harm will result from a person's conduct, but to the risk that the use of physical force against another might be required in committing a crime. * * *

Thus, while § 16(b) is broader than § 16(a) in the sense that physical force need not actually be applied, it contains the same formulation we found to be determinative in § 16(a): the use of physical force against the person or property of another. Accordingly, we must give the language in § 16(b) an identical construction, requiring a higher *mens rea* than the merely accidental or negligent conduct involved in a DUI offense. This is particularly true in light of § 16(b)'s requirement that the "substantial risk" be a risk of using physical force against another person "in the course of committing the offense." In no "ordinary or natural" sense can it be said that a person risks having to "use" physical force against another person in the course of operating a vehicle while intoxicated and causing injury.

In construing both parts of § 16, we cannot forget that we ultimately are determining the meaning of the term "crime of violence." The ordinary meaning of this term, combined with § 16's emphasis on the use of physical force against another person (or the risk of having to use such force in committing a crime), suggests a category of violent, active crimes that cannot be said naturally to include DUI offenses. * * *

Section 16 therefore cannot be read to include petitioner's conviction for DUI causing serious bodily injury under Florida law. * * *

This case does not present us with the question whether a state or federal offense that requires proof of the *reckless* use of force against a person or property of another qualifies as a crime of violence under 18 U.S.C. § 16. DUI statutes such as Florida's do not require any mental state with respect to the use of force against another person, thus reaching individuals who were negligent or less. Drunk driving is a nationwide problem, as evidenced by the efforts of legislatures to prohibit such conduct and impose appropriate penalties. But this fact does not warrant our shoehorning it into statutory sections where it does not fit. * * *

NOTES AND QUESTIONS ON CRIMES OF VIOLENCE

1. The *Leocal* Court concluded that the "crime of violence" definition in 18 U.S.C. § 16 was clear, but in a footnote added that it would have had to resolve any ambiguity in the noncitizen's favor:

> Although here we deal with § 16 in the deportation context, § 16 is a criminal statute, and it has both criminal and noncriminal applications. Because we must interpret the statute consistently, whether we encounter its application in a criminal or noncriminal context, the rule of lenity applies.

534 U.S. 1, 11 n.8. Both *Leocal* and *Fong Haw Tan*, p. 668, *supra*, involved a criminal statute relevant to an immigration case. Should the rule of lenity apply in an immigration case with no criminal law component?

2. *Leocal* applies a categorical approach, limiting its analysis to what the statute covers and not looking at the facts of the particular case. How if at all would the outcome have been different under a modified categorical approach? Some of the implications of this question emerge from posing a related question: if Josue Leocal and others convicted of driving under the influence of alcohol are not aggravated felons because the statute of conviction requires no greater mens rea than negligence, are they still deportable for having committed crimes involving moral turpitude?

The Ninth Circuit held in *Hernandez–Martinez v. Ashcroft*, 329 F.3d 1117 (9th Cir. 2003), that driving under the influence is not a crime involving moral turpitude because the conviction was under an Arizona statute that is divisible and covers conduct that is not base, vile, or depraved. The BIA held in *Matter of Torres–Varela*, 23 I & N Dec. 78 (BIA 2001) (en banc), that driving under the influence with two prior DUI offenses is not a crime of moral turpitude because the conviction was under an Arizona statute does not require a culpable mental state. In 2009, however, the Ninth Circuit, applying the same statute as in *Hernandez–Martinez*, held that DUI *is* a crime involving moral turpitude by applying a modified categorical approach. *Marmolejo–Campos v. Holder*, 558 F.3d 903 (9th Cir. 2009).

(ii) State Felonies That Are Federal Misdemeanors

State offenses may be aggravated felonies under INA § 101(a)(43), yet some states may criminalize behavior that other states do not, or one state may punish as a felony what other states call a misdemeanor. These disparities may make noncitizens deportable for acts in one state that would not have the same consequence if committed in another.

Did Congress intend state charges to count as an aggravated felony for INA purposes even though the underlying conduct would not be punishable as a federal felony? Is uniformity desirable, or does federalism mean that jurisdictions will have different criminal laws, and individuals can live where they agree with those judgments? The argument would continue that a jurisdiction's residents should follow its norms of behavior even if another state or the federal government adopts different norms. One counter might be that even if such considerations support differing degrees of criminal punishment, federal immigration law should adopt a national standard on the level of offensiveness of criminal conduct that warrants removal from the United States.

In the next case, the U.S. Supreme Court construed one important subparagraph of INA § 101(a)(43) not to apply to conduct punishable as a federal misdemeanor and a state felony.

LOPEZ v. GONZALES

Supreme Court of the United States, 2006.
549 U.S. 47, 127 S.Ct. 625, 166 L.Ed.2d 462.

JUSTICE SOUTER delivered the opinion of the Court.

* * *

[P]etitioner Jose Antonio Lopez entered the United States illegally in 1986, [and] in 1990 he became a legal permanent resident. In 1997, he was arrested on state charges in South Dakota, pleaded guilty to aiding and abetting another person's possession of cocaine, and was sentenced to five years' imprisonment. S.D. Codified Laws § 22–42–5 (1988); § 22–6–1 (Supp.1997); § 22–3–3 (1988). He was released for good conduct after 15 months.

After his release, the Immigration and Naturalization Service (INS) began removal proceedings against Lopez, on two grounds: that his state conviction was a controlled substance violation, see INA § 237(a)(2)(B)(i), and was also for an aggravated felony, see INA § 237(a)(2)(A)(iii). Lopez conceded the controlled substance violation but contested the aggravated felony determination, which would disqualify him from discretionary cancellation of removal. * * *

* * *

The INA makes Lopez guilty of an aggravated felony if he has been convicted of "illicit trafficking in a controlled substance ... including," but not limited to, "a drug trafficking crime (as defined in section 924(c) of title 18)." INA § 101(a)(43)(B). Lopez's state conviction was for helping someone else possess cocaine in South Dakota, which state law treated as the equivalent of possessing the drug, S.D. Codified Laws § 22–3–3, a state felony, § 22–42–5. Mere possession is not, however, a felony under the federal [Controlled Substances Act] although possessing more than what one person would have for himself will support conviction for the federal felony of possession with intent to distribute * * *.

Despite this federal misdemeanor treatment, the Government argues that possession's felonious character as a state crime can turn it into an aggravated felony under the INA. There, it says, illicit trafficking includes a drug trafficking crime as defined in federal Title 18. Title 18 defines "drug trafficking crime" as "any felony punishable" under the Controlled Substances Act and the CSA punishes possession, albeit as a misdemeanor. That is enough, says the Government, because § 924(c)(2) requires only that the offense be punishable, not that it be punishable as a federal felony. Hence, a prior conviction in state court will satisfy the felony element because the State treats possession that way.

There are a few things wrong with this argument, the first being its incoherence with any commonsense conception of "illicit trafficking," the term ultimately being defined. The everyday understanding of "trafficking" should count for a lot here, for the statutes in play do not define the term, and so remit us to regular usage to see what Congress probably meant. And ordinarily "trafficking" means some sort of commercial dealing. See Black's Law Dictionary 1534 (8th ed. 2004) * * *. Commerce, however, was no part of Lopez's South Dakota offense of helping someone else to possess, and certainly it is no element of simple possession, with which the State equates that crime. * * *

Reading § 924(c) the Government's way, then, would often turn simple possession into trafficking, just what the English language tells us not to expect, and that result makes us very wary of the Government's position. Which is not to deny that the Government might still be right; Humpty Dumpty used a word to mean " 'just what [he chose] it to mean— neither more nor less,' " and legislatures, too, are free to be unorthodox. Congress can define an aggravated felony of illicit trafficking in an unexpected way. But Congress would need to tell us so, and there are good reasons to think it was doing no such thing here.

First, an offense that necessarily counts as "illicit trafficking" under the INA is a "drug trafficking crime" under § 924(c), that is, a "felony punishable under the [CSA]," § 924(c)(2). And if we want to know what felonies might qualify, the place to go is to the definitions of crimes punishable as felonies under the Act; where else would one naturally look? Although the Government would have us look to state law, we suspect that if Congress had meant us to do that it would have found a much less misleading way to make its point. Indeed, other parts of § 924 expressly refer to guilt under state law, and the implication confirms that the reference solely to a "felony punishable under the [CSA]" in § 924(c)(2) is to a crime punishable as a felony under the federal Act. * * * Unless a state offense is punishable as a federal felony it does not count.

The Government stresses that the text does not read "punishable as a felony," and that by saying simply "punishable" Congress left the door open to counting state felonies, so long as they would be punishable at all under the CSA. But we do not normally speak or write the Government's way. We do not use a phrase like "felony punishable under the [CSA]" when we mean to signal or allow a break between the noun "felony" and the contiguous modifier "punishable under the [CSA]," let alone a break that would let us read the phrase as if it said "felony punishable under the CSA whether or not as a felony." Regular usage points in the other direction, and when we read "felony punishable under the . . . Act," we instinctively understand "felony punishable as such under the Act" or "felony as defined by the Act." * * *

* * *

Finally, the Government's reading would render the law of alien removal, and the law of sentencing for illegal entry into the country, dependent on varying state criminal classifications even when Congress has apparently pegged the immigration statutes to the classifications Congress itself chose. It may not be all that remarkable that federal consequences of state crimes will vary according to state severity classification when Congress describes an aggravated felony in generic terms, without express reference to the definition of a crime in a federal statute (as in the case of "illicit trafficking in a controlled substance"). But it would have been passing strange for Congress to intend any such result when a state criminal classification is at odds with a federal provision that the INA expressly provides as a specific example of an "aggravated felony" (like the § 924(c)(2) definition of "drug trafficking crime"). We cannot imagine that Congress took the trouble to incorporate its own statutory scheme of felonies and misdemeanors if it meant courts to ignore it whenever a State chose to punish a given act more heavily.

* * *

The dissenting opinion of JUSTICE THOMAS is omitted.

NOTES AND QUESTIONS ON LOPEZ

1. Justice Souter, writing for an 8–1 majority in *Lopez*, took an "ordinary meaning" approach to interpreting the statutory scheme involved in the aggravated felony definition. In *Leocal*, Justice Rehnquist took a similar approach, writing for a unanimous Court. Both construed the statutes in favor of the noncitizen, though the BIA and the federal appellate courts had concluded that criminal conduct in question constituted an aggravated felony.

What are the implications of the "ordinary meaning" approach for the *Chevron* doctrine, *Chevron U.S.A., Inc. v. Natural Resources Defense Council*, 467 U.S. 837, 104 S.Ct. 2778, 81 L.Ed.2d 694 (1984), discussed in Chapter Five, p. 338? Under *Chevron*, courts defer to the statutory interpretations adopted by the administrative agency, here the BIA, with expertise in enforcing the statute. Neither *Lopez* nor *Leocal* mentioned *Chevron*, though immigration cases often rely on it. Why was the Court silent on this point in *Lopez*? Would the same rationale apply to *Leocal*?

2. *Lopez* held that only a crime that is punishable as a federal felony can be an aggravated felony under INA § 101(a)(43)(B), which expressly refers to federal law in defining "illicit trafficking in a controlled substance" as an aggravated felony. *Lopez* left open the meaning of "punishable as a federal felony," as the next case explains.

CARACHURI–ROSENDO v. HOLDER

Supreme Court of the United States, 2010.
560 U.S. ＿＿, 130 S.Ct. 2577, 177 L.Ed.2d 68.

JUSTICE STEVENS delivered the opinion of the Court.

Petitioner Jose Angel Carachuri–Rosendo, a lawful permanent resident who has lived in the United States since he was five years old, faced deportation under federal law after he committed two misdemeanor drug possession offenses in Texas. For the first, possession of less than two ounces of marijuana, he received 20 days in jail. For the second, possession without a prescription of one tablet of a common antianxiety medication, he received 10 days in jail. After this second offense, the Federal Government initiated removal proceedings against him. He conceded that he was removable, but claimed he was eligible for discretionary relief from removal under INA § 240A(a).

To decide whether Carachuri–Rosendo is eligible to seek cancellation of removal or waiver of inadmissibility under § 240A(a), we must decide whether he has been convicted of an "aggravated felony," a category of crimes singled out for the harshest deportation consequences. * * *

Under the Immigration and Nationality Act (INA), a lawful permanent resident subject to removal from the United States may apply for discretionary cancellation of removal if, *inter alia,* he "has not been convicted of any aggravated felony," § 240A(a)(3). The statutory definition of the term "aggravated felony" includes a list of numerous federal offenses, one of which is "illicit trafficking in a controlled substance ... including a drug trafficking crime (as defined in section 924(c) of title 18)." § 101(a)(43)(B). Section 924(c)(2), in turn, defines a "drug trafficking crime" to mean "any felony punishable under," *inter alia,* "the Controlled Substances Act (21 U.S.C. 801 et seq.)." A felony is a crime for which the "maximum term of imprisonment authorized" is "more than one year." 18 U.S.C. § 3559(a).

* * * Except for simple possession of crack cocaine or flunitrazepam, a first-time simple possession offense is a federal misdemeanor; the maximum term authorized for such a conviction is less than one year. However, a conviction for a simple possession offense "after a prior conviction under this subchapter [or] under the law of any State ... has become final"—what we will call recidivist simple possession—may be punished as a felony, with a prison sentence of up to two years. Thus, except for simple possession offenses involving isolated categories of drugs not presently at issue, only *recidivist* simple possession offenses are "punishable" as a federal "felony" under the Controlled Substances Act. And thus only a conviction within this particular category of simple possession offenses might, conceivably, be an "aggravated felony" under INA § 101(a)(43).

For a subsequent simple possession offense to be eligible for an enhanced punishment, *i.e.,* to be punishable as a felony, the Controlled Substances Act requires that a prosecutor charge the existence of the prior simple possession conviction before trial, or before a guilty plea. Notice, plus an opportunity to challenge the validity of the prior conviction used to enhance the current conviction are mandatory prerequisites to obtaining a punishment based on the fact of a prior conviction. And they are also necessary prerequisites under federal law to "authorize" a felony punishment, for the type of simple possession offense at issue in this case.

* * * [I]n *Lopez v. Gonzales,* 549 U.S. 47, 56, 127 S.Ct. 625, 166 L.Ed.2d 462 (2006), we determined that, in order to be an "aggravated felony" for immigration law purposes, a state drug conviction must be punishable as a felony under *federal* law. * * *

In the case before us, the Government argues that Carachuri–Rosendo, despite having received only a 10–day sentence for his Texas misdemeanor simple possession offense, nevertheless has been "convicted" of an "aggravated felony" within the meaning of the INA. This is so, the Government contends, because had Carachuri–Rosendo been prosecuted in federal court instead of state court, he *could have been* prosecuted as a felon and received a 2–year sentence based on the fact of his prior simple possession offense. * * *

* * *

* * * This type of petty simple possession offense is not typically thought of as an "aggravated felony" or as "illicit trafficking." * * *

The same is true for the type of penalty at issue. We do not usually think of a 10–day sentence for the unauthorized possession of a trivial amount of a prescription drug as an "aggravated felony." A "felony," we have come to understand, is a "serious crime usu[ally] punishable by imprisonment for more than one year or by death." Black's Law Dictionary 694 (9th ed. 2009) (hereinafter Black's). An "aggravated" offense is one "made worse or more serious by circumstances such as violence, the presence of a deadly weapon, or the intent to commit another crime." *Id.,* at 75, 127 S.Ct. 625. The term "aggravated felony" is unique to Title 8, which covers immigration matters; it is not a term used elsewhere within the United States Code. * * *

* * *

The Government's position, like the Court of Appeals' "hypothetical approach," would treat all "conduct punishable as a felony" as the equivalent of a "conviction" of a felony whenever, hypothetically speaking, the underlying conduct could have received felony treatment under federal law. We find this reasoning—and the "hypothetical approach" itself—unpersuasive for the following reasons.

First, and most fundamentally, the Government's position ignores the text of the INA, which limits the Attorney General's cancellation power only when, *inter alia,* a noncitizen "has ... been *convicted* of a[n] aggravated felony." INA § 240A(a)(3) (emphasis added). The text thus indicates that we are to look to the conviction itself as our starting place, not to what might have or could have been charged. * * *

* * * Although a federal immigration court may have the power to make a recidivist finding in the first instance, it cannot, *ex post,* enhance the state offense of record just because facts known to it would have authorized a greater penalty under either state or federal law. Carachuri–Rosendo was not actually "convicted," § 240A(a)(3), of a drug possession offense committed "after a prior conviction ... has become final," § 844(a), and no subsequent development can undo that history.

* * *

Second, and relatedly, the Government's position fails to give effect to the mandatory notice and process requirements contained in 21 U.S.C. § 851. For federal law purposes, a simple possession offense is not "punishable" as a felony unless a federal prosecutor first elects to charge a defendant as a recidivist in the criminal information. The statute * * * speaks in mandatory terms, permitting "[n]o person" to be subject to a recidivist enhancement—and therefore, in this case, a felony sentence—

"unless" he has been given notice of the Government's intent to prove the fact of a prior conviction. Federal law also gives the defendant an opportunity to challenge the fact of the prior conviction itself. The Government would dismiss these procedures as meaningless, so long as they may be satisfied during the immigration proceeding.

But these procedural requirements have great practical significance with respect to the conviction itself and are integral to the structure and design of our drug laws. They authorize prosecutors to exercise discretion when electing whether to pursue a recidivist enhancement. * * *

* * *

Third, the Court of Appeals' hypothetical felony approach is based on a misreading of our decision in *Lopez*. We never used the term "hypothetical" to describe our analysis in that case. We did look to the "proscribe[d] conduct" of a state offense to determine whether it is "punishable as a felony under that federal law." 549 U.S. at 60, 127 S.Ct. 625. But the "hypothetical approach" employed by the Court of Appeals introduces a level of conjecture at the outset of this inquiry that has no basis in *Lopez*. * * *

Fourth, it * * * is quite unlikely that the "conduct" that gave rise to Carachuri–Rosendo's conviction would have been punished as a felony in federal court. Under the United States Sentencing Guidelines, Carachuri–Rosendo's recommended sentence, based on the type of controlled substance at issue, would not have exceeded one year and very likely would have been less than 6 months. * * *

Finally, as we noted in *Leocal v. Ashcroft,* 543 U.S. 1, 11 n.8, 125 S.Ct. 377, 160 L.Ed.2d 271 (2004), ambiguities in criminal statutes referenced in immigration laws should be construed in the noncitizen's favor. * * *

* * *

In sum, the Government is correct that to qualify as an "aggravated felony" under the INA, the conduct prohibited by state law must be punishable as a felony under federal law. But as the text and structure of the relevant statutory provisions demonstrate, the defendant must *also* have been *actually convicted* of a crime that is itself punishable as a felony under federal law. The mere possibility that the defendant's conduct, coupled with facts outside of the record of conviction, could have authorized a felony conviction under federal law is insufficient to satisfy the statutory command that a noncitizen be "convicted of a[n] aggravated felony" before he loses the opportunity to seek cancellation of removal. INA § 240A(a)(3). * * *

* * *

The concurring opinions of JUSTICE SCALIA and JUSTICE THOMAS are omitted.

(iii) State Misdemeanors as Aggravated Felonies

Lopez tells us that a state felony is not an aggravated felony under INA § 101(a)(43)(B)—which defines "illicit trafficking in a controlled substance" by referring to another federal statute—when the corresponding federal offense is a misdemeanor. But can a state misdemeanor be an aggravated felony? Many states define as a misdemeanor any criminal offense for which the sentence is one year or less. For example, New York classifies certain assaults as misdemeanors with a maximum one-year prison term. *See, e.g.,* N.Y. Penal Code, §§ 120.00, 70.15. Would such an assault be as an aggravated felony under INA § 101(a)(43)(F) because it is "a crime of violence * * * for which the term of imprisonment [is] at least one year"?

What about a guilty plea by a nineteen-year-old lawful permanent resident to a misdemeanor charge based on sexual intercourse with a fifteen-year-old female? Is this a conviction for the aggravated felony of sexual abuse of a minor, which would make the permanent resident ineligible for cancellation of removal under INA § 240A? Faced with these facts, the Seventh Circuit reasoned:

> * * * Congress decided to broaden INA § 101(a)(43)(A) from just murder to include rape and sexual abuse of a minor, implicitly signaling that it felt both of these latter two crimes were of similar severity and import. Murder and rape are widely recognized as felony crimes. Thus, grouping sexual abuse of a minor with these two acts, without explicitly limiting sexual abuse of a minor to the status of a misdemeanor, is a fairly strong indication, albeit a limited one because of the lack of definite legislative commentary on the subject, that Congress intended both misdemeanor and felony convictions for sexual abuse of a minor to be considered aggravated felonies.

> * * * [R]ather than leave the question of what constitutes an aggravated felony open-ended, Congress said, "The term 'aggravated felony' means— ..." and proceeded to list what crimes would be considered aggravated felonies. It is important to note that the term aggravated felony is placed within quotation marks and Congress then used the word "means" after this term. What is evident from the setting aside of aggravated felony with quotation marks and the use of the term "means" is that INA § 101(a)(43) serves as a definition section. * * * Congress had the discretion to use whatever term it pleased and define the term as it deemed appropriate. The statute functions like a dictionary, in that it provides us with Congress' definition of the term "aggravated felony." There is no explicit provision in the statute directing that the term "aggravated felony" is limited only to felony crimes. We therefore are constrained to conclude that Congress, since it did not specifically articulate that aggravated felonies cannot be misdemeanors, intended to have the term aggravated felony apply to the broad range of crimes listed in the statute, even if these include misdemeanors.

Guerrero–Perez v. INS, 242 F.3d 727, 736–37 (7th Cir. 2001). The BIA ultimately acceded to the Seventh Circuit's view in *Matter of Small*, 23 I & N Dec. 448 (BIA 2002), applying the rule nationwide.

SECTION C.   RELIEF FROM REMOVAL

In most removal proceedings, the noncitizen does not seriously challenge removability. Instead, the major issue is an application for relief from removal. For example, DHS records can prove an overstay violation. Proof of identity and alienage, plus a certification of the lack of a DHS record of valid admission, can establish entry without inspection. Criminal grounds of inadmissibility or deportability can be based on the record of conviction, which generally cannot be attacked collaterally in immigration court. Noncitizens often concede removability at the outset of the hearing and then request one or more forms of relief.

The longer a noncitizen has lived in the United States—legally or illegally—the greater the ties she is likely to have established and the greater the hardship that removal will entail. The burdens do not fall solely on the noncitizen: family and friends may be deprived of significant personal relationships, employers may lose productive employees, and neighborhoods may lose valued residents. Not surprisingly, then, a number of avenues of relief are available to noncitizens, especially those who have lived in the United States for a substantial period of time and have close relatives who are U.S. citizens or permanent residents.

Relief from removal can come in several forms. We start with the forms of relief that are most desirable from the noncitizen's perspective because they restore—or establish—lawful permanent resident status. (However, we defer until Chapter Eight our consideration of relief from removal based on protection from persecution and torture.) This chapter then examines types of relief from removal that do not confer permanent resident status and typically do not eliminate the underlying deportability ground.

As you study these materials on relief, ask yourself if it is sensible for the INA to have many different forms of relief. What policies and goals have led to the development of these avenues for some noncitizens to avoid expulsion? Is there are better way to organize and define these provisions? We will return to these fundamental questions later in this section.

1.   CANCELLATION OF REMOVAL

We start with a provision, INA § 240A, that allows noncitizens to regularize their status in the United States. Through a mechanism called cancellation of removal, § 240A grants lawful permanent resident status to noncitizens who are otherwise removable from the United States. This version of relief for permanent residents was enacted in 1996, but it has precursors that date back to the early 1900s.

Under § 240A, the Attorney General—typically acting through an immigration judge—may cancel the removal of a noncitizen and allow the noncitizen to remain as a permanent resident. Threshold eligibility for cancellation may extend not only to noncitizens are in the United States lawfully, but also to some noncitizens who are unlawfully present, even if they entered without inspection. The requirements for the actual grant of relief also vary, depending on the noncitizen's circumstances. Cancellation is easier for battered spouses and children to obtain.

Cancellation of removal confers permanent resident status for the first time on noncitizens who entered the United States without inspection or who were admitted as nonimmigrants. For noncitizens who are already permanent residents, cancellation maintains that status in spite of their removability (usually on the basis of a criminal conviction). For all noncitizens, cancellation of removal effectively erases the prior personal history for removability purposes, though it may still impair naturalization eligibility.[12]

a. Cancellation of Removal for Permanent Residents

If lawful permanent residents who are either inadmissible or deportable satisfy certain statutory prerequisites, § 240A(a) provides that the Attorney General *may* cancel their removal. (The statutory predecessor of § 240A(a) cancellation for permanent residents, known as § 212(c) relief, was repealed in 1996 but may still be available to certain individuals who are removable due to pre–1996 events. *See* p. 754, *infra*.)

(i) Continuous Residence

Eligibility for § 240A(a) cancellation for lawful permanent residents has two requirements concerned with time. A noncitizen must have (1) resided in the United States continuously for seven years after lawful admission, and (2) been a lawful permanent resident for at least five years. For example, individuals who have resided continuously in the United States since admission as a permanent resident seven or more years ago would satisfy both elements. So, too, would someone who has resided continuously in the United States since being admitted as a student seven years ago, and then adjusting to permanent resident status at least five years ago. For members of the military, the continuous residence requirement may not apply, *see* INA § 240A(d)(3).

Calculating the time period is pivotal for many applicants. Until 1996, time that accrued during deportation and exclusion proceedings counted toward the requirement. Now, the service of a notice to appear (NTA) in a removal proceeding stops the accrual of continuous residence. This is what is often called the stop-time rule in § 240A(d)(1)(A). (Prosecutorial discre-

---

12. Another form of relief from removal is adjustment of status, which a noncitizen can invoke in proceedings before an immigration judge. However, we considered adjustment in Chapter Six on admission procedures, because adjustment is sought most typically not defensively by noncitizens who are in removal proceedings, but rather affirmatively by noncitizens as a way of gaining permanent resident status without traveling abroad to obtain an immigrant visa at a U.S. consulate.

tion in the form of "repapering" may be exercised to cancel a notice to appear and then reissue it after the required time has accrued.)

The stop-time rule also applies "when the alien has committed an offense referred to in section 212(a)(2) that renders the alien inadmissible to the United States under section 212(a)(2) or removable from the United States under section 237(a)(2) or (4)." INA § 240A(d)(1)(B).

PROBLEMS ON QUALIFYING TIME PERIODS

Try applying the statutory provisions on residence and the accrual of time to the following situations.

1. J lawfully entered the United States as a nonimmigrant employee of the United Nations exactly eight years ago. Exactly three years later, she became a permanent resident. One month ago, she was served a notice to appear in a removal proceeding based on a deportability ground. (Assume that she committed no offense that under INA § 240A(d)(1)(B) would stop the accrual of qualifying time.) Is J eligible to apply for cancellation of removal?

2. Same facts as the previous problem, except that J is the battered spouse of a U.S. citizen. Is J eligible to apply for cancellation?

3. K was admitted as a student eight years ago and became a lawful permanent resident six years ago. Two years ago, she was charged with a crime involving moral turpitude, and two months thereafter she was convicted. Three months ago, K was served with a notice to appear in a removal proceeding. Is K eligible to apply for cancellation of removal?

4. Same facts as the previous problem, except that the crime is within the petty offense exception of § 212(a)(2)(A)(ii)(II), making K deportable under § 237(a)(2), but not inadmissible under § 212(a)(2). When does the clock stop?

(ii) Discretionary Factors

Long-term permanent residents do not need to establish a particular degree of hardship to be eligible for cancellation under § 240A(a)—although of course hardship is likely to figure into the exercise of discretion. In 1998, the BIA announced that the standards previously used in cases under its predecessor provision, former INA § 212(c), would guide the exercise of discretion for cancellation under § 240A(a):

> * * * [T]here is no inflexible standard for determining who should be granted discretionary relief, and each case must be judged on its own merits. Within this context, the Board ruled in *Matter of Marin*, [16 I & N Dec. 581 (BIA 1978),] that in exercising discretion under section 212(c) of the Act, an Immigration Judge, upon review of

the record as a whole, "must balance the adverse factors evidencing the alien's undesirability as a permanent resident with the social and humane considerations presented in his (or her) behalf to determine whether the granting of . . . relief appears in the best interest of this country." We find this general standard equally appropriate in considering requests for cancellation of removal under section 240A(a) of the Act.

We also find that the factors we have enunciated as pertinent to the exercise of discretion under section 212(c) are equally relevant to the exercise of discretion under section 240A(a) of the Act. For example, favorable considerations include such factors as family ties within the United States, residence of long duration in this country (particularly when the inception of residence occurred at a young age), evidence of hardship to the respondent and his family if deportation occurs, service in this country's armed forces, a history of employment, the existence of property or business ties, evidence of value and service to the community, proof of genuine rehabilitation if a criminal record exists, and other evidence attesting to a respondent's good character. Among the factors deemed adverse to an alien are the nature and underlying circumstances of the grounds of exclusion or deportation (now removal) that are at issue, the presence of additional significant violations of this country's immigration laws, the existence of a criminal record and, if so, its nature, recency, and seriousness, and the presence of other evidence indicative of a respondent's bad character or undesirability as a permanent resident of this country.

In some cases, the minimum equities required to establish eligibility for relief under section 240A(a) (i.e., residence of at least 7 years and status as a lawful permanent resident for not less than 5 years) may be sufficient in and of themselves to warrant favorable discretionary action. However, as the negative factors grow more serious, it becomes incumbent upon the alien to introduce additional offsetting favorable evidence, which in some cases may have to involve unusual or outstanding equities.

With respect to the issue of rehabilitation, a respondent who has a criminal record will ordinarily be required to present evidence of rehabilitation before relief is granted as a matter of discretion. However, applications involving convicted aliens must be evaluated on a case-by-case basis, with rehabilitation a factor to be considered in the exercise of discretion. We have held that a showing of rehabilitation is not an absolute prerequisite in every case involving an alien with a criminal record.

Matter of C–V–T–, 22 I & N Dec. 7, 11–12 (BIA 1998).

QUESTIONS ON THE EXERCISE OF DISCRETION

What would you add to or delete from this list of favorable and unfavorable factors identified in *C–V–T–*? What weight should be given to the listed factors? Should an adjudicator seek evidence on each factor? To what extent will evaluation of the factors depend on the perspective of the particular adjudicator? What mechanisms exist (or could be constructed) to promote uniformity among decisionmakers?

Now suppose you were an immigration judge to whom this power of discretion is assigned. How would you go about exercising it? Is it a grand power to dispense justice as you see fit? If it is the ultimate power to bestow mercy, can you act on hunches or your personal reaction to the noncitizen? How far does your discretion go? Can you grant relief to persons whose cases you find sympathetic, even if they do not meet the statutory eligibility criteria?

(iii) Waivers Under Former INA § 212(c)

Before 1996, when Congress established cancellation of removal by enacting INA § 240A(a), lawful permanent residents could seek what was known as "§ 212(c) relief." Former INA § 212(c) seemed to allow long-term lawful permanent residents to obtain waivers of what were then called *exclusion* grounds. A series of administrative and judicial decisions extended § 212(c) relief to permanent residents in *deportation* proceedings. If they had seven years of lawful domicile in the United States, permanent residents who were deportable—typically due to criminal convictions—could show countervailing equities to the immigration judge to ask for relief from deportation. *See Francis v. INS*, 532 F.2d 268 (2d Cir.1976); *see generally* Aleinikoff, Martin & Motomura, Immigration: Process and Policy 689–714 (3d ed. 1995).

Relief under § 212(c) still can be invoked by some noncitizens convicted before April 1997. The 1996 Act expressly allowed noncitizens who were in deportation proceedings before April 1, 1997 to use § 212(c). Moreover, in *INS v. St. Cyr*, 533 U.S. 289, 121 S.Ct. 2271, 150 L.Ed.2d 347 (2001), the U.S. Supreme Court held that § 212(c) remained available to noncitizens who pled guilty before April 1, 1997, even if their proceedings began after that date. Given the potentially severe effects of applying the repeal retrospectively, the Court invoked "[t]he presumption against retroactive application of ambiguous statutory provisions, buttressed by 'the longstanding principle of construing any lingering ambiguities in deportation statutes in favor of the alien.'" *Id*. at 320.

As we go to press in late 2011, a case pending in the U.S. Supreme Court, *Judulang v. Holder, cert. granted*, ___ U.S. ___, 131 S.Ct. 2093, 179 L.Ed.2d 889 (2011), is expected to decide questions about eligibility for § 212(c) relief when a conviction before April 1997 makes the noncitizen deportable. The federal circuits and the BIA have been divided on the key questions: whether the noncitizen applying for § 212(c) relief (1) must be deportable based on a ground for which there is a corresponding ground of inadmissibility, and (2) must have traveled outside the United States after his conviction.

b. Cancellation of Removal for Nonpermanent Residents

INA § 240A(b) outlines another form of cancellation of removal that is designed primarily to afford relief to noncitizens who have lived in the United States for an extended period, but who are not lawful permanent residents. An earlier version of this relief was known as "suspension of deportation," authorized by former INA § 244.

Cancellation of removal pursuant to § 240A(b) allows a noncitizen to become a lawful permanent resident. There is no requirement that the noncitizens have been admitted to the United States or that they be lawfully present, so unauthorized migrants may be eligible. Despite the provision's caption in the INA, which refers to nonpermanent residents, nothing bars permanent residents from seeking cancellation under § 240A(b). They may wish to do so if they are ineligible for § 240A(a) cancellation. You will see that this form of cancellation has threshold requirements that resemble those for cancellation for lawful permanent residents, but overall are much more demanding.

(i) Continuous Physical Presence

Ten years of continuous physical presence (not residence) is the minimum time period for § 240A(b) cancellation of removal. The INA does not define "presence," but § 240A(d)(2) sets out rules for determining if physical presence is "continuous." For members of the military, this requirement may not apply, *see* INA § 240A(d)(3). The same basic stop-time rule governs both subsections (a) and (b) of § 240A.

PROBLEMS ON QUALIFYING TIME PERIODS

5. L was admitted to the United States on a student visa twelve years ago, and became a permanent resident two years ago. She has returned home to France for the month of August every year since she first arrived as a student. Three months ago, L was served with a notice to appear (based on a deportability ground unrelated to any crime). Do the summer trips render L ineligible for cancellation of removal?

6. M has been working without authorization since clandestinely crossing the border from Mexico twelve years ago. Seven years ago, she took a two-month trip to Mexico to visit her dying grandmother. Three months ago, M was served with a notice to appear based on being in the United States without admission or parole. Does the two-month trip make M ineligible for § 240A(b) cancellation?

(ii) Good Moral Character

Under INA § 240A(b)(1)(B), a noncitizen who applies for cancellation must have been of "good moral character" for ten years immediately preceding the date of application. INA § 101(f), which Chapter Two discussed in the naturalization context, lists some persons who are *not* of "good moral character" (such as anyone convicted of an aggravated felony), but it does not define what "good moral character" is. Unsurprisingly, criminal activities constitute the major grounds for finding that a person lacks good moral character.

(iii) Exceptional and Extremely Unusual Hardship

For § 240A(b) cancellation, noncitizens must show that removal would result in "exceptional and extremely unusual hardship to the alien's spouse, parent, or child, who is a citizen of the United States or an alien lawfully admitted for permanent residence." This demanding requirement, adopted in 1996, was largely a response to the BIA decision in *Matter of O–J–O–*, 21 I & N Dec. 381 (BIA 1996), which granted suspension of deportation under former INA § 244 based on the pre–1996 extreme hardship standard. The applicant, a 24–year–old from Nicaragua, had lived in the United States since the age of thirteen. According to the Board:

> This is a close case on the issue of "extreme hardship" but one which, in the final analysis, meets the requirement of significant hardships over and above the normal economic and social disruptions involved in deportation. The respondent has lived in the United States during his critical formative years. He has significant church and community ties in the United States. He is fully assimilated into American culture and society. This assimilation makes the prospect of readjustment to life in Nicaragua much harder than would ordinarily be the case. He would also face difficult economic and political circumstances in his native country, including the possible loss of an ongoing business concern.

Against this backdrop, the legislative history explains the change in 1996:

> The managers have deliberately changed the required showing of hardship from "extreme hardship" to "exceptional and extremely unusual hardship" to emphasize that the alien must provide evidence of harm to his spouse, parent, or child substantially beyond that which ordinarily would be expected to result from the alien's deportation. The "extreme hardship" standard has been weakened by recent administrative decisions holding that forced removal of an alien who has become "acclimated" to the United States would constitute a hardship sufficient to support a grant of suspension of deportation. *See Matter of O–J–O–* (BIA 1996). Such a ruling would be inconsistent with the standard set forth in new section 240A(b)(1). Similarly, a showing that an alien's United States citizen child would fare less well in the alien's country of nationality than in the United States

does not establish "exceptional" or "extremely unusual" hardship and thus would not support a grant of relief under this provision. Our immigration law and policy clearly provide that an alien parent may not derive immigration benefits through his or her child who is a United States citizen. The availability in truly exceptional cases of relief under section 240A(b)(1) must not undermine this or other fundamental immigration enforcement policies.

H.R. Conf. Rep. 104–828, 104th Cong. 2d Sess. 230 (1996).

The BIA applies the new language in the next case.

MATTER OF GONZALEZ RECINAS

Board of Immigration Appeals, 2002.
23 I & N Dec. 467.

VILLAGELIU, BOARD MEMBER:

The respondents have appealed from the decision of an Immigration Judge dated December 18, 2000, denying their application for cancellation of removal pursuant to section 240A(b) of the Immigration and Nationality Act. The appeal will be sustained.

I. FACTUAL BACKGROUND

The adult respondent is a 39–year–old native and citizen of Mexico. She is the mother of four United States citizen children, aged 12, 11, 8, and 5, and the two minor respondents, aged 15 and 16, both of whom are natives and citizens of Mexico. Her parents are lawful permanent residents and her five siblings are United States citizens. She is divorced and has no immediate family in Mexico.

The three respondents entered the United States in 1988 on nonimmigrant visas and stayed longer than authorized. Except for a brief absence in 1992, they have remained in this country since their initial entry.

II. ISSUE

The sole issue on appeal is whether the Immigration Judge erred in finding that the respondent failed to demonstrate that her removal would result in exceptional and extremely unusual hardship to her four United States citizen children and/or her lawful permanent resident parents.[1]

III. ANALYSIS

* * *

A. *Exceptional and Extremely Unusual Hardship Standard*

In *Matter of Monreal*, 23 I & N Dec. 56 (BIA 2001), we first considered the "exceptional and extremely unusual" hardship standard in a prece-

---

1. As the Immigration Judge noted, the minor respondents do not have a qualifying relative for purposes of cancellation of removal. See section 240A(b)(1)(D) of the Act.

dent decision in the case of a 34–year–old Mexican national who was the father of three United States citizen children. We held that to establish exceptional and extremely unusual hardship under section 240A(b) of the Act, an alien must demonstrate that his or her spouse, parent, or child would suffer hardship that is substantially beyond that which would ordinarily be expected to result from the person's departure. We specifically stated, however, that the alien need not show that such hardship would be "unconscionable." We also noted that, in deciding a cancellation of removal claim, consideration should be given to the age, health, and circumstances of the qualifying family members, including how a lower standard of living or adverse country conditions in the country of return might affect those relatives.

After reviewing the case, we dismissed the respondent's appeal, finding that he had not satisfied the new hardship standard. We noted that the respondent had been working for 10 years at his uncle's business, but had a brother living in Mexico who also worked for the same business. Our decision emphasized that the respondent was in good health and would be able to work and support his United States citizen children in Mexico. We further found that, upon his return to Mexico, the respondent would be reunited with family members, including his wife (the mother of their three children), who had already returned to Mexico with one of the children. Finally, we noted that the respondent's children were in good health and that the eldest, who was 12 years old, could speak, read, and write Spanish.

We revisited the issue in *Matter of Andazola*, 23 I & N Dec. 319 (BIA 2002), finding that the exceptional and extremely unusual hardship standard was not met in the case of a single Mexican woman. The respondent had two United States citizen children, who were 11 and 6 years old. Their father (who apparently had authorization to remain in the United States) contributed financially to the family, was a presence in the lives of the children, and could continue to help support the family upon their return to Mexico. All of the respondent's siblings were living in the United States, but were without documentation. The respondent had not shown that her United States citizen children would be deprived of all schooling, or of an opportunity to obtain any education. In denying relief, we considered it "significant" that the respondent had accumulated assets, including $7,000 in savings and a retirement fund, and owned a home and two vehicles. We noted that these assets could help ease the family's transition to Mexico. Accordingly, we found that the case presented a common fact pattern that was insufficient to satisfy the exceptional and extremely unusual hardship standard.

While any hardship case ultimately succeeds or fails on its own merits and on the particular facts presented, *Matter of Andazola* and *Matter of Monreal* are the starting points for any analysis of exceptional and extremely unusual hardship. Cancellation of removal cases coming before the Immigration Judges and the Board must therefore be examined under the standards set forth in those cases.

B. Hardship Factors

In the present case, the adult respondent is a single mother of six children, four of whom are United States citizens. The respondent and her children have no close relatives remaining in Mexico. Her entire family lives in the United States, including her lawful permanent resident parents and five United States citizen siblings. As in *Matter of Andazola*, the respondent's mother serves as her children's caretaker and watches the children while the respondent manages her own motor vehicle inspection business.

The respondent is divorced from the father of her United States citizen children. Although the respondent's former husband at one point was paying $146.50 per month in child support, there is no indication that he remains actively involved in their lives. He is currently out of status and was in immigration proceedings in Denver as of the date of the respondent's last hearing.

The respondent has been operating her own business performing vehicle inspections for 2 years. The business has two employees. She reported having $4,600 in assets, which is apparently the value of an automobile she owns. The respondent testified that after 2 months in business her proceeds were $10,000 a month, but she was also repaying her mother and brother money that she and her former husband had borrowed from them. After meeting expenses, her net profits were $400–500 per month.

The respondent's four United States citizen children have all spent their entire lives in this country and have never traveled to Mexico. She and her family live 5 minutes away from her mother, with whom they have a close relationship. According to the respondent, her children, particularly two of her United States citizen children, experience difficulty speaking Spanish and do not read or write in that language.

Finally, the respondent has no alternative means of immigrating to the United States in the foreseeable future. There is a significant backlog of visa availability to Mexican nationals with preference classification. Therefore, the respondent has little hope of immigrating through her United States citizen siblings, or even her parents, should they naturalize.

C. Assessment of Hardship

While this case presents a close question, we find it distinguishable from both *Matter of Monreal* and *Matter of Andazola*. As we noted in those decisions, the exceptional and extremely unusual hardship standard for cancellation of removal applicants constitutes a high threshold that is in keeping with Congress' intent to substantially narrow the class of aliens who would qualify for relief. Nevertheless, the hardship standard is not so restrictive that only a handful of applicants, such as those who have a qualifying relative with a serious medical condition, will qualify for relief. We consider this case to be on the outer limit of the narrow spectrum of cases in which the exceptional and extremely unusual hardship standard will be met. Keeping in mind that this hardship standard must be assessed solely with regard to the qualifying relatives in this case, we find the following factors to be significant.

The respondent has raised her family in the United States since 1988, and her four United States citizen children know no other way of life. The respondent's children do not speak Spanish well, and they are unable to read or write in that language.

Unlike the children in *Monreal* and *Andazola*, the respondent's four United States citizen children are entirely dependent on their single mother for support. The respondent is divorced from the children's father, and there is no indication that he remains involved in their lives in any manner. This increases the hardship the children would face upon return to Mexico, as they would be completely dependent on their mother's ability, not only to find adequate employment and housing, but also to provide for their emotional needs.

The respondent has been able to leave her children in the care of her lawful permanent resident mother while she attended courses to obtain a vehicle inspector's certificate and established a business. This assistance from her mother has enabled her to support her children within a stable environment. The respondent's ability to provide for the needs of her family will be severely hampered by the fact that she does not have any family in Mexico who can help care for her six children. As a single mother, the respondent will no doubt experience difficulties in finding work, especially employment that will allow her to continue to provide a safe and supportive home for her children.

From the perspective of the United States citizen children, it is clear that significant hardship will result from the loss of the economic stake that their mother has gained in this country, coupled with the difficulty she will have in establishing any comparable economic stability in Mexico. We emphasize that the respondent is a single parent who is solely responsible for the care of six children and who has no family to return to in Mexico. These are critical factors that distinguish her case from many other cancellation of removal claims.

In addition to the hardship of the United States citizen children, factors that relate only to the respondent may also be considered to the extent that they affect the potential level of hardship to her qualifying relatives. In *Andazola* we found that similar factors were not sufficient to meet the high standard of exceptional and extremely unusual hardship. However, in this case, there are additional factors that we find raise the level of hardship, by a close margin, to that required to establish eligibility for relief.

The respondent's lawful permanent resident parents also are qualifying relatives. While we have not considered their hardship in assessing the respondent's claim, her parents form part of the strong system of family support that the respondent and the minor qualifying relatives would lose if they are removed from the United States.

Although the minor respondents lack a qualifying relative for purposes of cancellation of removal, their existence also cannot be ignored. In a family such as this, headed by a single parent, the hardship of their parent inherently translates into hardship on the rest of the family, in this case to all six children. In considering the hardship that the United States citizen children would face in Mexico, we must also consider the totality of the burden on the entire family that would result when a single mother must support a family of this size. Unlike the situation in *Monreal* and *Andazola*, all of the respondent's family, including her siblings, resides *lawfully* in the United States. We find this significant because they are unlikely to be subject to immigration enforcement and will probably remain in the United States indefinitely. The respondent's family members are very close and have been instrumental in helping her raise her children and obtain the necessary funds to establish her business. The loss of this support would further increase the hardship that she, and therefore her United States citizen children, would suffer if they are compelled to return to Mexico, where no support structure exists.

Finally, we note that the respondent's prospects for lawful immigration through her United States citizen siblings or lawful permanent resident parents are unrealistic due to the backlog of visa availability for Mexican nationals with preference classification. There are no other apparent methods of adjustment available to any of the respondents. These are factors we have previously found to be significant when considering an identical hardship standard for suspension of deportation.

The hardship factors present in this case are more different in degree than in kind from those present in *Monreal* and *Andazola*. For this reason, we see no need to depart from the analysis set forth in those cases. Part of that analysis requires the assessment of hardship factors in their totality, often termed a "cumulative" analysis. Here, the heavy financial and familial burden on the adult respondent, the lack of support from the children's father, the United States citizen children's unfamiliarity with the Spanish language, the lawful residence in this country of all of the respondent's immediate family, and the concomitant lack of family in Mexico combine to render the hardship in this case well beyond that which is normally experienced in most cases of removal. The level of hardship presented here is higher than that established in either *Monreal* or *Andazola* and, in our view, is sufficient to be considered exceptional and extremely unusual.

We emphasize, in conclusion, that this decision cannot be read in isolation from *Monreal* and *Andazola*. Those cases remain our seminal interpretations of the meaning of "exceptional and extremely unusual hardship" in section 240A(b)(1)(D) of the Act. The cumulative factors present in this case are indeed unusual and will not typically be found in most other cases, where respondents have smaller families and relatives who reside in both the United States and their country of origin.

IV. CONCLUSION

Given the unusual facts presented in this case, we find that the adult respondent has shown that her United States citizen children will suffer exceptional and extremely unusual hardship if she is removed from the United States. Accordingly, her appeal will be sustained and she will be granted cancellation of removal.

As the adult respondent has been granted relief and appears to have no impediment to adjusting her status, the minor respondents are likely to soon have a qualifying relative for purposes of establishing eligibility for cancellation of removal. Given this fact, we find it appropriate to remand their records to the Immigration Judge for their cases to be held in abeyance pending a disposition regarding the adult respondent's status.

NOTES AND QUESTIONS ON EXCEPTIONAL AND EXTREMELY UNUSUAL HARDSHIP

1. The BIA notes that the two noncitizen children lack a "qualifying relative" for purposes of § 240A(b). How can the mother have such a relationship while her children do not? (Read § 240A(b)(1)(D) closely.)

2. Is it sound policy to limit the class of qualifying relationships? The 1996 amendments eliminated a noncitizen's ability under prior law to meet the hardship requirement by showing hardship to herself. The statute also seems to preclude consideration of harm to extended family members (such as a grandparent or nephew) or to others for whom the noncitizen has acted like an immediate family member. Does the specific list of individuals rule out an expansive reading of the language?

In a pre–1996 suspension of deportation case, the U.S. Supreme Court held that the statute's plain meaning controls. The Third Circuit had ordered the BIA to decide if a noncitizen's relationship to her nieces was the "functional equivalent" of a parent-child relationship, and if so, to decide if deporting the noncitizen would cause extreme hardship to the nieces. The Supreme Court reversed, reasoning that "Congress has specifically identified the relatives whose hardship is to be considered, and then set forth unusually detailed and unyielding provisions defining each class of included relatives." Thus, "even if [the alien's] relationship with her nieces resembles a parent-child relationship, we are constrained to hold that Congress, through the plain language of the statute, precluded this functional approach to defining the term 'child.' " *INS v. Hector*, 479 U.S. 85, 88, 90, 107 S.Ct. 379, 93 L.Ed.2d 326 (1986) (per curiam).

(iv) Discretionary Factors

Once threshold eligibility is established, cancellation of removal under § 240A(b) still requires the favorable exercise of discretion by the Attorney General, delegated to an immigration judge presiding over a removal proceeding. *Matter of C–V–T–*, p. 752 *supra*, discussed the factors relevant to discretion when lawful permanent residents seek cancellation under

§ 240A(a). Should the same factors—or others—apply to § 240A(b) cancellation for noncitizens who are not permanent residents?

(v) Numerical Limits on Cancellation

INA § 240A(e) caps—at 4000 per fiscal year—the number of persons who may be granted cancellation of removal under INA § 240A(b) (and suspension of deportation where the old rules apply). Looking at the statutory text, can you see why the cap does not apply to § 240A(a)?

The Executive Office for Immigration Review has a procedure for reserving decisions in cancellation cases when, as in 2010, the number of grants approaches the cap. *See* Monger & Yankay, U.S. Legal Permanent Residents: 2010, at 3, table 2 (DHS Office of Immigration Statistics 2011). Once 3,800 cases have been granted, immigration judges and the BIA are instructed to delay final decisions until October 1 of the following fiscal year. *See Chief IJ O'Leary Issues Guidance on Handling Applications for Suspension or Cancellation when FY Numbers Used Up*, 88 Interp.Rel. 1302 (2011). The cap was reached for the first time in 2010.

Recall that applicants for § 240A(b) cancellation must establish that their removal would impose "exceptional and extremely unusual hardship" on certain U.S. citizen or permanent resident family members. Why let a cap cut off relief for persons otherwise fully qualified for cancellation and for whom there has been a favorable exercise of discretion?

———————

Now that you have worked through the basics of cancellation, assess the following facts and identify any further relevant information that you might need to obtain.

EXERCISE

Patricio Hernandez–Cordero and Maria Guadalupe Ortega de Hernandez are citizens of Mexico. The Hernandezes have four children: Victor (age 14), Patricio, Jr. (7), Lisa (5), and Veronica (2). Victor is a Mexican citizen; the youngest three children are United States citizens. Twelve years ago, Mr. Hernandez entered the United States without inspection and has not left the country since. Seven years ago, Mrs. Hernandez was lawfully admitted as a permanent resident. Two years after becoming a permanent resident, she returned to Mexico for four weeks, and three years after that, she took another trip to Mexico, this time for five months.

Last month, Mr. and Mrs. Hernandez were served with notices to appear (NTA). The NTA against Mrs. Hernandez alleges that she helped a cousin enter the United States illegally six months ago. (She is not facing criminal charges.) The NTA against Mr. Hernandez states that he is present in the United States without being admitted or paroled.

DHS has stipulated that, but for the immigration violations, the couple is "industrious, law-abiding, and the type of people that anyone would desire as next-door neighbors." The family lives in Georgetown, Texas, where Mr. Hernandez built a home on a lot purchased six years ago. Mr. Hernandez is a self-employed carpenter, earning about $30,000 a year; he has, through hard work and thrift, accumulated assets having a value of approximately $125,000. These assets include the family's home, a car, Mr. Hernandez's tools, and another piece of unimproved real estate for which they have paid in full.

The Hernandezes say that they would suffer hardship if removed to Mexico based on the following considerations:

(1) They would be forced to sell their home at a loss.

(2) The family would lose economic self-sufficiency because Mr. Hernandez would be unable to find in Mexico the kind of work at the same rate of remuneration that he has obtained in the United States. The evidence of economic hardship is supported by an affidavit from an economist who specializes in Latin America.

(3) Although the four children speak Spanish, they are currently enrolled in American schools, and none reads or writes Spanish. Three of the children have never visited or lived in Mexico. Six teachers have provided affidavits detailing the diminished educational opportunities available in Mexico and the serious emotional difficulty that the children would suffer if their parents were removed and they accompanied the family to Mexico.

(4) An affidavit from a licensed psychologist also concludes that the family would suffer severe emotional and psychological consequences if forced to return to Mexico.

(5) Lisa has a fairly rare form of blood disorder that requires treatment every four months. The family has, so far, been unable to identify a hospital in Mexico that could provide the necessary treatments.

(6) The family would leave behind many friends and relatives, a number of whom are prepared to vouch for the honesty and decency of the family. For example, Dan Johnson, the vice president of the bank that financed construction of the Hernandez home, would testify that "Patricio Hernandez and his family would be an asset to any country in which they chose to live. He takes pride in his work, and his word is his bond." And John Bryan, a ranch owner who employed both Mr. and Mrs. Hernandez in the past, would state: "I have had continuous contact with the Hernandez family over the past decade. I consider them to be outstanding people who would be a great asset to American society. They are hard working, and persons of the highest moral caliber. They have assimilated themselves well into our society."

In response, DHS argues:

(1) Economic opportunities in Mexico may not be as favorable in Mexico as in the United States, but Mr. Hernandez is an able-bodied skilled craftsman; furthermore, mere economic hardship cannot constitute "exceptional and extremely unusual hardship" under the statute.

(2) The hardships of loss of friends and schooling opportunities are real, but they are hardly exceptional or extreme. Such hardship is likely to attend the removal of any alien who has resided unlawfully in the United States for a number of years. Moreover, the Hernandezes have significant family ties in Mexico where their parents and most of their brothers and sisters live. The children are bilingual, which should significantly help them integrate into Mexican life.

You are the immigration judge. Are the Hernandezes eligible to apply for cancellation of removal? If so, how would you rule on their applications?

(vi) Cancellation for Battered Spouses or Children

The Violence Against Women Act of 1994 (VAWA), Pub.L. 103–322, § 40703, 108 Stat. 1796, 1955, added a special form of relief for battered spouses and children in INA § 240A(b)(2). However, VAWA cancellation applies only if the batterer is a U.S. citizen or lawful permanent resident. VAWA cancellation parallels cancellation of removal for nonpermanent residents, with relaxed requirements.

The hardship standard is "extreme," not exceptional and extremely unusual, and it may be hardship to the applicant, not just to the applicant's parent or child. To establish good moral character, a waiver is available for any otherwise disqualifying conduct or a conviction that connected to the abuse. The continuous physical presence requirement is only three years, which can accrue after the noncitizen has received a notice to appear, despite the general stop-time rule. Absences from the United States that are connected to the abuse do not count toward the 90/180–day periods that interrupt continuous physical presence.

Two VAWA cancellation cases follow. The first interprets some of the statutory elements, and the second illustrates the exercise of discretion.

LOPEZ–BIRRUETA v. HOLDER

United States Court of Appeals, Ninth Circuit, 2011.
633 F.3d 1211.

GRABER, CIRCUIT JUDGE:

Petitioner Maria Lopez–Birrueta petitions for review of the Board of Immigration Appeals' ("BIA") denial of special-rule cancellation of removal under the Violence Against Women Act of 1994 ("VAWA"). The BIA held that, although Petitioner's children were mistreated by their lawful-permanent-resident father, that mistreatment did not rise to the level of "battery" under INA § 240A(b)(2)(A). We disagree. * * *

FACTUAL AND PROCEDURAL HISTORY

Petitioner is a native and citizen of Mexico. She entered the United States without inspection in 1994 at the age of 14. In 2002, the government served her with a notice to appear. She conceded removability but applied for special-rule cancellation of removal under INA § 240A(b)(2)(A). To qualify, an alien must demonstrate (1) the existence of battery or extreme cruelty, (2) physical presence, (3) good moral character, (4) not being inadmissible for certain specified reasons, and (5) extreme hardship. Regarding the first requirement, Petitioner sought to demonstrate that she "is the parent of a child of an alien who is ... a lawful permanent resident and the child has been battered or subjected to extreme cruelty by such permanent resident parent."

At a merits hearing in 2008, Petitioner testified as follows. After arriving in the United States, and still at the age of 14, Petitioner began a sexual relationship with Gill Campos, who was then 36 years old. Campos is a legal permanent resident of the United States.

Petitioner and Campos had two children together. At age 16, Petitioner gave birth to E—. At age 18, she gave birth to G—. Petitioner and Campos lived together while the children were very young.

During that time, Campos repeatedly threatened Petitioner, insulted her, prohibited her from talking with others, acted aggressively toward her, and threatened to alert immigration officials if Petitioner disobeyed his orders. While they lived together, Campos was not a loving father. He was violent toward his children, yelled at them, and often took them for rides in his car when he was drunk.

Petitioner described one incident in detail. In front of his "drunken friends," Campos struck E—, then 3 years old, three times on the legs with a stick that was 24 inches long and one-half inch in diameter. The strikes caused red welts to appear on E—'s legs, which Petitioner treated with ointment and ice. That same form of beating occurred two to three times a week. Campos subjected G—to the same mistreatment. Asked why, Petitioner responded that Campos "probably want[ed] to control me through the children."

Twice, Petitioner left Campos but, both times, she returned after Campos convinced her that he had changed. Petitioner left for good in 1999 and moved to Yakima, Washington, with her children. Since Petitioner left, the children have visited Campos for one or two months at a time, and once for almost a year. Campos no longer strikes the children.

Both children testified at the hearing. At the time, E—was 12 years old, and G—was 11 years old. E—testified that he has not had any problems with his father in the past few years and that, although he did not love his father when he was younger, he loves him now. He remembers his father striking him, "for no reason," with a tree branch and with his hand. G—testified that he remembers that his father would beat him and E—with a stick, on the legs. When his father came home, G—was scared and hid to "try[ ] to get away." But he no longer feels that way about his father.

In a written decision, an immigration judge ("IJ") denied cancellation of removal. The IJ expressly found Petitioner credible but found that she failed to establish that the children had been "battered" or subjected to "extreme cruelty" under the statute. Because the IJ held that Petitioner did not meet the statutory requirement of battery or extreme cruelty, he did not reach any of the other statutory requirements for relief.

* * * [T]he BIA adopted and affirmed the IJ's decision. * * *

* * *

DISCUSSION

A. *Sources of Law*

* * *

Because Petitioner and Campos never married (legally or bigamously), Petitioner cannot claim protection under VAWA for Campos' mistreatment *of her*. Instead, Petitioner sought to demonstrate that she fell within the category protected by the parenthetical in subsection (II), that she "is the parent of a child of an alien who is . . . a lawful permanent resident and the child has been battered or subjected to extreme cruelty by such permanent resident parent." None of the other categories applies.

The statute does not define the phrase "has been battered or subjected to extreme cruelty." But the agency has promulgated a regulation at 8 C.F.R. § 204.2 that pertains to the topic. Although we ultimately agree with the BIA and the parties that the regulation's definitions of "battery or extreme cruelty" apply, some explanation is required.

The first seven subsections of the regulation pertain to a particular type of petitioner. For instance, subsection (a) is entitled "Petition for a spouse" and contains implementing regulations for petitions filed by a spouse of a citizen or legal permanent resident. Relevant here, subsection (c) is entitled "Self-petition by spouse of abusive citizen or lawful permanent resident," and subsection (e) is entitled "Self-petition by child of abusive citizen or lawful permanent resident." Both subsections (c) and (e) describe the requirements for special-rule cancellation of removal under VAWA, and both subsections contain a definition of "battery or extreme cruelty." Except for their respective final sentences, the two definitions are identical:

> Battery or extreme cruelty. For the purpose of this chapter, the phrase "was battered by or was the subject of extreme cruelty" includes, but is not limited to, being the victim of any act or threatened act of violence, including any forceful detention, which results or threatens to result in physical or mental injury. Psychological or

sexual abuse or exploitation, including rape, molestation, incest (if the victim is a minor), or forced prostitution shall be considered acts of violence. Other abusive actions may also be acts of violence under certain circumstances, including acts that, in and of themselves, may not initially appear violent but that are a part of an overall pattern of violence.

The final sentence in the two definitions varies depending on whether the petitioner is a spouse or child. The subsection concerning a petition for a spouse states: "The qualifying abuse must have been committed by the citizen or lawful permanent resident spouse, must have been perpetrated against the self-petitioner or the self-petitioner's child, and must have taken place during the self-petitioner's marriage to the abuser." The subsection concerning a petition for a child states: "The qualifying abuse must have been committed by the citizen or lawful permanent resident parent, must have been perpetrated against the self-petitioner, and must have taken place while the self-petitioner was residing with the abuser."

* * *

* * * [T]he definitions do not cover Petitioner's situation. Petitioner filed neither a petition from an abusive *spouse,* covered by the definition at § 204.2(c)(1)(vi), nor a petition from a *child,* covered by the definition at § 204.2(e)(1)(vi). Petitioner is the non-married parent of a child abused by the other parent. Even though the *statute* covers Petitioner's situation, it appears that the agency failed to promulgate regulations specifically covering that situation. Both the parties and the BIA assumed that the relevant part of the definitions, block-quoted above, applies to Petitioner's circumstances, even though the definitions on their face do not apply. We agree that the BIA permissibly extended the use of the definitions here. There is no indication in the statute or elsewhere that a different definition of battery or extreme cruelty should apply depending on the marital status of the petitioner.

B. *Battery Under VAWA*

"Congress's goal in enacting VAWA was to eliminate barriers to women leaving abusive relationships." *Hernandez v. Ashcroft,* 345 F.3d 824, 841 (9th Cir. 2003). The statute "was a generous enactment, intended to ameliorate the impact of harsh provisions of immigration law on abused women." *Id.* at 840. Accordingly, when interpreting this statute, we have "adhere[d] to the general rule of construction that when the legislature enacts an ameliorative rule designed to forestall harsh results, the rule will be interpreted and applied in an ameliorative fashion." *Id.*

"The text of the statute reveals that Congress distinguished between 'battery' and 'extreme cruelty,' reserving the term extreme cruelty for something other than physical assault, presumably actions in some way involving mental or psychological cruelty." *Id.* at 838. "Under [8 C.F.R. § 204.2(c)(1)(vi)], any act of physical abuse is deemed to constitute domestic violence without further inquiry, while 'extreme cruelty' describes all other manifestations of domestic violence." *Id.* at 840. Relevant here, the regulation states that battery "includes, but is not limited to, . . . any act or threatened act of violence, including any forceful detention, which results or threatens to result in physical or mental injury." 8 C.F.R. § 204.2(c)(1)(vi), (e)(1)(vi).

We acknowledge that those sources of law are somewhat open-ended: The regulation defines some conduct that qualifies as battery but leaves open the full scope of what "battery" encompasses and, in *Hernandez,* we did not elaborate on what constitutes an "act of physical abuse." But those sources provide more than adequate definitions for the challenged conduct here.

Campos struck his children with a stick two or three times a week, when they were 2 and 3 years old, in front of his "drunken friends," for no reason at all (that is, not as punishment), causing red welts that required home medical treatment of ointment and ice and causing his children to fear him. We are compelled to conclude that those regular, arbitrary beatings causing injury constituted an "act of physical abuse," *Hernandez,* 345 F.3d at 840, or an "act of violence . . . which results . . . in physical . . . injury," 8 C.F.R. § 204.2(c)(1)(vi), (e)(1)(vi). We therefore hold that the BIA erred in concluding otherwise.

* * *

C. *The BIA's Legal Errors*

[Because the BIA adopted the immigration judge's reasoning, the court reviewed the immigration judge's decision as if it were the BIA's.]

First, the IJ held that "[t]he regulatory definition of 'battery or extreme cruelty' requires a heightened level of violence that 'results or threatens to result in physical or mental injury.' " (Quoting 8 C.F.R. § 204.2(c)(1)(vi).) But the regulation states that battery "*includes, but is not limited to*" an act of violence resulting in injury. (emphasis added). The definition does not *require* that the violence be "heightened" or result in injury, though physically injurious acts of violence qualify per se as battery.

Second, and perhaps most egregious, the IJ turned to California's criminal-law definition of "battery" and its definition of "injury" for certain sentencing purposes. From that premise, the IJ held that the term "injury" in the federal regulation "means 'any physical injury which requires professional medical treatment.' " (Quoting Cal. Penal Code § 243(f)(5)). As an initial matter, nothing in the *federal* statute suggests that the acts required to constitute battery depend on *state* law. Given the strong uniformity sought by Congress in the area of immigration law and its remedial purpose in enacting VAWA, we doubt that acts of violence would qualify (or fail to qualify) as battery depending on locale.

In any event, examining the cited definitions in context reveals the fatal flaws of the IJ's analysis here. The definition of "injury" found in

California Penal Code section 243(f)(5) has a very limited application. It applies only if a state criminal defendant battered certain emergency workers (such as an ambulance driver or lifeguard) such that the battery caused an "injury." *Id.* § 243(c)(1). If the battery caused an "injury," then the defendant is subject to increased criminal penalties. It is wholly illogical to reason that Congress intended to import a narrow, specialized state-law sentencing enhancement definition as the proper definition of "injury" in the immigration context. * * *

Finally, the BIA also suggested (as does the government on appeal) that no battery occurred for reasons that, while facially appealing, are in fact irrelevant. For example, it is true that the children now love their father and that he no longer beats them. But Congress chose to provide protection for anyone who *"has been"* battered while residing with the abuser. Petitioner and the amicus point out that, in the context of an abusive relationship, the abuser may re-start the abuse when he or she once again has that opportunity, for instance, if Petitioner is removed and the children move in with their father again and, if they wish to remain in the United States, have no choice but to remain with their father. Congress chose to prevent that opportunity by granting relief to those who *had been* subjected to battery. The BIA's suggestion that no battery occurred *in the past* because of the state of the relationship *today* is irrelevant under the plain text of the statute.

CONCLUSION

We hold that Petitioner demonstrated that her children had been battered by Campos within the meaning of INA § 240A(b)(2)(A)(i)(II). We therefore grant the petition. The BIA also held that Petitioner failed to establish that the children had been subjected to extreme cruelty. Because we grant the petition on other grounds, we do not reach the issue of extreme cruelty.

The BIA did not reach the other four statutory requirements for relief. We remand for consideration of those requirements and any other issues not addressed by this opinion.

MATTER OF MARTINEZ
Board of Immigration Appeals, 2009.
25 I & N Dec. 66.

The record reflects that the respondent, a 41–year–old native and citizen of Mexico, married her ex-husband in Oaxaca, Mexico, in 1984. They have four children together, one of whom is a United States citizen. In 1989 the respondent's ex-husband was working in the United States and arranged for the respondent, who did not have lawful status, to join him. The record contains extensive documentation that the respondent's ex-husband abused her both physically and mentally for a number of years. The couple eventually separated in 1996, and the respondent stated that she has not seen her ex-husband since 1998. After their separation, the respondent filed a self-petition to adjust her status to that of a lawful permanent resident as the battered spouse of a lawful permanent resident pursuant to INA § 204(a). The former Immigration and Naturalization Service (now the DHS) approved the respondent's self-petition on September 25, 2001. Thereafter, the respondent and her ex-husband divorced on August 18, 2004, and she remarried in March 2006. Her current husband does not have lawful status in the United States.

The respondent was placed in removal proceedings on July 30, 2004, after she attempted to enter the United States from Mexico at the Otay Mesa port of entry in California with two minor children who were not her own. The respondent testified that she agreed to drive the children, who did not have lawful status or documentation to enter the United States, as a favor to their mother. There is no evidence in the record that she was criminally charged for this incident. The DHS issued a Notice to Appear (Form I–862), charging her as an arriving alien who is inadmissible under INA § 212(a)(6)(E)(i), for alien smuggling.

During her proceedings before the Immigration Judge, the respondent requested several forms of relief, including special rule cancellation for battered spouses under INA § 240A(b)(2). At a hearing on April 26, 2007, the parties stipulated that the respondent's ex-husband is a lawful permanent resident. The respondent also testified about the hardship that her United States citizen son, who is now 16 years old, would suffer if she were removed to Mexico. The respondent stated that he was born with a birth defect because his right ear is physically deformed, and he has hearing loss in that ear. She testified that her son is eligible for reconstructive surgery and that because of his hearing problems, he has been enrolled in special education classes since kindergarten.

* * *

[N]otwithstanding the heading of INA § 240A(b), which only refers to nonpermanent residents, we find that lawful permanent residents may be eligible to apply for special rule cancellation of removal for battered spouses under INA § 240A(b)(2). * * *

* * *

Cancellation of removal, like the relief available under former INA §§ 212(c) and 244(a), is a discretionary form of relief. In this case, the Immigration Judge found that the respondent was deserving of a discretionary grant of cancellation of removal. As previously noted, we have authority to review questions of discretion de novo.

* * *

The positive factors presented in the respondent's case include her residence in the United States since 1989, her three children with legal status living in the United States, and her gainful employment as a housekeeper. The Immigration Judge also found that her United States citizen son will suffer extreme hardship if she is removed and noted that she expressed remorse concerning the reasons for her removability. The negative factors include the circumstances underlying the respondent's removability, her failure to provide evidence that she filed income taxes, and her May 2003 conviction for driving under the influence.

Furthermore, given that the respondent is seeking relief as the battered spouse of a lawful permanent resident, we find that there are additional factors relevant to our consideration. Importantly, the Immigration Judge found that the respondent divorced her abusive ex-husband in 2004, and that she has already relied on her relationship with her ex-husband to adjust her status as a VAWA self-petitioner. Moreover, the respondent has been remarried since 2006 and is no longer in an abusive relationship with her ex-husband.

Given the underlying purpose of the battered spouse provisions of the Act, which is to enable aliens to leave their abusive citizen or lawful permanent resident spouses who may use the threat of deportation or sponsorship for an immigration benefit to maintain control over them, we find that these factors weigh heavily against granting the respondent's request for cancellation of removal under INA § 240A(b)(2). The respondent has already obtained a form of VAWA relief once, has become removable, and has not argued that she needs or is eligible for VAWA protection in her current relationship. The VAWA should not be invoked again to benefit an alien when the past abusive relationship has ended and the former abusive spouse no longer poses a threat. We recognize that the same factors, namely, the respondent's divorce, remarriage, and previous self-petition based on her abusive marriage, may not be equally relevant to other forms of discretionary relief. However, the respondent has requested cancellation of removal as a battered spouse, and such factors are significant to the nature and purpose of the relief she is seeking.

As a result, despite the respondent's equities, which are substantial, we find that on balance, given the adverse factors and the nature of the relief she is seeking, she has not shown that cancellation of removal under INA § 240A(b)(2) should be granted as a matter of discretion. Accordingly, we conclude that the Immigration Judge's grant of relief in the exercise of discretion was not appropriate.

* * *

NOTES AND QUESTIONS ON *VAWA* CANCELLATION

1. Under INA § 242(a)(2)(B)(I), "any judgment regarding the granting of relief under ... [§ 240A]" is not reviewable in federal court, with courts interpreting "judgment" to mean any discretionary decision. This provision bars judicial review of the BIA panel in *Martinez*. But if you were rearguing the discretionary aspect of VAWA cancellation on rehearing before the BIA en banc, could you argue persuasively that the panel erred by citing prior

adjustment of status as a VAWA self-petitioner and the fact that her "former abusive spouse no longer poses a threat"? How might the government respond to your arguments?

2. What is the small change in facts that would have persuaded the BIA panel in *Martinez* to affirm the immigration judge's decision?

3. The Ninth Circuit explains in *Lopez–Birrueta* that "Congress distinguished between 'battery' and 'extreme cruelty,' reserving the term extreme cruelty for something other than physical assault, presumably actions in some way involving mental or psychological cruelty." Though this alternative showing expands eligibility for VAWA cancellation, the majority of circuits have held that immigration judge and BIA determinations regarding the presence or absence of extreme cruelty are discretionary and under INA § 242(a)(2)(B)(I) are not reviewable in federal court. *Compare* Johnson v. Attorney General, 602 F.3d 508, 510–11 (3d Cir. 2010); *and Perales–Cumpean v. Gonzales*, 429 F.3d 977, 982 (10th Cir. 2005); *with Hernandez v. Ashcroft*, 345 F.3d 824, 833–35 (9th Cir.2003).

2. PRIVATE BILLS

When there is no other way to prevent removal, relief may still possible through federal legislation granting permanent resident status to one specific individual. In recent years, such private bills have been enacted in a tiny number of cases. *See* Lee, *Private Immigration Legislation*, Congressional Research Service Report to Congress (2007).

As we go to press in late 2011, only two private bills have been signed into law since 2005. One was for a Japanese citizen, Shigeru Yamada, who had been admitted to the United States at the age of ten, accompanying his mother and two sisters who were fleeing his physically abusive alcoholic father. His mother died in a car crash three years later, revoking his legal status. At the time, she was engaged to a U.S. citizen, and the marriage would have conferred legal status on him, but her death left him without options for lawful immigration status.

The other private bill was for Hotaru Nakama Ferschke, the Japanese widow of a U.S. marine who was killed in Iraq while she was pregnant with his child. Although they had met thirteen months previously, they did not marry until they held a ceremony by telephone during his deployment. She could not acquire lawful status through the marriage because of INA § 101(a)(35), which provides: "The term 'spouse', 'wife', or 'husband' do not include a spouse, wife, or husband by reason of any marriage ceremony where the contracting parties thereto are not physically present in the presence of each other, unless the marriage shall have been consummated." *See Congress Passes Two Private Immigration Relief Bills*, 87 Interp.Rel. 2414 (2010).

One reason for the decline is that mere introduction of a private bill does not automatically guarantee a stay of removal, as it did in earlier decades. Now, after introduction of a private bill, the House or Senate Judiciary Committee may ask the executive branch for a report on the noncitizen. If that happens, the immigration agencies will generally authorize a stay of removal, forestalling removal for a considerable period, irrespective of the private bill's ultimate chance for passage. However, relevant House and Senate subcommittee rules greatly limit requests for such reports. *See* Gallagher, *Remedies of Last Resort: Private Bills and Pardons*, 06–02 Imm. Briefings (Feb. 2006).

In earlier periods of federal immigration law—but unlike today— private bills were the primary form of relief from deportation. They were enacted in order to create humanitarian flexibility in a law that, if applied as written, would have produced harsh results. In this role, private bills frequently were the forerunners of significant legislative amendments. Here is one example:

> Before the Immigration and Nationality Act accorded "nonquota" status to spouses of American citizens irrespective of their ancestry, Asian spouses of American citizens were subject to quota restrictions. The stationing of American servicemen in the Far East and the resulting marriages between American citizens and alien spouses of Asian ancestry led to the introduction and passage of a considerable number of private bills according the individual Asian spouse "nonquota" status. The increasing volume of this type of private bills led eventually to public legislation giving "nonquota" status to the spouses of American servicemen irrespective of their ancestry and later led to the provision in the Immigration and Nationality Act which placed alien spouses of all American citizens on equal footing irrespective of race. Similarly, the provision of the Act of September 3, 1954 exempting petty offenders from the excluding provisions of the general law was preceded by a series of private bills seeking relief in cases of individual aliens, mostly alien wives of American servicemen who, during the post-war period, had been convicted for minor offenses.

E. Harper, Jr. & R. Chase, Immigration Laws of the United States 657–59 (1975).

A former General Counsel of the Senate Judiciary Committee cites the initial enactment of INA § 312(b)(2) as another illustration of this phenomenon:

> A perfect example is P.L. 95–579 of November 2, 1978. In embryonic form as S. 2247, it was a private bill to exempt an elderly female alien from the English literacy requirements in Section 312. After passing the Senate, it was amended by the House to provide a general statutory waiver of the literacy requirements for all naturalization applicants over 50 years of age with 20 or more years of lawful residence on the date of filing the petition. The Senate concurred in the House amendment, the President signed, and it became a law.

Rawitz, *In the Hands of Congress: Suspension of Deportation and Private Bills*, 57 Interp. Rel. 76, 80 (1980).

3. RETHINKING RELIEF FROM REMOVAL

Does it make sense for the INA to have so many different and overlapping forms of relief from removal? Current law may reflect historical happenstance more than legislative fine-tuning.

One set of issues concerns the overall structure of relief from removal, with the statutory eligibility criteria for each. Other issues concern the exercise of discretion. As we have seen, BIA decisions guide discretionary decisions, but administrative agencies could adopt regulations for this purpose, or Congress could provide guidance by statute. Daniel Kanstroom frames the role of discretion as follows:

> The roots of the deportation discretion problem are deeply intertwined with our understanding of the nature of law. One might distinguish discretion from rules: the core of the "rule of law." * * * Discretion, as Ronald Dworkin once famously put it, "like the hole in a doughnut, does not exist except as an area left open by a surrounding belt of restriction." A rough, pragmatic definition is simply "power to make a choice between alternative courses of action." The implication in either case is that there is no such thing as a uniquely correct discretionary decision. There may, however, certainly be *incorrect* discretionary decisions, such as those that are unauthorized or arbitrary. The most basic theoretical problems of discretion are thus how to define and restrain its abuse without destroying its nonrulelike character.

* * *

> One of the most well-known and best attempts to grapple with this problem is that of Judge Henry Friendly in a 1966 case, *Wong Wing Hang v. INS*. The case was an appeal from a denial of suspension of deportation relief. Judge Friendly * * * offered a useful formula: "The denial of suspension to an eligible alien would be an abuse of discretion if it were made without a rational explanation, inexplicably departed from established policies, or rested on an impermissible basis such as an invidious discrimination against a particular race. * * *

D. Kanstroom, Deportation Nation: Outsiders in American History 231–32 (2007).

Judge Friendly's reasoning in *Wong Wing Hang* offers further guidance on the exercise of discretion to grant relief from removal. The case raised questions of judicial review in light of the apparent tension between two provisions of the Administrative Procedure Act:

> Here we encounter the familiar conflict between the preamble of § 10 [of the Administrative Procedure Act, *excepting from judicial review*] "agency action [that] is by law committed to agency discretion," and the command of subsection (e) that *the reviewing court*

*shall "set aside agency action * * * found to be (1) arbitrary, capricious, an abuse of discretion,* or otherwise not in accordance with law." (Emphasis supplied.) Some help in resolving the seeming contradiction may be afforded by the distinction drawn by Professors Hart and Sacks between a discretion that "is not subject to the restraint of the obligation of reasoned decision and hence of reasoned elaboration of a fabric of doctrine governing successive decisions" and discretion of the contrary and more usual sort, see The Legal Process 172, 175–177 (Tent. ed. 1958); only in the rare—some say nonexistent—case where discretion of the former type has been vested, may review for "abuse" be precluded. An argument could be made that the change from the earlier versions of the suspension provision, "the Attorney General may suspend if he finds," 54 Stat. 672 (1940), 62 Stat. 1206 (1948), to its present form affords an indication that Congress meant to accord the Attorney General or his delegate ad hoc discretion of that sort. But the Attorney General himself has not thought so; applications for suspension of deportation * * * have long been subjected to various administrative hearing and appeal procedures, see the history recounted in *Jay v. Boyd,* 351 U.S. 345, 351– 352, 76 S.Ct. 919, 100 L.Ed. 1242 (1956), with their concomitants of "the obligation of reasoned decision."

Wong Wing Hang v. INS, 360 F.2d 715, 717–18 (2d Cir.1966) (Friendly, J.).

Shifting from the judicial to the legislative role, how much could you do in drafting statutes or regulations to resolve the tension between (a) avenues of relief flexible enough to respond to the particular facts, and (b) rules to enhance predictability and limit executive branch discretion? In assessing the optimal degrees of flexibility and precision, consider the arguments by Maurice Roberts, former Chairman of the BIA, for more guidelines for the exercise of discretion:

It should be possible to achieve greater uniformity of decision, while at the same time minimizing the opportunities for result-oriented adjudication based on an adjudicator's subjective feelings, by defining with greater precision not only the policies to be served but also the elements to be considered. It does not matter whether the guiding principles are laid down in published regulations or in the Board's published precedent decisions, which are binding on the Service. Certainly, greater care should be taken in thinking through and then defining those elements which should be considered "adverse" and those which can be properly juxtaposed in mitigation. Great [precision] need not completely strait-jacket the adjudicator or limit the range of elements which may properly be considered.

* * *

Uniformity of decision with mathematical precision is, of course, possible. Specific point values could be prescribed for each element deemed relevant, *e.g.,* so many minus points for a preconceived intent, so many for a wife abroad, so many for each minor child abroad, so many for being responsible for the break-up of the foreign marriage, so many for each intentional misstatement to the Service, etc. Plus points could be assigned for an American citizen or permanent resident wife, for each American child, for each year of the alien's residence here, and the like. An appropriate plus score could be fixed as a prerequisite to the favorable exercise of discretion. * * *

Any notion of such mechanical jurisprudence would, of course, be summarily rejected if seriously suggested. Yet, unless more realistic and specific guidelines are laid down, the opposite extreme becomes possible if it is left to each individual adjudicator to determine for himself, on the basis of his own subjective experiences and beliefs, just what factors in the alien's life should be determinative in exercising discretion and how much weight should be accorded each factor. An intolerant adjudicator could deny relief to aliens whose cultural patterns, political views, moral standards or life styles differed from his own. Worse still, a hostile or xenophobic adjudicator could vent his spleen on aliens he personally considered offensive without articulating the actual basis for his decision.

Unless standards are laid down which are not illusory and can be uniformly applied in the real world, we depart from even-handed justice and the rule of law. * * *

Roberts, *The Exercise of Administrative Discretion Under the Immigration Laws*, 13 San Diego L.Rev. 144, 164–65 (1975).

Several years after Roberts urged greater guidance, the INS issued proposed regulations to identify factors to be considered in the exercise of discretion under various INA provisions, including § 245 for adjustment of status. 44 Fed.Reg. 36187–93 (1979). The INS abandoned the project a year and a half later, explaining:

There is an inherent failure in any attempt to list those factors which should be considered in the exercise of discretion. It is impossible to list or foresee all of the adverse or favorable factors which may be present in a given set of circumstances. Listing some, even with the caveat that such list is not all inclusive, still poses a danger that the use of the guidelines may become so rigid as to amount to an abuse of discretion.

46 Fed.Reg. 9119 (1981).

Would guidance—whether in regulations, a precedent decision of the BIA, or in the statute itself—hamper the free exercise of discretionary authority? If discretion is meant to be exercised under a decisionmaking process that develops a "fabric of doctrine," isn't some hampering of an individual immigration judge's decisions inevitable? Is it desirable?

Now consider the legislative proposals in the following Exercise.

EXERCISE

Consider this hypothetical legislative proposal:

§ 1.   Except as provided in Section 2, all provisions for relief from removal are hereby repealed.

§ 2.   The Secretary of Homeland Security may waive any ground of inadmissibility or deportability and adjust the status of an alien on whose behalf the ground is waived to that of lawful permanent resident if the Secretary determines that such waiver and adjustment are justified by humanitarian concerns or are otherwise in the national interest.

§ 3.   A determination by the Secretary under Section 2 shall not be set aside by a court unless it is arbitrary or capricious.

Now consider an alternate (or additional) proposal:

§ 1.   There shall be a five year statute of limitations on removal.

§ 2.   All provisions for relief from removal are hereby repealed.

If you were a member of Congress, would you support these provisions by themselves or in some combination? If not, what amendments might win your support?

Would you distinguish between immigrants and nonimmigrants? Between noncitizens who were admitted and noncitizens who entered without inspection? Between noncitizens who have resided here for a short while and those who are long-time residents? How exactly would a statute of limitations apply to *presence* in the United States in violation of law (INA § 237(a)(1)(B)?

Would you provide for judicial review of a final administrative decision regarding relief under the first provision?

Would you provide guidance for the exercise of discretion in the statute, or would you prefer guidance to come from the agency administering the statute? If the latter option is preferable, what form(s) should that guidance take?

4.   PROSECUTORIAL DISCRETION

As compared to relief from removal that results in permanent resident status, prosecutorial discretion potentially confers benefits on a far larger number of noncitizens, though in ways that are far less advantageous or durable. If immigration authorities decide not to initiate removal proceedings against noncitizens who are removable, these noncitizens will avoid expulsion from the United States. This disposition grants them no formal lawful immigration status, though in some cases the exercise of prosecutorial discretion may lead to meaningful collateral benefits, such as work authorization.

a. Defining Prosecutorial Discretion

Exercises of "prosecutorial discretion" occur at both macro and micro levels. Macro-level decisionmaking to set enforcement priorities clearly influences which noncitizens are likely to be removed. For example, the INS focused in the 1990s on the removal of noncitizens convicted of crimes while greatly scaling back worksite enforcement actions. DHS decisions post-September 11 emphasized national security issues (and to noncitizens from particular countries of origin). The Obama administration has continued prior administrations' emphasis on border enforcement and reinvigorated efforts to remove noncitizens with criminal convictions.

This chapter's discussion of prosecutorial discretion adopts the term's more typical usage, referring to micro-level decisions that affect particular individuals. We generally defer discussion of macro-level discretion to Chapter Nine on Enforcement. At the individual level, the federal government may decide to not initiate removal proceedings against a noncitizen it has identified as removable, or to terminate ongoing removal proceedings. Or some noncitizens who are removable may come forward and ask that the government exercise prosecutorial discretion to refrain from enforcement.

Nonenforcement may sound counterintuitive or raise even deeper concerns. If DHS officials know that a person is unlawfully in the country, would they not as a matter of course initiate a removal proceeding and seek his or her expulsion? We know from general experience under the criminal law that authorities frequently exercise prosecutorial discretion in not bringing the force of the law against every known violator. Similarly, the range of immigration law violations is vast. Some are highly technical, such as a gap between two valid periods of student status, while others are more obvious, such as ignoring a final removal order. Resource limitations are also a key part of prosecutorial discretion in immigration enforcement. In June 2010, John Morton, the director of ICE, explained that given present funding levels, the maximum capacity of the civil removal system is about 400,000 removals per year—under 4 percent of the unauthorized population.[9] These limitations, combined with extra-statutory judgments about the seriousness of a particular offender's violation or the urgency of removing him from the United States, play a role in determining whether and which charges are actually brought.

Prosecutorial discretion can take several forms, or it can simply be an informal decision, or series of them, not to act against a particular

---

9. *See* Memorandum From John Morton, Assistant Sec'y, U.S. Immigration & Customs Enforcement, on Civil Immigration Enforcement (June 30, 2010), *available at* http://www.ice.gov/doclib/detention-reform/pdf/civil_enforcement_priorities.pdf. This memo was reissued in March 2011, to include a disclaimer that it does not create any enforceable rights or benefits. *See* Memorandum From John Morton, Assistant Sec'y, U.S. Immigration & Customs Enforcement, on Civil Immigration Enforcement (March 2, 2010), *available at* http://www.ice.gov/doclib/news/releases/2011/110302washingtondc.pdf

noncitizen. To the extent that prosecutorial discretion is crystallized in a specific bureaucratic act of classifying a particular case as worthy of the exercise of discretion, one specific form is deferred action. Originally known as "nonpriority enforcement status," this category has been in existence for many years. The initial guidelines used by INS to grant deferred action status came to light in the mid–1970s in the midst of INS attempts to remove former Beatle John Lennon for a British drug conviction.[10] Those granted deferred action may obtain work authorization upon a showing of need, 8 C.F.R. § 274a.12(c)(14), but they receive few other benefits. They have no family reunification rights, and the status is subject to withdrawal at any time. Significantly, deferred action is not considered a period of authorized stay for purposes of the three- and ten-year bars on future admission imposed by INA § 212(a)(9)(B). *See* Wildes, *The Deferred Action Program of the Bureau of Citizenship and Immigration Services: A Possible Remedy for Impossible Immigration Cases*, 41 San Diego L. Rev. 819 (2004).

Another specific form of prosecutorial discretion is a stay of removal, which would be issued at a later step in the process, after a removal order. In practical effect, it can provide the same type of relief to noncitizens as deferred action. Though a discretionary stay of removal was traditionally used to give the noncitizen a reasonable amount of time to make arrangements prior to removal, or to forestall removal pending the outcome of a motion to reopen removal proceedings, it can be used more broadly, as rough equivalent to deferred action for persons who already have an order of removal.

b. The Regularization of Prosecutorial Discretion

The modern story of prosecutorial discretion in immigration enforcement starts with concerns that surfaced after the 1996 Act drastically limited relief from removal. Press accounts began to appear reporting on highly sympathetic cases that earlier would have generated a grant of relief but for which removal now seemed inevitable. Congress felt the pressure; in 1999, 28 members of the House wrote a letter to the Attorney General and INS Commissioner Doris Meissner calling attention to the existence of cases where removal was "unfair and resulted in unjustifiable hardship." The signatories included some of the leaders in adopting the restrictive 1996 legislation, including Congressman Lamar Smith (R–TX), chair of the House immigration subcommittee. They urged the adoption of guidelines for the use of prosecutorial discretion to avoid the hardship inflicted in such cases. 76 Interp. Rel. 1720 (1999).

In November 2000, Meissner issued a memorandum to INS field offices with guidance on prosecutorial discretion, explaining:

---

10. *See* Wildes, *The Nonpriority Program of the Immigration and Naturalization Service Goes Public: The Litigative Use of the Freedom of Information Act*, 14 San Diego L. Rev. 42, 42–49 (1976). Lennon escaped deportation (but based on judicial interpretation of the removal ground with which he was charged) and eventually became a lawful permanent resident. *Lennon v. INS*, 527 F.2d 187 (2d Cir. 1975).

Service officers are not only authorized by law but expected to exercise discretion in a judicious manner at all stages of the enforcement process—from planning investigations to enforcing final orders. * * * [Furthermore] INS officers may decline to prosecute a legally sufficient immigration case if the Federal immigration enforcement interest that would be served by prosecution is not substantial.

77 Interp. Rel. 1661 (2000). The memo identified factors to be considered in the exercise of prosecutorial discretion, including immigration history and status, length of stay in the United States, criminal history, humanitarian concerns, likelihood of ultimately removing the alien, likelihood of achieving the enforcement goal by other means, the effect on future admissibility, cooperation with law enforcement officials, community attention, U.S. military service, and available INS resources.

After the INS was abolished and immigration enforcement became the responsibility of Immigration and Customs Enforcement (ICE) within DHS, its Principal Legal Advisor reiterated many of the same principles for the exercise of prosecutorial discretion, highlighting different stages at which discretion can be exercised, with examples of situations when government attorneys should refrain from proceeding. He concluded:

Prosecutorial discretion is a very significant tool * * * to deal with the difficult, complex and contradictory provisions of the immigration laws and cases involving human suffering and hardship. It is clearly DHS policy that national security violators, human rights abusers, spies, traffickers both in narcotics and people, sexual predators and other criminals are removal priorities. * * * [C]ases that do not fall within these categories sometimes require that we balance the cost of an action versus the value of the result. Our reasoned determination in making prosecutorial discretion decisions can be a significant benefit to the efficiency and fairness of the removal process.

William J. Howard, Memorandum, Principal Legal Advisor, DHS Immigration and Customs Enforcement, October 24, 2005.

In September 2009, Peter Vincent, ICE Principal Legal Advisor, announced that prosecutorial discretion would be available to terminate removal proceedings or stay the removal of noncitizens with prima facie eligibility for U visa status. In the same June 2010 memo that estimated annual enforcement capacity at 400,000 removals, ICE Director Morton issued further guidance by identifying the agency's enforcement priorities:

- Priority 1: aliens who pose a danger to national security or a risk to public safety

- Priority 2: recent illegal entrants

- Priority 3: aliens who are fugitives or otherwise obstruct immigration controls

The memo characterized Priority 1 as the highest priority and Priority 2 and Priority 3 as "equal but lower, priorities." It also provided a hierarchy of criminal convictions to use in implementing Priority 1. Level 1 offenders are those convicted of aggravated felonies or two or more other felonies. Level 2 offenders are those convicted of any felony or three or more misdemeanors, and Level 3 covers those with one or two misdemeanors. "Principal attention" is to be given to removal of Level 1 offenders.

Two months later, Morton issued a memo in August 2010 with guidelines for the exercise of prosecutorial discretion when noncitizens are in removal proceedings but have pending or approved applications for lawful immigration status.

In June 2011, ICE Director Morton issued two memoranda with more refined guidance for the exercise of prosecutorial discretion. One memo addressed "removal cases involving the victims and witnesses of crime, including domestic violence, and individuals involved in non-frivolous efforts related to the protection of their civil rights and liberties." It explained: "In these cases, ICE officers, special agents, and attorneys should exercise all appropriate prosecutorial discretion to minimize any effect that immigration enforcement may have on the willingness and ability of victims, witnesses, and plaintiffs to call police and pursue justice." The memo continued that absent special circumstances, it is against ICE policy "to initiate removal proceedings against an individual known to be the immediate victim or witness to a crime" or "to remove individuals in the midst of a legitimate effort to protect their civil rights or civil liberties." This would include "(for example, union organizing or complaining to authorities about employment discrimination or housing conditions) who may be in a non-frivolous dispute with an employer, landlord, or contractor." This was the first time that such civil rights-related factors appeared in official policy on prosecutorial discretion. Memorandum From John Morton, Assistant Sec'y, U.S. Immigration & Customs Enforcement, on Prosecutorial Discretion: Certain Victims, Witnesses, and Plaintiffs (June 17, 2011).

The other June 2011 memo, set out here, addressed prosecutorial discretion more generally, expanding in significant respects on Morton's earlier memo on civil enforcement priorities.

EXERCISING PROSECUTORIAL DISCRETION CONSISTENT WITH THE CIVIL IMMIGRATION ENFORCEMENT PRIORITIES OF THE AGENCY FOR APPREHENSION, DETENTION, AND REMOVAL OF ALIENS

Memorandum From John Morton, Assistant Sec'y, U.S. Immigration
& Customs Enforcement, June 17, 2011.

BACKGROUND

One of ICE's central responsibilities is to enforce the nation's civil immigration laws in coordination with U.S. Customs and Border Protection (CBP) and U.S. Citizenship and Immigration Services (USCIS). ICE, however, has limited resources to remove those illegally in the United

States. ICE must prioritize the use of its enforcement personnel, detention space, and removal assets to ensure that the aliens it removes represent, as much as reasonably possible, the agency's enforcement priorities, namely the promotion of national security, border security, public safety, and the integrity of the immigration system. * * *

* * *

In the civil immigration enforcement context, the term "prosecutorial discretion" applies to a broad range of discretionary enforcement decisions, including but not limited to the following:

- deciding to issue or cancel a notice of detainer;

- deciding to issue, reissue, serve, file, or cancel a Notice to Appear (NTA);

- focusing enforcement resources on particular administrative violations or conduct;

- deciding whom to stop, question, or arrest for an administrative violation;

- deciding whom to detain or to release on bond, supervision, personal recognizance, or other condition;

- seeking expedited removal or other forms of removal by means other than a formal removal proceeding in immigration court;

- settling or dismissing a proceeding;

- granting deferred action, granting parole, or staying a final order of removal;

- agreeing to voluntary departure, the withdrawal of an application for admission, or other action in lieu of obtaining a formal order of removal;

- pursuing an appeal;

- executing a removal order; and

- responding to or joining in a motion to reopen removal proceedings and to consider joining in a motion to grant relief or a benefit.

AUTHORIZED ICE PERSONNEL

Prosecutorial discretion in civil immigration enforcement matters is held by the Director and may be exercised, with appropriate supervisory oversight, by the following ICE employees according to their specific responsibilities and authorities:

- officers, agents, and their respective supervisors within Enforcement and Removal Operations (ERO) who have authority to institute immigration removal proceedings or to otherwise engage in civil immigration enforcement;

- officers, special agents, and their respective supervisors within Homeland Security Investigations (HSI) who have authority to institute immigration removal proceedings or to otherwise engage in civil immigration enforcement;

- attorneys and their respective supervisors within the Office of the Principal Legal Advisor (OPLA) who have authority to represent ICE in immigration removal proceedings before the Executive Office for Immigration Review (EOIR); and

- the Director, the Deputy Director, and their senior staff.

ICE attorneys may exercise prosecutorial discretion in any immigration removal proceeding before EOIR, on referral of the case from EOIR to the Attorney General, or during the pendency of an appeal to the federal courts, including a proceeding proposed or initiated by CBP or USCIS.
* * *

FACTORS TO CONSIDER WHEN EXERCISING PROSECUTORIAL DISCRETION

When weighing whether an exercise of prosecutorial discretion may be warranted for a given alien, ICE officers, agents, and attorneys should consider all relevant factors, including, but not limited to—

- the agency's civil immigration enforcement priorities;

- the person's length of presence in the United States, with particular consideration given to presence while in lawful status;

- the circumstances of the person's arrival in the United States and the manner of his or her entry, particularly if the alien came to the United States as a young child;

- the person's pursuit of education in the United States, with particular consideration given to those who have graduated from a U.S. high school or have successfully pursued or are pursuing a college or advanced degrees at a legitimate institution of higher education in the United States;

- whether the person, or the person's immediate relative, has served in the U.S. military, reserves, or national guard, with particular consideration given to those who served in combat;

- the person's criminal history, including arrests, prior convictions, or outstanding arrest warrants;

- the person's immigration history, including any prior removal, outstanding order of removal, prior denial of status, or evidence of fraud;

- whether the person poses a national security or public safety concern;

- the person's ties and contributions to the community, including family relationships;

- the person's ties to the home country and conditions in the country;

- the person's age, with particular consideration given to minors and the elderly;

- whether the person has a U.S. citizen or permanent resident spouse, child, or parent;

- whether the person is the primary caretaker of a person with a mental or physical disability, minor, or seriously ill relative;

- whether the person or the person's spouse is pregnant or nursing;

- whether the person or the person's spouse suffers from severe mental or physical illness;

- whether the person's nationality renders removal unlikely;

- whether the person is likely to be granted temporary or permanent status or other relief from removal, including as a relative of a U.S. citizen or permanent resident;

- whether the person is likely to be granted temporary or permanent status or other relief from removal, including as an asylum seeker, or a victim of domestic violence, human trafficking, or other crime; and

- whether the person is currently cooperating or has cooperated with federal, state or local law enforcement authorities, such as ICE, the U.S Attorneys or Department of Justice, the Department of Labor, or National Labor Relations Board, among others.

This list is not exhaustive and no one factor is determinative. ICE officers, agents, and attorneys should always consider prosecutorial discretion on a case-by-case basis. The decisions should be based on the totality of the circumstances, with the goal of conforming to ICE's enforcement priorities.

That said, there are certain classes of individuals that warrant particular care. As was stated in the Meissner memorandum on Exercising Prosecutorial Discretion, there are factors that can help ICE officers, agents, and attorneys identify these cases so that they can be reviewed as early as possible in the process.

The following positive factors should prompt particular care and consideration:

- veterans and members of the U.S. armed forces;

- long-time lawful permanent residents;

- minors and elderly individuals;

- individuals present in the United States since childhood;

- pregnant or nursing women;

- victims of domestic violence; trafficking, or other serious crimes;

- individuals who suffer from a serious mental or physical disability; and

- individuals with serious health conditions.

In exercising prosecutorial discretion in furtherance of ICE's enforcement priorities, the following negative factors should also prompt particular care and consideration by ICE officers, agents, and attorneys:

- individuals who pose a clear risk to national security;

- serious felons, repeat offenders, or individuals with a lengthy criminal record of any kind;

- known gang members or other individuals who pose a clear danger to public safety; and

- individuals with an egregious record of immigration violations, including those with a record of illegal re-entry and those who have engaged in immigration fraud.

TIMING

While ICE may exercise prosecutorial discretion at any stage of an enforcement proceeding, it is generally preferable to exercise such discretion as early in the case or proceeding as possible in order to preserve government resources that would otherwise be expended in pursuing the enforcement proceeding. * * * It is also preferable for ICE officers, agents, and attorneys to consider prosecutorial discretion in cases without waiting for an alien or alien's advocate or counsel to request a favorable exercise of discretion. Although affirmative requests from an alien or his or her representative may prompt an evaluation of whether a favorable exercise of discretion is appropriate in a given case, ICE officers, agents, and attorneys should examine each such case independently to determine whether a favorable exercise of discretion may be appropriate.

* * *

DISCLAIMER

As there is no right to the favorable exercise of discretion by the agency, nothing in this memorandum should be construed to prohibit the apprehension, detention, or removal of any alien unlawfully in the United States or to limit the legal authority of ICE or any of its personnel to enforce federal immigration law. Similarly, this memorandum, which may be modified, superseded, or rescinded at any time without notice, is not intended to, does not, and may not be relied upon to create any right or benefit, substantive or procedural, enforceable at law by any party in any administrative, civil, or criminal matter.

NOTES AND QUESTIONS ON THE JUNE 2011 MORTON MEMOS AND LATER DEVELOPMENTS

1. Around the same time that ICE issued the June 2011 Morton memos, pressure on prosecutorial discretion came from a different direction, arising in

the context of the DREAM Act. As discussed in Chapter Nine, p. 1117 *infra*, the DREAM Act is proposed federal legislation that would grant lawful immigration status to unauthorized migrants who were brought to the United States at a young age and attend college or serve in the military. As part of their advocacy for the legislation, some potential DREAM Act beneficiaries have deliberately made their identities known to the federal government, essentially daring ICE to arrest them and initiate removal proceedings. *See* Preston, *After a False Dawn, Anxiety for Illegal Immigrant Students*, N.Y. TIMES, Feb. 8, 2011, at A15. As the June 2011 Morton memo excerpted above suggests, noncitizens in this group are a low enforcement priority.

2. Both the DREAM Act advocacy through self-identification and the state and local involvement in immigration enforcement through Secure Communities and DREAM Act advocacy through self-identification have raised the stakes for the federal government. Contrast the diffuse macro-decisionmaking that leads to a small likelihood that any given individual who is among the 11 million unauthorized migrants in the United States will be arrested. Those who want the federal government to pursue enforcement more vigorously will protest, but their complaints may be scattered. In contrast, a government decision not to initiate a removal proceeding against a removable individual who not only has been identified by name, but also has been brought into custody leave the federal government much more politically exposed. The decision not to proceed—whether it reflects resource constraints or policy priorities—is much more likely to attract criticism, including the accusation that the government is disregarding the law. *See* Motomura, *The Discretion That Matters, Federal Immigration Enforcement, State and Local Arrests, and the Civil–Criminal Line*, 58 UCLA L. Rev. 1819, 1853–54 (2011) (explaining how this political exposure phenomenon constrains the exercise of prosecutorial discretion after an individual noncitizen has been identified and arrested).

3. Such criticism came in the summer of 2011 from several quarters. The National ICE Council of the American Federation of Government Employees, which represents over 7,000 ICE officers, agents, and employees, sharply criticized the June 2011 Morton memos. Chris Crane, the ICE Council president, said that the memos created a "law enforcement nightmare" for ICE agents, adding: "It appears if the Obama administration doesn't like some laws, they just ignore them." *See* Savage, *Gay Couples in Immigration Limbo*, L.A. Times, July 15, 2011, at 8.

Around the same time, Congressman Lamar Smith (R–TX), chair of the House immigration subcommittee (and leading legislative architect of many of the 1996 amendments to federal immigration law), introduced the Hinder the Administration's Legalization Temptation (HALT) Act, H.R. 2497, 112th Cong., 1st Sess. (2011). This legislation would suspend unlawful presence waivers, parole, cancellation under INA § 240A(b), and deferred action until January 13, 2013, thus through the current presidential term. *The New York Times* was quick to respond with a vigorous editorial. The *Times* noted that Smith had urged expanded use of prosecutorial discretion in 1999 because, as he put it then, "True hardship cases call for the exercise of discretion." The editorial speculated that "hypocrisy and rank opportunism" explained

Smith's opposition to the Obama administration's exercise of prosecutorial discretion. *See The Forgetful Mr. Smith*, N.Y. Times, July 12, 2011, at A26.

4. The Obama administration announced in August 2011 that it would initiate an interagency working group to implement the enforcement priorities outlined in June 2011 by ICE Director Morton. DHS Secretary Janet Napolitano explained on August 18, 2011, that the working group would review removal proceedings pending in immigration court (approximately 300,000), as well as "initiate a case-by-case review to ensure that new cases placed in removal proceedings similarly meet such priorities." The group will also "issue guidance on how to provide for appropriate discretionary consideration to be given to compelling cases involving a final order of removal." *See Administration Takes Action to Ease Deportation Policies*, 88 Interp.Rel. 1961 (2011).

The practical questions prompted by this announcement include:

- How will the announcement affect the day-to-day activities of ICE employees, and immigration judges?

- What administrative structure will be set up to review 300,000 individual cases?

- Will work authorization be available to some or all noncitizens whose cases are "low priority"?

- Will removable noncitizens and their attorneys have an opportunity to argue for "low priority" status?

- What should noncitizens do if they believe that they are removable and would be classified as low priority, but are not in removal proceedings?

- What should noncitizens do if they have received a final removal order but are still in the United States, and believe that they would be classified as low priority?

See generally Preston, U.S. *Issues New Deportation Policy's First Reprieves*, N.Y. Times, Aug. 22, 2011, at A15; Pear, *Fewer Youths to Be Deported in New Policy*, N.Y. Times, Aug. 19, 2011, at A1.

5. VOLUNTARY DEPARTURE

We conclude this chapter with voluntary departure, a form of relief from removal that does not permit noncitizen to stay in the United States indefinitely as cancellation of removal does, or prosecutorial discretion may. Relatively few removable noncitizens are eligible to maintain or establish permanent resident status, but many can obtain more limited forms of relief. By far the most common is voluntary departure, which allows the noncitizen a certain period of time, not exceeding 120 days, to leave the United States. As with other forms of relief, voluntary departure requires both statutory eligibility and a favorable exercise of discretion. For example, noncitizens removable for aggravated felonies or terrorist activities are not eligible to seek voluntary departure. INA § 240B(a)(1).

Though voluntary departure is typically considered a form of relief from removal, the statistical reports of the Executive Office for Immigration Review count voluntary departure as a form of removal, presumably because the practical result is supposed to be the noncitizen's departure. In each of the three fiscal years 2007–2009, 14 or 15 percent of total removal decisions in immigration courts—about 25,000 per year—were grants of voluntary departure, as compared with about 180,000 removal orders in each year. Executive Office for Immigration Review Statistical Yearbook 2009, table Q1. It is also important to put voluntary departure into the broader context of the number of noncitizens who are compelled in some way to leave the United States. As compared to the number of removal orders, in a much larger number of cases—476,405 in 2010—the noncitizen is returned to the home country without a removal order. DHS Office of Immigration Statistics, Immigration Enforcement Actions: 2010, at 4 (2011). Most of these cases, counted as "returns," are not voluntary departures under INA § 240B. A majority of those returns are accomplished by CBP based on apprehension at or near the border.

As the next case explains more fully, there are three types of voluntary departure. The first two types, under § 240B(a), are available before the conclusion of removal proceedings under terms more favorable than the third type, under § 240B(b). Voluntary departure under subsection (a) is the benefit extended in a kind of plea bargain, saving the government at least the expense of a full merits hearing in immigration court, and possibly any engagement with immigration court at all, if the noncitizen agrees with DHS to "voluntary departure in lieu of being subject to removal proceedings." Noncitizens identified or arrested by DHS agree to waive a full removal hearing—in which the government would bear the burden showing removability by clear and convincing evidence.

All three types of voluntary departure allow noncitizens to avoid a formal removal order. The negative consequences of a formal removal order include inadmissibility for ten years, unless the noncitizen obtains advance permission to reapply for admission. INA § 212(a)(9)(A). (The value of escaping this ten-year inadmissibility may be limited, however, now that mere departure often triggers a different ten-year bar under INA § 212(a)(9)(B).) Noncitizens with formal removal orders who later reenter unlawfully are also subject to a felony prosecution, INA § 276, whereas simple entry without inspection is a misdemeanor under § 275.

But if the noncitizen fails to meet the conditions of a grant of voluntary departure by an immigration judge, an alternate order of removal takes effect. That is, immigration court procedure accounts efficiently for the not infrequent situation where the noncitizen does not leave within the specified period. The immigration judge grants voluntary departure in an order that automatically becomes a fully enforceable removal order, without the need for further court proceedings, if the individual fails to depart in timely fashion. A noncitizen who fails to leave on time also faces a potential fine and a ten-year ineligibility period for voluntary departure, cancellation, registry, or adjustment of status. *See* INA § 240B(d). Further, if he leaves under voluntary departure embodied in an immigration court order, but later returns without advance permission, he can be quickly removed through a process called reinstatement. *See* INA § 241(a)(5), discussed in Chapter Ten, at p. 1212.

The following decision explains the statutory structure of voluntary departure and discusses the exercise of discretion. It also suggests how voluntary departure has become a docket management tool.

MATTER OF ARGUELLES–CAMPOS

Board of Immigration Appeals (en banc), 1999
22 I & N Dec. 811.

JONES, BOARD MEMBER:

* * *

The Immigration Judge denied the respondent's application for voluntary departure in the exercise of discretion. The Immigration Judge noted that the respondent has two United States citizen children and volunteers at his church. However, the Immigration Judge found the adverse factors in the respondent's case to greatly outweigh his equities. Weighing most in the Immigration Judge's decision was the fact that the respondent had already voluntarily departed the United States five times, only to reenter five times without inspection. The Immigration Judge also noted the respondent's traffic violations, including speeding and driving without a license for an extended period of time.

II.   VOLUNTARY DEPARTURE AND REMOVAL PROCEEDINGS

* * *

A.   *Relief Available in Lieu of Removal Proceedings or at Two Distinct Times During Removal Proceedings*

Under section 240B(a) of the Act, an alien may apply for voluntary departure either in lieu of being subject to proceedings under INA § 240, or before the conclusion of the removal proceedings, or voluntary departure may be requested at the conclusion of the removal proceedings under INA § 240B(b). An alien may seek to depart voluntarily from the United States in lieu of being subject to proceedings under INA § 240 by applying for voluntary departure with the Service. Alternatively, once removal proceedings have been initiated, an alien may apply for one of two types of voluntary departure with an Immigration Judge.

If the alien applies for voluntary departure before the conclusion of the proceedings, as the respondent has done in this case, he must make the request prior to or at the master calendar hearing at which the case is initially calendared for a merits hearing. It is not necessary that the alien request the relief at the first master calendar hearing. The Immigration Judge must then rule on the voluntary departure request within 30 days pursuant to 8 C.F.R. § 240.26(b)(1)(ii), or the Service may stipulate to a voluntary departure grant under INA § 240B(a) at any time prior to the completion of the removal proceedings under 8 C.F.R. § 240.26(b)(2).[2]

In the alternative, if the alien decides to apply for voluntary departure at the conclusion of the removal proceedings under INA § 240B(b), he may do so after the case is initially calendared for a merits hearing. Then, depending on when the alien requests the relief during proceedings, different eligibility requirements and conditions must be met.

1. Requirements and Conditions Under INA § 240B(a)
    (In Lieu of Being Subject to Removal Proceedings)

An alien who wishes to voluntarily depart the United States instead of being subject to removal proceedings may apply for voluntary departure with the Service. The authorized Service officer, in his or her discretion, shall specify the period of time permitted for voluntary departure. The Service officer may also grant extensions of the departure period, except that the total period permitted, including any extensions, cannot exceed 120 days. * * *

The Service may attach to the granting of voluntary departure any conditions it deems necessary to ensure the alien's timely departure from the United States, including the posting of a bond, continued detention pending departure, and removal under safeguards.

* * *

2. Requirements and Conditions Under INA § 240B(a)
    (Before the Conclusion of Removal Proceedings)

If an alien applies for voluntary departure before the conclusion of the removal proceedings, no additional relief may be requested. If additional relief has been requested, such a request must be withdrawn. The alien must also have conceded removability, waived appeal of all issues, and not been convicted of an aggravated felony or be deportable on national security grounds. INA § 240B(a)(1).

The Immigration Judge may not grant a voluntary departure period exceeding 120 days and may impose other conditions as deemed necessary to ensure the alien's departure, including the posting of a voluntary departure bond to be canceled upon proof that the alien has departed the United States within the time specified. INA §§ 240B(a)(2), (3). * * *

Finally, neither the Act nor the regulations require that the alien show good moral character under INA § 240B(a), although the alien must merit a favorable exercise of discretion. Therefore, in the case before us, we find that the Immigration Judge was incorrect in stating that the

---

2. Voluntary departure under INA § 240B(a) of the Act is not available to aliens arriving in the United States who are (or otherwise would be) placed in removal proceedings at the time of their arrival. However, INA § 240B(a)(4) of the Act should not be construed as preventing such aliens from withdrawing an application for admission and immediately departing the United States in accordance with INA § 235(a)(4).

respondent must demonstrate good moral character for a period of 5 years preceding his application for voluntary departure.

3. Requirements and Conditions Under INA § 240B(b) (At the Conclusion of Removal Proceedings)

Different requirements and conditions arise if an alien applies for voluntary departure at the conclusion of removal proceedings under INA § 240B(b). First, the alien must have been physically present in the United States for at least 1 year immediately preceding the date the Notice to Appear was served * * *. Second, the alien must show that he is, and has been, a person of good moral character for at least 5 years immediately preceding the application for voluntary departure. * * * The alien must also show by clear and convincing evidence that he has the means to depart the United States and intends to do so.

Like INA § 240B(a), section 240B(b) requires an applicant for voluntary departure to provide the Service with travel documents. However, unlike section 240B(a), under section 240B(b) the alien must also pay a mandatory voluntary departure bond of an amount sufficient to ensure the alien's departure, in no case less than $500. If the bond is not timely posted, the Immigration Judge's voluntary departure order is automatically vacated and the alternate order of removal takes effect the following day. The alien must also merit a favorable exercise of discretion. Finally, the Immigration Judge may impose other conditions as deemed necessary to ensure the alien's departure and may not grant a voluntary departure period exceeding 60 days.

B. Differences Between Requirements and Conditions Under INA §§ 240B(a) and 240B(b)

It is clear from the significant differences between voluntary departure under INA §§ 240B(a) and 240B(b) that Congress intended the two provisions to be used for different purposes. * * * [S]ection 240B(a) requires much less from the alien. Under section 240B(a), an alien need not show that he has good moral character or that he has the financial means to depart the United States. An alien must request section 240B(a) relief either in lieu of being subject to proceedings, or early in removal proceedings. He must also voluntarily forego all other forms of relief. Thus, Immigration Judges can use section 240B(a) relief to quickly and efficiently dispose of numerous cases on their docket, where appropriate. We accept the need for such a tool and support its purpose. However, we note that discretion remains a required element of voluntary departure under both INA §§ 240B(a) and 240B(b).

The Board ruled in *Matter of Gamboa,* 14 1 & N Dec. 244 (BIA 1972), that many factors may be weighed in exercising discretion with voluntary departure applications, including the nature and underlying circumstances of the deportation ground at issue; additional violations of the immigration laws; the existence, seriousness, and recency of any criminal record; and other evidence of bad character or the undesirability of the applicant as a permanent resident. We further stated that discretion may be favorably exercised in the face of adverse factors where there are compensating elements such as long residence here, close family ties in the United States, or humanitarian needs. We find that these factors, which we have enunciated as pertinent to the exercise of discretion under [pre–1996 law], are equally relevant to the exercise of discretion under section 240B of the Act in removal proceedings. However, an Immigration Judge has broader authority to grant voluntary departure in discretion under section 240B(a) than under section 240B(b) or [under pre–1996 law].

C. General Conditions Under INA § 240B (Both Before the Conclusion and at the Conclusion of Removal Proceedings)

Further restrictions and penalties also exist under both parts of INA § 240B. First, an alien is ineligible for voluntary departure under section 240B if the alien was previously permitted to so depart after having been found inadmissible under section 212(a)(6)(A). * * *

Also, if an alien is permitted to depart voluntarily under section 240B and fails to depart the United States within the time period specified, the alien shall be subject to a civil penalty of $1,000 to $5,000 and be ineligible for relief of cancellation of removal, voluntary departure, adjustment of status, change of nonimmigrant classification, and registry for a 10–year period. INA § 240B(d). We note that the order permitting the alien to depart voluntarily must inform the alien of these consequences. * * * [B]oth the Service and the alien may appeal issues of eligibility and discretion, as the respondent has done in this case.

III. RESPONDENT'S APPLICATION

The respondent applied for voluntary departure at his second master calendar hearing, at which point the case was not yet calendared for a merits hearing. Therefore, he applied for the relief before the conclusion of his removal proceedings and must meet the requirements under INA § 240B(a), as well as the federal regulations at 8 C.F.R. § 240.26, to be eligible for voluntary departure. Although the respondent initially indicated that he wanted to apply for cancellation of removal under INA § 240A(b), he properly withdrew that request and applied solely for voluntary departure. The respondent also conceded that he is inadmissible as charged under INA § 212(a)(6)(A)(i). In addition, the record of proceedings does not indicate that the respondent has been convicted of an aggravated felony or that he is removable on national security grounds. Finally, although the respondent was previously permitted to voluntarily depart the United States five times, he was granted each voluntary departure under [prior law], rather than under section 240B. Therefore, section 240B(c) does not currently render the respondent statutorily ineligible for voluntary departure under section 240B. * * *

While we note that Congress changed many of the requirements for the relief of voluntary departure in [the 1996 Act], including the elimination of good moral character in INA § 240B(a), an alien must still show that he merits voluntary departure in the exercise of discretion. Although the respondent appears statutorily eligible for voluntary departure under INA § 240B(a), we agree with the Immigration Judge that he does not merit the relief in the exercise of discretion.

In the case before us, the respondent first entered the United States in August 1987 but has departed this country several times. He lives with his two United States citizen children, volunteers at his church, and appears to have no criminal convictions. On the other hand, he has been working without authorization, driving in the United States without a license for a lengthy period of time, and most important, he has entered this country five times without inspection after being permitted to voluntarily depart five times. The record, in fact, reflects that within 3 months before the removal proceedings, the respondent had twice been granted voluntary departure within a matter of days and had immediately reentered the United States without inspection on both occasions. The respondent testified that he has returned to the United States without inspection because he belongs with his two children and their mother. The Immigration Judge could reasonably conclude on the facts of this case that the respondent simply viewed grants of voluntary departure as a means to avoid immigration proceedings, or bring them to a close, by leaving the United States briefly and reentering illegally in hopes of not being apprehended again.

We agree with the Immigration Judge that the respondent's equities are outweighed by his adverse factors, particularly his immigration history and the nature of his entries into this country. Given the respondent's past immigration history, it seems quite unlikely that he would remain in Mexico until he is afforded the opportunity to legally immigrate to this country. We therefore find that the Immigration Judge properly denied the application for voluntary departure in the exercise of discretion.

* * *

The appeal is dismissed.

[Concurring and dissenting opinions are omitted.]

NOTE ON VOLUNTARY DEPARTURE

As Chapter Ten will explain, noncitizens may move to reopen their removal proceedings, as for example in *Dada v. Mukasey*, 554 U.S. 1, 128 S.Ct. 2307, 171 L.Ed.2d 178 (2008), which presented these facts:

> Petitioner Samson Taiwo Dada, a native and citizen of Nigeria, came to the United States in April 1998 on a temporary nonimmigrant visa. He overstayed it. In 1999, petitioner alleges, he married an American citizen. Petitioner's wife filed an I–130 Petition for Alien Relative on his behalf. The necessary documentary evidence was not provided, however, and the petition was denied in February 2003.

> In 2004, the Department of Homeland Security (DHS) charged petitioner with being removable under § 237(a)(1)(B) of the Immigration and

Nationality Act (INA), for overstaying his visa. Petitioner's wife then filed a second I–130 petition. The Immigration Judge (IJ) denied petitioner's request for a continuance pending adjudication of the newly filed I–130 petition and noted that those petitions take an average of about three years to process. The IJ found petitioner to be removable but granted the request for voluntary departure. The BIA affirmed on November 4, 2005, without a written opinion. It ordered petitioner to depart within 30 days * * *.

Two days before expiration of the 30–day period, on December 2, 2005, petitioner sought to withdraw his request for voluntary departure. At the same time he filed with the BIA a motion to reopen removal proceedings under INA § 240(c)(7). He contended that his motion recited new and material evidence demonstrating a bona fide marriage and that his case should be continued until the second I–130 petition was resolved.

554 U.S. at 6–7, 128 S.Ct.at 2311.

Do you see Dada's dilemma? Ideally for him, the pendency of the motion to reopen would suspend the voluntary departure deadline. But if the motion has no such effect, can he withdraw his voluntary departure request? If not, he will violate the terms of voluntary departure, leading to other problems, as the U.S. Supreme Court explained:

On February 8, 2006, more than two months after the voluntary departure period expired, the BIA denied the motion to reopen on the ground that petitioner had overstayed his voluntary departure period. * * * [T]he BIA reasoned, [that] an alien who has been granted voluntary departure but fails to depart in a timely fashion is statutorily barred from applying for and receiving certain forms of discretionary relief, including adjustment of status. The BIA did not address petitioner's motion to withdraw his request for voluntary departure.

554 U.S. at 7, 128 S.Ct.at 2312.

Here is how the U.S. Supreme Court grappled with this dilemma:

Absent tolling or some other remedial action by the Court, then, the alien who is granted voluntary departure but whose circumstances have changed in a manner cognizable by a motion to reopen is between Scylla and Charybdis: He or she can leave the United States in accordance with the voluntary departure order; but, pursuant to regulation, the motion to reopen will be deemed withdrawn. Alternatively, if the alien wishes to pursue reopening and remains in the United States to do so, he or she risks expiration of the statutory period and ineligibility for adjustment of status, the underlying relief sought.

The purpose of a motion to reopen is to ensure a proper and lawful disposition. We must be reluctant to assume that the voluntary departure statute was designed to remove this important safeguard for the distinct class of deportable aliens most favored by the same law. * * *

* * *

Some solutions, though, do not conform to the statutory design. Petitioner, as noted, proposes automatic tolling of the voluntary departure period during the pendency of the motion to reopen. We do not find statutory authority for this result. Voluntary departure is an agreed-upon exchange of benefits, much like a settlement agreement. In return for anticipated benefits, including the possibility of readmission, an alien who requests voluntary departure represents that he or she "has the means to depart the United States and intends to do so" promptly. Included among the substantive burdens imposed upon the alien when selecting voluntary departure is the obligation to arrange for departure, and actually depart, within the 60-day period. If the alien is permitted to stay in the United States past the departure date to wait out the adjudication of the motion to reopen, he or she cannot then demand the full benefits of voluntary departure; for the benefit to the Government—a prompt and costless departure—would be lost. Furthermore, it would invite abuse by aliens who wish to stay in the country but whose cases are not likely to be reopened by immigration authorities.

* * *

We hold that, to safeguard the right to pursue a motion to reopen for voluntary departure recipients, the alien must be permitted to withdraw, unilaterally, a voluntary departure request before expiration of the departure period, without regard to the underlying merits of the motion to reopen. As a result, the alien has the option either to abide by the terms, and receive the agreed-upon benefits, of voluntary departure; or, alternatively, to forgo those benefits and remain in the United States to pursue an administrative motion.

If the alien selects the latter option, he or she gives up the possibility of readmission and becomes subject to the IJ's alternate order of removal. The alien may be removed by the Department of Homeland Security within 90 days, even if the motion to reopen has yet to be adjudicated. But the alien may request a stay of the order of removal and, though the BIA has discretion to deny the motion for a stay, it may constitute an abuse of discretion for the BIA to do so where the motion states nonfrivolous grounds for reopening.

554 U.S. at 18–21, 128 S.Ct.at 2318–20.

CHAPTER EIGHT

ASYLUM AND THE CONVENTION AGAINST TORTURE

■ ■ ■

SECTION A. HUMANITARIAN PROTECTION

People are forced to leave their homelands for many reasons. They flee war, persecution, natural disaster, environmental catastrophe, severe economic privation, and other intolerable conditions. Over the decades, U.S. policymakers have responded—selectively—to the need for humanitarian action via ad hoc programs, special legislation, and flexible administrative procedures. Congress has also adopted permanent legislation that provides for more enduring and less situational protection for specified categories of forced migrants, especially through sections 208 and 241(b)(3) of the Immigration and Nationality Act. In this chapter we provide an introduction to the laws and procedures, loosely known as humanitarian protection, that can provide legal status to noncitizens in extreme need.

In earlier chapters we examined the legal framework that authorizes noncitizens to enter the United States as permanent residents and as temporary visitors. In addition to immigration based on family ties and employment offers, the United States extends permanent resident status each year to refugees who are screened and selected overseas. Under the Refugee Act of 1980, Pub.L. 96–212, 94 Stat. 102 (1980), the President, in consultation with Congress, authorizes the resettlement of a specific number of refugees each year, and designates in broad terms which refugee situations will be the focus of resettlement. INA § 207. More specific information on the world refugee situation and the exact refugee groups who will be the primary recipients of refugee admissions are set forth in the materials sent to Congress as part of the annual consultations. This procedure allowed more than 100,000 refugees to come to the United States annually through much of the 1990s. In the post–2001 decade the yearly quota has fluctuated between 70,000 and 80,000, with heightened screening procedures sometimes resulting in fewer refugees arriving than were authorized. The latest formal Presidential Determination establishing refugee admission levels for the coming fiscal year is reprinted in the Statutory Supplement. Persons admitted as refugees can adjust status to lawful permanent resident after one year in the United States. INA § 209(a). *See generally* D. Martin, The United States Refugee Admission Program: Reforms for a New Era of Refugee Resettlement (2005).

In addition to admitting individuals from refugee camps overseas, the Refugee Act of 1980 also authorizes individuals to apply for asylum when they arrive at the U.S. borders (or from within U.S. territory). INA § 208. There are no numerical limits on grants of asylum in the United States every year, but asylum seekers—like refugees—must demonstrate that they have a well-founded fear of persecution.

Figure 8.1
Refugee Resettlement Ceilings and Numbers of Refugees
Admitted to the United States, FY 1980–2010

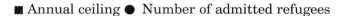

■ Annual ceiling ● Number of admitted refugees

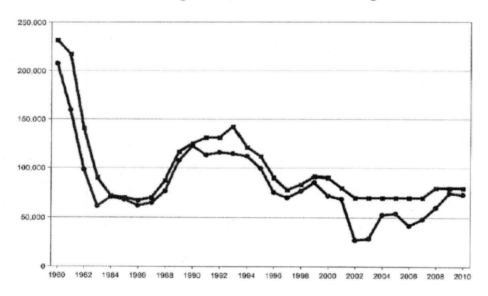

Source: http://www.migrationinformation.org/datahub/charts/historic3.cfm; based on DHS Office of Immigration Statistics, *Yearbook of Immigration Statistics (various years)*, http://www.dhs.gov/files/statistics/publications/yearbook.shtm.

What about those fleeing war or earthquake or a disaster at a nuclear plant? Such persons may find safe haven in the United States via temporary protected status (TPS). INA § 244. This program allows the Secretary of Homeland Security, in her discretion, to designate countries in which armed conflict, natural disaster, or other circumstances pose a serious threat to personal safety or to the ability of the home country to handle the return of its citizens. INA § 244(b)(1). The Secretary designates which countries' citizens are eligible for TPS, and TPS typically is authorized for one-year renewable increments. The TPS designation protects only individuals already in the United States. INA § 244(c)(1). This substantial limitation is meant to prevent TPS from creating a magnet effect. Since the enactment of the TPS statue in 1990, TPS has been granted to hundreds of thousands of citizens from roughly 20 countries, based sometimes on the existence of armed conflict, sometimes on environmental disasters. For a review of the first two decades of the TPS program, see Anchors, *Temporary Protected Status: Making the Designation Process More Credible, Fair, and Transparent*, 39 Ariz. St. L. J. 565 (2007).

In addition, the Victims of Trafficking and Violence Protection Act of 2000, Pub.L. 106–386, 114 Stat. 1464 (Oct. 28, 2000), created special programs for victims of trafficking offenses and for individuals who suffered substantial physical or mental abuse. As we discussed in Chapter Five, 5,000 T visas are available each year to protect trafficking victims who assist in the investigation and prosecution of the traffickers. INA § 101(a)(15)(T). Separately, 10,000 U visas per year for individuals who have suffered criminal abuse and assist law enforcement officers in prosecuting the offenders. INA § 101(a)(15)(U). After three years, both the T visa holders and the U visa holders may become lawful permanent residents.

Special juvenile immigrant status provides another route to lawful permanent residence for those in special need. This applies to individuals under the age of 21 who cannot be reunited with their parents due to abuse, neglect, or abandonment. They must have been placed in the custody of a state agency and there must be a determination that it would not be in the child's best interest to be returned to his or her homeland. INA § 101(a)(27)(J).

This snapshot of humanitarian protection in the United States sets the context for our further exploration of the core legal protections, asylum and withholding of removal based on threats of persecution or torture. We offer here merely an overview and introduction to this immensely complex area.

This chapter will acquaint you with the major procedures and substantive standards, and will deal selectively with a few of the central legal and policy issues: Who should receive asylum? What is persecution and when are fears of persecution well-founded? Which reasons for persecution are relevant for asylum? We will also consider bars to asylum that prevent relief even if there is a risk of persecution, and alternative relief that may be available under the Convention Against Torture (CAT). A full examination of this burgeoning area of law is beyond the scope of this chapter, but you can find a more in-depth treatment in our casebook on this subject, D. Martin, T.A. Aleinikoff, H. Motomura & M. Fullerton, Forced Migration: Law and Policy (2007).

SECTION B.   THE INTERNATIONAL LEGAL FRAMEWORK FOR REFUGEES

1.   THE REFUGEE DEFINITION

Narratives of flight from persecution or war evoke sympathetic images of refugees. Protection, however, is usually reserved for those who meet a specific legal definition. The law of many countries, including the United States, grants refugee status only to those who arrive at the borders or who enter the country and show they satisfy the definition adopted by Article 1(A)(2) the 1951 Convention Relating to the Status of Refugees, 189 U.N.T.S. 137, signed July 28, 1951, as modified by Article I of the 1967 Protocol, 1967 Protocol Relating to the Status of Refugees, done January 31, 1967, 19 U.S.T. 6223, T.I.A.S. No. 6577, 606 U.N.T.S. 267 (both reprinted in the Statutory Supplement):

> [T]he term "refugee" shall apply to any person who * * * owing to well-founded fear of being persecuted for reasons of race, religion, nationality, membership of a particular social group or political opinion, is outside the country of his nationality and is unable or, owing to such fear, is unwilling to avail himself of the protection of that country * * *.

When governments gathered to ratify the 1951 Convention, the Second World War was a recent memory. Millions of people had been uprooted; many had not returned and were likely never to go home. Responding to this reality, and reluctant to commit themselves to large obligations in the future, the governments crafted a limited definition: refugees had to have crossed an international border, to have a well-founded fear of persecution on account of one of five specified reasons, and to be unwilling to return home.

Before parsing the definition, it may be worthwhile to put it in context. The United Nations High Commissioner for Refugees placed the world's total of refugees and asylum seekers at 16.2 million at the beginning of 2011, in addition to 27.5 million individuals living in refugee-like situations within their own countries. A great many of these people would probably not satisfy the UN Convention definition, for they have not fled targeted persecution. Some of the largest concentrations of refugee populations (as they are popularly understood)—for example, Afghan refugees in Pakistan and Iran, Iraqi refugees in Syria and Jordan, Sudanese and Somalis in Chad, Congo, and Kenya, Burmese in Thailand, or Colombians in Latin America—consist primarily of people who fled civil war and ethnic strife, or perhaps some combination of natural disasters (such as drought) and human-caused suffering. The prevailing legal definition does not include such victims, and the readings that follow present various perspectives on which individuals should be defined as refugees.

ARISTIDE R. ZOLBERG, ASTRI SUHRKE, & SERGIO AGUAYO, ESCAPE FROM VIOLENCE: CONFLICT AND THE REFUGEE CRISIS IN THE DEVELOPING WORLD*

269–72 (1989).

Our analysis of contemporary refugee movements [has] delineated three sociological types of refugees: (1) the activist, (2) the target, and (3) the victim. * * * [T]he classic activists are dissenters and rebels whose actions contribute to the conflict that eventually forces them to flee. The targeted refugees are individuals who, through membership in a particular group, are singled out for violent action. And the victims are randomly caught in the cross fire or are exposed to generalized social violence. What all three have in common is fear of immediate violence—violence resulting from conflict between state and civil society, between opposing armies, or conflict among ethnic groups or class formations that the state is unable or unwilling to control. Whether the individuals are activists or passive bystanders simply caught in the conflict is immaterial from the point of view of their immediate security. Their need clearly could be the same regardless of the cause, and has demonstrably been so in many of the cases analyzed. It follows that in a historical and normative sense, the three types of refugees are equally deserving. The activist, the target, and the victim have an equally valid claim to protection from the international community.

The international refugee regime has to some extent recognized the moral equivalence of the three types. The U.N. Convention's definition accommodates the first two but has no provision for the victim. On the other hand, victims were in practice recognized as refugees in the European experience, both in earlier centuries and after World War II. The victims were also acknowledged in the institutional response to Third World refugees through the expanded mandate of the UNHCR in the 1960s and the general practices of first asylum countries in Asia, Africa, and Latin America. Legal codes in Africa and Latin America were also adjusted to allow for mere "victims" (in the 1969 OAU convention and the 1984 Cartagena Declaration). The UNHCR introduced the notion of "victims of violence" in the mid–1980s to plead for asylum seekers in other regions.

From this perspective, the restrictive tendencies evident in North American and West European asylum practices in the 1980s, toward a narrow interpretation of the convention's criterion of persecution as the basis for refugee status, are highly questionable and have been deplored by UNHCR officials. To deny "mere victims" the opportunity to escape from violence is not only morally untenable but runs counter to broader historical trends. It is also open to charges of discrimination on racial and political grounds, as the restrictive tendencies have been most clearly

---

evident with respect to spontaneous asylum seekers of non-European origin who come from noncommunist states.

* * *

An optimal policy would start from the explicit premise of moral equivalence among all three refugee types; the administration of protection and services should also be formal and explicit rather than leaving the beneficiary to an uncertain or semilegal status. Equally important, however, is the need to limit the number of prospective beneficiaries. It will be recalled that with the development toward a universal definition of refugees in the 1930s, it was stressed that some "exact definitions" were necessary to prevent the number of refugees from multiplying *ad infinitum*. Half a century later the point has, if anything, become more self-evident. Because it represents a privileged form of migration, refugee status can be given to only a limited number of people. The question then arises whether the concept of violence lends itself to discriminating interpretations that permit setting priorities.

We submit that it can and that the central ranking principle must be the immediacy and degree of life-threatening violence. Those most exposed must be given preferential access to protection, which becomes the most basic of rights. Farther along in the queue, relief could be given as far as resources and political will permit. More specifically, this would mean that priority be given to individuals or groups who find themselves in extremely threatening situations: civilians in battle areas, likely targets of death squads and pogroms, political prisoners under threat of torture, members of rebel or dissident groups on "wanted" lists, and the like. Proscription on cultural expressions such as lack of freedom of religion would come much farther down on the list, except when it is associated with life-threatening forms of violence.

Situations in which the economic prerequisites for sustaining life have suddenly been removed equally constitute life-threatening violence, and such victims need protection. This definition would include the poverty-stricken masses of the developing world, the victims of structural violence who are systematically pressed toward starvation levels, and the victims of drought and famine, with or without the compounded effect of warfare. It may be objected that such a definitional basis of refugee is totally unrealistic; in particular, the resource-rich countries of the North would not want to relieve famine or massive poverty in the South by means of a large-scale relocation of people.

The objection seems unfounded. Most victims of famine and starvation who today cross international borders remain in neighboring countries, where their claims to life-sustaining support generally are recognized by the international relief or refugee regime. Groups accused of being economic refugees who have claimed asylum in the industrialized countries are not the ones who are most economically destitute and would hardly be admitted as victims of violence even if economically based violence were included in the definition[.] * * *

The rule must be that victims of economic, that is, structural, violence must be helped first in their own country. Observance of the *in situ* clause, * * * is necessary to prevent neighboring and often poor developing countries from becoming overloaded by an influx of desperately poor people seeking relief and not to encourage an international restructuring of populations that in an age of nation-states is politically unacceptable.

In an earlier chapter, Zolberg, Suhrke, and Aguayo had discussed the *"in situ* clause" in these terms:

> [T]he key issue from the perspective of concerned humanitarians is not only whether the movement is involuntary and essentially political but also whether the immediate, intense suffering of the victims can be relieved by helping them in their own country—through policies of their own government or combined with favorable external initiatives—or if relief is possible only by enabling them to move abroad—that is, by providing them with a refuge. * * * [This approach makes it possible, for example,] to distinguish refugees from persons who move as a consequence of a natural disaster. Most victims of malnutrition and slow starvation in the developing world should not be considered as refugees because most of them can be assisted *in situ* in their own countries.

Id. at 33.

In the next article, David Martin constructs an approach to refugee protection based on the pragmatic observation that asylum is a politically scarce resource.

DAVID A. MARTIN, THE REFUGEE CONCEPT: ON DEFINITIONS, POLITICS, AND THE CAREFUL USE OF A SCARCE RESOURCE

Refugee Policy: Canada and the United States (H. Adelman ed. 1991). 30–51.

Contemporary commentary on refugee law, in both Canada and the United States, tends to be harshly critical of the reigning refugee definition, derived from the 1951 United Nations Convention Relating to the Status of Refugees. Especially objectionable, say many of the writers, is the dichotomy between political refugees on the one hand, who can claim a host of legal protections, and economic migrants or displaced persons on the other, who cannot. This dichotomy is said to be overly European—appropriate, perhaps, to the circumstances confronting the world in 1951 when the UN Convention was drafted, but insufficiently sensitive to what is really happening on our planet today. It is particularly inept, so runs this line of criticism, at addressing the travails of the developing world, the source of most of today's fifteen million refugees.

The tide of criticism is powerful. I intend, perhaps inadvisably, to swim against it. For I have become convinced that the Convention definition, understood narrowly but appropriately, may offer the best way to make sense of the precarious legal institution of political asylum in those haven countries where the rule of law enjoys sufficient strength and independence to draw a fairly sharp distinction between law and politics. My argument requires both a careful appreciation of the exact purposes of a definition in this context and an effort to maximize achievement of these purposes in the light of the political constraints confronting refugee protection. * * *

ASYLUM AS AN ENTITLEMENT

* * * Most of the detailed entitlements [in the 1951 Convention], it turns out, are available only to refugees "lawfully in" or "lawfully staying in" the host country. Nations retain complete discretion regarding the legalization of such aliens' status[.] * * * Merely proving that you are a refugee under the treaty definition, as arduous as that process can be, does not mean you achieve the requisite lawful status.

This is why the 1951 Convention is not a treaty about asylum and why, as refugee-law writings frequently repeat, there is no individual right of asylum in international law. The Convention is, as the title advertises, a treaty about the status of refugees—and primarily about the status of those refugees that the state has chosen, in its discretion, to treat as lawfully present. * * *

* * * Although the treaties do not pronounce a fully operative legal right of asylum—asylum in the sense of an indefinite right to stay, accompanied by a range of other rights that will facilitate a reasonably normal life in the new land—they do firmly establish protection against return to the persecuting state, even for those who are present illegally: the famous obligation of *nonrefoulement* of Article 33. This was no mean achievement.

More important, behold the significant edifice that has been constructed on this modest foundation, at least in most of those states that are parties to the treaties and have highly developed legal systems. It turns out in practice that the *nonrefoulement* obligation has been virtually transformed into * * * a de facto right of asylum, in the stronger sense given above [involving all the entitlements spelled out in the Convention], for those who manage to establish physical presence in an asylum country and prove that they meet the refugee definition.

* * * [Of course, to] a major extent governments are simply bowing to necessity when they act in this fashion. Although Article 33 prevents return only to the home country and usually poses no obstacles to sending the individual to some other state, in practice, wealthy Western countries almost never find other nations volunteering to take refugees off their hands. * * * [The treaty would still permit the host country to warehouse refugees in a camp.] Nevertheless, these Western countries, because of their own human rights traditions, find it politically unthinkable to keep these individuals—recognized refugees—in such enforced idleness and

detention. The domestic political climate simply would not tolerate such an approach.

In reality, then, and with very limited exceptions (having primarily to do with criminal misbehaviour), an asylum-seeker in these Western countries who proves that he or she is a refugee will have established a right to asylum. The political reality is that those who prove entitlement to *nonrefoulement* wind up also with an entitlement to asylum in the stronger sense. A legal obligation under Article 33, of what seems to be exceedingly modest proportions, thus becomes the centrepiece for important *political* consequences that do lead to highly significant protections. * * * Those protections attach for those who, first, establish physical presence, and, second, show that they meet the refugee definition.

The reader whose cynicism is undiminished may immediately focus on the enumerated qualifications. * * * That is, states that wish to minimize their exposure will try, first, to block the establishment of a claimant's physical presence on their national territory, and, second, to tighten the procedural and substantive requirements for satisfying the refugee definition.

Both these restrictionist processes are indeed under way, and I will have more to say about them later, for denial of access should be seen as much more disturbing than certain forms of tightening of the requirements. * * * [But for now we should simply recognize that restrictive pressures seek an outlet. Then,] armed with that recognition, we must learn how to shape our legal doctrine to sustain the political conditions that keep [the de facto entitlement to asylum] vital.

ASYLUM AS A SCARCE RESOURCE

If asylum is an entitlement, it carries its own special fragility, for it easily generates backlash when the press of claimants increases. * * * [A]sylum must respond to two different impulses, largely but somewhat paradoxically shared by much of the public in Western nations since World War II. On the one hand, they—we—genuinely wish to provide haven for the persecuted. On the other hand, we still value the reassurance that comes from reasonable control over the entry of aliens. When the number of asylum-seekers increases sharply, the ability to control appears increasingly threatened, at least in the absence of a convincing demonstration that the increase came from a real outbreak of implacable persecution— that is, evidence that most of the new arrivals are "true refugees".

* * *

Ironically, the fact that asylum has become an entitlement compounds the sense of threat to immigration control. An entitlement, in contrast to a discretionary bestowal of political grace, holds a unique immunity to the measures for deliberate decisions concerning intake that are available, at least in theory, in other subfields of immigration law. * * *

* * * [A] claim to refugee status trumps most of the other criteria for control, and for good reason, when applied to the truly threatened, but for reasons that appear decreasingly convincing when the radius of the definitional circle is expanded. We did not have to confront this built-in tension so baldly in earlier times, largely because physical distances and the cost of travel provided natural limitations on the numbers who might seek extra-regional asylum, but now that improved communication and transport have radically shrunk the globe, we cannot escape it. * * *

As the past decade has proven, asylum is a scarce resource. This might seem an odd claim to make in a volume focusing on the United States and Canada, two of the globe's wealthiest societies, and certainly among those with the greatest reserves of available land. Asylum's scarcity is political, however, not physical. The negative public reaction is not based on a sense that these societies are unable to absorb 150,000 or so needy people, newly arrived on North American soil; it is based instead on the fear that the intake will not remain at those levels. Asylum as an entitlement undermines confidence in immigration controls, at least when the numbers increase, because it lacks ready conceptual assurance that the entitlement will remain within reasonable limits. The actions of Western governments in recent years, building harsher deterrents and stronger barriers to arrival, afford support for this claim. We can talk ourselves hoarse in condemning these trends and exhorting greater generosity, but we might better expend our energies in accepting certain political limits and searching instead for ways to make the most of the scarce, but potent, legal resource we have at our disposal.

That will have to mean that asylum is available, as an entitlement rather than as an act of optional political grace, only to a relatively modest number of persons.* * *

* * * Nearly all countries seem joined in a parallel effort to narrow the standards and thereby minimize the loss of control that the asylum entitlement otherwise presages. In doing so, however, some very bad doctrine has emerged. Though narrowing may be politically necessary, not all forms of narrowing are appropriate. The task is to preserve as much as possible of the core purposes of asylum without overtaxing the system. This in turn requires a further exploration of these core purposes.

A DEFENCE OF THE UN DEFINITION: RELOCATION AND THE PRIMACY OF THE POLITICAL

* * *

The asylum system is not some kind of administrative referendum judging relative need or degree of elicited sympathy in * * * abstract terms. It is instead a system for assigning a very particular sort of scarce resource, a resource that is only one of many possible ways to respond to need or to compassionate claims. And what, stripped to its barest essentials, is that resource? It is an entitlement to relocation—or better an entitlement to continue one's relocation indefinitely—in a foreign country.

* * *

Relocation is not indispensable in responding to need in the realm of economic and social rights. As elemental and brutal as the need for food and shelter can be, it plainly can be met in situ, sometimes by provision of urgent relief supplies, sometimes by broader aid meant to improve general economic and social conditions. Urgent relief resources sent by outsiders are usually welcomed by the government in control of the territory. If not, then that resistance almost always bespeaks an element of political oppression that probably should itself bring the deprivation within the classic contours of the UN definition, as traditionally understood. Similar observations apply to earthquake and other natural disaster victims; in any event, the source of their needs tends to be of shorter duration than the socio-economic deprivations mentioned earlier.

Civil war poses more complex issues. Depending on the extent and intensity of the fighting, civilians' greatest need often is precisely for relocation. * * *

If justification [for their exclusion from the definition] is to be found, it must derive from a rough generalization about the need for *foreign* relocation, or at least foreign relocation as a matter of entitlement, as opposed to relocation elsewhere within the home country. Civil wars do usually have limited fronts, and civilians may flee to safer zones. Life may be extremely hard for them in these circumstances, having lost, at least for a time, their homes and perhaps all means of providing for their own livelihood, but the privations that result are of a kind that can be met, at least in principle, by urgent relief assistance provided from outside. Beyond this, where foreign flight is indispensable (as when the fighting cuts off access to other regions of the home country, or when no region is safe), such an option has usually been made available, as a matter of temporary political grace, in adjacent countries, again usually accompanied by substantial relief efforts mounted by the international community. The exclusion of such persons from the Convention definition then perhaps reflects a rough judgment that an entitlement system is not indispensable for affording such shelter in these circumstances, particularly because the need for such haven is more reliably temporary.

Contrast these situations with that faced by an "activist" targeted for political persecution, to use the first of the categories helpfully developed by Zolberg, Suhrke, and Aguayo [reprinted, *supra* pp. 801–803] The government recognizes that the activist is a political opponent and is bent on defeating both the individual and the cause. To effect this defeat, the government is likely to visit serious sanctions on the activist: jailing, beatings, perhaps even torture and death. Because of the nature of the government's political objectives, nothing we can send from outside addresses the individual's need. The case is the same with those Zolberg and his colleagues call "targets", that is, the racial, ethnic, or religious minorities singled out for violent government abuse because of that characteristic. Their plight is not addressed by material assistance or emergency relief crews sent from outside; it can be effectively relieved only by relocation outside the national borders.

In tacit recognition of this fact, the Western world has, haltingly and with many conceptual missteps, developed a system—today's asylum system—that provides relocation as an entitlement to individuals facing precisely these sorts of implacable *political* threats. The modern asylum system says, in effect, that it is too much to expect an ordinary mortal to return home in these particular kinds of threatening circumstances, facing dangers that cannot be propitiated in any other fashion, precisely because of their targeted political character.

* * *

ASYLUM AS PART OF AN INTEGRATED HUMAN RIGHTS STRATEGY

* * * [A]nother angle [of approach] * * * reveals more about the basic purposes of the asylum entitlement. * * *

If the home society is beset by serious human rights problems, it is not immediately apparent why individual escapes provide a response that is superior to changes that would benefit the whole community in the home country. That is, those who leave are, to some extent, turning their backs on continuing the struggle for a communal answer to the human rights abuses and instead simply seeking, through relocation, an improvement in their individual human rights situation. This is a perfectly natural and understandable human response, but whether it should be institutionally encouraged is more doubtful. * * *

* * * We should help point people toward struggling for community solutions, unless the danger at home is so great that it is too much to ask them to remain or return. The asylum standard thus must not be interpreted to require heroism of those to whom it denies shelter.[a] Return is too much to ask when the home government has targeted the individual (or a group to which he or she belongs) for severe mistreatment, for persecution. It is not too much to ask if the risk is less severe or less focused. Staying put in those circumstances is simply what we, too—ordinary, unheroic citizens—should expect of ourselves if our nations were beset by the same kinds of human rights abuses.

* * * This may mean that [those who stay home] have to keep their heads down until circumstances are more propitious or until the heroic actions, even martyrdom, of the bravest among their number create opportunities for radical changes. Having witnessed the dramatic and surprising changes of this past year in many parts of the globe, we should not underestimate the importance of such support from people of modest fortitude, who previously showed few signs of willingness or ability to work for human rights.

---

a. Relocated sentence—eds.

CONCLUSION

Refugee law, taken to extremes, ironically can demean those it means to benefit. Its focus is solely on haven, on sheltering people who fear their governments—as though governments never had anything to fear from the people. * * * With its "exilic bias" * * * ambitious refugee law tends to treat people as history's pawns, never its players: as objects always on the receiving end of home government action, not as subjects capable of acting in their own right.

A narrower political standard, of the kind I advocate here, respects this capacity in those persons. * * * [It] also husbands the limited political reserves that keep asylum vital in the haven countries for those who are in greatest jeopardy.

NOTES AND QUESTIONS ON THE REFUGEE DEFINITION

1. The readings take differing approaches toward economic deprivation as a basis for refugee-type protections. Under what circumstances should severe economic conditions result in mandated protection in a foreign country under Martin's approach? Under Zolberg, Suhrke, and Aguayo's formulation? When does the "*in situ* clause" the latter authors discuss take effect and justify a proposed haven state's rejection of the asylum seekers' claims? What if international relief in place is possible, but has not materialized? What if it is possible, but only if the world community would deploy military force?

2. Most of the time the safe haven provided to "victims" (as the word is used by Zolberg, Suhrke, and Aguayo) outside the borders of their countries of origin has resulted from ad hoc political efforts undertaken by the receiving states and international organizations, although an increasing number of countries have expanded legal provisions to cover some such persons. Receiving states, however, have often resisted efforts to characterize such practices as legally required. They prefer to speak of them as desirable measures that may be taken when conditions permit—including conditions having to do with the overall numbers and relative burdens imposed by the asylum seekers. Is it appropriate for states to refuse to consider themselves legally bound to these "victims" based on negative consequences on the receiving state? If a binding legal regime of this type appears advantageous, what legislative standards would you recommend?

3. Evolving regional norms have embraced broader refugee definitions than found in the 1951 Convention. In Africa, the Organization of African Unity (OAU) (since 2002 known as the African Union) Convention Governing the Specific Aspects of Refugee Problems in Africa, done Sept. 10, 1969, 1001 U.N.T.S. 45, defined its coverage to include both the 1951 Convention definition, as expanded by the Protocol, and the following (Art. I(2)):

The term "refugee" shall also apply to every person who, owing to external aggression, occupation, foreign domination or events seriously disturbing public order in either part or the whole of his country of origin or nationality, is compelled to leave his place of habitual residence in order to seek refuge in another place outside his country of origin or nationality.

In the Americas, the Organization of American States (OAS) General Assembly endorsed the refugee definition found in the Cartagena Declaration on Refugees, but in a form that does not have the legally binding effect of a treaty:

> * * * [T]he concept of a refugee * * * [should include] persons who have fled their country because their lives, safety or freedom have been threatened by generalized violence, foreign aggression, internal conflicts, massive violation of human rights or other circumstances which have seriously disturbed public order.

Legal Status of Asylees, Refugees, and Displaced Persons in the American Hemisphere, AG/RES 774/XV–0/85 (Dec. 9, 1985).

Does either of these formulations comport with Martin's view? With the approach of Zolberg, Suhrke, and Aguayo?

4.   There exists a rich and growing literature on the philosophical and legal conceptions of "refugee." For a very selective sampling *see, e.g.,* M. Price, Rethinking Asylum: History, Purposes, and Limits (2009); C. Bohmer & A. Shuman, Rejecting Refugees: Political Asylum in the 21st Century (2007); G. Goodwin–Gill & J. McAdam, The Refugee in International Law (3d ed., 2007); J. Hathaway, The Rights of Refugees Under International Law (2005), C. Boswell, The Ethics of Refugee Policy (2005); B.S. Chimni, ed., International Refugee Law: A Reader (2000); F. Nicholson & P. Twomey, eds., Refugee Rights and Realities: Evolving Concepts and Regimes 13–150 (1999); Carens, *The Philosopher and the Policymaker: Two Perspectives on the Ethics of Immigration with Special Attention to the Problem of Restricting Asylum, in* Immigration Admissions: The Search for Workable Policies in Germany and the United States 3 (K. Hailbronner et al., eds., 1997); J. Carlier et al., Who is a Refugee? (1997); Singer & Singer, *The Ethics of Refugee Policy,* in Open Borders? Closed Societies?: The Ethical and Political Issues 111 (M. Gibney, ed., 1988).

2.   ASYLUM AND *NONREFOULEMENT*

The 1951 Convention Relating to the Status of Refugees, despite the limitations that the previous readings explored, has remained the fundamental legal framework for protecting refugees, and many of the cases in this chapter will analyze the refugee definition. In addition to defining those who qualify as refugees, the Convention details specific protections furnished to those who fall within its scope. *See generally* J. Hathaway, The Rights of Refugees Under International Law (2005). Two concepts, asylum and *nonrefoulement*, are basic to understanding the legal ramifications of refugee status. Protection against *refoulement*, the French term often used to denote the return of refugees to persecution, is clearly the most basic need of a refugee. "Asylum" is subject to more varied understanding, but usually refers to a situation wherein the refugee is not merely shielded against return but also enjoys an ample array of rights, such as the rights to work and to reunite with family, that enables him or her to rebuild a normal life in the country of refuge.

Refugees from Kosovo wait at Blace to cross into Macedonia, March 1999.
(Photo: © Roger Le Moyne, UNHCR).

The drafting history of the treaty indicates that states were not necessarily expected to grant lawful status to persons simply because they meet the definition of "refugee." Most Convention rights, including work authorization (Article 17) and access to public relief or social security (Articles 23 and 24), are restricted to refugees "lawfully in" or "lawfully staying in" the territory. These rights, which we would associate with asylum—a term not used in the text of the Convention, are within the state's discretion. Nonetheless, core rights, including *nonrefoulement* and access to courts (Article 16), may be claimed by refugees even if they are not lawfully present.

Article 33 of the Convention provides:

No Contracting State shall expel or return ("*refouler*") a refugee in any manner whatsoever to the frontiers of territories where his life or freedom would be threatened on account of his race, religion, nationality, membership of a particular social group or political opinion.

This protection mandates only non-return; it does not require states to provide further rights. Indeed, it does not even require states to allow the individuals to remain—they can be sent away to any other state so long as they are not returned to a state where their life or freedom would be threatened. In practice, though, other states are unlikely to accept a person (not bearing their nationality) whom a sister state is trying to send away. Consequently, most states realize that they will not be able to expel a noncitizen who satisfies the *nonrefoulement* criteria. Developed countries (and many developing countries) therefore tend to give these individuals a legal status—in many countries known as asylum—that allows them to remain and earn a living.

Most of the practice concerning *nonrefoulement* developed in the context of Article 33 of the 1951 Convention, but the *nonrefoulement* concept is not so limited. A closely related protection derives from the Convention Against Torture and Other Cruel, Inhuman, or Degrading Treatment or Punishment (CAT), adopted Dec. 10, 1984, G.A. Res. 39/46, U.N. GAOR, 39th Sess., Supp. No. 51, U.N. Doc. A/39/51 (1985), entered into force, June 26, 1987. Article 3 bars return of a person to a state "where there are substantial grounds for believing that he would be in danger of being subjected to torture." The United States became a party to the treaty in 1994 and fully implemented this specific *nonrefoulement* protection by regulations adopted in 1999. We will consider CAT protection in Section F of this chapter.

SECTION C.   ASYLUM IN THE UNITED STATES

1.   HISTORICAL OVERVIEW

From the very beginning of federal immigration laws, Congress has recognized that special exemptions may be necessary for otherwise inadmissible or deportable noncitizens who have become political enemies of the government in the nation to which they would be sent. In 1875, when Congress first provided that convicts would be excludable, it exempted persons who had been convicted of political offenses. Similar exemptions appeared with regularity in later laws. *See, e.g.*, Act of March 3, 1875, Ch. 141, § 5, 18 Stat. 477; Act of August 3, 1882, Ch. 376, § 4, 22 Stat. 214; Act of March 3, 1891, Ch. 551, § 1, 26 Stat. 1084; Act of Feb. 20, 1907, Ch. 1134, § 2, 34 Stat. 898, 899; Immigration Act of 1917, Ch. 29, § 3, 39 Stat. 874, 877.

There was, however, little systematic attention in the United States to providing asylum to refugees prior to the end of World War II. Indeed, much of the impetus for new American and international efforts after the war derived from a recognition that pre-war efforts, especially on behalf of Jewish refugees, had been shamefully inadequate. *See generally* H. Feingold, The Politics of Rescue: The Roosevelt Administration and The Holocaust, 1938–1945 (1970). For the next three decades, most legislative attention was focused on the overseas refugee situation, and statutes mainly provided for bringing forced migrants from distant locations as part of a deliberate U.S. program. (This part of U.S. refugee protection is discussed briefly in Section A of this chapter and at length in the Forced Migration casebook, *supra*.)

There were special programs to deal with displaced persons left stranded by World War II, the Displaced Persons Act of 1948, Ch. 647, 62

Stat. 1009, refugees from the Hungarian revolution in 1956, and Cubans who fled to the United States after Fidel Castro came to power. Further, Congress enacted a statute in 1950 to exempt noncitizens from deportation "to any country in which the Attorney General shall find that such alien would be subjected to physical persecution." Internal Security Act of 1950, Ch. 1024, § 23, 64 Stat. 987, 1010. Two years later Congress rewrote this provision to authorize the Attorney General, *in his discretion*, to withhold deportation of a noncitizen who would be subject to physical persecution in his or her homeland. This *nonrefoulement* protection, which at that time appeared as § 243(h) of the INA, became known in the United States as "withholding of deportation" or, more recently, as "withholding of removal." It was administered for many years under the strong influence of Cold War assumptions. Successful claimants were, in overwhelming proportions, refugees from Communist countries, although the statute contained no such limitation.

In contrast, the landmark 1965 immigration legislation, which abolished the national origins quota system, adopted a provision to admit a certain number of refugees from overseas, and limited qualifying refugees to those who had "fled" persecution in a "Communist or Communist-dominated country" or a "country within the general area of the Middle East." Immigration and Nationality Act Amendments of 1965, Pub. L. No. 89–236, § 3, 79 Stat. 911, 913, amending § 203(a)(7) of the INA. Furthermore, the 1965 legislative scheme contained no new provisions concerning refugees who arrived in the United States on their own. The withholding provision, INA § 243(h), afforded basic protection, but gave no solid immigration status to its beneficiaries. Regulations and administrative guidance, sometimes stimulated by litigation, clarified some parts of the treatment of asylum seekers in the United States. See Martin, *Reforming Asylum Adjudication: On Navigating the Coast of Bohemia*, 138 U. Pa. L. Rev. 1247, 1294–98 (1990).

When Congress passed the Refugee Act of 1980, the flow of refugees from Indochina in the aftermath of the Vietnam War (which concluded in 1975) was at its peak, and Congress focused on reforming the overseas refugee admissions programs. Nevertheless, the Act made a few important improvements respecting asylum for those who came on their own to the United States. The 1980 Refugee Act added § 208 to the INA, establishing "asylum" (or "asylee") status for individuals who meet the statutory definition of refugee—that is, who have a well-founded fear of persecution on account of one of the five specified grounds if returned to their home countries.

In addition, the Refugee Act of 1980 amended INA § 243(h) to make its provisions mandatory. This brought the United States into line with its international treaty obligations as a party to the 1967 Protocol relating to the Status of Refugees. The 1996 amendments to the INA moved the *nonrefoulement* provision to INA § 241(b)(3), but without significant substantive change. (You will still see references in some cases in this chapter to the former numbering scheme.)

Since 1980, then, there have been two persecution-based forms of relief from removal, one discretionary and the other mandatory. Asylum, under INA § 208, requires a "well-founded fear of persecution;" the *nonrefoulement* provision, now in INA § 241(b)(3), requires that the individual's "life or freedom would be threatened." As Section D will explore, the Supreme Court has ruled that this difference in language signifies a difference in the risk level that the asylum seeker must prove.

Asylum status also affords more protections than withholding of removal status (frequently referred to by the short hand term "withholding" in immigration practice). Those granted asylum are allowed to work, to bring members of their immediate families to the United States, and to access some public assistance. Asylees also have a routine mechanism for adjusting to permanent resident status after one year in the United States, INA § 209(b).[1] While those granted withholding generally receive work authorization, 8 C.F.R. § 274a.12(a)(10), and can sometimes receive public assistance, they may not bring their immediate families to the United States. In principle, they could be removed at any time to a willing third country, though such offers rarely materialize. They may remain in this form of uncertain legal limbo for decades, as there is no provision for eventual adjustment of status to lawful permanent resident, although they are not precluded from adjusting their status if they otherwise qualify, such as through marriage or employment.

2. U.S. PROCEDURES FOR SEEKING ASYLUM AND *NONREFOULEMENT*

a. Applications for Protection

Applications for protection from persecution are automatically treated simultaneously as requests for both *nonrefoulement* and asylum in the United States. Asylum claims must generally be filed within one year of arriving in the United States, INA § 208(a)(2)(B), but there is no deadline for seeking withholding of removal. (See the discussion of the deadline, its exceptions, and its consequences in Section E of this chapter *infra*.)

The applications for protection follow three different paths, depending on whether the applicant is currently in removal proceedings, and, if so, in what type of proceeding. The two most important paths are usually called affirmative applications and defensive applications, to be described below. The third, through the expedited removal procedure described below and

---

1. In its initial form, this section expressly limited the number of asylee adjustments each year. This limitation eventually caused massive backlogs and was finally deleted from the statute in 2005. When it was in force, it was a ceiling on asylee adjustments only; there was never an annual limit on the number of initial grants of asylum.

in Chapter Six, applies to arriving aliens and to some narrow classes of applicants who are entrants without inspection. They must first clear the preliminary hurdle of "credible fear" screening, but if they do, their cases are thereafter handled as defensive claims.

Under regulations collected at 8 C.F.R. Part 208 and 1208, a noncitizen applies for protection under either INA § 208 or § 241(b)(3) (as well as under the Convention Against Torture) by filing Form I–589 (available in the Statutory Supplement). This form asks why the applicant is seeking protection and what he or she thinks would happen upon return to the home country. The form requires the applicant to provide other information that may throw further light on the claim, such as past activities and organizational affiliations, current whereabouts and condition of family members, and the circumstances of departure and travel to the United States. Many applicants also provide additional material, sometimes quite voluminous, including affidavits, news accounts, or human rights reports, including those from nongovernmental organizations like Amnesty International or Human Rights Watch.

The statute requires that applicants be advised of the privilege of being represented by counsel, that they be provided with a list of available pro bono representatives, that absent exceptional circumstances the initial interview or hearing shall take place within 45 days of filing, and the final adjudication (by the immigration judge) shall be completed within 180 days. INA § 208(d). Also, the applicant must be advised that knowingly filing a frivolous application makes him "permanently ineligible for any benefits under this Act." INA § 208(d)(6). The statute also states that asylum may not be granted until the applicant's identity is fully checked against law enforcement and national security databases. INA § 208(d)(5)(A)(I). As a result, an applicant approved by an asylum officer or immigration judge may receive only a preliminary grant of asylum, and may then have to wait weeks for completion of fingerprint and name checks before delivery of the final documents, including work authorization.

(i) Affirmative Applications

Applicants who are not currently in removal proceedings may file an affirmative application by mailing the I–589 to a regional service center (RSC), an arm of USCIS. The RSC staff checks that the application is complete and, if so, schedules the individual for an interview with an asylum officer, which is to be carried out in a "nonadversarial manner." 8 C.F.R. § 208.9. A specialized corps of full-time professional asylum officers, required by regulation to "receive special training in international human rights law, nonadversarial interview techniques, and other relevant national and international refugee laws and principles," 8 C.F.R. § 208.1(b), receives the application and interviews the applicant.

Asylum officers, also part of USCIS, are currently based in eight asylum offices located in cities throughout the country that have high concentrations of asylum applicants, and they ride circuit to hear claims at other places. Asylum officers make their decisions on the basis of the application form, the information presented during the interview, and possibly other information from the State Department or "other credible sources, such as international organizations, private voluntary agencies, news organizations, or academic institutions." 8 C.F.R. § 208.12(a). They are supported by their own central Resource Information Center, see *id.* § 208.1(b), which makes wide-ranging information about country conditions and legal developments available to the officers on-line.

Asylum officer grants of asylum in meritorious cases initially ran between 15 and 30 percent of affirmative filings, but in recent years have exceeded 40 percent. In general, asylum officers refer applicants not found to meet the standards for asylum to immigration court, rather than deny the applications. *See* 8 C.F.R. § 208.14(c)(1). The asylum officer does not have to explain in detail the reason for the referral. The immigration judge then considers the asylum claim further in the course of the removal proceeding. If the applicant was still in a lawful status at the time of the interview with the asylum officer, however, the officer issues a denial, stating reasons for the decision. Such applicants can renew the asylum claim later, if they are someday placed into removal proceedings.

(ii) Defensive Applications

If removal proceedings are already underway, the applicant can apply for asylum or withholding only by presenting a defensive application that is heard exclusively by the immigration judge. 8 C.F.R. § 208.2(b). Typically the noncitizen makes known at master calendar (the first appearance in immigration court) her wish to seek asylum (or withholding of removal) as a form of relief, and the judge then grants a specified period of time within which the I–589 must be completed and filed with the immigration court. The matter is then heard in the more formal setting of the immigration court, with examination and cross-examination by the noncitizen's counsel (if she has one) and the DHS trial attorney. (Removal proceedings will be discussed at greater length in Chapter Ten.)

Sometimes, the noncitizen is ordered removed from the United States, and only then applies for asylum, perhaps because the applicant did not have counsel until after the issuance of a removal order. In such cases, the asylum claim can only be raised by means of a motion to reopen filed with the immigration judge or BIA, depending on which forum last heard the matter. A motion to reopen is sometimes the first motion that a newly retained attorney files in a case. Many of the decisions that you will read in this chapter arose from motions to reopen. Chapter Ten will examine motions to reopen in more detail.

Figure 8.2
Affirmative and Defensive Asylum Claims, 1990–2009

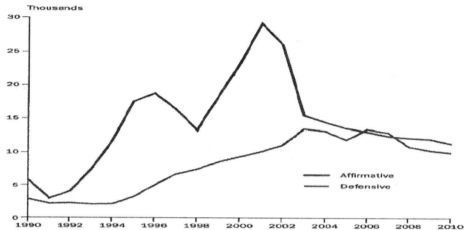

Source: DHS Annual Flow Report, Daniel C. Martin, *Refugees and Asylees: 2010*, May 2011, Figure 2, at 4.

(iii) Applications In Expedited Removal Proceedings

Under the expedited removal procedures, INA § 235(b)(1), described in Chapter Six, noncitizens arriving at the port of entry or brought to the United States after interdiction at sea (plus specified classes of entrants without inspection who have been in the country for less than two years) are subject to removal on the order of an immigration officer, not an immigration judge, if found inadmissible under INA § 212(a)(6)(C) or (7) (for having false or inadequate documents or for other fraud or misrepresentation, even at an unrelated time in the past). Those among this group who express a fear of return or ask for asylum are referred to an asylum officer who interviews them (no sooner than 48 hours later) to determine whether they have a "credible fear of persecution," defined in INA § 235(b)(1)(B)(v) as a "significant possibility * * * that the alien could establish eligibility for asylum." If found to have a credible fear, their claims are heard on the merits as defensive asylum claims, based upon a full hearing in immigration court.

Those not found to have a credible fear are ordered removed. They may request that an immigration judge review this negative determination in a special expedited procedure. Within seven days at the latest, and within 24 hours if practicable, an immigration judge considers the asylum officer's report and conducts a review in person, by video, or by telephone. INA § 235(b)(1)(B)(iii)(III). Judicial review of the immigration judge's decision on credible fear is available only in limited circumstances. INA §§ 242(a)(2)(A), 242(e). Of those who received a credible fear hearing by an asylum officer between 2006 and 2011, approximately 80% were found to have a credible fear. DHS, Briefing Paper on Expedited Removal and Credible Fear Process, Oct. 19, 2011.

(iv) Work Authorization

Prior to 1995, regulations authorized permission to work to all asylum seekers whose applications were not deemed "frivolous." 8 C.F.R. § 208.7(a) (1995). In effect, almost everyone who filed an asylum claim received employment authorization. Many argued that the easy acquisition of work authorization created an incentive to file asylum applications, whether or not there were grounds to support asylum. In 1995, new regulations postponed the issuance of work authorization until at least 180 days had elapsed—unless asylum is granted before then. They also provided that no authorization would issue if the application had been denied by an immigration judge within that time period. Asylum applications thereafter decreased significantly. These constraints are now written into the statute. INA § 208(d)(2). The government completes the asylum proceedings, both the asylum officer ruling and the immigration court hearing and judgment, within the 180 day period in the majority of cases. Delays requested by the asylum seeker do not count in accumulating the 180 days. *See generally* Martin, *Making Asylum Policy: The 1994 Reforms*, 70 Wash. L. Rev. 725, 733–37, 753–54 (1995).

b. Immigration Court

Immigration judges provide the initial evaluation of all the defensive applications for asylum and withholding, and they provide a second consideration of affirmative applications referred by asylum officers. In the latter case, the immigration judge receives the pre-existing I–589, with its attachments, from the asylum officer, along with copies of the charging document. Applicants of course can supplement their claims in immigration court and put on additional witnesses, but the use of the original application form in both settings is meant to enhance efficiency and save time. Immigration judges consider referred cases in much the same fashion as defensive claims, granting some asylum claims and giving rejected applicants a full statement of reasons as part of the decision in the case.

The immigration judge's decision on either a defensive asylum claim or a referred affirmative claim is appealable to the Board of Immigration Appeals (BIA). If the BIA rules against the claim for protection, judicial review may be available as part of the review of the removal order. For a more thorough discussion of judicial review and the applicable review standards, see Chapter Ten.

3. ASYLUM TRENDS AND STATISTICS

The number of asylum applications has ebbed and flowed over the years, with peaks in the early 1980s, late 1980s, and mid 1990s. The number of asylum claims substantially decreased after the 1995 regulations decoupled work authorization from the filing of an asylum application. Since 1995, as indicated above, work authorization is postponed until 180 days after filing an asylum application, unless asylum is granted earlier.

Figures 8.3 and 8.4 refer solely to asylum claims filed with DHS and do not take into account asylum decisions rendered by immigration judges. Figure 8.3 reports the number of affirmative asylum cases filed over the past 35 years. Figure 8.4 depicts the number of affirmative asylum cases filed with and approved by DHS during the past 14 years.

Figure 8.3
Asylum Cases Filed, 1973–2009

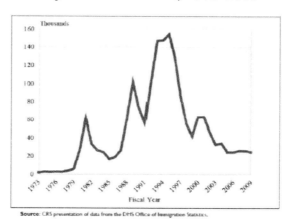

Source: CRS presentation of data from the DHS Office of Immigration Statistics.

Source: Congressional Research Service (CRS) Report for Congress, R. Wasem, *Asylum and "Credible Fear" Issues in U.S. Immigration Policy*, Apr. 6, 2011, Figure 1, at 3.

Figures 8.5, 8.6, and 8.7 report on asylum claims decided by immigration judges. These include those cases referred to immigration court by USCIS asylum officers, Figure 8.5, those filed initially in immigration court, Figure 8.6, and the overall grant rate, Figure 8.7.[2]

---

2. The immigration court statistics calculate the grant rate as a percentage of asylum claims decided on the merits. The calculation does not include the substantial number of asylum claims that are withdrawn, decided on procedural grounds, such as venue, or granted some other type of relief. EOIR, FY 2010 Statistical Year Book, K1. In FY 2010 EOIR reported 9,869 grants of asylum, 9,554 denials, 7,194 withdrawals, 1,799 abandoned, and 12,129 other dispositions. *Id.* at K3.

Figure 8.4
Affirmative Asylum Cases Filed and Approved, 1996–2009

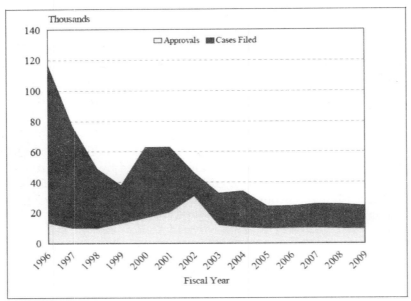

Source: CRS presentation of data from the USCIS Directorate of Refugee, Asylum, and International Operations.

Notes: Data represent cases not individuals.

Figure 8.5
Immigration Court Decisions on Asylum Claims Referred
by Asylum Officers, 2006–2010

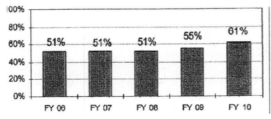

Immigration Court Affirmative Grant Rate			
	Grants	Denials	Grant Rate
FY 06	9,530	9,020	51%
FY 07	8,427	7,953	51%
FY 08	7,356	7,051	51%
FY 09	7,262	5,940	55%
FY 10	7,088	4,508	61%

Source: EOIR, FY 2010 Statistical Year Book, Figure 17, at K-2.

Figure 8.6
Immigration Court Decisions on Asylum Claims Filed Initially in Immigration Court, 2006–2010

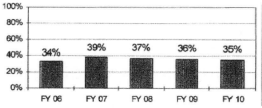

Immigration Court Defensive Grant Rate			
	Grants	Denials	Grant Rate
FY 06	3,774	7,457	34%
FY 07	4,426	6,921	39%
FY 08	3,520	6,116	37%
FY 09	3,030	5,394	36%
FY 10	2,771	5,046	35%

Source: EOIR, FY 2010 Statistical Year Book, Figure 18, at K-2.

Figure 8.7
Immigration Court Grant Rate on All Asylum Claims, 2006–2010

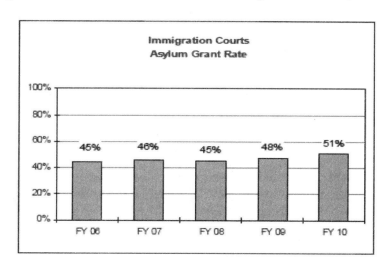

Source: EOIR, FY 2010 Statistical Year Book, Figure 16, at K–1.

Figure 8.8 compares the countries from which asylum seekers came in 2009, looking first at those who filed affirmative claims with USCIS, and then at those who raised asylum as a defense to removal in immigration court, which is part of EOIR. The graphs show that Chinese citizens file the largest number of asylum applications with both USCIS and EOIR.

Figure 8.8
Source Countries for Asylum Seekers, 2009

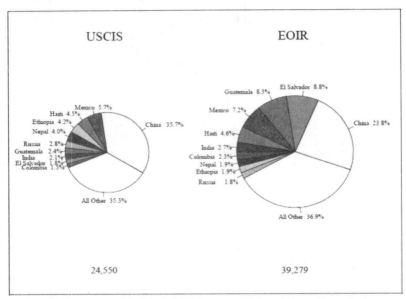

Source: CRS presentation of data from the USCIS Directorate of Refugee, Asylum, and International Operations and the Office of Planning, Analysis and Technology in the Executive Office for Immigration Review.

Notes: Data represent cases not individuals.

In comparison, Figure 8.9 shows the array of nationalities of individuals with successful asylum claims in 2009. Approximately 25 percent of the USCIS grants of asylum were to Chinese nationals, as were approximately 35 percent of the cases granted asylum by immigration judges.

Figure 8.9
Asylum Grants by Nationality, 2009

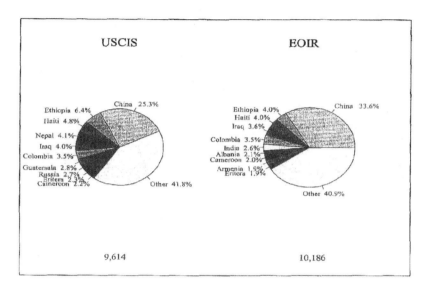

Source: Congressional Research Service (CRS) Report for Congress, R. Wasem, *Asylum and "Credible Fear" Issues in U.S. Immigration Policy*, Apr. 6, 2011, Figure 13, at 22.

Figure 8.10 shifts focus from asylum to withholding of removal. As you may recall from the prior section in this Chapter, individuals seeking protection in the United States file Form I–589, on which they can apply for asylum and withholding of removal. Immigration judges, not asylum officers, evaluate all applications for withholding. Figure 8.10 reports on the success rate for those seeking withholding of removal. Cases in which the applicant sought both asylum and withholding and was granted asylum have been omitted from this total.[3]

---

3. These successful asylum cases are reflected in Figure 8.7.

Figure 8.10
Immigration Courts: Withholding of Removal Grant Rate

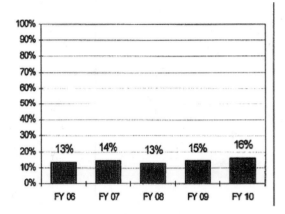

Immigration Court Withholding of Removal Grant Rate		
	Grants	Denials	Grant Rate
FY 06	2,571	16,778	13%
FY 07	2,554	15,343	14%
FY 08	2,055	14,013	13%
FY 09	1,984	11,680	15%
FY 10	1,874	9,894	16%

Source: EOIR, FY 2010 Statistical Year Book, Figure 19-A, at K-4.

Figure 8.11 combines the successful asylum grants with the successful withholding grants. Counting both forms of relief together, the graph shows that between 50 and 60 percent of applicants for protection who saw their cases through to a decision by the immigration judge have been successful in immigration court in recent years. Note, however, that immigration court statistics indicate that only 50 percent of the claims for protection reach a decision on the merits; the other 50 percent are withdrawn, abandoned, or result in another disposition. EOIR, FY 2010 Statistical Year Book, Figure 19, at K–3.

Figure 8.11
Immigration Courts: Asylum and Withholding of Removal

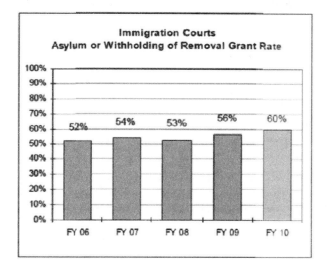

Immigration Court Asylum or Withholding of Removal Grant Rate				
	Asylum Grants	Withholding of Removal Grants	Denials of Both Asylum and Withholding of Removal	Grant Rate
FY 06	13,304	2,571	14,452	52%
FY 07	12,859	2,554	13,048	54%
FY 08	10,881	2,055	11,630	53%
FY 09	10,298	1,984	9,625	56%
FY 10	9,869	1,874	7,906	60%

Source: EOIR, FY 2010 Statistical Year Book, Figure 19-B, at K-5.

SECTION D.   THE SUBSTANTIVE CRITERIA FOR ASYLUM

Section 208 of the INA provides that the Attorney General may grant asylum in the United States to an applicant who satisfies the refugee definition provided in INA § 101(a)(42): an individual who has a well-founded fear of persecution on account of race, religion, nationality, membership in a particular social group, or political opinion. The *nonrefoulement* provision, § 241(b)(3), prohibits returning an individual to a country in which his or her life or freedom would be threatened on account of the individual's race, religion, nationality, membership in a particular social group, or political opinion. The concept of persecution is central to both forms of protection from removal, although the term itself does not appear in the latter statutory section.

The full framework for determining whether U.S. law will protect an individual requires not only that he or she be faced with "persecution," but also that any such persecution be "on account of race, religion, nationality, membership in a particular social group or political opinion."

Each of these five grounds is a term of art, as is the phrase "on account of," which requires a certain type of nexus among the persecutor, the individual being persecuted, and the reason for the persecution. We focus first on "persecution," but the lines between these issues—(1) persecution, (2) the five grounds, and (3) nexus—are often blurred in practical application. Many cases implicate more than one of these issues, and it is not always possible to tease them neatly apart. As you work through the material in this chapter, we urge you to remain aware of the interaction among these three issues, and to think holistically about the phrase "persecution on account of race, religion, nationality, membership in a particular social group or political opinion."

1. PERSECUTION

We start with the central concept: what is persecution? Neither the U.S. law, nor the 1951 Convention from which it is derived, defines persecution. Several courts have offered their views. The Ninth Circuit had this to say:

> Although the term "persecution" is not defined in the Act, we have explained it as "the infliction of suffering or harm upon those who differ (in race, religion or political opinion) in a way regarded as offensive." We have cautioned that "persecution is an extreme concept that does not include every sort of treatment our society regards as offensive." Discrimination on the basis of race or religion, as morally reprehensible as it may be, does not ordinarily amount to "persecution" within the meaning of the Act. *See Bastanipour v. INS*, 980 F.2d 1129, 1133 (7th Cir. 1992) (distinguishing persecution "from mere discrimination or harassment"). The Board has held that discrimination can, in extraordinary cases, be so severe and pervasive as to constitute "persecution" within the meaning of the Act. In a case such as the one before us, however, where private discrimination is neither condoned by the state nor the prevailing social norm, it clearly does not amount to "persecution" within the meaning of the Act.

Ghaly v. INS, 58 F.3d 1425, 1431 (9th Cir. 1995).

A more succinct definition comes from Judge Posner in *Osaghae v. INS*, 942 F.2d 1160, 1163 (7th Cir. 1991): " 'Persecution' means, in immigration law, punishment for political, religious, or other reasons that our country does not recognize as legitimate."

The task in this section is to identify a workable notion of when this country is prepared to declare another nation's punishments (or other harms) illegitimate such that our legal system should provide protection. Some cases are easy, but a great many fall at the margin and present surprisingly difficult issues.

a. Type of Harm

As the Ninth Circuit indicated above, persecution is generally described as harmful conduct that is more severe than discrimination or harassment. Frequently, persecution takes the form of physical violence or imprisonment, but it encompasses a wide array of harm. At issue in the following case is when economic measures rise to the level of persecution.

MIRISAWO v. HOLDER

United States Court of Appeals, Fourth Circuit, 2010.
599 F.3d 391.

Niemeyer, Circuit Judge:

* * *

Rosemary Mirisawo was born in Harare, Zimbabwe, in 1966 and lived there until she came to the United States in 1999. She came to the United States on a nonimmigrant G–5 visa[b] to work as a housekeeper, leaving her children with family members in Zimbabwe. Mirisawo has worked as a housekeeper, both in Zimbabwe and the United States, since she was 20 and, during this time, has lived in the homes of her employers. She has four children, as well as two brothers and eight sisters. * * * All of her children now live with family members in Harare, Zimbabwe.

Mirisawo remained in the United States, employed as a housekeeper, until August 2002, when she returned to Zimbabwe for a month to visit family and to provide better accommodations for her children and brother, Tobias. A few months prior to her visit—in March 2002—Tobias had been severely beaten by supporters of the Zimbabwean government because he was an active member of the Movement for Democratic Change ("MDC"), a political party that opposed Robert Mugabe, the leader of the ZANU–PF party and the president of Zimbabwe for the last 29 years. Tobias was hospitalized following the beating and continues to receive medical treatment for his injuries. To avoid being associated with Tobias and his political activities during her visit, Mirisawo stayed with her sister Maggie. During her stay, she purchased a home in Mabvuku, a suburb of Harare, for Tobias and her children.

While in Zimbabwe during this visit, Mirisawo did not experience any difficulties with the government—she was not stopped, questioned, harassed, or beaten. * * *

In May 2005, the Mugabe government began implementing Operation Restore Order, pursuant to which it destroyed thousands of homes and buildings in Harare for the officially stated purpose of cleaning out urban slums. It was widely believed, however, that the operation was retributive, targeting areas known by the government to have voted for the opposition in presidential and parliamentary elections. In the course of Operation

---

b. This is a type of nonimmigrant visa available for personal employees of staff members of international organizations.—eds.

Restore Order, the government bulldozed three of the four rooms in the house that Mirisawo had purchased for Tobias and her children. Tobias and Mirisawo's son continued to live in the remaining room, while her other children went to live with Mirisawo's sister, Maggie.

According to the country report prepared by the United States Department of State in 2006, the human rights record of the Zimbabwean government was "very poor." The report noted that persons perceived to be opposition supporters were tortured, raped, and abused by government-sanctioned youth militia and ruling-party supporters and that the government "routinely used selective violence to achieve its political objectives."

Despite these conditions, Tobias, Mirisawo's daughter Tsitsi, and Mirisawo's sister Maggie continue to be members of the MDC. Since his beating in 2002, Tobias has not experienced any further threats or abuses. Tsitsi has never been harmed, but she was threatened into purchasing a ZANU–PF identification card. Maggie also has never been harmed or even threatened, although she keeps her membership in the MDC secret and does not live in the area of Harare where Mirisawo claims the government presumes all residents to be MDC members.

On August 3, 2005, some three months before her G–5 visa was to expire, Mirisawo filed an application for asylum with the Department of Homeland Security. * * *

* * *

The immigration judge held that the destruction of Mirisawo's house did not amount to past persecution because Mirisawo had never lived in the house nor depended on it for her livelihood. The immigration judge also held that she was not likely to face future persecution because she had not been harassed upon her return to Zimbabwe in 2002 and because none of her family members who remained in Zimbabwe had been harmed since Tobias' beating in 2002. * * *

* * *

* * * [T]o establish eligibility for asylum, the applicant must demonstrate that she has suffered from past persecution or that she has a well-founded fear of future persecution. And to establish a well-founded fear of future persecution, the applicant must demonstrate that "(1) a reasonable person in the circumstances would fear persecution; and (2) that the fear has some basis in the reality of the circumstances and is validated with specific, concrete facts.". * * *

While "persecution" is often manifested in physical violence, "the harm or suffering [amounting to persecution] need not be physical, but may take other forms," so long as the harm is of sufficient severity. Among the forms of nonphysical harm amounting to persecution is that of "economic persecution," which includes the "deliberate deprivation of basic necessities" and the "deliberate imposition of severe economic disadvantage." Thus, to establish "economic persecution," an asylum applicant must demonstrate that, on account of one of the statutorily enumerated grounds, the applicant's life or freedom has been threatened by either (1) a deliberate and severe deprivation of basic necessities or (2) a deliberate imposition of severe financial disadvantage. It is important to emphasize that not every economic deprivation or disadvantage makes a person a "refugee." Rather, it must be a deprivation or disadvantage so severe that it threatens the person's very life or liberty.

* * *

Mirisawo contends that she is eligible for asylum and withholding of removal because she suffered past economic persecution when the government destroyed her house during Operation Restore Order. She claims that the destruction of her house constituted economic persecution either because a house is a basic necessity for survival or because its destruction caused her to suffer severe financial disadvantage. * * *

* * *

* * * At the time of the government's partial destruction of her house, Mirisawo had never lived in the house and was living and working in the United States as a live-in housekeeper. Nor is it likely that Mirisawo will ever need to live in the house, as she will likely continue to be employed as a live-in housekeeper if she returns to Zimbabwe. Mirisawo focuses on the facts that the property destroyed was a house and that the effect of Operation Restore was to deprive many Harare residents of the shelter necessary for their survival. But when evaluating the significance of the partial destruction of her house, we must focus not on the effect the government action had on the house itself or on others impacted by the government action, but on the effect the action had on *Mirisawo's* life and liberty. In this case, the record supports the conclusion that the destruction of Mirisawo's house in no way interfered with her ability to provide housing for herself, and therefore we cannot say that she was deprived of a basic necessity that threatened her "life or freedom."

With respect to Mirisawo's contention that the destruction of her house was "the deliberate imposition of severe economic disadvantage," the BIA found that the destruction of Mirisawo's house did not impose sufficiently severe financial harm to constitute economic persecution, mainly because Mirisawo did not depend on her house for her livelihood. Mirisawo spent her career employed as a housekeeper, and the destruction of her house in no way interfered with her ability to continue in this type of employment. Moreover, she never attempted to live in the house nor expressed any intention to live there. While the partial destruction of her house undoubtedly resulted in an investment loss, Mirisawo did not rely on that investment for current or future income and did not, nor does not, need a return on that investment to continue working as a housekeeper and living as she has. In these circumstances, we cannot say that the BIA erred in concluding that the harm imposed was not sufficiently severe to constitute a threat to Mirisawo's life or freedom. * * *

* * *

Mirisawo also contends that she has a well-founded fear of future persecution based on "a political opinion that may be imputed to her by virtue of her family ties or her status as an impoverished land-owner in Harare." She claims that the Zimbabwean government will believe that she is a member of the MDC because her brother Tobias, daughter Tsitsi, and sister Maggie are all members of the MDC and because it is widely believed that most of the residents of her neighborhood are members of the MDC.

While the BIA accepted Mirisawo's claim that she had a subjective fear of persecution, it rejected the notion that her fear was objectively reasonable. It reached its conclusion based in part on the fact that when Mirisawo returned to Zimbabwe in 2002, she faced no persecution of any type. It also noted that neither her oldest daughter nor her sister had ever suffered any persecution and that her brother Tobias, while having been beaten in 2002, has continued to live in Zimbabwe without further incident. We conclude that these facts provide substantial evidence to support the BIA's conclusion. The fact that family members whose political opinions Mirisawo fears will be imputed to her have not themselves faced harm fatally undermines her claim that she will suffer persecution because of her association with them. Moreover, the fact that she herself suffered no acts of persecution when she returned to Zimbabwe in 2002, shortly after her brother Tobias had been beaten, is highly probative.

For the foregoing reasons, we affirm the decision of the BIA and deny Mirisawo's petition for review.

Petition Denied.

GREGORY, CIRCUIT JUDGE, concurring in part and dissenting in part:

Petitioner Rosemary Mirisawo came to the United States in order to pursue a job; she had no illusions or desire that her residency here would become permanent. Rather, she accepted a G–5 visa and, for six years, worked as a household domestic in this country. In preparation for her eventual return to Zimbabwe, Mirisawo purchased a home in her native land. Her disabled brother and some of her children inhabited the house while she remained abroad. However, in 2005, the home, the only one she had ever owned, was destroyed by the Mugabe government in a show of force against the Movement for Democratic Change opposition. Therefore, now that Mirisawo's visa has not been renewed and she lacks status in this country, she has no shelter to which she may return. Given that destruction, Mirisawo has established past economic persecution and thus qualifies as a refugee for asylum purposes. For this reason, I dissent.

* * *

* * * Economic persecution may qualify as past persecution if it constitutes either the "deliberate deprivation of basic necessities" or the "deliberate imposition of severe economic disadvantage." Of the basic necessities of human life, shelter is certainly included. Along with food and water, housing is one of the components of fundamental human existence. Thus, its intentional deprivation constitutes past persecution.

The majority goes further, announcing for the first time that in this Circuit, for economic persecution to be shown, it must "be so severe that it threatens the life or freedom of the applicant" * * *. The majority's standard for economic persecution goes beyond our prior holding in *Li* [*v. Gonzales*, 405 F.3d 171 (4th Cir. 2005),], where we required that the economic harm "constitute a threat," not that the harm itself actually and currently threaten the individual's life or liberty. Further, the majority's requirement of a "severe" deprivation of basic necessities goes beyond any of our prior precedent which required only a "deliberate deprivation" of such essentials. * * *

* * *

There are two fundamental flaws in the majority's argument, one factual and one conceptual, both demonstrating that persecution was shown here. First, the majority unwarrantedly assumes that Mirisawo was not planning on returning to the home she purchased. Indeed, it assumes that Mirisawo was forever consigned to her role as a live-in domestic, continually inhabiting the homes and lives of other people, unable to forge her own way. Yet, there is direct evidence in the record to the contrary showing that Mirisawo was actively preparing for her return home. * * * At bottom, the majority's error is to assume that Mirisawo preferred to live in her employers' homes, when the evidence points to the fact that at the first chance she had, she purchased a home of her own that would be available for her return.

The second flaw in the majority's argument is more conceptual. It is erroneous to conclude that as a matter of law an individual who has not lived in his home cannot make out a claim of economic persecution. The logical flaw of the majority's opinion is quite clear in the following example. Imagine an alien in the United States who has secured a temporary work visa and who has no interest or reason to seek permanent resident status. As that person prepares to return home, he contacts a friend in his home country and asks him to dig a well at his house. In return, the alien will send him $1,000 via Western Union. The friend agrees, and within two weeks, the well is completed and the money transferred. Unfortunately, before the alien returns home, agents of the government come to his house and pour poison in his well, suspecting that he sympathizes with the opposition party, supporters of which live in his neighborhood. In response, the alien files an asylum claim in the United States, claiming past economic persecution which deprives him of the necessities of life: water. Confronted with that case, would this Court hold that merely because the alien had yet to drink from the well, he was not persecuted? That result is counter to logic and counter to law.

So too here the majority's decision is without basis in law or reason. Mirisawo was able to buy the house with her earnings in the United States. Like so many temporary workers, she used the money she earned abroad to provide for her future at home. Unfortunately Mirisawo was never able to enjoy the fruits of her labors because the house was bulldozed before she inhabited it. Yet, merely from her inability to occupy the house, how can we assume that Mirisawo never intended to live there in the first place? Fundamentally, it is without support in the law to hold that the destruction of the most significant investment a person has ever purchased, which is also a necessity of life, does not constitute persecution.

The majority opinion evinces some knowledge of a maid's life, but betrays no understanding of her dream. I must dissent.

NOTES AND QUESTIONS ON THE MEANING OF PERSECUTION

1.   Why is it significant to the majority that Mirisawo had not lived in the house she bought for her brother and children? Would it have mattered to the majority if the evidence had demonstrated that Mirisawo had lost her job as a housekeeper and no longer had the ability to live in the home of her employer? The dissent, in contrast, emphasized that Mirasawo had planned to return to Zimbabwe to live in her own home. Why should that matter if the government purposefully destroyed her major financial asset? On the other hand, although destruction of her home was almost surely a human rights violation, is asylum designed to afford relocation to all who have suffered such violations? Or is it meant to protect a narrower class of persons whose life on return would be so constricted that it would amount to persecution? Since Mirisawo's children have been able to live with her sister, has Mirisawo been able to make a showing of persecution?

2.   In *Borca v. INS*, 77 F.3d 210, 215 (7th Cir. 1996), the BIA ruled that economic persecution results in refugee status only when "the persecution is so severe as to deprive an applicant of all means of earning their living." Applying this doctrine, it found that the Romanian asylum applicant was not eligible for asylum, even though she had been fired from her job as a radiologist and apparently denied a license for any other government job except farm laborer. The Seventh Circuit reversed, applying a standard derived from *Kovac v. INS*, 407 F.2d 102, 107 (9th Cir. 1969): "deliberate imposition of substantial economic disadvantage for reasons of race, religion or political opinion" would suffice to justify political asylum. More recently, the Seventh Circuit ruled that government mistreatment of a Mormon in Ukraine might compel a finding of persecution: "the government prevented her from continuing her education in the Ph.D. physics program, denied her permission to live in Kiev and reduced her to working in menial jobs that required no education, training or acuity." *Koval v. Gonzales*, 418 F.3d 798, 805–06 (7th Cir. 2005). Do the court decisions in *Borca* and *Koval* both of which ruled for the asylum applicant, go too far? Is working in a menial job

really a form of persecution? If so for Koval, then why not for thousands of others who never had a shot at a Ph.D. program? At what point do economic sanctions rise to the level of persecution? In *Matter of T–Z–*, 24 I & N Dec. 163 (BIA 2007), the BIA acknowledged that there were two potentially inconsistent lines of cases dealing with economic persecution. Instead of choosing one line or the other, it sought to harmonize them by interpreting both to require "severe" and not merely "substantial" economic harm.

b. Uniform National Policy

As noted in the preceding case, the Zimbabwe government justified destroying private dwellings as a legitimate slum clearance project, but many characterized the actions as retribution against political opponents. What if a government applies criminal or other procedurally regular sanctions even-handedly in pursuit of a policy aim it deems legitimate, or indeed vital? If the asylum state does not share that view, it may have to pass judgment on the validity of the underlying policy. Ask yourself if it is possible to devise an approach that does not require value choices about the substantive rightness of the underlying policy—e.g., an approach that focuses only on procedural defects in implementation. Or is there anything wrong with the asylum state imposing its values, at least in this limited sense, on the policy choices of the other state?

"It Is Better to Have One Child Only." (Photo: © David Clark)

The Board of Immigration Appeals faced this issue in deciding whether China's coercive population control policy constituted persecution. The Board's reasoning is instructive, although Congress eventually overturned the result by changing the statute.

We do not find that the "one couple, one child" policy of the Chinese Government is on its face persecutive. China has adopted a policy whose stated objective is to discourage births through economic incentives, economic sanctions, peer pressure, education, availability of sterilization and other birth control measures, and use of propaganda. Chinese policymakers are faced with the difficulty of providing for China's vast population in good years and in bad. The Government is concerned not only with the ability of its citizens to survive, but also with their housing, education, medical services, and the other benefits of life that persons in many other societies take for granted. For China to fail to take steps to prevent births might well mean that many millions of people would be condemned to, at best, the most marginal existence. The record reflects that China was in fact encouraged by world opinion to take measures to control its population.

There is no evidence that the goal of China's policy is other than as stated, or that it is a subterfuge for persecuting any portion of the Chinese citizenry on account of one of the reasons enumerated in section 101(a)(42)(A) of the Act. The policy does not prevent couples from having children but strives to limit the size of the family. It appears that exceptions are made so that couples facing certain hardships may have another child. The policy applies to everyone but expressly protects, and indeed is more leniently applied to, minority (non-Han) peoples within China. It appears to impose stricter requirements on Party members (state cadres) than on some non-Party members. The Chinese Government has stated that it does not condone forced sterilizations and that its policy is to take action against local officials who violate this policy.

The population problem arising in China poses a profound dilemma. We cannot find that implementation of the "one couple, one child" policy in and of itself, even to the extent that involuntary sterilizations may occur, is persecution or creates a well-founded fear of persecution "on account of race, religion, nationality, membership in a particular social group, or political opinion." This is not to say that such a policy could not be implemented in such a way as to individuals or categories of persons so as to be persecution on account of a ground protected by the Act. To the extent, however, that such a policy is solely tied to controlling population, rather than as a guise for acting against people for reasons protected by the Act, we cannot find that persons who do not wish to have the policy applied to them are victims of persecution or have a well-founded fear of persecution within the present scope of the Act.

Matter of Chang, 20 I & N Dec. 38, 44 (BIA, 1989).

NOTES AND QUESTIONS ON COERCIVE POPULATION CONTROL

1.   Although serious consequences potentially awaited the applicant in *Chang*, including his forced sterilization or his wife's forced abortion, the BIA

appeared unwilling to find that this would amount to persecution on account of one of the five reasons stated in the definition. These harms could constitute persecution in some settings, but apparently not if they are applied to virtually all in the population who fail to go along with the national policy. Persecution, in this conception, apparently requires some sort of invidious discrimination. Do you agree? Consider how the definition would apply to people who escaped Cambodia under Pol Pot, whose Khmer Rouge, in power from 1975 to 1979, attempted to purge their country of all Western influence, and who killed over a million of their countrymen in the process (often in quite indiscriminate fashion). Should the need for a showing of invidious discrimination be reduced to the extent that the threatened harm is regarded as especially severe?

2. Do you think the BIA in *Chang* considered the scope of potential immigration from the most populous country in the world? Would any such attention to practical consequences and political limitations be a legitimate factor to consider in shaping the law of *nonrefoulement* and asylum?

Congress overruled the *Chang* decision in the 1996 Act by amending the statutory refugee definition, INA § 101(a)(42), to add this sentence:

> For purposes of determinations under this Act, a person who has been forced to abort a pregnancy or to undergo involuntary sterilization, or who has been persecuted for failure or refusal to undergo such a procedure or for other resistance to a coercive population control program, shall be deemed to have been persecuted on account of political opinion, and a person who has a well-founded fear that he or she will be forced to undergo such a procedure or subject to persecution for such failure, refusal, or resistance shall be deemed to have a well founded fear of persecution on account of political opinion.

At the same time, Congress placed a ceiling of 1,000 per year on the number of persons who could receive protection pursuant to this provision either by a grant of asylum or by admission through the overseas refugee program. Within a decade a backlog developed of close to 9,000 conditional grants of asylum, and Congress repealed the ceiling in 2005. *See Full Asylum Benefits for FY 2004 Available for Certain Conditional Grant Beneficiaries*, 10 Bender's Imm. Bull. 100 (2005); Pub. L. 109–13, 119 Stat. 231, 305, Div. B, § 101(g)(2).

Neither the 1996 nor 2005 amendments addressed withholding under § 241(b)(3). When the BIA faced this issue in *In re X–P–T–*, 21 I & N Dec. 634 (BIA 1996), it ruled that the 1996 amendment superseded *Chang* and applies in withholding cases (for which there was no ceiling) as well.

c. Prosecution Versus Persecution

Although the *Chang* case involved enforcement via economic and social sanctions, states often enforce uniform national policies via the criminal law. In the absence of uneven enforcement of the law, are there circumstances when the application of criminal penalties constitutes persecution? These questions have frequently arisen in cases challenging criminal sanctions imposed for violating a nation-wide requirement of military service, but they can also arise in many other situations. What if a state criminalized distribution of contraceptive drugs and devices? Barred all private ownership of firearms? Banned any use of languages other than the official language in all public settings?

The three excerpts below, all arising at different stages of the same case that began when a young man refused to join the Salvadoran army in 1982, analyze whether the punishment for evading military service constituted persecution or prosecution.

> The respondent * * * left El Salvador because he did not want to serve in the army on account of its violent record, but he feared he would be tortured and possibly killed as a sympathizer of the opposition if he refused to serve. He stated that one cousin, a former soldier, was killed in about 1981 by the army when he participated in an anti-government demonstration and that another cousin was drafted by the guerrillas and killed by them around 1980 after he killed a supervisor. A relative of his common-law wife was an officer in the guerrilla army. This man was killed in about 1980. The respondent himself was recruited by a friend to be an *oreja*, or spy, for the government, but he declined. A member of the civilian patrol allegedly threatened him but was executed himself shortly thereafter. The respondent also reported that he was beaten up by soldiers at a roadblock in 1981 and again in 1982. The brother of the respondent's brother-in-law was killed after the respondent had left El Salvador, apparently by a so-called death squad, for providing food to some guerrillas.

> * * *

> The issue before us is whether the respondent has made a prima facie case of at least a well-founded fear of persecution for one of the listed reasons, if he returns to El Salvador. * * * The respondent argues that he will refuse to serve in the "terrorist" military and that his refusal is based on his political beliefs. He then contends that he would likely suffer severe penalties including death at the hands of the death squads for his refusal, because he would be suspected of anti-government sympathies. He also argues that it would be against his moral values to serve in an army which has engaged in violations of human rights. * * *

> * * *

> We hold to the long-accepted position that it is not persecution for a country to require military service of its citizens. Exceptions to this rule may be recognized in those rare cases where a disproportionately severe punishment would result on account of one of the five grounds enumerated in section 101(a)(42)(A) of the Act, or where the

alien would necessarily be required to engage in inhuman conduct as a result of military service required by the government. *See* Office of the United Nations High Commissioner for Refugees, *The Handbook on Procedures and Criteria for Determining Refugee Status Under the 1951 Convention and the 1967 Protocol Relating to the Status of Refugees* 39–41 (Geneva, 1979). * * *

The respondent * * * asserts that the actions of the Salvadoran Army violate international law and have been condemned by the international community. Although incidents involving the Salvadoran Army have been reported, which undoubtedly involve the violation of the rights of noncombatants and international law, there is no evidence that these incidents represent the policy of the Salvadoran Government or that the respondent would be required to engage in such actions as a member of the armed forces. The statements of opinion of Americas Watch to the contrary in the record may indeed be the belief of those who represent that organization. Such statements of opinion of private unofficial bodies do not constitute evidence of condemnation by recognized international governmental bodies, which would be necessary at a minimum for us to accept this argument. For an example of a statement of opinion of a recognized international governmental body, see the resolution concerning the status of persons refusing service in military or police forces used to enforce apartheid. G.A. Res. 33/165, 33 U.N. GAOR Supp. (No. 45) at 154, U.N. Doc. A/33/45 (1979).

* * *

Accordingly, the appeal will be dismissed.

Matter of A–G–, 19 I & N Dec. 502, 503–08 (BIA 1987)

On appeal from the BIA decision, a three-judge panel of the U.S. Court of Appeals for the Fourth Circuit came to a different conclusion.

Failure to serve in the military may * * * be the expression of a political opinion, subjecting the evader to the same punishment as any other draft evader. When this occurs, the applicant should ordinarily be denied refugee status because the draft is generally recognized as lawful. There is, however, an exception to this general rule[.] * * * It is the possibility that an unwilling conscriptee may be associated with the commission of atrocities which places him in a different predicament from that of a conscriptee who merely disagrees with the political justification of a conflict.

* * *

We think that the Board has made the petitioner's burden unduly harsh. An applicant for political asylum should not be required to prove that he would be compelled to commit atrocities. It is unlikely that such a standard could ever be met. * * * Whether an individual will be associated with condemned conduct will depend largely on how widespread it has become, and it follows that the likelihood that an individual would be forced to participate in atrocities increases as the atrocities become more widespread. We therefore think that the appropriate inquiry is to consider the pervasiveness of atrocities. * * *

We also decline to adopt the Board's requirement that there be proof that the acts of atrocity with which M.A. does not want to be associated are the policies of the Salvadoran government. It is sufficient that M.A. show that the Salvadoran government is unwilling or unable to control the offending group, here, the armed forces. * * *

Similarly, we do not think that M.A. must wait for international bodies such as the United Nations to condemn officially the atrocities committed by a nation's military in order to be eligible for political asylum. Paragraph 171 of the [*UNHCR*] *Handbook* shelters those individuals who do not wish to be associated with military action "condemned by the international community as contrary to basic rules of human conduct...." These basic rules are well documented and readily available to guide the Board in discerning what types of actions are considered unacceptable by the world community. [The court cited and discussed the Geneva Conventions of 1949].

* * *

Reversed and remanded.

M.A. A26851062 v. INS, 858 F.2d 210, 215, 218 (4th Cir. 1988).

The government next petitioned for rehearing en banc. The full court of appeals vacated the panel's ruling and issued the following decision.

M.A. claims that the military in which he might be forced to serve has committed acts that are contrary to the basic rules of human conduct. The Board was within its discretion in rejecting this claim based on M.A.'s failure to present cognizable evidence that the alleged atrocities he wanted to avoid were perpetrated as a result of the policies of the Salvadoran military or government. Misconduct by renegade military units is almost inevitable during times of war, especially revolutionary war, and a country as torn as El Salvador will predictably spawn more than its share of poignant incidents. Without a requirement that the violence be connected with official governmental policy, however, any male alien of draft age from just about any country experiencing civil strife could establish a well-founded fear of persecution. The Refugee Act does not reach this broadly.

M.A. did, of course, bring forth evidence from prominent private organizations such as Amnesty International and Americas Watch.

These organizations have condemned the Salvadoran military and security forces for committing violent acts against all sectors of Salvadoran society. They report that the Salvadoran military engages in "extrajudicial execution on noncombatant civilians, individual death squad-style killings, 'disappearances,' arbitrary detention and torture." Moreover, they contend that the military violence is carried out pursuant to a deliberate policy of the Salvadoran government designed to further that government's political interests.

* * *

[But a] standard of asylum eligibility based solely on pronouncements of private organizations or the news media is problematic almost to the point of being non-justiciable. * * * Although we do not wish to disparage the work of private investigative bodies in exposing inhumane practices, these organizations may have their own agendas and concerns, and their condemnations are virtually omnipresent. Taken alone, they do not suffice to overturn the Board's judgment in M.A.'s case.

It is, of course, the role of private organizations and news reports to energize the political branches. But that is quite a different thing from requiring the courts in each instance to evaluate independently the accusations of private organizations to determine whether they set forth conditions adequate to overturn the Board's discretionary judgment. This responsibility would require us to make immigration decisions based on our own implicit approval or disapproval of U.S. foreign policy and the acts of other nations. Courts could be put in the position of ruling, as a matter of law, that a government whose actions have not been condemned by international governmental bodies engages in persecution against its citizens. * * * Such a role for the courts would transform the political asylum process from a method of individual sanctuary left largely to the political branches into a vehicle for foreign policy debates in the courts.

M.A. v. INS, 899 F.2d 304, 312–13 (4th Cir. 1990) (en banc).

NOTES AND QUESTIONS ON MILITARY SERVICE

1. What, if anything, makes military service (whether in the context of conscription or of following a superior officer's orders) different from the sort of government policy at issue in *Chang*? After all, governments have armed forces, and even if they have no conscription, they impose discipline within the ranks. And what, if anything, makes military discipline different from the general governmental interest in self-preservation by prosecuting anyone, civilian or military, who might try to overthrow it?

2. M.A. had not served in the military, nor had he had been specifically ordered to commit an act that would have been a human rights violation, and possibly a war crime or crime against humanity. In. *Ramos–Vasquez v. INS,* 57 F.3d 857, 861–64 (9th Cir. 1995), the asylum applicant had deserted from

the Honduran army after he had been punished for refusing to execute deserters. The court found that punishment for a deserter in these circumstances could be considered persecution. Should individual orders always be required? What about a person who fled before being conscripted into service in the Khmer Rouge forces of Pol Pot, which ultimately killed one million Cambodians? The army of Afghanistan's Taliban? The South African army before apartheid was abolished? The Libyan army ordered by Qaddafi to defeat the NATO-supported rebel uprising?

3.   The asylum applicant in *M.A.* is a "selective conscientious objector," to use the terminology applied in the United States during the Vietnam War and more recently in the war in Iraq. That is, he did not claim to be opposed to war in any form, but only to the particular uses of military force employed by the Salvadoran military at the time. U.S. conscription laws have usually allowed Americans who conscientiously oppose all war to avoid military service, subject to an obligation to perform alternative noncombatant service, while denying that option to selective objectors. For discussions of conscientious objection as a basis for asylum, see Musalo, *Conscientious Objection as a Basis for Refugee Status: Protection for the Fundamental Right of Freedom of Thought, Conscience and Religion*, 26 Ref. Survey Q. 69 (2007); Bailliet, *Assessing Jus Ad Bellum and Jus in Bello Within the Refugee Status Determination Process: Contemplations on Conscientious Objectors Seeking Asylum*, 20 Geo. Immigr. L.J. 337 (2006); Note, *Asylum for Unrecognized Conscientious Objectors: Is There a Right not to Fight?*, 31 Va. J. Int'l L. 447 (1991).

d.   Persecution by Nongovernmental Actors

U.S. law has accepted that harm or threats from non-state actors can provide a basis for asylum. As the Ninth Circuit explained in *McMullen v. INS*, 658 F.2d 1312, 1315 n. 2 (9th Cir. 1981), "persecution within the meaning of § 243(h) includes persecution by non-governmental groups * * * where it is shown that the government of the proposed country of deportation is unwilling or unable to control that group." The BIA agrees. *See, e.g., Matter of O–Z– and I–Z–*, 22 I & N Dec. 23 (BIA 1998) (affirming asylum grant to a Ukrainian Jew who had been beaten and threatened by an anti-Semitic ultranationalist group).

Ascertaining when a government is unable or unwilling to control a persecuting group is a more complicated question than it might initially seem. In all countries, violent crime occurs to a greater or lesser degree, despite control efforts by the government. No one can be completely guaranteed protection against all such criminal activity. If a threatened violent crime has a political cast to it, must the potential harm be considered persecution of a kind that might give rise to a valid asylum claim? In *Matter of O–Z–and I–Z–, supra*, the BIA emphasized the fact "that the respondent reported at least three of the incidents to the police, who took no action beyond writing a report" before finding that the nongovernmental acts were sufficiently condoned by the government to justify a grant of asylum. On the other hand, in *Matter of V–T–S–*, 21 I & N Dec. 792 (BIA 1997), the Board refused to grant asylum to a person who had been threatened with kidnapping by insurgent forces in the Philippines. In dictum, the BIA noted that the applicant had failed to show a sufficient government default to make the kidnapping a sound basis for asylum, in part because the government had mounted major efforts against the perpetrators when the applicant's siblings had been kidnapped.

The significance of nongovernmental persecutors arises frequently in situations where there is communal strife. For example, in *Singh v. INS*, 94 F.3d 1353 (9th Cir. 1996), the asylum applicant had fled from Fiji, where the population was evenly divided between ethnic Fijians and Indo–Fijians, and there had been considerable ethnic strife, including two coups. Singh and his family had been threatened and assaulted by groups of ethnic Fijians, and the court concluded that this constituted persecution by a group the government was unable or unwilling to control.

The infliction of harm by non-state actors also arises in many gender-related claims for asylum. For example, cases based on claims of female genital mutilation generally focus on family members who insist on compliance with the custom. Similarly, many cases raising claims of domestic violence allege that the spouse or intimate partner inflicted the harm. We will examine these further in pages 882–888 of this chapter.

It is important to note that the significance of nongovernmental actors is different in applications for protection under the Convention Against Torture (CAT). In contrast to asylum and withholding claims, requests for protection under the CAT require a showing of government participation or acquiescence. This CAT requirement is discussed in Section F of this chapter.

e. Past Persecution

Although there is no requirement that applicants for protection under the asylum and withholding statutes have already suffered persecution, some applicants have. In U.S. practice, these applicants are the beneficiaries of an express rebuttable presumption that they have a well-founded fear of future persecution. The regulations specify that applicants who establish that they faced persecution on one of the protected grounds in the past will be presumed to have a well-founded fear of persecution. 8 C.F.R. § 208.13(b)(1). The government can rebut this presumption in two ways: (1) by showing that a fundamental change in circumstances has occurred that removes any well-founded fear of persecution or (2) by showing that the asylum applicant could avoid future persecution by relocating to another part of the home country and that it would be reasonable to expect the applicant to do so. 8 C.F.R. § 208.13(b)(1)(i). A similar presumption operates in the context of withholding of removal. *Id.* § 208.16(b)(1).

In addition to the explicit evidentiary presumption, the regulations allow a humanitarian grant of asylum (but not withholding) for victims of past persecution even in the absence of fears of future persecution.

An applicant * * * may be granted asylum, in the exercise of the decision-maker's discretion, if the applicant has demonstrated compelling reasons for being unwilling * * * to return * * * arising out of the severity of the past persecution * * *.

8 C.F.R. § 208.13(b)(1)(iii)(A).

The BIA has indicated that such a grant is exceptional, because refugee protection is ordinarily forward-looking, intended to shield against future harm. *See Matter of Chen*, 20 I & N Dec. 16 (BIA 1989). But the broader practice is possible because Congress chose to write the INA definition of refugee in a way that departs from the Convention, to include as refugees persons outside their countries of origin "because of persecution *or* a well-founded fear of persecution." (Compare INA § 101(a)(42)(A) to Article 1 of the Convention.)

2. LEVEL OF RISK

In addition to exploring the meaning of persecution, many cases have examined another fundamental question: what *degree of threat* or level of risk in the homeland must an applicant prove before being found to meet the threshold qualification for protection under U.S. law? The asylum provision, INA § 208, and the withholding provision, § 241(b)(3), may seem on an early look to protect the same group of persons threatened with persecution in their homelands. But the statutory texts are not identical: asylum is predicated on a "well-founded fear" of persecution, while withholding is available when an individual's "life or freedom would be threatened." The meaning of these statutory sections was the subject of major debate for many years.

During the 1950s the BIA ruled that applicants for relief under § 243(h), the predecessor to § 241(b)(3), had to demonstrate a "clear probability of persecution." The BIA continued to use this formulation after the United States acceded to the UN Protocol in 1968 and withholding became, in effect, mandatory because of the treaty obligation under Article 33. *Matter of Dunar*, 14 I & N Dec. 310 (BIA 1973). Not long after the passage of the Refugee Act of 1980, the Supreme Court examined a case in which the applicant was seeking only withholding, not asylum. *INS v. Stevic*, 467 U.S. 407, 104 S.Ct. 2489, 81 L.Ed.2d 321 (1984). Justice Stevens, writing for a unanimous Court, made a sharp distinction between the two sections. Paying close attention to what he regarded as the plain language of § 243(h), Justice Stevens approved the Board's "clear probability" approach, but only for applying § 243(h). He concluded that this standard requires the applicant to show that persecution "is more likely than not." *Id.* at 424 and n. 19, 104 S. Ct. at 2498 and n. 19. The Court rejected the "premise that every alien who qualifies as a 'refugee' under the statutory definition [referred to in § 208] is also entitled to a withholding of deportation under § 243(h)," 467 U.S. at 428, 104 S.Ct. at 2500, and left the § 208 standard for consideration on another day.

Predictably, litigation resumed immediately, now carefully targeting the § 208 issue. The courts of appeals reached disparate results, but the BIA adhered to its position "that the standards for asylum and withholding of deportation are not meaningfully different and, in practical application, converge." *Matter of Acosta*, 19 I & N Dec. 211, 219 (BIA 1985). After the courts of appeals reached disparate results, the Supreme Court returned to these questions.

INS v. CARDOZA–FONSECA

Supreme Court of the United States, 1987.
480 U.S. 421, 107 S.Ct. 1207, 94 L.Ed.2d 434.

JUSTICE STEVENS delivered the opinion of the Court.

* * *

Respondent is a 38–year–old Nicaraguan citizen who entered the United States in 1979 as a visitor. After she remained in the United States longer than permitted, and failed to take advantage of the Immigration and Naturalization Service's (INS) offer of voluntary departure, the INS commenced deportation proceedings against her. Respondent conceded that she was in the country illegally, but requested withholding of deportation pursuant to § 243(h) and asylum as a refugee pursuant to § 208(a).

To support her request under § 243(h), respondent attempted to show that if she were returned to Nicaragua her "life or freedom would be threatened" on account of her political views; to support her request under § 208(a), she attempted to show that she had a "well-founded fear of persecution" upon her return. The evidence supporting both claims related primarily to the activities of respondent's brother who had been tortured and imprisoned because of his political activities in Nicaragua. Both respondent and her brother testified that they believed the Sandinistas knew that the two of them had fled Nicaragua together and that even though she had not been active politically herself, she would be interrogated about her brother's whereabouts and activities. Respondent also testified that because of her brother's status, her own political opposition to the Sandinistas would be brought to that government's attention. Based on these facts, respondent claimed that she would be tortured if forced to return.

* * *

Under [§ 208(a)], eligibility for asylum depends entirely on the Attorney General's determination that an alien is a "refugee," as that term is defined in § 101(a)(42), which was also added to the Act in 1980. [The Court then quotes the text of INA § 101(a)(42)(A).] Thus, the "persecution or well-founded fear of persecution" standard governs the Attorney General's determination whether an alien is eligible for asylum.[5]

---

5. It is important to note that the Attorney General is *not required* to grant asylum to everyone who meets the definition of refugee. Instead, a finding that an alien is a refugee does no

In addition to establishing a statutory asylum process, the 1980 Act amended the withholding of deportation provision, § 243(h). Prior to 1968, the Attorney General had discretion whether to grant withholding of deportation to aliens under § 243(h). In 1968, however, the United States agreed to comply with the substantive provisions of Articles 2 through 34 of the 1951 United Nations Convention Relating to the Status of Refugees. Article 33.1 of the Convention, which is the counterpart of § 243(h) of our statute, imposed a mandatory duty on contracting States not to return an alien to a country where his "life or freedom would be threatened" on account of one of the enumerated reasons. Thus, although § 243(h) itself did not constrain the Attorney General's discretion after 1968, presumably he honored the dictates of the United Nations Convention.[8] In any event, the 1980 Act removed the Attorney General's discretion in § 243(h) proceedings.

In *Stevic* we considered it significant that in enacting the 1980 Act Congress did not amend the standard of eligibility for relief under § 243(h). While the terms "refugee" and hence "well-founded fear" were made an integral part of the § 208(a) procedure, they continued to play no part in § 243(h).

* * *

[T]he language Congress used to describe the two standards conveys very different meanings. The "would be threatened" language of § 243(h) has no subjective component, but instead requires the alien to establish by objective evidence that it is more likely than not that he or she will be subject to persecution upon deportation.[10] *See Stevic.* In contrast, the reference to "fear" in the § 208(a) standard obviously makes the eligibility determination turn to some extent on the subjective mental state of the alien. "The linguistic difference between the words 'well-founded fear' and 'clear probability' may be as striking as that between a subjective and an objective frame of reference.... We simply cannot conclude that the standards are identical." *Guevara Flores v. INS*, 786 F.2d 1242, 1250 (C.A.5 1986) [*cert. denied*, 480 U.S. 930, 107 S.Ct. 1565, 94 L.Ed.2d 757 (1987)].

That the fear must be "well-founded" does not alter the obvious focus on the individual's subjective beliefs, nor does it transform the standard into a "more likely than not" one. One can certainly have a well-founded fear of an event happening when there is less than a 50% chance of the occurrence taking place. As one leading authority has pointed out:

more than establish that "the alien *may* be granted asylum *in the discretion of the Attorney General.*" § 208(a) [1987 version](emphasis added).

8. While the protocol constrained the Attorney General with respect to § 243(h) between 1968 and 1980, the Protocol does not require the granting of asylum to anyone, and hence does not subject the Attorney General to a similar constraint with respect to his discretion under § 208(a).

10. "The section literally provides for withholding of deportation only if the alien's life or freedom 'would' be threatened in the country to which he would be deported; it does not require withholding if the alien 'might' or 'could' be subject to persecution." *Stevic,* 467 U.S., at 422.

Let us ... presume that it is known that in the applicant's country of origin every tenth adult male person is either put to death or sent to some remote labor camp ... In such a case it would be only too apparent that anyone who has managed to escape from the country in question will have 'well-founded fear of being persecuted' upon his eventual return.

1 A. Grahl–Madsen. The Status of Refugees in International Law 180 (1966).

This ordinary and obvious meaning of the phrase is not to be lightly discounted.

* * *

In *Stevic*, we dealt with the issue of withholding of deportation, or *nonrefoulement*, under § 243(h). This provision corresponds to Article 33.1 of the Convention. Significantly though, Article 33.1 does not extend this right to everyone who meets the definition of "refugee." Rather, it provides that "[n]o Contracting State shall expel or return (*'refouler'*) a *refugee* in any manner whatsoever to the frontiers of territories *where his life or freedom would be threatened* on account of his race, religion, nationality, membership of a particular social group or political opinion." Thus, Article 33.1 requires that an applicant satisfy two burdens: first, that he or she be a "refugee," i.e., prove at least a "well-founded fear of persecution"; second, that the "refugee" show that his or her life or freedom "would be threatened" if deported. Section 243(h)'s imposition of a "would be threatened" requirement is entirely consistent with the United States' obligations under the Protocol.

Section 208(a), by contrast, is a discretionary mechanism which gives the Attorney General the *authority* to grant the broader relief of asylum to refugees. As such, it does not correspond to Article 33 of the Convention, but instead corresponds to Article 34. That Article provides that the contracting States "shall as far as possible facilitate the assimilation and naturalization of refugees...." Like § 208(a), the provision is precatory; it does not require the implementing authority actually to grant asylum to all those who are eligible. Also like § 208(a), an alien must only show that he or she is a "refugee" to establish eligibility for relief. No further showing that he or she "would be" persecuted is required.

Thus, as made binding on the United States through the Protocol, Article 34 provides for a precatory, or discretionary, benefit for the entire class of persons who qualify as "refugees," whereas Article 33.1 provides an entitlement for the subcategory that "would be threatened" with persecution upon their return.

* * *

INS repeatedly argues that the structure of the Act dictates a decision in its favor, since it is anomalous for § 208(a), which affords greater benefits than § 243(h), to have a less stringent standard of eligibility. This argument sorely fails because it does not take into account the fact that an alien who satisfies the applicable standard under § 208(a) does not have a *right* to remain in the United States; he or she is simply *eligible* for asylum, if the Attorney General, in his discretion, chooses to grant it. An alien satisfying § 243(h)'s stricter standard, in contrast, is automatically entitled to withholding of deportation. In *Matter of Salim*, 18 I. & N. Dec. 311 (1982), for example, the Board held that the alien was eligible for both asylum and withholding of deportation, but granted him the more limited remedy only, exercising its discretion to deny him asylum. We do not consider it at all anomalous that out of the entire class of "refugees," those who can show a clear probability of persecution are *entitled* to mandatory suspension of deportation and *eligible* for discretionary asylum, while those who can only show a well-founded fear of persecution are not *entitled* to anything, but are *eligible* for the discretionary relief of asylum.

* * *

This vesting of discretion in the Attorney General is quite typical in the immigration area. If anything is anomalous, it is that the INS now asks us to restrict its discretion to a narrow class of aliens. Congress has assigned to the Attorney General and his delegates the task of making these hard individualized decisions; although Congress could have crafted a narrower definition, it chose to authorize the Attorney General to determine which, if any, eligible refugees should be denied asylum.

* * *

The question whether Congress intended the two standards to be identical is a pure question of statutory construction for the courts to decide. Employing traditional tools of statutory construction, we have concluded that Congress did not intend the two standards to be identical. In *Chevron U.S.A. Inc. v. Natural Resources Defense Council, Inc.*, 467 U.S. 837 (1984), we explained:

> The judiciary is the final authority on issues of statutory construction and must reject administrative constructions which are contrary to clear congressional intent. [Citing cases.] If a court, employing traditional tools of statutory construction, ascertains that Congress had an intention on the precise question at issue, that intention is the law and must be given effect.

Id. at 843, n.9, 104 S.Ct., at 2782, n.9 (citations omitted).

The narrow legal question whether the two standards are the same is, of course, quite different from the question of interpretation that arises in each case in which the agency is required to apply either or both standards to a particular set of facts. There is obviously some ambiguity in a term like "well-founded fear" which can only be given concrete meaning through a process of case-by-case adjudication. In that process of filling " 'any gap left, implicitly or explicitly, by Congress,' " the courts must respect the interpretation of the agency to which Congress has delegated the responsibility for administering the statutory program. But our task today is much narrower, and is well within the province of the judiciary. We do not attempt to set forth a detailed description of how the "well-founded fear" test should be applied.[31] Instead, we merely hold that the Immigration Judge and the BIA were incorrect in holding that the two standards are identical.

* * *

Deportation is always a harsh measure; it is all the more replete with danger when the alien makes a claim that he or she will be subject to death or persecution if forced to return to his or her home country. In enacting the Refugee Act of 1980 Congress sought to "give the United States sufficient flexibility to respond to situations involving political or religious dissidents and detainees throughout the world." Our holding today increases that flexibility by rejecting the Government's contention that the Attorney General may not even consider granting asylum to one who fails to satisfy the strict § 243(h) standard. Whether or not a "refugee" is eventually granted asylum is a matter which Congress has left for the Attorney General to decide. But it is clear that Congress did not intend to restrict eligibility for that relief to those who could prove that it is more likely than not that they will be persecuted if deported.

The judgment of the Court of Appeals is affirmed.

[The concurring opinion of JUSTICE BLACKMUN is omitted.]

JUSTICE POWELL, with whom THE CHIEF JUSTICE and JUSTICE WHITE join, dissenting.

The Court's opinion seems to assume that the BIA has adopted a rigorous mathematical approach to asylum cases, requiring aliens to demonstrate an objectively quantifiable risk of persecution in their homeland that is more than 50%. The Court then argues that such a position is inconsistent with the language and history of the Act. But this has never been the BIA's position.

* * *

[T]he BIA does not contend that both the "well-founded fear" standard and the "clear probability" standard require proof of a 51% chance that the alien will suffer persecution if he is returned to his homeland. The BIA plainly eschews analysis resting on mathematical probabilities. Rather, the BIA has adopted a four-part test requiring proof of facts that demonstrate a realistic likelihood of persecution actually occurring. The heart of the Acosta decision is the BIA's empirical conclusion, based on its experience in adjudicating asylum applications, that if the facts establish such a basis for an alien's fear, it rarely will make a difference whether the judge asks if persecution is "likely" to occur or "more likely than not"

---

31. How "meaningful" the differences between the two standards may be is a question that cannot be fully decided in the abstract, but the fact that Congress has prescribed two different standards in the same Act certainly implies that it intended them to have significantly different meanings. * * *

to occur. If the alien can establish such a basis, he normally will be eligible for relief under either standard.

NOTES AND QUESTIONS ON LEVEL OF RISK

1. The *Cardoza–Fonseca* majority is convinced, *Chevron* notwithstanding, that the plain meaning of the two sections mandates a differential standard of proof for §§ 208 and 243(h). It emphasizes that the language of § 243(h) is "would," not " 'might' or 'could' be subject to persecution" (footnote 10, quoting *Stevic*). But this juxtaposition of the language is not fully responsive to the actual wording. The withholding provision extends its protection to noncitizens whose "life or freedom would be threatened" on the specified grounds, not "would be taken away." Consider the Court's own example of an individual facing return to a country where the government is killing or jailing every tenth adult male. Assuming that the asylum seeker is a male, obviously he has a well-founded fear of persecution on return. But how does the plain language apply here? Would we say that this man's life or freedom would be threatened on return?

2. Apparently the Supreme Court countenances returning a recognized "refugee" to her country of origin, provided that she falls short of the standard for § 243(h). Is this sound policy? Is it what Congress had in mind? Would the drafters of the UN treaties have intended to permit such a result? More fundamentally, does it make sense to have two different forms of protection, with two different levels of risk required for protection under U.S. law?

3. The BIA moved quickly in response to *Cardoza–Fonseca*. In *Matter of Mogharrabi*, 19 I & N Dec. 439 (BIA 1987), the BIA explained that the asylum applicant must show that a "reasonable person in [the asylum applicant's] circumstances would fear persecution." The current regulations, issued after the INA was amended in 1996, ask whether "there is a reasonable possibility of suffering such persecution if he or she were to return to [the home] country." 8 C.F.R. § 208.12(b)(2).

EXERCISE

The readings above have covered a variety of formulations of the standard for claiming asylum-type protections under § 208 or § 241(b)(3). We have grouped the alternative interpretations below in two categories, first for *nonrefoulement* and second for asylum. Within each category, they range from the most demanding to the least.

1. threat to life or freedom:

    A. clear probability of persecution

    B. persecution is more likely than not

2. well-founded fear of persecution:

    A. realistic likelihood of persecution

B.   reasonable possibility of persecution

C.   good reason to fear persecution

D.   a reasonable person in such circumstances would fear persecution upon return to the homeland.

Test your understanding of the various tests and their implications for concrete cases by applying them to the following hypotheticals, and keep them in mind as you consider the more detailed exploration of standards that follows these problems.

Hypothetical A.

(1) A was a local leader in a teacher's organization that began a campaign of criticism against the authoritarian government in Ruritania and called for democratic reforms. The government has denounced the protests, but so far has done nothing further.

(2) Same facts, but now the Ruritanian government has shown some signs that it will crack down on opponents. So far, however, it has arrested only labor union leaders.

(3) Same facts, but Ruritania now branches out beyond labor leaders and seizes three top officials at the national level in the teacher's organization, holding them without charge for 10 days, then releasing them. Local leaders have not been bothered.

Hypothetical B.

(1) Noncitizen B worked a two-acre farm in Montana province in Fredonia. That province has just come under the control of a local militia chief who has a reputation for ruling with an iron hand.

(2) Same facts, but now B adds that the bodies of two activists were found, decapitated, on the main street of the province's capital city shortly before he left for the United States.

(3) Same facts, but B adds that he attended an antigovernment demonstration three years ago at which the two activists gave a speech.

(4) Same facts, but B adds that he helped organize that demonstration, although he had been inactive since then.

(5) Same facts, but B adds that he was a lower-echelon leader in the organization to which the two activists belonged.

3. PROTECTED GROUNDS

Both the 1951 Convention and the U.S. statutes make it clear that a well-founded fear of persecution is not sufficient to trigger protection. Rather, individuals must prove that the persecution they fear is linked—in a certain way—to one of five grounds. Or, as much of the commentary frames it, there must be a connection, or a nexus, between the persecution and race, religion, nationality, membership in a particular social group, or political opinion.

On the face of it, this seems straightforward. All who fear persecution may desire protection, but under the express language of the treaty, refugee status is reserved for a subset of the persecuted. Persecution based solely on a personal grudge or persecution solely to secure financial gain will not result in refugee status. Some of this linkage between persecution and the five grounds is implicit in the very notion of "persecution." That is, harsh sanctions do not usually amount to persecution unless they are inflicted on the basis of some characteristic that is thought not to justify such a response. A person imprisoned at hard labor after a valid conviction for armed robbery is not being persecuted.

Out of this seemingly clear-cut element of the refugee definition, however, the developing law has uncovered many complex questions. What are the outer limits of each of the five specified grounds? The statute explicitly calls for attention to these linkages, and the BIA sometimes requires close connection between the allegedly persecuting act and the precise basis or motive for the oppression before the threat can serve as a valid foundation for asylum. What if a persecutor incorrectly believes the victim to belong to a certain racial or religious or political group? Whose political opinion is relevant—the persecutor's or the victim's? What kind of connection must there be between the persecution and the ground? What if multiple factors or mixed motives are involved?

This section offers an introductory examination of these questions, which are often difficult to separate neatly. We start our study of the law concerning the grounds of persecution by exploring what it means to be persecuted based on political opinion. After political opinion, we look at cases that involve some combination of race, nationality, and religion to define groups that face persecution. Finally, we survey the jurisprudence concerning persecution based on membership in a particular social group, a legal term that has presented a welter of conceptual difficulties.

a. Political Opinion

For many years the majority of asylum cases filed in the United States appeared to rely on fears of persecution based on political opinion. Many of these cases involved "classic" political opinion claims: the asylum seeker was a recognizable political dissident, the asylum seeker had participated in political demonstrations, and so on. The unfortunate growth of armed insurrections and civil wars in the late twentieth century generated new legal challenges in the asylum system as they spawned many claims of politically motivated persecution that did not fit within this paradigm. Two topics—imputed political opinion and neutrality—presented special difficulties. Sometimes persecutors think individuals have opinions or beliefs that the individuals may not, in fact, hold. For example, government officials might view young men who evade military conscription as sympathetic to a local guerrilla movement and impute to the draft evaders the political opinions of the guerrillas. Other times, particularly in civil war situations, the contending factions do not tolerate neutrality and insist that the population choose sides; they essentially impute opposition to those who want to be left alone. Imputed political opinion and neutrality pose difficult questions individually, and they interact in complex ways. The Supreme Court addressed these and related issues in the following opinion.

INS v. ELIAS–ZACARIAS

Supreme Court of the United States, 1992.
502 U.S. 478, 112 S.Ct. 812, 117 L.Ed.2d 38.

JUSTICE SCALIA delivered the opinion of the Court.

The principal question presented by this case is whether a guerrilla organization's attempt to coerce a person into performing military service necessarily constitutes "persecution on account of . . . political opinion" under § 101(a)(42) of the Immigration and Nationality Act.

I

Respondent Elias–Zacarias, a native of Guatemala, was apprehended in July 1987 for entering the United States without inspection. In deportation proceedings brought by petitioner Immigration and Naturalization Service (INS), Elias–Zacarias conceded his deportability but requested asylum and withholding of deportation.

The Immigration Judge summarized Elias–Zacarias' testimony as follows:

> [A]round the end of January in 1987 [when Elias–Zacarias was 18], two armed, uniformed guerrillas with handkerchiefs covering part of their faces came to his home. Only he and his parents were there. . . . [T]he guerrillas asked his parents and himself to join with them, but they all refused. The guerrillas asked them why and told them that they would be back, and that they should think it over about joining them.

> [Elias–Zacarias] did not want to join the guerrillas because the guerrillas are against the government and he was afraid that the government would retaliate against him and his family if he did join the guerrillas. [H]e left Guatemala at the end of March [1987] . . . because he was afraid that the guerrillas would return.

[The Immigration Judge denied asylum and withholding of deportation. The BIA affirmed, and the Court of Appeals for the Ninth Circuit reversed the BIA.]

II

* * * The BIA's determination that Elias–Zacarias was not eligible for asylum must be upheld if "supported by reasonable, substantial, and probative evidence on the record considered as a whole." INA § 106(a)(4). It can be reversed only if the evidence presented by Elias–Zacarias was

such that a reasonable factfinder would have to conclude that the requisite fear of persecution existed.[1]

The Court of Appeals found reversal warranted. In its view, a guerrilla organization's attempt to conscript a person into its military forces necessarily constitutes "persecution on account of ... political opinion," because "the person resisting forced recruitment is expressing a political opinion hostile to the persecutor and because the persecutors' motive in carrying out the kidnapping is political." The first half of this seems to us untrue, and the second half irrelevant.

Even a person who supports a guerrilla movement might resist recruitment for a variety of reasons—fear of combat, a desire to remain with one's family and friends, a desire to earn a better living in civilian life, to mention only a few. The record in the present case not only failed to show a political motive on Elias–Zacarias' part; it showed the opposite. He testified that he refused to join the guerrillas because he was afraid that the government would retaliate against him and his family if he did so. Nor is there any indication (assuming, *arguendo*, it would suffice) that the guerrillas erroneously *believed* that Elias–Zacarias' refusal was politically based.

As for the Court of Appeals' conclusion that the guerrillas' "motive in carrying out the kidnaping is political": It apparently meant by this that the guerrillas seek to fill their ranks in order to carry on their war against the government and pursue their political goals. But that does not render the forced recruitment "persecution on account of ... political opinion." * * * The ordinary meaning of the phrase "persecution on account of ... political opinion" in § 101(a)(42) is persecution on account of the victim's political opinion, not the persecutor's. If a Nazi regime persecutes Jews, it is not, within the ordinary meaning of language, engaging in persecution on account of political opinion; and if a fundamentalist Moslem regime persecutes democrats, it is not engaging in persecution on account of religion. Thus, the mere existence of a generalized "political" motive underlying the guerrillas' forced recruitment is inadequate to establish (and, indeed, goes far to refute) the proposition that Elias–Zacarias fears persecution on account of political opinion, as § 101(a)(42) requires.

Elias–Zacarias appears to argue that not taking sides with any political faction is itself the affirmative expression of a political opinion. That seems to us not ordinarily so, since we do not agree with the dissent that only a "narrow, grudging construction of the concept of 'political opinion'" would distinguish it from such quite different concepts as indifference, indecisiveness and risk-averseness. But we need not decide whether the evidence compels the conclusion that Elias–Zacarias held a political

---

1. Quite beside the point, therefore, is the dissent's assertion that "the record in this case is more than adequate to *support the conclusion* that this respondent's refusal [to join the guerrillas] was a form of expressive conduct that constituted the statement of a 'political opinion,'" (emphasis added). To reverse the BIA finding we must find that the evidence not only supports that conclusion, but *compels* it—and also compels the further conclusion that Elias–Zacarias had a well-founded fear that the guerrillas would persecute him *because of* that political opinion.

opinion. Even if it does, Elias–Zacarias still has to establish that the record also compels the conclusion that he has a "well-founded fear" that the guerrillas will persecute him because of that political opinion, rather than because of his refusal to fight with them. He has not done so with the degree of clarity necessary to permit reversal of a BIA finding to the contrary; indeed, he has not done so at all.[2]

Elias–Zacarias objects that he cannot be expected to provide direct proof of his persecutors' motives. We do not require that. But since the statute makes motive critical, he must provide some evidence of it, direct or circumstantial. And if he seeks to obtain judicial reversal of the BIA's determination, he must show that the evidence he presented was so compelling that no reasonable factfinder could fail to find the requisite fear of persecution. That he has not done.

The BIA's determination should therefore have been upheld in all respects, and we reverse the Court of Appeals' judgment to the contrary.

It is so ordered.

JUSTICE STEVENS, with whom JUSTICE BLACKMUN and JUSTICE O'CONNOR join, dissenting.

Respondent refused to join a guerrilla organization that engaged in forced recruitment in Guatemala. He fled the country because he was afraid the guerrillas would return and "take me and kill me." After his departure, armed guerrillas visited his family on two occasions searching for him. In testimony that the hearing officer credited, he stated that he is still afraid to return to Guatemala because "these people" can come back to "take me or kill me."

It is undisputed that respondent has a well-founded fear that he will be harmed, if not killed, if he returns to Guatemala. It is also undisputed that the cause of that harm, if it should occur, is the guerrilla organization's displeasure with his refusal to join them in their armed insurrection against the government. The question of law that the case presents is whether respondent's well-founded fear is a "fear of persecution on account of ... political opinion" within the meaning of § 101(a)(42) of the Immigration and Naturalization Act.

* * *

---

2. The dissent misdescribes the record on this point in several respects. For example, it exaggerates the "well-foundedness" of whatever fear Elias–Zacarias possesses, by progressively transforming his testimony that he was afraid the guerrillas would " 'take me or kill me,' " into, first, "the guerrillas' *implied threat* to 'take' him or to 'kill' him," (emphasis added), and, then, into the flat assertion that the guerrillas "*responded by threatening* to 'take' or to 'kill' him" (emphasis added). The dissent also erroneously describes it as "undisputed" that the cause of the harm Elias–Zacarias fears, if that harm should occur, will be "the guerrilla organization's displeasure with his refusal to join them in their armed insurrection against the government." The record shows no such concession by the INS, and all Elias–Zacarias said on the point was that he feared being taken or killed by the guerrillas. It is quite plausible, indeed likely, that the taking would be engaged in by the guerrillas in order to augment their troops rather than show their displeasure; and the killing he feared might well be a killing in the course of resisting being taken.

Today the Court holds that respondent's fear of persecution is not "on account of ... political opinion" for two reasons. First, he failed to prove that his refusal to join the guerrillas was politically motivated; indeed, he testified that he was at least in part motivated by a fear that government forces would retaliate against him or his family if he joined the guerrillas. Second, he failed to prove that his persecutors' motives were political. In particular, the Court holds that the persecutors' implicit threat to retaliate against respondent "because of his refusal to fight with them," is not persecution on account of political opinion. I disagree with both parts of the Court's reasoning.

I

A political opinion can be expressed negatively as well as affirmatively. A refusal to support a cause—by staying home on election day, by refusing to take an oath of allegiance, or by refusing to step forward at an induction center—can express a political opinion as effectively as an affirmative statement or affirmative conduct. Even if the refusal is motivated by nothing more than a simple desire to continue living an ordinary life with one's family, it is the kind of political expression that the asylum provisions of the statute were intended to protect.

As the Court of Appeals explained in *Bolanos–Hernandez v. INS*, 767 F.2d 1277 (9th Cir. 1985):

> Choosing to remain neutral is no less a political decision than is choosing to affiliate with a particular political faction. * * *

Id. at 1286.

The narrow, grudging construction of the concept of "political opinion" that the Court adopts today is inconsistent with the basic approach to this statute that the Court endorsed in *INS v. Cardoza–Fonseca*. In that case, relying heavily on the fact that an alien's status as a "refugee" merely makes him eligible for a discretionary grant of asylum—as contrasted with the entitlement to a withholding of deportation * * *—the Court held that the alien's burden of proving a well-founded fear of persecution did not require proof that persecution was more likely than not to occur. * * *

Similar reasoning should resolve any doubts concerning the political character of an alien's refusal to take arms against a legitimate government in favor of the alien. In my opinion, the record in this case is more than adequate to support the conclusion that this respondent's refusal was a form of expressive conduct that constituted the statement of a "political opinion" within the meaning of § 208(a).[5]

---

5. Here, respondent not only engaged in expressive conduct by refusing to join the guerrilla organization but also explained that he did so "[b]ecause they see very well, that if you join the guerrillas ... then you are against the government. You are against the government and if you join them then it is to die there. And, then the government is against you and against your family." Respondent thus expressed the political view that he was for the government and against the guerrillas. The statute speaks simply in terms of a political opinion and does not require that the view be well developed or elegantly expressed.

II

It follows as night follows day that the guerrillas' implied threat to "take" him or to "kill" him if he did not change his position constituted threatened persecution "on account of" that political opinion. As the Court of Appeals explained in *Bolanos–Hernandez, supra*:

> It does not matter to the persecutors what the individual's motivation is. The guerrillas in El Salvador do not inquire into the reasoning process of those who insist on remaining neutral and refuse to join their cause. They are concerned only with an act that constitutes an overt manifestation of a political opinion. Persecution because of that overt manifestation is persecution because of a political opinion.

It is important to emphasize that the statute does not require that an applicant for asylum prove exactly why his persecutors would act against him; it only requires him to show that he has a "well-founded fear of persecution on account of . . . political opinion." As we recognized in *INS v. Cardoza Fonseca*, the applicant meets this burden if he shows that there is a " 'reasonable possibility' " that he will be persecuted on account of his political opinion (quoting *INS v. Stevic*). Because respondent expressed a political opinion by refusing to join the guerrillas, and they responded by threatening to "take" or to "kill" him if he did not change his mind, his fear that the guerrillas will persecute him on account of his political opinion is well founded.[7]

Accordingly, I would affirm the judgment of the Court of Appeals.

NOTES AND QUESTIONS ON IMPUTED POLITICAL OPINION

1. The doctrine of imputed political opinion seemed at risk after *Elias–Zacarias*, but INS General Counsel Grover Joseph Rees issued a lengthy opinion in 1993 concluding that this doctrine was still viable. 70 Interp. Rel. 498 (1993). The BIA agreed, *see, e.g., In re T–M–B–*, 21 I & N Dec. 775 (1997), as do the courts, *see, e.g., Zhou v. Gonzales*, 437 F.3d 860, 868–70 (9th Cir. 2006); *Najjar v. Ashcroft*, 257 F.3d 1262, 1289 (11th Cir. 2001).

2. In *Mirisawo v. Holder*, 599 F.3d 391 (4th Cir. 2010), pp. 827–832, *supra*, the asylum applicant contended that the Zimbabwean government would impute membership in a political organization to her because her brother and sister were members and because her neighborhood was known to be home to many supporters of the organization. Are these facts a more compelling depiction of imputed political opinion than those put forth by *Elias Zacarias*? Is it relevant that the Zimbabwe government had often employed violence against political opponents and disrupted electoral campaigning? *See, e.g.,* Smith, *Pro–Mugabe Militias Blamed as Zimbabwe Violence Erupts*, The

---

7. In response to this dissent, the Court suggests that respondent and I have exaggerated the "well-foundedness" of his fear. The Court's legal analysis, however, would produce precisely the same result no matter how unambiguous the guerrillas' threatened retaliation might have been. Moreover, any doubts concerning the sinister character of a suggestion to "think it over" delivered by two uniformed masked men carrying machine guns should be resolved in respondent's favor.

Guardian, Feb. 3, 2011, <http://www.guardian.co.uk/world/2011/feb/03/pro-mugabe-militias-zimbabwe-violence>.

Mixed Motives

The imputed political opinion doctrine often arises in circumstances in which the persecutor may have mixed motives. In *Matter of S–P–*, 21 I & N Dec. 486 (BIA 1996), a Tamil from Sri Lanka had been beaten and detained by the Sri Lankan Army after the soldiers raided an insurgent camp where he had been conscripted to work as a welder. The BIA stated that the government may have punished the asylum applicant as a part of its intelligence gathering, for political views imputed to him, for criminal conduct, or for a mix of these and other motives. It concluded, however, that "the applicant ha[d] produced evidence from which it is reasonable to believe that those who harmed him were in part motivated by an assumption that his political views were antithetical to those of the Government," and that this was sufficient to support a well-founded fear of future persecution. *Id.* at 496. *See* also *Gafoor v. INS*, 231 F.3d 645 (9th Cir. 2000) (reprisals against Indo–Fijian police officer for arrest of ethnic Fijian army officer based in part on race and imputed political opinion).

Controversy surrounding the proper test for asylum when a persecutor acts from mixed motives led Congress, in the REAL ID Act of 2005, Pub. L. 109–13, § 101(a), 119 Stat. 231, 303 (2005), to add the following language to the asylum statute, INA § 208(b)(1)(B)(i):

> To establish that the applicant is a refugee * * *, the applicant must establish that race, religion, nationality, membership in a particular social group, or political opinion was or will be *at least one central reason* for persecuting the applicant.

Id. (emphasis added). The BIA's first precedent decision to consider the amendment, *Matter of J–B–N– & S–M–*, 24 I & N Dec. 208 (BIA 2007), stated:

> Having considered the conference report and the language of the REAL ID Act, we find that our standard in mixed motive cases has not been radically altered by the amendments. The prior case law requiring the applicant to present direct or circumstantial evidence of a motive that is protected under the Act still stands. As had previously been the case, the protected ground cannot play a minor role in the alien's past mistreatment or fears of future mistreatment. That is, it cannot be incidental, tangential, superficial, or subordinate to another reason for harm.

Id. at 214.

As the materials in the following section emphasize, persecution often involves a mixture of grounds, as well as a mixture of motives. Before we leave this topic, though, test your understanding by applying the legal standards to the scenario below.

EXERCISE

Before coming to the United States, where he has applied for asylum, Oleg worked as a tax auditor for the government of Ruritania, part of the former Soviet Union. During an audit of the Budro Corporation, Oleg uncovered an illegal tax-evasion scheme. Oleg discovered that Budro, founded by a high-ranking government official with close ties to the former communist leaders of Ruritania during Soviet days, had evaded the payment of automobile import duties. When Oleg reported his findings to officials at Budro, they tried to bribe him to change his report. Oleg refused the bribes and referred the matter to local prosecutors.

Oleg and his wife, Nicola, soon began receiving threats. Two men forcibly removed Nicola from a bus. Three days later, she suffered a miscarriage, which she attributed to this incident. Fearing for his safety, Oleg arranged for his cousin to drive him to work. While Oleg's cousin was driving alone in his car, equipped with tinted windows, he was shot. Oleg was supposed to be in the car but had cancelled at the last minute.

After Oleg and Nicola fled Ruritania for the United States, his apartment was vandalized, and some of Nicola's relatives were hurt in a suspicious car accident that Nicola suspects was caused by Budro officials.

You are the immigration judge in Oleg's case. How would you rule on his claim that he has a well-founded fear of persecution on account of political opinion if he is returned to Ruritania?

---

b. Race, Nationality, and Religion

Although the concepts of race, nationality, and religion are familiar, the meaning of these terms in the asylum statute frequently differs from that used in general conversation. The drafters of the 1951 Convention, the model for the U.S. statute, had the suffering involved with World War II still fresh in their minds. Did they think that the Nazi persecution of the Jews was based on race? On religion? What about Nazi persecution of the Roma? Of the Poles?

The 1951 Convention did not define the term "race," and it has been used to refer to ethnic groups identifiable by their shared culture as much as by any physical distinctiveness. In the absence of a 1951 Convention definition of "race," many look to the International Convention on the Elimination of All Forms of Racial Discrimination, G.A. Res. 2106 (XX), Annex, 20 U.N. GAOR Supp. (No. 14) at 47, U.N. Doc. A/6014 (1966), 660 U.N.T.S. 195, *entered into force* Jan. 4, 1969, and its formulation that the term "race" includes "race, color, descent, or national or ethnic origin." Article 1(1).

The 1951 Convention's reference to persecution based on nationality takes a similarly comprehensive approach. Nationality is sometimes used to refer to those who have the same citizenship as the persecutors, but who belong to a different linguistic or ethnic community. For example, in Romania under Ceausescu, the millions of Romanian citizens of Hungarian lineage were often considered to possess Romanian citizenship but Hungarian nationality. The lines between race and nationality have also often been blurred. Infamous persecutions of the past led to the expulsion of thousands of Ugandan citizens of Indian origin in 1972; multitudes of Vietnamese citizens of ethnic Chinese origin fled in 1975; the Tamils in Sri Lanka, the Tutsi in Rwanda; the Bosnians in the Balkans, and the Black Fulanis of Mauritania have all felt the scourge of ethnic cleansing and persecution.

Religion, too, often enters into the mix of ethnic and political conflict. In Sri Lanka the conflict between the Tamil minority, largely Hindu, and the Sinhalese majority, largely Buddhist, has led to years of bloodshed. There have been many recent cases involving civil disturbances and attacks on groups in Indonesia that are defined by a combination of ethnicity and religion. *See, e.g., Lie v. Ashcroft*, 396 F.3d 530 (3d Cir. 2005) (attacks on ethnic Chinese Christians in Indonesia not sufficient to constitute persecution); *Eduard v. Ashcroft*, 379 F.3d 182 (5th Cir. 2004) (pattern of violence against Christians in Indonesia constituted evidence of persecution).

Although the case law analyzing persecution concerning religious beliefs and practices was relatively sparse in the first years after the Refugee Act of 1980, this has begun to change in recent years, perhaps sparked, in part, by a congressional effort to give greater visibility to those suffering religious persecution. In 1998, the International Religious Freedom Act, Pub. L. 105–292, 112 Stat. 2787 (1998), established a new State Department Office on International Religious Freedom and created a U.S. Commission on International Religious Freedom to investigate and report on religious persecution around the world. The legislation requires training for all U.S. officials involved in refugee adjudication, and requires those who decide asylum cases to refer to annual reports on international religious freedom.

Several recent cases have analyzed the impact of Chinese laws against unregistered religious activities. *See., e.g., Chen v. INS*, 359 F.3d 121 (2d Cir. 2004) (reversing denial of asylum to lay leader of Roman Catholic Church detained for raising funds and distributing literature). Other religion-based asylum claims have included challenges to clothing requirements imposed on women in some Islamic societies. *See Matter of S–A–*, 22 I & N Dec. 1328 (BIA 2000) (Moroccan father's beating and burning of his daughter for wearing improper attire constitutes persecution based on religion).

The initial Fifth Circuit decision in *Xiadong Li v. Gonzales*, 420 F.3d 500, vacated as moot, 429 F.3d 1153 (5th Cir. 2005) set off a firestorm when it affirmed a BIA ruling that a Chinese participant in an underground church was not entitled to asylum because he had been subjected to punishment for his unregistered "religious activities," not on account of his religion. The U.S. Commission on International Religious Freedom sent a letter to the Attorney General voicing its concern about this conclusion, and the Department of Homeland Security eventually filed a motion with the BIA to reopen the case so that it could withdraw its appeal of the immigration court ruling in favor of the applicant. This led the Fifth Circuit to vacate its decision as moot. 429 F.3d 1153 (5th Cir. 2005). *See* Nelson, *Shaking the Pillars: An Asylum Applicant Shakes Loose Some Unusual Relief*, 83 Interp. Rel. 1 (2006); Martin, *Major Developments in Asylum Law Over the Past Year*, 83 Interp. Rel. 1889, 1896–97 (2006).

Test your understanding of the meaning of persecution, the significance of uniform national policies, the requirements of military service, and the idea of persecution based on religion in the following exercise.

EXERCISE

Garzeh testified at his asylum hearing that he fears returning to his country of Aridonia because the government there persecutes members of his church, the Jehovah's Witnesses. Garzeh presented evidence that Jehovah's Witnesses have been denied government jobs, housing assistance, and business licenses because they refuse on religious grounds to vote or participate in national service.

Garzeh further testified that he has been a Jehovah's Witness since 1984. He stated that Jehovah's Witnesses cannot participate in national service (which in Aridonia involves military service), because they "don't intend to kill anybody because we have to love each other." According to Garzeh, Jehovah's Witnesses were denied civil service positions and travel documents because they refused to participate in national service. Garzeh also testified that the Aridonian government arrested his brother for refusing to engage in national service. After a number of severe beatings in jail, Garzeh's brother was taken to a hospital where he eventually died.

Garzeh also said that he applied to the Aridonian government for a business license, but received a letter rejecting the application:

> You have applied for a business license to open a land irrigation consulting service. We have reviewed your application and found out that you are a follower of the Jehovah's Witnesses and have not registered or participated in the national service. We are obligated to follow the guidelines given to us by the government and have denied your application for the above reasons.

> Has Garzeh met his burden of establishing a well-founded fear of persecution on account of religion?

c.   Membership in a Particular Social Group

"Membership in a particular social group" may be the most elusive of the five factors listed in the Refugee Convention and in the U.S. statute. An early decision by the Board of Immigration Appeals construed this phrase to include individuals bound together by a characteristic that is either immutable or so fundamental to their identity that they should not be required to change it. *Matter of Acosta*, 19 I & N Dec. 211 (BIA 1985). The Ninth Circuit took a sharply different approach. It initially defined this term to refer to "a collection of people closely affiliated with each other, who are actuated by some common impulse or interest[;] * * * a voluntary associational relationship * * * which imparts some common characteristic that is fundamental to their identity." *Sanchez–Trujillo v. INS*, 801 F.2d 1571, 1576–77 (9th Cir. 1986). A later Ninth Circuit opinion expanded the definition to include groups united by a voluntary association or by an immutable characteristic or one fundamental to the members' identity. *Hernandez–Montiel v. INS*, 225 F.3d 1084, 1092–93 (9th Cir. 2000).

Successful "particular social group" asylum claims have included clan membership, *Matter of H–*, 21 I & N Dec. 337 (BIA 1996), women of the Tchamba–Kunsuntu Tribe who have not been subjected to female genital mutilation (FGM) and who oppose the practice, *Matter of Kasinga*, 21 I & N Dec. 357 (BIA 1996), sexual orientation, *Matter of Toboso–Alfonso*, 20 I & N Dec. 819 (BIA 1990), and former members of the Salvadoran national police, *Matter of Fuentes*, 19 I & N Dec. 658 (BIA 1988). Many recent cases raise the issue whether individuals connected in some way with gangs (sometimes as recruits, sometimes as former gang members, sometimes as opponents of gangs) constitute a particular social group. These issues have led the BIA to emphasize the social visibility of the group, as well as to examine whether groups are amorphous or "particular." The following decision explores these concepts in the context of unwilling gang members and informants against a smuggling ring.

MATTER OF S–E–G–

Board of Immigration Appeals, 2008
24 I & N Dec. 579.

GRANT, BOARD MEMBER:

* * *

In June 2004, the [Mara Salvatrucha–13 (MS–13)] stole money from * * * two brothers, harassed and beat them for refusing to join their gang, and threatened to rape or harm the female respondent. Neither of the brothers required medical treatment as a result of the beatings, but armed

MS–13 gang members warned the respondents that the brothers must join the gang or else their bodies might end up in a dumpster or in the street someday. Fearing retaliation and believing the police would not help them, the respondents never reported the beatings and threats to the two police officers in their neighborhood. Eventually, the MS–13 warned the respondents that they had been given sufficient time to make a decision about whether to join the gang, and they advised the respondents to take the gang seriously because the threats were not a game. A few months prior to their departure from El Salvador, the respondents also learned that the MS–13 shot and killed a young boy in the neighborhood after he refused to join the gang.

The respondent's expert witness, a professor at the Central American University, * * * testified that the MS–13, which originated in Los Angeles, California, and spread to Latin America, is comprised of youth who operate mainly in urban areas and who often commit serious crimes. * * * In the professor's opinion, the [Salvadoran] police are not capable of controlling the MS–13, which acquires members, in part, through the forcible recruitment of young males who live within an MS–13 controlled zone. * * * [The professor stated that an] individual who refuses recruitment by the MS–13 would have a reasonable fear of harm in El Salvador because it is a small country, there is a constant flow of information and communication within the country, and it would be very difficult to find a place where a person could be sure of not being identified by the MS–13. * * *

The Immigration Judge * * * determined that [the respondents] testimony was credible but concluded that they had failed to establish either past persecution or a well-founded fear of future persecution on account of a protected ground. The Immigration Judge ruled that the beatings and threats against the respondents were based on the gang's desire to recruit new members and fill their ranks, rather than to punish the respondents for their membership in a particular social group or their political opinion. * * *

The Immigration Judge also determined that the respondents failed to establish that the Government of El Salvador was unable or unwilling to control the criminal gangs. * * * The Immigration Judge also denied the respondents' claims under the Convention Against Torture * * * *.

* * *

A. PARTICULAR SOCIAL GROUP

We have not previously addressed whether either of the putative social groups described by the respondents—Salvadoran youths who have resisted gang recruitment, or family members of such Salvadoran youth—constitutes a "particular social group" cognizable under section 101(a)(42) of the Act. * * *

In deciding this question, we are guided by our recent decisions holding that membership in a purported social group requires that the group have particular and well-defined boundaries, and that it possess a recognized level of social visibility. *See Matter of A—M—E—*, 24 I & N Dec. 69 (BIA 2007), *aff'd, Ucelo–Gomez v. Mukasey*, 509 F.3d 70 (2d Cir. 2007); *Matter of C–A–*, 23 I & N Dec. 951 (BIA 2006), *aff'd, Castillo–Arias v. United States AG*, 446 F.3d 1190 (11th Cir. 2006), *cert. denied sub nom. Castillo–Arias v. Gonzales*, 127 S. Ct. 977 (2007). These concepts of "particularity" and "social visibility" give greater specificity to the definition of a social group, which was first determined in *Matter of Acosta*, to be a group whose members "share a common, immutable characteristic . . . that members of the group either cannot change, or should not be required to change because it is fundamental to their individual identities or consciences."

* * *

For the reasons stated below, we find that neither of the social groups proposed by the respondents satisfies the standards of "particularity" or "social visibility" that we have recently explicated. We agree with the Immigration Judge that "youth" is not an entirely immutable characteristic but is, instead, by its very nature, a temporary state that changes over time. The mutability of age is reflected in this case by the fact that the male respondents are now 18 years old, and the female respondent is 21. Therefore, the respondents are no longer considered "children," as that term is commonly understood. In saying this, however, we acknowledge that the mutability of age is not within one's control, and that if an individual has been persecuted in the past on account of an age-described particular social group, or faces such persecution at a time when that individual's age places him within the group, a claim for asylum may still be cognizable.

Furthermore, youth who have been targeted for recruitment by, and resisted, criminal gangs may have a shared past experience, which, by definition, cannot be changed. However, this does not necessarily mean that the shared past experience suffices to define a particular social group for asylum purposes. *See Gomez v. INS*, 947 F.2d 660, 663–64 (2d Cir. 1991) (finding that a woman who had been beaten and raped by guerrillas in her youth was not, for that reason, a member of a particular social group for asylum purposes); *see also Rreshpja v. Gonzales, supra*, at 556 (stating that "a social group may not be circularly defined by the fact that it suffers persecution"); *Castellano–Chacon v. INS, supra*, at 548; *Matter of C–A–, supra*, at 958. Further, we do not find that in this case the social group can be defined exclusively by the fact that its members have been subjected to harm in the past (i.e., forced gang recruitment and any violence associated with that recruitment), although this may be a relevant factor in considering the group's visibility in society, as discussed further in section 2 below.

1. PARTICULARITY

We held in *Matter of A–M–E– & J–G–U–*, that the respondents' proposed group of "wealthy" Guatemalans was not so readily "identifiable" or sufficiently defined to meet the requirements of a *particular* social group within the meaning of the refugee definition. *See also Davila–Mejia v. Mukasey*, 531 F.3d 624 (8th Cir. 2008) (finding that a proposed group of "competing family business owners" is too "amorphous" under Board and circuit court standards to constitute a "particular" social group). The essence of the "particularity" requirement, therefore, is whether the proposed group can accurately be described in a manner sufficiently distinct that the group would be recognized, in the society in question, as a discrete class of persons. While the size of the proposed group may be an important factor in determining whether the group can be so recognized, the key question is whether the proposed description is sufficiently "particular," or is "too amorphous ... to create a benchmark for determining group membership." *Davila–Mejia v. Mukasey, supra*, 531 F.3d 624, (citing *Matter of A–M–E– & J–G–U–, supra*, at 76). Under these standards, the respondents' proposed groups fail the particularity requirement of the refugee definition.

The male respondents attempt to limit or define their proposed group by claiming that it is comprised of male children who lack stable families and meaningful adult protection, who are from middle and low income classes, who live in the territories controlled by the MS–13 gang, and who refuse recruitment. However, these characteristics remain amorphous because "people's ideas of what those terms mean can vary." *Davila–Mejia v. Mukasey, supra*, 531 F.3d 624. Moreover, there is no evidence in the record to show that gang members limit recruitment efforts to male children who fit the above description, or do so in order to punish them for these characteristics, although these factors perhaps make the potential recruit an easier and more desirable target.

The female respondent contends that she belongs to a social group that includes "family members" of Salvadoran youth who have been subjected to recruitment efforts by MS–13 and who have rejected or resisted membership in the gang. The proposed group of "family members," which could include fathers, mothers, siblings, uncles, aunts, nieces, nephews, grandparents, cousins, and others, is also too amorphous a category.

Our conclusion is supported by the holdings of the circuit courts in analogous cases. The Second Circuit in *Ucelo–Gomez v. Mukasey, supra*, affirmed our findings that "wealth" and "affluence" are too subjective to serve as boundaries of a cognizable social group. As the court stated, "If 'wealth' defined the boundaries of a particular social group, a determination about whether any petitioner fit into the group (or might be perceived as a member of the group) would necessitate a sociological analysis as to how persons with various assets would have been viewed by others in their country.... Moreover, because money attracts thieves ... and more money attracts more and better thieves, it would be impractical for [Immigration Judges] to distinguish between petitioners who are targeted or held to ransom because of their class status or merely because that's where the money is." *Id.* at 73.

For similar reasons, the purported social groups in this case lack particularity. They make up a potentially large and diffuse segment of society, and the motivation of gang members in recruiting and targeting young males could arise from motivations quite apart from any perception that the males in question were members of a class. Similarly, in *Castillo–Arias v. United States Attorney General, supra*, at 1198, the Eleventh Circuit affirmed our finding that noncriminal informants working against a Colombian drug cartel did not constitute a particular social group, in part because the proposed group was potentially too numerous or inchoate.

The Eighth Circuit's decision in *Hassan v. Gonzales, supra*, is distinguishable because, while recognizing a social group that in other contexts might be considered broad and diffuse, and certainly is large, the defining characteristics of the group—being female and subject to FGM [female genital mutilation]—are sufficiently distinct in the context of Somali culture to meet the requirement of particularity. This case is far more analogous to the Ninth Circuit's decision in *Ochoa v. Gonzales*, 406 F.3d 1166 (9th Cir. 2005), which rejected the claim that Colombian business owners who refused demands from narcotics traffickers are a particular social group. Like the purported social group in *Ochoa*, the groups asserted here are too broad to qualify because "[t]here is no unifying relationship or characteristic to narrow this diverse and disconnected group." *Id.* at 1171.

2. SOCIAL VISIBILITY

We recently reaffirmed the importance of social visibility as a factor in the particular social group determination in *Matter of A–M–E– & J–G–U–, supra* (holding that "affluent Guatemalans" did not have sufficient social visibility to be perceived as a group by society), and *Matter of C–A–, supra* (holding that "noncriminal informants working against the Cali drug cartel" in Colombia were not a particular social group and addressing the importance of the social visibility of the claimed social group). n3 In reaffirming the requirement that the shared characteristic of the group should generally be recognizable by others in the community, we relied, in part, on the Second Circuit's view that " 'the attributes of a particular social group must be recognizable and discrete.' " *Matter of C–A–, supra*, at 956 (quoting *Gomez v. INS, supra*, at 664). In addition, we referred to the 2002 guidelines of the United Nations High Commissioner for Refugees, which endorse an approach in which an important factor is whether the members of the group are " 'perceived as a group by society.' " *Matter of C–A–, supra*, at 956 (quoting UNHCR, Guidelines on International Protection: "Membership of a particular social group" within the context of Article 1A(2) of the 1951 Convention and/or its 1967 Protocol relating to the Status of Refugees, U.N. Doc. HCR/GIP/02/02, P 11 (May 7, 2002)).

The question whether a proposed group has a shared characteristic with the requisite "social visibility" must be considered in the context of the country of concern and the persecution feared. *Matter of A–M–E– & J–*

G–U–, supra, at 74. The respondents in this case are victims of harassment, beatings, and threats from a criminal gang in El Salvador. There is little in the background evidence of record to indicate that Salvadoran youth who are recruited by gangs but refuse to join (or their family members) would be "perceived as a group" by society, or that these individuals suffer from a higher incidence of crime than the rest of the population.

The respondents assert that they have a specific reason (i.e., their refusal to join the gang) to fear that the MS–13 would subject them to more violence than the general population. We do not doubt, as the respondents' expert witness testified, that gangs such as the MS–13 retaliate against those who refuse to join their ranks. However, such gangs have directed harm against anyone and everyone perceived to have interfered with, or who might present a threat to, their criminal enterprises and territorial power. The respondents are therefore not in a substantially different situation from anyone who has crossed the gang, or who is perceived to be a threat to the gang's interests. *See Matter of C–A–, supra*, at 960.

* * * [G]ang violence and crime in El Salvador appear to be widespread, and the risk of harm is not limited to young males who have resisted recruitment, or their family members, but affects all segments of the population. * * *

While the respondents present sympathetic personal circumstances, victims of gang violence come from all segments of society, and it is difficult to conclude that any "group," as actually perceived by the criminal gangs, is much narrower than the general population of El Salvador. The respondents have provided no persuasive evidence, and we have no reason to believe, that the general societal perception would be otherwise. Accordingly, we conclude that the proposed group, which consists of young Salvadorans who have been subject to recruitment efforts by criminal gangs, but who have refused to join for personal, religious, or moral reasons, fails the "social visibility" test and does not qualify as a particular social group. The family members of such Salvadoran youth also do not constitute a particular social group.

* * *

The Social Visibility Test

Several federal appellate courts have adopted a "social visibility" requirement. *See, e.g., Ramos–Lopez v. Holder*, 563 F.3d 855, 859–61 (9th Cir. 2009) (Honduran men resisting gang recruitment); *Scatambuli v. Holder*, 558 F.3d 53, 58 (1st Cir. 2009) (drug informants); *Davila–Mejia v. Mukasey*, 531 F.3d 624, 628–29 (8th Cir. 2008) (competing family business owners). However, Judge Posner, writing for the Seventh Circuit, took forceful exception to this limitation on the definition of a particular social group in a case involving the Mungiki, a Kenyan group known to punish defectors severely. In response to one such defection, the group broke into the defector's house, killed a servant and the family pets, burned two cars, and kidnapped and tortured the defector. His asylum claim was rejected on the grounds that Mungiki defectors do not constitute a "particular social group."

* * *

The immigration statute does not define "particular social group," but the Board has defined it as a group whose members share "common characteristics that members of the group either cannot change, or should not be required to change because such characteristics are fundamental to their individual identities." *Sepulveda v. Gonzales,* 464 F.3d 770, 771–72 (7th Cir.2006) gives examples of qualifying groups: "the educated, landowning class of cattle farmers targeted by Colombian rebels, Christian women in Iran who oppose the Islamic dress code for women, parents of Burmese student dissidents, and children who escaped after being enslaved from Ugandan guerillas who had enslaved them." *Sepulveda* holds that former subordinates of the attorney general of Colombia who had information about the insurgents plaguing that nation were also a "particular social group." They had been targeted for assassination by the insurgents, and many had been assassinated. While an employee could resign from the attorney general's office, he could not resign from a group defined as former employees of the office; once a former employee, always a *former* employee (unless one is reemployed by one's former employer).

We cannot see how this case can be distinguished from *Sepulveda,* which the Board did not cite. Instead the Board cited cases which hold that a group must have "social visibility" to be a "particular social group," meaning that "members of a society perceive those with the characteristic in question as members of a social group." The Board said there was no evidence that Gatimi "possesses any characteristics that would cause others in Kenyan society to recognize him as a former member of Mungiki.... There is no showing that membership in a larger body of persons resistant to Mungiki is of concern to anyone in Kenya or that such individuals are seen as a segment of the population in any meaningful respect."

This formula cannot be squared with *Sepulveda.* More important, it makes no sense; nor has the Board attempted, in this or any other case, to explain the reasoning behind the criterion of social visibility. Women who have not yet undergone female genital mutilation in tribes that practice it do not look different from anyone else. A homosexual in a homophobic society will pass as heterosexual. If you are a member of a group that has been targeted for assassination or torture or some other mode of persecution, you will take pains to avoid being socially visible; and to the extent that the members of the target group are successful in remaining invisible, they will not be "seen" by other people in the society "as a segment of the population." Those former employees of the Colombian attorney general tried hard, one can be sure, to become invisible and, so far as appears, were unknown to Colombian society as a whole.

* * *

The Board has a legitimate interest in resisting efforts to classify people who are targets of persecution as members of a particular social group when they have little or nothing in common beyond being targets. * * * But like the lawyers in the *Sepulveda* case, the defectors from the Mungiki constitute a group with as much coherence as children of the bourgeoisie, or of the aristocracy, had in the Soviet Union: breakaway factions that were relentlessly persecuted.

Gatimi v. Holder, 578 F.3d 611, 614–615, 616 (7th Cir. 2009).

NOTES AND QUESTIONS ON PARTICULAR SOCIAL GROUP

1. *Matter of Acosta*, 19 I & N Dec. 211 (BIA 1985), quoted in *Matter of S–E–G–*, construed a "particular social group" to include individuals bound together by a characteristic that is either immutable or so fundamental to their identity that they should not be required to change it. Acosta himself was a taxi driver who helped to form a taxi cooperative that defied calls for a general strike; he received death threats afterwards. The Board rejected Acosta's assertion that members of this taxi cooperative constituted a social group, saying that driving a taxi was neither immutable nor a matter of conscience that individuals should not be forced to change. The Board also rejected Acosta's claim that the death threats were on account of his political opinion. Is the social group proffered in *Matter of S–E–G–* a stronger or weaker claim than the *Acosta* taxi drivers?

2. In *S–E–G–* the BIA rejected the proposed social group composed of urban young men who refused the MS–13 recruitment efforts, because it was too amorphous and lacked social visibility. What about the converse: is a gang itself a particular social group? Gang members often can be identified by their tattoos, the color of their clothes, or other insignia. In *Arteaga v. Mukasey*, 511 F.3d 940 (9th Cir. 2007), the court affirmed a BIA conclusion that membership in a criminal gang cannot constitute membership in a particular social group. Is that outcome consistent with *S–E–G–*? Gangs, typically, are groups that have high social visibility and consist of a defined membership. On the other hand, the treatment that gangs receive may be prosecution, not persecution, or gang members may be ineligible for asylum because they have committed criminal offenses.

Is gang membership a changeable characteristic, as that concept is described in *Matter of Acosta*? Could such membership be fundamental to identity? Even if it is, would it be permissible for U.S. law to insist that it be changed? In any event, do *former* gang members have an immutable characteristic? *See Ramos v. Holder*, 589 F.3d 426 (7th Cir. 2009) (former members of Mara Salvatrucha may constitute a particular social group).

3. Would Judge Posner agree or disagree with the following perspective offered by Alex Aleinikoff, who argues that the *Acosta* view on defining a "particular social group," sometimes known as the "protected characteristics" approach, can fit comfortably within a broader "social perception" approach:

> * * * What constitutes a particular social group is "a common attribute and a societal perception that they stand apart". The attribute must not only be shared, it must unite the group as a matter of self-perception or societal perception. That is to say, the shared characteristic must make "those who share it a cognisable group within their society".
> * * *

* * *

> * * * The social perception analysis would appear to encompass the groups currently recognized under the protected characteristics approach. This is primarily due to the fact that groups recognized under the protected characteristics analysis are likely to be perceived as social groups. Why is this the case? It is so because persons in groups that are the subject of persecutory, discriminatory treatment will avoid the shared characteristic that defines the group if they are able to; but groups defined by immutable characteristics cannot do so, and groups defined by characteristics fundamental to human dignity often choose not to do so, nor should they be required to do so. Thus, such groups are likely to maintain their membership despite unfavorable treatment, and generally will be perceived as social groups—defined by the characteristic for which the abuse is imposed.* * *

> While most "protected characteristics" groups are likely to be perceived as social groups, there may also be social groups perceived as such that are not based on protected characteristics. A social perception approach, therefore, moves beyond protected characteristics by recognizing that external factors can be important to a proper social group definition. Asking whether a group has been "marked as other" is not to collapse the social group and persecution issues, but rather to examine whether the group is a cognizable group in a particular cultural context.* * *

Aleinikoff, *Protected Characteristics and Social Perceptions: An Analysis of the Meaning of "Membership of a Particular Social Group"*, in Refugee Protection in International Law 263, 296–98. (E. Feller, V. Türk, & F. Nicholson eds., 2003).

4. Subsequent to the *S–E–G–* decision, DHS joined in a motion to reopen the case to allow the three young respondents in *S–E–G–* to apply for protection under the Wilberforce Trafficking Victims Protection Act (TVPRA), Pub.L. 110–457, reauthorization signed Dec. 23, 2008, another avenue for humanitarian protection for unaccompanied minors. INA § 208(b)(3)(C). The BIA granted the parties' joint motion to reopen and remand so the immigration judge could administratively close the proceedings. BIA, July 28, 2009,

<http://www.immigrantlawcentermn.org/litigation/SEG_Joint_Reopening _Documents.pdf>.

4. DISCRETION TO GRANT OR DENY PROTECTION

Thus far we have been exploring the elements of the refugee definition. Under both international and U.S. law, refugees are those who fear persecution, whose fear is well-founded, and whose threatened persecution is on account of one of the five protected grounds. Qualifying as a refugee is necessary, but not sufficient. The U.S. asylum statute provides that refugees are eligible for asylum, but the Secretary of Homeland Security and the Attorney General have discretion to decide which refugees receive asylum status. INA § 208(b)(1)(A). (As mentioned above, withholding of removal is not discretionary, but it is country-specific and entails fewer rights than asylum. This distinction in discretionary authority over asylum versus withholding is consistent with the 1951 Convention.) The Supreme Court emphasized the discretionary nature of asylum in *Cardoza–Fonseca, supra*. Subsequently, the BIA addressed factors that might warrant either a positive or negative exercise of discretion.

> * * * [T]he totality of the circumstances and actions of an alien in his flight from the country where he fears persecution should be examined in determining whether a favorable exercise of discretion is warranted. Among those factors which should be considered are whether the alien passed through any other countries or arrived in the United States directly from his country, whether orderly refugee procedures were in fact available to help him in any country he passed through, and whether he made any attempts to seek asylum before coming to the United States. In addition, the length of time the alien remained in a third country, and his living conditions, safety, and potential for long-term residency there are also relevant. For example, an alien who is forced to remain in hiding to elude persecutors, or who faces imminent deportation back to the country where he fears persecution, may not have found a safe haven even though he has escaped to another country. Further, whether the alien has relatives legally in the United States or other personal ties to this country which motivated him to seek asylum here rather than elsewhere is another factor to consider. In this regard, the extent of the alien's ties to any other countries where he does not fear persecution should also be examined. Moreover, if the alien engaged in fraud to circumvent orderly refugee procedures, the seriousness of the fraud should be considered. The use of fraudulent documents to escape the country of persecution itself is not a significant adverse factor while, at the other extreme, entry under the assumed identity of a United States citizen with a United States passport, which was fraudulently obtained by the alien from the United States Government, is very serious fraud.

In addition to the circumstances and actions of the alien in his flight from the country where he fears persecution, general humanitarian considerations, such as an alien's tender age or poor health, may also be relevant in a discretionary determination. A situation of particular concern involves an alien who has established his statutory eligibility for asylum but cannot meet the higher burden required for withholding of deportation. Deportation to a country where the alien may be persecuted thus becomes a strong possibility. In such a case, the discretionary factors should be carefully evaluated in light of the unusually harsh consequences which may befall an alien who has established a well-founded fear of persecution; the danger of persecution should generally outweigh all but the most egregious of adverse factors.

Matter of Pula, 19 I & N Dec. 467, 473–74 (BIA 1987).

Later, in *Matter of Kasinga,* 21 I & N Dec. 357, 367 (BIA 1996), the BIA noted that an asylum applicant bears the burden of proving that a favorable exercise of discretion is warranted, but stated that "[t]the danger of persecution will outweigh all but the most egregious adverse factors."

Despite the relatively routine practice, under *Pula* and *Kasinga,* of exercising discretion in favor of granting asylum when the applicant proves a well-founded fear of persecution, there have been a few notable cases in which discretion has been used to deny asylum. One such instance involved a leader in the Islamic Salvation Front (FIS) of Algeria. The FIS had ties to an armed group in Algeria that the U.S. Secretary of State had designated a "foreign terrorist organization." Attorney General Ashcroft personally took referral of the case from the BIA and ruled that asylum should be denied in the exercise of discretion.

I conclude that, taken together, the circumstances concerning respondent's links to the activities of the armed Islamist groups in Algeria, as outlined above, strongly weigh against a discretionary grant of asylum in this case, whether or not respondent has a well-founded fear of persecution if returned to Algeria. The United States has significant interests in combating violent acts of persecution and terrorism wherever they may occur, including in Algeria, and it is inconsistent with these interests to provide safe haven to individuals who have connections to such acts of violence. It is also in the national interest of the United States for Algeria to achieve a peaceful and stable resolution to the conflicts that have plagued that nation.

Moreover, certain additional factors weigh against asylum for respondent: Specifically, respondent testified that he received money from overseas for his political work, yet he never filed income tax returns in the United States and his children nevertheless received financial assistance from the Commonwealth of Virginia. Respondent's apparent tax violations and his abuse of a system designed to provide relief to the needy exhibit both a disrespect for the rule of law and a willingness to gain advantage at the expense of those who are more deserving. Although there are equities that weigh in respondent's favor—for example, his wife and children reside legally in the United States and three of his children are United States citizens— these equities do not outweigh the negative factors I have identified. My view, based on a thorough review of the record and considering the balance of factors discussed above, is that respondent is not entitled to become a lawful permanent resident of the United States. Therefore, I deny respondent's application for asylum in the exercise of my discretion.

Matter of A–H–, 23 I & N Dec. 774, 782–83 (AG 2005).

The Attorney General then remanded the case to the BIA to consider whether the applicant was eligible for withholding of removal or protection under the Convention Against Torture.

NOTES AND QUESTIONS ON DISCRETION AND ASYLUM

1. *Matter of A–H–* was a rare instance of a "referral" from the BIA to the Attorney General. As described in Chapter Four, regulations provide specific circumstances in which the Attorney General may personally review a BIA decision. 8 C.F.R. § 1003.1(h). Consider why Attorney General Ashcroft may have wished to use the referral procedure in this case.

2. Over the years, Congress has modified the statutory grounds for asylum, and in doing so has converted factors that formerly were matters to be taken into account in the exercise of discretion into factors that result in a mandatory denial of asylum. These factors include firm resettlement in another country and a growing list of criminal convictions. Congress has also imposed a one-year deadline for asylum applications. Although the one-year deadline does not apply to withholding, late-filers, who are excluded from asylum by the deadline, face the added barrier of a higher threat standard: they can win protection only if they show that persecution is more likely than not. We will consider the one-year deadline and mandatory bars to protection more thoroughly in Section E of this chapter.

3. Most of the attention regarding the role of discretion in asylum cases arises in circumstances when asylum applicants have established that they have a well-founded fear of persecution in the future, but they have engaged in other conduct that this country is likely to view as objectionable. Discretion to grant asylum also plays a significant role when eligibility for protection is based on a showing of past persecution and the applicant is not able to prove future persecution. See pp. 841–842, *supra.*

4. Congress wished to protect the exercise of discretion by the Secretary of Homeland Security and the Attorney General when it acted in 1996 to bar the courts from reviewing immigration decisions that are statutorily entrusted to the discretion of these officials. Congress stated, however, that judicial review remains available for discretionary asylum decisions. INA § 242(a)(2)(B)(ii). Congress went on to specify the following standard of review in such cases: "the * * * discretionary judgment whether to grant

relief under section 208(a) shall be conclusive unless manifestly contrary to the law and an abuse of discretion." *Id.* § 242(b)(4)(D). See Chapter Ten for a further discussion of judicial review.

5. GENDER–RELATED CLAIMS

Recent years have brought increasing attention to the impact of gender on refugee and asylum issues. Neither the 1951 Convention nor the U.S. statute specifies sex or gender as one of the grounds of persecution that trigger international protection, an omission that has been criticized. Others, however, such as Rodger Haines, a longtime member of the New Zealand Refugee Status Appeals Authority and renowned refugee law scholar, assert that there is no need for an express reference to sex or gender; they argue that, so long as the Convention is interpreted without discrimination against women, the refugee definition provides ample protection:

> The failure of decision makers to recognize and respond appropriately to the experiences of women stems not from the fact that the 1951 Convention does not refer specifically to persecution on the basis of sex or gender, but rather because it has often been approached from a partial perspective and interpreted through a framework of male experiences. The main problem facing women as asylum seekers is the failure of decision makers to incorporate the gender-related claims of women into their interpretation of the existing enumerated grounds and their failure to recognize the political nature of seemingly private acts of harm to women.

Haines, *Gender-related Persecution*, in Refugee Protection in International Law 319, 327 (E. Feller, V. Türk, & F. Nicholson eds., 2003).

Because states are unlikely to modify the 1951 Convention to add an additional ground, the reality is that courts and agencies will grapple with gender issues within the framework of the current specified grounds of persecution: race, religion, nationality, membership in a particular social group, and political opinion.

Most, though not all, of the gender issues that arise in refugee and asylum claims concern women. This is not surprising for two reasons. First, according to the UNHCR, women and children comprise more than 80 percent of the world-wide refugee population. Second, in many societies women are vulnerable, which makes them easy targets for persecution and other harm and also makes their difficulties easy for societies and governments to overlook. In contrast to the refugee population in general, asylum seekers, those who manage to travel to developed countries where they seek lawful residence, are predominantly male. As a consequence, asylum procedures have sometimes developed in ways that implicitly respond to experiences more common to men. This has led to calls for more awareness on the part of asylum adjudicators to the impact gender may have. On the other hand, there are some indications that women may not be disadvantaged in the asylum process. Thomas Spijkerboer's analysis of data concerning the approval rates of asylum applications in the Netherlands and Canada shows that in some respects women do better than men in the asylum application process. See T. Spijkerboer, Gender and Refugee Status 15–43 (2000).

The materials in this section highlight some of the situations in which decisionmakers and advocates have begun to address the role of gender in asylum cases. (Gender in this context refers to social roles assigned to men and women, whereas sex refers to biological differences. See H. Crawley, Refugees and Gender: Law and Process (2001).) Gender-related cases raise many complex legal issues, some of which we have touched upon in earlier discussions. For example, do women, or certain subsets of women, constitute a particular social group? Under what circumstances does harm inflicted by private individuals—nongovernmental actors—count as "persecution" within the meaning of asylum law? What kinds of imputed political opinions arise in cases involving gender roles? These issues, in turn, raise challenges in demonstrating that the persecution is "on account of" one of the five enumerated grounds. We will examine these issues in the context of asylum claims filed in three intensely litigated contexts: resistance to social norms regarding clothing, female genital mutilation, and domestic violence.

a.   Resistance to Social Norms

FATIN v. INS

United States Court of Appeals, Third Circuit, 1993.
12 F.3d 1233.

ALITO, CIRCUIT JUDGE.

* * *

The petitioner is a native and citizen of Iran. On December 31, 1978, approximately two weeks before the Shah left Iran, the petitioner entered the United States as a nonimmigrant student. She was then 18 years old. She attended high school in Philadelphia through May 1979, and the following September she enrolled in Spring Garden College, also in Philadelphia.

In May 1984, apparently while still attending college, she applied * * * for political asylum * * *. In response to question 31 on [the asylum application] form, which asked what she thought would happen to her if she returned to Iran, she wrote: "I would be interrogated, and I would be forced to attend religious sessions against my will, and I would be publicly admonished and even jailed." In answer to question 34, which asked about any organization in Iran to which she or any immediate family member had ever belonged, she wrote:

> I personally belonged to a student group that favored the Shah. We refused to demonstrate with the students who favored Khomeni. I

refused to wear a veil which was a sign or badge that I favor Khomeni. My cousin ... is now a refugee living in Paris France. He was formerly one of the guards for the Shah.

* * *

[In 1987, in proceedings before the immigration judge, she] reiterated and expanded upon the statements in her initial asylum application concerning the treatment of her relatives in Iran, adding that one of her cousins had subsequently been killed in a demonstration and that her brother was in hiding in order to avoid the draft. She also elaborated upon her political activities prior to coming to the United States, stating that she had been involved with a student political group and with a women's rights group associated with the Shah's sister.

When her attorney asked her why she feared going back to Iran, she responded: "Because of the government that is ruling the country. It is a strange government to me. It has different rules and regulation[s] th[a]n I have been used to." She stated that "anybody who [had] been a Moslem" was required "to practice that religion" or "be punished in public or be jailed," and she added that she had been "raised in a way that you don't have to practice if you don't want to." She subsequently stated that she would be required "to do things that [she] never had to do," such as wear a veil. When asked by her attorney whether she would wear a veil, she replied:

> A.   I would have to, sir.
>
> Q.   And if you didn't?
>
> A.   I would be jailed or punished in public. Public mean by whipped or thrown stones and I would be going back to barbaric years.

Later, when the immigration judge asked her whether she would wear a veil or submit to arrest and punishment, she stated:

> If I go back, I would try personally to avoid it as much as I could do. . . . I will start trying to avoid it as much as I could.

The petitioner also testified that she considered herself a "feminist" and explained:

> As a feminist I mean that I believe in equal rights for women. I believe a woman as a human being can do and should be able to do what they want to do. And over there in ... Iran at the time being a woman is a second class citizen, doesn't have any right to herself. . . .

After the hearing, the immigration judge denied the petitioner's applications for withholding of deportation, asylum, and suspension of deportation. * * *

Petitioner then appealed to the Board of Immigration Appeals. In her brief, she argued that she feared persecution "on account of her membership of a particular social group, and on the basis of her political opinion." Her brief identified her "particular social group" as "the social group of the upper class of Iranian women who supported the Shah of Iran, a group of educated Westernized free-thinking individuals." Her brief also stated that she had a "deep[ly] rooted belief in feminism" and in "equal rights for women, and the right to free choice of any expression and development of abilities, in the fields of education, work, home and family, and all other arenas of development." In addition, her brief observed that she would be forced upon return to Iran "to practice the Moslem religion." Her brief stated that "she would try to avoid practicing a religion as much as she could." Her brief added that she had "the personal desire to avoid as much practice as she could," but that she feared that "through religious ignorance and inexperience she would be unable to play the role of a religious Shi'ite woman." Her brief contained one passage concerning the requirement that women in Iran wear a veil in public:

> In April 1983, the government adopted a law imposing one year's imprisonment on any women caught in public without the traditional Islamic veil, the Chador. However, from reports, it is clear that in many instances the revolutionary guards ... take the law into their own hands and abuse the transgressing women....

Her brief did not discuss the question whether she would comply with the law regarding the wearing of a chador. Nor did her brief explain what effect submitting to that requirement would have upon her.

In the section of her brief devoted to political opinion, she mentioned her political activities while in Iran, as well as her current "deep-rooted beliefs in freedom of choice, freedom of expression [and] equality of opportunity for both sexes."

The Board of Immigration Appeals dismissed the petitioner's appeal. The Board * * * stated that there was no evidence that she would be "singled out" for persecution. Instead, the Board observed that she would be "subject to the same restrictions and requirements" as the rest of the population. The Board also noted that there had been "a considerable passage of time since [she] was in high school and participated in political activities." In addition, the Board stated that her claims were based on circumstances that had arisen since her entry into this country and that "[s]uch claims are dimly viewed."

After the Board issued its order requiring her voluntary departure or deportation, the petitioner filed the current petition for review.

* * *

Both courts and commentators have struggled to define "particular social group." Read in its broadest literal sense, the phrase is almost completely open-ended. Virtually any set including more than one person could be described as a "particular social group." Thus, the statutory language standing alone is not very instructive.

Nor is there any clear evidence of legislative intent. * * *

* * * When the Conference of Plenipotentiaries was considering the [UN Convention relating to the Status of Refugees] in 1951, the phrase "membership of a particular social group" was added to this definition as an "afterthought." The Swedish representative proposed this language, explaining only that it was needed because "experience had shown that certain refugees had been persecuted because they belonged to particular social groups," and the proposal was adopted. Conference of Plenipotentiaries on the Status of Refugees and Stateless Persons, Summary Rec. of the 3d Mtg., U.N. Doc. A/CONF.2/SR.3 at 14 (Nov. 19, 1951). Thus, neither the legislative history of the relevant United States statutes nor the negotiating history of the pertinent international agreements sheds much light on the meaning of the phrase "particular social group."

* * *

Here, the Board has interpreted the phrase "particular social group" [as] * * * "a group of persons all of whom share a common, immutable characteristic." * * * We have no doubt that this is a permissible construction of the relevant statutes, and we are consequently bound to accept it.

With this understanding of the phrase "particular social group" in mind, we turn to the elements that an alien must establish in order to qualify for withholding of deportation or asylum based on membership in such a group. We believe that there are three such elements. The alien must (1) identify a group that constitutes a "particular social group" within the interpretation just discussed, (2) establish that he or she is a member of that group, and (3) show that he or she would be persecuted or has a well-founded fear of persecution based on that membership.

In the excerpt from *Acosta* quoted above, the Board specifically mentioned "sex" as an innate characteristic that could link the members of a "particular social group." Thus, to the extent that the petitioner in this case suggests that she would be persecuted or has a well-founded fear that she would be persecuted in Iran simply because she is a woman, she has satisfied the first of the three elements that we have noted. She has not, however, satisfied the third element; that is, she has not shown that she would suffer or that she has a well-founded fear of suffering "persecution" based solely on her gender.

* * * [T]he BIA interpreted "persecution" to include threats to life, confinement, torture, and economic restrictions so severe that they constitute a threat to life or freedom. By contrast, the BIA suggested that "[g]enerally harsh conditions shared by many other persons" do not amount to persecution. * * *

In this case, the evidence in the administrative record regarding the way in which women in Iran are generally treated is quite sparse. We certainly cannot say that "a reasonable factfinder would have to conclude," based on that record, that the petitioner, if returned to Iran, would face treatment amounting to "persecution" simply because she is a woman. See *INS v. Elias–Zacarias*, 502 U.S. 478, 481, 112 S.Ct. 812, 815, 117 L.Ed.2d 38 (1992). While the amici supporting the petitioner have called to our attention articles describing the harsh restrictions placed on all women in Iran, the facts asserted in these articles are not part of the administrative record. * * *

The petitioner's primary argument, in any event, is not that she faces persecution simply because she is a woman. Rather, she maintains that she faces persecution because she is a member of "a very visible and specific subgroup: Iranian women who *refuse to conform* to the government's gender-specific laws and social norms." This definition merits close consideration. It does not include all Iranian women who hold feminist views. Nor does it include all Iranian women who find the Iranian government's "gender-specific laws and repressive social norms" objectionable or offensive. Instead, it is limited to those Iranian women who find those laws so abhorrent that they "refuse to conform"—even though, according to the petitioner's brief, "the routine penalty" for noncompliance is "74 lashes, a year's imprisonment, and in many cases brutal rapes and death."

Limited in this way, the "particular social group" identified by the petitioner may well satisfy the BIA's definition of that concept, for if a woman's opposition to the Iranian laws in question is so profound that she would choose to suffer the severe consequences of noncompliance, her beliefs may well be characterized as "so fundamental to [her] identity or conscience that [they] ought not be required to be changed." *Acosta*. The petitioner's difficulty, however, is that the administrative record does not establish that she is a member of this tightly defined group, for there is no evidence in that record showing that her opposition to the Iranian laws at issue is of the depth and importance required.

The Iranian restriction discussed most prominently in the petitioner's testimony was the requirement that women wear the chador or traditional veil, but the most that the petitioner's testimony showed was that she would find that requirement objectionable and would seek to avoid compliance if possible. When asked whether she would prefer to comply with that law or suffer the consequences of noncompliance, she stated only that she "would try to avoid" wearing a chador as much as she could. Similarly, her brief to the BIA stated only that she would seek to avoid Islamic practices "as much as she could." She never testified that she would refuse to comply with the law regarding the chador or any of the other gender-specific laws or social norms. Nor did she testify that wearing the chador or complying with any of the other restrictions was so deeply abhorrent to her that it would be tantamount to persecution. Instead, the most that emerges from her testimony is that she would find these requirements objectionable and would not observe them if she could avoid doing so. This testimony does not bring her within the particular social group that she has defined—Iranian women who refuse to conform with those requirements even if the consequences may be severe.

The "particular social group" that her testimony places her within is, instead, the presumably larger group consisting of Iranian women who find their country's gender-specific laws offensive and do not wish to comply with them. But if the petitioner's "particular social group" is defined in this way, she cannot prevail because the administrative record does not satisfy the third element described above, i.e., it does not show that the consequences that would befall her as a member of that group would constitute "persecution." According to the petitioner, she would have two options if she returned to Iran: comply with the Iranian laws or suffer severe consequences. Thus, while we agree with the petitioner that the indicated consequences of noncompliance would constitute persecution, we must still inquire whether her other option—compliance—would also constitute persecution.

In considering whether the petitioner established that this option would constitute persecution, we will assume for the sake of argument that the concept of persecution is broad enough to include governmental measures that compel an individual to engage in conduct that is not physically painful or harmful but is abhorrent to that individual's deepest beliefs. An example of such conduct might be requiring a person to renounce his or her religious beliefs or to desecrate an object of religious importance. Such conduct might be regarded as a form of "torture" and thus as falling within the Board's description of persecution in *Acosta*. Such a requirement could constitute "torture" or persecution, however, only if directed against a person who actually possessed the religious beliefs or attached religious importance to the object in question. Requiring an adherent of an entirely different religion or a non-believer to engage in the same conduct would not constitute persecution.

Here, while we assume for the sake of argument that requiring some women to wear chadors may be so abhorrent to them that it would be tantamount to persecution, this requirement clearly does not constitute persecution for all women. Presumably, there are devout Shi'ite women in Iran who find this requirement entirely appropriate. Presumably, there are other women in Iran who find it either inconvenient, irritating, mildly objectionable, or highly offensive, but for whom it falls short of constituting persecution. As we have previously noted, the petitioner's testimony in this case simply does not show that for her the requirement of wearing the chador or complying with Iran's other gender-specific laws would be so profoundly abhorrent that it could aptly be called persecution. Accordingly, we cannot hold that she is entitled to withholding of deportation or asylum based on her membership in a "particular social group."

* * *

* * * We therefore deny the petition for review.

NOTES AND QUESTIONS ON SOCIAL NORMS

1. Would Fatin's chances have improved if she had been a Christian? Should it matter if her rejection of a social norm were based on her religion rather than her views of women's roles in society? For contrasting views on punishment of women who defy norms regarding their attire, consider *Matter of S–A–,* 22 I & N Dec. 1328 (BIA 2000), where a father's beatings of his daughter for wearing a short skirt were deemed religious persecution of a woman because she did not subscribe to the father's strict interpretation of Islam. On the other hand, in *Fisher v. INS,* 79 F.3d 955, 964 (9th Cir. 1996) (en banc), the majority concluded that penalties for refusal to comply with the governing attire and other behavior for women were "routine punishment for violating generally applicable laws." Judge Noonan, who had written the earlier panel opinion that had ruled in favor of the applicant, 61 F.3d 1366 (9th Cir. 1994) (amended opinion) emphasized imputed religious and political grounds in dissent:

> [W]hat befell Saidel Hassib–Tehrani was not because she had demonstrated a sympathy for feminism or voiced a more tolerant interpretation of Islam than the Ayatollah's or expressed in Iran any dissent from the rigorist regime. The arrests and search occurred because the regime perceived her as a religious nonconformist. The way in which she led her daily life was enough to invite repression. It was on account of her religious opinion, as perceived by the regime viewing her unconventional routine behaviors, that she was arrested * * *. As Iran is a theocracy, the religious beliefs imputed to her by the regime were also political opinions, and the persecution she fears from the regime would also be "on account of" those imputed political opinions.

Id. at 970.

2. Under *Fatin's* reasoning, what exactly must gay or lesbian asylum seekers prove? That they are a recognized social group? That their status is immutable? That it is fundamental to their identity, whether or not immutable? That they should not be required to change it? That they are socially visible? What if they could avoid persecution by remaining closeted?

3. Although much of the *Fatin* opinion focused on the particular social group issue, the court also concluded that wearing a chador did not rise to the level of persecution, at least not for Fatin. What proof could Fatin present to demonstrate that being forced, on pain of whipping and prison, to wear traditional clothes with religious and political symbolism constituted persecution for her? Is Fatin's situation different from that of Saudi women arrested for driving cars? *See* Bakri, *Saudi Religious Police Detained 5 Women for Driving, Group Reports*, N.Y. Times, June 29, 2011. Does then-Judge Alito's opinion suggest that women have to engage in civil disobedience to demonstrate the sincerity of their belief? Under the court's reasoning, would Jews in Nazi Germany face persecution if they said they refused to wear yellow stars when they went out in public?

4. In *Al–Ghorbani v. Holder*, 585 F.3d 980, 995 (6th Cir. 2009), *petition for rehearing denied*, 594 F.3d 546 (6th Cir. 2010), the court granted with-

holding of removal to the applicants who sought protection as members of a social group of "young westernized people who have defied traditional Islamic values by marrying without paternal permission." The couple, who came from different social classes, had already married and traveled to the United States; they testified that they faced death threats and "honor" killings if returned to Yemen. Is the right to marry one's chosen partner fundamental to identity in a way that differs from the right to choose the type of clothing to wear in public? Do women who flee arranged marriages constitute a particular social group? Is it persecution to force an individual to marry someone that he or she does not love? *See Gao v. Gonzalez,* 440 F.3d 62 (2d Cir. 2006) (eligible for asylum and withholding as member of particular social group of women sold into marriage in a feudal society), *vacated and remanded sub nom. Keisler v. Gao,* 552 U.S. 801, 128 S.Ct. 345, 169 L.Ed.2d 2 (2007) (reconsideration warranted in light of recent precedent remanding case to BIA for evaluation of family as particular social group).

5.   Should prevailing social norms in a given country be viewed, for asylum and *nonrefoulement* purposes, as a "uniform national policy"? Are the moral codes regarding women's attire akin to the population control policy in *Matter of Chang,* discussed on pp. 833–835 of this chapter? Why or why not?

6.   The *Fatin* court betrays concern about the numerical consequences of expansive doctrine governing "particular social group" claims: "If persecution were defined that expansively, a significant percentage of the world's population would qualify for asylum in this country—and it seems most unlikely that Congress intended such a result." 12 F.3d at 1240. Are these consequentialist concerns legitimate in deciding doctrinal questions? In any event, does the court's doctrine, emphasizing "abhorrent" practices and "profound" objections, effectively guard against such an outcome?

b. Female Genital Mutilation

Many forms of sexual abuse, sexual harassment, dowry-related violence, and so-called "honor killings" of women can constitute persecution. Asylum claims based on the tradition of female genital mutilation, or genital cutting, raise complex issues. If performed by women in the society, who are under no government coercion, and whose intent is not to harm the young girls, does this constitute persecution? If it does, what particular social group is the target of harm, and has it been targeted because it is a social group? The BIA addressed many of these questions in *Matter of Kasinga,* 21 I & N Dec. 357 (BIA 1996). The asylum applicant was a teenage girl from Togo, who had fled a forced marriage to a middle-aged man and the genital cutting that she would have been forced to undergo at the time of the marriage. The BIA concluded that the scheduled female genital mutilation constituted persecution, even though the actors did not intend to punish the asylum seeker. The definition of the particular social group led to contrasting perspectives from the majority and the concurring opinions. First, the majority's analysis:

> In the context of this case, we find the particular social group to be the following: young women of the Tchamba–Kunsuntu Tribe who

have not had FGM, as practiced by that tribe, and who oppose the practice. * * *

* * *

In accordance with *Acosta*, the particular social group is defined by common characteristics that members of the group either cannot change, or should not be required to change because such characteristics are fundamental to their individual identities. The characteristics of being a "young woman" and a "member of the Tchamba–Kunsuntu Tribe" cannot be changed. The characteristic of having intact genitalia is one that is so fundamental to the individual identity of a young woman that she should not be required to change it.

* * *

We agree with the parties that, as described and documented in this record, FGM is practiced, at least in some significant part, to overcome sexual characteristics of young women of the tribe who have not been, and do not wish to be, subjected to FGM. We therefore find that the persecution the applicant fears in Togo is "on account of" her status as a member of the defined social group.

Id. at 366–67

In her concurrence, Board Member Rosenberg rejoined:

Unlike requests for asylum premised upon political opinion, social group claims, like those involving race, ethnicity, or religion, are status based and do not necessarily require a showing of the presence of an individual's opinions or activities which spurs the persecutor's wrath or otherwise motivates the harm or persecution. *Matter of H–*, [21 I & N Dec. 337 (BIA 1996)]. Rather, such requests involve a determination of whether the shared characteristics are those which motivate an agent of persecution to seek to overcome or otherwise harm the individual. Consequently, while not inaccurate, it is surplusage to define the social group in this case by including as an element the applicant's opposition to the practice of female genital mutilation.

It may be true that sometimes an individual woman's political opinion may overlap or coexist with her membership in a group designated as a particular social group; however, that does not detract from the fact that social group membership is a status-based ground protected under the Act, just as is religion or ethnicity. While it is not impossible that a political or social opinion, either actual or imputed, may be shared by persons whom, as a result, we would characterize as constituting a particular social group within the meaning of the Act, that is not the case here. As I have stated, the applicant's political or social views—her attitude or intent—is not relevant to our definition of the social group to which she belongs, but rather to whether the harm or abuse she faces constitutes persecution.

In *Matter of H–*, this Board found, without difficulty or the need to qualify, that a man who was a member of a tribe in Somalia whose members were being systematically attacked by other tribes in retribution for the corruption and brutality of former ruler and tribe member, Siad Barre, had established persecution based on his clan membership alone. * * * His attitude towards that persecution was neither examined nor relevant.

* * * Here, the applicant is a member of a group: girls and women of a given tribe, some perhaps of marriageable age, whose members are routinely subjected to the harm which the majority finds to constitute persecution. The applicant's opposition (which happens to be present in this case) or the lack of it, is neither determinative, nor necessary to define the social group in accordance with the statutory language.

Id. at 376.

c. Domestic Violence

A study conducted by the World Health Organization (WHO) and published in the medical journal *The Lancet* in October 2006 estimated the extent of physical and intimate sexual partner violence against women in 15 sites in ten countries: Bangladesh, Brazil, Ethiopia, Japan, Namibia, Peru, Samoa, Serbia and Montenegro, Thailand, and the United Republic of Tanzania. Based on interviews with nearly 25,000 women, the study found that the reported lifetime prevalence of physical or sexual partner violence, or both, varied from a low of 15 percent in Yokohama, Japan to a high of 71 percent in rural Ethiopia. Violence against women by their live-in spouses or partners, according to the study, is a widespread phenomenon, both in the developed and developing world, as well as in rural and urban areas. See Garcia–Moreno *et al., Prevalence of Intimate Partner Violence: Findings From the WHO Multi-country Study on Women's Health and Domestic Violence*, 368 The Lancet 1260 (2006); Rosenthal, *Women Face Greatest Threat of Violence at Home, Study Finds*, N.Y. Times, Oct. 6, 2006. Other studies have analyzed different types of domestic violence, and the circumstances that result in harm directed at men, as well as at women. See, e.g., Kelly & Johnson, *Domestic Violence: Differentiation Among Types of Intimate Partner Violence: Research Update and Implications for Interventions*, 46 Fam. Ct. Rev. 476 (2008).

Over the past decade a growing number of women have filed asylum claims based on domestic violence. Typically, they fear persecution at the hands of their male partner, who may not articulate a reason for his actions and may not act in this manner toward anyone else. These cases raise multiple legal questions. Does violence by individuals, as opposed to organized groups, constitute persecution? Is the violence "on account of" one of the specified grounds? What alternatives within her home country are available to the claimant? These issues are not unique to asylum claims based on domestic violence, but they pose particularly difficult conceptual puzzles in this developing area of the law.

Many cases outside the gender context have cast a skeptical eye on asylum claims founded on a risk of violence growing out of a private dispute, even when there was some political or governmental involvement. For example, courts have rejected asylum claims despite beatings that appeared to be in retaliation for reporting a supervisor for stealing supplies, *Kozulin v. INS*, 218 F.3d 1112 (9th Cir. 2000), denied asylum to an individual beaten for reporting the rape of his aunt by a prominent Salvadoran businessman and politician, *Molina–Morales v. INS*, 237 F.3d 1048 (9th Cir. 2001), and refused asylum to an applicant threatened based on charges and countercharges of corruption among prominent families and officials in Paraguay under the Stroessner dictatorship, *Zayas–Marini v. INS*, 785 F.2d 801 (9th Cir. 1986).

Lazo–Majano v. INS, 813 F.2d 1432 (9th Cir. 1987), appeared as an early exception to this pattern, in the specific setting of severe domestic abuse. The court ruled that Olimpia Lazo–Majano, a domestic servant who had been raped and battered and called a "subversive" by her employer, a sergeant in the Salvadoran army, had established persecution on account of political opinion. In general, though, courts were unsympathetic to asylum claims based on sexual violence. *E.g., Campos–Guardado v. INS*, 809 F.2d 285, 290 (5th Cir. 1987) (no asylum for Salvadoran woman raped and threatened by masked gunmen during that country's civil war because no "political implications" to the violence); *Gomez v. INS*, 947 F.2d 660 (2d Cir. 1991) (rejecting asylum for women "previously battered and raped by Salvadoran guerrillas").

Nonetheless, similar claims began to appear more often, and some decisionmakers showed greater acceptance. For example, in *Matter of D–V–*, 21 I & N Dec. 77 (BIA 1993), the BIA granted asylum to a Haitian woman who had been gang-raped and beaten by members of the Haitian military. *See also Angoucheva v. INS*, 106 F.3d 781 (7th Cir. 1997) (reversing and remanding to the BIA for more complete consideration of the claim that an interrupted sexual assault committed by a Bulgarian security officer during interrogation amounted to persecution on account of a protected ground).

The BIA faced the issue of domestic abuse as persecution in *Matter of R–A–*, 22 I & N Dec. 906 (BIA 2001). Rodi Alvarado had fled Guatemala and horrific abuse from her husband there. The BIA determined that she had suffered harm that clearly qualified as persecution, and that she had been unsuccessful in obtaining any protection from Guatemalan government officials. It concluded, however, that the persecution had not been on account of one of the protected grounds. With regard to political opinion the Board rejected the argument that Alvarado's husband necessarily imputed to her the political opinion that "women should not be controlled and dominated by men." *Id.* at 911. More importantly, according to the Board, it did not follow that he harmed Alvarado because she held those beliefs. *Id.* With regard to "particular social group," the Board stated:

Initially, we find that "Guatemalan women who have been involved intimately with Guatemalan male companions, who believe that women are to live under male domination" is not a particular social group. Absent from this group's makeup is "a voluntary associational relationship" that is of "central concern" in the Ninth Circuit [citing *Sanchez–Trujillo v. INS* and related cases].

Moreover, regardless of Ninth Circuit law, we find that the respondent's claimed social group fails under our own independent assessment of what constitutes a qualifying social group. [The social group] appears to have been defined principally, if not exclusively, for purposes of this asylum case, and without regard to the question of whether anyone in Guatemala perceives this group to exist in any form whatsoever. The respondent fits within the proposed group. But the group is defined largely in the abstract. It seems to bear little or no relation to the way in which Guatemalans might identify subdivisions within their own society or otherwise might perceive individuals either to possess or to lack an important characteristic or trait. * * * [There needs to be some showing] that the potential persecutors in fact see persons sharing the characteristic as warranting suppression or the infliction of harm.

* * *

In this case, even if we were to accept as a particular social group "Guatemalan women who have been involved intimately with Guatemalan male companions, who believe that women are to live under male domination," the respondent has not established that her husband has targeted and harmed the respondent because he perceived her to be a member of this particular social group. The record indicates that he has targeted only the respondent. The respondent's husband has not shown an interest in any member of this group other than the respondent herself. The respondent fails to show how other members of the group may be at risk of harm from him. If group membership were the motivation behind his abuse, one would expect to see some evidence of it manifested in actions toward other members of the same group.

* * *

The adequacy of state protection is obviously an essential inquiry in asylum cases. But its bearing on the "on account of" test for refugee status depends on the facts of the case and the context in which it arises. In this case, the independent actions of the respondent's husband may have been tolerated. But, as previously explained, this record does not show that his actions represent desired behavior within Guatemala or that the Guatemalan Government encourages domestic abuse.

Importantly, construing private acts of violence to be qualifying governmental persecution, by virtue of the inadequacy of protection, would obviate, perhaps entirely, the "on account of" requirement in the statute. We understand the "on account of" test to direct an inquiry into the motives of the entity actually inflicting the harm. *See INS v. Elias–Zacarias.* Further, the adoption of such an approach would represent a fundamental change in the analysis of refugee claims. We see no principled basis for restricting such an approach to cases involving violence against women. The absence of adequate governmental protection, it would seem, should equally translate into refugee status for other categories of persons unable to protect themselves.

Id. at 917–23.

* * *

Five members of the Board of Immigration Appeals disagreed with the majority's reasoning in *Matter of R–A–* and filed a dissent. They emphasized the complicity of the government of Guatemala. The record was clear that the government made no effort to protect Alvarado; this was evidence of the government's institutional bias against women, which appeared "to stem from a pervasive belief, common in patriarchal societies, that a man should be able to control a wife or female companion by any means he sees fit: including rape, torture, and beatings." *Id.* at 930.

With regard to "particular social group," the dissent said:

> The Immigration Judge found that the respondent was a member of a social group comprised of "Guatemalan women, who have been involved intimately with Guatemalan male companions, who believe that women are to live under male domination." In so finding, she carefully analyzed the facts of the case and correctly applied the law as set forth in *Matter of Acosta*, and, most recently, in *Matter of Kasinga*.

* * *

> Under *Acosta*, * * * immutability is of the essence. In a number of decisions, we have applied the Acosta immutability standard to recognize particular social groups. In each case, we recognized an immutable trait or past experience shared by the members of the social group. The shared past experience of former members of the national police force in El Salvador, for example, has been recognized as an immutable characteristic which makes such individuals members of a particular social group for asylum purposes. *Matter of Fuentes*, 19 I & N Dec. 658 (BIA 1988). Similarly, gay men and lesbians in Cuba have been found to constitute a particular social group. *Matter of Toboso–Alfonso*, 20 I & N Dec. 819 (BIA 1990). Members of the Darood clan and Marehan subclan in Somalia have been found to share immutable characteristics required for social group recognition, *Matter of H–*, 22 I & N Dec. 337 (BIA 1996) * * *.

* * *

The Immigration Judge decided the case before her consistent with our precedent decision in *Kasinga*. In both cases, the social group was defined by reference to gender in combination with one or more additional factors. In *Kasinga*, the social group was defined by gender, ethnic affiliation, and opposition to female genital mutilation ("FGM"). In the instant case, the social group is based on gender, relationship to an abusive partner, and opposition to domestic violence. As the Immigration Judge below correctly observed, the respondent's relationship to, and association with, her husband is something she cannot change. It is an immutable characteristic under the *Acosta* guidelines, which we affirmed in *Kasinga*. *Id.* at 366.

* * *

The international community has recognized that gender-based violence, such as domestic violence, is not merely a random crime or a private matter; rather, such violence is a violation of fundamental human rights. * * *

* * *

[I]n conjoined appeals involving women seeking asylum protection in the United Kingdom for domestic violence in Pakistan, the House of Lords found "women in Pakistan" to constitute a particular social group under the Convention's refugee definition, *Islam (A.P.) v. Secretary of State for the Home Dep't, supra.* Lord Steyn found "women in Pakistan" to be a "logical application of the seminal reasoning" of *Acosta.* Lord Hoffman recognized the importance of context in deciding whether a social group has been identified: "While persecutory conduct cannot define the social group, the actions of the persecutors may serve to identify or even cause the creation of a particular social group." *Id.* Citing the example of a Jew whose business was destroyed by a competitor in Nazi Germany, Lord Hoffman recognized that a persecutor's knowledge that he could act with impunity "for reasons of" (i.e., "on account of") his victim's religion went to the heart of the analysis of why the harm occurred. *Id.*

* * *

Like the persecutor who targets the Jewish shopkeeper because he knows he can act with impunity owing to his victim's religion, the respondent's husband knows he can commit his atrocities with impunity because of the respondent's gender and their relationship. * * *

Id., at 931–39 (Guendelsberger, Member, dissenting).

NOTES AND QUESTIONS ON DOMESTIC VIOLENCE

1. One year after *Matter of R–A–*, the BIA granted asylum to a 20 year old Moroccan whose father beat, punched, and kicked her frequently and once burned her thighs after she wore a short skirt outside the home. The BIA

distinguished *Matter of R–A–* by emphasizing the "religious element" in the later case. The Board characterized the persecution as acts taken on account of the daughter's religious beliefs with regard to the proper role of women, which were not as strict as those of her orthodox Muslim father. *Matter of S–A–*, 22 I & N Dec. 1328, 1337 (BIA 2000). At the INS' urging, *Matter of S–A–* was designated for publication as a precedent in June 2000, and we have mentioned it earlier in conjunction with persecution on account of religion on account of resistance to social norms. Can *Matter of R–A–* be reconciled with *Matter of S–A–*? Do you think that the BIA would have reached a different result if the father in *Matter of S–A–* had justified his actions against his daughter by "tradition" rather than by his religious beliefs?

2. Perhaps the distinction between *Matter of S–A–*and *Matter of R–A–* turns on the familial roles. Reading these decisions together, do they imply that the BIA thinks that young women cannot realistically protect themselves or leave their father's homes, but that wives can? Or do consequentialist concerns explain the distinction—that is, is parental abuse considered less likely to create a wave of asylum seekers because fewer parents severely abuse their daughters than husbands abuse their wives—or perhaps that fewer children will be able to escape and travel to a distant country to claim protection? Are these kinds of concerns legitimate when severe abuse and persecution is involved? Do they arise more frequently in cases involving gender than in cases involving other protected grounds?

3. The subsequent proceedings in *Matter of R–A–* lasted more than a decade and involved three different administrations. In December 2000, the Department published proposed amendments to the asylum regulations, including new definitions of "persecution," "on account of," and "membership in a particular social group." 65 Fed. Reg. 76588–98 (2000). The changes were intended, in major part, to make the doctrine more amenable to domestic violence claims. Attorney General Janet Reno vacated the BIA decision in *Matter of R–A–*, and remanded the case to the BIA. Reno directed the Board to wait until the new asylum regulations were final and then to reconsider the case in light of those regulations. See 78 Interp. Rel. 256, 335 (2001); Musalo & Knight, *Steps Forward and Steps Back: Uneven Progress in the Law of Social Group and Gender–Based Claims in the United States*, 13 Int'l J. Ref. L. 51 (2001).

The proposed regulations were handed to a new administration in January 2001. Internal debates persisted, however, and no final regulations appeared. Apparently, in light of this stalemate, Attorney General John Ashcroft directed that the *R–A–* case be referred to the Attorney General for reconsideration While the case was pending, the Department of Homeland Security filed a new brief generally supportive of domestic violence claims which proffered another description of the pertinent social group: "married women in Guatemala who are unable to leave the relationship." In the end, however, Ashcroft remanded the case to the BIA shortly before he left office. Nearly four years later, in 2008, with no new regulations in view, Attorney General Mukasey retook the case and directed the BIA to resolve it based on intervening BIA and judicial case law. See 81 Interp. Rel. 245 (2004); *Matter of R–A–*, 23 I & N Dec. 694 (AG 2005); *Matter of R–A–*, 24 I & N Dec. 629 (AG 2008). When the BIA then remanded the case to an immigration judge, DHS agreed that Alvarado was eligible for asylum as a member of this social group, and that she merited a favorable decision as a matter of discretion. The immigration judge granted asylum on December 10, 2009. Elias, *Domestic Violence Victim Granted Asylum in U.S.*, Associated Press, Dec. 18, 2009, <http://cgrs. uchastings.edu/news/>. For an overview of the litigation, see Musalo, *A Short History of Gender Asylum in the United States: Resistance and Ambivalence May Very Slowly Be Inching Towards Recognition of Women's Claims*, 29 Refugee Survey Quarterly 46, 56–60 (2010).

In July 2010, DHS issued a written statement expressly stating that women in these types of domestic relationships can be a particular social group, *DHS Written Clarification Regarding the Definition of "Particular Social Group,"* July 13, 2010, and the next month granted asylum to a Mexican woman who had been abused and beaten by her common law husband. Preston, *Asylum Granted to Mexican Woman in Case Setting Standard on Domestic Abuse*, N.Y. Times, Aug. 12, 2010. New regulations had not yet appeared as of late 2011.

SECTION E.   LIMITATIONS ON ASYLUM

1. FILING DEADLINE

Asylum applicants must file their claims within one year of their arrival in the United States. INA § 208(a)(2)(B). By statute, later-filed applications may be considered only if there are changed circumstances that materially affect the asylum seeker's eligibility for asylum or if there are extraordinary circumstances that are related to the delay. INA § 208(a)(2)(D). There is no judicial review of an administrative decision that the filing fails to comply with the statutory deadline provisions, INA § 208(a)(3), but a person denied by an asylum officer because of the deadline can obtain de novo consideration of that issue before the immigration judge, and can then appeal a deadline ruling to the BIA.

The regulations spell out more detailed standards. 8 C.F.R. §§ 208.4(a)(4), (5); 1208.4(a)(5). They provide that physical and mental conditions may constitute "extraordinary circumstances" if they are "directly related to the failure to meet the 1–year deadline." Certain legal obstacles, such as ineffective assistance of counsel, or the possession of another temporary legal status until a reasonable period before filing, may also satisfy the "extraordinary circumstances" exception. *Id.* The BIA issued a precedent decision holding that the late filing by a 16–year–old unaccompanied minor satisfied the exception because the applicant was under a legal disability (minority) during the first year of his time in the United States and submitted his asylum application within five months of his release by the INS into the custody of his uncle. *Matter of Y–C–*, 23 I & N Dec. 286 (BIA 2002).

In the first few years the agencies appeared to construe the deadline in a reasonably flexible manner, finding that roughly three-quarters of asylum applications were timely. Thereafter, according to a recent study, the deadline had a more pronounced effect, disqualifying 35 percent of the affirmative asylum applicants. Schrag, Schoenholtz, Ramji–Nogales, & Dombach, *Rejecting Refugees: Homeland Security's Administration of the One–Year Bar to Asylum*, 52 William & Mary L. Rev. 651 (2010). The study found that the rate of exceptions varies significantly among asylum officers and rejections based on the deadline vary significantly among asylum seekers from different countries. *Id.* at 713. It also suggested that the deadline precluded approximately 20,000 individuals from receiving asylum from DHS asylum officers, though it does not report how many ultimately received asylum or withholding of removal when their cases proceeded to immigration court. *Id.* at 704–06.

The filing deadline has been heavily criticized in the United States since its adoption in 1996. Many refugees appear to delay filing for asylum in the hope that things will improve at home before too long and they will be able to return. Some have suffered traumatic experiences that effectively disable them. For many, the difficulty of obtaining legal assistance dissuades them from acting in a timely way. The impediments of a foreign language and different cultural expectations compound the other difficulties. *See, e.g.*, Pistone, *Asylum Filing Deadlines: Unfair and Unnecessary*, 10 Geo. Imm. L. J. 95 (1996), Schrag & Pistone, *The 1996 Immigration Act: Asylum Application Deadlines and Expedited Removal—What the INS Should Do*, 73 Interp. Rel. 1565 (1996).

It is important to note that withholding of removal is not subject to any deadline. Because all asylum applications are simultaneously considered as requests for withholding, individuals who run afoul of the one-year deadline for asylum automatically will be screened for *nonrefoulement* protection. But because the standard of proof for withholding is higher, the impact of the asylum deadline remains significant.

2.   FIRM RESETTLEMENT

The INA precludes those who have been firmly resettled in another country from asylum in the United States. INA § 208(b)(2)(A)(vi). Withholding of removal is not barred in the case of firm resettlement, but recall that withholding is country-specific. A grant of withholding would not prevent sending the asylum seeker back to the third country—if that country will still accept the asylum seeker. If not, he or she is likely to remain in the United States, with the limited protections that accompany withholding of removal status.

The concept of firm resettlement is defined in 8 C.F.R. § 208.15:

An alien is considered to be firmly resettled if, prior to arrival in the United States, he or she entered into another nation with, or while in that nation received, an offer of permanent resident status, citizenship, or some other type of permanent resettlement * * *.

The regulation provides that a finding of firm resettlement can be overcome if the applicant shows either that "entry into that country was a necessary consequence of his or her flight from persecution, that he or she remained in that nation only as long as was necessary to arrange onward travel, and that he or she did not establish significant ties in that country" or that "the conditions of his or her residence in that country were so substantially and consciously restricted by the authority of the country of refuge that he or she was not in fact resettled." The regulation then lists factors to consider in making the second determination.

The BIA set forth a four-step analytical framework to determine whether an asylum seeker had been firmly resettled in *Matter of A—G—G—*. 25 I & N Dec. 486 (2011), a case involving a Mauritanian asylum seeker who had married a Senegalese wife and lived in Senegal for eight years without receiving permanent legal status. The Board ruled that the availability of a legal process by which an individual can obtain permanent residence may be prima facie evidence of firm resettlement, and that an individual's failure to apply for permanent residence is not dispositive. The Board then remanded the case to the immigration judge to determine whether the Senegalese law granting permanent residence to the spouses of Senegalese citizens applies to men marrying Senegalese women or only to foreign women marrying Senegalese men.

3. PERSECUTORS

Congress specified that persons who assisted in persecuting others must be excluded from asylum, INA § 208(b)(2)(A)(i), and withholding of removal. INA § 241(b)(3)(B)(i). The exclusion of persons who participated or assisted in persecution is written in very broad terms. Take a look at that statutory language. This breadth reflects the provision's provenance, for the language mirrors the language of former § 241(a)(19), now § 237(a)(4)(D), a rigorous provision originally directed at those who aided Nazi persecution in Germany. For many years the BIA interpreted these anti-Nazi provisions in a particularly strict manner, relying on a 1981 Supreme Court decision in a denaturalization case. *Fedorenko v. United States*, 449 U.S. 490, 101 S.Ct. 737, 66 L.Ed.2d 686 (1981). The BIA held that they provide for the removal of such persons, even if they assisted the persecution involuntarily or under duress. *See Matter of Fedorenko*, 19 I & N Dec. 57 (BIA 1984); *Matter of Laipenieks*, 18 I & N Dec. 433 (BIA 1983), reversed, *Laipenieks v. INS*, 750 F.2d 1427 (9th Cir.1985). *See generally* Creppy, *Nazi War Criminals in Immigration Law*, 12 Geo. Immigr. L.J. 443 (1998).

Some questioned whether the BIA's harsh construction, however appropriate it might have been for those who collaborated with the Nazis in the 1930s and 1940s, should continue to govern the persecutor exception to asylum and withholding of removal. The BIA faced this question in *Matter of Rodriguez–Majano*, 19 I & N Dec. 811 (BIA 1988), a case that arose in the civil war in El Salvador. The Board concluded that an individual's involuntary participation in persecution was a bar to asylum, but ruled that mere membership in an organization that persecuted others did not preclude a grant of asylum.

Ultimately, the availability of a duress exception to the asylum bar for those who participated in persecution reached the Supreme Court. Justice Kennedy, writing for the majority, contrasted the 1948 Displaced Persons Act at issue in *Fedorenko* with the 1980 Refugee Act provisions implicated in the case of an Ethiopian forced to work as a prison guard in Eritrea in 1998.

NEGUSIE v. HOLDER

Supreme Court of the United States, 2009.
555 U.S. 511, 129 S.Ct. 1159, 173 L.Ed.2d 20.

JUSTICE KENNEDY delivered the opinion of the Court.

* * *

Daniel Girmai Negusie, a dual national of Eritrea and Ethiopia, * * * left [Ethiopia] for Eritrea around the age of 18 to see his mother and find employment. The year was 1994. After a few months in Eritrea, state officials took custody of petitioner and others when they were attending a movie. He was forced to perform hard labor for a month and then was conscripted into the military for a time. War broke out between Ethiopia and Eritrea in 1998, and he was conscripted again.

When petitioner refused to fight against Ethiopia, his other homeland, the Eritrean Government incarcerated him. Prison guards punished petitioner by beating him with sticks and placing him in the hot sun. He was released after two years and forced to work as a prison guard, a duty he performed on a rotating basis for about four years. It is undisputed that the prisoners he guarded were being persecuted on account of a protected ground—*i.e.*, "race, religion, nationality, membership in a particular social group, or political opinion." Petitioner testified that he carried a gun, guarded the gate to prevent escape, and kept prisoners from taking showers and obtaining fresh air. He also guarded prisoners to make sure they stayed in the sun, which he knew was a form of punishment. He saw at least one man die after being in the sun for more than two hours. Petitioner testified that he had not shot at or directly punished any prisoner and that he helped prisoners on various occasions. Petitioner escaped from the prison and hid in a container, which was loaded on board a ship heading to the United States. Once here he applied for asylum and withholding of removal.

[T]he Immigration Judge * * * concluded that petitioner assisted in persecution by working as an armed guard. * * *

The BIA [relying on *Fedorenko*] affirmed the denial of asylum and withholding. It noted petitioner's role as an armed guard in a facility where "prisoners were tortured and left to die out in the sun ... on account of a protected ground." The BIA held that "[t]he fact that [petitioner] was compelled to participate as a prison guard, and may not have actively tortured or mistreated anyone, is immaterial." That is because " 'an alien's motivation and intent are irrelevant to the issue of whether he "assisted" in persecution ... [I]t is the objective effect of an alien's actions which is controlling.' " * * *

On petition for review the Court of Appeals agreed with the BIA that whether an alien is compelled to assist in persecution is immaterial for persecutor-bar purposes. * * *

* * *

The parties disagree over whether coercion or duress is relevant in determining if an alien assisted or otherwise participated in persecution. As there is substance to both contentions, we conclude that the statute has an ambiguity that the agency should address in the first instance.

Petitioner argues that the statute's plain language makes clear that involuntary acts do not implicate the persecutor bar because "persecution" presumes moral blameworthiness. He invokes principles of criminal culpability, concepts of international law, and the rule of lenity. Those arguments may be persuasive in determining whether a particular agency interpretation is reasonable, but they do not demonstrate that the statute is unambiguous. * * *

The Government, on the other hand, asserts that the statute does not allow petitioner's construction. "The statutory text," the Government says, "directly answers that question: there is no exception" for conduct that is coerced because Congress did not include one. We disagree. The silence is not conclusive. The question is whether the statutory text mandates that coerced actions must be deemed assistance in persecution. On that point the statute, in its precise terms, is not explicit. Nor is this a case where it is clear that Congress had an intention on the precise question at issue.

* * *

In *Fedorenko*, the Court interpreted the Displaced Persons Act of 1948 (DPA), 62 Stat. 1009, [and concluded that] "an individual's service as a concentration camp armed guard—whether voluntary or involuntary—made him ineligible for a visa" under § 2(a) of the IRO Constitution. That Congress did not adopt a voluntariness requirement for § 2(a), the Court noted, "is plain from comparing § 2(a) with § 2(b), which excludes only those individuals who '*voluntarily*' assisted the enemy forces.' " The Court relied on the principle of statutory construction that "the deliberate omission of the word 'voluntary' from § 2(a) compels the conclusion that the statute made *all* those who assisted in persecution of civilians ineligible for visas."

Fedorenko does not compel the same conclusion in the case now before us. The textual structure of the statute in *Fedorenko* ("voluntary" is in one subsection but not the other) is not part of the statutory framework considered here. Congress did not use the word "voluntary" in any subsection of the persecutor bar, so its omission cannot carry the same significance.

The difference between the statutory scheme in *Fedorenko* and the one here is confirmed when we "look not only to the particular statutory language, but to the design of the statute as a whole and to its object and policy." Both statutes were enacted to reflect principles set forth in international agreements, but the principles differ in significant respects.

As discussed, Congress enacted the DPA in 1948 as part of an international effort to address individuals who were forced to leave their homelands during and after the second World War. The DPA excludes those who "voluntarily assisted the enemy forces since the outbreak of the second world war," as well as all who "assisted the enemy in persecuting civil populations of countries." The latter exclusion clause makes no reference to culpability. The exclusion of even those involved in nonculpable, involuntary assistance in Nazi persecution, as an expert testified in *Fedorenko*, may be "[b]ecause the crime against humanity that is involved in the concentration camp puts it into a different category."

The persecutor bar in this case, by contrast, was enacted as part of the Refugee Act of 1980. Unlike the DPA, which was enacted to address not just the post war refugee problem but also the Holocaust and its horror, the Refugee Act was designed to provide a general rule for the ongoing treatment of all refugees and displaced persons. As this Court has twice recognized, "one of Congress' primary purposes' in passing the Refugee Act was to implement the principles agreed to in the 1967 United Nations Protocol Relating to the Status of Refugees," as well as the United Nations Convention Relating to the Status of Refugees.

These authorities illustrate why *Fedorenko*, which addressed a different statute enacted for a different purpose, does not control the BIA's interpretation of this persecutor bar. Whatever weight or relevance these various authorities may have in interpreting the statute should be considered by the agency in the first instance, and by any subsequent reviewing court, after our remand.

* * *

In denying relief in this case the BIA recited a rule that has developed in its own case law in reliance on *Fedorenko:* "[A]n alien's motivation and intent are irrelevant to the issue of whether he 'assisted' in persecution ... [I]t is the objective effect of an alien's actions which is controlling." The rule is based on three earlier decisions: *Matter of Laipenieks*, 18 I. & N. Dec. 433 (1983); *Matter of Fedorenko*, 19 I. & N. Dec. 57; and *Matter of Rodriguez–Majano*, 19 I. & N. Dec. 811 (1988).

* * *

Our reading of these decisions confirms that the BIA has not exercised its interpretive authority [in a manner that would command judicial deference under the *Chevron* doctrine, discussed in Chapter Five, pp. 332–

342, *supra*] but, instead, has determined that *Fedorenko* controls. This mistaken assumption stems from a failure to recognize the inapplicability of the principle of statutory construction invoked in *Fedorenko*, as well as a failure to appreciate the differences in statutory purpose. The BIA is not bound to apply the *Fedorenko* rule that motive and intent are irrelevant to the persecutor bar at issue in this case. Whether the statute permits such an interpretation based on a different course of reasoning must be determined in the first instance by the agency.

Having concluded that the BIA has not yet exercised its *Chevron* discretion to interpret the statute in question, "the proper course, except in rare circumstances, is to remand to the agency for additional investigation or explanation." * * *

NOTES AND QUESTIONS ON PERSECUTION UNDER DURESS

1. Despite the Supreme Court's invitation to the agency to consider afresh the relevance of a duress exception to the asylum bar against those who took part in the persecution of others, the BIA has not yet done so via its decisions. Nor, as of late 2011, has DHS issued regulations setting forth circumstances in which motive, intent, coercion, and related factors should be considered in evaluating when participation in persecution constitutes a bar to asylum.

2. In *Miranda Alvarado v. Gonzales*, 449 F.3d 915 (9th Cir. 2006), the Ninth Circuit sustained the exclusion from protection of a Peruvian who fled death threats from the Shining Path. Miranda had joined the Civil Guard at age 19 and served as an interpreter during interrogations of Shining Path guerrillas. He conceded that he had been present during the questioning, which included electric shock torture, but stated he had never participated in the torture and had frequently asked the interrogators to stop. Does *Negusie* suggest that this ruling was erroneous, or must the answer await new regulations or a definitive ruling by the BIA in wake of that decision? Did Miranda provide material support to terrorist activity, a topic we will consider in the next section?

3. A series of brutal insurgencies and civil wars in the last decades of the twentieth century, marked by large-scale conscription of children by warlords and rebel groups, have given rise to a growing number of asylum claims filed by former child soldiers. Many recount harrowing tales of persecution and torture they endured, as well as persecution and torture they were forced to inflict on others. The law is under-developed as to whether criminal and civil responsibility should be attributed to child soldiers and the significance their coerced conduct should have on their claims for asylum and withholding. Commentary on these issues can be found in White, *A Chance for Redemption: Revising the "Persecutor Bar" and the "Material Support Bar" in the Case of Child Soldiers*, 43 Vand. J. Transnat'l L. 191 (2010).

4. SECURITY DANGERS AND TERRORIST ACTIVITY

The statute prohibits asylum for those considered security dangers, INA § 208(b)(2)(A)(iv), and bars withholding when "there are reasonable grounds for regarding the alien as a danger to the security of the United States." INA § 241(b)(3)(B)(iv). This language is nearly identical to Article 33(2) of the Convention, which limits the coverage of the treaty's *nonrefoulement* protection. In addition, Congress has added a provision to the withholding statute that equates engaging in terrorist activity (and certain other connections with terrorism) with posing a security danger to the United States, INA § 241(b)(3)(B) (last sentence), and has added an explicit ban on asylum for those involved in terrorist activity, INA § 208(b)(2)(A)(v). These provisions employ intricate cross-references to various portions of a highly complex terrorist inadmissibility ground, INA § 212(a)(3)(B), which we examined earlier in Chapter Seven, at pp. 625–644.

Some of the litigation concerning bars based on terrorist activity has involved fairly well known armed groups and violence committed against political opponents. For example, a member of the Irish National Liberation Army was denied asylum and withholding based on several crimes involving firearms and a conspiracy to kill a Royal Ulster Constabulary officer, crimes for which he had been convicted and imprisoned in Northern Ireland. The BIA and the federal court concluded that he had engaged in terrorist activity, which constitutes reasonable grounds for being regarded a danger to the security of the United States. Consequently, he was ineligible for asylum and withholding, even though he had fully served out his prison sentence in the United Kingdom and there was no indication of further involvement in violent acts. *McAllister v. Attorney General*, 444 F.3d 178 (3d. Cir. 2006).

Since September 11, 2001, Congress has expanded the definition of engaging in terrorist activities to a wide array of conduct, including the provision of any type of material support "to any individual the actor knows, or reasonably should know, has committed or plans to commit a terrorist activity," or to terrorist organizations. INA § 212(a)(3)(B)(iv)(VI). The current definition of a terrorist organization includes any group of "two or more individuals, whether organized or not," INA § 212(a)(3)(B)(vi)(III), which makes the reach of the material support provision extraordinarily wide. Providing food and tents at religious meetings attended by unnamed members of militant groups can constitute material support for terrorism. *Singh–Kaur v. Ashcroft*, 385 F.3d 293 (3d Cir. 2004). As detailed in Chapter Seven, Section A, donating several hundred dollars to a group resisting the military dictatorship in Burma can constitute material support to terrorism, even though the group used armed force defensively and was allied with the U.S.-supported National League for Democracy led by Nobel Peace Prize winner Aung

San Suu Kyi. *Matter of S–K–,* 23 I & N Dec. 936 (BIA 2006). After subsequent legislation specified that certain Burmese resistance groups were not terrorist organizations, Consolidated Appropriations Act, 2008, Pub. L. 110–161, 121 Stat. 1844, Div. J, § 691, the BIA concluded that S–K– herself was entitled to asylum, but stated that its earlier analysis of the material support provisions remained precedential, 24 I & N Dec. 475 (BIA 2008).

DHS and the Department of Justice have construed the terrorist provisions broadly, to include even minimal support given under duress, a stance that has provoked heated debate. Critics have pointed out that the broad reach of this interpretation leads to perverse consequences. For example, refugees who had been extorted to provide food and drink to armed groups, and then fled precisely to avoid future such threats and exactions, are precluded from protection under this reading of U.S. law.

Indeed, although the material support bar applies to all persons seeking to come to the United States, it has had at various times especially negative effects on the asylum and overseas refugee resettlement program. Resettlement initiatives during the past decade were frequently stalled because the State Department wished to resettle a group that included many members who had provided support of some form to armed groups. As *S–K–* demonstrates, it makes no difference that the government they resisted was tyrannical (absent a discretionary exemption from the terrorism bars, discussed below). In addition, the expanded material support bar has also stalled the adjustment of status to lawful permanent residence of refugees or asylees who had been admitted in earlier years before the terrorist bars were expanded. See Human Rights First, *Denial and Delay: The Impact of the Immigration Law's "Terrorist Bars" on Asylum Seekers and Refugees in the United States*, Human Rights First Report, p. 22, <http://www.humanrightsfirst.org/wp-content/uploads/pdf/RPP–Denialand Delay–FULL–111009–web.pdf>.

In 2010 the Supreme Court upheld against First Amendment challenges a broad material support provision that criminalized conduct by U.S. citizens intended to promote peaceful dispute resolution and charitable efforts involving organizations deemed terrorist. *Holder v. Humanitarian Law Project,* 561 U.S. ___, 130 S.Ct. 2705, 177 L.Ed.2d 355 (2010), which is treated at greater length in Chapter Seven, did not arise in the context of immigration and asylum, but its rationale suggests that the material support bar will continue to pose a substantial hurdle for many refugees, asylum seekers, and other immigrants.

Despite the manifest problems caused by the breadth of the terrorism-related bars, especially (but not exclusively) in their impact on refugees and asylum seekers, Congress has resisted narrowing the scope of those provisions. Instead it has provided and then unevenly expanded a provision that gives the Secretary of State or the Secretary of Homeland Security, after consulting together and with the Attorney General, the discretionary authority to exempt individuals or groups from many of the applicable bars. INA § 212(d)(3)(B). The statute emphasizes that such exemptions are provided in the "sole unreviewable discretion" of the Secretary. (Consider why Congress might have chosen this type of procedure, instead of amending the bars themselves.)

Early uses of this authority by the Secretary of State facilitated the admission of specific refugee groups as part of the U.S. resettlement program. Later decisions by the Secretary of Homeland Security have exempted specific resistance groups from the broad coverage of the definition of terrorist organization, and group exemptions continue to be considered and issued. A significant pair of DHS exemptions in 2007 cover person who provided material support under duress, with certain qualifications. USCIS officers consider the individual case to decide whether the person acted under duress and to apply the further standards set forth by the Secretary. *See* 72 Fed. Reg. 9954, 9958 (Mar. 6, 2007) and *id.* at 26,138 (May 8, 2007). *See also* 84 Interp. Rel. 191–192 (Jan. 22, 2007).

These waiver provisions have provided some reprieve from overbroad legislation, but significant problems still remain. The waiver process can be time-consuming and lengthy; waivers are decided by USCIS officers, not by immigration judges; and the waiver decision is discretionary and unreviewable. USCIS, *Department of Homeland Security Implements Exemption Authority for Certain Terrorist–Related Inadmissibility Grounds for Cases with Administratively Final Orders of Removal*, USCIS Fact Sheet, 23 Oct. 2008. *See generally* Fullerton, *Terrorism, Torture, and Refugee Protection in the United States*, 29 Refugee Survey Quarterly 4 (2010).

5. SERIOUS CRIMES

The asylum statute and the withholding statute both expressly prohibit relief to (1) those who committed a serious nonpolitical crime outside the United States prior to arrival, INA §§ 208(b)(2)(A)(iii); 241(b)(3)(B)(iii) (wording slightly different in § 241); and to (2) those who have been convicted of a particularly serious crime in the United States. INA §§ 208(b)(2)(A)(ii); 241(b)(3)(B)(ii). Both of these bars are drawn from provisions of the 1951 Convention (*see* Arts. 1(F), 33(2)), but the U.S. statute may apply them in somewhat different fashion from their deployment under the treaty. It is easy to confuse these statutory terms: what is a "serious nonpolitical crime" and how is it different from a "particularly serious crime"? Focusing on when and where the criminal activity occurred helps to clarify which portion of the statute applies.

a. Prior to Arrival in the United States

In recognition that governments frequently label their dissidents as criminals, the bar related to criminal acts outside the United States prior to arrival refers only to nonpolitical crimes. Many of the difficult challenges in analyzing this barrier to protection involve determining whether certain criminal conduct should be characterized as political or nonpolitical. For example, an asylum applicant from Guatemala had participated in political protests that involved burning buses, using force to remove passengers, breaking store windows, and attacking police cars. The Supreme Court ruled that these were serious nonpolitical crimes even though done in support of political objectives. *INS v. Aguirre–Aguirre*, 526 U.S. 415, 119 S.Ct. 1439, 143 L.Ed.2d 590 (1999). The Court approved the BIA's approach, which examined whether the political aspect of the criminal conduct outweighed its common law character, whether atrocious acts were involved, and whether there was a gross disproportion between the means and the ends.

Determining whether criminal conduct is political or nonpolitical can also arise in extradition proceedings, because most of the applicable treaties bar extradition if the crime charged is considered a "political offense" (or similar wording). A substantial case law has grown up interpreting that concept for extradition purposes, and that doctrine is sometimes consulted by courts considering what is a serious nonpolitical crime under the 1951 Convention. But care must be taken in using such guidance, because the treaty language diverges, and the policy concerns are also of a different nature. For a discussion of the interrelationship of these concepts in the two legal realms, see *McMullen v. INS*, 788 F.2d 591 (9th Cir. 1986). A look at the interplay between asylum, extradition, and rendition procedures can be found in Fitzpatrick, *The Post–Exclusion Phase: Extradition, Prosecution and Expulsion*, 12 Int'l J. Refugee Law (special issue) 272 (2000).

Even conduct determined to be nonpolitical will bar individuals from asylum and withholding only if it amounts to a serious crime. To determine whether an offense is sufficiently serious to bar protection, the UN High Commissioner for Refugees has articulated a "balancing" approach:

> [I]t is necessary to strike a balance between the nature of the offence presumed to have been committed by the applicant and the degree of persecution feared. If a person has well-founded fear of very severe persecution, e.g. persecution endangering his life or freedom, a crime must be very grave in order to exclude him. If the persecution feared is less serious, it will be necessary to have regard to the nature of the crime * * * in order to establish whether * * * his criminal character does not outweigh his character as a *bona fide* refugee.

Office of the United Nations Commissioner of Refugees, Handbook on Procedures and Criteria for Determining Refugee Status ¶ 156 (Geneva, 1979).

The *Aguirre–Aguirre* Court rejected the "balancing" approach, explaining that the UN Handbook is a useful, but nonbinding, interpretive aid, and stated: "As a matter of plain language [of the INA provision], it is not obvious that an already-completed crime is somehow rendered less serious by considering the further circumstance that the alien may be subject to persecution if returned to his home country." 526 U.S. at 426.

In contrast, courts in other countries have applied the "serious nonpolitical crime" term in the 1951 Convention by weighing the asylum applicant's criminal acts against the gravity of the persecution risked if returned home. In an Australian case, for example, the tribunal considered the asylum applicant's participation in armed raids on civilian villages as one factor in deciding whether to grant him asylum. Refugee Review Tribunal Reference N96/1201 (1996).

b. Within the United States

Individuals convicted of particularly serious crimes within the United States are also ineligible to apply for relief under the asylum and withholding statutes. The text of the statute refers not only to the seriousness of the conduct, but also to dangerousness: asylum is barred to an individual who "having been convicted by a final judgment of a particularly serious crime, constitutes a danger to the community of the United States," INA § 208(b)(2)(A)(ii). This wording gave rise to arguments that the statute requires asylum adjudicators to make two separate findings: (1) a prior conviction of a particularly serious crime, and (2) a present danger to the community. In examining the parallel bar to protection under the withholding statute, the BIA concluded:

> We find section 243(h)(2)(B) of the Act does not require that two separate and distinct factual findings be made in order to render an alien ineligible for withholding of deportation. It must be determined that an applicant for relief constitutes a danger to the community of the United States to come within the purview of section 243(h)(2)(B). However, the statute provides the key for determining whether an alien constitutes such a danger. That is, those aliens who have been finally convicted of particularly serious crimes are presumptively dangers to this country's community.

Matter of Carballe, 19 I & N Dec. 357, 360 (BIA 1986).

The BIA approach is not universal. Many countries and commentators have concluded that there should be a separate investigation into whether the individual convicted of a particularly serious crime is, in fact, an ongoing danger to the local community. *See, e.g.,* G. Goodwin–Gill & J. McAdam, The Refugee in International Law 238–239 (3d ed. 2007); Keller, *A Comparative and International Law Perspective on the United States (Non) Compliance with its Duty of Non-refoulement*, 2 Yale Hum. Rts. & Dev. L.J. 183 (1999) (surveying decisions in Sweden, Germany, and Belgium).

Nonetheless, under U.S. case law those convicted in this country of a "particularly serious crime" are deemed a danger to the community. Therefore, the interpretation of "particularly serious crime" is a matter of great importance. The 1951 Convention itself does not define this phrase, but commentators agree that a "particularly serious crime" refers to more heinous conduct than a "serious crime." The UNHCR Handbook concludes that a "serious crime" refers to "a capital crime or a very grave punishable act." Office of the United Nations High Commissioner for Refugees, Handbook on Procedures and Criteria for Determining Refugee Status ¶ 155 (Geneva, 1979).

In the early 1980s the BIA examined the meaning of "particularly serious crime" and adopted a case by case approach. In *Matter of Frentescu*, 18 I & N Dec. 244, 247 (BIA 1982), the Board held that burglary with intent to commit theft did not constitute a "particularly serious crime." It noted: "[A] 'particularly serious crime' is more serious than a 'serious nonpolitical crime,' although many crimes may be classified [as] both. * * * Crimes against persons are more likely to be categorized as 'particularly serious' * * * [yet] there may be instances where crimes * * * against property will be considered as such crimes."

Over the years, Congress has amended the statutes in order to expand the application of the criminal bars and has increasingly legislated bright-line rules. The 1990 Act added language to the withholding provision providing that an aggravated felony, as defined in INA § 101(a)(43), is to be considered per se a "particularly serious crime." It also barred asylum for anyone convicted of an aggravated felony. The 1996 Act greatly expanded the catalog of aggravated felonies in INA § 101(a)(43) by adding new offenses to the list and by reducing the minimum sentence necessary to render many crimes aggravated felonies. For example, theft offenses formerly required a five-year sentence to be counted as an aggravated felony. Now a one-year sentence will suffice.

Asylum remains barred for all aggravated felonies. INA § 208(b)(2)(B)(i). The Attorney General is expressly authorized to consider other offenses as well to be particularly serious crimes. INA § 208(b)(2)(B)(ii). With regard to withholding of removal, in apparent recognition that a complete ban for this wider class might violate the Convention—or at least that it might be overly harsh—the 1996 Act provided in INA § 241(b)(3)(B) a threshold of a five-year aggregate sentence for automatic preclusion:

> For purposes of [the clause excluding those convicted of particularly serious crimes], an alien who has been convicted of an aggravated felony (or felonies) for which the alien has been sentenced to an aggregate term of imprisonment of at least 5 years shall be considered to have committed a particularly serious crime. The previous sentence shall not preclude the Attorney General from determining that, notwithstanding the length of sentence imposed, an alien has been convicted of a particularly serious crime.

INA § 241(b)(3)(B).

Litigation arose involving individuals convicted of aggravated felonies but sentenced to less than five years in prison. In those cases, the BIA ruled that there is no presumption that the crime is particularly serious; instead a case-by-case inquiry is necessary. *See Matter of L–S–*, 22 I & N Dec. 645 (BIA 1999) (noncitizen convicted of bringing an undocumented alien into the United States and sentenced to 3 ½ months, held not barred from withholding); *Matter of S–S–*, 22 I & N Dec. 458 (BIA 1999) (noncitizen convicted of robbery in the first degree while armed with a handgun and sentenced to 55 months in prison held barred).

Attorney General Ashcroft overruled at least parts of the BIA's approach when he reviewed the case excerpted below. It involved three applicants for withholding who had been convicted of drug trafficking offenses; they had been sentenced, respectively, to confinement of a year and a day, 24 months, and 25 months.

MATTER OF Y–L–

Attorney General, 2002.
23 I & N Dec. 270.

[ASHCROFT, ATTORNEY GENERAL:]

* * * According to the BIA, the 1996 INA amendments—which eliminated a provision declaring that *all* aggravated felonies are "particularly serious crimes"—reflected Congress' desire to replace classifications based on the "category or type of crime that resulted in the conviction" with classifications "based on the length of sentence imposed." *See In re S–S–, supra*. I do not concur. The BIA's interpretation of these amendments places far too much weight on the first sentence of section 241(b)(3)'s final clause (the mandatory designation) and far too little weight on the final clause's second sentence (the grant of discretionary authority to the Attorney General). The fact that Congress designated as per se "particularly serious" every aggravated felony resulting in a term of incarceration of at least five years hardly reflects an intent to subordinate the nefarious or harmful *character* of a crime to mere secondary consideration, let alone remove it from the equation. While the imposition of certain harsh sentences may obviate the need to probe the underlying circumstances of a particular crime, the discretionary authority reserved to the Attorney General with respect to offenses from which less severe sentences flow is clearly intended to enable him to emphasize factors *other than* length of sentence. * * *

[After discussing the seriously negative effects of the drug trade, the Attorney General went on:] I might be well within my discretion to conclude that all drug trafficking offenses are per se "particularly serious crimes" under the INA. I do not consider it necessary, however, to exclude entirely the possibility of the very rare case where an alien may be able to demonstrate extraordinary and compelling circumstances that justify treating a particular drug trafficking crime as falling short of that standard. While this opinion does not afford the occasion to define the precise boundaries of what those unusual circumstances would be, they would need to include, at a *minimum*: (1) a very small quantity of controlled substance; (2) a very modest amount of money paid for the drugs in the offending transaction; (3) merely peripheral involvement by the alien in the criminal activity, transaction, or conspiracy; (4) the absence of any violence or threat of violence, implicit or otherwise, associated with the offense; (5) the absence of any organized crime or terrorist organization involvement, direct or indirect, in relation to the offending activity; and (6) the absence of any adverse or harmful effect of the activity or transaction on juveniles. Only if *all* of these criteria were demonstrated by an alien would it be appropriate to consider whether other, more unusual circumstances (e.g., the prospective distribution was solely for social purposes, rather than for profit) might justify departure from the default interpretation that drug trafficking felonies are "particularly serious crimes." I emphasize here that such commonplace circumstances as cooperation with law enforcement authorities, limited criminal histories, downward departures at sentencing, and post-arrest (let alone post-conviction) claims of contrition or innocence do not justify such a deviation.

* * *

[The Attorney General reversed the BIA and ruled that none of the applicants was entitled to relief.]

Notes and Questions on Particularly Serious Crimes

1. Do you agree that it is within the Attorney General's discretion to conclude that *all* drug trafficking offenses are particularly serious crimes? Is such a conclusion consistent with the 1951 Convention?

2. Around the same time as the *Y–L–* opinion, Attorney General Ashcroft handed down another decision greatly restricting the favorable exercise of discretion over asylum and related waivers. *Matter of Jean*, 23 I & N Dec. 373 (AG 2002). After refusing to exercise his discretion in favor of a mother of five who had been convicted of manslaughter, the Attorney General added: "I am highly disinclined to exercise my discretion—except * * * in extraordinary circumstances, such as those involving national security or foreign policy considerations, or cases in which an alien clearly demonstrates that the denial of relief would result in exceptional and extremely unusual hardship—on behalf of dangerous or violent felons seeking asylum." *Id.* at 385.

Exercise

As you consider these scenarios, you should have a copy of INA §§ 208(b)(2) and 241(b)(3)(B) at hand so that you identify the specific statutory section that applies and the precise statutory language that is relevant.

A. Crimes Outside the United States

1. Suppose your client, an asylum seeker, was convicted of extortion and murder in Fredonia, which caused her to flee to the United States to seek protection. She has convincing proof that she is a member of an ethnic group that the Fredonian government has traditionally persecuted. Is she eligible for asylum or withholding? What additional facts would you need to learn to assess the bars to protection that she might face?

2.   Same facts as above, except your client fled as soon as she learned that criminal charges had been filed against her and she has not been convicted of any crimes.

3.   Same facts as scenario 2, and your client has proof that she is a prominent member of the pro-democracy opposition to the military government.

4.   Same facts as scenario 3, and your client says the murder charge arose when she shot her former boyfriend, a police officer, to stop him from beating her.

B.   Crimes Within the United States

1.   Suppose your client, an asylum seeker, has been convicted of extortion in the United States and sentenced to three years in prison. Nonetheless, she has strong proof that she would likely be persecuted if returned to her home country of Ruritania. She acknowledged that her erratic behavior was a result of substance abuse, and she entered a rehabilitation program. She has now been sober for two years, and her psychiatrist will testify that a relapse is extremely unlikely. Is she eligible for asylum or withholding?

2.   Same facts as scenario 1, but she was sentenced to five years in prison.

3.   Suppose your client had been charged with extortion in the United States but had been acquitted. During the trial she testified that she had been a substance abuser, but had been sober since she finished a rehabilitation program two years ago.

SECTION F.   CONVENTION AGAINST TORTURE

The Convention Against Torture and Other Cruel, Inhuman, or Degrading Treatment or Punishment (CAT, reprinted in the Statutory Supplement), to which the United States became a party in 1994, provides another avenue of humanitarian protection. The centerpiece of the Convention is the agreement that torture is illegitimate, and most of the articles of the treaty impose specific obligations on state parties to prevent and punish torture committed on their territory. But it also forbids governments from returning individuals to situations where they will face torture. In short, the Convention imposes a *nonrefoulement* obligation:

> No State Party shall expel, return ("*refouler*") or extradite a person to another State where there are substantial grounds for believing that he would be in danger of being subjected to torture.

Art. 3, CAT. This provision, rather than the direct prevention and punishment provisions, has given rise to the greatest volume of litigation implicating the CAT.

Many acts that constitute torture give rise to a well-founded fear of persecution. Accordingly, the protection that arises under the 1951 Refugee Convention, as implemented by INA §§ 208 and 241(b)(3), substantially overlaps with the *nonrefoulement* protection afforded by the CAT. As a consequence, the asylum and withholding machinery we examined earlier in this chapter ordinarily suffices to honor Article 3 of the CAT in practice. But in certain circumstances the protections do not coincide. For example, torture routinely meted out as part of the punishment of common criminals would not be inflicted on account of one of the five grounds specified in the refugee treaties. Thus, it would not trigger protection under asylum or withholding, but it would implicate the *nonrefoulement* obligations of the CAT. Moreover, as the discussion in the prior section emphasized, certain criminal and other conduct disqualifies even those with a clear probability of persecution from asylum or withholding of removal. In contrast, the Torture Convention does not include a similar disqualification; the CAT *nonrefoulement* provision applies to everyone— including criminals—who would face torture.

The following excerpt provides a succinct account of the relationships between CAT protection and asylum:

> * * * In an important sense, then, the [CAT's] reach is both broader and narrower than that of a claim for asylum or withholding of deportation: coverage is broader because a petitioner need not show that he or she would be tortured "on account of" a protected ground; it is narrower, however, because the petitioner must show that it is "more likely than not" that he or she will be tortured, and not simply persecuted upon removal to a given country.

Kamalthas v. INS, 251 F.3d 1279, 1283 (9th Cir.2001).

Despite the conceptual differences, torture, in the modern world, is most commonly administered in campaigns against political opponents or against groups disfavored on account of race or religion. Therefore, potential victims of torture frequently are eligible to seek asylum. Those who qualify for both forms of protection—under the CAT and under the asylum provisions in INA § 208—clearly would prefer the latter. If they receive asylum, they will not be expelled and compliance with the CAT will be assured. And they will receive a status that allows the immediate family to immigrate and also opens a direct path to LPR status. In contrast, CAT protection consists, at best, of a form of withholding of removal. Hence, as a practical matter, the Torture Convention is likely to be relied on by those excluded from the normal asylum or withholding protections by the exception clauses—primarily individuals with criminal convictions.

1. APPLICATIONS FOR PROTECTION UNDER THE TORTURE CONVENTION

In recognition of the potential overlap in eligibility for CAT protection and asylum, applicants for protection under the CAT file their claims on the I–589 form, the same form used for asylum claims. By regulation, 8

C.F.R. § 208.16, immigration judges, not asylum officers, decide applications for protection under the CAT. (If the applicant simultaneously files an affirmative claim for asylum, an asylum officer will first review the file and determine whether to grant asylum. An officer who does not grant asylum will refer the case to immigration court.) The immigration judge will examine all the requests for protection together and decide whether to grant asylum, withholding of removal under § 241(b)(3), or withholding of removal under the CAT. Generally, the immigration judge will determine the applicability of protection under the Torture Convention only if the person fails to qualify for asylum or regular withholding.

The expedited removal procedure, discussed in Chapter Six, also incorporates consideration of claims of torture, as well as persecution, into the credible fear determinations. A noncitizen found there to have a credible fear of torture will ordinarily be placed in full removal proceedings before an immigration judge to have the CAT claim determined. 8 C.F.R. § 235.3(b)(4).

In the 1998 legislation implementing CAT article 3, Pub.L. 105–277, Div. G., Title XXII, § 2242, 112 Stat. 2681–822 (1998) (reprinted in the Statutory Supplement), Congress manifested unhappiness with the prospect of providing CAT protection to persons barred from regular withholding under INA § 241(b)(3)(B) because of crimes, involvement in persecution of others, or other threatening behavior. It therefore directed the agency to exclude such persons "to the maximum extent consistent with the obligations of the United States under the Convention." The agency concluded that no one facing the specified risk of torture could be excluded from protection, however, because the CAT's *nonrefoulement* protection is absolute. But it responded to the congressional mandate by providing two forms of CAT relief: withholding and deferral of removal.

Generally, those entitled to protection under the CAT receive withholding of removal, essentially equivalent to the protection developed in response to the persecution-based *nonrefoulement* requirement of INA § 241(b)(3). But those entitled to CAT protection who have persecuted others, committed particularly serious crimes or serious nonpolitical crimes, or who constitute a security danger to the United States are given a lesser form of protection, "deferral of removal." 8 C.F.R. § 208.16(d). This status carries many of the same features as withholding, including eligibility for work authorization, but it can be terminated somewhat more easily than asylum or withholding of removal in the event that conditions change in such a way as to permit lawful deportation to the country of origin or a third country. *Compare* 8 C.F.R. § 208.17(d) with § 208.24(f). Furthermore, the regulations contemplate that such persons might be held in detention, even if granted deferral of removal. *Id.* at § 208.17(c). The exact basis for this potential detention is not made clear; apparently, any such power has not been exercised.

As the table below shows, fewer than 500 of the 25,000 CAT applicants received protection in the United States under the Convention

Against Torture in 2010. Roughly 80 percent of the successful CAT applicants received withholding of removal, with the remaining 20 percent receiving deferral of removal.

Table 8.1
Convention Against Torture Cases by Disposition, 2010

Granted			Denied	Other	Withdrawn	Abandoned	Total
Withholding	Deferral	Total					
395	94	489	9,082	8,501	5,877	805	24,754

Source: EOIR, FY 2010 Statistical Year Book, Table 9, at M-1.

Those denied protection under the CAT can appeal to the BIA. In limited circumstances, they can appeal from BIA decisions denying CAT claims to the federal courts.

The regulations provide that the U.S. Secretary of State may forward to the Attorney General diplomatic assurances from the government of another country that a specified individual would not be tortured if returned to that country. 8 C.F.R. § 208.18(c). The Attorney General must assess "whether the assurances are sufficiently reliable to allow the alien's removal to that country consistent with Article 3" of the CAT. Only a limited list of high-level officials of Cabinet or immediate sub-Cabinet rank are authorized to make this assessment. Once the determination is made, the diplomatic assurances override any withholding or deferral granted by an immigration judge. The Third Circuit has ruled, however, that a noncitizen has the right to a hearing to challenge the government's reliance on diplomatic assurances as a basis for removal from the United States. *Khouzam v. Attorney General*, 549 F.3d 235 (3d Cir. 2008).

Other countries have, on occasion, also relied on diplomatic assurances in returning noncitizens to their homelands. *See, e.g., Agiza v. Sweden*, Committee Against Torture, Communication No. 233/2003, U.N. Doc. CAT/C/34/D/233/203 (May 24, 2005) (Sweden's reliance on diplomatic assurances from Egypt breached CAT); A. Deeks, *Promises Not To Torture: Diplomatic Assurances in U.S. Courts*, ASIL Discussion Paper Series, Dec. 2008, at 49–70 (review of European and Canadian uses of diplomatic assurances), <http://www.asil.org/files/ASIL–08–DiscussionPaper.pdf>. The reliance on diplomatic assurances has been controversial. *See* Jones, *Damned Lies and Diplomatic Assurances: The Misuse of Diplomatic Assurances in Removal Proceedings*, 8 Eur. J. of Migration & Law 9 (2006).

2. THE DEFINITION OF TORTURE

The Convention outlaws cruel, inhuman, or degrading treatment or punishment, in addition to torture, but its central focus is on preventing and punishing torture, and the *nonrefoulement* provision, Article 3, provides protection only against return to torture. Article 1 of the treaty sets forth a detailed definition of torture:

> any act by which severe pain or suffering, whether physical or mental, is intentionally inflicted on a person for such purposes as obtaining from him or a third person information or a confession, punishing him for an act he or a third person has committed or is suspected of having committed, or intimidating or coercing him or a third person, or for any reason based on discrimination of any kind when such pain and suffering is inflicted by or at the instigation of or with the consent or acquiescence of a public official or other person acting in an official capacity. It does not include pain or suffering arising only from, inherent in or incidental to lawful sanctions.

Art. 1, CAT.

In its resolution approving ratification of the Convention Against Torture, U.S. Resolution of Advice and Consent (With Reservations, Understandings and Declarations), 136 Cong. Rec. 36198–99 (1990), reprinted in the Statutory Supplement, the Senate included the following guidance for implementation of the Convention.

> The Senate's advice and consent is subject to the following understandings, which shall apply to the obligations of the United States under this Convention:

> * * *

> (1)(d) * * * the term "acquiescence" requires that the public official, prior to the activity constituting torture, have awareness of such activity and thereafter breach his legal responsibility to intervene to prevent such activity.

> * * *

> (2) * * * the United States understands the phrase, "where there are substantial grounds for believing that he would be in danger of being subjected to torture," as used in article 3 of the Convention, to mean "if it is more likely than not that he would be tortured."

a. Government Involvement or Acquiescence in Torture

Article 1 of the CAT defines torture to mean certain acts that inflict severe pain or suffering, but only "when such pain or suffering is inflicted by or at the instigation of or with the consent or acquiescence of a public official or other person acting in an official capacity." There is no similar government actor requirement in asylum, although, as we have seen in the discussion of domestic abuse cases above in Section D, purely private infliction of harm can raise difficult issues.

In 2000, the BIA confronted a CAT application filed by a citizen of Colombia, who after 17 years as a lawful permanent resident of the United States, had been convicted of grand theft, robbery, and driving with a suspended license, and was sentenced to four years in prison. He sought protection from *refoulement* because he feared that he would be a target of kidnapping by nongovernmental guerrilla, narcotrafficking, and paramilitary groups in Colombia. The BIA ruled that his criminal conviction and sentence made him ineligible for withholding of removal, and then proceeded to consider his claim for relief under the CAT:

> A public official's acquiescence to torture "requires that the public official, prior to the activity constituting torture, have awareness of such activity and thereafter breach his or her legal responsibility to intervene to prevent such activity." 8 C.F.R. § 208.18(a)(7). In its resolution of advice and consent to the Convention Against Torture, the United States Senate included an understanding replacing the word "knowledge" in this definition of acquiescence with the word "awareness," indicating that actual knowledge of activity constituting torture is not required. See 136 Cong. Rec. S17,486, 17,491–2 (daily ed. Oct. 27, 1990). This revision is also reflected in the regulations. The Senate Committee on Foreign Relations clarified the point by stating that "(t)he purpose of this condition is to make it clear that both actual knowledge and 'willful blindness' fall within the definition of the term 'acquiescence.' " Consequently, the definition of "torture" "includes only acts that occur in the context of governmental authority." Regulations Concerning the Convention Against Torture, 64 Fed. Reg. 8478, 8483 (1999) (citing S. Treaty Doc. No. 100–20, at 19).

> * * * To demonstrate "acquiescence" by Colombian Government officials, the respondent must do more than show that the officials are aware of the activity constituting torture but are powerless to stop it. He must demonstrate that Colombian officials are willfully accepting of the guerrillas' torturous activities. * * * Accordingly, we consider that a government's inability to control a group ought not lead to the conclusion that the government acquiesced to the group's activities.

Matter of S–V–, 22 I & N Dec. 1306, 1311–13 (BIA 2000).

Several years later, Attorney General Ashcroft issued the following opinion, *Matter of Y–L–*, as a precedent to guide future application of the CAT. The decision applies the acquiescence requirement of the Torture Convention to several individuals who had been convicted of drug trafficking and so were precluded from withholding of removal under INA § 241(b)(3). (This excerpt discusses the CAT claims of two individuals; another portion of the opinion concluding that they were not entitled to regular withholding of removal appeared above in Section E.5.)

MATTER OF Y–L

Attorney General, 2002.
23 I & N Dec. 270.

[Ashcroft, Attorney General:]

* * *

Although the respondents are statutorily ineligible for withholding of removal by virtue of their convictions for "particularly serious crimes," the regulations implementing the Convention Against Torture allow them to obtain a deferral of removal notwithstanding the prior criminal offenses if they can establish that they are "entitled to protection" under the Convention. *See* 8 C.F.R. § 208.17(a). To secure such relief, the respondents must demonstrate that, if removed to their country of origin, it is more likely than not they would be tortured by, or with the acquiescence of, government officials acting under color of law. None of the respondents has come close to making such a showing.

A. Y–L–

Y–L–, who was paroled into the United States in 1979, maintains that he will be killed if sent back to his native Haiti. He testified at his removal hearing that two months prior to his arrival in America, members of the Ton Ton Macoutes—a private army of Haitian death squads organized by former president Francois Duvalier and nurtured by his successor, Jean Claude Duvalier—murdered his father and aunt, and broke his cousin's leg as retribution for his father's unspecified criticism of the Duvalier government. Y–L–further insisted that the same group of people responsible for the death of his father killed his cousin in 1998, approximately twenty years after Y–L–initially left the country.

Y–L–'s claim for relief under the Convention Against Torture fails on at least two different levels. First, as the immigration judge correctly found, Y–L–produced no reliable evidence that he would likely be subjected to torture if returned to Haiti. While voluntarily visiting Haiti on two prior occasions, he was never personally harmed or threatened. * * * [The Attorney General concluded that the violence of earlier years was unlikely to threaten the applicant now.]

Second, even assuming Y–L–'s various allegations have some basis in fact, and even if his own alleged fears of torture are genuine, he is not entitled to deferral of removal under the Convention Against Torture because he has not established that current government officials acting in an official capacity would be responsible for such abuse. The regulations implementing the Convention allow for relief only if torture would be "inflicted by or at the instigation of or with the consent or acquiescence of a public official or other person acting in an official capacity." 8 C.F.R. § 208.18(a)(1) (emphasis added). Violence committed by individuals over whom the government has no reasonable control does not implicate the treaty. *See In re S–V–*, 22 I & N Dec. 1306, 1312 (BIA 2000) * * * The State Department's asylum profile on Haiti underscores that the Ton Ton Macoutes have effectively disbanded and neither play a role in, nor enjoy the tacit support of, the current Haitian government. Both Y–L–and his counsel conceded this point. If, by some chance—which has certainly not been proven to be more likely than not—former Ton Ton Macoute elements seek revenge on Y–L–because of his relationship to his father, there is no competent evidence in the record indicating that the current

Haitian administration would either participate in, or turn a blind eye to, such violence. In short, Y–L–has failed to sustain his burden of establishing entitlement to deferral of removal.

B. A–G–

The evidence advanced by A–G–similarly falls far short of what is required to obtain relief under the Convention Against Torture. At some point following his entry into the United States, A–G–decided to supplement his income as a maintenance worker by trafficking in illegal narcotics. His supplier was his long-time friend and roommate, K–C–, who had a drug-dealing base in Jamaica. As so often happens to those in the drug trade, A–G–was ultimately arrested by the FBI, charged with unlawful distribution of cocaine, and convicted on multiple counts of cocaine trafficking. To minimize his exposure to prison, he agreed to assist federal law enforcement officials by participating in a number of controlled drug purchases designed to implicate K–C–.

During a period in which both K–C–and A–G–were temporarily incarcerated at the same facility, K–C–allegedly delivered a message to A–G– that he would be killed if he returned to Jamaica. In addition, according to A–G–'s brothers and sisters, two or three men came to the family residence in Jamaica in either 1998, 1999, or 2000—the dates and other key particulars diverged sharply among these witnesses—and inquired as to A–G–'s whereabouts. At least one sibling claimed that these men were armed and made threats that A–G–would be murdered by K–C–or others if he returned to Jamaica.

Citing these apparent threats to his life, A–G–seeks to avoid removal pursuant to the Convention Against Torture. The main problem with his claim is that the record is devoid of credible evidence suggesting that the Jamaican government would bear any responsibility—either direct or through passive acquiescence—for physical harm visited upon A–G–. In fact, several of the witnesses candidly acknowledged at the hearing that no one in the family even reported the alleged threats to Jamaican authorities.

* * *

Although there are indications that corruption and brutality affect some elements of Jamaican law enforcement, the national government has undertaken substantial efforts at reform. * * * The State Department has further reported that the Jamaican government does not encourage or facilitate the illicit production or distribution of narcotics. While acknowledging that abuses by some members of the security forces occasionally occur, the State Department's 2000 Country Report for Jamaica makes clear that "[c]ivilian authorities generally maintain effective control of the security forces" * * *.

Ultimately, of course, it is impossible to say with certainty whether A–G–will be exposed to torture by particular individuals upon his return to Jamaica. Those who engage in the illegal drug trade quite commonly expose themselves to the risk of violence; it is an occupational hazard. The relevant inquiry under the Convention Against Torture, however, is whether governmental authorities would approve or "willfully accept" atrocities committed against persons in the respondent's position. *See In re S–V–, supra.* To suggest that this standard can be met by evidence of isolated rogue agents engaging in extrajudicial acts of brutality, which are not only in contravention of the jurisdiction's laws and policies, but are committed despite authorities' best efforts to root out such misconduct, is to empty the Convention's volitional requirement of all rational meaning. As the courts have clearly recognized, relief is available only if the torture would "occur[] in the context of governmental authority," not "as a wholly private act." *Ali v. Reno,* 237 F.3d 591, 597 (6th Cir.2001). There being no such credible evidence in the case at bar, A–G–'s request for deferral must be denied.

NOTES AND QUESTIONS ON GOVERNMENT INVOLVEMENT OR ACQUIESCENCE

1. Some courts take a different approach from Attorney General Ashcroft's. In particular, the Ninth Circuit has expressly disapproved the "willful acceptance" interpretation of the concept of acquiescence, as propounded in *Matter of S–V–* and *Matter of Y–L–.*

> * * * The Convention does not require, as the INS purports, the government to "knowingly acquiesce" to such torture. * * *

> [T]o qualify for relief under the Convention, Zheng has to prove that the torture inflicted by the snakeheads would be carried out with the awareness of the Chinese government officials. That awareness includes "both actual knowledge and 'willful blindness.' " * * *

> In *Matter of S–V–,* the BIA en banc * * * "interpreted the regulation at 8 C.F.R. § 208.8(a) [defining acquiescence] to be limiting"—more limiting than the Senate's just quoted intent to require awareness and not actual knowledge. Creating a standard more stringent than Congress clearly intended, the BIA held that to demonstrate acquiescence "the respondent *must do more than show that the officials are aware* of the activity constituting torture but are powerless to stop it. He must demonstrate that the Colombian officials are *willfully accepting* of the guerillas' torturous activities." (emphases added). * * *

> * * * The BIA's interpretation and application of acquiescence impermissibly requires more than awareness and instead requires that a government be willfully accepting of a third party's tortuous activities. There is nothing in the understandings to the Convention approved by the Senate, or the INS's regulations implementing the Convention, to suggest that anything more than awareness is required. * * * The correct inquiry as intended by the Senate is whether a respondent can show that public officials demonstrate "willful blindness" to the torture of their

citizens by third parties, or as stated by the Fifth Circuit, whether public officials "would turn a blind eye to torture."

Zheng v. Ashcroft, 332 F.3d 1186, 1194–96 (9th Cir. 2003). *Accord Khouzam v. Ashcroft*, 361 F.3d 161 (2d Cir. 2004) (only knowledge or willful blindness of government officials required).

2. CAT obliges states to protect only against torture with which the government is involved or in which it acquiesces. This is in contrast to the approach taken with regard to asylum and withholding; as noted in Section D of this chapter, U.S. law grants protection if the agents of persecution are private groups that the government is "unwilling or unable" to control. Why do you think that the Convention against Torture imposes a "state action" requirement?

3. Should the actions of "isolated rogue [police] agents" be dismissed as a "wholly private act"? Would the agents be acting under color of law? Should that be the test? On the other hand, if the authorities really are applying "their best efforts to root out [corrupt law enforcement] conduct," should the harm be seen as state action? Or is this mixing two separate issues: (1) government involvement and (2) likelihood of risk? Would evidence of such best efforts more appropriately be considered in making the factual determination of whether torture is more likely than not?

4. Look back at the facts of *Matter of S–V–*. Even if *Zheng* were now to provide the controlling doctrine, would that decision come out differently? That is, was the Colombian government willfully blind to torture committed by paramilitary groups or simply unable to control it? If the latter, is S–V– covered by CAT protection?

EXERCISE

The CAT defines torture as severe pain or suffering inflicted for improper purposes "at the instigation of or with the consent or acquiescence of a public official or a person acting in an official capacity." In interpreting the reach of the statute, the BIA, the Attorney General, and the Ninth Circuit have discussed different degrees of involvement by government officials: actual knowledge, willful blindness, willful acceptance, or awareness. Under the opinions you have read, which of the following situations would fall within the statutory requirement?

A. Torture in the presence of the police chief:

1. Torture by a private person and the police chief says nothing.

2. Torture by a private person and the police chief protests, but initiates no investigation or prosecution.

B. Torture outside the presence of the police chief:

1. The police chief learns that torture might occur and takes no action to prevent it.

2.   The police chief learns that torture has occurred and says nothing.

3.   The police chief learns that torture has occurred and expresses disapproval, but takes no action because he believes the government is unable to control the torturer.

4.   The police chief hears rumors that torture might have occurred, but considers the rumors unreliable and does nothing.

5.   The police chief hears rumors that torture occurred and investigates, but the prosecutor thinks the evidence is insufficient and refuses to bring charges.

6.   The police chief hears rumors that torture occurred, arrests the alleged torturer, prosecution is initiated, but the violator escapes from jail.

7.   Same as scenario 6 except that a corrupt jail official "erroneously" releases the alleged torturer.

C.   Would any of your answers change if the government official involved were a low-level police officer rather than the police chief? Several low-level police officers?

b.   Burden of Proof and Level of Risk

The text of Article 3 of the Torture Convention forbids governments to return individuals if there are "substantial grounds" for believing they will face torture. The U.S. Senate's resolution of advice and consent to the Torture Convention, reprinted in the Statutory Supplement, specified that the Senate understood "substantial grounds" to mean that torture is "more likely than not" to occur. The subsequent CAT regulations reiterate this standard, set forth the burden of proof, and acknowledge the importance of uncorroborated evidence in some cases.

> The burden of proof is on the applicant for withholding of removal under this paragraph to establish that it is more likely than not that he or she would be tortured if removed to the proposed country of removal. The testimony of the applicant, if credible, may be sufficient to sustain the burden of proof without corroboration.

8 C.F.R. § 208.16(c)(2).

The next case addresses the level of risk the CAT applicant must show and the role that the burden of proof plays. Note that this individual was concerned that she would be jailed when returned from the United States. For her, as for many applicants for CAT relief, prison conditions in her homeland are a focal point of the CAT litigation. The BIA had earlier established a rebuttable presumption that mistreatment in prison is not torture. *See Matter of J–E–*, 23 I & N Dec. 291 (BIA 2002).

MATTER OF M–B–A

Board of Immigration Appeals, 2002.
23 I & N Dec. 474.

HOLMES, BOARD MEMBER:

The respondent is a 40–year–old native and citizen of Nigeria who * * * was convicted of importation of a controlled substance and possession of heroin with intent to distribute. * * * She was initially sentenced to 121 months' imprisonment, but her sentence was later reduced to 78 months as a result of her assistance to Government controlled substances investigations.

* * *

The Immigration Judge concluded that the respondent's conviction and sentence precluded her from establishing eligibility for any relief other than deferral of removal under Article 3 of the Convention Against Torture * * **

In her application for protection under the Convention Against Torture, the respondent stated that if she is returned to Nigeria she would be imprisoned and tortured as a result of her drug conviction in this country. In support of this claim, the respondent submitted a detailed affidavit, evidence of country conditions in Nigeria, and a copy of a 1990 Nigerian federal military government decree which, in part, criminalized the conduct of Nigerians who are convicted of narcotic drug offenses in a foreign country and bring the name of Nigeria into disrepute, or who are detected carrying a narcotic drug into a foreign country after a journey originating from Nigeria. *See* National Drug Law Enforcement Agency (Amendment) Decree 1990, Decree No. 33 (Oct. 10, 1990) ("Decree No. 33").

During proceedings before the Immigration Judge on December 14, 1999, the respondent testified that she had traveled to Nigeria in 1993 to meet her then-fiancé's family and had been unwillingly involved in drug trafficking by his relatives and associates when she traveled back to the United States. She testified that because of this conviction she would be immediately turned over to drug enforcement authorities and imprisoned if she is returned to Nigeria, that she would be in jail for years before she would be able to see a judge, that she was subject to a mandatory 5–year term of imprisonment, and that she would be subjected to torture while jailed.

When asked how she knew that this would occur, the respondent referred to Decree No. 33 and also testified that some years before she had communicated with an unnamed Nigerian friend who had been convicted of a drug offense in this country and then returned to Nigeria. The respondent indicated that she spoke by telephone to her friend and her friend's parents in 1995. She was told that her friend had been detained upon her return to Nigeria in 1995, that her family had had to bring food and medication to the jail and pay money for her protection, that she slept on the floor, and that "you probably get raped and beat down" by the guards because they have authority to do "whatever they can do." Her friend remained in jail for 2 months until her family paid a bribe to get her released. The respondent did not know whether her friend had gone before a judge before being incarcerated or whether she had been raped in prison.* * *

The respondent further testified that there was no one to help her in Nigeria if she were jailed. * * *

The respondent testified, and provided supporting medical evidence, that she suffers from depression, a chronic ulcer, and asthma. She stated that she had no one to rely on to supply her with medicine if she were jailed in Nigeria. In addition, the respondent testified that she would probably be beaten and raped by prison guards. She stated that most women are subjected to such treatment in prison and that the government does not have the ability to protect them. She also claimed that she would be particularly vulnerable because her ex-fiancé would pay prison guards to harm her because of her cooperation with drug enforcement authorities in this country. The respondent indicated that her ex-fiancé was now in Nigeria, but she did not testify to any communications from or about him, or otherwise identify a specific basis for her claim that he had the ability and intent to cause her harm if she were detained in Nigeria.

* * *

In order to establish eligibility for deferral of removal, the respondent must show that it is more likely than not that she will be subject to torture by a public official, or at the instigation or with the acquiescence of such an official. * * *

* * *

The actual status of Decree No. 33 is not entirely clear on the record before us, but we will assume that it has not been repealed and is enforceable. However, even assuming that such is the case, there is little evidence of record on which to base any meaningful conclusion regarding the extent to which this provision is presently enforced, and how and against whom it is enforced. The fact that the decree is written in mandatory terms is not in itself determinative because it is common to couch criminal provisions in such terms. * * *

The respondent's own evidence concerning the present manner of enforcement of Decree No. 33 does not go much beyond conjecture, and her reference to the circumstances that were related to her by her friend and her friend's parents in 1995 involved one individual some 7 years ago under a different regime in Nigeria. * * *

In this regard, we do not find it sufficient for the respondent simply to cite the existence of Decree No. 33 and her unnamed friend's experiences in 1995. The respondent must provide some current evidence, or at least more meaningful historical evidence, regarding the manner of enforcement of the provisions of Decree No. 33 on individuals similarly situated to herself.* * *

The respondent's eligibility for deferral of removal rests upon a finding that it is more likely than not that she will be identified as a convicted drug trafficker upon her return to Nigeria; that, as a result, she will be detained on arrival; that, when detained, she will be held in detention without access to bail or judicial oversight; that she will be detained for a significant period of time; and that, as a result of this detention, she will suffer mistreatment that rises to the level of torture at the hands of prison guards or authorities. Given the evidence of harsh and life-threatening prison conditions in Nigeria and the serious drug trafficking problems that Nigerian authorities are attempting to address, the respondent's fear of return to her home country is understandable. On the record before us, however, we find that the respondent's case is based on a chain of assumptions and a fear of what might happen, rather than evidence that meets her burden of demonstrating that it is *more likely than not* that she will be subjected to torture by, or with the acquiescence of, a public official or other person acting in an official capacity if she is returned to her home country.

* * *

[The BIA dismissed the appeal.]

ROSENBERG, BOARD MEMBER, concurring and dissenting:

* * *

In my view, the majority imposes a standard far beyond that required to qualify for relief under the statutory and regulatory provisions of the Convention Against Torture. * * * The majority dismisses proof of Decree No. 33, the respondent's status as a convicted drug trafficker, her forcible return to Nigeria, and evidence of the mistreatment of a similarly situated friend some years earlier, and it demands either more "current evidence" or "meaningful historical evidence" before the respondent can establish that it is more likely than not that she will be identified, imprisoned, and tortured. If we actually quantify and apply the standard imposed by the majority, we must conclude that the respondent is charged with establishing the likelihood of torture *beyond a reasonable doubt*. However repugnant noncitizens convicted of criminal offenses may be, that is not the proper standard.

* * *

SCHMIDT, BOARD MEMBER, dissenting [joined by four other Board Members]:

I respectfully dissent.

I agree with Board Member Rosenberg's conclusion that the respondent has shown that it is more likely than not that she will be imprisoned under Decree No. 33 upon return to Nigeria.* * * I write separately to address the question the majority avoids: whether the respondent more likely than not will be tortured while in prison. I find that she will be tortured.

* * *

B.   PRISON CONDITIONS AS TORTURE

In Matter of J–E– [23 I & N Dec. 291 (BIA)], we effectively established a presumption that mistreatment in prison is not torture under the Convention Against Torture, but merely "cruel, inhuman or degrading treatment"—reprehensible, worthy of condemnation, but not a basis for relief.

To rebut this presumption, a respondent who is likely to be imprisoned upon removal must show that: (1) "torture" exists in the foreign prison system; and either (2) it is probable that any prisoner detained in the system will be tortured, or (3) he or she possesses individual characteristics making it more likely than not he or she will be tortured.

* * *

III.

A.   TORTURE EXISTS IN THE NIGERIAN PRISON SYSTEM

The most recent Department of State country report on Nigeria describes the abuses that are rampant in the Nigerian prison system. Bureau of Democracy, Human Rights, and Labor, U.S. Dep't of State, *Nigeria Country Reports on Human Rights Practices—2001 (Mar. 2002), available at http:// www.state.gov/g/drl/rls/hrrpt/2001/af/8397.htm ("Country Reports")*. At least one aspect of that abuse, intentional withholding of needed medical treatment for improper purposes, which is relevant to this respondent's situation, constitutes "torture" under the test set forth in *Matter of J–E–, supra.*

The respondent is a chronic asthmatic with no family in Nigeria who could provide food or proper medical treatment while she is in jail. The Country Reports state that "[p]rison officials, police, and security forces often denied inmates food and medical treatment as a form of punishment or to extort money from them." Country Reports, supra, at 6 (emphasis added).

* * *

Clearly, death caused at least in part by intentional withholding of medical treatment for improper purposes is common in the Nigerian prison system. The extent of the problem probably is understated because of the difficulty in obtaining accurate documentation from the Nigerian system.

* * *

B. RESPONDENT'S PERSONAL CHARACTERISTICS MAKE TORTURE LIKELY

The respondent is a woman, suffering from chronic asthma, without family to support and assist her in Nigeria, returning from the United States with a drug conviction. Decree No. 33, discussed by the majority, shows, at a minimum, that the Nigerian Government has a particular interest in those returning with foreign drug convictions.

The respondent's combination of personal traits places her in a particularly high-risk category to suffer torture through the intentional denial of medical treatment for her chronic asthma by Nigerian prison officials bent upon improperly punishing or extorting her.* * * Consequently, I find that the respondent more likely than not will be tortured if imprisoned in Nigeria.

NOTES AND QUESTIONS ON LEVEL OF RISK

1. Article 3 of the CAT forbids *refoulement* where there are "substantial grounds for believing that [a person] would be in danger of being subjected to torture." In its Understanding 2 to the resolution of advice and consent to the CAT, reprinted in the Statutory Supplement, the Senate made a point of expressly adopting the *Stevic* standard—that the harm is more likely than not—for assessing the threat level that triggers protection. Recall that the *Stevic* standard, discussed in Section D of this chapter, is more difficult to satisfy than the well-founded fear standard applied in the asylum determination.

2. What is the heart of the dispute between the majority and the dissents in *Matter of M–B–A–*? Does the majority believe that it is unlikely that the woman in question will be jailed in Nigeria or is the majority simply agnostic as to the likelihood of detention? What evidence could sway the majority on this point? In contrast, the dissents believe it is more likely than not that this Nigerian woman will be jailed and will have her asthma medication withheld. The Country Reports state that withholding of food or medication often occurs. Does "often" equate to "more likely than not"?

––––––––––

In addition to establishing a higher standard concerning the risk that torture will occur, the legislation implementing the Convention Against Torture provides that courts can review CAT claims only "as part of the review of a final order of removal pursuant to INA § 242." INA § 242(a)(4) (added in 2005). Essentially, the petition for review procedure, whereby judicial review occurs in the federal courts of appeals following exhaustion of appeals before the BIA, is the only avenue for judicial review of CAT claims. As Chapter Ten will discuss in more detail, Congress has limited judicial review in many instances when removal is based on criminal offenses, INA § 242(a)(2)(C), although in those circumstances it has preserved judicial review insofar as the challenge raises constitutional claims or questions of law. INA § 242(a)(2)(D). Nonetheless, challenges involving the Convention Against Torture and the U.S. implementing legislation do reach the courts, and it is a safe bet that the jurisprudence interpreting the Convention Against Torture will continue to expand.

CHAPTER NINE

ENFORCEMENT

■ ■ ■

The last couple of decades have witnessed polarized and often shrill debate over immigration enforcement. Proponents on one side point to the presence of 10 to 11 million unauthorized migrants as proof that the laws are badly underenforced. They call for the agencies to toughen their stands and expand their efforts, and for Congress to provide greater resources. Others contend that there is too much immigration enforcement, emphasizing that removal often splits families that include U.S. citizen children, or at least results in the deportation of otherwise law-abiding and hard-working people who had become well-established in their local communities. Several states and cities have stepped into this arena, with measures that span a wide spectrum. Some have adopted their own immigration crackdown laws meant to involve their personnel in direct immigration enforcement or to deny work or housing to the undocumented. At the opposite pole, other municipalities and a few states have restricted cooperation with federal immigration agencies, even to the point where some localities declare themselves "sanctuary cities."

Congress's primary response has been a substantial expansion in the funding for immigration enforcement, but it has tended to favor border enforcement (in general, the domain of CBP) over enhancements directed toward interior enforcement (roughly speaking, the domain of ICE), for reasons we will explore. And it has provided an array of new statutory tools and programs that can expedite or streamline removal for certain categories of violators, or improve the effectiveness of other control measures, such as visa screening or the verification of work authorization. Meantime, DHS has experimented with its own administrative initiatives to improve enforcement. Sometimes these changes expand the reach of enforcement or make certain procedures more efficient. Other changes emphasize a smarter use of prosecutorial discretion in an effort to narrow the focus, using limited resources to target more effectively the more dangerous or egregious violators of the immigration laws, while making sure that they not only receive a removal order but actually leave the country.

This chapter will first survey, in Section A, the array of federal tools and programs used by DHS and the Department of State in accomplishing immigration enforcement, with particular attention given to selected legal and policy issues that these tools, especially employer sanctions, can present for government attorneys and those advising private clients. Section B explores constitutional limitations on searches, arrests, interrogation and prosecutions, including whether or when ethnicity may be used in making enforcement choices. It also addresses issues raised by the use of immigration enforcement in the struggle against terrorism. Section C then considers the state and local role, both direct and indirect, in immigration enforcement. Section D concludes the chapter with a broad look at immigration reform proposals. These reform proposals range well beyond measures dealing in the strictest sense with enforcement, but to a significant extent all these elements are linked, at least in the view of many participants in the debate. As they assess the situation, the United States cannot achieve an effective enforcement regime unless we (1) reform legal migration provisions so as to better accommodate demand for immigration (temporary and permanent) and (2) provide some way to legalize the unauthorized population now illegally present. Although the material in Section D links to many chapters in this book, we place it here because much of the reform effort over the last several years has been pushed along by the desire to transition to an immigration control regime that can be—and deserves to be—enforced effectively.

SECTION A. CONTROLLING ILLEGAL MIGRATION

1. INTRODUCTION AND AN OVERVIEW

The Immigration Reform and Control Act of 1986 (IRCA) announced a national policy dedicated to staunching the flow of undocumented immigration. According to the House Report:

> While there is no doubt that many who enter illegally do so for the best of motives—to seek a better life for themselves and their families—immigration must proceed in a legal, orderly, and regulated fashion. As a sovereign nation, we must secure our borders.

H.R.Rep. No. 682(I), 99th Cong., 2d Sess. 46 (1986).

How were we to gain control of our borders? IRCA adopted a multi-prong strategy, including legalization of most of the undocumented aliens then resident in the United States and a limited program for admitting temporary agricultural workers legally in the future. On the enforcement side, some additional resources were made available to the Immigration and Naturalization Service, but IRCA's strategy was primarily one of *private* enforcement: it required employers to verify whether new hires were authorized to work in the United States. The basic reasoning was that jobs are what attract most migrants to the United States; if their access to the labor market could be blocked up front, it would deter the attempt to migrate unlawfully.

By the early 1990s it became apparent that IRCA had not succeeded in controlling illegal migration (though its legalization programs did produce legal status for nearly 2.7 million people who had been unlawfully present in 1986). Employer verification, it turned out, could be easily defeated by the use of false documents. Since then, the nation has engaged in sporadic rounds of new initiatives and increased funding meant to bring us closer to IRCA's enforcement promise. Initially the lawmakers' attention focused primarily on the objective highlighted in the quote above: reining in large-scale illegal movement of those who are mainly economic migrants. After September 11, 2001, a great deal of additional funding and innovation was fueled by a second and more targeted objective: improving security screening and enhancing the ability to exclude or remove persons involved in terrorism. Nonetheless, many of the new post–9/11 programs, especially those that enable improved identity checks and provide for durable electronic records linked to biometrics (at present, this means fingerprints), have also contributed to improved capabilities for enforcement against violators who are not in any way security threats.

The Illegal Immigration Reform and Immigrant Responsibility Act of 1996 (IIRIRA), along with related measures also adopted that year, represented the first major post-IRCA round of statutory changes meant to toughen enforcement. For example, IIRIRA substantially restricted the availability of discretionary relief (reflected in the current provisions for cancellation of removal) and added the three- and ten-year bars to the inadmissibility grounds, applicable to noncitizens who had been unlawfully present for six months or more. These changes were covered in Chapter Seven.

IIRIRA also enacted streamlined removal procedures applicable to specified categories of persons at the border or unlawfully present in the interior. These procedures can result in a removal order issued by an immigration officer rather than an immigration judge, or allow an officer to determine that an earlier order remains in effect, permitting removal of the noncitizen without a new appearance before a judge. The primary new procedures are: expedited removal for inadmissible aliens who lack documents or present fraudulent documents, INA § 235(b)(1); a speedy procedure to remove noncitizens who return without permission following an earlier order of removal or voluntary departure, known as reinstatement of removal, INA § 241(a)(5); and "administrative removal" for non-LPRs who have been convicted of an aggravated felony, INA § 238(b). Because these procedures are discussed in detail in Chapters Six and Ten, we do not further describe them here, but their growing importance to enforcement is reflected in Table 9.1 and Figure 9.1, which are based on a chart published by DHS. They indicate that over 62 percent of removals in 2010 resulted from expedited removal or reinstatement. (The DHS publication did not provide data on administrative removals under § 238(b).)

Table 9.1
Trends in Total Removals, Expedited Removals,
and Reinstatements, FY 2001–2010

Fiscal year	Total removals	Expedited removals	Reinstate-ments	All other removals
2001	189,026	69,923	38,943	80,160
2002	165,168	34,624	46,436	84,108
2003	211,098	43,920	66,713	100,465
2004	240,665	51,014	84,347	105,304
2005	246,431	87,888	43,137	115,406
2006	280,974	110,663	49,539	120,772
2007	319,382	106,196	77,696	135,490
2008	359,795	112,716	91,318	155,761
2009	395,165	106,025	116,903	172,237
2010	387,242	111,116	130,840	145,286

Source: DHS Office of Immigration Statistics, Immigration Enforcement Actions: 2010, table 2 (June 2011).

Figure 9.1
Trends in Total Removals, Expedited Removals,
and Reinstatements, FY 2001–2010

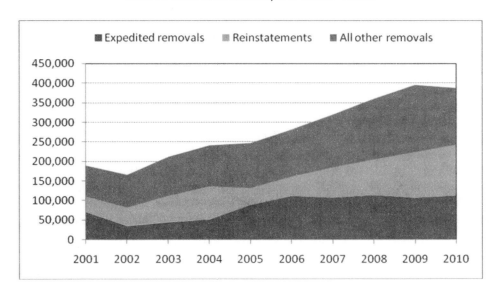

Table 9.1 shows that removals increased considerably over the past decade. But removals—the compulsory departure of a noncitizen on the basis of a removal order—tell only part of the enforcement story. Many apprehended individuals wind up leaving the country as a result of governmental action, usually under some type of DHS supervision or oversight, but without waiting for a formal order. (This kind of action

requires the individual's consent, but it also requires DHS agreement. There are times when DHS would prefer a formal order, for example because it permits the application of more serious sanctions if the person later returns without permission.) Therefore, DHS now reports overall totals of "removals and returns" as one metric indicating its enforcement performance. *See* Table 9.2 and Figure 9.2.

Table 9.2

Removals and Returns, FY 1990–2010

Fiscal year	Removals	Returns	Total
1990	30,039	1,022,533	1,054,562
1991	33,189	1,061,105	1,096,285
1992	43,671	1,105,829	1,151,492
1993	42,542	1,243,410	1,287,945
1994	45,674	1,029,107	1,076,775
1995	50,924	1,313,764	1,366,683
1996	69,680	1,573,428	1,645,104
1997	114,432	1,440,684	1,557,113
1998	174,813	1,570,127	1,746,938
1999	183,114	1,574,863	1,759,976
2000	188,467	1,675,876	1,866,343
2001	189,026	1,349,371	1,540,398
2002	165,168	1,012,116	1,179,286
2003	211,098	945,294	1,158,395
2004	240,665	1,166,576	1,409,245
2005	246,431	1,096,920	1,345,356
2006	280,974	1,043,381	1,326,361
2007	319,382	891,390	1,212,779
2008	359,795	811,263	1,173,066
2009	395,165	580,107	977,281
2010	387,242	476,405	865,657

Source: DHS Office of Immigration Statistics, 2009 Yearbook of Immigration Statistics 95, table 36; Immigration Enforcement Actions 2010, at 4 & table 2 (2011).

In reporting these statistics, DHS uses the following distinctions: Removals are "the compulsory and confirmed movement of an inadmissible or deportable alien out of the United States based on an order of removal." Returns are "the confirmed movement of an inadmissible or deportable alien out of the United States not based on an order of removal." 2009 DHS Statistical Yearbook 95, table 36 nn.1 & 2. Because a majority of returns in these figures are accomplished by the Border Patrol shortly after apprehending an individual at or near the border, most returnees have not spent much time on U.S. territory, at least not on this particular attempt at entry. (Border Patrol apprehension totals are summarized in Table 9.3 below.) As you can see from Table 9.2, removals increased significantly in 1997 and 1998, when the new streamlined removal procedures enacted by IIRIRA took effect. Since about 2000, the combined number of removals and returns has generally declined, primarily reflecting a noticeable drop in the number of returns, initially in 2001–03, and then more steeply since 2008. According to DHS, this most recent drop is "primarily due to decreases in Southwest border apprehensions." DHS Office of Immigration Statistics, Immigration Enforcement Actions 2010, at 4 (2011). This pattern calls attention to a further element in controlling unauthorized immigration—deterrence, whether it comes from a tipping point in the impact of compulsory enforcement measures or instead via employer screening, increased smuggler fees, or a distressed economy with higher U.S. unemployment.

Figure 9.2
Removals and Returns, FY 1990–2010

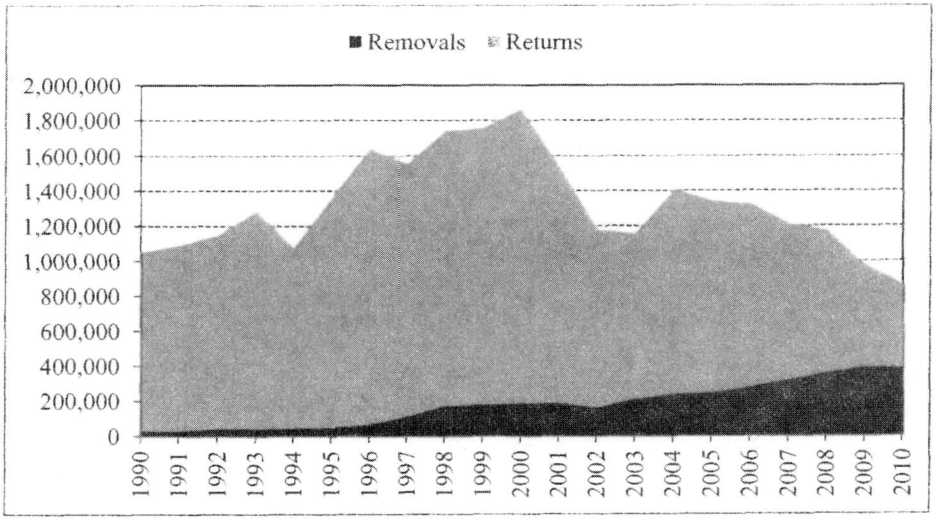

The materials that follow survey the various enforcement tools and initiatives now available to the immigration agencies (primarily the Departments of State and Homeland Security). We begin with a look at tools applied beyond U.S. territory, which received a major upgrade and revision since the September 11 attacks, and then move to border enforcement and finally to measures applied in the interior of the country, directly through U.S. government officials and indirectly through employer screening.

EXERCISE ON ENFORCEMENT TOOLS TO CONTROL ILLEGAL MIGRATION

Assume that you are an intern for a Washington think tank dedicated to improving law enforcement in the United States. In the past your organization has primarily focused its research and advocacy on issues faced by police departments, but because of its expertise in that field, the executive director has been asked to testify before the Senate Judiciary Committee at a hearing on Enhancing Immigration Enforcement. She has asked you to help prepare that testimony and wants you to begin by listing the principal goals or objectives that an immigration enforcement system should serve, as a way of framing her remarks. Drawing on the following materials, outline what you believe the testimony should highlight, for both short-term and long-term steps. What are the most pressing problems? What tools or methods show greatest promise for overall impact, even if they would not necessarily meet the most immediate problems? Which arena or arenas of enforcement deserve primary attention? What are the primary obstacles to success?

---

2. "PUSHING OUT THE BORDER," INCLUDING MORE EFFECTIVE IDENTITY CHECKS

DAVID A. MARTIN, REFINING IMMIGRATION LAW'S ROLE IN COUNTERTERRORISM

Legislating the War on Terror: An Agenda for Reform,
Chap. 6, pp. 185–90 (B.Wittes ed. 2009).

The U.S. admissions system historically has deployed a double layer of screening: scrutiny by a consular officer overseas of a person's eligibility for admission before a visa is issued and a second and potentially equally demanding review by an immigration inspector at the port of entry, even if the person holds a duly issued visa. One of the major responses to September 11 has been to "push out the borders"—that is, to try to maximize successful and rigorous screening well before a person embarks on a trip or shows up at the port of entry. That means designing systems to support more effective consular work or, for persons allowed to travel without a visa, to maximize the data available to U.S. officials well before the individual arrives on U.S. soil—ideally, before he or she even boards the plane. * * *

Some of the September 11 hijackers had obtained temporary visas, known as nonimmigrant visas, for travel to the United States without undergoing a face-to-face interview before a U.S. consular officer. In response, in May 2003, the State Department issued a new policy requiring a personal interview for nearly all categories of applicants for nonimmigrant or immigrant visas. Congress tightened that requirement and wrote it into the statute in the 2004 Intelligence Reform Act. * * *

More important to successful screening than face-to-face interviews is enhancing the timely availability to consular officers and immigration inspectors at the border of the best intelligence possible. That is, policymakers should not expect consular officers and immigration inspectors to play more than an occasional and adventitious role in actually detecting or unearthing terrorist plots through their questioning of applicants. What they should expect, however, is that those officers will have the best possible intelligence and law enforcement information about the people before them. * * *

Linking databases and providing user-friendly and comprehensive systems to frontline decisionmakers has been a significant focus of both statutory changes and administrative adjustments since September 11—a daunting task because the databases had developed in a haphazard and disconnected fashion. Disparate agencies used different and inconsistent systems and, before September 2001, jealously guarded their own information, only grudgingly yielding morsels to immigration officials. Reforms have made considerable headway over the last six years in improving the situation, driven in part by congressional mandates for consolidation and interoperability but also by administrative innovation in centralizing key processes and efficiently allocating the time of skilled analysts through an automated targeting system. * * *

DETECTING FRAUD AND COLLECTING BIOMETRIC IDENTIFYING INFORMATION

If a terrorist can successfully use another person's identity, then he or she can obviously defeat even the best systems for prompt checking of available intelligence and law enforcement information. Skilled questioning by an inspector or consular officer, as discussed above, can help spot inconsistencies or oddities that will trigger closer scrutiny of identity fraud. Beyond that, the increasing use of biometric identifiers, as required in many pieces of immigration-related legislation since September 11, helps guard against such fraud, as does increasing international standardization of identity documents with counterfeit-resistant features and embedded machine-readable biometric data.

One element of the U.S. Visitor and Immigrant Status Indicator Technology (US–VISIT) screening system—planned to become eventually a comprehensive DHS system monitoring aliens' entry and exit—provides an important protection against a specific kind of fraud. Under the earliest system component widely deployed (beginning in 2004), aliens arriving at a port of entry have had to submit to facial photographing and the electronic capture of two fingerprints (of the right and left index fingers), conducted right at the primary inspection booth—a procedure that added about 15 seconds to each inspection. At about that time, consular officers began to capture the same two fingerprints (photos having long been required) at the time of visa issuance. The system thus permits prompt comparison of the two sets of fingerprints, to ensure that the person applying for admission is the same person cleared to receive a visa.

The database that provides the foundation for US–VISIT, known as IDENT, also affords swift access to key watchlist information on possible terrorists and increasingly to the FBI's comprehensive fingerprint system, known as the Integrated Automated Fingerprint Identification System (IAFIS). * * * The decision of former DHS secretary Michael Chertoff in 2005 to alter US–VISIT so that the fingerprint readers [at ports of entry] will capture all ten fingerprints, rather than just the index fingers, also represents a significant security gain. That change will increase the chances of detecting terrorists [and criminals] by comparing the full fingerprint set against latent prints * * * collected by [the FBI or] the Department of Defense. Though challenges remain, US–VISIT has generally proven itself to be a gratifyingly successful technological venture.

THE VISA WAIVER PROGRAM

Some critics have urged an end to the statutorily authorized visa waiver program—which allows short-term visa-free travel (lasting no more than ninety days) to citizens of selected countries—seeing it as an especially vulnerable entry point for dangerous individuals. As of December 31, 2008, thirty-five countries were on the visa waiver list, most of them European democracies that accord a reciprocal privilege to U.S. citizens. But critics point out that some noted terrorists, including Richard Reid (the "shoe bomber") and Zacarias Moussaoui (the "twentieth hijacker"), were nationals of visa waiver countries. They allege that a border inspector's quick query of the databases in the primary inspection line at an airport affords an insufficient opportunity to detect dangerous travelers. Pressure for a speedy decision is even higher at the border or at ports of entry than at consulates, and even if a given person is referred for secondary inspection, he or she is already on U.S. soil and therefore must be either detained or released on bond here if a protracted inquiry ensues.

Although those concerns have some merit, * * * [r]equiring all nationals from the 35 high-volume countries involved to obtain visas, even for short trips, would deter some travel, sow ill will, probably reduce U.S. travel opportunities, and create a monumental additional workload on an already taxed consular corps. Nonetheless, Congress needs to take advantage of innovations that can reduce the vulnerabilities inherent in the visa waiver system. Statutory changes have already gone some distance in that direction. Visa waiver travelers must now have machine-readable passports, thus facilitating accurate and speedy database checks by airport inspectors. Under a separate initiative, airlines are now required to send data on all passengers to U.S. border authorities well before a plane arrives from an overseas location. This Advance Passenger Information System (APIS) affords Customs and Border Protection (CBP) officers additional time before landing for checking passenger names [and other identifying information, such as Passenger Name Record (PNR) information received from airlines] against databases in order to identify those whom CBP should either reject or at least subject to more intensive review at the border. * * * [Furthermore, the prospect of inclusion in the visa waiver program has proven to be a major inducement the United States can deploy to persuade other countries to share critical information usable in the screening and selection of persons for closer scrutiny, whether they are traveling with or without a visa. In] order to join the visa waiver program, countries must agree to cooperate fully in sharing terrorist-related intelligence and also in following other security-enhancing practices.

* * * [Since 2009, visa waiver passengers are also required to obtain advance clearance through an automated electronic system for travel authorization (ESTA).] Under ESTA, a prospective traveler from a visa waiver country must apply, ordinarily through the Internet many days or weeks before the flight, for travel authorization, providing at that time specified biographical information that allows DHS to check for "law enforcement or security risk." If none is found, the person will receive a code indicating eligibility for travel to the United States without a visa. * * * [Airlines are required] to check the code through an automated system before permitting the individual to board the aircraft for the United States. All such persons will still be subject to inspection and a new database check at the port of entry.

NOTES AND QUESTIONS ON ENHANCED ADMISSION SCREENING AND IDENTITY CHECKS

1. **More about IDENT.** DHS's IDENT database stores the biometric, biographic, and photo information obtained not only from persons applying for visas at a consulate or for admission at a port of entry but also from nearly all noncitizens encountered by any part of DHS. For example, persons apprehended by ICE or the Border Patrol (and in some circumstances the Coast Guard) are interviewed, fingerprinted, and photographed even if they are likely to be bused back to Mexico or returned to Haiti within a few hours. This information, along with whatever name and other biographical information the person provides, is shared with IDENT, matched against its extensive records, and stored for future use. (For a glimpse of the primitive record-keeping employed three decades ago by the Border Patrol, which relied on the name given by the apprehended noncitizen as well as paper storage, see the first edition of this casebook, T.A. Aleinikoff & D. Martin, Immigration: Process and Policy 466 (1985).) In this way, the relevant officer can identify whether the person may be more dangerous or have additional immigration violations, thus perhaps meriting criminal prosecution or removal under a formal order, which would make future U.S. entry a felony. The sharing also generates a readily retrievable record to be consulted if the person either applies for a benefit in later years or is picked up in further enforcement actions. Applicants to USCIS for immigration benefits are also fingerprinted and checked against IDENT, as a safeguard against identity fraud or misrepresentation of previous immigration history. IDENT therefore is building up an extensive, biometrically based record of all encounters with immigration authorities, thus permitting speedy access to all DHS information on the person, including any aliases the person may have used. For more information

on IDENT, see the US–VISIT website, <http://www.dhs.gov/files/programs/usv.shtm>.

2. **Tracking overstayers: a biometric exit tracking system?** US–VISIT provides a thorough biometric check of persons who *enter* the United States. It covers nearly all arriving air passengers, with very limited exceptions, mainly those under 14 or over 80 years of age. At land border ports, where high volumes and physical logistics complicate the use of biometric checks in primary inspection, the coverage is more selective, but nonetheless widely used in secondary inspection (the area to which cases are referred if they appear to merit further inquiry or if admissibility cannot be resolved at the primary inspection lane).

What about checks at time of *exit*? The 9/11 Commission recommended the creation of comprehensive biometric exit screening system as well, primarily to provide better information about overstayers—nonimmigrants who fail to depart by the end of their admission period. Congress has supported this aim in authorizing legislation since at least 1996, but has not provided the extensive funding that a comprehensive system would demand. That is, in order to be truly useful in determining who did *not* depart, the system would have to cover every departure , whether by air, land or sea. DHS estimated in July 2011 that the infrastructure to permit such checks on departing passengers would cost $3.5 billion over 10 years. *See US–VISIT backlog reduced by more than half, says Beers,* <http://www.fiercehomelandsecurity.com/story/us-visit-backlog-reduced-more-half-says-beers/2011–07–13>.

Under pressure from Congress, DHS attempted to launch an initial version of such exit monitoring at international airports in April 2008, by issuing proposed rules that would impose the requirement to take fingerprints of departing passengers on air carriers. This provoked such a strong reaction from the airlines that Congress stepped in to delay the program until different biometric exit pilot programs could be conducted, only one of which would involve airline personnel. As it happened, the airlines did not cooperate even in the pilot test—and the other two pilot programs, one involving biometric collection by CBP and the other by the officers of the Transportation Security Administration, provided limited and inconclusive information. *See* Testimony of Richard M. Stana, Government Accountability Office, *Visa Security: Additional Actions Needed to Strengthen Overstay Enforcement and Address Risks in the Visa Process* (GAO–11–910T, Sept. 13, 2011).

In 2011 DHS undertook a closer review of exit screening, especially to compare the expected benefits of a biometric exit system against the costs. In September 2011, in congressional testimony, DHS signaled that it would concentrate on using already collected biographical information (i.e., name-based rather than fingerprint-based) to expand its identification of suspected overstayers. It promised to refer all identified overstayers for some sort of action, most to the State Department to cancel the current visa and to enter the person on a lookout that would at least require extra vetting before any new visa is issued and might block future travel. DHS will also refer a growing percentage of overstayers identified in this fashion to ICE officers for follow-up enforcement action, according to a priority system that emphasizes criminal or security risks. *See* Testimony of John D. Cohen, DHS Principal

Deputy Counterterrorism Coordinator, before the House Committee on Homeland Security, Subcommittee on Border and Maritime Security, Sept. 13, 2011. This biographic-based exit monitoring system relies primarily on creative use of existing processes rather than costly new investments. Though it has gaps, so too would a biometric system until it achieved virtually 100 percent coverage of all exit points and all departing travelers. Improved biographic-based exit tracking in this manner has been made possible by advances in some of the other systems described above, particularly the regular collection and analysis of detailed passenger manifests from all carriers involved in international travel. *See generally* Testimony of Edward Alden, Council on Foreign Relations, before the House Committee on Homeland Security, *Visa Overstay Tracking: Progress, Prospects and Pitfalls*, March 25, 2010, <http://www.cfr.org/immigration/visa-overstay-tracking---progress-pitfalls/p21734> (describing biographic tracking capabilities and questioning the cost-effectiveness of biometric exit tracking).

In your view, should Congress fund and DHS implement a biometric exit monitoring system? Where exactly would the exit biometrics be taken—so as to assure that the persons thus recorded actually do leave the country? Once such a system identifies a visa overstayer, exactly what enforcement steps should be taken? By whom? Does the exit tracking system provide you with information that would help you to find the violator at that point? What other changes in record-keeping and filing requirements imposed on nonimmigrants would be needed to develop such a locator system?

3. **REAL ID and WHTI.** Over the past decade, Congress has also pressed for other improvements in identification systems. The REAL ID Act of 2005, Pub.L. No. 109–13, 119 Stat. 231 (2005), established detailed minimum requirements for states to meet in improving the issuance and quality of driver's licenses and other identity documents. Complaints over an unfunded federal mandate eventually erupted in stronger resistance from some state governors or legislatures. Nineteen states have passed legislation stating that they will not bring their systems into full compliance with REAL ID, essentially daring DHS to pull the only real enforcement trigger the act provides—namely, denying persons (citizens or noncitizens) who lack a complying document access to federal buildings and, more potently, to all air travel. (To date, DHS has successively postponed the deadline for full compliance.) Nonetheless, behind all the grumbling, all states have made substantial improvements to their ID issuance systems since 9/11, and they more readily share information among themselves. These steps have made it significantly harder to produce counterfeit IDs or to obtain genuine state identification documents through fraud. *See* J. Kephart, REAL ID Implementation: Less Expensive, Doable, and Helpful in Reducing Fraud (Center for Imm. Studies Backgrounder, Jan. 2011). *But see* Halsey, *Latest Counterfeit IDs Are So Good They're Dangerous,* Wash. Post, July 30, 2011 (reporting on ability to overcome some of these measures through sophisticated fraudulent cards, many of them purchased from a purveyor in China). On the debate over REAL ID, see Vijayan, *Obama will inherit a real mess on Real ID*, Computer World, Dec. 22, 2008, <http://www.infoworld.com/d/security-central/obama-will-inherit-real-mess-real-id–528?page=0,1>; AFSA, *The REAL ID Act: State Implementation & Effects* (March 2009), <http://www.afsaonline.org/CMS/file

REPOSITORY/The%20REAL%20ID%20Act%20Final.pdf>   (includes   chart
showing detailed status of state implementation and of state blocking legislation).

Congress also acted to guard against ID fraud that could result in
unauthorized access to the United States, when it enacted the Western
Hemisphere Travel Initiative (WHTI) in 2004. Before WHTI, persons entering
from Canada and some nearby islands could enter the United States by
presenting a birth certificate or other non-secure documents. Under WHTI,
which took full effect in 2009, all arriving passengers, both U.S. citizens and
foreigners, must show a passport or a limited list of other secure documents,
including driver's licenses from a few states that have agreed to especially
rigorous anti-fraud controls. Intelligence Reform and Terrorism Prevention
Act of 2004 (IRTPA), Pub. L. 108–458, § 7209, 118 Stat. 3638.

4. **Additional information.** Useful detailed information on the systems discussed in the Martin reading above may be found in two works by
former staff members of the 9/11 Commission: J. Kephart, Border Watchlist-
ing a Decade After 9/11 (Center for Imm. Studies Backgrounder, Aug. 2011);
S. Ginsburg, Securing Human Mobility in the Age of Risk: New Challenges for
Travel, Migration and Borders (2010). An engagingly written and comprehensive critical overview of the changes made after the September 11 attacks
appears in E. Alden, The Closing of the American Border: Terrorism, Immigration, and Security Since 9/11 (2008).

3.   BORDER ENFORCEMENT

Increased border enforcement has drawn solid support from both
political parties and from successive Presidential administrations. Particularly in recent years, Congress has rapidly increased funding for the
Border Patrol, so that its ranks grew to over 20,700 officers by summer
2011, more than double the total in 2004. About 85 percent of those
officers are deployed along the southwest border. This section recounts the
history of this buildup and of border control efforts generally. It also
summarizes various critiques and defenses of the expansion from the
standpoint of 2011, a time when political claims about both the wisdom
and the success or failure of "securing the border" contend for public
acceptance.

PETER ANDREAS, BORDER GAMES: POLICING
THE U.S.–MEXICO DIVIDE
85–86, 89–90, 92–93, 95, 111–12 (2000).

During much of the twentieth century, the United States and Mexico
not only quietly tolerated but actively facilitated and encouraged the
influx of cheap labor across the border; until recent decades the rising
level of illegal immigration commanded little national political attention.
For example, the platform of the Republican Party did not even mention
immigration control until 1980, and only four years later did it affirm the
country's right to control its borders and express concern about illegal
immigration.

Congressional debate over how to deal with illegal immigration culminated in the passage of the Immigration Reform and Control Act of 1986, which introduced employer sanctions for the first time, as well as a limited legalization program. But although IRCA provided a temporary sedative, the law exacerbated the very problem it purported to remedy. Rather than discouraging illegal immigration, the main impact of legalization under IRCA was to reinforce and expand already well-established cross-border migration networks. * * * Meanwhile, the primary impact of the poorly designed and minimally enforced employer sanctions was to create a booming business in fraudulent documents.

IRCA's perverse consequences helped set the stage for a powerful backlash against illegal immigration in the 1990s, most acute in California, which was home to nearly half of the unauthorized immigrants estimated to be in the country. * * * The new restrictionist mood was embodied in the passage of Proposition 187 by California voters in 1994, which sought to bar illegal immigrants from receiving social services. Proposition 187 was self-consciously designed and promoted as a symbolic gesture to express frustration and "send a message" to the federal government. Even though it was subsequently declared unconstitutional (as its proponents expected), its passage by a three-to-two margin sent shock waves across the country and through the halls of Congress.

* * *

Although border control was a low priority for President Clinton when he first took office, he soon became an enthusiastic proponent of tighter controls in order keep up with Republican initiatives in Congress. In late July 1993 he held a news conference to announce aggressive new measures against illegal immigration: "Today we send a strong and clear message. We will make it tougher for illegal aliens to get into our country." These measures included hiring 600 more Border Patrol agents * * *. Officials of the Border Patrol (the uniformed enforcement wing of the INS), long accustomed to being outside the political spotlight and marginalized within the criminal justice system, were suddenly brought center stage—and indeed were even invited for the first time to the White House for press announcements with the president.

The heightened status of immigration control has been reflected in the unprecedented expansion of the INS. * * * [The Border Patrol's] annual budget jumped from $354 million in 1993 to $877 million in 1998—a 148 percent increase.

* * * From 1993 to October 1999 the number of Border Patrol agents in the Southwest more than doubled, from 3,389 to some 8,200. * * * To "thicken" the border, the Border Patrol has also expanded its checkpoints on the roads leading north. * * *

The administration's border control offensive is based on a strategy developed by the INS in 1993–94 called "prevention through deterrence." The objective of increased fencing, surveillance equipment, penalties, and law enforcement personnel is to inhibit illegal entry and thus avoid having to apprehend entrants after they've crossed the border. Massive injections of law enforcement resources at the most popular points of unauthorized entry are designed to disrupt the human traffic, forcing migrants to attempt the crossing in more difficult, remote areas or at official ports of entry (which, the INS says, are easier to control). The result, U.S. border control strategists argue, is that many would-be border crossers are discouraged from trying, and those who do try fail repeatedly and eventually give up because of frustration and depleted resources.

Such a strategy was first tested with the launching of Operation Blockade (later given the more diplomatic name of Hold-the-Line) in El Paso in September 1993. Silvestre Reyes, the El Paso Border Patrol chief who was the architect of the plan, faced initial resistance from his superiors at INS headquarters. There was concern that such a concentrated deployment of force would lead to violent confrontations and strain U.S. relations with Mexico on the eve of NAFTA [the North American Free Trade Agreement]. Moreover, the emphasis on deterring entry rather than apprehending migrants as they crossed contradicted the Border Patrol's traditional reliance on high apprehension numbers to justify budget requests. Nevertheless, an enabling political climate and his own bureaucratic entrepreneurialism made it possible for Reyes to secure the overtime pay he needed to deploy 450 agents for intensive coverage of a twenty-mile stretch of the border.

As hoped, the operation led to a sharp drop in attempted entries in the El Paso sector. Previously, there had been up to 10,000 illegal border crossers per day, and only one of eight had been apprehended. The high profile show of force quickly reduced this flow to a trickle, drawing the immediate attention of Washington, the media, and California politicians eager to replicate the El Paso experience. * * * Chief Reyes became an overnight hero, and would later even be elected to Congress. The powerful appeal of Operation Hold-the-Line was that the results were both immediate and highly visible. Once it had achieved national attention, the INS had little choice but to promote it and take credit for its success. One consequence was that the rewards system within the Border Patrol was suddenly turned upside down, prevention rather than number of apprehensions becoming the new enforcement goal.

In consultation with the Defense Department's Center for Low Intensity Conflict, in 1994 the INS developed a comprehensive plan to apply "prevention through deterrence" across the rest of the border. The strategy would first focus on the busiest points of illegal entry: the El Paso and San Diego sectors, which in FY 1993 had accounted for 68 percent of all apprehensions. Thus, in October 1994, El Paso's Operation Hold-the-Line was joined by Operation Gatekeeper south of San Diego, which targeted the fourteen westernmost miles of the border. * * *

The tightening of controls in El Paso and San Diego predictably pushed migrants to attempt entry elsewhere; consequently, apprehensions remain far below previous levels in the El Paso sector but have jumped in New Mexico and Arizona. Similarly, apprehensions in the Imperial Beach sector south of San Diego have declined sharply since Gatekeeper began, but arrests have skyrocketed in the remote parts of eastern San Diego County.

* * *

The expanding Border Patrol presence in areas between the ports of entry, meanwhile, has sparked a surge in attempted illegal entries through the ports of entry themselves, and the INS has responded with an infusion of new port inspectors. Their number rose from 1,117 to 1,865 between FY 1994 and 1997, representing a 67 percent increase. At some crossing points, such as Calexico and San Ysidro in California, the number of inspectors has more than doubled. * * * The increase in staffing has been matched by stiffer penalties: those who attempt entry through the fraudulent use of documents are being prosecuted for repeat violations, and vehicles may also be confiscated. In addition, to inhibit the use of forged documents, officials are moving to replace the old border-crossing cards with high-tech visas containing a digital fingerprint.

* * *

High-profile immigration control initiatives * * * have transformed the landscape of the southwestern border. * * * [T]he most visible form of clandestine entry—groups of illegal migrants openly crossing the border near urban areas—is no longer politically tolerable. Thus, for the border crossers, evading apprehension has become a longer and more complex game requiring greater patience and stealth. * * * In other words, the old game between border enforcers and clandestine border crossers persists, but the game strategy of the enforcers has changed to maximize the appearance of control. Projecting a "winning image," it seems, has so far provided a politically viable alternative to actually winning the game.

That image has come at an enormous cost: more intensive border policing has brought with it more (and more organized) professional smuggling, greater corruption, and many border deaths. But at least for now, these negative consequences have been obscured by the powerful political and symbolic appeal of a border that appears more orderly and secure. At the same time, however, it should be emphasized that the deterrence effort has created the conditions for its own expansion, since the shifts in the methods and location of illegal border crossings have in turn placed new demands on the law enforcement system to adjust and keep up. Indeed, as envisioned by the Border Patrol, current enforcement levels are just the beginning of a long-term buildup. * * * As one agent put it, "We are taking back the border, piece by piece."

Further Evolution of Border Controls

Andreas describes the dramatic buildup at the border, which has continued over the succeeding decade, along with a less robust enforcement effort in the interior (discussed below). David Martin summarizes the practical and political considerations that help account for the choices that Congress and the executive branch have made about where to devote enforcement resources:

> Interior enforcement, through sending investigators out to track down and remove persons already illegally present, is costly and inefficient. It is also unglamorous and unpopular work in the eyes of most of Homeland Security's enforcement personnel; those officers who are successful at it regularly gain less administrative credit and prestige than others who are involved in criminal alien apprehension or participation in antiterrorist initiatives.

> A different specialty within internal enforcement focuses on employer compliance with the law's workplace screening requirements. Enhancing this type of enforcement should be far more efficient than one-by-one apprehensions at deterring illegal migration, but ramping up worksite enforcement carries other salient disadvantages. Primarily, it imposes visible burdens on business. As a result, significant interest group pressure quietly helps push Congress toward underfunding these enforcement endeavors, and there has been no equivalently organized constituency pushing back. Moreover, though employers may not like the current I–9 verification process, involving the examination of work authorization documents of all new hires (albeit according to a very lax standard of scrutiny), they have become accustomed to it. Proposed revisions in the employers' obligations generate determined resistance among a highly influential interest group. Border measures, in contrast, step on almost no influential toes. Border crackdowns are therefore used to demonstrate enforcement seriousness, alienating few and placating many.

Martin, *Eight Myths About Immigration Enforcement*, 10 N.Y.U. J. Legis. & Pub. Pol'y 525, 544–45 (2007).

Through the first decade or so of this buildup, from the early 1990s to the mid–2000s, the flow of illegal migration continued a general and sometimes dramatic rise, as measured by Border Patrol apprehension numbers (an imperfect metric for these purposes, but conventionally relied upon, in the absence of better measures). Moreover, estimates of the resident unauthorized population rose significantly. *See* Figure 5.6, *supra*, p. 452 (Pew Hispanic Center estimates of undocumented population showing growth from approximately 4 million in 1994 to 11 million in 2005). Noting these statistics, some critics assailed the border buildup as a political gesture that could not succeed against the economic realities that account for illegal migration. Writing in 2005, sociologist Douglas Massey leveled the following critique:

Not only have U.S. policies failed to reduce the inflow of people from Mexico, they have perversely reduced the outflow to produce an unprecedented increase in the undocumented population of the United States. America's unilateral effort to prevent a decades-old flow from continuing has paradoxically transformed a circular flow of Mexican workers into a settled population of families and dependents.

* * * Rather than choosing not to enter the United States illegally, undocumented migrants quite rationally invested more money to minimize the risks and maximize the odds of a successful border crossing. * * * [S]mugglers on the Mexican side upgraded the package of services they offered. Instead of simply accompanying small parties of undocumented migrants on foot across well-trod pathways from Tijuana to San Diego and delivering them to an anonymous urban setting, smugglers now had to transport people to remote sectors of the border, guide them across, and have them met on the other side by personnel who would arrange transport to destinations throughout the United States.

The net effect of U.S. policies, in other words, was to increase the quality but also the price of border-smuggling services. * * * The extent of this increase is indicated by estimates of the average amount of money that undocumented migrants paid someone to smuggle them into the United States by year. From 1980 to 1992 the cost of hiring a coyote, or *pollero* (as smugglers are colloquially labeled) was relatively flat, averaging around $400 per crossing. With the launching of the new strategy of prevention through deterrence in 1993, however, the cost of purchasing a smuggler's services rose to around $1,200 in 1999, before leveling off.

* * * If the first order of business on any trip to the United States is to recover that cost, then holding constant the rate of remuneration and hours worked per week, the stay would have to be three times as long.

D. Massey, Backfire at the Border: Why Enforcement without Legalization Cannot Stop Illegal Immigration 6–8 (Cato Institute Policy Analysis, 2005).

Other critics focused on the increased dangers to the migrants. The Border Patrol strategy of closing traditional entry routes near major U.S. cities such as San Diego and El Paso, plus later large deployments along other main routes in Texas, pushed unauthorized migrants to more dangerous paths through deserts and mountains. The result has been increases in the flow through remote areas, particularly in Arizona, and a significant increase in migrant deaths from exposure. By 2010, roughly 4300 migrants had died trying to cross into the United States since 1998, according to Border Patrol estimates. (The Patrol has expanded its capacities for search and rescue in response.) *See* S. Anderson, Death at the Border (National Foundation for American Policy, May 2010); M. Jimenez.

Humanitarian Crisis: Migrant Deaths at the U.S.-Mexico Border (ACLU and Mexico's National Comm'n of Human Rights, Oct. 1, 2009).

Supporters of the border buildup, in response, pointed out that this decade had been a period of economic boom and record low unemployment. Continued increases in migration proved nothing; the question was whether, under such circumstances, migration was lower than it would have been without the expanded enforcement. Congress sided with this camp and sustained the momentum of major annual funding increases for border enforcement by DHS. As indicated above, the Border Patrol's ranks doubled in size from 2004 to 2010, exceeding 20,700 in 2011. In 2006 and again in 2010, the executive branch augmented these increases with temporary deployments of the National Guard. Consistent with the laws governing domestic deployment of the military, they were not assigned direct enforcement responsibilities. Instead, they assisted in constructing barriers, training agents, conducting surveillance, and providing intelligence.

Congress also supported the addition of sophisticated technology, including the deployment of hundreds of seismic sensors, thermal imaging systems, remote video surveillance equipment, and even a fleet of Predator drone aircraft that now provides coverage from California to Texas. DHS has also centralized Southwest border intelligence gathering and evaluation at a center in El Paso, and has coordinated more closely with Mexican authorities, with a special emphasis on disrupting human and drug smuggling operations and prosecuting the smugglers and traffickers in both countries. *See* Testimony of Janet Napolitano, Secretary of Homeland Security, on Securing the Border: Progress at the Federal Level, before the Senate Committee on Homeland Security and Governmental Affairs 6–8 (May 4, 2011) [hereafter Napolitano Testimony]. And Congress passed the Secure Fence Act of 2006, Pub. L. 109–367, 120 Stat. 2368, calling for approximately 700 miles of additional fencing on the southern border. In 2008, in order to complete such fencing on an urgent basis, Secretary Chertoff exercised an expansive waiver authority granted to DHS in the REAL ID Act to waive the requirements of a host of environmental and other statutes, including the Administrative Procedure Act, that had been invoked to slow fence construction. By mid–2011, 649 miles of DHS's planned 653 miles of fencing had been completed.

Of perhaps greater impact, Congress and DHS made far more detention spaces available to the Border Patrol during this period, so that it could end in 2006 an earlier policy known derisively as "catch and release." That is, in earlier years many border-crossers (especially those from countries other than Mexico) who contested return were released pending their immigration court hearings, owing to limited detention space. Many had failed to show up in court. By keeping such persons in detention, DHS obviously was able to ensure the execution of removal orders issued in these cases. The new policy also rested on the belief that the prospect of sustained detention would help deter new migrants.

The picture of relentlessly rising illegal migration despite border buildups, which had fueled the mid-decade criticism, began to change in 2007, when Border Patrol apprehensions fell by 20 percent from the 2006 total. Succeeding years have seen a clear continuation of this trend. In fiscal year 2010, there were only 463,382 apprehensions, the lowest total since 1972 and a figure that is less than 30 percent of the highest total recorded, ten years earlier. *See* Table 9.3 *infra.* (This number fell to 327,577 in FY 2011.) Also, in 2007, the leading estimates of the undocumented population in the United States reported a decline for the first time since 1988, a pattern that continued for two years before leveling off in 2010. *See* Chapter Five, Section C, Figure 5.6 and pp. 452, 469–78 above. Many attribute this trend simply to the damaged U.S. economy and the accompanying jump in unemployment. But others see signs that the more extensive enforcement deployments are also playing a role. Edward Alden states:

> Much of this of course is the weak economy. * * * But if you go back and look at the data during the similarly deep recession of 1980 to '81 when unemployment was actually slightly higher than it is currently, there was nothing like the same decline in illegal crossings. And in fact, during that recession, the total unauthorized population continued to grow.

Alden, The Future of Immigration Reform (transcript, Council on Foreign Relations, April 29, 2010), <http://www.cfr.org/immigration/future-immigration-reform/p22038>. *See also* Alden and Roberts, *Are U.S. Borders Secure? Why We Don't Know and How to Find Out,* 90 Foreign Affairs 19 (2011).

Table 9.3
Border Patrol Agents Deployed and Apprehensions Recorded
FY 1990–2010

Fiscal Year	*Number of Border Patrol Agents*	*Number of Apprehensions*
1990	3,715	1,103,353
1995	4,876	1,324,202
2000	9,078	1,676,438
2005	11,156	1,189,075
2006	12,349	1,089,092
2007	14,923	876,704
2008	17,499	723,825
2009	20,119	556,041
2010	20,558	463,382

Sources: For all apprehensions data: U.S. CBP, Nationwide Illegal Alien Apprehensions FY 1925–FY 2010; for Border Patrol agent totals: TRAC, Syracuse University, National Trends in Apprehensions and Staffing (2006), <http://trac.syr.edu> (for years through 2005); U.S. CBP, 2006: A Year of Accomplishment (for 2006); Securing America's Borders (for 2007–2009); Snapshot: A Summary of CBP Facts and Figures (2011) (for 2010). All U.S. CBP documents cited here are available through the CBP website, <http://www.cbp.gov>.

Meantime, DHS and the Border Patrol continue to adjust enforcement strategies in an effort to respond to changes in migration patterns. Some of the change involves enhanced deployment of CBP and ICE resources to Arizona, which has seen major increases in illegal migration flows since the launch of the prevention-through-deterrence policy in California and Texas. DHS also has sought to thwart return migration attempts following successful enforcement action, through what CBP sometimes calls "consequence delivery." One strand of this effort is Operation Streamline, discussed in Section A4b below. In the districts where this Operation has been employed, U.S. Attorneys' offices prosecute a high percentage of apprehended noncitizens, even for the misdemeanor of simple illegal entry. INA § 275(a). Another important strand is the Alien Transfer Exit Program (ATEP), which returns noncitizens to Mexico in a way that "breaks the smuggling cycle by repatriating [them] into regions further east or west of their entry location and, thus, preventing them from immediately coordinating with their smugglers for re-entry." Napolitano Testimony, *supra*, at 10. *See also Successful Border Program Ensures Consequences*, Homeland Security Newswire, Feb. 10, 2011, <http://www.homelandsecuritynewswire.com/successful-border-program-ensures-consequences> (quoting CBP Commissioner Alan Bersin: "No mas. * * * No more returns without consequences."). A further measure with similar effect in reducing return migration, although it was agreed to by the Mexican government largely for humanitarian reasons, is the Mexico Interior Repatriation Program (MIRP). Persons apprehended during the brutally hot summer months in high-risk areas, who voluntarily accept this procedure, are flown back to the interior of Mexico nearer their home regions. Napolitano Testimony, *supra*, at 11.

The decline in border apprehensions and the stabilization of the unauthorized population has not dampened criticism of government enforcement efforts from those who want to see far more vigorous or draconian measures. Some of that criticism has relied heavily on the dramatic increase in brutal killings by drug cartels within Mexico in recent years. The argument is made that stronger steps are needed against illegal migration in order to prevent spillover violence in the United States. Other criticism takes the form of suggesting that there can be no consideration of immigration reform efforts until the border has been "secured"—or some say "sealed."

In response, DHS states that it, along with other law enforcement agencies, remains vigilant against spillover violence, but that there is little evidence that such violence is occurring. In fact, "[v]iolent crimes in Southwest border counties have dropped by more than 30 percent and are currently among the lowest per capita in the Nation. Crime rates in Arizona border towns have remained essentially flat for the past decade, even as drug-related violence has dramatically increased in Mexico." *Id.* at 12. Others see the call to delay immigration reform until the border is fully controlled as a politically convenient way to postpone difficult decisions. *See, e.g.,* C.S. Verdery, *Brick by Brick: A Half–Decade of Immigra-*

tion Enforcement and the Need for Comprehensive Immigration Reform (Center for American Progress, Jun. 2010), <http://www.american progress.org/issues/2010/06/pdf/dhs_enforcement.pdf>.

As noted in the report of a Task Force convened by the Council on Foreign Relations, excerpted at length in Section D below, most of the benchmarks for enforcement success set out in the 2007 reform legislation that stalled in the Senate that year have been achieved. (These included several thousand more Border Patrol agents, more fencing, improved collection and sharing of information among federal agencies, and the procurement of technological assets such as drones, sensors, and surveillance units.) Beyond this, Alden and Roberts urge DHS to help promote a more constructive debate by developing better measures than raw apprehension totals to assess the success of border enforcement. Alden and Roberts, *supra,* at 24–26. Secretary Napolitano launched such an effort in 2011. Napolitano Testimony, *supra,* at 15–17.

4. INTERIOR ENFORCEMENT

Even with the enormous increase in resources for CBP, border enforcement has to be supplemented or backstopped by interior enforcement. Border barriers may be more daunting now, but if it appears that anyone who once makes it past the Border Patrol has little risk of being caught thereafter and will enjoy good access to the U.S. job market, a substantial incentive exists to keep attempting clandestine entry. Further, visa overstayers constitute an estimated 25–40 percent of the unauthorized population. Interior enforcement is also needed to address other violations of the terms of entry, and to remove those who commit crimes that make them deportable. Interior enforcement addresses all these groups of noncitizens, as well as smugglers and traffickers who facilitate illegal entry or illegal travel to the final destination, or who extort additional fees and payments from migrants and family members before completing their human deliveries.

Interior enforcement, which is largely the domain of ICE, comprises both direct apprehension and removal (and possible prosecution) of persons who are unlawfully present as well as efforts to prevent unauthorized noncitizens from accessing U.S. employment. This subsection addresses both aspects.

a. Apprehension and Removal of Unauthorized Migrants

(i) *Background and Overview: Area Control and Worksite Operations*

With 10 to 11 million unauthorized residents, DHS would seem to have plenty of scope for interior enforcement, particularly because the statute gives immigration officers the authority, without a warrant, "to interrogate any alien or person believed to be an alien as to his right to be or to remain in the United States." INA § 287(a)(1). But such a framework raises immediate questions. How should enforcement be shaped to minimize adverse impact on other policy objectives, either those of DHS (such as facilitating legal migration) or those of other agencies (such as promoting international business and tourism, or encouraging community-based policing by state and local law enforcement)? For example, using the interrogation power delegated by § 287(a) to its maximum would surely antagonize and alienate many citizens as well as lawfully present visitors; administrative policy must therefore guide the prudent and targeted use of such authority. Further, given that ICE resources permit successful enforcement against only a modest percentage of the violator population, how should DHS focus its efforts to optimize its overall effectiveness? What are the benchmarks of effectiveness? What strategies would maximize deterrence or self-imposed compliance (such as timely departure by nonimmigrants) so as to reduce the burdens of direct enforcement?

For much of federal immigration control history, there was little central attention to these questions, because key decisions were left largely to the discretion of the roughly 30 INS district directors around the country. Some INS offices employed street sweeps or "area control operations" to identify, arrest, and charge randomly encountered immigration violators. *See* E. Harwood, In Liberty's Shadow: Illegal Aliens and Immigration Law Enforcement 96–124 (1986). Because such tactics often prompted local criticism and community opposition, by the 1980s and 1990s INS was focusing its apprehension efforts on the workplace—at farms, factories, construction sites, restaurants and hotels. This approach, with increasing efforts at centralized direction, continued through much of the Clinton administration, which reported a high of 17,500 workplace apprehensions in 1997—still a tiny number compared to the Border Patrol's million-plus apprehensions. Most of those apprehended were put into removal proceedings, though a small percentage were prosecuted for crimes. But in the later Clinton years, and continuing into the George W. Bush administration, such enforcement actions dropped off considerably. Worksite apprehensions during the first four years of the Bush administration averaged about 500 annually.

A significant change in approach was apparent by 2006, evidently meant to show a determined enforcement effort as part of the push to persuade Congress to pass a comprehensive immigration reform bill. The Bush administration initiated well-publicized worksite enforcement operations that apprehended several hundred unauthorized workers at a time, placing them into removal proceedings or sometimes (as in a widely publicized raid on a meatpacking plant in Postville, Iowa, in 2008, discussed in Section A4b below) charging most workers (and some supervisors) with crimes. Worksite enforcement arrests rose to 5,184 in FY 2008. ICE Fiscal Year 2008 Annual Report: Protecting National Security and Upholding Public Safety 17 (2008).

These worksite enforcement operations, as DHS calls them—raids in the parlance of their critics—generated substantial criticism, and the

Obama administration embarked on a different course. Under a policy adopted in April 2009, the new focus was to be on employer violators, as well as employment sites deemed to be critical infrastructure (such as military bases or chemical plants). ICE now focuses on both criminal and civil charges against egregious employers, rather than on widespread civil arrests of workers, because, in its current judgment, "[e]nforcement efforts focused on employers effectively target the root causes of illegal migration." Testimony of Kumar Kibble, ICE Deputy Director, before the Subcommittee on Immigration Policy and Enforcement of the House Judiciary Committee 2 (Jan. 26, 2011). Under this approach, ICE makes much greater use of I–9 audits, discussed below, which may result in the firing of unauthorized employees but usually not their placement into removal proceedings. The policy change resulted in record numbers of employer prosecutions, fines, forfeitures and restitutions, as well as debarments of violator companies from federal contracts in FY 2010. *Id.* at 3. In this fashion, DHS aimed to put deliberate management-level violators out of business and also to induce more extensive and careful observance of the law by other employers. As part of this process, it encouraged companies to use both compliance assistance programs offered by ICE and the E–Verify system for electronic checking of the employment authorization of new hires.

(ii) Focus on Aliens Involved in Crime

Although apprehensions in the worksite or through more random interior encounters thus dropped considerably, ICE still exceeded in FY 2009 and 2010 any earlier year's totals for removals and enforced returns. How did this come about? Under the Obama administration, ICE has done much more to focus interior enforcement on the removal of noncitizens with criminal convictions. *See* Table 9.4 *infra*.[1] This does not mean that the conviction is necessarily the formal basis for the removal charge; such charges are ordinarily relied on only with regard to lawful permanent residents—for the obvious reason that LPRs are essentially not otherwise deportable. In the majority of the cases counted as criminal removals, ICE can charge entrance without inspection or overstay, which is less cumbersome to prove in immigration court than a criminal conviction. The conviction remains relevant to mark the individual as a higher enforcement priority. Further, ICE increasingly relies on noncitizen encounters with the criminal justice system as a way to identify persons who are a priority for removal and to take them into custody.

---

1. Table 9.4 sets forth *ICE's* removals and returns, as reported based on ICE databases. These are a subset of the overall *DHS* removals and returns set forth in Table 9.2 above, and ICE uses essentially the same definitions of removals and returns described in connection with that Table. ICE reports its totals separately from the broad DHS numbers to help indicate its own interior enforcement accomplishments. These ICE numbers sometimes show higher totals of criminals than the combined DHS figure because of enhanced capacities to track criminal convictions in ICE databases as well as minor differences in the way that late-reported statistics (received weeks or months after the end of the fiscal year) are captured.

Table 9.4
Total Removals and Returns by ICE, FY 2007–2011

Fiscal year	Total	Convicted criminal	Non-criminal
2007	291,060	102,024	189,036
2008	369,221	114,415	254,806
2009	389,834	136,343	253,491
2010	392,862	195,772	197,090
2011(thru 7/31)	324,719	164,345	160,374

Source: ICE Total Removals through July 31, 2011, <http://www.ice.gov/doclib/about/offices/ero/pdf/ero-removals.pdf> (visited Sept. 24, 2011).

We explored in Chapter 7C4 *supra* the priority-setting process that ICE has used to direct this change in focus, along with a variety of issues it presents. This section considers the history behind this evolution, in order to understand the situation driving much of today's effort to apprehend and remove unauthorized migrants through interior enforcement, and also to summarize the specific programs ICE uses to achieve these ends.

CAP and IRP. For decades, the immigration agencies' ability to initiate removal of noncitizens convicted of crimes rested almost entirely on informal cooperative relations with state, local, and federal law enforcement agencies (LEAs), which varied greatly among cities or regions. As a result, in the 1980s and 1990s even some persons convicted of serious crimes might not come to the attention of INS before release, but if they were placed in proceedings, INS would typically take custody at the end of the person's criminal sentence and initiate removal proceedings at that time.[2] The resulting costs, plus the unsystematic character of the enforcement efforts directed at noncitizens convicted of crimes, attracted the criticism of Congress and stimulated legal and administrative reforms in the 1980s and 1990s.

Early reforms focused on persons confined in state and federal prison—the more serious offenders, serving lengthy sentences. INS began to develop more systematic relationships with prisons (under what later became known as the Criminal Alien Program, CAP) that would allow the timely identification and charging of those inmates who were noncitizens and therefore might be removable. It also worked to make arrangements with such facilities to hold removal proceedings for such persons while they were still confined in state or federal criminal custody. Some states even made room for (or constructed) immigration courtrooms in their prisons. This Institutional Hearing Program, later called the Institutional Removal Program (IRP), was designed to produce a final enforceable

---

2. The statute generally provides that DHS shall not remove someone sentenced to prison until he or she has finished the sentence of imprisonment, not counting any term of parole or probation. INA §§ 236(c), 241(a)(4). The latter section permits an exception when the noncitizen has committed only a nonviolent offense and the relevant state or federal official determines that earlier removal is "in the best interest" of the government concerned.

removal order before the person's release from his criminal sentence into INS custody. Instead of incurring many months of detention costs, INS thus might need to hold the person only for a few days while securing travel documents from the country of nationality and making transport arrangements. Congress approved this procedure and called for its expansion. INA § 238(a).

Jail programs. These steps left untouched those offenders who did not serve time in the major prison facilities, but instead were confined in local jails, both before and after conviction. In such cases, local INS offices tried to develop working relationships with state and local LEAs, but the pattern was quite uneven throughout the country, in part because INS did not even have offices in some states until the late 1990s. INS therefore often relied on receiving a call from the local law enforcement agency when it had apprehended a person believed to be illegally present, requesting that INS pick up the individual and place him into removal proceedings. INS's ability to respond was constrained by limited detention and officer resources or other factors such as distance from the jail to the nearest INS officer or facility. Consequently INS often had to decline such requests to take custody—to the consternation of the LEA, which was convinced it had a criminal violator who was also present in the country unlawfully. INS field offices made response decisions based on resource constraints and on the available information about the individual and the seriousness of his crime. Reliance on this patchwork of informal relations also meant that many noncitizens would escape INS's attention, even though they might have been a high priority for removal owing to the nature or number of their offenses.

In the 1990s and 2000s, with enhanced appropriations and various congressional urgings or mandates focused on removing criminal aliens, the immigration enforcement agencies worked to expand and systematize cooperation with local jails. Some jail initiatives involved stationing federal officers at high-volume booking locations in cities like Los Angeles or New York, to determine alienage and deportability via regular federal database checks and, as necessary, to conduct an interview of persons believed to be foreign born (information on place of birth is routinely collected as part of the booking process).

The focus of these jail programs has been intake or booking, not the far end of the process following disposition of the criminal charge, for several reasons. First, most persons thus identified could be charged as removable (as an EWI or overstayer) without relying on the current criminal charge or conviction. Second, a high percentage of the in-processed jail population, in contrast to those serving long sentences in state prisons, might be released shortly after arrest or their initial appearance in court. The prosecutor might choose to drop the charges or the judge might impose a sentence that amounted to time already served. If identification and preliminary immigration enforcement decisions, including the issuance of a detainer, were not done at the booking stage, the noncitizen could easily be freed before immigration enforcement action could occur. Some of these might be individuals with serious earlier convictions, issued at a time when DHS was not equipped to seek custody, or they could be persons with a history of the more serious immigration violations, such as returning without permission to the United States after an earlier deportation. Such a return could be charged as a federal felony (INA § 276(a)), but more often simply results in the noncitizen being treated as a higher priority for removal.

When DHS does seek a particular person in a local jail for removal (even if identified separately by federal officials without the LEA's involvement), it typically sends an ICE detainer to the current custodian—in line with a practice common among law enforcement agencies. A detainer is a formal request that the requesting law enforcement agency be notified when the individual is about to be released from the receiving agency's custody, along with a request that he or she be held for an additional reasonable period to permit travel and transfer arrangements. (ICE detainers ask for a period of 48 hours, not counting weekends and holidays). In the jail setting, the time taken to complete state or local confinement on the criminal charge could range from a few hours to months, years, or decades, depending on the length of any trial proceedings and the duration of the sentence, if the person is convicted.

Jail programs of this type are typically resource-intensive, for both federal authorities and the LEA. The latter had to cooperate to make space for the federal activity, to provide preliminary information in an agreed manner, perhaps to select persons to be referred for closer immigration status scrutiny, and to schedule inmates for interview. Over time INS and ICE introduced further efficiencies, for example through LEA agreement to install and maintain computer and video equipment that would permit a centrally located federal staff to perform these checking and interview functions in connection with several jail facilities. The federal agencies continued to seek improvements, in part to reduce training and operational burdens on LEAs and also to make the process less dependent on subjective local decisions to refer particular inmates for a closer look by federal officers.

Section 287(g). The 287(g) program offered one possibility. As discussed in Section C2a below, INA § 287(g), enacted in 1996, permits ICE to delegate certain immigration officer functions "in relation to the investigation, apprehension, or detention" of noncitizens to state and local officers, pursuant to a detailed agreement with the state or local LEA. The statute requires specific training and ongoing supervision by the federal agency of the participating officers. State and local officers could be given wide authority to arrest and detain suspected immigration violators (the task force model, as described in Section C2a), but a majority of the roughly 70 § 287(g) agreements focused instead on jails, training local officers to do the interview and database-checking functions described above, which could lead to the lodging of immigration charges and the eventual transfer of custody to federal officers for removal proceedings.

Secure Communities. In part because 287(g) agreements cover only a small fraction of the nearly 18,000 state and local law enforcement agencies nationwide, Congress pressed for still more systematic action against noncitizens convicted of crimes. Under specific directives contained in appropriations bills enacted from 2007 onward, ICE developed the Secure Communities program. Secure Communities at its core is a data-sharing process between the FBI and DHS. The computer interface involved takes information submitted to the FBI as part of an LEA's routine and familiar transmission of the fingerprints of arrested individuals and sends it on to be checked against information in IDENT, DHS's biometrics-based immigration database. For most arrestees, not surprisingly, there is no match with any IDENT record. When there is a match—for example revealing that the person just arrested had been encountered two earlier times near the border and returned by CBP to Mexico—the information is sent on to ICE officials for a decision on further action. Typically the ICE field office near the booking facility makes the determination whether to proceed with enforcement action. If so, it normally sends a detainer to the LEA.

Once a jurisdiction is activated for Secure Communities, all fingerprints transmitted to the FBI are checked against IDENT; no state or local officer makes a preliminary decision whether the person is a noncitizen subject to DHS jurisdiction. Moreover, only the fingerprints of persons who have been arrested and booked are transmitted. ICE has emphasized the importance of these features of the system design. Requiring the check of all fingerprints was intended to minimize any risk of selective or discriminatory referrals to ICE, for example based on ethnicity, appearance or language skills. The limitation to arrested persons was also one way of assuring that victims and witnesses would not be identified to ICE through the Secure Communities links. Only persons actually arrested and fingerprinted are checked against IDENT.

Moreover, DHS considered that Secure Communities had other efficiency advantages over earlier processes, particularly including 287(g). No special training or supervision of local officers is required. At the front end, the process is essentially invisible to the LEA officer doing the booking. No extra forms are completed, and no special or separate communication with DHS is required to initiate a check of immigration status. Nonetheless, ICE does seek to maintain working relationships with the booking LEA to help fill in gaps in the Secure Communities system. Some illegally present noncitizens will not generate a hit in IDENT, particularly those who successfully entered without inspection and never encountered DHS officers. If the person states a foreign place of birth in response to the standard booking questions but generates no hit in IDENT, he or she may warrant an ICE interview to determine current status. Also, federal encounter records from before about 2005 may not be in IDENT, though DHS is working to incorporate more and more of the earlier data into the automated system. The public controversy over Secure Communities is discussed in Section C2a below.

b. Prosecuting Immigration Violations as Crimes

One of the most significant recent enforcement trends has been a sharp increase in the number of federal criminal prosecutions for immigration law violations. No longer can a discussion of immigration enforcement confine itself to the process that may lead to a noncitizen's removal from the United States. The trend toward prosecuting immigration law violators with new intensity has several major components, as sketched in the following excerpt.

INGRID V. EAGLY, PROSECUTING IMMIGRATION

102 Nw. U. L. Rev. 1281, 1301–04, 1326–30 (2009).

A roadmap to the criminal-immigration system emerges from the exploration of a 2008 prosecution that took place in Postville, Iowa. In one of the largest immigration crime prosecutions in history, immigration officers raided a meatpacking plant and arrested hundreds of factory workers. Immigration authorities then brought these workers to an enclosed cattle fairground set up as a makeshift courtroom. There, the arrestees were assigned to counsel in groups of ten or more. Within four days, 270 workers had signed "exploding" plea agreements, entered binding felony guilty pleas in court, and received criminal sentences.

Postville's large-scale prosecution received enormous media attention, far overshadowing the broader story of immigration crime prosecutions dominating the federal docket. Criminal defense attorneys called into question whether the compressed time period to accept the pleas violated due process. Immigration lawyers, who were denied access to the fairground while the workers were being interrogated, charged that the defendants had been placed on a "new high-speed judicial railroad," where they were not advised of their immigration rights prior to signing the speedy plea agreements. A federal Spanish language interpreter assigned to the Postville hearings came forward, bringing national attention to a day he critiqued as "the saddest procession [he had] ever witnessed, which the public would never see." Two months later, Congressional hearings were held to examine the propriety of the criminal proceedings.

A close analysis of the Postville prosecution reveals many aspects of the interaction between the criminal prosecutor and the administrative apparatus of immigration. First, the Postville defendants were informed that they were ineligible for bail—not because of the formal criminal bail rules, but instead because the immigration agency had lodged an immigration detainer. Despite the fact that many defendants had bail equities—including long-term residence in the United States, dependent children, friends, and family in the community, and no criminal record—not a single defendant had a bail hearing. Even if hearings had been held and bond granted, the immigration detainers would have resulted in transfer into ICE custody rather than release to the community. This functional denial of bail is consequential because of how it impacted plea-bargain dynamics. The Postville defendants would have spent a longer time in pretrial detention awaiting a trial (six to eight months) than they would serve in prison by convicting themselves (most were offered a binding sentence of five months).

Prosecutors also threatened the slaughterhouse workers with aggravated identity theft charges (carrying a mandatory two-year sentence) unless they accepted the government's "fast-track" plea. Although the exact terms of specific pleas varied, most defendants pleaded guilty to false use of a document as evidence of authorized employment. Under the written plea offer, the defendants received a very short timetable for deciding whether to accept the plea or face the enhanced charges. In addition, once they accepted the pleas, prosecutors drastically abbreviated the normal time between the plea and sentencing. The standard sentencing process can take months, but the Postville defendants pleaded guilty and were sentenced on the same day. The fast-tracked pleas were entered en masse on the rented fairground, based on a uniform plea "script" written in advance by prosecutors. By the time the Supreme Court, in an unrelated case, interpreted the aggravated identity theft statute so that it could not be used to prosecute garden-variety false-document cases (as prosecutors did in Postville), the Postville defendants had already served their time and had been deported.

Postville prosecutors also insisted on a "stipulated removal order" as a mandatory term of the plea agreements. Although the slaughterhouse workers were alleged to be undocumented, any individual defendant might have been eligible to remain legally in the United States under established immigration law. For example, laws such as cancellation of removal, adjustment of status, asylum, and U or T visas provide avenues for undocumented persons to remain legally within the United States despite having entered and lived in the country without permission. However, as a practical matter, the short-fuse exploding plea offer precluded meaningful evaluation by defense attorneys of whether such immigration relief might be possible. And with stipulated orders of removal, the defendants abandoned any and all immigration claims in the criminal plea.

Looking back at Postville, two stories emerge. The simple story tells of overcharging and overzealous prosecution. That story may well be true. A less obvious, but equally important, story contemplates the Postville prosecution as emblematic of the blending of our criminal and immigration systems. * * *

* * *

* * * After a surge in immigration prosecution in the 1950s, the immigration agency lobbied Congress to establish a misdemeanor court that would allow for criminal immigration enforcement "at less expense and with a greater amount of effectiveness" than was possible with Article III courts. Foreshadowing the anticipated creation of such a court, immigration authorities convinced Congress in 1952 to amend the Immigration and Nationality Act to reduce the penalty for the crime of simple illegal entry from one year to six months. With this change in place, illegal entry

met the federal definition of "petty offense." This reduction in maximum sentence was critical because it meant that illegal entry cases could proceed before magistrate judges without the right to trial by jury or grand jury indictment.

A fundamental realignment of the immigration prosecution regime stemmed from the creation of a simple illegal entry crime that could be prosecuted without grand jury indictment or jury trial in a separate track court system. Removal of the jury screen disconnected immigration crime from the traditional system of checks and balances on prosecutorial overreaching. Along the southwest border, juries could be powerful; grand jury members would often not indict in immigration crime cases because such laws were "locally unpopular." For example, in El Paso, Texas in the late 1940s, over 90% of immigration crime cases sent to the grand jury were returned as "no bills." After the implementation of the magistrate court in 1971, petty illegal entry cases soon accounted for nearly 90% of federal criminal enforcement of immigration, virtually eliminating any form of jury screen from the charging or trial process for immigration crime. The volume of immigration crime also rose dramatically. Nation-wide, criminal immigration prosecutions increased by over 700%, from 2536 in the year that the Federal Magistrate Act was passed to 17,858 in 1974.

More recently, a border prosecution program known as Operation Streamline, or simply "Streamline," has exclusively used the magistrate courts. Under Streamline, the government has adopted a zero-tolerance stance, prosecuting every noncitizen arrested sneaking across certain portions of the Mexican border, primarily with the crime of entry without inspection. Defendants in Streamline waive rights, enter guilty pleas, and are sentenced in proceedings that may last only minutes. Frequently, Streamline proceedings include multiple defendants in the same hearing. As Chief Judge Martha Vasquez of the District of New Mexico has explained, defendants are being asked to give up critical rights in hearings that are conducted "in a way that we've never had to conduct them before": "We put them in a courtroom full of people that are not always charged with the same offense" and ask them to "waive important constitutional rights."

The Ninth Circuit recently considered whether the en masse plea hearings that typify Streamline violate federal law and found that they do. Bulk plea processing of fifty or more defendants in a single plea colloquy does not, according to the Ninth Circuit, comport with the Federal Rules of Criminal Procedure. No judge overseeing such mass proceedings could possibly determine that each defendant in the packed courtroom volun-tarily and knowingly pleaded guilty, as required under federal law.

The guilty plea rate for immigration crime in magistrate court has increased significantly under the Streamline program—from 63% in 2004 to 97% in 2009. With sentences as short as time served and trials not likely to be held for months, defendants would spend more time in custody by demanding a trial than by simply pleading guilty. The logical result is an almost perfect guilty plea rate.

Under Streamline, not only are first-time entrants processed through the magistrate court, but more serious offenders are "flopped" into magistrate proceedings. With the "flip-flop" plea agreement, smugglers or illegal entrants with prior removal orders are charged with both unlawful reentry (a felony) and unlawful entry (a misdemeanor). If the defendant pleads guilty to the lesser charge within an expedited time period, the case is resolved as a misdemeanor before an Article I magistrate judge.

Between 1992 and 2009, the proportion of the total U.S. Attorney workload processed by magistrate judges increased from 24% to 47%. Furthermore, within the magistrate caseload, the percentage of immigration-related matters rose during the same period from 24% to 82%. In other words, immigration prosecution has shifted much of the work of the federal criminal system into a separate system that is governed by distinct procedural rules. In the process, the magistrate criminal court has been defined, especially in the Southwest, as a separate adjudicatory system reserved almost exclusively for immigration crime.

NOTES AND QUESTIONS ON CRIMINAL PROSECUTION OF IMMIGRATION VIOLATIONS

1. *United States v. Roblero–Solis*, 588 F.3d 692, 693 (9th Cir. 2009), is the Ninth Circuit decision mentioned by Eagly that found en masse pleas to violate federal law, specifically that they are inconsistent with Federal Rule of Criminal Procedure 11, which governs the taking of pleas from criminal defendants in federal court. In practice, the response to *Roblero–Solis* has been to take pleas in smaller groups, to permit more individual attention by the judge to each defendant's responses. The decision has modestly altered the pace and processing in Operation Streamline, but the basic program continues in many border areas.

2. As described above and in Section A4c below, the Obama administration decided to focus interior enforcement on building criminal and civil cases against employers rather than on arresting and deporting large numbers of employees. Consequently, no Postville-style mass use of criminal charges against employees has been seen since 2008. Does the current administration's increased use of felony indictments against employers who knowingly employ unauthorized workers (often including criminal charges based on other worker-protection laws as well) raise any of the same issues identified by Eagly?

3. Addressing evolving practices of obtaining guilty pleas to criminal violations of immigration laws, Jennifer Chacón offers this critique:

> The ongoing erosion of the procedural rights of these criminal defendants thus far has been effectively normalized. Such procedural moves can be framed as nothing more than an extension of longstanding limitations on the due process rights of noncitizens in immigration proceedings. However, it is important not to lose sight of the legal

distinctions that separate the criminal from the civil realm. The prosecution of these offenses should not be allowed to reshape the criminal sphere to look more like the less rights-protective civil system where immigration enforcement has typically been centered. Unfortunately, at the moment, this is exactly what is happening.

Chacón, *Managing Migration Through Crime*, 109 Colum. L. Rev. Sidebar 135 (2009).

But consider this possible response: what is wrong with a special streamlined criminal justice system for criminal violations of immigration law, where penalties are less severe than in much of federal criminal law, and where defendants by definition are not citizens of the United States?

Or consider a different possible response, coming from the standpoint of the enforcing agencies. Congress has greatly increased the resources for enforcement over the last decade and has been loudly demanding meaningful results—not just tally sheets with increased numbers of removal orders or deportations, but a real impact in shrinking the unauthorized population or at least retarding its growth. A classic law enforcement approach toward achieving such objectives is to enhance deterrence by increasing the de facto sanctions experienced by violators. Hence the decision to add criminal prosecution to the normal response of a simple civil deportation. As part of this effort, the agencies also have been seeking ways to thwart the revolving door phenomenon—deported persons who simply attempt to enter again the following night. Instead of a quick bus trip back to the border, where the individual may just meet up with the *coyote* who will help him make another try, why not adopt a criminal procedure that involves several days of detention, a more august proceeding before a federal criminal judge or magistrate (which might more deeply impress upon some of the migrants the gravity of the violation), and a stern judicial warning that return can result in a felony prosecution and a much longer sentence? (In this connection, consider the materials in Section A3 above regarding CBP's efforts to improve "consequence delivery.")

4. Alan Bersin, U.S. Attorney for the Southern District of California (San Diego) during the Clinton administration and later the Commissioner of CBP under Obama, co-authored an article discussing an early initiative to bring criminal charges for more serious immigration-related offenses, see Bersin & Feigin, *The Rule of Law at the Border: Reinventing Prosecution Policy in the Southern District of California*, 12 Geo. Immigr. L.J. 285 (1998). For further analysis of Operation Streamline, see Lydgate, Comment, *Assembly–Line Justice: A Review of Operation Streamline*, 98 Calif. L. Rev. 481, 511 (2010).

c. Employer Sanctions and Antidiscrimination Provisions

(i) Employer Sanctions and the Verification Process

Interior enforcement—at least in theory—seeks to counteract unauthorized migration not only by removing persons unlawfully in the country but also by deterring illegal entry in the first place. The primary tool of deterrence is the employer sanctions regime, added to the INA by IRCA in 1986. The Senate Report on an earlier version of the bill that became IRCA made the case for employer sanctions as follows:

As long as greater job opportunities are available to foreign nationals who succeed in physically entering this country, intense illegal immigration pressure on the United States will continue. This pressure will decline only if the availability of United States employment is eliminated, or the disparity in wages and working conditions is reduced, through improvement in the Third World or deterioration in the United States.

The United States should, of course, assist Third World development, but the achievement of substantially higher living standards there is a prospect only for the long run, and in the short run Third World development may actually increase migration to the United States. Since deterioration in the United States is certainly not an attractive resolution, only one approach remains: To prohibit the knowing employment of illegal aliens.

S.Rep. No. 62, 98th Cong., 1st Sess. 7–8 (1983).

Take a careful look at INA § 274A, which (1) prohibits the hiring of "unauthorized aliens" (the categories of aliens authorized to work, either incident to status or by specific permission, are listed in 8 C.F.R. § 274a.12); and (2) requires that employers use form I–9 (reprinted in the Statutory Supplement) to verify the lawful status of all new hires. Good faith compliance with the I–9 procedure provides the employer an affirmative defense against a charge that it knowingly hired unauthorized workers. DHS may initiate a proceeding on either type of violation before an administrative law judge (ALJ) within the Office of the Chief Administrative Hearing Officer (OCAHO), which is part of the Executive Office for Immigration Review (EOIR). An employer who loses before the ALJ may seek a limited form of discretionary review by the Chief Administrative Hearing Officer; judicial review lies in the federal courts of appeals. *See generally* INA § 274A(e); 28 C.F.R. ch.1, part 68.

The debate over employer sanctions in the early 1980s was long and intense. Some members of Congress argued that the program might place an undue burden on employers. Not only would all employers be subject to new paperwork obligations, but a regime of employer sanctions also raised the specter that employers would have to become experts in immigration law in order to identify which categories of aliens were authorized to work. Another area of special concern was the question of what kind of documentation would suffice to establish eligibility for employment. Congress was aware of the huge market in fraudulent documents, and some proponents argued that a form of counterfeit-proof documentation ought to be devised to ensure the effectiveness of the program. The risk that this might lead to a "national identity card," however, caused many members of Congress to shy away from such a requirement. Those opposed to an identity card won. See INA § 274A(c).

Kitty Calavita describes another feature of the overall compromise that won passage of the 1986 law after years of debate:

[P]olicymakers faced an apparently irresolvable dilemma grounded in [a] political-economic contradiction * * *. Confronted on one hand by the political pressure for an employer sanctions law, and on the other by the impossibility of passing such a law over the objection of employers who derived significant economic benefits from undocumented migration, the outcome was an employer sanctions law that would be easy to comply with.* * * [T]he law in effect made *violations* "pragmatically easy." Through the affirmative defense and good faith provisions, Congress guaranteed that conformity with the [I–9] paperwork requirements would be taken as an indication of compliance, thereby ensuring that violations of the "knowing hire" provision—the real meat of the law—would be virtually risk-free.

Calavita, *Employer Sanctions Violations: Toward a Dialectical Model of White–Collar Crime*, 24 Law & Society Review 1041, 1057, 1060 (1990).

Section A4a(i) above describes changes in worksite enforcement strategies and patterns through recent presidential administrations—varying combinations of employer penalties and arrests of unauthorized workers themselves. Early in its tenure, the Obama administration reoriented the focus toward prosecuting or fining violator employers and away from the large-scale arrests of unauthorized workers that marked the last three years of the George W. Bush administration, which was itself a shift from the very limited worksite enforcement activity in President Bush's first term. For FY 2010 ICE reported criminal arrests of 196 employers for worksite-related violations, up from a previous high of 135 in 2008. In 2010 ICE initiated actions that resulted in administrative fines on employers of over $6.9 million, as well as judicially-imposed fines, forfeitures and restitutions totaling over $36.6 million. Kibble Testimony, *supra,* at 3. (This compares with a low of just $37,514 in administrative and criminal fines in 2003.) Because a great many of these investigations result in agreed settlements with employers or else are handled through the criminal justice system, relatively few civil fine proceedings are brought before EOIR's administrative law judges. Such civil fine filings, including both employer sanctions and antidiscrimination charges, totaled 91 in FY 2010, up from 23 in FY 2006. EOIR, FY 2010 Statistical Year Book, at Z1 (Jan. 2011).

(ii) Antidiscrimination Provisions

One major concern during the 1986 debate over IRCA was that employer sanctions would lead to employment discrimination against Hispanic–Americans, Asian–Americans, or others who "looked foreign," and that existing fair employment laws would provide no remedy. For example, Title VII of the Civil Rights Act of 1964, 42 U.S.C.A. § 2000e–2, applied only to employers with fifteen or more full-time employees; and it barred national origin discrimination but not discrimination based solely on alienage. *See Espinoza v. Farah Manufacturing Co.*, 414 U.S. 86, 94 S.Ct. 334, 38 L.Ed.2d 287 (1973).

As a result, Congress enacted INA § 274B as part of IRCA. That section established a Special Counsel for Immigration–Related Unfair Employment Practices in the Department of Justice to investigate and pursue charges of employment discrimination based on national origin or citizenship status. As to the latter, § 274B covers citizenship status discrimination only against citizens and certain classes of aliens, *viz.* lawful permanent resident aliens, newly legalized aliens, refugees, and asylees. Lawful permanent residents are not covered if they fail to initiate the naturalization process within six months after satisfying the residency requirement for citizenship. INA § 274B(a). Nonimmigrants (even those authorized to work) and parolees are not covered. Congress also supplemented Title VII protections by applying to employers with four or more employees the prohibitions of § 274B against national origin discrimination in hiring.

IRCA permits discrimination based on citizenship status when lawfully required under federal, state, or local governmental authority. And an employer may hire a U.S. citizen in preference to an alien if the two are "equally qualified." INA § 274B(a)(2), (4). Also, IRCA, unlike Title VII, applies only to hiring, referral for a fee, and firing, and thus offers no remedy for discrimination on the job. *See Ortega v. Vermont Bread*, 3 O.C.A.H.O. 475 (1992).

A sharp dispute over the coverage of the new § 274B surfaced shortly after the enactment of IRCA. Did the provision bar practices having a disparate impact on different groups or only actions motivated by discriminatory intent? Congress resolved the controversy by amending the INA in 1996 to supply an explicit intent test for discrimination claims arising out of employer verification practices. Section 274B(a)(6) now provides that requiring more or different documents in order to establish authorization to work or refusing to honor facially valid documents constitutes "an unfair immigration-related employment practice" only "if made for the purpose or with the intent of discriminating against an individual." What does this amendment mean? (Consider this provision in connection with Question 5 below.)

If the Special Counsel has not filed a complaint within 120 days after receiving an allegation of unlawful discrimination, a private party may also initiate an enforcement action. INA § 274B(d)(2). Administrative law judges hear complaints and may impose civil penalties, order equitable relief, and award attorney fees. *See* § 274B(e)–(h), 28 C.F.R. Part 44. An order of the ALJ is reviewable by the Chief Administrative Hearing Officer, and may be appealed to a federal court of appeals. *See* INA § 274B(i), 28 C.F.R. § 68.53.

You have XYZ Widget Co. as a client. The President of XYZ has come to you for advice. How would you answer the following questions? (You may need to consult §§ 274A and 274B, the implementing regulations in 8 C.F.R. Part 274a, and the following parts of this Section.)

1. "I think that illegal aliens are harder workers and more reliable than U.S. citizens. May I restrict hiring to noncitizens? Even if I can't, I intend to do so; and if I get caught I'll treat the penalty as a tax. How much could it cost me?" (What ethical problems do you confront as you contemplate answering this question?)

2. "I have recently received a letter from the Social Security Administration informing me that the social security number that one of my employees gave me when I hired her does not match SSA's records. I am worried that she is an unauthorized worker. May I ask her for additional documentation at this point to make sure she is eligible for work in the United States?"

3. "Do I have to ask you for identification before hiring you as my lawyer?"

4. "I want to make sure my employees can communicate with my customers. Can I refuse to hire anyone who doesn't speak English?"

5. "I have an employee who says he is a U.S. citizen but he speaks with an accent, so I really want to see a birth certificate before hiring him." Is that unlawful discrimination?

(iii) The Issue of Constructive Knowledge

The employer sanctions provisions of the INA prohibit the knowing hire of a noncitizen unauthorized to work in the United States. INA § 274A. Most employers comply with the prescribed verification process, examining documents supplied by employees and recording information on the I–9 form. Because of the widespread existence of fraudulent documents that pass as genuine—at least to employers not trained as immigration officers—the verification process, as presently constructed, does little to deter the hiring of unauthorized workers. Indeed, the statutory provisions were written expressly to establish a largely ministerial, form-filling role for employers, so as not to unduly burden them with immigration enforcement tasks and to protect against discrimination that might be occasioned by a more active employer role. The statute requires the employer to accept a document tendered by the employee if it "reasonably appears on its face to be genuine." INA § 274A(b)(1)(A). Rather than serving as an effective deterrent against the hiring of unauthorized workers, the I–9 process is more likely to serve the role of protecting the employer against charges of unlawful hiring: the employer points to the completed form as evidence that he or she has met statutory responsibilities.

But what if facts surrounding the employment situation would have led a reasonably alert employer to believe that the papers proffered by an employee were in fact fraudulent? Or suppose an employer has heard a rumor at the workplace that an employee is an unauthorized employee. May an employer be deemed to have *constructive knowledge* of the employment of an authorized worker and thereby be subject to sanctions?

In 1990, the INS adopted by regulation a definition of "knowing" that included "constructive knowledge":

> The term "knowing" includes not only actual knowledge but also knowledge which may fairly be inferred through notice of certain facts and circumstances which would lead a person, through the exercise of reasonable care, to know about a certain condition.

55 Fed Reg. 25,928 (1990) (amending 8 C.F.R. 274A).

The following case examines a situation in which the INS claimed that an employer had constructive knowledge that one of its employers was an unauthorized worker.

COLLINS FOODS INTERNATIONAL, INC. v. INS

United States Court of Appeals, Ninth Circuit, 1991.
948 F.2d 549.

CANBY, CIRCUIT JUDGE:

* * *

Ricardo Soto Gomez (Soto), an employee at a Phoenix Sizzler Restaurant,[a] is authorized to hire other Sizzler employees for that location. Soto extended a job offer to Armando Rodriguez in a long-distance telephone conversation; Soto was in Phoenix and Rodriguez was in California. Rodriguez said nothing in the telephone conversation to indicate that he was not authorized to work in the United States. Rodriguez was working for Sizzler in California at the time Soto extended the offer of employment in Phoenix.

When Rodriguez came to Phoenix, he reported to Sizzler for work. Before allowing Rodriguez to begin work, Soto asked Rodriguez for evidence of his authorization to work in the United States. Rodriguez informed Soto that he did not have the necessary identification with him. At that point, Soto did not let Rodriguez begin work, but sent him away with the understanding that he would return with his qualifying documents.

Rodriguez returned with a driver's license and what appeared to be a Social Security card. Soto looked at the face of the documents and copied information from them onto a Form I–9. Soto did not look at the back of the Social Security card, nor did he compare it with the example in the INS handbook. After Soto completed the necessary paperwork, Rodriguez began work at the Sizzler in Phoenix. Rodriguez, it turned out, was an

---

a. Collins Foods operates retail establishments under the name of Sizzler Restaurant—eds.

alien not authorized to work in the United States, and his "Social Security card" was a forgery.

DISCUSSION

The INS charged Collins Foods with one count of hiring an alien, knowing him to be unauthorized to work in the United States, in violation of INA § 274A(a)(1)(A). * * * Inasmuch as it was uncontroverted that Rodriguez was unauthorized to work in the United States, the only issue to be decided at the hearing was whether Collins Foods knew that Rodriguez was unauthorized at the time of hire. The ALJ declined to decide that Collins Foods had actual knowledge of the fact that Rodriguez was an illegal alien, but decided instead that it had "constructive knowledge." The ALJ based his "constructive knowledge" conclusion on two facts: first, that Soto offered the job to Rodriguez over the telephone without having seen Rodriguez' documentation; and, second, that Soto failed to compare the back of the Social Security card with the example in the INS manual. While we do not disturb the factual determinations made by the ALJ, we hold that these two facts cannot, as a matter of law, establish constructive knowledge under INA § 274A(a)(1)(A).

I. *Job Offer Prior to Verification of Documents*

The first of these facts, as a matter of law, cannot support a finding of constructive knowledge. Nothing in the statute prohibits the offering of a job prior to checking the documents; indeed, the regulations contemplate just such a course of action.

The statute that Collins Foods is charged with violating prohibits "a person or other entity [from] hir[ing] for employment" an alien not authorized to work. INA § 274A(a)(1)(A). The Regulations define "hiring" as "the actual commencement of employment of an employee for wages or other remuneration." 8 C.F.R. § 274a.1(c). As Rodriguez had not commenced employment for wages at the time Soto extended a job offer to him over the telephone, Rodriguez was not yet "hired" for purposes of section 274A. Soto was therefore not required to verify Rodriguez' documentation at that time.

Another regulation addresses the issue of the timeliness of verification, and it suggests the same result. Under 8 C.F.R. § 274a.2(b)(1)(ii), employers are required to examine an employee's documentation and complete Form I–9 "within three business days of the hire." Because Soto had examined Rodriguez' documents and completed the necessary paperwork by the time Rodriguez began work for wages, Soto was not delinquent in verifying Rodriguez' documentation.

There are additional, highly cogent reasons for rejecting the ALJ's reliance on the fact that Soto "told Rodriguez he would be hired long before Soto ever saw, or had any opportunity to verify, *any* evidence of Rodriguez' work authorization." To hold such a failure of early verification against the employer, as the ALJ did, places the employer in an impossible position. Pre-employment questioning concerning the applicant's national origin, race or citizenship exposes the employer to charges of discrimination if he does not hire that applicant. The Equal Employment Opportunity Commission has held that pre-employment inquiries concerning a job applicant's race, color, religion, national origin, or citizenship status "may constitute evidence of discrimination prohibited by Title VII." EEOC, *Pre–Employment Inquiries* (1981), *reprinted in* 2 Employment Practices Guide ¶ 4120, 4163 (CCH 1985). An employer who makes such inquiries will have the burden of proving that the answers to such inquiries "are not used in making hiring and placement decisions in a discriminatory manner prohibited by law." Id. ¶ 4120 at 4166. For that reason, employers attempting to comply with the Immigration Reform and Control Act of 1986 ("IRCA"), are well advised not to examine documents until after an offer of employment is made * * *.

The ultimate danger, of course, is that many employers, faced with conflicting commands from the EEOC and the INS, would simply avoid interviewing any applicant whose appearance suggests alienage. The resulting discrimination against citizens and authorized aliens would frustrate the intent of Congress embodied in both Title VII of the Civil Rights Act of 1964, 42 U.S.C. § 2000e et seq., and the 1986 Immigration Reform Act itself. We discuss below some of the legislative history of the latter Act. The legislative history cannot be squared with the ruling of the ALJ regarding Soto's telephone offer of employment to Rodriguez.

* * *

II. *Verification of Documents*

The portion of the statute that Collins Foods allegedly violated prohibits the hiring of an alien while "knowing" the alien is not authorized to work. The statute also prohibits the hiring of an individual without complying with the verification requirements outlined in the statute at INA § 274A(b)(1)(A). These two actions, failing properly to verify an employee's work-authorization documents, and hiring an alien knowing him to be unauthorized to work, constitute separate offenses under the IRCA. Nevertheless, the INS argues, and the ALJ held, that Collins Foods' failure to comply with the verification provisions of the statute establishes the knowledge element of subsection (a)(1)(A), hiring an alien knowing him to be unauthorized. We need not decide, however, whether a violation of the verification requirement establishes the knowledge element of section (a)(1)(A); Collins Foods complied with the verification requirement.

The statute, at INA § 274A(b)(1)(A), provides that an employer will have satisfied its verification obligation by examining a document which "reasonably appears on its face to be genuine." Soto examined the face of both Rodriguez' false Social Security card and his genuine driver's license, but failed to detect that the Social Security card was invalid. But as the ALJ acknowledged, even though Rodriguez was spelled "Rodriquez" on the front of the social security card, at a glance the card on its face did not appear to be false.

* * * [T]he ALJ held that Collins Foods did not satisfy its verification obligation because Soto did not compare the back of Rodriguez' social security card with the example in the INS handbook. We can find nothing in the statute that requires such a comparison. Moreover, even if Soto had compared the card with the example, he still may not have been able to discern that the card was not genuine. The handbook contains but one example of a Social Security card, when numerous versions exist. The card Rodriguez presented was not so different from the example that it necessarily would have alerted a reasonable person to its falsity. * * *

* * *

Congress carefully crafted INA § 274A to limit the burden and the risk placed on employers. The ALJ's holding in this case places on employers a verification obligation greater than that intended by Congress and beyond that outlined in the narrowly-drawn statute.

In addition, the ALJ's holding extends the constructive knowledge doctrine far beyond its permissible application in IRCA employer sanction cases. IRCA, as we have pointed out, is delicately balanced to serve the goal of preventing unauthorized alien employment while avoiding discrimination against citizens and authorized aliens. The doctrine of constructive knowledge has great potential to upset that balance, and it should not be expansively applied. * * * When the scope of liability is expanded by the doctrine of constructive knowledge, the employer is subject to penalties for a range of undefined acts that may result in knowledge being imputed to him. To guard against unknowing violations, the employer may, again, avoid hiring anyone with an appearance of alienage. To preserve Congress' intent in passing the employer sanctions provisions of IRCA, then, the doctrine of constructive knowledge must be sparingly applied.

Indeed, the only federal cases we have found that have allowed constructive knowledge to satisfy the knowledge element of section 1324a(a)(1)(A) are two recent decisions of this court. A comparison of those cases with the one before us illustrates why constructive knowledge cannot be found here.

In *Mester Mfg. Co. v. INS*, 879 F.2d 561 (9th Cir.1989), the INS had visited the employer's plant and obtained a list of employees. It then notified the employer that certain employees were suspected unlawful aliens, and if their green cards matched the numbers listed in the INS' letter to the employer, then they were using false cards or cards belonging to someone else. The employer did not take any corrective action, and continued to employ the unlawful aliens. We found constructive knowledge.

New El Rey Sausage Co. v. INS, 925 F.2d 1153 (9th Cir.1991), is essentially the same case. The INS visited the employer to inspect paperwork. After running checks on the alien registration numbers of the workers, the INS found several using improper or borrowed numbers. The INS then hand-delivered a letter to the employer reciting the results of its investigation and saying: "Unless these individuals can provide valid employment authorization from the United States Immigration and Naturalization Service, they are to be considered unauthorized aliens, and are therefore not authorized to be employed in the United States. Their continued employment could result in fine proceedings. . . ." *Id.* at 1155. The employer simply accepted the word of the aliens as to their legal status, and continued to employ them. We found constructive knowledge.

These cases lead us to conclude that a finding of constructive knowledge under the hiring violation statute requires more than the ALJ found to exist here. Failure to compare the back of a Social Security card with the example in the INS handbook, when neither statute nor regulation requires the employer to do so, falls far short of the "willful blindness" found in *Mester* and *New El Rey Sausage*.[17] To expand the concept of constructive knowledge to encompass this case would not serve the intent of Congress, and is certainly not required by the terms of ICRA.

Conclusion

Collins Foods did not have the kind of positive information that the INS had provided in *Mester* and *New El Rey Sausage* to support a finding of constructive knowledge. Neither the failure to verify documentation before offering employment, nor the failure to compare the back of the applicant's Social Security card with the example in the INS manual, justifies such a finding. There is no support in the employer sanctions provisions of IRCA or in their legislative history to charge Collins Foods, on the basis of the facts relied on by the ALJ here, with constructive knowledge of Rodriguez' unauthorized status. Accordingly, we reverse.

NOTES AND QUESTIONS ON CONSTRUCTIVE KNOWLEDGE

1. The court states that, in order to maintain the balance adopted by Congress, the doctrine of constructive knowledge "should not be expansively applied." It contrasts the facts in the case with those in *Mester Manufacturing Co. v. INS* and *New El Rey Sausage Co. v. INS*. Can you derive a legal standard for what constitutes constructive knowledge from the facts in these cases?

2. Between the time *Collins* was argued and decided, the INS amended the regulation to provide several examples of what circumstances might constitute constructive knowledge:

> Constructive knowledge may include, but is not limited to, situations where an employer:

---

17. Both *Mester* and *New El Rey Sausage* relied on *United States v. Jewell*, 532 F.2d 697, 698 (9th Cir.), *cert. denied*, 426 U.S. 951, 96 S.Ct. 3173, 49 L.Ed.2d 1188 (1976), for its application of the constructive knowledge standard. In *Jewell*, the constructive knowledge finding was based upon "a mental state in which the defendant is aware that the fact in question is highly probable but consciously avoids enlightenment," *id.* at 704, or the defendant evidenced willful blindness.

(i) Fails to complete or improperly completes the Employment Eligibility Verification Form, I–9;

(ii) Has information available to it that would indicate that the alien is not authorized to work, such as Labor Certification and/or an Application for Prospective Employer; or

(iii) Acts with reckless and wanton disregard for the legal consequences of permitting another individual to introduce an unauthorized alien into its work force or to act on its behalf.

56 FR 41,767 (August 23, 1991) (amending 8 C.F.R. § 274a.1(*l*)(1)). Had the court in *Collins* applied this regulation, would it have affected the result?

3. Suppose an employer is suspicious of the documents presented to him. May he ask for more? The Office of Special Counsel (which is responsible for enforcing the anti-discrimination provisions) has advised that an employer with "constructive knowledge" that an alien lacks work authorization must inquire further, notwithstanding the antidiscrimination provisions. *See* 70 Interp.Rel. 906 (1993); Gordon, Mailman & Yale–Loehr, Imm. Law and Procedure, § 7.07(2)(b).

Social Security No-match Letters

As part of their normal course of doing business—and not as part of any obligations under the immigration laws—employers send to the Social Security Administration (SSA) employee W–2 forms, which the SSA uses to credit employees' social security accounts. In some cases, the names or numbers on the W–2s do not match SSA records. SSA routinely sends employers notification of these discrepancies, known as "no-match letters," asking the employer for additional or corrected information. Perhaps the name has been misspelled by the employer, or the employee has changed his or her name, or digits in the social security number (SSN) have been inadvertently transposed in the preparation of the W–2. Sometimes the employer's information fails to match SSA records, however, because the employee has submitted, as part of the I–9 process, fraudulent information—either a false name, a fictitious number or both. SSA, of course, based solely on its records, cannot distinguish an unauthorized work situation from mere clerical errors or unreported name changes. The SSA no-match letter is the same in either case. Upon receipt of the SSA letter, employers are likely to go to the employee for the information, which employees usually provide in order to make sure that their wages are properly credited to their accounts, because such crediting affects their ultimate retirement payments from SSA.

Now suppose that an employer returns to the employee asking for clarifying information and that the employee provides none. Might these circumstances give rise to a finding of constructive knowledge on the part of the employer that the employee is not authorized to work? If so, must the employer terminate the employee or face possible employer sanctions?

In August 2007, DHS revised its regulations to deal with the issue of SSA no-match letters. 72 Fed. Reg. 45611–24 (2007). This change came at a time when the Bush administration was toughening its enforcement measures generally, in partial response to the defeat of its broader reform legislation—possibly to tighten the screws on business so that its leaders would feel a greater stake in trying to get that legislation revived. (Business had been at best a lukewarm supporter of reform at the crucial stages in 2007.) The new regulations added examples of situations where employers may be deemed to have constructive knowledge that an employee is not authorized to work, including where the employer "[f]ails to take reasonable steps after receiving" a social security no-match letter. The regulation then stated in detail what steps would be considered reasonable. The employer must first check whether the discrepancy was the result of a clerical error, and if so, act to correct it in a resubmission to SSA. If there was no clerical error, the employer must then request that the employee contact SSA to resolve the discrepancy, and the regulation essentially allowed 90 days for the resolution. In the absence of a timely resolution properly notified to the employer, the employer could be deemed to have constructive knowledge, provided of course that the worker was in fact unauthorized. On the other hand, an employer who followed the stated steps after receiving a social security no-match letter would enjoy a safe-harbor from a finding that it knowingly employed an unauthorized employee.

A coalition of business, labor and advocacy groups challenged the regulations in court, primarily on the basis of alleged flaws under the Administrative Procedure Act. In October 2007, District Judge Charles Breyer granted plaintiffs' request for a preliminary injunction. *American Federation of Labor v. Chertoff*, 2007 WL 2972952 (N.D. Cal. 2007). Before the court hearing on whether to issue a permanent injunction, the Obama administration announced that it would rescind the challenged regulation, as part of its overall change in strategy regarding worksite enforcement. 74 Fed.Reg. 41801 (2009) (proposed rescission rule); 74 Fed.Reg. 51447 (2009) (final rule). The final regulations restored the language of 8 C.F.R. § 274a.1(*l*)(1) to read as quoted in Note 2 above.

The preamble to the 2009 final regulations, however, preserved a possible role for SSA no-match letters in judging employer compliance.

> Receipt of a No–Match letter, when considered with other probative evidence, is a factor that may be considered in the totality of the circumstances and may in certain situations support a finding of "constructive knowledge." A reasonable employer would be prudent, upon receipt of a No–Match letter, to check their own records for errors, inform the employee of the no-match letter, and ask the employee to review the information. Employers would be prudent also to allow employees a reasonable period of time to resolve the no-match with SSA. * * *

> * * * Employers should not use No–Match letters, without more, as a basis for firing employees without resolution of the mis-match, and DHS has never countenanced such a practice.

74 Fed.Reg. at 51449–50. *See also Aramark Facility Services v. SEIU*, 530 F.3d 817 (2008) (upholding a labor arbitrator's award of reinstatement and backpay based on the employer's wrongful firing—before the 2007 regulations were issued—of 33 employees who were notified of no-match letters but were given only three days to initiate a correction with SSA).

The Increasing Use of I–9 Audits

Despite the quoted warning in the rule's preamble, SSA no-match letters have played a minimal role in interior enforcement in recent years. What has proven far more important is the increasing use of I–9 audits by ICE. Using authority provided in IRCA, ICE issues a notice of inspection to an employer, and the employer must produce its I–9 records within three days. ICE initiated such audits for over 4,600 businesses between January 2009 and May 2011. Napolitano Testimony, *supra,* at 14 (May 4, 2011). This nearly quadrupled the inspection pace from 2008, when 503 notices of inspection were issued. Fialkowski, *The Administration's New Work Site Enforcement Initiatives,* Business Law Today 17, 18 (Jan/Feb. 2010).

ICE typically assesses fines if it finds paperwork violations in the course of an audit. It also communicates to the employer the names of workers it suspects are not authorized to work, even if the paperwork was properly filled out by the employer based on the documents the employee presented. Such notices are equivalent to the information INS gave to the employers in the *Mester Manufacturing* and *New El Rey Sausage* cases, which are discussed by the court in the *Collins Food* decision above. Employers basically must ask the named employees for an explanation of their status and fire them if no satisfactory explanation is provided. Otherwise the employer will almost certainly be subject to the more serious sanctions that apply to those who continue employing a noncitizen despite constructive knowledge of the worker's unauthorized status.

Some have sharply criticized the extensive recent use of I–9 audits by ICE, calling them "paper raids" or "silent raids" that are just as damaging and unfair as the highly publicized worksite operations of the Bush administration, which resulted in the arrest and deportation of hundreds of workers. *See, e.g.,* Arrieta, *'Silent Raids': ICE's New Tactic Quietly Wreaks Havoc on Immigrant Workers,* In These Times, Jan. 27, 2011, <http://inthesetimes.com/working/entry/6895/silent_raids/>. Other critics deem the audits insufficient, arguing that without arrest and deportation of the workers, they will simply go out and take up other work in a depressed job market. *See House Judiciary Subcommittee on Immigration Policy and Enforcement Holds Hearing on ICE Worksite Enforcement,* 88 Interp.Rel. 556 (2011). ICE has defended the audits as a prudent use of the resources Congress directs toward worksite enforcement, and a strategy that is consistent with the administration's emphasis on employer violations as the root cause of the problem. *Id.*

(iv) E–Verify and the Ongoing Verification Debate

The preceding materials suggest the following paradox: the employer sanctions provisions have produced a fairly high degree of compliance but a relatively low degree of deterrence. The main cause is the ready availability of fraudulent papers and the minimal obligations placed on employers to verify the authenticity of documents presented to them. When one factors in the cost to businesses of the hiring paperwork and the increase in discrimination that was documented in studies conducted in the first few years after IRCA, one might well question the wisdom of continuing the current enforcement scheme. But repeal has not been a real part of the political discussion of immigration reform over the last decade. Instead, employer checking of work authorization enjoys wide support across the political spectrum as a key component of reform proposals—but with additional steps meant to overcome current problems so as to provide a real deterrent to unauthorized migration.

Most of the attention for improvements has focused on an electronic verification system that would check the documents an employee presents against government databases. The idea is that a verification program could defeat unauthorized hiring by detecting fraudulent documents and also decrease discrimination (by providing more reliable assurance to employers that the persons they have hired are in fact authorized to work in the United States). In the mid–1990s, the statutorily chartered Commission on Immigration Reform was a leading proponent of testing such an approach. *See* U.S. Commission on Immigration Reform, U.S. Immigration Policy: Restoring Credibility 52–63 (1994).

The 1996 immigration legislation (IIRIRA § 403(b)) planted the seeds for today's electronic verification system by requiring the Attorney General to establish a verification pilot program by September 30, 1997. Employer participants in the program, initially known as the "Basic Pilot," were to obtain confirmation of work authorization through means that would check the name and number shown on the documents presented by the employee against Social Security Administration and INS databases. (The most heavily used documents to establish work authorization have been either a Social Security card or an immigration document.)

The Basic Pilot program was set to last four years, but Congress has regularly passed successive extensions, has authorized its expansion to all 50 states, and has provided considerable funding to DHS, which inherited these functions from INS in 2003, for the operation and improvement of the system. It is now open to all employers, but the statute states that the Secretary of Homeland Security may not require any employer to participate (with very limited exceptions, primarily for employers found guilty of earlier illegal hiring). In August 2007, DHS renamed the Basic Pilot "E–Verify," as part of a major campaign to encourage employers to join.

The effort to expand employer participation in E–Verify received a significant boost from a series of state laws enacted from 2006–2010 in 14 states. They required such participation on the part of governmental agencies in the state or of state contractors—and in four cases, of all employers in the state. M. Rosenblum, E–Verify: Strengths, Weaknesses, and Proposals for Reform 3–4 (Migration Policy Institute Insight, Feb. 2011). (The Supreme Court's decision upholding the broad Arizona E–Verify law is considered in Section C below.) President George W. Bush also issued an executive order in 2008 requiring U.S. government contractors (with limited exceptions) to use E–Verify to check both their new hires and all of their existing employees. *See* E.O. 13465, 73 Fed. Reg. 33,285 (2008); 73 *id.* 67,651 (Nov. 14, 2008) (amendments to the Federal Acquisition Rule to implement the Executive Order). The implementing regulations did not take full effect until after President Bush left office, but the Obama administration decided to leave them and the executive order in place. The courts have rejected challenges to their validity. *See Chamber of Commerce v. Napolitano,* 648 F.Supp.2d 726 (D.Md. 2009).

E–Verify's growth has been dramatic. In March 2007, 15,663 employers were registered under the Basic Pilot; by October 2010, DHS counted 216,721 registered employers in E–Verify. *See* A. Bruno, Unauthorized Employment in the United States: Issues and Options 5 (Congressional Research Service 2007); M. Rosenblum, *supra,* at 2. Participation is especially high among large-scale employers. Though only about four percent of employers were using the system in 2010, over 20 percent of all new hires in the United States were checked through E–Verify that year, by means of 13.4 million queries. *Id.* at 2.

An employer's query usually generates a response within a matter of seconds. E–Verify will either confirm that the document matches the appropriate records or else state that further action is needed—a response known as a tentative nonconfirmation (TNC). The system does not generate an immediate negative response because the match failure could result from a host of other reasons besides lack of work authorization, such as clerical error in entering the data on the query screen, or a name or status change for the employee that has not yet been recorded in Social Security records. The employer is not authorized to fire the new employee based on a TNC; such an action could be an unfair employment practice actionable by the Special Counsel's office under the antidiscrimination provisions of INA § 274B. Instead, the employer is supposed to give the employee notice of the TNC along with instructions referring her to the appropriate agency (either SSA or USCIS, depending on the type of document involved), in order to correct any problems. The employee must contact the agency within eight days from the referral. If the employee tells the employer that she will not contest the TNC or does not document timely resolution of the issue, the TNC becomes a final nonconfirmation. The employer then is supposed to terminate employment, upon pain of being found to have knowingly continued the employment of an unauthorized worker.

Since 2005, successive Congresses have given serious consideration to proposed bills that would make E–Verify a mandatory national program. Such a system was a central component in the major comprehensive immigration reform bills that stalled in 2006 and 2007 despite gaining substantial support in Congress and the executive branch, and it remained a key element of most discussions of comprehensive reform since the election of President Obama. But there have also been repeated efforts from 2008 through 2011 to expand E–Verify to a mandatory national program as stand-alone legislation, without the provisions for legalizing much of the current undocumented workforce that balanced out the 2006 and 2007 bills.

The technology holds promise, but experts have identified difficulties in the current system and considerable challenges that must be surmounted if the E–Verify system is made mandatory for all employers. The 2006 report of a bipartisan Migration Policy Institute Task Force, chaired by former Senator Spencer Abraham and former Representative Lee Hamilton, noted these problems:

> The Basic Pilot searches both Social Security and immigration databases. The accuracy of the system must be dramatically improved if it is to be reliable. The problems that need to be corrected include delayed entry of data reflecting admission or status changes, data entry errors, the ability of individuals to view and correct their records, and alternate spellings and word order of foreign names.
>
> * * * [The Basic Pilot] excels in detecting fake identity cards because they are not in the databases, but it fails to detect the fraudulent use of borrowed or stolen documents that are in the databases.
>
> Equally important, the system generates an unacceptably high level of secondary verification responses. Twenty percent of noncitizens and 13 percent of US citizens are initially not confirmed and can only be confirmed if they contact SSA or USCIS. Ninety percent of these tentatively non-confirmed applicants fail to pursue their cases because employers mishandle their applications, workers find it easier to change employment than to correct their records, or they do not have legal status and are not authorized to work.

Immigration and America's Future: A New Chapter, Report of the Independent Task Force on Immigration and America's Future 48, 49 (Migration Policy Institute 2006) [hereafter MPI Task Force Report].

In succeeding years, USCIS worked to introduce design changes that would greatly reduce inaccurate TNCs. These included system changes to require employers to doublecheck data entry before the system would register a TNC, better links with government passport records, and an automatic link enabling a check of USCIS's naturalization database before a TNC would issue based on a citizenship status mismatch initially identified by SSA. (It appeared that SSA was slow to enter into its system generic information regularly transmitted from USCIS after it conducts naturalization ceremonies.) As a result of these changes, the rate of tentative nonconfirmations dropped to 2.6 percent in FY 2009—meaning that 97.4 percent of queries resulted in an immediate confirmation. M.

Rosenblum, *supra,* at 6–7. Despite this substantial progress, the obstacles to correcting an erroneous TNC remain problematic, and USCIS systems are not yet effective at monitoring whether employers properly notify employees about TNCs and allow them the specified time to correct any problems. These difficulties would compound in a nationwide system, particularly because such a change would bring in millions of small employers who, to put it mildly, lack a sophisticated human resources department. *See id.*

There is increasing attention as well to another set of potential errors in E–Verify—false positives, incorrectly confirming workers even though they are not authorized to work. Such errors arise when the person either borrows or steals the identity of another who is work-authorized. E–Verify basically checks the validity of *the document*: do the name and number, plus a limited amount of additional data, actually match what is shown in the central databases? But it lacks solid means to ensure that *the person* presenting the document is in fact the person to whom it was properly issued. This is a crucial failing, because the ultimate point of the verification system is of course not to check documents; it is to check whether the human being standing in the hiring office is actually authorized to work. USCIS has been working to minimize these kinds of errors as well, but it has not made nearly as much progress as against false negatives. Its primary means for addressing false identities is through the increasing use of a photo-matching tool that displays to the employer on the E–Verify screen the actual photo that should appear on the identity document presented by the employee. But at present this capacity is available only for DHS-issued documents and U.S. passports, whereas a majority of workers use driver's licenses to establish identity in the I–9 process. USCIS is working to get agreement from states to provide equivalent driver's license photo-sharing, but so far without success.

The 2006 MPI Task Force Report laid out some of the problems to be faced in dealing with these issues.

> Legislation that requires universal participation in an electronic verification system without first addressing the flaws in the Basic Pilot program will fail. In particular, it will create unacceptable burdens for prospective workers and businesses alike, particularly small businesses, which constitute the largest overall number of employers in the country. Task Force discussions with knowledgeable government officials led to the conclusion that three years' preparation time should be provided for implementation of mandatory verification. It might be possible to pilot the program in industries of particular sensitivity to terrorism concerns, such as chemical plants or transportation facilities. However, without the time and resources to make changes properly, the rush to *appear* tough on workplace enforcement will harm innocent workers, disrupt hiring practices and productivity, encourage non-compliance, and further undermine the legitimacy of immigration enforcement. * * *

In addition to confirming that job applicants are eligible to work, an effective verification system must also assure that individuals have valid, secure identification documents that tie the cardholder to the information on the card. The Task Force believes that it is time to develop a secure, biometric, machine-readable Social Security card that allows citizens to easily establish both their identity and eligibility to work. Currently, citizens have less secure documentation than noncitizens. Government agencies already issue such cards for noncitizens in the form of work authorization and "green" cards for LPRs. Citizens need analogous documents for a new system to work.

The objective of the REAL ID Act, scheduled for implementation by May 2008, is to create a secure identity document by mandating uniform federal standards and anti-fraud technology for state driver's licenses. But it seems unlikely that the REAL ID provisions alone will solve the document problem for workplace enforcement purposes. Non-secure breeder documents, such as birth certificates or Social Security cards, are used to obtain drivers' licenses, thus making them subject to fraud.

* * *

The importance of reliable documents is broadly accepted as one aspect of a layered security system in the post–9/11 era. Standard, federally issued documents that prove identity and eligibility to work in the United States should be treated as an important layer of this new system. Secure documents are also the best antidote to the potential for discrimination based on ethnicity or national origin in hiring practices. Along with "green" cards and work authorization cards, they are existing documents already used to obtain work. Making the Social Security card secure upgrades and safeguards the reliability of a document whose purpose is directly tied to employment and work eligibility.

MPI Task Force Report, *supra*, at 50–53.

As noted earlier in this chapter, state resistance to the REAL ID Act requirements has forced successive postponements in the full implementation of that statute's requirements for driver's licenses. In any event, as a way of responding to this identity-assurance problem, several recent bills have included a requirement that the federal government develop a biometric identifier to be used in the verification process. There are many possible variations, but here is one prominent proposal, along with a brief description of its privacy safeguards, championed by the Chair and Ranking Member of the Senate Judiciary Committee in 2010, Senators Charles Schumer (D–NY) and Lindsey Graham (R–SC):

We would require all U.S. citizens and legal immigrants who want jobs to obtain a high-tech, fraud-proof Social Security card. Each card's unique biometric identifier would be stored only on the card; no government database would house everyone's information. The cards would not contain any private information, medical information or tracking devices. The card would be a high-tech version of the Social Security card that citizens already have.

Prospective employers would be responsible for swiping the cards through a machine to confirm a person's identity and immigration status. Employers who refused to swipe the card or who otherwise knowingly hired unauthorized workers would face stiff fines and, for repeat offenses, prison sentences.

Schumer and Graham, *The Right Way To Mend Immigration*, Wash. Post, Mar. 19, 2010.

Tamar Jacoby, who supports a version of the swipe card as part of a national mandatory verification program, recognizes the costs:

Improving the databases, connecting the computers, purchasing the card readers, revamping and reissuing Social Security cards or drivers' licenses or both: together, it will cost billions of dollars—no one yet knows how many. Employers can help with some of it: it might not be unreasonable, for example, to ask that they buy their own simple swipe machines or * * * contribute toward maintaining the computerized system. (Business will, after all, be saving considerably—both time and money—when the possibility of swiping a card renders the I–9 process unnecessary.) But most of the expense will fall to government. And there can be no cutting corners: not in the startup costs or to maintain the system once it is in place. For unless the program is workable—streamlined, reliable, user-friendly, and fast—many employers will not use it, preferring, for the sake of business efficiency, to risk operating on the wrong side of the law.

Jacoby, *An Idea Whose Time Has Finally Come? The Case for Employment Verification*, Migration Policy Institute Policy Brief No. 9, at 11 (Nov. 2005).

In a thorough survey and critique of the current status of E–Verify and its future prospects, Marc Rosenblum reflects on what will be needed for a successful transition to a nationwide system:

* * * [T]o require broader participation in E–Verify without creating legal opportunities for employers to hire immigrant workers is a risky strategy because the downstream impact of enhanced worksite enforcement is impossible to predict. Indeed, after IRCA made it illegal to employ unauthorized immigrants, unauthorized employment remained widespread (because of the proliferation of false documents), but wages fell and discrimination against Latino workers increased, regardless of their legal status. New E–Verify mandates *may* produce their desired effect and cause employers who now hire unauthorized immigrants to replace them with legal workers; but poorly crafted mandates could lead instead to more identity fraud and off-the-books employment, resulting in lost revenues and deteriorating working conditions. Alternatively, the higher cost of

doing business and the difficulty of replacing unauthorized immigrants with legal workers could lead some employers to go out of business or to move their operations abroad, in which case new E–Verify mandates without broader immigration reforms would undermine the economic recovery.

* * *

* * * [A]ny new E–Verify mandates and/or biometric or other identification technology should be phased in gradually and should be evaluated on an ongoing basis against clearly articulated performance benchmarks. Time and again, the history of US immigration policy— and the history of worksite immigration enforcement in particular— finds that well-intentioned reforms may produce complex unintended consequences, often leaving stakeholders worse off than they were before. In the case of E–Verify, we have just early analyses of the effects of the dramatic growth that has occurred in the program since 2006. Moreover, much of that growth has occurred in the exceptional climate of low or negative employment growth, so little is known about how the program actually affects US labor markets.

Finally, the most promising strategy for expanding E–Verify is to link new mandates to a targeted or general legalization program for unauthorized workers and/or to employment-based visa reform. While a mandatory E–Verify requirement without such reforms would create incentives for employers and workers to look for work-arounds that undermine effective verification, linking E–Verify mandates to legalization and visa reform would have the opposite effect: encouraging the most problematic workers and employers to opt in to the system and to scrupulously comply with its requirements as a condition for earning legal status (in the case of workers) and for access to employment-based visa programs (in the case of employers). Making legalization for certain workers a building block for E–Verify growth also would dovetail with tough identification requirements likely to be included in any legalization program, and so could be a testing ground for new biometric or other identification technology.

M. Rosenblum, E–Verify: Strengths, Weaknesses, and Proposals for Reform 12–13, 15 (Migration Policy Institute Insight, Feb. 2011).

NOTES AND QUESTIONS ON ELECTRONIC VERIFICATION

1. Given the various considerations discussed above, should Congress adopt a nationwide mandate that all new hires be checked against E–Verify? What are the primary arguments for and against such a change? What modifications would you seek or require for such a nationwide system?

2. Should Congress require a federal biometric identifier as part of the E–Verify system? If adopted, how should such a system be phased in? What are the obstacles you foresee in getting the full U.S. workforce (over 150 million people) properly enrolled? Remember that a biometric identification

system is only as good as its enrollment process; any biometric system, whether run by the states or the federal government, has to start with some other way of authenticating identity before linking the claimed name to the fingerprint of the person sitting in the enrollment office. Who would perform the initial authentication? On what information or documentation regarding identity (what the MPI report called "breeder documents") should such enrolling officers rely?

5. EMPLOYER SANCTIONS AND WORKPLACE LAWS

How do employer sanctions affect the workplace rights and protections of workers who managed to secure employment but who are in fact not authorized to work? Suppose, for example, they present false documents, or an employer fails to ask for proof of identity and work authorization. If they are discharged for union organizing, or allege unlawful discrimination, does their unauthorized employment diminish their rights or remedies? The U.S. Supreme Court addressed this question in the following case.

HOFFMAN PLASTIC COMPOUNDS, INC. v. NLRB

Supreme Court of the United States, 2002.
535 U.S. 137, 122 S.Ct. 1275, 152 L.Ed.2d 271.

CHIEF JUSTICE REHNQUIST delivered the opinion of the Court.

The National Labor Relations Board (Board) awarded backpay to an undocumented alien who has never been legally authorized to work in the United States. We hold that such relief is foreclosed by federal immigration policy, as expressed by Congress in the Immigration Reform and Control Act of 1986 (IRCA).

Petitioner Hoffman Plastic Compounds, Inc. (petitioner or Hoffman), custom-formulates chemical compounds for businesses that manufacture pharmaceutical, construction, and household products. In May 1988, petitioner hired Jose Castro to operate various blending machines that "mix and cook" the particular formulas per customer order. Before being hired for this position, Castro presented documents that appeared to verify his authorization to work in the United States. In December 1988, the United Rubber, Cork, Linoleum, and Plastic Workers of America, AFL–CIO, began a union-organizing campaign at petitioner's production plant. Castro and several other employees supported the organizing campaign and distributed authorization cards to co-workers. In January 1989, Hoffman laid off Castro and other employees engaged in these organizing activities.

Three years later, in January 1992, respondent Board found that Hoffman unlawfully selected four employees, including Castro, for layoff "in order to rid itself of known union supporters" in violation of § 8(a)(3) of the National Labor Relations Act (NLRA).[1] To remedy this violation, the Board ordered that Hoffman (1) cease and desist from further violations of the NLRA, (2) post a detailed notice to its employees regarding the remedial order, and (3) offer reinstatement and backpay to the four affected employees. * * *

In June 1993, the parties proceeded to a compliance hearing before an Administrative Law Judge (ALJ) to determine the amount of backpay owed to each discriminatee. On the final day of the hearing, Castro testified that he was born in Mexico and that he had never been legally admitted to, or authorized to work in, the United States. He admitted gaining employment with Hoffman only after tendering a birth certificate belonging to a friend who was born in Texas. He also admitted that he used this birth certificate to fraudulently obtain a California driver's license and a Social Security card, and to fraudulently obtain employment following his layoff by Hoffman. * * * Based on this testimony, the ALJ found the Board precluded from awarding Castro backpay or reinstatement as such relief would be contrary to *Sure–Tan, Inc. v. NLRB*, 467 U.S. 883 (1984), and in conflict with IRCA, which makes it unlawful for employers knowingly to hire undocumented workers or for employees to use fraudulent documents to establish employment eligibility.

In September 1998, four years after the ALJ's decision, and nine years after Castro was fired, the Board reversed with respect to backpay. Citing its earlier decision in *A.P.R.A. Fuel Oil Buyers Group, Inc.*, 320 N.L.R.B. 408 (1995), the Board determined that "the most effective way to accommodate and further the immigration policies embodied in [IRCA] is to provide the protections and remedies of the [NLRA] to undocumented workers in the same manner as to other employees." The Board thus found that Castro was entitled to $66,951 of backpay, plus interest. It calculated this backpay award from the date of Castro's termination to the date Hoffman first learned of Castro's undocumented status, a period of 4 1/2 years. * * *

* * * [T]he Court of Appeals denied [Hoffman's] petition for review.

* * *

This case exemplifies the principle that the Board's discretion to select and fashion remedies for violations of the NLRA, though generally broad, is not unlimited. Since the Board's inception, we have consistently set aside awards of reinstatement or backpay to employees found guilty of serious illegal conduct in connection with their employment. In [*NLRB v. Fansteel Metallurgical Corp.*, 306 U.S. 240, 255 (1939)], the Board awarded reinstatement with backpay to employees who engaged in a "sit down strike" that led to confrontation with local law enforcement officials. We set aside the award, saying:

---

1. Section 8(a)(3) of the NLRA prohibits discrimination "in regard to hire or tenure of employment or any term or condition of employment to encourage or discourage membership in any labor organization."

We are unable to conclude that Congress intended to compel employers to retain persons in their employ regardless of their unlawful conduct, to invest those who go on strike with an immunity from discharge for acts of trespass or violence against the employer's property, which they would not have enjoyed had they remained at work.

Though we found that the employer had committed serious violations of the NLRA, the Board had no discretion to remedy those violations by awarding reinstatement with backpay to employees who themselves had committed serious criminal acts. Two years later, in [*Southern S.S. Co. v. NLRB*, 316 U.S. 31, 47 (1942)], the Board awarded reinstatement with backpay to five employees whose strike on shipboard had amounted to a mutiny in violation of federal law. We set aside the award, saying:

> It is sufficient for this case to observe that the Board has not been commissioned to effectuate the policies of the Labor Relations Act so single-mindedly that it may wholly ignore other and equally important [c]ongressional objectives.

Although the Board had argued that the employees' conduct did not in fact violate the federal mutiny statute, we rejected this view, finding the Board's interpretation of a statute so far removed from its expertise merited no deference from this Court. Since *Southern S.S. Co.,* we have accordingly never deferred to the Board's remedial preferences where such preferences potentially trench upon federal statutes and policies unrelated to the NLRA. * * *

Our decision in *Sure–Tan* followed this line of cases and set aside an award closely analogous to the award challenged here. There we confronted for the first time a potential conflict between the NLRA and federal immigration policy, as then expressed in the Immigration and Nationality Act (INA). Two companies had unlawfully reported alien-employees to the Immigration and Naturalization Service (INS) in retaliation for union activity. Rather than face INS sanction, the employees voluntarily departed to Mexico. The Board investigated and found the companies acted in violation of §§ 8(a)(1) and (3) of the NLRA. The Board's ensuing order directed the companies to reinstate the affected workers and pay them six months' backpay.

We affirmed the Board's determination that the NLRA applied to undocumented workers, reasoning that the immigration laws "as presently written" expressed only a " 'peripheral concern' " with the employment of illegal aliens. 467 U.S., at 892, 104 S.Ct. 2803 (quoting *De Canas v. Bica,* 424 U.S. 351, 360, 96 S.Ct. 933, 47 L.Ed.2d 43 (1976)). "For whatever reason," Congress had not "made it a separate criminal offense" for employers to hire an illegal alien, or for an illegal alien "to accept employment after entering this country illegally." *Sure–Tan, supra,* at 892–893, 104 S.Ct. 2803. Therefore, we found "no reason to conclude that application of the NLRA to employment practices affecting such aliens would necessarily conflict with the terms of the INA." 467 U.S., at 893, 104 S.Ct. 2803.

With respect to the Board's selection of remedies, however, we found its authority limited by federal immigration policy. See *id.,* at 903, 104 S.Ct. 2803 ("In devising remedies for unfair labor practices, the Board is obliged to take into account another 'equally important Congressional objective'" (quoting *Southern S.S. Co., supra,* at 47, 62 S.Ct. 886)). For example, the Board was prohibited from effectively rewarding a violation of the immigration laws by reinstating workers not authorized to reenter the United States. *Sure–Tan,* 467 U.S., at 903, 104 S.Ct. 2803. Thus, to avoid "a potential conflict with the INA," the Board's reinstatement order had to be conditioned upon proof of "the employees' legal reentry." *Ibid.* "Similarly," with respect to backpay, we stated: "[T]he employees must be deemed 'unavailable' for work (and the accrual of backpay therefore tolled) during any period when they were not lawfully entitled to be present and employed in the United States." *Ibid.* "[I]n light of the practical workings of the immigration laws," such remedial limitations were appropriate even if they led to "[t]he probable unavailability of the [NLRA's] more effective remedies." *Id.,* at 904, 104 S.Ct. 2803.

* * *

* * * The parties and the lower courts focus much of their attention on *Sure–Tan,* particularly its express limitation of backpay to aliens "lawfully entitled to be present and employed in the United States." 467 U.S., at 903, 104 S.Ct. 2803. All agree that as a matter of plain language, this limitation forecloses the award of backpay to Castro. Castro was never lawfully entitled to be present or employed in the United States, and thus, under the plain language of *Sure–Tan,* he has no right to claim backpay. The Board takes the view, however, that read in context, this limitation applies only to aliens who left the United States and thus cannot claim backpay without lawful reentry. The Court of Appeals agreed with this view. Another Court of Appeals, however, agrees with Hoffman, and concludes that *Sure–Tan* simply meant what it said, *i.e.,* that any alien who is "not lawfully entitled to be present and employed in the United States" cannot claim backpay. See *Del Rey Tortilleria, Inc. v. NLRB,* 976 F.2d 1115, 1118–1121 (C.A.7 1992). We need not resolve this controversy. For whether isolated sentences from *Sure–Tan* definitively control, or count merely as persuasive dicta in support of petitioner, we think the question presented here better analyzed through a wider lens, focused as it must be on a legal landscape now significantly changed.

The *Southern S.S. Co.* line of cases established that where the Board's chosen remedy trenches upon a federal statute or policy outside the Board's competence to administer, the Board's remedy may be required to yield. Whether or not this was the situation at the time of *Sure–Tan,* it is precisely the situation today. In 1986, two years after *Sure–Tan,* Congress enacted IRCA, a comprehensive scheme prohibiting the employment of illegal aliens in the United States. As we have previously noted, IRCA "forcefully" made combating the employment of illegal aliens central to "[t]he policy of immigration law." *INS v. National Center for Immigrants' Rights, Inc.,* 502 U.S. 183, 194, and n. 8, 112 S.Ct. 551, 116 L.Ed.2d 546 (1991). * * * IRCA mandates that employers verify the identity and eligibility of all new hires by examining specified documents before they begin work. If an alien applicant is unable to present the required documentation, the unauthorized alien cannot be hired.

Similarly, if an employer unknowingly hires an unauthorized alien, or if the alien becomes unauthorized while employed, the employer is compelled to discharge the worker upon discovery of the worker's undocumented status. Employers who violate IRCA are punished by civil fines, and may be subject to criminal prosecution. IRCA also makes it a crime for an unauthorized alien to subvert the employer verification system by tendering fraudulent documents. It thus prohibits aliens from using or attempting to use "any forged, counterfeit, altered, or falsely made document" or "any document lawfully issued to or with respect to a person other than the possessor" for purposes of obtaining employment in the United States. INA §§ 274C(a)(1)–(3). Aliens who use or attempt to use such documents are subject to fines and criminal prosecution. There is no dispute that Castro's use of false documents to obtain employment with Hoffman violated these provisions.

Under the IRCA regime, it is impossible for an undocumented alien to obtain employment in the United States without some party directly contravening explicit congressional policies. Either the undocumented alien tenders fraudulent identification, which subverts the cornerstone of IRCA's enforcement mechanism, or the employer knowingly hires the undocumented alien in direct contradiction of its IRCA obligations. The Board asks that we overlook this fact and allow it to award backpay to an illegal alien for years of work not performed, for wages that could not lawfully have been earned, and for a job obtained in the first instance by a criminal fraud. We find, however, that awarding backpay to illegal aliens runs counter to policies underlying IRCA, policies the Board has no authority to enforce or administer. Therefore, as we have consistently held in like circumstances, the award lies beyond the bounds of the Board's remedial discretion.

The Board contends that awarding limited backpay to Castro "reasonably accommodates" IRCA, because, in the Board's view, such an award is not "inconsistent" with IRCA. The Board argues that because the backpay period was closed as of the date Hoffman learned of Castro's illegal status, Hoffman could have employed Castro during the backpay period without violating IRCA. The Board further argues that while IRCA criminalized the misuse of documents, "it did not make violators ineligible for backpay awards or other compensation flowing from employment secured by the misuse of such documents." This latter statement, of course, proves little: The mutiny statute in *Southern S.S. Co.,* and the INA in *Sure–Tan,* were likewise understandably silent with respect to such things as backpay awards under the NLRA. What matters here, and what sinks both of the

Board's claims, is that Congress has expressly made it criminally punishable for an alien to obtain employment with false documents. There is no reason to think that Congress nonetheless intended to permit backpay where but for an employer's unfair labor practices, an alien-employee would have remained in the United States illegally, and continued to work illegally, all the while successfully evading apprehension by immigration authorities. Far from "accommodating" IRCA, the Board's position, recognizing employer misconduct but discounting the misconduct of illegal alien employees, subverts it.

Indeed, awarding backpay in a case like this not only trivializes the immigration laws, it also condones and encourages future violations. The Board admits that had the INS detained Castro, or had Castro obeyed the law and departed to Mexico, Castro would have lost his right to backpay. Castro thus qualifies for the Board's award only by remaining inside the United States illegally. Similarly, Castro cannot mitigate damages, a duty our cases require, without triggering new IRCA violations, either by tendering false documents to employers or by finding employers willing to ignore IRCA and hire illegal workers. The Board here has failed to even consider this tension. See 326 N.L.R.B., at 1063, n. 10 (finding that Castro adequately mitigated damages through interim work with no mention of ALJ findings that Castro secured interim work with false documents).

We therefore conclude that allowing the Board to award backpay to illegal aliens would unduly trench upon explicit statutory prohibitions critical to federal immigration policy, as expressed in IRCA. * * *

Lack of authority to award backpay does not mean that the employer gets off scot-free. The Board here has already imposed other significant sanctions against Hoffman—sanctions Hoffman does not challenge. These include orders that Hoffman cease and desist its violations of the NLRA, and that it conspicuously post a notice to employees setting forth their rights under the NLRA and detailing its prior unfair practices. Hoffman will be subject to contempt proceedings should it fail to comply with these orders. We have deemed such "traditional remedies" sufficient to effectuate national labor policy regardless of whether the "spur and catalyst" of backpay accompanies them. *Sure–Tan,* 467 U.S., at 904, 104 S.Ct. 2803. As we concluded in *Sure–Tan,* "in light of the practical workings of the immigration laws," any "perceived deficienc[y] in the NLRA's existing remedial arsenal" must be "addressed by congressional action," not the courts. *Id.,* at 904, 104 S.Ct. 2803. In light of IRCA, this statement is even truer today.

The judgment of the Court of Appeals is reversed.

JUSTICE BREYER, with whom JUSTICE STEVENS, JUSTICE SOUTER, and JUSTICE GINSBURG join, dissenting.

I cannot agree that the backpay award before us "runs counter to," or "trenches upon," national immigration policy. As *all* the relevant agencies (including the Department of Justice) have told us, the National Labor Relations Board's limited backpay order will *not* interfere with the implementation of immigration policy. Rather, it reasonably helps to deter unlawful activity that *both* labor laws *and* immigration laws seek to prevent. Consequently, the order is lawful.

* * *

The Court does not deny that the employer in this case dismissed an employee for trying to organize a union—a crude and obvious violation of the labor laws. And it cannot deny that the Board has especially broad discretion in choosing an appropriate remedy for addressing such violations. Nor can it deny that in such circumstances backpay awards serve critically important remedial purposes. Those purposes involve more than victim compensation; they also include deterrence, *i.e.,* discouraging employers from violating the Nation's labor laws.

Without the possibility of the deterrence that backpay provides, the Board can impose only future-oriented obligations upon law-violating employers—for it has no other weapons in its remedial arsenal. And in the absence of the backpay weapon, employers could conclude that they can violate the labor laws at least once with impunity. Hence the backpay remedy is necessary; it helps make labor law enforcement credible; it makes clear that violating the labor laws will not pay.

Where in the immigration laws can the Court find a "policy" that might warrant taking from the Board this critically important remedial power? Certainly not in any statutory language. The immigration statutes say that an employer may not knowingly employ an illegal alien, that an alien may not submit false documents, and that the employer must verify documentation. They provide specific penalties, including criminal penalties, for violations. But the statutes' language itself does not explicitly state how a violation is to effect the enforcement of other laws, such as the labor laws. What is to happen, for example, when an employer hires, or an alien works, in violation of these provisions? Must the alien forfeit all pay earned? May the employer ignore the labor laws? More to the point, may the employer violate those laws with impunity, at least once—secure in the knowledge that the Board cannot assess a monetary penalty? The immigration statutes' language simply does not say.

Nor can the Court comfortably rest its conclusion upon the immigration laws' purposes. For one thing, the general purpose of the immigration statute's employment prohibition is to diminish the attractive force of employment, which like a "magnet" pulls illegal immigrants toward the United States. H.R.Rep. No. 99–682, pt. 1, p. 45 (1986), U.S. Code Cong. & Admin. News 1986, p. 5649. To permit the Board to award backpay could not significantly increase the strength of this magnetic force, for so speculative a future possibility could not realistically influence an individual's decision to migrate illegally.

To *deny* the Board the power to award backpay, however, might very well increase the strength of this magnetic force. That denial lowers the cost to the employer of an initial labor law violation (provided, of course, that the only victims are illegal aliens). It thereby increases the employer's incentive to find and to hire illegal-alien employees. Were the Board forbidden to assess backpay against a *knowing* employer—a circumstance not before us today—this perverse economic incentive, which runs directly contrary to the immigration statute's basic objective, would be obvious and serious. But even if limited to cases where the employer did not know of the employee's status, the incentive may prove significant—for, as the Board has told us, the Court's rule offers employers immunity in border-line cases, thereby encouraging them to take risks, *i.e.,* to hire with a wink and a nod those potentially unlawful aliens whose unlawful employment (given the Court's views) ultimately will lower the costs of labor law violations. The Court has recognized these considerations in stating that the labor laws must apply to illegal aliens in order to ensure that "there will be no advantage under the NLRA in preferring illegal aliens" and therefore there will be "fewer incentives for aliens themselves to enter." *Sure–Tan,* [467 U.S.] at 893–894, 104 S.Ct. 2803. The Court today accomplishes the precise opposite.

The immigration law's specific labor-law-related purposes also favor preservation, not elimination, of the Board's backpay powers. As I just mentioned and as this Court has held, the immigration law foresees application of the Nation's labor laws to protect "workers who are illegal immigrants." And a policy of *applying* the labor laws must encompass a policy of *enforcing* the labor laws effectively. Otherwise, as Justice Kennedy once put the matter, "we would leave helpless the very persons who most need protection from exploitative employer practices." *NLRB v. Apollo Tire Co.,* 604 F.2d 1180, 1184 (C.A.9 1979) (concurring opinion). That presumably is why those in Congress who wrote the immigration statute stated explicitly and unequivocally that the immigration statute does *not* take from the Board *any* of its remedial authority. H.R.Rep. No. 99–682, at 58, U.S. Code Cong. & Admin. News 1986, pp. 5649, 5662 (IRCA does not "undermine or diminish in any way labor protections in existing law, or . . . limit the powers of federal or state labor relations boards . . . to remedy unfair practices committed against undocumented employees").

* * *

* * * [T]he two earlier cases upon which the Court relies, *NLRB v. Fansteel Metallurgical Corp.,* 306 U.S. 240, 59 S.Ct. 490, 83 L.Ed. 627 (1939), and *Southern S.S. Co. v. NLRB,* 316 U.S. 31, 47, 62 S.Ct. 886, 86 L.Ed. 1246 (1942), offer little support for its conclusion. The Court correctly characterizes both cases as ones in which this Court set aside the Board's remedy (more specifically, reinstatement). But the Court does not focus upon the underlying circumstances—which in those cases were very different from the circumstances present here. In both earlier cases, the employer had committed an independent unfair labor practice—in the one by creating a company union, in the other by refusing to recognize the employees' elected representative. In both cases, the employees had responded with unlawful acts of their own—a sit-in and a mutiny. And in both cases, the Court held that the employees' own unlawful conduct provided the employer with "good cause" for discharge, severing any connection to the earlier unfair labor practice that might otherwise have justified reinstatement and backpay.

By way of contrast, the present case concerns a discharge that was not for "good cause." The discharge did not sever any connection with an unfair labor practice. Indeed, the discharge *was* the unfair labor practice. Hence a determination that backpay was inappropriate in the former circumstances (involving a *justifiable* discharge) tells us next to nothing about the appropriateness as a legal remedy in the latter (involving an *un*justifiable discharge), the circumstances present here.

The Court also refers to the statement in *Sure–Tan, Inc. v. NLRB,* 467 U.S., at 903, 104 S.Ct. 2803, that "employees must be deemed 'unavailable' for work (and the accrual of backpay therefore tolled) during any period when they were not lawfully entitled to be present and employed in the United States." The Court, however, does not rely upon this statement as determining its conclusion. And it is right not to do so. *Sure–Tan* involved an order reinstating (with backpay) illegal aliens who had left the country and returned to Mexico. In order to collect the backpay to which the order entitled them, the aliens would have had to reenter the country illegally. Consequently, the order itself could not have been enforced without leading to a violation of criminal law. Nothing in the Court's opinion suggests that the Court intended its statement to reach to circumstances different from and not at issue in *Sure–Tan,* where an order, such as the order before us, does not require the alien to engage in further illegal behavior.

Finally, the Court cannot reasonably rely upon the award's negative features taken together. The Court summarizes those negative features when it says that the Board "asks that we . . . award backpay to an illegal alien [1] for years of work not performed, [2] for wages that could not lawfully have been earned, and [3] for a job obtained in the first instance by a criminal fraud." The first of these features has little persuasive force, given the facts that (1) backpay ordinarily and necessarily is awarded to a discharged employee who may not find other work, and (2) the Board is able to tailor an alien's backpay award to avoid rewarding that alien for his legal inability to mitigate damages by obtaining lawful employment elsewhere.

Neither can the remaining two features—unlawfully earned wages and criminal fraud—prove determinative, for they tell us only a small portion of the relevant story. After all, the same backpay award that compensates an employee in the circumstances the Court describes *also* requires an employer who has violated the labor laws to make a meaningful monetary payment. Considered from this equally important perspective, the award simply requires that employer to pay an employee whom the employer believed could lawfully have worked in the United States, (1) for years of work that he would have performed, (2) for a portion of the wages that he would have earned, and (3) for a job that the employee would have held—had that employer not unlawfully dismissed the employee for union organizing. In ignoring these latter features of the award, the Court undermines the public policies that underlie the Nation's labor laws.

Of course, the Court believes it is necessary to do so in order to vindicate what it sees as conflicting immigration law policies. I have explained why I believe the latter policies do not conflict. But even were I wrong, the law requires the Court to respect the Board's conclusion, rather than to substitute its own independent view of the matter for that of the Board. The Board reached its conclusion after carefully considering both labor law and immigration law. In doing so the Board has acted "with a discriminating awareness of the consequences of its action" on the immigration laws. *Burlington Truck Lines, Inc. v. United States,* 371 U.S. 156, 174, 83 S.Ct. 239, 9 L.Ed.2d 207 (1962). The Attorney General, charged with immigration law enforcement, has told us that the Board is right. See INA § 274A(e) (Immigration and Naturalization Service placed within the Department of Justice, under authority of Attorney General who is charged with responsibility for immigration law enforcement). And the Board's position is, at the least, a reasonable one. Consequently, it is lawful. *Chevron U.S.A. Inc. v. Natural Resources Defense Council, Inc.,* 467 U.S. 837, 842–843, 104 S.Ct. 2778, 81 L.Ed.2d 694 (1984) (requiring courts to uphold reasonable agency position).

For these reasons, I respectfully dissent.

NOTES AND QUESTIONS ON HOFFMAN PLASTIC COMPOUNDS

1. The majority concludes that the NLRB's reading of the statutes encourages unlawful behavior. But doesn't the majority's interpretation also encourage illegality by providing incentives to employers both to hire unauthorized migrants and to violate federal labor law?

Perhaps the core underlying problem is the artificially limited remedial arsenal that the NLRA gives to the NLRB. Except for backpay, the NLRB can impose only future-oriented remedies, such as required posting of notices and a cease-and-desist order—steps that the dissenters do not regard as meaningful deterrents against employer violators. If Congress were to expand the range of remedies, could it create a better balanced remedial regime, providing deterrence against both types of illegal actions—by employer or employee? For example, it could provide that employers who violate NLRA-based rights of undocumented workers pay out the full amount of a backpay award, but the funds would go to the U.S. treasury, not the unauthorized worker. What would be the advantages and disadvantages of such an amendment? Why do you think that such an idea has not gained serious consideration in the decade since the Supreme Court's decision? How would such a change affect incentives for unauthorized workers to initiate or participate in NLRA-based cases?

2. Compare *Hoffman Plastic* with *Agri Processor Co. v. NLRB,* 514 F.3d 1 (D.C. Cir.), *cert. denied,* 129 S.Ct. 594, 172 L.Ed.2d 455 (2008). In *Agri*

Processor, employees had voted to join the United Food and Commercial Workers Union, but the company refused recognition on the ground that most of those who voted were not authorized to work. Are unauthorized workers "employees" for purposes of establishing an employer's duty to bargain under the NLRA. Judge David Tatel, the author of the court of appeals decision in *Hoffman Plastic* later reversed by the U.S. Supreme Court, wrote for the *Agri Processor* majority, holding that unauthorized workers must be included in the NLRA and that the same bargaining unit may include both authorized and unauthorized workers. Judge Tatel explained:

> * * * [W]e think the company's reliance on *Hoffman Plastic* is entirely misplaced. In that case, the Supreme Court addressed only what remedies the Board may grant undocumented aliens when employers violate their rights under the NLRA. Nowhere in *Hoffman Plastic* did the Court hold that IRCA leaves undocumented aliens altogether unprotected by the NLRA. * * *

> * * * Leaving undocumented workers without the NLRA's protections would "create[] a subclass of workers without a comparable stake in the collective goals of their legally resident co-workers, thereby eroding the unity of all the employees and impeding effective collective bargaining." [*Sure–Tan, Inc. v. NLRB*, 467 U.S. 883, 892 (1984)].

> * * *

> This brings us to Agri Processor's second argument—that the Board may not place undocumented aliens and legal workers in the same bargaining unit. * * * "[I]n defining bargaining units, [the Board's] focus is on whether the employees share a 'community of interest.'" [*NLRB v. Action Auto., Inc.*, 469 U.S. 490, 494 (1985).] The community of interests test turns "on the interests of employees *as employees*, not their interests more generally." *Speedrack Prods. Group, Ltd. v. NLRB*, 114 F.3d 1276, 1280 (D.C. Cir. 1997). The Board, moreover, has "broad discretion in making unit determinations, and its unit determinations are accorded particular deference by a reviewing court." *Id.* at 1278.

> * * *

> * * * "[T]o determine if a community of interest exists," the Board typically looks at "the similarity of wages, benefits, skills, duties, working conditions, and supervision of the employee." *Id.* at 1278. With regard to each of these factors, undocumented workers and legal workers in a bargaining unit are identical. While undocumented aliens may face penalties for violating immigration laws, they receive the same wages and benefits as legal workers, face the same working conditions, answer to the same supervisors, and possess the same skills and duties.

514 F.3d at 7–9. On the general idea that unauthorized workers can successfully assert workplace rights by showing that harming them can harm coworkers who are U.S. citizens, lawful permanent residents, or otherwise working lawfully, see Motomura, *The Rights of Others: Legal Claims and Immigration Outside the Law*, 59 Duke L.J. 1723, 1751–56 (2010).

3. The majority in *Hoffman Plastic* states that unauthorized work in the United States is impossible without either the employee or the employer directly contravening congressional policies, and that the Board's opinion "asks us to overlook this fact and allow it to award backpay to an illegal alien for years of work not performed, for wages that could not lawfully have been earned, and for a job obtained in the first instance by a criminal fraud."

Are all three of these elements crucial to the Court's conclusion? Suppose an unauthorized migrant seeks enforcement of minimum wages under the federal Fair Labor Standards Act (FLSA) for work she has done. Should she, according to the majority, be able to recover—though she seeks wages that "could not lawfully have been earned"?

Following *Hoffman Plastic*, the Solicitor of Labor, Eugene Scalia, stated that the Labor Department would continue to enforce the FLSA minimum wage and overtime rules irrespective of a worker's immigration status. He offered these reasons:

> A first important difference between *Hoffman Plastic* and the FLSA is the nature of the statute at issue. The National Labor Relations Act permits back pay as a remedy, but does not expressly require it. This prompted the Supreme Court in *Hoffman* to look to congressional policies external to the NLRA to identify limits on the Board's discretion to award back pay. The FLSA, by contrast, exists for the very purpose of ensuring payment of wages. The immigration laws should not trump the plain text and command of the FLSA in the way they limited NLRA remedies in *Hoffman Plastic*.
>
> A second important distinction * * * is that *Hoffman* was about hours the employee did not work, whereas FLSA by definition is about hours that were worked. One of the factors the Supreme Court emphasized in its decision was that the NLRB was seeking pay for "years of work not performed." * * * [A]warding back wages for work performed by an undocumented alien is analogous to allowing recovery in *quantum meruit* as courts have done for years for services rendered under an unenforceable contract.

Speech before the Industrial Relations Research Association, June 20, 2002, available on-line at: <http://www.irra.uiuc.edu/meetings/NPF2002/Scalia's IRRASpeech6–20–02.pdf>. Is a majority of the Supreme Court—including Scalia *pere*—likely to agree with Scalia *fils*? More recently, the prevailing view has emerged that working without authorization does not bar recovery for wages under the FLSA. *See, e.g., Zavala v. Wal–Mart Stores,* 393 F. Supp.2d 295 (D.N.J. 2005) (*Hoffman Plastic* notwithstanding, unauthorized workers may recover under FLSA for minimum wage and overtime violations relating to work already performed).

4. *Discrimination claims.* After *Hoffman Plastic*, the U.S. Equal Employment Opportunity Commission announced that it would continue to protect immigrant workers from prohibited workplace discrimination—on such grounds as race, national origin, gender and religion—without inquiring into a worker's immigration status. At the same time, however, it rescinded 1999 guidance that had permitted awards of post-termination backpay to unauthorized migrants for federal antidiscrimination law violations. *EEOC*

Reaffirms Commitment to Protecting Undocumented Workers from Discrimination, EEOC Press Release, June 28, 2002.

In *Rivera v. NIBCO, Inc.*, 364 F.3d 1057, *reh'g en banc denied*, 384 F.3d 822 (9th Cir. 2004), *cert. denied*, 544 U.S. 905, 125 S.Ct. 1603, 161 L.Ed.2d 279 (2005), the plaintiffs asserted national origin discrimination claims under federal law (Title VII of the 1964 Civil Rights Act) and state law (the California Fair Employment and Housing Act). During discovery, the defendant sought information from the plaintiffs regarding their immigration status and their eligibility for employment; it asserted that such information, after *Hoffman Plastic*, could be relevant to potential remedies. The plaintiffs sought a protective order, which the federal magistrate granted and the district court sustained. The Court of Appeals affirmed. Writing for the majority, Judge Reinhardt reasoned:

> * * * While documented workers face the possibility of retaliatory discharge for an assertion of their labor and civil rights, undocumented workers confront the harsher reality that, in addition to possible discharge, their employer will likely report them to [DHS] and they will be subjected to deportation proceedings or criminal prosecution.
>
> As a result, most undocumented workers are reluctant to report abusive or discriminatory employment practices. Granting employers the right to inquire into workers' immigration status in cases like this would allow them to raise implicitly the threat of deportation and criminal prosecution every time a worker, documented or undocumented, reports illegal practice or files a Title VII action. * * *
>
> Even documented workers may be chilled by the type of discovery at issue here. Documented workers may fear that their immigration status would be changed, or that their status would reveal the immigration problems of their family and friends; similarly, new legal residents or citizens may feel intimidated by the prospect of having their history examined in a public proceeding. Any of these individuals, failing to understand the relationship between their litigation and immigration status, might choose to forego civil rights litigation.

Id. at 1064–65.

The defendant argued that *Hoffman Plastic* foreclosed any backpay award to the plaintiffs and therefore discovery of immigration status and employment authorization was crucial to its defense. The Court of Appeals concluded that it was "unlikely" the case applied to Title VII cases because (1) Title VII, unlike the NLRA, relies primarily upon private causes of action for enforcement; (2) Title VII plaintiffs have a wide range of available remedies, evidencing Congress' intent that the law be strongly enforced; and (3) in *Hoffman Plastic*, the Supreme Court noted that the NLRB could enforce only the NLRA and had limited power to interpret other federal statutes; courts, however, had authority to balance Title VII against IRCA if the two are found to conflict. (The court stated that it need not issue a definitive ruling on the issue because no backpay award had yet been authorized in the case and other remedies, should a violation be found, were available.) Are you persuaded? Why don't the considerations quoted above regarding Title VII apply with equal force to enforcement of the federal labor laws?

5. *State law responses.* After *Hoffman Plastic*, California adopted legislation in 2002 stating that:

(a) All protections, rights, and remedies available under state law, except any reinstatement remedy prohibited by federal law, are available to all individuals regardless of immigrant status who applied for employment, or who are or who have been employed, in this state;

(b) For purposes of enforcing state labor and employment laws, a person's immigration status is irrelevant to the issue of liability, and in proceedings or discovery undertaken to enforce those state laws no inquiry shall be permitted into a person's immigration status except where the person seeking to make this inquiry has shown by clear and convincing evidence that the inquiry is necessary in order to comply with federal immigration law.

Ann. Calif. Labor Code § 1171.5 (added by Stats. 2002, c. 1071, § 4).

California law provides workers with a cause of action for an employer's violation of prevailing wage rules applied to state construction statutes. May an undocumented employee sue under the statute, citing § 1171.5? Or is the California law guaranteeing rights and remedies irrespective of immigration status pre-empted by federal law as interpreted in *Hoffman Plastic*? *See Reyes v. Van Elk, Ltd.*, 148 Cal.App.4th 604, 56 Cal.Rptr.3d 68 (2007) (holding no preemption; California Labor Code § 1171.5 is not an obstacle to accomplishing purposes of federal employer sanctions).

6. Assume an unauthorized worker is injured on the job and sues the employer for lost future wages. Would *Hoffman Plastic* limit the employee's right to recover? *Compare Balbuena v. IDR Realty LLC*, 6 N.Y.3d 338, 812 N.Y.S.2d 416, 845 N.E.2d 1246 (2006) (recovery allowed; no evidence that plaintiffs produced false work documents in violation of IRCA) and *Madeira v. Affordable Housing Foundation. Inc.*, 469 F.3d 219 (2d Cir. 2006) (same) *with Ambrosi v. 1085 Park Avenue LLC*, 2008 WL 4386751 (S.D.N.Y. 2008) ("Plaintiff's claim for lost wages must be dismissed because Plaintiff is an undocumented alien who knowingly used fraudulent documentation to obtain employment . . . in violation of IRCA."). On the general idea that unauthorized workers can successfully assert workplace rights against more culpable employers, see Motomura, *The Rights of Others: Legal Claims and Immigration Outside the Law*, 59 Duke L.J. 1723, 1749–51 (2010).

7. For a detailed discussion of the background, reasoning and impact of *Hoffman Plastic*, see Fisk & Wishnie, Hoffman Plastic Compounds, Inc. v. NLRB: *The Rules of the Workplace for Undocumented Immigrants*, in Immigration Stories (D. Martin & P. Schuck eds. 2005).

SECTION B. ENFORCEMENT CHOICES

Immigration law is not self-executing. Every removal of a noncitizen from the United States reflects complex choices resulting in the enforcement of immigration law against that person. Every removal also is the product of an intricate procedural system with multiple opportunities for accuracy or error. In Chapter Seven, Section C on Relief From Removal looked at enforcement choices concerning specific individuals, for example when the federal government exercises prosecutorial discretion by deciding not to place someone in removal proceedings. This chapter studies enforcement choices that are more macro-level or systemic, whether to enforce at the border or in the interior, to conduct searches in certain patterns, to base enforcement priorities in part on nationality, or to include or exclude state and local governments in federal immigration enforcement. We defer to Chapter Ten our study of the removal procedures, including immigration court proceedings.

1. PERSPECTIVES ON ENFORCEMENT AND ENFORCEMENT DISCRETION

Any examination of enforcement must start by recognizing how immigration law is underenforced. Recall from Chapter Seven that John Morton, director of the Bureau of Immigration and Customs Enforcement (ICE) in the Department of Homeland Security, explained in June 2010 that given present funding levels, the maximum capacity of the civil removal system is about 400,000 removals per year—under 4 percent of the unauthorized population. There are many ways of understanding how this state of affairs came to be. Here is one perspective:

> [C]hronic and intentional underenforcement of immigration law has been de facto federal policy for over a century, even if enforcement is sometimes visible and severe. Much of this policy emerged in the American Southwest around the turn of the twentieth century, when growers began to rely heavily on Mexican immigrants to satisfy new labor demands generated by the irrigation of new croplands and the invention of the refrigerated railroad car. Many Mexicans entered legally, often as commuters or temporary farmworkers rather than as lawful immigrants. Others came outside the law.

> Formal regulation of Mexican immigration in the first part of the twentieth century consisted of qualitative exclusion grounds, not the numerical limits that have become familiar in modern admissions. Mexicans were exempt from some of these grounds—such as the literacy test—and other grounds were applied to them only selectively. Border control was scant. The minimal enforcement at that time primarily targeted Chinese immigrants who tried to evade the Chinese exclusion laws by entering the United States from Mexico.

> The hallmark of enforcement against Mexican immigrants was discretion that reflected the needs of employers, who often preferred to hire Mexican workers with temporary legal status or no legal status at all. They were a flexible, disposable workforce, ready to work when needed, but as compared to Europeans, more easily sent home when they were not. Heavily influenced by a variety of racial perceptions that cast Mexicans as a subordinate, expendable, and nonassimilable labor force, economically driven fluctuations gave rise to a de facto

policy of discretionary enforcement and partial tolerance of unlawful immigration that continues today.

* * *

Broad tolerance of immigration outside the law prevails today, even if enforcement puts on a strong public face and frequently results in harsh practices that visit severe hardships on the particular migrants who are targeted at the border and in the interior. Powerful interests oppose any law that would stanch the flow of unauthorized workers who are paid less, laid off more easily, and have fewer workplace protections. The jobs of citizen workers often depend on the availability of immigrant coworkers, without whom their companies cannot survive, let alone prosper. Consumers want lower prices. The remittances sent home by workers are not only a vital part of U.S. foreign aid, but also a tolerated alternative to initiatives that might foster economic development in migrants' home countries.

This de facto policy also reflects resistance to a more regulated labor market, and to intrusive monitoring and detection mechanisms—as for example, a national identity card—that may affect citizens as well. Tolerance of a substantial undocumented population may even be a rational admissions scheme. Inviting immigrants outside the law and then periodically legalizing those with strong work histories—an approach that relies heavily on a flexible notion of unlawful presence—may be more accurate and efficient than trying to identify ex ante who the best economic contributors will be. Today, even more than a generation ago, the resources devoted to immigration law enforcement are a mere fraction of what would be needed to significantly reduce immigration outside the law. At the same time, conditions in migrants' home countries make them more willing than ever to brave burning deserts and suffocating truck trailers in search of a better life in the United States.

Motomura, *Immigration Outside the Law*, 108 Colum. L. Rev. 2037, 2049–54 (2008). *See also* Calavita, *The Immigration Policy Debate: Critical Analysis and Future Options*, in Mexican Migration to the United States: Origins, Consequences, and Policy Options 151, 155–59 (W. Cornelius & J. Bustamante, eds. 1989); Massey, Goldring, & Durand, *Continuities in Transnational Migration: An Analysis of Nineteen Mexican Communities*, 99 Am. J. Soc. 1492, 1496–1502 (1994), both excerpted in Chapter Five, pp. 462–69 *supra*.

In turn, underenforcement combined with limited removal capacity means that government discretion in immigration law enforcement matters a great deal. Where, when, and how will enforcement resources be brought to bear on immigration law violators?

2. LIMITS ON GOVERNMENT ENFORCEMENT ACTIVITIES

a. Searches and Seizures

No matter whether enforcement involves civil immigration proceedings or criminal prosecution, the question arises of when and how the law limits what federal, state, or local law enforcement officers may do by way of searches, seizures, stops, or arrests. Each of these four words is a term of art that has generated controversy and case law.

Suppose that ICE agents want to arrest unauthorized migrants suspected of working at a local factory? Or suppose they believe that other unauthorized migrants are living in a certain house? Or suppose Border Patrol agents spot a car heading north on a dirt road in southern Arizona and think that the occupants have just crossed the border surreptitiously?

The most basic sources of limits are the Fourth and Fifth Amendments to the U.S. Constitution. Because they apply to both criminal procedure and civil immigration enforcement, the substantive limits on law enforcement that have developed in one area governs the other as well. But as we shall see, remedies may be more limited in civil removal proceedings than in criminal prosecution.

Besides the Constitution, the Immigration and Nationality Act, other statutes, and regulations impose requirements on officers and employees of DHS. These statutes and regulations may mirror constitutional commands, or they may demand more of the government. Even when they are substantively identical, they may allow remedies that would be unavailable for violations of the Constitution alone.

(i) When Do Fourth Amendment Protections Apply?

Immigration enforcement typically involves a physical encounter between a government official and an individual—at a land border or other port of entry, at a traffic stop or some other highway encounter, or perhaps in a raid at a workplace or home. In these encounters, immigration officers often stop and question persons suspected of being in the country unlawfully. Under INA § 287(a)(1) and (2), respectively, officers may "interrogate any alien or person believed to be an alien as to his right to be or remain in the United States," and arrest aliens unlawfully entering, attempting to enter, or in the United States.

Does the Fourth Amendment limit this authority? Yes, but only if the encounter amounts to a search or seizure. The first question, then, is how are these terms defined.

INS v. DELGADO

Supreme Court of the United States, 1984.
466 U.S. 210, 104 S.Ct. 1758, 80 L.Ed.2d 247.

JUSTICE REHNQUIST delivered the opinion of the Court.

* * *

Acting pursuant to two warrants, in January and September, 1977 the INS conducted a survey of the work force at Southern California Davis Pleating Co. (Davis Pleating) in search of illegal aliens. The warrants were issued on a showing of probable cause by the INS that numerous illegal aliens were employed at Davis Pleating, although neither of the search warrants identified any particular illegal aliens by name. A third factory survey was conducted with the employer's consent in October, 1977, at Mr. Pleat, another garment factory.

At the beginning of the surveys several agents positioned themselves near the buildings' exits, while other agents dispersed throughout the factory to question most, but not all, employees at their work stations. The agents displayed badges, carried walkie-talkies, and were armed, although at no point during any of the surveys was a weapon ever drawn. Moving systematically through the factory, the agents approached employees and, after identifying themselves, asked them from one to three questions relating to their citizenship. If the employee gave a credible reply that he was a United States citizen, the questioning ended, and the agent moved on to another employee. If the employee gave an unsatisfactory response or admitted that he was an alien, the employee was asked to produce his immigration papers. During the survey, employees continued with their work and were free to walk around within the factory.

Respondents are [two U.S. citizen and two lawful permanent resident] employees questioned in one of the three surveys. In 1978 respondents and their union representative, the International Ladies Garment Workers' Union, filed two actions * * * challenging the constitutionality of INS factory surveys and seeking declaratory and injunctive relief. * * *

* * *

The Fourth Amendment does not proscribe all contact between the police and citizens, but is designed "to prevent arbitrary and oppressive interference by enforcement officials with the privacy and personal security of individuals." *United States v. Martinez–Fuerte*, 428 U.S. 543, 554, 96 S.Ct. 3074, 3081, 49 L.Ed.2d 1116 (1976). Given the diversity of encounters between police officers and citizens, however, the Court has been cautious in defining the limits imposed by the Fourth Amendment on encounters between the police and citizens. As we have noted elsewhere: "Obviously, not all personal intercourse between policemen and citizens involves 'seizures' of persons. Only when the officer, by means of physical force or show of authority, has restrained the liberty of a citizen may we conclude that a 'seizure' has occurred." *Terry v. Ohio*, [392 U.S. 1, 19, n.16, 88 S.Ct. 1868, 1879 n.16, 20 L.Ed.2d 889 (1968)]. While applying such a test is relatively straightforward in a situation resembling a traditional arrest, the protection against unreasonable seizures also extends to "seizures that involve only a brief detention short of traditional arrest." *United States v. Brignoni–Ponce*, 422 U.S. 873, 878, 95 S.Ct. 2574, 2578, 45 L.Ed.2d 607 (1975). What has evolved from our cases is a determination that an initially consensual encounter between a police officer and a citizen can be transformed into a seizure or detention within the meaning of the Fourth Amendment, "if, in view of all the circumstances surrounding the incident, a reasonable person would have believed that he was not free to leave." [*United States v. Mendenhall*, 446 U.S. 544, 554, 100 S.Ct. 1870, 1877, 64 L.Ed.2d 497 (1980)].

* * *

* * * [P]olice questioning, by itself, is unlikely to result in a Fourth Amendment violation. While most citizens will respond to a police request, the fact that people do so, and do so without being told they are free not to respond, hardly eliminates the consensual nature of the response. Unless the circumstances of the encounter are so intimidating as to demonstrate that a reasonable person would have believed he was not free to leave if he had not responded, one cannot say that the questioning resulted in a detention under the Fourth Amendment. But if the persons refuses to answer and the police take additional steps * * * to obtain an answer, then the Fourth Amendment imposes some minimal level of objective justification to validate the detention or seizure.

* * * In support of the decision below, respondents argue that the INS created an intimidating psychological environment when it intruded unexpectedly into the workplace with such a show of officers. Besides the stationing of agents near the exits, respondents add that the length of the survey and the failure to inform workers they were free to leave resulted in a Fourth Amendment seizure of the entire work force.

We reject the claim that the entire work forces of the two factories were seized for the duration of the surveys when the INS placed agents near the exits of the factory sites. Ordinarily, when people are at work their freedom to move about has been meaningfully restricted, not by the actions of law enforcement officials, but by the workers' voluntary obligations to their employers. The record indicates that when these surveys were initiated, the employees were about their ordinary business, operating machinery and performing other job assignments. While the surveys did cause some disruption, including the efforts of some workers to hide, the record also indicates that workers were not prevented by the agents from moving about the factories.

Respondents argue, however, that the stationing of agents near the factory doors showed the INS's intent to prevent people from leaving. But there is nothing in the record indicating that this is what the agents at the doors actually did. The obvious purpose of the agents' presence at the factory doors was to insure that all persons in the factories were questioned. The record indicates that the INS agents' conduct in this case consisted simply of questioning employees and arresting those they had probable cause to believe were unlawfully present in the factory. This conduct should have given respondents no reason to believe that they would be detained if they gave truthful answers to the questions put to them or if they simply refused to answer. If mere questioning does not constitute a seizure when it occurs inside the factory, it is no more a seizure when it occurs at the exits.

A similar conclusion holds true for all other citizens or aliens lawfully present inside the factory buildings during the surveys. The presence of agents by the exits posed no reasonable threat of detention to these workers while they walked throughout the factories on job assignments. Likewise, the mere possibility that they would be questioned if they sought to leave the buildings should not have resulted in any reasonable apprehension by any of them that they would be seized or detained in any meaningful way. Since most workers could have had no reasonable fear that they would be detained upon leaving, we conclude that the work forces as a whole were not seized.

* * * [S]ince there was no seizure of the work forces by virtue of the method of conducting the factory surveys, the only way the issue of individual questioning could be presented would be if one of the named respondents had in fact been seized or detained. Reviewing the deposition testimony of respondents, we conclude that none were.

The questioning of each respondent by INS agents seems to have been nothing more than a brief encounter. None of the three Davis Pleating employees were questioned during the January survey. During the September survey at Davis Pleating, respondent Delgado was discussing the survey with another employee when two INS agents approached him and asked him where he was from and from what city. When Delgado informed them that he came from Mayaguez, Puerto Rico, the agent made an innocuous observation to his partner and left. Respondent Correa's experience in the September survey was similar. Walking from one part of the factory to another, Correa was stopped by an INS agent and asked where she was born. When she replied "Huntington Park, [California]," the agent walked away and Correa continued about her business. Respondent Labonte, the third Davis Pleating employee, was tapped on the shoulder and asked in Spanish, "Where are your papers?". Labonte responded that she had her papers and without any further request from the INS agents, showed the papers to the agents, who then left. Finally, respondent Miramontes, the sole Mr. Pleat employee involved in this case, encountered an agent en route from an office to her worksite. Questioned concerning her citizenship, Miramontes replied that she was a resident alien, and on the agent's request, produced her work permit. The agent then left.

Respondents argue that the manner in which the surveys were conducted and the attendant disruption caused by the surveys created a psychological environment which made them reasonably afraid they were not free to leave. Consequently, when respondents were approached by INS agents and questioned concerning their citizenship and right to work, they were effectively detained under the Fourth Amendment, since they reasonably feared that refusing to answer would have resulted in their arrest. But it was obvious from the beginning of the surveys that the INS agents were only questioning people. Persons such as respondents who simply went about their business in the workplace were not detained in any way; nothing more occurred than that a question was put to them. While persons who attempted to flee or evade the agents may eventually have been detained for questioning, respondents did not do so and were not in fact detained. The manner in which respondents were questioned, given its obvious purpose, could hardly result in a reasonable fear that respondents were not free to continue working or to move about the factory. Respondents may only litigate what happened to them, and our review of their description of the encounters with the INS agents satisfies us that the encounters were classic consensual encounters rather than Fourth Amendment seizures.

* * *

[The concurring opinions of JUSTICES STEVENS AND POWELL are omitted.]

JUSTICE BRENNAN, with whom JUSTICE MARSHALL joins, concurring in part and dissenting in part.

* * *

At first blush, the Court's opinion appears unremarkable. But what is striking about today's decision is its studied air of unreality. Indeed, it is only through a considerable feat of legerdemain that the Court is able to arrive at the conclusion that the respondents were not seized. The success of the Court's sleight of hand turns on the proposition that the interrogations of respondents by the INS were merely brief, "consensual encounters," that posed no threat to respondents' personal security and freedom. The record, however, tells a far different story.

* * *

* * * I have no difficulty concluding that respondents were seized within the meaning of the Fourth Amendment when they were accosted by the INS agents and questioned concerning their right to remain in the United States. Although none of the respondents was physically restrained by the INS agents during the questioning, it is nonetheless plain beyond cavil that the manner in which the INS conducted these surveys demonstrated a "show of authority" of sufficient size and force to overbear the will of any reasonable person. Faced with such tactics, a reasonable person could not help but feel compelled to stop and provide answers to the INS agents' questions. The Court's efforts to avoid this conclusion are rooted more in fantasy than in the record of this case. The Court goes astray, in my view, chiefly because it insists upon considering each interrogation in isolation as if respondents had been questioned by the INS in a setting similar to an encounter between a single police officer and a lone passerby that might occur on a street corner. * * *

The surrounding circumstances in this case are far different from an isolated encounter between the police and a passerby on the street. Each of the respondents testified at length about the widespread disturbance among the workers that was sparked by the INS surveys and the intimidating atmosphere created by the INS's investigative tactics. First, as the respondents explained, the surveys were carried out by surprise by relatively large numbers of agents, generally from 15 to 25, who moved systematically through the rows of workers who were seated at their work stations. Second, as the INS agents discovered persons whom they suspected of being illegal aliens, they would handcuff these persons and lead them away to waiting vans outside the factory. Third, all of the factory exits were conspicuously guarded by INS agents, stationed there to prevent anyone from leaving while the survey was being conducted. Finally, as the INS agents moved through the rows of workers, they would show their badges and direct pointed questions at the workers. In light of these circumstances, it is simply fantastic to conclude that a reasonable person could ignore all that was occurring throughout the factory and, when the INS agents reached him, have the temerity to believe that he was at liberty to refuse to answer their questions and walk away.

* * *

* * * [T]he respondents' testimony paints a frightening picture of people subjected to wholesale interrogation under conditions designed not to respect personal security and privacy, but rather to elicit prompt answers from completely intimidated workers. Nothing could be clearer than that these tactics amounted to seizures of respondents under the Fourth Amendment.

* * *

* * * [W]e have explained that brief detentions may be justified on "facts that do not amount to the probable cause required for an arrest." *United States v. Brignoni–Ponce*, 422 U.S. 873, 880, 95 S.Ct. 2574, 2580, 45 L.Ed.2d 607 (1975). Nevertheless, * * * we have insisted that police may not detain and interrogate an individual unless they have reasonable grounds for suspecting that the person is involved in some unlawful activity. In *United States v. Brignoni–Ponce*, for instance, the Court held that "[Border Patrol] officers on roving patrol may stop vehicles only if they are aware of specific articulable facts, together with rational inferences from those facts, that reasonably warrant suspicion that the vehicles contain aliens who may be illegally in the country." 422 U.S., at 884, 95 S.Ct., at 2581.

* * * [A]ll workers, irrespective of whether they were American citizens, permanent resident aliens, or deportable aliens, were subjected to questioning by INS agents concerning their right to remain in the country. By their own admission, the INS agents did not selectively question persons in these surveys on the basis of any reasonable suspicion that the persons were illegal aliens. That the INS policy is so indiscriminate should not be surprising, however, since many of the employees in the surveyed factories who are lawful residents of the United States may have been born in Mexico, have a Latin appearance, or speak Spanish while at work. What this means, of course, is that the many lawful workers who constitute the clear majority at the surveyed workplaces are subjected to surprise questioning under intimidating circumstances by INS agents who have no reasonable basis for suspecting that they have done anything wrong. To say that such an indiscriminate policy of mass interrogation is constitutional makes a mockery of the words of the Fourth Amendment.

* * *

Furthermore, even if the INS agents had pursued a firm policy of stopping and interrogating only those persons whom they reasonably suspected of being aliens, they would still have failed, given the particular circumstances of this case, to safeguard adequately the rights secured by the Fourth Amendment. The first and in my view insurmountable problem with such a policy is that, viewed realistically, it poses such grave problems of execution that in practice it affords virtually no protection to lawful American citizens working in these factories. This is so because, as the Court recognized in *Brignoni–Ponce*, 422 U.S., at 886, 95 S.Ct., at 2582, there is no reliable way to distinguish with a reasonable degree of accuracy between native-born and naturalized citizens of Mexican ancestry on the one hand, and aliens of Mexican ancestry on the other. Indeed, the record in this case clearly demonstrates this danger, since respondents Correa and Delgado, although both American citizens, were subjected to questioning during the INS surveys.

Moreover, the mere fact that a person is believed to be an alien provides no immediate grounds for suspecting any illegal activity. * * *In contexts such as these factory surveys, where it is virtually impossible to distinguish fairly between citizens and aliens, the threat to vital civil rights of American citizens would soon become intolerable if we simply permitted the INS to question persons solely on account of suspected alienage. Therefore, in order to protect both American citizens and lawful resident aliens, who are also protected by the Fourth Amendment, the INS must tailor its enforcement efforts to focus only on those workers who are reasonably suspected of being illegal aliens.

Relying upon *United States v. Martinez–Fuerte*, 428 U.S. 543, 96 S.Ct. 3074, 49 L.Ed.2d 1116 (1976), however, Justice POWELL would hold that the interrogation of respondents represented a "reasonable" seizure under the Fourth Amendment, even though the INS agents lacked any particularized suspicion of illegal alienage to support the questioning. In my view, reliance on that decision is misplaced. In *Martinez–Fuerte*, the Court held that when the intrusion upon protected privacy interests is extremely limited, the INS, in order to serve the pressing governmental interest in immigration enforcement, may briefly detain travelers at fixed checkpoints for questioning solely on the basis of "apparent Mexican ancestry." 428 U.S., at 563, 96 S.Ct., at 3085. In so holding, the Court was careful to distinguish its earlier decision in *Brignoni–Ponce*, which held that Border Patrol agents conducting roving patrols may not stop and question motorists solely on the basis of apparent Mexican ancestry, and may instead make such stops only when their observations lead them "reasonably to suspect that a particular vehicle may contain aliens who are illegally in the country." *Id.*, 422 U.S., at 881, 95 S.Ct., at 2580. The "crucial distinction" between the roving patrols and the fixed checkpoints * * * was "the lesser intrusion upon the motorist's Fourth Amendment interests" caused by the checkpoint operations. * * *

* * *

In my view, therefore, the only acceptable alternatives that would adequately safeguard Fourth Amendment values in this context are for the INS either (a) to adopt a firm policy of stopping and questioning only those workers who are reasonably suspected of being illegal aliens, or (b) to develop a factory survey program that is predictably and reliably less intrusive than the current scheme under review. The first alternative would satisfy the requirement of particularized suspicion enunciated in *Terry*—a principle that must control here because the specific conditions that permitted exception to that requirement in *Martinez–Fuerte* are simply not present. The second alternative would seek to redesign the factory survey techniques used by the INS in order to bring them more closely into line with the characteristics found in *Martinez–Fuerte*. * * *

* * *

NOTES AND QUESTIONS ON SEARCHES AND SEIZURES

1. Part of the reasoning in *Delgado* is that neither asking an individual for identification, nor its production in response, are sufficient to turn an encounter into a seizure to which the Fourth Amendment would apply. *See also Muehler v. Mena*, 544 U.S. 93, 100–01, 125 S.Ct. 1465, 1471, 161 L.Ed.2d 299 (2005) (holding that questioning a lawfully detained individual about her name, date and place of birth, or immigration status is not a discrete seizure that must independently satisfy the Fourth Amendment); *Hiibel v. Sixth Judicial District Court of Nevada*, 542 U.S. 177, 185–89, 124 S.Ct. 2451, 2458–60, 159 L.Ed.2d 292 (2004) (holding constitutional a Nevada statute requiring an individual, once stopped by a police officer based on reasonable suspicion, to disclose his name).

2. In addition to defining "seizure" over vigorous dissent, *Delgado* surveys a number of concepts and doctrines that figure prominently in defining Fourth Amendment limits on immigration enforcement. The basic

idea is that the Fourth Amendment requires searches and seizures to be reasonable, and that the definition of "reasonable" is subdivided into two scenarios.

A search or seizure pursuant to a judicial warrant (not an administrative warrant) is presumed to be reasonable, whereas a warrantless search or seizure is presumed not to be reasonable. But a warrantless search or seizure may be consistent with the Fourth Amendment if any one of several conditions is met, including several that are especially relevant to immigration law enforcement:

> a. the officer making an arrest has "probable cause" to believe that the individual has violated the law, *see United States v. Watson*, 423 U.S. 411, 417, 96 S.Ct. 820, 824–25, 46 L.Ed.2d 598 (1976).

> b. short of making a traditional arrest, the officer may engage in a brief investigatory stop of an individual or a vehicle based on "reasonable suspicion" (which is less than "probable cause") that unlawful activity "may be afoot" based on whether the officer has a particularized and objective basis for suspecting wrongdoing based on the totality of circumstances, *see Terry*, cited in *Delgado*; *see also United States v. Arvizu*, 534 U.S. 266, 273, 122 S.Ct. 744, 750, 151 L.Ed.2d 740 (2002);

> c. the search is incident to an arrest that has already taken place, *see Chimel v. California*, 395 U.S. 752, 762–63, 89 S.Ct. 2034, 2040, 23 L.Ed.2d 685 (1969);

> d. a search is based on consent. *see Schneckloth v. Bustamonte*, 412 U.S. 218, 222, 93 S.Ct. 2041, 2045, 36 L.Ed.2d 854 (1973);

> e. exigent circumstances, such as intervening in a fight to prevent serious injury, see *Brigham City v. Stuart*, 547 U.S. 398, 406, 126 S.Ct. 1943, 1949, 164 L.Ed.2d 650 (2006); or

> f. the search or seizure takes place at or near the border, where law enforcement activity is less constrained, *see Brignoni–Ponce* and *Martinez–Fuerte*, both cited in *Delgado*.

3. In keeping with the traditional border-interior distinction in due process analysis (compare *Knauff* with *Yamataya*), the U.S. Supreme Court has recognized that law enforcement officials have far greater power to search persons and property at the border than inside the country. Thus, a routine search at an official border inspection post may occur without probable cause or reasonable suspicion. *See United States v. Ramsey*, 431 U.S. 606, 619, 97 S.Ct. 1972, 52 L.Ed.2d 617 (1977). Intrusive searches that go beyond a normal border search require some degree of reasonable belief that illegal activity is occurring. In *United States v. Montoya de Hernandez*, 473 U.S. 531, 105 S.Ct. 3304, 87 L.Ed.2d 381 (1985), the Court upheld the sixteen-hour detention of a traveler seeking to enter the United States based on customs officials' "reasonable suspicion" that she was smuggling swallowed contraband.

The Supreme Court has applied the Fourth Amendment near the border more vigorously than at the border itself, but less vigorously than in the interior. Near but not at the border, the Court has distinguished between stops made at "fixed checkpoints" and those made by "roving patrols" (that is, officers traveling in cars).

At fixed immigration control checkpoints, brief stops are allowed even without reasonable suspicion, *United States v. Martinez–Fuerte*, 428 U.S. 543, 561–62, 96 S.Ct. 3074, 49 L.Ed.2d 1116 (1976). But once a car and its riders have been held for secondary inspection at a fixed check point, a search requires probable cause or consent. *United States v. Ortiz*, 422 U.S. 891, 896–97, 95 S.Ct. 2585, 45 L.Ed.2d 623 (1975).

In contrast, roving patrols may conduct brief stops and questioning only if an officer has a reasonable suspicion (the *Terry* standard) that the vehicle is involved in unlawful activity. *See United States v. Brignoni–Ponce*, 422 U.S. 873, 881–82, 95 S.Ct. 2574, 45 L.Ed.2d 607 (1975). Roving patrols may conduct arrests and full-scale searches only based on probable cause. *Almeida–Sanchez, supra*, 413 U.S. at 273.

4. Compare the facts in *Delgado* with *LaDuke v. Nelson*, 762 F.2d 1318 (9th Cir. 1985):

> The armed Border Patrol agents periodically cordoned off migrant housing during early morning or late evening hours, surrounded the residences in emergency vehicles with flashing lights, approached the homes with flashlights, and stationed officers at all doors and windows. The agents would then conduct house-to-house searches either without consent or with the alleged "knowing" consent of the occupants.

762 F.2d at 1321.

> Distinguishing *Delgado*, the Ninth Circuit found a "seizure":

> * * * First, unlike *Delgado*, the INS agents do not obtain any form of warrant for ranch and farm checks. As the district court found, the INS agents base their decision to check on a random basis without any current articulable suspicion that particular units will contain illegal aliens. Also unlike *Delgado*, the INS systematically fails to obtain the consent of the owner of the farm housing. A second distinction between the factory surveys in *Delgado* and farm checks is the materially different forum in which these searches take place—the workplace versus the home. Although the INS persists in contending that farm housing is part and parcel of the workplace and should be treated similarly, the simple truth is that the INS itself has recognized that they are dissimilar. If the INS truly thought that the occupants of farm housing were living at the workplace then the INS would be obliged to seek the consent of the employer—not the occupant—to obtain access. The measure of protection accorded the home under the Fourth Amendment is qualitatively different from that afforded the workplace under *Delgado*. * * * Significantly, the *Delgado* opinion's reliance on the permissibility of questioning within the open interior of the workplace to justify questioning at the workplace exits is clearly inapplicable to the home setting.

Id. at 1328–29.

5. Was there a seizure of the four respondents in *Delgado*, such that the Fourth Amendment would apply? Devon Carbado and Cheryl Harris observe that "at no point in Justice Rehnquist's opinion does he engage race" even though respondent Herman Delgado, a U.S. citizen, argued in his brief that "innocuous conduct does not become suspect merely because the person

observed is non-white. Yet that is precisely what occurs during these raids. Every Latin [sic] is suspected of being an undocumented alien due to his or her race." Carbado & Harris, *Undocumented Criminal Procedure*, 58 UCLA L. Rev. 1543, 1559 (2011).

Why should the omission of race from the Court's analysis in *Delgado* be troubling? What would be a sound basis for the plaintiff's assertion that every Latino is "suspected of being an undocumented alien"? How can the use of apparent race or ethnicity in enforcement decisions be monitored and controlled, perhaps through mechanisms within the executive branch, or by means of legal standards applied by courts? Beyond the answers to these questions that may emerge from your reading of *Delgado*, the next subsection continues this line of inquiry.

(ii) Enforcement and Ethnicity

In determining what the Fourth Amendment requires, a topic that sometimes arises is ethnicity. Should courts craft strict standards to protect noncitizens—and citizens—who may appear "foreign" to some law enforcement officers, leading them to believe they have reasonable suspicion or probable cause? Or given enforcement imperatives, should officials have some authority to consider ethnicity in carrying out their functions? Besides addressing the general standard for roving patrols near the border, the U.S. Supreme Court's 1975 decision in *Brignoni–Ponce* also held that "apparent Mexican ancestry" plus presence in an area where undocumented migrants frequently travel are not enough to justify a vehicle stop. The next year, the Court held in *Martinez–Fuerte* that motorists at a fixed checkpoint may be referred to secondary inspection (where they will be questioned at greater length) "largely on the basis of apparent Mexican ancestry." But *Martinez–Fuerte* also seemed to reconfirm the Court's holding in *Ortiz* that a search during secondary inspection at a fixed check point requires probable cause or consent. In the next case, the Ninth Circuit addressed whether the Fourth Amendment allows "Hispanic appearance" to play *any* role in enforcement near the border.

UNITED STATES v. MONTERO–CAMARGO

United States Court of Appeals, Ninth Circuit, en banc, 2000.
208 F.3d 1122, cert. denied, 531 U.S. 889, 121 S.Ct. 211, 148 L.Ed.2d 148.

REINHARDT, CIRCUIT JUDGE.

* * *

On the afternoon of October 15, 1996, a passing driver told border patrol agents at the Highway 86 permanent stationary checkpoint in El Centro, California, that two cars heading north, with Mexicali license plates, had just made U-turns on the highway shortly before the checkpoint. Upon receiving the tip, two Border Patrol Agents, Brian Johnson and Carl Fisher, got into separate marked patrol cars and headed south to investigate. Approximately one minute later (and about one mile from the checkpoint), the two agents saw a blue Chevrolet Blazer and a red Nissan sedan, both with Mexicali plates, pull off the shoulder and re-enter the highway heading south.

According to the agents, the area where they first observed the cars is used by lawbreakers to drop off and pick up undocumented aliens and illegal drugs, while evading inspection. Its use for such purposes is due in part to the fact that the view of that part of the highway area from the Border Patrol checkpoint is blocked. * * *

Both agents testified that almost all of the stops made by the Border Patrol at the turnaround site resulted in the discovery of "a violation of some sort . . ." involving either illegal aliens or narcotics. * * *

The place where the agents saw that the vehicles had stopped following the U-turn was a deserted area on the side of the southbound highway located opposite the large sign on the northbound side advising drivers that the checkpoint was open. As Agent Johnson testified, the sign was the first indication to northbound drivers that the Border Patrol's facility was operational. The checkpoint in question had been closed for some time and had reopened only a day or two earlier.

* * * Agent Johnson * * * testified that as he pulled behind the Blazer, he noted that both the driver and the passenger appeared to be Hispanic. Johnson stated that when the driver and passenger noticed him behind them, the passenger picked up a newspaper and began reading. This, according to Agent Johnson, further aroused his suspicions. Johnson then stopped the Blazer, identified himself as a Border Patrol agent, and asked about the citizenship of the two occupants. In response to Johnson's inquiries, the driver, Lorenzo Sanchez–Guillen, and his passenger, Sylvia Renteria–Wolff, showed Agent Johnson [their border crossing] cards, which allow Mexican citizens to travel up to 25 miles inside the United States for no longer than 72 hours at a time. As the Blazer had been stopped approximately 50 miles from the border, Johnson then brought the two occupants to the checkpoint for processing.

In the meantime, Agent Fisher continued to follow the second car, a red Nissan sedan. According to Fisher, when he and Agent Johnson first drew near the two cars, the Nissan began to accelerate. As Fisher caught up with the vehicle, he could see that the second driver also appeared to be Hispanic. Fisher ultimately pulled the Nissan over after following it for approximately four miles. Appellant German Espinoza Montero–Camargo was the driver. After stopping the car, Agent Fisher, with the aid of Agent Johnson, who had returned to help him, searched the trunk and found two large bags of marijuana. A subsequent search of the Blazer back at the checkpoint turned up a loaded .32 caliber pistol in the glove compartment and an ammunition clip that fit the pistol in the passenger's purse.

* * *

1. THE REASONABLE SUSPICION CALCULUS

* * *

* * * Although the level of suspicion required for a brief investigatory stop is less demanding than that for probable cause, the Fourth Amendment nevertheless requires an objective justification for such a stop. As a result, the officer in question "must be able to articulate more than an 'inchoate and unparticularized suspicion' or 'hunch' of criminal activity." *Illinois v. Wardlow,* 528 U.S. 119, 120 S.Ct. 673, 676, 145 L.Ed.2d 570 (2000). Rather, reasonable suspicion exists when an officer is aware of specific, articulable facts which, when considered with objective and reasonable inferences, form a basis for *particularized* suspicion.

The requirement of *particularized* suspicion encompasses two elements. First, the assessment must be based upon the totality of the circumstances. Second, that assessment must arouse a reasonable suspicion that *the particular person being stopped* has committed or is about to commit a crime. Accordingly, we have rejected profiles that are "likely to sweep many ordinary citizens into a generality of suspicious appearance...." *United States v. Rodriguez,* 976 F.2d 592, 595–96 (9th Cir. 1992) (concluding that the factors cited in the case—namely, a Hispanic man carefully driving an old Ford with a worn suspension who looked in his rear view mirror while being followed by agents in a marked car— described "too many individuals to create a reasonable suspicion that this particular defendant was engaged in criminal activity").

* * *

2. THE FACTORS CONSIDERED BY THE DISTRICT COURT

As noted above, the district court based its determination that reasonable suspicion existed on a series of factors: 1) the U-turn made before the checkpoint by the two cars; 2) the driving in tandem and the Mexicali license plates; 3) the area at which the U-turn occurred included a well-known drop-off point for smugglers; 4) the Hispanic appearance of the three defendants; and 5) Renteria–Wolff's picking up the newspaper after glancing back at the patrol cars. Although we agree with the district court that reasonable suspicion did exist to justify an investigatory stop, we conclude that some of the factors on which the district court relied are not relevant or appropriate to the reasonable suspicion analysis. We begin by considering the factors in that category, before turning to address those which the district court properly considered.

In concluding that reasonable suspicion existed, both the district court and the panel majority relied in part upon the Hispanic appearance of the three defendants. We hold that they erred in doing so. We first note that Agent Johnston testified at the suppression hearing that the majority of people who pass through the El Centro checkpoints are Hispanic, and thus, presumably have a Hispanic appearance.

As we stressed earlier, reasonable suspicion requires *particularized* suspicion. Where, as here, the majority (or any substantial number) of people share a specific characteristic, that characteristic is of little or no probative value in such a particularized and context-specific analysis. * * *

The likelihood that in an area in which the majority—or even a substantial part—of the population is Hispanic, any given person of Hispanic ancestry is in fact an alien, let alone an illegal alien, is not high enough to make Hispanic appearance a relevant factor in the reasonable suspicion calculus. As we have previously held, factors that have such a low probative value that no reasonable officer would have relied on them to make an investigative stop must be disregarded as a matter of law. Moreover, as we explain below, Hispanic appearance is not, in general, an appropriate factor.

* * *

In arriving at the dictum suggesting that ethnic appearance could be relevant, the Court [in *Brignoni–Ponce*] relied heavily on now-outdated demographic information. * * * *Brignoni–Ponce* was handed down in 1975, some twenty-five years ago. Current demographic data demonstrate that the statistical premises on which its dictum relies are no longer applicable. The Hispanic population of this nation, and of the Southwest and Far West in particular, has grown enormously—at least five-fold in the four states referred to in the Supreme Court's decision. According to the U.S. Census Bureau, as of January 1, 2000, that population group stands at nearly 34 million. Furthermore, Hispanics are heavily concentrated in certain states in which minorities are becoming if not the majority, then at least the single largest group, either in the state as a whole or in a significant number of counties. According to the same data, California has the largest Hispanic population of any state—estimated at 10,112,986 in 1998, while Texas has approximately 6 million

One area where Hispanics are heavily in the majority is El Centro, the site of the vehicle stop. As Agent Johnson acknowledged, the majority of the people who pass through the El Centro checkpoint are Hispanic. His testimony is in turn corroborated by more general demographic data from that area. * * * [A]ccording to census data, five Southern California counties are home to more than a fifth of the nation's Hispanic population. * * * Accordingly, Hispanic appearance is of little or no use in determining which particular individuals among the vast Hispanic populace should be stopped by law enforcement officials on the lookout for illegal aliens. * * *[22]

---

22. * * * Hispanic appearance, or any other racial or ethnic appearance, including Caucasian, may be considered when the suspected perpetrator of a specific offense has been identified as having such an appearance. Even in such circumstances, however, persons of a particular racial or ethnic group may not be stopped and questioned because of such appearance, unless there are other individualized or particularized factors which, together with the racial or ethnic appearance identified, rise to the level of reasonable suspicion or probable cause. To the extent that our prior

Moreover, the demographic changes we describe have been accompanied by significant changes in the law restricting the use of race as a criterion in government decision-making. The use of race and ethnicity for such purposes has been severely limited. Relying on the principle that " '[o]ur Constitution is color-blind, and neither knows nor tolerates classes among citizens,' " *City of Richmond v. J.A. Croson Co.,* 488 U.S. 469, 521, 109 S.Ct. 706, 102 L.Ed.2d 854 (1989) (Scalia, J., concurring) (quoting *Plessy v. Ferguson,* 163 U.S. 537, 559, 16 S.Ct. 1138, 41 L.Ed. 256 (1896) (Harlan, J., dissenting)), the Supreme Court has repeatedly held that reliance "on racial or ethnic criteria must necessarily receive a most searching examination to make sure that it does not conflict with constitutional guarantees." *Wygant v. Jackson Bd. of Ed.,* 476 U.S. 267, 273, 106 S.Ct. 1842, 90 L.Ed.2d 260 (1986). In invalidating the use of racial classifications used to remedy past discrimination in *Croson,* the Court applied strict scrutiny, stating that its rigorousness would ensure that:

> the means chosen "fit" this compelling goal so closely that there is little or no possibility that the motive for the classification was illegitimate racial prejudice or stereotype. Classifications based on race carry a danger of stigmatic harm. Unless they are strictly reserved for remedial settings, they may in fact promote notions of racial inferiority and lead to a politics of racial hostility.

Croson, 488 U.S. at 493, 109 S.Ct. 706. The danger of stigmatic harm of the type that the Court feared overbroad affirmative action programs would pose is far more pronounced in the context of police stops in which race or ethnic appearance is a factor. So, too, are the consequences of "notions of racial inferiority" and the "politics of racial hostility" that the Court pointed to. Stops based on race or ethnic appearance send the underlying message to all our citizens that those who are not white are judged by the color of their skin alone. Such stops also send a clear message that those who are not white enjoy a lesser degree of constitutional protection—that they are in effect assumed to be potential criminals first and individuals second. It would be an anomalous result to hold that race may be considered when it harms people, but not when it helps them.

We decide no broad constitutional questions here. Rather, we are confronted with the narrow question of how to square the Fourth Amendment's requirement of individualized reasonable suspicion with the fact that the majority of the people who pass through the checkpoint in question are Hispanic. In order to answer that question, we conclude that, at this point in our nation's history, and given the continuing changes in our ethnic and racial composition, Hispanic appearance is, in general, of such little probative value that it may not be considered as a relevant factor where particularized or individualized suspicion is required. Moreover, we conclude, for the reasons we have indicated, that it is also not an appropriate factor.

* * *

cases have approved the use of Hispanic appearance as a factor where there was no particularized, individual suspicion, they are overruled. * * *

In this case, the two cars driven in tandem by Montero–Camargo and Sanchez–Guillen made U-turns on a highway, at a place where the view of the border officials was obstructed, and stopped briefly at a locale histori- cally used for illegal activities, before proceeding back in the direction from which they had come. The U-turn occurred at a location where it was unlikely that the cars would have reversed directions because they had missed an exit. Moreover, the vehicles in question bore Mexicali license plates and the U-turn occurred just after a sign indicating that a Border Patrol checkpoint that had been closed for some time was now open. We conclude that these factors, although not overwhelming, are sufficient to constitute reasonable suspicion for the stop. In reaching that result, however, we firmly reject any reliance upon the Hispanic appearance or ethnicity of the defendants. * * *

* * *

[The concurring opinion of KOZINSKI, CIRCUIT JUDGE, joined by JUDGES T.G. NELSON, KLEINFELD and SILVERMAN, is omitted.]

NOTES AND QUESTIONS ON ENFORCEMENT AND ETHNICITY

1. In a leading pre-September 11 discussion, Kevin Johnson tied profil- ing in immigration law enforcement to broader immigration policy:

> Unfortunately, core features of immigration law in addition to race profiling contribute to less than full membership in U.S. society for persons of Latin American ancestry. The public charge exclusion, which bars admission of immigrants "likely at any time to become a public charge," has a disparate impact on working class and low income citizens and lawful immigrants of Latin American ancestry who seek to bring family members to the United States. The annual per-country ceilings impose a longer waiting period for potential Mexican immigrants, many of whom seek to join family members residing lawfully in the country, than that faced by similarly situated immigrants from other nations. For the most part, the diversity visa system excludes Mexican immigrants and favors potential immigrants from Europe. By diminishing the rights of Mexican American citizens and lawful immigrants seeking to bring family members to this country, these measures conflict with fundamental equality principles.

Johnson, *The Case Against Racial Profiling in Immigration Enforcement*, 78 Wash. U.L.Q. 675, 728–29 (2000).

And yet, more new lawful permanent residents come from Mexico than from any other country, accounting for about 13 percent of new green cards holders in 2010. *See* Monger & Yankay, U.S. Legal Permanent Residents: 2010, at 4 table 3 (DHS Office of Immigration Statistics 2011). But what does "equality" mean in this setting? For analyses of the complexities of this question, see Legomsky, *Immigration, Equality, and Diversity*, 31 Colum. J. Transnat'l L. 319, 332–33 (1993); Motomura, *Whose Alien Nation?: Two Models of Constitutional Immigration Law*, 94 Mich. L. Rev. 1927, 1939–42 (1996).

2. Beyond the immigration context, Frank Wu has outlined a useful framework for thinking about profiling. The first question, he suggests, is whether law enforcement uses profiling based on race, ethnicity, or other factors. The second question is whether it is rational, *e.g.*, whether persons of Asian ancestry are more likely than Caucasians to be foreign-born. And the third is whether profiling, even if rational, is morally right. Wu emphasizes that the second and third questions are quite separate, so that racial profiling might be rational and yet wrong. *See generally* F. Wu, Yellow: Race in America Beyond Black and White 173–213 (2002).

With Wu's framework in mind, why does Judge Reinhardt conclude in *Montero–Camargo* that "Hispanic appearance" is not a relevant factor in "reasonable suspicion"? Would he have reached the same result in a border area sparsely populated by Latinos? *See United States v. Manzo–Jurado*, 457 F.3d 928, 935 n.6 (9th Cir. 2006) (noting that the holding in *Montero–Camargo* "is inapplicable here because Havre, Montana, is sparsely populated with Hispanics" and citing U.S. Census data "indicating that Hispanics comprise 1.5 percent of the Havre population").

(iii) Remedies for Fourth Amendment Violations

Is evidence admissible in removal proceedings even if the government obtained it in violation of the Fourth Amendment? Generally yes, said the U.S. Supreme Court in *INS v. Lopez–Mendoza*, 468 U.S. 1032, 1043–50, 104 S.Ct. 3479, 82 L.Ed.2d 778 (1984). Distinguishing criminal prosecution, Justice O'Connor's majority opinion weighed "the likely social benefits of excluding unlawfully seized evidence against the likely costs." She was skeptical about the benefits, noting that deportation would still be possible in many cases without evidence derived from the arrest, that few officers would expect challenges to the circumstances of the arrest, that the government has its own scheme to deter Fourth Amendment violations, and that alternative private remedies are available. O'Connor noted that an exclusionary rule would have "unusual and significant" costs, including that it would "require the courts to close their eyes to ongoing violations of the law" and complicate the system of deportation proceedings.

Four Justices dissented. Justices Brennan and Marshall rejected the majority's balancing, arguing that "the basis of the exclusionary rule does not derive from its effectiveness as a deterrent, but is instead found in the requirements of the Fourth Amendment itself." Justice White, joined in substantial part by Justice Stevens, argued that "the costs and benefits of applying the exclusionary rule in civil deportation proceedings do not differ in any significant way from the costs and benefits of applying the rule in ordinary criminal proceedings."

But in a part of the opinion that only three other Justices joined, Justice O'Connor added:

> Our conclusions concerning the exclusionary rule's value might change, if there developed good reason to believe that Fourth Amendment violations by INS officers were widespread. Finally, we do not

deal here with egregious violations of Fourth Amendment or other liberties that might transgress notions of fundamental fairness and undermine the probative value of the evidence obtained.

Counting the four dissenters, eight justices seemed to recognize an egregious violation exception. When might this exception mean that unlawfully obtained evidence will be suppressed in removal proceedings?

LOPEZ–RODRIGUEZ v. MUKASEY

United States Court of Appeals, Ninth Circuit, 2008.
536 F.3d 1012.

Canby, Circuit Judge.

* * *

In October 2000, the Immigration and Naturalization Service ("INS") received a tip that a female by the name of Fabiola was fraudulently using a birth certificate belonging to Sugeyra Torres–Carillo, a citizen of the United States, to obtain employment. The tip also indicated that the suspect lived at a specified address in Fresno, California. [Fabiola Gastelum–Lopez ("Gastelum") and Luz Lopez–Rodriguez ("Lopez")], niece and aunt, resided at that address. Gastelum was seventeen years old at the time.

Three INS agents decided to act on the tip and visit the residence to investigate the matter. They did not obtain an arrest or search warrant prior to conducting their visit. * * * Once inside, the three INS agents questioned Gastelum. They asked her whether she was "Sugeyra." She answered that she was. They asked her to provide the names of her parents. She complied. They asked her where she had been born, and she responded that she was born in Texas. They asked where in Texas she was born, and she did not reply. They asked, "Who is Fabiola?" She said she was Fabiola. They immediately handcuffed her. The agents also arrested Lopez on suspicion of being an alien unlawfully present in the United States.

While in INS custody, Gastelum and Lopez were questioned about, among other things, their country of origin and immigration status in the United States. On the basis of the information they obtained, the INS agents prepared individual Forms I–213, Record of Deportable/ Inadmissible Aliens, for Gastelum and Lopez. * * * According to the forms, both Gastelum and Lopez are natives and citizens of Mexico not authorized to be in the United States. The forms also show that neither Gastelum nor Lopez had a criminal record.

The INS agents also produced a Record of Sworn Statement by Gastelum. In her sworn statement, Gastelum acknowledged that she was a native and citizen of Mexico. She also admitted that she had received a birth certificate in the name of Sugeyra from a 43–year–old foreman, Francisco Lopez–Fuentes (Fuentes), who had supervised her when she worked in the fields. Fuentes did not ask Gastelum for any money in exchange for the birth certificate.

The government issued Notices to Appear in removal proceedings to both Gastelum and Lopez. In joint proceedings, Gastelum and Lopez moved to suppress the Forms I–213 as well as Gastelum's sworn statement. They submitted an affidavit by Gastelum asserting that she did not consent to the INS agents' entry into their home. In the Forms I–213, the INS agents asserted that she had in fact consented. The IJ required Gastelum to testify at the removal hearing in support of her motion to suppress. She testified that, when the agents arrived, she was asleep in her bedroom. Her aunt Lopez woke her up to let her know that some individuals were calling her. Gastelum went to the door, which was "slightly open and not locked," "opened it a little more and . . . peeked outside." She saw two men standing outside the door. They asked her if her name was "Sugeyra." She did not open the door for them and did not allow them to enter. She testified that the two men pushed the door and entered, accompanied by a third, female agent. Once inside, the agents proceeded to interrogate her as described above. After Gastelum answered several questions and was being handcuffed, the INS agents finally identified themselves.

* * *

* * * We conclude that, on the facts developed before the IJ, the evidence of alienage[5] contained in these documents was obtained in violation of Gastelum's and Lopez's Fourth Amendment rights and that the violation was "egregious." Because the government did not produce any other evidence tending to show the petitioners' alienage in the proceedings before the IJ, we grant their petition for review and reverse the order of removal.

1. FOURTH AMENDMENT

* * * The presumption of unconstitutionality that accompanies "the [warrantless] entry into a home to conduct a search or make an arrest" may be overcome only by showing "consent or exigent circumstances." *Steagald v. United States,* 451 U.S. 204, 211, 101 S.Ct. 1642, 68 L.Ed.2d 38 (1981).

The government does not dispute that the INS agents entered the residence of Gastelum and Lopez and, after briefly questioning Gastelum, arrested both in their home. It is also evident that, prior to entering the premises, the INS agents did not obtain a warrant to arrest either Gastelum or Lopez or, for that matter, to conduct a search of their residence. The government makes no claim of exigent circumstances.

---

5. "[T]he INS must show only identity and alienage; the burden then shifts to the respondent to prove the time, place, and manner of his entry." *INS v. Lopez–Mendoza,* 468 U.S. 1032, 1039, 104 S.Ct. 3479, 82 L.Ed.2d 778 (1984). Because the identity of an alien in removal proceedings is "never itself suppressible as a fruit of an unlawful arrest, even if it is conceded that an unlawful arrest, search, or interrogation occurred," *id.,* the only suppressible evidence at issue here is that pertaining to alienage.

Thus, in order to overcome the presumption of unconstitutionality attaching to the agents' entry, the government must show that the petitioners gave legally sufficient consent.

In relevant part, the IJ summarized her factual findings as follows:

> [Gastelum] evidently came to the door when they knocked and, upon establishing a verbal contact with her, [the agents] pushed the door open and entered and continued to talk to her. At no time did she tell them to leave or tell them she did not want to talk to them, although, apparently from what she recalls, they did not identify themselves until they were handcuffing her.

* * *

* * * As we have made clear, "the government may not show consent to enter from the defendant's failure to object to the entry." *United States v. Shaibu,* 920 F.2d 1423, 1427 (9th Cir.1990). We have sustained an *inference* of consent to enter a residence only under very limited circumstances—i.e., where the officers have verbally requested permission to enter and the occupant's action suggests assent, or where prior collaborative interactions between the suspect and the officers make the inference of consent unequivocal. Here, there is no indication that the officers made any request to enter or that Gastelum collaborated with the INS officers in any way when they were at the door. Accordingly, the bare fact that Gastelum neither refused to speak to them nor ordered them to leave after they pushed the door open and entered her home is insufficient to establish consent. As a consequence, the arrest of the petitioners in their home violated their Fourth Amendment rights.

The government contends that it had a right to detain Gastelum for questioning because it had a reasonable suspicion that she had used a false birth certificate. * * * This argument misses the point. The question is not whether the agents could have detained Gastelum for questioning had they encountered her outside of her residence. The issue is whether they could enter her home without a warrant or consent. In the absence of exigent circumstances, they could not. * * *

2. APPLICABILITY OF THE EXCLUSIONARY RULE FOR "EGREGIOUS" VIOLATIONS

The statements sought to be suppressed were obtained from Gastelum and Lopez in the custody immediately following the unconstitutional entry of their residence. The government has made no attempt to bear its burden of showing any change in circumstances or attenuation that would prevent the statements from qualifying as fruits of the Fourth Amendment violation. The statements would therefore be excludible in a criminal case. In the present proceeding, however, we must next consider whether "the violations were sufficiently egregious to warrant the application of the exclusionary rule in these civil deportation proceedings." *Orhorhaghe* [*v. INS,* 38 F.3d 488, 501 (9th Cir. 1994).] A Fourth Amendment violation is "egregious" if "evidence is obtained by deliberate violations of the [F]ourth [A]mendment, or by conduct a *reasonable officer should [have* *known]* is in violation of the Constitution." *Gonzalez–Rivera v. INS,* 22 F.3d 1441, 1449 (9th Cir. 1994) (quoting *Adamson [v. Commissioner,* 745 F.2d, 541, 545 (1984)]) (emphasis and final alteration original). * * *

Few principles in criminal procedure are as well established as the maxim that "the Fourth Amendment has drawn a firm line at the entrance to the house. Absent exigent circumstances, that threshold may not reasonably be crossed without a warrant." *Payton [v. New York,* 445 U.S. 573, 590, 100 S.Ct. 1371, 1382, 63 L.Ed. 2d 639 (1980)]. Accordingly, although the voluntary consent of a party who has authority over the premises renders the warrantless entry of a person's home by law enforcement personnel constitutionally valid, exceptions to the warrant requirement are "jealously and carefully drawn," *Jones v. United States,* 357 U.S. 493, 499, 78 S.Ct. 1253, 2 L.Ed.2d 1514 (1958). As we have already noted, in keeping with the narrow scope of the consent exception, we "ha[ve] never sanctioned entry to the home based on inferred consent" in the absence of a request by the officers or ongoing, affirmative cooperation by the suspect. *Shaibu,* 920 F.2d at 1426 (citing *United States v. Impink,* 728 F.2d 1228, 1233–34 (9th Cir.1984)). * * *

Against this unequivocal doctrinal backdrop, reasonable officers would not have thought it lawful to push open the door to petitioners' home simply because Gastelum did not "tell them to leave or [that] she did not want to talk to them." * * * Nor has the government pointed to any authority in our Fourth Amendment jurisprudence suggesting that the warrant requirement applies with any less force in the administrative context. We conclude that reasonable INS agents should have known that they were violating the Fourth Amendment when they entered Gastelum's and Lopez's residence. * * * Thus, the INS agents' Fourth Amendment violation was "egregious" under this Circuit's controlling interpretation of the term. The fruits of the constitutional violation accordingly should have been suppressed.

* * *

BYBEE, CIRCUIT JUDGE, concurring:

I concur fully in the majority opinion. I write separately to caution that our precedent has set us on a collision course with the Supreme Court.

* * *

* * * In our circuit, the exclusionary rule must be applied in a deportation proceeding if the agents violated the Fourth Amendment and "the agents committed the violations deliberately or by conduct a reasonable officer should have known would violate the Constitution." *Orhorhaghe,* 38 F.3d at 493. If I am reading our decisions correctly, we have linked the exclusionary rule in civil cases to the qualified immunity standard: any constitutional violation for which an officer would lose immunity from suit is sufficient to trigger the exclusionary rule in a civil deportation proceeding. Regardless of how we arrived at this definition of

"egregious," it is a definition of an exception that is almost certain, over time, to swallow up the rule.[1] Moreover, I suspect it is a definition which might even include the unseemly conduct of the INS agents in *Lopez–Mendoza,* which the Court held did *not* warrant applying the exclusionary rule in that petitioner's immigration proceedings. *See Lopez–Mendoza,* 468 U.S. at 1036–37, 104 S.Ct. 3479 (describing how INS agents created a chaotic mass exodus of workers from a processing plant and then positioned themselves at the plant exits to observe which fleeing workers could not speak English and which averted their eyes).

* * * Our case law appears destined to import the exclusionary rule, with all of its attendant costs, back into immigration proceedings, after the Court has taken it out. At some point, we may wish to revisit our position.

NOTES AND QUESTIONS ON REMEDIES FOR FOURTH AMENDMENT VIOLATIONS

1. As the court observes in its footnote 5, *Lopez–Mendoza* made clear that motions to suppress cannot be used to exclude the identity of the respondent in a removal proceedings, but rather must seek to exclude or suppress specific evidence, such as evidence of alienage, which is essential to establishing removability.

2. Some Ninth Circuit decisions have granted suppression motions based on egregious violations when the enforcement was based on apparent ethnicity. For example, *Gonzalez–Rivera v. INS,* 22 F.3d 1441, 1449 (9th Cir. 1994), suppressed evidence from a vehicle stop based *solely* on the passengers' Hispanic appearance. The court held that this was an egregious Fourth Amendment violation because it was committed in bad faith when the law enforcement officer knew or reasonably should have known that his conduct would violate the Constitution. Another Ninth Circuit decision, *Orhorhaghe v. INS,* 38 F.3d 488, 501–04 (9th Cir. 1994), found it egregious to investigate a noncitizen because of his "Nigerian-sounding name" and then seize him outside of his apartment and conduct a nonconsensual, warrantless entry. Several Second Circuit decisions have indicated that it would consider race-based violations to be egregious. *See, e.g., Pinto–Montoya v. Mukasey,* 540 F.3d 126, 131 (2d Cir. 2008).

3. As Judge Bybee notes, the other circuits that have recognized and applied the egregious violation exception have interpreted it more narrowly. In addition to the First and Second Circuits mentioned in his opinion, *see also Puc–Ruiz v. Holder,* 629 F.3d 771 (8th Cir. 2010) (denying suppression). *Cf. Almeida–Amaral v. Gonzales,* 461 F.3d 231, 237 (2d Cir. 2006) ("Because of

---

1. The First and Second Circuits appear to have adopted a more stringent definition of "egregious." A mere violation—even an obvious violation—is not grounds for excluding the evidence without some additional aggravating circumstance. *See Kandamar v. Gonzales,* 464 F.3d 65, 71 (1st Cir. 2006) (requiring "specific evidence of … government misconduct by threats, coercion, or physical abuse" to demonstrate egregiousness); *Almeida–Amaral v. Gonzales,* 461 F.3d 231, 236 (2d Cir. 2006) ("*Lopez–Mendoza* requires more than a violation to justify exclusion. It demands "egregiousness." … Thus, the exclusion may well be proper where the seizure itself is gross or unreasonable *in addition to* being without a plausible legal ground…." (emphasis added)).

the absence of evidence that the stop was race-based, we conclude that Almeida–Amaral has not established that the Fourth Amendment violation was an egregious one."). Is he correct is suggesting that the egregious violation exception, as interpreted and applied by the Ninth Circuit, will swallow the rule in *Lopez–Mendoza*?

4. Justice O'Connor wrote in *Lopez–Mendoza*: "Our conclusions concerning the exclusionary rule's value might change, if there developed good reason to believe that Fourth Amendment violations by INS officers were widespread." What does this mean? For an argument based on this statement for applying the exclusionary rule to removal proceedings, see Elias, *"Good Reason to Believe": Widespread Constitutional Violations in the Course of Immigration Enforcement and the Case for Revisiting* Lopez–Mendoza, 2008 Wis. L. Rev. 1109. In *Melnitsenko v. Mukasey*, 517 F.3d 42, 47 (2d Cir. 2008), the Second Circuit declined to reconsider on this basis for failure to raise the argument before the BIA.

5. DHS regulations provide as follows:

(1) Interrogation is questioning designed to elicit specific information. An immigration officer, like any other person, has the right to ask questions of anyone as long as the immigration officer does not restrain the freedom of an individual, not under arrest, to walk away.

(2) If the immigration officer has a reasonable suspicion, based on specific articulable facts, that the person being questioned is, or is attempting to be, engaged in an offense against the United States or is an alien illegally in the United States, the immigration officer may briefly detain the person for questioning.

(3) Information obtained from this questioning may provide the basis for a subsequent arrest * * *.

8 C.F.R. § 287.8(b).

Evidence obtained in violation of this regulation or others can be suppressed, according to the BIA in *Matter of Garcia–Flores*, 17 I & N Dec. 325, 327 (BIA 1980), if the regulation was promulgated to benefit the alien and the violation resulted in prejudice.

6. Suppose federal immigration officers raid a workplace after receiving a tip about unauthorized workers from the employer, who wanted to disrupt union organizing, in clear violation of federal labor law. Should the evidence obtained in the raid be suppressed when the apprehended workers are put in removal hearings? Here is one answer:

[The apprehended worker] next argues that * * * the INS knew or should have known that it was being used by [the company] to defeat union-organizing activities.

* * *

We decline [his] invitation to fashion an exclusionary rule for evidence obtained in violation of an individual's First Amendment rights. Beyond violations of the Fourth Amendment, it is clear from *Lopez–Mendoza* that the exclusionary rule is applicable, if at all, only to deprivations that affect the fairness or reliability of the deportation proceeding. However, there is nothing inherently unfair about utilizing evidence obtained during a labor dispute, nor does the existence of a labor dispute make that evidence any less reliable. Thus, this case does not present us with the type of situation to which the exclusionary rule even arguably is applicable.

Montero v. INS, 124 F.3d 381, 385–86 (2d Cir. 1997).

The INS apparently did not know of the labor dispute when it began to investigate unauthorized workers at the worksite, but then learned before the raid that the tip came from the employer. What if the government had known this from the start? Or should immigration officers stay away worksites with labor disputes?

In March 2011, ICE and the Department of Labor entered into a new memorandum of understanding, available at <http://www.dol.gov/_sec/media/reports/hispaniclaborforce/dhs-dol-mou.pdf> meant to "deconflict" their investigation and enforcement activities at worksites. Further, ICE for many years has implemented a standard format for recording tips and complaints. Officers receiving the information are to inquire into whether the informant is engaged in a dispute or conflict with the individual involved. Finding that there is such a dispute does not preclude further investigation or enforcement, but it enables ICE officers to make better informed decisions about the validity of the tip and the appropriate response.

Compare article 36 of the Vienna Convention on Consular Relations, April 24, 1963, 21 U.S.T. 77, 5596 U.N.T.S. 261, which requires notification of consular officials of any arrested noncitizen's home country. The U.S. Supreme Court declined to adopt suppression of evidence as a remedy for a violation in *Sanchez–Llamas v. Oregon*, 548 U.S. 331, 343–50, 126 S.Ct. 2669, 2677–82, 165 L.Ed.2d 557 (2006).

b. Interrogations

Under the famous case of *Miranda v. Arizona*, 384 U.S. 436, 86 S.Ct. 1602, 16 L.Ed.2d 694 (1966), failure to inform an individual who is in custody of her rights to remain silent and to have a lawyer renders any statements she makes during a custodial interrogation inadmissible in her criminal trial. The courts have not read the Constitution to require such warnings in the removal context. Under current law, failure to give warnings means that any admissions by the noncitizen could be excluded from subsequent criminal proceedings, but the admissions would not be excluded automatically from the removal proceeding itself. *See, e.g., Bustos–Torres v. INS*, 898 F.2d 1053, 1056–57 (5th Cir. 1990).

This conclusion, like *Lopez–Mendoza*, relies heavily on the characterization of removal proceedings as civil rather than criminal, as well as on the following considerations:

A principal purpose of the *Miranda* warnings is to permit the suspect to make an intelligent decision as to whether to answer the government agent's questions. In deportation proceedings, however—in light of the alien's burden of proof, the requirement that the alien answer non-incriminating questions, the potential adverse consequences to the alien of remaining silent, and the fact that an alien's statement is admissible in the deportation hearing despite his lack of counsel at the preliminary interrogation—*Miranda* warnings would be not only inappropriate but could also serve to mislead the alien.

Chavez–Raya v. INS, 519 F.2d 397, 402 (7th Cir. 1975).

The current regulations provide:

> Except in the case of an alien subject to the expedited removal provisions of section 235(b)(1)(A) of the Act, an alien arrested without warrant and placed in formal proceedings under section 238 or 240 of the Act will be advised of the reasons for his or her arrest and the right to be represented at no expense to the Government. The examining officer will provide the alien with a list of the available free legal services provided by organizations and attorneys qualified under 8 CFR part 1003 and organizations recognized under § 292.2 of this chapter or 8 CFR 1292.2 that are located in the district where the hearing will be held. The examining officer shall note on Form I–862 [Notice to Appear] that such a list was provided to the alien. The officer will also advise the alien that any statement made may be used against him or her in a subsequent proceeding.

8 C.F.R. § 287.3(c). Interestingly, however, The regulation also requires a notation on the NTA that a list of free legal services was provided to the alien. This seems to presuppose that the list is provided before the NTA is filed. However, to the extent that "formal proceedings" commence with the filing of the NTA in immigration court, this regulation suggests that notifications are required only after the NTA is filed, and the BIA so held in *Matter of E–R–M–F– & A–S–M–*, 25 I & N Dec. 580, 582 (BIA 2011).

Whether warnings are given or not, the courts and the BIA will sometimes order the exclusion of prior statements on due process grounds where the government's behavior violated fundamental fairness, or the circumstances of the interrogation rendered the statements involuntary, or the noncitizen was prejudiced by the government's violation of regulations promulgated for his benefit. *See Navia–Duran v. INS*, 568 F.2d 803, 805 (1st Cir. 1977) (ordering evidence excluded where agents searched noncitizen's apartment without warrant or consent, took her into custody for questioning that lasted several hours until 2:00 a.m., and insisted that she had no choice but to agree to depart in two weeks).

For suppression motions, does the due process test, by being more flexible, provide a better accommodation between law enforcement needs and the rights of noncitizens than application of a strict *Miranda* rule?

c. Other Constitutional Violations: Equal Protection and First Amendment

Enforcement efforts also must not violate equal protection. This is the key issue in the next case, which does not involve suppression of evidence but instead is a civil suit under 42 U.S.C. § 1983 seeking damages from government officials for violating an individual's constitutional rights.

FARM LABOR ORGANIZING COMMITTEE
v. OHIO STATE HIGHWAY PATROL

United States Court of Appeals, Sixth Circuit, 2002.
308 F.3d 523.

MOORE, CIRCUIT JUDGE.

* * *

Plaintiffs Jose Aguilar and Irma Esparza ("plaintiffs") are lawfully admitted permanent resident aliens. On Sunday, March 26, 1995, Aguilar and Esparza were driving from their home in Chicago, Illinois, to Toledo, Ohio, to visit family members. During this trip, an Ohio State Highway Patrol ("OSHP") trooper, Kevin Kiefer, stopped Aguilar and Esparza for driving with a faulty headlight. After the plaintiffs pulled over, Trooper Kiefer approached the plaintiffs' car and asked to see Aguilar's driver's license. Aguilar provided Trooper Kiefer with a valid Illinois driver's license. Trooper Kiefer then ordered Aguilar out of the car and placed him in the back of his cruiser.

Almost immediately thereafter, a second OSHP cruiser arrived. A trooper from the second cruiser walked a drug-sniffing dog around the outside of the plaintiffs' vehicle. The dog "alerted," indicating that the vehicle contained narcotics.[2]

The second trooper then asked Esparza for identification. She offered the trooper an Illinois identification card, but the trooper reportedly grabbed her wallet and removed her green card. The trooper then instructed Esparza to step out of the vehicle. She was locked in the back of Trooper Kiefer's cruiser next to Aguilar. Trooper Kiefer then demanded to see Aguilar's green card. The green cards of both Aguilar and Esparza were valid and in force at the time of this encounter.

After examining the green cards, the troopers asked Aguilar and Esparza where they had obtained their green cards and whether they had paid for them. The troopers were attempting to inquire whether the documents were forged, since green cards are not offered for sale. Aguilar and Esparza speak limited English, however, and believed that the troopers were asking whether they had paid the required processing fees. They responded that they had paid for the cards, meaning that they had paid all required fees. Trooper Kiefer interpreted the plaintiffs' response as an indication that the cards were likely forged, and retained the green cards for authentication.

Trooper Kiefer was unable to contact the INS to verify the authenticity of plaintiffs' green cards at the time of the encounter, because it was a Sunday, so he took the green cards and let the plaintiffs go. * * *

The next day (Monday), the plaintiffs retained an attorney. That day, paralegal Arturo Ortiz contacted the OSHP on behalf of Aguilar and

---

2. It was later determined that the dog had alerted in error, and that neither of the plaintiffs were carrying drugs.

Esparza, but was unable to obtain assistance because he lacked information regarding the incident. On Thursday, Ortiz again contacted OSHP and spoke to Trooper Kiefer. Kiefer returned the green cards personally that same day, four days after the initial seizure. When asked in his deposition why it took so long to verify the green cards, Trooper Kiefer explained that he had taken a few days off from work and was unable to reach the INS during that time.

The plaintiffs contend that Trooper Kiefer's actions were, in part, the product of a pattern and practice by the OSHP of questioning motorists about their immigration status on the basis of their Hispanic appearance. From the record, it appears that the OSHP—particularly its Traffic and Drug Interdiction Team (TDIT)—began taking a more active role in immigration enforcement in 1995. Pursuant to this role, OSHP troopers have been known to inquire into motorists' immigration status during routine traffic stops. When these inquiries lead an OSHP trooper to conclude that an individual may be an illegal immigrant, the trooper will contact the Border Patrol and detain the suspect until the Border Patrol arrives. * * * Although the OSHP maintains that it does not do so frequently, troopers sometimes seize alien registration cards of suspected illegal immigrants and deliver them to federal authorities.

* * *

Plaintiffs allege that Trooper Kiefer violated their rights under the Equal Protection Clause of the Fourteenth Amendment by targeting them for investigation concerning immigration status and seizing their green cards because of their Hispanic appearance. * * * Trooper Kiefer contends that he is entitled to qualified immunity because the undisputed facts show that his inquiries into the plaintiffs' immigration status were motivated by the plaintiffs' difficulties speaking and understanding English, which he contends is a legitimate race-neutral reason for the investigative steps taken.

* * * The plaintiffs allege that Trooper Kiefer singled them out for inquiry into their immigration status on the basis of their Hispanic appearance during the course of a lawful traffic stop. The plaintiffs do not challenge the validity of their initial stop for a faulty headlight. Nor do they assert that the questioning exceeded the permissible scope of the stop under the Fourth Amendment. Nevertheless, as this court has recognized, "[t]he Equal Protection Clause of the Fourteenth Amendment provides citizens a degree of protection independent of the Fourth Amendment protection against unreasonable searches and seizures." *United States v. Avery,* 137 F.3d 343, 352 (6th Cir. 1997). * * * [I]f the plaintiffs can show that they were subjected to unequal treatment based upon their race or ethnicity during the course of an otherwise lawful traffic stop, that would be sufficient to demonstrate a violation of the Equal Protection Clause. *Cf. United States v. Montero–Camargo,* 208 F.3d 1122, 1135 (9th Cir.) (*en banc*) (holding that equal protection principles precluded use of Hispanic appearance as a relevant factor for Fourth Amendment individualized

suspicion requirement), *cert. denied,* 531 U.S. 889, 121 S.Ct. 211, 148 L.Ed.2d 148 (2000).

The Supreme Court has explained that a claimant alleging selective enforcement of facially neutral criminal laws must demonstrate that the challenged law enforcement practice "had a discriminatory effect and that it was motivated by a discriminatory purpose." *Wayte v. United States,* 470 U.S. 598, 608, 105 S.Ct. 1524, 84 L.Ed.2d 547 (1985). "To establish discriminatory effect in a race case, the claimant must show that similarly situated individuals of a different race were not prosecuted." *United States v. Armstrong,* 517 U.S. 456, 465, 116 S.Ct. 1480, 134 L.Ed.2d 687 (1996). * * * Determining whether official action was motivated by intentional discrimination "demands a sensitive inquiry into such circumstantial and direct evidence of intent as may be available." *Village of Arlington Heights v. Metro. Hous. Dev. Corp.,* 429 U.S. 252, 266, 97 S.Ct. 555, 50 L.Ed.2d 450 (1977). "[A]n invidious discriminatory purpose may often be inferred from the totality of the relevant facts, including the fact, if it is true, that the [practice] bears more heavily on one race than another." *Washington v. Davis,* 426 U.S. 229, 242, 96 S.Ct. 2040, 48 L.Ed.2d 597 (1976).

* * *

In its April 20, 2000, order, the district court determined that the plaintiffs had presented sufficient evidence to prove the requisite facts for a prima facie case of intentional discrimination under the selective prosecution framework. * * * The court noted that the record contained a range of circumstantial evidence supporting such a finding of intent. Perhaps most significantly, the court cited the deposition testimony of Kiefer and other OSHP officials:

> Trooper Kiefer . . . testified that when he found Hispanic passengers hiding under a blanket, he called the Border Patrol, but that if he found white people hiding under a blanket, he would not. Sgt. Elling likewise testified that he would not call the Border Patrol regarding a motorist . . . unless ["he] would think that they would probably be Hispanic in nature." And Trooper Pahl admitted that she once had contacted the Border Patrol after coming across two Hispanic men whose car had broken down, but that she wouldn't do the same for a white man.

The court also cited additional circumstantial evidence of discriminatory intent. The court noted that over ninety percent of OSHP's immigration inquiries concerned Hispanic motorists. The court also appears to have credited plaintiffs' argument that "[g]iven defendants' admitted lack of training in the identification of illegal immigrants, the only reasoned basis on which to question a motorist about immigration status . . . is the motorist's Hispanic appearance coupled with indicators of Hispanic ethnicity." * * *

As to the discriminatory effect prong, the district court observed that "[t]he burden rests on plaintiffs to show, by a preponderance of the evidence, that they were treated differently than similarly situated non-minorities." The court considered, and rejected, defendants' argument that "no evidence presented thus far indicates that Hispanic motorists are treated differently than non-Hispanic motorists." * * * The district court noted that "most motorists . . . [who were] asked about their green cards were Hispanic-looking" and defendants' misinformation and lack of training concerning what facts give rise to reasonable suspicion of immigration violations.

* * *

* * * The selective enforcement framework does not require a plaintiff to show that the defendant had *no* race-neutral reasons for the challenged enforcement decision. Instead, it is enough to show that the challenged action was taken "at least *in part* 'because of' . . . its adverse effects upon an identifiable group." *Wayte,* 470 U.S. at 610, 105 S.Ct. 1524 (quoting *Feeney,* 442 U.S. at 279, 99 S.Ct. 2282).

* * *

[W]e disagree with Trooper Kiefer's contention that the plaintiffs' difficulty speaking English necessarily establishes a valid race-neutral basis for initiating an immigration investigation. Kiefer relies on *United States v. Ortiz,* 422 U.S. 891, 897, 95 S.Ct. 2585, 45 L.Ed.2d 623 (1975), in which Supreme Court identified one's "inability to speak English" as one of many factors that may be taken into account in deciding whether there is probable cause to search a private vehicle for illegal aliens. * * *

We think *Ortiz* provides little guidance in the instant case. *Ortiz* was a Fourth Amendment case involving automobile searches at a Border Patrol checkpoint less than 100 miles from the U.S.–Mexican border. The respondent in *Ortiz* did not raise a Fourteenth Amendment claim and the Court mentioned the use of one's English-speaking ability as a basis for selection only once in a laundry list of factors that might be used in deciding whether there is probable cause to refer an automobile for further inspection. * * * Moreover, the Supreme Court has cautioned against extending the logic of border enforcement cases to situations remote from the border, where the government interest in immigration policing may be less compelling. *See United States v. Martinez–Fuerte,* 428 U.S. 543, 564 n.17, 96 S.Ct. 3074, 49 L.Ed.2d 1116 (1976); *accord United States v. Brignoni–Ponce,* 422 U.S. 873, 881, 95 S.Ct. 2574, 45 L.Ed.2d 607 (1975).

The Supreme Court did consider the equal protection implications of using language as a basis for selection in *Hernandez v. New York,* 500 U.S. 352, 111 S.Ct. 1859, 114 L.Ed.2d 395 (1991). In *Hernandez,* the Court cautioned that when a government official uses as a criterion for decision a person's ability to speak a *particular* language that is closely associated with a specific ethnic group, that fact may "raise . . . a plausible, though not a necessary, inference that language might be a pretext for what in fact were race-based" actions. *Id.* at 363, 111 S.Ct. 1859. * * *

Considering *Ortiz* in light of *Hernandez,* we think that an officer's reliance upon a suspect's *inability to speak English* may be a proper race-neutral factor, but that fact questions as to pretext are necessarily present where an officer acts based upon the fact that a suspect speaks *Spanish* due to the close connection between the Spanish language and a specific ethnic community, such as the large migrant labor community in Northwest Ohio. In light of this principle, it may be that genuine issues of material fact exist as to whether Trooper Kiefer's reliance on plaintiffs' inability to speak English was a legitimate race-neutral reason or a mere pretext for discrimination. * * *

[The court found that the relevant law was clearly established at the time of the encounter, and that therefore the district court correctly denied Kiefer's motion for summary judgment on his qualified immunity defense to the plaintiffs' equal protection claims. The court then found that Kiefer violated the plaintiffs' Fourth Amendment rights by detaining their green cards for four days without probable cause, that this law was clearly established, and that therefore the district court properly denied his summary judgment motion on qualified immunity as to these claims.]

* * *

KENNEDY, CIRCUIT JUDGE, dissenting.

* * *

[T]he majority would adopt a standard shifting to the defendant the burden of establishing that the same decision would have resulted even if the impermissible purpose had not been considered, relying on *Wayte* and *Armstrong.* The effect of the majority's holding would greatly diminish the protection of qualified immunity in equal protection claims. It would be a rare case involving a minority where plaintiff could not assert an issue of fact as to an officer's intent no matter how strong the non-discriminatory motive may be. * * *

* * *

NOTES AND QUESTIONS ON OTHER CONSTITUTIONAL VIOLATIONS

1. In *Farm Labor Organizing Committee,* suppression of evidence would have been no remedy at all, so plaintiffs pursued another remedy, seeking an award of damages for the constitutional violation. Other remedies include *Bivens* suits directly against a federal officer in his private capacity for the violation of an individual's constitutional rights, also resulting in a damages award if successful. *See Bivens v. Six Unknown Agents of the Federal Bureau of Narcotics,* 403 U.S. 388, 91 S.Ct. 1999, 29 L.Ed.2d 619 (1971). Another potential remedy is an action under the Federal Tort Claims Act, 28 U.S.C. §§ 1346(b), 2671–2680. Attorneys' fees may be available in lawsuits successfully seeking some of these remedies.

2. The U.S. Supreme Court briefly addressed selective prosecution in the First Amendment context in *Reno v. American–Arab Anti–Discrimination Committee*, 525 U.S. 471, 119 S.Ct. 936, 142 L.Ed.2d 940 (1999), which we encountered earlier in the materials on deportability in Chapter Seven, p. 677 *supra*. The respondents, eight noncitizens who belonged to the Popular Front for the Liberation of Palestine, alleged that the INS selectively enforced immigration laws against them in violation of their First and Fifth Amendment rights. The district court issued a preliminary injunction stopping the deportation proceedings against some of the noncitizens as amounting to unlawful selective prosecution.

The issue that reached the Supreme Court was jurisdiction, since INA § 242(b)(9) seems to require a final removal order before decisions in proceedings may be challenged, and § 242(g) seems to eliminate federal court jurisdiction over decisions or actions "to commence proceedings, adjudicate cases, or execute removal orders." The noncitizens sought immediate review, arguing that selective prosecution would otherwise unconstitutionally chill their exercise of First Amendment rights. They claimed that under the doctrine of constitutional avoidance, the Court should read the jurisdictional statute to allow immediate review to avoid serious constitutional questions concerning the First Amendment.

Finding that § 242(g) deprived the district court of jurisdiction, the Court, in a majority opinion by Justice Scalia, addressed selective prosecution:

> * * * As a general matter—and assuredly in the context of claims such as those put forward in the present case—an alien unlawfully in this country has no constitutional right to assert selective enforcement as a defense against his deportation.

> Even in the criminal-law field, a selective prosecution claim is a *rara avis*. Because such claims invade a special province of the Executive—its prosecutorial discretion—we have emphasized that the standard for proving them is particularly demanding, requiring a criminal defendant to introduce "clear evidence" displacing the presumption that a prosecutor has acted lawfully. *United States v. Armstrong*, 517 U.S. 456, 463–465, 116 S.Ct. 1480, 134 L.Ed.2d 687 (1996). We have said:

>> This broad discretion [afforded the Executive] rests largely on the recognition that the decision to prosecute is particularly ill-suited to judicial review. Such factors as the strength of the case, the prosecution's general deterrence value, the Government's enforcement priorities, and the case's relationship to the Government's overall enforcement plan are not readily susceptible to the kind of analysis the courts are competent to undertake. Judicial supervision in this area, moreover, entails systemic costs of particular concern. Examining the basis of a prosecution delays the criminal proceeding, threatens to chill law enforcement by subjecting the prosecutor's motives and decisionmaking to outside inquiry, and may undermine prosecutorial effectiveness by revealing the Government's enforcement policy. All of these are substantial concerns that make the courts properly hesitant to examine the decision whether to prosecute.

Wayte v. United States, 470 U.S. 598, 607–608, 105 S.Ct. 1524, 84 L.Ed.2d 547 (1985).

These concerns are greatly magnified in the deportation context. Regarding, for example, the potential for delay: Whereas in criminal proceedings the consequence of delay is merely to postpone the criminal's receipt of his just deserts, in deportation proceedings the consequence is to permit and prolong a continuing violation of United States law. Postponing justifiable deportation (in the hope that the alien's status will change—by, for example, marriage to an American citizen—or simply with the object of extending the alien's unlawful stay) is often the principal object of resistance to a deportation proceeding, and the additional obstacle of selective-enforcement suits could leave the INS hard pressed to enforce routine status requirements. * * * The Executive should not have to disclose its "real" reasons for deeming nationals of a particular country a special threat—or indeed for simply wishing to antagonize a particular foreign country by focusing on that country's nationals—and even if it did disclose them a court would be ill equipped to determine their authenticity and utterly unable to assess their adequacy. Moreover, the consideration on the other side of the ledger in deportation cases—the interest of the target in avoiding "selective" treatment—is less compelling than in criminal prosecutions. While the consequences of deportation may assuredly be grave, they are not imposed as a punishment. * * * Even when deportation is sought because of some act the alien has committed, in principle the alien is not being punished for that act (criminal charges may be available for that separate purpose) but is merely being held to the terms under which he was admitted. And in all cases, deportation is necessary in order to bring to an end *an ongoing violation* of United States law. The contention that a violation must be allowed to continue because it has been improperly selected is not powerfully appealing.

To resolve the present controversy, we need not rule out the possibility of a rare case in which the alleged basis of discrimination is so outrageous that the foregoing considerations can be overcome. Whether or not there be such exceptions, the general rule certainly applies here. When an alien's continuing presence in this country is in violation of the immigration laws, the Government does not offend the Constitution by deporting him for the additional reason that it believes him to be a member of an organization that supports terrorist activity.

525 U.S. at 489–92.

Justice Ginsburg agreed that § 242(g) deprived the court of jurisdiction notwithstanding First Amendment considerations, but on selective enforcement itself, she wrote:

It is well settled that "[f]reedom of speech and of press is accorded aliens residing in this country." *Bridges v. Wixon,* 326 U.S. 135, 148, 65 S.Ct. 1443, 89 L.Ed. 2103 (1945). Under our selective prosecution doctrine, "the decision to prosecute may not be deliberately based upon an unjustifiable standard such as race, religion, or other arbitrary classification, including the exercise of protected statutory and constitutional rights." *Wayte v. United States,* 470 U.S. 598, 608, 105 S.Ct. 1524, 84 L.Ed.2d 547 (1985). I am not persuaded that selective enforcement of deportation laws should be exempt from that prescription.

525 U.S. at 497–98, 119 S.Ct. at 950 (Ginsburg, J., concurring in part and concurring in the judgment).

3. IMMIGRATION LAW AS ANTI–TERRORISM LAW

a. Responses to September 11

Starting right after the attacks of September 11, 2001, the U.S. government adopted a variety of anti-terrorism initiatives. For example, the Department of Justice set out to interview about 7,600 nonimmigrants, focusing on Middle Eastern men ages 18 to 46, to discover what knowledge these interviewees had of terrorists and planned terrorist activities.

Other initiatives reflected the exercise of government discretion in immigration law enforcement. In October 2001 Attorney General Ashcroft announced that the Department of Justice would, as an antiterrorism strategy, detain and remove noncitizens for minor immigration violations. Several measures included a focus on noncitizens from predominantly Arab or Muslim countries. For example, the DHS announced in May 2003 that it would search for noncitizens who had violated the terms of their student visas, concentrating on potential national security risks, defined partly by nationality. Many hundreds of noncitizens were arrested and detained on the basis of generally minor crimes and immigration violations, but with the apparent purpose of preventing further acts of terrorism and aiding in the investigation of acts of terrorism that had already occurred. Many of these detainees were held for long periods, even exceeding one year.

Starting in September 2002, the National Security Entry–Exit Registration System (NSEERS) required certain nonimmigrants from listed countries (and some nonimmigrants from other countries as well, identified by individual characteristics deemed to signal risk) who arrive at U.S. ports of entry to undergo "special registration." As outlined in Chapter Six, special registration was designed to subject their stay in the United States to greater scrutiny than normal. In November 2002, NSEERS expanded to include individuals already in the United States through "call-in registration." This part of NSEERS was limited to certain nonimmigrant males at least 16 years of age who were nationals of 25 listed countries—all predominantly Arab or Muslim except for North Korea. Registrants were photographed, fingerprinted, interviewed under oath, and sometimes asked for credit card and banking information, and personal information, for example about political groups, places of worship, and roommates. Noncompliance with the call-in was deemed a deportable failure to maintain nonimmigrant status under INA § 237(a)(1)(C)(i), as well as a criminal violation under § 266.

Of about 84,000 noncitizens who complied with call-in registration, almost 14,000 were unlawfully present and faced removal proceedings as a result of the program. *See* U.S. Immigration and Customs Enforcement, Changes to National Security Entry/Exit Registration System (NSEERS) (2006). Implementation appeared to be uneven, especially for registrants with minor violations or approvable pending applications for lawful status. In some districts, these individuals were free to go, but about 2900 were detained, sometimes for long periods in squalid isolation. *See* Eggen & Aizenman, *Registration Stirs Panic, Worry*, Washington Post, Jan. 10, 2003. The government reported that call-in registration identified 11 noncitizens with links to terrorism, plus about 400 persons sought on criminal charges or barred from the United States. *See* Swarns, *More Than 13,000 May Face Deportation*, N.Y. Times, June 7, 2003. Call-in registration was terminated in December 2003, and the other reporting and review requirements were greatly scaled back at that time. The entire NSEERS program was ended in April 2011.

Very soon after the post-September 11 detentions began, allegations surfaced that the detainees were being mistreated. Two reports by the Office of the Inspector General of the Department of Justice on the treatment of detainees at the special high-security unit, known as the ADMAX SHU, at the Metropolitan Detention Center in Brooklyn detailed prolonged detention as well as patterns of physical and verbal abuse by guards that included: (1) slamming detainees against walls; (2) bending or twisting detainees' arms, hands, wrists, and fingers; (3) lifting restrained detainees off the ground by their arms, and pulling their arms and handcuffs; (4) stepping on detainees' leg restraint chains; and (5) using restraints improperly. Office of the Inspector General, Department of Justice, Supplemental Report on September 11 Detainees' Allegations of Abuse at the Metropolitan Detention Center in Brooklyn, NY 6 (2003); *see also* Office of the Inspector General, Department of Justice, The September 11 Detainees: A Review of the Treatment of Aliens Held on Immigration Charges in Connection with the Investigation of the September 11 Attacks (2003).

Some of the abused detainees sued the federal government and numerous federal officials, seeking damages for violations of rights under the First (freedom of speech and free exercise of religion), Fourth, Fifth (due process), and Fourteenth (equal protection) Amendments and claims under the Federal Tort Claims Act. In November 2009, five of the plaintiffs agreed to a $1.26 million settlement against the federal government. As we go to press in late 2011, litigation by other plaintiffs suing for damages is continuing.

b. Historical Background

U.S. history includes precedents for focusing immigration law enforcement on noncitizens from certain countries. In November 1979, a crowd of militant student followers of the Ayatollah Khomeini stormed the U.S. Embassy in Tehran, Iran. They took hostage over 60 Americans and held over 50 of them for 444 days, with backing from the government of Iran. Attorney General Benjamin Civiletti ordered all Iranians admitted as nonimmigrant students to report to INS district offices to demonstrate that they were in a lawful status (*e.g.,* still in the school they were authorized to attend). 44 Fed. Reg. 65728 (1979), *amended,* 44 Fed. Reg. 75165 (1979), *rescinded,* 46 Fed. Reg. 25599 (1981). More than 50,000 Iranian students reported. Although the vast majority were found to be lawfully in the country, those who were out of status were placed into deportation proceedings. This regulation of nonimmigrants was challenged as beyond the Attorney General's authority and a violation of equal protection.

NARENJI v. CIVILETTI

United States Court of Appeals, District of Columbia Circuit, 1979.
617 F.2d 745, cert. denied, 446 U.S. 957, 100 S.Ct. 2928, 64 L.Ed.2d 815 (1980).

ROBB, CIRCUIT JUDGE.

This is an appeal from a judgment of the District Court declaring unconstitutional a regulation promulgated by the Attorney General at the direction of the President. * * *

Regulation 214.5 requires all nonimmigrant alien post-secondary school students who are natives or citizens of Iran to report to a local INS office or campus representative to "provide information as to residence and maintenance of nonimmigrant status." * * * The regulation provides that failure to comply with the reporting requirement will be considered a violation of the conditions of the nonimmigrant's stay in the United States and will subject him to deportation proceedings under section 241(a)(9) of the Act.[a]

The regulation is within the authority delegated by Congress to the Attorney General under the Immigration and Nationality Act. That statute charges the Attorney General with "the administration and enforcement" of the Act, INA § 103(a), and directs him to "establish such regulations ... and perform such other acts as he deems necessary for carrying out his authority under the provisions of" the Act. He is directed to prescribe by regulation the time for which any nonimmigrant alien is admitted to the United States, and the conditions of such an admission. Finally, the Act authorizes the Attorney General to order the deportation of any nonimmigrant alien who fails to maintain his nonimmigrant status or to comply with the conditions of such status. * * *

* * *

The District Court concluded that even if authorized by statute regulation 214.5 is unconstitutional because it violates the Iranian students' right to equal protection of the laws. The court found no basis for the "discriminatory classification" of the students established by the

---

a. The substance of this provision is now in INA § 237(a)(1)(C)(i).—eds.

regulation. Here again we must differ. Distinctions on the basis of nationality may be drawn in the immigration field by the Congress or the Executive. *See Mathews v. Diaz*, 426 U.S. 67, 81–82, 96 S.Ct. 1883, 48 L.Ed.2d 478 (1976); *Fiallo v. Bell*, 430 U.S. 787, 97 S.Ct. 1473, 52 L.Ed.2d 50 (1977). So long as such distinctions are not wholly irrational they must be sustained.

By way of an affidavit from the Attorney General we are informed that his regulation was issued "as an element of the language of diplomacy by which international courtesies are granted or withdrawn in response to actions by foreign countries. The action implemented by these regulations is therefore a fundamental element of the President's efforts to resolve the Iranian crisis and to maintain the safety of the American hostages in Tehran." The Attorney General refers of course to the lawless seizure of the United States Embassy in Tehran and the imprisonment of the embassy personnel as hostages. Those actions denied to our embassy and citizens the protection to which they are entitled under the Amity Treaty in force between the United States and Iran (284 U.N.T.S. 93), and under international law. The lawlessness of this conduct of the Iranian government was recognized by the decision of the World Court on December 15, 1979. *United States v. Iran*, General List No. 64 (Int'l Ct. Justice, Dec. 15, 1979). Thus the present controversy involving Iranian students in the United States lies in the field of our country's foreign affairs and implicates matters over which the President has direct constitutional authority. *Mathews v. Diaz, supra.*

The District Court perceived no "overriding national interest" justifying the Attorney General's regulation: it found that "although defendants' regulation is an understandable effort designed to somehow reply to the Iranian attack upon this nation's sovereignty and the seizure of its citizens, it is one that does not support a legitimate national interest." In this we think the District Court erred.

As we have said, classifications among aliens based upon nationality are consistent with due process and equal protection if supported by a rational basis. *Mathews v. Diaz, supra; Fiallo v. Bell, supra*. The Attorney General's regulation 214.5 meets that test; it has a rational basis. To reach a contrary conclusion the District Court undertook to evaluate the policy reasons upon which the regulation is based. In doing this the court went beyond an acceptable judicial role. Certainly in a case such as the one presented here it is not the business of courts to pass judgment on the decisions of the President in the field of foreign policy. Judges are not expert in that field and they lack the information necessary for the formation of an opinion. The President on the other hand has the opportunity of knowing the conditions which prevail in foreign countries, he has his confidential sources of information and his agents in the form of diplomatic, consular and other officials. *United States v. Curtiss–Wright Export Corp.*, 299 U.S. 304, 320, 57 S.Ct. 216, 81 L.Ed. 255 (1936). As the Supreme Court said in *Mathews v. Diaz, supra*, 426 U.S. at 81, 82, 96 S.Ct. at 1892:

For reasons long recognized as valid, the responsibility for regulating the relationship between the United States and our alien visitors has been committed to the political branches of the Federal Government. Since decisions in these matters may implicate our relations with foreign powers, and since a wide variety of classifications must be defined in the light of changing political and economic circumstances, such decisions are frequently of a character more appropriate to either the Legislature or the Executive than to the Judiciary. This very case illustrates the need for flexibility in policy choices rather than the rigidity often characteristic of constitutional adjudication.... Any rule of constitutional law that would inhibit the flexibility of the political branches of government to respond to changing world conditions should be adopted only with the greatest caution. The reasons that preclude judicial review of political questions also dictate a narrow standard of review of decisions made by the Congress or the President in the area of immigration and naturalization.

And in *Harisiades v. Shaughnessy*, 342 U.S. 580, 588–89, 72 S.Ct. 512, 519, 96 L.Ed. 586 (1952), Mr. Justice Jackson wrote for the Court:

It is pertinent to observe that any policy toward aliens is vitally and intricately interwoven with contemporaneous policies in regard to the conduct of foreign relations, the war power, and the maintenance of a republican form of government. Such matters are so exclusively entrusted to the political branches of government as to be largely immune from judicial inquiry or interference.

This court is not in a position to say what effect the required reporting by several thousand Iranian students, who may be in this country illegally, will have on the attitude and conduct of the Iranian government. That is a judgment to be made by the President and it is not for us to overrule him, in the absence of acts that are clearly in excess of his authority.

* * *

MACKINNON, CIRCUIT JUDGE concurring.

I concur completely in the court's opinion but write separately to add additional support for its ruling.

First, to indicate that this is not an isolated act of diplomacy in the international crisis that faces the United States I would stress that the record also reflects that, as part of the same diplomatic effort, the President by order prohibited "crude oil produced in Iran (from entering) the ... United States" (Defendant's Ex. 3) and blocked all property and interests of the Government of Iran subject to United States jurisdiction. I also take judicial notice of the reports that substantial forces of the United States Navy have been moved to the Indian Ocean and the President has ordered the Iranian Embassy and consulate to return approximately 85% of its diplomatic staff to Iran.

It is also significant that Regulation 214.5 seeks "to identify Iranian students in the United States who are not maintaining status and to take immediate steps to commence deportation proceedings against such persons" (44 Fed. Reg. 65727) "in accordance with constitutional due process requirements." (Defendant's Ex. 3).

The disparity in treatment afforded the appellee nonimmigrant alien students who are in violation of our immigration laws is based upon the fact that the Government of their home country has committed, and is committing, a number of violent lawless acts against the United States and its citizens. That unlawful conduct against the United States places appellees, and others similarly situated who owe their allegiance to that country, in a different class for immigration purposes from the nonimmigrants of any other country. Therefore, since their government has made appellees part of a distinctly separate class, the United States under our Constitution may treat them differently because of the reasons that separate them from other aliens in the United States. The different treatment they may receive under subject regulation is directly related to the reasons for their different classification.

The status of Iranian aliens cannot be disassociated from their connection with their mother country since the alien "leaves outstanding a foreign call on his loyalties which international law not only permits our Government to recognize but commands it to respect." *Harisiades v. Shaughnessy*, 342 U.S. 580, 585–586, 72 S.Ct. 512, 517, 96 L.Ed. 586 (1951). The connection with the home country also means that the power of the United States Government to terminate the alien's stay is a necessary corollary to that observation * * *.

* * *

NOTES AND QUESTIONS ON NARENJI

1. In an article criticizing the nationality-based rule in *Narenji* as constitutionally impermissible, they also argued that race or ethnicity-based enforcement decisions are even more troubling. They pointed out that targeting Arabs and Muslims is not as narrowly tailored and more subject to abuse. Akram & Johnson, *Race, Civil Rights, and Immigration After September 11, 2001: The Targeting of Arabs and Muslims*, 58 N.Y.U. Ann. Surv. Am. L. 295, 338 (2002). Do you agree?

2. Do some or all of the government's post-September 11 immigration enforcement initiatives constitute profiling by ethnicity, religion, or race? More fundamentally, what if anything is objectionable about any of them? Consider the following framework for analysis.

c. Profiling and Immigration Law as Anti–Terrorism Law

SAMUEL R. GROSS & DEBRA LIVINGSTON, RACIAL PROFILING UNDER ATTACK

102 Colum. L. Rev. 1413, 1413, 1415, 1417–18, 1420–25, 1427, 1429–30 (2002).

We had just reached a consensus on racial profiling. By September 10, 2001, virtually everyone, from Jesse Jackson to Al Gore to George W. Bush to John Ashcroft, agreed that racial profiling was very bad. We also knew what racial profiling was: Police officers would stop, question, and search African American and Hispanic citizens disproportionately, because of their race or ethnicity, in order to try to catch common criminals. All this has changed in the wake of the September 11 attacks on the World Trade Center and the Pentagon. Now racial profiling is more likely to mean security checks or federal investigations that target Muslim men from Middle Eastern countries, in order to try to catch terrorists. And now lots of people are for it. In the fall of 1999, 81% of respondents in a national poll said they disapproved of "racial profiling," which was defined as the practice by some police officers of stopping "motorists of certain racial or ethnic groups because the officers believe that these groups are more likely than others to commit certain types of crimes." Two years later, 58% said they favored "requiring Arabs, including those who are U.S. citizens, to undergo special, more intensive security checks before boarding airplanes in the U.S." This new attitude has emerged across the political spectrum. Even as stalwart a civil libertarian as Floyd Abrams, the celebrated First Amendment lawyer, has said that under the circumstances we now face, "it seems entirely appropriate to look harder at such people. Remember, Justice [Robert] Jackson said 'the Constitution is not a suicide pact.' "

* * *

As we use the term, "racial profiling" occurs whenever a law enforcement officer questions, stops, arrests, searches, or otherwise investigates a person because the officer believes that members of that person's racial or ethnic group are more likely than the population at large to commit the sort of crime the officer is investigating. The essence of racial profiling is a global judgment that the targeted group—before September 11, usually African Americans or Hispanics—is more prone to commit crime in general, or to commit a particular type of crime, than other racial or ethnic groups. If the officer's conduct is based at least in part on such a general racial or ethnic judgment, it does not matter if she uses other criteria as well in deciding on her course of action. It is racial profiling to target young black men on the basis of a belief that they are more likely than others to commit crimes, even though black women and older black men are not directly affected.

It is not racial profiling for an officer to question, stop, search, arrest, or otherwise investigate a person because his race or ethnicity matches information about a perpetrator of a specific crime that the officer is investigating. That use of race—which usually occurs when there is a racially specific description of the criminal—does not entail a global judgment about a racial or ethnic group as a whole. Likewise, a deliberate practice of discrimination between known suspects of different races— stopping all speeders but giving tickets to black drivers only, and warnings to whites—is a violation of the Equal Protection Clause of the Fourteenth Amendment, but it is not racial profiling. Racial profiling can occur in almost any type of criminal investigation. It has received particular attention in the context of highway drug interdiction, and more recently, of course, in investigations of terrorism.

* * *

We will focus our discussion of racial and ethnic profiling on a concrete example. In November 2001, the Department of Justice began efforts to interview "more than 5,000 people nationwide—the majority Middle Eastern men ages eighteen to thirty-three who came here within the last two years on nonimmigrant visas—in search of information on terrorist organizations such as al Qaeda."[14] Four months later, the Justice Department announced that it would seek to interview 3,000 additional men, ages eighteen to forty-six, who entered the United States on nonim- migrant visas, between October 2001 and February 2002, from countries with an al Qaeda presence. The Department said that these men are not suspected of crimes but "might, either wittingly or unwittingly, be in the same circles, communities, or social groups as those engaged in terrorist activities."

Is the Justice Department's interview campaign an ethnic profiling program? Some civil libertarians, Arab American organizations, and local police departments say it is; the Department of Justice says it is not. Who is right? And would answering this question tell us whether the Justice Department's program is appropriate? We will discuss these questions in the context of five factors. Some are staples of racial profiling debates; in fact, the first factor we address is generally treated as the sole defining issue. Others, however, are usually ignored, or are treated as involving background information rather than critical facts. In actual cases—as we will see in the discussion of several concrete examples—these factors are often inextricably intertwined.

A. Is the Investigation Based on Race or Ethnicity?

* * *

[I]s the Justice Department's interview program ethnic profiling? The answer is not clear even assuming that ethnicity was a central factor in the selection of subjects. By our definition, it is not ethnic profiling for

---

14. * * * See Memorandum from the Deputy Attorney General, to All United States Attor- neys and All Members of the Anti–Terrorism Task Forces (Nov. 9, 2001) (describing the manner of conducting interviews and topics to be covered), available at <http:// www.freepress. com/gal- lery/2001/ interviews/index.htm>.

officers to focus their attention on people of a given ethnicity because the police have information that the specific crime they are investigating was committed by someone of that ethnic group. There is plenty of information that Middle Eastern men, some of whom remain at large, engaged in a conspiracy to commit acts of mass terror in the United States on September 11, 2001. Granted, the concept of a "specific crime" grows somewhat hazy when the crime at issue is an ongoing conspiracy of indeterminate size—and one that potentially involves not just Middle Eastern men, but also others, from different racial or ethnic groups. Nevertheless, if the sole purpose for this interview program was to determine whether any of the thousands to be interviewed was involved in this conspiracy, or had information that might lead to those who were, this would not be ethnic profiling. (Which is not to say that such a broad brush investigation would be unproblematic; that's a different question, as we will see). On the other hand, the Justice Department's program would involve ethnic profiling if it was undertaken even in part based upon a general belief that Middle Eastern men are more likely to commit acts of terrorism than people of other ethnic groups—if it was based upon a global assumption about the criminal propensities of people of Middle Eastern descent. In practice, it is probably impossible to make that distinction in a case like this, involving the protracted investigation of a far-flung conspiracy.

B. IS RACE (OR ETHNICITY) A STRONG PREDICTOR OF CRIMINAL BEHAVIOR?

* * *

Before September 11, 2001, a few conservative commentators were the only people who publicly defended racial profiling on practical grounds. That has changed. Journalists, politicians, and pollsters have all expressed and documented a widespread sentiment that in order to win the "war on terrorism" we must focus our scrutiny on Middle Eastern Muslim men. The Justice Department's interview program may not be expressly aimed at such individuals, but it has this effect. It is explicitly aimed at individuals from Middle Eastern countries and other countries with an al Qaeda presence—and for good reason. Although other groups and individuals have committed terrorist acts in the United States, before September 11 and probably after, it is very likely true that al Qaeda, an organization that consists entirely of Muslim men, primarily from the Middle East, poses the greatest immediate threat of mass terrorist killings.

Fortunately, it is also no doubt true that only a tiny proportion of Middle Eastern men are affiliated with al Qaeda. A similar pattern can occur in other settings: Even if race or ethnicity is a strong predictor of criminal behavior, an individual member of the relevant groups is very unlikely to be a criminal. For example, it could simultaneously be true that 90% of major cocaine traffickers on I–95 are black and Hispanic, and that 99.9% of black and Hispanic motorists on that highway are not drug traffickers of any description. When this type of juxtaposition does occur—

and we rarely, if ever, have information this definitive—choosing suspects by race will increase the efficiency of the police. But the benefit to law enforcement may be slight, and it will come at a price that may be very steep, depending on the other factors we consider.

C. What Does the Government Do Based on Race or Ethnicity?

Southeastern Michigan has the largest concentration of Arab Americans and Near Eastern visitors in the country, perhaps 300,000 or more, including 521 of the 600 or so Michigan residents on the Justice Department's initial interview list. These subjects were contacted by letters from the local United States Attorney that said:

> Your name was brought to our attention because, among other things, you came to Michigan on a visa from a country where there are groups that support, advocate, or finance international terrorism. We have no reason to believe that you are, in any way, associated with terrorist activities. Nevertheless, you may know something that could be helpful in our efforts.

They were then asked to call the United States Attorney's office by a given date to set up an appointment for an interview.

* * *

Perhaps the worst instance of ethnic profiling in American history began on February 19, 1942, when President Franklin Delano Roosevelt signed Executive Order 9066, giving the Secretary of War the power to order over 110,000 Japanese Americans on the west coast to be "resettle[d]" in "relocation centers" for the duration of the war. The Japanese internment was a disgraceful episode in American history. It is frequently cited as the prime example of the evil things we might do if we pursue racial profiling in response to the attacks of September 11. But what if, instead of being forced to sell their property for pennies on the dollar, to leave their homes, schools, farms, jobs, and communities, and to spend three and a half years behind barbed wire, Japanese Americans had been asked to report for interviews with the FBI? What if in addition they were required—because of their ethnicity—to report their whereabouts to the police periodically, but were otherwise allowed to lead their lives as they wished? Perhaps these policies, especially the second, would also have been unjustified, even during an all out war. Certainly both programs—like the actual internment program—would have involved ethnic profiling. Under any name, however, these sorts of ethnic profiling would have been far preferable to the relocation and imprisonment that were in fact ordered.

* * *

D. How Strong Is the Evidence of a Racially Identified Suspect's Guilt or Innocence?

Our normal operating assumption about racial profiling is that the typical individual who is profiled is very unlikely to be guilty. (Certainly no more than a tiny proportion of the men interviewed by the FBI are members of al Qaeda, if any.) The less likely the guilt of any individual, the higher the proportion of innocent people among those affected, and the higher the social cost of the practice. But what if the evidence of individual guilt becomes much stronger? Would this change our view on the use of profiling? The New York City Police Department's anti-gun campaign is a good illustration. From January 1998 through March 1999, guns were found on only 2.5% of the nearly 60,000 people who were stopped for suspected gun possession—one person in 40. Assuming the police did use race to decide whom to stop and frisk, would we feel differently about the practice if they had found weapons on 90% of those they searched? How about 30%?

* * *

E. What are the Likely Benefits of Racial Profiling?
* * *

* * * If we thought we could reduce the risk of hijacking by 15%, would that justify searching every Middle Eastern man who boards a plane? This may well be within the current national consensus that we must take strong measures to protect ourselves. On the other hand, the same people who would accept severe measures (including ones based on race) that offered any promise of reducing a genuine threat of nuclear terrorism, might still readily condemn a racial profiling program that efficiently combats the threat of marijuana possession or ticket scalping. And even people who favor the Justice Department's post-September 11 interview program might be angry if the Department sent out letters to 5000 Mexican nationals, almost all of them law abiding, asking them to come in for interviews because:

> Your name was brought to our attention because, among other things, you came to the United States on a visa from a country where there are groups that engage in or finance international drug trafficking. We have no reason to believe that you are, in any way, associated with drug trafficking. Nevertheless, you may know something that could be helpful in our efforts.

There are two parts to this calculation: How great is the harm we are fighting? And how likely is our conduct to be useful? When the danger is extreme, we may accept unpleasant methods that have only a slight chance of success. But it is one thing to sketch out these calculations on paper, and quite another to do so in a real emergency. We never actually know either the magnitude of the danger or the effectiveness of possible countermeasures. Urgency and fear do not improve our judgment. They may lead us to overestimate the danger, or the value of preventive steps, or both. Racism and ethnic prejudice may color every step of the process. Most Americans probably feel particularly threatened because the September 11 suicide hijackers were foreign, and some may be especially fearful because they were Arabs. This fear may cause us to exaggerate the danger of future attacks in general, and of attacks by Middle Eastern terrorists in particular. As a result, we may overestimate the effect of racially specific security measures. And unfortunately, we are more willing to accept aggressive measures when they target small and politically disempowered groups, specifically racial and ethnic minorities, and foreign nationals.

* * *

Additional Perspectives on Profiling and Anti–Terrorism Law

1. When the Department of Justice published the final NSEERS rule in 2002, it responded to the charge that NSEERS targets specific minority ethnic groups and members of a specific religion:

> The Department strongly disagrees with the premise of the comments that the rule is invidiously discriminatory. Congressional enactments and regulations concerning immigration have historically drawn distinctions on the basis of nationality and related criteria. The political branches of the government have plenary authority in the immigration area. *See Fiallo v. Bell*, 430 U.S. 787, 792 (1977); *Mathews v. Diaz*, 426 U.S. 67, 80–82 (1976). In the context of immigration and nationality laws, the Supreme Court has particularly "underscore[d] the limited scope of judicial inquiry." *Fiallo*, 430 U.S. at 792. * * * The substantive decision to relax requirements for only specified nationals, while excluding all others, is among those political decisions that are "wholly outside the concern and competence of the Judiciary," *Harisiades v. Shaughnessy*, 342 U.S. 580, 596 (1952) (Frankfurter, J., concurring). * * * The distinctions drawn by the rule are appropriate in the context of immigration law and national security.

> The Department recognizes that a few individuals in the United States have questioned the loyalty of some Muslim Americans to the United States. The Department also recognizes that some American Muslims have been targets of discrimination. Some mosques have been damaged and desecrated. A number of Muslim Americans—and others wrongly believed to be Muslims—have been threatened or attacked. These attacks against Muslim Americans and the Muslim communities are not only reprehensible; like terrorism, they are also attacks against the United States and humanity. The Federal Bureau of Investigation (FBI) has investigated such attacks and threats against Arab, Muslim, and Sikh Americans. The FBI has initiated more than 360 investigations in concert with state and local law enforcement authorities. More than 100 individuals have already been charged with federal, state, and local crimes relating to such attacks. The Department continues to treat such crimes as civil rights violations and will vigorously prosecute these violations.

67 Fed. Reg. 52585 (2002).

2. Leti Volpp has argued that the post-September 11 focus on Arabs and Muslims has precursor episodes in which other racial groups were similarly targeted as foreign threats, often regardless of citizenship status:

> Edward Said describes Orientalism as a master discourse of European civilization that constructs and polarizes the East and the West. Western representations of the East serve not only to define those who are the objects of the Orientalizing gaze, but also the West, which is defined through its opposition to the East. Thus, for example, the West is defined as modern, democratic, and progressive, through the East being defined as primitive, barbaric, and despotic.[41] Similar discourses sustain American national identity. American Orientalism references North Africa, the Middle East, and Turkey, as well as East Asia. Collectively, and often indistinguishably, they function as the "East" to America's democratic and progressive "West." September 11 gave this discourse new currency in relation to what are depicted as the barbaric regions of the world that spawn terror.

* * *

> There are obviously enormous resonances in what has been happening to the treatment of Japanese Americans during World War II, whereby the fungibility of members of a racially defined community was considered to make it impossible to screen individually loyal citizens from enemy aliens. Recently, the publisher of the Sacramento Bee attempted to deliver a graduation speech at Cal State Sacramento. Booed and heckled, she was unable to finish her speech about the need for the protection of civil liberties; when she wondered what would happen if racial profiling became routine, the audience cheered. Witnesses described the event as terrifying; the president of the faculty senate was quoted in the New York Times as stating, " 'For the first time in my life, I can see how something like the Japanese internment camps could happen in our country.' "[67]

> And, in fact, a Gallup poll found that one-third of the American public surveyed thought that we should intern Arab Americans. Motivation for the internment of over 120,000 Japanese Americans was fear of what we today might call sleeper cells. The fact that the Japanese Americans did not attack after Pearl Harbor was understood to mean that they were patiently waiting to strike and therefore must be interned. Japanese American internment constituted a pivotal moment in American Orientalism; the present moment is another.

* * *

---

41. *See generally* Edward Said, Orientalism (1978); Edward Said, Culture and Imperialism (1993). * * *

67. Timothy Egan, *In Sacramento, a Publisher's Questions Draw the Wrath of the Crowd*, N.Y. Times, Dec. 21, 2001, at B1 (quoting Bob Buckley, computer science professor at California State University, Sacramento).

The shift in perceptions of racial profiling is clearly grounded in the fact that those individuals who are being profiled are not considered to be part of "us." Many of those racially profiled in the sense of being the targets of hate violence or being thrown off airplanes are formally citizens of the United States, through birth or naturalization. But they are not considered citizens as a matter of identity, in that they in no way represent the nation.

* * *

In the American imagination, those who appear "Middle Eastern, Arab, or Muslim" may be theoretically entitled to formal rights, but they do not stand in for or represent the nation. Instead, they are interpellated as antithetical to the citizen's sense of identity. Citizenship in the form of legal status does not guarantee that they will be constitutive of the American body politic. In fact, quite the opposite: The consolidation of American identity takes place against them.

* * *

Thus, the boundaries of the nation continue to be constructed through excluding certain groups. The "imagined community"[79] of the American nation, constituted by loyal citizens, is relying on difference from the "Middle Eastern terrorist" to fuse its identity at a moment of crisis. Discourses of democracy used to support the U.S. war effort rest on an image of anti-democracy, in the form of those who seek to destroy the "American way of life." The idea that there are norms that are antithetical to "Western values" of liberty and equality helps solidify this conclusion.

Volpp, *The Citizen and the Terrorist*, 49 UCLA L. Rev. 1575, 1586–95 (2002).

3. Compare these comments from Eric Muller:

We might roll our eyes when our government today defends its interrogation program as ethnicity-neutral. After all, while the five thousand young men may not have been selected because they are Arab, we do know that they were selected because they arrived recently from countries where al Qaeda operates, and that certainly sounds like a pretext for anti-Arab discrimination. But on closer examination, especially in the comparative light of the interrogation of the ethnically Japanese during World War II, the government's defense of its program is plausible. The 1990 census counted about 940,000 people of Arab ancestry in the United States, about eighteen percent of whom were non-citizens. This made for a total of about 170,000 aliens of Arab ancestry living in the United States in 1990. The numbers in the year 2001 were naturally a good deal higher * * *. Still, 5,000 is just under three percent of 170,000, a number so small as to suggest that the government did in fact target people for

---

79. *See* Benedict Anderson, Imagined Communities 7 (1991) (writing that the nation is "an imagined political community"). * * *

questioning on the basis of criteria other than the raw fact of their origin in an Arab country. The additional criteria that the government announced—age of between eighteen and thirty-three years and recent arrival from a country believed to have been a way-station for members of al Qaeda—certainly seem to describe a major subset of those who might have some information, perhaps to them entirely innocent-seeming, that would help the government fend off future al Qaeda attacks.

Most importantly, despite dire predictions that the supposedly information-gathering interviews would be mere pretext for coercive criminal interrogations, this turned out not to be so. After a somewhat clumsy start, the FBI quickly responded to suggestions and complaints from the Arab American community and ran interviews that lawyers in attendance called "polite, even solicitous." The FBI's New Jersey office invited a prominent lawyer in the Muslim community to give a sensitivity training session to federal agents and local police, and the event was standing-room-only. In the meantime, the response rate from those the government asked to interview was around ninety percent, and the Attorney General reported when the interviews were through that they had produced "several leads." Of course, the government now also has a list of those who declined to be interviewed, and it remains to be seen what use the government will make of that information. On the whole, though, the program of interrogation, if it was ethnic profiling at all, was ethnic profiling with a decidedly light touch.

Muller, *12/7 and 9/11: War, Liberties, and the Lessons of History*, 104 W. Va. L. Rev. 571, 575–77 (2002). Does Muller's view apply more to some aspects of the government's antiterrorism campaign than to others?

4. A key question in assessing the uses of immigration law as antiterrorism law is to ask how citizenship matters. David Cole has argued that while noncitizen status accounts for the harshness of many of the recent measures taken in the struggle against terrorism, how we treat nonmembers may ultimately have an impact on rights of full members:

Some argue that a "double standard" for citizens and noncitizens is perfectly justified. The attacks of September 11 were perpetrated by 19 Arab noncitizens, and we have reason to believe that other Arab noncitizens are associated with the attackers and will seek to attack again. Citizens, it is said, are presumptively loyal; noncitizens are not.
* * *

* * *

[W]hat we are willing to allow our government to do to immigrants creates precedents for how it treats citizens. In 1798, for example, Congress enacted the Enemy Alien Act, which remains on the books to this day and authorizes the President during wartime to detain, deport, or otherwise restrict the liberties of any citizen over 14 years of age of a country with which we are at war, without any individualized showing of disloyalty, criminal conduct, or even suspicion. In World War II, the government extended that logic to intern 110,000 persons of Japanese ancestry, about two-thirds of whom were U.S. citizens. Similarly, while we think of the McCarthy era as beginning in the 1940s, it was in fact preceded by several decades of targeting immigrants for their purportedly subversive political associations using immigration law. Joe McCarthy simply applied to citizens techniques developed in the 1910s under the leadership of a young J. Edgar Hoover, head of the Justice Department's "Alien Radical" division. Measures initially targeted at noncitizens may well come back to haunt us all.

Cole, *Enemy Aliens*, 54 Stan. L. Rev. 953, 957–59 (2002).

Cole focuses on future consequences, but consider this comment on the present-day connection between how we treat citizens and noncitizens:

[M]any noncitizens caught up in today's dragnets are * * * the mothers and fathers and husbands and wives of U.S. citizens. These noncitizens are vital members of ethnic communities composed of citizens and noncitizens, and these noncitizens were targeted because of their race, ethnicity, or nationality. The administration acts as if it is possible to affect noncitizens without also affecting U.S. citizens and communities, when in fact, U.S. citizens and communities have been devastated. * * *

In the time since the September 11 attacks, the government has tightened the circle in ways that leave many U.S. citizens and communities on the outside if they are the wrong race, ethnicity, or nationality. When enforcement measures are based on these factors, it is only natural for U.S. citizens and noncitizens in Arab and South Asian communities in the United States to feel real fear in these terms. To identify U.S. citizens by race, ethnicity, or nationality has taken away a vital part of what these citizens thought it meant to be a U.S. citizen in the first place. Profiling by race begets fear by race— fear on the part of citizens and noncitizens alike.

Motomura, *Immigration and We the People After September 11*, 66 Albany L. Rev. 413, 422–24 (2003).

SECTION C. STATE AND LOCAL ENFORCEMENT

We now expand our inquiry to the enforcement facet of immigration federalism—a shorthand reference to state and local involvement in matters relating to immigration and immigrants. Today, state and local roles in enforcement can take several forms. We start with the stage that began in the 1970s. State and local governments tried to mitigate the perceived costs of nonenforcement and drive out unauthorized migrants by limiting their access to education, jobs, or housing. In a second stage, states and localities have become directly involved in specific elements of immigration law enforcement under express authority from the federal government. Most recently, some states and localities have asserted a role in directly enforcing federal immigration law without express federal authorization. State laws like Arizona's SB 1070, enacted in April 2010, seem to be in this third group, though the boundaries between categories can sometimes blur. Indeed, classification is often heavily contested, for putting state and local activity into a particular category may effectively decide whether it is permitted.

1. INDIRECT ENFORCEMENT BY STATE AND LOCAL GOVERNMENTS

a. The Foundation Cases

(i) *Graham v. Richardson*

We start with excerpts from three U.S. Supreme Court decisions from the 1970s that are foundational to modern immigration federalism. In *Graham v. Richardson*, 403 U.S. 365, 91 S.Ct. 1848, 29 L.Ed.2d 534 (1971), the plaintiffs were lawful permanent residents who objected to laws that limited eligibility for state welfare programs. Pennsylvania required U.S. citizenship, and Arizona limited eligibility to citizens and noncitizens who had lived in the United States for fifteen years. The Court found these laws unconstitutional, explaining in one part of its analysis:

> Under traditional equal protection principles, a State retains broad discretion to classify as long as its classification has a reasonable basis. * * * But the Court's decisions have established that classifications based on alienage, like those based on nationality or race, are inherently suspect and subject to close judicial scrutiny. Aliens as a class are a prime example of a "discrete and insular" minority (*see United States v. Carolene Products Co.*, 304 U.S. 144, 152–153, n.4, 58 S.Ct. 778, 783–784, 82 L.Ed. 1234 (1938)) for whom such heightened judicial solicitude is appropriate. * * *

403 U.S. at 371–72, 91 S.Ct. 1852.

As an "additional reason" for invalidity, the Court cited preemption:

> Congress has broadly declared as federal policy that lawfully admitted resident aliens who become public charges for causes arising after their entry are not subject to deportation, and that as long as they are here they are entitled to the full and equal benefit of all state laws for the security of persons and property. * * *

> * * * [I]n the ordinary case an alien, becoming indigent and unable to work, will be unable to live where, because of discriminatory denial of public assistance, he cannot "secure the necessities of life, including food, clothing and shelter." State alien residency requirements that either deny welfare benefits to noncitizens or condition

them on longtime residency [shorter than applicable federal requirements], equate with the assertion of a right, inconsistent with federal policy, to deny entrance and abode. Since such laws encroach upon exclusive federal power, they are constitutionally impermissible.

403 U.S. at 378–80, 91 S.Ct. 1856.

Graham suggests two sets of distinctions, the first being between equal protection and preemption. The complexities of this distinction are suggested by this intriguing statement at the end of the decision, addressing this relationship: "Although the Federal Government admittedly has broad constitutional power to determine what aliens shall be admitted to the United States, the period they may remain, and the terms and conditions of their naturalization, Congress does not have the power to authorize the individual States to violate the Equal Protection Clause." 403 U.S. at 382, 91 S.Ct. 1857. The other distinction—also exceedingly complex—is between noncitizens with lawful immigration status like the permanent residents in *Graham* and the unauthorized migrants in the next one.

(ii) *De Canas v. Bica*

In *De Canas v. Bica*, 424 U.S. 351, 96 S.Ct. 933, 47 L.Ed.2d 43 (1976), the question was whether states had the authority to penalize employers who hired someone who was in the United States unlawfully. Or did federal immigration law preempt any such authority? The case was decided ten years before the Immigration Reform and Control Act (IRCA) introduced federal employer sanctions in 1986.

The plaintiffs were migrant farmworkers who alleged they had lost their jobs because the defendant farm labor contractors hired unauthorized migrants. The plaintiffs sought reinstatement and a permanent injunction against the hiring practices, citing California Labor Code § 2805(a), which provided "(n)o employer shall knowingly employ an alien who is not entitled to lawful residence in the United States if such employment would have an adverse effect on lawful resident workers."

The central issue was whether federal law preempted the California statute. No, said the Court in a unanimous decision that established several propositions still central to immigration federalism. The Court started by emphasizing it is not enough to ask if state regulation affects noncitizens:

> Power to regulate immigration is unquestionably exclusively a federal power. But the Court has never held that every state enactment which in any way deals with aliens is a regulation of immigration and thus per se pre-empted by this constitutional power, whether latent or exercised. * * * [S]tanding alone, the fact that aliens are the subject of a state statute does not render it a regulation of immigration, which is essentially a determination of who should or should not be admitted into the country, and the conditions under which a legal entrant may remain. Indeed, there would have been no need, in cases

such as *Graham* * * * , even to discuss the relevant congressional enactments in finding pre-emption of state regulation if all state regulation of aliens was *ipso facto* regulation of immigration, for the existence *vel non* of federal regulation is wholly irrelevant if the Constitution of its own force requires pre-emption of such state regulation. * * * [A]bsent congressional action, § 2805 would not be an invalid state incursion on federal power.

424 U.S. at 354–56, 96 S.Ct. 936.

The Court acknowledged that "States possess broad authority under their police powers to regulate the employment relationship to protect workers within the State." 424 U.S. at 356, 96 S.Ct. 937. But it added:

> Of course, even state regulation designed to protect vital state interests must give way to paramount federal legislation. But we will not presume that Congress, in enacting the INA, intended to oust state authority to regulate the employment relationship covered by § 2805(a) in a manner consistent with pertinent federal laws. Only a demonstration that complete ouster of state power including state power to promulgate laws not in conflict with federal laws was " 'the clear and manifest purpose of Congress' " would justify that conclusion. *Florida Lime & Avocado Growers v. Paul, supra,* at 146, 83 S.Ct., at 1219, quoting *Rice v. Santa Fe Elevator Corp.,* 331 U.S. 218, 230, 67 S.Ct. 1146, 1152, 91 L.Ed. 1447 (1947). Respondents have not made that demonstration. They fail to point out, and an independent review does not reveal, any specific indication in either the wording or the legislative history of the INA that Congress intended to preclude even harmonious state regulation touching on aliens in general, or the employment of illegal aliens in particular.
>
> Nor can such intent be derived from the scope and detail of the INA. The central concern of the INA is with the terms and conditions of admission to the country and the subsequent treatment of aliens lawfully in the country. The comprehensiveness of the INA scheme for regulation of immigration and naturalization, without more, cannot be said to draw in the employment of illegal aliens as "plainly within . . . (that) central aim of federal regulation." *San Diego Unions v. Garmon,* 359 U.S. 236, 244, 79 S.Ct. 773, 779, 3 L.Ed.2d 775 (1959).

424 U.S. at 357–59, 96 S.Ct. 937–38.

Applying this analysis to the facts, the Court asked "whether, although the INA contemplates some room for state legislation, § 2805(a) is nevertheless unconstitutional because it 'stands as an obstacle to the accomplishment and execution of the full purposes and objectives of Congress' in enacting the INA." Concluding that the answer to this question required first giving California courts the opportunity to interpret § 2805(a), the Court remanded the case.

(iii) Mathews v. Diaz

The third foundation case is *Mathews v. Diaz,* 426 U.S. 67, 96 S.Ct. 1883, 48 L.Ed.2d 478 (1976), decided three months after *De Canas.* The plaintiffs were three Cuban refugees who did not meet the federal Medicare eligibility requirement that noncitizens be permanent residents who have lived in the United States for five years. All were lawfully present, one as a permanent resident and two after being been paroled into the country. They argued that the requirement violated equal protection.

The Supreme Court rejected this challenge in an analysis that started by addressing constitutional protections for noncitizens generally:

> The fact that all persons, aliens and citizens alike, are protected by the Due Process Clause does not lead to the further conclusion that all aliens are entitled to enjoy all the advantages of citizenship or, indeed, to the conclusion that all aliens must be placed in a single homogeneous legal classification. * * *

> In the exercise of its broad power over naturalization and immigration, Congress regularly makes rules that would be unacceptable if applied to citizens. The exclusion of aliens and the reservation of the power to deport have no permissible counterpart in the Federal Government's power to regulate the conduct of its own citizenry. The fact that an Act of Congress treats aliens differently from citizens does not in itself imply that such disparate treatment is "invidious."

> In particular, the fact that Congress has provided some welfare benefits for citizens does not require it to provide like benefits for all aliens. Neither the overnight visitor, the unfriendly agent of a hostile foreign power, the resident diplomat, nor the illegal entrant, can advance even a colorable constitutional claim to a share in the bounty that a conscientious sovereign makes available to its own citizens and some of its guests. The decision to share that bounty with our guests may take into account the character of the relationship between the alien and this country: Congress may decide that as the alien's tie grows stronger, so does the strength of his claim to an equal share of that munificence.

426 U.S. at 78–80, 96 S.Ct. 1890–92.

The Court distinguished *Graham*:

> Of course, the latter ground of decision actually supports our holding today that it is the business of the political branches of the Federal Government, rather than that of either the States or the Federal Judiciary, to regulate the conditions of entry and residence of aliens. The equal protection analysis also involves significantly different considerations because it concerns the relationship between aliens and the States rather than between aliens and the Federal Government.

426 U.S. at 84–85, 96 S.Ct. 1893–94.

These passages from *Diaz* have prompted a variety of explanations for the differences in outcome between *Graham* and *Diaz*. It is clear that the federal government can treat noncitizens less well than citizens, and that states and localities have less constitutional authority to do so. Less clear is whether this greater federal authority reflects a preemption analysis, *see* Perry, *Modern Equal Protection: A Conceptualization and Appraisal,* 79 Colum. L. Rev. 1023, 1061–63 (1979), or an equal protection analysis that requires less to justify federal line-drawing than state or local line-drawing, *see* Koh, *Equality With a Human Face: Justice Blackmun and the Equal Protection of Aliens,* 8 Hamline L. Rev. 51, 98–102 (1985).

(iv) Plyler v. Doe

The three foundation cases suggest two facts that will make a constitutional difference: (1) the source of regulation—federal versus state or local; and (2) the noncitizen's status—lawfully in the United States or not. This is the context in which the Supreme Court decided *Plyler v. Doe.*

PLYLER v. DOE

Supreme Court of the United States, 1982.
457 U.S. 202, 102 S.Ct. 2382, 72 L.Ed.2d 786.

JUSTICE BRENNAN delivered the opinion of the Court.

* * *

In May 1975, the Texas Legislature revised its education laws to withhold from local school districts any state funds for the education of children who were not "legally admitted" into the United States. The 1975 revision also authorized local school districts to deny enrollment in their public schools to children not "legally admitted" to the country. Tex. Educ. Code Ann. § 21.031. These cases involve constitutional challenges to those provisions.

* * *8

II

* * * Appellants argue at the outset that undocumented aliens, because of their immigration status, are not "persons within the jurisdiction" of the State of Texas, and that they therefore have no right to the equal protection of Texas law. We reject this argument. Whatever his status under the immigration laws, an alien is surely a "person" in any ordinary sense of that term. Aliens, even aliens whose presence in this country is unlawful, have long been recognized as "persons" guaranteed due process of law by the Fifth and Fourteenth Amendments. *Shaughnessy v. Mezei,* 345 U.S. 206, 212, 73 S.Ct. 625, 629, 97 L.Ed. 956 (1953); *Wong Wing v. United States,* 163 U.S. 228, 238, 16 S.Ct. 977, 981, 41 L.Ed. 140 (1896); *Yick Wo v. Hopkins,* 118 U.S. 356, 369, 6 S.Ct. 1064, 1070, 30 L.Ed. 220 (1886). Indeed, we have clearly held that the Fifth Amendment protects aliens whose presence in this country is unlawful from invidious

---

8. Appellees * * * continue to press the argument that § 21.031 is pre-empted by federal law and policy. In light of our disposition of the Fourteenth Amendment issue, we have no occasion to reach this claim.

discrimination by the Federal Government. *Mathews v. Diaz*, 426 U.S. 67, 77, 96 S.Ct. 1883, 1890, 48 L.Ed.2d 478 (1976).

* * *

III

* * * In applying the Equal Protection Clause to most forms of state action, we * * * seek only the assurance that the classification at issue bears some fair relationship to a legitimate public purpose.

But we would not be faithful to our obligations under the Fourteenth Amendment if we applied so deferential a standard to every classification. The Equal Protection Clause was intended as a restriction on state legislative action inconsistent with elemental constitutional premises. Thus we have treated as presumptively invidious those classifications that disadvantage a "suspect class," or that impinge upon the exercise of a "fundamental right." With respect to such classifications, it is appropriate to enforce the mandate of equal protection by requiring the State to demonstrate that its classification has been precisely tailored to serve a compelling governmental interest. In addition, we have recognized that certain forms of legislative classification, while not facially invidious, nonetheless give rise to recurring constitutional difficulties; in these limited circumstances we have sought the assurance that the classification reflects a reasoned judgment consistent with the ideal of equal protection by inquiring whether it may fairly be viewed as furthering a substantial interest of the State. * * *

Sheer incapability or lax enforcement of the laws barring entry into this country, coupled with the failure to establish an effective bar to the employment of undocumented aliens, has resulted in the creation of a substantial "shadow population" of illegal migrants—numbering in the millions—within our borders. This situation raises the specter of a permanent caste of undocumented resident aliens, encouraged by some to remain here as a source of cheap labor, but nevertheless denied the benefits that our society makes available to citizens and lawful residents. The existence of such an underclass presents most difficult problems for a Nation that prides itself on adherence to principles of equality under law.

The children who are plaintiffs in these cases are special members of this underclass. Persuasive arguments support the view that a State may withhold its beneficence from those whose very presence within the United States is the product of their own unlawful conduct. These arguments do not apply with the same force to classifications imposing disabilities on the minor *children* of such illegal entrants. At the least, those who elect to enter our territory by stealth and in violation of our law should be prepared to bear the consequences, including, but not limited to, deportation. But the children of those illegal entrants are not comparably situated. Their "parents have the ability to conform their conduct to societal norms," and presumably the ability to remove themselves from the State's jurisdiction; but the children who are plaintiffs in these cases "can affect neither their parents' conduct nor their own status." *Trimble v. Gordon*, 430 U.S. 762, 770, 97 S.Ct. 1459, 1465, 52 L.Ed.2d 31 (1977). Even if the State found it expedient to control the conduct of adults by acting against their children, legislation directing the onus of a parent's misconduct against his children does not comport with fundamental conceptions of justice. * * *

Of course, undocumented status is not irrelevant to any proper legislative goal. Nor is undocumented status an absolutely immutable characteristic since it is the product of conscious, indeed unlawful, action. But § 21.031 is directed against children, and imposes its discriminatory burden on the basis of a legal characteristic over which children can have little control. It is thus difficult to conceive of a rational justification for penalizing these children for their presence within the United States. Yet that appears to be precisely the effect of § 21.031.

Public education is not a "right" granted to individuals by the Constitution. But neither is it merely some governmental "benefit" indistinguishable from other forms of social welfare legislation. Both the importance of education in maintaining our basic institutions, and the lasting impact of its deprivation on the life of the child, mark the distinction. * * * [E]ducation provides the basic tools by which individuals might lead economically productive lives to the benefit of us all. In sum, education has a fundamental role in maintaining the fabric of our society. We cannot ignore the significant social costs borne by our Nation when select groups are denied the means to absorb the values and skills upon which our social order rests.

In addition to the pivotal role of education in sustaining our political and cultural heritage, denial of education to some isolated group of children poses an affront to one of the goals of the Equal Protection Clause: the abolition of governmental barriers presenting unreasonable obstacles to advancement on the basis of individual merit. Paradoxically, by depriving the children of any disfavored group of an education, we foreclose the means by which that group might raise the level of esteem in which it is held by the majority. But more directly, "education prepares individuals to be self-reliant and self-sufficient participants in society." *Wisconsin v. Yoder, supra*, 406 U.S., at 221, 92 S.Ct., at 1536. Illiteracy is an enduring disability. The inability to read and write will handicap the individual deprived of a basic education each and every day of his life. The inestimable toll of that deprivation on the social, economic, intellectual, and psychological well-being of the individual, and the obstacle it poses to individual achievement, make it most difficult to reconcile the cost or the principle of a status-based denial of basic education with the framework of equality embodied in the Equal Protection Clause. What we said 28 years ago in *Brown v. Board of Education*, 347 U.S. 483, 74 S.Ct. 686, 98 L.Ed. 873 (1954), still holds true:

> * * * In these days, it is doubtful that any child may reasonably be expected to succeed in life if he is denied the opportunity of an

education. Such an opportunity, where the state has undertaken to provide it, is a right which must be made available to all on equal terms.

These well-settled principles allow us to determine the proper level of deference to be afforded § 21.031. Undocumented aliens cannot be treated as a suspect class because their presence in this country in violation of federal law is not a "constitutional irrelevancy." Nor is education a fundamental right; a State need not justify by compelling necessity every variation in the manner in which education is provided to its population. But more is involved in these cases than the abstract question whether § 21.031 discriminates against a suspect class, or whether education is a fundamental right. Section 21.031 imposes a lifetime hardship on a discrete class of children not accountable for their disabling status. The stigma of illiteracy will mark them for the rest of their lives. By denying these children a basic education, we deny them the ability to live within the structure of our civic institutions, and foreclose any realistic possibility that they will contribute in even the smallest way to the progress of our Nation. In determining the rationality of § 21.031, we may appropriately take into account its costs to the Nation and to the innocent children who are its victims. In light of these countervailing costs, the discrimination contained in § 21.031 can hardly be considered rational unless it furthers some substantial goal of the State.

IV

* * * [I]n the State's view, Congress' apparent disapproval of the presence of these children within the United States, and the evasion of the federal regulatory program that is the mark of undocumented status, provides authority for its decision to impose upon them special disabilities. Faced with an equal protection challenge respecting the treatment of aliens, we agree that the courts must be attentive to congressional policy; the exercise of congressional power might well affect the State's prerogatives to afford differential treatment to a particular class of aliens. But we are unable to find in the congressional immigration scheme any statement of policy that might weigh significantly in arriving at an equal protection balance concerning the State's authority to deprive these children of an education.

The Constitution grants Congress the power to "establish an uniform Rule of Naturalization." Art. I., § 8, cl. 4. Drawing upon this power, upon its plenary authority with respect to foreign relations and international commerce, and upon the inherent power of a sovereign to close its borders, Congress has developed a complex scheme governing admission to our Nation and status within our borders. The obvious need for delicate policy judgments has counseled the Judicial Branch to avoid intrusion into this field. But this traditional caution does not persuade us that unusual deference must be shown the classification embodied in § 21.031. The States enjoy no power with respect to the classification of aliens. This power is "committed to the political branches of the Federal Government." *Mathews*, 426 U.S., at 81, 96 S.Ct., at 1892. Although it is "a routine and normally legitimate part" of the business of the Federal Government to classify on the basis of alien status, *id.*, at 85, 96 S.Ct., at 1894, and to "take into account the character of the relationship between the alien and this country," *id.*, at 80, 96 S.Ct., at 1891, only rarely are such matters relevant to legislation by a State.

As we recognized in *De Canas v. Bica*, 424 U.S. 351, 96 S.Ct. 933, 47 L.Ed.2d 43 (1976), the States do have some authority to act with respect to illegal aliens, at least where such action mirrors federal objectives and furthers a legitimate state goal. In *De Canas*, the State's program reflected Congress' intention to bar from employment all aliens except those possessing a grant of permission to work in this country. In contrast, there is no indication that the disability imposed by § 21.031 corresponds to any identifiable congressional policy. The State does not claim that the conservation of state educational resources was ever a congressional concern in restricting immigration. More importantly, the classification reflected in § 21.031 does not operate harmoniously within the federal program.

To be sure, like all persons who have entered the United States unlawfully, these children are subject to deportation. But there is no assurance that a child subject to deportation will ever be deported. An illegal entrant might be granted federal permission to continue to reside in this country, or even to become a citizen. In light of the discretionary federal power to grant relief from deportation, a State cannot realistically determine that any particular undocumented child will in fact be deported until after deportation proceedings have been completed. It would of course be most difficult for the State to justify a denial of education to a child enjoying an inchoate federal permission to remain.

We are reluctant to impute to Congress the intention to withhold from these children, for so long as they are present in this country through no fault of their own, access to a basic education. In other contexts, undocumented status, coupled with some articulable federal policy, might enhance state authority with respect to the treatment of undocumented aliens. But in the area of special constitutional sensitivity presented by these cases, and in the absence of any contrary indication fairly discernible in the present legislative record, we perceive no national policy that supports the State in denying these children an elementary education. * * * We therefore turn to the state objectives that are said to support § 21.031.

V

Appellants argue that the classification at issue furthers an interest in the "preservation of the state's limited resources for the education of its lawful residents." Of course, a concern for the preservation of resources standing alone can hardly justify the classification used in allocating those resources. *Graham v. Richardson*, 403 U.S. 365, 374–375, 91 S.Ct. 1848, 1853, 29 L.Ed.2d 534 (1971). The State must do more than justify its classification with a concise expression of an intention to discriminate. Apart from the asserted state prerogative to act against undocumented children solely on the basis of their undocumented status—an asserted prerogative that carries only minimal force in the circumstances of these cases—we discern three colorable state interests that might support § 21.031.

First, appellants appear to suggest that the State may seek to protect itself from an influx of illegal immigrants. While a State might have an interest in mitigating the potentially harsh economic effects of sudden shifts in population,[23] § 21.031 hardly offers an effective method of dealing with an urgent demographic or economic problem. There is no evidence in the record suggesting that illegal entrants impose any significant burden on the State's economy. To the contrary, the available evidence suggests that illegal aliens underutilize public services, while contributing their labor to the local economy and tax money to the state fisc. The dominant incentive for illegal entry into the State of Texas is the availability of employment; few if any illegal immigrants come to this country, or presumably to the State of Texas, in order to avail themselves of a free education. Thus, even making the doubtful assumption that the net impact of illegal aliens on the economy of the State is negative, we think it clear that "[c]harging tuition to undocumented children constitutes a ludicrously ineffectual attempt to stem the tide of illegal immigration," at least when compared with the alternative of prohibiting the employment of illegal aliens. 458 F. Supp., at 585.

Second, * * * appellants suggest that undocumented children are appropriately singled out for exclusion because of the special burdens they impose on the State's ability to provide high-quality public education. But the record in no way supports the claim that exclusion of undocumented children is likely to improve the overall quality of education in the State. * * * Of course, even if improvement in the quality of education were a likely result of barring some *number* of children from the schools of the State, the State must support its selection of *this* group as the appropriate target for exclusion. * * *

Finally, appellants suggest that undocumented children are appropriately singled out because their unlawful presence within the United States renders them less likely than other children to remain within the boundaries of the State, and to put their education to productive social or political use within the State. Even assuming that such an interest is legitimate, it is an interest that is most difficult to quantify. The State has no assurance that any child, citizen or not, will employ the education provided by the State within the confines of the State's borders. In any

---

23. Although the State has no direct interest in controlling entry into this country, that interest being one reserved by the Constitution to the Federal Government, unchecked unlawful migration might impair the State's economy generally, or the State's ability to provide some important service. Despite the exclusive federal control of this Nation's borders, we cannot conclude that the States are without any power to deter the influx of persons entering the United States against federal law, and whose numbers might have a discernible impact on traditional state concerns. See *De Canas v. Bica*, 424 U.S., at 354–356, 96 S.Ct., at 935–936.

event, the record is clear that many of the undocumented children disabled by this classification will remain in this country indefinitely, and that some will become lawful residents or citizens of the United States. It is difficult to understand precisely what the State hopes to achieve by promoting the creation and perpetuation of a subclass of illiterates within our boundaries, surely adding to the problems and costs of unemployment, welfare, and crime. It is thus clear that whatever savings might be achieved by denying these children an education, they are wholly insubstantial in light of the costs involved to these children, the State, and the Nation.

* * *

JUSTICE MARSHALL, concurring.

While I join the Court's opinion, I do so without in any way retreating from my opinion in *San Antonio Independent School District v. Rodriguez*, 411 U.S. 1, 70–133, 93 S.Ct. 1278, 1315–1348, 36 L.Ed.2d 16 (1973) (dissenting opinion). I continue to believe that an individual's interest in education is fundamental, and that this view is amply supported "by the unique status accorded public education by our society, and by the close relationship between education and some of our most basic constitutional values." *Id.*, at 111, 93 S.Ct., at 1336. * * * It continues to be my view that a class-based denial of public education is utterly incompatible with the Equal Protection Clause of the Fourteenth Amendment.

JUSTICE BLACKMUN, concurring.

* * *

* * * Children denied an education are placed at a permanent and insurmountable competitive disadvantage, for an uneducated child is denied even the opportunity to achieve. * * * Other benefits provided by the State, such as housing and public assistance, are of course important; to an individual in immediate need, they may be more desirable than the right to be educated. But classifications involving the complete denial of education are in a sense unique, for they strike at the heart of equal protection values by involving the State in the creation of permanent class distinctions. In a sense, then, denial of an education is the analogue of denial of the right to vote: the former relegates the individual to second-class social status; the latter places him at a permanent political disadvantage.

* * *

* * * [T]he structure of the immigration statutes makes it impossible for the State to determine which aliens are entitled to residence, and which eventually will be deported. Indeed, any attempt to do so would involve the State in the administration of the immigration laws. * * * [T]he statute at issue here sweeps within it a substantial number of children who will in fact, and who may well be entitled to, remain in the

United States. Given the extraordinary nature of the interest involved, this makes the classification here fatally imprecise. * * *

* * *

JUSTICE POWELL, concurring.

* * *

Our review in a case such as these is properly heightened. The classification at issue deprives a group of children of the opportunity for education afforded all other children simply because they have been assigned a legal status due to a violation of law by their parents. These children thus have been singled out for a lifelong penalty and stigma. A legislative classification that threatens the creation of an underclass of future citizens and residents cannot be reconciled with one of the fundamental purposes of the Fourteenth Amendment. In these unique circumstances, the Court properly may require that the State's interests be substantial and that the means bear a "fair and substantial relation" to these interests.

* * * [T]he interests relied upon by the State would seem to be insubstantial in view of the consequences to the State itself of wholly uneducated persons living indefinitely within its borders. By contrast, access to the public schools is made available to the children of lawful residents without regard to the temporary nature of their residency in the particular Texas school district. * * * [T]he exclusion of appellees' class of children from state-provided education is a type of punitive discrimination based on status that is impermissible under the Equal Protection Clause.

In reaching this conclusion, I am not unmindful of what must be the exasperation of responsible citizens and government authorities in Texas and other States similarly situated. Their responsibility, if any, for the influx of aliens is slight compared to that imposed by the Constitution on the Federal Government. So long as the ease of entry remains inviting, and the power to deport is exercised infrequently by the Federal Government, the additional expense of admitting these children to public schools might fairly be shared by the Federal and State Governments. But it hardly can be argued rationally that anyone benefits from the creation within our borders of a subclass of illiterate persons many of whom will remain in the State, adding to the problems and costs of both State and National Governments attendant upon unemployment, welfare, and crime.

CHIEF JUSTICE BURGER, with whom JUSTICE WHITE, JUSTICE REHNQUIST, and JUSTICE O'CONNOR join, dissenting.

Were it our business to set the Nation's social policy, I would agree without hesitation that it is senseless for an enlightened society to deprive any children—including illegal aliens—of an elementary education. I fully agree that it would be folly—and wrong—to tolerate creation of a segment of society made up of illiterate persons, many having a limited or no command of our language. However, the Constitution does not constitute us as "Platonic Guardians" nor does it vest in this Court the authority to strike down laws because they do not meet our standards of desirable social policy, "wisdom," or "common sense." We trespass on the assigned function of the political branches under our structure of limited and separated powers when we assume a policymaking role as the Court does today.

* * *

The dispositive issue in these cases, simply put, is whether, for purposes of allocating its finite resources, a state has a legitimate reason to differentiate between persons who are lawfully within the state and those who are unlawfully there. The distinction the State of Texas has drawn—based not only upon its own legitimate interests but on classifications established by the Federal Government in its immigration laws and policies—is not unconstitutional.

The Court acknowledges that, except in those cases when state classifications disadvantage a "suspect class" or impinge upon a "fundamental right," the Equal Protection Clause permits a state "substantial latitude" in distinguishing between different groups of persons. Moreover, the Court expressly—and correctly—rejects any suggestion that illegal aliens are a suspect class, or that education is a fundamental right. Yet by patching together bits and pieces of what might be termed quasi-suspect-class and quasi-fundamental-rights analysis, the Court spins out a theory custom-tailored to the facts of these cases.

* * *

The Court first suggests that these illegal alien children, although not a suspect class, are entitled to special solicitude under the Equal Protection Clause because they lack "control" over or "responsibility" for their unlawful entry into this country. Similarly, the Court appears to take the position that § 21.031 is presumptively "irrational" because it has the effect of imposing "penalties" on "innocent" children. However, the Equal Protection Clause * * * protects against arbitrary and irrational classifications, and against invidious discrimination stemming from prejudice and hostility; it is not an all-encompassing "equalizer" designed to eradicate every distinction for which persons are not "responsible."

The Court does not presume to suggest that appellees' purported lack of culpability for their illegal status prevents them from being deported or otherwise "penalized" under federal law. Yet would deportation be any less a "penalty" than denial of privileges provided to legal residents? Illegality of presence in the United States does not—and need not—depend on some amorphous concept of "guilt" or "innocence" concerning an alien's entry. Similarly, a state's use of federal immigration status as a basis for legislative classification is not necessarily rendered suspect for its failure to take such factors into account.

* * * This Court has recognized that in allocating governmental benefits to a given class of aliens, one "may take into account the character of the relationship between the alien and this country." *Mathews v. Diaz*, 426 U.S. 67, 80, 96 S.Ct. 1883, 1891, 48 L.Ed.2d 478 (1976). When that "relationship" is a federally prohibited one, there can, of course, be no presumption that a state has a constitutional duty to include illegal aliens among the recipients of its governmental benefits.[7]

* * *

The importance of education is beyond dispute. Yet we have held repeatedly that the importance of a governmental service does not elevate it to the status of a "fundamental right" for purposes of equal protection analysis. * * * Moreover, the Court points to no meaningful way to distinguish between education and other governmental benefits in this context. Is the Court suggesting that education is more "fundamental" than food, shelter, or medical care?

* * *

The central question in these cases, as in every equal protection case not involving truly fundamental rights "explicitly or implicitly guaranteed by the Constitution," *San Antonio Independent School Dist., supra*, 411 U.S., at 33–34, 93 S.Ct., at 1296–1297, is whether there is some legitimate basis for a legislative distinction between different classes of persons. The fact that the distinction is drawn in legislation affecting access to public education—as opposed to legislation allocating other important governmental benefits, such as public assistance, health care, or housing—cannot make a difference in the level of scrutiny applied.

Once it is conceded—as the Court does—that illegal aliens are not a suspect class, and that education is not a fundamental right, our inquiry should focus on and be limited to whether the legislative classification at issue bears a rational relationship to a legitimate state purpose.

The State contends primarily that § 21.031 serves to prevent undue depletion of its limited revenues available for education, and to preserve the fiscal integrity of the State's school-financing system against an ever-increasing flood of illegal aliens—aliens over whose entry or continued presence it has no control. Of course such fiscal concerns alone could not justify discrimination against a suspect class or an arbitrary and irrational denial of benefits to a particular group of persons. Yet I assume no Member of this Court would argue that prudent conservation of finite state revenues is *per se* an illegitimate goal. Indeed, the numerous classifications this Court has sustained in social welfare legislation were invariably related to the limited amount of revenues available to spend on any given program or set of programs. The significant question here is whether the requirement of tuition from illegal aliens who attend the public schools—as well as from residents of other states, for example—is a

---

7. It is true that the Constitution imposes lesser constraints on the Federal Government than on the states with regard to discrimination against lawfully admitted aliens. * * * However, the same cannot be said when Congress has decreed that certain aliens should not be admitted to the United States at all.

rational and reasonable means of furthering the State's legitimate fiscal ends.[10]

Without laboring what will undoubtedly seem obvious to many, it simply is not "irrational" for a state to conclude that it does not have the same responsibility to provide benefits for persons whose very presence in the state and this country is illegal as it does to provide for persons lawfully present. By definition, illegal aliens have no right whatever to be here, and the state may reasonably, and constitutionally, elect not to provide them with governmental services at the expense of those who are lawfully in the state. In *De Canas v. Bica*, 424 U.S. 351, 357, 96 S.Ct. 933, 937, 47 L.Ed.2d 43 (1976), we held that a State may protect its "fiscal interests and lawfully resident labor force from the deleterious effects on its economy resulting from the employment of illegal aliens." * * *

It is significant that the Federal Government has seen fit to exclude illegal aliens from numerous social welfare programs, such as the food stamp program, the old-age assistance, aid to families with dependent children, aid to the blind, aid to the permanently and totally disabled, and supplemental security income programs, the Medicare hospital insurance benefits program, and the Medicaid hospital insurance benefits for the aged and disabled program. Although these exclusions do not conclusively demonstrate the constitutionality of the State's use of the same classification for comparable purposes, at the very least they tend to support the rationality of excluding illegal alien residents of a state from such programs so as to preserve the state's finite revenues for the benefit of lawful residents.

The Court maintains—as if this were the issue—that "barring undocumented children from local schools would not necessarily improve the quality of education provided in those schools." However, the legitimacy of barring illegal aliens from programs such as Medicare or Medicaid does not depend on a showing that the barrier would "improve the quality" of medical care given to persons lawfully entitled to participate in such programs. Modern education, like medical care, is enormously expensive, and there can be no doubt that very large added costs will fall on the State or its local school districts as a result of the inclusion of illegal aliens in the tuition-free public schools. The State may, in its discretion, use any savings resulting from its tuition requirement to "improve the quality of education" in the public school system, or to enhance the funds available for other social programs, or to reduce the tax burden placed on its residents; each of these ends is "legitimate." * * *

* * *

---

10. The Texas law might also be justified as a means of deterring unlawful immigration. While regulation of immigration is an exclusively federal function, a state may take steps, consistent with federal immigration policy, to protect its economy and ability to provide governmental services from the "deleterious effects" of a massive influx of illegal immigrants. *De Canas v. Bica*, 424 U.S. 351, 96 S.Ct. 933, 47 L.Ed.2d 43 (1976). * * *

NOTES AND QUESTIONS ON PLYLER v. DOE

1. Several sources richly tell of the origins, backstory, and aftermath of *Plyler*. For a perceptive analysis of the role of the Mexican–American Legal Defense and Educational Fund (MALDEF) and the myriad lawyering choices, see Olivas, *Plyler v. Doe, the Education of Undocumented Children, and the Polity*, in Immigration Stories 197–220 (D. Martin & P. Schuck eds., 2005). Looking at the families and offering a fascinating glimpse of the justices' deliberations, Barbara Belejack unearths this intriguing fact:

> The day the opinion was issued, a little-known Department of Justice lawyer co-wrote a memo chastising the U.S. solicitor general for not filing a brief taking Texas' side. Had such a brief been filed, future Supreme Court Chief Justice John Roberts suggested, Powell might have voted differently.

Belejack, *A Lesson in Equal Protection: The Texas cases that opened the schoolhouse door to undocumented immigrant children*, 99 Texas Observer no. 14 (July 13, 2007).

2. Is *Plyler* consistent with *De Canas*, which figures prominently in both majority and dissent in *Plyler*? Why does depriving undocumented children of an education differ from depriving their parents of a job?

3. In *De Canas*, the argument for federal preemption of California's employer sanctions was made by employers who, the plaintiffs contended, were maintaining an illegal workforce that excluded authorized workers. In *Plyler*, the federal preemption argument was made by migrant children. Did this difference affect the outcomes?

4. Justice Brennan relies in part on the "[s]heer incapability or lax enforcement of the laws barring entry into this country, coupled with the failure to establish an effective bar to the employment of undocumented aliens." Quoting the district court, Brennan adds that "[c]harging tuition to undocumented children constitutes a ludicrously ineffectual attempt to stem the tide of illegal immigration," at least when compared with the alternative of prohibiting the employment of illegal aliens. And he notes "[t]here is no evidence in the record suggesting that illegal entrants impose any significant burden on the State's economy." Do these observations remain valid today? If not, what follows?

5. The majority and dissenting opinions display remarkably different renderings of societal membership. Justice Brennan appears to find attributes of membership for the plaintiff children. He holds that the Constitution applies irrespective of status, and he argues that the denial of education to the plaintiff children would "deny them the ability to live within the structure of our civic institutions" and would "foreclose any realistic possibility that they will contribute in even the smallest way to the progress of our Nation." To Chief Justice Burger, the permissibility of excluding unauthorized alien children from public schools is self-evident: "By definition, illegal aliens have no right whatever to be here, and the state may reasonably, constitutionally, elect not to provide them with governmental services." Which account do you find more persuasive? Why? For thoughtful arguments for recognizing resi-

dent undocumented aliens as members of the U.S. community, see Bosniak, *Exclusion and Membership: The Dual Identity of the Undocumented Worker under United States Law,* 1988 Wis. L. Rev. 955; Lopez, *Undocumented Mexican Migration: In Search of a Just Immigration Law and Policy,* 28 UCLA L. Rev. 615 (1981).

6. Contrast the Court's equal protection analysis in *Plyler* with *Graham* and *Diaz.* Despite the significance of *Plyler* for educational access, Michael Olivas has commented on the decision's limited doctrinal reach outside this realm: "*Plyler*'s incontestably bold reasoning has not substantially influenced subsequent Supreme Court immigration jurisprudence in the twenty-plus years since it was decided." Olivas, *supra,* at 210–11.

Addressing the decision not as doctrine but as a window on policy debates about immigration outside the law, Hiroshi Motomura "sketches the three key themes that explain the wide gulf between the majority and the dissent and which have become central to current debates":

> The first theme is the meaning of unlawful presence: Is immigration outside the law a matter of egregious lawbreaking, or does it represent an invited contribution to the U.S. economy and society that the government tolerates? The second theme is the role of states and cities: Can states and cities try to force out unlawful migrants by making it hard to find work or housing, or may they welcome immigrants who come outside the law? The third theme is the integration of immigrants: Should unlawful immigrants be given access to education, work, lawful immigration status, or even a path to formal citizenship? What measures—if any—should we take to foster their integration into American society?

Motomura, *Immigration Outside the Law,* 108 Colum. L.Rev. 2037, 2039 (2008).

7. What if a *federal* law directly barred unauthorized migrant children from public K–12 education? Would it be constitutional, given the broader scope of federal authority suggested in *Diaz*? But what did this sentence in *Graham* mean: "Although the Federal Government admittedly has broad constitutional power to determine what aliens shall be admitted to the United States, the period they may remain, and the terms and conditions of their naturalization, Congress does not have the power to authorize the individual States to violate the Equal Protection Clause."

Does it matter if Congress acts directly, or authorizes the states to act? During debate on the 1996 Act, Congress considered an amendment sponsored by Congressman Elton Gallegly (R–CA) that would have authorized states to bar unauthorized children from public education. After strong opposition from the Clinton administration, the proposal was removed from the final version of the 1996 Immigration Act and was ultimately passed by the House 254–175 as a separate bill. It never came up for a Senate vote. What if the Gallegly amendment had been enacted and Texas re-adopted the statute invalidated in *Plyler*? Is there a constitutional difference between a federal law that allows states to deny public education and a federal law that does so directly?

Proposition 187

In November 1994, California voters approved Proposition 187, re-printed in the Statutory Supplement. This "Save Our State" initiative was intended to "provide for cooperation between [the] agencies of state and local government with the federal government, and to establish a system of required notification by and between such agencies to prevent illegal aliens in the United States from receiving benefits or public services in the State of California." Republican Governor Pete Wilson, one of its most prominent champions, argued that illegal aliens would "self-deport."

As drafted, Proposition 187 restricted unauthorized migrants' access to public services, including education and non-emergency health care. It also required state and local law enforcement, social services, health care and education officials to verify the immigration status of persons with whom they came in contact and to report to the INS persons suspected of being unlawfully in the United States. And it imposed criminal penalties for the manufacture, distribution, sale, or use of false citizenship or permanent residence documents.

Lawsuits immediately challenged Proposition 187, and a federal district court held that the federal immigration power preempted the requirements that state officials ascertain immigration status and report suspected unauthorized migrants to federal authorities. *League of United Latin American Citizens v. Wilson*, 908 F.Supp. 755 (C.D. Cal. 1995). Applying *Plyler*, the court also found it unconstitutional to deny public education to children without lawful immigration status, but it upheld the new criminal provisions relating to false documents.

Did federal law preempt California's denial of state benefits to unauthorized migrants? This was unresolved until 1996, when the federal 1996 Welfare Act pervasively regulated noncitizen eligibility for state and federal benefits. Interestingly, it addressed access to public schools as follows: "Nothing in this chapter [limiting federal and state benefits for unauthorized migrants] may be construed as addressing alien eligibility for a basic public education as determined by the Supreme Court of the United States under *Plyler v. Doe*." 8 U.S.C. § 1643. The district court ruled that the federal Welfare Act preempted the public benefits provisions of Proposition 187. *League of United Latin American Citizens v. Wilson*, 997 F.Supp. 1244, 1261 (C.D.Cal.1997).

The Proposition 187 litigation was ultimately settled after Democratic Governor Gray Davis took office. The state dropped its appeal. The public school access bar and the requirements that state employees check status and report suspected unauthorized migrants never took effect, though the false documents provisions did. With the settlement, Proposition 187 never gave the U.S. Supreme Court a chance to revisit *Plyler*.

From one perspective, Proposition 187 accomplished little. Before the initiative, unauthorized migrants were already ineligible for most benefit programs. To the extent that it tried to adopt policies that would deter the entry and residence of unauthorized migrants, it is reasonable to ask if the denial of benefits would have substantially reduced the flow of unauthorized migrants into California.

From another perspective, California may have lost the battle but won the war. Despite a holding of near total preemption, it accomplished—through federal welfare legislation—much its goal of excluding unauthorized migrants from benefit programs. This may remind you of another relationship between state and federal legislative activity over a century before—the enactment of the federal Chinese exclusion laws after similar state laws had been found unconstitutional as beyond the power of state authority. Moreover, Proposition 187 opened up the political landscape for similar efforts to address unauthorized migration through making it harder to live in a state or locality without lawful immigration status.

Support for Proposition 187 came from many quarters. There was concern over the fiscal and social consequences of unauthorized migration, a fear among some voters of a loss of control over culture and language, and anger at the federal government for failure to enforce immigration laws effectively. But Kevin Johnson adds: "it is difficult to refute the claim that the ethnicity of the stereotypical undocumented immigrant played at least *some* role in the passage of Proposition 187." Johnson, *An Essay on Immigration Politics, Popular Democracy, and California's Proposition 187: The Political Relevance and Legal Irrelevance of Race*, 70 Wash. L. Rev. 629, 651 (1995). What would it take to persuade you that Proposition 187—or any similar measure—does or does not reflect racial or ethnic animus?

The opposition to Proposition 187 also deserves comment. "What is striking," writes Linda Bosniak, "is the relatively narrow range of arguments that were made against Prop. 187." She continues:

> Especially notable was the near-complete omission from the public debate of one particular opposing argument which might have seemed, in theory, an obvious one to make: * * * that Prop. 187 should be rejected on grounds that its treatment of undocumented immigrants is unjust. * * * Prop. 187 is, after all, a law that specifically targets undocumented immigrants for social exile from the most basic institutions of our society; to say it imposes on them a comprehensive form of legal apartheid is hardly mere hyperbole.

* * *

* * * [T]he question of how to articulate what is wrong with [Proposition 187] poses an important intellectual challenge for progressive thought. Certainly, progressives can, and do, criticize policies which mandate the wholesale social exclusion of a class of people who reside and work here as normatively intolerable. But the problem is that undocumented immigrants are not entirely like other classes of

subordinated people whose condition progressives have addressed and whose inclusion they have championed. * * * [T]he full story of their subordination * * * [includes] the efforts by government to keep them from coming in the first place and to remove them once they are here. Yet progressives' normative nationalism—whether tacit or explicit—makes them far less able and less likely to criticize the immigrants' exclusion from territory in the first place. The result is a gap—between a politics of inclusion within the national society, and a politics of exclusion, or acquiescence to exclusion, at the society's boundaries.

Bosniak, *Opposing Prop. 187: Undocumented Immigrants and the National Imagination*, 28 Conn. L. Rev. 555, 567, 617–18 (1996).

b. Current Controversies

Starting in earnest about ten years after Proposition 187, a new wave of state and local laws emerged with vehemence, targeting unauthorized migrants and prompting court challenges. Many of these laws have tried to limit access to housing and work. Compare the next two decisions with each other in reasoning and outcome. The first is a Third Circuit decision that struck down local housing and employment ordinances enacted in 2006 in Hazleton, Pennsylvania. In the second decision, *Chamber of Commerce v. Whiting*, 564 U.S. ___, 131 S.Ct. 1968, 179 L.Ed.2d 1031 (2011), the U.S. Supreme Court upheld a 2007 Arizona state employment law. The Court then vacated the Third Circuit's *Hazleton* decision for reconsideration in light of *Whiting*. We will consider later in the chapter the better known and more restrictive Arizona law, SB 1070, that was enacted in 2010.

LOZANO v. CITY OF HAZLETON

United States Court of Appeals for the Third Circuit, 2010.
620 F.3d 170.

McKEE, CHIEF JUDGE:

* * *

The City of Hazleton is located in Luzerne County in northeastern Pennsylvania. * * *

Hazleton's population was only 23,000 in 2000. Between 2000 and the time of trial, however, its population increased to between 30,000 and 33,000. Much of this growth was due to an influx of Latino families who migrated from New York and New Jersey to Pennsylvania in the early 2000s. These newcomers included United States citizens and lawful permanent residents, as well as persons lacking lawful immigration status, who are often referred to as "undocumented immigrants" or "illegal aliens."

Hazleton's mayor, as well as other local officials, subsequently concluded that aliens lacking lawful status were to blame for certain social problems in the City, and that the federal government could not be relied upon to prevent such aliens from moving into the City, or to remove them. Accordingly, City officials decided to take independent action to regulate the local effects of unlawful immigration. Beginning on July 13, 2006, Hazleton's City Council began enacting a series of ordinances designed to address these concerns.

* * *

1. The Illegal Immigration Relief Act Ordinance

The IIRAO begins with a statement of findings and a declaration of purpose, which asserts:

> [t]hat unlawful employment, the harboring of illegal aliens in dwelling units in the City of Hazleton, and crime committed by illegal aliens harm the health, safety and welfare of authorized U.S. workers and legal residents in the City of Hazleton. Illegal immigration leads to higher crime rates, subjects our hospitals to fiscal hardship and legal residents to substandard quality of care, contributed to other burdens on public services, increasing their cost and diminishing their availability to legal residents, and diminishes our overall quality of life.

IIRAO § 2C. * * *

Section 4 of the IIRAO asserts that it is unlawful "for any business entity" to "recruit, hire for employment, or continue to employ" or "permit, dispatch, or instruct any person" who is an "unlawful worker" to perform work within Hazleton. Under the IIRAO, an "unlawful worker" is defined as: "a person who does not have the legal right or authorization to work due to an impediment in any provision of federal, state or local law, including but not limited to a minor disqualified by nonage, or an unauthorized alien as defined by [INA § 274A(h)(3)]." IIRAO § 3E. Section 4A requires "[e]very business entity that applies for a business permit" to "sign an affidavit ... affirming that they do not knowingly utilize the services or hire any person who is an unlawful worker."

Section 4 also provides for public monitoring, prosecution, and sanctions. Any City resident may submit a complaint to Hazleton's Code Enforcement Office alleging that a local business entity is violating the section's prohibition on utilizing the services of an unlawful worker. Upon receipt of such complaint, the Code Enforcement Office requests identity information about the alleged unlawful worker from the employing business, and that business must provide the information within three business days, or Hazleton will suspend its business license. If the worker is alleged to be an unauthorized alien, the Code Enforcement Office submits any identity information received from the business to the federal government, pursuant to 8 U.S.C. § 1373, for verification of "the immigration status of such person(s)."

If the Code Enforcement Office confirms that the worker lacks authorization to work in the United States, the business must terminate that person within three business days or the City will suspend its business license. Safe harbor from this sanction is provided to businesses that verify the work authorization of its workers through use of the "Basic Pilot Program" (which has since been named "E–Verify"). E–Verify is a federal program for verifying work authorization which Congress has authorized for use on a trial basis.

* * *

The IIRAO further creates a private cause of action against businesses that employ unlawful workers. Section 4E of the IIRAO makes it "an unfair business practice" for a business entity to discharge "an employee who is not an unlawful worker," if, on the date of the discharge, "the business entity was not participating in [E–Verify] and the business entity was employing an unlawful worker." An employee discharged under these conditions may sue the business entity under the IIRAO for treble actual damages, as well as reasonable attorney's fees and costs.

The IIRAO also addresses the "harboring" of persons lacking lawful immigration status. Section 5 makes it "unlawful for any person or business entity that owns a dwelling unit in the City to harbor an illegal alien in the dwelling unit, knowing or in reckless disregard of the fact that an alien has come to, entered, or remains in the United States in violation of law." "Harboring" is broadly defined. The ordinance states: "to let, lease, or rent a dwelling unit to an illegal alien ... shall be deemed to constitute harboring." Additionally, Section 7 of the IIRAO makes legal immigration status a condition precedent to entering into a valid lease. All leases entered into by persons lacking lawful status are deemed breached.

The mechanisms for enforcing the housing provisions of the IIRAO are similar to those set forth above for enforcing the employment provisions. Thus, any City resident may file a complaint with Hazleton's Code Enforcement Office alleging that a property owner is illegally "harboring" a tenant who is an "illegal alien." Once such a complaint is received, the Code Enforcement Office may request identifying information about the named tenant from the property owner, and the property owner must provide that information within three days. The City then verifies the legality of the tenant's immigration status with the federal government, pursuant to 8 U.S.C. § 1373(c).

If the federal government confirms that the tenant lacks lawful immigration status, the IIRAO gives the property owner five business days to evict that tenant. If the owner fails to do so, the City suspends the owner's rental license and bars the owner from collecting any rent for the applicable dwelling unit. * * *

2. *The Rental Registration Ordinance*

The RO operates in conjunction with the anti-harboring provisions of the IIRAO. Section 7 of the RO requires that *any* prospective occupant of rental housing over the age of eighteen apply for and receive an occupancy permit. To receive that permit, the prospective occupant must pay a ten-dollar fee and must submit certain documents, including "[p]roper identification showing proof of legal citizenship and/or residency" to Hazleton's Code Enforcement Office. Hazleton landlords are required to inform all prospective occupants of this requirement, and they are prohibited from allowing anyone over the age of eighteen to rent or occupy a rental unit, unless that person has a permit.

Section 10 of the RO provides that a landlord found guilty of renting to someone without a permit must pay an initial fine of $1000 per unauthorized occupant, and an additional fine of $100 per day per unauthorized occupant until the violation is corrected. An authorized occupant of rental housing who is found guilty of permitting someone without a rental permit to live in her/his apartment must pay the same fine.

* * *

In deciding whether to permit those Plaintiffs with concerns about the legality of their immigration status to proceed anonymously, * * * the court found that ethnic tensions had escalated in Hazleton since enactment of the ordinances, and that the named Plaintiffs had been harassed and intimidated for their involvement in this litigation.[19] The court concluded that the Doe Plaintiffs, because of their unlawful status, would face an "exponentially greater" risk of harassment, and even physical danger, if their identities were revealed. * * * [G]iven the environment in Hazleton following enactment of these ordinances, the court did not abuse its discretion in permitting the Doe Plaintiffs to proceed using pseudonyms.

VI. DISCUSSION

* * *

As we noted at the outset, state and local attempts to regulate issues related to immigration have skyrocketed in recent years. According to the National Conference of State Legislatures ("NCSL"), 300 bills pertaining to immigration were introduced in state legislatures in 2005, and thirty-eight of them were enacted into law. Less than five years later, these numbers had increased more than five-fold: in 2009, over 1,500 bills

---

19. Lozano, for example, testified that hate mail was sent to his home three separate times. One letter "contained a clipping from a newspaper describing the [alleged] effects of illegal immigration as well as a picture of a 'warrior' wearing 'a huge Mexican hat.' Scrawled near this picture were the phrases, '[s]ubhuman spic scum' and '[i]f it is brown, flush it down.' " This letter also contained a link to a website proclaiming itself "the Official Home Page of the National Socialist Movement, an organization dedicated to the preservation of our Proud Aryan Heritage, and the creation of a National Socialist Society in America and around the world." The district court noted that this sort of harassment extended even to people who were merely perceived as being connected to the lawsuit, even if this perception was not rooted in fact. Amilcar Arroyo, a United States citizen who publishes a Hazleton-based Spanish-language newspaper, was publically harassed when he tried to cover a rally in support of the ordinances. Based on a rumor that he was a plaintiff in this suit, rally participants gathered around him shouting, "get out of the country" and "traitor." Police escorted Arroyo from the rally for his own protection.

pertaining to immigration were introduced. From these, 222 laws were enacted, and 131 resolutions adopted.

A number of these laws contain provisions that are either identical, or similar, to provisions in Hazleton's ordinances. In their brief filed on behalf of Plaintiffs, *Amici Curiae* Chambers of Commerce note that Arizona, Mississippi, Oklahoma, Utah, Tennessee, Louisiana, West Virginia, Colorado, Minnesota, Georgia, and Rhode Island, as well as the municipalities of Valley Park, Missouri; Mission Viejo, California; Beaufort County, South Carolina; and Apple Valley, California, have all enacted laws that in some way regulate either the procedures employers must undertake in order to avoid hiring unauthorized aliens, or the penalties that can be imposed for doing so. In addition, Plaintiffs call our attention to several localities, including Escondido, California and the City of Farmers Branch, Texas, which have passed ordinances regulating the provision of rental housing to aliens not lawfully present in the United States.

Various challenges have been leveled at these enactments—most commonly, attacks rooted in the Supremacy Clause—and the resulting body of case law informs our analysis. * * *

* * *

* * * The pre-emption doctrine is a necessary outgrowth of the Supremacy Clause. It ensures that when Congress either expresses or implies an intent to preclude certain state or local legislation, offending enactments cannot stand.

As this Court has recently noted, "the Supreme Court has recognized three types of pre-emption: express pre-emption, implied conflict pre-emption, and field pre-emption." *Bruesewitz v. Wyeth Inc.,* 561 F.3d 233, 238–239 (3d Cir.2009) (citing *Hillsborough County, Fla. v. Automated Med. Labs., Inc.,* 471 U.S. 707, 713, 105 S.Ct. 2371, 85 L.Ed.2d 714 (1985)). Both conflict pre-emption and field pre-emption are types of implied pre-emption. * * *

* * *

Express pre-emption occurs when Congress expressly declares a law's pre-emptive effect. *See Lorillard Tobacco Co. v. Reilly,* 533 U.S. 525, 541, 121 S.Ct. 2404, 150 L.Ed.2d 532 (2001). In such cases, "our task is to identify the domain expressly pre-empted." *Id.* * * *

Implied field pre-emption occurs when state or local governments attempt regulation in a field which Congress has implied an intent to exclusively occupy. Congress's intent to occupy a field can be inferred where a federal regulatory scheme is "so pervasive as to make reasonable the inference that Congress left no room for the States to supplement it," *Gade v. Nat'l Solid Wastes Mgmt. Ass'n,* 505 U.S. 88, 98, 112 S.Ct. 2374, 120 L.Ed.2d 73 (1992), or where an Act of Congress "touch[es] a field in which the federal interest is so dominant that the federal system will be assumed to preclude enforcement of state laws on the same subject," *Rice v. Santa Fe Elevator Corp.*, 331 U.S. 218, 230, 67 S.Ct. 1146, 91 L.Ed. 1447 (1947).

Implied conflict pre-emption occurs where it is "impossible ... to comply with both state and federal law," *Geier v. Am. Honda Motor Co.*, 529 U.S. 861, 873, 120 S.Ct. 1913, 146 L.Ed.2d 914 (2000) (internal quotation marks omitted), or where state law "stands as an obstacle to the accomplishment and execution of the full purposes and objectives of Congress," *Hines v. Davidowitz*, 312 U.S. 52, 67, 61 S.Ct. 399, 85 L.Ed. 581 (1941). * * *

1. *Employment Provisions*
[The court struck down the employment provisions.]

2. *Housing Provisions*

* * *

Although we realize that a state certainly can, and presumably should, regulate rental accommodations to ensure the health and safety of its residents, and that such regulation may permissibly affect the rights of persons in the country unlawfully, we cannot bury our heads in the sand ostrich-like ignoring the reality of what these ordinances accomplish. Through its housing provisions, Hazleton attempts to regulate residence based solely on immigration status. Deciding which aliens may live in the United States has always been the prerogative of the federal government. * * *

The rest of our analysis flows directly from our conclusion that Hazleton's housing provisions regulate which aliens may live there. Under *De Canas,* a state or locality may not "regulate immigration," which the Supreme Court has defined as any attempt to determine "who should or should not be admitted into the country, and the conditions under which a legal entrant may remain." *De Canas,* 424 U.S. at 355. Such power is delegated by the Constitution exclusively to the federal government, and even if Congress had never acted in the field, states and localities would be precluded from doing so. * * *

The housing provisions of the IIRAO and the RO are also field pre-empted by the INA. As the Supreme Court explained in *De Canas,* the central concern of the INA is with "the terms and conditions of admission to the country and the subsequent treatment of aliens lawfully in the country." 424 U.S. at 359. The "comprehensiveness of the INA scheme for regulation of immigration and naturalization," *id.,* plainly precludes state efforts, whether harmonious or conflicting, to regulate residence in this country based on immigration status.

We recognize, of course, that Hazleton's housing provisions neither control actual physical entry into the City, nor physically expel persons from it. Nonetheless, "[i]n essence," that is precisely what they attempt to do. *Bonito Boats [Inc. v. Thunder Craft Boats, Inc.,* 489 U.S. 141, 160, 109

S.Ct. 971, 103 L.Ed.2d 118 (1989)], "It is difficult to conceive of a more effective method" of ensuring that persons do not enter or remain in a locality than by precluding their ability to live in it.

At oral argument, Hazleton posited that aliens lacking lawful status could still reside in the City through purchasing a home, or through staying with friends. The response is as disingenuous as it is unrealistic. There is nothing on this record that suggests that the people whom the residential provisions are aimed at could avail themselves of such options. Even if they were viable alternatives for some, however, many others still would be excluded, and that is sufficient for these provisions to be preempted.

We also recognize that Hazleton's housing provisions regulate presence only within its city limits, not the entire country. This does not change the analysis. To be meaningful, the federal government's exclusive control over residence in this country must extend to any political subdivision. Again, it is not only Hazleton's ordinance that we must consider. If Hazleton can regulate as it has here, then so could every other state or locality. * * *

The housing provisions of the IIRAO and the RO are also conflict preempted by the INA. As the district court explained, these provisions attempt to effectively "remove" persons from Hazleton based on a snapshot of their current immigration status, rather than based on a federal order of removal. This is fundamentally inconsistent with the INA.

Hazleton goes to great lengths to defend its housing provisions as providing for an accurate assessment of tenants' immigration status, and only denying housing to those whom the federal government confirms are here unlawfully. Even assuming Hazleton is correct, this argument does not advance Hazleton's cause; rather, it highlights the fundamental misconception at the heart of these ordinances. Through its housing provisions, Hazleton attempts to remove persons from the community based on *current* immigration status. However, as Justice Blackmun explained in *Plyler:* "the structure of the immigration statutes makes it impossible for the State to determine which aliens are entitled to residence, and which eventually will be deported." 457 U.S. at 236 (Blackmun, J., concurring).

Under federal law, an unlawful immigration status does not lead instantly, or inevitably, to removal. Under most circumstances, a federal removal hearing under section 240 of the INA is required. Absent certain limited exceptions, this proceeding is the "sole and exclusive procedure for determining whether an alien may be admitted to the United States or, if the alien has been so admitted, removed from the United States." As we explained in detail above, knowing whether the government will decide to initiate proceedings against a particular alien is as impossible as trying to predict the outcome of such a proceeding once initiated.

The federal government has discretion in deciding whether and when to initiate removal proceedings. As the district court found, the government purposefully exercises its discretion not to prosecute in certain instances, and thereby tacitly allows the presence of those whose technical status remains "illegal." Furthermore, once the government initiates these proceedings, whether they will result in removal is far from certain. A judge may award discretionary relief saving a removable alien from removal, or even adjusting that alien's status to that of lawful permanent resident. * * *

Stitched into the fabric of Hazleton's housing provisions, then, is either a lack of understanding or a refusal to recognize the complexities of federal immigration law. Hazleton would effectively remove from its City an alien college student the federal government has purposefully declined to initiate removal proceedings against. So too would Hazleton remove an alien battered spouse, currently unlawfully present, but eligible for adjustment of status to lawful permanent resident under the special protections Congress has afforded to battered spouses and children. In each of these instances, as in every single instance in which Hazleton would deny residence to an alien based on immigration status rather than on a federal order of removal, Hazleton would act directly in opposition to federal law.

Hazleton attempts to avoid this result by again relying on the concept of "concurrent enforcement" to defend its housing provisions. According to Hazleton, its housing provisions mirror the INA's prohibition against "harboring," * * * INA § 274(a)(1)(A)(iii). Hazleton contends that since federal courts have consistently found that providing housing to aliens lacking lawful immigration status constitutes unlawful "harboring," its housing provisions do no more than concurrently enforce federal law. Hazleton is wrong.

As we have explained, Hazleton's housing provisions operate in a field which the federal government exclusively occupies. Therefore, even if Hazleton's housing provisions did concurrently enforce federal law, this would not save them; even harmonious regulation is pre-empted here. However, Hazleton is also plainly incorrect in claiming that its housing provisions "mirror" federal law. The federal prohibition against harboring has never been interpreted to apply so broadly as to encompass the typical landlord/tenant relationship.

* * *

In sum, we find the housing provisions of Hazleton's ordinances pre-empted as regulations of immigration, and both field and conflict pre-empted by the INA.

* * *

CHAMBER OF COMMERCE v. WHITING

Supreme Court of the United States, 2011
564 U.S. ___, 131 S.Ct. 1968, 179 L.Ed.2d 1031.

ROBERTS, C. J., delivered the opinion of the Court, except as to Parts II–B and III–B. SCALIA, KENNEDY, and ALITO, JJ., joined that opinion in full, and THOMAS, J., joined as to Parts I, II–A, and III–A and concurred in the judgment.

Federal immigration law expressly preempts "any State or local law imposing civil or criminal sanctions (other than through licensing and similar laws) upon those who employ ... unauthorized aliens." INA § 274A(h)(2). A recently enacted Arizona statute—the Legal Arizona Workers Act—provides that the licenses of state employers that knowingly or intentionally employ unauthorized aliens may be, and in certain circumstances must be, suspended or revoked. The law also requires that all Arizona employers use a federal electronic verification system to confirm that the workers they employ are legally authorized workers. The question presented is whether federal immigration law preempts those provisions of Arizona law. * * *

I

* * * Originally known as the "Basic Pilot Program," E–Verify "is an internet-based system that allows an employer to verify an employee's work-authorization status." *Chicanos Por La Causa, Inc. v. Napolitano,* 558 F.3d 856, 862 (9th Cir. 2009). An employer submits a request to the E–Verify system based on information that the employee provides similar to that used in the I–9 process. In response to that request, the employer receives either a confirmation or a tentative nonconfirmation of the employee's authorization to work. An employee may challenge a nonconfirmation report. If the employee does not do so, or if his challenge is unsuccessful, his employment must be terminated or the Federal Government must be informed.

In the absence of a prior violation of certain federal laws, IIRIRA [Illegal Immigration Reform and Immigrant Responsibility Act of 1996, also referred to in this casebook as "the 1996 Act"] prohibits the Secretary of Homeland Security from "requir[ing] any person or ... entity" outside the Federal Government "to participate in" the E–Verify program, [IIRIRA] § 402(a), (e) [8 U.S.C.A. § 1324a, Note]. To promote use of the program, however, the statute provides that any employer that utilizes E–Verify "and obtains confirmation of identity and employment eligibility in compliance with the terms and conditions of the program ... has established a rebuttable presumption" that it has not violated IRCA's unauthorized alien employment prohibition, [IIRIRA] § 402(b)(1).

Acting against this statutory and historical background, several States have recently enacted laws attempting to impose sanctions for the employment of unauthorized aliens through, among other things, "licensing and similar laws," INA § 274A(h)(2). Arizona is one of them. The Legal Arizona Workers Act of 2007 allows Arizona courts to suspend or revoke the licenses necessary to do business in the State if an employer knowingly or intentionally employs an unauthorized alien.

Under the Arizona law, if an individual files a complaint alleging that an employer has hired an unauthorized alien, the attorney general or the county attorney first verifies the employee's work authorization with the Federal Government pursuant to 8 U.S.C. § 1373(c). Section 1373(c) provides that the Federal Government "shall respond to an inquiry by a" State "seeking to verify or ascertain the citizenship or immigration status of any individual ... by providing the requested verification or status information." The Arizona law expressly prohibits state, county, or local officials from attempting "to independently make a final determination on whether an alien is authorized to work in the United States." If the § 1373(c) inquiry reveals that a worker is an unauthorized alien, the attorney general or the county attorney must notify United States Immigration and Customs Enforcement officials, notify local law enforcement, and bring an action against the employer.

When a complaint is brought against an employer under Arizona law, "the court shall consider only the federal government's determination pursuant to" 8 U.S.C. § 1373(c) in "determining whether an employee is an unauthorized alien." Good-faith compliance with the federal I–9 process provides employers prosecuted by the State with an affirmative defense.

A first instance of "knowingly employ[ing] an unauthorized alien" requires that the court order the employer to terminate the employment of all unauthorized aliens and file quarterly reports on all new hires for a probationary period of three years. The court may also "order the appropriate agencies to suspend all licenses ... that are held by the employer for [a period] not to exceed ten business days." A second knowing violation requires that the adjudicating court "permanently revoke all licenses that are held by the employer specific to the business location where the unauthorized alien performed work."

For a first intentional violation, the court must order the employer to terminate the employment of all unauthorized aliens and file quarterly reports on all new hires for a probationary period of five years. The court must also suspend all the employer's licenses for a minimum of 10 days. A second intentional violation requires the permanent revocation of all business licenses.

* * *

The Arizona law also requires that "every employer, after hiring an employee, shall verify the employment eligibility of the employee" by using E–Verify. "[P]roof of verifying the employment authorization of an employee through the e-verify program creates a rebuttable presumption that an employer did not knowingly employ an unauthorized alien."

The Chamber of Commerce of the United States and various business and civil rights organizations (collectively Chamber of Commerce or Chamber) filed a preenforcement suit in federal court against those charged with administering the Arizona law * * *. The Chamber argued that the Arizona law's provisions allowing the suspension and revocation of business licenses for employing unauthorized aliens were both expressly and impliedly preempted by federal immigration law, and that the mandatory use of E–Verify was impliedly preempted.

* * *

II

* * *

IRCA expressly preempts States from imposing "civil or criminal sanctions" on those who employ unauthorized aliens, "other than through licensing and similar laws." INA 274A(h)(2). The Arizona law, on its face, purports to impose sanctions through licensing laws. The state law authorizes state courts to suspend or revoke an employer's business licenses if that employer knowingly or intentionally employs an unauthorized alien. * * *

* * *

A license is "a right or permission granted in accordance with law ... to engage in some business or occupation, to do some act, or to engage in some transaction which but for such license would be unlawful." Webster's Third New International Dictionary 1304 (2002). Articles of incorporation and certificates of partnership allow the formation of legal entities and permit them as such to engage in business and transactions "which but for such" authorization "would be unlawful." *Ibid.* * * * Moreover, even if a law regulating articles of incorporation, partnership certificates, and the like is not itself a "licensing law," it is at the very least "similar" to a licensing law, and therefore comfortably within the savings clause.

* * *

* * * Whatever the usefulness of relying on legislative history materials in general, the arguments against doing so are particularly compelling here. Beyond verbatim recitation of the statutory text, all of the legislative history documents related to IRCA save one fail to discuss the savings clause at all. The Senate Judiciary Committee Report on the Senate version of the law does not comment on it. Only one of the four House Reports on the law touches on the licensing exception, and we have previously dismissed that very report as "a rather slender reed" from "one House of a politically divided Congress." *Hoffman [Plastic Compounds, Inc. v. NLRB,* 535 U.S. 137, 149–150, n.4, 122 S.Ct. 1275, 152 L.Ed.2d 271 (2002)]. And the Conference Committee Report does not discuss the scope of IRCA's preemption provision in any way.

IRCA expressly preempts some state powers dealing with the employ-ment of unauthorized aliens and it expressly preserves others. We hold that Arizona's licensing law falls well within the confines of the authority Congress chose to leave to the States and therefore is not expressly preempted.

As an alternative to its express preemption argument, the Chamber contends that Arizona's law is impliedly preempted because it conflicts with federal law. At its broadest level, the Chamber's argument is that Congress "intended the federal system to be exclusive," and that any state system therefore necessarily conflicts with federal law. But Arizona's procedures simply implement the sanctions that Congress expressly al-lowed Arizona to pursue through licensing laws. Given that Congress specifically preserved such authority for the States, it stands to reason that Congress did not intend to prevent the States from using appropriate tools to exercise that authority.

And here Arizona went the extra mile in ensuring that its law closely tracks IRCA's provisions in all material respects. The Arizona law begins by adopting the federal definition of who qualifies as an "unauthorized alien."

Not only that, the Arizona law expressly provides that state investiga-tors must verify the work authorization of an allegedly unauthorized alien with the Federal Government, and "shall not attempt to independently make a final determination on whether an alien is authorized to work in the United States." * * *

The federal determination on which the State must rely is provided under 8 U.S.C. § 1373(c). That provision requires the Federal Govern-ment to "verify or ascertain" an individual's "citizenship or immigration status" in response to a state request. Justice BREYER is concerned that this information "says nothing about work authorization." Justice SOTO-MAYOR shares that concern. But if a § 1373(c) inquiry reveals that someone is a United States citizen, that certainly answers the question whether that individual is authorized to work. The same would be true if the response to a § 1373(c) query disclosed that the individual was a lawful permanent resident alien or, on the other hand, had been ordered re-moved. In any event, if the information provided under § 1373(c) does not confirm that an employee is an unauthorized alien, then the State cannot prove its case.

From this basic starting point, the Arizona law continues to trace the federal law. Both the state and federal law prohibit "knowingly" employ-ing an unauthorized alien. * * *

The Arizona law provides employers with the same affirmative de-fense for good-faith compliance with the I-9 process as does the federal law. And both the federal and Arizona law accord employers a rebuttable presumption of compliance with the law when they use E-Verify to validate a finding of employment eligibility.

Apart from the mechanics of the Arizona law, the Chamber argues more generally that the law is preempted because it upsets the balance that Congress sought to strike when enacting IRCA. In the Chamber's view, IRCA reflects Congress's careful balancing of several policy considerations—deterring unauthorized alien employment, avoiding burdens on employers, protecting employee privacy, and guarding against employment discrimination. According to the Chamber, the harshness of Arizona's law " 'exert[s] an extraneous pull on the scheme established by Congress' " that impermissibly upsets that balance.

* * *

The Chamber and Justice BREYER assert that employers will err on the side of discrimination rather than risk the " 'business death penalty' " by "hiring unauthorized workers." That is not the choice. License termination is not an available sanction simply for "hiring unauthorized workers." Only far more egregious violations of the law trigger that consequence. The Arizona law covers only knowing or intentional violations. The law's permanent licensing sanctions do not come into play until a second knowing or intentional violation at the same business location, and only if the second violation occurs while the employer is still on probation for the first. These limits ensure that licensing sanctions are imposed only when an employer's conduct fully justifies them. An employer acting in good faith need have no fear of the sanctions.

As the Chamber points out, IRCA has its own anti-discrimination provisions; Arizona law certainly does nothing to displace those. Other federal laws, and Arizona anti-discrimination laws, provide further protection against employment discrimination—and strong incentive for employers not to discriminate.

All that is required to avoid sanctions under the Legal Arizona Workers Act is to refrain from knowingly or intentionally violating the employment law. Employers enjoy safe harbors from liability when they use the I–9 system and E–Verify—as Arizona law requires them to do. The most rational path for employers is to obey the law—both the law barring the employment of unauthorized aliens and the law prohibiting discrimination—and there is no reason to suppose that Arizona employers will choose not to do so.

As with any piece of legislation, Congress did indeed seek to strike a balance among a variety of interests when it enacted IRCA. Part of that balance, however, involved allocating authority between the Federal Government and the States. The principle that Congress adopted in doing so was not that the Federal Government can impose large sanctions, and the States only small ones. IRCA instead preserved state authority over a particular category of sanctions—those imposed "through licensing and similar laws."

Of course Arizona hopes that its law will result in more effective enforcement of the prohibition on employing unauthorized aliens. But in preserving to the States the authority to impose sanctions through licensing laws, Congress did not intend to preserve only those state laws that would have no effect. The balancing process that culminated in IRCA resulted in a ban on hiring unauthorized aliens, and the state law here simply seeks to enforce that ban.

* * *

III

The Chamber also argues that Arizona's requirement that employers use the federal E–Verify system to determine whether an employee is authorized to work is impliedly preempted. * * *

We begin again with the relevant text. The provision of IIRIRA setting up the program that includes E–Verify contains no language circumscribing state action. It does, however, constrain federal action: absent a prior violation of federal law, "the Secretary of Homeland Security may not require any person or other entity [outside of the Federal Government] to participate in a pilot program" such as E–Verify. IIRIRA § 402(a), 110 Stat. 3009–656. That provision limits what the Secretary of Homeland Security may do—nothing more.

* * *

Arizona's use of E–Verify does not conflict with the federal scheme. The Arizona law requires that "every employer, after hiring an employee, shall verify the employment eligibility of the employee" through E–Verify. That requirement is entirely consistent with the federal law. And the consequences of not using E–Verify under the Arizona law are the same as the consequences of not using the system under federal law. In both instances, the only result is that the employer forfeits the otherwise available rebuttable presumption that it complied with the law.

Congress's objective in authorizing the development of E–Verify was to ensure reliability in employment authorization verification, combat counterfeiting of identity documents, and protect employee privacy. Arizona's requirement that employers operating within its borders use E–Verify in no way obstructs achieving those aims.

In fact, the Federal Government has consistently expanded and encouraged the use of E–Verify. When E–Verify was created in 1996, it was meant to last just four years and it was made available in only six States. Congress since has acted to extend the E–Verify program's existence on four separate occasions, the most recent of which ensures the program's vitality through 2012. And in 2003 Congress directed the Secretary of Homeland Security to make E–Verify available in all 50 States. * * *

The Chamber contends that "if the 49 other States followed Arizona's lead, the state-mandated drain on federal resources would overwhelm the federal system and render it completely ineffective, thereby defeating Congress's primary objective in establishing E–Verify." Whatever the legal significance of that argument, the United States does not agree with the factual premise. According to the Department of Homeland Security, "the E–Verify system can accommodate the increased use that the Arizona statute and existing similar laws would create." Brief for United States as *Amicus Curiae* 34. And the United States notes that "[t]he government continues to encourage more employers to participate" in E–Verify.

The Chamber has reservations about E–Verify's reliability, but again the United States disagrees. The Federal Government reports that "E–Verify's successful track record ... is borne out by findings documenting the system's accuracy and participants' satisfaction." Brief for United States as *Amicus Curiae* 31. Indeed, according to the Government, the program is "the best means available to determine the employment eligibility of new hires." U.S. Dept. of Homeland Security, U.S. Citizenship and Immigration Services, E–Verify User Manual for Employers 4 (Sept. 2010).

* * *

IRCA expressly reserves to the States the authority to impose sanctions on employers hiring unauthorized workers, through licensing and similar laws. In exercising that authority, Arizona has taken the route least likely to cause tension with federal law. It uses the Federal Government's own definition of "unauthorized alien," it relies solely on the Federal Government's own determination of who is an unauthorized alien, and it requires Arizona employers to use the Federal Government's own system for checking employee status. If even this gives rise to impermissible conflicts with federal law, then there really is no way for the State to implement licensing sanctions, contrary to the express terms of the savings clause.

Because Arizona's unauthorized alien employment law fits within the confines of IRCA's savings clause and does not conflict with federal immigration law, the judgment of the United States Court of Appeals for the Ninth Circuit is affirmed.

JUSTICE KAGAN took no part in the consideration or decision of this case.

JUSTICE BREYER, with whom JUSTICE GINSBURG joins, dissenting.

* * *

I

* * *

Essentially, the federal Act requires employers to verify the work eligibility of their employees. And in doing so, the Act balances three competing goals. First, it seeks to discourage American employers from hiring aliens not authorized to work in the United States.

Second, Congress wished to avoid "placing an undue burden on employers," *id.*, at 90, and the Act seeks to prevent the "harassment" of "innocent employers," S.Rep. No. 99–132, p. 35 (1985).

Third, the Act seeks to prevent employers from disfavoring job applicants who appear foreign. * * *

The Act reconciles these competing objectives in several ways:

First, the Act prohibits employers from hiring an alien knowing that the alien is unauthorized to work in the United States. INA § 274A(a)(1)(A).

Second, the Act provides an easy-to-use mechanism that will allow employers to determine legality: the I–9 form. * * *

A later amendment to the law also allows an employer to verify an employee's work eligibility through an Internet-based federal system called E–Verify. If the employer does so, he or she will receive the benefit of a rebuttable presumption of compliance.

Third, the Act creates a central enforcement mechanism. The Act directs the Attorney General to establish a single set of procedures for receiving complaints, investigating those complaints that "have a substantial probability of validity," and prosecuting violations. INA § 274A(e)(1). * * *

Fourth, the Act makes it "an unfair immigration-related employment practice . . . to discriminate against any individual" in respect to employment "because of such individual's national origin." INA § 274B(a).

Fifth, the Act sets forth a carefully calibrated sanction system. * * *

As importantly, the Act limits or removes any incentive to discriminate on the basis of national origin by setting antidiscrimination fines at equivalent levels: $375–$3,200 per worker for first-time offenders, and $3,200–$16,000 per worker for repeat offenders. The Act then ties its unlawful employment and antidiscrimination provisions together by providing that, should the antihiring provisions terminate, the antidiscrimination provisions will also terminate "the justification for them having been removed," H.R. Conf. Rep. No. 99–1000, p. 87 (1986).

* * *

* * * [T]he state statute seriously threatens the federal Act's antidiscriminatory objectives by radically skewing the relevant penalties. For example, in the absence of the Arizona statute, an Arizona employer who intentionally hires an unauthorized alien for the second time would risk a maximum penalty of $6,500. But the Arizona statute subjects that same employer (in respect to the same two incidents) to mandatory, permanent loss of the right to do business in Arizona—a penalty that Arizona's Governor has called the "business death penalty." At the same time, the state law leaves the other side of the punishment balance—the antidiscrimination side—unchanged.

This is no idle concern. Despite the federal Act's efforts to prevent discriminatory practices, there is evidence that four years after it had become law, discrimination was a serious problem. * * *

Second, Arizona's law subjects lawful employers to increased burdens and risks of erroneous prosecution. In addition to the Arizona law's severely burdensome sanctions, the law's procedures create enforcement risks not present in the federal system. The federal Act creates one centralized enforcement scheme, run by officials versed in immigration law and with access to the relevant federal documents. * * *

Contrast the enforcement system that Arizona's statute creates. Any citizen of the State can complain (anonymously or otherwise) to the state attorney general (or any county attorney), who then "*shall* investigate," Ariz. Rev. Stat. Ann. § 23–212(B) (emphasis added), and, upon a determination that that the "complaint is not false and frivolous ... shall notify the appropriate county attorney to bring an action," § 23–212(C)(3). * * *

Again, this matter is far from trivial. Studies of one important source of Government information—the E–Verify system—describe how the federal administrative process *corrected* that system's tentative "unemployable" indications *18% of the time.* * * *

* * *

Why would Congress, after deliberately limiting ordinary penalties to the range of a few thousand dollars per illegal worker, want to permit far more drastic state penalties that would directly and mandatorily destroy entire businesses? Why would Congress, after carefully balancing sanctions to avoid encouraging discrimination, want to allow States to destroy that balance? Why would Congress, after creating detailed procedural protections for employers, want to allow States to undermine them? Why would Congress want to write into an express pre-emption provision—a provision designed to prevent States from undercutting federal statutory objectives—an exception that could so easily destabilize its efforts? The answer to these questions is that Congress would not have wanted to do any of these things. And that fact indicates that the majority's reading of the licensing exception—a reading that would allow what Congress sought to forbid—is wrong.

* * *

III

I would therefore read the words "licensing and similar laws" as covering state licensing systems applicable primarily to the licensing of firms in the business of recruiting or referring workers for employment, such as the state agricultural labor contractor licensing schemes in existence when the federal Act was created. This reading is consistent with the provision's history and language, and it minimizes the risk of harm of the kind just described.

* * *

In 1986, Congress (when enacting the Act now before us) focused directly upon the earlier federal agricultural labor contractor licensing system. And it changed that earlier system by including a series of conforming amendments in the Act. One amendment removes from the earlier statutes the specific prohibition against hiring unauthorized aliens. It thereby makes agricultural labor contractors subject to the Act's similar general prohibition against such hiring. IRCA § 101(b)(1)(C) (repealing AWPA § 106). Another amendment takes from the Secretary of Labor most of the Secretary's enforcement powers in respect to the hiring of unauthorized aliens. It thereby leaves agricultural labor contractors subject to the same single unified enforcement system that the immigration Act applies to all employers. A third amendment, however, leaves with the Secretary of Labor the power to withdraw the federal registration certificate from an agricultural labor contractor that hired unauthorized aliens. Thus, the Act leaves this subset of employers (*i.e.,* agricultural labor contractors but not other employers) subject to a federal licensing scheme.

So far, the conforming amendments make sense. But have they not omitted an important matter? Prior to 1986, States as well as the Federal Government could license agricultural labor contractors. Should the 1986 statute not say whether Congress intended that dual system to continue? The answer is that the 1986 Act does not omit this matter. It answers the coexistence question directly with the parenthetical phrase we are now considering, namely, the phrase, "other than through licensing and similar laws," placed in the middle of the Act's pre-emption provision. INA § 274A(h)(2). That phrase refers to agricultural labor contractors, and it says that, in respect to those licensing schemes, dual state/federal licensing can continue.

* * *

IV

Another section of the Arizona statute requires "every employer, after hiring an employee," to "verify the employment eligibility of the employee" through the Federal Government's E–Verify program. This state provision makes participation in the federal E–Verify system *mandatory* for virtually all Arizona employers. The federal law governing the E–Verify program, however, creates a program that is *voluntary.* * * *

* * *

Congress had strong reasons for insisting on the voluntary nature of the program. E–Verify was conceived as, and remains, a pilot program. Its database consists of tens of millions of Social Security and immigration records kept by the Federal Government. These records are prone to error. And making the program mandatory would have been hugely expensive.

* * *

In co-opting a federal program and changing the key terms under which Congress created that program, Arizona's mandatory state law simply ignores both the federal language and the reasoning it reflects, thereby posing an " 'obstacle to the accomplishment' " of the objectives Congress' statute evinces. *Crosby [v. National Foreign Trade Council,* 530 U.S. 363, 373, 120 S.Ct. 2288, 147 L.Ed.2d 352 (2000) (quoting *Hines v. Davidowitz,* 312 U.S. 52, 67, 61 S.Ct. 399, 85 L.Ed. 581 (1941))].

* * *

JUSTICE SOTOMAYOR, dissenting.

* * * Having constructed a federal mechanism for determining whether someone has knowingly employed an unauthorized alien, and having withheld from the States the information necessary to make that determination, Congress could not plausibly have intended for the saving clause to operate in the way the majority reads it to do. When viewed in context, the saving clause can only be understood to preserve States' authority to impose licensing sanctions after a final federal determination that a person has violated IRCA by knowingly employing an unauthorized alien. Because the Legal Arizona Workers Act instead creates a separate state mechanism for Arizona state courts to determine whether a person has employed an unauthorized alien, I would hold that it falls outside the saving clause and is pre-empted.

I would also hold that federal law preempts the provision of the Arizona Act making mandatory the use of E–Verify, the federal electronic verification system. By requiring Arizona employers to use E–Verify, Arizona has effectively made a decision for Congress regarding use of a federal resource, in contravention of the significant policy objectives motivating Congress' decision to make participation in the E–Verify program voluntary.

I

* * *

Under the majority's reading of the saving clause, state prosecutors decide whether to commence licensing-related proceedings against a person suspected of employing an unauthorized alien. * * * The Arizona Act illustrates the problems with reading the saving clause to permit such state action. The Act directs prosecutors to verify an employee's work authorization with the Federal Government pursuant to § 1373(c), and the state court "shall consider only the federal government's determination pursuant to [§]1373(c)" in "determining whether an employee is an unauthorized alien." Putting aside the question whether § 1373(c) actually provides access to work authorization information, § 1373(c) did not exist when IRCA was enacted in 1986. Arizona has not identified any avenue by which States could have accessed work authorization information in the first decade of IRCA's existence. The absence of any such avenue at the time of IRCA's enactment speaks volumes as to how Congress would have understood the saving clause to operate: If States had no access to information regarding the work authorization status of aliens, how could state courts have accurately adjudicated the question whether an employer had employed an unauthorized alien?

The Arizona Act's reliance on § 1373(c) highlights the anomalies inherent in state schemes that purport to adjudicate whether an employee is an authorized alien. Even when Arizona prosecutors obtain information regarding an alien's *immigration* status pursuant to § 1373(c), the prosecutors and state court will have to determine the significance of that information to an alien's *work authorization* status, which will often require deciding technical questions of immigration law. * * *

* * *

Furthermore, given Congress' express goal of "unifor[m]" enforcement of "the immigration laws of the United States," IRCA § 115, 100 Stat. 3384, I cannot believe that Congress intended for the 50 States and countless localities to implement their own distinct enforcement and adjudication procedures for deciding whether employers have employed unauthorized aliens. * * *

In sum, the statutory scheme as a whole defeats Arizona's and the majority's reading of the saving clause. Congress would not sensibly have permitted States to determine for themselves whether a person has employed an unauthorized alien, while at the same time creating a specialized federal procedure for making such a determination, withholding from the States the information necessary to make such a determination, and precluding use of the I–9 forms in nonfederal proceedings.

To render IRCA's saving clause consistent with the statutory scheme, I read the saving clause to permit States to impose licensing sanctions following a final federal determination that a person has violated § 274A(a)(1)(A) by knowingly hiring, recruiting, or referring for a fee an unauthorized alien. This interpretation both is faithful to the saving clause's text, and best reconciles the saving clause with IRCA's "careful regulatory scheme," [*United States v. Locke,* 529 U.S. 89, 106, 120 S.Ct. 1135, 146 L.Ed.2d 69 (2000)]. It also makes sense as a practical matter. In enacting IRCA's pre-emption clause, Congress vested in the Federal Government the authority to impose civil and criminal sanctions on persons who employ unauthorized aliens. Licensing and other types of business-related permissions are typically a matter of state law, however. * * *

* * *

NOTES AND QUESTIONS ON LOZANO V. CITY OF HAZLETON AND CHAMBER OF COMMERCE V. WHITING

1. What does it mean for state or local activity to be consistent with federal immigration law? Why isn't Hazleton's housing ordinance consistent with federal immigration law? Compare the reliance on federal law as it is practically enforced in *City of Hazleton* with the reliance on the letter of federal law in *Chamber of Commerce v. Whiting.* When the federal govern-

ment makes immigration-related decisions, must it do so in certain ways so that it is federal "law" for preemption purposes? *Compare Erie RR. v. Tompkins*, 304 U.S. 64, 58 S.Ct. 817, 82 L.Ed. 1188 (1938), *with Swift v. Tyson*, 41 U.S. 1, 10 L.Ed. 865 (1842).

2. The complaint in *Lozano v. City of Hazleton*, alleged equal protection violations in counts that the district court dismissed and were not at issue on appeal. Both the district court and the Third Circuit mentioned the racially charged atmosphere, yet their analyses relied entirely on preemption. Why? Did the court disregard the evidence relevant to discrimination? Consider this explanation:

> The * * * meaning of unlawful presence is heavily contested. Some observers view determinations of federal immigration status as largely ministerial, and they urge state and local officials to act on these straightforward findings of illegality by impeding access to work and housing, and even by arresting unauthorized migrants. But according to the view of unlawful presence in * * * *City of Hazleton*, a noncitizen's actual removal from the United States and other facets of immigration law enforcement reflect complex, highly discretionary choices. It matters who allocates resources and picks enforcement targets and who balances enforcement goals against competing concerns.

> What are these competing concerns? * * * [T]he most forceful and often repeated criticism of state and local involvement in immigration enforcement is improper reliance on race and ethnicity. * * * [T]he concern is that not only unauthorized migrants, but also lawfully present U.S. citizens and noncitizens, will suffer targeting and discrimination by race and ethnicity.

> In this setting, preemption-based skepticism of state and local enforcement can give expression to concerns about discrimination. An equal protection challenge would require proof of discriminatory intent, but a preemption challenge can persuade some judges based on reasonable possibility of discriminatory intent. One wonders if the court in *City of Hazleton* would have found preemption if the plaintiffs had not introduced so much evidence on race and ethnicity. Though that evidence was insufficient to sustain an equal protection claim, it is hard to read [the district court judge's] discussion of local variance from federal enforcement in his preemption analysis without also considering his discussions of demographic shifts in Hazleton, his analysis of the atmosphere of intimidation of local Latino residents, and his appendix on U.S. immigration history, which emphasized the historical role of racial exclusion.

> Put differently, preemption and equal protection can function roughly as alternative vehicles for expressing concern about racial and ethnic discrimination. Plaintiffs will likely lose an equal protection argument because of the law's requirement of discriminatory intent and its presumption against finding it. A preemption argument can manage doubt differently by shifting the risk of uncertain knowledge from the plaintiff to state and local governments. Courts may sustain preemption challenges out of concern that state and local laws addressing unauthorized

migration give state and local actors a zone of discretion that is too broad because it enables improper reliance on race and ethnicity.

Motomura, *The Rights of Others: Legal Claims and Immigration Outside the Law*, 59 Duke L.J. 1723, 1742–44 (2010).

3. In June 2011, the U.S. Supreme Court vacated *Lozano v. City of Hazleton*, remanding to the Third Circuit for further consideration in light of *Chamber of Commerce v. Whiting*. How controlling is the Supreme Court's analysis of the Arizona employment law on the preemption of the Hazleton provisions on employment? On housing?

4. Is the real conflict not between federal and state/local government, but between two groups of states—those that act against unauthorized migration, and those that do not? Consider this comment, originally about Proposition 187, but applicable to any state effort to diminish the perceived costs of unauthorized migration, either by securing federal reimbursement or more directly by reducing the unauthorized population itself:

> If California and similar states secure increased federal reimbursement, they will have succeeded in harnessing the power of the federal budget to shift immigration-related costs to the other group of states. Proposition 187 is a more direct means to the same end. If it works as intended and reduces the undocumented population in California, it will likely do so as much by shifting the undocumented population to other states as by deterring its entry into the United States as a whole.

Motomura, *Immigration and Alienage, Federalism and Proposition 187*, 35 Va. J. Int'l L. 201 (1994). *See also* Delaney, Note, *In the Shadow of Article I: Applying a Dormant Commerce Clause Analysis to State Laws Regulating Aliens*, 82 NYU L. Rev. 1821 (2007). If this is true, should the federal government equalize the fiscal effects of unauthorized migration among the several states? How could a fair accounting of the benefits and costs be reached?

2. DIRECT STATE AND LOCAL ENFORCEMENT

State and local officers may be active in the direct enforcement of federal immigration law. The overall DHS administrative umbrella for the thirteen programs serving this function is ICE ACCESS (Agreements of Cooperation in Communities to Enhance Safety and Security). We sketch some of the major programs here. For a fuller account, see Chacón, *A Diversion of Attention: Immigration Courts and the Adjudication of Fourth and Fifth Amendment Rights*, 58 Duke L.J. 1563, 1586–98 (2010).

a. With Express Federal Authorization

§ 287(g) Agreements. Under INA § 287(g), enacted in 1996, the federal government may authorize state and local law enforcement officials to carry out immigration law enforcement functions "in relation to the investigation, apprehension, or detention of aliens in the United States (including the transportation of such aliens * * * to detention centers),'' under an agreement with DHS that provides for training and ongoing federal supervision of the state and local officers involved (though the cost is usually borne by the nonfederal agency). The agreement spells out the specific functions expected of the cooperating state or local agency; it is not a blanket deputization of state and local officers to act as federal immigration enforcers.

Agreements follow two basic models. The "jail model" authorizes trained state officers to carry out immigration enforcement only in local jails, interviewing detainees and querying immigration databases to determine deportability, issuing charging documents, and then possibly transporting the person to ICE custody. The "task force model" authorizes immigrant status determination as part of a wider range of state or local policing activities in the field. Ninety percent of detainers issued under the 287(g) program in 2010 derived from jail programs. *See* R. Capps, M. Rosenblum, C. Rodríguez, & M. Chishti, Delegation and Divergence: A Study of 287(g) State and Local Immigration Enforcement (Migration Policy Institute, 2011).

In July 2002, Florida and the Department of Justice entered into the first such agreement, allowing 35 state law enforcement officers to enforce federal immigration laws. As of October 2010, DHS had § 287(g) agreements with sixty-nine jurisdictions in twenty-four states. *See Fact Sheet: Delegation of Immigration Authority Section 287(g) Immigration and Nationality Act*, U.S. Immigr. & Customs Enforcement, http://www.ice. gov/news/library/factsheets/287g.htm.

The Criminal Alien Program (CAP). Under this program, ICE officers screen arrestees in local jails—sometimes in-person and sometimes through remote electronic means—to identify and issue detainers against noncitizens in local custody who lack authorization to be in the United States. CAP also operates in state and federal prisons, where longer sentences often permit the completion of removal proceedings (rather than the simple issuance of a detainer) while the person is incarcerated. If ruled removable, ICE will then have an enforceable final order at the point of release and will incur only limited detention expenses before removal. For a critical examination of CAP's operation in one Texas city, see Gardner & Kohli, The C.A.P. Effect: Racial Profiling in the ICE Criminal Alien Program (2009), available at http://www.law.berkeley.edu/files/policybrief_ irving_0909_v9.pdf.

Secure Communities. DHS' Secure Communities initiative contrasts with 287(g) as an approach to state and local involvement in federal immigration enforcement. The initiative calls for anyone arrested by state and local law enforcement to have fingerprints checked—as part of the booking process—against IDENT, the DHS biometrics-based immigration database, to determine any criminal history and immigration status. No state or local officer makes a preliminary decision whether the person is a noncitizen subject to DHS jurisdiction, and only persons actually arrested and fingerprinted are checked against the DHS. The stated purpose is to facilitate the removal of aliens with criminal convictions, with more serious crimes as the priority. Secure Communities has much broader coverage than 287(g) agreements—as of October 2011, Secure Communities covered over 1515 jurisdictions in 44 states, with priority given to areas with large unauthorized populations, and nationwide coverage planned by 2013. *See* Department of Homeland Security, *Testimony of Secretary Janet Napolitano Before the United States House of Representatives Committee on the Judiciary*, Oct. 26, 2011.

Secure Communities has been heavily criticized, especially in 2011, as it increased the number of noncitizens brought into contact with federal immigration enforcement. A principal objection was that the program was in fact targeting noncitizens who were not serious criminal offenders at all. Critics argued that Secure Communities undermined immigrants' trust in law enforcement. This and related concerns led Illinois, Massachusetts, and New York to move to end or curtail their participation. *See* Preston, *U.S. Pledges to Raise Deportation Threshold*, N.Y. Times, June 18, 2011, at A14. Localities in other states tried to opt out, though their ability to do so was typically constrained by state law and existing state-federal cooperative arrangements. Partly in response to these criticisms, ICE director John Morton issued two memoranda in June 2011 to regularize the exercise of prosecutorial discretion as to individuals identified through Secure Communities and other ICE enforcement programs, available at <http://www.ice.gov/doclib/secure-communities/pdf/prosecutorial-discretion-memo.pdf>, discussed in detail in Chapter Seven, p. 782. On August 5, 2011, Morton sent a letter to all governors stating that the agreements with states initially used to activate the Secure Communities program were not legally necessary and had led to confusion. Therefore all existing agreements would be terminated, and Secure Communities would proceed thenceforth as an information-sharing program between two federal agencies, the FBI and DHS. Under the ICE policy reflected in the letters, states would not have to make an affirmative decision to participate in Secure Communities, but they would also not have the choice to opt out, so long as they continue sending fingerprints of arrested persons to the FBI. *See* Semple & Preston, *Deal to Share Fingerprints Is Dropped, Not Program*, N.Y. Times, Aug. 6, 2011.

b. Without Express Federal Authorization

May state and local officials enforce federal immigration laws without express federal authorization? INA § 103(a)(10) allows the federal government to authorize state or local law enforcement officers to perform the duties of federal immigration officers or employees if "an actual or imminent influx" of aliens off the coast or near a land border presents "urgent circumstances requiring an immediate Federal response." What about state and local authority in less extraordinary circumstances? The various responses to this question led up to Arizona's enactment of Senate Bill 1070 in April 2010, followed by similar laws in other states.

Analysis has traditionally started with the view that state and local law enforcement officers do not require express federal authorization to make arrests for criminal violations of federal immigration law. This conclusion is consistent with a long-standing judicial acceptance, manifest in numerous nonimmigration cases, of inherent state authority to arrest persons for violation of federal criminal law. *See, e.g. Miller v. United States*, 357 U.S. 301, 305, 78 S.Ct. 1190, 1193, 2 L.Ed.2d 1332 (1958) (narcotics case: the lawfulness of an arrest for a federal violation by state peace officers is to be determined by reference to state law).

An influential Ninth Circuit case, *Gonzales v. City of Peoria*, 722 F.2d 468 (9th Cir. 1983), drew a sharp distinction between criminal and civil enforcement, offering this rationale for this civil/criminal line:

> Plaintiffs correctly assert that an intent to preclude local enforcement may be inferred where the system of federal regulation is so pervasive that no opportunity for state activity remains. We assume that the civil provisions of the Act regulating authorized entry, length of stay, residence status, and deportation, constitute such a pervasive regulatory scheme, as would be consistent with the exclusive federal power over immigration. However, this case does not concern that broad scheme, but only a narrow and distinct element of it—the regulation of criminal immigration activity by aliens. The statutes relating to that element are few in number and relatively simple in their terms. They are not, and could not be, supported by a complex administrative structure. It therefore cannot be inferred that the federal government has occupied the field of criminal immigration enforcement.

722 F.2d at 474–75.

Whether or not this reasoning is persuasive, the authority of state and local officers to make arrests for criminal violations of federal immigration law has come to be assumed. Violators subject to state arrest would potentially include any unauthorized migrant who entered without inspection at a port of entry, who would thereby commit a misdemeanor criminal offense under INA § 275. In contrast, unauthorized migrants who were admitted lawfully but then have overstayed or otherwise violated a condition of admission are likewise deportable, but without more they have committed no federal crime.

Gonzales became background for a much more controversial issue: Do state and local officers have inherent authority to make arrests for *civil* violations of federal immigration law? The spectrum of answers was defined by two opinions issued by the Office of Legal Counsel (OLC) of the Department of Justice, the first in 1996 under President Clinton. The OLC explained that state and local law officers may enforce the criminal, but not the civil, provisions of federal immigration law.

ASSISTANCE BY STATE AND LOCAL POLICE
IN APPREHENDING ILLEGAL ALIENS

Teresa Wynn Roseborough, Deputy Assistant Attorney General, Office of Legal
Counsel, Memorandum Opinion for the United States Attorney, Southern
District of California, February 5, 1996.

* * *

A. VALIDITY AND SCOPE OF STATE POLICE PARTICIPATION
IN ENFORCING FEDERAL IMMIGRATION LAWS

It is well-settled that state law enforcement officers are permitted to enforce federal statutes where such enforcement activities do not impair federal regulatory interests. This general principle extends to state enforcement of the Immigration and Naturalization Act as well. In *Gonzales v. City of Peoria*, 722 F.2d 468 (9th Cir. 1983), for example, the Ninth Circuit held that "federal law does not preclude local enforcement of the criminal provisions of the [Immigration and Naturalization] Act."

* * *

B. CIVIL ENFORCEMENT/DEPORTABLE ALIENS

Whether state officers may assist in enforcing the *civil* component of federal immigration law raises a separate issue. Deportation of aliens under the INA is a civil proceeding. * * *

In *Gonzales*, the Ninth Circuit held that the authority of state officials to enforce the provisions of the INA "is limited to criminal violations." The court based this distinction between the civil and criminal provisions of the INA on the theory that the former constitute a pervasive and preemptive regulatory scheme, whereas the latter do not. Application of this rule would seem to preclude detentions by state officers based solely on suspicion of deportability (as opposed to *criminal* violations of the INA).

In an opinion issued in 1989, this Office similarly recognized the distinction between the civil and criminal provisions of the INA for purposes of state law enforcement authority. We first expressed our belief that "the mere existence of a warrant of deportation for an alien does not provide sufficient probable cause to conclude that the criminal provisions [of the INA] have in fact been violated." We then concluded:

> Because INA § 241[1] makes clear that an alien who has lawfully entered this country, lawfully registered, and who has violated no criminal statute may still be deported for noncompliance with the noncriminal or civil immigration provisions, the mere existence of a warrant of deportation does not enable all state and local law enforcement officers to arrest the violator of those civil provisions.

---

1. INA § 241 at the time contained the grounds of deportability. As amended and reorganized, those grounds now appear in INA § 237.—eds.

Id. at 9.

In that regard, INA § 287(a)(2) imposes substantial restrictions even upon the authority of *federal* officers to make warrantless arrests for purposes of civil deportation. It requires that the arresting officer reasonably believe the alien is in the United States illegally and that he is "likely to escape before a warrant can be obtained for his arrest." *See Mountain High Knitting, Inc. v. Reno*, 51 F.3d 216, 218 (9th Cir. 1995) (asserting that even INS agents have no legitimate basis for a warrantless arrest of aliens subject to civil deportation unless the arresting officer reasonably believes that the alien is likely to escape before an arrest warrant can be obtained).

Taking all these authorities into account, we conclude that state and local police lack recognized legal authority to stop and detain an alien *solely on suspicion of civil deportability*, as opposed to a criminal violation of the immigration laws or other laws.

* * *

In 2002, an OLC opinion issued under President George W. Bush withdrew the part of the 1996 opinion that addressed civil enforcement.

NON–PREEMPTION OF THE AUTHORITY OF STATE AND LOCAL LAW ENFORCEMENT OFFICIALS TO ARREST ALIENS FOR IMMIGRATION VIOLATIONS

Memorandum for the Attorney General
Jay S. Bybee, Assistant Attorney General, Office of Legal Counsel, April 3, 2002.

* * *

We first address whether, in the absence of any affirmative authorization under federal law, States have inherent power (subject to federal preemption) to make arrests for violation of federal law. Otherwise stated, may state police, exercising state law authority only, lawfully make arrests for violation of federal law, or do they have power to make such arrests only insofar as they are exercising delegated federal executive power?

We believe that the answer to this question rests ultimately on the States' status as sovereign entities. The Declaration of Independence proclaims that the States are "FREE AND INDEPENDENT STATES ... and that as FREE AND INDEPENDENT STATES, they have full Power to levy War, conclude Peace, contract Alliances, establish Commerce, *and to do all other Acts and Things which INDEPENDENT STATES may of right do.*" (Emphasis added.) The United States Constitution conferred on Congress only the powers "herein granted," U.S. Const. art. I, § 1, and "reserved to the States respectively, or to the people," the "powers not delegated to the United States by the Constitution, nor prohibited by it to the States," amend. X. Thus, although the Constitution did impose some disabilities on the States, it did not purport to confer, or otherwise be the source of their affirmative authority. The original States that ratified the Constitution instead obtained their authority from state constitutions or charters that preceded the federal Constitution. And States that entered the Union after 1789 did so on "equal footing" with the original States and thus enjoy the same sovereign status as the original States.

We therefore do not believe that the authority of state police to make arrests for violation of federal law is limited to those instances in which they are exercising delegated federal power. We instead believe that such arrest authority inheres in the States' status as sovereign entities. In the same way that police in Canada do not exercise delegated Article II power when they arrest someone who has violated U.S. law and turn him over to U.S. authorities, state police, too, need not be exercising such federal power when they make arrests for violation of federal law. Instead, the power to make such arrests inheres in the ability of one sovereign to accommodate the interests of another sovereign.

* * *

On re-examination, we believe that the authorities we cited in the 1996 OLC Opinion provide no support for our conclusion that state police lack the authority to arrest aliens solely on the basis of civil deportability. First, our assertion that "the Ninth Circuit [in *Gonzales*] held that the authority of state officials to enforce the provisions of the INA 'is limited to criminal violations,' " confuses the court's *holding* on the state-law question of "what authority the State of Arizona has conferred on its police officers with the court's mere *assumption in dictum* that the civil provisions of the INA preempt state enforcement." * * * [T]he 1989 OLC Opinion, notwithstanding its apparent confusion over the need for affirmative federal authorization for state arrests for federal offenses, goes no further than to conclude that "it is *not clear* under current law that local police may enforce non-criminal federal statutes"—a conclusion that falls well short of the 1996 OLC Opinion's conclusion that it is clear that local police may not enforce non-criminal federal statutes. Finally, the restrictions imposed on INS employees by INA § 287(a)(2) * * * apply equally to warrantless arrests for criminal violations as to warrantless arrests for civil violations. We therefore fail to see how § 287(a)(2) bears in any way on the question whether state police may arrest aliens for civil deportability.

* * *

More fundamentally, we believe that the 1996 OLC Opinion failed to appreciate the extremely limited and unusual nature of the preemption question posed with respect to state arrests for violation of federal law. Unlike the typical preemption scenario, this question does not involve an attempt by States to enact *state* laws, or to promulgate regulations pursuant to state laws, that arguably conflict with federal law or intrude into a field that is reserved to Congress or that federal law has occupied. What this question instead presents is whether States can assist the federal government by arresting aliens who have violated *federal* law and by turning them over to federal authorities. In this context, we believe that the question posed in dictum by the Ninth Circuit in *Gonzales*— whether the civil provisions of the INA constitute a pervasive regulatory scheme—was entirely misplaced. We instead believe that the principle governing our construction of federal law in this context should have been that voiced by Judge Learned Hand in *Marsh* [*v. United States*, 29 F.2d 172 (2d Cir. 1928)]: that "it would be unreasonable to suppose that [the United States'] purpose was to deny to itself any help that the states may allow." Consistent with this principle, we believe that the 1996 OLC Opinion should have applied a strong presumption against preemption of state arrest authority. Had it done so, it should have concluded that federal law did not preempt state police from arresting aliens on the basis of civil deportability.

We therefore withdraw the 1996 OLC Opinion's advice that federal law precludes state police from arresting aliens on the basis of civil deportability.

* * *

NOTES AND QUESTIONS ON DIRECT ENFORCEMENT BY STATES AND LOCALITIES

1. It is useful to ask exactly what is involved in any state and local authority to enforce the immigration laws, whether civil or criminal. None of the cases or memoranda contemplates full operation of a state-run deportation or criminal punishment system. The state authority, whether under the 2002 OLC memorandum or even under § 287(g), involves authority only during the earliest stages of enforcement. In the criminal realm, state and local officers would not prosecute cases in federal court. Instead, after making an arrest (for any federal criminal offense), they would simply present the case for prosecution to a U.S. Attorney's office, which would decide whether to accept it based on the office's own assessment of the facts and law, and on its own prosecutorial discretion guidelines. A declination would result in the person's release—and thus exert pressure on state and local officers not to persist in presenting weak or insignificant cases that federal prosecutors will not pursue.

Similarly, in the civil domain under the 2002 OLC opinion, state or local officers would have authority only to arrest and offer the person to federal authorities for further action. They would not be authorized to run their own immigration courts, nor even to file a charging document or conduct the removal case. ICE, like the U.S. attorney, retains the authority to decline to proceed with enforcement. Section 287(g) agreements permit state activity a bit further along the enforcement pipeline, but only to the point of issuing charging documents and transporting to ICE detention facilities. The statute by its terms permits delegation only of functions relating to investigation, apprehension, detention and transportation of persons believed to be present in violation of the immigration laws, not the prosecution or adjudication of charges.

2. Michael Wishnie, one of a number of critics of the 2002 OLC opinion and of state and local enforcement generally, has argued, among other things, that "the permanent involvement of state and local police in routine immigration enforcement raises the further risk of racial profiling and selective immigration enforcement beyond moments of real or perceived national threat." Wishnie, *State and Local Police Enforcement of Immigration Laws*, 6 U. Pa. J. Const. L. 1084, 1104 (2004). Huyen Pham has advanced a different argument: "DOJ's invitation for local enforcement will result in a "thousand borders" problem, violating the constitutional mandate for uniform immigration laws as local authorities will enforce federal immigration laws differently, creating, in effect, different immigration laws." Pham, *The Inherent Flaws in the Inherent Authority Position: Why Inviting Local Enforcement of Immigration Laws Violates the Constitution*, 31 Fla. St. U. L. Rev. 965, 995 (2004). For an opposing view from Kris Kobach, who served as Counsel to Attorney General Ashcroft when the OLC issued its 2002 opinion, see Kobach, *The Quintessential Force Multiplier: The Inherent Authority of Local Police to Make Immigration Arrests*, 69 Alb. L. Rev. 179, 183 (2005–06) (adopting analysis that generally tracks the 2002 OLC opinion). For a comprehensive analysis of various conceptual approaches to preemption of state and local immigration authority, see Huntington, *The Constitutional Dimension of Immigration Federalism*, 61 Vand. L. Rev. 787 (2008).

3. Can concerns about profiling and nonuniformity be weighty even if state and local authority is confined to the arrest stage and can be offset by federal prosecutorial discretion? Consider this argument, that because the arrest of any given unauthorized migrant is highly unlikely, but those arrested are much more likely to be put in removal proceedings, the discretion to arrest has been the "discretion that matters":

> * * * even an expansion in federal enforcement discretion would not neutralize the more fundamental changes in immigration enforcement that may result from *Gonzales* arrests, § 287(g) agreements, and Secure Communities. In subtle but effective ways, these forms of state and local involvement threaten to usurp basic aspects of federal control over immigration enforcement. The core problem is that state and local decisionmakers will act as gatekeepers, filling the enforcement pipeline with cases of their choice for civil removal and possibly criminal prosecution as well. Even assuming that more federal post-arrest discretion becomes available and actually offsets the state and local choices made by exercising arrest discretion, any such federal discretion is fundamentally reactive.

Motomura, *The Discretion That Matters: Federal Immigration Enforcement, State and Local Arrests, and the Civil–Criminal Line*, 58 UCLA L. Rev. 1819, 1856 (2011).

4. A related issue is that some states and localities decide affirmatively that they do *not* wish to cooperate or otherwise be involved in the enforcement of federal immigration law. In the 1996 Act, Congress took aim at local

regulations that prohibited officials from communicating with federal authorities about the immigration status of persons with whom they came in contact, by providing in 8 U.S.C.A. § 1373(a):

> Notwithstanding any other provision of Federal, State, or local law, a Federal, State, or local government entity or official may not prohibit, or in any way restrict, any government entity or official from sending to, or receiving from, the Immigration and Naturalization Service information regarding the citizenship or immigration status, lawful or unlawful, of any individual.

See also 8 U.S.C.A. § 1644 (setting out the same prohibition). Rudy Giuliani, then mayor of New York City, challenged the federal statute in court, alleging that it violated the U.S. Constitution because it usurped the City's administration of core functions of government. The case was dismissed on the ground that "the effect on local policy is not the type of intrusion that is sufficient to violate the Tenth Amendment of principles of federalism." *City of New York v. United States*, 971 F.Supp. 789 (S.D.N.Y.1997).

As an example of local skepticism—if not outright opposition—to federal immigration law enforcement, the City of Seattle adopted an ordinance in January 2003 that bars city employees from "inquir[ing] into the immigration status of any person, or engag[ing] in activities designed to ascertain the immigration status of any person." The City noted that the September 11th attacks "have left immigrants of color afraid to access benefits to which they are entitled, for fear of being reported to the [INS]." Police officers are exempted from the prohibition with respect to a person whom the officer has a "reasonable suspicion" has previously been removed from the U.S. and is committing or has committed a felony. No doubt with an eye to 8 U.S.C.A. § 1373, the ordinance states that it shall not be construed to prohibit any city employee from cooperating with federal immigration authorities as required by law.

Though such measures are sometimes referred to as "sanctuary" policies, they generally do not inhibit cooperation with federal immigration authorities in enforcement priority cases, especially those involving noncitizens arrested for crimes. Many policies are limited to assurances that government officials will not as a general matter ask about an individual's immigration status nor report any such information to the federal government absent an affirmative federal request. In Los Angeles, for example, Special Order 40, issued by police chief Daryl Gates in 1979, provides that "officers shall not initiate police action with the objective of discovering the alien status of a person," but it does not keep officers from turning over arrested individuals to federal authorities.

Instructive is a series of developments in San Francisco, which in 1989 adopted one of the country's most far-reaching sanctuary policies, providing that no municipal resources would be used to assist federal immigration enforcement. There was an express exception to accommodate cooperation required by federal law, such as reporting of adults arrested for felonies. The city did not refer arrested minors to federal immigration authorities. In June 2008, it came to light that the alleged gunman in a triple homicide had been in the United States unlawfully and had earlier been released by authorities after a juvenile arrest without notifying the federal government. The publicity also brought heavy criticism of related city policies. One led some arrested minors to be flown at public expense to their home countries rather than handed over to federal authorities for formal removal proceedings. The city had also sent other arrested juveniles to group homes from which they escaped. Mayor Gavin Newsom responded by rescinding the prior policy and calling for police to report any juvenile arrested of a felony to federal immigration authorities. *See* McKinley, *San Francisco at Crossroads Over Immigration*, N.Y. Times, June 12, 2009, at A12. In October 2009, the Board of Supervisors overrode Newsom's veto to enact an ordinance requiring a conviction before a juvenile would be reported to federal authorities. Newsom refused to implement the restriction. In May 2011, his successor, Edwin Lee, announced that the City would not report juveniles arrested on felony charges if they have family ties to the Bay Area, are enrolled in school, and are not repeat offenders. *See* Gordon, *Stance on Illegal Youths Is Revised*, S.F. Chron. May 11, 2011, at A1.

Such local controversies illustrate the political pressure on state and localities to engage in immigration law enforcement against noncitizens in the criminal justice system, even if their general policies appear to preclude inquiry into a noncitizen's immigration status. Moreover, the implementation of Secure Communities nationwide would moot these questions of local case-by-case cooperation, since any arrest would trigger reporting to the federal government regardless of the state or local government's position.

Other local policies address unauthorized migration from a different angle. For example, a few cities, most prominently San Francisco and New Haven, Connecticut, issue identification cards for unauthorized migrants. *See* Knight, *Hundreds Wait for Hours to Buy ID Card*, San Francisco Chronicle, Jan. 16, 2009, at B1; Medina, *New Haven Approves Program To Issue Illegal Immigrants IDs*, N.Y. Times, June 5, 2007, at B6. For discussions of local laws and policies that involve nonenforcement or integration, and thus may run counter to federal immigration law enforcement, see Villazor, *What is a "Sanctuary"?*, 61 SMU L.Rev. 133 (2008); Motomura, *Immigration Outside the Law*, 108 Colum. L.Rev. 2037, 2075–83 (2008); Rodriguez, *The Significance of the Local in Immigration Regulation*, 106 Mich. L. Rev. 567 (2008).

———————

In April 2010, Arizona Governor Janice Brewer signed Senate Bill 1070, which appears in the Statutory Supplement as amended one week later by House Bill 2162. SB 1070 differs from the emphases on employment and housing in the earlier Arizona statute (*Chamber of Commerce v. Whiting*) and the Hazelton ordinances (*Lozano v. Hazelton*). SB 1070 authorized state and local activity that was more directly—or at least less indirectly—involved in federal immigration enforcement.

Soon after enactment, individual and organizational plaintiffs filed lawsuits to invalidate SB 1070 as unconstitutional and to seek preliminary injunctions to block it from taking effect. The federal government then took the highly unusual step of filing its own lawsuit to block implementation and invalidate the law, asserting preemption but not the individual rights challenges in the private party lawsuits. On July 28, 2010, the day before SB 1070 was to take effect, District Judge Susan Bolton issued a preliminary injunction against many of the law's provisions, and the state of Arizona soon appealed.

The Ninth Circuit's decision below summarizes the legislation and addresses the preemption issue that was central to *De Canas v. Bica*, *Lozano v. City of Hazleton*, and *Chamber of Commerce v. Whiting*, including the scope of inherent state and local authority to enforce the civil provisions of federal immigration law.

UNITED STATES v. ARIZONA

United States Court of Appeals for the Ninth Circuit, 2011.
641 F.3d 339.

PAEZ, CIRCUIT JUDGE:

In April 2010, in response to a serious problem of unauthorized immigration along the Arizona–Mexico border, the State of Arizona enacted its own immigration law enforcement policy. Support Our Law Enforcement and Safe Neighborhoods Act, as amended by H.B. 2162 ("S.B. 1070"), "make[s] attrition through enforcement the public policy of all state and local government agencies in Arizona." S.B. 1070 § 1. The provisions of S.B. 1070 are distinct from federal immigration laws. To achieve this policy of attrition, S.B. 1070 establishes a variety of immigration-related state offenses and defines the immigration-enforcement authority of Arizona's state and local law enforcement officers.

Before Arizona's new immigration law went into effect, the United States sued the State of Arizona in federal district court alleging that S.B. 1070 violated the Supremacy Clause on the grounds that it was preempted by the Immigration and Nationality Act ("INA"), and that it violated the Commerce Clause. * * *

The district court granted the United States' motion for a preliminary injunction in part, enjoining enforcement of S.B. 1070 Sections 2(B), 3, 5(C), and 6, on the basis that federal law likely preempts these provisions. * * * [T]he United States' likelihood of success on its federal preemption argument against these four sections is the central issue this appeal presents.

* * *

Even if Congress has not explicitly provided for preemption in a given statute, the Supreme Court "ha[s] found that state law must yield to a congressional Act in at least two circumstances." *Crosby [v. Nat'l Foreign Trade Council,* 530 U.S. 363, 372, 120 S.Ct. 2288, 147 L.Ed.2d 352 (2000)]. First, "[w]hen Congress intends federal law to 'occupy the field,' state law in that area is preempted." *Id.* (quoting *California v. ARC America Corp.,* 490 U.S. 93, 100, 109 S.Ct. 1661, 104 L.Ed.2d 86 (1989)). Second, "even if Congress has not occupied the field, state law is naturally preempted to the extent of any conflict with a federal statute." *Id.* Conflict preemption, in turn, has two forms: impossibility and obstacle preemption. Impossibility preemption exists "where it is impossible for a private party to comply with both state and federal law." *Id.* Obstacle preemption exists "where 'under the circumstances of [a] particular case, [the challenged state law] stands as an obstacle to the accomplishment and execution of the full purposes and objectives of Congress.' " *Id.* at 373, 120 S.Ct. 2288 (quoting *Hines v. Davidowitz,* 312 U.S. 52, 67, 61 S.Ct. 399, 85 L.Ed. 581 (1941)). To determine whether obstacle preemption exists, the Supreme Court has instructed that we employ our "judgment, to be informed by examining the federal statute as a whole and identifying its purpose and intended effects." *Id.*

* * *

II. SECTION 2(B)

S.B. 1070 Section 2(B) provides, in the first sentence, that when officers have reasonable suspicion that someone they have lawfully stopped, detained, or arrested is an unauthorized immigrant, they "shall" make "a reasonable attempt . . . when practicable, to determine the immigration status" of the person. Section 2(B)'s second and third sentences provide that "[a]ny person who is arrested shall have the person's immigration status determined before the person is released," and "[t]he person's immigration status shall be verified with the federal government." The Section's fifth sentence states that a "person is presumed to not be an alien who is unlawfully present in the United States if the person provides" a form of identification included in a prescribed list.

A. *Interpretation of Section 2(B)*

To review the district court's preliminary injunction of Section 2(B), we must first determine how the Section's sentences relate to each other. Arizona argues that Section 2(B) does not require its officers to determine the immigration status of every person who is arrested. * * * That is, Arizona argues that its officers are only required to verify the immigration status of an arrested person before release if reasonable suspicion exists that the person lacks proper documentation.

On its face, the text does not support Arizona's reading of Section 2(B). The second sentence is unambiguous: "*Any* person who is arrested *shall* have the person's immigration status *determined* before the person is released" (emphasis added). The all-encompassing "any person," the mandatory "shall," and the definite "determined," make this provision incompatible with the first sentence's qualified "reasonable attempt . . . when practicable," and qualified "reasonable suspicion."

* * *

We agree with the district court that the reasonable suspicion requirement in the first sentence does not modify the plain meaning of the second sentence. Thus, Section 2(B) requires officers to verify—with the federal government—the immigration status of *all* arrestees before they are released, regardless of whether or not reasonable suspicion exists that the arrestee is an undocumented immigrant. Our interpretation gives effect to "arrest" in the first sentence and "arrest" in the second sentence. * * *

B. Preemption of Section 2(B)

* * * The states have not traditionally occupied the field of identifying immigration violations so we apply no presumption against preemption for Section 2(B).

We begin with "the purpose of Congress" by examining the text of INA § 287(g). In this section of the INA, titled "Performance of immigration officer functions by State officers and employees," Congress has instructed under what conditions state officials are permitted to assist the Executive in the enforcement of immigration laws. * * *

These provisions demonstrate that Congress intended for states to be involved in the enforcement of immigration laws under the Attorney General's close supervision.[a] Not only must the Attorney General approve of each *individual* state officer, he or she must delineate which functions each individual officer is permitted to perform, as evidenced by the disjunctive "or" in subsection (g)(1)'s list of "investigation, apprehension, or detention," and by subsection (g)(5). An officer might be permitted to help with investigation, apprehension *and* detention; or, an officer might be permitted to help only with one or two of these functions. Subsection (g)(5) also evidences Congress' intent for the Attorney General to have the discretion to make a state officer's help with a certain function permissive or mandatory. In subsection (g)(3), Congress explicitly required that in enforcing federal immigration law, state and local officers "shall" be directed by the Attorney General. This mandate forecloses any argument that state or local officers can enforce federal immigration law as directed by a mandatory state law.

We note that in subsection (g)(10), Congress qualified its other INA § 287(g) directives:

> Nothing in this subsection shall be construed to require an agreement ... in order for any officer or employee of a State ... (A) to communicate with the Attorney General regarding the immigration status of any individual ... or (B) otherwise to cooperate with the Attorney General in the identification, apprehension, detention, or removal of aliens not lawfully present.

INA § 287(g)(10). Although this language, read alone, is broad, we must interpret Congress' intent in adopting subsection (g)(10) in light of the rest of § 287(g). Giving subsection (g)(10) the breadth of its isolated meaning would completely nullify the rest of § 287(g), which demonstrates that Congress intended for state officers to aid in federal immigra-

---

a. The court echoes the INA in referring to the Attorney General in this case as the official to supervise § 287(g) agreements, but under the Homeland Security Act of 2002 this authority is now exercised by the Secretary of Homeland Security.—eds.

tion enforcement only under particular conditions, including the Attorney General's supervision. Subsection (g)(10) does not operate as a broad alternative grant of authority for state officers to systematically enforce the INA outside of the restrictions set forth in subsections (g)(1)–(9).

The inclusion of the word "removal" in subsection (g)(10)(B) supports our narrow interpretation of subsection (g)(10). Even state and local officers authorized under § 287(g) to investigate, apprehend, or detain immigrants do not have the authority to remove immigrants; removal is exclusively the purview of the federal government. By including "removal" in § 287(g)(10)(B), we do not believe that Congress intended to grant states the authority to remove immigrants. Therefore, the inclusion of "removal" in the list of ways that a state may "otherwise [ ] cooperate with the Attorney General," indicates that subsection (g)(10) does not permit states to opt out of subsections (g)(1)–(9) and systematically enforce the INA in a manner dictated by state law, rather than by the Attorney General. We therefore interpret subsection (g)(10)(B) to mean that when the Attorney General calls upon state and local law enforcement officers—or such officers are confronted with the necessity—to cooperate with federal immigration enforcement on an incidental and as needed basis, state and local officers are permitted to provide this cooperative help without the written agreements that are required for *systematic* and *routine* cooperation. Similarly, we interpret subsection (g)(10)(A) to mean that state officers can communicate with the Attorney General about immigration status information that they obtain or need in the performance of their regular state duties. But subsection (g)(10)(A) does not permit states to adopt laws dictating how and when state and local officers must communicate with the Attorney General regarding the immigration status of an individual. Subsection (g)(10) does not exist in a vacuum; Congress enacted it alongside subsections (g)(1)–(9) and we therefore interpret subsection (g)(10) as part of a whole, not as an isolated provision with a meaning that is unencumbered by the other constituent parts of § 1357(g).

* * * Section 2(B) sidesteps Congress' scheme for permitting the states to assist the federal government with immigration enforcement. Through Section 2(B), Arizona has enacted a mandatory and systematic scheme that conflicts with Congress' explicit requirement that in the "[p]erformance of immigration officer functions by State officers and employees," such officers "shall be subject to the direction and supervision of the Attorney General." INA § 287(g)(3). Section 2(B) therefore interferes with Congress' scheme because Arizona has assumed a role in directing its officers how to enforce the INA. * * *

Arizona argues that in another INA provision, "Congress has expressed a clear intent to *encourage* the assistance from state and local law enforcement officers," citing 8 U.S.C. § 1373(c). Section 1373(c) creates an obligation, on the part of the Department of Homeland Security ("DHS"), to "respond to an inquiry by a Federal, State, or local government agency, seeking to verify or ascertain the citizenship or immigration status of any individual ... for any purpose authorized by law."

We agree that § 1373(c) demonstrates that Congress contemplated state assistance in the identification of undocumented immigrants. We add, however, that Congress contemplated this assistance within the boundaries established in § 287(g), not in a manner dictated by a state law that furthers a state immigration policy. Congress passed § 1373(c) at the same time that it added subsection (g) to § 287. Thus, Congress directed the appropriate federal agency to respond to state inquiries about immigration status at the same time that it authorized the Attorney General to enter into § 287(g) agreements with states. * * *

* * *

By imposing mandatory obligations on state and local officers, Arizona interferes with the federal government's authority to implement its priorities and strategies in law enforcement, turning Arizona officers into state-directed DHS agents. As a result, Section 2(B) interferes with Congress' delegation of discretion to the Executive branch in enforcing the INA. * * *

In light of this guidance, Section 2(B)'s interference with Congressionally-granted Executive discretion weighs in favor of preemption. Section 2(B)'s "unyielding" mandatory directives to Arizona law enforcement officers "undermine[ ] the President's intended statutory authority" to establish immigration enforcement priorities and strategies. *Crosby* 530 U.S. at 377. * * * Through Section 2(B), Arizona has attempted to hijack a discretionary role that Congress delegated to the Executive.

In light of the above, S.B. 1070 Section 2(B) "stands as an obstacle to the accomplishment and execution of the full purposes and objectives of Congress" as expressed in the aforementioned INA provisions. *Hines,* 312 U.S. at 67, 61 S.Ct. 399. * * *

In addition to Section 2(B) standing as an obstacle to Congress' statutorily expressed intent, the record unmistakably demonstrates that S.B. 1070 has had a deleterious effect on the United States' foreign relations, which weighs in favor of preemption. In *[Am. Ins. Ass'n v.] Garamendi*, [539 U.S. 396, 123 S.Ct. 2374, 156 L.Ed.2d 376 (2003),] the Court stated that "even ... the *likelihood* that state legislation will produce something more than *incidental* effect in conflict with express foreign policy of the National Government would require preemption of the state law." 539 U.S. at 420, 123 S.Ct. 2374 (emphasis added).

The record before this court demonstrates that S.B. 1070 does not threaten a *"likelihood* ... [of] produc[ing] something more than *incidental* effect;"* rather, Arizona's law has created *actual* foreign policy problems of a magnitude far greater than incidental. *Garamendi,* 539 U.S. at 419, 123 S.Ct. 2374 (emphasis added). Thus far, the following foreign leaders and bodies have publicly criticized Arizona's law: The Presidents of Mexico, Bolivia, Ecuador, El Salvador, and Guatemala; the governments of Brazil, Colombia, Honduras, and Nicaragua; the national assemblies in Ecuador and Nicaragua and the Central American Parliament; six human rights experts at the United Nations; the Secretary General and many permanent representatives of the Organization of American States; the Inter–American Commission on Human Rights; and the Union of South American Nations.

* * *

Finally, the threat of 50 states layering their own immigration enforcement rules on top of the INA also weighs in favor of preemption. In *Wis. Dep't of Indus., Labor and Human Relations v. Gould Inc.,* 475 U.S. 282, 288, 106 S.Ct. 1057, 89 L.Ed.2d 223 (1986), where the Court found conflict preemption, the Court explained that "[e]ach additional [state] statute incrementally diminishes the [agency's] control over enforcement of the [federal statute] and thus further detracts from the integrated scheme of regulation created by Congress." (internal citations omitted).

* * *

III. SECTION 3

S.B. 1070 Section 3 provides: "In addition to any violation of federal law, a person is guilty of willful failure to complete or carry an alien registration document if the person is in violation of [INA § 264(e) or § 266(a)]." The penalty for violating Section 3 is a maximum fine of one hundred dollars, a maximum of twenty days in jail for a first violation, and a maximum of thirty days in jail for subsequent violations. Section 3 "does not apply to a person who maintains authorization from the federal government to remain in the United States." Section 3 essentially makes it a state crime for unauthorized immigrants to violate federal registration laws.

Starting with the touchstones of preemption, punishing unauthorized immigrants for their failure to comply with federal registration laws is not a field that states have "traditionally occupied." Therefore, we conclude that there is no presumption against preemption of Section 3.

Determining Congress' purpose, and whether Section 3 poses an obstacle to it, first requires that we evaluate the text of the federal registration requirements in INA §§ 264 or 266. These sections create a comprehensive scheme for immigrant registration, including penalties for failure to carry one's registration document at all times, INA § 264(e), and penalties for willful failure to register, failure to notify change of address, fraudulent statements, and counterfeiting. INA § 266(a)–(d). These provisions include no mention of state participation in the registration scheme. By contrast, Congress provided very specific directions for state participation in INA § 287, demonstrating that it knew how to ask for help where it wanted help; it did not do so in the registration scheme.

* * *

In addition, S.B. 1070 Section 3 plainly stands in opposition to the Supreme Court's direction: "where the federal government, in the exercise of its superior authority in this field, has enacted a complete scheme of regulation and has therein provided a standard for the registration of aliens, states cannot, inconsistently with the purpose of Congress, conflict or interfere with, curtail or complement, the federal law, or enforce additional or auxiliary regulations." *Hines,* 312 U.S. at 66–67, 61 S.Ct. 399. * * *

* * *

IV. SECTION 5(C)

S.B. 1070 Section 5(C) provides that it "is unlawful for a person who is unlawfully present in the United States and who is an unauthorized alien to knowingly apply for work, solicit work in a public place or perform work as an employee or independent contractor in this state." Violation of this provision is a class 1 misdemeanor, which carries a six month maximum term of imprisonment. Thus, Section 5(C) criminalizes unauthorized work and attempts to secure such work.

* * *

In *National Center [for Immigrants' Rights, Inc. v. I.N.S.,* 913 F.2d 1350 (9th Cir.1990), *rev'd on other grounds,* 502 U.S. 183, 112 S.Ct. 551, 116 L.Ed.2d 546 (1991)],* we * * * concluded that "[w]hile Congress initially discussed the merits of fining, detaining or adopting criminal sanctions against the *employee,* it ultimately rejected all such proposals ... Congress quite clearly was willing to deter illegal immigration by making jobs less available to illegal aliens but not by incarcerating or fining aliens who succeeded in obtaining work." *Id.* at 1367–68.

* * *

The text of the relevant IRCA statutory provision—INA § 274A—also supports this conclusion. Section 274A establishes a complex scheme to discourage the employment of unauthorized immigrants—primarily by penalizing employers who knowingly or negligently hire them. The statute creates a system through which employers are obligated to verify work authorization. * * *

In addition, other provisions in INA § 274A provide affirmative protections to unauthorized workers, demonstrating that Congress did not intend to permit the criminalization of work. * * *

Subsection 274A(g)(1) demonstrates Congress' intent to protect unauthorized immigrant workers from financial exploitation—a burden less severe than incarceration. This section provides that "[i]t is unlawful for a person or other entity, in the hiring ... of any individual, to require the individual to post a bond or security, to pay or agree to pay an amount, or otherwise to provide a financial guarantee or indemnity, against any potential liability arising under this section relating to such hiring . . . of the individual." * * *

* * *

* * * As Arizona states, "Section 5(C) clearly furthers the strong federal policy of prohibiting illegal aliens from seeking employment in the United States." The Supreme Court has cautioned, however, that "conflict in technique can be fully as disruptive to the system Congress erected as conflict in overt policy." *Gould,* 475 U.S. at 286, 106 S.Ct. 1057 (quoting *Motor Coach Emps. v. Lockridge,* 403 U.S. 274, 287, 91 S.Ct. 1909, 29 L.Ed.2d 473 (1971)). In *Crosby,* the Court explained that "a common end hardly neutralizes conflicting means." 530 U.S. at 379–80, 120 S.Ct. 2288. Similarly, in *Garamendi,* the Court explained that a state law was preempted because "[t]he basic fact is that California seeks to use an iron fist where the President has consistently chosen kid gloves." 539 U.S. at 427, 123 S.Ct. 2374. The problem with a state adopting a different technique in pursuit of the same goal as a federal law, is that "[s]anctions are drawn not only to bar what they prohibit but to allow what they permit, and the inconsistency of sanctions . . . undermines the congressional calibration of force." *Crosby,* 530 U.S. at 380, 120 S.Ct. 2288.

* * * By criminalizing work, S.B. 1070 Section 5(C) constitutes a substantial departure from the approach Congress has chosen to battle this particular problem. Therefore, Arizona's assertion that this provision "furthers the strong federal policy" does not advance its argument against preemption. Sharing a goal with the United States does not permit Arizona to "pull[ ] levers of influence that the federal Act does not reach." *Crosby,* 530 U.S. at 376, 120 S.Ct. 2288. By pulling the lever of criminalizing work—which Congress specifically chose not to pull in the INA—Section 5(C) "stands as an obstacle to the accomplishment and execution of the full purposes and objectives of Congress." *Hines,* 312 U.S. at 67, 61 S.Ct. 399. It is therefore likely that federal law preempts Section 5(C).

In addition, as detailed with respect to Section 2(B) above, S.B. 1070's detrimental effect on foreign affairs, and its potential to lead to 50 different state immigration schemes piling on top of the federal scheme, weigh in favor of the preemption of Section 5(C).

V. SECTION 6

S.B. 1070 Section 6 provides that "[a] peace officer, without a warrant, may arrest a person if the officer has probable cause to believe . . . [t]he person to be arrested has committed any public offense that makes the person removable from the United States."

* * * [W]e conclude, as the district court did, that Section 6 "provides for the warrantless arrest of a person where there is probable cause to believe the person *committed a crime in another state* that would be considered a crime if it had been committed in Arizona and that would subject the person to removal from the United States." 703 F.Supp.2d at 1005 (emphasis in original). Section 6 also allows for warrantless arrests

when there is probable cause to believe that an individual committed a removable offense in Arizona, served his or her time for the criminal conduct, and was released; and when there is probable cause to believe that an individual was arrested for a removable offense but was not prosecuted.

Thus, the question we must decide is whether federal law likely preempts Arizona from allowing its officers to effect warrantless arrests based on probable cause of removability. Because arresting immigrants for civil immigration violations is not a "field which the States have traditionally occupied," we do not start with a presumption against preemption of Section 6. *Wyeth [v. Levine,* 555 U.S. 555, 129 S.Ct. 1187, 1194, 173 L.Ed.2d 51 (2009)].

We first turn to whether Section 6 is consistent with Congressional intent. As authorized by 8 U.S.C. § 1252c, state and local officers may, "to the extent permitted by relevant State ... law," arrest and detain an individual who:

> (1) is an alien illegally present in the United States; and

> (2) has previously been convicted of a felony in the United States and deported or left the United States after such conviction, *but only after* the State or local law enforcement officials obtain appropriate confirmation from the Immigration and Naturalization Service of the status of such individual.

8 U.S.C. § 1252c (emphasis added). Nothing in this provision permits warrantless arrests, and the authority is conditioned on compliance with a mandatory obligation to confirm an individual's status with the federal government prior to arrest. Moreover, this provision only confers state or local arrest authority where the immigrant has been convicted of a felony. Section 6, by contrast, permits warrantless arrests if there is probable cause that a person has "committed any public offense that makes the person removable." Misdemeanors, not just felonies, can result in removability. Thus, Section 6 authorizes state and local officers to effectuate more intrusive arrests than Congress has permitted in Section 1252c. Moreover, none of the circumstances in which Congress has permitted federal DHS officers to arrest immigrants without a warrant are as broad as Section 6. Absent a federal officer actually viewing an immigration violation, warrantless arrests under INA § 287(a) require a likelihood that the immigrant will escape before a warrant can be obtained. INA §§ 287(a)(2), (a)(4), (a)(5). Section 6 contains no such requirement and we are not aware of any INA provision indicating that Congress intended state and local law enforcement officers to enjoy greater authority to effectuate a warrantless arrest than federal immigration officials.

Thus, Section 6 significantly expands the circumstances in which Congress has allowed state and local officers to arrest immigrants. Federal law does not allow these officers to conduct warrantless arrests based on probable cause of *civil* removability, but Section 6 does. Therefore, Section 6 interferes with the carefully calibrated scheme of immigration enforcement that Congress has adopted, and it appears to be preempted. Arizona suggests, however, that it has the inherent authority to enforce federal *civil* removability without federal authorization, and therefore that the United States will not ultimately prevail on the merits. We do not agree. Contrary to the State's view, we simply are not persuaded that Arizona has the authority to unilaterally transform state and local law enforcement officers into a state-controlled DHS force to carry out its declared policy of attrition.

We have previously suggested that states do not have the inherent authority to enforce the civil provisions of federal immigration law. In *Gonzales v. City of Peoria*, 722 F.2d 468, 475 (9th Cir.1983), *overruled on other grounds by Hodgers–Durgin v. de la Vina*, 199 F.3d 1037 (9th Cir.1999), we held that "federal law does not preclude local enforcement of the *criminal* provisions of the [INA]." (Emphasis added). There, we "assume[d] that the *civil* provisions of the [INA] regulating authorized entry, length of stay, residence status, and deportation, constitute such a pervasive regulatory scheme, as would be consistent with the exclusive federal power over immigration." *Id.* at 474–75 (emphasis added). We are not aware of any binding authority holding that states possess the inherent authority to enforce the civil provisions of federal immigration law—we now hold that states do not have such inherent authority.

* * *

Subsection [287](g)(10) neither grants, nor assumes the preexistence of, inherent state authority to enforce civil immigration laws in the absence of federal supervision. If such authority existed, all of INA § 287(g)—and § 1252c for that matter—would be superfluous, and we do not believe that Congress spends its time passing unnecessary laws.

In sum, we are not persuaded that Arizona has the inherent authority to enforce the *civil* provisions of federal immigration law. Therefore, Arizona must be federally-authorized to conduct such enforcement. Congress has created a comprehensive and carefully calibrated scheme—and has authorized the Executive to promulgate extensive regulations—for adjudicating and enforcing civil removability. S.B. 1070 Section 6 exceeds the scope of federal authorization for Arizona's state and local officers to enforce the civil provisions of federal immigration law. Section 6 interferes with the federal government's prerogative to make removability determinations and set priorities with regard to the enforcement of civil immigration laws. Accordingly, Section 6 stands as an obstacle to the full purposes and objectives of Congress.

In addition, as detailed with respect to Section 2(B) above, S.B. 1070's detrimental effect on foreign affairs, and its potential to lead to 50 different state immigration schemes piling on top of the federal scheme, weigh in favor of the preemption of Section 6.

* * *

Accordingly, we find that as to the S.B. 1070 Sections on which the United States is likely to prevail, the district court did not abuse its discretion in finding that the United States demonstrated that it faced irreparable harm and that granting the preliminary injunction properly balanced the equities and was in the public interest.

CONCLUSION

For the foregoing reasons, we affirm the preliminary injunction enjoining enforcement of S.B. 1070 Sections 2(B), 3, 5(C), and 6.

NOONAN, CIRCUIT JUDGE, concurring:

I concur in the opinion of the court. I write separately to emphasize the intent of the statute and its incompatibility with federal foreign policy.

[Section 1] of the act constitutes an authoritative statement of the legislative purpose. The purpose is "attrition," a noun which is unmodified but which can only refer to the attrition of the population of immigrants unlawfully in the state. The purpose is to be accomplished by "enforcement," also unmodified but in context referring to enforcement of law by the agencies of Arizona. The provisions of the act are "intended to work together." Working together, the sections of the statute are meant "to discourage and deter the unlawful entry and presence of aliens and economic activity by persons unlawfully present in the United States."

It would be difficult to set out more explicitly the policy of a state in regard to aliens unlawfully present not only in the state but in the United States. The presence of these persons is to be discouraged and deterred. Their number is to be diminished. Without qualification, Arizona establishes its policy on immigration.

* * *

Federal foreign policy is a pleonasm. What foreign policy can a federal nation have except a national policy? That fifty individual states or one individual state should have a foreign policy is absurdity too gross to be entertained. In matters affecting the intercourse of the federal nation with other nations, the federal nation must speak with one voice.

That immigration policy is a subset of foreign policy follows from its subject: the admission, regulation and control of foreigners within the United States. By its subject, immigration policy determines the domestication of aliens as American citizens. It affects the nation's interactions with foreign populations and foreign nations. It affects the travel of foreigners here and the trade conducted by foreigners here. It equally and reciprocally bears on the travel and trade of Americans abroad. As the declarations of several countries or governmental bodies demonstrate in this case, what is done to foreigners here has a bearing on how Americans will be regarded and treated abroad.

* * *

The Arizona statute before us has become a symbol. For those sympathetic to immigrants to the United States, it is a challenge and a chilling foretaste of what other states might attempt. For those burdened by unlawful immigration, it suggests how a state could tackle that problem. It is not our function, however, to evaluate the statute as a symbol. We are asked to assess the constitutionality of five sections on their face integrated by the intent stated in Section 1. If we read Section 1 of the statute, the statute states the purpose of providing a solution to illegal immigration into the United States. So read, the statute is a singular entry into the foreign policy of the United States by a single state. The district court properly enjoined implementation of the four sections of the statute.

BEA, CIRCUIT JUDGE, concurring in part and dissenting in part:

* * *

I dissent from the majority's determination that Section 2(B) of Arizona S.B. 1070 is preempted by federal law and therefore is unconstitutional on its face. As I see it, Congress has clearly expressed its intention that state officials *should* assist federal officials in checking the immigration status of aliens, *see* 8 U.S.C. § 1373(c), and in the "identification, apprehension, detention, or removal of aliens not lawfully present in the United States," INA § 287(g)(10)(B). The majority comes to a different conclusion by minimizing the importance of § 1373(c) and by interpreting § 287(g)(10) precisely to invert its plain meaning "*Nothing* in this subsection shall be construed to require an agreement . . . to communicate with the Attorney General regarding the immigration status of any individual" (emphasis added) to become "*Everything* in this subsection shall be construed to require an agreement." Further, the majority mischaracterizes the limited scope of Section 2(B), misinterprets the Supreme Court's cases on foreign relations preemption to allow any complaining foreign country to preempt a state law, and holds that the prospect of all 50 states assisting the federal government in identifying illegal aliens is—to Congress—an unwanted burden. * * *

* * *

The majority's error is to read § 287(g)(1)–(9), which provides the precise conditions under which the Attorney General *may* enter into written agreements to "deputize" officers, as the *exclusive* authority which Congress intended state officials to have in the field of immigration enforcement. That reading is made somewhat awkward in view of § 287(g)(10), which explicitly carves out certain immigration activities by state and local officials as *not* requiring a written agreement. But, the majority opinion reasons that since state officials cannot themselves *remove* illegal aliens, the natural reading of § 287(g)(10) is that state officials cannot *act at all* in immigration enforcement matters, absent an explicit written agreement, unless:

1. They are "called upon" by the Attorney General; OR

2.   There is a "necessity"; AND

3.   Such cooperation is "incidental," rather than "systematic and routine."

I concede the majority's insertion of the quoted terms into § 287(g)(10) is quite original, which perhaps explains why no legal basis is cited for any of it.* * *

* * *

Next, the majority seems to believe that when a state officer (1) initiates the identification of an illegal alien by checking the alien's immigration status with federal officials pursuant to § 1373(c), and (2) has the alien identified to him by federal authorities, the state officer has somehow *usurped* the federal role of immigration enforcement. Section 2(B)'s scope, however, is not so expansive. Section 2(B) does not purport to authorize Arizona officers to remove illegal aliens from the United States—Section 2(B) merely requires Arizona officers to inquire into the immigration status of suspected illegal aliens during an otherwise lawful encounter. Section 2(B) does not govern any other action taken by Arizona officers once they discover an alien is illegally present in the United States. Further, Section 2(B) does not require that ICE accept custody or initiate removal of the illegal alien from the United States. Federal authorities are merely obligated to respond to the immigration status inquiry pursuant to § 1373(c). Once this occurs, federal authorities are free to refuse additional cooperation offered by the state officers, and frankly to state their lack of interest in removing the illegal alien. The federal authorities can stop the illegal alien removal process at any point after responding to the state immigration status request.

* * *

The majority also finds that state officers reporting illegal aliens to federal officers, Arizona would interfere with ICE's "priorities and strategies." It is only by speaking in such important-sounding abstractions—"priorities and strategies"—that such an argument can be made palatable to the unquestioning. How can simply informing federal authorities of the presence of an illegal alien, which represents the full extent of Section 2(B)'s limited scope of state-federal interaction, possibly interfere with federal priorities and strategies—unless such priorities and strategies are to avoid learning of the presence of illegal aliens? What would we say to a fire station which told its community not to report fires because such information would interfere with the fire station's "priorities and strategies" for detecting and extinguishing fires?

* * *

* * * The majority would have us believe that Congress has provided the Executive with the power to veto any state law which happens to have some effect on foreign relations, as if Congress had not weighed that possible effect in enacting laws permitting state intervention in the immigration field. To the contrary, here Congress *has* established—through its enactment of statutes such as INA § 287(g)(10), 1373(c), and 1644—a policy which encourages the free flow of immigration status information between federal and local governments. * * * Second, the Executive's desire to appease foreign governments' complaints cannot override Congressionally-mandated provisions—as to the free flow of immigration status information between states and federal authorities—on grounds of a claimed effect on foreign relations any more than could such a foreign relations claim override Congressional statutes for (1) who qualifies to acquire residency in the United States, or (2) who qualifies to become a United States citizen.

* * *

I concur with the majority that Section 3, which penalizes an alien's failure to carry documentation as required by federal immigration statutes, impermissibly infringes on the federal government's uniform, integrated, and comprehensive system of registration which leaves no room for its enforcement by the state. I also concur with the majority that Section 5(C), which penalizes an illegal alien for working or seeking work, conflicts with Congress's intent to focus on employer penalties * * *.

* * *

* * * [T]he majority misrepresents Arizona's attempt to assist the federal government as "unilaterally transform[ing] state and local law enforcement officers into a state-controlled DHS force to carry out its declared policy of attrition." Section 6 is not, and could not, be so broad. Instead, Section 6 merely authorizes Arizona police officers to make warrantless arrests when they cooperate in the enforcement of federal immigration law—as invited to do by Congress. *See* INA § 287(g)(10).

* * *

The majority contends that § 287(g)(10) "neither grants, nor assumes the preexistence of, inherent state authority to enforce civil immigration laws in the absence of federal supervision." What, then, does § 287(g)(10) do? We must read 287(g)(10) in context of § 287(g) as a whole. Section 287(g) created, for the first time, the authority of the Attorney General to enter into agreements with states and localities to deputize their officers as 287(g) immigration officers. Subsections (g)(1)–(9) set out the specifics of the explicit written agreements—state officers are paid by the state, trained by the federal government, supervised by the Attorney General, and should be treated as federal employees for purposes of liability and immunity. However, § 287(g)(10) states clearly that this new method of state involvement—287(g) deputized officers—is not the *only* way state officers may cooperate in the enforcement of federal immigration law. Subsection (g)(10) preserves the preexisting authority of state officers to participate in enforcing immigration law, without the requirement of any formal, written agreement as envisioned by § 287(g)(1)–(9).

* * *

NOTES AND QUESTIONS ON *SB 1070*

1. The U.S. Supreme Court declined to review the Ninth Circuit's decision affirming the preliminary injunction blocking implementation of SB 1070. In the meantime, the federal government and private lawsuits proceeded in district court and remain pending as we go to press in late 2011. In October 2010, Judge Bolton, ruled on defendants' motions to dismiss in one of the private lawsuits, *Friendly House v. Whiting*, CV 10–1061–PHX-SRB (D. Ariz. Oct. 7, 2010).

Her ruling addressed several constitutional claims that the federal government had not asserted. She denied Arizona's motions to dismiss plaintiffs' claims that SB 1070 violates their rights under the Equal Protection Clause and 42 U.S.C. § 1981 (for race and national origin discrimination); under the Due Process Clause by denying procedural due process and section 6 is void for vagueness; and under the Fourth Amendment by requiring state and local officers to conduct unreasonable searches and seizures of individuals.

Judge Bolton granted Arizona's motions to dismiss plaintiffs' claims that SB 1070 violated the First Amendment (for restricting employment solicitation speech and infringing on the First Amendment rights of non-English speakers and individuals who speak English with an accent), and that sections 2 and 5 are void for vagueness.

2. As a matter of the options that a state could consider to address unauthorized migration, what are the key differences between (a) focus on checks of federal immigration status and the enactment of state criminal penalties for immigration violations, and (b) state and local laws that target unauthorized migration more indirectly by addressing housing and employment? Does this contrast make a constitutional difference for preemption purposes?

To put the second question more concretely, consider that the Ninth Circuit decided *United States v. Arizona* six weeks before the U.S. Supreme Court decided *Chamber of Commerce v. Whiting*. Suppose the Supreme Court reviews the preliminary injunction, or the Ninth Circuit revisits the same issues after a district court decides the merits of the case. How does the Supreme Court's decision in *Chamber of Commerce v. Whiting* affect *United States v. Arizona*?

3. Though litigation over the intergovernmental issues in SB 1070 has concerned federal-state relations, Rick Su reminds us that SB 1070 is at least as significant for its effects on state-local relations:

> [SB 1070] threatens to drastically alter the state-local relationship. Indeed, most of the recent discussions regarding S.B. 1070 have overlooked one of its central objectives: to eliminate local discretion with respect to immigration enforcement. In that regard, the law is inherently restrictive, not empowering, and it is through these restrictions on counties, cities, and towns that S.B. 1070 most directly encourages abusive profiling and harassment. The fact is, the purpose of S.B. 1070 is not to *allow* state and local law enforcement officials to enforce federal immigration laws. Rather it *requires* such officials and their departments to do so,

even if—perhaps especially if—they would ordinarily refrain out of concerns about relations with immigrant neighborhoods, competing local priorities, or lack of fiscal resources. Thus, S.B. 1070 not only targets undocumented immigrants and those who may be suspected of being such, but also local law enforcement agencies and the counties, cities, and towns that they serve.

Su, *The Overlooked Significance of Arizona's New Immigration Law*, 108 Mich. L.Rev. First Impressions 76 (2010).

4. Why did the federal government rely entirely on preemption rather than asserting the individual rights claims that other lawsuits have raised as part of their challenges to SB 1070?

State Legislation After SB 1070

As we go to press in late 2011, legislatures in more than half of the states have considered bills that would make E–Verify mandatory for all employers in the state, and would include some of the more controversial provisions of Arizona's SB 1070, including local police enforcement of immigration laws. Sixteen such state legislative proposals that included many provisions mirroring SB 1070 were defeated, but several became law—legislation in Utah, Georgia, South Carolina, and Alabama that closely resemble SB 1070, as well as a more limited law in Indiana. Other proposals remain pending. The defeated bills will likely be reintroduced in future sessions, and other states may consider similar proposals.

The newly enacted state laws replicate key aspects of SB 1070, but several went further in noteworthy respects. For example, Utah HB 497 enacted provisions that resemble section 2 of SB 1070, but other Utah legislation purported to provide guestworker status under state law. The Alabama law, HB 56, incorporated many provisions similar to those in SB 1070, but it also requires public schools to check the immigration status of new students, though for the stated purpose of merely ascertaining the fiscal impact of unauthorized students. Other provisions of the Alabama law would make contracts with unauthorized migrants unenforceable under certain circumstances, and would make it a felony for an "alien not lawfully present in the United States" to conduct a business transaction with the state of Alabama or any political subdivision thereof. The South Carolina law, S 20, and the Indiana law, SEA 590, limit the use of identification documents issued by foreign governments.

Unsurprisingly, lawsuits have tried to block the implementation of all of these new state laws, making substantially the same arguments deployed against SB 1070 by the federal government in *United States v. Arizona* and the private plaintiffs in *Friendly House v. Whiting*. Federal district courts issued preliminary injunctions in lawsuits brought by private plaintiffs against implementation of many of the provisions of the Georgia and Indiana legislation. The reasoning in these decisions generally followed the Ninth Circuit in *United States v. Arizona. See Georgia Latino Alliance for Human Rights v. Deal*, 2011 WL 2520752 (N.D. Ga.

2011); *Buquer v. City of Indianapolis*, 2011 WL 2532935 (S.D. Ind. 2011). A motion for a preliminary injunction against Utah HB 497 is pending as we go to press.

The federal government and various private plaintiffs filed suits to block implementation of the Alabama, South Carolina, and Utah laws. In Alabama, U.S. District Judge Blackburn initially allowed many of the more controversial provisions to go into effect, expressly rejecting the reasoning in the Arizona and Georgia preliminary injunction decisions. *See United States v. Alabama*, 2011 WL 4469941 (N.D.Ala. 2011). In October 2011, the Eleventh Circuit, hearing appeals in both the federal government and private plaintiff suits, issued a preliminary injunction against two of the Alabama law's most controversial provisions: the immigration status check for public school children, and another section that would make it a state crime not to carry an alien registration document as required under federal law. The appeals court allowed several other provisions to take effect. One of them, like Arizona SB 1070, requires law enforcement officers to check the immigration status of any person who is lawfully stopped, detained, or arrested if "reasonable suspicion" of unlawful presence exists. The Eleventh Circuit also declined to block the provision making contracts with unauthorized migrants unenforceable under certain circumstances. *See United States v. Alabama*, 2011 WL 4863957 (11th Cir. Oct. 14, 2011). As of late 2011, the litigation remains pending in the Eleventh Circuit.

Concluding Question on State and Local Enforcement

This chapter has examined two areas in which states and cities have addressed matters relating to immigration and immigrants: (1) laws that target unauthorized migrants; and (2) enforcement of (or refusal to enforce) federal immigration law. How do you assess the overall authority of states and cities in this area of law? Too much authority, or too little? If it depends on the issue, how and why does it depend? Are states different from cities? If so, how and why?

SECTION D. PROPOSALS TO REFORM THE LEGAL IMMIGRATION SYSTEM

Today, widespread agreement that the current U.S. immigration system is broken coexists with dramatically different notions about how to fix it—and a discouragingly polarized debate among the contending camps. For some the key feature of the breakdown is the ineffectiveness of enforcement. For others the central breakdown is manifested in hardships that the current system imposes on existing and prospective migrants, either through deportation that can divide families or the enforcement strategies that have diverted entry patterns through dangerous deserts. And for still others, particularly in influential sectors of the U.S. business community, the key is the mismatch of temporary and permanent immigration opportunities with the claimed needs of the U.S. economy or the desires of prospective immigrants.

Many of those in the first camp favor legislative and administrative changes that deal with enforcement only. Those in the latter camps either embrace or acquiesce in the argument that improved enforcement must be part of any new regime, and they have tried to develop legislative proposals that would include enhanced enforcement but also take steps to address the other concerns. They push for "comprehensive immigration reform," in contrast to an enforcement-only package. Comprehensive reform proposals include three major components: (1) enforcement—both through enhanced resources and new approaches at the border, in the interior, and through improved employer screening; (2) reform of legal immigration categories, especially to satisfy perceived labor market needs—often including proposals for an expansive guest-worker program; and (3) legalization, with conditions, of most of the current population present without authorization (opponents call this element "amnesty"; proponents favor "earned legalization" or "path to citizenship").

Since 2005 there has been steady interest in reform, with key votes in the House and the Senate on legislation in 2005 through 2007—though without success in uniting enough support from the various camps to get legislation enacted. The Obama administration has also strongly supported comprehensive immigration reform, but as of late 2011 has not been able to muster the appropriate forces to obtain serious consideration in either chamber of Congress. As we go to press, it is widely assumed that no comprehensive immigration reform measures will be taken up until—at the earliest—after the 2012 elections.

You should be familiar with the main elements of the enforcement proposals in recent immigration reform measures from the preceding parts of this chapter. New proposals are usually refinements and expansions of the strategies and mechanisms discussed above—more resources for ICE and CBP, expanded application of summary removal procedures and of penalties for violations, and (in some proposals) greater use of state and local coordination to enhance enforcement capacities. The most important single enforcement measure would be the phased deployment of nationwide mandatory use of E–Verify or some similar electronic employment verification system, in an effort to block job opportunities for unauthorized workers. You may want to review the material in Section A, pp. 968–71, *supra*, on E–Verify and the challenges that would face a mandatory system (especially the identity authentication issue) before proceeding further.

The balance of this Section provides a selective introduction to the other two main components of reform proposals: legalization and changes to legal immigration procedures and categories, both permanent and temporary. (A more extensive discussion of the pros and cons of guest worker programs, both high-skilled and low-skilled, appears in chapter 5B, *supra,* pp. 408–16 and 428–51.)

EXERCISE ON IMMIGRATION REFORM

To frame and focus your reading of the following material, assume that you are a legislative aide to a newly elected member of Congress. She wants to devote much of her legislative effort to fixing the immigration system and she has asked you to outline preliminary ideas for her legislative initiatives in this field. Therefore, keep track of the policy issues you regard as the most important to be addressed in any new round of reform, and note which of the competing proposals on each of the elements seem most promising. Pay attention to the assumptions you make about the underlying goals that the system should serve and also about what the political climate will bear.

---

1. A SURVEY AND INTRODUCTION

We begin with excerpts from the 2009 report of an independent and bipartisan task force chartered by the Council on Foreign Relations. The Task Force was chaired by former Republican Governor Jeb Bush of Florida and Thomas (Mac) McLarty, who served as Chief of Staff to Democratic President Bill Clinton. The report, which argued for a version of comprehensive immigration reform, lays out the issues and also provides an indication of the salient history, going back to the previous attempt at comprehensive reforms in the 1986 Immigration Reform and Control Act (IRCA), which contained both legalization and new enforcement measures. It also makes reference to the legislative efforts in 2006–2007, providing some indication of what proponents put into their reform packages, and what have been the main political considerations and obstacles.

JEB BUSH, THOMAS F. McLARTY III, & EDWARD ALDEN, U.S. IMMIGRATION POLICY

Independent Task Force Report No. 63; Council on Foreign Relations, 2009.
Chapter on "The Need for Comprehensive Immigration Reform," pp. 44–69, 76–79.

The task of making U.S. immigration policies better serve America's national interests is an urgent one facing the current administration and Congress. * * *

It has been said many times before, but it is also the conclusion of this Task Force that the current immigration system is badly broken. It will take both changes to the law and changes to current practices to make the system function more effectively. *The Task Force recommends that a new effort to pass a comprehensive immigration reform bill be a first-tier priority for the Obama administration and Congress * * *.*

Congress has tried repeatedly to address some of the problems in the immigration system, passing significant legislation in 1986, 1990, and 1996. Yet the conclusions of the congressionally established Jordan Commission in 1994 remain as true today as they were then. "Serious problems undermine present immigration policies, their implementation, and their credibility: people who should get in find a cumbersome process that often impedes their entry; people who should not get in find it all too easy to enter; and people who are here without permission remain with impunity."

The Bush administration and Congress made efforts to overhaul U.S. immigration laws in 2006 and 2007, but in the face of strong opposition from both sides of the debate, a compromise could not be found. * * * Although there was considerable support for the 2007 Senate bill, little of it was enthusiastic, with many backers considering it only marginally preferable to the status quo. In addition, opponents of the legislation were strong and vocal in their denunciations. And, though the principles of the congressional proposals were generally sound, by the time of its eventual defeat, the Senate bill had become so complex that effective implementation by the Department of Homeland Security and other agencies would likely have been impossible. *The Task Force believes that the administration and Congress must be careful that a legislative reform effort does not simply impose a huge additional mandate on an already overburdened bureaucracy. It is not enough to pass comprehensive immigration reform; this time, reform must work.* Further, even if a compromise can be reached, the United States must break out of the pattern in which Congress revisits immigration policy every decade or so, approves what is claimed at the time to be a lasting fix, and then washes its hands of the issue until the problems again become too big to ignore.

Since 2007, the administration's primary response to the failure of comprehensive immigration reform has been to escalate enforcement at the border and to toughen measures to stop companies from employing unauthorized migrants. In an effort to keep out illegal immigrants, the United States has expanded the Border Patrol into the nation's largest law enforcement agency, spent billions on deploying high-tech virtual barriers, and is close to completing construction of nearly seven hundred miles of pedestrian and vehicle fences along its southern border with Mexico. * * *

Although many in the media, and some in Congress, continue to insist that U.S. borders are out of control and insecure, the Task Force believes that the border enforcement efforts of the past several years are impressive and not well enough understood by the public. * * * Along with increased border enforcement, DHS last year removed nearly 350,000 illegal immigrants apprehended inside the United States, a 20 percent increase over 2007 and by far the highest number on record. The United States has also used intelligence gathering and modern technologies to help target terrorists, criminals, and others it wants to exclude from the country.

The Task Force finds that these measures represent determined, expansive efforts to control America's borders and enforce U.S. immigration laws. But no amount of enforcement can eliminate the underlying problem, which is that aggressively enforcing a broken regime does not fix it. Unless the United States has a more sensible and efficient system for admitting legal migrants who come to take advantage of work opportunities, no reasonable level of enforcement is likely to be enough to resolve the illegal immigration problem.

* * *

Comprehensive immigration reform is likely to be no easier in the current Congress than it was in the previous one. In some ways, it could be harder because the deep recession in the U.S. economy will leave many lawmakers with little appetite for measures aimed at making it easier for foreigners to come and work legally in the United States. But there may also be a window of opportunity. Although millions of illegal immigrants are still in the United States, the number trying to enter is falling rapidly, due to a combination of economic weakness and tougher enforcement. The construction industry, for example, which has employed many unauthorized migrants, was one of the earliest sectors hit by the economic downturn. Illegal immigrants are also easier for employers to dismiss, and thus tend to be the first let go as the economy weakens. It is too soon to know whether illegal immigrants are returning home in large numbers, but there is no question that illegal migration to the United States has slowed significantly. By the best estimates available, the total number of illegal immigrants living in the United States began to decline in 2007, and may have already fallen by as many as 500,000. Although a recession is never an easy time to consider reforming immigration laws, the decline in illegal immigration has the benefit of allowing Congress and the administration to focus on the broader set of issues raised in this report and elsewhere, rather than solely on the issue of controlling illegal immigration. * * * An effective immigration system that provides timelier processing for immigrant workers who will be needed as the economy returns to growth is a critical component of the larger economic recovery package.

There are improvements to the immigration system that can and should be undertaken without legislation, but a piecemeal effort at reform is unlikely to make anything other than modest progress, given the flaws in the current legal regime and the complexity of the competing interests and concerns. * * * [This] report will discuss the four central elements of any immigration reform effort: improvements in the legal immigration system, more effective enforcement to discourage illegal immigration, a plan for dealing with those already living illegally in this country, and, finally, a strategy for ensuring successful integration of the growing number of immigrants who are arriving and settling in the United States.[a]

---

a. The immigrant integration discussion is omitted from this excerpt.—eds.

ENCOURAGING LEGAL IMMIGRATION

Most immigrants come to the United States to work. * * *

As is being demonstrated by the current recession, the quickest way to discourage illegal migration is to stop creating jobs for migrants and everyone else. When the economy recovers, the demand for new immigrants, whether legal or illegal, will also recover. The current slowdown, therefore, should be seen as an opportunity to overhaul U.S. immigration policies to better serve U.S. economic needs as the economy regains its footing.

It is the view of the Task Force that getting legal immigration right is the most critical immigration policy challenge facing the administration and Congress. Although not enough on its own, the most effective way to combat illegal immigration is to have an immigration policy that provides adequate and timely means for the United States to admit legal immigrants.

Three central principles should guide the reform of the legal immigration system: first, the United States should be admitting immigrants (and their close family members) in the number and range of skills that reflect the demands from its economy; second, it needs a much simpler and more transparent system for admitting both migrants and temporary workers; and finally, the government must invest in making the legal immigration system work more efficiently.

Immigrant numbers

The current immigration system does not respond well to supply and demand in the U.S. labor market. Economics should not be the only factor shaping American immigration policy decisions, but neither can the United States simply ignore the vast economic forces that drive international migration. The effort to gain control of illegal migration is certain to fail unless the supply of foreign workers and the demand for them in the United States are brought more closely into line. That for much of this decade roughly 800,000 migrants could come to the United States illegally each year and find jobs is a clear indicator that the legal migration system has not remotely reflected market demand. Indeed, one of the reasons illegal immigration is so attractive not only to the migrants but also to U.S. employers is that it responds quickly to market pressures. The lengthy waits and substantial expense required for hiring most foreign workers through existing legal channels have discouraged many employers from using those channels, except for the most highly skilled workers.

Labor market needs currently get far too little attention in deciding who gets priority to immigrate. For the past half century, most new immigrants coming to the United States have been family members of legal migrants or U.S. citizens. In 2008, nearly 700,000 people acquired green cards on the basis of family ties. By contrast, only just over 166,000 did so on the basis of employment, 76,000 to the employees and the remaining 90,000 to their spouses and children. There has long been a debate over whether the strong preference for family reunification in U.S. immigration law serves American interests. There are clearly some good reasons for maintaining the policy—the family is a core unit of American society, and strong families are critical for the education, financial support, and social integration of newcomers to the country. Families can also serve as an information network, alerting relatives at home to job prospects in the United States, and providing them with support after they arrive. * * *

The current system for family-based immigration, however, is exceedingly slow, and does not work well even in bringing families together. As a result of quotas designed to limit immigrants from a handful of countries such as Mexico, India, and China, waits for sponsoring family members can stretch to a decade or more. * * * Even the waiting times for spouses and minor children of legal immigrants from anywhere in the world are often more than five years—a delay that is so long as to make a mockery of the concept of family reunification.

However, the system for admitting immigrants with needed skills but without family connections is even worse. Changes to the quotas as part of the 1990 Immigration Act raised the number of green cards for employment-based immigrants and their families from 56,000 to 140,000, but this remains a fraction of the numbers available for family members. In addition, most of the employment-based slots are claimed by individuals already living in the United States under some sort of temporary status. At the higher-skilled end, the main temporary visa available for bringing skilled workers to the United States and putting them on a path to permanent residence has been the H–1B visa program, though that same program has also been used heavily by Indian companies bringing over strictly temporary workers to support their business model of outsourcing back-office work for U.S. companies. American high technology companies are the main users of the H–1B program, although universities and other educational institutions as well as financial services companies are also significant employers. * * * [The H–1B cap has been changed by Congress several times over the past decade,] but it is clear that the [current] quota [of 65,000] is inadequate in anything but a deep recession.

The logic of the current quotas is that hiring more foreign technology workers will mean fewer jobs for American technology workers. There is little evidence, however, that those restrictions end up creating more jobs for American workers. * * * A recent survey by the National Venture Capital Association found that one-third of privately held venture capital-backed U.S. companies—the most innovative firms in the United States—had been increasing hiring abroad due to restrictions that prevented them from hiring foreign workers in this country.

A number of other advanced industrialized nations have implemented policies that explicitly target immigrants whose skills the government believes are valuable to the economy, or are thought to be in short supply. Canada, Britain, Australia, and New Zealand all have what are known as points-based systems for selecting immigrants. They use factors such as education, occupation, work experience, age, and language skills to decide which immigrants to admit. The system is implemented by the government, in contrast to the U.S. scheme, which depends more on private companies identifying and hiring particular foreign workers.

In 2007, in the final throes of the debate over immigration reform, the Senate introduced a compromise bill crafted by senators Jon Kyl (R–AZ) and Edward Kennedy (D–MA) that would have introduced a points system in the United States. At the same time, it would have increased the percentage of employment-based green cards significantly and reduced family preferences, particularly for parents and siblings. The proposal generated strong opposition from many immigrant rights groups, who objected to the reduction in family preferences. But it also drew surprisingly strong hostility from business, which feared it would compromise the ability of companies to seek out and hire the best foreign workers and would instead place greater authority in the hands of the government. The danger of a points system is that it can become delinked from the actual labor market, bringing in employment-based workers for whom no employment actually exists. Despite the arguments in favor of a points system, the United States, under its current system, has been the most successful country in the world in attracting the most highly skilled immigrants—a record that calls for reforming the current system to make it more efficient, easier to use, and more responsive to market demand, rather than adopting a different system wholesale.

U.S. policies for attracting low-skilled workers have also been divorced from the realities of supply and demand. The current legal quota for green cards for unskilled laborers and their families, for example, is just ten thousand each year, a miniscule number that does not begin to reflect actual demand. The H–2A visa program for temporary agricultural workers tends to be underused by employers because of its cost and complexity, whereas the H–2B program for seasonal workers has a quota that is normally too low to meet demand. * * *

There has long been serious consideration given to expanding temporary worker programs, especially for low-skilled migrants from Mexico who would otherwise be likely to enter the United States illegally. A temporary worker program was a central feature of the failed immigration reform efforts in both 2006 and 2007. Temporary and seasonal work programs have been the only mechanism that has allowed the cross-border flow of workers from Mexico to the United States to be funneled into a program that can be monitored by government authorities. The biggest dilemma has been how to enforce labor certification, minimum wage, and labor rights provisions in an effort to ensure that migrant workers are not being exploited, and are not used by employers to drive down wages and standards for American workers. * * *

Temporary worker programs have never been a panacea, and the U.S. experience with such schemes has been decidedly mixed. The biggest of these was the Bracero Program for Mexican agricultural workers[, which] * * * became notorious for widespread labor rights abuses and was shut down by Congress in 1965. * * *

The United States is not alone in its mixed experiences. Other countries have generally been unsuccessful in creating smoothly functioning guest worker programs for at least two reasons. First, except in certain industries, such as agriculture and tourism, which have large seasonal employment fluctuations, temporary work is something of a misnomer. Many temporary work permits are for full-time, year-round jobs, but with the assumption that at the end of a certain period, usually three years, the individual will return home. The assumption collides with too much of what is known about human nature and economic realities. Someone who leaves home for three years almost invariably puts down some roots in the new community, and is unlikely to leave voluntarily at the end of that period. The employee may have come to depend on the higher wage, much of which is often sent back home to families as remittances. An employer may also be reluctant to lose a good employee. * * * As a result, many temporary workers try to find legal channels to remain permanently in their adopted countries or, failing that, often remain illegally.

The second problem is that the conditions of employment for temporary workers tend to be substandard, with employers sometimes paying workers below the legal minimum wage and withholding normal employment benefits. In cases where an individual's legal status in the host country depends on a particular job, as is frequently the case, those workers have little or no ability to seek better wages or working conditions. Unions have found it particularly difficult, and usually impossible, to organize foreign workers enrolled in such programs. The United States has attempted to deal with these criticisms by requiring that employers attest that they have been unable to find enough workers domestically, and that they will offer foreign workers the same wages and working conditions as domestic employees. But in practice such labor certification requirements have been extremely difficult to enforce, particularly with the inadequate resources devoted to the task.

Complexity

The current legal immigration system is inordinately complex and cumbersome. Lengthy delays in processing routine requests make it difficult, if not impossible, to carry out an immigration policy that serves the nation's interests. According to the U.S. Citizenship and Immigration Services (USCIS) ombudsman, many of the "pervasive and serious problems" in the handling of legal immigration and visa claims "stem from the complexity and opaque nature of the immigration rules and the agency administering them." The basic law underlying U.S. immigration policy was written in 1952, and since that time most of the changes approved by Congress have simply layered additional burdens on an already inadequate law and an ineffective bureaucracy. * * *

Although it will never be easy to simplify a system that must deal with such a huge volume and diversity of individual cases, the Task Force believes that the government must begin moving in that direction. For more than half a century, the United States has made the system more and more complicated; it is time to begin reversing course.

The current template for legal immigration to the United States also bears little resemblance to how most immigration actually takes place. The assumption on which the laws are written is that most aspiring immigrants will apply from their home countries for permission to immigrate to the United States, and then wait their turn in line. That may once have been an accurate reflection of the reality, but currently most who immigrate permanently to the United States spend many years living here first on some kind of temporary visa.

In theory, almost everyone who comes to the United States on a temporary visa—whether as a tourist, a student, or an employee—is expected to demonstrate the intent to return home after the visa expires. * * * Yet in practice, the distinction between temporary employees and permanent immigrants has utterly broken down. Because permanent visas are so difficult to obtain, temporary ones have become a substitute. Far more temporary work visas are therefore issued each year than employment-based green cards. In 2008, for instance, more than 166,000 employment-based green cards were issued to both employees and their family members; in comparison, more than 600,000 temporary work visas were issued, many to people living in the United States for years and waiting for a green card. More than 60 percent of those seeking green cards each year are already in the United States; that figure is nearly 90 percent for employment-based immigrants.

There are good arguments in favor of an immigration system that allows many people to come here first on some sort of temporary basis. The process permits a potential immigrant to experience living and working in the United States before making the more consequential decision to immigrate. The student visa program, for instance, has been an enormously important channel for attracting young, highly skilled individuals who often end up living permanently in the United States. On the demand side, temporary schemes are also easier for the government to adjust upward and downward as economic conditions in the United States change, a flexibility that does not exist with family-based permanent immigration.

* * * In simplifying the immigration system, the United States needs to move to a scheme that more closely resembles how migration actually occurs in the world today.

Government Investment

Even if the current system can be simplified, it will not work properly without a more effective funding system for facilitating legal immigration. *The Task Force finds that some of the recent operational problems in the*

U.S. legal immigration system are a result of the way in which the system is financed. * * *

Congress has mandated that USCIS be self-funded. Under the current system, the cost of immigration processing is paid for entirely by a series of fees levied on visa applicants, temporary immigrants, green-card applicants, and those seeking U.S. citizenship. Certain types of visa applications are particularly expensive.

* * *

The underlying message is that America as a country believes that immigration serves only the interests of immigrants, and therefore they should pay the entire cost themselves. Further, the refusal to use any taxpayer money to pay for immigration services indicates that the United States does not believe that facilitating legal immigration is a significant national priority. One of the consequences is that USCIS is simply not held to the same accountability and performance standards by Congress as are other functions of the U.S. government, including immigration enforcement, which are paid for by taxpayers. *The Task Force believes that both facilitating legal immigration and preventing unlawful entry should be considered equally important priorities, and should receive the funding and oversight to ensure they perform at an optimal level.*

In particular, Congress should be prepared to appropriate funds to support the development of a modern infrastructure for processing immigrant and temporary visa applications. USCIS has recently launched a long-overdue Transformation Initiative to create a paperless processing system that should improve efficiency and customer service as it reduces fraudulent applications and speeds security checks. Although USCIS is budgeting to fund the initiative out of fee revenue, infrastructure investment cannot be a single initiative, but requires ongoing budgetary support.

* * *

DISCOURAGING ILLEGAL IMMIGRATION

The United States has the right, and the duty, to control and secure its borders. It is an affront to the rule of law that hundreds of thousands of people each year can enter the country unannounced or pose as visitors when their intention is to live here permanently. It is also true that, except for the small percentage who come here as drug smugglers or with the intention of committing other crimes, the vast majority of illegal immigrants have broken the law only in pursuit of a dream shared by many, to make better lives for themselves and for their families. But a central feature of the American dream is the idea that success comes from playing by the rules; that so many who wish to come here now try to succeed by violating the rules is a sad distortion of that ideal. *The Task Force believes that in any effort to reform immigration laws, the rule of law must be reasserted. No reform will be accepted by the American people, nor should it be, unless it restores respect for the law.* This means that alongside reform of its legal immigration system, the United States must assert greater control over its borders, assure compliance with terms of admission, and sharply reduce the number of jobs available to persons not authorized to work in this country.

Comprehensive immigration reform would substantially lower the flow of illegal migrants by providing alternative legal channels for migrants to live and work in the United States. * * * Reducing the flow would also allow for a much higher apprehension rate, which would in turn discourage others who might be thinking about trying to enter the United States illegally. There is a law enforcement tipping point at which the costs and difficulty of entering illegally would become a powerful disincentive, particularly given the existence of new legal options. The sharp reduction in illegal entry into the United States over the past two years as the economy has softened and enforcement has grown indicates that it is possible to reach this tipping point in a recession; the challenge is to do so when the economy recovers and the demand for new employees again rises.

The Task Force believes that an effective enforcement regime centers on three elements: first, a comprehensive and accurate system that discourages employers from hiring unauthorized migrants; second, tougher enforcement at the borders that stops those who should not be admitted at a U.S. land border or port of entry; and, third, closer cooperation among federal, state, and local law enforcement officials in enforcing immigration laws.[b]

Employment Enforcement

Since the 1986 Immigration Reform and Control Act, the biggest missing piece in the enforcement effort has been the absence of any serious attempt to discourage employers from hiring undocumented workers. The grand bargain of 1986 was supposed to offer legalization for those already here in exchange for much tougher enforcement measures to bar the employment of illegal workers in the future. In practice, for both political and technological reasons, the employer sanctions provisions have not been adequately enforced, particularly not in recent years. * * * The result was that rather than discouraging illegal immigration, the 1986 act almost certainly accelerated it. That has left the American public rightly cynical of any similar grand bargain in the future. But the egregious failure of the U.S. government to carry out what had been promised in the 1986 legislation should not be used to discredit the entire approach. The failure was not conception; it was implementation.

Employment opportunities are the magnet that pulls most illegal migrants to the United States; if those opportunities can be diminished, illegal immigration will also diminish. *The Task Force believes employer sanctions need to be strengthened to discourage employers from hiring*

---

b. The discussion of cooperation with state and local law enforcement is omitted from this excerpt.—eds.

unauthorized workers; there should be clear guidelines to enable employers to comply with employer sanctions law, and these laws should be enforced to achieve optimal deterrence. Such measures are the most effective and humane way to discourage illegal migration to the United States. There will always be a certain degree of gray-market employment, and in sectors like agriculture and construction it will be particularly difficult to end all such hiring. But far more can be done. The government must strengthen the penalties it levies against employers who hire unauthorized migrants and make it easier for willing employers to comply with the law. In particular, the government needs to improve and expand what is still a fledgling electronic verification system, E–Verify, which will permit employers to avoid prosecution by verifying against a government database that the employee applying for a job is legally entitled to work in the United States. In addition, the agency in charge of enforcing employer sanctions—Immigration and Customs Enforcement—must have adequate resources to conduct investigations and to initiate prosecutions for employers who violate the law.

Why should enforcement at the work site be any more effective than it was after 1986? In some ways, the problem is more difficult because the hiring of unauthorized migrants is so pervasive that many employers have a strong incentive to continue the practice. On the other hand, the U.S. government now has the capability to use information technologies that allow for quicker and more accurate verification that new employees are authorized to work in the United States. The E–Verify system, begun on a pilot basis in 1997, has gradually been expanded to encompass many more employers. * * * Overall, about one in eight new hires in the United States is now being checked through the E–Verify system.

Although still in its infancy, the E–Verify system shows considerable promise. * * *

* * *

Generally, employer sanctions have been almost an afterthought in the U.S. enforcement regime, even as all other aspects of enforcement have been ramped up significantly in recent years. * * *

The limited enforcement of employer sanctions can be explained by the ubiquity of the violations, lack of resources, the rampant use of fraudulent documents, the lack of clarity in government guidelines, and the weakness of the sanctions for those who get caught. Much like traffic cops who have taken to ticketing only dangerous drivers rather than all speeders, routine and widespread violation of the law makes enforcement extremely difficult and challenging. It will take strengthened employer sanctions, along with a robust electronic verification system that provides immunity from prosecution for employers who use it, to achieve compliance by the vast majority of U.S. employers. This, in turn, would permit focused and targeted investigations and prosecution of noncompliant employers, further increasing the deterrent effect of the strengthened law. There is a tipping point where violations become the exception, but getting to it will require tougher sanctions. Both the carrot and the stick are needed.

The Task Force believes that as more legal immigrant workers become available, and as the government increasingly puts in place tools to encourage and to make it easier for legitimate companies to comply with the law, tough enforcement against violations by employers needs to become routine.

Border Enforcement

The United States has made impressive strides in the past several years in strengthening its border enforcement measures. Border enforcement is vital to safeguarding the nation against those who would do it harm, particularly terrorists and serious criminals, and for keeping out those trying to enter the United States illegally. Along with a comprehensive reform of the immigration system that allows new legal paths for immigrants, border enforcement is needed for deterring and catching those who would still try to enter the United States illegally. As the experience of the 1986 legislation has shown, there cannot be meaningful and lasting reform of U.S. legal immigration policies without an effective system to secure the borders.

The fundamental goal of border enforcement is to permit the United States to know, to the fullest extent possible, who is entering the country, but to do so in a way that does not disrupt legitimate cross-border movement.

* * *

EARNED LEGALIZATION

The toughest issue is what to do with the millions already living illegally in the United States. This, more than any other issue, led to the failure of congressional efforts at immigration reform in 2006 and 2007. By the best estimates, slightly fewer than twelve million unauthorized immigrants are thought to be living currently in the United States, though that number is likely shrinking as a result of the weakening economy and tougher enforcement. Public opinion polls, perhaps surprisingly, show that about two-thirds of Americans support finding a way for those who live illegally in the United States to gain lawful status, providing they develop English-language skills, pass background checks, and pay some sort of restitution. But deep suspicion rightly remains that a mass legalization will simply repeat the 1986 experience and do nothing to stem the problem of illegal migration in the future.

Language matters a great deal in the debate over immigration, but it matters here particularly. The legalization provisions in many of the bills considered by Congress from 2004 to 2007 were denounced by some critics as amnesty. More than any other single argument, it was the amnesty claim that did the most to kill the legislation. By any reasonable definition, however, the use of the term *amnesty* to describe the proposed reforms was a gross misstatement. The *Merriam-Webster Dictionary* defines amnesty as the "the act of an authority (as a government) by which pardon is granted to a large group of individuals." In other words, amnesty means wiping a transgressor's record clean—it is a free ride. Moreover, amnesty implies a serious threat of criminal prosecution and conviction. Like it or not, for the millions of illegal immigrants in the United States, there has never been a serious threat of criminal prosecution. * * *

* * * [In contrast, even] the most generous bills [considered in Congress recently] would have required those living in the United States unlawfully to earn their legalization. Illegal migrants would have had to demonstrate a long, virtually uninterrupted period of gainful employment, pass criminal and national security background checks, pay substantial fines, and demonstrate basic mastery of English. In a number of versions of the legislation, those who qualified would only be eligible initially for a temporary work visa, and would need to live and work in the United States for another significant period before being permitted to seek permanent residence.

Other, more targeted bills such as the Development, Relief, and Education for Alien Minors (DREAM) Act were aimed at providing some path to legalization for children who were brought to the United States illegally by their parents and thus had no active part in the decision to violate U.S. immigration laws. Those who had been present in the United States for at least five years, had earned a high school diploma, had been admitted to a postsecondary program, and had demonstrated good moral character would be eligible to adjust to permanent residence. The Agricultural Job Opportunities, Benefits, and Security (AgJOBS) Act would similarly have offered temporary status to those already employed as farm workers. If they remained in good standing for the following three to six years, those individuals could seek permanent residence.

* * *

The strongest argument against some form of earned legalization is that it will simply set the United States up for further illegal immigration and another round of legalization one or two or three decades from now. The experience of 1986 serves as a stark warning, and there is indeed a degree of moral hazard in any legalization scheme. There is no question that earned legalization creates an incentive for others to try to enter the United States illegally in the hope that they too will be allowed to stay by a future act of legalization. *The Task Force believes it is critical that any legalization program be accompanied both by more realistic immigration and temporary worker quotas and by stringent enforcement.*

Weighed against those arguments are the stronger, practical, ethical, economic, and national security arguments in favor of earned legalization. Practically, the difficulties in deporting so many illegal immigrants are extraordinary. Although not impossible, by any measure the undertaking would be extremely costly. For all the resources already been dedicated to increasing the number of removals, and the weak economy that has encouraged some to leave on their own, there appears to have been only a small decline in the number of illegal migrants living in the United States. Given both the expense and the further damage mass deportation would do to America's economy and to its reputation as a nation of immigrants, such an effort would not be in the country's interest.

The United States has long been a country that believes in second chances. The alternative—to break up families and wrench people away from communities where they have lived for many years, and in some cases even decades—is morally unacceptable. In many cases, it would require breaking up families in which some of the members are undocumented, others are legal residents, and others, particularly children, were born in the United States and are therefore U.S. citizens. * * *

Economically, the existence of a kind of shadow workforce that comprises more than 5 percent of the U.S. workforce makes little sense. Given the danger of deportation, it is impossible for these workers to press for better wages or working conditions. The result is an unfair advantage to employers who hire undocumented immigrants rather than native-born workers or legal migrants. Normalizing the status of undocumented workers in the United States could help improve both wages and working conditions for all those in lower-skilled jobs, and create fairer competition for American workers.

* * *

As unsatisfactory as it is to many from a rule-of-law perspective, including members of this Task Force, we believe there is little choice but to find some way to bring illegal migrants already in the United States who wish to remain out of the shadows and to offer them an earned pathway to legal status. It is the right policy choice—for economic reasons, for security reasons, and for the simply pragmatic reason that the United States should not attempt to deport people who have lived here for a long time, raised their families here, worked hard, and otherwise obeyed the law.

NOTES ON REFORM PROPOSALS

1. The Council on Foreign Relations (CFR) Task Force reached conclusions similar to an earlier independent task force convened by the Migration Policy Institute (MPI). Doris Meissner, Deborah W. Myers, Demetrios Papademetriou & Michael Fix, Immigration and America's Future: A New Chapter (Report of the Independent Task Force on Immigration and America's Future, Migration Policy Institute, Sept. 2006). The MPI report included a detailed proposal for substantially revising and simplifying the immigrant preference system and the nonimmigrant categories. We reprint later in this section a portion of its report, proposing a new mechanism of "provisional visas."

The Brookings Institution, along with Duke's Kenan Institute for Ethics, also convened a bipartisan roundtable in 2008 to consider immigration reform. Its conclusions were somewhat more cautious or restrictive than CFR's or MPI's. This report recommended that overall permanent immigration be held to roughly the current level of 1.1 million annually, but with changes to allocate more admissions to high-skilled migration. Also, family migration should be narrowed to admit just the nuclear family of citizens and lawful permanent residents. Enforcement should focus on workplace verification, and legalization should be phased in based on demonstrated progress in deploying such a verification system. Furthermore, any legalization program should be limited to persons who had been unlawfully present for at least five years. Brookings–Duke Immigration Policy Roundtable, Breaking the Immigration Stalemate: From Deep Disagreements to Constructive Proposals (2009).

2. During 2009 and 2010, the Obama administration worked behind the scenes to refine legislative proposals and to build support for comprehensive reform, primarily seeking cooperation with the chairman and ranking member of the Senate subcommittee having jurisdiction over immigration, Charles Schumer (D–NY) and Lindsey Graham (R–SC). The inability to find another Republican who would join Graham as a cosponsor and strong proponent of reform helped to stymie those efforts. As frustration over the delays built in 2010, the two senators did publish an op-ed essay with the outlines of their reform plans. Graham & Schumer, *The Right Way to Mend Immigration,* Wash. Post, Mar. 19, 2010. Nonetheless, progress remained stalled as the 2010 elections neared. In the House, Rep. Luis Gutierrez (D–IL), joined by 91 other members, introduced his own generous version of comprehensive reform in late 2009. Comprehensive Immigration Reform for America's Security and Prosperity Act (CIR ASAP), H.R. 4231, 111th Cong. (2009). *See* 86 Interp.Rel. 3064 (2009). Senator Robert Menendez (D–NJ) introduced a similar measure in the Senate, but neither bill moved.

In the absence of legislative progress, the White House published in 2011 a 29–page "blueprint" of the President's overall vision for immigration reform. Building a 21st Century Immigration System (May 2011), <http://www.whitehouse.gov/sites/default/files/rss_viewer/immigration_blueprint.pdf>. Meantime, in the new congressional session that began in January 2011, various members introduced their own proposals for accomplishing portions of the reform agenda in piecemeal fashion. Several focused exclusively on new or expanded enforcement measures, especially to make E–Verify into a national mandatory screening system. Others addressed the admissions or legalization side. Most prominent was the effort to pass the DREAM Act, legalizing persons who had come to the United States as children. It is discussed in more detail at the end of this chapter. Other bills looked to expand the admission opportunities for high-skilled migrants (including a catchy proposal described as "stapling" a green card to the diploma of any student obtaining an advanced degree from a U.S. university in scientific and technical (STEM) fields). Still others sought to expand and streamline the system for admitting temporary agricultural workers.

2. REFORMS TO LEGAL MIGRATION CATEGORIES

a. Reforms to Family–Sponsored Immigration

Family reunification has obviously been a key element of permanent immigration to the United States. But the lengthy backlogs that now characterize all family categories except immediate relatives of U.S. citizens, in the words of the Council on Foreign Relations task force, "make a mockery of the concept of family reunification." How could those categories be reformed to serve the goal more closely?

For decades, various proposals have sought to provide sufficient admission numbers to have a reasonable chance at keeping current with the demand in the family categories deemed most important by eliminating certain admission categories. Diversity visas and the fourth preference, for siblings of U.S. citizens, have been primary targets for elimination. Removing the fourth preference met strong political resistance from within the immigrant advocacy community, however. Opponents of such a change argued that the fourth preference is needed to recognize and honor certain ethnic traditions about family relations (particular reference was often made to Asian Americans). As a result, several family reform proposals were adjusted to provide for a transition period and usually for the grandfathering of applicants already in line. Other proposals retained a significant cutback on the fourth preference, but would have preserved immigration rights for unmarried or never-married siblings of U.S. citizens.

The congressionally chartered Commission on Immigration Reform, chaired by former Congresswoman Barbara Jordan, however, went further. It recommended in 1995 that several current categories (family-sponsored preferences 1, 2B, 3, and 4) be eliminated so as to focus on what it regarded as the highest priority, the nuclear family. It thus proposed changing to just three family preference categories: (1) spouses and minor children of U.S. citizens; (2) parents of U.S. citizens; and (3) spouses and minor children, plus adult physically or mentally dependent offspring of lawful permanent residents. It also favored a true preference system: numbers would be available to a lower preference only if the preceding category did not make full use of that year's family numbers (which the Commission recommended be set at 550,000 for a transition period, with possible lowering later). U.S. Commission on Immigration Reform, Legal Immigration: Setting Priorities xi-xix (1995).

The 2006 legislation passed by the Senate is representative of proposals that have taken a much different approach. S. 2611, 109th Cong., 2d Sess. (as passed by the Senate on May 25, 2006). It proposed to increase the ceilings in virtually all the family categories, and effectively to raise total annual family admissions for the preference categories to 480,000 from the normal current level of 226,000. Because the immediate relative category would remain uncapped, this could produce nearly a million family-based admissions each year. Other proposals regard as the most objectionable feature of current family migration the long separation that the present four- to five-year backlogs in category 2A can impose on lawful permanent residents seeking the admission of their spouses and minor children. They propose to remedy that delay by making spouses and children of LPRs also eligible for quota-free immediate relative status.

After the 2006 comprehensive immigration reform bill failed to win passage in the House, the 2007 "grand bargain" reform bill, S. 1639, 110th Cong., 1st Sess. (2007), tacked back in a restrictive direction. Like the Commission on Immigration Reform's proposal above, it would have eliminated family preferences 1, 2B, 3, and 4, and even taken parents of U.S. citizens out of the quota-free immediate relative category. Instead parents of U.S. citizens would have their own capped preference category with 40,000 permanent admissions annually, plus a new nonimmigrant category for parental visits to the United States, but with safeguards to help assure departure at the end. The maximum admission period for this nonimmigrant category would be 30 days, and overstaying would result in a permanent bar for the parent.

QUESTIONS ON FAMILY IMMIGRATION

Obviously there are many ways in which family categories could be revised. What would be the primary goals that a revision should serve? Once you have pondered that question and identified your own priorities, what changes to family migration would you favor? For a comprehensive discussion of policy considerations relevant to family reunification, see Motomura, *The Family and Immigration: A Roadmap for the Ruritanian Lawmaker*, 43 Am.J.Comp.L. 511 (1995).

b. Reforms to Employment–Based Immigration

Dissatisfaction with the employment-based portion of our immigration system comes from many directions and covers a wide range of issues, including selection criteria and procedures (including concerns about the labor certification and attestation processes), admission levels, the effectiveness of protections for both the imported workers and the wage levels and working conditions of U.S. workers in the same field, the need for flexibility to respond to changes in the labor market without having to wait for Congress to amend the levels and categories by statute, and claims for either more or less reliance on temporary worker programs. This book's primary treatment of temporary worker categories and programs, for both high-skilled and low-skilled workers, appears in Chapter Five, supra, pp. 402–16 and 428–51. The readings in this subsection deal primarily with other questions in the reform debate over employment-related immigration.

(i) High–Skilled Versus Low–Skilled Immigration

Many of those who favor reorienting immigration toward more high-skilled admissions rely on the findings of an extensive study carried out by the National Research Council (NRC). The New Americans: Economic, Demographic, and Fiscal Effects of Immigration (James P. Smith and Barry Edmonston, eds. 1997). Its findings about the overall long-term fiscal impacts of immigration have been summarized as follows:

> * * *[An] immigrant's fiscal balance—the taxes paid minus the cost of services consumed—depends primarily on the immigrant's earnings. A third of immigrants have not graduated from high school, and if they live in high-service states such as California, a combination of low taxes and extensive services means that households headed by U.S.-born persons pay higher taxes to provide services to immigrant-headed households. * * *

> Fiscal-balance studies are snapshots. However, immigrant earnings tend to rise with time in the United States, and so do immigrant tax contributions. The NRC attempted to construct a motion picture of immigrant integration, projecting future patterns of immigrant and native earnings, taxes paid and use of government services, and the earnings and taxes-benefit ratios for the children and grandchildren of immigrants and natives.

> The lifetime contribution of an immigrant was estimated at $80,000 in 1996, reflecting a negative $3,000 for the immigrant, but a positive $83,000 for the immigrant's children. The NRC found that immigrants with more education earn more and thus have a more favorable fiscal balance. Immigrants with more than a high-school diploma make a lifetime contribution of $105,000, and if the benefits from their children are included, a benefit for the United States of $198,000. However, immigrants with less than a high-school diploma impose a lifetime cost of $89,000 and, even with the gain of $76,000 from their children, the net effect is a $13,000 loss. The NRC concluded: "If the policy goal were to maximize the positive contribution of immigration to public sector budgets, that could be achieved by policies favoring highly educated immigrants and not admitting immigrants over age 50."

Philip Martin and Elizabeth Midgley, Immigration: Shaping and Reshaping America 22–23 (Population Reference Bureau, revised and updated 2d ed., 2006).

The Commission on Immigration Reform pointed to the NRC study in the course of making its core recommendations in 1997, which strongly favored high-skilled admissions:

> [The Commission recommends:] Skill-based admissions policies that enhance opportunities for the entry of highly-skilled immigrants, particularly those with advanced degrees, and eliminate the category for admission of unskilled workers. The Commission continues to recommend that immigrants be chosen on the basis of the skills they contribute to the U.S. economy. Only if there is a compelling national interest—such as nuclear family reunification or humanitarian admissions—should immigrants be admitted without regard to the economic

contributions they can make. The reunification of adult children and siblings of adult citizens solely because of family relationship is not as compelling.

A number of the * * * findings [of the NRC report] argue for increasing the proportion of immigrants who are highly-skilled and educated so as to maximize fiscal contributions, minimize fiscal impacts, and protect the economic opportunities of unskilled U.S. workers. The NRC research shows that education plays a major role in determining the impacts of immigration. Immigration of unskilled immigrants comes at a cost to unskilled U.S. workers, particularly established immigrants for whom new immigrants are economic substitutes. Further, the difference in estimated fiscal effects of immigrants by education is striking: using the same methodology to estimate net costs and benefits, immigrants with a high school education or more are likely to be net contributors while those without a high school degree are likely to be net costs to taxpayers.

Shifting priorities to higher skilled employment-based immigrants will have a beneficial multiplier effect. The highly-skilled are, in effect, new seed immigrants who will petition for their family members. The educational level of the spouses and children of highly-educated persons tends to be in the same range. Hence, our society benefits not only from the entry of highly-skilled immigrants themselves, but also from the entry of their family.

The Commission's framework for legal skills-based admissions includes two broad categories. The first category would cover individuals who are exempt from labor market tests because their entry will generate economic growth and/or significantly enhance U.S. intellectual and cultural strength without undermining the employment prospects and remuneration of U.S. workers: aliens with extraordinary ability, multinational executives and managers, entrepreneurs, and ministers and religious workers. The second category covers individuals subject to labor market tests, including professionals with advanced degrees, professionals with baccalaureate degrees, and skilled workers with specialized work experience.

U.S. Commission on Immigration Reform, Becoming an American: Immigration and Immigrant Policy 67–68 (1997 Report to Congress).

By the time the reform debate was seriously rejoined in the middle of the following decade, however, one heard far more arguments for large numbers of unskilled or low-skilled workers (though proposals varied with regard to whether they should come on temporary visas or as permanent immigrants). The following passage from Tamar Jacoby, written in 2006, is representative:

Arguably the most important statistic for anyone seeking to understand the immigration issue is this: in 1960, half of all American men dropped out of high school to look for unskilled work, whereas less than ten percent do so now. [And half of the 56 million jobs expected to be created in 2002–2012 will require no more than a high school education, but U.S. workers are becoming more educated.]

The resulting shortfall of unskilled labor—estimated to run to hundreds of thousands of workers a year—is showing up in sector after sector. The construction industry creates some 185,000 jobs annually, and although construction workers now earn between $30,000 and $50,000 a year, employers in trades such as masonry and dry-walling report that they cannot find enough young Americans to do the work. The prospects for the restaurant business are even bleaker. With 12.5 million workers nationwide, restaurants are the nation's largest private-sector employer, and their demand for labor is expected to grow by 15 percent between 2005 and 2015. But the native-born work force will grow by only ten percent in that period, and the number of 16- to 24-year-old job seekers—the key demographic for the restaurant trade—will not expand at all. So unless the share of older Americans willing to bus tables and flip hamburgers increases—and in truth, it is decreasing—without immigrants, the restaurant sector will have trouble growing through the next decade.

Fortunately for the United States, economic changes south of the border are freeing up a supply of unskilled labor to meet these growing needs in a timely way. * * *

The market mechanisms that connect U.S. demand with foreign supply, particularly from Latin America, are surprisingly efficient. Immigrants already here communicate to their compatriots still at home that the job market in, say, Detroit is flat, while that in Las Vegas is booming—and this produces a just-in-time delivery of workers wherever they are most needed. The vast majority of the immigrants who make the trip to the United States do so in order to work: if you are going to be unemployed, it is better to be unemployed at home in Mexico than in New York or Chicago. * * *

These facts are stark, and those who buy into the comprehensive [reform] vision see no point in quarreling with them. Rather than seeking to repeal the laws of supply and demand—or trying futilely to block them, as current policy does—reformers want an immigration policy that acknowledges and makes the most of these realities. * * *

This is the paradox at the heart of the comprehensive consensus. The best way to regain control is not to crack down but to liberalize— to expand quotas, with a guest-worker program or some other method, until they line up with labor needs. The analogy is Prohibition: an unrealistic ban on alcohol was all but impossible to enforce. Realistic limits, in contrast, are relatively easy to implement.

Jacoby, Immigration Nation, 85 Foreign Affairs 50, 52–54, 60 (2006).

Labor economist Vernon Briggs, in a book published in 2003, reached very different conclusions from Jacoby's about the need for and impact of low-skilled immigrant labor. Though he would support focused use of high-skilled admissions, managed by an administrative body that would have much greater flexibility in adjusting numbers and criteria, he argues that low-skilled immigration should be curtailed:

* * * The employment trends associated with the transformation of the nation's labor market are patently clear. On the demand side, occupations that stress skill and educational achievement are expanding, and those that do not are contracting. The number of skilled and educated workers is increasing, and, despite extensive corporate downsizing in the early 2000s, the trend should be a need for more in the future. As for unskilled and poorly educated workers, their ranks continue to swell. With their unemployment rates being consistently double the national rate, there is no apparent shortage of unskilled job seekers now or on the horizon. To the contrary, the major domestic economic policy challenge confronting the nation is what to do with so many poorly skilled workers at a time when the demand for their services is contracting. Since 1990, immigration has increased the number of high school dropouts in the labor force by 21 percent while increasing the supply of all other workers by only 5 percent.* * *

The nation is at an economic crossroad. It must choose between being a nation of high wages, made possible by a highly productive labor force, or becoming a nation of low wages, the consequence of a lowly productive labor force. * * *

* * * While there is no prospect for a general labor shortage as the twenty-first century begins, there may be spot shortages. This is a normal byproduct of a dynamic economy. These shortages will most likely be in occupations that require extensive training and educational preparation. In the technologically driven and internationally competitive economic setting of contemporary times, no industrialized nation with as many functionally illiterate adults as the United States has need have any short-run fear of a shortage of unqualified workers. There is no need for immigration to add to this surplus of illiterate adult job seekers. * * *

In this economic environment, an immigration policy designed to admit a flexible number of highly skilled and educated workers is what is required. The Immigration Act of 1990 was ostensibly intended to move public policy in this direction. But, as has been shown, it actually expanded the nepotistic family reunification focus that had been the [predominant] feature of the law it replaced and only marginally increased employment-based immigration. * * *

Already having an abundance of unskilled and poorly educated adults, the last thing that the nation needs is to continue to allow more such persons to immigrate into the United States. It is always possible for more highly skilled and educated persons to do unskilled work. * * * But the reverse is not possible. * * *

If the prevailing policy of mass and unguided immigration continues, it is unlikely that there will be sufficient pressure to enact the long-term human resource development policies needed to prepare and to incorporate these citizens from minority groups into the mainstream economy. Instead, by providing both competition and alternatives, the large and unplanned influx of immigrant labor will serve to maintain the social marginalization of many blacks and Hispanics who are citizens and permanent resident aliens. It will also mean that job opportunities will be reduced for the growing numbers of older workers who may wish to prolong their working years and for the vast pool of disabled citizens who were extended employment protection by the Americans with Disabilities Act of 1990. In other words, a substantial human reserve of potential citizen workers already exists. If their latent human resource development needs were addressed comprehensively, they could provide an ample supply of workers for most of the labor force needs in the foreseeable future.

V. Briggs, Jr., Mass Immigration and the National Interest: Policy Directions for the New Century 274–80 (3d ed. 2003).

NOTES AND QUESTIONS ON THE SKILLS DEBATE

The second decade of the 21st century, following the Great Recession of 2008–09, presents a far different U.S. employment picture from the one that formed the backdrop to Jacoby's 2006 article. What conclusions do you draw from those changes? What reforms to the employment-based categories, both temporary and permanent, would you favor?

(ii) Different Ways to Select Employment–Based Immigrants

Discontent with the labor certification system has been manifest for many years. One complaint is that the system is highly artificial, asking employers to go through expensive maneuvers ostensibly seeking U.S. workers when the whole point and true motivation of their efforts is to hire the targeted noncitizen. As a result, labor certification (and perhaps even more so with any system relying on attestations) fails to provide realistic safeguards to protect the job prospects or wages and working conditions of U.S. workers. Moreover, there is no guarantee that workers who enter on a labor certification will remain with that employer for any significant period—or even in the same field of employment.

In *Balancing Interests: Rethinking U.S. Selection of Skilled Immigrants* (1996). Demetrios Papadametriou and Stephen Yale–Loehr offered these observations on the core shortcomings of the current approach:

> [T]he labor certification system focuses on only a short-term goal: the immediate needs of the labor market. Immigrants are *permanent* additions to the labor force. It makes little sense to admit them (using the labor certification or any similar system) *solely* on the basis of a specific job opening that may quickly become redundant or for a

function that may offer few long-term benefits for either the employer or the country. Instead, a key goal of the economic immigrant selection system should be to satisfy ourselves that those who are admitted into the United States as presumptive members of our society have a proper mix of skills and other attributes, such as experience, education, and language, that maximizes the probability of long-term success in the labor force. Even if it worked perfectly, the existing labor certification process would have no more than a haphazard relationship to that goal.

Id. at 145.

The authors proposed abolishing the labor certification process and instituting a system that would include three requirements: (1) that the noncitizen have a job offer from a U.S. employer; (2) that the noncitizen have three years of experience in the occupation for which he or she is being sponsored; and (3) that the sponsoring employer attest that it will pay the higher of the prevailing wage for the occupation or the actual wage it pays to similarly situated employees. In addition, building on the experience of other countries such as Canada and Australia with points-based selection systems, the authors proposed that a noncitizen would have to qualify under a selection formula that would award value points for certain "human capital attributes." Specifically, points would be awarded for English language proficiency, education level, age (25 to 50 scoring highest), and "adaptability" (indicated, e.g., by prior work or study in the United States or another foreign country or having taken advantage of avenues for personal or professional development). A noncitizen would have to cumulate a specified number of points to be eligible for admission.

The 2006 reform bill passed by the Senate stayed largely with the current system for employment-based immigration, but with some enhancement in the numbers. As mentioned in the Council on Foreign Relations Task Force report above, however, the 2007 compromise Senate bill departed suddenly and unexpectedly from that approach. It would have abolished the first three employment-based preferences (including all admission categories based on labor certification), implementing instead an elaborate point system that shared some features with the earlier point system proposal by Papademetriou and Yale–Loehr. Unlike that proposal, the Senate version did not require a job offer from a U.S. employer, but did give a few extra points for workers who had such an offer. Would a point system be superior to the current arrangements? In the following paper, the authors discuss the advantages and disadvantages of a point system for admissions and also describe other variations on a selection system. The paper reflects some evolution in the views of Papademetriou from the 1996 paper quoted above.

DEMETRIOS G. PAPADEMETRIOU AND MADELEINE SUMPTION, RETHINKING POINTS SYSTEMS AND EMPLOYER–SELECTED IMMIGRATION

Migration Policy Institute, 2011, pp. 1, 3–7.

Two competing models for selecting economic-stream immigrants are now widely used in advanced industrialized economies: points-based and employer-led selection. Points-based systems admit immigrants who have a sufficient number of qualifications and experiences from a list that typically includes language skills, work experience, education, and age. Points systems appeal to policymakers because they are transparent, flexible, and can be adjusted to meet evolving economic needs or respond to evidence on immigrants' integration outcomes. But since employers are not involved in selection, points systems often admit immigrants who are unable to find work at their skill level once they arrive. This undermines both integration and the long-term economic benefits of immigration.

Employer-driven systems, by contrast, allow employers to select the workers they need, subject to government regulations. Being selected by an employer is evidence that immigrants' skills are needed and thus guarantees that they will have a job when they arrive. However, it also raises concerns that employers may manipulate the system in order to access cheaper labor or that workers will be too dependent on their employers (and hence vulnerable to exploitation).

Hybrid selection systems combine the best ideas from both points-based and employer-driven models. Immigrant-receiving countries that once selected foreign workers using purely points-based or purely employer-led systems have increasingly opted to borrow from the competing model, developing hybrid systems that bring some of the advantages of both. The resulting selection systems have much of the flexibility of points systems, typically providing several routes to permanent residence and giving foreign workers more freedom to move between employers. Crucially, however, they prioritize employer demand, in the form of a job offer or a good track record of employment in the host country. As a result, some of the most successful immigrant-selection models rely on temporary-to-permanent visa pathways that admit workers initially on temporary work permits but provide a clear and predictable path to permanent residence to those with good integration prospects.

* * *

POINTS SYSTEMS

* * * [Although policymakers are often attracted to points systems, evidence] of problems with points-based selection formulae * * * abounds. Perhaps the greatest single flaw of the traditional points-based model is that immigrants arrive without a job offer and there is no guarantee that they will find work easily at their skill level. Points systems can only assess quantifiable skills and credentials, and have difficulty distinguishing between qualifications of different quality or utility. They are also ill equipped to reward "soft" attributes that employers care about, such as interpersonal skills or informal on-the-job training. Research from Canada and Australia points to substantial un- and underemployment among points-selected foreign workers—giving credence to the concern that points systems often lead to "brain waste" and do not identify workers with skills that local employers value. Integration suffers accordingly.

* * *

EMPLOYER-LED SYSTEMS

The demand-driven, employer-led system resolves many of these problems. As a direct policy vehicle for economic growth and firms' competitiveness, this selection system has no equal, responding directly to the needs of firms and allowing employers to find workers who meet their specific needs from within the enormous global talent pool.

Second, employer selection ensures a level of immigrant integration that points systems have struggled to achieve. * * * And even though employers select workers, governments can still require minimum levels of education, language proficiency, or earnings to ensure that workers qualify as highly skilled. Evidence from countries that admit economic-stream immigrants both with and without job offers is compelling: employer-selected immigrants fare better.

Concerns about employer-led immigration focus primarily on the risk that employers will manipulate the system to access cheaper labor. Unlike points systems, employer-driven systems tend to tie workers to specific jobs, making it difficult for them to stand up to exploitative employers or respond to changing labor demand by moving jobs. Crucially, this may allow employers to pay them below-market wages. Meanwhile, there is a risk that open access to a foreign labor pool will allow employers to pay lower wages or avoid responsibility for training domestic workers—or indeed the foreign workers that they hire—thus doing little to reduce the scarcity of skills that economic-stream immigration is in part designed to address. Finally, there is a gnawing fear that temporary employer-driven immigration may spill over into illegal immigration if workers lose their jobs.

Moreover, many of the regulations that governments create to shape employers' use of the system are viewed with suspicion by some advocates, who argue that they fail to prevent employers from discriminating against local workers or from paying immigrants lower wages. Ultimately, one of the most effective safeguards against these problems is visa "portability": that is, worker's ability to move between employers, perhaps after a probationary period. Freedom of movement between employers is one of the benefits of the points system and has also been incorporated into hybrid immigration systems, described next.

HYBRID SELECTION SYSTEMS: ALTERNATIVES THAT
COMBINE THE BEST OF BOTH SYSTEMS

* * * [P]olicymakers in several immigrant-receiving nations have experimented with ways of combining the best ideas from both. Led by Australia, countries dependent on points systems have come to appreciate and accommodate the unparalleled advantages that employer selection brings in terms of both immigrant integration and firms' competitiveness. Meanwhile, some governments with demand-driven systems have also seen the value of giving workers more independence from their employers and of raising the "quality" of employer-selected immigrants using a flexible set of criteria such as a points test.

* * *

* * * [One] way that points systems can accommodate employer demand is by *awarding points for job offers*. This approach, used in both Canada and New Zealand, helps to prioritize the admission of immigrants who have already found employment, without making a job offer compulsory. Canada also provides priority processing for applicants who have a job offer[.] * * *

[Second,] hybrid systems can be created by *developing temporary-to-permanent visa pathways*. Increasing proportions of skilled workers in both points and demand-driven systems now enter on temporary visas that can be converted into permanent ones if their holders meet certain conditions. In many cases, these workers are initially employer selected. In New Zealand, for example, employer-driven visas are explicitly designed as an initial entry route for workers who hope to qualify for permanent residence under the points system. In the United Kingdom, almost all economic-stream immigrants must now have an employer sponsor to enter the country, but those who pass a points test from within the country can apply to become independent of their sponsor. In Sweden, work-based immigration is employer selected but work authorization becomes fully portable after two years, and the temporary visa can be converted into permanent residence after four years. * * *

Several countries now emphasize *foreign students* as a pool from which temporary foreign workers are recruited. This policy has some obvious advantages. Foreign students' graduation, particularly in fields of study that the host economy values, is a direct measure of both language competence and qualifications. Many students are also preselected by universities that have high standards.[14] Graduating students can be required to have an employer sponsor to stay on, making the credential-recognition and employability issue moot. And the fact that the initial period of work authorization is temporary creates a transitional period

---

14. Of course, not all educational institutions have high standards, as policymakers in Australia and the United Kingdom recently discovered. In both countries, a lack of quality control over sponsoring colleges led to the growth of "diploma mills" that attracted students whose real interest was in the labor market. This phenomenon has prompted policymakers to rethink the student-to-worker pathway and to make it more selective.

during which a real vetting of the worker can assuage most concerns about his or her employability and ability to integrate.

Finally, systems that rely on employers to select most or even all immigrants can *require that their workers pass a points test*. This approach allows governments to raise the skill profile of economic-stream immigrants by requiring them to meet a flexible set of criteria that may include language proficiency, education level, and prospective earnings.

c. Provisional Visas

Papademetriou and Sumption speak of the possibility of greater use of "temporary-to-permanent" visas, an idea that has gained increasing attention. A high-level task force gathered by the Migration Policy Institute in 2005, chaired by former Rep. Lee Hamilton (D–Indiana) and former Senator Spencer Abraham (R–Michigan), devoted considerable attention to this idea (using the terminology of "provisional visas") in its 2006 report on ways to fix the overall immigration system. That report, excerpted immediately below, also championed a new mechanism that would provide for greater flexibility in adjusting immigration categories and levels, through the work of a permanent government commission on immigration. Many other reform proposals have embraced variations of the commission idea.

DORIS MEISSNER, DEBORAH W. MYERS, DEMETRIOS PAPADEMETRIOU & MICHAEL FIX, IMMIGRATION AND AMERICA'S FUTURE: A NEW CHAPTER

Report of the Independent Task Force on Immigration and America's Future,
Migration Policy Institute, Sept. 2006, pp. 21–23, 33, 35–39, 41–42.

TEMPORARY IMMIGRATION

Along with illegal immigration, nonimmigrant (temporary) immigration programs constitute the primary ways immigration has adapted to meet new conditions and labor market demands.

Temporary immigration programs have increasingly been used as a step to permanent immigration. Traditionally, the purpose of temporary immigration visas has been to meet seasonal or transitory needs and shortages. Increasingly, however, temporary workers and visa categories are meeting standing, ongoing labor market needs and employer preferences. In response, there has been explosive growth in the categories and numbers of temporary immigration programs, creating a patchwork system of visas tailored to specific types of workers or entrants. As a result, illegal immigration is meeting the nation's low-skill demands, and temporary visa programs in the legal immigration system are meeting the demands for mostly high-skilled immigration.

* * *

Of the 980,000 persons granted lawful permanent resident status on average each year between FY 2001 and 2005, 61 percent were already in the country and adjusting their status. In the case of employment-based immigrants, the rate was 80 percent. Thus, permanent immigration to the United States is largely a product of the adjustment of status of persons who have already established strong ties to jobs and labor markets in the country while in various temporary statuses or here illegally.

Employers have learned to rely on the temporary system to gain access to workers because it is faster and less cumbersome than the permanent immigration system. * * *

THE LEGAL IMMIGRATION SELECTION SYSTEM

The immigration selection system rarely realizes its core goals of meeting family reunification and labor market demands. Immigration critics often call for intending immigrants to "play by the rules." However, the rules do not work effectively.

Immigrants who try to immigrate legally (and family members and employers who sponsor them) quickly are constrained by immigration category caps, as well as caps that limit each country to no more than 7 percent (approximately 25,600) of the total number of annual worldwide visas. * * * [The caps have] led to unreasonable delays for employers and family unification applicants * * *.

Delays in employment-based immigration mean that the system often fails to meet labor market needs. Inflexible statutory ceilings, limits in allocation of numbers to high-demand countries, and overly complex procedures all contribute to employers not getting workers when they need them. * * *

* * *

A core principle of the current system, which has been in place since 1952, has been separating temporary (non-immigrant) and permanent (immigrant) visas, as temporary visas were not intended to lead to permanent immigration. Yet through incremental changes in law and practice, many temporary visas are now temporary in name only. * * * In addition, those with temporary visas who are de facto immigrants are not counted in official estimates of permanent annual immigration until the year of their formal adjustment to permanent status.

* * *

The immigration system should provide legal channels for effectively regulating employment-based immigration—regardless of skill levels—so that immigration can function as a strategic national resource. Sufficient opportunities for legal immigration to meet labor market needs will reduce pressures for illegal immigration, providing the opportunity for border enforcement and other controls to become more effective.

A PROPOSAL FOR A NEW SYSTEM

The Task Force proposal sets immigration levels of approximately 1.5 million annually as a starting point. That number would be adjusted every two years on the basis of the analysis and recommendations of a new agency, The Standing Commission on Immigration and Labor Markets, described below. The starting point of 1.5 million is about 300,000 less than the true annual levels of immigration, 1.8 million, that the United States is experiencing. * * *

In addition, the proposal rationalizes an outdated selection system, provides legal channels of entry for immigration that is occurring illegally in response to legitimate labor market demands, and envisions regular numerical adjustments in response to changing economic and demographic conditions. Because family-based immigrants work and employment-based immigrants bring their families, family and employment-based immigration overlap. Nonetheless, the crisis in immigration policy turns on labor market issues. Thus, the policy focus of the proposal is primarily on employment-based immigration.

* * *

The proposal has the following key features:

- It creates a new immigration stream called provisional visas. Provisional visas allow for lengthier stays than temporary visas and for the opportunity of bridging to permanent immigration after several years, based on meeting employment and other criteria.

- It provides opportunities for employment-based immigration of all skill types in the permanent stream.

- It provides a new type of visa—strategic growth visas—in the permanent stream to help the United States compete more effectively for international talent.

- It organizes employment-based immigration around streamlined employer recruitment procedures as the best way to allocate immigrant labor efficiently, consistent with appropriate rights and protections of all workers.

- It provides for biennial adjustments of immigration levels, based on ongoing analysis of the impact of immigration on labor markets and the economy.

Such a system would respond to a broad set of current and future labor market needs by providing for legal, regulated flows in a flexible, transparent fashion. It would eliminate the rationale for large, guest-worker programs from an earlier era that tie workers to a single employer with no opportunity to qualify for permanent immigration.

* * *

PROVISIONAL IMMIGRATION

The new provisional visa bridges the false divide that now exists between certain forms of temporary and permanent immigration, creating an integrated system that organizes immigration around the ways in which immigration and labor markets work in practice.

Provisional visas would allow employers to recruit workers for permanent jobs who may eventually be interested in permanent immigration and applying for a "green" card. Such visas provide both employers and workers the flexibility to exercise choices before committing to permanent immigration. The visas would act as a tool to attract the best and brightest at all skill levels, many of whom are shopping for the best offer in a competitive international marketplace.

Provisional visas would also be suitable for large numbers of workers who are not in temporary or seasonal jobs across the occupational spectrum. Such a program would meet employer needs for foreign-born workers in jobs that are more permanent than envisioned by the temporary immigration stream. In combination with temporary visas, the new provisional visa category ensures that sufficient opportunities would exist to meet the current and longer term needs of the economy in ways well-tailored to individuals and the labor market.

* * * This category provides for applicants of all skill levels who have employer sponsors. Provisional visa holders would be admitted for three-year periods, renewable once. Provisional visa holders would work in permanent or year-round jobs and transition into permanent residence after three years if they qualify and so choose. Provisional visas would be issued to workers with extraordinary ability, workers in jobs that require a BA or more, and workers in low- and semi-skilled jobs who currently have no real chance for legal immigration. Provisional visa holders would be able to bring dependent family members with them.

Employers of most provisional workers would be required to participate in an attestation process or become pre-certified as a licensed employer of foreign-born workers. * * * Those with provisional visas would be eligible to change employers after an initial period and would have the same labor protections as similarly employed US workers.

The number of provisional visas would initially be set to approximate current flows of such workers who enter both legally and illegally. The numbers would then be adjusted according to recommendations made by The Standing Commission.

In addition to an employment offer, qualifications for adjusting to permanent status would include evidence of continued employment in the occupation or field for which the applicant's educational or professional credentials served as the basis for the provisional visa, ability to speak English, and renewed clearance of a security and background check.

* * *

FLEXIBILITY IN THE IMMIGRATION SYSTEM: THE STANDING COMMISSION ON IMMIGRATION AND LABOR MARKETS

To harness the benefits of immigration, policy must be responsive to changing economic, political, and social conditions instead of residing within a rigid framework that dates back to the 1950s.

* * *

Establishing appropriate immigration levels is a powerful policy tool that contains some of the characteristics of monetary policy. Yet in contrast to setting interest rates, which are formally reviewed eight times a year on the basis of calculations by over 400 professional economists working for the Federal Reserve Board, immigration limits are locked into statutes that have been revisited, on average, less than once per decade. When immigration levels are changed, they are the product of political compromises made during contentious legislative debates.

Managing immigration in the national interest requires a parallel institutional capacity to monitor and analyze information as the basis for making changes. This capacity does not exist. The Task Force proposes creating a new independent federal agency called The Standing Commission on Immigration and Labor Markets. The Standing Commission would be charged with making recommendations to the president and the Congress for adjustments to levels and categories of immigration. Its mandate would be to propose changes that support economic growth while maintaining low unemployment and preventing wage-depression. Baseline immigration levels would be set in the immigration statutes, with the requirement that The Standing Commission conduct ongoing analysis of labor market conditions and trends and propose adjustments to these levels.

* * *

The Standing Commission would be required to submit a report and recommendations every odd-numbered (non-election) year. After a specified period for Congressional consultation, unless Congress enacted legislation to maintain the statutory baseline levels, the president would issue a formal Determination of New Levels and other adjustments in immigration categories for the coming two years. A somewhat similar procedure has been successfully used in setting annual refugee admissions levels and has achieved timely changes with full involvement of both the executive and legislative branches. In addition to recommendations for adjustments in immigration levels, The Standing Commission would prepare an annual report for the president, Congress, and the public. It would also make its research reports and data publicly available.

NOTES AND QUESTIONS ON PROVISIONAL VISAS

1. Which of the following occupational fields would qualify for provisional visas under the MPI Task Force proposal? Which should—that is, which are the most logical to bring within a provisional visa system? Why? What criteria guide your judgment? Consider these occupations: nannies, gardeners, high-tech engineers, law professors, high school teachers, managers or supervisors being transferred within a global company, chefs, waiters, construction workers.

2. The Task Force states that provisional visas "provide both employers and workers the flexibility to exercise choices before committing to permanent

immigration.'' This sounds like a balanced benefit with comparable advantages for both sides. But are provisional visas really superior from the standpoint of the worker? With a green card, wouldn't she have the same flexibility to change her mind about the permanency of the work after a few months or even years on the job? After all, no lawful permanent resident is required to remain in the United States, and historically a significant percentage of LPRs do return to their home countries rather than live their entire lives in the United States. Moreover, a worker with a green card rather than a provisional visa would almost always have a wider range of choices to exercise. How could the proposal be revised to minimize the classic difficulty with all temporary visas—that the employee remains vulnerable to unfair practices by managers or supervisors because the employer holds the key to any future permanent status?

3. The Task Force suggests that the number of provisional visas should initially be set to approximate the flows of comparable workers who enter both legally and illegally. Is this realistic? Even with the seemingly strong support for guest worker programs in Congress in 2006 and 2007, the totals of such visas to be permitted were cut substantially before final consideration of the legislation, to 200,000 annual admissions—far below the estimated 500–800,000 flow of unauthorized workers at that time. Further, recall that the CFR report above opined that ''[c]omprehensive immigration reform would substantially lower the flow of illegal migrants by providing alternative legal channels for migrants to live and work in the United States.'' How high would admissions have to be in order to provide a sufficient alternative to dissuade future migrants from coming without authorization? *See generally* Martin, *Eight Myths About Immigration Enforcement*, 10 N.Y.U.J. Legis. & Pub. Pol'y 525, 532–34 (2006–07) (expressing skepticism about any such channeling effect and suggesting that substantial enforcement efforts will still be needed after comprehensive reform).

The MPI report was written during flush economic times with low unemployment. By 2011, following the major economic slowdown and deployment of additional enforcement resources, the flow of undocumented migration appears to be considerably lower and the overall population of the unauthorized has plateaued and may be declining. What then should be the benchmark for setting the level of provisional visas? Does this slowdown suggest the need for other revisions to any such plan?

Ex Ante vs. Ex Post Immigration Screening

Legal scholars Adam Cox and Eric Posner offer a more theoretical approach to admission issues, but reach a conclusion that provides support for the MPI Task Force's idea of expanding the use of provisional visas—an ex post system that allows the ultimate governmental decision on permanent immigration to be made after gaining more knowledge of the immigrant. Cox & Posner, *The Second–Order Structure of Immigration Law*, 59 Stan. L.Rev. 809 (2007). Analogizing a nation's immigration decisions to the process whereby employers choose employees, they write:

     * * * [I]mmigration screening presents an information problem[.] The main screening advantage of the ex post system is that it uses

more information (both about the immigrants and about the country's current needs) than the ex ante system does, which minimizes errors. The main advantage of the ex ante system is that it reduces the risk faced by potential immigrants that they will be deported, so that risk-averse noncitizens are more likely to enter and invest in the country than they are under the ex post system. * * *

Our framework clarifies numerous positive and normative questions about immigration law. * * * [P]ort-of-entry exclusion systems (which are predominantly ex ante) result in poorer screening than post-entry deportation systems (which are predominantly ex post), but also encourage risk-averse immigrants to make country-specific investments of value to the host country, and may be cheaper to enforce. The choice between the two systems turns in part on trade-offs among these variables. We also argue that although the U.S. de jure system is highly (although not entirely) ex ante, the U.S. de facto system is predominantly ex post—this is the "illegal immigration system" that results from deliberate underenforcement of immigration law plus periodic amnesties.

59 Stan. L.Rev. at 811–14.

In a commentary on the Cox & Posner article, Hiroshi Motomura finds much that is valuable in the basic analytical approach, but adds words of caution:

The real effects of ex post screening are part of the complex process of immigrant integration. All else being equal, immigrants who face ex post screening will feel less attached to and accepted by the host country, and immigrants will feel more attached and accepted where ex ante screening is the norm. * * * The probationary message that would be inherent in a decision by the United States to rely heavily on ex post screening is easily read as an enduring message of exclusion, especially in light of the long history of racial and ethnic exclusion in U.S. immigration law.

* * * The exclusionary message inherent in ex post screening applies more to lawful nonimmigrants. And most importantly, the exclusionary message applies even more directly and profoundly to permanent residents, for whom naturalization is the next point of ex post screening. Putting them on probation, even if the chances of failure are remote, makes them less likely to integrate and perhaps even less likely to naturalize. In short, immigrant integration depends on a wider variety of factors than [the Cox and Posner article] discusses. It is important not to read its reasoning to justify ex post screening in a broad range of settings. As potentially applied to lawfully present nonimmigrants through adjustment of status and to lawful permanent residents through naturalization, ex post screening deserves special caution.

* * * [The article, however,] is quite correct in observing that the "illegal immigration system ... can be seen as a de facto ex post

screening system operated under the guise of an ex ante system." * * * In this zone of underenforced law, government officials make many discretionary immigration law decisions that add up to ex post screening.

* * *

For [lawful migrants, especially permanent residents], the question with the most consequences is whether they progress toward citizenship, so for them it is important to adopt a citizenship frame.

Modern European experience provides a cautionary tale about adopting an immigration rather than a citizenship frame when dealing with noncitizens who come lawfully and whose natural concern is the transition to permanent residence and in turn to citizenship. The industrialized European countries recruited foreign workers in the 1960s and 1970s as if they were employers picking employees. The incomplete integration of these immigrant communities into their adopted countries has been a social problem of very troubling dimensions. As Swiss writer Max Frisch put it: "We asked for workers, but people came." In fortunate contrast, the principal legislative proposals in the United States for the legalization of undocumented immigrants include a "path to citizenship." This reflects an important understanding of the dangers of choosing immigrants without making citizens. Though it makes sense initially to approach undocumented immigration as a matter of choosing immigrants, it would be a mistake to adopt it as an overall frame of reference for immigration law.

Motomura, *Choosing Immigrants, Making Citizens*, 59 Stan. L. Rev. 857, 864–70 (2007).

3. LEGALIZATION

The last major round of what might be described as comprehensive immigration reform, in the Immigration Reform and Control Act of 1986, offered legalization to a significant portion of the undocumented population then living in the United States. Approximately 2.7 million persons were legalized, and later, after obtaining full LPR status or even citizenship, a great many of the legalized noncitizens petitioned for family members to join them. In bringing vulnerable individuals out of the shadows and recognizing the connections they had built with their communities during their years in the United States, IRCA's legalization program was a success.

But because the enforcement portions of IRCA proved ineffective, many view IRCA as a failure and voice skepticism of another round of legalization. It would only reward lawbreaking, they maintain, and would entice a new generation of unlawful migrants to come in the hopes of yet another legalization in the future. Proponents of legalization, as reflected in the Council on Foreign Relations Task Force report that opened this section, respond that the current enforcement capacity of the government is now much stronger, and that added enforcement innovations and resources in a comprehensive bill can help strengthen future enforcement. Some also argue that the new enforcement measures themselves are likely to fail if they have to be applied not only to new arrivals but also to the 10 to 11 million persons already long-resident here. In addition to sheer cost of such measures, sympathetic cases of that type lead both to bad publicity that helps to discredit resolute enforcement and to case law that strains to find interpretive loopholes, potentially weakening the new enforcement push in a different fashion.

MARSHALL FITZ, GEBE MARTINEZ, & MADURA WIJE-WARDENA, THE COSTS OF MASS DEPORTATION: IMPRACTICAL, EXPENSIVE, AND INEFFECTIVE

Center for American Progress (March 2010), pp. 1–3.

* * * [The] legislative battle for immigration reform now looms again on the horizon. There are three options for restoring order to our immigration system:

- Live with the dysfunctional status quo, pouring billions of dollars into immigration enforcement programs at the worksite, in communities, and on the border without reducing the numbers of undocumented immigrants in the country

- Double down on this failed enforcement strategy in an attempt to apprehend and remove all current undocumented immigrants

- Combine a strict enforcement strategy with a program that would require undocumented workers to register, pass background checks, pay their full share of taxes, and earn the privilege of citizenship while creating legal channels for future migration flows

The first alternative would leave in place policies that have allowed 5 percent of our nation's workforce—approximately 8.3 million workers in March 2008—to remain undocumented in our country. This is clearly an unsustainable position in a democratic society—permitting a class of workers to operate in a shadow economy subject to exploitation and undermining all workers' rights and opportunities.

The second option, mass deportation of undocumented immigrants, is essentially the enforcement-only status quo on steroids. As this paper demonstrates, this option would be prohibitively expensive and trigger profound collateral consequences. Our analysis is comprised of a detailed review of all federal spending to prevent unauthorized immigration and deport undocumented immigrants in FY 2008, the last fiscal year (ending in October 2008) for which there is complete data. It shows that the total cost of mass deportation and continuing border interdiction and interior enforcement efforts would be $285 billion (in 2008 dollars) over five years.

Specifically, this report calculates a price tag of $200 billion to enforce a federal dragnet that would snare the estimated 10.8 million undocumented immigrants in the United States over five years [$158 billion for apprehension, $29 billion for detention, $7 billion for legal processing, and $6 billion for transportation]. That amount, however, does not include the annual recurring border and interior enforcement spending that will necessarily have to occur. It would cost taxpayers at least another $17 billion annually (in 2008 dollars) to maintain the status quo at the border and in the interior, or a total of nearly $85 billion over five years. That means the total five-year immigration enforcement cost under a mass deportation strategy would be approximately $285 billion.

* * * Spending $285 billion would require $922 in new taxes for every man, woman, and child in this country.

* * *

That leaves the third course, comprehensive immigration reform, as the only rational alternative. The solution to our broken immigration system must combine tough border and workplace enforcement with practical reforms that promote economic growth, protect all workers, and reunite immediate family members. Among other things, that means we must establish a realistic program to require undocumented immigrants to register with the government while creating legal immigration channels that are flexible, serve the national interest, and curtail future illegal immigration.

Some proponents of the second option—a deportation-only strategy—contend that the Great Recession and heightened unemployment justify mass deportation. * * * The patently erroneous analysis behind this contention—that unemployed Americans are a perfect substitute for undocumented workers in the workforce—ignores the devastating impact such an approach would have on economic growth.

In fact, a recent study by the Center for American Progress and the Immigration Policy Center demonstrates how legalization of undocumented immigrants and more flexible immigration channels would significantly expand the economy—by a cumulative $1.5 trillion in gross domestic product over 10 years—through increased consumer spending, higher tax receipts, and other related factors. A deportation approach, by contrast, would have the cumulative effect of draining $2.5 trillion over 10 years from the U.S. economy. That is a $4 trillion swing in GDP depending on which policy approach we adopt.

Once policymakers in Congress and their constituents across the country weigh the unrealistic five-year immigration enforcement costs of pursuing a deportation-only strategy—$285 billion—against the progressive alternative they will recognize once and for all that mass deportation is fiscally untenable. * * *

Mark Krikorian has provided one of the most often-invoked critiques of arguments like those that appear in the preceding reading.

MARK KRIKORIAN, DOWNSIZING ILLEGAL IMMIGRATION: A STRATEGY OF ATTRITION THROUGH ENFORCEMENT

Center for Immigration Studies Backgrounder (May 2005),
<http://www.cis.org/articles/2005/back605.html>.

Senators John McCain and Edward Kennedy recently unveiled a major bipartisan immigration proposal backed by a coalition of business, labor, and ethnic organizations. Unfortunately, this plan, like other suggested immigration plans (including President Bush's) is based on a false premise: Since the federal government can't quickly deport the 10–12 million illegal aliens, the only alternative is legalization—*i.e., amnesty.*

But there is a third way that rejects this false choice, and it is the only approach that can actually work: Shrink the illegal population through consistent, across-the-board enforcement of the immigration law. By deterring the settlement of new illegals, by increasing deportations to the extent possible, and, most importantly, by increasing the number of illegals already here who give up and deport themselves, the United States can bring about an annual decrease in the illegal-alien population, rather than allowing it to continually increase. The point, in other words, is not merely to curtail illegal immigration, but rather to bring about a steady reduction in the total number of illegal immigrants who are living in the United States. The result would be a shrinking of the illegal population to a manageable nuisance, rather than today's looming crisis.

This is analogous to the approach a corporation might take to downsizing a bloated workforce: a hiring freeze, some layoffs, plus new incentives to encourage excess workers to leave on their own.

* * *

A Realistic Goal

This strategy of attrition is not a pipe dream, or the idle imaginings of a policy wonk. The central insight is that there is already significant churn in the illegal population, which can be used to speed the decline in overall numbers. According to a 2003 report from the Immigration and Naturalization Service, thousands of people are subtracted from the illegal population each year. From 1995 to 1999, an average of 165,000 a year went back home on their own after residing here for at least a year; the same number got some kind of legal status, about 50,000 were deported, and 25,000 died, for a total of more than 400,000 people each year subtracted from the resident illegal population. The problem is that the average annual inflow of new illegal aliens over that same period was nearly 800,000, swamping the outflow and creating an average annual increase of close to 400,000.

A strategy of attrition would seek to reverse this relationship, so that the outflow from the illegal population is much larger than the number of new illegal settlers from abroad. This would be a measured approach to the problem, one that doesn't aspire to an immediate, magical solution to a long-brewing crisis, but also does not simply declare surrender, as the Bush and McCain/Kennedy amnesty proposals do.

* * *

NOT INEVITABLE

* * *

Granted, interrupting such networks is harder than creating them, but it is not impossible—after all, the trans-Atlantic immigration networks from the turn of the last century were successfully interrupted, and atrophied completely. And, to move beyond theory, the few times we actually tried to enforce the immigration law, it worked—until we gave up for political reasons.

During the first several years after the passage of the IRCA, illegal crossings from Mexico fell precipitously, as prospective illegals waited to see if we were serious. Apprehensions of aliens by the Border Patrol—an imperfect measure but the only one available—fell from more than 1.7 million in FY 1986 to under a million in 1989. But then the flow began to increase again as the deterrent effect of the hiring ban dissipated, when word got back that we were not serious about enforcement and that the system could be easily evaded through the use of inexpensive phony documents.

That showed that reducing new illegal immigration is possible; but what about increasing the number of illegals already here who give up and leave? That, too, has already been demonstrated. After the 9/11 attacks, immigration authorities undertook a "Special Registration" program for visitors from Islamic countries. The affected nation with the largest illegal-alien population was Pakistan, with an estimated 26,000 illegals here in 2000. Once it became clear that the government was getting more serious about enforcing the immigration law—at least with regard to Middle Easterners—Pakistani illegals started leaving on their own in large numbers. The Pakistani embassy estimated that more than 15,000 of its illegal aliens left the United States, and the Washington Post reported the "disquieting" fact that in Brooklyn's Little Pakistan the mosque was one-third empty, business was down, there were fewer want ads in the local Urdu-language paper, and "For Rent" signs sprouted everywhere.

* * *

ENFORCEMENT PLUS VERIFICATION

What would a policy of attrition look like? It would combine an increase in conventional enforcement—arrests, prosecutions, deportations, asset seizures, etc.—with expanded use of verification of legal status at a variety of important points, to make it as difficult and unpleasant as possible to live here illegally.

* * *

An important point about using verification of legal status as a way to downsize the illegal population is that its effects would be felt gradually, rather than all at once. A new, functional verification system for employment, for instance, would be applied mainly to new hires (though employers should have the option of checking existing employees as well). The same is true for getting a driver's license or a mortgage—these are not things people do every day, so the effects of verifying legal status would unfold over a period of time.

Attrition requires not only implementing policies to force illegals to deport themselves, but also avoiding policies that would trigger more illegal immigration. This has two main policy implications: First, streamline the legal immigration system to make it less likely to promote illegal immigration, by eliminating the [diversity] visa lottery and the preference category for adult siblings of U.S. citizens. And second, under no circumstances undertake any new guestworker programs, the inevitable result of which would be to stimulate even more illegal immigration.

And finally, legalization (i.e., amnesty) isn't even a legitimate topic for discussion until *after* the broken immigration system is fixed. * * *

An effective strategy of immigration law enforcement requires no booby traps, no tanks, no tattoos on arms—none of the cartoonish images invoked in the objections raised routinely by supporters of loose borders. The consistent application of ordinary law-enforcement tools is all we need. "Consistent," though, is the key word. Enforcement personnel—whether they are Border Patrol agents, airport inspectors, or plainclothes investigators—need to know that their work is valued, that their superiors actually want them to do the jobs they've been assigned, and that they will be backed up when the inevitable complaints roll in.

* * *

Krikorian relies in part on expanded use of electronic verification of work authorization as part of his attrition through enforcement strategy. David Martin also views deployment of an ambitious mandatory employment verification system as a key measure in creating a successful immigration enforcement and management system, but reaches very different conclusions from Krikorian. He argues that a broad legalization program is needed precisely in order to facilitate implementation of nationwide E–Verify and other long-term enforcement improvements:

> If such an employment verification system can be built and sustained, we can get away from the current wrong-headed paradigm of immigration enforcement: catching people and incarcerating them

until they are removed one-by-one. No law enforcement system is healthy if assuring compliance must rely primarily on direct enforcement through the personal attention of the police. Healthy systems are based on widespread voluntary compliance, leaving police to target misbehavior around the margins.

In immigration enforcement, we are miles away from such a system, but the crucial leverage for getting there lies in the workplace. If, after full implementation of a verification system, new unauthorized arrivals cannot readily find work in the American workplace, far fewer will attempt the journey. That audience—people who have not yet migrated—must remain the crucial focus of the endeavor. Deterring such new migration through strong workplace screening is an achievable goal. The transition to an effective workplace screening system will go far more smoothly, and win wider support from the employers who must implement it, if we do not at the same time ask employers to sever pre-existing relationships. This means * * * that realism in immigration reform counsels incorporating some mechanism for legalizing most of those currently present, so as to minimize business opposition to new enforcement measures.

Martin, *Eight Myths About Immigration Enforcement*, 10 N.Y.U.J. Legis. & Pub. Pol'y 525, 549–50 (2006–07). For further reflections on legalization, see Motomura, *What is "Comprehensive Immigration Reform"?: Taking the Long View*, 63 Ark.L.Rev. 225 (2010).

The DREAM Act and Wider Perspectives on Legalization

With progress on comprehensive immigration reform stalled, advocates have focused considerable effort on passing the Development, Relief and Education for Alien Minors (DREAM) Act. It would provide legal status and eventual lawful permanent resident status for persons who were brought to the United States as children. Proponents believe in the justice of such a measure, to provide stable status (as well as improved access to higher education) for members of the U.S. community who have little or no acquaintance with life in another country. But they also have thought it would be easier to pass than a wider legalization measure, because it would benefit only those who should not be held responsible for their illegal presence.

A version of the DREAM Act was included in the Comprehensive Immigration Reform Act of 2006 (S. 2611), which passed the Senate in May 2006 but was never voted on in the House. That version covered students who (a) initially entered the United States before the age of 16; (b) were physically present in the United States for five years immediately preceding enactment; and (c) earned a high school diploma or the equivalent in the United States, or had been admitted to an institution of higher education in the United States. These persons would be eligible for cancellation of removal, which would lead first to conditional permanent resident status, then, after six years, to permanent residence upon the fulfillment of certain other conditions. The most important such condition was the earning of a college degree, the completion of at least two years of college, or two years of service in the U.S. armed forces.

The DREAM Act was reintroduced regularly in later Congresses. The House finally passed a version during the lame-duck congressional session in December 2010. To gain passage, sponsors had to tighten up the provisions considerably, especially in light of concerns about the federal budgetary impact, given new estimates of the population eligible for DREAM Act-based legalization, which by then had climbed to 2.1 million persons. Covered individuals would receive only conditional *nonimmigrant* status for five years, subject to further extensions in five-year increments, provided they had by then completed the requisite two years of college study or military service. Only after 10 years could they seek LPR status. High fees were also imposed (in addition to processing costs): $525 for the initial application, and an additional $2,000 at the time of each extension. *See* Bruno, Congressional Research Service, Unauthorized Alien Students: Issues and "DREAM Act" Legislation (Dec. 14, 2010). Even with these stringent limits and exactions, the bill failed on an unsuccessful procedural vote in the Senate. *See* 87 Interp. Rel. 2334, 2419 (2010).

In reflecting on the DREAM Act and related measures, Hiroshi Motomura summarizes various perspectives that have been brought to bear in making judgments about legalization. (He draws on the Supreme Court's decision in *Plyler v. Doe,* reprinted in Section 9C *supra.*) Consider what conclusions each such perspective suggests about the appropriate criteria and scope of legalization (if it is justified at all).

Opponents of the DREAM Act and other legalization programs often voice their objections in "rule of law" terms. They characterize any program that confers lawful status on unauthorized migrants as unacceptable amnesty that rewards lawbreakers by letting them "jump the line" over immigrants who "play by the rules" in coming to America. From this vantage point emphasizing illegality in the present, the predicament of students without lawful immigration status becomes a straightforward matter of illegal aliens whose unlawful presence compels their removal. This emphasis on illegality today supports uncompromising enforcement as the most effective way of ensuring that no illegitimate claims to future integration can ripen. This view of unlawful presence, combined with skepticism about integrating illegal immigrants, thus emphasizes the present over the past and future, equating any form of legalization with "amnesty."

* * *

* * * [R]hetoric supporting the DREAM Act and other forms of legalization * * * subdivides into two broad categories, depending on how they see the connection between unlawful presence and integration, and on why they favor recognition of historical patterns and future integration over present illegality. Some argue pragmatically that lawmakers should concede to enforcement realities and recognize that unlawfully present children will inevitably remain in the United States. Immigration outside the law may be susceptible to some regulation at the margins, but efforts to control its fundamental contours are doomed to failure. From this pragmatic perspective on the future, it does not matter if we think of the unlawfully present as bad people—as illegal aliens, as lawbreakers, and even as criminals. We still must accept and regulate unlawful migration, for example by putting less stock in enforcement and expanding the number of immigrants who are granted lawful status. And we should take seriously the need to integrate these immigrants.

In contrast, other DREAM Act supporters see the future differently. They make moral arguments that emphasize an asserted obligation to migrants who came to America as an intended consequence of past or present de facto U.S. immigration policy to tolerate and even encourage immigration outside the law to provide U.S. employers with a flexible, disposable labor force. These arguments for the DREAM Act and other forms of legalization emphasize in turn that integration is a compelling priority as a moral imperative.

The *Plyler* majority's combined approach to unlawful presence and integration blended pragmatic and moral arguments. Reasoning pragmatically, it adopted the Attorney General's description of unauthorized migrants as "productive and law-abiding" individuals who had a "permanent attachment" to the United States, and who were "unlikely to be displaced from our territory." But the core of *Plyler* was a moral argument: "Even if the State found it expedient to control the conduct of adults by acting against their children, legislation directing the onus of a parent's misconduct against his children does not comport with fundamental conceptions of justice." Though the majority emphasized the innocence of children brought here by their parents, its understanding of unlawful presence as the consequence of U.S. government policies suggests that its moral argument also applies, if less powerfully, to adults who immigrate outside the law. This approach argues against barriers to the integration of the students who would benefit from the DREAM Act. More generally, it maintains that denying educational opportunity to anyone whose unlawful presence is inherently ambiguous and historically contingent is especially unjust. From this perspective, a shift to airtight enforcement, even if it were possible, would disserve justice.

Motomura, *Immigration Outside the Law,* 108 Colum.L.Rev. 2037, 2087–91 (2008).

CHAPTER TEN

REMOVAL, DETENTION, AND JUDICIAL REVIEW

■ ■ ■

Removal from the United States constitutes the central and most powerful element of immigration enforcement. We consider in this chapter the administrative procedures employed in adjudicating a noncitizen's removability (Section A) and then two closely related topics. Section B examines the substantive provisions and procedures that govern detention of noncitizens, both during removal proceedings and after an order becomes final, while the Department of Homeland Security works to carry out the removal. Section C surveys the complex statutes and case law governing judicial review of removal orders and related actions.

SECTION A. REMOVAL PROCEEDINGS

The primary form of enforcement deployed against noncitizen violators of the immigration laws is physical expulsion from the United States, and the statute ordinarily requires that such a sanction be imposed as a result of a *removal proceeding*. INA § 240(a)(3). The Immigration and Nationality Act adopted this nomenclature in 1996 as an umbrella term to describe the procedure used to remove noncitizens. Until then, the INA had separately authorized *deportation proceedings* for those who had entered the United States, and *exclusion proceedings* for noncitizens whose eligibility was questioned at the border before entry (essentially the class now called by the statute "arriving aliens"). Today charges against either category of noncitizen are to be heard in a unified form of removal proceeding. Some noncitizens in removal proceedings have been admitted but have since become deportable. Others have not been admitted to the United States at all; these noncitizens may have entered surreptitiously, or they may have been stopped at a port of entry. The removal proceeding, conducted by an immigration judge, constitutes the forum for the government to establish the basic charges of either inadmissibility or deportability and for the alien to contest the charges and make any claims for relief from removal.

Each topic in this section has at least two dimensions. One is what the statute and regulations provide. The other is what constitutional due process requires at a minimum—a question typically answered by applying the constitutional framework explored in Chapter Six, Section C. Recall that *Yamataya*, *Knauff*, *Chew*, *Mezei*, and *Plasencia* are key to deciding whether procedural due process applies. And if it does, courts typically apply the three-factor analysis in *Mathews v. Eldridge,* 424 U.S. 319, 335, 96 S.Ct. 893, 47 L.Ed.2d 18 (1976) to decide whether the procedures are sufficient.

We begin with the standard removal procedures in § 240, but we also note that in recent years a significant trend has been the expanded availability and use of special removal procedures for specified categories of cases, largely to minimize reliance on standard removal procedures that Congress has perceived as inefficient or excessive. We review those procedures, which are conducted by immigration officers rather than immigration judges, in Section A6 below.[1]

1. OVERVIEW

If the Department of Homeland Security chooses to initiate removal, it serves a charging document that commands appearance before an immigration judge for a hearing at a designated time and place. For many years, the charging document in deportation was an Order to Show Cause (you will see this term in some of the cases in this chapter), but today all removal proceedings employ a form called a Notice to Appear (NTA). The NTA is Form I–862 (in the Statutory Supplement). INA § 239 sets out the contents of the NTA and the requirements for service.

The NTA may be served in person or by mail. *See Matter of M–D–*, 23 I & N Dec. 540, 542–45 (BIA 2002) (summarizing law on mail service). In order to give the respondent a chance to obtain counsel, a hearing may not be scheduled until at least ten days after service, unless the respondent requests an earlier date in writing. (In practice, a respondent who wants to be represented by counsel can typically obtain one or more continuances to locate and engage counsel.) The NTA includes a warning that anything the respondent says may be used against her (but not that she has the right to remain silent), and a paragraph that addresses representation by counsel. Proceedings formally commence when the government files the NTA with the clerk of the immigration court.

Although many NTAs are served without the respondent being arrested, the power of arrest remains. After arrest, a DHS officer ordinarily examines the case and determines whether the noncitizen can be released on bond or on her own recognizance. Unless she is an arriving alien, she can obtain speedy review (sometimes conducted telephonically) of the release decision before an immigration judge, in what is known as a "bond redetermination" hearing.

---

1. These summary procedures are sometimes referred to as "removal proceedings," but we will ordinarily reserve that term in this chapter for a § 240 proceeding before an immigration judge.

INA § 236(a) governs arrest with a warrant. Under INA § 287(a), immigration officers may arrest without a warrant an alien who the officer believes (1) is entering, or attempting to enter the United States in violation of the immigration laws, or (2) is present in the United States in violation of the immigration laws and is likely to escape before an arrest warrant can be obtained. An alien arrested under § 287 must be brought before another immigration officer for examination. If the examining officer is satisfied that there is a *prima facie* case against the respondent, formal removal proceedings are initiated (unless the officer decides to permit the respondent to depart the country voluntarily). In certain circumstances, this examination may be made by the arresting officer. *See* 8 C.F.R. § 287.3(b). By regulation, the decision to begin removal proceedings must be made within 48 hours of the arrest, "except in the event of an emergency or other extraordinary circumstance in which case a determination will be made within an additional reasonable period of time." 8 C.F.R. § 287.3(d).

The majority of noncitizens who are apprehended are not served with NTAs, particularly those apprehended at or near the land borders who agree to a quick return to Mexico or Canada (after fingerprinting and basic paperwork). Also, those who are served may receive permission for voluntary departure, from the DHS officer or from an immigration judge. INA § 240B. By departing without a removal order, they avoid certain penalties and future disabilities associated with formal removal.

Removal proceedings are typically conducted in two stages: the master calendar hearing and the individual merits hearing. The master calendar hearing is similar to a civil calendar call or a criminal arraignment. It serves to determine whether an individual merits hearing is even required, and in many cases it is not. For example, the respondent may admit the allegations in the NTA and waive any relief, except perhaps voluntary departure, permitting the judge to issue an appropriate order and dispose of the case right at the first master calendar appearance. But if issues of fact are disputed, if inadmissibility or deportability is contested, or if the respondent seeks asylum, cancellation of removal, or other forms of relief besides voluntary departure, the immigration judge will set an individual merits hearing for a future date.

For noncitizens in removal, a very important question is whether they are released or detained while removal proceedings are pending. Besides meaning incarceration for months until a removal hearing, detention may impair a noncitizen's ability to present her case, especially if she is held far from family, friends, or counsel. On the other hand, a significant number of noncitizens ordered removed do not voluntarily present themselves for removal (or leave the country on their own) after losing before the immigration judge or on appeal. The total number of "fugitive aliens"—most of whom are noncitizens with final removal orders who fail to leave the United States—increased steadily from 331,734 in September 2001 to 623,292 in August 2006. *See* Office of the Inspector General, Department of Homeland Security, An Assessment of United States Immigration and Customs Enforcement's Fugitive Operations Teams 12 (2007). By August 2009, ICE's enhanced efforts to locate and arrest fugitives had brought the estimate down to 535,000. Fact Sheet: ICE Fugitive Operations Program (Aug. 19, 2009), <http://www.ice.gov/news/library/fact sheets/fugops.htm>. Hence, detention plays a key role in securing actual enforcement of removal orders.

2. RIGHT TO COUNSEL

Aliens in removal proceedings "shall have the privilege of being represented, at no expense to the Government, by counsel of the alien's choosing who is authorized to practice in such proceedings." INA § 240(b)(4)(A), *see also id.* § 292. Noncitizens who cannot afford an attorney must be informed of free legal services in the area. *Id.* § 239(b)(2); 8 C.F.R. § 240.10(a)(2). Volunteer lawyers may be hard to find, however, especially for noncitizens detained in remote locations. From FY 2007 through FY 2010, 57–60 percent of noncitizens who appeared in immigration court were unrepresented. Before the BIA, representation is more common, but here too 25–30 percent are unrepresented. *See* Executive Office for Immigration Review, Department of Justice, FY 2010 Statistical Year Book, at G1, V1.

Does the Constitution require the government to provide counsel for indigent noncitizens? The Sixth Amendment's guarantee of appointed counsel is unavailable in removal proceedings, because they are not criminal proceedings. Any right to appointed counsel must be found in the Fifth Amendment's Due Process Clause. The next case predates *Eldridge*, but it remains a leading discussion of the constitutional right to counsel in removal proceedings.

AGUILERA–ENRIQUEZ v. INS

United States Court of Appeals, Sixth Circuit, 1975.
516 F.2d 565, cert. denied, 423 U.S. 1050, 96 S.Ct. 776, 46 L.Ed.2d 638 (1976).

CELEBREZZE, CIRCUIT JUDGE.

Petitioner, Jesus Aguilera–Enriquez, seeks reversal of a deportation order on the ground that he was constitutionally entitled to but was not afforded the assistance of counsel during his deportation hearing. * * *

A thirty-nine-year-old native and citizen of Mexico, Petitioner has resided in the United States since December 18, 1967, when he was admitted for permanent residence. He is a married farm worker, living with his wife and three daughters in Saginaw, Michigan.

In December 1971, Petitioner traveled to Mexico for a vacation. An officer of the Saginaw, Michigan Police Department notified federal customs officers at the Mexican border that he had reason to believe that Petitioner would be returning with a quantity of heroin. When Petitioner crossed the border on his return, he was subjected to a search which produced no heroin but did reveal two grams of cocaine.

On April 12, 1972, Petitioner pleaded guilty in the United States District Court for the Western District of Texas, on one count of knowingly possessing a quantity of cocaine, a Schedule II controlled substance, in violation of 21 U.S.C. § 844(a) (1970). Petitioner received a suspended one-year sentence, was placed on probation for five years, and was fined $3,000, to be paid in fifty-dollar monthly installments over the five-year probationary period. Neither Petitioner's appointed counsel nor the District Court informed him that a narcotics conviction would almost certainly lead to his deportation.

On December 7, 1972, the Immigration and Naturalization Service issued an Order to Show Cause and Notice of Hearing, charging that because of his narcotics conviction, Petitioner should be deported under * * * the Immigration and Nationality Act.

On February 6, 1973 Petitioner appeared before the Immigration Judge and requested appointed counsel. The Immigration Judge refused this request. After a hearing Petitioner was ordered deported and was not afforded the option of voluntary departure.

Shortly after the Immigration Judge's ruling, Petitioner engaged as counsel a Michigan legal assistance attorney, who in turn secured the services of a Texas attorney.

On February 14, 1973, Petitioner filed an appeal to the Board of Immigration Appeals, stating that the validity of the Texas conviction was being challenged.

On May 23, 1973, Petitioner's Texas counsel filed a motion to withdraw his guilty plea under Rule 32(d), F.R. Crim. P. The motion asserted that the District Court had not followed Rule 11 in accepting the plea because it had not properly determined that there was a factual basis for the plea and that the plea was made with a full understanding of the probable consequences.

On February 1, 1974, after full briefing and oral argument by counsel for Petitioner and the Government, the Board of Immigration Appeals dismissed Petitioner's appeal. A petition for review was timely filed in this Court.

The issue Petitioner raises here is whether an indigent alien has the right to appointed counsel in a deportation proceeding. He attacks the constitutional validity of INA § 242(b)(2), which gives an alien facing deportation proceedings "the privilege of being represented (at no expense to the Government) by such counsel, authorized to practice in such proceedings, as he shall choose."[a] The Immigration Judge held that this section prevented appointment of counsel at Government expense. Since he could not afford to hire a lawyer, he did not have one before the Immigration Judge.

The courts have been vigilant to ensure that aliens receive the protections Congress has given them before they may be banished from

---

a. This is now in INA § 240(b)(4)(A). *See also* INA § 292.—eds.

our shores. As this Circuit noted in *United States ex rel. Brancato v. Lehmann*, 239 F.2d 663, 666 (6th Cir. 1956),

> Although it is not penal in character, * * * deportation is a drastic measure, at times the equivalent of banishment or exile, for which reason deportation statutes should be given the narrowest of the several possible meanings.

The Supreme Court has held that once an alien has been admitted to lawful residence, "not even Congress may expel him without allowing him a fair opportunity to be heard." *Kwong Hai Chew v. Colding*, 344 U.S. 590, 598, 73 S.Ct. 472, 478, 97 L.Ed. 576 (1953). Thus, if procedures mandated by Congress do not provide an alien with procedural due process, they must yield, and the constitutional guarantee of due process must provide adequate protection during the deportation process. *Yamataya v. Fisher (The Japanese Immigrant Case)*, 189 U.S. 86, 100, 23 S.Ct. 611, 47 L.Ed. 721 (1903).

The test for whether due process requires the appointment of counsel for an indigent alien is whether, in a given case, the assistance of counsel would be necessary to provide "fundamental fairness—the touchstone of due process." *Gagnon v. Scarpelli*, 411 U.S. 778, 790, 93 S.Ct. 1756, 1763, 36 L.Ed.2d 656 (1973).[3]

In Petitioner's case the absence of counsel at his hearing before the Immigration Judge did not deprive his deportation proceeding of fundamental fairness.

Petitioner was held to be deportable under section 241(a)(11) of the Immigration and Nationality Act, which states in relevant part:

> (a) Any alien in the United States ... shall, upon the order of the Attorney General, be deported who—

> (11) ... at any time has been convicted of a violation of ... any law or regulation relating to the illicit possession of or traffic in narcotic drugs....[b]

Before the Immigration Judge, Petitioner raised no defense to the charge that he had been convicted in April 1972 of a violation of 21 U.S.C. § 844(a). Thus, he was clearly within the purview of section 241(a)(11) of the Act, and no defense for which a lawyer would have helped the argument was presented to the Immigration Judge for consideration. After the decision of the Immigration Judge, Petitioner moved to withdraw his guilty plea in the Texas District Court under Rule 32(d), F.R. Crim. P. He then urged before the Board of Immigration Appeals that this motion took him outside the reach of section 241(a)(11), because the likelihood of

---

3. The Supreme Court's holdings in *Gagnon, Morrissey v. Brewer*, 408 U.S. 471, 92 S.Ct. 2593, 33 L.Ed.2d 484 (1972), and *In re Gault*, 387 U.S. 1, 87 S.Ct. 1428, 18 L.Ed.2d 527 (1967), have undermined the position that counsel must be provided to indigents only in criminal proceedings. * * * Where an unrepresented indigent alien would require counsel to present his position adequately to an immigration judge, he must be provided with a lawyer at the Government's expense. Otherwise, "fundamental fairness" would be violated.

b. The current version is in INA § 237(a)(2)(B)(i).—eds.

success on that motion meant that he had not been "convicted" of a narcotics offense. He was effectively represented by counsel before the Board, and his argument was considered upon briefing and oral argument. The lack of counsel before the Immigration Judge did not prevent full administrative consideration of his argument. Counsel could have obtained no different administrative result. "Fundamental fairness," therefore, was not abridged during the administrative proceedings, and the order of deportation is not subject to constitutional attack for a lack of due process.

* * *

The petition for review is denied.

DeMascio, District Judge, dissenting.

A deportation proceeding so jeopardizes a resident alien's basic and fundamental right to personal liberty that I cannot agree due process is guaranteed by a "fundamental fairness" analysis on a case-by-case basis. *Gagnon v. Scarpelli*, 411 U.S. 778, 93 S.Ct. 1756, 36 L.Ed.2d 656 (1973). I think a resident alien has an unqualified right to the appointment of counsel. *In re Gault*, 387 U.S. 1, 87 S.Ct. 1428, 18 L.Ed.2d 527 (1967). When the government, with plenary power to exclude, agrees to allow an alien lawful residence, it is unconscionable for the government to unilaterally terminate that agreement without affording an indigent resident alien assistance of appointed counsel. Expulsion is such lasting punishment that meaningful due process can require no less. Assuredly, it inflicts punishment as grave as the institutionalization which may follow an *In re Gault* finding of delinquency. A resident alien's right to due process should not be tempered by a classification of the deportation proceeding as "civil", "criminal", or "administrative." No matter the classification, deportation is punishment, pure and simple.

In *Gagnon*, the Supreme Court acknowledged that it was affording parolees and probationers less due process than it afforded juveniles in *In re Gault*. It reached this result because a parolee or probationer is in that position solely because he was previously convicted of a crime. The court reasoned that parolees and probationers should be required to demonstrate that an attorney would serve a useful purpose prior to compelling the government to provide counsel at government expense. But, in a deportation proceeding, the respondent need not necessarily be before the immigration judge because of a prior conviction.[2] The fact of conviction is only one of numerous grounds for deportation outlined in the statute. Similar to the juvenile, an alien may only stand accused of an offense.

* * *

---

2. If the court wishes to extend *Gagnon*, perhaps a better approach is to limit the case-by-case appointment of counsel to proceedings where respondent is being deported because he has a previous conviction and is, therefore, entitled to less due process. In all other instances, counsel should be appointed as a matter of right under the due process clause. * * *

Further, a probation revocation hearing is a non-adversary proceeding. The government is not represented by a prosecutor. There are no procedural rights which may be lost as in a criminal trial. A deportation hearing on the other hand is always an adversary proceeding. *Gagnon* does not go so far as to hold that in adversary proceedings due process may be afforded on a case-by-case basis by retrospective determination that the hearing was characterized by "fundamental fairness."

The court today has fashioned a test to resolve whether a resident alien's due-process right requires appointment of counsel. That test is whether ". . . in a given case, the assistance of counsel would be necessary to provide 'fundamental fairness—the touchstone of due process.' " *Gagnon, supra.* The majority concludes that lack of counsel before the immigration judge did not prevent full consideration of petitioner's sole argument and no different result would have been obtained had counsel been appointed. Accordingly, the court holds the hearing was fundamentally fair. These conclusions are reached by second guessing the record—a record made without petitioner's meaningful participation.

In my view, the absence of counsel at respondent's hearing before the immigration judge inherently denied him fundamental fairness. Moreover, I do not believe that we should make the initial determination that counsel is unnecessary; or that lack of counsel did not prevent full administrative consideration of petitioner's argument; or that counsel could not have obtained a different administrative result. We should not speculate at this stage what contentions appointed counsel could have raised before the immigration judge. For example, a lawyer may well have contended that § 241(a)(11) is an unconstitutional deprivation of the equal protection of the laws by arguing that alienage was the sole basis for the infliction of punishment, additional to that imposed by criminal law; that since the government elected to rely upon the criminal law sanctions, it may not now additionally exile petitioner without demonstrating a compelling governmental interest.

I do not intend to imply such a contention has validity. I cite this only to emphasize the danger of attempting to speculate at this stage whether counsel could have obtained a different result and to show that it is possible that the immigration judge did not fully consider all of petitioner's arguments.

Because the consequences of a deportation proceeding parallel punishment for crime, only a per se rule requiring appointment of counsel will assure a resident alien due process of law. In this case, the respondent, a resident alien for seven years, committed a criminal offense. Our laws require that he be punished and he was. Now, he must face additional punishment in the form of banishment. He will be deprived of the life, liberty, and pursuit of happiness he enjoyed by governmental consent.[6] It

---

6. Of course, what I have said applies only to a resident alien. I readily agree that an alien who enters illegally is entitled to less due process, if any at all. It is interesting to note that the Immigration Act seems to treat all aliens alike.

may be proper that he be compelled to face the consequences of such a proceeding. But, when he does, he should have a lawyer at his side and one at government expense, if necessary. When the government consents to grant an alien residency, it cannot constitutionally expel unless and until it affords that alien due process. Our country's constitutional dedication to freedom is thwarted by a watered-down version of due process on a case-by-case basis.

I would reverse and remand for the appointment of counsel before the immigration judge.

NOTES AND QUESTIONS ABOUT THE RIGHT TO COUNSEL

1. In *Lassiter v. Department of Social Services*, 452 U.S. 18, 101 S.Ct. 2153, 68 L.Ed.2d 640 (1981), the Supreme Court, in a five-to-four decision, rejected the claim that indigent defendants have a right to appointed counsel in a proceeding to terminate their parental status. The Court summarized its prior right to counsel decisions as follows: "The pre-eminent generalization that emerges from this Court's precedents on an indigent's right to appointed counsel is that such a right has been recognized to exist only where the litigant may lose his physical liberty if he loses the litigation." *Lassiter*, 452 U.S. at 25, 101 S.Ct. at 2158. Is removal a loss of physical liberty, or does it simply mean that noncitizens must pursue their liberty in their home countries?

In *Turner v. Rogers*, ___ U.S. ___, 131 S.Ct. 2507, 180 L.Ed.2d 452 (2011), Turner faced imprisonment for up to one year in a civil contempt proceeding held to enforce a child support order that Turner had failed to pay. Justice Breyer's opinion for the Court (in another five-to-four decision) surveyed *Lassiter* and other Court precedents, and suggested that loss of physical liberty is a necessary condition for requiring counsel in a civil proceeding, but not always a sufficient condition. The court vacated Turner's conviction and remanded, but held that alternative safeguards could often satisfy the due process clause in such cases without requiring paid counsel. In applying the *Eldridge* analysis here, one central factor was that the key factual determination, Turner's ability to pay, can be "sufficiently straightforward to warrant determination *prior* to providing a defendant with counsel." 131 S.Ct. at 2519 (emphasis in original). Alternative safeguards, such as explicit warnings and well-designed questioning or forms that elicit relevant financial information, might provide an appropriate substitute, though counsel could conceivably be required based on the specific circumstances. Are the issues in *Aguilera* also "straightforward" so that alternative safeguards would suffice? In other typical removal cases?

2. Research reveals no published decision applying the test set forth in *Aguilera–Enriquez* to require government-paid counsel in a deportation or removal proceeding, though many cases reiterate the fundamental fairness standard.

a. Would it matter if the noncitizens in proceedings were children? In *Perez–Funez v. District Director*, 619 F.Supp. 656, 664–65 (C.D. Cal. 1985), the court struck down, on due process grounds, voluntary departure procedures as applied to unaccompanied minors. Given their "limited understanding and decision-making ability," as well as "the critical importance of the decisions, and the inherently coercive nature of INS processing," the court found that "legal counsel certainly would be the best insurance against a deprivation of rights." But the court stopped short of holding that unaccompanied minors have a right to appointed counsel, instead noting that an alternative would be "to have children contact a parent, close adult relative, or adult friend who can put the child on a more equal footing with the INS."

b.   In 2010 the appointed counsel issue was raised anew in a class action complaint filed on behalf of noncitizens held in DHS custody for removal proceedings who suffered from serious mental disabilities that rendered them mentally incompetent to represent themselves. The district court granted a preliminary injunction in the cases of two named plaintiffs, barring future removal proceedings unless the person is represented by a "qualified representative," though it did not expressly require DHS or EOIR to pay for counsel. Although the court noted the plaintiffs' due process claims, it rested its holding on § 504 of the Rehabilitation Act, which requires reasonable accommodations to the disabled. *Franco–Gonzales v. Holder*, 767 F.Supp.2d 1034 (C.D. Cal. 2010). As of late 2011, this litigation continues.

c.   The BIA recently issued a precedent decision in a case involving alleged mental incompetency. After specifically outlining the procedures and standards to be used in assessing such claims, the decision noted that safeguards are required by statute when the respondent is incompetent. INA § 240(b)(3). The ruling discussed the various safeguards available, including those specified in statute or regulation, and then remanded the case to the immigration judge for further proceedings. Among the safeguards are the appearance of a friend, custodian, or attorney on behalf of the noncitizen, but the decision does not expressly mention the possibility of appointed counsel. *Matter of M–A–M–*, 25 I & N Dec. 474 (BIA 2011).

3.   Alternative sources of representation may affect your thinking on any right to appointed counsel. Consider these factors:

a.   The statute requires that everyone placed into removal proceedings shall receive a list, updated at least quarterly, of persons in the area who are available to represent aliens on a pro bono basis. INA § 239(b)(2). This section codifies a practice developed administratively several decades ago to address the representation issue. *See also* 8 C.F.R. § 1240.10(a)(2), (3). Immigration judges regularly grant continuances, sometimes multiple continuances, to enable a noncitizen to find pro bono counsel willing to take his or her case. The regulations also permit representation in immigration court by EOIR-accredited representatives who are not attorneys, and under certain circumstances by "reputable individuals." *Id.*, § 1292.1, .2.

b.   Law students and law graduates not yet admitted to practice may represent noncitizens before federal agencies in immigration matters under certain circumstances and with permission of the official before whom they wish to appear. *See* 8 C.F.R. §§ 292.1(a)(2), 1292.1(a)(2). Law students must be directly supervised by a faculty member, attorney, or accredited representative in a legal aid program or clinic conducted by a law school or non-profit organization. Law graduates (who are not yet admitted to the bar) must appear under the supervision of an attorney or accredited representative. Law students and law graduates must appear without direct or indirect remuneration from the noncitizen whom they represent.

c. Since 1983, the federally funded Legal Services Corporation (LSC) generally may not fund any person or entity providing legal assistance—even using non-LSC funds—to noncitizens who are not permanent residents, immediate relatives of U.S. citizens who have applied for adjustment of status, noncitizens granted refugee status or asylum, or noncitizens granted withholding of removal under INA § 241(b)(3). An exception allows entities receiving LSC funds to use non-LSC funds for legal assistance to noncitizen victims of domestic abuse. *See* 45 C.F.R. §§ 1626.4, 1626.5. Would expanded availability of LSC funds be a meaningful alternative to appointed counsel?

d. Since 2003, the Legal Orientation Program of the Executive Office for Immigration Review has funded pre-hearing "legal orientation presentations" by private non-profit agencies to all detainees in certain facilities, in cooperation with federal immigration officials. *See* Vera Institute, Improving Efficiency and Promoting Justice in the Immigration System: Lessons from the Legal Orientation Program (May 2008). Many detainees then choose not to contest removal, and their cases are usually completed that day at a master calendar hearing before the immigration judge. Others are then ordinarily able to meet privately after the presentation with lawyers or paralegals from the organization to discuss the case or at least provide information that may help line up appropriate pro bono representation. With this further advice, some choose not to contest, while others are given written materials and counseling that will help them to pursue their claims themselves, and still others may obtain full pro bono representation. As of October 2010, EOIR was funding LOP programs at 27 detention sites around the country, servicing 60,000 detainees that year. *See* U.S. Dept of Justice, Recent Initiatives for EOIR's Legal Orientation and Pro Bono Program (Oct. 4, 2010), <http://www.justice.gov/eoir/press/2010/RecentInitiativesforLOP10042010.htm>.

e. Under the Equal Access to Justice Act (EAJA), 5 U.S.C.A. § 504, a "prevailing party" in an "adversary adjudication" against the government is entitled to recover attorneys' fees if the government's position was "not substantially justified." EAJA does not apply to deportation hearings, according to the Supreme Court in *Ardestani v. INS*, 502 U.S. 129, 112 S.Ct. 515, 116 L.Ed.2d 496 (1991). The Court reasoned that a deportation hearing is not an "adversary adjudication" for EAJA purposes, even though it is identical in key respects to administrative hearings that are. Attorneys' fees may be available under EAJA for successful review of removal orders in federal court, and for certain other sorts of court challenges to immigration decisions or practices. Would allowing EAJA fees in removal proceedings be a sound alternative to appointed counsel?

4. A 2005 study found that represented, non-detained noncitizens obtained relief in 34 percent of their cases, in contrast to 23 percent of non-detained noncitizens who were unrepresented. Represented detainees received relief in 24 percent of their cases, compared to 15 percent for unrepresented detainees. *See* Kerwin, *Revisiting the Need for Appointed Counsel*, Migration Policy Institute Insight 6 (April 2005). The difference in approval rates was

even greater between represented and unrepresented asylum applicants—a result echoed in several other studies over the past decade. (The disparity between represented and unrepresented cases may not be surprising, given that many respondents must rely on counsel willing to serve on a pro bono basis, and pro bono attorneys typically interview prospective clients carefully so as to focus their limited resources on cases they believe to be meritorious.) Several studies have offered their own suggestions for reforms that would improve representation. *See, e.g.,* American Bar Association Commission on Immigration, Reforming the Immigration System: Proposals to Promote Independence, Fairness, Efficiency, and Professionalism in the Adjudication of Removal Cases, chap. 5 (2010); Katzmann, *The Legal Profession and the Unmet Needs of the Immigrant Poor,* 21 Geo. J. Legal Ethics 3 (2008).

5. Note that the neither the BIA nor the court in *Aguilera–Enriquez* waited to learn the outcome of the noncitizen's efforts to have his convictions vacated. Should they have? Consider what arguments could be marshaled for and against such a delay. Today, counsel's failure to advise Aguilera of the deportation consequences of his guilty plea to the cocaine charge would raise serious questions under *Padilla v. Kentucky,* ___ U.S. ___, 130 S.Ct. 1473, 176 L.Ed.2d 284 (2010), discussed in Chapter Seven. Those questions would be litigated initially in the context of a challenge to the criminal conviction. Does the potential *Padilla* remedy reduce or enhance the claim to counsel in a removal proceeding of this type?

EXERCISE

You work for a member of Congress who wants to make appointed counsel available in removal proceedings, but is concerned about the cost of appointing counsel for every indigent noncitizen. Your assignment is to redraft INA § 240(b)(4)(A) and § 292 to provide appointed counsel for some indigent noncitizens in some cases, and write a memorandum explaining your policy and drafting decisions. If there is additional information that you would like to have before finalizing your recommendation, describe the needed information. Would other changes to the INA be needed to implement your recommendation?

---

3. THE IMMIGRATION JUDGE

For most of the twentieth century, the federal officials who conducted exclusion and deportation hearings were officers of INS or its predecessor agencies. Soon after the McCarran–Walter Act became law in 1952, the U.S. Supreme Court in *Marcello v. Bonds,* 349 U.S. 302, 311, 75 S.Ct. 757, 762, 99 L.Ed. 1107 (1955), summarily rejected a constitutional challenge to the adjudicator's ties to INS, but criticism continued. It was not until 1983 that this arrangement ended with the creation of the Executive Office for Immigration Review (EOIR). *See* 8 C.F.R. § 1003.0. Now, immigration judges are under the general supervision of the Director of EOIR, which remains in the Department of Justice after INS functions were moved to the Department of Homeland Security.

INA § 240(b)(1) provides that an immigration judge "shall administer oaths, receive evidence, interrogate, examine, and cross-examine the alien and any witnesses." It further provides: "The immigration judge may issue subpoenas for the attendance of witnesses and presentation of evidence." While this language may suggest an inquisitorial model—conferring both prosecuting and judging functions on an immigration judge—in fact immigration court hearings generally conform to the more familiar adversarial model, with the government represented by a specialized staff of trial attorneys. But some special removal procedures, discussed later in this section, do not involve an immigration judge at all.

Within this scheme, what do constitutional due process requirements and the statute require an immigration judge to do? Consider the next case.

JACINTO v. INS

United States Court of Appeals, Ninth Circuit, 2000.
208 F.3d 725.

BRIGHT, CIRCUIT JUDGE.

Norma Antonia Jacinto Carrillo ("Jacinto") and her son, Ronald Garcia, are natives and citizens of Guatemala. On behalf of herself and her son, Jacinto petitions this court for review of the Board of Immigration Appeals' ("Board") decision denying her application for asylum and withholding of deportation. She also contests the Board's denial of voluntary departure * * *. We have jurisdiction over this petition * * *.

I

In December, 1994, Jacinto filed an affirmative asylum application with the Immigration and Naturalization Service ("INS"). Therein she alleged that members of the Guatemalan military were persecuting her and her family, including her common-law husband who is a former member of the Guatemalan military. In March, 1995, the INS issued an Order to Show Cause and Notice of Hearing.

Following two hearings, one on August 25, 1995, and the second on January 11, 1996, the immigration judge denied Jacinto's application for asylum, withholding of deportation, and voluntary departure. The immigration judge found that Jacinto did not have a well-founded fear of persecution because she could not explain why members of the military were pursuing her and her husband and had not demonstrated a subjective fear of persecution. In addition, the immigration judge found that Jacinto's testimony throughout the proceedings was not credible.

* * *

II

This court reviews claims of due process violations in deportation proceedings *de novo*.

The Fifth Amendment guarantees that individuals subject to deportation proceedings receive due process. Due process requires that an alien receive a full and fair hearing. In addition to constitutional protections, there are statutory and regulatory safeguards as well. For example, individuals in deportation proceedings are entitled to present personal testimony in their behalf. When these protections are denied and such denial results in prejudice, the constitutional guarantee of due process has been denied. Prejudice occurs when the rights of the alien have been transgressed in such a way as is likely to impact the results of the proceedings.

The case record consisted of two hearings with different immigration judges presiding at each hearing. * * *

* * *

We start with the initial hearing of August 24, 1995, concerning [Jacinto's] son Ronald Garcia. At that hearing, the immigration judge discussed her son's right to an attorney. The transcript of this matter is reproduced below:

Q. At this hearing he has a right to an attorney at his own expense, at his family's expense. You are now being handed a Form I–618 and also a copy of the local legal aid list which contains the names of organizations and attorneys who may be able to help him for little or not [sic] fee. Do you understand all that I've said so far, Ms. Jacinto Carrillo?

A. Yes.

Q. All right. Do you wish the Court to give you additional time to get an attorney to speak for you, rather for your son, in these proceedings, or do you wish to speak for him?

A. Yes.

Q. Which one?

A. The problem is—

Q. Which one? I don't want to hear about the problems, I just want to know whether you want to speak for him or whether you want time to get an attorney to speak for him?

A. I want to speak for him.

Q. All right. At this hearing, your son has certain rights, one, to present evidence in his own behalf; two, to examine and object to evidence presented against him; and three, to question any witnesses brought into hearing. Do you understand the rights that your son enjoys?

A. Yes.

The likely misunderstanding surfaces in Jacinto's answer "The problem is—" A reasonable interpretation of this colloquy is that Jacinto was given a choice: either she could get an attorney to speak for her son or she could speak for her son, but not both.

This is not the rule. She could have obtained an attorney and she also could have spoken for her son as a witness (and as an adviser to the attorney). This was never clearly explained to her. In other words, from the standpoint of this unsophisticated witness, the court gave her the choice of either being silent or getting somebody else to speak for her son.

Her general misunderstanding about the hearing process and the matters to be resolved is reflected in various places throughout the record. For example, the confusion regarding voluntary departure[c] is indicated in the following excerpt from the transcript of the initial hearing:

Q. All right. In his behalf, do you admit that he [Ronald Garcia] is deportable and that he entered the United States without inspection?

A. That's if I admit?

Q. Yes, do you concede that your son, Ronald, in behalf of your son that he is deportable, that is, that he could be sent out of the United States because he entered this country illegally, that is that he entered the United States without inspection?

A. Yes.

Q. All right. If deportation becomes necessary, your son has the right to choose the country to which he will be sent. In that event, what, if any, country does he choose?

A. Well, it's safe here.

Q. Well, if he's ordered to leave here, what, if any, country does he wish to be sent, deported to?

A. Any other country but Guatemala.

Q. All right, well, does he wish to name a country, yes or no?

A. Like, Washington or—

Q. Country.

A. Any other place.

Q. Does he wish to name a country, yes or no? Yes or no?

A. Washington.

Q. What country is Washington?

A. I don't know, but—

Q. I don't either.

---

c. This colloquy actually does not relate to voluntary departure. The immigration judge was discussing what might happen if the person were subjected to a formal removal order. Even when ruled removable, noncitizens other than arriving aliens have the authority, within limits, to designate the country to which removal will occur. INA § 241(b)(2).—eds.

A. But we don't want to leave here.

Q. Yes. Well, I'll show that the Respondent declined to name a country . . . .

These responses make clear that Jacinto never actually understood what she was being asked to do with respect to voluntary departure.

The ambiguity of the language explaining self-representation or having an attorney continued during the latter part of this initial hearing. The immigration judge stated that Jacinto was scheduled for a hearing the same day as her son, and the following inquiry occurred:

Q. Do you remember everything that I told you regarding your son's right to an attorney?

A. Yes.

Q. The same thing applies for you. Do you understand?

A. Yes.

Q. And you've already been given a Form I–618 and a legal aid list and we'll give you another one right now. Do you want time to get an attorney to speak for you or do you want to speak for yourself?

A. I'd like to speak for myself.

Q. All right. As I advised you a moment ago of the rights that your son had as far as presenting evidence in his own behalf. The same rights apply to you. Do you recall?

A. Yes.

The ambiguity is apparent. Jacinto may well have believed that she was being given a choice between speaking for herself at the proceedings or having an attorney. The court never adequately explained to her that she could have an attorney and also speak for herself, by being a witness, or that if she took the part of the attorney herself, she could still present her own testimony in narrative form, in addition to acting as an advocate.

We turn next to the deportation hearing conducted on January 11, 1996. * * *

Jacinto's confusion immediately surfaced when the court asked if Jacinto intended to introduce documentary evidence in support of her application. The record indicates that Jacinto did not comprehend the nature of the evidence that was requested:

Q. All right. Very well. At these hearings you also have the right to present any documentary evidence in support of your claim for asylum. Do you have any documents that you wish to submit at this time in support of your case?

A. Documents for, yes, I think I have some right here.

Q. Okay.

A. No.

Jacinto produced no documentary evidence at this time but offered to present documentary evidence later in the hearing. When Jacinto did offer to show the immigration judge such evidence in the form of photographs, the judge stated that it was not necessary to view them. He thus denied her the opportunity to present evidence that could have been relevant to her application, particularly given his finding that she was not credible.

The manner of conducting the asylum hearing placed Jacinto at a considerable disadvantage. The asylum hearing in this case began with the immigration judge asking preliminary questions. Rather than permitting Jacinto to present her own testimony, the immigration judge then turned questioning over to the INS attorney. The questioning of Jacinto then alternated between the immigration judge and the INS attorney. At no point was she afforded the opportunity to present her own affirmative testimony, in narrative form or otherwise.

* * *

The immigration judge, in the questioning of Jacinto, focused on a number of matters where Jacinto did not fully respond. During questioning of Jacinto by the INS attorney, the immigration judge would interrupt frequently and ask questions and then turn the questioning back to the government attorney. The examination of Jacinto went back and forth between the immigration judge and the government attorney with some of the questions relating to the credibility of Jacinto's statements. For example, the following colloquy occurred between the INS attorney and Jacinto:

Q. Ma'am, if they came to your house so often, and you were so afraid, why did you stay there for two years?

A. In the house?

Q. Why didn't you leave Guatemala earlier?

A. It's that we, they started, like I said, they started to bother us because he told them if they continued [to] bother him he was going to say everything he knew because he knew all the bad things that they did. That's when they started to persecute him to kill him.

Q. See, but, ma'am, please answer my question. If you were so afraid of these people and they were bothering you so often, why did you wait two years to leave Guatemala?

A. I did not wait that long. They threatened him, but they did not bother me, just at the end that they would come and bother me.

At the end of the examination on the merits, the immigration judge did not afford Jacinto any opportunity to explain her answers, but turned to the government counsel and inquired, "Anything further, counsel?"

At that point counsel indicated that he wished to inquire about voluntary departure. However, at no time did the immigration judge explain that Jacinto could testify further with respect to the asylum claim, could explain or add to her previous answers, or offer additional evidence. Thus, Jacinto was never at any time given the opportunity to present directly, or fully detail, her account supporting her claim for asylum.

After the government completed its inquiry relating to voluntary departure, the court called Jacinto's only witness, [her common-law husband] Francisco Javier Lopez. Lopez made some statements that one might deem to be harmful to the cause of the petitioner. For instance, he stated that initially Jacinto wanted to return to Guatemala until recently when he convinced her that it would be dangerous for her to return and that the family should stay together.

After the immigration judge and the INS attorney finished questioning Lopez, the immigration judge asked Jacinto the following:

Q. To the Respondent, do you have any questions that you would like for the witness to answer?

A. No.

The immigration judge did not explain to Jacinto that she could use this opportunity to clarify any matters, dispel any conclusions, highlight certain facts, or present additional evidence supporting her right to remain in the country. For instance, Jacinto never asked Lopez to further expound upon his statement that he knew of several instances of killings of Guatemalan citizens by the Guatemalan army. Jacinto failed to amplify this matter, and there is no indication that she recognized the importance of showing a political motivation for the adverse action taken against her and Lopez while in Guatemala that served as the reason to leave Guatemala.

* * *

In *Fisher* [*v. INS*, 79 F.3d 955, 972 (9th Cir. 1996) (*en banc*) (Noonan, J., dissenting)], Judge Noonan noted that the statutory and regulatory obligations required, in short, the immigration judge to fully develop the record. Reciting the statutory and regulatory mandates of the immigration judge, Judge Noonan observed that the duty of the immigration judge is analogous to that of the administrative law judge in social security disability cases. In social security disability cases, the administrative law judge has a duty to "fully and fairly develop the record. . . ." *Brown v. Heckler,* 713 F.2d 441, 443 (9th Cir. 1983). We agree.

Both administrative settings have the common feature of determining the applicant's eligibility for certain benefits. The benefit sought in social security disability cases is, of course, monetary. The benefit sought in deportation hearings is the permission of the United States government for the alien to stay in the United States because the individual has suffered past persecution or has a well-founded fear of persecution in her homeland.

In addition, both social security and deportation hearings are likely to be unfamiliar settings for the applicant, and, as the Supreme Court has noted, such procedures "should be understandable to the layman claimant . . . and not strict in tone and operation." *Richardson v. Perales,* 402 U.S. 389, 400, 91 S.Ct. 1420, 28 L.Ed.2d 842 (1971). When an applicant appears pro se, this rationale is all the stronger, and the administrative law judge must "scrupulously and conscientiously probe into, inquire of, and explore for all the relevant facts. [The judge] must be especially diligent in ensuring that favorable as well as unfavorable facts and circumstances are elicited." *Key v. Heckler,* 754 F.2d 1545, 1551 (9th Cir. 1985).

While the rationale for full development of the record in social security cases lies in the non-adversarial nature of the proceedings, the rationale in deportation proceedings is at least as important.

Like in social security cases, applicants for asylum often appear without counsel and may not possess the legal knowledge to fully appreciate which facts are relevant. Yet a full exploration of all the facts is critical to correctly determine whether the alien does indeed face persecution in their homeland. Thus, in such circumstances, the immigration judge is in a good position to draw out those facts that are relevant to the final determination.

Further, aliens often lack proficiency in English, the language in which the proceedings are typically conducted. Despite the presence of a translator, the language barrier presents the potential to affect the ability of the alien to communicate and the ability of the immigration judge to understand what is being stated.

Moreover, while the proceedings are adversarial in nature, the implication of the proceedings is that an individual is required to leave this country. Thus, the petitioner could face a significant threat to his or her life, safety, and well-being. Should the immigration judge fail to fully develop the record, information crucial to the alien's future remains undisclosed.

Thus, under the statute and regulations previously cited, and for the reasons we have stated here, immigration judges are obligated to fully develop the record in those circumstances where applicants appear without counsel, as is this case.

In this case, Jacinto represented herself under circumstances in which the court did not clearly explain either that she had the right to testify even if she was represented by a lawyer or that she could present evidence, in the form of affirmative testimony, even while representing herself. Thus, not only did she not have the assistance of counsel, but she suffered because her rights were not adequately outlined for her. Her testimony was the product of an examination conducted by parties somewhat adverse to her position. Further, and perhaps most important, the immigration judge never gave her the opportunity to present her own additional narrated statement that might have added support to her claim. These combined failures resulted in a denial of a full and fair hearing.

The lack of a full and fair hearing, however, will not alone establish a due process violation. The alien must establish that she suffered prejudice. Prejudice is apparent and pervasive in this case as demonstrated by an examination of the immigration judge's determinations regarding credibility and by the testimony relating to voluntary departure.

It was important for Jacinto to establish that her persecution or her well-founded fear of persecution rested on one of these factors: race, religion, nationality, membership in a particular social group or political opinion. However, this was not developed in the proceedings because the immigration judge never explained this requirement to her, and never gave her an opportunity to testify fully in her own behalf. Instead, Jacinto only was permitted to "testify" through an examination conducted by the immigration judge and the INS attorney.

Interestingly, the immigration judge observed "the Respondent herself did not know the reason why these individuals were actually after her husband." Yet it appears from the record that Jacinto's husband, Lopez, indicated they had information that members of the military were involved in murders of other persons. Had the immigration judge attempted to elicit more information from Lopez on this subject, the questions could well have led to some additional information about the relationship between military abuses and political opinions that would have lent support to Jacinto's application.

Perhaps not surprisingly, the immigration judge did not believe some of Jacinto's testimony. Yet, with further information, the credibility issue might have been resolved differently. * * * These matters might have been better resolved if Jacinto had received the necessary information about her right to present her own direct narrative testimony in explanation of her circumstances in Guatemala.

More than that however, Jacinto's inability to understand the hearing process and the questions presented to her from the immigration judge is reflected in the dialogue concerning voluntary departure. The record shows that Jacinto did not understand her privilege of a voluntary departure. The immigration judge questioned Jacinto as to whether she would agree to depart voluntarily should her asylum application be denied. In response, Jacinto replied, "I'm afraid to go over there," "I'm afraid to return to my country." The immigration judge continued:

Q: All right, ma'am, so, are you saying that if I do grant you a period in which to leave voluntarily, you will not leave. Is that what you're saying?

A: If you give me permission?

Q: To leave voluntarily, would you leave?

A: I don't know where I would go, but not to Guatemala.

Q: Well, you could go wherever you wanted to go, but you could leave, you would have to leave the United States.

A: How's that?

Q: You would have to leave the United States. You would not have to go back to Guatemala, but you would have to leave the United States. Are you willing to do that, yes or no?

A: No. I cannot answer that question.

Jacinto's desire to depart voluntarily should her asylum application be denied is obvious from the fact that she applied for voluntary departure in the first instance. Despite the clear advantage in agreeing to voluntarily depart, Jacinto repeatedly stated that she would not go back to Guatemala. Her responses to the immigration judge's questioning, and her failure to supplement the adverse inferences against her in the record as developed by the immigration judge and the INS attorney demonstrate that Jacinto did not understand the procedures in which she was engaged or the implications of her answers. These examples are sufficient to demonstrate that Jacinto suffered prejudice not only as to the issue of voluntary departure but as to the merits as well.

We do not decide the merits of Jacinto's application for asylum. We hold only that Jacinto did not receive a full and fair hearing, that she suffered prejudice, and thus was denied due process. Accordingly, we vacate the Board's decision, and we remand the case to the Board with instructions to remand to the immigration judge for a new hearing consistent with this opinion.[6]

TROTT, CIRCUIT JUDGE, dissenting.

I respectfully disagree with the majority opinion's conclusions (1) that Jacinto did not receive a full and fair hearing, (2) that the immigration judges failed in their responsibilities, (3) that Jacinto did not understand her rights with respect to the hearing procedure, (4) that she was denied a reasonable opportunity to present evidence, and (5) that she was the subject of two cross-examinations. Thus, I conclude that she was not denied due process.

Before the hearings, Jacinto received written notice of her rights. Then, on August 24, 1995, *after* her son's right to an attorney was explained, I.J. Martin asked, "Do you understand all that I've said so far, Ms. Jacinto Carillo?" Answer, "Yes." When she said she wished to speak for her son at the initial deportability hearing, the I.J. explained her son's rights—to present evidence in his own behalf, to examine and object to evidence, and to question any witnesses. He asked her, "Do you understand the rights that your son enjoys?" Her answer was, "Yes." At the same hearing, the I.J. told her that she had the same rights as did her son, including the rights to an attorney and to present evidence on her own behalf. He said, "The same thing applies to you. Do you understand?" Her answer was, "Yes." At the end of that hearing, the I.J. again asked, "Do

---

6. Because Jacinto received representation from counsel on this appeal, we assume on remand that she will have the assistance of an attorney.

you understand all that I've said?" Her answer was, "Yes, Your Honor." Then, she had over four months to get ready for the hearings.

At the January 11, 1996, asylum hearing, she was again given an opportunity to have a lawyer, but she chose "to speak for herself." She submitted documents on her behalf and called a witness, Francisco Lopez, who made her case.

Where I do agree with the majority opinion is on its conclusion that Jacinto did not understand voluntary departure. But I cannot in good conscience fault the I.J.s for depriving this petitioner of due process. The I.J. presiding at the asylum hearing was *helping* her. If he had simply said, "Okay, your case, go ahead," I think we would fault the I.J. for throwing Jacinto to the wolves.

Accordingly, I would restrict the remand in this case to the issue of voluntary departure.

NOTES AND QUESTIONS ON DUE PROCESS AND THE IMMIGRATION JUDGE'S ROLE

1. Why isn't it enough due process for Jacinto that she received written notice of her rights, including the right to have a lawyer represent her, plus a list of attorneys available to do so at little or no cost? Shouldn't she have to live with the consequences of declining representation?

2. *Aguilera–Enriquez* says there is no automatic right to appointed counsel, but *Jacinto* finds a due process violation because the immigration judge failed to assist the noncitizen adequately. Do *Jacinto* and *Aguilera–Enriquez* reflect complementary or conflicting views of the right to counsel in removal proceedings? Do they reflect complementary or conflicting understandings of the nature of removal proceedings?

3. Although counsel is not required at government expense (absent a truly exceptional showing that fundamental fairness would require such a step), it is accepted that the government must pay for translation if the respondent is not capable of understanding the proceedings in English. Courts have held that an incompetent translation deprives a noncitizen of due process when prejudice results. *See, e.g., Amadou v. INS*, 226 F.3d 724, 726–28 (6th Cir. 2000) (interpreter's faulty translation likely played a significant part in the judge's credibility determination). Current practice is to provide translation only of those questions directed at those who cannot speak English. *See El Rescate Legal Services, Inc. v. EOIR*, 959 F.2d 742, 752 (9th Cir. 1991) (generally approving this practice). *Cf. United States v. Leon–Leon*, 35 F.3d 1428, 1431–32 (9th Cir. 1994) (no prejudice resulted from failure to translate other crucial parts of hearing).

4. Applying *Eldridge*, courts have developed an elaborate body of case law that defines constitutional due process in removal proceedings. Many such decisions arise, like *Jacinto*, on immediate, direct review of a removal order. Other rulings arise—as we will see later in this section—when the noncitizen seeks a second chance through a motion to reopen or to reconsider a prior removal order. Still later on, a noncitizen might raise due process as part of a

collateral attack on an earlier removal order. *See, e.g., Chacon–Corral v. Weber*, 259 F.Supp.2d 1151, 1160–64 (D. Colo. 2003) (invalidating, because of multiple procedural defects, prior deportation order on which government relied in seeking removal). Also, the government may prosecute a noncitizen for the crime of illegal reentry after removal under INA § 276. One defense to that charge may be that the prior removal proceeding violated due process. The Supreme Court held in *United States v. Mendoza–Lopez*, 481 U.S. 828, 837–38, 107 S.Ct. 2148, 95 L.Ed.2d 772 (1987), that in a criminal reentry prosecution, a collateral attack on the earlier deportation order is allowed when the prior proceeding was fundamentally unfair *and* the respondent was effectively denied the opportunity for meaningful judicial review. Congress essentially codified the standards of *Mendoza–Lopez* in 1996, in INA § 276(d). The circuits apply varying standards in determining whether a flaw in the earlier proceeding (1) prejudiced the noncitizen or (2) prevented meaningful judicial review. For a survey of the case law, see Kurzban, *Criminalizing Immigration Law,* in Practicing Law Institute, 42nd Annual Immigration and Naturalization Institute 321, 344–61 (2009).

5. Statutory amendments in 1996 authorized the use of video teleconferencing (VTC) to conduct removal proceedings. INA § 240(b)(2)(A). EOIR has used this option in selected locations, soon to expand to all 59 immigration courts, and has made efforts to improve its practices in response to criticism and as the technology has improved. Such a procedure could mean that the judge and interpreter and ICE attorney are in one location, but the respondent and his counsel are at a remote location, perhaps at an ICE detention facility. Under some variations, the respondent's counsel is collocated with the immigration judge instead. Some proponents see such technology as a welcome efficiency that can reduce immigration court backlogs (and perhaps improve the availability of counsel in remote locations). *See generally* Olorunnipa, Agency Use of Video Hearings: Best Practices and Possibilities for Expansion 25–38 (Administrative Conference of the United States In–House Research Report 2011). Other studies have identified practical and procedural problems with VTC. *See, e.g.,* Walsh & Walsh, *Effective Processing or Assembly–Line Justice?: The Use of Teleconferencing in Asylum Removal Hearings,* 22 Geo. Imm. L.J. 259 (2008); Note, *Access to Courts,* 122 Harv. L.Rev. 1151, 1181–92 (2009).

4. EVIDENTIARY RULES

As with most administrative proceedings, the formal rules of evidence do not apply in removal hearings. Hearsay and unauthenticated documents may be admitted if the immigration judge deems them material and relevant. *See* 8 C.F.R. § 1240.7(a), *Felzcerek v. INS*, 75 F.3d 112, 115–16 (2d Cir. 1996). However, courts have ordered the exclusion of evidence if its admission would be unfair, or set aside a removal order based on unauthenticated documents. *See, e.g., Ezeagwuna v. Ashcroft*, 325 F.3d 396, 405–08 (3d Cir. 2003) (finding due process violation where denial of asylum was based almost entirely on letter that was multiple hearsay and unreliable); *Cunanan v. INS*, 856 F.2d 1373, 1374–75 (9th Cir. 1988) (fundamentally unfair to rely on affidavit of noncitizen's wife where INS had not attempted to produce her as witness). Why aren't removal hearings run according to the Federal Rules of Evidence? Should they be?

a. Burden of Proof, Silence, and Adverse Inferences

In a removal proceeding, who has the burden of proof; *i.e.,* who must prove what, and to what degree of likelihood or certainty? When Congress in 1996 created a unified removal proceeding governing both allegedly inadmissible and deportable noncitizens, the statute spelled out by issue some of the allocation of the burden and also the relevant standard of proof. INA § 240(c). On certain other issues, these questions are answered by the regulations or by case law.

Because the immigration laws obviously do not apply to citizens, the government initially bears the burden of proof on the threshold issue of whether an individual is in fact a noncitizen. The regulations provide: "In the case of a respondent charged as being in the United States without being admitted or paroled, the Service must first establish the alienage of the respondent." 8 C.F.R. § 1240.8(c). If the individual is an alien, she must establish either "by clear and convincing evidence" that she is "lawfully present in the United States pursuant to a prior admission" or that she "is clearly and beyond doubt entitled to be admitted and is not inadmissible under section 212." INA § 240(c)(2). If the noncitizen has been admitted, the government then has the burden to establish deportability "by clear and convincing evidence." INA § 240(c)(3)(A). In some cases, it can matter a great deal who has the burden of proof on key issues. But often there is no real contest over alienage or whether the person had been admitted. Moreover in the majority of contested cases, the noncitizen concedes removability, and the hearing focuses instead on relief from removal, where the noncitizen has the burden. INA § 240(c)(4).

Noncitizens have a Fifth Amendment right to refuse to provide answers in a removal hearing that could be used against them in a criminal proceeding. Note that unlawful entry is not just a ground for removal but a potential criminal offense as well, *see* INA §§ 275, 276. The Board of Immigration Appeals has held that when the government introduces no evidence at all, the noncitizen's silence is insufficient by itself to meet the government's burden to show deportability by clear, unequivocal, and convincing evidence. *See Matter of Guevara*, 20 I & N Dec. 238 (BIA 1991). The situation is different, however, once the government introduces evidence of, for example, alienage or the circumstances of entry. Then silence may leave the noncitizen open to adverse inferences. *See United States ex rel. Bilokumsky v. Tod*, 263 U.S. 149, 153–54, 44 S.Ct. 54, 55–56, 68 L.Ed. 221 (1923): "Conduct which forms a basis for inference is evidence. Silence is often evidence of the most persuasive character. * * * [T]here is no rule of law which prohibits officers charged with the administration of the immigration law from drawing an inference from the silence of one who is called upon to speak." Similarly, the Court in

Baxter v. Palmigiano, 425 U.S. 308, 316–20, 96 S.Ct. 1551, 1557–59, 47 L.Ed.2d 810 (1976), allowed the drawing of an adverse inference from a prisoner's silence after invocation of the Fifth Amendment in a prison disciplinary proceeding, on the basis that the privilege applies only "in a criminal case." *See also INS v. Lopez–Mendoza*, 468 U.S. 1032, 1044, 104 S.Ct. 3479, 3486, 82 L.Ed.2d 778 (1984) (holding that the exclusionary rule does not apply to civil deportation proceedings; the case is discussed in Chapter 9B *supra*). *See generally* Kanstroom, *Hello Darkness: Involuntary Testimony and Silence as Evidence in Deportation Proceedings*, 4 Geo. Immig. L.J. 599 (1990) (analyzing "the complex relationship between the fifth amendment self-incrimination clause and civil deportation proceedings").

b. Standard of Proof

Under INA § 240(c)(3)(A), the government must show deportability by "clear and convincing evidence." To understand the rationale for this standard, it may be useful to consider the reasoning used by the Supreme Court in establishing the practically indistinguishable "clear, unequivocal, and convincing evidence" standard for deportability under the pre–1996 statute, which did not itself specify a standard of proof.

> The petitioners urge that the appropriate burden of proof in deportation proceedings should be that which the law imposes in criminal cases—the duty of proving the essential facts beyond a reasonable doubt. The Government, on the other hand, points out that a deportation proceeding is not a criminal case, and that the appropriate burden of proof should consequently be the one generally imposed in civil cases and administrative proceedings—the duty of prevailing by a mere preponderance of the evidence.

> To be sure, a deportation proceeding is not a criminal prosecution. *Harisiades v. Shaughnessy*, 342 U.S. 580, 72 S.Ct. 512, 96 L.Ed. 586. But it does not syllogistically follow that a person may be banished from this country upon no higher degree of proof than applies in a negligence case. This Court has not closed its eyes to the drastic deprivations that may follow when a resident of this country is compelled by our Government to forsake all the bonds formed here and go to a foreign land where he often has no contemporary identification. * * *

> In denaturalization cases the Court has required the Government to establish its allegations by clear, unequivocal, and convincing evidence. The same burden has been imposed in expatriation cases. That standard of proof is no stranger to the civil law.

> No less a burden of proof is appropriate in deportation proceedings. The immediate hardship of deportation is often greater than that inflicted by denaturalization, which does not, immediately at least, result in expulsion from our shores. And many resident aliens have lived in this country longer and established stronger family,

social, and economic ties here than some who have become natural-ized citizens.

We hold that no deportation order may be entered unless it is found by clear, unequivocal, and convincing evidence that the facts alleged as grounds for deportation are true. * * *

Woodby v. INS, 385 U.S. 276, 284–86, 87 S.Ct. 483, 487–88, 17 L.Ed.2d 362 (1966).

Looking more broadly at the standard of proof, it is important to recognize that opting for a heightened standard does more than simply ensure that fewer noncitizens are wrongfully removed. It also means that more noncitizens who should be removed will not be removed, because the government will not be able to meet the higher standard. Justice Harlan, addressing the constitutionally required standard of proof in a juvenile delinquency determination, explained this trade-off as follows:

In a lawsuit between two parties, a factual error can make a difference in one of two ways. First, it can result in a judgment in favor of the plaintiff when the true facts warrant a judgment for the defendant. The analogue in a criminal case would be the conviction of an innocent man. On the other hand, an erroneous factual determina-tion can result in a judgment for the defendant when the true facts justify a judgment in plaintiff's favor. The criminal analogue would be the acquittal of a guilty man.

The standard of proof influences the relative frequency of these two types of erroneous outcomes. If, for example, the standard of proof for a criminal trial were a preponderance of the evidence rather than proof beyond a reasonable doubt, there would be a smaller risk of factual errors that result in freeing guilty persons, but a far greater risk of factual errors that result in convicting the innocent. Because the standard of proof affects the comparative frequency of these two types of erroneous outcomes, the choice of the standard to be applied in a particular kind of litigation should, in a rational world, reflect an assessment of the comparative social disutility of each.

In re Winship, 397 U.S. 358, 370–71, 90 S.Ct. 1068, 1075–76, 25 L.Ed.2d 368 (1970) (Harlan, J., concurring).

QUESTIONS ABOUT STANDARDS OF PROOF AND OTHER PROCEDURAL PROTECTIONS

1. How would you allocate the risk of error in removal? Making a reasonable decision requires you to consider at least these issues: (a) by how much will wrongful non-removals increase by imposing a higher standard of proof on the government?; (b) how do you (or the American public, or Congress) value a wrongful removal as compared to a wrongful non-removal?; and (c) how might other procedural protections—such as appointed counsel—affect the error rate? Does it matter what the reason for removal is? Does it matter whether the respondent is a lawful permanent resident as opposed to a

nonimmigrant or someone who was never admitted? What role do the stakes for the individual play in your determination? How should one assess those stakes?

2. How are the immigration judge's role (*see Jacinto*), the right to counsel (*see Aguilera–Enriquez*), the burden of proof, and the standard of proof all related to each other? For example, does a demanding standard of proof compensate for the absence of appointed counsel? If you were a noncitizen in removal proceedings, which procedural protections would you find more important? Which would you find less important?

c. Secret Evidence

In some removal proceedings, the government tries to limit disclosure of evidence that it regards as sensitive national security information. Here we address three situations in which the INA authorizes nondisclosure or limited disclosure.

(i) Removal Proceedings Under INA § 235(c)

In 1952, Congress provided explicit statutory authority for the kinds of secret procedures that had been employed, on the authority of regulations alone, against the two applicants for admission in the *Knauff* and *Mezei* cases (considered in detail in Chapter Six, pp. 531–35 and 542–54). INA § 235(c) permits the Attorney General to order removal—but of arriving aliens only—on most of the national security inadmissibility grounds without a further hearing on the basis of "confidential information," the disclosure of which "would be prejudicial to the public interest, safety, or security." Section 235(c) does not preclude an asylum claim or other possible relief.

This procedure is invoked less frequently today than it was in the 1950s, but it is still employed. *See, e.g., Avila v. Rivkind*, 724 F.Supp. 945 (S.D. Fla. 1989) (sustaining summary exclusion of Orlando Bosch, who had often been involved in violent anti-Castro activity); *El–Werfalli v. Smith*, 547 F.Supp. 152 (S.D.N.Y.1982) (sustaining exclusion based on confidential information of Libyan student coming to attend classes in aircraft training, applying exclusion ground making excludable those noncitizens believed likely to "engage in activities which would be prejudicial to the public interest, or endanger the welfare, safety, or security of the United States"); *Arar v. Ashcroft*, 532 F.3d 157, 162 (2d Cir. 2008) (describing the use of § 235(c) in 2002 in the internationally controversial case of Maher Arar, who was summarily removed to Jordan and later sent to Syria, where he was allegedly subjected to torture), *vacated and superseded on rehearing en banc*, 585 F.3d 559 (2d Cir. 2009), *cert. denied*, ___ U.S. ___, 130 S.Ct. 3409, 177 L.Ed.2d 349 (2010). A leading case, *Rafeedie v. INS*, 880 F.2d 506 (D.C. Cir. 1989), *on remand*, 795 F.Supp. 13, 18–20 (D.D.C. 1992)—which is sketched in the next principal case in this section—held that a returning permanent resident is entitled to more procedural due process than § 235(c) provides.

(ii) Removal Proceedings Under § 240

Outside the situation of arriving aliens addressed in § 235(c), INA § 240(b)(4)(B) guarantees the respondent in a removal hearing "a reasonable opportunity to examine the evidence against the alien, to present evidence on the alien's own behalf, and to cross-examine witnesses presented by the Government." But it expressly exempts national security information offered in opposition to a noncitizen's admission or to an application for discretionary relief from this guarantee. Importantly, this provision thus does not allow the use of undisclosed evidence as part of the government's case-in-chief for inadmissibility or deportability. But it is worth noting that only a very small number of noncitizens are formally charged on the terrorism grounds in removal proceedings, for a straightforward practical reason: terrorism grounds are difficult to prove. Even if the government focuses on a noncitizen because it believes he is involved in terrorist activity, if the person is removable on another ground, those charges will suffice.

In many if not most cases, moreover, relief issues take up most of the time at merits hearings, because ordinarily the government can easily prove entry without inspection, overstaying a nonimmigrant admission, or deportability based on a criminal conviction. For example, if a nonimmigrant has clearly overstayed his authorized admission period, the central issue in immigration court will be relief from removal. This is precisely when § 240(b)(4)(B) applies to limit the noncitizen's access to classified evidence. *See* Martin, *Graduated Application of Constitutional Protections for Aliens: The Real Meaning of Zadvydas v. Davis*, 2001 Sup. Ct. Rev. 47, 132–33.

Is the exemption in § 240(b)(4)(B)—or its application in certain cases—unconstitutional? The next case gives one answer and a useful survey of the precedents. The district court's conclusions subsequently triggered a strong reaction from the court of appeals in related litigation. The appellate court's decision, issued shortly after the attacks of September 11, is summarized following the district court's opinion.

KIARELDEEN v. RENO

United States District Court for the District of New Jersey, 1999.
71 F.Supp.2d 402.

WALLS, DISTRICT JUDGE.

This matter is before the court on the petition for a writ of habeas corpus brought by Hany Mahmoud Kiareldeen, who, since March 1998, has been in the custody of the Immigration and Naturalization Service (INS) pending the resolution of his removal proceedings. His petition alleges [two primary] grounds for release: (1) the petitioner's detention violates the Due Process Clause because it is based on secret evidence that he has not had the opportunity to examine or confront; (2) his continued detention violates his due process rights because the government's evidence consists of uncorroborated hearsay accusations which he has rebutted[.] * * *

FACTUAL BACKGROUND

Hany Kiareldeen is a Palestinian who has resided continuously in the United States since 1990, when he entered from Israel on a student visa. In 1994, Kiareldeen married Amal Kamal, with whom he had a daughter. That marriage had ended in a bitter divorce. And in 1997, Kiareldeen married an United States citizen, Carmen Negron, who soon after submitted a relative petition to adjust his status to a conditional legal permanent resident.

In March 1998, INS and FBI agents arrested the petitioner and charged him as deportable for overstaying the time period of his student visa after his completion of his studies. He has been detained without bond pending the outcome of the deportation hearing. * * * Kiareldeen conceded that he had overstayed his visa, but sought discretionary adjustment of status and mandatory relief pursuant to the asylum provisions of the INA and the United Nations Convention Against Torture.

In opposition to the petitioner's applications for relief, the INS presented classified evidence *ex parte* and *in camera* to the Immigration Judge which allegedly demonstrated that Kiareldeen was a suspected member of a terrorist organization and a threat to the national security. Throughout the proceedings, the INS never presented any evidence in open court. According to [the immigration judge (IJ)], the INS did not call a single witness from the FBI's Joint Terrorism Task Force (the "JTTF"), which produced the unclassified documentary evidence that the petitioner has submitted to this court. * * *

On April 2, 1999, the IJ issued two opinions: the first granted the petitioner's request for adjustment of status, and the second allowed his release from custody on $1500 bond. That day, the INS appealed the decision to the Board of Immigration Appeals ("BIA"), which stayed execution of the IJ's release order. Kiareldeen moved to dissolve the stay. On June 29, 1999, a panel of BIA judges by a divided 2–1 decision denied his request for release.

* * * [T]he BIA affirmed the IJ's decision to grant the petitioner permanent resident status. Normally, this decision would moot the habeas petition because the petitioner would be released from custody upon receipt of his green card. In this case, however, the INS has applied to the BIA for a stay of execution of its order until October 29, 1999, to give the agency time to file a motion to reconsider or to request that the case be referred to the Attorney General for review. Pending the resolution of the INS' application, the petitioner still remains in custody.

The petitioner has never been charged with violation of any criminal laws. And in July 1999, the FBI closed its criminal investigation. The government has disclosed that it does not intend to reopen the investigation unless it receives new information that Kiareldeen is involved in terrorist activity.

ANALYSIS

* * *

At the threshold, the court notes that several of the decisions relied on by the respondents to demonstrate that secret evidence passes constitutional muster provide no support. *United States ex rel. Knauff v. Shaughnessy,* 338 U.S. 537, 70 S.Ct. 309, 94 L.Ed. 317 (1950), and *Shaughnessy v. U.S. ex rel. Mezei,* 345 U.S. 206, 73 S.Ct. 625, 97 L.Ed. 956 (1953), address the due process implications of secret evidence used to exclude nonresident aliens who seek admission to the country.

There is no doubt that the legislative and executive branches have plenary power to exclude nonresident aliens from the United States [citing the *Chinese Exclusion Case,* 130 U.S. 581, 9 S.Ct. 623, 32 L.Ed. 1068 (1889); and *Mezei.*] Moreover, such exclusion may employ one-sided procedures and be based on discriminatory distinctions offensive to the Constitution if applied to citizens or resident aliens. *See, e.g., Fiallo v. Bell,* 430 U.S. 787, 97 S.Ct. 1473, 52 L.Ed.2d 50 (1977); *Kleindienst v. Mandel,* 408 U.S. 753, 92 S.Ct. 2576, 33 L.Ed.2d 683 (1972). Precisely because Congressional power over alien exclusion is so broad, the respondents' reliance on exclusion cases such as *Knauff* and *Mezei* is somewhat disingenuous. The limited judicial inquiry undertaken in alien exclusion cases stands in marked contrast to the searching scrutiny required of governmental actions taken against resident aliens such as Kiareldeen, which are clearly circumscribed by the bounds of the Constitution. *See, e.g., Kwong Hai Chew v. Colding,* 344 U.S. 590, 596–97, 73 S.Ct. 472, 97 L.Ed. 576 (1953) (holding that because resident aliens are guaranteed due process rights by the Fifth Amendment, INS procedures applied to permanent residents must meet a higher standard than government actions taken to exclude nonresidents).

The respondents contend that even if the petitioner is entitled to constitutional protections, he "forfeited" his due process rights by "conceding deportability." They assert that, because the petitioner conceded that he overstayed his student visa, he has no more due process rights than an excludable alien. This argument ignores the axiomatic, constitutional premise that aliens, once legally admitted into the United States, are entitled to the shelter of the Constitution. *See, e.g., Yick Wo v. Hopkins,* 118 U.S. 356, 369, 6 S.Ct. 1064, 30 L.Ed. 220 (1886); *Landon v. Plasencia,* 459 U.S. 21, 31, 103 S.Ct. 321, 74 L.Ed.2d 21 (1982).

* * * Although Kiareldeen conceded that he had overstayed his student visa, he did not concede deportability.[d] In reality, at his removal

---

d. The judge's use of the concept of "conceding deportability" departs from the normal usage of the term in immigration practice, which generally distinguishes baseline deportability from questions of relief from removal. One may concede deportability (i.e., that a relevant ground of deportability in INA § 237(a) applies) without conceding that an order of removal is appropri-

hearings, Kiareldeen applied for several forms of relief from deportation, including discretionary adjustment of status, and mandatory relief under the asylum provisions of the INA and the United Nations Convention Against Torture. Moreover, the IJ granted the petitioner's application for discretionary adjustment of status pursuant to INA § 245(a), and this decision was recently affirmed by the BIA.

* * *

With this in mind, the court turns to the merits of the constitutional issues present. The essence of the petitioner's constitutional claim is that the INS' reliance on evidence never disclosed to the petitioner violated "every tenet of due process." The petitioner claims that the government's use of secret evidence denied him meaningful notice of the charges against him, rendered illusory any opportunity to defend himself, and carried with it a high risk of error.

The government relies principally on two decisions that the use of secret evidence in immigration proceedings raises no constitutional concerns: first, *Jay v. Boyd*, 351 U.S. 345, 76 S.Ct. 919, 100 L.Ed. 1242 (1956), where the Supreme Court considered a habeas corpus petition brought by a resident alien whose application for suspension of deportation had been denied by the Board of Immigration Appeals. There, as here, a regulation promulgated by the Attorney General expressly authorized the use of confidential information where the disclosure of such information would be "prejudicial to the public interest, safety, or security." In a sharply divided decision, Justice Reed, writing for the majority, found the regulation to be consistent with the plain meaning of the INA provision, and affirmed the INS' reliance on confidential information to deny the petitioner relief.[5]

That case does not further the government's argument for a simple reason: the petitioner there did not raise a constitutional challenge to the statute or the regulation, the *Jay* decision answers a question of statutory interpretation. Although the Court remarked, by a footnote, that "the constitutionality of § 244 [of the INA] as herein interpreted gives us no difficulty," Justice Reed recognized that the petitioner had requested only a favorable construction of the applicable statutory and regulatory provisions. In short, the *Jay* Court did not reach the constitutional question presented by Kiareldeen today.

* * *

---

ate—because relief from removal should be granted. But the key point for the judge is that contested issues remain.—eds.

5. The *Jay* majority never described the information that had been proffered by the government in opposition to the petitioner's application. However, in his habeas petition, Cecil Jay alleged that, "upon information and belief," the government had relied on nothing more than the fact that Jay's name had appeared on a list circulated by American Committee for the Protection of the Foreign Born, an organization which had been deemed subversive by the Attorney General. *Jay*, 351 U.S. at 350 n. 6, 76 S.Ct. 919. In his dissent, Justice Black asserted that Jay was "banished because he was a member of the Communist Party from 1935 to 1940," which was not illegal during the period of his alleged participation. *Id.* at 362, 76 S.Ct. 919 (Black, J., dissenting).

Instead, the court finds guidance from several recent decisions which have considered the constitutional implications of the use of confidential information in immigration proceedings. In *Rafeedie v. INS,* 688 F. Supp. 729 (D.D.C. 1988), the District Court addressed the INS' use of a special summary proceeding to exclude a permanent resident from re-entry into the United States. The underlying statute authorized the Attorney General to rely upon confidential information and to issue an order of exclusion and deportation without giving the alien an opportunity to cross-examine witnesses, to consider the government's evidence, or to appeal the decision. The INS had invoked the summary procedure because of allegations (vehemently contested) that the resident alien was a high-ranking member of a purportedly terrorist organization, the Popular Front for the Liberation of Palestine ("PFLP"). Because the circumscribed process provided no opportunity to the resident alien to confront the INS or the evidence against him directly, the District Court granted him a preliminary injunction that barred the government from employing the summary proceeding.

On appeal, the District of Columbia Circuit Court affirmed the preliminary injunction, held that "[t]here can be no doubt that, as a permanent resident alien, Rafeedie has a liberty interest in remaining in the United States, which is protected by the Due Process Clause of the Fifth Amendment," and remanded the case to the District Court for further exploration of the due process issues. *Rafeedie,* 880 F.2d 506, 524 (D.C. Cir. 1989). That Circuit Court noted that Rafeedie, like Joseph K. in Kafka's allegory *The Trial,* was in the untenable position of being forced to prove that he was not a terrorist in face of the Government's confidential information: "It is difficult to imagine how even someone innocent of all wrongdoing could meet such a burden."

On remand, the District Court ruled that because the plaintiff had been given only one opportunity to argue his case, and because that sole opportunity had been "exercised in ignorance of the confidential information with which he [had] been charged," the summary proceedings in his case did not satisfy the "basic and fundamental standard" of due process. *Rafeedie,* 795 F. Supp. 13, 20 (D.D.C.1992).

The Ninth Circuit joined in this conclusion in *American–Arab Anti–Discrimination Committee v. Reno,* 70 F.3d 1045 (9th Cir. 1995). Two permanent resident aliens applied for adjustment of their status pursuant to a provision of the INA which the INS claimed authorized the use of secret evidence in legalization proceedings. The INS had earlier arrested the immigrants, charged them with membership in the allegedly communist PFLP, and denied the applications on the basis of undisclosed classified information. After examination of the government's evidence, the District Court had found that the government's reliance on the information would constitute a due process violation and granted the plaintiffs a permanent injunction against its use.

The Ninth Circuit affirmed. Applying the constitutional balancing test of *Mathews v. Eldridge,* 424 U.S. 319, 96 S.Ct. 893, 47 L.Ed.2d 18 (1976), the Court weighed the following factors in regard to the INS' use of secret evidence: (1) the private interest affected; (2) the risk of erroneous deprivation of the interest and the value of additional or alternative procedural safeguards; and (3) the government's interest in utilizing the procedure.

The appellate court found that after ten years' residence in the United States, the immigrants had a strong liberty interest in remaining in their homes and at their work, even though they had committed technical visa violations. Next, the Court discussed the "immutable principle" that the government's evidence must be disclosed in adversary proceedings so that individuals have an opportunity to disprove the government's case against them. The Court determined that because secret procedures deprive individuals of their rights of confrontation and cross-examination, the use of undisclosed information presented an "exceptionally high risk of erroneous deprivation." Finally, the Court recognized the legitimate governmental interest in removing persons deemed to be threats to the national security while protecting its confidential sources. However, it determined that the government's failure to produce evidence that the targeted individuals had personally advocated prohibited doctrines or participated in terrorist activities belied its claim that they constituted a national security threat. Because the government was free to institute deportation proceedings or deny immigration benefits on the basis of non-secret evidence, the claimed governmental interest in choosing not to reveal its sources was outweighed. The Court concluded: "Because of the danger of injustice when decisions lack the procedural safeguards that form the core of constitutional due process, the *Mathews* balancing suggests that use of undisclosed information in adjudications should be presumptively unconstitutional. Only the most extraordinary circumstances could support one-sided process."

* * * Review of the Service's procedures involving Kiareldeen leads the court to believe that the petitioner's case is an example of the dangers of secret evidence. The petitioner came to the United States to attend a language program at Rutgers University, and continued his studies until he married for the first time and no longer could afford to work [*sic*]. He has supported himself and his family by working at a pizzeria and an electronics store in New Jersey. He has lived in the United States for almost a decade, married an American citizen, and applied to become a permanent resident. In March 1998, INS and FBI agents arrested the petitioner without warning and placed him in indefinite detention. Kiareldeen has presented evidence on his own behalf at two separate bond hearings and a removal proceeding that spanned seven months. He has subpoenaed the only government witness that he is able to identify: his ex-wife Amal Kamal, whom he suspects may be the source of the accusations against him. The Immigration Judge who presided over his removal proceedings and second bond hearing determined that "[a]n evaluation of

the evidence by a person of ordinary prudence and caution cannot sustain a finding that this respondent has engaged in terrorist activity" and ordered his release from custody * * *.

The unclassified evidence that the government made available to the petitioner to support these extraordinary measures consists of five separate "summaries" of information gathered by the FBI's Joint Terrorism Task Force, which the agency assures was "obtained from multiple reliable sources who have provided reliable information in the past." The most detailed of these identifies not a single source and is barely over two pages.

To assay the constitutionality of the INS procedures applied to the petitioner, the court considers the three factors enunciated in *Mathews v. Eldridge.* The first, the petitioner's private interest in his physical liberty, must be accorded the utmost weight. * * * The second, the risk of erroneous deprivation, also militates in the petitioner's favor. Use of secret evidence creates a one-sided process by which the protections of our adversarial system are rendered impotent. The petitioner has been compelled by the government to attempt to prove the negative in the face of anonymous "slurs of unseen and unsworn informers." *Jay,* 351 U.S. at 365, 76 S.Ct. 919 (Warren, J., dissenting). * * *

Finally, the court considers the government's interest in relying on secret evidence. Even if the interest is deemed to be the unarguably weighty one of national security, as the government maintains, the court must inquire "whether that interest is so all-encompassing that it requires that [the petitioner] be denied virtually every fundamental feature of due process." *Rafeedie,* 795 F. Supp. at 19.

The court does not, however, necessarily accept at face value the government's contentions that the national security is implicated by the petitioner's alleged misdeeds. The court has considered the government's unclassified "summary" evidence and finds it lacking in either detail or attribution to reliable sources which would shore up its credibility. More important, however, is the apparent conclusion that even the government does not find its own allegations sufficiently serious to commence criminal proceedings. The petitioner asserts, unchallenged, that the FBI recently closed its criminal investigation of Kiareldeen, and does not intend to reopen the investigation unless it receives new information that he is involved in terrorist activity. Under these circumstances, the government's claimed interest in detaining the petitioner cannot be said to outweigh the petitioner's interest in returning to freedom.

Here, the government's reliance on secret evidence violates the due process protections that the Constitution directs must be extended to all persons within the United States, citizens and resident aliens alike. * * * [T]he court finds this failure to be sufficient basis to grant the petitioner's writ of habeas corpus and direct his release from custody.

* * *

The Court of Appeals Considers the *Kiareldeen* Issues

The federal government filed a notice of appeal and sought an emergency stay of the decision on secret evidence that you have just read. But Kiareldeen was released, and the government eventually dropped its appeal. *See Kiareldeen v. Ashcroft*, 273 F.3d 542, 547 (3d Cir. 2001). The district court later issued a separate decision awarding attorneys' fees and costs to Kiareldeen. The government appealed this second district court decision to the Court of Appeals for the Third Circuit, which vacated the award. Although the appeal was theoretically limited to the award of fees and costs, the governing standard—whether the government's position on secret evidence was "substantially justified," 28 U.S.C. § 2412(d)—allowed the appeals court to revisit the merits.

The Third Circuit, writing less than two months after the attacks of September 11, 2001, bluntly criticized the district court's analysis:

> * * * The district court * * * attacked the credibility of the summaries directly, describing them as "lacking in either detail or attribution to reliable sources." *Kiareldeen v. Reno*, 71 F. Supp. 2d at 414. That the FBI would be unwilling to compromise national security by revealing its undercover sources, is both understandable and comforting. That a court would then choose to criticize the FBI for being unwilling to risk undermining its covert operations against terrorists is somewhat unnerving.

> The district court also criticized the government for its apparent unwillingness to also bring criminal charges against Kiareldeen. It stated that "even the government does not find its own allegations sufficiently serious to commence criminal proceedings."

> This statement illustrates both a simplistic and entirely uninformed view of the processes by which the Justice Department investigates and deals with suspected terrorists within our borders. It completely disregards the often complex determinations involved in releasing confidential counter-terrorism intelligence into the public arena through its introduction into both administrative hearings and court proceedings. Such a criticism implies that the government may only utilize information against an individual in a civil context, such as in deportation procedures, if it also intends to commence criminal proceedings against that same individual. Such a fettering of the Executive Branch has no support in either case law or statute.

> * * *

> We are not inclined to impede investigators in their efforts to cast out, root and branch, all vestiges of terrorism both in our homeland and in far off lands. As the Court has stated:

> > Few interests can be more compelling than a nation's need to ensure its own security. It is well to remember that freedom as

we know it has been suppressed in many countries. Unless a society has the capability and will to defend itself from the aggressions of others, constitutional protections of any sort have little meaning.

Wayte v. United States, 470 U.S. 598, 611–612, 105 S.Ct. 1524, 84 L.Ed.2d 547 (1985). The district court, in its fact finding process, understandably felt shackled by the government's unwillingness to provide Kiareldeen the names and addresses of its counter-terrorism personnel, both in uniform and in civilian clothes. Nonetheless, the public fisc should not lightly be exposed to financial penalties when the war on terrorism is transferred from the domestic battlefield that our country has become, to the vacuum-sealed environment of a federal courtroom, with such civilized accouterments as burdens of proof and axioms of evidence.

Kiareldeen v. Ashcroft, 273 F.3d 542, 552–53, 555–56 (3d Cir. 2001), *rev'g Kiareldeen v. Reno*, 92 F. Supp. 2d 403 (D.N.J. 2000).

NOTES AND QUESTIONS ON THE USE OF SECRET EVIDENCE

1.   The district court relies heavily on *Rafeedie*. Is that reliance appropriate? Rafeedie had been admitted as a lawful permanent resident. Kiareldeen had several years of de facto residence in the United States, but most of his ties, including his employment, were acquired only after he violated the terms of his nonimmigrant admission. For an argument that immigration status should be considered in the *Eldridge* due process balance, and that the interest of LPRs should be given the greatest weight (while still affording some protections for other noncitizens), see Martin, *Graduated Application, supra*, 2001 Sup. Ct. Rev. at 84–101. *See also* Ramji–Nogales, *A Global Approach to Secret Evidence: How Human Rights Law Can Reform Our Immigration System*, 39 Colum. Hum. Rts. L.Rev. 287 (2008); Akram, *Scheherezade Meets Kafka: Two Dozen Sordid Tales of Ideological Exclusion*, 14 Geo. Immig. L.J. 51 (1999); Frenzen, *National Security and Procedural Fairness: Secret Evidence and the Immigration Laws*, 76 Interp. Rel. 1677 (1999) (arguing against the use of secret evidence or for greater protections).

2.   How do you evaluate the competing visions of the government's interest, in *Eldridge* terms, offered by the district court and the court of appeals? Which has the better view? Even if you are persuaded by the higher court's assessment of the weight of the government's interest, how should the *Eldridge* balance come out? Some of the answer to this question may depend on the possibility and nature of alternative safeguards for the individual, even if direct access to the classified information is denied. Part (iii) below explores certain possible alternatives.

3.   In 2002, the regulations were amended to provide more precise procedures for the submission of evidence under seal, including in national security-related cases, and for the issuance of a protective order forbidding respondent and counsel, as well as others, from disclosing the covered information. 8 C.F.R. § 1003.46.

(iii) The Alien Terrorist Removal Court

The Alien Terrorist Removal Court (ATRC) represents one possible alternative framework for the use of secret evidence. *See* INA §§ 501–507. Because classified information can be withheld from the respondent under INA § 235(c) for an "arriving alien," and under § 240 to contest discretionary relief for any noncitizen, the government has no need to invoke the more complex arrangements of the ATRC unless it needs the information to prove baseline removability for an alien who is not an arriving alien.

Practically, this means that the ATRC will likely be used only to remove a permanent resident, or possibly a nonimmigrant in valid immigration status (though in the latter case the government might choose to wait until that nonimmigrant status expires before initiating removal proceedings). As of this writing no case has ever been brought in the ATRC, but the structure merits close examination, not only because the court may be convened in the future, but also because of the vision these provisions set forth of an alternative set of procedures to protect important individual interests while still meeting core government security objectives. In fact, procedures roughly along the lines set forth for the ATRC have in fact been used increasingly since 2001 in judicial settings, mentioned in the notes below, where a government seeks to shelter classified information.

The ATRC consists of five federal district judges appointed to this court by the Chief Justice of the United States for five-year terms. INA § 502(a). These judges are full life-tenured Article III judges; when not conducting ATRC business, they retain their normal district court responsibilities. The ATRC hears cases only if the Attorney General submits an application under INA § 503. The special ATRC procedures apply if the Attorney General certifies, and a single judge of the removal court determines: that the charged noncitizen is an "alien terrorist," that the person is physically present in the United States, and that his removal under normal procedures "would pose a risk to the national security of the United States." INA § 503(a), (c). An "alien terrorist" is any alien deportable under § 237(a)(4)(B), which now includes any admitted alien described in the broad terrorism inadmissibility ground, INA § 212(a)(3)(B). The Attorney General may take into custody any person who is the subject of such certification. Permanent residents are given a hearing to decide on release while the case is pending. *See* INA § 506.

A public hearing follows "as expeditiously as practicable." *See* INA § 504. The respondent must be given notice, including "a general account of the basis for the charges." He has the right to be present and to be represented by counsel, including appointed counsel for any person financially unable to obtain counsel. Information may not be disclosed "if disclosure would present a risk to the national security of the United States." Where removal is to be based on any such information, the judge must examine it *ex parte* and *in camera*. The respondent generally receives only an unclassified summary of the classified information. But he does not get even that summary if the judge finds that "(I) the continued presence of the alien in the United States would likely cause serious and irreparable harm to the national security or death or serious bodily injury to any person, and (II) the provision of the summary would likely cause serious and irreparable harm to the national security or death or serious bodily injury to any person." INA § 504(e)(3). In such cases, if the respondent is a lawful permanent resident, the judge appoints a "special attorney" to represent the individual, an attorney who has received an appropriate clearance to examine secret information. *See* § 502(e). That attorney's role is to review and challenge the classified information *in camera*. A special attorney who discloses the information "to the alien or to any other attorney representing the alien" is subject to substantial criminal penalties. INA § 504(e)(3)(F).

NOTES AND QUESTIONS ON SAFEGUARDS WHEN SECRET EVIDENCE IS USED

1. What are the strengths and weaknesses of the ATRC? Do its procedures satisfy due process, especially as applied to lawful permanent residents? Should the statute be amended to permit using this procedure in a wider class of cases where secret evidence is involved? Which cases? Consider, for example, asylum cases where the government submits classified information for the immigration judge's *in camera* review as part of its evidence in opposition to the claim. The regulations already provide that when the government uses classified information in an asylum case, it shall provide an unclassified summary that is "as detailed as possible, in order that the applicant may have an opportunity to offer opposing evidence." 8 C.F.R. § 1240.33(c)(4). What other protections would the ATRC procedures entail?

2. It may be useful to compare due process requirements in criminal prosecutions:

> In proceedings where the fullest measure of due process protection unmistakably applies, criminal trials, secret evidence simply cannot be used as the basis for a prosecution. The Fifth and Sixth Amendments generally require giving the defendant the details of the government's case and affording the right to cross-examine adverse witnesses. If the classified information is needed for the case in chief, the government is put to a choice whether to "burn the asset"—that is, pull in the informant and shield him in other ways after he testifies in open court, thereby losing future information—or else abandon the prosecution. Should a similar rule apply to immigration proceedings? The black-letter law holds that deportation is not punishment, thereby making criminal law protections not directly applicable. But it also provides that deportable aliens are entitled to procedural due process protection, superintended by the courts, in removal proceedings. If the potential for unfairness is so great, perhaps results similar to those in criminal proceedings should obtain. [The author goes on to explore other "middle ground" arrangements that might be more appropriate for various types of immigration proceedings.]

Martin, *Graduated Application, supra,* 2001 Sup. Ct. Rev. at 129–30.

For certain matters that do not go to the heart of the criminal charges, however, provision has been made for sheltering the classified information while making available to the accused unclassified summaries or other substitutes. Congress provided for such procedures, identifying the circumstances in which they would be appropriate, in the Classified Information Procedures Act (CIPA). 18 U.S.C. App. 3 §§ 1–16. In the prosecution of Zacarias Moussaoui, who was charged with conspiracy with the September 11 plotters, the court crafted procedures by analogy to CIPA that gave the accused access to unclassified summaries of classified statements by detainees at Guantánamo, as a substitute for interviewing those witnesses to seek information that might help in his defense. *United States v. Moussaoui,* 365 F.3d 292, 312–17 (4th Cir. 2004).

3. In a related arena, the cases challenging the detention of U.S. prisoners at Guantánamo have often involved the use of classified evidence. The Supreme Court in *Boumediene v. Bush,* 553 U.S. 723, 128 S.Ct. 2229, 171 L.Ed.2d 41 (2008), held that the constitutional guarantee of habeas corpus applies at Guantánamo, but left most of the substantive and procedural details to be resolved by the district courts hearing these cases. The district court has proceeded by way of requiring the government to prepare an unclassified summary, reviewed for adequacy by the judge, who has access to the unredacted information. Moreover, the executive branch, after background checks, has granted secret-level security clearances to certain counsel for the petitioners, so that they can have access to much of the evidence and can thus challenge the validity or significance of the secret information before the judge *in camera,* even when it cannot be disclosed to the client. *See In re Guantanamo Bay Detainee Litigation,* 577 F.Supp.2d 143 (D.D.C. 2008). *See also* Barak–Erez & Waxman, *Secret Evidence and the Due Process of Terrorism Detentions,* 48 Colum.J. Transnat'l L. 3 (2009) (comparative study involving United Kingdom, Canadian, Israeli and U.S. procedures, finding common components, albeit with many variations: requirements that the individual receive the core or gist of the information in unclassified form, that the judge take an expanded management role *in camera,* and that some form of special advocate with security clearance have access to the information on behalf of the individual).

4. Surprisingly, despite the various avenues available for the use of secret evidence in removal proceedings, the government has rarely even attempted to employ such information since 2001. *See* Eggen, *U.S. Uses Secret Evidence in Secrecy Fight with ACLU,* Wash. Post, Aug. 20, 2004, at A17 (reporting expert views that secret evidence has been rarely used since the late 1990s). This may result from far more rigorous internal review procedures, adopted by the Justice Department in 1999 following several court setbacks, including the initial ruling in *Kiareldeen,* but no public explanation has been offered. *See* Martin, *Offshore Detainees and the Role of Courts after Rasul v. Bush,* 25 Boston Coll. Third World L.J. 125, 157 (2005).

d. Public Access

A related issue came to a head in 2002. The regulations give an immigration judge the discretion to limit attendance or to close a removal hearing to the public "[f]or the purpose of protecting witnesses, parties, or the public interest." 8 C.F.R. § 1003.27. Though this power has long been exercised case by case, soon after the September 11 attacks, the Department of Justice issued a directive to close off access on a blanket basis to several hundred removal proceedings involving noncitizens determined by the Department to be of "special interest," going so far as to order employees not to confirm or deny whether such cases were even on the docket. The practice was challenged, primarily by press organizations, claiming violation of a First Amendment right of access. The Court of Appeals for the Sixth Circuit held that access was required:

> Democracies die behind closed doors. The First Amendment, through a free press, protects the people's right to know that their government acts fairly, lawfully, and accurately in deportation proceedings. When government begins closing doors, it selectively controls information rightfully belonging to the people. Selective information is misinformation. The Framers of the First Amendment "did not trust any government to separate the true from the false for us." *Kleindienst v. Mandel.* They protected the people against secret government.

* * *

> Under the two-part "experience and logic" test from *Richmond Newspapers [Inc. v. Virginia*, 448 U.S. 555, 100 S.Ct. 2814, 65 L.Ed.2d 973 (1980)], we conclude that there is a First Amendment right of access to deportation proceedings. Deportation hearings, and similar proceedings, have traditionally been open to the public, and openness undoubtedly plays a significant positive role in this process.

* * *

> The Government's ongoing anti-terrorism investigation certainly implicates a compelling interest. However, the [closure] directive is neither narrowly tailored, nor does it require particularized findings. Therefore, it impermissibly infringes on the Newspaper Plaintiffs' First Amendment right of access.

Detroit Free Press v. Ashcroft, 303 F.3d 681, 683, 700, 705 (6th Cir. 2002).

Shortly thereafter, the Third Circuit reached the opposite result in *North Jersey Media Group v. Ashcroft*, 308 F.3d 198 (3d Cir. 2002), *cert. denied*, 538 U.S. 1056, 123 S.Ct. 2215, 155 L.Ed.2d 1106 (2003). The court found no historical right of access:

> We ultimately do not believe that deportation hearings boast a tradition of openness sufficient to satisfy *Richmond Newspapers* * * * [especially in light of] evidence that some deportation proceedings were, and are, explicitly closed to the public or conducted in places unlikely to allow general public access. * * *

Id. at 212. Continuing to apply *Richmond Newspapers*, the court next considered "whether public access plays a significant role in the functioning of the particular process in question." The court acknowl-edged that "a number of newspapers have editorialized favorably upon Judge Keith's eloquent language in the *Detroit Free Press* case." But the court continued:

> Others have been less impressed. Michael Kelly has written in the Washington Post:
>
>> *"Democracies die behind closed doors."* So they do, some-times. But far more democracies have succumbed to open assaults of one sort or another—invasions from without, military coups and totalitarian revolutions from within—than from the usurpa-tion-by-in-camera-incrementalism that Judge Keith fears.
>>
>> Democracy in America does at this moment face a serious threat. But it is not the threat the judge has in mind, at least not directly. It is true that last September's unprecedented mass-slaughter of American citizens on American soil inevitably forced the government to take security measures that infringed on some rights and privileges. But these do not in themselves represent any real threat to democracy. A real threat could arise, however, should the government fail in its mission to prevent another September 11. If that happens, the public will demand, and will get, immense restrictions on liberties.
>
> Although Mr. Kelly ultimately sided with openness on a case-by-case basis, we find his quoted statements powerful. They certainly seem appropriate to the decision to close the deportation hearings of those who may have been affiliated with the persons responsible for the events of September 11th, all of the known perpetrators of which were aliens. And they are consonant with the reality that the persons most directly affected by the [closure directive] are the media, not the aliens who may be deported. As always, these aliens are given a heavy measure of due process—the right to appeal the decision of the Immigration Judge (following the closed hearing) to the Board of Immigration Appeals (BIA) and the right to petition for review of the BIA decision to the Regional Court of Appeals.

308 F.3d at 220.

By the time the issue was presented to the Supreme Court, nearly all the closed removal hearings had been concluded and most of the respon-dents deported. The Court denied certiorari. Thereafter, blanket closure ceased, and the immigration courts have returned to the practice of infrequent case-by-case closure.

5. A SECOND CHANCE?

a. Introduction

So far we have examined what happens from the NTA to a final removal order. Is there any chance to revisit what happened in the proceeding and correct errors? Of course, direct appeal is available, first to the Board of Immigration and Appeals and then in most circumstances to a federal court of appeals. But in a surprisingly large number of cases (though still a modest percentage), a noncitizen finds good reason to present new evidence or argument after losing on direct appeal or after the appeal time has already run. Often this discovery is associated with obtaining new counsel—or obtaining counsel for the first time—perhaps shortly before the date when removal is scheduled.

Noncitizens board an ICE removal flight from Buffalo, New York,
to Liberia, Ghana, and Nigeria, August 2007.
(Photo: Department of Homeland Security)

To fill out our picture of removal proceedings, we explore here two cases from the courts of appeals, *Saakian* and *Anin*, which set forth three linked issues: (1) *in absentia* removal orders, (2) ineffective assistance of counsel, and (3) motions to reopen. These issues may seem analytically distinct from each other, but they often arise together, and they share this fundamental question: what is the best balance between the need for finality in immigration court decisions and the need for confidence that those decisions are accurate?

Before reading the two cases, take a look at the general statutory provisions governing motions to reopen or to reconsider, INA §§ 240(c)(6) and (7). The statute and the regulations provide the following basic framework for these motions. (There are additional and specialized rules governing several details of motions to reopen in order to challenge an *in* absentia removal order; those details are addressed in the *Saakian* and *Anin* decisions below, and in the notes following those cases.) Motions to reopen are used to offer previously unavailable, material evidence; here INA § 240(c)(7) and 8 C.F.R. § 1003.2 govern. A motion to reconsider is different; it asks for review of claimed errors in an earlier appraisal of the law or the facts. *See* INA § 240(c)(6). These motions are to be filed with either the immigration judge or the BIA—whichever adjudicating body last considered the case. Filing a motion to reopen or reconsider does not automatically stay the execution of a removal order (unless it is a motion to reopen an *in absentia* order). But immigration judges, the BIA, and certain DHS officers have discretion to stay removal pending a decision. 8 C.F.R. §§ 241.6, 1003.2(f), 1003.23(b)(1)(v).

Generally, only one motion to reopen and one motion to reconsider may be filed. A motion to reconsider must be filed within 30 days and a motion to reopen within 90 days of entry of a final removal order. The statute sets out exceptions to the 90–day deadline, primarily for battered spouses, changed circumstances affecting an asylum claim, and challenges to *in absentia* removal orders. INA § 240(c)(7)(C). Importantly, the statute's numerical and time limits apply only to motions filed by the noncitizen, not DHS. Therefore respondent's counsel seeking to file a belated motion often seeks to persuade the ICE attorney that a gross mistake was made, and that ICE should therefore agree to file a joint motion to reopen, which would obviate any late filing problem. In addition, the Board or immigration judge may at any time reopen *sua sponte*, though this power is to be used in "exceptional situations," and not "as a general cure for filing defects or to otherwise circumvent the regulations, where enforcing them might result in hardship." *Matter of J–J–*, 21 I & N Dec. 976, 984 (1997). *See* 8 C.F.R. §§ 1003.2(a), 1003.23(b)(1). Judicial review of a motion to reopen must be consolidated with review of the underlying order. INA § 242(b)(6).

In *INS v. Abudu*, 485 U.S. 94, 108 S.Ct. 904, 99 L.Ed.2d 90 (1988), the U.S. Supreme Court discussed the standards for judicial review of decisions to grant or deny a motion to reopen. Abudu, a citizen of Ghana, had overstayed his student visa. After he pleaded guilty to drug charges in 1981, Abudu was ordered deported in 1982, and in 1984 the BIA dismissed his appeal. In 1985, Abudu moved to reopen so that he could apply for asylum, seeking to introduce new facts that he believed would show his life and freedom would be threatened if he returned to Ghana. In upholding the BIA's denial of Abudu's motion, the Court explained:

> There are at least three independent grounds on which the BIA may deny a motion to reopen. First, it may hold that the movant has not established a *prima facie* case for the underlying substantive relief sought. * * *. Second, the BIA may hold that the movant has not introduced previously unavailable, material evidence, or, in an asylum application case, that the movant has not reasonably explained his failure to apply for asylum initially. * * * We decide today that the appropriate standard of review of such denials is abuse of discretion.[e] Third, in cases in which the ultimate grant of relief is discretionary, * * * the BIA may leap ahead, as it were, over the two threshold

---

e. Abuse of discretion is a standard of review that is generally highly deferential to the administrative determination. We will consider standards for judicial review in Section C of this chapter.—eds.

concerns (prima facie case and new evidence/reasonable explanation), and simply determine that even if they were met, the movant would not be entitled to the discretionary grant of relief. We have consistently held that denials on this third ground are subject to an abuse-of-discretion standard.

485 U.S. at 104–05, 108 S.Ct. at 912.

SAAKIAN v. INS

United States Court of Appeals, First Circuit, 2001.
252 F.3d 21.

STAHL, SENIOR CIRCUIT JUDGE.

* * *

I. BACKGROUND

Saakian, a native and citizen of Armenia, entered the United States on November 13, 1993, as a non-immigrant visitor for pleasure. He was accompanied by his father and stepmother. The family's visas authorized them to remain in the United States until May 12, 1994. On January 12, 1994, Saakian's father applied for asylum on behalf of the three of them. The record is silent as to the disposition of this application.

On June 26, 1996, Saakian filed his own individual request for asylum, about which he was interviewed by the Immigration and Naturalization Service (INS) on September 17, 1996. His request was denied on September 30, 1996, and an Order to Show Cause issued, stating that Saakian was deportable because he had stayed in the United States beyond the time allowed by his visa. This Order was served on Saakian on October 16, 1996, and it directed him to appear before an IJ on November 20, 1996. When Saakian appeared on that date, he was told to return for a full hearing on March 19, 1997.

Saakian thereafter retained Connie Frentzos, of the Khmer Humanitarian Organization in Los Angeles, to represent him in the proceeding. Frentzos is not an attorney, though Saakian alleges that he believed that she was one at the time he retained her. Despite her non-attorney status, Frentzos is authorized by the Executive Office for Immigration Review to represent aliens in deportation proceedings. On March 4, 1997, Frentzos filed a motion to change venue from Boston to Los Angeles because Saakian intended to relocate there. According to Saakian, Frentzos thereafter advised him that the motion rendered it unnecessary for him to appear at the March 19 hearing. Saakian, allegedly acting on this advice, did not appear at the hearing. The IJ subsequently ordered him deported *in absentia.*

On April 18, 1997, Saakian filed with the IJ a motion to reopen, stating that his failure to appear was caused by his belief that he did not have to show up because of the pending motion to change venue. He filed this motion *pro se,* near the beginning of the 180–day period provided by law for filing such a motion. The INS filed its opposition to this motion on April 25, 1997, arguing that the motion to change venue did not excuse Saakian's absence. On April 28, 1997, only ten days after Saakian had filed his motion, he filed a supporting affidavit, in which he stated that his erroneous belief was the result of bad advice from Frentzos, who had told him not to appear. He did not specifically allege "ineffective assistance of counsel" at this stage, but he did allege facts which, if true, could be defined as ineffective assistance.

On June 19, 1997, the IJ denied Saakian's motion to reopen. In that order, the IJ construed Saakian's claim as one of ineffective assistance of counsel, and proceeded to note that only one of the three evidentiary requirements for such claims, as set forth in *Matter of Lozada,* 19 I & N Dec. 637, 639 (BIA 1988), had been met by Saakian. Although Saakian had filed his motion *pro se,* and was well within the 180–day window for filing motions to reopen, the IJ did not give him an opportunity to satisfy the other two *Lozada* requirements. Instead, he denied the motion in language suggesting that Saakian was foreclosed from remedying the deficiencies in his motion.

Saakian timely appealed to the BIA. In his appellate papers Saakian requested, and was granted, additional time to retain an attorney before briefing the appeal. The appeal alleged, *inter alia,* that the IJ's *de facto* denial with prejudice of his motion to reopen deprived him of due process under the circumstances of this case. Along with his appellate brief, counsel submitted to the BIA the remaining documents required by *Lozada.*

On May 26, 2000, the BIA dismissed Saakian's appeal. It noted that, because Saakian had not met all three *Lozada* requirements when he initially filed his motion to reopen, the IJ had properly denied it. The BIA did not address Saakian's due process claim on the merits. Saakian now petitions us to review the BIA's decision.

II. DISCUSSION

In his petition, Saakian argues that, under the facts of this case, the IJ and BIA denied him due process by denying his motion to reopen with prejudice. In Saakian's view, due process required that he be afforded the opportunity to satisfy the *Lozada* requirements and have his ineffective assistance claim heard on the merits. We agree.

Deportation is a civil, not a criminal, proceeding; as such, there is no Sixth Amendment right to counsel. Nonetheless, "[i]t is well established that the Fifth Amendment entitles aliens to due process of law in deportation proceedings." *Reno v. Flores,* 507 U.S. 292, 306, 113 S.Ct. 1439, 123 L.Ed.2d 1 (1993) (citing *The Japanese Immigrant Case,* 189 U.S. 86, 100–101, 23 S.Ct. 611, 47 L.Ed. 721 (1903)).

In *Bridges v. Wixon,* the Supreme Court emphasized the importance of strictly protecting an alien's right to procedural due process:

Here the liberty of an individual is at stake.... We are dealing here with procedural requirements prescribed for the protection of the alien. Though deportation is not technically a criminal proceeding, it visits a great hardship on the individual and deprives him of the right to stay and live and work in this land of freedom. That deportation is a penalty—at times a most serious one—cannot be doubted. Meticulous care must be exercised lest the procedure by which he is deprived of that liberty not meet the essential standards of fairness.

326 U.S. 135, 154, 65 S.Ct. 1443, 89 L.Ed. 2103 (1945).

Aliens have a statutory right to be represented by counsel, at their own expense, in deportation proceedings. That right is "an integral part of the procedural due process to which the alien is entitled." *Batanic v. INS,* 12 F.3d 662, 667 (7th Cir. 1993). Ineffective assistance of counsel exists where, as a result of counsel's actions (or lack thereof), "the proceeding was so fundamentally unfair that the alien was prevented from reasonably presenting his case." *Bernal–Vallejo v. INS,* 195 F.3d 56, 63 (1st Cir. 1999). It is generally also expected that the alien show at least a reasonable probability of prejudice. The BIA has held, however, that the prejudice requirement does not apply in cases where an order was issued on the basis of a hearing held *in absentia.*

As a procedural matter, a claim of ineffective assistance of counsel is typically raised through a motion to reopen, which can be brought before either the BIA or the IJ directly. * * * [W]here an order has been entered against the alien *in absentia,* the alien has 180 days from that order to file any motions to reopen, assuming the alien can demonstrate that the failure to appear was caused by exceptional circumstances beyond his control. The BIA has stated that incompetent representation qualifies as an "exceptional circumstance." *In re Grijalva–Barrera,* 21 I & N Dec. 472, 473–74 (BIA 1996). Moreover, there is no numerical limit on the number of motions to reopen an alien may file pursuant to this provision. Saakian thus was entitled to file multiple motions to reopen during the 180–day period.

As to the contents of a motion to reopen, the regulation requires that the motion "state the new facts that will be proven at a hearing to be held if the motion is granted and ... be supported by affidavits and other evidentiary material." 8 C.F.R. § 1003.23(b)(3). "Claims of ineffective assistance of counsel satisfy the general requirement that motions to reopen present 'new facts' that are 'material and [were] not available and could not have been discovered or presented at the former hearing.'" *Iavorski v. INS,* 232 F.3d 124, 129 (2d Cir. 2000) (brackets in original).

In *Matter of Lozada,* the BIA specified the documents an alien is expected to file with a motion to reopen founded upon ineffective assistance of counsel. 19 I & N Dec. 637, 639 (BIA 1988). There, the BIA stated that when an alien makes such a claim to the Board, the motion should be supported by 1) an affidavit setting forth "in detail the agreement that was entered into with former counsel with respect to the actions to be taken," as well as any representations made by counsel to the alien; 2) proof that the movant has informed former counsel of the allegations in writing, as well as any response received; and 3) a statement detailing "whether a complaint has been filed with appropriate disciplinary authorities regarding such representation, and if not, why not."

* * *

We have not had occasion to decide whether a failure to satisfy the *Lozada* requirements in an initial motion to reopen justifies a denial of the motion with prejudice to its being subsequently refiled. But the Ninth Circuit has consistently held that, "[a]lthough the BIA acts within its discretion to impose the heightened *Lozada* procedural requirements, it may not impose the *Lozada* requirements arbitrarily." *Ontiveros–Lopez v. INS,* 213 F.3d 1121, 1124–25 (9th Cir. 2000) (internal citations omitted). We agree. Furthermore, we regard this as a case involving an arbitrary application of *Lozada.*

As we have noted, Saakian filed his *Lozada*-deficient motion a mere one month into the 180–day period provided for filing a motion to reopen an *in absentia* deportation order. Despite this fact, and despite Saakian's *pro se* status, the IJ denied the motion without either inviting Saakian to remedy its deficiencies or noting Saakian's entitlement to file a second, properly supported motion. Moreover, in ruling as he did, the IJ actually used language seeming to suggest that, by filing a deficient motion, Saakian had lost his one and only opportunity to allege ineffective assistance of counsel. Elevating form over substance, the BIA then upheld this course of conduct without analysis. As a result, Saakian's ineffective assistance of counsel claim has not been examined, despite Saakian's persistent efforts to have it heard. This violates due process.

* * *

Here, the BIA did not analyze the merits of Saakian's claim based on the *Lozada* materials he had submitted, even though he was entitled, as an in absentia deportee, to more than one bite at the apple. The BIA's refusal to consider his newly formed *Lozada* claim was also despite the fact that Saakian had not been provided with an adequate opportunity to fulfill *Lozada*'s requirements with the IJ. As a result, Saakian did what he was supposed to do in order to be heard on the merits (prepared an affidavit, notified Frentzos, and filed complaints against her), but, nonetheless, his claim never was heard on the merits.

III. CONCLUSION

For the reasons stated, we grant Saakian's petition for review, and remand to the BIA for further proceedings consistent with this opinion.

ANIN v. RENO

United States Court of Appeals, Eleventh Circuit, 1999.
188 F.3d 1273.

PER CURIAM:

* * *

I

Petitioner Alexis Anin, a native of Burkina–Faso, entered the United States on October 30, 1991 with a C–1 visa as an "alien in transit." The visa gave him permission to remain in the United States only until the next day. However, Anin did not depart as required and remained in the United States without seeking approval from the Immigration and Naturalization Service ("INS"). During this time he met Linda McSwain, a United States citizen, and married her on January 14, 1994. On July 26, 1994, the INS concluded that Anin had entered into a sham marriage for the purpose of obtaining immigration benefits and issued an order to show cause * * *. While in custody, pursuant to the order to show cause, Anin filed an application for asylum. His wife also filed an I–130 Visa Petition seeking permanent residence status for Anin.

On November 16, 1994, the Immigration Court scheduled a February 21, 1995 hearing on these matters, and sent notice of the hearing by certified mail to Anin's attorney of record. The notice was received and signed by someone in the office of Anin's attorney. Neither Anin nor his attorney appeared at the February hearing. At the hearing, a deportation order for Anin was entered *in absentia.* Later, after being notified of an interview for the I–130 Visa Petition, Anin and his wife appeared at the INS office in Atlanta and Anin was taken into custody. At that point, Anin's counsel of record claimed that he had not received notice of the deportation hearing. The attorney then informed Anin that he would be able to reopen the case. This conversation marked the first time that Anin learned of the deportation order entered *in absentia* against him.

A motion then was filed to reopen the deportation proceedings on account of the attorney's lack of notice. The Immigration Court denied the motion after Anin's attorney admitted that a member of his staff received and signed for the notice of the deportation hearing. Anin's lawyer never informed his client that his firm actually had received notice of the hearing. Moreover, he advised Anin that the case would be reopened as soon as his wife's I–130 Petition was approved. The BIA denied Anin's appeal on March 7, 1996. Anin was never informed of this adverse decision by his lawyer.

In December 1996, Anin learned for the first time that his appeal to the BIA had been denied by way of a "bag and baggage" letter ordering Anin to report for deportation on February 1, 1997. Anin then went to his attorney's office and examined his case file where he learned that the original notice of hearing had been received by his attorney. Anin then sought the assistance of new counsel. On February 20, 1997, almost two years after the *in absentia* deportation order was issued, Anin filed a new motion to reopen his deportation order alleging lack of notice, and for the first time, exceptional circumstances of ineffective assistance of counsel, and a denial of due process. Anin and his wife also filed affidavits which outlined his ineffective assistance of counsel claim as required by law. *See Matter of Lozada,* 19 I & N Dec. 637 (BIA 1988).

On July 16, 1998, a majority of the BIA, with four members dissenting and two members not participating, denied the motion. The BIA held that Anin was time-barred * * * from advocating an "exceptional circumstance" exception to a denial of a motion to reopen a deportation order. The court ruled that the 180 day filing deadline was unambiguous and that even an ineffective assistance of counsel claim did not justify a statutory exemption. On August 10, 1998, Anin filed a petition to this Court for review of this decision.

II

This Court reviews the BIA's denial of Anin's motion to reopen his deportation order for abuse of discretion. *See INS v. Doherty,* 502 U.S. 314, 323–24, 112 S.Ct. 719, 116 L.Ed.2d 823 (1992). In this particular area, the BIA's discretion is quite " 'broad.' " *Id.* (quoting *INS v. Rios–Pineda,* 471 U.S. 444, 449, 105 S.Ct. 2098, 85 L.Ed.2d 452 (1985)). An immigration judge may conduct a scheduled deportation hearing *in absentia* if an alien fails to appear at the appointed time. However, a deportation order entered *in absentia* may be rescinded if a petitioner proves that his failure to appear resulted from exceptional circumstances or a lack of proper notice. Under this statutory framework, we evaluate Anin's petition to reopen his deportation proceedings.

The INA's plain language clearly allows the INS to fulfill its notice requirement in deportation proceedings by notifying an alien's attorney through certified mail. Anin concedes that his attorney of record at the time received notice of the February deportation hearing by certified mail in accordance with this provision of the INA. Furthermore, no statutory provision requires an alien to receive *actual* notice of a deportation proceeding. Indeed, the Code of Federal Regulations instructs that notice be provided to the attorney of record rather than the alien.

* * * The statute unambiguously holds Anin responsible for his lawyer's actions and omissions. Therefore, despite the fact that Anin may not have received actual notice, the BIA did not abuse its discretion in denying his motion to reopen his deportation proceeding.

Additionally, the fact that Anin did not receive actual notice of the deportation hearing does not present a violation of the Due Process Clause. Although procedural due process in the deportation context requires a meaningful and fair hearing with a reasonable opportunity to be heard, *see Landon v. Plasencia,* 459 U.S. 21, 32–33, 103 S.Ct. 321, 74

L.Ed.2d 21 (1982), it does not demand that an alien receive actual notice. Due process is satisfied if notice is accorded "in a manner 'reasonably calculated' to ensure that notice reaches the alien." *Farhoud v. INS,* 122 F.3d 794, 796 (9th Cir. 1997) (quoting *United States v. Estrada–Trochez,* 66 F.3d 733, 736 & 736 n.1 (5th Cir. 1995)); *cf. Mullane v. Central Hanover Bank & Trust Co.,* 339 U.S. 306, 318, 70 S.Ct. 652, 94 L.Ed. 865 (1950) (finding that "notice must be such as is reasonably calculated to reach interested parties"). In this case, the INS simply followed the INA statute and chose a method of notice authorized by the statute—a method Congress itself determined was reasonably calculated to ensure proper notice. This method of notification does not violate an alien's due process rights. So long as the method of notification was "reasonably calculated" to procure notice, the notice requirements of due process are satisfied. *Id.* For this reason, the BIA's refusal to reopen Anin's deportation proceeding did not violate due process.

The BIA also did not err in refusing to reopen Anin's deportation order based on an ineffective assistance claim. Section [240(b)(5)(C)(i)] of the INA contains a 180 day filing deadline to contest deportation orders if "exceptional circumstances" arise such as ineffective assistance. All exceptional circumstances claims must be filed 180 days from the date of the deportation order. Notably, Anin filed his exceptional circumstances appeal almost two years after the *in absentia* deportation order was issued. As a result, Anin's appeal is statutorily time-barred. Congressional filing deadlines are given a literal reading by federal courts. * * * The provision is jurisdictional and mandatory. As a result, no exceptions have been carved into the 180 day filing deadline by federal courts. More generally, no exception to an INA deadline has been found even where an alien acts blamelessly.

Filing deadlines inherently are arbitrary and harsh. As the Supreme Court has explained, "filing deadlines, like statutes of limitations, necessarily operate harshly and arbitrarily with respect to persons who fall just on the other side of them, but if the concept is to have any content, the deadline must be enforced." [*United States v. Locke,* 471 U.S. 84, 91, 105 S.Ct. 1785, 85 L.Ed.2d 64 (1985).] Here, Anin did not even narrowly miss the filing deadline. He filed late not by a day or so but by almost two years. To allow an exception in this case would stretch the filing provisions too far. As the Supreme Court has instructed, "with respect to filing deadlines a literal reading of Congress' words is generally the only proper reading of those words." *Id.* Based on these authorities, the statute's plain language, and general principles of statutory construction, we can find no exception to the 180 day filing deadline.

Lastly, the BIA did not abuse its discretion by not reopening Anin's deportation order under 8 C.F.R. [§ 1003.2(a)]. The provision reposes very broad discretion in the BIA "to reopen or reconsider" any motion it has rendered at any time or, on the other hand, "[to] deny a motion to reopen." The discretion accorded in this provision is so wide that "even if the party moving has made out a prima facie case for relief," the BIA can deny a motion to reopen a deportation order. No language in the provision requires the BIA to reopen a deportation proceeding under any set of particular circumstances. Instead, the provision merely provides the BIA the discretion to reopen immigration proceedings as it sees fit. Federal circuit courts consistently have interpreted the provision in this way. They have read 8 C.F.R. [§ 1003.2(a)] to give the BIA the discretion to reopen immigration proceedings in situations where federal courts lack the legal authority to mandate reopening. In short, the provision gives the BIA non-reviewable discretion to dismiss Anin's claim. We can find no abuse of discretion here.

Accordingly, we affirm.

NOTES AND QUESTIONS ON THE ISSUES RAISED BY SAAKIAN AND ANIN

1. Both *Saakian* and *Anin* ask: what is the best balance between fairness and finality? On the one hand, it seems unfair—and arguably a violation of due process—to burden a noncitizen with representation that is incompetent or even deceptive. But when does the system's interest in finality justify the response that clients must live with their choice of lawyers and that at some point it is simply too late to contest removal? What is your assessment of the answers provided by each of these decisions?

One difference between the two cases is that the 180 days had run before the motion was filed in *Anin* but not in *Saakian*. Does this explain the different outcomes? Does it justify them? Or do the differences that matter run deeper?

2. Both cases discuss the constitutional underpinnings of ineffective assistance of counsel doctrine. Addressing this issue, an oft-cited decision held that a noncitizen "must show not merely ineffective assistance of counsel, but assistance which is so ineffective as to have impinged upon the fundamental fairness of the hearing in violation of the fifth amendment due process clause." *Magallanes–Damian v. INS*, 783 F.2d 931, 933 (9th Cir. 1986) *See also Dakane v. U.S. Att'y Gen.*, 399 F.3d 1269, 1273–74 (11th Cir. 2005).

b. *In Absentia* Orders

Background and statistics. Bond and detention may help ensure that noncitizens appear at removal hearings, but a 1989 study by the General Accounting Office partly attributed a nonappearance rate of 27 percent to INS' inadequate notification of the time or place of hearings, and to the absence of serious penalties (other than forfeiture of bond) for failure to appear. General Accounting Office, Immigration Control: Deporting and Excluding Aliens from the United States 3 (1989). These findings led Congress in 1990 to adopt detailed provisions meant to provide for more effective use of *in absentia* orders.

In FY 2002, about 25 percent of immigration judge decisions involved noncitizens who failed to appear, which led to the issuance of an *in absentia* order in over 80 percent of these cases. This non-appearance rate held steady through FY 2004. In both FY 2005 and FY 2006, the nonappearance rate rose to 39 percent, with an *in absentia* order issued in over 90 percent of these cases; in FY 2006 this totaled 102,834 *in absentia* orders. *See* Executive Office for Immigration Review, Department of Justice, FY 2006 Statistical Year Book, at H1–H2. In FY 2007, the non-appearance rate fell to 16 percent, and has slowly declined since then, to 12 percent in FY 2010. (Much of the decline can probably be attributed to DHS's decision in 2006 to end the "catch and release" policy, meaning that the agency provided sufficient detention space to hold virtually all persons apprehended at or near the land borders, rather than releasing many to await an immigration court hearing months later.) In FY 2010, immigration judges issued 26,790 *in absentia* orders, constituting 12 percent of their total decisions. FY 2010 Statistical Year Book, at H1–H–3. But the lower nonappearance figures may be somewhat misleading in view of the greater use of detention. The nonappearance rate for nondetained aliens has remained at around the 30 percent level since FY 2007, after peaking at 60 percent in 2005 and 2006.

A noncitizen ordered removed—whether *in absentia* or not—is inadmissible for ten years after removal or departure (for arriving aliens formally removed, the period is five years). *See* INA § 212(a)(9)(A). Moreover, a noncitizen ordered removed *in absentia* is ineligible for ten years for discretionary relief, *i.e.,* voluntary departure, cancellation of removal, adjustment of status, change of nonimmigrant classification, and registry. *See* INA § 240(b)(7). And under § 212(a)(6)(B), "an alien who without reasonable cause fails or refuses to attend or remain in attendance at a proceeding to determine the alien's inadmissibility or deportability" is inadmissible for five years after her departure or removal.

Rescission and equitable tolling of the deadline. INA § 240(b)(5) provides for *in absentia* orders against respondents who fail to appear at a removal hearing after receiving the notice required by statute. To rescind an *in absentia* order, the noncitizen must move to reopen by showing (1) lack of notice, (2) custody in a state or federal facility, or (3) "exceptional circumstances" (defined in INA § 240(e)(1)). A motion alleging grounds (1) or (2) can be filed at any time; for an exceptional circumstances claim, the statute requires filing within 180 days.

Anin reads the 180–day deadline as mandatory and jurisdictional, but several other circuits have found that the deadline is subject to equitable tolling to permit a late filing in cases where ineffective assistance of counsel is alleged, if the noncitizen moves with due diligence after learning of the entry of the order. *See, e.g., Iavorski v. INS,* 232 F.3d 124 (2d Cir. 2000); *Pervaiz v. Gonzales,* 405 F.3d 488 (7th Cir. 2005). *Anin's* stance against equitable tolling would appear to be bolstered by the U.S. Supreme Court's ruling in *Bowles v. Russell,* 551 U.S. 205, 127 S.Ct. 2360, 168 L.Ed.2d 96 (2007), which held that time limits *set by statute* for appealing judgments in civil cases to federal courts of appeals are jurisdictional and do not allow equitable exceptions. *Khan v. Gonzales,* 494 F.3d 255, 257–59 (2d Cir. 2007), distinguished *Bowles* in allowing an equitable exception to the 30–day deadline for appeals to the BIA, because that time limit was established in regulations. But the 180–day deadline for filing to rescind an *in absentia* order is provided by statute. Nonetheless, the Second Circuit has stated after *Bowles* that equitable tolling is still available, without mentioning that Supreme Court decision. *Aris v. Mukasey,* 517 F.3d 595, 599 (2d Cir. 2008). Other circuit rulings after *Bowles* have similarly indicated the continued availability of equitable tolling of deadlines for motions to reopen, though often in dicta. *See, e.g., Valencia v. Holder,* 657 F.3d 745 (8th Cir. 2011). (Interestingly, Attorney General Mukasey's ruling in *Compean,* described below, also permitted equitable tolling and ignored *Bowles.*)

Assuming a motion to reopen is timely, what besides incompetent representation could constitute "exceptional circumstances"? Look at the statutory definition in INA § 240(e)(1), and then consider these facts:

> On January 11, de Morales left his home in Boerne, Texas at approximately 7:00 a.m. to travel sixty miles to his 8:30 a.m. deportation hearing in San Antonio. The engine of his car died on the way to the hearing. Because de Morales was unable to repair the car himself or pay to have it towed to San Antonio and fixed there, he decided to try to get a ride home so that a relative could repair the car.

> At approximately 8:00 a.m., de Morales obtained a ride from a passing driver who took him to a grocery store in Boerne. From there, he called a relative who picked him up and drove him home. De Morales arrived home at approximately 8:50 a.m.

> De Morales attempted to call the immigration court in San Antonio when he arrived home but was unable to locate the phone number in the San Antonio phone book or in his notice of hearing. De Morales did not attempt any further correspondence with the immigration court until he received notice of the order of deportation entered against him. At that time, de Morales contacted an attorney who filed a motion to reopen the proceedings on his behalf.

Are these "exceptional circumstances"? *See de Morales v. INS,* 116 F.3d 145, 146–47, 148–49 (5th Cir. 1997). (Also try finding the phone number of the immigration court with jurisdiction over your residence.) *See generally* G. Seipp, *In Absentia* Removal Orders: Consequences and Remedies, 09–11 Imm. Briefings (2009).

c. Ineffective Assistance of Counsel

As *Saakian* notes, the BIA decision in *Matter of Lozada,* 19 I & N Dec. 637 (BIA 1988), sets forth procedural requirements for motions to reopen based on ineffective assistance of counsel. (Chapter Seven addressed ineffective assistance of counsel in a different setting associated with the Supreme Court case of *Padilla v. Kentucky*: when ineffective assistance in a prior criminal proceeding can be the basis for withdrawing a guilty plea.) In *Lozada,* the Board explained the reason for imposing its threefold requirements:

Where essential information is lacking, it is impossible to evaluate the substance of such a claim. * * * [T]he potential for abuse is apparent where no mechanism exists for allowing former counsel, whose integrity or competence is being impugned, to present his version of events if he so chooses, thereby discouraging baseless allegations. The requirement that disciplinary authorities be notified of breaches of professional conduct not only serves to deter meritless claims of ineffective representation but also highlights the standards which should be expected of attorneys who represent persons in immigration proceedings, the outcome of which may, and often does, have enormous significance for the person.

Id. at 639. Courts' insistence on compliance with *Lozada* has varied. *Compare Castillo–Perez v. INS,* 212 F.3d 518, 525–26 (9th Cir. 2000) (*Lozada* requirements should not be rigidly enforced); *and Yang v. Gonzales,* 478 F.3d 133, 142–43 (2d Cir. 2007) (only substantial compliance is necessary); *with Stroe v. INS,* 256 F.3d 498, 501–04 (7th Cir. 2001) (upholding denial of motion to reopen for failure to comply with *Lozada*).

In *Matter of Assaad,* 23 I & N Dec. 553 (BIA 2003), the BIA considered a challenge to *Lozada* that was based on the U.S. Supreme Court's decision in *Coleman v. Thompson,* 501 U.S. 722, 752–54, 111 S.Ct. 2546, 2566–68, 115 L.Ed.2d 640 (1991). The Court had held that where there is no constitutional right to appointed counsel in a criminal proceeding, there is no constitutional basis for a claim of ineffective assistance of counsel. In *Assaad,* the government argued that this reasoning from *Coleman* applies in removal proceedings and conflicts with *Lozada.* The BIA disagreed, distinguishing the Fifth Amendment due process underpinnings of ineffective assistance of counsel claims in removal proceedings. 23 I & N Dec. at 557–60.

Despite the BIA's ruling, DHS and the DOJ Office of Immigration Litigation remained interested in pressing the *Coleman* issue. In 2009, these lingering questions came to a head in a case that prompted the rare intervention of two attorneys general of the United States, one of whom reversed his predecessor. The case grew out of three separate removal proceedings. All three respondents were unlawfully in the United States, but each claimed some form of relief from removal. After an adverse ruling in his removal proceeding, each respondent moved to reopen, arguing that his attorney had rendered ineffective assistance of counsel by failing to present highly relevant evidence or failing to file an appellate brief. Applying prevailing law based on *Lozada,* the three immigration judges denied these motions, and the Board of Immigration Appeals (BIA) affirmed all three.

Attorney General Michael Mukasey then certified the cases to himself for consolidated review, in order, as he put it, to "review the Board's position on both the constitutional question and the question of how best to resolve an alien's claim that his removal proceeding was prejudiced by his lawyer's errors." *Matter of Compean,* 24 I & N Dec. 710, 714 (Att'y

Gen. 2009). His ultimate decision in *Compean* was handed down two weeks before President Bush left office.

Noting that several federal appeals courts in the six years since *Assaad* had found no constitutional right to effective assistance of counsel in removal proceedings, Mukasey overruled *Lozada* and *Assaad*. His reasoning went through three main steps. First, because deportation is civil, not criminal, the Fifth Amendment's Due Process Clause is the source of any constitutional right to counsel. Second, the performance of private counsel does not constitute state action, which is normally required for a due process violation. Third, and most directly addressing the central issue in the case, the Constitution does not guarantee counsel at all, so there is no constitutional right to effective assistance of counsel. Nonetheless, "as a matter of sound discretion," *id.* at 727, the Attorney General directed that there be remedies for noncitizens who could show egregious errors by counsel and clear prejudice: "In extraordinary cases, where a lawyer's deficient performance likely changed the outcome of an alien's removal proceedings, the Board may reopen those proceedings notwithstanding the absence of a constitutional right to such relief." *Id.* at 714. He went on to outline procedures and requirements for such filings, tracking much of *Lozada,* but imposing more detailed and rigorous requirements.

In the fifth month of the Obama administration, Attorney General Eric Holder vacated his predecessor's decision.

MATTER OF COMPEAN

Attorney General of the United States, 2009
25 I & N Dec. 1.

ATTORNEY GENERAL HOLDER:

On January 7, 2009, Attorney General Mukasey overruled in part the decisions of the Board of Immigration Appeals in *Matter of Lozada*, 19 I. & N. Dec. 637 (BIA 1988), and *Matter of Assaad*, 23 I. & N. Dec. 553 (BIA 2003), and affirmed the Board's orders denying reopening [in the three cases now before me.] * * * The [earlier] *Compean* decision acknowledged that the *Lozada* framework had "largely stood the test of time," having been expressly reaffirmed by the Board 15 years after its initial adoption. Nonetheless, *Compean* both rejected *Lozada's* constitutional reasoning and ordered the Board not to rely upon the *Lozada* framework, even as a discretionary matter. Instead, *Compean* set forth, as an exercise of the Attorney General's administrative discretion, a new substantive and procedural framework for reviewing all such claims and a formulation of the prejudice showing different from that followed by many courts, despite the limited discussion of the *Lozada* framework in the briefs submitted in *Compean* by the parties and amici curiae. *Compean* further provided that this new administrative framework should apply "henceforth," even though the decision acknowledged it might conflict with the *Lozada-based* approach taken by a number of Federal Courts of Appeals.

For the reasons stated herein, I have determined that it is appropriate to reconsider the January 7, 2009 decision.

Establishing an appropriate framework for reviewing motions to reopen immigration proceedings based on claims of ineffective assistance of counsel is a matter of great importance. I do not believe that the process used in *Compean* resulted in a thorough consideration of the issues involved, particularly for a decision that implemented a new, complex framework in place of a well-established and longstanding practice that had been reaffirmed by the Board in 2003 after careful consideration. The preferable administrative process for reforming the *Lozada* framework is one that affords all interested parties a full and fair opportunity to participate and ensures that the relevant facts and analysis are collected and evaluated.

Accordingly, I direct the Acting Director of the Executive Office for Immigration Review to initiate rulemaking procedures as soon as practicable to evaluate the *Lozada* framework and to determine what modifications should be proposed for public consideration. After soliciting information and public comment, through publication of a proposed rule in the Federal Register, from all interested persons * * *, the Department of Justice may, if appropriate, proceed with the publication of a final rule.

In *Compean*, * * * Attorney General Mukasey [concluded] that there is no constitutional right to effective assistance of counsel in removal proceedings. Because that conclusion is not necessary either to decide these cases under *pre-Compean* standards or to initiate a rulemaking process, this Order vacates *Compean* in its entirety. To ensure that there is an established framework in place pending the issuance of a final rule, the Board and Immigration Judges should apply the *pre-Compean* standards to all pending and future motions to reopen based upon ineffective assistance of counsel, regardless of when such motions were filed. The litigating positions of the Department of Justice will remain unaffected by this Order.

Finally, prior to *Compean*, the Board itself had not resolved whether its discretion to reopen removal proceedings includes the power to consider claims of ineffective assistance of counsel based on conduct of counsel that occurred after a final order of removal had been entered. * * * I resolve the question in the interim by concluding that the Board does have this discretion, and I leave it to the Board to determine the scope of such discretion.

Turning to the merits of the particular cases at issue, I find that * * * the orders denying reopening of the three matters reviewed in *Compean* were appropriate under the *Lozada* framework and standards as established by the Board before *Compean*. On that basis, I concur with Attorney General Mukasey's decision to affirm the Board's decisions denying reopening of these matters.

As of late 2011, no proposed rules implementing the Holder decision had been published, but the semiannual rulemaking agenda for the Department of Justice indicates that such rules are in the works.

d. Motions to Reopen or Reconsider

In practice, many noncitizens who may benefit from a motion to reopen have been granted voluntary departure, which allows them a stated period of time to leave the United States to avoid a formal removal and its adverse consequences. See Chapter Seven, pp. 788–90. The statute imposes disabilities, however, on persons who do not leave within the allowed period. In particular, they become ineligible for 10 years for specified forms of relief, including for adjustment of status under § 245. *See* INA § 240B(d). If such a noncitizen moves to reopen in order to apply for one of the listed forms of relief, does the pendency of the motion suspend the voluntary departure deadline? If the answer is no, can she withdraw the voluntary departure request, to avoid incurring the ineligibility (and thus wholly defeating the purpose of the desired reopening)? Addressing the significance of motions to reopen and voluntary departure, the Supreme Court grappled with this dilemma in the following case.

DADA v. MUKASEY

Supreme Court of the United States, 2008.
554 U.S. 1, 128 S.Ct. 2307, 171 L.Ed.2d 178.

KENNEDY, J., delivered the opinion of the Court.

* * *

Petitioner Samson Taiwo Dada, a native and citizen of Nigeria, came to the United States in April 1998 on a temporary nonimmigrant visa. He overstayed it. In 1999, petitioner alleges, he married an American citizen. Petitioner's wife filed an I–130 Petition for Alien Relative on his behalf. The necessary documentary evidence was not provided, however, and the petition was denied in February 2003.

In 2004, the Department of Homeland Security (DHS) charged petitioner with being removable under § 237(a)(1)(B) of the Immigration and Nationality Act (INA), for overstaying his visa. Petitioner's wife then filed a second I–130 petition. The Immigration Judge (IJ) denied petitioner's request for a continuance pending adjudication of the newly filed I–130 petition * * *. The IJ found petitioner to be removable but granted the request for voluntary departure. The BIA affirmed on November 4, 2005, without a written opinion. [The Board granted a voluntary departure period of 30 days.] * * *

Two days before expiration of the 30–day period, on December 2, 2005, petitioner sought to withdraw his request for voluntary departure. At the same time he filed with the BIA a motion to reopen removal proceedings under INA § 240(c)(7). He contended that his motion recited new and material evidence demonstrating a bona fide marriage and that his case should be continued until the second I–130 petition was resolved.

On February 8, 2006, more than two months after the voluntary departure period expired, the BIA denied the motion to reopen on the ground that petitioner had overstayed his voluntary departure period. * * * [T]he BIA reasoned [that] an alien who has been granted voluntary departure but fails to depart in a timely fashion is statutorily barred from applying for and receiving certain forms of discretionary relief, including adjustment of status. The BIA did not address petitioner's motion to withdraw his request for voluntary departure.

* * *

Resolution of the questions presented turns on the interaction of two statutory schemes—the statutory right to file a motion to reopen in removal proceedings; and the rules governing voluntary departure.

* * *

Voluntary departure, under the current structure, allows the Government and the alien to agree upon a *quid pro quo*. From the Government's standpoint, the alien's agreement to leave voluntarily expedites the departure process and avoids the expense of deportation—including procuring necessary documents and detaining the alien pending deportation. The Government also eliminates some of the costs and burdens associated with litigation over the departure. With the apparent purpose of assuring that the Government attains the benefits it seeks, the Act imposes limits on the time for voluntary departure, and prohibits judicial review of voluntary departure decisions.

Benefits to the alien from voluntary departure are evident as well. He or she avoids extended detention pending completion of travel arrangements; is allowed to choose when to depart (subject to certain constraints); and can select the country of destination. And, of great importance, by departing voluntarily the alien facilitates the possibility of readmission. * * * Under the current Act, an alien involuntarily removed from the United States is ineligible for readmission for a period of 5, 10, or 20 years, depending upon the circumstances of removal. * * * An alien who makes a timely departure under a grant of voluntary departure, on the other hand, is not subject to these restrictions—although he or she otherwise may be ineligible for readmission based, for instance, on an earlier unlawful presence in the United States.

* * *

The Government argues that, by requesting and obtaining permission to voluntarily depart, the alien knowingly surrenders the opportunity to seek reopening. Further, according to the Government, petitioner's proposed rule for tolling the voluntary departure period would undermine the "carefully crafted rules governing voluntary departure," including the statutory directive that these aliens leave promptly.

* * *

Reading the Act as a whole, and considering the statutory scheme governing voluntary departure alongside the statutory right granted to the alien to pursue "one motion to reopen proceedings," the Government's position that the alien is not entitled to pursue a motion to reopen if the alien agrees to voluntarily depart is unsustainable. It would render the statutory right to seek reopening a nullity in most cases of voluntary departure. (And this group is not insignificant in number; between 2002 and 2006, 897,267 aliens were found removable, of which 122,866, or approximately 13.7%, were granted voluntary departure.) It is foreseeable, and quite likely, that the time allowed for voluntary departure will expire long before the BIA issues a decision on a timely filed motion to reopen.

* * *

Absent tolling or some other remedial action by the Court, then, the alien who is granted voluntary departure but whose circumstances have changed in a manner cognizable by a motion to reopen is between Scylla and Charybdis: He or she can leave the United States in accordance with the voluntary departure order; but, pursuant to regulation, the motion to reopen will be deemed withdrawn. Alternatively, if the alien wishes to pursue reopening and remains in the United States to do so, he or she risks expiration of the statutory period and ineligibility for adjustment of status, the underlying relief sought.

The purpose of a motion to reopen is to ensure a proper and lawful disposition. We must be reluctant to assume that the voluntary departure statute was designed to remove this important safeguard for the distinct class of deportable aliens most favored by the same law. * * *

It is necessary, then, to read the Act to preserve the alien's right to pursue reopening while respecting the Government's interest in the *quid pro quo* of the voluntary departure arrangement.

Some solutions, though, do not conform to the statutory design. Petitioner, as noted, proposes automatic tolling of the voluntary departure period during the pendency of the motion to reopen. We do not find statutory authority for this result. Voluntary departure is an agreed-upon exchange of benefits, much like a settlement agreement. In return for anticipated benefits, including the possibility of readmission, an alien who requests voluntary departure represents that he or she "has the means to depart the United States and intends to do so" promptly. Included among the substantive burdens imposed upon the alien when selecting voluntary departure is the obligation to arrange for departure, and actually depart, within the 60–day period. If the alien is permitted to stay in the United States past the departure date to wait out the adjudication of the motion to reopen, he or she cannot then demand the full benefits of voluntary departure; for the benefit to the Government—a prompt and costless departure—would be lost. Furthermore, it would invite abuse by aliens who wish to stay in the country but whose cases are not likely to be reopened by immigration authorities.

* * *

We hold that, to safeguard the right to pursue a motion to reopen for voluntary departure recipients, the alien must be permitted to withdraw, unilaterally, a voluntary departure request before expiration of the departure period, without regard to the underlying merits of the motion to reopen. As a result, the alien has the option either to abide by the terms, and receive the agreed-upon benefits, of voluntary departure; or, alternatively, to forgo those benefits and remain in the United States to pursue an administrative motion.

If the alien selects the latter option, he or she gives up the possibility of readmission and becomes subject to the IJ's alternate order of removal. The alien may be removed by the Department of Homeland Security within 90 days, even if the motion to reopen has yet to be adjudicated. But the alien may request a stay of the order of removal and, though the BIA has discretion to deny the motion for a stay, it may constitute an abuse of discretion for the BIA to do so where the motion states nonfrivolous grounds for reopening.

Though this interpretation still confronts the alien with a hard choice, it avoids both the quixotic results of the Government's proposal and the elimination of benefits to the Government that would follow from petitioner's tolling rule. Contrary to the Government's assertion, the rule we adopt does not alter the *quid pro quo* between the Government and the alien. If withdrawal is requested prior to expiration of the voluntary departure period, the alien has not received benefits without costs; the alien who withdraws from a voluntary departure arrangement is in the same position as an alien who was not granted voluntary departure in the first instance. Allowing aliens to withdraw from their voluntary departure agreements, moreover, establishes a greater probability that their motions to reopen will be considered. At the same time, it gives some incentive to limit filings to nonfrivolous motions to reopen; for aliens with changed circumstances of the type envisioned by Congress in [authorizing motions to reopen] are the ones most likely to forfeit their previous request for voluntary departure in return for the opportunity to adjudicate their motions. * * *

A more expeditious solution to the untenable conflict between the voluntary departure scheme and the motion to reopen might be to permit an alien who has departed the United States to pursue a motion to reopen postdeparture, much as Congress has permitted with respect to judicial review of a removal order. As noted previously, 8 CFR § 1003.2(d) provides that the alien's departure constitutes withdrawal of the motion to reopen. This regulation, however, has not been challenged in these proceedings, and we do not consider it here.

* * *

JUSTICE SCALIA, with whom THE CHIEF JUSTICE and JUSTICE THOMAS join, dissenting.

The statutory provision at issue here authorizes the Attorney General to permit an alien who has been found deportable, if he so requests, to depart the country voluntarily * * * [and states] that failure to depart within the prescribed period causes the alien to be ineligible for certain relief, including adjustment of status, for 10 years. * * * All of these provisions were in effect when petitioner agreed to depart, and the Court cites no statute or regulation currently in force that permits an alien who has agreed voluntarily to depart to change his mind. * * * I respectfully dissent.

* * *

It seems to me that the BIA proceeded just as it should have, and just as petitioner had every reason to expect. To be sure, the statute provides for the right to file (and presumably to have ruled upon in due course) a petition to reopen. But it does not forbid the relinquishment of that right in exchange for other benefits that the BIA has discretion to provide. Nor does it suggest any weird departure from the ancient rule that an offer (the offer to depart voluntarily in exchange for specified benefits, and with specified consequences for default) cannot be "withdrawn" after it has been accepted and after the *quid pro quo* promise (to depart) has been made.

* * *

The Court is quite right that the Act does not allow us to require that an alien who agrees to depart voluntarily must receive the benefits of his bargain without the costs. But why does it allow us to convert the alien's statutorily required promise to depart voluntarily into an "option either to abide by the terms, and receive the agreed-upon benefits, of voluntary departure; or, alternatively, to forgo those benefits and remain in the United States to pursue an administrative motion"? And why does it allow us to nullify the provision of § 240B(d)(1) that failure to depart within the prescribed and promised period causes the alien to be ineligible for certain relief, including adjustment of status (which is what petitioner seeks here) for 10 years?

* * *

JUSTICE ALITO, dissenting.

* * *

Neither the BIA nor the Fifth Circuit addressed petitioner's motion to withdraw, and therefore the ground for the Board's decision is unclear. I would affirm if the BIA either chose as a general matter not to permit the withdrawal of requests for voluntary departure or decided that permitting withdrawal was not appropriate under the facts of this case. However, if the BIA rejected the withdrawal request on the ground that it lacked the statutory authority to permit it, the Board erred. Because the ground for the BIA's decision is uncertain, I would vacate and remand.

NOTES AND QUESTIONS ON DADA V. MUKASEY

1. The majority reaches its result in order to avoid "render[ing] the statutory right to seek reopening a nullity." It characterizes the motion to reopen as an "important safeguard" meant "to ensure a proper and lawful disposition." And it even suggests that denial of a related motion for a stay of removal might constitute an abuse of discretion if the movant has offered "nonfrivolous grounds for reopening." These statements stand in some tension with concerns the Court expressed in *INS v. Abudu, supra,* where Justice Stevens wrote for the Court:

> The reasons why motions to reopen are disfavored in deportation proceedings are comparable to those that apply to petitions for rehearing, and to motions for new trials on the basis of newly discovered evidence. There is a strong public interest in bringing litigation to a close as promptly as is consistent with the interest in giving the adversaries a fair opportunity to develop and present their respective cases.

> * * *

> We have never suggested that all ambiguities in the factual averments must be resolved in the movant's favor [as the lower court had ruled], and we have never analogized such a motion to a motion for summary judgment. The appropriate analogy is a motion for a new trial in a criminal case on the basis of newly discovered evidence, as to which courts have uniformly held that the moving party bears a heavy burden.

INS v. Abudu, 485 U.S. 94, 107, 109–10, 108 S.Ct. 904, 913–15, 99 L.Ed.2d 90 (1988). Which is the better view of motions to reopen? Why?

2. The *Dada* Court suggested that the executive branch should consider a "more expeditious solution" to the dilemma it faced: changing the current regulation that now forbids the consideration of a motion to reopen filed after the respondent has departed from the country (either voluntarily or pursuant to a removal order). 8 C.F.R. § 1003.2(d); *see Matter of Armendarez–Mendez,* 24 I & N Dec. 646 (BIA 2008). Since then, several courts have ruled that this regulation is in conflict with the statute or that the BIA at least retains jurisdiction to consider in its discretion motions to reopen or reconsider filed by persons who have been removed, notwithstanding the regulation. *See, e.g., Pruidze v. Holder,* 632 F.3d 234 (6th Cir. 2011); *Marin–Rodriguez v. Holder,* 612 F.3d 591 (7th Cir. 2010). Other judicial decisions have upheld the departure bar as a jurisdictional limitation on consideration of some or all such motions. *See, e.g. Zhang v. Holder,* 617 F.3d 650 (2d Cir. 2010) (collecting and discussing cases from many circuits). If that regulation is amended, or if the BIA applies these court rulings nationwide to permit consideration of motions to reopen filed from abroad, could the BIA revert to the practice of refusing permission to withdraw from a voluntary departure agreement? Should it?

6. REMOVAL PROCEEDINGS WITHOUT IMMIGRATION COURT

For decades the immigration laws have provided for summary determinations of removability, by immigration officers rather than immigration judges, in certain classes of cases deemed especially in need of speedy resolution. In 1996, Congress significantly expanded the set of summary proceedings. Each provision has its own specific procedures and scope of application.

Consider as you read this subsection several related questions: Why was this particular abbreviated procedure adopted? What policy goals support these provisions? Which other policy goals are undercut or hampered by their operation? Could they be refined to do a better job of serving each of the counterpoised goals? What changes would you make?

a. Overview

The statute for decades has prescribed summary procedures for *stowaways* and *crewmen*. *See* INA §§ 235(a)(2) (stowaways); 252(b), 8 C.F.R. § 252.2 (crewmen). These procedures currently spark little controversy. Why do you think that is?

Also, since 1986, when the visa waiver provision, INA § 217, was initially adopted, denial of admission and determination of deportability for *visa waiver travelers* have been placed within the sole authority of immigration officers. *See* 8 C.F.R. § 217.4; *Bingham v. Holder*, 637 F.3d 1040 (9th Cir. 2011) (upholding constitutional validity of such procedures). In each of these cases, more complete consideration, sometimes involving an immigration judge, is available when the individual claims asylum or protection from torture.

Five other procedures that entail little or no direct involvement by immigration judges have been adopted or else refined and greatly expanded over the last 20 years.

One, *expedited removal*, under INA § 235(b)(1), applicable primarily to arriving aliens who lack documents or are judged to be committing or to have committed immigration fraud, was considered in some detail in Chapter Six, pp. 569–81. It has also been applied to certain entrants without inspection, primarily persons apprehended within 100 miles of the border and within 14 days of entry.

A second, *judicial removal*, was initially authorized by statute in 1994. *See* INA § 238(c) (there are two subsections (c) in § 238; this is the second). It empowers federal district courts to order removal when sentencing noncitizens for conviction of a crime that makes them deportable. Judicial removal is available only when the U.S. Attorney seeks it with the concurrence of federal immigration authorities, and the court has discretion to decide whether to hear the removal case. If not, the removal charges can still be heard via the more customary removal procedures.

The defendant must receive notice and be given an opportunity to establish eligibility for relief from removal. The judicial removal procedure did not meet with welcome from federal judges, who often expressed misgivings about dealing with such specialized matters, especially when the defendant made a request for relief from removal that required the exercise of discretion. *See, e.g., United States v. Qadeer*, 953 F.Supp. 1570, 1583 (S.D. Ga. 1997). The procedure is rarely used today (in part because of the growth of stipulated removals, considered below, which are sometimes negotiated as part of a plea agreement in a criminal case.) For a thoughtful discussion of judicial removal and possible reforms that could be built on that framework, see Taylor & Wright, *The Sentencing Judge as Immigration Judge*, 51 Emory L.J. 1131, 1175–76 (2002).

Third, *stipulated removals* are authorized by INA § 240(d), which permits "the entry by an immigration judge of an order of removal stipulated to by the alien * * * [and DHS]. A stipulated determination shall constitute a conclusive determination of the alien's removability from the United States." See 8 C.F.R. § 1003.25(b). As described in guidance issued by the Chief Immigration Judge, this procedure "allows interested respondents * * * to have their cases adjudicated expeditiously and without an in-person hearing. For interested respondents, stipulated removal orders reduce their time in detention and expedite their return to their homeland." Procedures for Handling Requests for a Stipulated Removal Order (OPPM 10–01, Sept. 15, 2010), <http://www.justice.gov/eoir/efoia/ocij/oppm10/10–01.pdf>. Critics have charged that ICE officers pressure detained noncitizens into signing such stipulations, and that those who sign are usually unrepresented by counsel. Some immigration judges have also been resistant to approving orders on the basis of the papers, voicing doubts about whether the waivers are voluntary, knowing, and intelligent. *See* J. Koh, J. Srikantiah, & K. Tumlin, Deportation Without Due Process (2011) <http://www.nilc.org/pubs/news-releases/nr097.htm> (also reporting that over 40,000 stipulated orders were issued in FY 2008, declining to approximately 30,000 in 2010). The guidance in EOIR's OPPM 10–01, quoted above, clarifies the procedures and also includes a template for an 8–page stipulation form that ICE is expected to use going forward. The questions on the template, in both English and Spanish, appear designed to help provide more information to the individual about his or her rights and the nature of the waiver, as well as more complete information to the immigration judge who must decide whether to issue the stipulated order without direct contact with the noncitizen.

We consider the remaining two summary procedures at somewhat greater length.

b. Administrative Removal Under INA § 238(b)

Administrative removal under INA § 238(b) applies to certain persons convicted of an aggravated felony. Because of the caption to § 238, some reviewing courts refer to this procedure as "expedited removal." Immigration officers, however, refer to it as "administrative removal," and we follow this terminology. In any event, it is important to distinguish the § 238(b) process from expedited removal under § 235(b)(1), discussed above and in Chapter Six.

Administrative removal applies to two groups of noncitizens charged with deportability under the aggravated felony ground, INA § 237(a)(2)(A)(iii)—those who are not lawful permanent residents, and those who are conditional permanent residents under § 216 based on marriage. The statute prescribes in some detail the required procedures to be followed by the deciding immigration officer. INA § 238(b)(4). Judicial review is available in the courts of appeals, subject to the scope restrictions that apply generally to aliens with criminal convictions (considered in Section C below). So that the respondent can seek judicial review, the order cannot be executed for fourteen days from entry. The first of the two subsections (c) of § 238 provides the substantive basis for removal: "An alien convicted of an aggravated felony shall be conclusively presumed to be deportable from the United States." The statute also provides that covered persons are not eligible for any discretionary relief from removal. § 238(b)(5). The regulations provide for an initial "reasonable fear" screening by an asylum officer for anyone in administrative removal who claims to be eligible for withholding of removal under INA § 241(b)(3) or for protection under the Convention Against Torture. Those who pass this screening are referred to immigration court for full consideration of the claim. 8 C.F.R. § 208.31.

Courts have uniformly rejected arguments that administrative removal violates constitutional due process. Typical is *United States v. Benitez–Villafuerte*, 186 F.3d 651, 657 (5th Cir. 1999), *cert. denied*, 528 U.S. 1097, 120 S.Ct. 838, 145 L.Ed.2d 704 (2000). This was a criminal prosecution for illegal reentry under § 276. One of the elements of the offense was prior removal. The defendant cited procedural due process in collaterally attacking his prior removal, which had been an administrative removal under § 238(b). The court rejected this argument, finding that § 238(b) satisfies the requirements of notice of charges, a hearing before an executive or administrative tribunal, and a fair opportunity to be heard.

Statistics on the number of administrative removals are hard to find. A 2007 study found that about half of the removal orders issued on the basis of the aggravated felony charge from 2002 to 2006 were administrative removal orders issued under § 238(b), a rough average of 11,000 administrative removal orders a year. Transactional Records Access Clearinghouse (TRAC), Syracuse University, New Data on the Processing of Aggravated Felons, <http://trac.syr.edu/immigration/reports/175/>. It appears likely that usage has increased since then.

Would it be constitutional to expand § 238(b) to include any noncitizen, including permanent residents, convicted of an aggravated felony? Would it be sound policy? What about extending coverage to include conviction of any felony? Of any drug offense? Is the application of current § 238(b) to conditional permanent residents under § 216 constitutional?

On the other hand, even if a permanent resident has substantial stake in the United States, why require more procedure, if the substantive law forecloses any relief from removal?

c. Reinstatement of Removal Orders

INA § 241(a)(5) provides for the reinstatement of removal orders against noncitizens who illegally reenter the United States after having been removed or after having departed voluntarily under a removal order. As amended in 1996, the statute also provides explicitly that the original order is not subject to being reopened or reviewed, and that the noncitizen is ineligible for any discretionary relief under the INA. This procedure is highly useful from an enforcement perspective, because an individual subject to reinstatement can ordinarily be removed within a few days of apprehension. As we saw in Chapter 9A (Table 9.1), reinstatements have accounted for a quarter to a third of all removals in recent years.

The regulations provide that an immigration officer will make the relevant determinations—prior order, identity, and unlawful reentry—without review by an immigration judge. *See* 8 C.F.R. § 241.8. If the noncitizen expresses a fear of returning to the country designated in the prior removal order, however, the case will be referred to an asylum officer to initiate a procedure for "reasonable fear" screening and possible referral to an immigration judge to consider withholding of removal. *Id.* § 208.31.

Are reinstatements consistent with the INA and with the Constitution's due process guarantee? A panel of the Ninth Circuit initially found the procedure constitutionally dubious and therefore applied the constitutional avoidance canon to interpret the INA to require a hearing before an immigration judge as part of the reinstatement process. But upon rehearing en banc, the court reversed course. *Morales–Izquierdo v. Gonzales,* 486 F.3d 484 (9th Cir. 2007) (en banc). The case involved a previously deported Mexican citizen who returned without permission, married an American citizen, and was subjected to the reinstatement procedure when he and his wife came to an INS office to pursue her I–130 petition on his behalf.

The majority, in an opinion by Judge Kozinski, first signaled its view that the statute is properly construed to establish a more summary procedure conducted by an immigration officer. But because other circuits had found the statute to be ambiguous on this point, the court went on to apply *Chevron's* step two, which directs courts to defer to the implementing agency's construction of an ambiguous statute, provided that the construction is a permissible one. (We considered the *Chevron* doctrine and its two-step analysis at length in Chapter Five, *supra,* pp. 338–42.) Finding the regulation's assignment of decisionmaking to an immigration officer a reasonable interpretation, the majority then turned to consider the constitutional question:

Morales first argues that the regulation violates due process because it assigns the reinstatement determination to an immigration officer—an official not qualified to resolve disputed questions as to the factual predicates for reinstatement. But reinstatement only requires proof that (1) petitioner is an alien, (2) who was subject to a prior removal order, and (3) who illegally reentered the United States. * * *

We note at the outset that the regulation provides significant procedural safeguards against erroneous reinstatements. First, the immigration officer must verify the identity of the alien. "In disputed cases, verification of identity shall be accomplished by a comparison of fingerprints." If no fingerprints are available, the removal order cannot be reinstated under 8 C.F.R. § 241.8. Second, the immigration officer "must obtain the prior order of exclusion, deportation, or removal relating to the alien." Without this documentation, 8 C.F.R. § 241.8 cannot be used and the matter is referred to an immigration judge. And, third, the officer must determine whether the alien reentered the United States illegally. "In making this determination, the officer shall consider all relevant evidence, including statements made by the alien and any evidence in the alien's possession. The immigration officer shall attempt to verify an alien's claim, if any, that he or she was lawfully admitted, which shall include a check of Service data systems available to the officer." 8 C.F.R. § 241.8(a)(3).

We need not determine whether these procedures are adequate as to all aliens in all cases because Morales does not dispute that he satisfies the statutory predicates for reinstatement. * * * Because none of the grounds Morales raises would have been a proper basis for relief during the reinstatement process, he suffered no prejudice by being denied access to an official who could adjudicate facts that might support these claims. * * *

We are satisfied, moreover, that the regulation provides sufficient procedural safeguards to withstand a facial challenge for patent procedural insufficiency. Given the narrow and mechanical determinations immigration officers must make and the procedural safeguards provided by 8 C.F.R. § 241.8, the risk of erroneous deprivation is extremely low. * * * [Therefore,] any additional or substitute procedural safeguards—including those Morales seeks—would produce marginal protections, if any, against erroneous determinations, while the cost in terms of resources and delay would be substantial. Due process does not require such a poor bargain. *See Mathews v. Eldridge,* 424 U.S. 319, 335, 96 S.Ct. 893, 47 L.Ed.2d 18 (1976).

* * *

Morales also claims that a removal order may not constitutionally be reinstated if the underlying removal proceeding itself violated due process. * * *

* * * [We hold that reinstatement] of a prior removal order—regardless of the process afforded in the underlying order—does not offend due process because reinstatement of a prior order does not change the alien's rights or remedies. The *only* effect of the reinstatement order is to cause Morales' removal, thus denying him any benefits from his latest violation of U.S. law, committed when he reentered the United States without the Attorney General's permission in contravention of INA § 212(a)(9). The reinstatement order imposes no civil or criminal penalties, creates no new obstacles to attacking the validity of the removal order, and does not diminish petitioner's access to whatever path for lawful entry into the United States might otherwise be available to him under the immigration laws.

The Supreme Court noted this very point in *Fernandez–Vargas* [*v. Gonzales*, 548 U.S. 30, 126 S.Ct. 2422 (2006)]:

> While the [reinstatement] law looks back to a past act in its application to "an alien [who] has reentered . . . illegally," INA § 241(a)(5), the provision does not penalize an alien for reentry (criminal and civil penalties do that); it establishes a process to remove him "under the prior order at any time after the reentry." *Ibid.* . . . [T]he statute applies to stop an indefinitely continuing violation that the alien himself could end at any time by voluntarily leaving the country.

126 S.Ct. at 2432 (second alteration in original). While aliens have a right to fair procedures, they have no constitutional right to force the government to re-adjudicate a final removal order by unlawfully reentering the country. Nor is the government required to expend vast resources on extraneous procedures before reinstating a removal order that has already been finalized and executed.

Or, to put it differently, an alien who respects our laws and remains abroad after he has been removed should have no fewer opportunities to challenge his removal order than one who unlawfully reenters the country despite our government's concerted efforts to keep him out. If Morales has a legitimate basis for challenging his prior removal order, he will be able to pursue it after he leaves the country, just like every other alien in his position. If he has no such basis, nothing in the Due Process Clause gives him the right to manufacture for himself a new opportunity to raise such a challenge. The contrary conclusion would create a new and wholly unwarranted incentive for aliens who have previously been removed to reenter the country illegally in order to take advantage of this self-help remedy. * * * Nothing in the Constitution requires such a perverse result.

* * *

486 F.3d, at 495–98.

Judge Thomas, joined by three colleagues, said this about the due process issue in his dissent:

When we examine the reinstatement procedures more closely, the constitutional concerns expressed by our court and others become apparent. It is well-settled that the due process clause of the Fifth Amendment applies to aliens in removal proceedings. Due process requires "a full and fair hearing of [the alien's] claims and a reasonable opportunity to present evidence on his behalf[.]" * * *

First, purely on a facial analysis, the reinstatement process itself approaches the "constitutional danger zone" because it does not provide any opportunity for the alien to challenge the legality of a prior removal order. * * * Thus, an alien that previously has been removed *in absentia* and without due process [as the respondent claims here] has no means of raising his due process claim.

* * * The reinstatement procedure does not provide adequate means to contest the predicates to reinstatement. As we observed in [an earlier case,] "an alien cannot receive a full and fair hearing unless he has the right to place information into the administrative record." Under the regulation, however, the alien is afforded the ability only to make "a written or oral statement contesting the determination" to the officer who has already decided to reinstate the order. * * * [The] alien has no right to introduce documents or other evidence to be considered by the officer; the officer alone determines what will constitute the administrative record. Furthermore, the alien has no right to a hearing at which he or she could call witnesses to testify, and the alien is not afforded the right to review the immigration file upon which the charges are based or to confront the evidence assembled by the government in support of reinstatement.

* * *

Because the reinstatement procedures fall within the constitutional danger zone, both facially and as applied to Morales, the doctrine of constitutional avoidance requires a presumption that Congress intended to afford Morales a full § 240 hearing before an immigration judge. This statutory construction, which is consistent with the plain words of § 240 and with the overall structure of the INA, necessarily means that the reinstatement regulation is *ultra vires* to the statute and must be invalidated.

* * *

Id. at 505–08.

Notes and Questions on Reinstatement of Removal

1. As the Ninth Circuit notes, the U.S. Supreme Court held in *Fernandez–Vargas v. Gonzales*, 548 U.S. 30, 126 S.Ct. 2422, 165 L.Ed.2d 323 (2006), that reinstatement of removal pursuant to § 241(a)(5) applies to noncitizens

who unlawfully reentered the United States before the 1997 effective date of § 241(a)(5). The Court reasoned that applying the statute in these circumstances is not retroactive because it did not attach new consequences to past acts. Section 241(a)(5) "applies to Fernandez–Vargas today not because he reentered in 1982 or at any other particular time, but because he chose to remain after the new statute became effective." *Id.* at 2431. Moreover, according to the Court, the six-month delay between the provision's enactment date and its effective date "shows that Fernandez–Vargas had an ample warning of the coming change in the law, but chose to remain until the old regime expired and § 241(a)(5) took its place." *Id.*

2. Section 241(a)(5) requires that the noncitizen have "reentered the United States illegally after having been removed." What if she reenters through a port of entry and her inadmissibility is not discovered there? Would reinstatement still apply? One circuit has said yes. *Cordova–Soto v. Holder,* 659 F.3d 1029 (10th Cir. 2011) (a procedurally regular entry can count as an illegal reentry for purposes of the reinstatement statute, even if it is sufficient to constitute an "admission" for purposes of INA § 101(a)(13), as construed in *Matter of Quilantan,* 25 I & N Dec. 285 (BIA 2010)).

3. *Morales–Izquierdo* involves several interlocking issues: statutory authority for an agency regulation, *Chevron* deference, constitutional avoidance, and due process. And the court decides the case against the backdrop of *Fernandez–Vargas,* where the U.S. Supreme Court addressed another topic: retroactivity. Each of these issues—and all of them in combination—may turn on a decisionmaker's view of what it means for Morales–Izquierdo (or Fernandez–Vargas) to have returned unlawfully, lived in the United States, married a U.S. citizen, and carried on his life. How do the majority and dissent in *Morales–Izquierdo* differ in this fundamental respect? Which view is more persuasive?

SECTION B.   DETENTION

Detention serves multiple purposes in a system of removal procedures. In a perfect procedural world, removal decisions are error-free and carried out immediately, and detention is unnecessary. But in reality, detention has come to provide part of the answer to several important, unavoidable questions.

First, what happens when a noncitizen arrives in the United States and her admissibility is in doubt? Should she be provisionally allowed into the country while her status is being decided? Second, what happens if a noncitizen already in the United States appears to be deportable? Should he be taken into custody while his status is being decided? Third, what if a final removal order has issued? Should the noncitizen be detained until she actually leaves the United States? Fourth, what if a noncitizen is ordered removed, but no other country will take her? Should she be detained indefinitely, released as if she had never been ordered removed, or something in between?

Each of these questions might call for a different answer, but they have much in common. Detention is an obvious restraint on personal liberty that should not be imposed without good reason. To a visitor to an immigration detention facility and especially to a detainee, detention may seem indistinguishable from a prison sentence for a criminal conviction. Especially for a detainee who has lived in the United States for a while, detention may mean separation from family and friends, and the loss of a job. Detention is costly, both to the government and to the detainee, for whom the harm is greatly magnified if he turns out not to be removable. Detention, particularly in remote locations, can severely limit a noncitizen's ability to obtain legal representation, especially if she must rely on volunteer counsel, and to present her case. *See* Taylor, *Promoting Legal Representation for Detained Aliens: Litigation and Administrative Reform*, 29 Conn. L. Rev. 1647 (1997) (exploring implications of detention practices for access to legal representation).

But there are good—sometimes even compelling—reasons to detain noncitizens in each of the four situations that we have sketched. Detention can be important to make sure that noncitizens appear for removal hearings, and that they will actually leave the United States if ordered removed. Moreover, some noncitizens are removable because they are deemed to pose a risk to society; detaining them pending removal minimizes that risk. Detention also plays a more general role in any system of immigration enforcement. If arriving noncitizens are seldom detained, noncitizens who are clearly inadmissible may have a strong incentive to come to the United States to stay as long as they can before being removed. Without detention, immigration laws are difficult if not impossible to enforce. *See generally* Legomsky, *The Detention of Aliens: Theories, Rules, and Discretion*, 30 Univ. Miami Inter–Am. L. Rev. 531 (1999). Beyond these practical imperatives, the federal government may sometimes use detention to crack down on certain groups of violators, or to "restore credibility" to the entire immigration enforcement system. *See* Taylor, *Symbolic Detention*, 20 In Defense of the Alien 153 (1998) (criticizing this use of detention policy).

1. OVERVIEW

a. The Statutory Framework

Arriving aliens. The statutory provisions on detention provide different coverage and procedures for arriving aliens as distinguished from other noncitizens. Under INA § 235(b)(2), arriving aliens not in expedited removal "shall be detained," but the immigration authorities have consistently interpreted this provision to leave open a noncitizen's eligibility for release on parole under § 212(d)(5). The regulations prescribe these circumstances for such paroles: (1) serious medical conditions; (2) pregnant women; (3) certain juveniles; (4) witnesses in government proceedings in the United States; and (5) aliens "whose continued detention is not in the public interest." 8 C.F.R. § 212.5. ICE field office directors decide about release and any conditions (e.g., amount of bond, electronic monitoring, or periodic reporting requirements). Immigration judges lack jurisdiction to review bond decisions regarding arriving aliens, including lawful permanent residents who fall into that category. *See* 8 C.F.R. §§ 236.1(c)(11), 1003.19(h)(2)(i)(B).

Noncitizens within the United States. Different rules apply to noncitizens who are not arriving aliens. They may be detained or released either on their own recognizance or on bond (minimum $1500). *See* INA § 236(a); 8 C.F.R. § 236.1(c). Here, too, the ICE field office director makes the initial decision regarding any release and its terms, but then the noncitizen may ask an immigration judge for "bond redetermination"—a process that allows the judge to revise the bond or order release without bond. The judge has limited authority to change the other terms of release as well. *See Matter of Aguilar–Aquino*, 24 I & N Dec. 747 (BIA 2009); *Matter of Garcia–Garcia*, 25 I & N Dec. 93 (BIA 2009). The central criteria for release decisions, whether done by an ICE officer or an immigration judge, are flight risk and possible danger to the community. *See Matter of Guerra*, 24 I & N Dec. 37 (BIA 2006). Bond hearings should consider the noncitizen's employment history, length of residence in the community, family ties, record of appearance or nonappearance at court proceedings, and previous criminal or immigration law violations. *See id.; Matter of Sugay*, 17 I & N Dec. 637, 638–39 (BIA 1981). Both the noncitizen and DHS may appeal the judge's decision to the BIA, which may stay release until it decides. But if a field office director originally ordered detention without bond or a bond of at least $10,000, an immigration judge orders release, and the government promptly files its appeal, the order is automatically stayed until the BIA rules. *See* 8 C.F.R. §§ 236.1(d)(4), 1003.19(i).

Janet Gilboy's empirical study of the Chicago district office found that immigration judges in de novo bond redeterminations reduced the original bonds set by an INS officer by an average of over two-thirds. Gilboy suggests that at the heart of the "interinstitutional differences" lies a "value dissensus." The INS (and now ICE) focuses on immigration enforcement, in which bail is an important tool, especially in "the difficult environment in which INS investigators see themselves operating—one that contains immigration court delays and BIA appeals, extensive reliance on aliens leaving the country voluntarily on their own, and limited resources for locating absconders." Gilboy, *Administrative Review in a System of Conflicting Values*, 13 Law & Soc. Inquiry 515, 523–25 (1988). In contrast, immigration judges can strike a different balance between effective immigration law enforcement and protection of the liberty interests of the individual noncitizens because they "do not face the same pressures, constraints, and responsibilities." *Id.* For an analysis of "bureaucratic biases" favoring detention over release of asylum seekers, see Pistone, *Justice Delayed Is Justice Denied: A Proposal for Ending the Unnecessary Detention of Asylum Seekers*, 12 Harv. Human Rights L.J. 197, 239–47 (1999). But consider this contrasting view: "Compared to the [immigration judges], the [field office director] almost certainly faces an array of incentives, responsibilities, and constraints * * * that are more balanced, more comprehensive, and more reflective of the full benefits and costs (social, fiscal, political, and otherwise) of detention and bonding decisions." Schuck, *INS Detention and Removal: A White Paper*, 11 Geo. Immig. L.J. 667, 684 (1997).

Mandatory detention. None of the foregoing possibilities for release from detention are available to noncitizens who are subject to mandatory detention while removal proceedings are pending. Under INA § 236(c), the following aliens must be detained and may not be released: aliens covered by the terrorist grounds and aliens removable on the following criminal grounds: multiple crimes of moral turpitude, aggravated felonies, controlled substance offenses, firearms offenses, "miscellaneous crimes," or, in some cases, single crimes of moral turpitude. The only statutory exceptions are release for witness protection or cooperation, and then only if the detainee is neither a security risk nor a flight risk. We will consider court-imposed limits on mandatory detention later in this section.

A more targeted mandatory detention provision is INA § 236A, enacted in 2011 as part of the USA PATRIOT Act, which requires detention of specified noncitizens reasonably believed to be involved in terrorism or other activity, for up to seven days before placing them in removal proceedings or filing criminal charges, and then throughout proceedings. But this form of detention requires a certification, signed personally by either the Attorney General or the Deputy Attorney General, which must be reviewed every six months. As of late 2011, this power has not been used.

b. ICE's Detention System

Capacities. As of 2011, immigration detainees are housed in about 250 detention facilities, including one dedicated solely for families. Twenty-one large facilities hold about 50 percent of the detained population. Of these 21, seven are ICE-owned, though generally operated under contract with private companies, seven more facilities are owned and operated by private contractors, and seven are dedicated county jail facilities with which ICE maintains intergovernmental service agreements (IGSAs). The other 50 percent are detained in state and local detention facilities also operated under IGSAs. The number of individuals held in immigration detention over the course of a fiscal year was approximately 100,000 in FY 2001. That number rose steeply over the succeeding decade, peaking at over 383,000 in FY 2009, before declining to 363,064 in FY 2010. *See* Schriro, Immigration Detention Overview and Recommendations 2, 10–11 (ICE report, Oct. 6, 2009); 2007 Immigration Enforcement Actions, Dept. of Homeland Security (Dec. 2008); 2008 *id.* (July 2009); 2009 *id.* (Aug. 2010); 2010 *id.* (June 2011); 86 Interp. Rel. 3088(2009); ICE, Detention Reform Accomplishments (2011), <http://www.ice.gov/detention-reform/detention-reform.htm>. Higher annual detention numbers are a product of both more detention beds and shorter lengths of stay. ICE's detention capacity, which was under 20,000 beds in FY 2005, rose to 30,000 in FY 2007, and to 33,000 as of July 2011, while the average length of stay declined from 37.2 days in 2007 to 29.0 in 2011. ICE Total Removals

Through July 31, 2011, <http://www.ice.gov/doclib/about/offices/ero/pdf/ero-removals.pdf>. Within those averages, of course, there are many uncontested cases that lead to release or removal within a few days, whereas some detainees remain incarcerated for months or even years. In FY 2005, 29 percent of completed cases in immigration court involved detained noncitizens; that number rose to 44 percent by FY 2010. *See* Executive Office for Immigration Review, Department of Justice, FY 2005 Statistical Year Book, at O1; FY 2010 Statistical Year Book, at O1.

Reforms. Significant concerns about the immigration detention system have been heard for decades, and numerous reports and studies have documented problems and complaints. *See, e.g.,* Amnesty International, Jailed without Justice: Immigration Detention in the USA, (2009) <http://www.amnestyusa.org/pdfs/JailedWithoutJustice.pdf>; M. Dow, American Gulag: Inside U.S. Immigration Prisons (2004). Some of the concerns go to the conditions in the facilities, which have traditionally been designed based on American Correctional Association standards that were developed to cover facilities in the criminal justice system. Oversight of contract and IGSA facilities has been decentralized and inconsistent, with what critics saw as insufficient responses to poor performance or even major violations of applicable performance standards. Medical care for detainees drew many complaints, and a few notorious incidents of delayed responses to serious medical conditions over the past decades apparently contributed to detainee deaths (and ensuing litigation). *See, e.g.,* Hernandez, *Denied Medication, AIDS Patient Dies in Custody*, L.A. Daily Journal, Aug. 9, 2007; Bernstein, *Before Deaths that Caught Public's Eye, Others Stayed Hidden*, N.Y. Times, Jan. 10, 2010. Critics also noted that many of the largest facilities are distant from major urban areas where legal assistance might be more readily found, and arrested noncitizens have often been transferred to one of these facilities, far from family and friends.

In its earliest weeks, the Obama administration initiated an internal process meant to lead to significant detention reform. DHS Secretary Janet Napolitano engaged an experienced expert on detention management, Dr. Dora Schriro, to study the detention system and suggest specific reforms. Her report, Schriro, *supra,* documented problems and urged multi-year changes to shift from the criminal model to a civil detention system, with greater outside access by family and counsel, contact visits, enhanced recreational opportunities, and permission for more detainees to wear their own clothing. The Secretary and ICE Director John Morton accepted the report and launched an ambitious reform process in October 2009. *See* DHS Fact Sheet, ICE Detention Reform: Principles and Next Steps (Oct. 6, 2009).

Changes are still in the early stages, and many critics remain skeptical of the pace of progress, waiting to judge the extent of DHS's commitment to reform, but ICE has initiated work on many fronts. Under the lead of a new Office of Detention Policy and Planning, it has begun acquisition of new facilities appropriate to a civil detention model, looking especially at converted hotels (emulating a pioneering facility of this sort, which has been in operation in Broward County, Florida, for several years), nursing homes, and other residential facilities. It has also begun the process of building an entirely new facility designed for civil detention. ICE has terminated several detention contracts and consolidated existing facilities, reducing the number from 341 to 255 by October 2010, while centralizing management to help assure more uniform performance. It has opened large new facilities in underserved areas, such as California and the northeast corridor, in order to move toward better alignment between the location of detention space and the location of enforcement activity. This is meant to cut down on distant transfers. In the meantime, ICE developed a well-received online detainee locator system, launched in July 2010, which can be used by family, friends and counsel.

Other changes include the development of a detainee assessment tool, to facilitate and standardize decisions on whether to detain, and if so, in what level of security. Supervision of medical care was overhauled, and clinical directors at the facilities received greater autonomy to approve medical requests and thus speed the provision of needed treatment. To achieve improved accountability, ICE doubled the staff of ICE officers (to 50) who now provide full-time on-site oversight at the largest detention facilities (covering 80 percent of detainees). It also created a centralized Office of Detention Oversight as part of the Office of Professional Responsibility, which reports directly to the head of ICE and is independent of the ICE division that manages detention. ICE has also developed, in wide consultations that included NGOs, a new set of Performance Based National Detention Standards, with clearer benchmarks for judging contractor performance and imposing sanctions for failures. *See* ICE Detention Reform Accomplishments, *supra*; Human Rights First, Jails and Jumpsuits: Transforming the U.S. Immigration Detention System—A Two–Year Review (2011), <http://www.humanrightsfirst.org>.

Juveniles. Separate standards apply to the detention of juveniles, which has been an area of special concern at least as far back as the U.S. Supreme Court decision in *Reno v. Flores*, 507 U.S. 292, 113 S.Ct. 1439, 123 L.Ed.2d 1 (1993). That case led to a settlement on detention, processing, and release of minors, which provided standards and procedures that governed juvenile detention for many years. Further reforms ensued. The Homeland Security Act of 2002 transferred most responsibility for detention of minors to the Office of Refugee Resettlement in the Department of Health and Human Services, and the William Wilberforce Trafficking Victims Protection Reauthorization Act of 2008 strengthened the procedures and protections applicable to unaccompanied children who come into the immigration system. *See* Bhabha & Schmidt, *From Kafka to Wilberforce: Is the U.S. Government's Approach to Child Migrants Improving?*, 11–02 Imm. Briefings (2011); DHS Office of Inspector General, CBP's Handling of Unaccompanied Alien Children (OIG–10–117, Sept. 2010).

Alternatives to detention. ICE has also made increasing use in recent years of what are called alternatives to detention (ATDs). These are programs that enable release of the individual, but provide enhanced supervision, periodic reporting, and usually either telephone or ankle bracelet (GPS) monitoring. These steps are meant to help assure that the noncitizen appears for proceedings and will be reachable for removal if an order becomes final, but without the need for physical incarceration. Congress has mandated a nationwide plan to expand the use of ATDs, in part because such a system can be more humane, affording greater opportunity for the individual to prepare his case and consult with counsel and others, but also because ATDs are generally less expensive. A 2009 estimate placed the cost of the most expensive version of ATD at $14 per individual per day, while detention runs $100 per day or more. Detained cases have typically been prioritized for expeditious resolution by EOIR, and ICE was concerned that the savings from ATDs would be undercut if those cases remained on the slower track followed by ordinary nondetained cases. ICE therefore has negotiated arrangements with EOIR to provide a separate expedited track for ATD cases. *See generally* Schriro, *supra,* at 20–21; D. Kerwin, Testimony on "Moving Toward More Effective Immigration Detention Management," Hearing before the House Subcommittee on Border, Maritime, and Global Counterterrorism [hereafter Detention Management Hearing], Dec. 10, 2009, at 4–5; Detention Watch Network & Mills Legal Clinic, Stanford Law School, Community–Based Alternatives to Immigration Detention 7–11 (Aug. 2010), <http://www. law.stanford.edu/program/clinics/immigrantsrights/pdf/DWN_ATD_ Report_FINAL.pdf>.

Though there is broad support in the NGO community for increasing use of ATDs, another witness at the same hearing on effective detention management in 2009 voiced this opposition, in testimony that reflected more broadly on the use of immigration detention:

> [A] majority of removable aliens who promise to appear for their court dates are simply lying to the immigration authorities [citing statistics on nonappearance rates, including a DHS Inspector General report that 62 percent of released aliens who receive a final order fail to surrender for removal]. This is the reason immigration detention must not only continue, but must be expanded significantly. The only way to ensure that illegal aliens actually appear before an immigration court is to physically compel them to do so through detention. * * *

> Furthermore, alternatives to detention are not even plausible subjects for experiment unless the criminal penalties for failing to appear are employed. * * * The pervasive unwillingness of illegal aliens to comply with immigration law in the absence of detention is not surprising. Unlike in the criminal justice setting, where failing to appear often results in additional penalties, a final order of removal is all an illegal alien realistically faces, whether he shows up to immigration court or not. Though the law provides for imprisonment of up to 10 years for aliens who fail to appear at their hearings, the chances

that an immigration absconder not involved in additional crimes will be prosecuted are vanishingly small.

M. Krikorian, Testimony at Detention Management Hearing, *supra*, at 2–3 (paragraphing altered).

2. LIMITS ON DETENTION

Are there constitutional or statutory limits on detention? We consider this in two settings: (1) indefinite detention when a removal order has issued but the noncitizen cannot be removed; and (2) mandatory detention pending removal proceedings. It might seem more logical to consider detention pending proceedings first, but because indefinite detention reached the Supreme Court before the other procedures were litigated there, we take them in this order.

a. Indefinite Detention After a Final Removal Order

Under INA § 241(a), removal must normally take place within the 90–day "removal period" after the order becomes final. During these 90 days, the Attorney General "shall detain the alien," and may not release those found inadmissible or deportable under the criminal or certain national security grounds. *See* INA § 241(a)(2). If removal does not occur during this period, the Attorney General has discretion to release the noncitizen under supervision. *See* INA § 241(a)(3), (6); 8 C.F.R. §§ 241.4, 241.5.

Noncitizens almost always have somewhere to be sent. Indeed, international law usually obligates countries to permit its nationals to return. The Universal Declaration of Human Rights states: "Everyone has the right to leave any country, including his own, and to return to his country." Art. 13(2), UNGA Res. 217 (III), UN Doc. A/801 (1948). But what if the noncitizen cannot be removed because no country will take him? Can the government detain him indefinitely? In *Shaughnessy v. United States ex rel. Mezei*, 345 U.S. 206, 73 S.Ct. 625, 97 L.Ed. 956 (1953), considered in Chapter Six, the Supreme Court approved indefinite detention of an excludable alien, without any judicial testing of the substantive merits or even the procedural validity of the detention order. But *Wong Wing v. United States*, 163 U.S. 228, 16 S.Ct. 977, 41 L.Ed. 140 (1896), excerpted in Chapter Three, may limit *Mezei*, if the noncitizen succeeds in characterizing his detention as criminal punishment.

Succeeding years presented few opportunities to rethink the *Mezei* approach to indefinite detention. But cases of prolonged, perhaps indefinite detention began to reach the federal courts in the 1990s because a small but significant group of countries would not take back their own citizens who received final orders for removal from the United States. Other indefinite detainees were either stateless or of uncertain citizenship, and no country would accept them. In the following case, the U.S. Supreme Court considered whether indefinite detention is lawful.

ZADVYDAS v. DAVIS

Supreme Court of the United States, 2001.
533 U.S. 678, 121 S.Ct. 2491, 150 L.Ed.2d 653.

JUSTICE BREYER delivered the opinion of the Court.

When an alien has been found to be unlawfully present in the United States and a final order of removal has been entered, the Government ordinarily secures the alien's removal during a subsequent 90–day statutory "removal period," during which time the alien normally is held in custody.

A special statute authorizes further detention if the Government fails to remove the alien during those 90 days. It says:

> An alien ordered removed [1] who is inadmissible ... [2] [or] removable [as a result of violations of status requirements or entry conditions, violations of criminal law, or reasons of security or foreign policy] or [3] who has been determined by the Attorney General to be a risk to the community or unlikely to comply with the order of removal, may be detained beyond the removal period and, if released, shall be subject to [certain] terms of supervision....

INA § 241(a)(6).

In these cases, we must decide whether this post-removal-period statute authorizes the Attorney General to detain a removable alien *indefinitely* beyond the removal period or only for a period *reasonably necessary* to secure the alien's removal. We deal here with aliens who were admitted to the United States but subsequently ordered removed. Aliens who have not yet gained initial admission to this country would present a very different question. Based on our conclusion that indefinite detention of aliens in the former category would raise serious constitutional concerns, we construe the statute to contain an implicit "reasonable time" limitation, the application of which is subject to federal court review.

I

* * *

We consider two separate instances of detention. The first concerns Kestutis Zadvydas, a resident alien who was born, apparently of Lithuanian parents, in a displaced persons camp in Germany in 1948. When he was eight years old, Zadvydas immigrated to the United States with his parents and other family members, and he has lived here ever since.

Zadvydas has a long criminal record, involving drug crimes, attempted robbery, attempted burglary, and theft. He has a history of flight, from both criminal and deportation proceedings. Most recently, he was convicted of possessing, with intent to distribute, cocaine; sentenced to 16 years' imprisonment; released on parole after two years; taken into INS custody; and, in 1994, ordered deported to Germany.

In 1994, Germany told the INS that it would not accept Zadvydas because he was not a German citizen. Shortly thereafter, Lithuania refused to accept Zadvydas because he was neither a Lithuanian citizen nor a permanent resident. In 1996, the INS asked the Dominican Republic (Zadvydas' wife's country) to accept him, but this effort proved unsuccessful. In 1998, Lithuania rejected, as inadequately documented, Zadvydas' effort to obtain Lithuanian citizenship based on his parents' citizenship; Zadvydas' reapplication is apparently still pending.

* * *

The second case is that of Kim Ho Ma. Ma was born in Cambodia in 1977. When he was two, his family fled, taking him to refugee camps in Thailand and the Philippines and eventually to the United States, where he has lived as a resident alien since the age of seven. In 1995, at age 17, Ma was involved in a gang-related shooting, convicted of manslaughter, and sentenced to 38 months' imprisonment. He served two years, after which he was released into INS custody.

In light of his conviction of an "aggravated felony," Ma was ordered removed. The 90–day removal period expired in early 1999, but the INS continued to keep Ma in custody, because, in light of his former gang membership, the nature of his crime, and his planned participation in a prison hunger strike, it was "unable to conclude that Mr. Ma would remain nonviolent and not violate the conditions of release."

* * *

III

The post-removal-period detention statute applies to certain categories of aliens who have been ordered removed, namely inadmissible aliens, criminal aliens, aliens who have violated their nonimmigrant status conditions, and aliens removable for certain national security or foreign relations reasons, as well as any alien "who has been determined by the Attorney General to be a risk to the community or unlikely to comply with the order of removal." It says that an alien who falls into one of these categories "may be detained beyond the removal period and, if released, shall be subject to [certain] terms of supervision." INA § 241(a)(6).

The Government argues that the statute means what it literally says. It sets no "limit on the length of time beyond the removal period that an alien who falls within one of the Section 241(a)(6) categories may be detained." Hence, "whether to continue to detain such an alien and, if so, in what circumstances and for how long" is up to the Attorney General, not up to the courts.

"[I]t is a cardinal principle" of statutory interpretation, however, that when an Act of Congress raises "a serious doubt" as to its constitutionality, "this Court will first ascertain whether a construction of the statute is fairly possible by which the question may be avoided." *Crowell v. Benson*, 285 U.S. 22, 62 (1932). We have read significant limitations into other immigration statutes in order to avoid their constitutional invalidation. For similar reasons, we read an implicit limitation into the statute before us. In our view, the statute, read in light of the Constitution's demands, limits an alien's post-removal-period detention to a period reasonably necessary to bring about that alien's removal from the United States. It does not permit indefinite detention.

A

A statute permitting indefinite detention of an alien would raise a serious constitutional problem. The Fifth Amendment's Due Process Clause forbids the Government to "depriv[e]" any "person ... of ... liberty ... without due process of law." Freedom from imprisonment—from government custody, detention, or other forms of physical restraint—lies at the heart of the liberty that Clause protects. And this Court has said that government detention violates that Clause unless the detention is ordered in a *criminal* proceeding with adequate procedural protections, *see United States v. Salerno*, 481 U.S. 739, 746 (1987), or, in certain special and "narrow" non-punitive "circumstances," *Foucha* [*v. Louisiana*, 504 U.S. 71, 80 (1992)], where a special justification, such as harm-threatening mental illness, outweighs the "individual's constitutionally protected interest in avoiding physical restraint." *Kansas v. Hendricks*, 521 U.S. 346, 356 (1997). The proceedings at issue here are civil, not criminal, and we assume that they are nonpunitive in purpose and effect. There is no sufficiently strong special justification here for indefinite civil detention—at least as administered under this statute. The statute, says the Government, has two regulatory goals: "ensuring the appearance of aliens at future immigration proceedings" and "[p]reventing danger to the community." But by definition the first justification—preventing flight—is weak or nonexistent where removal seems a remote possibility at best. * * *

The second justification—protecting the community—does not necessarily diminish in force over time. But we have upheld preventive detention based on dangerousness only when limited to specially dangerous individuals and subject to strong procedural protections. [Citing *Hendricks*, *Salerno*, and *Foucha*.] In cases in which preventive detention is of potentially *indefinite* duration, we have also demanded that the dangerousness rationale be accompanied by some other special circumstance, such as mental illness, that helps to create the danger.

* * * [O]nce the flight risk justification evaporates, the only special circumstance present is the alien's removable status itself, which bears no relation to a detainee's dangerousness.

Moreover, the sole procedural protections available to the alien are found in administrative proceedings, where the alien bears the burden of proving he is not dangerous, without (in the Government's view) significant later judicial review. * * * The serious constitutional problem arising out of a statute that, in these circumstances, permits an indefinite, perhaps permanent, deprivation of human liberty without any such protection is obvious.

The Government argues that, from a constitutional perspective, alien status itself can justify indefinite detention, and points to *Shaughnessy v. United States ex rel. Mezei*, 345 U.S. 206 (1953), as support. * * *

Although *Mezei*, like the present cases, involves indefinite detention, it differs from the present cases in a critical respect. As the Court emphasized, the alien's extended departure from the United States required him to seek entry into this country once again. His presence on Ellis Island did not count as entry into the United States. Hence, he was "treated," for constitutional purposes, "as if stopped at the border." And that made all the difference.

The distinction between an alien who has effected an entry into the United States and one who has never entered runs throughout immigration law. It is well established that certain constitutional protections available to persons inside the United States are unavailable to aliens outside of our geographic borders. But once an alien enters the country, the legal circumstance changes, for the Due Process Clause applies to all "persons" within the United States, including aliens, whether their presence here is lawful, unlawful, temporary, or permanent. *See Plyler v. Doe*, 457 U.S. 202, 210 (1982); *Mathews v. Diaz*, 426 U.S. 67, 77 (1976); *Kwong Hai Chew v. Colding*, 344 U.S. 590, 596–598, and n.5 (1953); *Yick Wo v. Hopkins*, 118 U.S. 356, 369 (1886); *cf. Mezei, supra*, at 212 ("[A]liens who have once passed through our gates, even illegally, may be expelled only after proceedings conforming to traditional standards of fairness encompassed in due process of law"). Indeed, this Court has held that the Due Process Clause protects an alien subject to a final order of deportation, *see Wong Wing v. United States*, 163 U.S. 228, 238 (1896), though the nature of that protection may vary depending upon status and circumstance, *see Landon v. Plasencia*, 459 U.S. 21, 32–34 (1982).

In *Wong Wing, supra*, the Court held unconstitutional a statute that imposed a year of hard labor upon aliens subject to a final deportation order. That case concerned substantive protections for aliens who had been ordered removed, not procedural protections for aliens whose removability was being determined. * * * And contrary to Justice Scalia's characterization, in *Mezei* itself, both this Court's rejection of Mezei's challenge to the procedures by which he was deemed excludable and its rejection of his challenge to continued detention rested upon a basic territorial distinction.

* * *

The Government also looks for support to cases holding that Congress has "plenary power" to create immigration law, and that the judicial branch must defer to executive and legislative branch decisionmaking in that area. But that power is subject to important constitutional limitations. In these cases, we focus upon those limitations. In doing so, we nowhere deny the right of Congress to remove aliens, to subject them to supervision with conditions when released from detention, or to incarcerate them where appropriate for violations of those conditions. The question before us is not one of " 'confer[ring] on those admitted the right to remain against the national will' " or " 'sufferance of aliens' " who should be removed. Rather, the issue we address is whether aliens that the Government finds itself unable to remove are to be condemned to an indefinite term of imprisonment within the United States.

Nor do the cases before us require us to consider the political branches' authority to control entry into the United States. Hence we leave no "unprotected spot in the Nation's armor." *Kwong Hai Chew*, *supra*, at 602. Neither do we consider terrorism or other special circumstances where special arguments might be made for forms of preventive detention and for heightened deference to the judgments of the political branches with respect to matters of national security. The sole foreign policy consideration the Government mentions here is the concern lest courts interfere with "sensitive" repatriation negotiations. But neither the Government nor the dissents explain how a habeas court's efforts to determine the likelihood of repatriation, if handled with appropriate sensitivity, could make a significant difference in this respect.

Finally, the Government argues that, whatever liberty interest the aliens possess, it is "greatly diminished" by their lack of a legal right to "liv[e] at large in this country." The choice, however, is not between imprisonment and the alien "living at large." It is between imprisonment and supervision under release conditions that may not be violated. And, for the reasons we have set forth, we believe that an alien's liberty interest is, at the least, strong enough to raise a serious question as to whether, irrespective of the procedures used, the Constitution permits detention that is indefinite and potentially permanent.

B

Despite this constitutional problem, if "Congress has made its intent" in the statute "clear, 'we must give effect to that intent.' " *Miller v. French*, 530 U.S. 327, 336 (2000) (quoting *Sinclair Refining Co. v. Atkinson*, 370 U.S. 195, 215 (1962)). We cannot find here, however, any clear indication of congressional intent to grant the Attorney General the power to hold indefinitely in confinement an alien ordered removed. * * *

The Government points to the statute's word "may." But while "may" suggests discretion, it does not necessarily suggest unlimited discretion. In that respect the word "may" is ambiguous. Indeed, if Congress had meant to authorize long-term detention of unremovable aliens, it certainly could have spoken in clearer terms. Compare INA § 507(b)(2)(C) ("If no country is willing to receive" a terrorist alien ordered removed, "the Attorney General may, notwithstanding any other provision of law, retain the alien in custody" and must review the detention determination every six months).

* * *

We have found nothing in the history of [the] statutes [that are precursors of § 241(a)(6)] that clearly demonstrates a congressional intent to authorize indefinite, perhaps permanent, detention. Consequently, interpreting the statute to avoid a serious constitutional threat, we conclude that, once removal is no longer reasonably foreseeable, continued detention is no longer authorized by statute. *See* 1 E. Coke, Institutes *70b ("*Cessante ratione legis cessat ipse lex*") (the rationale of a legal rule no longer being applicable, that rule itself no longer applies).

IV

* * *

[A court considering a habeas corpus petition] must ask whether the detention in question exceeds a period reasonably necessary to secure removal. It should measure reasonableness primarily in terms of the statute's basic purpose, namely assuring the alien's presence at the moment of removal. Thus, if removal is not reasonably foreseeable, the court should hold continued detention unreasonable and no longer authorized by statute. In that case, of course, the alien's release may and should be conditioned on any of the various forms of supervised release that are appropriate in the circumstances, and the alien may no doubt be returned to custody upon a violation of those conditions. And if removal is reasonably foreseeable, the habeas court should consider the risk of the alien's committing further crimes as a factor potentially justifying confinement within that reasonable removal period.

* * *

Ordinary principles of judicial review in this area recognize primary Executive Branch responsibility. They counsel judges to give expert agencies decisionmaking leeway in matters that invoke their expertise. They recognize Executive Branch primacy in foreign policy matters. And they consequently require courts to listen with care when the Government's foreign policy judgments, including, for example, the status of repatriation negotiations, are at issue, and to grant the Government appropriate leeway when its judgments rest upon foreign policy expertise.

We realize that recognizing this necessary Executive leeway will often call for difficult judgments. In order to limit the occasions when courts will need to make them, we think it practically necessary to recognize some presumptively reasonable period of detention. We have adopted similar presumptions in other contexts to guide lower court determinations.

While an argument can be made for confining any presumption to 90 days, we doubt that when Congress shortened the removal period to 90 days in 1996 it believed that all reasonably foreseeable removals could be accomplished in that time. We do have reason to believe [based on the legislative history of a precursor statute], however, that Congress previously doubted the constitutionality of detention for more than six months.

Consequently, for the sake of uniform administration in the federal courts, we recognize that period. After this 6–month period, once the alien provides good reason to believe that there is no significant likelihood of removal in the reasonably foreseeable future, the Government must respond with evidence sufficient to rebut that showing. And for detention to remain reasonable, as the period of prior post-removal confinement grows, what counts as the "reasonably foreseeable future" conversely would have to shrink. This 6–month presumption, of course, does not mean that every alien not removed must be released after six months. To the contrary, an alien may be held in confinement until it has been determined that there is no significant likelihood of removal in the reasonably foreseeable future.

* * *

JUSTICE SCALIA, with whom JUSTICE THOMAS joins, dissenting.

I join Part I of Justice Kennedy's dissent, which establishes the Attorney General's clear statutory authority to detain criminal aliens with no specified time limit. I write separately because I do not believe that, as Justice Kennedy suggests in Part II of his opinion, there may be some situations in which the courts can order release. * * * A criminal alien under final order of removal who allegedly will not be accepted by any other country in the reasonably foreseeable future claims a constitutional right of supervised release into the United States. This claim can be repackaged as freedom from "physical restraint" or freedom from "indefinite detention," but it is at bottom a claimed right of release into this country by an individual who *concededly* has no legal right to be here. There is no such constitutional right.

Like a criminal alien under final order of removal, an inadmissible alien at the border has no right to be in the United States. *The Chinese Exclusion Case*, 130 U.S. 581, 603 (1889). In *Shaughnessy v. United States ex rel. Mezei*, 345 U.S. 206 (1953), we upheld potentially indefinite detention of such an inadmissible alien whom the Government was unable to return anywhere else. We said that "we [did] not think that respondent's continued exclusion deprives him of any statutory or constitutional right." While four members of the Court thought that Mezei deserved greater procedural protections (the Attorney General had refused to divulge any information as to why Mezei was being detained), no Justice asserted that Mezei had a substantive constitutional right to release into this country. * * * Insofar as a claimed legal right to release into this country is concerned, an alien under final order of removal stands on an equal footing with an inadmissible alien at the threshold of entry: He has no such right.

The Court expressly declines to apply or overrule *Mezei*, but attempts to distinguish it—or, I should rather say, to obscure it in a legal fog. First, the Court claims that "[t]he distinction between an alien who has effected an entry into the United States and one who has never entered runs throughout immigration law." True enough, but only where that distinction makes perfect sense: with regard to the question of what *procedures* are necessary to prevent entry, as opposed to what *procedures* are necessary to eject a person already in the United States. See, *e.g., Landon v. Plasencia*, 459 U.S. 21, 32 (1982) ("Our cases have frequently suggested that a continuously present resident alien is entitled to a fair hearing *when threatened with deportation*" (emphasis added)). The Court's citation of *Wong Wing v. United States*, 163 U.S. 228 (1896), for the proposition that we have "held that the Due Process Clause protects an alien subject to a final order of deportation," is arguably relevant. That case at least involved aliens under final order of deportation.* But all it held is that they could not be subjected to the punishment of hard labor without a judicial trial. I am sure they cannot be tortured, as well—but neither prohibition has anything to do with their right to be released into the United States. Nor does *Wong Wing* show that the rights of detained aliens subject to final order of deportation are different from the rights of aliens arrested and detained at the border—unless the Court believes that the detained alien in *Mezei could* have been set to hard labor.

Mezei thus stands unexplained and undistinguished by the Court's opinion. We are offered no justification why an alien under a valid and final order of removal—which has *totally extinguished* whatever right to presence in this country he possessed—has any greater due process right to be released into the country than an alien at the border seeking entry. * * *

JUSTICE KENNEDY, with whom THE CHIEF JUSTICE joins, and with whom JUSTICE SCALIA and JUSTICE THOMAS join as to Part I, dissenting.

The Court says its duty is to avoid a constitutional question. It deems the duty performed by interpreting a statute in obvious disregard of congressional intent; curing the resulting gap by writing a statutory amendment of its own; committing its own grave constitutional error by arrogating to the Judicial Branch the power to summon high officers of the Executive to assess their progress in conducting some of the Nation's most sensitive negotiations with foreign powers; and then likely releasing into our general population at least hundreds of removable or inadmissible aliens who have been found by fair procedures to be flight risks, dangers to the community, or both. * * *

I

* * *

The Court, it is submitted, misunderstands the principle of constitutional avoidance which it seeks to invoke. The majority gives a brief bow to the rule that courts must respect the intention of Congress, but then waltzes away from any analysis of the language, structure, or purpose of the statute. Its analysis is not consistent with our precedents explaining the limits of the constitutional doubt rule. The rule allows courts to

---

* The Court also cites *Landon v. Plasencia*, 459 U.S. 21 (1982), * * * [b]ut that case is entirely inapt because it did not involve an alien subject to a final order of deportation. * * *

choose among constructions which are "fairly possible," *Crowell v. Benson*, 285 U.S. 22, 62 (1932), not to " 'press statutory construction to the point of disingenuous evasion even to avoid a constitutional question,' " *Salinas v. United States*, 522 U.S. 52, 60 (1997) (quoting *Seminole Tribe of Fla. v. Florida*, 517 U.S. 44, 57, n.9 (1996)). Were a court to find two interpretations of equal plausibility, it should choose the construction that avoids confronting a constitutional question. The majority's reading of the statutory authorization to "detai[n] beyond the removal period," however, is not plausible. * * *

Other provisions in § 241 itself do link the requirement of a reasonable time period to the removal process [citing §§ 241(c)(1)(A), § 241(c)(3)(A)(ii)(II)]. That Congress chose to impose the limitation in these sections and not in § 241(a)(6) is evidence of its intent to measure the detention period by other standards. When Congress has made express provisions for the contingency that repatriation might be difficult or prolonged in other portions of the statute, it should be presumed that its omission of the same contingency in the detention section was purposeful. * * *

The 6–month period invented by the Court, even when modified by its sliding standard of reasonableness for certain repatriation negotiations, makes the statutory purpose to protect the community ineffective. The risk to the community exists whether or not the repatriation negotiations have some end in sight; in fact, when the negotiations end, the risk may be greater. The authority to detain beyond the removal period is to protect the community, not to negotiate the aliens' return. The risk to the community survives repatriation negotiations. To a more limited, but still significant, extent, so does the concern with flight. It is a fact of international diplomacy that governments and their policies change; and if repatriation efforts can be revived, the Attorney General has an interest in ensuring the alien can report so the removal process can begin again.

* * *

The majority's unanchored interpretation ignores another indication that the Attorney General's detention discretion was not limited to this truncated period. Section 241(a)(6) permits continued detention not only of removable aliens but also of inadmissible aliens, for instance those stopped at the border before entry. Congress provides for detention of both categories within the same statutory grant of authority. Accepting the majority's interpretation, then, there are two possibilities, neither of which is sustainable. On the one hand, it may be that the majority's rule applies to both categories of aliens, in which case we are asked to assume that Congress intended to restrict the discretion it could confer upon the Attorney General so that all inadmissible aliens must be allowed into our community within six months. On the other hand, the majority's logic might be that inadmissible and removable aliens can be treated differently. Yet it is not a plausible construction of § 241(a)(6) to imply a time limit as to one class but not to another. The text does not admit of this possibility. As a result, it is difficult to see why "[a]liens who have not yet gained initial admission to this country would present a very different question."

* * * It is reasonable to assume, then, and it is the proper interpretation of the INA and § 241(a)(6), that when Congress provided for detention "beyond the removal period," it exercised its considerable power over immigration and delegated to the Attorney General the discretion to detain inadmissible and other removable aliens for as long as they are determined to be either a flight risk or a danger to the Nation.

The majority's interpretation, moreover, defeats the very repatriation goal in which it professes such interest. * * * One of the more alarming aspects of the Court's new venture into foreign affairs management is the suggestion that the district court can expand or contract the reasonable period of detention based on its own assessment of the course of negotiations with foreign powers. The Court says it will allow the Executive to perform its duties on its own for six months; after that, foreign relations go into judicially supervised receivership.

* * *

II

The aliens' claims are substantial; their plight is real. They face continued detention, perhaps for life, unless it is shown they no longer present a flight risk or a danger to the community. In a later case the specific circumstances of a detention may present a substantial constitutional question. That is not a reason, however, for framing a rule which ignores the law governing alien status.

As persons within our jurisdiction, the aliens are entitled to the protection of the Due Process Clause. Liberty under the Due Process Clause includes protection against unlawful or arbitrary personal restraint or detention. The liberty rights of the aliens before us here are subject to limitations and conditions not applicable to citizens, however. See, *e.g., Mathews v. Diaz*, 426 U.S. 67, 79–80 (1976) ("In the exercise of its broad power over naturalization and immigration, Congress regularly makes rules that would be unacceptable if applied to citizens"). No party to this proceeding contests the initial premise that the aliens have been determined to be removable after a fair hearing under lawful and proper procedures. * * *

* * *

When an alien is removable, he or she has no right under the basic immigration laws to remain in this country. The removal orders reflect the determination that the aliens' ties to this community are insufficient to justify their continued presence in the United States. An alien's admission to this country is conditioned upon compliance with our laws, and removal is the consequence of a breach of that understanding.

* * * Removable and excludable aliens are situated differently before an order of removal is entered; the removable alien, by virtue of his continued presence here, possesses an interest in remaining, while the excludable alien seeks only the privilege of entry.

Still, both removable and inadmissible aliens are entitled to be free from detention that is arbitrary or capricious. Where detention is incident to removal, the detention cannot be justified as punishment nor can the confinement or its conditions be designed in order to punish. *See Wong Wing v. United States*, 163 U.S. 228 (1896). * * * It is neither arbitrary nor capricious to detain the aliens when necessary to avoid the risk of flight or danger to the community.

Whether a due process right is denied when removable aliens who are flight risks or dangers to the community are detained turns, then, not on the substantive right to be free, but on whether there are adequate procedures to review their cases, allowing persons once subject to detention to show that through rehabilitation, new appreciation of their responsibilities, or under other standards, they no longer present special risks or danger if put at large. The procedures to determine and to review the status-required detention go far toward this objective.

By regulations, promulgated after notice and comment, the Attorney General has given structure to the discretion delegated by the INA in order to ensure fairness and regularity in INS detention decisions. First, the INS provides for an initial postcustody review, before the expiration of the 90–day removal period, at which a district director conducts a record review. 8 CFR § 241.4 (2001). The alien is entitled to present any relevant information in support of release, and the district director has the discretion to interview the alien for a personal evaluation. § 241.4(h)(1). At the end of the 90–day period, the alien, if held in custody, is transferred to a postorder detention unit at INS headquarters, which in the ordinary course will conduct an initial custody review within three months of the transfer. § 241.4(k)(2)(ii). If the INS determines the alien should remain in detention, a two–member panel of INS officers interviews the alien and makes a recommendation to INS headquarters. §§ 241.4(i)(1)–(3). The regulations provide an extensive, nonexhaustive list of factors that should be considered in the recommendation to release or further detain. Those include: "[t]he nature and number of disciplinary infractions"; "the detainee's criminal conduct and criminal convictions, including consideration of the nature and severity of the alien's convictions, sentences imposed and time actually served, probation and criminal parole history, evidence of recidivism, and other criminal history"; "psychiatric and psychological reports pertaining to the detainee's mental health"; "[e]vidence of rehabilitation"; "[f]avorable factors, including ties to the United States such as the number of close relatives"; "[p]rior immigration violations and history"; "[t]he likelihood that the alien is a significant flight risk or may abscond to avoid removal, including history of escapes"; and any other probative information. § 241.4(f). Another review must occur within one year, with mandatory evaluations each year thereafter; if the alien requests, the INS has the discretion to grant more frequent reviews. § 241.4(k)(2)(iii). The INS must provide the alien 30–days advance, written notice of custody reviews; and it must afford the alien an opportunity to submit any relevant materials for consideration. § 241.4(i)(3)(ii). The alien may be assisted by a representative of his choice during the review, §§ 241.4(i)(3)(i), (ii), and the INS must provide the alien with a copy of its decision, including a brief statement of the reasons for any continued detention, § 241.4(d).

* * *

* * * [T]he procedural protection here is real, not illusory; and the criteria for obtaining release are far from insurmountable. Statistics show that between February 1999 and mid-November 2000 some 6,200 aliens were provided custody reviews before expiration of the 90–day removal period, and of those aliens about 3,380 were released. As a result, although the alien carries the burden to prove detention is no longer justified, there is no showing this is an unreasonable burden.

* * *

* * * The majority instead would have the Judiciary review the status of repatriation negotiations, which, one would have thought, are the paradigmatic examples of nonjusticiable inquiry. * * * The Court's rule is a serious misconception of the proper judicial function, and it is not what Congress enacted.

* * *

NOTES AND QUESTIONS ON ZADVYDAS V. DAVIS

1. Justice Scalia not only endorses *Mezei*; he believes it should control the result in *Zadvydas*, because both detainees had final removal orders that ended their permanent resident status:

> We are offered no justification why an alien under a valid and final order of removal—which has *totally extinguished* whatever right to presence in this country he possessed—has any greater due process right to be released into the country than an alien at the border seeking entry.

Is there a good response to this argument?

2. How persuasive is the Court's reading of the statute? If it is unconvincing, why did the Court adopt it? Consider the view that "[t]he principal decisions that have contributed to [the] expansion of judicial review in immigration cases have not been decisions of constitutional immigration law. Instead, they reached results favorable to noncitizens by interpreting statutes, regulations, or other forms of subconstitutional immigration law." Motomura, *Immigration Law After a Century of Plenary Power: Phantom Constitutional Norms and Statutory Interpretation*, 100 Yale L.J. 545, 560 (1990). Motomura continues:

> In immigration law, the "constitutional" norms that actually inform statutory interpretation—which are norms borrowed from public norms

generally—conflict with the expressly articulated constitutional norm—unreviewable plenary power. The former are "phantom" rather than "real" constitutional norms in the sense that they do not serve the first function of "constitutional" norms—namely, direct application to constitutional issues raised in immigration cases. * * * But "phantom constitutional norms" are "constitutional" in the sense that they, having been at least seriously entertained as a constitutional argument and in many cases actually adopted as an expressly constitutional decision in other areas of law, then carry over to immigration cases, where they are substantial enough to serve the limited function of informing interpretation of immigration statutes and other subconstitutional texts. Or, to use an image from the physical sciences, they have enough gravitational force to exercise a pull on these other sources of law. In this context, phantom norms produce results that are much more sympathetic to aliens than the results that would follow from the interpretation of statutes in light of * * * plenary power.

Id. at 564–65. *Cf.* Aleinikoff, *Detaining Plenary Power: The Meaning and Impact of Zadvydas v. Davis*, 16 Geo. Immig. L.J. 365, 369 (2002) ("the Court has moved beyond invoking a 'phantom' constitutional norm"; characterizing *Zadvydas* as a decision of constitutional law).

3. The Court wants to distinguish noncitizens in the United States from those who are not here, and it cites *Mezei* as a prime example of a case involving a noncitizen on the wrong side of the constitutional borderline. But what line does *Zadvydas* draw? Is it based on physical presence in the United States, on having been admitted, or having entered? (Recall from Chapter Six that entry marked the pre–1996 line between exclusion and deportation proceedings, and that entry generally included physically present noncitizens who had crossed the border surreptitiously.) All three lines appear in *Zadvydas*, though they did not matter on the facts, because both Zadvydas and Ma were physically present, had been admitted, and had entered the United States. *See* Bosniak, *A Basic Territorial Distinction*, 16 Geo. Immig. L.J. 407 (2002).

Although many immigrants' rights groups hailed *Zadvydas* as a victory, the Court reaffirmed the vitality of their old nemesis, *Mezei*. "In an odd and unfortunate way, the case reaffirms what most scholars thought constitutional law was moving beyond: a distinction between the constitutional rights of non-citizens at the U.S border and those located inside the country." Aleinikoff, *Detaining Plenary Power, supra*, 16 Geo. Immig. L.J. at 366. Ironically, the dissenters Kennedy and Rehnquist "would not let the substantive liberty decision turn on the exclusion-deportation line" and thus implied their disagreement with *Mezei's* approval of indefinite detention of a returning permanent resident. *See* Martin, *Graduated Application of Constitutional Protections for Aliens: The Real Meaning of* Zadvydas v. Davis, 2001 Sup. Ct. Rev. 47, 78.

4. Is *Zadvydas* best understood (and defended) as a decision distinguishing once-permanent residents from other noncitizens?

If we focus on LPRs, we can perhaps recast the majority as saying something important about the deep structure or the trans-statutory understanding of just what lawful permanent residence really means. Historically and psychologically, admission in this category amounts to an invitation to full membership in the society and eventually the polity. Immigrants—that is, aliens selected for lawful permanent resident status—pass through the most rigorous screening our immigration system imposes. But having done so, they are then invited to become part of our community, to sink roots—permanent roots—and to chart out life plans in reliance on enduring rights to remain. With minimal additional effort, an LPR can also graduate to the highest level of membership, by becoming a naturalized citizen after five years residence. And in general it is fair to say that our reigning national mythology, bolstered by certain practical inducements, reflects an expectation that immigrants should and will naturalize. The exact holding in *Zadvydas*, which involved only LPRs, could be understood as saying that roots or connections established in that fashion, on the basis of such an invitation, simply count for more when calculating the constitutional limits on future treatment—even if the initially favorable legal status, for valid reasons, has been terminated. The historical paths these two aliens followed to a removal order leave them in a genuinely different constitutional position from [someone detained at the time of initial entry].

Martin, Graduated Application, supra, 2001 Sup. Ct. Rev. at 101–02.

5. Detention and release issues related to *Mezei* arose in one branch of the judicial battles over the detention at Guantánamo of prisoners apprehended by the United States during its military operations in Afghanistan. After early rounds of litigation, the U.S. government conceded that 17 ethnic Uighur detainees from China, captured in late 2001, were not enemy combatants and so had to be released. But because the government agreed not to send them to China, where they were at risk of torture, they remained at Guantánamo, under slightly better conditions of detention, for a lengthy period thereafter, while the U.S. government sought to resettle them in other countries. In late 2008 the district court, frustrated at the slow pace, ordered that they be released into the United States, in view of the "exceptional" circumstances of the case and the need to safeguard "an individual's liberty from unbridled executive fiat." The D.C. Circuit reversed, holding that no law authorized the release of these detainees into the United States. The dissent suggested that the habeas corpus statute, as construed by the Supreme Court in *Boumediene v. Bush,* 553 U.S. 723, 128 S.Ct. 2229, 171 L.Ed.2d 41 (2008), justified such a step. But the majority disagreed. The issue was not whether they should be released—the issue that habeas opens up—but where. Under *Knauff* and *Mezei, t*he political branches retain authority over any entry into the United States. *Kiyemba v. Obama,* 555 F.3d 1022 (D.C.Cir.2009), *opinion reinstated as amended, after remand from Supreme Court,* 605 F.3d 1046 (D.C.Cir. 2010).

The D.C. Circuit ruling carries echoes of Justice Scalia's comment in *Zadvydas.* "I am sure they cannot be tortured, as well—but neither prohibition has anything to do with their right to be released into the United States." Scalia was in dissent. Under the *Zadvydas* majority's approach, how should the Uighur's claims have been treated? Are there relevant differences between those detainees and Zadvydas or Ma?

As the Uighur case unfolded, the Supreme Court granted certiorari to review the D.C. Circuit's ruling described above, but the U.S. government's efforts to find resettlement offers in third countries then found success for all 17. Twelve of the Uighurs accepted the offers and are now living in Palau or Switzerland. When the Supreme Court remanded the case for reconsideration of the five remaining petitions in light of the resettlement offers, the D.C. Circuit reinstated its earlier ruling, and the Supreme Court then denied certiorari. *Kiyemba v. Obama,* 605 F.3d 1046 (D.C. Cir. 2010), *cert. denied,* ___ U.S. ___, 131 S.Ct. 1631, 179 L.Ed.2d 925 (2011).

b. Detention Pending Removal Proceedings

Much more common than lengthy detention after a final removal order is detention during removal proceedings. INA § 236(c) requires detention of certain categories of aliens in removal proceedings, not excluding lawful permanent residents. There is no individual bond hearing. Is this constitutional? The U.S. Supreme Court addressed this question two years after *Zadvydas*.

DEMORE v. KIM

Supreme Court of the United States, 2003.
538 U.S. 510, 123 S.Ct. 1708, 155 L.Ed.2d 724.

CHIEF JUSTICE REHNQUIST delivered the opinion of the Court.

* * * Respondent is a citizen of the Republic of South Korea. He entered the United States in 1984, at the age of six, and became a lawful permanent resident of the United States two years later. In July 1996, he was convicted of first-degree burglary in state court in California and, in April 1997, he was convicted of a second crime, "petty theft with priors." The Immigration and Naturalization Service (INS) charged respondent with being deportable from the United States in light of these convictions, and detained him pending his removal hearing. We hold that Congress, justifiably concerned that deportable criminal aliens who are not detained continue to engage in crime and fail to appear for their removal hearings in large numbers, may require that persons such as respondent be detained for the brief period necessary for their removal proceedings.

* * * In conceding that he was deportable, respondent forwent a hearing at which he would have been entitled to raise any nonfrivolous argument available to demonstrate that he was not properly included in a mandatory detention category. See 8 CFR [§ 1003.19(h)(2)(ii)] (2002); *Matter of Joseph,* 22 I & N Dec. 799 (1999).[3] Respondent instead filed a habeas corpus action pursuant to 28 U.S.C. § 2241 in the United States District Court for the Northern District of California challenging the

---

3. This "*Joseph* hearing" is immediately provided to a detainee who claims that he is not covered by § 236(c). At the hearing, the detainee may avoid mandatory detention by demonstrating that he is not an alien, was not convicted of the predicate crime, or that the INS is otherwise substantially unlikely to establish that he is in fact subject to mandatory detention. Because respondent conceded that he was deportable because of a conviction that triggers § 236(c) and thus sought no *Joseph* hearing, we have no occasion to review the adequacy of *Joseph* hearings generally in screening out those who are improperly detained * * *.

constitutionality of § 236(c) itself. He argued that his detention under § 236(c) violated due process because the INS had made no determination that he posed either a danger to society or a flight risk.

* * *

II

* * * Section 236(c) mandates detention during removal proceedings for a limited class of deportable aliens—including those convicted of an aggravated felony. Congress adopted this provision against a backdrop of wholesale failure by the INS to deal with increasing rates of criminal activity by aliens. Criminal aliens were the fastest growing segment of the federal prison population, already constituting roughly 25% of all federal prisoners, and they formed a rapidly rising share of state prison populations as well. Congress' investigations showed, however, that the INS could not even *identify* most deportable aliens, much less locate them and remove them from the country. One study showed that, at the then-current rate of deportation, it would take 23 years to remove every criminal alien already subject to deportation. Making matters worse, criminal aliens who were deported swiftly reentered the country illegally in great numbers.

The agency's near-total inability to remove deportable criminal aliens imposed more than a monetary cost on the Nation. First, as Congress explained, "[a]liens who enter or remain in the United States in violation of our law are effectively taking immigration opportunities that might otherwise be extended to others." Second, deportable criminal aliens who remained in the United States often committed more crimes before being removed. One 1986 study showed that, after criminal aliens were identified as deportable, 77% were arrested at least once more and 45%—nearly half—were arrested multiple times before their deportation proceedings even began. Hearing on H.R. 3333 before the Subcommittee on Immigration, Refugees, and International Law of the House Committee on the Judiciary, 101st Cong., 1st Sess., 54, 52 (1989) (hereinafter 1989 House Hearing).

Congress also had before it evidence that one of the major causes of the INS' failure to remove deportable criminal aliens was the agency's failure to detain those aliens during their deportation proceedings. * * *

Once released, more than 20% of deportable criminal aliens failed to appear for their removal hearings. * * *

* * *

* * * Some studies presented to Congress suggested that detention of criminal aliens during their removal proceedings might be the best way to ensure their successful removal from this country. It was following those Reports that Congress enacted INA § 236, requiring the Attorney General to detain a subset of deportable criminal aliens pending a determination of their removability.

"In the exercise of its broad power over naturalization and immigration, Congress regularly makes rules that would be unacceptable if applied to citizens." *Mathews v. Diaz,* 426 U.S. 67, 79–80, 96 S.Ct. 1883, 48 L.Ed.2d 478 (1976). * * *

In his habeas corpus challenge, respondent did not contest Congress' general authority to remove criminal aliens from the United States. Nor did he argue that he himself was not "deportable" within the meaning of § 236(c).[6] Rather, respondent argued that the Government may not, consistent with the Due Process Clause of the Fifth Amendment, detain him for the brief period necessary for his removal proceedings. The dissent, after an initial detour on the issue of respondent's concession, ultimately acknowledges the real issue in this case.

"It is well established that the Fifth Amendment entitles aliens to due process of law in deportation proceedings." *Reno v. Flores,* 507 U.S. 292, 306, 113 S.Ct. 1439, 123 L.Ed.2d 1 (1993). At the same time, however, this Court has recognized detention during deportation proceedings as a constitutionally valid aspect of the deportation process. As we said more than a century ago, deportation proceedings "would be vain if those accused could not be held in custody pending the inquiry into their true character." *Wong Wing v. United States,* 163 U.S. 228, 235, 16 S.Ct. 977, 41 L.Ed. 140 (1896).

In *Carlson v. Landon,* 342 U.S. 524, 72 S.Ct. 525, 96 L.Ed. 547 (1952), the Court considered a challenge to the detention of aliens who were deportable because of their participation in Communist activities. The detained aliens did not deny that they were members of the Communist Party or that they were therefore deportable. Instead, like respondent in the present case, they challenged their detention on the grounds that there had been no finding that they were unlikely to appear for their deportation proceedings when ordered to do so. Although the Attorney General ostensibly had discretion to release detained Communist aliens on bond, the INS had adopted a policy of refusing to grant bail to [them]. * * *

* * * The Court noted that Congress had chosen to make such aliens deportable based on its "understanding of [Communists'] attitude toward the use of force and violence ... to accomplish their political aims." And it concluded that the INS could deny bail to the detainees "by reference to the legislative scheme" even without any finding of flight risk. * * *

* * *

Despite this Court's longstanding view that the Government may constitutionally detain deportable aliens during the limited period necessary for their removal proceedings, respondent argues that the narrow detention policy reflected in § 236(c) violates due process. Respondent,

---

6. * * * Lest there be any confusion, we emphasize that by conceding he is "*deportable*" and, hence, subject to mandatory detention under § 236(c), respondent did not concede that he *will ultimately be deported.* As the dissent notes, respondent has applied for withholding of removal.

like the four Courts of Appeals that have held § 236(c) to be unconstitutional, relies heavily upon our recent opinion in *Zadvydas v. Davis,* 533 U.S. 678, 121 S.Ct. 2491, 150 L.Ed.2d 653 (2001).

* * *

But *Zadvydas* is materially different from the present case in two respects.

First, in *Zadvydas,* the aliens challenging their detention following final orders of deportation were ones for whom removal was "no longer practically attainable." * * *

In the present case, the statutory provision at issue governs detention of deportable criminal aliens *pending their removal proceedings.* Such detention necessarily serves the purpose of preventing deportable criminal aliens from fleeing prior to or during their removal proceedings, thus increasing the chance that, if ordered removed, the aliens will be successfully removed. Respondent disagrees, arguing that there is no evidence that mandatory detention is necessary because the Government has never shown that individualized bond hearings would be ineffective. But as discussed above, in adopting § 236(c), Congress had before it evidence suggesting that permitting discretionary release of aliens pending their removal hearings would lead to large numbers of deportable criminal aliens skipping their hearings and remaining at large in the United States unlawfully.

Respondent argues that these statistics are irrelevant and do not demonstrate that individualized bond hearings "are ineffective or burdensome." It is of course true that when Congress enacted § 236, individualized bail determinations had not been tested under optimal conditions, or tested in all their possible permutations. But when the Government deals with deportable aliens, the Due Process Clause does not require it to employ the least burdensome means to accomplish its goal. The evidence Congress had before it certainly supports the approach it selected even if other, hypothetical studies might have suggested different courses of action.

Zadvydas is materially different from the present case in a second respect as well. While the period of detention at issue in *Zadvydas* was "indefinite" and "potentially permanent," the detention here is of a much shorter duration.

Zadvydas distinguished the statutory provision it was there considering from § 236 on these very grounds, noting that "post-removal-period detention, *unlike detention pending a determination of removability . . . ,* has no obvious termination point." *Id.,* at 697, 121 S.Ct. 2491 (emphasis added). Under § 236(c), not only does detention have a definite termination point, in the majority of cases it lasts for less than the 90 days we considered presumptively valid in *Zadvydas.* The Executive Office for Immigration Review has calculated that, in 85% of the cases in which aliens are detained pursuant to § 236(c), removal proceedings are completed in an average time of 47 days and a median of 30 days. In the remaining 15% of cases, in which the alien appeals the decision of the Immigration Judge to the Board of Immigration Appeals, appeal takes an average of four months, with a median time that is slightly shorter.

These statistics do not include the many cases in which removal proceedings are completed while the alien is still serving time for the underlying conviction. In those cases, the aliens involved are never subjected to mandatory detention at all. In sum, the detention at stake under § 236(c) lasts roughly a month and a half in the vast majority of cases in which it is invoked, and about five months in the minority of cases in which the alien chooses to appeal. Respondent was detained for somewhat longer than the average—spending six months in INS custody prior to the District Court's order granting habeas relief, but respondent himself had requested a continuance of his removal hearing.

For the reasons set forth above, respondent's claim must fail. * * *

JUSTICE KENNEDY, concurring.

While the justification for INA § 236(c) is based upon the Government's concerns over the risks of flight and danger to the community, the ultimate purpose behind the detention is premised upon the alien's deportability. As a consequence, due process requires individualized procedures to ensure there is at least some merit to the Immigration and Naturalization Service's (INS) charge and, therefore, sufficient justification to detain a lawful permanent resident alien pending a more formal hearing. * * *

As the Court notes, these procedures were apparently available to respondent in this case. Respondent was entitled to a [*Joseph*] hearing in which he could have "raise[d] any nonfrivolous argument available to demonstrate that he was not properly included in a mandatory detention category." * * * Respondent, however, did not seek relief under these procedures, and the Court had no occasion here to determine their adequacy.

For similar reasons, since the Due Process Clause prohibits arbitrary deprivations of liberty, a lawful permanent resident alien such as respondent could be entitled to an individualized determination as to his risk of flight and dangerousness if the continued detention became unreasonable or unjustified. *Zadvydas,* 533 U.S., at 684–686, 121 S.Ct. 2491; *id.,* at 721, 121 S.Ct. 2491 (Kennedy, J., dissenting) ("[A]liens are entitled to be free from detention that is arbitrary or capricious"). Were there an unreasonable delay by the INS in pursuing and completing deportation proceedings, it could become necessary then to inquire whether the detention is not to facilitate deportation, or to protect against risk of flight or dangerousness, but to incarcerate for other reasons. That is not a proper inference, however, either from the statutory scheme itself or from the circumstances of this case. The Court's careful opinion is consistent with these premises, and I join it in full.

[JUSTICE O'CONNOR, with JUSTICE SCALIA and JUSTICE THOMAS, joined the Court's opinion on the merits but would have found that the federal courts lacked jurisdiction to hear the case.]

* * *

JUSTICE SOUTER, with whom JUSTICE STEVENS and JUSTICE GINSBURG join, concurring in part and dissenting in part.

* * *

* * * The Court's holding that the Constitution permits the Government to lock up a lawful permanent resident of this country when there is concededly no reason to do so forgets over a century of precedent acknowledging the rights of permanent residents, including the basic liberty from physical confinement lying at the heart of due process. The INS has never argued that detaining Kim is necessary to guarantee his appearance for removal proceedings or to protect anyone from danger in the meantime. Instead, shortly after the District Court issued its order in this case, the INS, *sua sponte* and without even holding a custody hearing, concluded that Kim "would not be considered a threat" and that any risk of flight could be met by a bond of $5,000. He was released soon thereafter, and there is no indication that he is not complying with the terms of his release.

* * *

At the outset, there is the Court's mistaken suggestion that Kim "conceded" his removability. The Court cites no statement before any court conceding removability, and I can find none. At the first opportunity, Kim applied to the Immigration Court for withholding of removal, and he represents that he intends to assert that his criminal convictions are not for removable offenses and that he is independently eligible for statutory relief from removal. * * *

* * *

II

A

It has been settled for over a century that all aliens within our territory are "persons" entitled to the protection of the Due Process Clause. Aliens "residing in the United States for a shorter or longer time, are entitled, so long as they are permitted by the government of the United States to remain in the country, to the safeguards of the Constitution, and to the protection of the laws, in regard to their rights of person and of property, and to their civil and criminal responsibility." *Fong Yue Ting v. United States,* 149 U.S. 698, 724, 13 S.Ct. 1016, 37 L.Ed. 905 (1893). *The Japanese Immigrant Case* [*Yamataya v. Fisher*], 189 U.S. 86, 100–101, 23 S.Ct. 611, 47 L.Ed. 721 (1903), settled any lingering doubt that the Fifth Amendment's Due Process Clause gives aliens a right to challenge mistreatment of their person or property.

The constitutional protection of an alien's person and property is particularly strong in the case of aliens lawfully admitted to permanent residence (LPRs). The immigration laws give LPRs the opportunity to establish a life permanently in this country by developing economic, familial, and social ties indistinguishable from those of a citizen. In fact, the law of the United States goes out of its way to encourage just such attachments by creating immigration preferences for those with a citizen as a close relation, and those with valuable professional skills or other assets promising benefits to the United States.

Once they are admitted to permanent residence, LPRs share in the economic freedom enjoyed by citizens: they may compete for most jobs in the private and public sectors without obtaining job-specific authorization, and apart from the franchise, jury duty, and certain forms of public assistance, their lives are generally indistinguishable from those of United States citizens. That goes for obligations as well as opportunities. Unlike temporary, nonimmigrant aliens, who are generally taxed only on income from domestic sources or connected with a domestic business, LPRs, like citizens, are taxed on their worldwide income. Male LPRs between the ages of 18 and 26 must register under the Selective Service Act of 1948. "Resident aliens, like citizens, pay taxes, support the economy, serve in the Armed Forces, and contribute in myriad other ways to our society." *In re Griffiths,* 413 U.S. 717, 722, 93 S.Ct. 2851, 37 L.Ed.2d 910 (1973). And if they choose, they may apply for full membership in the national polity through naturalization.

The attachments fostered through these legal mechanisms are all the more intense for LPRs brought to the United States as children. They grow up here as members of the society around them, probably without much touch with their country of citizenship, probably considering the United States as home just as much as a native-born, younger brother or sister entitled to United States citizenship. * * * Kim is an example. He moved to the United States at the age of six and was lawfully admitted to permanent residence when he was eight. His mother is a citizen, and his father and brother are LPRs. LPRs in Kim's situation have little or no reason to feel or to establish firm ties with any place besides the United States.

* * * [I]n *Kwong Hai Chew v. Colding,* 344 U.S. 590, 73 S.Ct. 472, 97 L.Ed. 576 (1953), we read the word "excludable" in a regulation as having no application to LPRs, since such a reading would have been questionable given "a resident alien's constitutional right to due process." *Id.,* at 598–599, 73 S.Ct. 472. *Kwong Hai Chew* adopted the statement of Justice Murphy, concurring in *Bridges* [*v. Wixon,* 326 U.S. 135, 65 S.Ct. 1443, 89 L.Ed. 2103 (1945)], that " 'once an alien lawfully enters and resides in this country he becomes invested with the rights guaranteed by the Constitution to all people within our borders. Such rights include those protected by the First and the Fifth Amendments and by the due process clause of the Fourteenth Amendment. None of these provisions acknowledges any distinction between citizens and resident aliens. They extend their inalien-

able privileges to all "persons" and guard against any encroachment on those rights by federal or state authority.' " 344 U.S., at 596–597, n.5, 73 S.Ct. 472 (quoting *Bridges, supra,* at 161, 65 S.Ct. 1443).

The law therefore considers an LPR to be at home in the United States, and even when the Government seeks removal, we have accorded LPRs greater protections than other aliens under the Due Process Clause [citing *Landon v. Plasencia,* 459 U.S. 21, 103 S.Ct. 321, 74 L.Ed.2d 21 (1982).]

Although LPRs remain subject to the federal removal power, that power may not be exercised without due process, and any decision about the requirements of due process for an LPR must account for the difficulty of distinguishing in practical as well as doctrinal terms between the liberty interest of an LPR and that of a citizen. In evaluating Kim's challenge to his mandatory detention under INA § 236(c), the only reasonable starting point is the traditional doctrine concerning the Government's physical confinement of individuals.

B

Kim's claim is a limited one: not that the Government may not detain LPRs to ensure their appearance at removal hearings, but that due process under the Fifth Amendment conditions a potentially lengthy detention on a hearing and an impartial decisionmaker's finding that detention is necessary to a governmental purpose. He thus invokes our repeated decisions that the claim of liberty protected by the Fifth Amendment is at its strongest when government seeks to detain an individual. The Chief Justice wrote in 1987 that "[i]n our society liberty is the norm, and detention prior to trial or without trial is the carefully limited exception." *United States v. Salerno,* 481 U.S. 739, 755, 107 S.Ct. 2095, 95 L.Ed.2d 697.

* * *

[Our prior cases on physical confinement, *Salerno, supra; Foucha v. Louisiana,* 504 U.S. 71, 112 S.Ct. 1780, 118 L.Ed.2d 437 (1992); *Addington v. Texas,* 441 U.S. 418, 99 S.Ct. 1804, 60 L.Ed.2d 323 (1979); *Kansas v. Hendricks,* 521 U.S. 346, 117 S.Ct. 2072, 138 L.Ed.2d 501 (1997); *Jackson v. Indiana,* 406 U.S. 715, 92 S.Ct. 1845, 32 L.Ed.2d 435 (1972)] yield a simple distillate that should govern the result here. Due process calls for an individual determination before someone is locked away. In none of the cases cited did we ever suggest that the government could avoid the Due Process Clause by doing what § 236(c) does, by selecting a class of people for confinement on a categorical basis and denying members of that class any chance to dispute the necessity of putting them away. The cases, of course, would mean nothing if citizens and comparable residents could be shorn of due process by this sort of categorical sleight of hand. Without any "full-blown adversary hearing" before detention, *Salerno, supra,* at 750, 107 S.Ct. 2095, or heightened burden of proof, *Addington, supra,* or other procedures to show the government's interest in committing an individual, *Foucha, supra*; *Jackson, supra*, procedural rights would amount to nothing but mechanisms for testing group membership. And if procedure could be dispensed with so expediently, so presumably could the substantive requirements that the class of detainees be narrow and the detention period strictly limited.

C

We held as much just two Terms ago in *Zadvydas v. Davis*, which stands for the proposition that detaining an alien requires more than the rationality of a general detention statute; any justification must go to the alien himself. * * *

The *Zadvydas* opinion opened by noting the clear applicability of general due process standards: physical detention requires both a "special justification" that "outweighs the 'individual's constitutionally protected interest in avoiding physical restraint' " and "adequate procedural protections." 533 U.S., at 690, 121 S.Ct. 2491 (quoting *Hendricks*, 521 U.S. at 356, 117 S.Ct. 2072). Nowhere did we suggest that the "constitutionally protected liberty interest" in avoiding physical confinement, even for aliens already ordered removed, was conceptually different from the liberty interest of citizens considered in *Jackson, Salerno, Foucha*, and *Hendricks*. On the contrary, we cited those cases and expressly adopted their reasoning, even as applied to aliens whose right to remain in the United States had already been declared forfeited.

* * *

Our individualized analysis and disposition in *Zadvydas* support Kim's claim for an individualized review of his challenge to the reasons that are supposed to justify confining him prior to any determination of removability. In fact, aliens in removal proceedings have an additional interest in avoiding confinement, beyond anything considered in *Zadvydas:* detention prior to entry of a removal order may well impede the alien's ability to develop and present his case on the very issue of removability * * * [because they could be transferred and isolated] away from their lawyers, witnesses, and evidence. * * *

In fact, the principal dissenters in *Zadvydas*, as well as the majority, accepted a theory that would compel success for Kim in this case. The dissent relied on the fact that Zadvydas and Ma were subject to a "final order of removal" and had "no right under the basic immigration laws to remain in this country," 533 U.S., at 720, 121 S.Ct. 2491 (opinion of KENNEDY, J.), in distinguishing them "from aliens with a lawful right to remain here," which is Kim's position. The dissent recognized the right of all aliens, even "removable and inadmissible" ones, to be "free from detention that is arbitrary or capricious," and the opinion explained that detention would pass the "arbitrary or capricious" test "when necessary to avoid the risk of flight or danger to the community."

* * * The references to the "necessity" of an individual's detention and the discussion of the procedural requirements show that the principal

Zadvydas dissenters envisioned due process as individualized review, and the Court of Appeals in this case correctly held that Kim's mandatory detention without benefit of individualized enquiry violated due process as understood by both the *Zadvydas* majority and Justice Kennedy in dissent.

D

* * *

By these standards, Kim's case is an easy one. * * * Detention is not limited to dangerous criminal aliens or those found likely to flee, but applies to all aliens claimed to be deportable for criminal convictions, even where the underlying offenses are minor. *E.g., Michel v. INS*, 206 F.3d 253, 256 (C.A.2 2000) (possession of stolen bus transfers); *Matter of Bart*, 20 I & N Dec. 436 (BIA 1992) (issuance of a bad check). Detention under § 236(c) is not limited by the kind of time limit imposed by the Speedy Trial Act, and while it lasts only as long as the removal proceedings, those proceedings have no deadline and may last over a year. * * *

Kim's detention without particular justification in these respects, or the opportunity to enquire into it, violates both components of due process, and I would accordingly affirm the judgment of the Court of Appeals requiring the INS to hold a bail hearing to see whether detention is needed to avoid a risk of flight or a danger to the community. This is surely little enough, given the fact that INA § 506 gives an LPR charged with being a foreign terrorist the right to a release hearing pending a determination that he be removed.

III

* * *

A

The Court spends much effort trying to distinguish *Zadvydas*, but even if the Court succeeded, success would not avail it much. *Zadvydas* was an application of principles developed in over a century of cases on the rights of aliens and the limits on the government's power to confine individuals. While there are differences between detention pending removal proceedings (this case) and detention after entry of a removal order (*Zadvydas*), the differences merely point up that Kim's is the stronger claim. In any case, the analytical framework set forth in *Salerno, Foucha, Hendricks, Jackson*, and other physical confinement cases applies to both, and the two differences the Court relies upon fail to remove Kim's challenge from the ambit of either the earlier cases or *Zadvydas* itself.[16]

* * *

The Court's closest approach to a reason justifying class-wide detention without exception here is a Senate Report stating that over 20% of

---

16. The Court tellingly does not even mention *Salerno, Foucha, Hendricks*, or *Jackson*.

nondetained criminal aliens failed to appear for removal hearings. To begin with, the Senate Report's statistic treats all criminal aliens alike and does not distinguish between LPRs like Kim, who are likely to have developed strong ties within the United States, and temporary visitors or illegal entrants. Even more importantly, the statistic tells us nothing about flight risk at all because, as both the Court and the Senate Report recognize, the INS was making its custody determinations not on the ground of likelihood of flight or dangerousness, but "in large part, according to the number of beds available in a particular region." Senate Report, at 23. * * * Four former high-ranking INS officials explained the Court's statistics as follows: "Flight rates were so high in the early 1990s not as a result of chronic discretionary judgment failures by [the] INS in assessing which aliens might pose a flight risk. Rather, the rates were alarmingly high because decisions to release aliens in proceedings were driven overwhelmingly by a lack of detention facilities." Brief for T. Alexander Aleinikoff et al. as *Amici Curiae* 19.

* * *

The Court's second effort is its claim that mandatory detention under § 236(c) is generally of a "much shorter duration" than the incarceration at issue in *Zadvydas*. While it is true that removal proceedings are unlikely to prove "indefinite and potentially permanent," they are not formally limited to any period, and often extend beyond the time suggested by the Court[.] * * *

* * * As the Solicitor General conceded, the length of the average detention period in great part reflects the fact that the vast majority of cases involve aliens who raise no challenge to removability at all. LPRs like Kim, however, will hardly fit that pattern. Unlike many illegal entrants and temporary nonimmigrants, LPRs are the aliens most likely to press substantial challenges to removability requiring lengthy proceedings. Successful challenges often require several months of proceedings; detention for an open-ended period like this falls far short of the "stringent time limitations" held to be significant in *Salerno*. The potential for several months of confinement requires an individualized finding of necessity under *Zadvydas*.

* * *

IV

This case is not about the National Government's undisputed power to detain aliens in order to avoid flight or prevent danger to the community. The issue is whether that power may be exercised by detaining a still lawful permanent resident alien when there is no reason for it and no way to challenge it. The Court's holding that the Due Process Clause allows this under a blanket rule is devoid of even ostensible justification in fact and at odds with the settled standard of liberty. I respectfully dissent.

JUSTICE BREYER, concurring in part and dissenting in part.

* * *

This case * * * is not one in which an alien concedes deportability. As Justice Souter points out, Kim argues to the contrary. Kim claims that his earlier convictions were neither for an " 'aggravated felony,' " nor for two crimes of " 'moral turpitude.' " And given shifting lower court views on such matters, I cannot say that his arguments are insubstantial or interposed solely for purposes of delay.

That being so—as long as Kim's legal arguments are neither insubstantial nor interposed solely for purposes of delay—then the immigration statutes, interpreted in light of the Constitution, permit Kim (if neither dangerous nor a flight risk) to obtain bail. For one thing, Kim's constitutional claims to bail in these circumstances are strong. Indeed, they are strong enough to require us to "ascertain whether a construction of the statute is fairly possible by which the [constitutional] question may be avoided." *Crowell v. Benson*, 285 U.S. 22, 62, 52 S.Ct. 285, 76 L.Ed. 598 (1932); accord, *Zadvydas, supra,* at 689, 121 S.Ct. 2491.

For another, the relevant statutes literally say nothing about an individual who, armed with a strong argument against deportability, might, or might not, fall within their terms. INA § 236(c) tells the Attorney General to "take into custody any alien who . . . *is* deportable" (emphasis added), not one who may, or may not, fall into that category. Indeed, the Government now permits such an alien to obtain bail if his argument against deportability is significantly *stronger* than substantial, *i.e.,* strong enough to make it "substantially unlikely" that the Government will win. *In re Joseph,* 22 I & N Dec. 799 (1999).

Finally, bail standards drawn from the criminal justice system are available to fill this statutory gap. Federal law makes bail available to a criminal defendant after conviction and pending appeal provided (1) the appeal is "not for the purpose of delay," (2) the appeal "raises a substantial question of law or fact," and (3) the defendant shows by "clear and convincing evidence" that, if released, he "is not likely to flee or pose a danger to the safety" of the community. 18 U.S.C. § 3143(b). These standards give considerable weight to any special governmental interest in detention (*e.g.,* process-related concerns or class-related flight risks). The standards are more protective of a detained alien's liberty interest than those currently administered in the INS' *Joseph* hearings. And they have proved workable in practice in the criminal justice system. Nothing in the statute forbids their use when § 236(c) deportability is in doubt.

I would interpret the (silent) statute as imposing these bail standards. So interpreted, the statute would require the Government to permit a detained alien to seek an individualized assessment of flight risk and dangerousness as long as the alien's claim that he is not deportable is (1) not interposed solely for purposes of delay and (2) raises a question of "law or fact" that is not insubstantial. And that interpretation, in my view, is consistent with what the Constitution demands. * * *

NOTES AND QUESTIONS ON DEMORE V. KIM

1. Chief Justice Rehnquist and Justice Souter clearly disagree on the significance of a noncitizen's concession that he is "deportable." Rehnquist places great weight on deportability, while Souter regards it as much less significant than Kim's application for discretionary relief. Who is right on this point? *See* Taylor, *Judicial Deference to Congressional Folly: The Story of Demore v. Kim*, in Immigration Stories 343, 357 (D. Martin & P. Schuck eds., 2005) ("the *Demore* majority equated an apparent concession of baseline deportability—an admission that Kim's convictions fit within some deportation ground—with a concession that the government had properly classified him as an aggravated felon, rendering him ineligible for discretionary relief from removal").

If you agree with Justice Souter, how likely must it be that a noncitizen will be granted discretionary relief before mandatory detention is unconstitutional? How does Justice Breyer's approach differ on this point? After *Demore*, can a noncitizen avoid mandatory detention under § 236(c) simply by contesting deportability?

2. As between the majority and Justice Souter's dissent, which analysis is more faithful to *Zadvydas*? How can Justice O'Connor be consistent and join the majority in both *Zadvydas* and *Demore*? In particular, how can she rely on the *Salerno–Foucha* line of cases in *Zadvydas*, but agree to an opinion that does not even mention them in *Demore*?

3. Why isn't Chief Justice Rehnquist correct in noting that Kim did get an individualized hearing, namely to determine whether he falls within the category of noncitizens subject to mandatory detention? Justice Souter seems to reply that this is not a truly individualized determination. But doesn't *all* decisionmaking, even decisions that seem to focus on an individual, ultimately depend on generalizations based on categories? If so, what is Justice Souter's basis for believing that the Congress overstepped its authority in enacting § 236(c)?

4. What does Justice Kennedy, writing separately, have in mind when he suggests that he might differently approach detention in another case, if intended "not to facilitate deportation, or to protect against risk of flight or dangerousness, but to incarcerate for other reasons"? Does he cast constitutional doubt on mandatory detention that lasts much longer than the usual period of removal proceedings? How much longer?

5. How plausible is the reading of INA § 236 that Justice Breyer proposes? Is it as plausible as the Court's reading of § 241(a)(6) in *Zadvydas*?

6. How would the dissenters rule on a constitutional challenge to mandatory detention of a noncitizen who is *not* a permanent resident?

c. Defining the Scope of *Zadvydas*

Zadvydas left undefined its implications for detained noncitizens who had never been admitted. DHS regulations adopted the view that *Zadvy-*

das applied only to noncitizens who had been admitted or were in the United States after having entered without inspection. *See* 8 C.F.R. § 241.13(b). This meant that it would not require release of excludable aliens (as they were called before 1996) or arriving aliens (as they are now known) who faced indefinite detention because they could not be readily removed. As of mid–2002, about 2000 such noncitizens were believed to be in federal custody, of which about 1700 were Mariel Cubans, and the rest arriving aliens. *See* Joyce, *INS Detention Practices Post–Zadvydas v. Davis*, 79 Interp. Rel. 809, 813 (2002).

The Mariel Cubans (or "Marielitos") arrived in 1980 from the port of Mariel, opened by the Cuban government with an invitation to relatives in the United States to come pick up their family members. In this sudden and chaotic process, Cuban officials also forced returning boats to carry thousands of others whom the Cuban government wished to remove, including hundreds escorted from prisons or mental hospitals to the docks. The 125,000 Marielitos were undocumented, but the vast majority were paroled into the United States shortly after arrival. Most eventually obtained LPR status under special legislation. But a different outcome ensued if the person committed a crime in the United States while released. INS then revoked parole and took the person back into custody. These detainees were nearly all found excludable, but Cuba generally refused to take them back. The pattern of Cuban acceptance was erratic, however, and Washington continued trying to negotiate conditions for their return. Meanwhile, wishing to avoid the expense of lengthy detentions, but also not wanting to release dangerous criminals, the U.S. government undertook various screening measures to decide who would be released while the diplomacy continued. Some who were released in this fashion committed new offenses and found themselves back in custody. Over the course of 20–plus years, thousands of Cubans encountered lengthy incarceration—physically in the United States, inadmissible because of criminal convictions, and detained indefinitely because they failed to secure release through the review process and because Cuba would not take them back.

Many Marielitos brought statutory and constitutional challenges to their detention, but their claims were rejected by most of the federal appeals courts that heard them. *See, e.g., Carrera–Valdez v. Perryman*, 211 F.3d 1046, 1048 (7th Cir. 2000); *Barrera–Echavarria v. Rison*, 44 F.3d 1441 (9th Cir.) (en banc), *cert. denied*, 516 U.S. 976, 116 S.Ct. 479, 133 L.Ed.2d 407 (1995); *but see Rosales–Garcia v. Holland*, 238 F.3d 704, 725–27 (6th Cir.), *vacated*, 534 U.S. 1063, 122 S.Ct. 662, 151 L.Ed.2d 577 (2001), *on remand, Rosales–Garcia v. Holland*, 322 F.3d 386 (6th Cir.), *cert. denied*, 539 U.S. 941, 123 S.Ct. 2607, 156 L.Ed.2d 627 (2003).

Then came the U.S. Supreme Court decision in *Zadvydas*. Did that case—which involved detainees who had been admitted to the United States as lawful permanent residents—have implications for the indefinite detention of arriving aliens and parolees?

CLARK v. MARTINEZ

Supreme Court of the United States, 2005.
543 U.S. 371, 125 S.Ct. 716, 160 L.Ed.2d 734.

JUSTICE SCALIA delivered the opinion of the Court.

[The petitioners, Sergio Suarez Martinez and Daniel Benitez, had arrived in the United States from Cuba as part of the Mariel boatlift in June 1980, and had been paroled into the United States under INA § 212(d)(5). Because of criminal convictions that made them inadmissible, they never became permanent residents. Their convictions also led to revocation of their parole and ultimately to final removal orders.]

* * *

* * *By its terms, [INA § 241(a)(6)] applies to three categories of aliens: (1) those ordered removed who are inadmissible under § 212, (2) those ordered removed who are removable under § 237(a)(1)(C), 237(a)(2), or 237(a)(4), and (3) those ordered removed whom the Secretary determines to be either a risk to the community or a flight risk. In *Zadvydas v. Davis,* the Court interpreted this provision to authorize the Attorney General (now the Secretary [of Homeland Security]) to detain aliens in the second category only as long as "reasonably necessary" to remove them from the country. * * * The Court further held that the presumptive period during which the detention of an alien is reasonably necessary to effectuate his removal is six months; after that, the alien is eligible for conditional release if he can demonstrate that there is "no significant likelihood of removal in the reasonably foreseeable future."

The question presented by these cases, and the question that evoked contradictory answers from the Ninth and Eleventh Circuits, is whether this construction of § 241(a)(6) that we applied to the second category of aliens covered by the statute applies as well to the first—that is, to the category of aliens "ordered removed who are inadmissible under [§]212." We think the answer must be yes. The operative language of § 241(a)(6), "may be detained beyond the removal period," applies without differentiation to all three categories of aliens that are its subject. To give these same words a different meaning for each category would be to invent a statute rather than interpret one. As the Court in *Zadvydas* recognized, the statute can be construed "literally" to authorize indefinite detention, or (as the Court ultimately held) it can be read to "suggest [less than] unlimited discretion" to detain. It cannot, however, be interpreted to do both at the same time.

* * *

The Government, joined by the dissent, argues that the statutory purpose and the constitutional concerns that influenced our statutory construction in *Zadvydas* are not present for aliens, such as Martinez and Benitez, who have not been admitted to the United States. Be that as it may, it cannot justify giving the *same* detention provision a different meaning when such aliens are involved. It is not at all unusual to give a statute's ambiguous language a limiting construction called for by one of the statute's applications, even though other of the statute's applications, standing alone, would not support the same limitation. The lowest common denominator, as it were, must govern. In other words, when deciding which of two plausible statutory constructions to adopt, a court must consider the necessary consequences of its choice. If one of them would raise a multitude of constitutional problems, the other should prevail— whether or not those constitutional problems pertain to the particular litigant before the Court.

The dissent takes issue with this maxim of statutory construction on the ground that it allows litigants to "attack statutes as constitutionally invalid based on constitutional doubts concerning other litigants or factual circumstances" and thereby to effect an "end run around black-letter constitutional doctrine governing facial and as-applied constitutional challenges." This accusation misconceives—and fundamentally so—the role played by the canon of constitutional avoidance in statutory interpretation. The canon is not a method of adjudicating constitutional questions by other means. Indeed, one of the canon's chief justifications is that it allows courts to *avoid* the decision of constitutional questions. It is a tool for choosing between competing plausible interpretations of a statutory text, resting on the reasonable presumption that Congress did not intend the alternative which raises serious constitutional doubts. The canon is thus a means of giving effect to congressional intent, not of subverting it. And when a litigant invokes the canon of avoidance, he is not attempting to vindicate the constitutional rights of others, as the dissent believes; he seeks to vindicate his own *statutory* rights. We find little to recommend the novel interpretive approach advocated by the dissent, which would render every statute a chameleon, its meaning subject to change depending on the presence or absence of constitutional concerns in each individual case. * * *

* * *

The Government fears that the security of our borders will be compromised if it must release into the country inadmissible aliens who cannot be removed. If that is so, Congress can attend to it. But for this Court to sanction indefinite detention in the face of *Zadvydas* would establish within our jurisprudence, beyond the power of Congress to remedy, the dangerous principle that judges can give the same statutory text different meanings in different cases.

[JUSTICE O'CONNOR's concurring opinion is omitted.]

JUSTICE THOMAS, with whom THE CHIEF JUSTICE joins as to Part I–A, dissenting.

* * *

[I–A]

The *Zadvydas* Court * * * tethered its reading of § 241(a)(6) to the specific class of aliens before it. The term this Court read into the statute was not simply a presumptive 6–month period, but a presumptive 6–month period for admitted aliens. Its reading of the statute "in light of the Constitution's demands," that is, depended on the constitutional considerations at work in *"the cases before [it],"* (emphasis added). * * *

* * * The Court [today] says that its reading [in this case] is necessary to avoid "invent[ing] a statute rather than interpret[ing] one"; to preclude "giving the *same* detention provision a different meaning" depending on the aliens before the Court (emphasis in original); and to forestall establishing "the dangerous principle that judges can give the same statutory text different meanings in different cases." I agree that we should adopt none of these principles, but this is no warrant for the reading of *Zadvydas* that the majority advocates. *Zadvydas* established a single and unchanging, if implausible, meaning of § 241(a)(6): that the detention period authorized by § 241(a)(6) depends not only on the circumstances surrounding a removal, but also on the type of alien ordered removed.

I grant that this understanding of *Zadvydas* could result in different detention periods for different classes of aliens—indefinite detention for some, limited detention for others. But it does not follow that this reads the meaning of the statute to "change" depending on the alien involved, any more than the meaning of the statute could be said to "change" simply because the time that is "reasonably necessary to effect removal" may differ depending on the type of alien involved, as both the Court's opinion, and Justice O'Connor's concurring opinion, concede it may. A statute's sense is the same even if what it requires depends on factual context.

* * *

d. Detention After *Zadvydas*, *Demore*, and *Clark*

(i) Repatriation

Repatriation agreements are useful in setting the framework for return of the nationals of the contracting state (in both directions) when a person is ruled removable by the authorities. But such agreements are not indispensable; arrangements can be made ad hoc with a focus on a particular case. *See Kassama v. DHS,* 553 F.Supp.2d 301, 305 (W.D.N.Y. 2008). With or without a broad or formal repatriation agreement, ICE removal officers frequently deal with consular officers from the country of nationality at the retail level to overcome specific problems, supply or obtain necessary documents, or make precise travel arrangements. Shortly after the Supreme Court's ruling in *Zadvydas,* the U.S. government concluded a long-sought repatriation agreement with Cambodia, signed in March 2002, and soon thereafter the Cambodian government accepted the return of Kim Ho Ma. *See* Stansell, *The Deportation of Kim Ho Ma*, 7 Bender's Imm. Bull. 1500 (2002).

But repatriation can face a variety of barriers beyond a foreign government's refusal to accept its own citizens. Sometimes, the citizenship of a removable noncitizen is not clear. And what if the country has no functioning government? This question reached the U.S. Supreme Court in *Jama v. Immigration & Customs Enforcement*, 543 U.S. 335, 125 S.Ct. 694, 160 L.Ed.2d 708 (2005). Justice Scalia, writing for a five-to-four majority, rejected Keyse Jama's statute-based argument that he could not be removed to Somalia, where he remained a citizen, on the grounds that "Somalia has no functioning government, that Somalia therefore could not consent in advance to his removal, and that the Government was barred from removing him to Somalia absent such advance consent." Justice Scalia reasoned that in view of the limits on detention and removal in *Clark* and *Zadvydas*, "there is every reason to refrain from reading restrictions into that process that do not clearly appear." He also observed: "To infer an absolute rule [requiring explicit governmental] acceptance where Congress has not clearly set it forth would run counter to our customary policy of deference to the President in matters of foreign affairs." 543 U.S. at 348, 125 S.Ct. at 704.

After the Supreme Court's decision, the U.S. government tried to remove Jama to Somalia in April 2005 by flying him first to Kenya, where he was turned over to a private security company that then flew him to the city of Bosasso in Puntland, a self-declared autonomous region of Somalia. There, however, local officials refused to accept Jama, and he was flown back to Kenya and then back to the United States. A federal district court ordered his release, but that order was stayed pending the government's appeal, which the Eighth Circuit rejected in July 2005. The government then released Jama under supervision while it continued in its efforts to remove him to Somalia. *See* Tillotson, *A free man, at least for now*, Minneapolis Star Tribune, July 17, 2005, at 3B. Soon thereafter, Jama moved to Canada. He was later convicted in Winnipeg of aggravated assault and robbery for an armed home invasion where he stabbed a man. Canada eventually deported him to Somalia based on his long criminal record. Jama reported that he was trapped on the plane when it landed in Somalia by armed men who threatened to kill him. *Deported Somali Says "Extremists" Shot at Plane*, CBC News, Sept. 15, 2010. Later reporting discredited that claim. Brodbeck, *Refugee's Safety Not Our Problem*, Winnipeg Sun, Sept. 18, 2010.

(ii) Post–Order Custody Review

According to a February 2007 report by the Office of Inspector General of the Department of Homeland Security, approximately 80 percent of those detained following a final order are either removed or released within the 90–day removal period. DHS Office of Inspector General, ICE's Compliance with Detention Limits for Aliens with a Final Order of Removal from the United States 10 (2007). The remainder are entitled to prompt review of their situation to determine whether removal can be effectuated within the time frame set out by the Supreme Court or whether continued detention is justified, in accordance with a post-order custody review (POCR) process set forth in regulations adopted shortly after *Zadvydas*. 8 C.F.R. §§ 241.4, 241.13, 241.14. *See* 66 Fed. Reg. 38433 (2001).

The detainee must first show that he has cooperated in trying to obtain travel documents and that there is no significant likelihood of removal in the reasonably foreseeable future. *See* 8 C.F.R. § 241.4(g). If the detainee makes these showings, he is generally to be released under conditions designed "to protect the public safety and to promote the ability of the Service to effect the alien's removal as ordered." 8 C.F.R. § 241.13(h). He may still be detained, however, subject to stated procedures and review, if he falls into any of four categories: (1) aliens with a highly contagious disease that is a threat to public safety; (2) aliens detained on account of serious adverse foreign policy consequences if they are released; (3) aliens detained on account of security and terrorism concerns; and (4) aliens determined to be specially dangerous because they have been convicted of a crime of violence and have a mental condition or personality disorder indicating that they are likely to commit acts of violence in the future. *See* 8 C.F.R. §§ 241.13(e)(6), 241.14. The overwhelming majority of this remaining population is then either removed or released, subject to supervision, before the 180–day mark. Courts have divided on whether these regulations permitting extended detention in the four specific circumstances are consistent with the statute. *Compare Tran v. Mukasey,* 515 F.3d 478 (5th Cir. 2008), *and Tuan Thai v. Ashcroft,* 366 F.3d 790 (9th Cir. 2004) (finding regulation invalid), *with Hernandez–Carrera v. Carlson,* 547 F.3d 1237 (10th Cir. 2008) (upholding regulation).

In testimony given in May 2011, the head of ICE's Office of Enforcement and Removal Operations singled out four countries for being "very slow to issue travel documents to ICE"—the main reason for lengthy post-order detention: China, India, Iran, and Laos. He also listed 19 other countries that are "recalcitrant" in accepting return of their nationals, setting forth the average time required to obtain travel documents from each, ranging from 52 days to 344 days. ICE is working with the Department of State to work out better arrangements with each such country to facilitate return. G. Mead, Testimony at Hearing on "H.R. 1932, The Keep Our Communities Safe Act," House Comm. on the Judiciary, May 24, 2011.

A number of court decisions since *Zadvydas* have addressed the question whether removal in an individual case is "reasonably foreseeable," in which case continued detention would be authorized by INA § 241(a)(6). *Compare Lema v. United States INS*, 341 F.3d 853, 856 (9th Cir. 2003) ("when an alien refuses to cooperate fully and honestly with officials to secure travel documents from a foreign government, the alien cannot meet his or her burden to show there is no significant likelihood of removal in the reasonably foreseeable future"); *with Seretse–Khama v.*

Ashcroft, 215 F. Supp. 2d 37, 50 (D.D.C.2002) ("the INS has made only the faintest efforts to seek petitioner's removal, despite the fact that he has already been in INS detention for close to four years"). *Diouf v. Napolitano*, 634 F.3d 1081 (9th Cir. 2011) also found the regulations deficient for failing to provide a hearing before an immigration judge on the issue of whether removal is reasonably foreseeable.

Another post–*Zadvydas* issue concerns the conditions placed upon release under § 241(a)(3), which lists specific forms of allowed supervision. According to the Ninth Circuit, the government may also require a bond even though that is not listed in § 241(a)(3), but it stated that "serious questions may arise concerning the reasonableness of the amount of the bond if it has the effect of preventing an alien's release." *Doan v. INS*, 311 F.3d 1160, 1162 (9th Cir. 2002).

Would the same "serious questions" arise in the case of bond that was set under § 236(a), which governs pre-final-order detention pending a hearing or an appeal? The Ninth Circuit has suggested that they do not. In *Prieto–Romero v. Clark*, 534 F.3d 1053 (9th Cir. 2008), three bond hearings before immigration judges had not resulted in the release of the respondent, a lawful permanent resident, while he awaited the court's decision on his petition for review of his removal order. (Though he had been convicted of an aggravated felony, his conviction occurred before the mandatory detention provision of § 236(c) took full effect.) The first two hearings resulted in a denial of release because Prieto–Romero was judged dangerous and a flight risk. At the third, the IJ set a $15,000 bond, which the respondent said he could not pay. The court ruled that "*Doan* does not license us to review the reasonableness of the amount of bond, even if Prieto–Romero cannot afford to post it," citing the tight limits on judicial review of pre-order release decisions in INA § 236(e) (the discretionary judgment regarding application of § 236 "shall not be subject to review").

e. Limits on Government Authority to Detain

Though details are still contested, *Zadvydas* establishes a reasonably clear framework for deciding on the validity of lengthy detention after the removal period has begun and INA § 241(a)(6) comes into play. But under what circumstances is detention before that point subject to challenge? Somewhat surprisingly, the lower courts have found significant constraints on lengthy detention under the mandatory detention provision in § 236(c), despite the Supreme Court's apparent endorsement of that provision in *Demore. See* G. Seipp & S. Feal, The Mandatory Detention Dilemma: The Role of the Federal Courts in Tempering the Scope of INA § 236(c), 10–07 Imm. Briefings (2010). The cases essentially proceed by reading back into the pre-final-order custody determination some of the reasoning that *Zadvydas* applied to § 241(a)(6). But the decisions take differing views of when such limits take effect, what the government must do once a limit is reached, and what precise statutory authority provides the basis for these conclusions.

CASAS–CASTRILLON v. DHS

United States Court of Appeals, Ninth Circuit, 2008.
535 F.3d 942.

FISHER, CIRCUIT JUDGE:

This appeal concerns whether the government may detain an alien who is a legal permanent resident of the United States for seven years without providing him with an adequate opportunity to contest the necessity of his detention before a neutral decision maker. We conclude that a prolonged detention must be accompanied by appropriate procedural safeguards, including a hearing to establish whether releasing the alien would pose a danger to the community or a flight risk.

Luis Felipe Casas–Castrillon ("Casas") is a native and citizen of Colombia and has been a legal permanent resident of the United States since 1990. He was served with a notice to appear and detained by the Immigration and Naturalization Service in August 2001, following his release from a state prison for a conviction on an auto burglary charge. An immigration judge ("IJ") found that Casas was a removable alien because he had been convicted of two crimes involving moral turpitude. Casas appealed this determination to the Board of Immigration Appeals ("BIA"), which affirmed the removal order in July 2002.

From that time until the present, Casas has remained in the continuous custody of the federal government while he has pursued various avenues of relief from removal in the federal district court and the court of appeals, some successful and some not. While he has sought judicial review, his removal has been stayed by court orders for much of the period from 2002 to the present. As of the time that this opinion is filed, Casas is now back before the BIA after this court granted his petition for review of his final order of removal. During this nearly seven-year period of detention, it is unclear what, if any, opportunity Casas has had to argue to a neutral decision maker that his detention is unnecessary because he does not pose a danger to the community or a flight risk.

Casas filed the instant petition for habeas corpus under 28 U.S.C. § 2241 on August 4, 2005. At that time, his administrative proceedings had been complete for approximately three years, but he was awaiting our court's review of his timely filed petition for review of his final removal order. In his pro se habeas petition to the district court, Casas argued that his detention had become indefinite and was therefore not authorized by any statute, and that his prolonged detention without a meaningful opportunity to contest the necessity of continued detention violated his right to procedural due process. The district court denied Casas' petition on August 15, 2007, and we granted expedited review * * * and [now] reverse.

As we explained in *Prieto–Romero v. Clark*, [534 F.3d 1053 (9th Cir.2008)], Casas' entitlement to relief turns in part on locating him within the statutory framework of detention authority provided by Sections 236 and 241 of the Immigration and Nationality Act. This is because "[w]here an alien falls within this statutory scheme can affect whether his detention is mandatory or discretionary, as well as the kind of review process available to him if he wishes to contest the necessity of his detention." *Id.* Casas and the government vigorously dispute which statutory provision governs his detention. We conclude that Congress has provided the Attorney General with authority to detain Casas under § 236(a), which gives the Attorney General a broad grant of discretionary authority to detain an alien "pending a decision on whether the alien is to be removed from the United States."

A.

The statutory scheme governing the detention of aliens in removal proceedings is not static; rather, the Attorney General's authority over an alien's detention shifts as the alien moves through different phases of administrative and judicial review. * * * Casas' own case presents this problem, because we have considered, granted and remanded Casas' petition for review of his removal order during the same period that we have been considering on appeal his habeas corpus challenge, actions that arguably affect the Attorney General's statutory authority over his detention.

To determine by what authority the Attorney General currently may detain Casas, it is helpful to begin with the Attorney General's authority to detain Casas initially—detention authority Casas does not dispute. Casas was charged with being removable for having committed two crimes involving moral turpitude, and Congress has mandated that such aliens must be taken into custody at the time they are charged. See § 236(c)(1)(B). The Attorney General may release an alien detained under § 236(c) only for narrow reasons not implicated here. See § 236(c)(2). Unlike noncriminal aliens, who are detained under § 236(a), aliens detained under § 236(c) are not given a bond hearing before an IJ. Thus these aliens do not have the opportunity to show—as noncriminal aliens would—that their detention is unnecessary because they do not pose a danger to the community or a flight risk.

Although the Attorney General's initial statutory authority to detain Casas is undisputed, both parties agree that § 236(c) at some point no longer governed Casas' detention. As Casas' case ably demonstrates, aliens challenging an order of removal may languish in the system for years. Even after the BIA has entered a final order of removal, an alien may petition for review of that removal order with the court of appeals in the judicial circuit in which his immigration proceedings occurred. See § 242(b). Before Congress enacted the REAL ID Act ("RIDA") in May 2005, Pub.L. No. 109–13, Div. B, 199 Stat. § 231 (2005), certain aliens could also obtain judicial review of constitutional questions or questions of law raised by their final orders of removal through a petition for habeas corpus brought in the district court. Even post-RIDA, aliens may continue to bring collateral legal challenges to the Attorney General's detention authority—such as in this case—through a petition for habeas corpus. See *Nadarajah v. Gonzales*, 443 F.3d 1069, 1075 (9th Cir.2006) (holding that "the jurisdiction-stripping provision [of RIDA] does not apply to federal habeas corpus petitions that do not involve final orders of removal"). The courts of appeals have the authority to enter judicial stays of removal for aliens who have petitions for review or habeas corpus petitions pending. See § 242(b)(3)(B). This means that many aliens may continue to be detained for months, if not years, after their removal order is finalized by the agency, while they seek review of the legal or factual basis for their removal.

Casas has himself explored all of these possible avenues of review and relief. * * *

* * * In June 2006, we entered a stay of removal pending our disposition of his petition. We eventually granted Casas' petition for review in January 2008 and remanded to the BIA. Our mandate in that case issued in March 2008.

B.

* * * The government argues that aliens awaiting judicial review of their petitions for review become subject to continued detention under the Attorney General's grant of authority in § 241(a), which provides for detention "during" and "beyond" the "removal period." As we explained in *Prieto–Romero*, we disagree. If an alien has filed a petition for review with this court and received a judicial stay of removal, the "removal period" under § 241(a) does not begin until this court "denies the petition and withdraws the stay of removal." Therefore, Casas was not subject to detention under § 241(a) at the time he filed his petition for habeas corpus while his petition for review was pending in this court.

Because § 241(a) does not govern Casas' detention, we must determine which statute does. The statutory scheme presents two possible options: either Casas has remained in detention throughout this seven-year period under § 236(c), which requires mandatory detention of criminal aliens, or at some point the detention authority shifted to § 236(a), which gives the Attorney General general discretionary authority to detain an alien "pending a decision on whether the alien is to be removed from the United States." We reject the government's suggestion that § 236(c) mandates Casas' detention for the duration of his now seven-year confinement. As we explained in *Tijani v. Willis*, 430 F.3d 1241, 1242 (9th Cir.2005), § 236(c)'s mandatory detention provision applies only to "expedited removal of criminal aliens."[f] The Supreme Court similarly recognized in *Demore v. Kim*, 538 U.S. 510, 123 S.Ct. 1708, 155 L.Ed.2d 724 (2003), that § 236(c) was intended only to "govern[ ] detention of deportable criminal aliens *pending their removal proceedings*," (emphasis added),

---

f. In that opinion the court was referring to Congress' general desire for speed in the removal process, not to "expedited removal" under either INA 235(b) or 238(b).—eds.

which the Court emphasized typically "lasts roughly a month and a half in the vast majority of cases in which it is invoked, and about five months in the minority of cases in which the alien chooses to appeal" his removal order to the BIA. The Department of Homeland Security ("DHS") has similarly interpreted § 236(c) to apply only "during removal proceedings." See 8 C.F.R. § 236.1(c)(1)(i). The "conclusion of proceedings" occurs upon the dismissal of the alien's appeal by the BIA. *See id.* § 1241.1(a).

Because neither § 241(a) nor § 236(c) governs the prolonged detention of aliens awaiting judicial review of their removal orders, we conclude that Casas' detention was authorized during this period under the Attorney General's general, discretionary detention authority under § 236(a). Section 236(a) authorizes the Attorney General to detain an alien "pending a decision on whether the alien is to be removed from the United States." Again, as we explained in *Prieto–Romero*, "[i]t is reasonable to consider the judicial review of a removal order as part of the process of making an ultimate 'decision' as to whether an alien 'is to be removed.'" Once Casas' proceedings before the BIA were complete, the Attorney General's authority to detain him under § 236(c) ended and that authority shifted instead to § 236(a).

We lastly reject the government's suggestion that, even if Casas was not subject to detention under § 236(c) while his petition for review was pending on appeal, he became subject to such custody again after we granted his petition for review and remanded his case to the BIA. An alien whose case is being adjudicated before the agency for a second time—after having fought his case in this court and won, a process which often takes more than a year—has not received expeditious process. We therefore conclude that the mandatory, bureaucratic detention of aliens under § 236(c) was intended to apply for only a limited time and ended in this case when the BIA affirmed Casas' order of removal in July 2002. Thereafter, the Attorney General's detention authority rests with § 236(a) until the alien enters his "removal period," which occurs only after we have rejected his final petition for review or his time to seek such review expires.

II.

Having determined that the government's authority to detain Casas falls under § 236(a), we now turn to the question of whether Casas is entitled to any habeas corpus relief.

A.

Casas first argues that he is entitled to release from detention because his detention has become prolonged and is potentially indefinite and Congress has not statutorily authorized such detention. Although Casas' nearly seven-year detention certainly qualifies as prolonged by any measure, we hold that the government retains authority to detain him under § 236(a) because Casas faces a significant likelihood of removal to Colombia once his judicial and administrative review process is complete.

In *Prieto–Romero*, we concluded that an alien whose removal had been delayed "while he pursues judicial review of his administratively final order of removal" had failed to show that his detention was unauthorized by statute, where there was "nothing, such as a lack of a repatriation agreement with his home country or a finding that he merit[ed] mandatory relief from removal, that would prevent [his] removal . . . if he is ultimately unsuccessful in his petition for review." * * *

B.

* * * Casas raises a second challenge to the legality of his detention—whether the government may detain him for such a prolonged period without providing an individualized determination as to the necessity of his detention. Even though Casas' detention is permitted by statute because keeping him in custody could serve a legitimate immigration purpose, Casas may nonetheless have the right to contest before a neutral decision maker whether the government's purported interest is actually served by detention in his case. There is a difference between detention being authorized and being necessary as to any particular person. We hold that the government may not detain a legal permanent resident such as Casas for a prolonged period without providing him a neutral forum in which to contest the necessity of his continued detention.

* * *

The Supreme Court upheld § 236(c)'s mandatory detention provision in *Demore*, but did so with the specific understanding that § 236(c) authorized mandatory detention only for the "limited period of [the alien's] removal proceedings," which the Court estimated "lasts roughly a month and a half in the vast majority of cases in which it is invoked, and about five months in the minority of cases in which the alien chooses to appeal" his removal order to the BIA. References to the brevity of mandatory detention under § 236(c) run throughout *Demore*. * * * Casas' nearly seven-year detention, if unaccompanied by meaningful, individualized review, would clearly be a far longer period of detention than the "brief" period of mandatory detention during administrative review that the Supreme Court approved in Demore.

The question before us, therefore, is whether legal permanent residents such as Casas, who have been subjected to prolonged detention pending judicial review of their final order of removal or agency reconsideration on remand, may continue to be detained by the Attorney General without receiving an individualized determination of the necessity of detention before a neutral decision maker, such as an immigration judge. We conclude that prolonged detention without adequate procedural protections would raise serious constitutional concerns. * * * Detention during judicial review—like the detention during removal proceedings that *Demore* considered—may serve the purpose of "preventing deportable . . . aliens from fleeing[,] . . . thus increasing the chance that, if ordered removed, the alien will be successfully removed." Even where detention is permissible, however, due process requires "adequate procedural protections" to ensure that the government's asserted justification for physical confinement "outweighs the individual's constitutionally protected interest in avoiding physical restraint." *Zadvydas*. We are skeptical that *Demore's* limited holding that Congress could permissibly authorize "brief" detention without procedural protections can be extended to encompass the nearly seven-year detention at issue here.

We need not resolve this constitutional question, however, because we find no evidence that Congress intended to authorize the long-term detention of aliens such as Casas without providing them access to a bond hearing before an immigration judge. In *Tijani*, we held that an alien initially detained under § 236(c) could not continue to be detained during his judicial review process unless he was afforded an individualized hearing before an IJ. *See* 430 F.3d at 1242. Like Casas, Tijani was a legal permanent resident. By the time we issued our decision in his case, he had been detained for two years and eight months, with approximately 20 months of his detention occurring during his removal proceedings. Also like Casas, Tijani had filed a petition for review with our court—which accounted for 10 months of his 30–month detention—and we noted that Tijani could be expected to be detained for another "year or more" while we completed our review of his removal order. We then concluded that Tijani's mandatory detention throughout this period was not authorized under § 236(c), because § 236(c) applies only to "expedited removal of criminal aliens," and "[t]wo years and eight months of process is not expeditious." Applying the doctrine of constitutional avoidance, we concluded that Tijani's prolonged mandatory detention was not authorized by that statute. We therefore held that the government must provide Tijani "a hearing ... before an Immigration Judge with the power to grant him bail unless the government establishes that he is a flight risk or will be a danger to the community."

Although its reasoning was sparse, we believe *Tijani* was correct that § 236(c) does not authorize prolonged mandatory detention after an alien's administrative proceedings are complete. Rather, these aliens are detained under the Attorney General's broader grant of discretionary authority under § 236(a). * * * Section 236(a), unlike § 236(c), provides * * * authority for the Attorney General to conduct a bond hearing and release the alien on bond or detain him if necessary to secure his presence at removal. *See* § 236(a)(2). Because the prolonged detention of an alien without an individualized determination of his dangerousness or flight risk would be "constitutionally doubtful," we hold that § 236(a) must be construed as *requiring* the Attorney General to provide the alien with such a hearing. *See Tijani*, 430 F.3d at 1242. * * *

* * *

Because the parties did not develop an adequate record of the procedural review that Casas has received, we cannot determine whether the government has afforded him a bond hearing that complies with the requirements of *Tijani*. We therefore reverse the district court and remand with instructions to grant the writ unless, within 60 days, the government provides Casas with "a hearing . . . before an Immigration Judge with the power to grant him bail unless the government establishes that he is a flight risk or will be a danger to the community," or shows that he has already received such a bond hearing.

Reversed and remanded.

DIOP v. ICE/HOMELAND SECURITY

United States Court of Appeals for the Third Circuit, 2011.
656 F.3d 221.

FUENTES, CIRCUIT JUDGE.

A 1996 law requires that the Executive Branch take into custody any person who is removable from this country because he has committed, among other things, a crime involving moral turpitude or a crime involving a controlled substance. [INA § 236(c).] Detention under this authority is mandatory, does not provide for the possibility of release on bond, and does not require that the Executive Branch at any time justify its conduct. Pursuant to this law, the petitioner in this case, Cheikh Diop, was detained for 1,072 days—two years, eleven months, and five days. The District Court concluded that such prolonged detention was lawful. We disagree. For the following reasons, we conclude that the statute authorizes only detention for a reasonable period of time. After that, the Due Process Clause of the Fifth Amendment to the Constitution requires that the Government establish that continued detention is necessary to further the purposes of the detention statute.

I.

Although the merits of the immigration case against Diop are not before us, we chronicle his journey through our complex immigration system in order to illustrate how individual actions by various actors in the immigration system, each of which takes only a reasonable amount of time to accomplish, can nevertheless result in the detention of a removable alien for an unreasonable, and ultimately unconstitutional, period of time. [The court then recounts the delays, which resulted from, inter alia, multiple continuances in immigration court to enable Diop to find counsel; DHS's filing of new charges during that time; belated claims for withholding of removal under INA § 241(b)(3) filed by Diop; successive remands from the BIA for the IJ to clarify or correct his rulings; new hearings in criminal court, in the wake of *Padilla v. Kentucky,* 130 S.Ct. 1473 (2010) on Diop's claims of ineffective assistance of counsel there, resulting in vacatur of the underlying criminal conviction, which was then appealed by the state of Pennsylvania and remains pending; a concession by DHS that the vacatur made him eligible for withholding pending the state appeal; a subsequent grant of withholding by the IJ; and ICE's decision not to appeal that grant, though it reserved the right to revisit the issue if the criminal conviction were reinstated. Diop was released when ICE decided not to appeal.]

II.

[The controversy has not been mooted by Diop's release, because the] issues raised are capable of repetition and are the kinds of issues that would almost always evade review by this court. * * *

[III. A.]

We begin with the argument that neither of Diop's prior criminal convictions authorizes his detention because, if they do not, then his detention is unlawful independent of any constitutional concerns. * * *

* * *

The dispute over whether Diop's conviction is, as a definitive legal matter, one involving moral turpitude, is irrelevant. If the statute required certitude that an alien was deportable before that alien could be detained, then no alien could ever be detained because the question of removability cannot be answered until after proceedings in the immigration courts are resolved. The appropriate question is whether applicable regulations, and interpretations of the governing statutes by the BIA, allow ICE to detain Diop with some level of suspicion, but no definitive legal conclusion, that he is covered by § 236(c). They do. According to the regulations and the commentary accompanying them, an authorized ICE agent may detain an alien if there is "reason to believe that this person was convicted of a crime covered by the statute." 8 C.F.R. § 236.1. Immigration judges then have the authority to review the ICE agent's initial determination that a person is subject to detention at a *Joseph* hearing. *See In re Joseph II,* 22 I. & N. Dec. 799, 800 (B.I.A.1999); *see also Demore,* 538 U.S. at 514 n. 3, 123 S.Ct. 1708 (explaining that a *Joseph* hearing gives an alien the opportunity to avoid mandatory detention by establishing that he is not an alien, was not convicted of a crime requiring mandatory detention, or is otherwise not subject to mandatory detention). Because neither party attacks the constitutionality of these regulations, or the BIA's interpretation of the applicable statutes, we will assume, without deciding, that they are valid and that they authorize Diop's pre-removal detention because "there is reason to believe"—even if we do not know for sure—that the 2005 conviction was for a crime involving moral turpitude.[8]

B.

The Government asserts that § 236(c) says that aliens can be detained for as long as removal proceedings are "pending," even if they are "pending" for prolonged periods of time. * * * Applying [the constitution-

---

8. * * * We note, however, that the issue is an open one, and that at least one circuit judge has expressed grave doubts as to whether *Joseph* is consistent with due process of law, *see Tijani v. Willis,* 430 F.3d 1241, 1244 (9th Cir.2005) (Tashima, J., concurring).

al avoidance] principle, we conclude that the statute implicitly authorizes detention for a reasonable amount of time, after which the authorities must make an individualized inquiry into whether detention is still necessary to fulfill the statute's purposes of ensuring that an alien attends removal proceedings and that his release will not pose a danger to the community.

1.

* * *

The Supreme Court has concluded that [§ 236(c) is constitutional], at least on its face. Reading through the legislative history in *Demore v. Kim,* the Supreme Court noted that Congress was concerned with the immigration authorities' "wholesale failure" to "deal with the increasing rates of criminal activity by aliens." Section 236(c) was intended to remedy this perceived problem by ensuring that aliens convicted of certain crimes would be present at their removal proceedings and not on the loose in their communities, where they might pose a danger.

The Supreme Court's opinion emphasized Congress's broad power to pass laws relating to immigration. It reasoned that, although Congress's powers are limited by the Due Process Clause, aliens' due process rights are not necessarily violated when they are initially detained without a specific, individualized, finding that a particular alien poses a flight risk or a risk of danger to the community [citing *Carlson v. Landon*].

Justice Kennedy concurred in the Supreme Court's opinion, but highlighted an important limitation on the scope of its holding. In his view, Congress's broad immigration powers allow it to pass a law authorizing an alien's initial detention, so long as those implementing the statute provide individualized procedures through which an alien might contest the basis of his detention—a requirement satisfied in *Demore* when the petitioner, Hyung Joon Kim, received a *Joseph* hearing. Critically, Justice Kennedy added that even if an alien is given an initial hearing, his detention might still violate the Due Process Clause if "the continued detention became unreasonable or unjustified." "Were there to be an unreasonable delay * * * in pursuing and completing deportation proceedings, it would become necessary then to inquire whether the detention is not to facilitate deportation, or to protect against risk of flight or dangerousness, but to incarcerate for other reasons."

Justice Kennedy's opinion provides helpful guidance[.] * * * [T]he Executive Branch *must* detain an alien at the beginning of removal proceedings, without a bond hearing—and may do so consistent with the Due Process Clause—so long as the alien is given some sort of hearing when initially detained at which he may challenge the basis of his detention. However, the constitutionality of this practice is a function of the length of the detention. At a certain point, continued detention becomes unreasonable and the Executive Branch's implementation of § 236(c) becomes unconstitutional unless the Government has justified its actions at a hearing inquiring into whether continued detention is consistent with the law's purposes of preventing flight and dangers to the community. This will necessarily be a fact-dependent inquiry that will vary depending on individual circumstances. We decline to establish a universal point at which detention will always be considered unreasonable.

* * *

In short, when detention becomes unreasonable, the Due Process Clause demands a hearing, at which the Government bears the burden of proving that continued detention is necessary to fulfill the purposes of the detention statute.

2.

This leaves us with the question of whether Diop's prolonged detention in this case was unconstitutionally unreasonable and, therefore, a violation of the Due Process Clause. We conclude that it was. *Demore* emphasized that mandatory detention pursuant to § 236(c) lasts only for a "very limited time" in the vast majority of cases. * * * Indeed, the petitioner in *Demore* had been detained for only slightly longer than the average (6 months) when his habeas petition was decided. Assuming, without deciding, that this was a presumably reasonable period of detention, and comparing it to Diop's 35 months of detention, which was nearly six times longer, leads us to conclude that Diop's detention, without any post-*Joseph* hearing inquiry into whether it was necessary to accomplish the purposes of § 236(c), was unreasonable.

The Government argues that there was no "unreasonable delay" in Diop's proceedings because he was given continuances to find an attorney, to draft an application for asylum and withholding of removal, and because he took several appeals. Diop responds that the delay is attributable to the immigration judge's continued errors, which necessitated the appeals and remands. We agree with the Government that the reasonableness determination must take into account a given individual detainee's need for more or less time, as well as the exigencies of a particular case. But we also conclude that reasonableness must take into account errors in the proceedings that cause unnecessary delay. No system of justice can be error-free, and those errors require time to fix. Nevertheless, in this case the immigration judge's numerous errors, combined with the Government's failure to secure, at the earliest possible time, evidence that bore directly on the issue of whether Diop was properly detained, resulted in an unreasonable delay.

* * * In *Zadvydas,* the Supreme Court adopted a presumption that six months of detention pursuant to the post-removal statute was reasonable. * * * Amicus ACLU urges us to adopt a similar position in this case. We decline to adopt such a one-size-fits-all approach. Reasonableness, by its very nature, is a fact-dependent inquiry requiring an assessment of all of the circumstances of any given case. * * * In this case, there can be no question that Diop's detention for nearly three years without further inquiry into whether it was necessary to ensure his appearance at the removal proceedings or to prevent a risk of danger to the community, was unreasonable and, therefore, a violation of the Due Process Clause.

3.

* * * We do not believe that Congress intended to authorize prolonged, unreasonable, detention without a bond hearing. * * * Accordingly we conclude that § 236(c) contains an implicit limitation of reasonableness: the statute authorizes only mandatory detention that is reasonable in length. After that, § 236(c) yields to the constitutional requirement that there be a further, individualized, inquiry into whether continued detention is necessary to carry out the statute's purpose. *Cf. Zadvydas.*

* * *

NOTES AND QUESTIONS ON THE JUDICIAL NARROWING OF MANDATORY DETENTION

1. The *Casas–Castrillon* court emphasizes that both Casas and Tijani, the respondent in an earlier case the court often cites, were lawful permanent residents. Are the release rulings here applicable only to LPRs? Should they be?

2. After the 1996 Immigration Reform Act, a removed noncitizen can still pursue his judicial appeal from abroad. Should that have been seen as a sufficient answer to Casas–Castrillon's and Diop's argument for release from detention, at least after the BIA had ruled? Each could apparently have ended his detention by accepting removal in the interim, without jeopardizing his right to judicial review of the issues he was raising on appeal.

3. In *Nadarajah v. Gonzales,* 443 F.3d 1069 (9th Cir. 2006), the court ruled that DHS's five-year detention of the respondent, who had been detained as an arriving alien, was unreasonable, and it directly ordered his release, even though administrative appeals were still pending. This outcome differs from the remedy ordered by most courts considering post-*Demore* issues involving persons at least initially covered by § 236(c); the ordinary remedy is not release, but an individualized bond determination by an immigration judge, applying the standard criteria of flight risk and dangerousness. *See, e.g., Diouf v. Napolitano,* 634 F.3d 1081, 1091 (9th Cir. 2011) (generally requiring a bond hearing before an immigration judge at which the government bears the burden of proof after six months of detention). But perhaps the more extreme remedy is explained by the government behavior that led to the delays. Nadarajah had been found, by both an IJ and the BIA in two separate rounds of consideration, entitled to withholding of removal and protection under the Convention Against Torture, thus precluding his removal to his native Sri Lanka. But DHS continued his detention while it pursued the rarely invoked referral procedure to take the case before the Attorney General. The court also found that *Zadvydas* principles applied even though there was as yet no final order, because the rulings on withholding and CAT protection meant that removal was not reasonably foreseeable.

4. Surveying recent cases, one district court compiled a non-exclusive list of factors that go into determining whether the length of detention is reasonable (and hence whether an individualized bond hearing is required): (1) whether detention has extended beyond the average time ordinarily necessary for completion of removal proceedings; (2) the probable extent of future removal proceedings; (3) the likelihood that removal proceedings will actually result in removal; and (4) the conduct of both the alien and the government—essentially, who bears the primary responsibility for any delays. *Alli v. Decker*, 644 F.Supp.2d 535, 543–45 (M.D.Pa. 2009), *rev'd in part on other grounds*, 650 F.3d 1007 (3d Cir. 2011).

5. *Casas–Castrillon* finds that a noncitizen subject to mandatory detention under § 236(c) reverts to the discretionary detention regime of § 236(a) once the BIA has ruled on the appeal and a petition for review is pending before the courts. Can that reading be squared with the policy reasons cited by the *Demore* majority in explaining why Congress adopted mandatory detention in the first place (e.g., "detention of criminal aliens * * * might be the best way to ensure their successful removal from the country"). Isn't the risk of absconding heightened once the person has already lost before both the immigration court and the BIA? Is there really "no evidence that Congress intended to authorize the long-term detention of aliens [with criminal convictions] without providing them access to a bond hearing before an immigration judge"? Wasn't that Congress's precise purpose in enacting § 236(c) in 1996? What sort of evidence is the court seeking?

6. In view of the widespread judicial resistance to mandatory detention, basically giving *Demore* its narrowest possible application, should the detention statutes be changed? Wouldn't it be simpler and more efficient just to provide for an individualized release procedure in each case, in which a past criminal record would of course be given weight in assessing flight risk and dangerousness? On the other hand, are the courts placing too much faith in the capacity for individualized assessment of flight risk? Recall from our discussion of *in absentia* orders in Section A5 *supra* that the nonappearance rate in immigration court for nondetained aliens has been 30 percent in recent years, down from 60 percent in 2006 and 2007. Though some of the no-shows can be attributed to problems with notifications about the time and place of the hearing, this statistic still reflects a serious problem of noncompliance on the part of people once deemed appropriate for release. There is further attrition in compliance after a removal order becomes final. A 2006 report from the DHS Office of Inspector General stated that "historical trends indicate that 62 percent of the aliens released will eventually be issued final orders of removal * * * and later fail to surrender for removal or abscond." Detention and Removal of Illegal Aliens (OIG–06–33, April 2006).

7. There have been several legislative efforts, so far unsuccessful, to revise the statutes construed in *Demore* and *Zadvydas* to clarify the authorization for wider use of detention. Some would overrule *Clark v. Martinez* to permit indefinite detention of arriving aliens. Other proposed legislation would amend INA § 241(a)(6) to authorize indefinite detention for certain admitted aliens, based on a wider set of factors such as past convictions for crimes of violence or aggravated felonies. Additional proposed changes would specify that mandatory detention under § 236(c) applies from initial ICE

arrest to either removal or a ruling that the individual is not removable. *See, e.g.,* S. 1984, 110th Cong., § 202 (2007); H.R.1932, 112th Cong. (2011). For a description of the latter bill, the "Keep Our Communities Safe Act," as approved by the House Judiciary Committee, see 88 Interp.Rel. 1680 (2011).

EXERCISE

If you were a member of Congress, how would you vote to alter the provisions governing decisions on release? Should the system release more or fewer respondents? Set higher bonds? Make more use of ATDs? Deploy more intensive supervision, perhaps including GPS ankle bracelets? Specify the categories to which your changes would apply, or at least identify factors that could give more precise guidance to the DHS officers and immigration judges who have to make release decisions and stand accountable for each such release.

SECTION C. JUDICIAL REVIEW

Decisions under the immigration laws can carry the most telling personal consequences known to the federal administrative process. To be sure, a ratemaking order or a broadcast licensing proceeding might mean millions of dollars in profit or loss to the contending parties—sums far beyond what one encounters in the immigration field. But those on the losing side, even in such titanic administrative battles, can go home and relieve their disappointment among family and friends. Immigration decisions, in contrast, often bear directly on just where home will be, and on which relatives and friends will share in life's triumphs and defeats.

Given the potential stakes, both the noncitizen and the government have the strongest reasons for wanting to be sure that such decisions are reached correctly. To this end, complex mechanisms for administrative review have evolved, as we have seen, that vary considerably depending on the precise application or decision at issue. But Americans have probably always harbored a measure of distrust for bureaucrats, even those who serve in purely corrective or appellate roles. With the growth of the modern administrative state, the federal courts, staffed with life-tenured judges, have come to be seen as the ultimate guarantors of administrative reliability. Whether or not this great faith in the bench is always well-placed, this judicial role is a well-entrenched feature of modern life. Under doctrines worked out over the last fifty years or so, federal agency actions—not just agencies concerned with immigration—are now presumptively subject to review in the courts, *Abbott Laboratories v. Gardner*, 387 U.S. 136, 140–41, 87 S.Ct. 1507, 1510, 1511, 18 L.Ed.2d 681 (1967). The Supreme Court has emphasized, however, that this is "just a presumption" that can be overcome if Congress has foreclosed review in a given category of cases. *See Lincoln v. Vigil,* 508 U.S. 182, 190, 113 S.Ct. 2024, 2030, 124 L.Ed.2d 101 (1993).

The immigration caseload in the federal courts grew dramatically over the past decade. In 2001, such cases constituted only three percent of the caseload in the courts of appeals. By 2006, they accounted for nearly 18 percent, and then slowly declined to 12 percent in 2010. The volume varies considerably by circuit. Over the past decade, roughly two-thirds of appeals from the BIA went to the Second and Ninth Circuits. In FY 2010, the Ninth received 3,169 cases (down from 5,862 in 2006), and the Second 1,299. The Third Circuit ranked third with 484, followed closely, as might be expected, by the Fifth and Eleventh. The Tenth Circuit had the lightest load, with 69 cases. *See* Judicial Business of the United States Courts, Table B–3 (2010 Annual Report of the Director, Administrative Office of the United States Courts); Caplow, *After the Flood: The Legacy of the "Surge" of Federal Immigration Appeals,* Northwestern J. L. & Social Pol'y (forthcoming 2011).

In considering judicial review, we encounter a familiar tension. We do not want to foster manipulation by noncitizens who might use judicial review only to prolong a stay to which they are not entitled. At the same time, we do not want to stint on measures to assure accurate and humane application of the laws. What is the right balance?

1. A BRIEF HISTORY

At least since 1891, federal statutes have regularly provided that orders of executive branch officers in deportation and exclusion cases are "final." Some early Supreme Court decisions seemed to read this in its harshest literal sense, as precluding any possible judicial role. But that phase did not last long. Soon the courts began to entertain cases challenging the decisions of the administrators in exclusion and deportation cases. Often the substantive standard for review was extraordinarily deferential to the administrators, when viewed from a modern perspective, but the immigration authorities did not always prevail. In any event, the mere fact of judicial consideration was significant, in the face of the statute's command of finality. Many of the cases that you have read throughout this book—the *Chinese Exclusion Case, Fong Yue Ting, Knauff, Mezei,* and *Yamataya,* to mention just a few—reached the courts, even if the outcome on the merits was to uphold the government decision in question.

These cases present an apparent puzzle. Federal courts are courts of limited jurisdiction, and they must ordinarily trace their power to hear a case to a specific congressional authorization. The early immigration statutes merely set forth the administrative arrangements and purported to make the resulting orders final. Clearly *they* bestowed no review authority on the courts. Indeed, it was not until 1961 that any general provisions for judicial review appeared in our immigration laws. Just how did the courts manage to assume jurisdiction?

The answer derives from the brute requirements of the removal process. No unwilling noncitizen can be removed without being physically restrained at some point. Classically, such physical restraint—custody—is the foundation for issuance of the Great Writ, the writ of habeas corpus, a remedy guaranteed in the text of the Constitution. Article I, section 9, clause 2 states: "The privilege of the Writ of Habeas Corpus shall not be suspended, unless when in Cases of Rebellion or Invasion the public Safety may require it." The habeas corpus remedy was also the subject of federal statutes well before the first immigration acts were passed, and sometimes it is not clear whether particular features of habeas practice derived from constitutional command or from statutory refinement. Until 1955, habeas review was the standard basis of court jurisdiction to review agency immigration decisions.

Litigants still sought other ways into court, for a simple reason. The very foundation of the high regard Anglo–American jurisprudence has maintained for the habeas corpus remedy—its availability at the moment when a person was restrained of his or her liberty—also resulted in its major disadvantage. As habeas was understood until recent decades, the noncitizen could not petition for the writ until he was actually in physical custody. By then he may have had to sell his belongings, bid farewell to family and friends, and wait from his jail cell for the court's decision.

Could noncitizens get to court without using habeas, and thus obtain review without having to undergo physical custody? Noncitizens tried different statutes for this purpose. They did not succeed with the 1934 Declaratory Judgment Act, 28 U.S.C.A. § 2201, or the 1946 Administrative Procedure Act (APA), as applied to pre-existing immigration laws. In 1955, however, the Supreme Court held that under the 1946 APA, combined with the then-new INA, declaratory and injunctive relief would thenceforth be available to test deportation orders. *Shaughnessy v. Pedreiro*, 349 U.S. 48, 75 S.Ct. 591, 99 L.Ed. 868 (1955). The next year, the Court reached the same conclusion for exclusion. *Brownell v. Shung*, 352 U.S. 180, 77 S.Ct. 252, 1 L.Ed.2d 225 (1956). Noncitizens could at last contest exclusion and deportation orders without having to wait until they were detained. But Congress grew concerned that the court access opened up by *Pedreiro* and *Brownell* would be abused to string out review beyond reasonable bounds. *See, e.g.*, H.R. Rep. No. 1086, 87th Cong., 1st Sess. 28–32 (1961).

In 1961, Congress enacted INA § 106, the first statute specifically governing review of exclusion and deportation orders. For exclusion cases, § 106(b) reestablished habeas corpus as the exclusive means for review. Habeas petitions were almost invariably filed in the federal district courts, with appeal available in the court of appeals and certiorari in the Supreme Court. For deportation, § 106(a) took a wholly new approach. Rather than return to the pre–1955 reliance on habeas, Congress made the Hobbs Act, 28 U.S.C.A. §§ 2341–2351, the "sole and exclusive" procedure for judicial review of final deportation orders. The Hobbs Act, which governs review for several other administrative agencies such as the Federal Communications Commission, takes review out of the district courts and puts it in the courts of appeals, through a procedure known as a petition for review.

Another subsection, INA § 106(a)(10), provided that "any alien held in custody pursuant to an order of deportation may obtain judicial review thereof by habeas corpus proceedings." Just how this provision fit with INA § 106(a)'s designation of the Hobbs Act as the "sole and exclusive procedure" for reviewing deportation orders posed some knotty issues that we will spare you, except to generalize that courts adopted several different (and sometimes inconsistent) ways of limiting the reach of (a)(10), so that habeas review of deportation was available only under specific circumstances.

The 1961 scheme remained intact until 1996, when, first, the Antiterrorism and Effective Death Penalty Act of 1996 (AEDPA), Pub. L. 104–132, 110 Stat. 1214, significantly amended the 1961 scheme. Later that year, the 1996 Illegal Immigration Reform and Immigrant Responsibility Act (IIRIRA) adopted an entirely new judicial review scheme that appears in the current INA § 242, but this scheme did not take effect immediately. In the interim, review was governed by transitional rules that were not codified in the INA. Many of the transitional rules and the permanent rules in INA § 242 carried forward themes from AEDPA—for example, barring judicial review in certain types of cases—but crucial differences in the three texts sometimes led courts to construe them differently.

New INA § 242 eliminates separate systems of judicial review for exclusion and deportation orders. There is now a single scheme for removal orders, explicitly made the "sole and exclusive means for judicial review of an order of removal" by § 242(a)(5)—namely the Hobbs Act procedure that the 1961 Act had applied to deportation orders. *See* INA § 242(a)(1). Under § 242(b), review is exclusively in the court of appeals and is obtained by filing a petition for review with the court for the circuit in which the immigration court proceedings were completed. Section 242(b) also sets out rules for service and a filing deadline of 30 days after the date of the final order.

Under § 242(b)(3)(B), removal orders are no longer stayed automatically pending court review, as they had been before 1996, but a noncitizen may apply for a discretionary stay. Also, he may initiate or continue court review even after leaving the United States, in contrast with pre–1996 law, which barred review after the noncitizen's departure from the United States.

As this historical sketch suggests, Congress has worked since 1961 to channel, limit, or expedite review in the immigration field, but its focus in those efforts has been on removal orders. What about judicial review of agency decisions or actions other than removal orders? Here the path for review, when it exists, has been guided by the Administrative Procedure Act, which provides: "A person suffering a legal wrong because of agency action, or adversely affected or aggrieved by agency action within the meaning of a relevant statute, is entitled to judicial review thereof." 5

U.S.C. § 702. Review is to be had through any special statutory review proceeding, if one is provided. (That is why review of removal orders must follow § 242.) But in the "absence or inadequacy" of such special proceeding, "any applicable form of legal action," including injunction, declaratory judgment, and habeas corpus, may be pursued. *Id.* § 703. The APA is not a jurisdictional statute, but 28 U.S.C.A. § 1331 would provide federal subject matter jurisdiction based on a federal question.

APA review, typically an action for injunctive or declaratory relief in federal district court, would be the avenue to challenge, for example, a denial of a visa petition, *see Soltane v. USDOJ*, 381 F.3d 143, 148 (3d Cir. 2004); *Fred 26 Importers v. U.S. DHS*, 445 F. Supp. 2d 1174, 1178–79 (C.D. Cal. 2006), or a denial *by USCIS* of an application for adjustment of status, *see Pinho v. Gonzales*, 432 F.3d 193 (3d Cir. 2005).[2] One further wrinkle must be kept in mind. Many applications denied by USCIS (primarily adjustment of status or asylum) can be renewed in removal proceedings for de novo consideration by an immigration judge. If such a removal process is underway for, say, a denied adjustment applicant, a district court would ordinarily dismiss APA review of the USCIS denial, leaving review to the court of appeals if the IJ does not provide the relief. *See Ibarra v. Swacina,* 628 F.3d 1269 (11th Cir. 2010). Denial of an application for relief from removal by an immigration judge in the course of a removal proceeding is reviewable only on petition for review in the court of appeals.

Judicial review of immigration decisions could take up a book of its own, but this section will focus selectively on a few key issues. First, under what circumstances must noncitizens wait until the end of agency decisionmaking before going to court? Second, § 242(a)(2) limits or eliminates review in certain categories of cases. When and how does it do so? Third, when is a stay of removal appropriate while judicial review proceeds? And finally, when may multiple litigants combine their cases to challenge a government practice or policy?

2. LIMITING JUDICIAL REVIEW

Section 242 of the INA significantly curtails judicial review in a variety of ways, of which the most important are treated below. (There are also other jurisdiction-limiting provisions sprinkled elsewhere within the INA. *See, e.g.,* INA § 208(a)(3), (b)(2)(D). We touch upon only a few of them in this chapter.)

a. Exhaustion of Administrative Remedies

Reflecting a traditional prerequisite to judicial review, INA § 242(d)(1) provides: "A court may review a final order of removal only if

---

2. There are conflicting court rulings, however, as to whether INA § 242(b)(2)(B), discussed below, may apply to bar review of such USCIS decisions in visa petition and adjustment of status cases, because they are seen—by the courts that restrict review—as discretionary. *See* G. Seipp, Federal Court Jurisdiction to Review Immigration Decisions: A Tug of War Between the Three Branches, 07–04 Imm. Briefings 6–7, 9–10 (2007).

* * * the alien has exhausted all administrative remedies available to the alien as of right." The exhaustion rule "is based on the need to allow agencies to develop the facts, to apply the law in which they are particularly expert, and to correct their own errors. The rule ensures that whatever judicial review is available will be informed and narrowed by the agencies' own decisions. It also avoids duplicative proceedings, and often the agency's ultimate decision will obviate the need for judicial intervention." *Schlesinger v. Councilman*, 420 U.S. 738, 756–57, 95 S.Ct. 1300, 1312–13, 43 L.Ed.2d 591 (1975). Courts have found limited exceptions to the statutory requirement, such as when a particular available procedure cannot be considered a remedy, *see Castro–Cortez v. INS*, 239 F.3d 1037, 1044–45 (9th Cir. 2001), *overruled on other grounds by Fernandez–Vargas v. Gonzales*, 548 U.S. 30, 126 S.Ct. 2422, 165 L.Ed.2d 323 (2006), but exceptions to a statutory exhaustion requirement are infrequent.

If the noncitizen is not challenging a final removal order, however, the § 241(d) restriction is usually considered not to apply. Courts still impose a prudential exhaustion requirement, but a wider range of traditional exceptions may be available, for example, that pursuing an administrative remedy would be futile. *See Gonzalez v. O'Connell*, 355 F.3d 1010, 1015–18 (7th Cir. 2004).

b. Discretionary Relief

Section 242(a)(2)(B)(i) bars judicial review of "any judgment regarding the granting of relief" under the waiver provisions in § 212(h) and § 212(i), cancellation of removal, voluntary departure, and adjustment of status. INA § 242(a)(2)(B)(ii) bars judicial review of any other "decision or action" that is specified under Title II of the INA (therefore not applicable to Title III, which concerns Nationality and Naturalization) to be in the discretion of the Attorney General or Secretary of Homeland Security. An exception leaves judicial review available for asylum decisions, but the statute specifies a highly deferential standard of review, *see* INA § 242(b)(4)(D).

What review is precluded? Suppose a noncitizen seeks review of a decision denying discretionary relief. Does § 242(a)(2)(B)(i) bar review only of the decision's discretionary elements, or also of the decision's nondiscretionary elements, such as whether he meets threshold eligibility requirements for the relief sought? One might have thought that the Congress that passed the highly restrictive IIRIRA in 1996 intended to bar all such review, and the government so argued. But most courts have construed the bar narrowly. In *Montero–Martinez v. Ashcroft,* 277 F.3d 1137, 1141–44 (9th Cir. 2002), the Ninth Circuit held that under § 242(a)(2)(B)(i) it still could review nondiscretionary eligibility issues—in particular, whether Montero–Martinez was ineligible for cancellation of removal because his adult daughter was no longer a "child." *See also Morales–Morales v. Ashcroft*, 384 F.3d 418, 423 (7th Cir. 2004) (jurisdiction exists to review legal standards applied in determining whether an applicant for cancellation had been continuously physically present). On the other hand, whether "exceptional and extremely unusual hardship" exists for purposes of cancellation of removal is a discretionary determination beyond judicial review. *See Romero–Torres v. Ashcroft*, 327 F.3d 887, 889–92 (9th Cir. 2003).

Some circuits also consider "good moral character" to be a discretionary determination. Judge Easterbrook has explained this conclusion:

> Eligibility must be a question of law, [respondent] insists, and therefore must be open to plenary judicial review. This argument reflects a confusion that we thought had been cleared up * * *. "Good moral character" is a statutory requirement—that is, a condition of eligibility—for cancellation of removal. But the Immigration and Nationality Act does not define "good moral character." Hence the decision *whether* an alien has the required character reflects an exercise of administrative discretion. * * * Neither the immigration judge nor the Board compared Portillo–Rendon's driving record against a rule. For the purpose of § 242(a)(2)(D), "law" means a dispute about the meaning of a legal text, so that the alien wins if the text means one thing and loses if it means something else. * * * There is no dispute about a controlling text here; there is only a (potential) dispute about whether Portillo–Rendon's driving infractions are serious and frequent enough to show that he lacks good moral character, as opposed to making isolated mistakes. The IJ and BIA thought that this record shows poor moral fiber; that is a discretionary call and thus is not subject to judicial review.

Portillo-Rendon v. Holder, ___ F.3d ___, 2011 WL 5319855 (7th Cir. 2011) (paragraphing altered).

Essentially the early judicial readings of § 242(a)(2)(B) marked out this rough dividing line: legal determinations are subject to review, while factual findings and discretionary decisions are not. *See, e.g., Pareja v. Attorney General*, 615 F.3d 180, 187–88 (3d Cir. 2010) (though "exceptional and extremely unusual hardship" is a discretionary determination, jurisdiction exists to review the legal standard the BIA employs in making that decision). After the enactment of INA § 242(a)(2)(D) in the REAL ID Act of 2005, which expressly preserved judicial review over "constitutional claims and questions of law" (discussed in Section C3 below), the statute now provides more directly for using this same general line to differentiate reviewable from nonreviewable issues.

Who defines what is discretionary? What if a decision is made discretionary by agency regulation, not by statute? Does INA § 242(a)(2)(B) bar judicial review? The Supreme Court said no, in *Kucana v. Holder*, ___ U.S. ___, 130 S.Ct. 827, 175 L.Ed.2d 694 (2010). At issue in *Kucana* was denial of a motion to reopen an asylum proceeding. The relevant regulation places a decision to grant or deny a motion to reopen "within the discretion of the Board." 8 C.F.R. § 1003.2(a). The core of the Supreme Court's reasoning follows:

To the clause (i) enumeration of administrative judgments that are insulated from judicial review [under § 242(a)(2)(B)], Congress added in clause (ii) a catchall provision covering "any other decision . . . the authority for which is specified under this subchapter [to be within administrative discretion]." * * * Read harmoniously, both clauses convey that Congress barred court review of discretionary decisions only when Congress itself set out the Attorney General's discretionary authority in the statute.

* * *

Any lingering doubt about the proper interpretation of § 242(a)(2)(B)(ii) would be dispelled by a familiar principle of statutory construction: the presumption favoring judicial review of administrative action. When a statute is "reasonably susceptible to divergent interpretation, we adopt the reading that accords with traditional understandings and basic principles: that executive determinations generally are subject to judicial review." * * * It therefore takes "clear and convincing evidence" to dislodge the presumption. There is no such evidence here.

Finally, we stress a paramount factor in the decision we render today. By defining the various jurisdictional bars by reference to other provisions in the INA itself, Congress ensured that it, and only it, would limit the federal courts' jurisdiction. To read § 242(a)(2)(B)(ii) to apply to matters where discretion is conferred on the Board by regulation, rather than on the Attorney General by statute, would ignore that congressional design. If the [contrary] construction * * * were to prevail, the Executive would have a free hand to shelter its own decisions from abuse-of-discretion appellate court review simply by issuing a regulation declaring those decisions "discretionary." Such an extraordinary delegation of authority cannot be extracted from the statute Congress enacted.

130 S.Ct. at 836–40.

c. Review Standards

Statutes and case law prescribe the scope and standard of review of various kinds of decisions taken by administrative agencies. The standard ranges from the most intrusive form of appellate review, de novo consideration of findings of fact and rulings of law (which applies, for example, to a denial of naturalization, INA § 310(c)), to others that are far more deferential. Examples of the latter include standards that permit the setting aside of agency decisions only on a judicial determination that they were "arbitrary and capricious" or amounted to an "abuse of discretion." *See generally* C. Koch, 3 Admin. L. & Prac. § 9:21 (3d ed. 2010).

Section 242(b)(4) sets the general judicial review standards governing orders of removal, formulations clearly designed to elicit deference to the administrative agency. For example, "administrative findings of fact are conclusive unless any reasonable adjudicator would be compelled to conclude the contrary," and "a decision that an alien is not eligible for admission to the United States is conclusive unless manifestly contrary to law." Asylum, as noted above, is one of the few discretionary decisions that remains subject to judicial review after IIRIRA. For asylum decisions, however, the "discretionary judgment whether" to grant asylum "shall be conclusive unless manifestly contrary to the law and an abuse of discretion."

d.   Removal Based on Criminal Convictions

Among the most far-reaching limits on court review are those that purport to bar judicial review completely in certain cases, based not on the issues raised but the characteristics of the person raising them. The central example is INA § 242(a)(2)(C), which, as originally enacted in IIRIRA in 1996, provided:

> Notwithstanding any other provision of law, no court shall have jurisdiction to review any final order of removal against an alien who is removable by reason of having committed a criminal offense covered in [the subsections dealing with criminal grounds of inadmissibility or deportability, with a limited exception for a person convicted only of a single crime involving moral turpitude].

This provision, along with a similar provision in the Antiterrorism and Effective Death Penalty Act (AEDPA), § 440(a), enacted earlier that same year, triggered a massive round of constitutional challenges. The litigants claimed that such a broad bar to judicial review violates the due process clause, the principle of separation of powers, or the clause generally forbidding suspension of the privilege of habeas corpus (Art. I, § 9, cl. 2).

The 1996 restrictions on judicial review in immigration cases also launched wide-ranging commentary in the law journals, because this jurisdiction-stripping provision fit into a long line of congressional attempts over the preceding decades to restrict federal court jurisdiction in response to judicial decisions Congress found objectionable. All such attempts raise a classic question of constitutional law and the law of federal courts: what are the limits, if any, on Congress's power under the Constitution (U.S. Const. Art. III, § 1, and § 2, cl. 2) to restrict the jurisdiction of the federal courts? *See* Hart, *The Power of Congress to Limit the Jurisdiction of Federal Courts: An Exercise in Dialectic*, 66 Harv. L. Rev. 1362, 1395–1397 (1953).

Earlier attempts of this sort have included proposals to strip the courts of jurisdiction over cases involving school prayer, abortions, or prison litigation. During the McCarthy era of the 1950s, members of Congress rallied support for bills to strip court authority over laws requiring loyalty oaths. In the 1960s, *Miranda v. Arizona* spawned proposals to deny jurisdiction over state rules governing the voluntariness of admissions for use in a criminal prosecution. More recently, some members proposed to prevent federal courts from hearing challenges to the

Pledge of Allegiance or to the Defense of Marriage Act. *See* E. Chemerinsky, Federal Jurisdiction 174–77 (5th ed. 2007). Erwin Chemerinsky commented on those earlier efforts: "The obvious purpose of these jurisdiction stripping bills is to achieve a change in the substantive law by a procedural device." *Id.* at 177. Despite the many proposals of this sort over the years, however, Congress has only rarely managed to enact jurisdiction-stripping provisions. Consequently, courts have only rarely examined their constitutionality, leaving considerable room for rich debate over the constitutional issues presented by the 1996 restrictions on judicial review of removal orders.

What is the relationship between constitutional challenges based on due process and separation of powers? Are they identical, overlapping, or distinct? Can the government respond in the same way to both? Or are there responses that rebut only one type of challenge or the other? For discussions of due process, separation of powers, and habeas corpus as constitutional sources of court review of immigration decisions, see Neuman, *Jurisdiction and the Rule of Law After the 1996 Immigration Act*, 113 Harv. L. Rev. 1963, 1969–75 (2000); Cole, *Jurisdiction and Liberty: Habeas Corpus and Due Process as Limits on Congress's Control of Federal Jurisdiction*, 86 Geo. L.J. 2481, 2489–2506 (1998); Fallon, *Applying the Suspension Clause to Immigration Cases*, 98 Colum. L. Rev. 1068, 1077–91 (1998).

Why is judicial review important in the first place? For answers to this question, a discussion of the costs of judicial review, and analysis of congressional skepticism of judicial review, see Legomsky, *Fear and Loathing in Congress and the Courts*, 78 Tex. L. Rev. 1615 (2001). For a discussion of the general objectives that Congress and the administration had in mind in channeling and recasting court review in the 1996 Act, and an assessment of their legitimacy, see Martin, *Behind the Scenes on A Different Set: What Congress Needs to Do in the Aftermath of* St. Cyr *and* Nguyen, 16 Geo. Immig. L.J. 313, 314–32 (2002).

Most of the early decisions on INA § 242(a)(2)(C) or its statutory predecessor in AEDPA upheld the restrictions, but on the basis that an individual thus barred from the ordinary petition for review in the court of appeals could still obtain judicial consideration under the general habeas corpus statute, 28 U.S.C. § 2241. *See, e.g., Kolster v. INS,* 101 F.3d 785 (1st Cir. 1996); *Duldulao v. INS,* 90 F.3d 396 (9th Cir. 1996). That statute gives federal courts jurisdiction to hear petitions for habeas corpus filed by persons "in custody * * * under the authority of the United States," and the writ may issue if the petitioner is "in custody in violation of the Constitution or laws or treaties of the United States." The government fought this conclusion, in part because it would mean that persons with criminal convictions who are barred from the normal petition for review process would have more rounds of judicial access than other respondents; habeas petitions are typically heard in district court and the decision can then be appealed to the court of appeals. The government urged that the preclusion of review be read to apply as well to habeas, but it did concede that the statute would have to be read to permit barred individuals to use the petition for review process if they presented "substantial" constitutional claims.

The issue ultimately came to the Supreme Court in the following case.

INS v. ST. CYR

Supreme Court of the United States, 2001.
533 U.S. 289, 121 S.Ct. 2271, 150 L.Ed.2d 347.

Justice Stevens delivered the opinion of the Court.

* * *

Respondent, Enrico St. Cyr, is a citizen of Haiti who was admitted to the United States as a lawful permanent resident in 1986. Ten years later, on March 8, 1996, he pled guilty in a state court to a charge of selling a controlled substance in violation of Connecticut law. That conviction made him deportable. Under pre-AEDPA law applicable at the time of his conviction, St. Cyr would have been eligible for a waiver of deportation at the discretion of the Attorney General [under former INA § 212(c)].[g] However, removal proceedings against him were not commenced until April 10, 1997, after both AEDPA and IIRIRA became effective, and, as the Attorney General interprets those statutes, he no longer has discretion to grant such a waiver.

* * *

The first question we must consider is whether the District Court retains jurisdiction under the general habeas corpus statute, 28 U.S.C. § 2241, to entertain St. Cyr's challenge. His application for a writ raises a pure question of law. He does not dispute any of the facts that establish his deportability or the conclusion that he is deportable. Nor does he contend that he would have any right to have an unfavorable exercise of the Attorney General's discretion reviewed in a judicial forum. Rather, he contests the Attorney General's conclusion that, as a matter of statutory interpretation, he is not eligible for discretionary relief.

The District Court held, and the Court of Appeals agreed, that it had jurisdiction to answer that question in a habeas corpus proceeding. The INS argues, however, that four sections of the 1996 statutes * * * stripped the courts of jurisdiction to decide the question of law presented by respondent's habeas corpus application.

For the INS to prevail it must overcome both the strong presumption in favor of judicial review of administrative action and the longstanding rule requiring a clear statement of congressional intent to repeal habeas jurisdiction. *See Ex parte Yerger*, 8 Wall. 85, 102 (1869) ("We are not at liberty to except from [habeas corpus jurisdiction] any cases not plainly excepted by law"); *Felker v. Turpin*, 518 U.S. 651, 660–661 (1996).

---

g. Discretionary relief under former § 212(c) is discussed in Chapter Seven.—eds.

Implications from statutory text or legislative history are not sufficient to repeal habeas jurisdiction; instead, Congress must articulate specific and unambiguous statutory directives to effect a repeal.

In this case, the plain statement rule draws additional reinforcement from other canons of statutory construction. First, as a general matter, when a particular interpretation of a statute invokes the outer limits of Congress' power, we expect a clear indication that Congress intended that result. Second, if an otherwise acceptable construction of a statute would raise serious constitutional problems, and where an alternative interpretation of the statute is "fairly possible," *see Crowell v. Benson*, 285 U.S. 22, 62 (1932), we are obligated to construe the statute to avoid such problems.

A construction of the amendments at issue that would entirely preclude review of a pure question of law by any court would give rise to substantial constitutional questions. Article I, § 9, cl. 2, of the Constitution provides: "The Privilege of the Writ of Habeas Corpus shall not be suspended, unless when in Cases of Rebellion or Invasion the public Safety may require it." Because of that Clause, some "judicial intervention in deportation cases" is unquestionably "required by the Constitution." *Heikkila v. Barber*, 345 U.S. 229, 235 (1953).

* * *

At its historical core, the writ of habeas corpus has served as a means of reviewing the legality of executive detention, and it is in that context that its protections have been strongest. In England prior to 1789, in the Colonies, and in this Nation during the formative years of our Government, the writ of habeas corpus was available to nonenemy aliens as well as to citizens. It enabled them to challenge executive and private detention in civil cases as well as criminal. Moreover, the issuance of the writ was not limited to challenges to the jurisdiction of the custodian, but encompassed detentions based on errors of law, including the erroneous application or interpretation of statutes. It was used to command the discharge of seamen who had a statutory exemption from impressment into the British Navy, to emancipate slaves, and to obtain the freedom of apprentices and asylum inmates. Most important, for our purposes, those early cases contain no suggestion that habeas relief in cases involving executive detention was only available for constitutional error.

* * *

[E]ven assuming that the Suspension Clause protects only the writ as it existed in 1789, there is substantial evidence to support the proposition that pure questions of law like the one raised by the respondent in this case could have been answered in 1789 by a common law judge with power to issue the writ of habeas corpus. It necessarily follows that a serious Suspension Clause issue would be presented if we were to accept the INS's submission that the 1996 statutes have withdrawn that power from federal judges and provided no adequate substitute for its exercise. * * *

* * *

Until the enactment of the 1952 Immigration and Nationality Act, the sole means by which an alien could test the legality of his or her deportation order was by bringing a habeas corpus action in district court. In such cases, other than the question whether there was some evidence to support the order, the courts generally did not review factual determinations made by the Executive. *See Ekiu v. United States*, 142 U.S. 651, 659 (1892). However, they did review the Executive's legal determinations. * * * In case after case, courts answered questions of law in habeas corpus proceedings brought by aliens challenging Executive interpretations of the immigration laws.

Habeas courts also regularly answered questions of law that arose in the context of discretionary relief. *See, e.g., United States ex rel. Accardi v. Shaughnessy*, 347 U.S. 260 (1954); *United States ex rel. Hintopoulos v. Shaughnessy*, 353 U.S. 72, 77 (1957). Traditionally, courts recognized a distinction between eligibility for discretionary relief, on the one hand, and the favorable exercise of discretion, on the other hand. *See* Neuman, 113 Harv. L. Rev., at 1991 (noting the "strong tradition in habeas corpus law . . . that subjects the legally erroneous failure to exercise discretion, unlike a substantively unwise exercise of discretion, to inquiry on the writ"). Eligibility that was "governed by specific statutory standards" provided "a right to a ruling on an applicant's eligibility," even though the actual granting of relief was "not a matter of right under any circumstances, but rather is in all cases a matter of grace." *Jay v. Boyd*, 351 U.S. 345, 353–354 (1956). Thus, even though the actual suspension of deportation authorized by § 19(c) of the Immigration Act of 1917 was a matter of grace, in *United States ex rel. Accardi v. Shaughnessy*, 347 U.S. 260 (1954), we held that a deportable alien had a right to challenge the Executive's failure to exercise the discretion authorized by the law. The exercise of the District Court's habeas corpus jurisdiction to answer a pure question of law in this case is entirely consistent with the exercise of such jurisdiction in *Accardi*.

Thus, under the pre–1996 statutory scheme—and consistent with its common-law antecedents—it is clear that St. Cyr could have brought his challenge to the Board of Immigration Appeals' legal determination in a habeas corpus petition under 28 U.S.C. § 2241. The INS argues, however, that AEDPA and IIRIRA contain four provisions that express a clear and unambiguous statement of Congress' intent to bar petitions brought under § 2241, despite the fact that none of them mention that section. [The Court then examines those four sections in detail and concludes that none provides a sufficiently clear statement of Congress' intent to bar habeas corpus relief.]

* * *

If it were clear that the question of law [presented by the petitioner regarding the availability of § 212(c) relief] could be answered in another judicial forum, it might be permissible to accept the INS' reading of § 242. But the absence of such a forum, coupled with the lack of a clear, unambiguous, and express statement of congressional intent to preclude judicial consideration on habeas of such an important question of law, strongly counsels against adopting a construction that would raise serious constitutional questions. Accordingly, we conclude that habeas jurisdiction under § 2241 was not repealed by AEDPA and IIRIRA.

[On the substantive legal issue, the Court concluded: "§ 212(c) relief remains available for aliens, like respondent, whose convictions were obtained through plea agreements and who, notwithstanding those convictions, would have been eligible for § 212(c) relief at the time of their plea under the law then in effect." For more on this part of *St. Cyr*, see Chapter Seven.]

[The dissenting opinion of JUSTICE O'CONNOR is omitted.]

JUSTICE SCALIA, with whom THE CHIEF JUSTICE and JUSTICE THOMAS join, and with whom JUSTICE O'CONNOR joins [in part], dissenting.

* * *

In categorical terms that admit of no exception, the Illegal Immigration Reform and Immigrant Responsibility Act of 1996 (IIRIRA), unambiguously repeals the application of 28 U.S.C. § 2241 (the general habeas corpus provision), and of all other provisions for judicial review, to deportation challenges brought by certain kinds of criminal aliens. * * * I will begin by * * * explaining IIRIRA's jurisdictional scheme. It begins with what we have called a channeling or " 'zipper' clause," *Reno v. American–Arab Anti–Discrimination Comm.*, 525 U.S. 471, 483 (1999)— namely, § 242(b)(9). This provision, entitled "Consolidation of questions for judicial review," provides as follows:

> Judicial review of *all* questions of law and fact, including interpretation and application of constitutional and statutory provisions, arising from *any action taken or proceeding brought to remove an alien* from the United States under this subchapter shall be available *only* in judicial review of a final order under this section.

(Emphases added.)

In other words, *if* any review is available of any "questio[n] of law ... arising from any action taken or proceeding brought to remove an alien from the United States under this subchapter," it is available "only in judicial review of a final order under this section [§ 242]." What kind of review does that section provide? That is set forth in § 242(a)(1) * * *. In other words, *if* judicial review is available, it consists *only* of the modified Hobbs Act review specified in § 242(a)(1).

In some cases (including, as it happens, the one before us), there can be no review at all, because IIRIRA categorically and unequivocally rules out judicial review of challenges to deportation brought by certain kinds of criminal aliens. Section 242(a)(2)(C) provides:

> Notwithstanding *any* other provision of law, *no court* shall have jurisdiction to review any final order of removal against an alien who

is removable by reason of having committed [one or more enumerat-ed] criminal offense[s] [including drug-trafficking offenses of the sort of which respondent had been convicted].

(Emphases added.)

* * *

Unquestionably, unambiguously, and unmistakably, IIRIRA expressly supersedes § 2241's general provision for habeas jurisdiction. The Court asserts that *Felker v. Turpin*, 518 U.S. 651 (1996), and *Ex parte Yerger*, 8 Wall. 85 (1869), reflect a "longstanding rule requiring a clear statement of congressional intent to repeal habeas jurisdiction." They do no such thing. Those cases simply applied the general principle—not unique to habeas—that "[r]epeals by implication are not favored." * * * In the present case, unlike in *Felker* and *Yerger*, none of the statutory provisions relied upon * * * requires us to imply from one statutory provision the repeal of another. All *by their terms* prohibit the judicial review at issue in this case.

* * *

* * * By authorizing § 2241 habeas review in the district court but foreclosing review in the court of appeals, the Court's interpretation routes all legal challenges to removal orders brought by criminal aliens to the district court, to be adjudicated under that court's § 2241 habeas authority, which specifies no time limits. After review by that court, criminal aliens will presumably have an appeal as of right to the court of appeals, and can then petition this Court for a writ of certiorari. In contrast, noncriminal aliens seeking to challenge their removal orders— for example, those charged with having been inadmissible at the time of entry, with having failed to maintain their nonimmigrant status, with having procured a visa through a marriage that was not bona fide, or with having become, within five years after the date of entry, a public charge, will still presumably be required to proceed directly to the court of appeals by way of petition for review, under the restrictive modified Hobbs Act review provisions set forth in § 242(a)(1), including the 30–day filing deadline, *see* § 242(b)(1). * * * The Court has therefore succeeded in perverting a statutory scheme designed to *expedite* the removal of criminal aliens into one that now affords them *more* opportunities for (and layers of) judicial review (and hence more opportunities for delay) than are afforded *non*-criminal aliens—and more than were afforded criminal aliens prior to the enactment of IIRIRA. This outcome speaks for itself; no Congress ever imagined it.

* * *

In the remainder of this opinion I address the question the Court *should* have addressed: Whether these provisions of IIRIRA are unconsti-tutional.

* * *

Even if one were to assume that the Suspension Clause, despite its text * * *, guarantees some constitutional minimum of habeas relief, that minimum would assuredly not embrace the rarified right asserted here: the right to judicial compulsion of the exercise of Executive *discretion* (which may be exercised favorably or unfavorably) regarding a prisoner's release. * * *

[One possible reading is] that the Suspension Clause guarantees the common-law right of habeas corpus, as it was understood when the Constitution was ratified. [But there] is no doubt whatever that this did not include the right to obtain discretionary release. * * *

All the other Framing-era or earlier cases cited in the Court's opinion—indeed, *all the later Supreme Court cases until United States ex rel. Accardi v. Shaughnessy*, 347 U.S. 260, *in 1954*—provide habeas relief from executive detention only when the custodian had no legal authority to detain. * * * [C]ourts understood executive discretion as lying entirely beyond the judicial ken. * * *

* * *

The Due Process Clause does not "[r]equir[e] [j]udicial [d]etermination [o]f" respondent's claim. Respondent has no legal entitlement to suspension of deportation, no matter how appealing his case. "[T]he Attorney General's suspension of deportation [is] 'an act of grace' which is accorded pursuant to her 'unfettered discretion,' *Jay v. Boyd*, 351 U.S. 345, 354 (1956) ..., and [can be likened, as Judge Learned Hand observed,] to 'a judge's power to suspend the execution of a sentence, or the President's to pardon a convict,' " *INS v. Yueh–Shaio Yang*, 519 U.S. 26, 30 (1996). * * *

* * * The notion that Article III requires every Executive determination, on a question of law or of fact, to be subject to judicial review has no support in our jurisprudence. Were it correct, the doctrine of sovereign immunity would not exist, and the APA's general permission of suits challenging administrative action, *see* 5 U.S.C. § 702, would have been superfluous. * * *

* * *

The Court has created a version of IIRIRA that is not only unrecognizable to its framers (or to anyone who can read) but gives the statutory scheme precisely the *opposite* of its intended effect, affording criminal aliens *more* opportunities for delay-inducing judicial review than others have, or even than criminal aliens had prior to the enactment of this legislation. Because § 2241's exclusion of judicial review is unmistakably clear, and unquestionably constitutional, both this Court and the courts below were without power to entertain respondent's claims. I would set aside the judgment of the court below and remand with instructions to have the District Court dismiss for want of jurisdiction. I respectfully dissent from the judgment of the Court.

On the same day the Supreme Court issued the *St. Cyr* opinion, it also decided *Calcano–Martinez v. INS,* 533 U.S. 348, 121 S.Ct. 2268, 150 L.Ed.2d 392 (2001), upholding the constitutionality of INA § 242(a)(2)(C). That section's restrictions on judicial review, the court held, were permissible because any constitutionally required court scrutiny remained available through habeas corpus, as described in *St. Cyr.*

3. THE REAL ID ACT

The REAL ID Act of 2005, Pub. L. No. 109–13, Div. B, § 106, 119 Stat. 231, 310–11, responded to *St. Cyr* and revised the system for court review of immigration decisions. In the legislative history, Congress focused on the problem that Justice Scalia identified: that noncitizens with criminal convictions would have more layers of review than others involved in removal proceedings. Even for other respondents with no criminal records, the system was deeply confusing. Some issues, particularly denials of relief from removal, would have to go to the district court on habeas because of § 242(a)(2)(B), whereas any challenge to baseline deportability by the same respondent would go to the court of appeals directly on a petition for review. *See* H.R. Rep. No. 109–72, at 173–74 (2005), reprinted in 2005 U.S.C.C.A.N. 240 (Conference Report).

The REAL ID Act re-established petitions for review in the courts of appeals as the principal vehicle for court review of final removal orders and certain other immigration decisions by the government. The Act did this by making it clear that the various provisions that had previously eliminated judicial review also eliminated habeas corpus jurisdiction, mandamus jurisdiction, and jurisdiction under the All Writs Act, 28 U.S.C. § 1651. The amendments made by the REAL ID Act expressly provided that these forms of jurisdiction no longer exist for review of removal orders. *See, e.g.,* the current version of INA § 242(a)(2)(A)–(C), and (a)(5).

At the same time, Congress minimized possible constitutional confrontation with the Supreme Court by adding a provision that preserves judicial review, in the courts of appeals, of the major kinds of immigration issues that had been considered via habeas corpus in federal district courts since 1996. The REAL ID Act did this by adding section 242(a)(2)(D) to the INA:

> Nothing in subparagraph (B) or (C), or in any other provision of this Act (other than this section) which limits or eliminates judicial review, shall be construed as precluding review of constitutional claims or questions of law raised upon a petition for review filed with an appropriate court of appeals in accordance with this section.

As courts interpret the various provisions of the REAL ID Act in the coming years, much attention will be devoted to two broad areas of inquiry: (1) what sort of review is now available in the courts of appeals, and (2) whether habeas corpus jurisdiction remains, and if so, what sort? *See generally* Motomura, *Immigration Law and Federal Court Jurisdic-*

tion Through the Lens of Habeas Corpus, 91 Corn.L.Rev. 459 (2006). The next decision grapples with these questions.

a. "Questions of Law"

CHEN v. GONZALES

United States Court of Appeals, Second Circuit, 2006.
471 F.3d 315.

JOSÉ A. CABRANES, CIRCUIT JUDGE.

* * *

Petitioner Xiao Ji Chen, a native and citizen of China, seeks review of a September 25, 2002 order of the Board of Immigration Appeals ("BIA") affirming the November 17, 2000 decision of Immigration Judge ("IJ")[.]
* * *

* * *

In her removal hearing before the IJ, petitioner alleged past and future persecution based on her opposition to the Chinese family planning policy, testifying that she had been forced to undergo an abortion in October 1997 and that she would be sterilized were she to return to China.

* * *

Rather than [report to a doctor] for sterilization, as she had been instructed [by local birth control officials], petitioner states that she made arrangements to flee to the United States, where she arrived on or about May 21, 1998. Petitioner gave birth in the United States to a second child in April 2000.

On April 27, 1999, approximately eleven months after her arrival in the United States, petitioner was detained for approximately 5–6 hours by INS officials and was ordered to appear at a removal hearing in August 1999. Petitioner filed her written application for asylum with the immigration court on October 13, 1999, nearly fifteen months after her arrival in the United States, and a merits hearing was held before the IJ on November 17, 2000.

In a decision issued at the conclusion of petitioner's hearing, the IJ rejected petitioner's application for asylum on the grounds that she had failed to file her application within one year of her arrival in the United States, as required by INA § 208(a)(2)(B), and that she had failed to establish either "changed circumstances" materially affecting her eligibility for asylum or "extraordinary circumstances" excusing her untimely filing. The IJ then concluded that, even if petitioner's asylum application was not in fact time-barred, she had failed to establish a credible case of past or future persecution entitling her either to asylum or withholding of removal under the INA or the CAT [Convention Against Torture]. * * *

* * *

In this case, we consider first whether we have jurisdiction to review the IJ's discretionary and factual determination, with respect to petitioner's asylum claim, that petitioner failed to establish either changed or extraordinary circumstances under INA § 208(a)(2)(D). We then evaluate petitioner's claim that the IJ improperly rejected her request for withholding of removal under both the INA and the CAT.

I. Asylum

INA 208(a)(1) provides, in relevant part, that "[a]ny alien who is physically present in the United States or who arrives in the United States . . . may apply for asylum." That statutory provision, however, is limited by § 208(a)(2)(B), which states that § 208(a)(1) "shall not apply to an alien unless the alien demonstrates by clear and convincing evidence that the application [for asylum] has been filed within 1 year after the date of the alien's arrival in the United States." A discretionary exception to § 208(a)(2)(B)'s one-year bar is created by § 208(a)(2)(D), which provides that

> [a]n application for asylum of an alien *may be considered,* notwithstanding [an alien's failure to apply for asylum within one year of the alien's arrival or the denial of a prior asylum application], if the alien demonstrates *to the satisfaction of the Attorney General* either the existence of changed circumstances which materially affect the applicant's eligibility for asylum or extraordinary circumstances relating to the delay in filing an application within the [one-year] period[.]

§ 208(a)(2)(D) (emphases added). Finally, § 208(a)(3) provides that "[n]o court shall have jurisdiction to review any determination of the Attorney General under [§ 208(a)(2)]."

* * *

* * * [Section 106 of] the REAL ID Act restored the jurisdiction of courts to review even factual and discretionary decisions of the Attorney General (and his representatives) under the INA, but only to the limited extent that the petition for review of such decisions raises a constitutional claim or a question of law. * * *

The term "constitutional claims" clearly relates to claims brought pursuant to provisions of the Constitution of the United States. By contrast, "questions of law" does not have a similarly clear meaning, and the terms of the REAL ID Act provide no guidance as to the precise content of that phrase, which is subject to countless interpretations. Construed in the broadest sense possible, "questions of law" would encompass any question related to law or having any legal dimension—that is, anything pertaining to the work in which courts are engaged, including virtually all decisions in the immigration field. For the reasons that follow, we conclude that "questions of law" could not have been intended to expand our jurisdiction in such a boundless fashion.

We find ambiguity in the meaning of this term. First, "questions of law" would include all constitutional claims, which by definition raise legal questions. Yet the statute refers to two separate categories: "constitutional claims or questions of law." Had Congress intended "questions of law" to be understood as *all* questions pertaining to law generally, it would have been redundant to include "constitutional claims" in Section 106. Because, as a matter of statutory construction, we do not assume Congress intended to include pure "surplusage" in its enactments, we are left with uncertainty as to the meaning of "questions of law."

Second, the broadest meaning of "questions of law" would bring within our jurisdiction certain kinds of claims that the INA otherwise removes from our jurisdiction. *See, e.g.,* § 242(a)(2)(B)(i) (depriving courts of jurisdiction to review *"any judgment* regarding the granting of relief under section 212(h), 212(i), 240A, 240B, or 245 of this title") (emphasis added); *id.* § 242(a)(2)(B)(ii) (depriving courts of jurisdiction to review *"any other decision or action* of the Attorney General . . . the authority for which is specified under this subchapter to be *in the discretion* of the Attorney General") (emphases added); § 208(a)(3) ("No court shall have jurisdiction to review *any determination* of the Attorney General under [§ 208(a)(2)].") (emphasis added). *All* questions arising in the context of such claims, however, could not have been included in the meaning of Section 106, for this would suggest that Congress intended to repeal the jurisdiction-denying provisions of the INA *in their entirety,* rather than modify in part the *reach* of such provisions. Although it is clear that Congress has expressly limited the effect of the jurisdiction-denying provisions of the INA by restoring our jurisdiction to review "questions of law," *see* § 242(A)(2)(D) (applying to "any . . . provision of [the INA] (other than this section) which limits or eliminates judicial review"), nothing in the text of Section 106 suggests that Congress intended to engage effectively in a wholesale repeal of these jurisdiction-denying provisions by adopting the broadest meaning of "questions of law." As a result, we are left with uncertainty as to the meaning of the phrase.

Third, in light of our obligation to interpret "questions of law" in the context of the REAL ID Act as a whole, we are mindful of the fact that the title of the subsection containing the phrase "questions of law" is "JUDICIAL REVIEW OF *CERTAIN* LEGAL CLAIMS," thereby suggesting that not all legal claims are included within the phrase "questions of law."
* * *

Accordingly, because the statutory text is ambiguous, we turn to the legislative history of the REAL ID Act in order to ascertain Congress's intent.

As Committee Reports are the most authoritative sources on the meaning of legislation, we look to the House Conference Committee Report on the REAL ID Act. That report explains that the original draft of the statute used the phrase "pure questions of law," but that the word "pure" was later deleted because "it is superfluous." H.R. Rep. No. 109–

72, at 175 (2005), U.S. Code Cong. & Admin. News 2005, at pp. 240, 300 ("Conference Report"). "The word 'pure' add[ed] no meaning" because "[t]he purpose of section 106(a)(1)(A)(iii) is to permit judicial review over those issues that were historically reviewable on habeas—constitutional and statutory-construction questions, not discretionary or factual questions." A "question of law," the Conference Report thus concluded, "is a question regarding the construction of a statute."

* * *

The Conference Report makes clear that Congress, in enacting the REAL ID Act, sought to avoid the constitutional concerns outlined by the Supreme Court in *St. Cyr,* which stated that as a result of the Suspension Clause, *"some* judicial intervention in deportation cases is unquestionably required by the Constitution." In *St. Cyr,* the Supreme Court expressed doubts as to whether stripping the courts of habeas corpus jurisdiction to review deportation orders would pass constitutional muster. In response to the Court's doubts, Congress passed the REAL ID Act providing, according to the summary in the Conference Report, that "all aliens who are ordered removed by an immigration judge will be able to appeal to the BIA and then raise constitutional and legal challenges in the courts of appeals." Congress intended to "provide a scheme [of judicial review] which is an 'adequate and effective' substitute for habeas corpus."

While the Conference Report refers to "statutory construction questions," we do not interpret that reference to be exhaustive, but merely illustrative. We construe the intent of Congress's restoration under the REAL ID Act rubric of "constitutional claims or questions of law" to encompass the same types of issues that courts traditionally exercised in habeas review over Executive detentions. As stated in the Conference Report, "the Supreme Court recognized that 'Congress could, without raising any constitutional questions, provide an adequate substitute through the courts of appeals.' " *Id.* (quoting *St. Cyr,* 533 U.S. at 314 n.38, 121 S.Ct. 2271). While the Supreme Court in *St. Cyr* did not define the exact scope of constitutional protection required, it said that "at the absolute minimum, the Suspension Clause protects the writ [of habeas corpus] 'as it existed in 1789.' "

Traditionally, habeas review for Executive detention had encompassed both constitutional claims and questions of law. In *St. Cyr,* the Supreme Court noted that historically, habeas review of Executive detentions was broader than habeas review over other types of detentions resulting from judicial determinations. "While habeas review of a court judgment was limited to the issue of the sentencing court's jurisdictional competency, an attack on an executive order could raise *all issues* relating to the legality of detention." (emphasis added). This was because "[a]t its historical core, the writ of habeas corpus has served as a means of reviewing the legality of Executive detention, and it is in that context that its protections have been strongest."

As part of its historical review of the scope of habeas jurisdiction, the Supreme Court did not expressly limit its analysis to issues of "statutory construction," but instead stated that such review traditionally had "encompassed detentions based on *errors of law*, including the erroneous *application or interpretation* of statutes," (emphases added), as well as challenges to "Executive interpretations of the immigration laws," and determinations regarding an alien's "statutory eligibility for discretionary relief." Furthermore, one of the habeas corpus cases on which *St. Cyr* relied—*United States ex rel. Accardi v. Shaughnessy*, 347 U.S. 260, 74 S.Ct. 499, 98 L.Ed. 681 (1954)—involved the application and interpretation of a *regulation*, not a statute.

With respect to determinations committed to the discretion of the Attorney General, the Supreme Court found that "[h]abeas courts also regularly answered *questions of law* that arose in the context of discretionary relief." *St. Cyr*, 533 U.S. at 307, 121 S.Ct. 2271 (emphasis added). At the same time, the Supreme Court emphasized in both *St. Cyr* and *Accardi* that habeas jurisdiction is not without limits. In *St. Cyr*, the Court wrote:

> [St. Cyr] does not dispute any of the *facts* that establish his deportability or the conclusion that he is deportable. Nor does he contend that he would have any right to have an unfavorable *exercise* of the Attorney General's discretion reviewed in a judicial forum. Rather, he contests the Attorney General's conclusion that, *as a matter of statutory interpretation*, he is not *eligible* for discretionary relief.

Id. at 298, 121 S.Ct. 2271 (emphases added). In *Accardi*, the Court emphasized that it was not "reviewing and reversing the *manner* in which discretion was exercised," stating that any such review would have required "discussing the evidence in the record supporting or undermining the alien's claim to discretionary relief." *Accardi*, 347 U.S. at 268, 74 S.Ct. 499. Rather, the applicant there raised a reviewable claim because he had challenged the BIA's "alleged *failure to exercise* its own discretion, contrary to existing valid regulations." (emphasis added).

In another habeas corpus case on which *St. Cyr* relied, *United States ex rel. Hintopoulos v. Shaughnessy*, 353 U.S. 72, 77 S.Ct. 618, 1 L.Ed.2d 652 (1957), the BIA denied petitioners' request for relief under the Immigration Act of 1917 as a matter of administrative discretion, but also said "[i]t is crystal clear that Congress intended to greatly restrict the granting of suspension of deportation by the change of phraseology which was used in Section 244(a) of the Immigration and Nationality Act [of 1952] as well as the Congressional comment at the time this provision was enacted." *Id.* at 76, 77 S.Ct. 618 (alteration in original). The Supreme Court, upon habeas review, considered the petitioners' argument that the BIA *"abused its discretion* in denying their application for suspension of deportation" and *"applied an improper standard* when exercising its discretion" by taking into account the congressional policy underlying a "concededly inapplicable" statute (emphases added). Because the petition for review raised questions of law, *i.e.,* abuse of discretion and an argument about the standard of law applied by the BIA in its exercise of discretion, the Supreme Court exercised jurisdiction over the petition, notwithstanding that the decision being challenged was one within the Attorney General's discretion. Having exercised jurisdiction, the Court rejected the claim because "the reasons relied on by the Hearing Office and the Board . . . were neither capricious nor arbitrary" and "we cannot say that it was improper or arbitrary for the Board to be influenced, in exercising that discretion, by its views as to congressional policy."

In deciding this case, we need not determine the precise outer limits of the term "questions of law" under the REAL ID Act, nor need we define the full extent of "those issues that were historically reviewable on habeas," or what the Suspension Clause itself requires on direct, non-habeas review of a removal order. Rather, it is enough for us to hold simply that, although the REAL ID Act restores our jurisdiction to review "constitutional claims or questions of law," § 242(a)(2)(D), we remain deprived of jurisdiction to review decisions under the INA when the petition for review essentially disputes the correctness of an IJ's fact-finding or the wisdom of his exercise of discretion and raises neither a constitutional claim nor a question of law. To determine whether a reviewing court has jurisdiction under Section 106 to consider a petition for review, especially one challenging the agency's fact-finding or its exercise of discretion, the court would need to study the arguments asserted. The court would need to determine, regardless of the rhetoric employed in the petition, whether it merely quarrels over the correctness of the factual findings or justification for the discretionary choices, in which case the court would lack jurisdiction, or whether it instead raises a "constitutional claim" or "question of law," in which case the court could exercise jurisdiction to review those particular issues. Such an issue would arise for example in fact-finding which is flawed by an error of law, such as might arise where the IJ states that his decision was based on petitioner's failure to testify to some pertinent fact when the record of the hearing reveals unambiguously that the petitioner *did* testify to that fact. Such an issue would also arise where a discretionary decision is argued to be an abuse of discretion because it was made without rational justification or based on a legally erroneous standard. But when analysis of the arguments raised by the petition for judicial review reveals that they do not in fact raise any reviewable issues, the petitioner cannot overcome this deficiency and secure review by using the rhetoric of a "constitutional claim" or "question of law" to disguise what is essentially a quarrel about fact-finding or the exercise of discretion.[8]

---

8. In so holding, we emphasize the particular role played by Section 106 of the REAL ID Act— namely, to *restore* some of the jurisdiction that is otherwise *denied* by another provision of the INA. *See* § 242(a)(2)(D) ("Nothing in subparagraph (B) or (C), or in any other provision of this chapter (other than this section) *which limits or eliminates judicial review,* shall be construed as precluding review of constitutional claims or questions of law raised upon a petition for *review* . . . .") (emphasis added). By contrast, where no jurisdiction-denying provision of the INA is implicated, a reviewing court need not resort to the jurisdictional terms of Section 106, but is instead presumed to have the authority to consider "*all* questions of law and fact, including

Petitioner here argues that the IJ erred in either his fact-finding or in his exercise of discretion in rejecting petitioner's contention that changed or extraordinary circumstances excused the untimeliness of her petition for asylum. In her effort to establish such changed or extraordinary circumstances, petitioner argued changed circumstances because the government of China had recently cracked down on political dissidents and extraordinary circumstances because petitioner made an oral request to file for asylum when she was detained by the INS. The IJ rejected these contentions, finding that "nothing had changed" in China's family planning policies that would have affected her eligibility for asylum, and that she had "ample opportunity" to file her asylum application within one year as required, notwithstanding her "very brief" detention in April 1999. Petitioner's challenge to the IJ's rulings are just the kind of quarrels with fact-finding determinations and with exercises of discretion that courts continue to have no jurisdiction to review, notwithstanding the REAL ID Act's restoration of jurisdiction over constitutional claims and questions of law.

In an effort to come within the restored jurisdiction for constitutional claims and questions of law, petitioner asserts that the IJ "fail[ed] to apply the law," and argues that a claim of failure to apply the law raises a question of law, if not also a constitutional claim of violation of due process. A petitioner cannot overcome the lack of jurisdiction to review by invocation of such rhetoric.

To determine whether the petition for review in fact raises a constitutional claim or question of law, we examine the precise arguments of the petition. The conclusory assertion that the IJ and the BIA "fail[ed] to apply the law" presents neither a constitutional claim nor a question of law within the meaning of the REAL ID Act. Indeed, were we to exercise jurisdiction based on a petitioner's talismanic statement that an IJ "fail[ed] to apply the law," without more, a petitioner would have no need to raise a specific "constitutional claim[ ] or question[ ] of law" to obtain the court's jurisdiction. Although, as we have pointed out, a "question of law" may be found in some instances in petitions to review an IJ's discretionary denial of relief, a petitioner's mere resort to the terms conventionally used in describing constitutional claims and questions of law will not overcome Congress's decision to deny jurisdiction over claims which in reality consist of nothing more than quarrels over the correctness of fact-finding and of discretionary decisions. Accordingly, we conclude that, on this record, petitioner's mere assertion that the IJ and the BIA "fail[ed] to apply the law" does not convert a mere disagreement with the IJ's factual findings and exercise of discretion into a constitutional claim or a question of law.

Moreover, we emphasize that our jurisdiction in this case is not restored by the REAL ID Act on the ground that the IJ's decision involved

---

interpretation and application of constitutional and statutory provisions" in reviewing a final order of removal. *See* INA § 242(b)(9) (emphasis added).

the allegedly erroneous "application" of a statute—here, INA § 208(a)(2)(B) and (D). While the term "questions of law" undeniably can encompass claims of "erroneous *application* or interpretation of statutes," *St. Cyr*, 533 U.S. at 302, 121 S.Ct. 2271 (emphasis added), every discretionary determination under the INA can in some sense be said to reflect an "application" of a statute to the facts presented. The mere use of the term "erroneous application" of a statute will not, however, convert a quarrel over an exercise of discretion into a question of law.[11] We must look to the *nature of the argument* being advanced in the petition and determine whether the petition raises "constitutional claims or questions of law" or merely objects to the IJ's fact-finding or exercise of discretion. This petitioner's challenge is merely an objection to the IJ's factual findings and the balancing of factors in which discretion was exercised. Accordingly, for the reasons stated above, we dismiss the petition for review of the denial of asylum because we lack jurisdiction to hear it.

[The court also denied the petition for review of the immigration judge's denial of withholding of removal.]

* * *

NOTES AND QUESTIONS ON THE SCOPE OF REVIEW AFTER THE *REAL ID* ACT

1. With regard to the one-year deadline on applying for asylum, most other circuits have agreed with the general approach in *Chen* and have concluded that the timeliness of an asylum application and the decision whether the lateness is excused by "changed circumstances" or "extraordinary circumstances" are factual or discretionary decisions over which review is barred. *See, e.g., Gomis v. Holder,* 571 F.3d 353, 358–359 (4th Cir. 2009) (collecting cases), *rehearing and rehearing en banc denied,* 585 F.3d 197 (4th Cir. 2009), *cert. denied,* ___ U.S. ___, 130 S.Ct. 1048, 175 L.Ed.2d 881 (2010).

2. In another case involving a question of late filing for asylum, the Ninth Circuit announced a more expansive understanding of what is open to review under INA § 242(a)(2)(D):

> * * * [T]he phrase "questions of law" as it is used in section 106 of the Real ID Act includes review of the application of statutes and

---

11. We emphasize, however, that our analysis above does not foreclose the possibility of a case in which the "application" of a statute actually presents a "question of law" within the meaning of the REAL ID Act. Although we need not specify here any precise dividing line between the "application or interpretation" of a statute, on the one hand, and the "exercise of discretion," on the other, we note that the Fourth Circuit's analysis in *Jean v. Gonzales,* 435 F.3d 475 (4th Cir.2006), is instructive on this score. In that case, the Court held that the BIA's decision that the petitioner was *"statutorily precluded* from demonstrating good moral character" was "not a discretionary decision," but rather, was "essentially a legal determination involving the application of law to factual findings."

At the same time, however, the Fourth Circuit declined to review the BIA's discretionary denial of a waiver of inadmissibility under 8 U.S.C. § 1182(h), noting that the petitioner "argue[d] only that the immigration judge drew the wrong *factual* conclusions from the evidence and then determined these conclusions outweighed any factors supporting a favorable exercise of *discretion.*" *Id.* at 480 (emphases added). Because the petitioner had in that respect failed to present a "question of law" under the REAL ID Act, the Court lacked jurisdiction to review the claim.

regulations to undisputed historical facts. This construction is amply supported by the statute and legislative history, and a narrower interpretation would pose a serious Suspension Clause issue.

* * *

* * * [W]e dispute the government's characterization of the changed circumstances determination as "not only a 'predominately factual' inquiry, but also a discretionary determination," relying on the statutory requirement that changed circumstances be established "to the satisfaction of the Attorney General."

The words "to the satisfaction of the Attorney General" do not render the changed circumstances determination discretionary. Instead, this phrase is a specification of *who* is to make the decision, rather than a characterization of that decision itself. * * * We have explicitly held that "to the satisfaction of the Attorney General" does *not* render a determination discretionary.

* * *

We now turn to Ramadan's claims. Ramadan's challenge to the IJ's determination that Ramadan failed to show changed circumstances is a reviewable mixed question of law and fact. The Supreme Court has defined such questions as those in which "the historical facts are admitted or established, the rule of law is undisputed, and the issue is whether the facts satisfy the statutory standard." Here, the factual basis of Ramadan's petition is undisputed; we only review whether the IJ appropriately determined that the facts did not constitute "changed circumstances" as defined by immigration law. * * * [W]e have jurisdiction to hear Ramadan's petition * * *.

Ramadan v. Gonzales, 479 F.3d 646, 654–57 (9th Cir. 2007).

The Seventh Circuit, however, announced its strong disagreement with the approach in *Ramadan*:

The panel in *Ramadan* held that § 242(a)(2)(D) authorizes judicial review of all "mixed questions of law and fact," including all applications of law to fact. Only pure findings of fact are outside the scope of subsection (D), the panel concluded. Because no administrative case can be decided without applying some law to some facts, that understanding of § 242(a)(2)(D) vitiates all clauses in the statute, including § 208(a)(3), that limit judicial review of particular classes of decisions. * * * The panel in *Ramadan* conceded that § 242(a)(2)(D) does not say that "mixed" or "ultimate" questions are reviewable—and * * * the legislative history of § 242(a)(2)(D) is incompatible with extending that proviso beyond pure questions of law—but adopted its interpretation to avoid any need to consider constitutional objections to § 242(a)(2)(D).

It is hard to appreciate what those objections might be; the Constitution itself allows Congress to create exceptions to the jurisdiction of the federal courts. Provisions foreclosing judicial review of particular administrative decisions are common. The most famous such exclusion is in the Administrative Procedure Act of 1946, 5 U.S.C. § 701(a)(2) (decisions "committed to agency discretion by law" are not judicially reviewable), and to our knowledge no serious argument has ever been made that § 701(a)(2) is unconstitutional. * * *

Nine judges dissented from the denial of rehearing en banc in *Ramadan.* * * * [T]he ninth circuit stands alone: at least eight circuits read § 242(a)(2)(D) as limited to pure questions of law. * * *

Viracacha v. Mukasey, 518 F.3d 511, 515–16 (7th Cir.), *cert. denied,* 129 S.Ct. 451 (2008).

3. In confronting the issues with which *Chen* grapples, patterns vary among circuits (and sometimes within circuits) regarding when § 242(a)(2)(D) is judged to preserve review. Those courts that are inclined to preserve as much review as possible tend to find ways to subdivide the questions presented and locate a separately identifiable question of law, or possibly a due process issue. Other courts are more resistant to such arguments by the petitioner. Here are some recent examples in which the court found jurisdiction—or not—under § 242(a)(2)(D) based on an asserted constitutional claim or question of law:

a. A claim that a statute that gives the Attorney General the discretion to remove an aggravated felon under either the administrative removal procedure in INA § 238 or standard removal proceeding under INA § 240 violates equal protection?

Held: jurisdiction. *Flores–Ledezma v. Gonzales*, 415 F.3d 375, 380 (5th Cir. 2005) (statute upheld).

b. A claim that the immigration judge failed to consider adequately a waiver applicant's daughter's U.S. citizenship in making the factual determination that she would not suffer hardship?

Held: no jurisdiction. *Rodrigues–Nascimento v. Gonzales*, 485 F.3d 60, 62 (1st Cir. 2007).

c. A claim that the Board of Immigration Appeals violated the noncitizen's right to due process when it (1) overturned the immigration judge's finding that the asylum applicant was a "persecutor" but (2) did not overturn the immigration judge's denial of voluntary departure that had been based solely on the "persecutor" finding.

Held: jurisdiction. *Patel v. Gonzales*, 470 F.3d 216, 219–20 (6th Cir. 2006) (remanded to BIA so that it can exercise discretion on voluntary departure).

d. A claim that the Board of Immigration Appeals applied the wrong standard of review when it reversed the immigration judge's discretionary grant of the waiver of removal under former INA § 212(c).

Held: no jurisdiction. *Guevara v. Gonzales*, 472 F.3d 972, 974–75 (7th Cir. 2007).

e. A claim that the BIA improperly denied cancellation of removal when it found that petitioner had not established "exceptional and extremely unusual hardship."

Held: no jurisdiction to consider claim that BIA improperly assumed that the U.S. citizen child would return to Mexico with petitioner (because not a colorable claim in light of the record), but jurisdiction exists to consider whether the legal interpretation in the controlling BIA precedent was valid, and whether the BIA improperly attached weight to the number of qualifying relatives in its hardship determination. *Pareja v. Attorney General*, 615 F.3d 180, 188 (3d Cir. 2010) (sustaining BIA legal interpretation under *Chevron*; but remanding for BIA to clarify its decision in light of court's holding on weight to be given the number of qualifying relatives).

4. For a thorough discussion of what it means for an immigration decision to be "discretionary," see D. Kanstroom, Deportation Nation: Outsiders in American History 228–40 (2007).

b. Immigration Habeas After the REAL ID Act

Because the REAL ID Act significantly expanded court of appeals jurisdiction, most of the review that would have been available via habeas corpus before the REAL ID Act may now take place through petitions for review in the courts of appeals. At the same time, most of the review that was available via habeas before the REAL ID Act *must* take place through petitions for review in the courts of appeals. As noted above, this is because the jurisdiction-limiting provisions in the amended INA now explicitly provide that habeas corpus jurisdiction under 28 U.S.C. § 2241 is unavailable for review of removal orders, *see* INA § 242(a), or for consideration of certain other specified issues, *see, e.g.,* INA § 208(a)(3), (b)(2)(D).

After the REAL ID Act, what habeas corpus jurisdiction remains? The Conference Report stated that the Act's changes to the INA's jurisdictional provisions were not intended to "preclude habeas review over challenges to detention that are independent of challenges to removal orders." H.R. Conf. Rep. No. 109–72, at 175 (2005). Although this conclusion sits somewhat uneasily with the actual text of INA § 242 as amended, especially in view of § 242(b)(9) (a consolidation provision discussed later in this chapter), it is now well-settled that habeas corpus is available to consider challenges to detention before, during or after removal proceedings. *See, e.g., Kellici v. Gonzales*, 472 F.3d 416, 419–20 (6th Cir. 2006);, *Hernandez v. Gonzales*, 424 F.3d 42, 42 (1st Cir. 2005). Thus *Zadvydas* and *Demore,* were they to arise today, would still be habeas actions, because they challenge the validity of pre-hearing or post-order detention, and the issues are independent of the validity of the removal charges.

What, if any, habeas jurisdiction remains to review final removal orders? When might petitions for review in the courts of appeals fail to provide the "adequate substitute" for habeas corpus that *St. Cyr* said would be necessary to avoid Suspension Clause problems? Consider two situations, both discussed in Neuman, *On the Adequacy of Direct Review After the REAL ID Act of 2005*, 51 N.Y.L. Sch. L. Rev. 133 (2006–07); and Kusin, Yale–Loehr, & Rosenberg, *Habeas Corpus Restrictions Under the REAL ID Act: The Case Law So Far*, 10–19 Bender's Immigr. Bull. 1 (2005).

(i) Missing the 30–Day Deadline for Filing a Petition for Review

Assume that a noncitizen who has a final removal order misses the 30–day deadline for filing a petition for review in the courts of appeals. He asserts that this default occurred because of ineffective assistance of counsel, and argues that the law should be read to permit a late filing or some other remedy. The REAL ID Act would seem to repeal habeas and thus leave him with no court review at all. In *Wang v. Department of Homeland Security*, 484 F.3d 615, 618 (2d Cir. 2007), the Second Circuit quoted *Chen, supra,* in acknowledging that, given the constitutional concerns raised by the Supreme Court in *St. Cyr,*

> [i]t is possible that in some future case, the particular circumstances that prevented a petitioner from seeking review within the 30-day time limit of § 242(b)(1) would require us to reexamine whether that limit ought to be treated as jurisdictional now that the petition for review is the exclusive means of obtaining "judicial intervention in deportation cases."

The court held, however, that this was not such a case because Wang had failed to challenge his final order of removal for almost four years, and because he offered no explanation for the delay. *See also Luna v. Holder,* 637 F.3d 85, 95–97 (2d Cir. 2011) (habeas not required; statutory procedure permitting motion to reopen before the BIA is an adequate and effective substitute allowing noncitizen to raise claim that ineffective assistance of counsel had prevented timely filing of a petition for review).

(ii) Inadequate Factual Record

What about cases in which effective review requires the development of a factual record? According to INA § 242(a)(1), "the court may not order the taking of additional evidence under 28 U.S.C. § 2347(c)," and according to INA § 242(b)(4)(A), "the court of appeals shall decide the petition only on the administrative record on which the order of removal is based." The only exception permitting further factual development in district court (upon transfer from the court of appeals) is found in INA § 242(b)(5)(B), applicable only to claims that the respondent is a U.S. national.

In *Rafaelano v. Wilson*, 471 F.3d 1091 (9th Cir. 2006), the Ninth Circuit had before it a petition for review that turned on whether the noncitizen had voluntarily departed the country under a previously unappealed 1995 alternate order, which, by its terms, became an enforceable deportation order if she did not timely depart. She said she had complied. DHS, which had discovered her in this country in 2003, claimed she had not, and it was now acting to remove her summarily based on the 1995 order. The court described its factfinding dilemma:

> [W]e are left in a situation where we cannot review the decision of the district court [owing to the REAL ID Act's transitional rules] and yet have no BIA decision to review nor any administrative record

regarding the relevant factual issue * * *. Further, we cannot adjudicate Rafaelano's claims in the first instance, as our review is generally limited to what is contained in the administrative record.

The court chose this solution: "In light of these unusual circumstances, we find it necessary and appropriate to transfer this matter to the BIA to permit the executive agency to consider the contested issues and conduct any necessary fact-finding." 471 F.3d at 1097–98. (The matter was sent to the BIA even though it had apparently never heard the case before.) Judge Rawlinson, dissenting, would have appointed a special master "to recommend factual findings and disposition" as authorized by Rule 48 of the Federal Rules of Appellate Procedure. 471 F.3d at 1099 (Rawlinson, J., dissenting).

The Supreme Court has addressed the question of what constitutes an inadequate factual record in an agency case, and what to do about it, but in a non-immigration setting. In *Florida Power & Light Co. v. Lorion*, 470 U.S. 729, 105 S.Ct. 1598, 84 L.Ed.2d 643 (1985), the Nuclear Regulatory Commission had decided—without a hearing—not to initiate enforcement action requested by a petitioner. Partly for lack of a hearing before the agency, the court of appeals ruled that the petitioner must seek judicial review in the district court, where evidence could be presented and evaluated, notwithstanding the Hobbs Act court of appeals review that ordinarily applies to the Commission's decisions. The Supreme Court reversed, expressing concern that the lower court's approach would result in a counterproductive bifurcation of review:

> Perhaps the only plausible justification for linking initial review in the court of appeals to the occurrence of a hearing before the agency would be that, absent a hearing, the reviewing court would lack an adequate agency-compiled factual basis to evaluate the agency action and a district court with factfinding powers could make up that deficiency. Such a justification cannot, however, be squared with fundamental principles of judicial review of agency action. * * *

> If the record before the agency does not support the agency action, if the agency has not considered all relevant factors, or if the reviewing court simply cannot evaluate the challenged agency action on the basis of the record before it, the proper course, except in rare circumstances, is to remand to the agency for additional investigation or explanation. * * * Moreover, a formal hearing before the agency is in no way necessary to the compilation of an agency record. * * * The APA specifically contemplates judicial review on the basis of the agency record compiled in the course of informal agency action in which a hearing has not occurred.

Id. at 743–44, 105 S.Ct. at 1606–07. *Cf. Mohamed v. Gonzales*, 477 F.3d 522, 526 (8th Cir. 2007) (rejecting a constitutional challenge based on an allegedly inadequate factual record for petition for review, because the noncitizen could have introduced the missing evidence before the BIA); *Aguilar v. U.S. ICE*, 510 F.3d 1, 15–16 (1st Cir. 2007) ("immigration judges possess ample fact-gathering faculties"; habeas not needed to develop sufficient record of claim of inadequate access to counsel).

4. THE STANDARDS FOR A STAY PENDING JUDICIAL REVIEW

INA § 242(f)(2) provides that "no court shall enjoin the removal of any alien pursuant to a final order * * * unless the alien shows by clear and convincing evidence that the entry or execution of such order is prohibited as a matter of law." Is this also the standard that must be met to obtain a stay of a final removal order pending appeal? The courts of appeals divided on this question, until the Supreme Court resolved the issue in *Nken v. Holder*, 556 U.S. 418, 129 S.Ct. 1749, 173 L.Ed.2d 550 (2009). Nken had been unsuccessful on his asylum and withholding of removal claims before the immigration judge and the BIA. He sought a stay of the order while the court of appeals considered his petition for review. The Fourth Circuit denied a stay, applying § 242(f)(2). The U.S. Supreme Court reversed, 7–2, in an opinion by Chief Justice Roberts:

> * * * Nken argues that the "traditional" standard for a stay applies. Under that standard, a court considers four factors: "(1) whether the stay applicant has made a strong showing that he is likely to succeed on the merits; (2) whether the applicant will be irreparably injured absent a stay; (3) whether issuance of the stay will substantially injure the other parties interested in the proceeding; and (4) where the public interest lies." *Hilton v. Braunskill,* 481 U.S. 770, 776 (1987).

> The Government disagrees, arguing that a stay is simply a form of injunction, or alternatively that the relief petitioner seeks is more accurately characterized as injunctive, and therefore that the limits on injunctive relief set forth in subsection (f)(2) apply.

> * * *

> An injunction and a stay have typically been understood to serve different purposes. The former is a means by which a court tells someone what to do or not to do. When a court employs "the extraordinary remedy of injunction," it directs the conduct of a party, and does so with the backing of its full coercive powers.

> * * *

> By contrast, instead of directing the conduct of a particular actor, a stay operates upon the judicial proceeding itself. It does so either by halting or postponing some portion of the proceeding, or by temporarily divesting an order of enforceability.

> * * *

> Applying the subsection (f)(2) standard to stays pending appeal would not fulfill the historic office of such a stay. The whole idea is to

hold the matter under review in abeyance because the appellate court lacks sufficient time to decide the merits. Under the subsection (f)(2) standard, however, a stay would only be granted after the court in effect *decides* the merits, in an expedited manner. The court would have to do so under a standard—"clear and convincing evidence"— that does not so much preserve the availability of subsequent review as render it redundant. Subsection (f)(2), in short, would invert the customary role of a stay, requiring a definitive merits decision earlier rather than later.

129 S. Ct. at 1756–58, 1760. The Court went on to provide further guidance on the appropriate stay standards, including a critical review of the standards used by some of the lower courts that had earlier been applying the traditional four-part test:

> "A stay is not a matter of right, even if irreparable injury might otherwise result." * * * The party requesting a stay bears the burden of showing that the circumstances justify an exercise of that discretion.

> The fact that the issuance of a stay is left to the court's discretion "does not mean that no legal standard governs that discretion. . . . '[A] motion to [a court's] discretion is a motion, not to its inclination, but to its judgment; and its judgment is to be guided by sound legal principles.' " * * *

> The first two factors of the traditional standard are the most critical. It is not enough that the chance of success on the merits be "better than negligible." *Sofinet v. INS*, 188 F.3d 703, 707 (C.A.7 1999). Even petitioner acknowledges that "[m]ore than a mere 'possibility' of relief is required." By the same token, simply showing some "possibility of irreparable injury," *Abbassi v. INS*, 143 F.3d 513, 514 (C.A.9 1998), fails to satisfy the second factor. As the Court pointed out earlier this Term, the " 'possibility' standard is too lenient."

> Although removal is a serious burden for many aliens, it is not categorically irreparable, as some courts have said. * * *

> The automatic stay prior to IIRIRA reflected a recognition of the irreparable nature of harm from removal before decision on a petition for review, given that the petition abated upon removal. Congress's decision in IIRIRA to allow continued prosecution of a petition after removal eliminated the reason for categorical stays * * *. It is accordingly plain that the burden of removal alone cannot constitute the requisite irreparable injury. Aliens who are removed may continue to pursue their petitions for review, and those who prevail can be afforded effective relief by facilitation of their return, along with restoration of the immigration status they had upon removal.

> Once an applicant satisfies the first two factors, the traditional stay inquiry calls for assessing the harm to the opposing party and weighing the public interest. These factors merge when the Govern-

ment is the opposing party. In considering them, courts must be mindful that the Government's role as the respondent in every removal proceeding does not make the public interest in each individual one negligible, as some courts have concluded.

Of course there is a public interest in preventing aliens from being wrongfully removed, particularly to countries where they are likely to face substantial harm. But that is no basis for the blithe assertion of an "absence of any injury to the public interest" when a stay is granted. There is always a public interest in prompt execution of removal orders: The continued presence of an alien lawfully deemed removable undermines the streamlined removal proceedings IIRIRA established, and "permit[s] and prolong[s] a continuing violation of United States law." [*Reno v. American–Arab Anti–Discrimination Committee*], 525 U.S. [471], at 490, 119 S.Ct. 936. The interest in prompt removal may be heightened by the circumstances as well—if, for example, the alien is particularly dangerous, or has substantially prolonged his stay by abusing the processes provided to him. *See ibid.* ("Postponing justifiable deportation (in the hope that the alien's status will change—by, for example, marriage to an American citizen—or simply with the object of extending the alien's unlawful stay) is often the principal object of resistance to a deportation proceeding"). A court asked to stay removal cannot simply assume that "[o]rdinarily, the balance of hardships will weigh heavily in the applicant's favor."

Id. at 1760–62.

PROBLEMS ON STAYS PENDING APPEAL

Applying these standards from *Nken*, how would you, as a judge, assess a request for a stay pending appeal in each of the following cases? (Consider each of the lettered scenarios separately.) Your answers may require addressing whether the substantive issue being raised is reviewable at all. Identify what additional information you would find useful or indispensable in order to reach a final conclusion.

1. A lawful permanent resident found removable on the basis of convictions for a crime involving moral turpitude; the LPR contends that his convictions were not properly considered to be a CIMT.

2. A visa overstayer who sought cancellation of removal, which was denied: (a) on a finding that she lacked good moral character; (b) on a finding that she had not shown exceptional and extremely unusual hardship; or (c) in the exercise of discretion, based on a judgment that the negative factors outweighed the positive factors in her case, even though she was statutorily eligible.

3. An entrant without inspection whose asylum claim was denied: (a) on a finding that the noncitizen lacked credibility; (b) on the

basis of nexus—a ruling that the claimed persecution would not be on one of the five prescribed statutory grounds; (c) on a finding that the person had shown past persecution but that conditions have changed in the country of origin; or (d) on the ground that the claim was filed more than one year after arrival and that no exceptions to the deadline apply.

5. CONSOLIDATING ISSUES FOR REVIEW

Beyond the questions of whether a court may review, which court may review, what issues it may review and by what procedural vehicle, and when a stay of removal is appropriate pending review, further questions address how review is packaged. There are two general types of such consolidation issues. One concerns timing: for example, does court review take place only after all issues relating to a single removal proceeding are reduced to a final removal order, or are issues reviewable as they arise along the way? The other type of consolidation issue concerns multiple parties. When a noncitizen goes to court to challenge a government immigration decision, must she limit her suit to her own case, or may she join forces with others to challenge a pattern or practice of government decisionmaking? We will take these two areas in turn.

a. Timing of Review in an Individual Case

Should a reviewing court take up issues individually or consolidate them after a final order? And once a court undertakes review of a final removal order, exactly what issues are reviewable? Just the removal order? All decisions on potential relief from removal, or only those decided by an immigration judge? Should the court resolve all complaints the removable noncitizen might have about decisions under the immigration laws that at any time have gone against him—such as a denial of an extension of a nonimmigrant stay (leaving him in violation of status and thus deportable), or a visa petition denial that prevents his filing for adjustment? Or should the court limit review to those matters that arose before or during the immigration court hearing, leaving resolution of other issues to another forum?

Section 242(a)(1) makes the petition for review in the courts of appeals the "sole and exclusive" procedure for reviewing removal orders. Section 242 contains two other provisions that look toward consolidating issues for judicial consideration on a petition for review in the court of appeals. INA § 242(g) forbids review, "[e]xcept as provided in this section," of "any cause or claim * * * arising from the decision or action * * * to commence proceedings, adjudicate cases, or execute removal orders." INA § 242(b)(9) consolidates all questions of law or fact "arising from any action taken or proceeding brought to remove an alien from the United States" for review in the court of appeals when it considers a final order of removal.

The first of these provisions was construed by the Supreme Court in *Reno v. American–Arab Anti–Discrimination Committee*, 525 U.S. 471, 119 S.Ct. 936, 142 L.Ed.2d 940 (1999). That case involved a collateral attack on deportation proceedings which alleged that the immigration authorities had selectively targeted the respondents for removal in violation of their First and Fifth Amendment rights. *See* Chapter Seven, pp. 675–77 (considering this element of the *AADC* litigation). This separate litigation had begun well before enactment of the 1996 amendments. The Supreme Court ruled that the lower courts lacked jurisdiction because of § 242(g). It explained that Congress had enacted § 242(g) partly to bar judicial review of certain matters, and partly to require consolidation of court challenges. As to the latter purpose, the Court said this:

> There was good reason for Congress to focus special attention upon, and make special provision for, judicial review of the Attorney General's discrete acts of "commenc[ing] proceedings, adjudicat[ing] cases, [and] execut[ing] removal orders"—which represent the initiation or prosecution of various stages in the deportation process. At each stage the Executive has discretion to abandon the endeavor, and at the time IIRIRA was enacted the INS had been engaging in a regular practice (which had come to be known as "deferred action") of exercising that discretion for humanitarian reasons or simply for its own convenience. * * * Since no generous act goes unpunished, however, the INS's exercise of this discretion opened the door to litigation in instances where the INS chose *not* to exercise it. * * * Such litigation was possible because courts read [the former INA] § 106's prescription that the Hobbs Act shall be "the sole and exclusive procedure for the judicial review of all final orders of deportation" to be inapplicable to various decisions and actions leading up to or consequent upon final orders of deportation, and relied on other jurisdictional statutes to permit review. Section 242(g) seems clearly designed to give some measure of protection to "no deferred action" decisions and similar discretionary determinations, providing that if they are reviewable at all, they at least will not be made the bases for separate rounds of judicial intervention outside the streamlined process that Congress has designed.

> Of course *many* provisions of IIRIRA are aimed at protecting the Executive's discretion from the courts—indeed, that can fairly be said to be the theme of the legislation. It is entirely understandable, however, why Congress would want only the discretion-protecting provision of § 242(g) applied even to pending cases: because that provision is specifically directed at the deconstruction, fragmentation, and hence prolongation of removal proceedings.

525 U.S. at 483–87, 119 S.Ct. at 943–45.

Justice Ginsburg, concurring along with Justice Breyer, agreed with the majority's reading of § 242(g):

Here, Congress has established an integrated scheme for deportation proceedings, channeling judicial review to the final order, and deferring issues outside the agency's authority until that point. Given Congress' strong interest in avoiding delay of deportation proceedings, I find the opportunity to raise a claim during the judicial review phase sufficient.

525 U.S. at 495, 119 S.Ct. at 949 (Ginsburg, J., concurring).

For illustrative applications of § 242(g), see *Elgharib v. Napolitano,* 600 F.3d 597 (6th Cir. 2010) (no jurisdiction to consider application for writ of prohibition to bar removal based on *in absentia* order); *Chapinski v. Ziglar,* 278 F.3d 718, 720–21 (7th Cir. 2002) (no jurisdiction to hear a class action to compel government to commence removal proceedings so that noncitizens could have immigration judges adjudicate their applications for relief).

INA § 242(g) applied to the facts of *American–Arab Anti–Discrimination Committee,* but § 242(b)(9) did not, because (g) applied to all pending cases once the 1996 Act took effect, while (b)(9) had a deferred effective date. The Court still briefly addressed § 242(b)(9), calling it an "unmistakable 'zipper' clause"—that is, a more far-reaching consolidation provision that would apply once the IIRIRA judicial review scheme became fully effective. 525 U.S. at 482–83, 119 S.Ct. at 943. The eventual applicability of this provision, in Justice Scalia's view, helped to explain why § 242(g) reaches only three discrete steps that constitute simply part, but not all, of the deportation process.

INA § 242(b)(9) thus seems to defer review until a final removal order has issued, but what does it mean when it refers to questions of law or fact "arising from any action taken or proceeding brought to remove an alien"? Courts have often found quite perplexing the task of distinguishing between issues that have to be consolidated and those which are not covered by § 242(b)(9) and therefore could be raised on a separate habeas petition. *See, e.g., Luna v. Holder,* 637 F.3d 85, 87 (2d Cir. 2011). Their results and applicable tests cover a spectrum.

The Ninth Circuit takes a narrow view of the issues covered by the zipper clause, permitting separate review (often by habeas) if the issue being raised is characterized as independent of a challenge to the removal order. It has included in that category challenges claiming that no enforceable removal order exists, that the noncitizen did not receive notice of a removal order, that he could not be sent to a particular country because it lacked a functioning government, and that ineffective assistance of counsel led to late filing of a petition for review with the court of appeals (because by the time of the late filing, the removal order was final and any remedy would not challenge that order but merely send the matter back to the BIA for reentry of the order so that he could have his day in court). *See Singh v. Gonzales,* 499 F.3d 969, 978–79 (9th Cir. 2007).

The First Circuit takes a more stringent approach toward requiring consolidation:

In enacting section 242(b)(9) Congress plainly intended to put an end to the scattershot and piecemeal nature of the review process that previously had held sway in regard to removal proceedings. * * * [N]othing in the statute limits its reach to claims arising from extant removal proceedings.

[But we do not] imply that section 242(b)(9) is limitless in its scope. * * * [T]hese words cannot be read to swallow all claims that might somehow touch upon, or be traced to, the government's efforts to remove an alien. * * * Congress's choice of phrase suggests that it did not intend section 242(b)(9) to sweep within its scope claims with only a remote or attenuated connection to the removal of an alien. * * *

We thus read the words "arising from" in section 242(b)(9) to exclude claims that are independent of, or wholly collateral to, the removal process. Among others, claims that cannot effectively be handled through the available administrative process fall within that purview.

Aguilar v. U.S. ICE, 510 F.3d 1, 9–11 (1st Cir. 2007) (paragraphing altered).

See generally Motomura, *Judicial Review in Immigration Cases After AADC: Lessons From Civil Procedure*, 14 Geo. Immig. L.J. 385, 409–30 (2000) (urging a narrow reading of (b)(9) that allows review of significant independent matters). *But cf.* Martin, *Behind the Scenes on a Different Set: What Congress Needs to Do in the Aftermath of* St. Cyr *and* Nguyen, 16 Geo. Immigr. L.J. 313, 321, 327 (2002) (arguing for strong consolidation provisions that are nonetheless designed to "keep open a real and meaningful chance for judicial consideration of all issues").

Use the following exercise to test your overall understanding of consolidation issues and also the preceding material on judicial review under INA § 242. You may also want to draw upon Section A above, which covered the removal hearing itself and various motions and procedures available there.

EXERCISE

Sakha Mamadou has been a lawful permanent resident of the United States since immigrating with his parents in 1980, when he was six years old. Mamadou was convicted in early 2002 for a theft that he admitted to committing in October 2001 in Pueblo, Colorado. After spending thirty days in jail and having the remaining months of his sentence suspended, he was served with a Notice to Appear.

At a removal proceeding in Denver in which Mamadou was unrepresented (because he could not afford an attorney and could not find pro bono counsel), the judge ruled that the conviction made

Mamadou deportable and ineligible for discretionary relief, and in any event that his equities were insufficient to warrant the favorable exercise of discretion. The judge ordered Mamadou removed. Mamadou then paid a lawyer recommended by a friend. The lawyer told him that he had filed an appeal to the BIA. Mamadou has heard almost nothing from his attorney about the progress of the case thereafter. He is now in custody in a detention facility in Florence, Arizona, and has just learned that the BIA ruled against him summarily. You work with an Arizona pro bono organization, which has just asked you to represent Mamadou to ask a court to review the immigration judge's rulings.

(a) On what issues could you expect to get court review?

(b) What procedural vehicle (petition for review or petition for a writ of habeas corpus) would you use to seek review?

(c) In what court (court of appeals or district court, and where) would you seek review of the BIA decision?

Now assume that before your first interview with Mamadou the time for motions to reopen and reconsider had already expired. Answer each of the three questions above in light of this changed assumption. (You may need to give consideration to new administrative filings, in addition to any judicial options).

b. Multi–Party Litigation

One final aspect of judicial review deserves analysis. What if a group of plaintiffs allege that the government has adopted a practice in its enforcement or administration of immigration law that violates a statute or is unconstitutional? This happened in *McNary v. Haitian Refugee Center, Inc.*, 498 U.S. 479, 111 S.Ct. 888, 112 L.Ed.2d 1005 (1991), a class action in which the plaintiffs alleged a pattern or practice of procedural due process violations in INS administration of the special agricultural worker (SAW) legalization program in the Immigration Reform and Control Act of 1986, INA § 210. The plaintiffs argued that the interview process implemented by the INS deprived them of due process because they were not allowed to present witnesses on their behalf, competent interpreters were not provided, and no verbatim recordings of the interviews were made. The plaintiffs sought injunctive relief in the district court.

INA § 210(e), governing court jurisdiction over SAW denials, provided in relevant part: "There shall be no administrative or judicial review of a determination respecting an application for [legalization] under this section except in accordance with this subsection," and "There shall be judicial review of such a denial only in the judicial review of an order of exclusion or deportation under [the former] section 106."

The U.S. Supreme Court read this language to constrain only direct review of individual denials of SAW status, not general challenges to agency practices and policies used in processing applications. The Court's explanation included reference to language that Congress might have adopted to foreclose jurisdiction more sweepingly:

> [H]ad Congress intended the limited review provisions of § 210(e) of the INA to encompass challenges to INS procedures and practices, it could easily have used broader statutory language. Congress could, for example, have modeled § 210(e) on the more expansive language in the general grant of district court jurisdiction under Title II of the INA by channeling into the Reform Act's special review procedures "all causes . . . arising under any of the provisions" of the legalization program. It moreover could have modeled § 210(e) on 38 U.S.C. § 211(a), which governs review of veterans' benefits claims, by referring to review "on all questions of law and fact" under the SAW legalization program.

498 U.S. at 494.

The Court was also troubled by the consequences of reading the statute to preclude jurisdiction to hear the challenge:

> Several aspects of this statutory scheme would preclude review of respondents' application denials if we were to hold that the District Court lacked jurisdiction to hear this challenge. Initially, administrative or judicial review of an agency decision is almost always confined to the record made in the proceeding at the initial decisionmaking level, and one of the central attacks on INS procedures in this litigation is based on the claim that such procedures do not allow applicants to assemble adequate records. As the District Court found, because of the lack of recordings or transcripts of LO [Legalization Office] interviews and the inadequate opportunity for SAW applicants to call witnesses or present other evidence on their behalf, the administrative appeals unit of the INS, in reviewing the decisions of LOs and regional processing facilities, and the courts of appeals, in reviewing SAW denials in the context of deportation proceedings, have no complete or meaningful basis upon which to review application determinations.

> Additionally, because there is no provision for direct judicial review of the denial of SAW status unless the alien is later apprehended and deportation proceedings are initiated, most aliens denied SAW status can ensure themselves review in courts of appeals only if they voluntarily surrender themselves for deportation. Quite obviously, that price is tantamount to a complete denial of judicial review for most undocumented aliens.

> Finally, even in the context of a deportation proceeding, it is unlikely that a court of appeals would be in a position to provide meaningful review of the type of claims raised in this litigation. To establish the unfairness of the INS practices, respondents in this case adduced a substantial amount of evidence, most of which would have been irrelevant in the processing of a particular individual applica-

tion. Not only would a court of appeals reviewing an individual SAW determination therefore most likely not have an adequate record as to the pattern of INS' allegedly unconstitutional practices, but it also would lack the factfinding and record-developing capabilities of a federal district court. * * * It therefore seems plain to us, as it did to the District Court and the Court of Appeals, that restricting judicial review to the courts of appeals as a component of the review of an individual deportation order is the practical equivalent of a total denial of judicial review of generic constitutional and statutory claims.

498 U.S. at 496–97.

The key question under new § 242 is how much of the *McNary* reasoning survives. One potential limit on multi-party litigation is § 242(b)(9), which we have already considered. Compare the language of § 242(b)(9) with the models the *McNary* majority noted that Congress could have followed if it really wanted to block all review outside the one designated channel. Does (b)(9) deprive a federal court of jurisdiction to hear multi-party litigation against the government until after final removal orders have issued in those cases? For analysis suggesting that (b)(9) does not erect such a bar and therefore does not supersede *McNary*, see Motomura, *Judicial Review in Immigration Cases After AADC: Lessons From Civil Procedure*, 14 Geo. Immig. L.J. 385, 434–38 (2000). *See also id.* at 440 (characterizing (b)(9) as an exhaustion requirement). *But cf.* Martin, *Behind the Scenes, supra*, 16 Geo. Immig. L.J., at 321.

Another part of INA § 242 that may affect multi-party litigation is subsection (f)(1), which provides:

> Regardless of the nature of the action or claim or of the identity of the party or parties bringing the action, no court (other than the Supreme Court) shall have jurisdiction or authority to enjoin or restrain the operation of the provisions of chapter 4 of title II [INA §§ 231–244], as amended by the Illegal Immigration Reform and Immigrant Responsibility Act of 1996, other than with respect to the application of such provisions to an individual alien against whom proceedings under such chapter have been initiated.

Does (f)(1) also bar a declaratory judgment against the government with regard to a particular policy or practice? The district court in *Alli v. Decker,* 644 F.Supp.2d 535 (M.D.Pa. 2009) held that it does. "The practical effect of the class-based declaration that the petitioners seek would be indistinguishable from the effect of a class-based injunction." The court invoked *California v. Grace Brethren Church,* 457 U.S. 393, 102 S.Ct. 2498, 73 L.Ed.2d 93 (1982), in support of its conclusion. There the Supreme Court held that a provision of the Tax Injunction Act stating that the district courts "shall not enjoin, suspend or restrain" state tax collection also applies to bar declaratory relief: "[B]ecause there is little practical difference between injunctive and declaratory relief, we would be hard pressed to conclude that Congress intended to prohibit taxpayers from seeking one form of anticipatory relief * * *, while permitting them to seek another, thereby defeating the principal purpose of the Tax Injunction Act: 'to limit drastically federal district court jurisdiction to interfere with so important a local concern as the collection of taxes.' " 457 U.S., at 408–09.

A divided Third Circuit reversed. *Alli v. Decker,* 650 F.3d 1007 (3d Cir. 2011). Relying on the principle that "statutes limiting equitable relief are to be construed narrowly," the court held that "restrain" in § 242(f)(1) does not cover declaratory relief. It distinguished *Grace Brethren* on the ground that principles of federalism supported a wider reading of the limits on federal intervention at issue in that case. Here Congress had a "plausible basis" for differentiating between injunctive and declaratory relief. Judge Fuentes dissented. Emphasizing the first line of the statute, which applies the bar "[r]egardless of the nature of the action or claim," he argued that "declaratory relief alone [would have] virtually the same practical impact as a formal injunction," *Id.* at 1018, quoting *Samuels v. Mackell,* 401 U.S. 66, 72, 91 S.Ct. 764, 27 L.Ed.2d 688 (1971).

Why would Congress forbid class-wide injunctions but permit class-wide declaratory relief? In *Grace Brethren,* the Supreme Court focused on the "principal purpose" of the statute at issue. In *Reno v. American–Arab Anti–Discrimination Committee, supra,* the Supreme Court said of the 1996 IIRIRA, which created § 242: "protecting the Executive's discretion from the courts * * * can fairly be said to be the theme of the legislation." 525 U.S. at 487, 119 S.Ct. at 945. For general discussions favorable to finding that declaratory relief is not barred by § 242(f)(1), see Neuman, *Federal Courts Issues in Immigration Law,* 78 Tex. L. Rev. 1661, 1684–87 (2001); Motomura, *Judicial Review, supra,* 14 Geo. Immig. L.J. at 438–39.

In broader perspective, what are the advantages of multi-party litigation, including class actions, for those who wish to challenge the government on immigration matters? What are the disadvantages, particularly with regard to the values traditionally served by the exhaustion of remedies requirement? What kinds of problems does such a ruling pose to an efficient legalization or general enforcement system? *See* Martin, *Behind the Scenes, supra,* 16 Geo. Immig. L.J. at 320–23 (interlocutory orders in some post-IRCA class actions stayed in effect for seven years and probably provided benefits to large numbers who did not qualify under IRCA). Consider the impact of decisions like *McNary* on the work of pro bono lawyers who wish to challenge government policies. One factor is finding a more sympathetic judge: "The availability of class actions creates opportunities for forum shopping. A class action may, at least provisionally, project the legal views of a sympathetic district judge beyond the district, and a nationwide class action may project favorable circuit precedent beyond the circuit." Neuman, *Federal Courts Issues, supra,* 78 Tex. L. Rev. at 1681. *See also Naranjo–Aguilera v. INS,* 30 F.3d 1106, 1114 (9th Cir. 1994) (commenting on impact on counsel of disallowing class action challenge to SAW regulations). And yet, why is forum shopping—by either side—something that any system of judicial review should tolerate, let alone foster?

Other factors are financial. Recall that appointed counsel is unavailable in individual deportation proceedings, and that even if the noncitizen prevails in that forum, she cannot, unlike most other litigants against the government, obtain government reimbursement of attorney's fees under the Equal Access to Justice Act, 28 U.S.C.A. § 2412. *See Ardestani v. INS,* 502 U.S. 129, 112 S.Ct. 515, 116 L.Ed.2d 496 (1991). EAJA has been available in class action challenges, however, sometimes leading to awards of several hundred thousand dollars. In fact, plaintiffs in the original *HRC v. McNary* litigation were later awarded fees amounting to $441,000 plus interest. *See Haitian Refugee Center v. Meese,* 791 F.2d 1489, 1501 (11th Cir. 1986), *opinion amended,* 804 F.2d 1573 (11th Cir. 1986).

What would you think of a bill in Congress to amend the statutes to adopt this trade-off: curtail immigration class actions, but (a) allow EAJA awards to noncitizens who prevail in deportation cases, or (b) provide the funding for appointed counsel, as needed, in removal proceedings?

Finally, consider three aspects of the reasoning in *McNary.* First, is it true that without jurisdiction over the class action that there would be no meaningful review of due process claims, because no adequate record could be created? Suppose you had represented a SAW applicant during the legalization process. At the time of application you of course could not be certain whether class actions in the district court would ultimately be allowed (because the Supreme Court did not issue its decision in *McNary* until after the application period had closed). If you believed that your client was being denied the statutory and constitutional rights at issue, could you have created some basis for later pursuit of those claims? What steps could you take?

This might prompt a second question: how sound is the assumption that adequate administrative records will be available only when factual issues were first aired in the quasi-judicial forum of the immigration court or the BIA, or else before a district court? Factual issues are routinely resolved in a variety of administrative settings that do not conform to classic trial-type procedures, and the APA certainly contemplates judicial review, on the available administrative record, of most such "informal" decisionmaking. *See Florida Power & Light Co. v. Lorion,* 470 U.S. 729, 743–44, 105 S.Ct. 1598, 84 L.Ed.2d 643 (1985), excerpted p. 1299 *supra;* Martin, *Mandel, Cheng Fan Kwok and Other Unappealing Cases: The Next Frontier of Immigration Reform,* 27 Va. J. Int'l L. 803, 809 (1987).

Third, is it true that the statute permitting judicial review of a SAW denial only upon review of a later removal order is "tantamount to a complete denial of judicial review for most undocumented aliens"? Consider a perspective that may underpin the particular structure for judicial review in IRCA (*see generally* Martin, *Judicial Review of Legalization Denials,* 65 Interp.Rel. 757, 760 (1988)): IRCA (which enacted the SAW program) was intended to end the presence of undocumented workers, both through two legalization programs and through enhanced enforcement. Bluntly stated, Congress wanted people unlawfully present either to legalize or to leave. Channeling access to judicial review through removal proceedings is precisely adapted to this two-pronged objective. Someone who believes he was wrongfully denied legalization has a genuine, even if potentially costly, avenue to correction by the courts. If he wins, Congress is fine with his remaining here. If he is wrong on the law, the removal order facilitates what the law requires—his departure.

EXERCISE

Hundreds of ICE agents took part in "Operation United Front" in New Bedford, Massachusetts. About 360 employees of Bianco, a Department of Defense subcontractor, were taken into custody. Most were taken to a holding facility at Ft. Devens in Ayer, Massachusetts. Within forty-eight hours, 210 of the detainees were flown to detention centers in Harlingen and El Paso, Texas.

In planning the sweep, ICE had taken steps to determine whether arrestees had minor dependents and had asked the Massachusetts Department of Social Services (DSS) to help address any issues of unattended children. The coordination with DSS, however, proved inadequate. Logistical difficulties and failed communications resulted in minor children being stranded without adult supervision.

The detained employees have sued ICE in federal district court, asking the court to order ICE to transfer them back to Massachusetts for removal proceedings. They allege: that ICE seized them with the intention of promptly transferring them to isolated locations where ICE knew, or should have known, that they could not effectively exercise their rights, that ICE restricted access to counsel during their detention in Fort Devens, that ICE did not coordinate with the DSS to address issues concerning the welfare of their children and families and allow the employees to make meaningful decisions concerning the care of their children, that their transfer to remote locations in Texas resulted in their inability to retain counsel of their choice or any counsel at all, that restricted access to counsel has prevented them from obtaining advice concerning potential grounds for asylum or other forms of relief, and that their transfer to Texas has severely prejudiced their ability to demonstrate ties to the community and otherwise present evidence on their behalf in bond hearings.

ICE has responded that it transferred the detainees from Massachusetts because of a shortage of bed space. ICE also contends that the detainees would receive the same procedural protections in immigration proceedings in Texas as they would in Massachusetts.

Does the court have jurisdiction to hear the employees' class-wide claims and grant the relief that they seek? If not, what avenues do they have to seek redress?

6. CONCLUDING QUESTIONS ON JUDICIAL REVIEW

In the 1996 Act, Congress responded to a judicial review scheme that it perceived as too elaborate or time-consuming with measures intended to consolidate review in many situations and to bar review altogether in others.

After a series of judicial correctives—most prominently the U.S. Supreme Court decision in *INS v. St. Cyr*—INA § 242 now sets out (1) a general scheme for judicial review via petitions for review in the federal courts of appeals, (2) a repeal of habeas corpus for most challenges that noncitizens might raise in immigration cases, (3) ostensible bars to judicial review for certain categories of persons or issues, but (4) exceptions to those bars for constitutional claims and questions of law.

Are there elements of this scheme that trouble you? If so, how would you change them? What consequences would your proposed changes have? In what ways do you think your proposed changes and their consequences would result in a more effective, efficient, and fair immigration management system?

CHAPTER ELEVEN

CONSTITUTIONAL PROTECTION
IN ALIENAGE LAW

■ ■ ■

Chapter Three noted how the Supreme Court, in the late nineteenth century, appeared to separate the questions of noncitizens entering and remaining in the United States from the questions of their constitutional protection on matters other than admission and expulsion itself. Thus arose the contrast between the Court's severe rulings in *Fong Yue Ting* and the *Chinese Exclusion Case*, on the one hand, and other rulings that protected Chinese noncitizens in other ways while they were in the United States—particularly the landmark *Yick Wo* and *Wong Wing* decisions.

This chapter examines constitutional protection of noncitizens after admission to the United States. Our focus is principally on permanent residents: how do we treat citizens and permanent residents differently? But we also consider how the constitutional treatment of permanent residents might apply to noncitizens who are lawfully present in the United States as nonimmigrants, especially if they remain for extended periods.

As we have seen in previous chapters, some differences are matters of *immigration law*, which, as traditionally defined, concerns the admission of noncitizens to the United States and the terms under which they may remain. A citizen must be admitted to the United States, while a noncitizen may be refused admission. Permanent residents also have fewer opportunities than citizens to sponsor their relatives for admission as immigrants. A citizen may not be removed from the United States, unless she first loses her citizenship through renunciation or denaturalization. In contrast, noncitizens may be removed on various deportability grounds set forth in INA § 237.

Other differences between citizens and permanent residents are part of *alienage law*, which as traditionally defined is distinguished from immigration law and addresses other matters relating to the legal status of noncitizens. In fact, noncitizens largely enjoy the same substantive rights as citizens. For instance, access to the civil courts is not contingent on citizenship status, nor is protection under a wide variety of regulatory schemes. And as Chapter Nine explained, laws governing the workplace protect not only permanent residents but sometimes even the undocumented. But there are differences between the rights of citizens and noncitizens. For example, noncitizens generally may not vote in public elections, nor hold federal civil service jobs. Their access to some state and local public employment and to federal welfare and other public benefits is limited. These distinctions between citizens and noncitizens raise constitutional law and public policy issues as to equal treatment, and also questions as to when federal, state, or local government may legitimately employ such distinctions. Chapter Two discussed who is a citizen of the United States; in this chapter, we ask: what does it mean to be (or not to be) a citizen of the United States?

SECTION A.   PUBLIC BENEFITS

1.   THE FOUNDATION CASES

From *Yick Wo* onward, a steady stream of U.S. Supreme Court decisions addressed the issue of constitutional protection of noncitizens in the United States. The next case, *Graham v. Richardson*, comments on the most important among these decisions. But first some background.

One idea that figured prominently from *Yick Wo* to *Graham* was that under the U.S. federal system a state could constitutionally treat citizens and noncitizens differently in order to protect a "special public interest" in its common property or resources. This idea drew support from *Truax v. Raich*, 239 U.S. 33, 36 S.Ct. 7, 60 L.Ed. 131 (1915), which struck down an Arizona employment statute as violating equal protection.

The statute challenged in *Truax* required any employer of more than five employees to employ at least 80 percent "qualified electors or native-born citizens of the United States or some sub-division thereof." Central to the Court's holding was that a state statute denying work would be tantamount to a denial of entry and abode, and therefore would be inconsistent with exclusive federal authority to "admit or exclude aliens." But later in the same opinion, the Court left open the possibility that if alienage classifications were needed to protect a "special public interest," states could adopt them in contexts other than employment in the general labor market.

After *Truax*, the Supreme Court applied the special public interest doctrine or similar reasoning to uphold other state alienage classifications. One was a New York state law barring the employment of noncitizens on public works projects, where the state's "special public interest" was to devote public funds to employ its own citizens. *Crane v. New York*, 239 U.S. 195, 198, 36 S.Ct. 85, 85–86, 60 L.Ed. 218 (1915). In *Patsone v. Pennsylvania*, 232 U.S. 138, 143–46, 34 S.Ct. 281, 282–83, 58 L.Ed. 539 (1914), the Court upheld a Pennsylvania law that barred noncitizens from hunting wild game and also "to that end" from owning shotguns or rifles. The Court explained that the ownership ban was intended to protect wildlife, "which the state may preserve for its own citizens if it pleases," and that the state legislature's choice of methods was entitled to great deference. Additional Court decisions adopted other rationales in rejecting constitutional challenges to state and local alienage classifications. For example, *State ex rel. Clarke v. Deckebach*, 274 U.S. 392, 394, 396, 47 S.Ct. 630, 631, 71 L.Ed. 1115 (1927), upheld a Cincinnati city ordinance under which only citizens were allowed to operate pool halls. The Court said it was not unreasonable for the city to conclude that noncitizens were not as well-qualified to run businesses that were "meeting places of idle and vicious persons," and that therefore required "strict police surveillance."

The Supreme Court declined to apply the special public interest doctrine in *Takahashi v. Fish & Game Comm'n*, 334 U.S. 410, 68 S.Ct. 1138, 92 L.Ed. 1478 (1948). In 1943, California barred the issuance of a commercial fishing license to any "alien Japanese." In 1945, this language was changed to bar any "person ineligible to citizenship," which the legislature intended to refer to Japanese noncitizens. The Court struck down the 1945 statute, rejecting the argument that the State of California was the owner-trustee of all fish in its coastal waters. Rather, the Court reasoned, a nondiscrimination principle applies to residence in any state by "all persons lawfully in this country."

Takahashi differed from the earlier cases in one key respect. The Court clearly understood that the phrase "ineligible to citizenship" made the California statute a race-based law, rather than a law that discriminated against noncitizens generally. Indeed, Justice Black's majority opinion explained:

> It does not follow, as California seems to argue, that because the United States regulates immigration and naturalization in part on the basis of race and color classifications, a state can adopt one or more of the same classifications to prevent lawfully admitted aliens within its borders from earning a living in the same way that other state inhabitants earn their living.

334 U.S. at 418–19, 68 S.Ct. at 1142.

Yet, *Takahashi* distinguished (without overruling) several decisions that had upheld state laws barring land ownership by aliens "ineligible to citizenship." *See Terrace v. Thompson*, 263 U.S. 197, 44 S.Ct. 15, 68 L.Ed. 255 (1923); *Porterfield v. Webb*, 263 U.S. 225, 44 S.Ct. 21, 68 L.Ed. 278 (1923); *Webb v. O'Brien*, 263 U.S. 313, 44 S.Ct. 112, 68 L.Ed. 318 (1923); *Frick v. Webb*, 263 U.S. 326, 44 S.Ct. 115, 68 L.Ed. 323 (1923).

Takahashi left important questions unanswered: How much was it a decision about race? What did it say about alienage classifications in general? And what was left of the special public interest doctrine?

a. State Laws

In 1971, a few years before the Court rejected a constitutional challenge to the federal immigration statute in *Fiallo v. Bell*, in Chapter Five, p. 293, it issued a landmark decision that struck down state laws limiting permanent residents' access to welfare benefits.

GRAHAM v. RICHARDSON

Supreme Court of the United States, 1971.
403 U.S. 365, 91 S.Ct. 1848, 29 L.Ed.2d 534.

MR. JUSTICE BLACKMUN delivered the opinion of the Court.

* * * The issue here is whether the Equal Protection Clause of the Fourteenth Amendment prevents a State from conditioning welfare benefits either (a) upon the beneficiary's possession of United States citizenship, or (b) if the beneficiary is an alien, upon his having resided in this country for a specified number of years. The facts are not in dispute.

I

No. 609. This case, from Arizona, concerns the State's participation in federal categorical assistance programs. * * * Arizona Rev. Stat. Ann., Tit. 46, Art. 2, as amended, provides for assistance to persons permanently and totally disabled (APTD). Arizona Rev. Stat. Ann. § 46–233, as amended in 1962, reads:

> A. No person shall be entitled to general assistance who does not meet and maintain the following requirements:
>
> 1. Is a citizen of the United States, or has resided in the United States a total of fifteen years. . . .

A like eligibility provision conditioned upon citizenship or durational residence appears in § 46–252(2), providing old-age assistance, and in § 46–272(4), providing assistance to the needy blind.

Appellee Carmen Richardson, at the institution of this suit in July 1969, was 64 years of age. She is a lawfully admitted resident alien. She emigrated from Mexico in 1956 and since then has resided continuously in Arizona. She became permanently and totally disabled. She also met all other requirements for eligibility for APTD benefits except the 15–year residency specified for aliens by § 46–233(a)(1). * * *

No. 727. This case, from Pennsylvania, concerns that portion of a general assistance program that is not federally supported. The relevant statute is § 432(2) of the Pennsylvania Public Welfare Code, [which] * * * provides that those eligible for assistance shall be (1) needy persons who qualify under the federally supported categorical assistance programs and (2) those other needy persons who are citizens of the United States. * * *

Appellee Elsie Mary Jane Leger is a lawfully admitted resident alien. She was born in Scotland in 1937. She came to this country in 1965 at the age of 28 under contract for domestic service with a family in Havertown. She has resided continuously in Pennsylvania since then and has been a taxpaying resident of the Commonwealth. In 1967 she left her domestic employment to accept more remunerative work in Philadelphia. She entered into a common-law marriage with a United States citizen. In 1969 illness forced both Mrs. Leger and her husband to give up their employment. They applied for public assistance. Each was ineligible under the federal programs. Mr. Leger, however, qualified for aid under the state program. Aid to Mrs. Leger was denied because of her alienage. * * *

Appellee Beryl Jervis was added as a party plaintiff to the Leger action. She was born in Panama in 1912 and is a citizen of that country. In March 1968, at the age of 55, she came to the United States to undertake domestic work under contract in Philadelphia. She has resided continuously in Pennsylvania since then and has been a taxpaying resident of the Commonwealth. After working as a domestic for approximately one year, she obtained other, more remunerative, work in the city. In February 1970 illness forced her to give up her employment. She applied for aid. However, she was ineligible for benefits under the federally assisted programs and she was denied general assistance solely because of her alienage. * * *

It was stipulated that "the denial of General Assistance to aliens otherwise eligible for such assistance causes undue hardship to them by depriving them of the means to secure the necessities of life, including food, clothing and shelter," and that "the citizenship bar to the receipt of General Assistance in Pennsylvania discourages continued residence in Pennsylvania of indigent resident aliens and causes such needy persons to remove to other States which will meet their needs."

* * *

II

The appellants argue initially that the States, consistent with the Equal Protection Clause, may favor United States citizens over aliens in the distribution of welfare benefits. It is said that this distinction involves no "invidious discrimination" for the State is not discriminating with respect to race or nationality.

The Fourteenth Amendment provides, "[N]or shall any State deprive any person of life, liberty, or property, without due process of law; nor deny to any person within its jurisdiction the equal protection of the laws." It has long been settled, and it is not disputed here, that the term "person" in this context encompasses lawfully admitted resident aliens as well as citizens of the United States and entitles both citizens and aliens to the equal protection of the laws of the State in which they reside. *Yick Wo v. Hopkins*, 118 U.S. 356, 369, 6 S.Ct. 1064, 1070, 30 L.Ed. 220 (1886); *Truax v. Raich*, 239 U.S. 33, 39, 36 S.Ct. 7, 9, 60 L.Ed. 131 (1915); *Takahashi v. Fish & Game Comm'n*, [334 U.S. 410, 420, 68 S.Ct. 1138, 1143, 92 L.Ed. 1478 (1948)]. Nor is it disputed that the Arizona and Pennsylvania statutes in question create two classes of needy persons, indistinguishable except with respect to whether they are or are not citizens of this country. Otherwise qualified United States citizens living in Arizona are entitled to federally funded categorical assistance benefits without regard to length of national residency, but aliens must have lived in this country for 15 years in order to qualify for aid. United States citizens living in Pennsylvania, unable to meet the requirements for federally funded benefits, may be eligible for state-supported general assistance, but resident aliens as a class are precluded from that assistance.

Under traditional equal protection principles, a State retains broad discretion to classify as long as its classification has a reasonable basis. This is so in "the area of economics and social welfare." *Dandridge v. Williams*, 397 U.S. 471, 485, 90 S.Ct. 1153, 1161, 25 L.Ed.2d 491 (1970). But the Court's decisions have established that classifications based on alienage, like those based on nationality or race, are inherently suspect and subject to close judicial scrutiny. Aliens as a class are a prime example of a "discrete and insular" minority (*see United States v. Carolene Products Co.*, 304 U.S. 144, 152–153, n.4, 58 S.Ct. 778, 783–784, 82 L.Ed. 1234 (1938)) for whom such heightened judicial solicitude is appropriate. Accordingly, it was said in *Takahashi*, that "the power of a state to apply its laws exclusively to its alien inhabitants as a class is confined within narrow limits."

Arizona and Pennsylvania seek to justify their restrictions on the eligibility of aliens for public assistance solely on the basis of a State's "special public interest" in favoring its own citizens over aliens in the distribution of limited resources such as welfare benefits. It is true that this Court on occasion has upheld state statutes that treat citizens and noncitizens differently, the ground for distinction having been that such laws were necessary to protect special interests of the State or its citizens. Thus, in *Truax v. Raich*, 239 U.S. 33, 36 S.Ct. 7, 60 L.Ed. 131 (1915), the Court, in striking down an Arizona statute restricting the employment of aliens, emphasized that "[t]he discrimination defined by the act does not pertain to the regulation or distribution of the public domain, or of the common property or resources of the people of the state, the enjoyment of which may be limited to its citizens as against both aliens and the citizens of other states." 239 U.S., at 39–40, 36 S.Ct., at 10. And in *Crane v. New York*, 239 U.S. 195, 36 S.Ct. 85, 60 L.Ed. 218 (1915), the Court affirmed the judgment in *People v. Crane*, 214 N.Y. 154, 108 N.E. 427 (1915), upholding a New York statute prohibiting the employment of aliens on public works projects. * * * On the same theory, the Court has upheld statutes that, in the absence of overriding treaties, limit the right of noncitizens to engage in exploitation of a State's natural resources, restrict the devolution of real property to aliens, or deny to aliens the right to acquire and own land.

Takahashi, however, cast doubt on the continuing validity of the special public-interest doctrine in all contexts. There the Court held that California's purported ownership of fish in the ocean off its shores was not such a special public interest as would justify prohibiting aliens from making a living by fishing in those waters while permitting all others to do so. It was said:

> The Fourteenth Amendment and the laws adopted under its authority thus embody a general policy that all persons lawfully in this country

shall abide 'in any state' on an equality of legal privileges with all citizens under nondiscriminatory laws.

334 U.S., at 420, 68 S.Ct., at 1143.

Whatever may be the contemporary vitality of the special public-interest doctrine in other contexts after *Takahashi*, we conclude that a State's desire to preserve limited welfare benefits for its own citizens is inadequate to justify Pennsylvania's making noncitizens ineligible for public assistance, and Arizona's restricting benefits to citizens and long-time resident aliens. First, the special public interest doctrine was heavily grounded on the notion that "[w]hatever is a privilege, rather than a right, may be made dependent upon citizenship." *People v. Crane*, 214 N.Y., at 164, 108 N.E., at 430. But this Court now has rejected the concept that constitutional rights turn upon whether a governmental benefit is characterized as a "right" or as a "privilege." Second, as the Court recognized in *Shapiro* [*v. Thompson*]:

> [A] State has a valid interest in preserving the fiscal integrity of its programs. It may legitimately attempt to limit its expenditures, whether for public assistance, public education, or any other program. But a State may not accomplish such a purpose by invidious distinctions between classes of its citizens.... The saving of welfare costs cannot justify an otherwise invidious classification.

[394 U.S. 618, 633, 89 S.Ct. 1322, 1330, 22 L.Ed.2d 600 (1969).] Since an alien as well as a citizen is a "person" for equal protection purposes, a concern for fiscal integrity is no more compelling a justification for the questioned classification in these cases than it was in *Shapiro*.

* * * The classifications involved in the instant cases * * * are inherently suspect and are therefore subject to strict judicial scrutiny whether or not a fundamental right is impaired. * * *

We agree with the three-judge court in the Pennsylvania case that the "justification of limiting expenses is particularly inappropriate and unreasonable when the discriminated class consists of aliens. Aliens like citizens pay taxes and may be called into the armed forces. Unlike the short-term residents in *Shapiro*, aliens may live within a state for many years, work in the state and contribute to the economic growth of the state." There can be no "special public interest" in tax revenues to which aliens have contributed on an equal basis with the residents of the State.

Accordingly, we hold that a state statute that denies welfare benefits to resident aliens and one that denies them to aliens who have not resided in the United States for a specified number of years violate the Equal Protection Clause.

III

An additional reason why the state statutes at issue in these cases do not withstand constitutional scrutiny emerges from the area of federal-state relations. The National Government has "broad constitutional powers in determining what aliens shall be admitted to the United States, the period they may remain, regulation of their conduct before naturalization, and the terms and conditions of their naturalization." *Takahashi v. Fish & Game Comm'n*, 334 U.S., at 419, 68 S.Ct., at 1142. Pursuant to that power, Congress has provided, as part of a comprehensive plan for the regulation of immigration and naturalization, that "[a]liens who are paupers, professional beggars, or vagrants" or aliens who "are likely at any time to become public charges" shall be excluded from admission into the United States, and that any alien lawfully admitted shall be deported who "has within five years after entry become a public charge from causes not affirmatively shown to have arisen after entry...." Admission of aliens likely to become public charges may be conditioned upon the posting of a bond or cash deposit. But Congress has not seen fit to impose any burden or restriction on aliens who become indigent after their entry into the United States. Rather, it has broadly declared: "All persons within the jurisdiction of the United States shall have the same right in every State and Territory ... to the full and equal benefit of all laws and proceedings for the security of persons and property as is enjoyed by white citizens...." 42 U.S.C. § 1981. The protection of this statute has been held to extend to aliens as well as to citizens. *Takahashi*, 334 U.S., at 419 n.7, 68 S.Ct., at 1142. Moreover, this Court has made it clear that, whatever may be the scope of the constitutional right of interstate travel, aliens lawfully within this country have a right to enter and abide in any State in the Union "on an equality of legal privileges with all citizens under nondiscriminatory laws." *Takahashi*, 334 U.S., at 420, 68 S.Ct., at 1143.

State laws that restrict the eligibility of aliens for welfare benefits merely because of their alienage conflict with these overriding national policies in an area constitutionally entrusted to the Federal Government. In *Hines v. Davidowitz*, 312 U.S., at 66–67, 61 S.Ct., at 403–404, where this Court struck down a Pennsylvania alien registration statute (enacted in 1939, as was the statute under challenge in No. 727) on grounds of federal pre-emption, it was observed that "where the federal government, in the exercise of its superior authority in this field, has enacted a complete scheme of regulation ... states cannot, inconsistently with the purpose of Congress, conflict or interfere with, curtail or complement, the federal law, or enforce additional or auxiliary regulations." And in *Takahashi* it was said that the States

> can neither add to nor take from the conditions lawfully imposed by Congress upon admission, naturalization and residence of aliens in the United States or the several states. State laws which impose discriminatory burdens upon the entrance or residence of aliens lawfully within the United States conflict with this constitutionally derived federal power to regulate immigration, and have accordingly been held invalid.

334 U.S., at 419, 68 S.Ct., at 1142.

Congress has broadly declared as federal policy that lawfully admitted resident aliens who become public charges for causes arising after their entry are not subject to deportation, and that as long as they are here they are entitled to the full and equal benefit of all state laws for the security of persons and property. The state statutes at issue in the instant cases impose auxiliary burdens upon the entrance or residence of aliens who suffer the distress, after entry, of economic dependency on public assistance. Alien residency requirements for welfare benefits necessarily operate, as did the residency requirements in *Shapiro*, to discourage entry into or continued residency in the State. Indeed, in No. 727 the parties stipulated that this was so.

In *Truax* the Court considered the "reasonableness" of a state restriction on the employment of aliens in terms of its effect on the right of a lawfully admitted alien to live where he chooses:

> * * * The authority to control immigration—to admit or exclude aliens—is vested solely in the Federal Government.... The assertion of an authority to deny to aliens the opportunity of earning a livelihood when lawfully admitted to the state would be tantamount to the assertion of the right to deny them entrance and abode, for in ordinary cases they cannot live where they cannot work. And, if such a policy were permissible, the practical result would be that those lawfully admitted to the country under the authority of the acts of Congress, instead of enjoying in a substantial sense and in their full scope the privileges conferred by the admission, would be segregated in such of the states as chose to offer hospitality.

239 U.S., at 42, 36 S.Ct., at 11. The same is true here, for in the ordinary case an alien, becoming indigent and unable to work, will be unable to live where, because of discriminatory denial of public assistance, he cannot "secure the necessities of life, including food, clothing and shelter." State alien residency requirements that either deny welfare benefits to noncitizens or condition them on longtime residency, equate with the assertion of a right, inconsistent with federal policy, to deny entrance and abode. Since such laws encroach upon exclusive federal power, they are constitutionally impermissible.

IV

Arizona suggests, finally, that its 15–year durational residency requirement for aliens is actually authorized by federal law. Reliance is placed on § 1402(b) of the Social Security Act of 1935. That section provides:

> The Secretary shall approve any plan which fulfills the conditions specified in subsection (a) of this section, except that he shall not approve any plan which imposes, as a condition of eligibility for aid to the permanently and totally disabled under the plan—

. . .

(2) Any citizenship requirement which excludes any citizen of the United States.

The meaning of this provision is not entirely clear. On its face, the statute does not affirmatively authorize, much less command, the States to adopt durational residency requirements or other eligibility restrictions applicable to aliens; it merely directs the Secretary not to approve state-submitted plans that exclude citizens of the United States from eligibility.

* * * [I]f § 1402(b), as well as the identical provisions for old-age assistance and aid to the blind, were to be read so as to authorize discriminatory treatment of aliens at the option of the States, *Takahashi* demonstrates that serious constitutional questions are presented. Although the Federal Government admittedly has broad constitutional power to determine what aliens shall be admitted to the United States, the period they may remain, and the terms and conditions of their naturalization, Congress does not have the power to authorize the individual States to violate the Equal Protection Clause. *Shapiro v. Thompson*, 394 U.S., at 641, 89 S.Ct., at 1335. Under Art. I, § 8, cl. 4, of the Constitution, Congress' power is to "establish an uniform Rule of Naturalization." A congressional enactment construed so as to permit state legislatures to adopt divergent laws on the subject of citizenship requirements for federally supported welfare programs would appear to contravene this explicit constitutional requirement of uniformity.[14] Since "statutes should be construed whenever possible so as to uphold their constitutionality," *United States v. Vuitch*, 402 U.S. 62, 70, 91 S.Ct. 1294, 1298, 28 L.Ed.2d 601 (1971), we conclude that § 1402(b) does not authorize the Arizona 15–year national residency requirement.

The judgments appealed from are affirmed.

It is so ordered.

Affirmed.

MR. JUSTICE HARLAN joins in Parts III and IV of the Court's opinion, and in the judgment of the Court.

NOTES AND QUESTIONS ON GRAHAM V. RICHARDSON

1. The famous footnote four in *Carolene Products*, from which *Graham* takes the "discrete and insular minority" idea, reads as follows:

There may be narrower scope for operation of the presumption of constitutionality when legislation appears on its face to be within a specific prohibition of the Constitution, such as those of the first ten Amendments, which are deemed equally specific when held to be embraced within the Fourteenth.

It is unnecessary to consider now whether legislation which restricts those political processes which can ordinarily be expected to bring about

---

14. We have no occasion to decide whether Congress, in the exercise of the immigration and naturalization power, could itself enact a statute imposing on aliens a uniform nationwide residency requirement as a condition of federally funded welfare benefits.

repeal of undesirable legislation, is to be subjected to more exacting judicial scrutiny under the general prohibitions of the Fourteenth Amendment than are most other types of legislation.

Nor need we enquire whether similar considerations enter into the review of statutes directed at particular religious, or national, or racial minorities; whether prejudice against discrete and insular minorities may be a special condition, which tends seriously to curtail the operation of those political processes ordinarily to be relied upon to protect minorities, and which may call for a correspondingly more searching judicial inquiry.

United States v. Carolene Products Co., 304 U.S. 144, 152–153, n.4, 58 S.Ct. 778, 783–784 n.4, 82 L.Ed. 1234 (1938) (citations omitted).

2. *Graham* involved permanent residents, not nonimmigrants or the undocumented. Even with his reasoning so cabined, is Justice Blackmun correct that "aliens as a class" are a discrete and insular minority? Are aliens as a class truly discrete? Are they insular? Are they politically powerless? Does the possibility of diplomatic intervention by their home governments undercut this argument? And why can't they overcome their relative lack of political power by naturalizing?

Arguing that aliens are a "relatively easy case" of a discrete and insular minority, John Hart Ely explained:

Aliens cannot vote in any state, which means that any representation they receive will be exclusively "virtual." That fact should at the very least require an unusually strong showing of a favorable environment for empathy, something that is lacking here. Hostility toward "foreigners" is a time-honored American tradition. Moreover, our legislatures are composed almost entirely of citizens who have always been such. Neither, finally, is the exaggerated stereotyping to which that situation lends itself ameliorated by any substantial degree of social intercourse between recent immigrants and those who make the laws.

J.H. Ely, Democracy and Distrust 161–62 (1980). But consider this, from Aleinikoff, *Citizens, Aliens, Membership and the Constitution*, 7 Const. Comm. 9, 24 n.58 (1990): "To be sure, discrimination against aliens has a persistent and ugly history in this country; but generally such hatred has been based on racial or ethnic backgrounds, not the fact of 'alienage.' Aliens, as a class, are remarkably diverse and not particularly 'insular.' "

3. A related question is whether certain groups of noncitizens are discrete and insular minorities, even if noncitizens in general are not. Kevin Johnson has argued that "restriction of benefits and services, besides affecting persons with a certain immigration status, has a disparate impact on people of color ..., women ..., and the poor...." Johnson, *Public Benefits and Immigration: The Intersection of Immigration Status, Ethnicity, Gender, and Class*, 42 UCLA L. Rev. 1509, 1516 (1995).

4. Is there any other explanation for the outcome in *Graham* besides the idea that noncitizens are a discrete and insular minority? Suppose we assume that noncitizens cannot be so described, and therefore are not a defenseless group needing judicial protection. Consider this analysis of the next-to-last paragraph of Justice Blackmun's equal protection discussion (near the end of

Part II, in the paragraph beginning "We agree with the three-judge court ...."):

> Although Blackmun does not appear to recognize the tension this paragraph creates for his opinion, in these lines he actually flips the justification of invalidating discriminatory state laws. The statutes in *Graham* should be invalidated not because aliens are a defenseless group needing judicial protection, but rather because—at least from the state's perspective—they are indistinguishable from other residents of the state. State laws excluding aliens from opportunities should be seen as no more legitimate than laws excluding redheads. Both would be invalid, not because such groups are downtrodden but because the state can offer no legitimate reason for singling them out.

Aleinikoff, *Citizens, Aliens, Membership and the Constitution*, *supra*, at 24. Is this approach to alienage classifications more persuasive than the discrete and insular minority approach?

b. Federal Laws

In footnote 14 of *Graham*, the Court noted that it was not addressing the validity of a citizenship requirement for *federal* benefits. For equal protection analysis—assuming that was what the Court applied in *Graham*—why should it matter if the federal government or a state adopts an alienage classification? Recall from Chapter Two that in *Bolling v. Sharpe*, 347 U.S. 497, 74 S.Ct. 693, 98 L.Ed. 884 (1954), a companion case to *Brown v. Board of Education*, the Court held that segregated schools in the District of Columbia violated the Due Process Clause of the Fifth Amendment. It has been accepted since *Bolling* that as a general rule "[e]qual protection analysis in the Fifth Amendment area is the same as that under the Fourteenth Amendment." *Buckley v. Valeo*, 424 U.S. 1, 93, 96 S.Ct. 612, 670, 46 L.Ed.2d 659 (1976) (per curiam). Combining *Bolling* with *Graham*, are federal laws limiting noncitizen access to public benefits unconstitutional? Read the next case.

MATHEWS v. DIAZ

Supreme Court of the United States, 1976.
426 U.S. 67, 96 S.Ct. 1883, 48 L.Ed.2d 478.

MR. JUSTICE STEVENS delivered the opinion of the Court.

* * *

Each of the appellees is a resident alien who was lawfully admitted to the United States less than five years ago. Appellees Diaz and Clara are Cuban refugees who remain in this country at the discretion of the Attorney General; appellee Espinosa has been admitted for permanent residence. All three are over 65 years old and have been denied enrollment in the Medicare Part B supplemental medical insurance program * * *. * * * [T]hey attack 42 U.S.C. § 1395o(2), which grants eligibility to resident citizens who are 65 or older but denies eligibility to comparable aliens unless they have been admitted for permanent residence and also have resided in the United States for at least five years. Appellees Diaz and Clara meet neither requirement; appellee Espinosa meets only the first.

* * *

II

There are literally millions of aliens within the jurisdiction of the United States. The Fifth Amendment, as well as the Fourteenth Amendment, protects every one of these persons from deprivation of life, liberty, or property without due process of law. *Wong Yang Sung v. McGrath*, 339 U.S. 33, 48–51, 70 S.Ct. 445, 453–455, 94 L.Ed. 616, 627–629; *Wong Wing v. United States*, 163 U.S. 228, 238, 16 S.Ct. 977, 981, 41 L.Ed. 140, 143; *see Russian Fleet v. United States*, 282 U.S. 481, 489, 51 S.Ct. 229, 231, 75 L.Ed. 473, 476. Even one whose presence in this country is unlawful, involuntary, or transitory is entitled to that constitutional protection.

The fact that all persons, aliens and citizens alike, are protected by the Due Process Clause does not lead to the further conclusion that all aliens are entitled to enjoy all the advantages of citizenship or, indeed, to the conclusion that all aliens must be placed in a single homogeneous legal classification. For a host of constitutional and statutory provisions rest on the premise that a legitimate distinction between citizens and aliens may justify attributes and benefits for one class not accorded to the other;[12] and the class of aliens is itself a heterogeneous multitude of persons with a wide-ranging variety of ties to this country.

In the exercise of its broad power over naturalization and immigration, Congress regularly makes rules that would be unacceptable if applied to citizens. The exclusion of aliens and the reservation of the power to deport have no permissible counterpart in the Federal Government's power to regulate the conduct of its own citizenry. The fact that an Act of Congress treats aliens differently from citizens does not in itself imply that such disparate treatment is "invidious."

In particular, the fact that Congress has provided some welfare benefits for citizens does not require it to provide like benefits for all

---

12. The Constitution protects the privileges and immunities only of citizens, Amdt. 14, § 1; see Art. IV, § 2, cl. 1, and the right to vote only of citizens. Amdts. 15, 19, 24, 26. It requires that Representatives have been citizens for seven years, Art. I, § 2, cl. 2, and Senators citizens for nine, Art. I, § 3, cl. 3, and that the President be a "natural born Citizen." Art. II, § 1, cl. 5.

A multitude of federal statutes distinguish between citizens and aliens. The whole of Title 8 of the United States Code, regulating aliens and nationality, is founded on the legitimacy of distinguishing between citizens and aliens. A variety of other federal statutes provide for disparate treatment of aliens and citizens. These include prohibitions and restrictions upon Government employment of aliens, upon private employment of aliens, and upon investments and businesses of aliens, statutes excluding aliens from benefits available to citizens, and from protections extended to citizens; and statutes imposing added burdens upon aliens. Several statutes treat certain aliens more favorably than citizens. Other statutes, similar to the one at issue in this case, provide for equal treatment of citizens and aliens lawfully admitted for permanent residence. Still others equate citizens and aliens who have declared their intention to become citizens. Yet others condition equal treatment of an alien upon reciprocal treatment of United States citizens by the alien's own country.

aliens. Neither the overnight visitor, the unfriendly agent of a hostile foreign power, the resident diplomat, nor the illegal entrant, can advance even a colorable constitutional claim to a share in the bounty that a conscientious sovereign makes available to its own citizens and some of its guests. The decision to share that bounty with our guests may take into account the character of the relationship between the alien and this country: Congress may decide that as the alien's tie grows stronger, so does the strength of his claim to an equal share of that munificence.

The real question presented by this case is not whether discrimination between citizens and aliens is permissible; rather, it is whether the statutory discrimination within the class of aliens—allowing benefits to some aliens but not to others—is permissible. We turn to that question.

III

For reasons long recognized as valid, the responsibility for regulating the relationship between the United States and our alien visitors has been committed to the political branches of the Federal Government.[17] Since decisions in these matters may implicate our relations with foreign powers, and since a wide variety of classifications must be defined in the light of changing political and economic circumstances, such decisions are frequently of a character more appropriate to either the Legislature or the Executive than to the Judiciary. This very case illustrates the need for flexibility in policy choices rather than the rigidity often characteristic of constitutional adjudication. Appellees Diaz and Clara are but two of over 440,000 Cuban refugees who arrived in the United States between 1961 and 1972. And the Cuban parolees are but one of several categories of aliens who have been admitted in order to make a humane response to a natural catastrophe or an international political situation. Any rule of constitutional law that would inhibit the flexibility of the political branches of government to respond to changing world conditions should be adopted only with the greatest caution. The reasons that preclude judicial review of political questions[21] also dictate a narrow standard of review of decisions made by the Congress or the President in the area of immigration and naturalization.

---

17. "(A)ny policy toward aliens is vitally and intricately interwoven with contemporaneous policies in regard to the conduct of foreign relations, the war power, and the maintenance of a republican form of government. Such matters are so exclusively entrusted to the political branches of government as to be largely immune from judicial inquiry or interference." *Harisiades v. Shaughnessy*, supra, 342 U.S., at 588–589, 72 S.Ct. 512, 519, 96 L.Ed. 586, 598 (footnote omitted). *Accord, e.g. Kleindienst v. Mandel*, supra, 408 U.S., at 765–767, 92 S.Ct. 2576, 2582–2584, 33 L.Ed.2d 683, 693–695; *Fong Yue Ting v. United States*, 149 U.S. 698, 711–713, 13 S.Ct. 1016, 1021–1022, 37 L.Ed. 905, 912–913.

21. "It is apparent that several formulations which vary slightly according to the settings in which the questions arise may describe a political question, although each has one or more elements which identify it as essentially a function of the separation of powers. Prominent on the surface of any case held to involve a political question is found a textually demonstrable constitutional commitment of the issue to a coordinate political department; or a lack of judicially discoverable and manageable standards for resolving it; or the impossibility of deciding without an initial policy determination of a kind clearly for nonjudicial discretion; or the impossibility of a court's undertaking independent resolution without expressing lack of the respect due coordinate branches of government; or an unusual need for unquestioning adherence to a political decision

Since it is obvious that Congress has no constitutional duty to provide all aliens with the welfare benefits provided to citizens, the party challenging the constitutionality of the particular line Congress has drawn has the burden of advancing principled reasoning that will at once invalidate that line and yet tolerate a different line separating some aliens from others. In this case the appellees have challenged two requirements—first, that the alien be admitted as a permanent resident, and, second, that his residence be of a duration of at least five years. But if these requirements were eliminated, surely Congress would at least require that the alien's entry be lawful; even then, unless mere transients are to be held constitutionally entitled to benefits, some durational requirement would certainly be appropriate. In short, it is unquestionably reasonable for Congress to make an alien's eligibility depend on both the character and the duration of his residence. Since neither requirement is wholly irrational, this case essentially involves nothing more than a claim that it would have been more reasonable for Congress to select somewhat different requirements of the same kind.

We may assume that the five-year line drawn by Congress is longer than necessary to protect the fiscal integrity of the program. We may also assume that unnecessary hardship is incurred by persons just short of qualifying. But it remains true that some line is essential, that any line must produce some harsh and apparently arbitrary consequences, and, of greatest importance, that those who qualify under the test Congress has chosen may reasonably be presumed to have a greater affinity with the United States than those who do not. In short, citizens and those who are most like citizens qualify. Those who are less like citizens do not.

The task of classifying persons for medical benefits, like the task of drawing lines for federal tax purposes, inevitably requires that some persons who have an almost equally strong claim to favored treatment be placed on different sides of the line; the differences between the eligible and the ineligible are differences in degree rather than differences in the character of their respective claims. When this kind of policy choice must be made, we are especially reluctant to question the exercise of congressional judgment. In this case, since appellees have not identified a principled basis for prescribing a different standard than the one selected by Congress, they have, in effect, merely invited us to substitute our judgment for that of Congress in deciding which aliens shall be eligible to participate in the supplementary insurance program on the same conditions as citizens. We decline the invitation.

IV

The cases on which appellees rely are consistent with our conclusion that this statutory classification does not deprive them of liberty or property without due process of law.

---

already made; or the potentiality of embarrassment from multifarious pronouncements by various departments on one question." *Baker v. Carr*, 369 U.S. 186, 217, 82 S.Ct. 691, 710, 7 L.Ed.2d 663, 685.

Graham v. Richardson, 403 U.S. 365, 91 S.Ct. 1848, 29 L.Ed.2d 534, provides the strongest support for appellees' position. That case holds that state statutes that deny welfare benefits to resident aliens, or to aliens not meeting a requirement of durational residence within the United States, violate the Equal Protection Clause of the Fourteenth Amendment and encroach upon the exclusive federal power over the entrance and residence of aliens. Of course, the latter ground of decision actually supports our holding today that it is the business of the political branches of the Federal Government, rather than that of either the States or the Federal Judiciary, to regulate the conditions of entry and residence of aliens. The equal protection analysis also involves significantly different considerations because it concerns the relationship between aliens and the States rather than between aliens and the Federal Government.

Insofar as state welfare policy is concerned,[24] there is little, if any, basis for treating persons who are citizens of another State differently from persons who are citizens of another country. Both groups are noncitizens as far as the State's interests in administering its welfare programs are concerned. Thus, a division by a State of the category of persons who are not citizens of that State into subcategories of United States citizens and aliens has no apparent justification, whereas, a comparable classification by the Federal Government is a routine and normally legitimate part of its business. Furthermore, whereas the Constitution inhibits every State's power to restrict travel across its own borders, Congress is explicitly empowered to exercise that type of control over travel across the borders of the United States.

* * *

We hold that § 1395o(2)(B) has not deprived appellees of liberty or property without due process of law.

* * *

NOTES AND QUESTIONS ON MATHEWS V. DIAZ

1. How analytically helpful is it to say that the classification in *Mathews v. Diaz* was a classification among aliens rather than between aliens and citizens? What classifications that distinguish between aliens and citizens do not also somehow distinguish between groups of aliens?

2. Does *Mathews v. Diaz* silently repudiate—even with regard to state alienage classifications—the idea in *Graham* that alienage classifications should prompt close judicial scrutiny because aliens are a discrete and insular minority? Some aspects of *Diaz* might be read as so suggesting, yet the

---

24. We have left open the question whether a State may prohibit aliens from holding elective or important nonelective positions or whether a State may, in some circumstances, consider the alien status of an applicant or employee in making an individualized employment decision. *See Sugarman v. Dougall*, 413 U.S. 634, 646–649, 93 S.Ct. 2842, 2849–2851, 37 L.Ed.2d 853, 862–864; *In re Griffiths*, 413 U.S. 717, 728–729 and n.21, 93 S.Ct. 2851, 2858–2859, 37 L.Ed.2d 910, 919–920.

Supreme Court persisted in applying *Graham* in later cases to strike down some state alienage classifications. *See* the cases on citizenship requirements for state public employment in Section B of this chapter.

3. One of the most often quoted sentences from *Diaz* is: "In the exercise of its broad power over naturalization and immigration, Congress regularly makes rules that would be unacceptable if applied to citizens." But does this mean that the plenary power doctrine operates with as much force in alienage law as in immigration law? Compare the judicial deference in *Diaz* with the judicial deference in *Fiallo v. Bell*, 430 U.S. 787, 97 S.Ct. 1473, 52 L.Ed.2d 50 (1977), in Chapter Five p. 293. Would the *Diaz* Court have upheld a Medicare eligibility rule that restricted noncitizen access by gender or illegitimacy? Is *Diaz* correct when it bases Congress' power to classify by alienage on its "broad power over naturalization and immigration," citing the power to refuse admission and to remove noncitizens?

Should we approach alienage classifications and immigration rules in similar fashion, and if so, why? Does it follow from the judicial deference to an immigration statute in *Fiallo* that courts should likewise defer to a statute—like the Medicare statute in *Diaz*—that disadvantages noncitizens after their admission?

4. To understand the immigration-alienage line, consider the following comment on California's Proposition 187, approved by California voters in 1994. As explained in Chapter Nine, pp. 1053–55, the principal effect of that ballot initiative would have been to deny public education and non-emergency medical services to the undocumented, but constitutional challenges in court kept almost all of its provisions from being implemented.

> * * * "Alienage" rules may be surrogates for "immigration" rules. Often, the intended and/or actual effect of an alienage rule is to affect immigration patterns. California's * * * Proposition 187 is a good example. It does not purport to regulate admission to the United States directly; instead, its principal effect is to deny public education and non-emergency medical services to undocumented aliens. However, Proposition 187 is clearly meant to deter undocumented aliens from entering California and to encourage the voluntary exit of those already there. Governor Wilson has expressed his hope that undocumented aliens, once denied access to public benefits, will "self-deport."

> Similarly, "immigration" rules may be surrogates for "alienage" rules. For example, the law governing deportation traditionally belongs to "immigration law." This understanding makes sense in that deportation grounds allow the government to undo an alien's original admission (or surreptitious entry or parole) into the United States. Yet the intended and actual effect of deportation grounds is to regulate the everyday lives of aliens in the United States no less than do rules governing their access to public benefits.

Motomura, *Immigration and Alienage, Federalism and Proposition 187*, 35 Va. J. Int'l L. 201, 202–03 (1994).

5. Linda Bosniak explains why it isn't enough to distinguish immigration law from alienage law. She discusses the issues that persist even if we assume that an issue is a matter of alienage law:

> * * * [T]he law has constructed alienage as a hybrid legal status category that lies at the nexus of two legal—and moral—worlds. It lies, first of all, in the world of borders, sovereignty, and national community membership; this is the world of the government's immigration power, which regulates decisions about the admission and exclusion of outsiders and which places conditions on their entry and residence. The very existence of alienage is a product of this world because the government designates aliens as such in the exercise of its immigration power. In the broader landscape of American public law, this power remains exceptionally unconstrained.

> Yet alienage as a legal category also lies in the world of social relationships among territorially present persons. In this world, government power to impose disabilities on people based on their status is substantially constrained. Formal commitments to norms of equal treatment and to the elimination of caste-like status have importantly shaped American public law, particularly during the past several decades. From this perspective, aliens appear to be at once indistinguishable from citizens and precisely the sort of social group that requires the law's protection.

> Because alienage lies at the nexus of these two legal worlds—because it is a hybrid legal status that is the creature of both—the question of when and whether a person's status as an alien legitimately matters in determining the allocation of rights and benefits in our society tends to take the form of what can best be described as a "jurisdictional" dispute in case law. This dispute concerns the question of which of the two worlds (or regulatory domains) that define alienage—I will call them the domains of membership and equal personhood, respectively—properly controls in any given case. Alternatively, when the law assumes the relevance of both domains, the dispute concerns the question of how they are to be accommodated and where the boundary between them rightfully lies.

Bosniak, *Membership, Equality, and the Difference That Alienage Makes*, 69 N.Y.U. L. Rev. 1047, 1056–57 (1994).

c. Preemption or Equal Protection?

To explore the relationship between equal protection and preemption-based approaches to state alienage laws, compare the analysis in *Graham*, which relied on both equal protection and preemption, with the exclusive reliance on preemption in the next case.

TOLL v. MORENO

Supreme Court of the United States, 1982.
458 U.S. 1, 102 S.Ct. 2977, 73 L.Ed.2d 563.

JUSTICE BRENNAN delivered the opinion of the Court.

The state-operated University of Maryland grants preferential treatment for purposes of tuition and fees to students with "in-state" status.

Although citizens and immigrant aliens may obtain in-state status upon a showing of domicile within the State, nonimmigrant aliens, even if domiciled, are not eligible for such status. * * *

* * *

In 1975, when this action was filed, respondents Juan Carlos Moreno, Juan Pablo Otero, and Clare B. Hogg were students at the University of Maryland. Each resided with, and was financially dependent on, a parent who was a nonimmigrant alien holding a "G–4" visa. Such visas are issued to nonimmigrant aliens who are officers or employees of certain international organizations, and to members of their immediate families. Despite respondents' residence in the State, the University denied them in-state status pursuant to its policy of excluding all nonimmigrant aliens. Seeking declaratory and injunctive relief, the three respondents filed a class action against the University of Maryland and its President. They contended that the University's policy violated various federal laws, the Due Process and Equal Protection Clauses of the Fourteenth Amendment, and the Supremacy Clause.

* * *

[T]he University adopted a "clarifying resolution" concerning its in-state policy. * * * The interests assertedly served by the policy were described in the following terms [in that resolution]:

(a) limiting the University's expenditures by granting a higher subsidy toward the expenses of providing educational services to that class of persons who, as a class, are more likely to have a close affinity to the State and to contribute more to its economic well-being;

(b) achieving equalization between the affected classes of the expenses of providing educational services;

(c) efficiently administering the University's in-state determination and appeals process; and

(d) preventing disparate treatment among categories of nonimmigrants with respect to admissions, tuition, and charge-differentials.

* * *

* * * For the reasons that follow, we hold that the University of Maryland's in-state policy, as applied to G–4 aliens and their dependents, violates the Supremacy Clause of the Constitution, and on that ground affirm the judgment of the Court of Appeals. We therefore have no occasion to consider whether the policy violates the Due Process or Equal Protection Clauses.

II

Our cases have long recognized the preeminent role of the Federal Government with respect to the regulation of aliens within our borders. See, *e.g., Mathews v. Diaz,* 426 U.S. 67, 96 S.Ct. 1883, 48 L.Ed.2d 478

(1976); *Graham v. Richardson*, 403 U.S. 365, 377–380, 91 S.Ct. 1848, 1854–1856, 29 L.Ed.2d 534 (1971); *Takahashi v. Fish & Game Comm'n*, 334 U.S. 410, 418–420, 68 S.Ct. 1138, 1142–1143, 92 L.Ed. 1478 (1948); *Hines v. Davidowitz*, 312 U.S. 52, 62–68 (1941); *Truax v. Raich*, 239 U.S. 33, 42, 36 S.Ct. 7, 11, 60 L.Ed. 131 (1915). Federal authority to regulate the status of aliens derives from various sources, including the Federal Government's power "[t]o establish [a] uniform Rule of Naturalization," U.S. Const., Art. I, § 8, cl. 4, its power "[t]o regulate Commerce with foreign Nations", *id.*, cl. 3, and its broad authority over foreign affairs, see *United States v. Curtiss–Wright Export Corp.*, 299 U.S. 304, 318, 57 S.Ct. 216, 220, 81 L.Ed. 255 (1936); *Mathews v. Diaz, supra*, at 81, n.17, 96 S.Ct., at 1892, n.17; *Harisiades v. Shaughnessy*, 342 U.S. 580, 588–589, 72 S.Ct. 512, 518–519, 96 L.Ed. 586 (1952).

Not surprisingly, therefore, our cases have also been at pains to note the substantial limitations upon the authority of the States in making classifications based upon alienage. In *Takahashi v. Fish & Game Comm'n*, we considered a California statute that precluded aliens who were "ineligible for citizenship under federal law" from obtaining commercial fishing licenses, even though they "met all other state requirements" and were lawful inhabitants of the State. In seeking to defend the statute, the State argued that it had "simply followed the Federal Government's lead" in classifying certain persons as "ineligible for citizenship." We rejected the argument, stressing the delicate nature of the federal-state relationship in regulating aliens * * *.[16]

The decision in *Graham v. Richardson* followed directly from *Takahashi*. In *Graham* we held that a State may not withhold welfare benefits from resident aliens "merely because of their alienage." Such discrimination, the Court concluded, would not only violate the Equal Protection Clause, but would also encroach upon federal authority over lawfully admitted aliens. * * *

Read together, *Takahashi* and *Graham* stand for the broad principle[17] that "state regulation not congressionally sanctioned that discriminates against aliens lawfully admitted to the country is impermissible if it imposes additional burdens not contemplated by Congress." *De Canas v. Bica*, 424 U.S. 351, 358, n.6, 96 S.Ct. 933, 938, n.6, 47 L.Ed.2d 43 (1976).[18]

16. * * * While pre-emption played a significant role in the Court's analysis in *Takahashi*, the actual basis for invalidation of the California statute was apparently the Equal Protection Clause of the Constitution. Commentators have noted, however, that many of the Court's decisions concerning alienage classifications, such as *Takahashi*, are better explained in pre-emption than in equal protection terms. See, *e.g.*, Perry, *Modern Equal Protection: A Conceptualization and Appraisal*, 79 Colum. L.Rev. 1023, 1060–1065 (1979); Note, *The Equal Treatment of Aliens: Preemption or Equal Protection?*, 31 Stan. L.Rev. 1069 (1979).

17. Our cases do recognize, however, that a State, in the course of defining its political community, may, in appropriate circumstances, limit the participation of noncitizens in the States' political and governmental functions. See, *e.g.*, *Cabell v. Chavez–Salido*, 454 U.S. 432, 102 S.Ct. 735, 70 L.Ed.2d 677 (1982); *Ambach v. Norwick*, 441 U.S. 68, 72–75, 99 S.Ct. 1589, 1592–1593, 60 L.Ed.2d 49 (1979); *Foley v. Connelie*, 435 U.S. 291, 295–296, 98 S.Ct. 1067, 1070, 55 L.Ed.2d 287 (1978); *Sugarman v. Dougall*, 413 U.S. 634, 646–649, 93 S.Ct. 2842, 2849–2851, 37 L.Ed.2d 853 (1973).

18. In *De Canas*, we considered whether a California statute making it unlawful in some circumstances to employ *illegal* aliens was invalid under the Supremacy Clause. We upheld the

To be sure, when Congress has done nothing more than permit a class of aliens to enter the country temporarily, the proper application of the principle is likely to be a matter of some dispute. But the instant case does not present such a situation, and there can be little doubt regarding the invalidity of the challenged portion of the University's in-state policy.

The Immigration and Nationality Act represents "a comprehensive and complete code covering all aspects of admission of aliens to this country, whether for business or pleasure, or as immigrants seeking to become permanent residents." *Elkins v. Moreno*, [435 U.S. 647, 664, 98 S.Ct. 1338, 1348, 55 L.Ed.2d 614 (1978)]. The Act recognizes two basic classes of aliens, immigrant and nonimmigrant. With respect to the nonimmigrant class, the Act establishes various categories, the G–4 category among them. For many of these nonimmigrant categories, Congress has precluded the covered alien from establishing domicile in the United States. But significantly, Congress has allowed G–4 aliens—employees of various international organizations, and their immediate families—to enter the country on terms permitting the establishment of domicile in the United States. In light of Congress' explicit decision not to bar G–4 aliens from acquiring domicile, the State's decision to deny "in-state" status to G–4 aliens, *solely* on account of the G–4 alien's federal immigration status, surely amounts to an ancillary "burden not contemplated by Congress" in admitting these aliens to the United States. We need not rely, however, simply on Congress' decision to permit the G–4 alien to establish domicile in this country; the Federal Government has also taken the additional affirmative step of conferring special tax privileges on G–4 aliens.

As a result of an array of treaties, international agreements, and federal statutes, G–4 visaholders employed by the international organizations described in INA § 101(a)(15)(G)(iv) are relieved of federal and, in many instances, state and local taxes on the salaries paid by the organizations. * * *

In affording G–4 visaholders such tax exemption, the Federal Government has undoubtedly sought to benefit the employing international organizations by enabling them to pay salaries not encumbered by the full panoply of taxes, thereby lowering the organizations' costs. The tax benefits serve as an inducement for these organizations to locate significant operations in the United States. By imposing on those G–4 aliens who are domiciled in Maryland higher tuition and fees than are imposed on other domiciliaries of the State, the University's policy frustrates these federal policies. * * *

JUSTICE BLACKMUN, concurring.

---

statute. Justice Rehnquist's dissent in the present case suggests that the pre-emption claim was rejected in *De Canas* because "the Court found no strong evidence that Congress intended to pre-empt" the State's action. Justice Rehnquist has misread *De Canas*. We rejected the pre-emption claim not because of an absence of congressional intent to pre-empt, but because Congress *intended* that the States be allowed, "to the extent consistent with federal law, [to] regulate the employment of illegal aliens." 424 U.S., at 361, 96 S.Ct., at 939.

I join the Court's opinion. Its action today provides an eloquent and sufficient answer to Justice Rehnquist's dissent: despite the vehemence with which his opinion is written, Justice Rehnquist has persuaded only one Justice to his position. But because the dissent attempts to plumb the Court's psyche,[1] I feel compelled to add comments addressed to Justice Rehnquist's ruminations on equal protection. In particular, I cannot leave unchallenged his suggestion that the Court's decisions holding resident aliens to be a "suspect class" no longer are good law.

Justice Rehnquist's analysis on this point is based on a simple syllogism. Alienage classifications have been subjected to strict scrutiny, he suggests, because "aliens [are] barred from asserting their interests in the governmental body responsible for imposing burdens upon them." But "[m]ore recent decisions," he continues, have established that "the political powerlessness of aliens is itself the consequence of distinctions on the basis of alienage that are constitutionally permissible." This prompts Justice Rehnquist to pose what one supposes to be a rhetorical question: "whether political powerlessness is any longer a legitimate reason for treating aliens as a 'suspect class' deserving of 'heightened judicial solicitude.'" The reader would infer from this analysis that Justice Rehnquist would uphold state enactments disadvantaging aliens unless those enactments are wholly irrational.

With respect, in my view it is Justice Rehnquist's analysis that is wholly irrational; simply to state his proposition is to demonstrate its logical flaws. Most obviously, his exegesis of the Court's reasons for according aliens "suspect class" status is simplistic to the point of caricature. By labeling aliens a " 'discrete and insular' minority," *Graham v. Richardson*, 403 U.S. 365, 372, 91 S.Ct. 1848, 1852, 29 L.Ed.2d 534 (1971), the Court did something more than provide an historical description of their political standing. That label also reflected the Court's considered conclusion that for most legislative purposes there simply are no meaningful differences between resident aliens and citizens, so that aliens and citizens are "persons similarly circumstanced" who must "be treated alike." *F. S. Royster Guano Co. v. Virginia*, 253 U.S. 412, 415, 40 S.Ct. 560, 562, 64 L.Ed. 989 (1920). At the same time, both common experience and the unhappy history reflected in our cases demonstrate that aliens often have been the victims of irrational discrimination.

In combination, these factors—disparate treatment accorded a class of "similarly circumstanced" persons who historically have been disabled by the prejudice of the majority led the Court to conclude that alienage classifications "in themselves supply a reason to infer antipathy," *Personnel Administrator of Massachusetts v. Feeney*, 442 U.S. 256, 272, 99 S.Ct. 2282, 2292, 60 L.Ed.2d 870 (1979), and therefore demand close judicial scrutiny. This understanding, which is at the heart of the Court's modern alienage decisions, was unreservedly reaffirmed this Term in *Cabell v.*

---

1. The Justice opines that "[i]f the Court has eschewed strict scrutiny in the 'political process' [alienage-equal protection] cases, it may be because the Court is becoming uncomfortable with the categorization of aliens as a suspect class."

Chavez–Salido, 454 U.S. [432], 438, 102 S.Ct. [735], 739 (1982) ("citizenship is not a relevant ground for the distribution of economic benefits").

* * *

Justice Rehnquist nevertheless suggests that the Court's original understanding somehow has been undercut by "more recent decisions" recognizing that aliens may be excluded from the governmental process. * * * Again, with all due respect, Justice Rehnquist is simply wrong. The idea that aliens may be denied political rights is not a recently discovered concept or a newly molded principle that can be said to have eroded the prior understanding. To the contrary, the Court always has recognized that aliens may be denied use of the mechanisms of self-government, and *all* of the alienage cases have been decided against the backdrop of that principle. * * *

Finally, even were I to accept Justice Rehnquist's view that powerlessness is the end-all of alienage-equal protection doctrine, I would find preposterous his further suggestion that, because States do not violate the Constitution when they exclude aliens from participation in the government of the community, the alien's powerlessness therefore is constitutionally irrelevant. From the moment the Court began constructing modern equal protection doctrine in *United States v. Carolene Products Co.*, 304 U.S. 144, 58 S.Ct. 778, 82 L.Ed. 1234 (1938), it never has been suggested that the *reason* for a discrete class' political powerlessness is significant; instead, the *fact* of powerlessness is crucial, for in combination with prejudice it is the minority group's inability to assert its political interests that "curtail[s] the operation of those political processes ordinarily to be relied upon to protect minorities." *Id.*, at 152–153, n.4, 58 S.Ct., at 783–784, n.4. * * *

* * *

Justice O'Connor, concurring in part and dissenting in part.

I concur in the Court's opinion insofar as it holds that the State may not charge out-of-state tuition to nonimmigrant aliens who, under federal law, are exempt from both state and federal taxes, and who are domiciled in the State. Imposition of out-of-state tuition on such aliens conflicts with federal law exempting them from state taxes, since, after all, the University admits that it seeks to charge the higher tuition in order to recover costs that state income taxes normally would cover.

I cannot join the remainder of the Court's opinion, however, for it wholly fails to address the criticisms leveled in Justice Rehnquist's dissenting opinion. As Justice Rehnquist makes clear, the class of G–4 aliens is not homogenous: some G–4 aliens are exempt under federal law from state taxes, while other G–4 aliens are not. * * * Thus, I disagree with the Court when it states that the "State may not recoup indirectly from respondents' parents the taxes that the Federal Government has expressly barred the State from collecting," for in fact Congress has not barred the State from collecting state taxes from many G–4 aliens. Accordingly, I conclude that the Supremacy Clause does not prohibit the University from charging out-of-state tuition to those G–4 aliens who are exempted by federal law from federal taxes only.

JUSTICE REHNQUIST, with whom THE CHIEF JUSTICE joins, dissenting.

* * *

Unquestionably, federal power over immigration and naturalization is plenary and exclusive. Our decision in *De Canas v. Bica*, 424 U.S. 351, 96 S.Ct. 933, 47 L.Ed.2d 43 (1976), however, unambiguously forecloses any argument that this power, either unexercised or as manifested in the Immigration and Nationality Act, preempts the field of regulations affecting aliens once federal authorities have admitted them into this country. * * * In *De Canas* the Court also held that Congress' enactment of the Immigration and Nationality Act (INA) was insufficient to oust "harmonious state regulation touching on aliens in general."

Thus, neither Congress' unexercised constitutional power over immigration and naturalization, nor its exercise of that power in passing the INA, precludes the States from enforcing laws and regulations that prove burdensome to aliens. Under our precedents, therefore, state law is invalid only if there is "such actual conflict between the two schemes of regulation that both cannot stand in the same area," *Florida Lime & Avocado Growers, Inc. v. Paul*, [373 U.S. 132,] 141, 83 S.Ct., [1210,] 1217, 10 L.Ed.2d 248 (1963), or if Congress has in some other way unambiguously declared its intention to foreclose the state law in question. In the absence of a conflict, "we are not to conclude that Congress legislated the ouster of [a state law] in the absence of an unambiguous congressional mandate to that effect." *Florida Lime & Avocado Growers*, 373 U.S., at 146–147, 83 S.Ct., at 1219.

Notwithstanding these settled principles, the Court suggests in dicta that any state law which discriminates against lawfully admitted aliens is void, presumably without regard to the strength of the State's justification, if Congress did not contemplate such a law. This standard seems to me clearly to reverse the presumption that normally prevails when state laws are challenged under the Supremacy Clause. * * *

[In *Takahashi v. Fish & Game Comm'n*, 334 U.S. 410, 68 S.Ct. 1138, 92 L.Ed. 1478 (1948); *Truax v. Raich*, 239 U.S. 33, 36 S.Ct. 7, 60 L.Ed. 131 (1915); and *Hines v. Davidowitz*, 312 U.S. 52, 61 S.Ct. 399, 85 L.Ed. 581 (1941);] the Court found either a clear encroachment on exclusive federal power to admit aliens into the country or a clear conflict with a specific congressional purpose. It was with these cases in mind that the Court in *Takahashi* condemned "[s]tate laws which impose discriminatory burdens upon the entrance or residence of aliens lawfully within the United States." 334 U.S., at 419, 68 S.Ct., at 1142. It is most unlikely, therefore, that the Court intended with one stroke of the pen to reverse the normal presumption applicable in cases challenging state enactments under the Supremacy Clause, and to declare such laws invalid without regard to the existence of a conflict with federal statutes or a usurpation of federal power over immigration.

The Court also relies on *Graham v. Richardson*, 403 U.S. 365, 91 S.Ct. 1848, 29 L.Ed.2d 534 (1971), which struck down as a denial of equal protection a California law that withheld welfare benefits from lawfully resident aliens. As an alternative ground, the Court also declared the law invalid as an encroachment on federal power. On the basis of specific federal statutes barring the admission of aliens likely to become public charges, and providing for the deportation of aliens who become public charges because of factors that existed prior to entry, the Court inferred a congressional purpose not "to impose any burden or restriction on aliens who become indigent after their entry into the United States." The Court also concluded, relying on *Truax, supra,* that the law denied indigent aliens the "necessities of life," and therefore "equate[d] with the assertion of a right, inconsistent with federal policy, to deny entrance and abode." The holding in *Graham,* therefore, offers no support for a presumption that *all* state laws burdening aliens conflict with amorphous federal power over immigration.

* * *

The Court relies on two features of federal law. First, it notes that Congress has permitted nonimmigrant aliens holding G–4 visas to establish domicile in the United States. It then reasons that denying these aliens in-state tuition conflicts with Congress' decision. The Court offers no evidence that Congress' intent in permitting respondents to establish "domicile in the United States" has any bearing at all on the tuition available to them at state universities. Federal law does not require the States to make residence or domicile the determinant of their tuition policies, and as the Court recognizes, Maryland has chosen not to do so in the case of nonimmigrant aliens. * * *

The second feature of federal law on which the Court relies consists of certain statutes and treaties that affect the tax liability of G–4 visaholders. The Court considers these statutes and treaties as an amorphous whole and concludes that the University's policy "frustrates" the policies embodied in them. "The State may not recoup indirectly from respondents' parents the taxes that the Federal Government has expressly barred the State from collecting." There are two serious flaws in this argument. First, the Federal Government has not barred the States from collecting taxes from many, if not most, G–4 visaholders. Second, as to those G–4 nonimmigrants who *are* immune from state income taxes by treaty, Maryland's tuition policy cannot fairly be said to conflict with those treaties in a manner requiring its pre-emption.

* * *

The lower courts' principal basis for invalidating Maryland's tuition policy was not the Supremacy Clause, but the Equal Protection Clause. Those courts interpreted the State's policy as a classification based on alienage, and therefore subjected it to "strict scrutiny" on the authority of *Graham v. Richardson*, 403 U.S. 365, 91 S.Ct. 1848, 29 L.Ed.2d 534 (1971), and later cases. In light of several recent decisions, however, it is clear that not every alienage classification is subject to strict scrutiny. In my view, the classification relied upon by the State in this case cannot fairly be called "suspect," and therefore I would ask only whether it rests upon a rational basis. Because I believe it does, I cannot agree with the lower courts that it denies the equal protection of the laws.

* * *

In the vast majority of cases our judicial function permits us to ask only whether the judgment of relevance made by the State is rational. In a very few other cases, we have required that the State pass a more demanding test because of the judgment that the classification drawn by the State is virtually never permissible from a constitutional perspective. Such classifications are deemed "suspect" and strictly scrutinized. Until 1971, only race and national origin had been so classified by the Court.

In *Graham v. Richardson,* the Court added alienage to this select list. Apart from the abbreviated conclusion that "[a]liens as a class are a prime example of a 'discrete and insular' minority," the Court did not elaborate on the justification for "heightened judicial solicitude." Subsequently, the Court observed that aliens, unlike other members of the community, were subject to the particular disadvantage of being unable to vote, and thus were barred from participating formally in the process of self-government. *Hampton v. Mow Sun Wong*, 426 U.S. 88, 102, 96 S.Ct. 1895, 1905, 48 L.Ed.2d 495 (1976). One could infer that rigorous judicial scrutiny normally was necessary because aliens were barred from asserting their interests in the governmental body responsible for imposing burdens upon them.

More recent decisions have established, however, that the political powerlessness of aliens is itself the consequence of distinctions on the basis of alienage that are constitutionally permissible. [Justice Rehnquist discussed cases—in Section B of this chapter—that upheld the exclusion of noncitizens from the states' political and governmental functions.]

If the exclusion of aliens from the political processes is legitimate, as it clearly is, there is reason to doubt whether political powerlessness is any longer a legitimate reason for treating aliens as a "suspect class" deserving of "heightened judicial solicitude." * * * In my view, these decisions merely reflect the judgment that alienage, or the other side of the coin, citizenship, is for certain important state purposes a constitutionally relevant characteristic and therefore cannot always be considered invidious in the same manner as race or national origin.

IV

The State's policy in this case is to provide in-state tuition to residents of the State who are citizens and immigrant aliens lawfully admitted for permanent residence. In-state tuition is not available to certain students, however, regardless of whether they have established residence within the State. Within this class are citizens who are financially dependent either on parents or on a spouse who is not domiciled in the State, as well as citizens who are members of the Armed Forces and have been assigned by the military to attend the University. Also within the class are nonimmigrant aliens, who have not been admitted to this country for permanent residence.

In each case in which the Court has tested state alienage classifications under the Equal Protection Clause, the question has been the extent to which the States could permissibly distinguish between citizens and permanent resident aliens. In this case, however, the question is whether the State can distinguish between two groups, each of which consists of citizens and aliens. For two reasons, the State's classification should not be deemed "suspect" and subjected to strict scrutiny.

First, unlike immigrant aliens, nonimmigrants such as G–4 visaholders are significantly different from citizens in certain important respects. Our previous decisions have emphasized that immigrant aliens have been lawfully admitted to this country for permanent residence and share many of the normal burdens of citizenship, such as the duty to pay taxes and to serve in the Armed Forces. * * *

Second, the State's tuition policy, as it applies to G–4 visaholders, simply cannot be broadly characterized as a classification that discriminates on the basis of alienage. It is more accurately described as a policy that classifies on the basis of financial contribution toward the costs of operating the University. In one class are citizens and permanent resident aliens, all of whom have lived in the State and have contributed to state revenues through the payment of income taxes. * * *

In the other class is an equally mixed group of citizens and aliens. Some of these citizens do not reside in the State and therefore do not pay state taxes. Others do reside in the State, but are financially dependent on parents or a spouse who is domiciled elsewhere and therefore do not help finance the operation of the University through income taxes. Nonimmigrant aliens holding G–4 visas also reside in the State but, like citizens in this class, do not pay state income taxes. To all members of this class the State charges a higher, so-called "out-of-state" tuition, although one that still does not fully cover the cost of education. * * *

Consequently, for either of these reasons, the "strict scrutiny" authorized by *Graham v. Richardson*, even if it is still applicable to discrimination against permanent resident aliens, has no proper application to the State's policy in this case. The only question, therefore, is whether "the State's classification rationally furthers the purpose identified by the State." *Massachusetts Board of Retirement v. Murgia*, 427 U.S. 307, 314, 96 S.Ct. 2562, 2567, 49 L.Ed.2d 520 (1976). The State has articulated several purposes for its policy of denying in-state tuition to nonimmigrant aliens. One purpose is roughly to equalize the cost of higher education borne by those students who do and those who do not financially contribute to the University through income tax payments. The purpose surely is a legitimate one, and I should think it evident that the State's classification rationally furthers that purpose.

* * *

NOTES AND QUESTIONS ON TOLL v. MORENO, EQUAL PROTECTION, AND PREEMPTION

1. Are the different outcomes in *Graham* and *Diaz* attributable to a distinction between state and federal alienage classifications? And if it matters whether a state or the federal government classifies by alienage, *why* does it matter? These questions have prompted debate over whether we should understand *Graham* and *Diaz* as preemption cases or equal protection cases.

In other words, were the Arizona and Pennsylvania welfare requirements constitutionally defective because they either conflicted with federal law and its objectives or were state laws in an area reserved for federal decisionmaking, or did the substance of those requirements violate equal protection regardless of their source? In *Graham*, for example, how are we to understand Part III's opening sentence, which explains that the area of federal-state relations yields an "additional reason" to strike down the state statutes?

Does footnote 16 in the *Toll* majority opinion help you formulate answers to these questions?

2. If, under either preemption or equal protection, states have less authority than the federal government to adopt alienage classifications, do states have *any* authority to treat citizens and noncitizens differently? How far do *Graham*, *Diaz*, and *Toll*, taken together, go to reduce state authority?

Footnote 17 of the majority opinion in *Toll* and footnote 24 in *Mathews v. Diaz* recognize that a state can constitutionally exclude a lawfully present noncitizen from political and governmental functions, such as voting or public offices. Does *Toll* say that outside this exception, every distinction between citizens and lawfully present noncitizens is unconstitutional if it "imposes additional burdens not contemplated by Congress." When does a state law that treats lawfully present noncitizens differently *not* impose such an "additional burden"?

3. Would it matter if the alienage classifications were benefits rather than burdens? For example, would it be constitutional for a state to give cash grants to new immigrants, in order to aid their integration into American society? Would it be constitutional for a state to organize and finance classes to help permanent residents prepare for naturalization? Does this suggest a distinction between the broad category of alienage *classification* and a more constitutionally suspect subset of alienage *discrimination*? But what would justify drawing such a distinction? Is the line between burdens and benefits always clear?

4. What would the Court have said if it had reached the equal protection issue in *Toll*? What would Justice Rehnquist say?

2. PUBLIC BENEFITS, IMMIGRATION, AND CITIZENSHIP

What basic principles—constitutional law and policy considerations—should guide legislators as they decide eligibility for public benefits? To explore these questions, we turn now to the rules for federal welfare eligibility.

a. The 1996 Welfare Reform Act

Before 1996, the major federally-funded public benefits programs were open to citizens, lawful permanent residents, and noncitizens who were "otherwise permanently residing in the United States under color of law" (PRUCOL). PRUCOL was defined somewhat differently under the regulations for different programs. The concept generally excluded unauthorized migrants, but even they were considered PRUCOL for most programs if they were in the United States "with the knowledge and permission of the Immigration and Naturalization Service and the agency does not contemplate enforcing [their] departure." *See, e.g.,* 20 C.F.R. § 416.1618 (Supplemental Security Income [SSI]).

In August 1996, Congress enacted major welfare reform legislation, the Personal Responsibility and Work Opportunity Reconciliation Act, Pub. L. 104–193, 110 Stat. 2105 ("the Welfare Act" or PRWORA). It generally limited all welfare recipients to five years of benefits and required them to work within two years of receiving aid. Abandoning the PRUCOL language, the Welfare Act barred undocumented noncitizens from nonemergency assistance programs. In contrast, some "qualified aliens," as defined in the Act, could receive assistance, but subject to significant restrictions, as explained in *City of Chicago v. Shalala*, 189 F.3d 598 (7th Cir. 1999), *cert. denied*, 529 U.S. 1036, 120 S.Ct. 1530, 146 L.Ed.2d 345 (2000):

> * * * Section 402(a) of the Act provides that, subject to certain exceptions, "qualified alien[s]" are not eligible to receive SSI or Food Stamp benefits. As defined in § 431 of the Act, qualified aliens include permanent resident aliens, asylees, refugees, aliens who are paroled into the United States, aliens whose deportation is being withheld, aliens who have been granted conditional entry, certain Cuban and Haitian entrants, and certain "battered" aliens.

Id. at 600–01. Besides SSI and food stamps, the Welfare Act also barred anyone who became a "qualified alien" on or after August 22, 1996, from Medicaid and any other "federal means-tested public benefits" for five years. *See* § 403, 8 U.S.C.A. § 1613.

These bars did not apply to permanent residents who had worked for 40 quarters, some recipients who were 65 or older, under 18, or blind and disabled, certain refugees, asylees, noncitizens granted withholding of removal, veterans and active duty military personnel and their families, and some other exempt groups. Nor did the bars apply to some programs, including emergency Medicaid, child nutrition programs, Head Start, and community programs that provide in-kind assistance (domestic violence protection services, homeless shelters, food banks, and the like). *See* § 403(c)(2).

After the five-year bar expires, immigrants with financial sponsors generally stay ineligible for public assistance due to provisions that deem a sponsor's income to be the immigrant's for deciding eligibility. Deeming (also discussed in Chapter Seven, p. 601) generally continues until the noncitizen naturalizes or has worked 40 quarters without receiving federal means-tested benefits. *See* § 421, 8 U.S.C.A. § 1631. At the time of passage, the Act was slated to save the federal government $54 billion in the first six years, 44 percent of which was expected to be the direct result of cutting benefits for noncitizens. *See* Fix & Passel, The Scope and Impact of Welfare Reform's Immigrant Provisions (Urban Institute 2002).

The constitutionality of these benefits cutoffs was challenged in several cases. All upheld the statute. In *City of Chicago*, for example, the individual plaintiffs were lawful immigrants who were receiving or were eligible to receive federal SSI and food stamps in August 1996. Their co-plaintiff, the city of Chicago, claimed that the cutoffs imposed substantial financial burdens on it. Rejecting plaintiffs' argument that it was uncon-stitutional to take federal benefits away from lawful immigrants who had been eligible, the court first found that the controlling precedent was *Mathews v. Diaz*, not *Graham v. Richardson*:

> [I]n *Mathews v. Diaz*, 426 U.S. 67, 96 S.Ct. 1883, 48 L.Ed.2d 478 (1976), the Court made clear that the standard of scrutiny applied to state legislation in *Richardson* does not govern judicial review of federal legislation involving alienage. * * * Although the Court did not adopt explicitly the "rational basis" standard of scrutiny, it in effect applied rational basis review, upholding the legislation because it was not "wholly irrational." The Court explicitly distinguished the *Richardson* case and explained that state and federal alienage classifi-cations must be treated differently because of Congress' plenary authority to regulate the conditions of entry and residence of aliens. In short, we believe that the *Diaz* case is directly on point on the issue of what level of scrutiny should be applied to Congressional regulation of aliens' welfare benefits.

Id. at 603–04. Applying rational basis review, the court upheld the statute:

> * * * First, Congress stated that the Act's provisions are intend-ed to foster the legitimate governmental purpose of encouraging aliens' self-sufficiency. * * *
>
> * * * In Congress' view, such aliens ought to rely on their families, sponsors, or private organizations for support, rather than on the public welfare rolls. The statute is reasonably related to that goal. Indeed, even if some aliens have no access to support from these alternate sources, the citizenship requirement is still rationally relat-

ed to the goal of encouraging aliens to rely on private, not public, resources to meet their needs.

Congress has stated its policy that "the availability of public benefits not constitute an incentive for immigration to the United States." 8 U.S.C. § 1601(2)(B). Although reasonable individuals certainly can disagree on the wisdom of controlling immigration through such a policy, we must conclude that the provisions of the Welfare Reform Act are rationally related to the legitimate governmental goal of discouraging immigration that is motivated by the availability of welfare benefits. * * *

Section 1612 also declares that Congress wanted to preserve the public fisc by reducing the rising costs of operating federal benefits programs. * * * [W]e cannot say that it was irrational for Congress to decide to achieve its budget objectives by eliminating aliens from these programs. * * *

The Executive Branch, defending the constitutionality of the statute before this court, offers a further justification not found in Congress' statement of policy. It submits that the Act's provisions are rationally related to the legitimate governmental purpose of encouraging naturalization. The Act gives resident aliens in need of welfare benefits a strong economic incentive to become naturalized citizens. * * * This court and other courts of appeals have recognized the legitimacy of this governmental interest in encouraging naturalization. The Supreme Court assumed in *Hampton v. Mow Sun Wong*, 426 U.S. 88, 96 S.Ct. 1895, 48 L.Ed.2d 495 (1976), that the "national interest in providing an incentive for aliens to become naturalized" would justify a citizenship requirement for federal civil service employment. *Id.* at 105. We cannot say, therefore, that it would be irrational for Congress to conclude that restricting the availability of welfare benefits to aliens would provide incentive for aliens to seek naturalization. As we have already mentioned, rational basis scrutiny does not require a perfect fit between this legitimate governmental purpose and the means chosen to achieve it.

The plaintiffs submit finally that the Act fails rational basis review because it was motivated by impermissible animus toward noncitizens. We disagree. As the Supreme Court made clear in *Diaz*, "it is obvious that Congress has no constitutional duty to provide all aliens with the welfare benefits provided to citizens." *Diaz*, 426 U.S. at 82, 96 S.Ct. 1883. * * *

Finally, we note that the Welfare Reform Act also contains a number of exceptions to its general exclusion of aliens from the welfare programs. Like the situation that confronted the Supreme Court in *Diaz*, therefore, we have a statutory scheme that, strictly speaking, distinguishes not between citizens and aliens but rather among subclasses within the alien population. * * *

Id. at 606–08. For similar reasoning, see *Aleman v. Glickman*, 217 F.3d 1191, 1197–1202 (9th Cir. 2000); *Rodriguez v. United States*, 169 F.3d 1342, 1346–53 (11th Cir. 1999).

Notice that two of the reasons advanced by the court in *Shalala* would appear to contradict each other. One reason was to save money. Another reason was to encourage naturalization. Yet naturalization of permanent residents would eliminate the intended fiscal savings. Does this apparent contradiction mean that the statute lacks a rational basis?

Since 1996, Congress has modified the original bars several times. *See* Pub. L. 105–33, 111 Stat. 251 (1997); Pub. L. No. 105–185, 112 Stat. 523 (1998); Pub. L. No. 105–306, 112 Stat. 2926 (1998). In 2002, Congress restored food stamps to (1) new permanent residents, refugees, asylees, and certain battered spouses and children after they have resided in the United States for five years; (2) all "qualified alien" children regardless of arrival date; and (3) noncitizens lawfully residing in the United States and receiving benefits under specified disability-based programs. *See* § 4401, Pub. L. 107–171, 116 Stat. 134. These changes have combined to restore SSI to virtually all noncitizens receiving benefits on August 22, 1996, and restored food stamps to most noncitizens receiving benefits on that date and to future permanent residents after five years. Undocumented noncitizens remain ineligible for both SSI and food stamps.

b. The Significance of Citizenship

As a way of evaluating federal welfare eligibility, and more generally as a way of thinking about distinctions that lawmakers might draw between citizens and noncitizens, first consider this argument for including permanent residents within the circle of membership:

> [I]t is never explained why *citizenship* is the appropriate category for the development of a communitarian ethos. Why wouldn't we seek the formation of a sense of reciprocal obligations among all persons living and working within the territory of the United States? We know, as an empirical matter, that strong bonds between citizens and resident aliens exist. These ties, based on familial relationship, ethnicity, religion, race, or location may be far more powerful than those that can be fostered among citizens who share nothing but American nationality.

Aleinikoff, *Citizens, Aliens, Membership and the Constitution*, 7 Const. Comm. 9, 30–31 (1990). *See also* Legomsky, *Immigration, Federalism, and the Welfare State*, 42 UCLA L. Rev. 1453, 1462–68 (1995). *Cf.* Scaperlanda, *Who is My Neighbor?: An Essay on Immigrants, Welfare Reform, and the Constitution*, 29 Conn. L. Rev. 1587, 1599 (1997) (arguing that discrimination against permanent residents "violates a Judeo–Christian and specifically Catholic Christian perspective of our constitutional heritage").

(i) A Comparative Side–Glance: The European Union

As an example of an approach that deemphasizes citizenship, the European Union adopted a Council Directive in 2003 that addressed "the status of third-country nationals who are long-term residents." ("Third-country" nationals means nationals of a country other than the host country or other EU country.) The Directive, which entered into force on February 12, 2004, provides:

Article 11: Equal treatment

1. Long-term residents shall enjoy equal treatment with nationals as regards:

(a) access to employment and self-employed activity, provided such activities do not entail even occasional involvement in the exercise of public authority, and conditions of employment and working conditions, including conditions regarding dismissal and remuneration;

(b) education and vocational training, including study grants in accordance with national law;

(c) recognition of professional diplomas, certificates and other qualifications, in accordance with the relevant national procedures;

(d) social security, social assistance and social protection as defined by national law;

(e) tax benefits;

(f) access to goods and services and the supply of goods and services made available to the public and to procedures for obtaining housing;

(g) freedom of association and affiliation and membership of an organisation representing workers or employers or of any organisation whose members are engaged in a specific occupation, including the benefits conferred by such organisations, without prejudice to the national provisions on public policy and public security;

(h) free access to the entire territory of the Member State concerned, within the limits provided for by the national legislation for reasons of security.

2. With respect to the provisions of paragraph 1, points (b), (d), (e), (f) and (g), the Member State concerned may restrict equal treatment to cases where the registered or usual place of residence of the long-term resident, or that of family members for whom he/she claims benefits, lies within the territory of the Member State concerned.

3. Member States may restrict equal treatment with nationals in the following cases:

(a) Member States may retain restrictions to access to employment or self-employed activities in cases where, in accordance with existing national or Community legislation, these activities are reserved to nationals, EU or EEA citizens;

(b) Member States may require proof of appropriate language proficiency for access to education and training. Access to university may be subject to the fulfilment of specific educational prerequisites.

4. Member States may limit equal treatment in respect of social assistance and social protection to core benefits.

Member States may also decide to grant equal treatment with regard to areas not covered in paragraph 1.

Council Directive 2003/109/EC of 25 November 2003 concerning the status of third-country nationals who are long-term residents, Official Journal L 016, 23/01/2004 P. 0044–0053.

The official commentary to the Proposal that led to this Directive set out this basic rationale for equal treatment of long-term residents:

> [I]t is ... essential to create a welcoming society and to recognise that integration is a two-way process involving adaptation on the part of both the immigrant and of the host society. The European Union is by its very nature a pluralistic society enriched by a variety of cultural and social traditions, which will in the future become even more diverse. There must, therefore be respect for cultural and social differences but also of our fundamental shared principles and values: respect for human rights and human dignity, appreciation of the value of pluralism and the recognition that membership of society is based on a series of rights but brings with it a number of responsibilities for all of its members be they nationals or migrants. The provision of equality with respect to conditions of work and access to services, together with the granting of civic and political rights to longer-term migrant residents brings with it such responsibilities and promotes integration.

¶ 5.1, Proposal for a Council Directive concerning the status of third-country nationals who are long-term residents, Brussels, 13.3.2001 COM(2001) 127 final 2001/0074 (CNS) (quoting Communication From the Commission to the Council and the European Parliament on a Community Integration Policy, Commission of the European Communities, Brussels, 22.11.2000 COM(2000)) 757 final.

On the provisions most analogous to those at issue in *Graham*, *Diaz*, and *Shalala*, the official commentary to the Proposal explained further:

> (d) Long-term residents must have the same social protection entitlements as nationals. This would include family allowances, retirement pensions, sickness insurance and unemployment benefits.

> (e) All forms of social assistance provided by the State for its nationals must be available to long-term residents. This would include the minimum income support or retirement pensions and free healthcare.

> (f) The social benefits covered here are the economic or cultural benefits given in the Member States by public authorities or private

bodies * * *. They include concessionary public transport fares, reduced admission charges for cultural and other events and subsidised meals for children of low-income families. The tax reliefs are those given by the State: long-term residents must be eligible for them on the same terms as nationals.

Proposal for a Council Directive concerning the status of third-country nationals who are long-term residents, *supra*, at 18–19.

(ii) Distinguishing Citizens From Noncitizens

How might we think about drawing lines between citizens and noncitizens? The next excerpt identifies several answers to this question in U.S. law and policy by drawing on the framework, introduced in Chapter Seven, p. 669, that choices in immigration and immigrant policy may reflect immigration as contract, affiliation, or transition.

HIROSHI MOTOMURA, AMERICANS IN WAITING: THE LOST STORY OF IMMIGRATION AND CITIZENSHIP IN THE UNITED STATES*

52–53, 85–87, 154–55, 199–200 (2006).

The welfare law's preamble declared: "Self-sufficiency has been a basic principle of United States immigration law since this country's earliest immigration statutes." Along the same lines, President Bill Clinton explained, "when an immigrant comes to America, . . . they have to promise that they won't try to get on welfare and they won't take any public money." The Senate report had similar words: "immigrants make a promise to the American people that they will not become a financial burden," and "It was only on the basis of the assurance of the immigrant and the sponsor that the immigrant would not at any time become a public charge that the immigrant was allowed in this country." And in the debate over the immigration law changes in 1996, proponents of binding [sponsor] affidavits made a contract-based argument that they were needed to enforce each immigrant's promise of financial self-sufficiency.

But the debates about welfare eligibility and affidavits also made clear that contract-based arguments do not always disfavor noncitizens. It all depends on the terms of the contract. * * * [I]mmigration as contract can also be cited *against* the welfare bars and the affidavit requirement. * * * When supporters of the welfare bars and affidavit invoked contract-based arguments, opponents countered that *taking away* public benefits was the real breach of promise. Congress was changing the rules of the game, disappointing the settled expectations of lawful immigrants who had arrived when they were eligible for the safety net. * * *

Immigration as contract also played an important role in shaping litigation that challenged the constitutionality of the 1996 welfare bars.

The plaintiffs were only the lawful immigrants with the strongest constitutional claims: those already in the United States and receiving welfare in August 1996. No lawsuit raised the constitutional claims of future lawful immigrants. The plaintiffs' acquiescence in the validity of a cutoff date reflected their acquiescence in casting the controversy in contract terms.

* * *

Supporters of [the post–1996] restorations also drew on immigration as contract and the rhetoric of broken promises. Thus Senator Frank Lautenberg: "Congress pulled the rug out from under these people and eliminated their disability benefits." One newspaper editorial argued for restorations: "More and more Republicans are starting to publicly agree that the welfare reform bill goes too far in punishing poor and elderly legal immigrants who had every right to believe American promises that they would not be left homeless and hungry." Opponents of the restorations countered with their own version of promises, as in one editorial: "Noncitizens who reap welfare benefits and their sponsors are breaking their pledge to the American people—the people who granted them the privilege of coming to the U.S.... The government did not promise to feed and care for the struggling immigrant; the sponsor did." This, too, shows the strong influence of immigration as contract in alienage law.

* * * But immigration as affiliation played just as large a role * * *. Affiliation shaped Congress's decision first to enact the 1996 bars, then the legal challenges, and later the laws restoring eligibility for some noncitizens. Like contract, affiliation was crucial to arguments on both sides. In the original legislation, for example, noncitizen eligibility depended partly on ties; the bars never applied to noncitizens who had worked ten years in the United States without receiving federal welfare.

Affiliation next became the conceptual basis for the many court decisions that sustained the bars as constitutional. Typical is the 1999 federal appeals court decision in *City of Chicago v. Shalala*. * * *

Like the Supreme Court in *Diaz*, the appeals court in *City of Chicago* saw the issue not as a line between citizens and noncitizens, but between two groups of noncitizens. Then, to explain the constitutionality of the line that Congress had drawn, *City of Chicago* relied heavily on ties and immigration as affiliation. Congress could rationally extend benefits to noncitizens who had made "special contributions to this country," either to "reward such service or to encourage other aliens to make similar contributions in the future." Other federal court decisions that rejected similar constitutional challenges also emphasized ties to distinguish some noncitizens from others. And in Congress, many of the critics of the 1996 cutbacks made affiliation-based arguments that Congress had not recognized ties adequately. These arguments led to the restoration of many of the benefits taken away in 1996.

* * * Immigration as affiliation * * * says that new arrivals have only minimal ties but should be treated more like citizens as they build a life in the United States. Affiliation-based equality is to be earned. Permanent residence gradually resembles citizenship but does not equal it, although a few advocates of immigration as affiliation urge what amounts to automatic naturalization of longtime permanent residents. Immigration as affiliation recognizes that a group of newly arrived lawful immigrants will always be treated unlike citizens, but addresses the problem of defining equality in immigration and citizenship by letting individual lawful immigrants gradually earn near-equality through an approximation of citizenship.

* * *

In contrast, immigration as transition means treating lawful immigrants as Americans in waiting from their first day in this country. This means weakening distinctions between them and citizens. Generally, taking transition seriously means that equality is presumed and that lawful immigrants should be treated like citizens until they have been here long enough to naturalize. As a corollary, immigration as transition also allows sharper distinctions between prenaturalization lawful immigrants and other noncitizens, whether lawfully or unlawfully present.

The real difference between affiliation and transition thus lies in their end points. Affiliation works gradually toward equal citizenship but does not get all the way there. In this sense, immigration as affiliation represents a way to treat lawful immigrants well without citizenship. Though immigration as transition gives new lawful immigrants immediate near-equality with citizens, that is not transition's conceptual essence. Rather, immigration as transition recognizes that even the best treatment of lawful immigrants is always something less than citizenship, and instead tries to give them the best chance to reach complete equality in the future through the acquisition of citizenship itself.

This basic difference between affiliation and transition flips the relevance of time. Affiliation gives a lawful immigrant nothing on arrival, but gradually confers a favored status that approaches but never equals citizenship. Transition protects them during an earlier period—when they are Americans in waiting—that starts with arrival and ends with eligibility to naturalize.

* * *

[A]ffiliation-based benefits and protections for longtime lawful immigrants reduce naturalization incentives. For example, a lawful immigrant currently gains Medicare and food stamp eligibility after five years, but at that point he has satisfied the naturalization residency requirement. A law that denies him Medicare and food stamp eligibility even after five years would give him a tangible incentive to naturalize. But if he can get the same benefits without naturalizing, he may decide not to. Immigration as transition produces a very different incentive pattern, because its logic confines near-equal treatment of citizens and lawful immigrants to the prenaturalization years. Once a lawful immigrant does not naturalize, he can no longer invoke transition-based rationales for treatment as an American in waiting. The prospect of losing near-equal treatment can create significant naturalization incentives.

If transition were the *only* rationale for protecting lawful immigrants, then those who do not naturalize would suffer a precipitous drop in protection. This threat might be enough to turn incentives into coercion. But transition is not the only rationale for protecting lawful immigrants, as long as immigration as affiliation and immigration as contract offer complementary protections for non-naturalizing permanent residents. * * *

NOTES AND QUESTIONS ON THE SIGNIFICANCE OF CITIZENSHIP

1. Would the EU Directive make sense as a set of guidelines for treatment of permanent residents in the United States? Why or why not?

2. As a distinct alternative to what Motomura calls "immigration as affiliation," Linda Bosniak has analyzed what she calls "ethical territoriality": that regardless of acquired ties or stake, the mere fact of a person's territorial presence should serve as the basis for rights and recognition. This perspective would support significant claims by a broader group of unauthorized migrants. *See* Bosniak, *Being Here: Ethical Territoriality and the Rights of Immigrants*, 8 Theoretical Inquiries L. 389 (2007).

3. Does the option to naturalize make the 1996 welfare bars more justifiable? What about those who cannot naturalize, because they cannot afford the application fees, or because they cannot pass the English-language and civics test? More fundamentally, does it trouble you that access to welfare benefits—not deeper attachments to the United States—is the primary motivation for many permanent residents to naturalize?

If this troubles you, then should you reject a greater role for immigration as transition—*i.e.*, for aiding integration by treating permanent residents like citizens until they can naturalize? After all, such policies would give them incentives to naturalize, but those incentives arguably dilute the meaning of citizenship. Or do such policies give meaning to citizenship by making it worthwhile to become a citizen?

4. For thoughtful discussions of the value of citizenship, see Schuck, *Membership in the Liberal Polity: The Devaluation of American Citizenship*, 3 Geo. Immig. L.J. 1 (1989); Abraham, *The Good of Banality?: The Emergence of Cost–Benefit Analysis and Proportionality in the Treatment of Aliens in the U.S. and Germany*, 4 Citizenship Studies 237 (2000).

3. LIMITS ON FEDERAL ALIENAGE LAWS

After *Mathews v. Diaz* and the 1996 Welfare Act cases, when (if ever) is a federal alienage classification unconstitutional? For one answer, see the next case. It was decided the same day as *Diaz*, with Justice Stevens writing for the Court in both cases.

HAMPTON v. MOW SUN WONG

Supreme Court of the United States, 1976.
426 U.S. 88, 96 S.Ct. 1895, 48 L.Ed.2d 495.

MR. JUSTICE STEVENS delivered the opinion of the Court.

Five aliens, lawfully and permanently residing in the United States, brought this litigation to challenge the validity of a policy, adopted and enforced by the Civil Service Commission and certain other federal agencies, which excludes all persons except American citizens and natives of American Samoa from employment in most positions subject to their respective jurisdictions. * * *

Each of the five plaintiffs was denied federal employment solely because of his or her alienage. They were all Chinese residents of San Francisco and each was qualified for an available job. * * *

* * * In their brief, the petitioners rephrased the question presented as "(w)hether the Civil Service Commission's regulation . . . is within the constitutional powers of Congress and the President and hence not a constitutionally forbidden discrimination against aliens."

This phrasing of the question assumes that the Commission regulation is one that was mandated by the Congress, the President, or both. On this assumption, the petitioners advance alternative arguments to justify the discrimination as an exercise of the plenary federal power over immigration and naturalization. First, the petitioners argue that the equal protection aspect of the Due Process Clause of the Fifth Amendment is wholly inapplicable to the exercise of federal power over aliens, and therefore no justification for the rule is necessary. Alternatively, the petitioners argue that the Fifth Amendment imposes only a slight burden of justification on the Federal Government, and that such a burden is easily met by several factors not considered by the District Court or the Court of Appeals. Before addressing these arguments, we first discuss certain limitations which the Due Process Clause places on the power of the Federal Government to classify persons subject to its jurisdiction.

The federal sovereign, like the States, must govern impartially. The concept of equal justice under law is served by the Fifth Amendment's guarantee of due process, as well as by the Equal Protection Clause of the Fourteenth Amendment. Although both Amendments require the same type of analysis, the Court of Appeals correctly stated that the two protections are not always coextensive. Not only does the language of the two Amendments differ, but more importantly, there may be overriding national interests which justify selective federal legislation that would be unacceptable for an individual State. On the other hand, when a federal rule is applicable to only a limited territory, such as the District of Columbia, or an insular possession, and when there is no special national interest involved, the Due Process Clause has been construed as having the same significance as the Equal Protection Clause.

* * *

We do not agree * * * with the petitioners' primary submission that the federal power over aliens is so plenary that any agent of the National Government may arbitrarily subject all resident aliens to different substantive rules from those applied to citizens. We recognize that the petitioners' argument draws support from both the federal and the political character of the power over immigration and naturalization. Nevertheless, countervailing considerations require rejection of the extreme position advanced by the petitioners.

The rule enforced by the Commission has its impact on an identifiable class of persons who, entirely apart from the rule itself, are already subject to disadvantages not shared by the remainder of the community.[22] Aliens are not entitled to vote and, as alleged in the complaint, are often handicapped by a lack of familiarity with our language and customs. The added disadvantage resulting from the enforcement of the rule—ineligibility for employment in a major sector of the economy—is of sufficient significance to be characterized as a deprivation of an interest in liberty. Indeed, we deal with a rule which deprives a discrete class of persons of an interest in liberty on a wholesale basis. By reason of the Fifth Amendment, such a deprivation must be accompanied by due process. It follows that some judicial scrutiny of the deprivation is mandated by the Constitution.

Respondents argue that this scrutiny requires invalidation of the Commission rule under traditional equal protection analysis. It is true that our cases establish that the Due Process Clause of the Fifth Amendment authorizes that type of analysis of federal rules and therefore that the Clause has a substantive as well as a procedural aspect. However, it is not necessary to resolve respondents' substantive claim, if a narrower inquiry discloses that essential procedures have not been followed.

When the Federal Government asserts an overriding national interest as justification for a discriminatory rule which would violate the Equal Protection Clause if adopted by a State, due process requires that there be a legitimate basis for presuming that the rule was actually intended to serve that interest. If the agency which promulgates the rule has direct responsibility for fostering or protecting that interest, it may reasonably be presumed that the asserted interest was the actual predicate for the rule. That presumption would, of course, be fortified by an appropriate statement of reasons identifying the relevant interest. Alternatively, if the rule were expressly mandated by the Congress or the President, we might presume that any interest which might rationally be served by the rule did in fact give rise to its adoption.

---

22. Some of these disadvantages stem directly from the Constitution itself, see *Sugarman v. Dougall*, 413 U.S., at 651–653, 93 S.Ct., at 2862–2863, 37 L.Ed.2d, at 865–866 (Rehnquist, J., dissenting). The legitimacy of the delineation of the affected class buttresses the conclusion that it is "a 'discrete and insular' minority," see *In re Griffiths*, 413 U.S., at 721, 93 S.Ct., at 2854, 37 L.Ed.2d, at 915 and, of course is consistent with the premise that the class is one whose members suffer special disabilities.

In this case the petitioners have identified several interests which the Congress or the President might deem sufficient to justify the exclusion of noncitizens from the federal service. They argue, for example, that the broad exclusion may facilitate the President's negotiation of treaties with foreign powers by enabling him to offer employment opportunities to citizens of a given foreign country in exchange for reciprocal concessions—an offer he could not make if those aliens were already eligible for federal jobs. Alternatively, the petitioners argue that reserving the federal service for citizens provides an appropriate incentive to aliens to qualify for naturalization and thereby to participate more effectively in our society. They also point out that the citizenship requirement has been imposed in the United States with substantial consistency for over 100 years and accords with international law and the practice of most foreign countries. Finally, they correctly state that the need for undivided loyalty in certain sensitive positions clearly justifies a citizenship requirement in at least some parts of the federal service, and that the broad exclusion serves the valid administrative purpose of avoiding the trouble and expense of classifying those positions which properly belong in executive or sensitive categories.

The difficulty with all of these arguments except the last is that they do not identify any interest which can reasonably be assumed to have influenced the Civil Service Commission, the Postal Service, the General Service Administration, or the Department of Health, Education, and Welfare in the administration of their respective responsibilities or, specifically, in the decision to deny employment to the respondents in this litigation. We may assume with the petitioners that if the Congress or the President had expressly imposed the citizenship requirement, it would be justified by the national interest in providing an incentive for aliens to become naturalized, or possibly even as providing the President with an expendable token for treaty negotiating purposes; but we are not willing to presume that the Chairman of the Civil Service Commission, or any of the other original defendants, was deliberately fostering an interest so far removed from his normal responsibilities. * * *

It is the business of the Civil Service Commission to adopt and enforce regulations which will best promote the efficiency of the federal civil service. That agency has no responsibility for foreign affairs, for treaty negotiations, for establishing immigration quotas or conditions of entry, or for naturalization policies. Indeed, it is not even within the responsibility of the Commission to be concerned with the economic consequences of permitting or prohibiting the participation by aliens in employment opportunities in different parts of the national market. On the contrary, the Commission performs a limited and specific function.

The only concern of the Civil Service Commission is the promotion of an efficient federal service. In general it is fair to assume that its goal would be best served by removing unnecessary restrictions on the eligibility of qualified applicants for employment. With only one exception, the interests which the petitioners have put forth as supporting the Commission regulation at issue in this case are not matters which are properly the business of the Commission. That one exception is the administrative desirability of having one simple rule excluding all noncitizens when it is manifest that citizenship is an appropriate and legitimate requirement for some important and sensitive positions. Arguably, therefore, administrative convenience may provide a rational basis for the general rule.

For several reasons that justification is unacceptable in this case. The Civil Service Commission, like other administrative agencies, has an obligation to perform its responsibilities with some degree of expertise, and to make known the reasons for its important decisions. There is nothing in the record before us, or in matter of which we may properly take judicial notice, to indicate that the Commission actually made any considered evaluation of the relative desirability of a simple exclusionary rule on the one hand, or the value to the service of enlarging the pool of eligible employees on the other. Nor can we reasonably infer that the administrative burden of establishing the job classifications for which citizenship is an appropriate requirement would be a particularly onerous task for an expert in personnel matters; indeed, the Postal Service apparently encountered no particular difficulty in making such a classification. Of greater significance, however, is the quality of the interest at stake. Any fair balancing of the public interest in avoiding the wholesale deprivation of employment opportunities caused by the Commission's indiscriminate policy, as opposed to what may be nothing more than a hypothetical justification, requires rejection of the argument of administrative convenience in this case.

In sum, assuming without deciding that the national interests identified by the petitioners would adequately support an explicit determination by Congress or the President to exclude all noncitizens from the federal service, we conclude that those interests cannot provide an acceptable rationalization for such a determination by the Civil Service Commission. * * * By broadly denying this class substantial opportunities for employment, the Civil Service Commission rule deprives its members of an aspect of liberty. Since these residents were admitted as a result of decisions made by the Congress and the President, implemented by the Immigration and Naturalization Service acting under the Attorney General of the United States, due process requires that the decision to impose that deprivation of an important liberty be made either at a comparable level of government or, if it is to be permitted to be made by the Civil Service Commission, that it be justified by reasons which are properly the concern of that agency. We hold that § 338.101(a) of the Civil Service Commission Regulations has deprived these respondents of liberty without due process of law and is therefore invalid.

* * *

Mr. Justice Brennan, with whom Mr. Justice Marshall joins, concurring.

I join the Court's opinion with the understanding that there are reserved the equal protection questions that would be raised by congressional or Presidential enactment of a bar on employment of aliens by the Federal Government.

MR. JUSTICE REHNQUIST, with whom THE CHIEF JUSTICE, MR. JUSTICE WHITE, and MR. JUSTICE BLACKMUN join, dissenting.

* * *

[The majority's] holding overlooks the basic principle that a decision to exclude aliens from the civil service is a political decision reserved to Congress, the wisdom of which may not be challenged in the courts. Once it is determined that the agency in question was properly delegated the power by Congress to make decisions regarding citizenship of prospective civil servants, then the reasons for which that power was exercised are as foreclosed from judicial scrutiny as if Congress had made the decision itself. The fact that Congress has delegated a power does not provide a back door through which to attack a policy which would otherwise have been immune from attack.

For this Court to hold that the agency chosen by Congress, through the President, to effectuate its policies, has "no responsibility" in that area is to interfere in an area in which the Court itself clearly has "no responsibility": the organization of the Executive Branch. Congress, through the President, obviously gave responsibility in this area to the Civil Service Commission. The wisdom of that delegation is not for us to evaluate. * * *

* * *

The Rest of the Story

Soon after the Supreme Court decided *Mow Sun Wong*, President Ford issued Executive Order No. 11935, which limited the federal civil service to U.S. citizens and nationals. Lower courts upheld the Order. *See, e.g., Mow Sun Wong v. Campbell*, 626 F.2d 739, 744–45 (9th Cir. 1980), *cert. denied*, 450 U.S. 959, 101 S.Ct. 1419, 67 L.Ed.2d 384 (1981).

Documents in the Gerald R. Ford Library provide a fascinating glimpse into the process by which the Civil Service Commission's order, once invalidated by the Supreme Court, reemerged as an Executive Order. Of particular interest is a memorandum from the General Counsel of the Office of Management and Budget to the White House when the matter came before President Ford. This excerpt briefly discusses comments from various federal agencies:

> [The Civil Service Commission (CSC)] suggested various reasons related to the national interest which might serve as justification for the issuance of [the] order. Agency comments, although generally

favoring or having no objection to such an order, indicate that CSC's suggested justifications (*e.g.,* need for undivided loyalty; consistency with the practices of foreign states) are more apparent than real. Further, the Postal Service advises that its recent practice of employing aliens in nonsensitive and nonpolicy-making positions has not presented any policy difficulties. Nevertheless, there is a widespread visceral feeling that Government jobs should be reserved for citizens, at least where there are qualified citizen applicants.

The Department of Justice is of the opinion that the Congress, pursuant to its constitutional authority over immigration, has the authority to broadly prohibit aliens from employment in the competitive civil service. Although the Supreme Court left open the question whether the President could exclude aliens from the competitive service, there are Presidential concerns (*e.g.,* foreign policy) which would lend some support to [a] Presidential order barring aliens from government employment. The Department of Justice concludes, based on the *Wong* decision, that an Executive order barring aliens would probably be upheld by a divided Supreme Court.

Memorandum from William N. Nichols, General Counsel, Office of Management and Budget, to Robert D. Linden, White House Chief Executive Clerk, Aug. 30, 1976 (on file, Gerald R. Ford Library, Ann Arbor, Michigan).

What does this memorandum tell you about the value of the Court's apparent insistence that an institutionally competent unit of the federal government articulate any federal interests offered in support of an alienage classification?

EXERCISE: FARM LOANS

A federal statute reads as follows:

The Secretary [of Agriculture] is authorized to make and insure loans under this subchapter to farmers and ranchers in the United States, and to farm cooperatives and private domestic corporations, partnerships, joint operations, trusts, and limited liability companies that are controlled by farmers and ranchers and engaged primarily and directly in farming or ranching in the United States, subject to the conditions specified in this section. To be eligible for such loans, applicants who are individuals, or, in the case of cooperatives, corporations, partnerships, joint operations, trusts, and limited liability companies, individuals holding a majority interest such entity, must be citizens of the United States.

Antonio Lopez has been a permanent resident of the United States since 1968, but he has never applied for naturalization. His application for a farm operating loan under this statute has been denied because he is not a U.S. citizen. What policy arguments can you muster to persuade your Congressional delegation that this citizenship requirement is not sound policy? How might you argue that this statute is unconstitutional? What are the best counter-arguments at both policy and constitutional levels?

4. BLURRING THE FEDERAL–STATE LINE

For lawfully present noncitizens, the 1996 Welfare Act gave states new authority to decide eligibility for jointly funded federal-state programs (*e.g.*, TANF, non-emergency Medicaid), and for state-funded public benefits. *See* § 412, 8 U.S.C.A. § 1622. In fact, more than half of the states provide benefits to at least some noncitizens who are ineligible for federal services. *See* National Immigration Law Center, *Update Page: Guide to Immigrant Eligibility for Federal Programs*, <www.nilc.org/pubs/Guide_update.htm>. The result has been a substantial shift in costs from the federal government to the states and localities. (For unauthorized migrants, the Act allowed states and localities to grant certain public benefits, but this generally requires them to enact new state legislation to that effect. *See* § 411, 8 U.S.C.A. § 1621.)

The grant of authority by the federal government to the states to draw lines for benefits eligibility raises several questions. Assuming the federal government has much more power than the states to treat citizens and noncitizens differently, could it delegate all or part of this power to the states? What if anything limits such delegation? What does this statement near the end of *Graham* mean: "Congress does not have the power to authorize the individual States to violate the Equal Protection Clause"? The next two cases give different answers to these questions.

ALIESSA v. NOVELLO

New York Court of Appeals, 2001.
96 N.Y.2d 418, 754 N.E.2d 1085, 730 N.Y.S.2d 1.

ROSENBLATT, J.

* * *

Plaintiffs are 12 aliens who lawfully reside in New York State. They immigrated to the United States from various countries, including Bangladesh, Belorussia, Ecuador, Greece, Guyana, Haiti, Italy, Malaysia, the Philippines, Syria and Turkey. As legal aliens, they fall into two groups. Some are lawfully admitted permanent residents of the United States under the Immigration and Nationality Act (i.e., green card holders) the rest are permanently residing in the United States under color of law (PRUCOLs). All suffer from potentially life-threatening illnesses and, but for the exclusion under Social Services Law § 122, would allegedly qualify for Medicaid benefits funded solely by the State.

* * *

In response to PRWORA, New York enacted Social Services Law § 122, terminating Medicaid for non-qualified aliens—including PRUCOL plaintiffs. New York did, however, maintain Medicaid for otherwise eligible PRUCOLs who, as of August 4, 1997, were receiving Medicaid and were diagnosed with AIDS or residing in certain licensed residential health care facilities.

As for qualified aliens, section 122 provides Medicaid to all otherwise eligible qualified aliens who entered the United States before August 22, 1996 and continuously resided in the United States until attaining qualified status. Those entering on or after August 22, 1996, however, are no longer immediately eligible for State Medicaid, but must now wait five years for coverage. This group includes the lawfully admitted permanent resident plaintiffs. Finally, all plaintiffs (both PRUCOLs and qualified aliens) may receive safety net assistance and emergency medical treatment.

* * *

In *Graham v. Richardson*, the Supreme Court held that as a class, aliens are a "prime example of a 'discrete and insular' minority * * * for whom such heightened judicial solicitude is appropriate." Lawful resident aliens benefit our country in a great many ways. Like citizens, they contribute to our economy, serve in the Armed Forces and pay taxes including, of course, taxes that fund State Medicaid. Nevertheless, aliens may not vote, which has historically inhibited their ability to protect their interests.

The State does not attempt to justify section 122 under a strict scrutiny standard. Nor has it identified any "compelling governmental interest" that section 122 promotes. Instead, the State argues that strict scrutiny does not apply here. It contends that section 122 implements [the 1996 Welfare Act's] Federal immigration policy and should therefore be evaluated under the less stringent "rational basis" standard. To address this argument, we must compare State and Congressional legislative authority in the context of immigration and naturalization.

The Constitution empowers Congress to "establish [a] uniform Rule of Naturalization," "regulate Commerce with foreign Nations," "declare War," approve treaties, and legislate over foreign affairs. In entertaining challenges to Federal immigration and naturalization statutes, the Supreme Court has interpreted these sources of authority to accord Congress—as distinguished from the States—considerable latitude (*see, Fiallo v. Bell,* 430 U.S. 787, 792–797, 97 S.Ct. 1473, 52 L.Ed.2d 50; *Hampton v. Mow Sun Wong,* 426 U.S. 88, 100–105, 96 S.Ct. 1895; *Kleindienst v. Mandel,* 408 U.S. 753, 765–770, 92 S.Ct. 2576, 33 L.Ed.2d 683). The Court has explained that "over no conceivable subject is the legislative power of Congress more complete" (*Oceanic Steam Nav. Co. v. Stranahan,* 214 U.S. 320, 339, 29 S.Ct. 671, 53 L.Ed. 1013).

When allocating Federal welfare benefits, the Constitution does not prohibit Congress from distinguishing between aliens and citizens. In *Mathews v. Diaz,* a group of aliens challenged a Federal statute that denied aliens Medicare eligibility unless they had been admitted for permanent residence and resided in the United States for at least five years. The Court held that the "decision to share [our] bounty with our guests may take into account the character of the relationship between the alien and this country: Congress may decide that as the alien's tie grows stronger, so does the strength of his claim to an equal share of that munificence" (*id.* at 80, 96 S.Ct. 1883). * * *

Graham v. Richardson is at the center of our analysis. There, the State of Arizona administered a Federal disability program under Federal guidelines much the same as New York administers Medicaid. Arizona argued that because its 15–year residency period for aliens was impliedly authorized by Federal law, it did not violate the Fourteenth Amendment. The Supreme Court rejected this contention, holding that a Federal statute authorizing "discriminatory treatment of aliens *at the option of States*" would present "serious constitutional questions." The Court recognized that although the Federal government has broad constitutional power to distinguish among aliens in setting the rules for their admission and naturalization, "Congress does not have the power to authorize the individual States to violate the Equal Protection Clause." Indeed, the Court went on to state that a "congressional enactment construed so as to permit state legislatures to adopt divergent laws on the subject of citizenship requirements for federally supported welfare programs would appear to contravene this explicit constitutional requirement of uniformity."

Additional Supreme Court decisions reinforce *Graham*'s requirement for uniformity in immigration policy (*see, Plyler v. Doe,* 457 U.S. 202, 219 n.19, 102 S.Ct. 2382 ["(I)f the Federal Government has by *uniform* rule prescribed what it believes to be appropriate standards for the treatment of an alien subclass, the States may, of course, follow the federal direction"] [emphasis added]). Moreover, in *Mathews v. Diaz,* the Court recognized that when it comes to State welfare policy, "there is little, if any, basis for treating persons who are citizens of another State differently from persons who are citizens of another country." In distinguishing between Federal and State powers, the Court held that a "division by a State of the category of persons who are not citizens of that State into subcategories of United States citizens and aliens has no apparent justification, whereas, a comparable classification by the Federal Government is a routine and normally legitimate part of its business."

Finally, in *Hampton v. Mow Sun Wong,* the Supreme Court drew limits on the power of entities other than Congress or the President to make alienage classifications in furtherance of Federal immigration policy. In addressing whether Federal agencies could make such classifications for civil service eligibility, the Court concluded that if Congress or the President had created the classification, it could be justifiable as a valid exercise of immigration authority in the national interest. When, however, it came to Federal agencies that did not deal directly with immigration, the Court was not willing to presume they would deliberately foster national immigration interests, which are "so far removed from [their] normal responsibilities." Surely this is also true of the States.

Title IV [of the 1996 Welfare Act] does not impose a *uniform* immigration rule for States to follow. Indeed, it expressly authorizes States to enact laws extending "any State or local public benefit" even to those aliens not lawfully present within the United States. The converse is also true and exacerbates the lack of uniformity: Section 1622(a) provides that, subject to certain exceptions, States are authorized to withhold State Medicaid from even those qualified aliens who are eligible for Federal Medicaid * * *. Thus, in administering their own programs, the States are free to discriminate in either direction—producing not uniformity, but potentially wide variation based on localized or idiosyncratic concepts of largesse, economics and politics. Considering that Congress has conferred upon the States such broad discretionary power to grant or deny aliens State Medicaid, we are unable to conclude that title IV reflects a uniform national policy. If the rule were uniform, each State would carry out the same policy under the mandate of Congress—the only body with authority to set immigration policy.

In exercising its discretion under title IV, New York has chosen to continue Medicaid coverage for any PRUCOL who, as of August 4, 1997, was receiving Medicaid and was either diagnosed with AIDS or residing in certain licensed residential health care facilities. This demonstrates that New York—along with every other State—with Congressional permission is choosing its own policy with respect to health benefits for resident, indigent legal aliens. Thus, we address this case outside the context of a Congressional command for nationwide uniformity in the scope of Medicaid coverage for indigent aliens as a matter of federal immigration policy.

We conclude that section 122 is subject to—and cannot pass—strict scrutiny, notwithstanding title IV's authorization. Because title IV authorizes each State to extend the ineligibility period for Federal Medicaid beyond the mandatory five years and terminate Federal Medicaid eligibility for certain refugees and asylees after seven years, it is directly in the teeth of *Graham* insofar as it allows the States to "adopt divergent laws on the subject of citizenship requirements for *federally* supported welfare programs." Moreover, title IV goes significantly beyond what the *Graham* Court declared constitutionally questionable. In the name of national immigration policy, it impermissibly authorizes each State to decide whether to disqualify many otherwise eligible aliens from State Medicaid. Section 122 is a product of this authorization. In light of *Graham* and its progeny, title IV can give section 122 no special insulation from strict scrutiny review. Thus, section 122 must be evaluated as any other State statute that classifies based on alienage. * * *

SOSKIN v. REINERTSON

United States Court of Appeals, Tenth Circuit, 2004.
353 F.3d 1242.

HARTZ, CIRCUIT JUDGE.

* * *

The PRWORA does * * * allow states to provide optional Medicaid coverage to legal aliens not included within Congress's definition of "qualified aliens." § 1612(b). In essence, states may redefine "qualified aliens" to cover additional legal aliens, so long as they do not cover those aliens explicitly excluded by the PRWORA (e.g., most aliens who have not lived in the United States for five years).

Initially Colorado opted to provide coverage beyond that mandated by the PRWORA. In 1997 Colorado responded to the PRWORA by enacting legislation that maintained the optional Medicaid coverage it had previously provided to all lawfully present aliens who were otherwise eligible. But Colorado policy changed in March of 2003. Faced with an enormous budget shortfall, the state looked to its Medicaid program for savings. The Colorado legislature passed and the governor signed SB 03–176, which removed the optional Medicaid coverage Colorado had been providing to legal aliens. After SB 03–176 takes effect, only those aliens that Congress defined in the PRWORA as "qualified aliens" will be eligible for Medicaid in Colorado. The state estimates that it will save $5.9 million annually by eliminating optional alien coverage.

* * *

On March 27, 2003, Plaintiffs filed this class-action lawsuit to enjoin the implementation of SB 03–176. Class members include legal aliens who rely on Medicaid to cover important medical services, including chemotherapy, nursing home care, home health care, surgical care, and life-sustaining prescription drug coverage. Without Medicaid, Plaintiffs claim, they will be unable to afford these necessary services and will suffer serious injuries and irreparable harm. Plaintiffs contend that in some cases the loss of medical care could be life threatening.

Plaintiffs' suit seeks a judgment declaring that SB 03–176's eligibility requirements violate the Equal Protection Clause of the Fourteenth Amendment because they discriminate against legal aliens, and that Defendant's procedures for terminating benefits are inadequate under Medicaid law and the Due Process Clause of the Fourteenth Amendment. Plaintiffs also seek an injunction permanently enjoining termination of benefits under SB 03–176.

* * *

The parties appear to agree that SB 03–176 would not survive strict scrutiny but would satisfy the rational-basis test. Thus, the constitutionality of SB 03–176 depends on the level of scrutiny to which the law is subject. We turn to Supreme Court precedent for guidance.

[The court summarized *Graham v. Richardson* and *Mathews v. Diaz.*]

Neither *Graham* nor *Mathews* determines the result in this case. Unlike *Graham,* here we have specific Congressional authorization for the state's action, the PRWORA. Unlike *Mathews,* here we have a state-administered program, and the potential for states to adopt coverage restrictions with respect to aliens that are not mandated by federal law.

The fact of state administration in itself is not a distinction from *Mathews* that has impressed the circuits that have addressed the matter. Following *Mathews,* several circuits have applied rational-basis review to uphold federal statutes restricting state-administered welfare benefits to legal aliens.

The potential for states to adopt coverage restrictions for aliens that are not federally mandated is, however, more problematic. The difficulty is illustrated by opinions addressing non-mandated state restrictions—one each from the high courts of New York and Massachusetts. We discuss each in turn.

[The court summarized the holding and analysis in *Aliessa.*]

The Massachusetts Supreme Judicial Court addressed similar issues in *Doe v. Comm'r of Transitional Assistance,* 437 Mass. 521, 773 N.E.2d 404 (2002), but reached a different result. It concluded that state-made intra-alien classifications are subject only to rational-basis review. *Doe* involved a state-only supplemental-benefits program that was enacted to provide coverage to certain aliens who, based on the PRWORA, were going to lose the joint state-federal benefits they had previously received. But the benefits provided by the supplemental program were restricted to aliens who had resided in Massachusetts for at least six months.

The plaintiffs in *Doe* argued that the six-month residency requirement violated the Equal Protection Clause because it imposed the requirement on some legal aliens, but not on other legal aliens and citizens. Here again, the dispute hinged on whether strict scrutiny or rational-basis review applied.

The court first emphasized that the benefits provided by the program went only to aliens (not citizens), meaning that the six-month residency requirement did not discriminate between citizens and aliens, but rather only amongst aliens. Then, after reviewing *Graham, Mathews,* and other relevant law, the court turned to the standard of review:

> * * * [T]he proper standard of review is rational basis. We reach this conclusion because we find that the operative classification for equal protection purposes in the setting of this case is not alienage, but residency.

* * *

The Supreme Court precedents establish two propositions. First, states on their own cannot treat aliens differently from citizens without a compelling justification. *See Graham,* 403 U.S. at 371–72, 376, 91 S.Ct. 1848. Second, the federal government can treat aliens differently from citizens so long as the difference in treatment has a rational basis. *See Mathews,* 426 U.S. at 78–83, 96 S.Ct. 1883. This case fits somewhere in between. Plaintiffs claim that its location is clear, because *Graham* said that "Congress does not have the power to authorize the individual States to violate the Equal Protection Clause." But we think the issue is more nuanced than the quoted proposition indicates.

We do not read *Graham* as being as categorical as Plaintiffs claim it is regarding the effect of Congressional authorization of state discrimination against aliens. If the Court had definitively decided that the distinctions made in Arizona law would be unconstitutional regardless of Congressional authorization, there would have been no cause for the Court to examine the legislative history of the federal statute that Arizona relied upon. Nor would the Court have needed to rely on a rule of construction—construing the statute to avoid constitutional concerns—to resolve the case before it. As we read *Graham,* the Court was, in essence, insisting on a clear expression of Congressional intent to permit states to discriminate against aliens before it would tackle the constitutional issue.

We recognize that *Graham* said that "Congress does not have the power to authorize the individual States to violate the Equal Protection Clause." But that proposition is almost tautological. The question is not whether Congress can authorize such a constitutional violation. The question is what constitutes such a violation when Congress has (clearly) expressed its will regarding a matter relating to aliens. After all, Congress has extensive powers with respect to aliens derived from specific constitutional provisions as well as from the inherent powers of a sovereign nation. *See, e.g., Chae Chan Ping v. United States,* 130 U.S. 581, 609, 9 S.Ct. 623, 32 L.Ed. 1068 (1889) (stating that Congress's immigration power is "an incident of sovereignty"); *Harisiades v. Shaughnessy,* 342 U.S. 580, 588–89, 72 S.Ct. 512, 96 L.Ed. 586 (1952) ("'[A]ny policy toward aliens is vitally and intricately interwoven with contemporaneous policies in regard to the conduct of foreign relations, the war power, and the maintenance of a republican form of government.'").

When Congress exercises these powers to legislate with regard to aliens, the proper standard of judicial review is rational-basis review. That is the lesson of *Mathews.* Although *Mathews* involved Medicare, a program administered and funded by the federal government, while the PRWORA involves a program administered and partially funded by the states, that difference, as noted above, is immaterial in assessing the constitutionality of the federal legislation itself.

There is, however, one significant difference between the federal law at issue here and the one at issue in *Mathews.* The present law gives the states a measure of discretion. Some benefits for aliens are required, some are prohibited. In between, the states are permitted to be more restrictive (or, depending on one's point of view, more generous). Relying on *Graham,* one could say, as Plaintiffs do, that when a state elects not to provide aliens with the maximum benefits permitted by federal law, it is discriminating against aliens and the federal government's imprimatur for such discrimination cannot reduce the level of scrutiny to which the state's choice is subjected under the Equal Protection Clause. This is the view adopted by the New York Court of Appeals in *Aliessa.*

We do not share that view. The reason for applying rational-basis review to federal law regarding aliens is that such laws reflect national policy that Congress has the constitutional power to enact. Once Congress has expressed that policy, the courts must be deferential. What Plaintiffs fail to consider is that a state's exercise of discretion can also effectuate national policy. Recall that the PRWORA does not give the states unfettered discretion. Some coverage must be provided to aliens; some coverage is forbidden. State discretion is limited to the remaining optional range of coverage. In exercising that discretion each state is to make its own assessment of whether it can bear the burden of providing any optional coverage. When a state determines that the burden is too high and decides against optional coverage, it is addressing the Congressional concern (not just a parochial state concern) that "individual aliens not burden the public benefits system." 8 U.S.C. § 1601(4). This may be bad policy, but it is Congressional policy; and we review it only to determine whether it is rational.

One way of regarding the impact of Congressional policy is to view the PRWORA in a way suggested by the analysis of the Massachusetts Supreme Judicial Court in *Doe.* What Congress has done in the PRWORA is, in essence, create two welfare programs, one for citizens and one for aliens. Within the aliens-only program, states have the option of including more or fewer aliens. The decision to have separate programs for aliens and citizens is a Congressional choice, subject only to rational-basis review. *See Mathews.* A state's exercise of the option to include fewer aliens in its aliens-only program, then, should not be treated as discrimination against aliens as compared to citizens. That aspect of the discrimination is Congress's doing—by creating one program for citizens and a separate one for aliens. Rather, what the state is doing is discriminating within the aliens-only program against one class of aliens as compared to other classes of aliens. This discrimination among subclassifications of aliens is not based on a suspect classification (such as alienage). The discrimination, rather, is based on nonsuspect classifications such as work history or military service. We follow the Massachusetts Supreme Judicial Court's *Doe* decision in applying rational-basis review to such distinctions.

Furthermore, we reject the argument that the PRWORA's authorization to the states to provide or deny Medicaid benefits to certain aliens runs afoul of the uniformity requirement of the Constitution's Naturalization Clause. * * *

* * * To begin with, we note that Congressional power over aliens derives from more than just the Naturalization Clause. Other sources of Congressional authority include "its plenary authority with respect to foreign relations and international commerce, and ... the inherent power of a sovereign to close its borders." *Plyler v. Doe,* 457 U.S. 202, 225, 102 S.Ct. 2382, 72 L.Ed.2d 786 (1982) (Equal Protection Clause is violated by state law authorizing local school districts to deny enrollment to children not legally admitted into the United States).

Indeed, it is not at all clear how the authority "[t]o establish an uniform Rule of Naturalization" is being exercised when Congress restricts welfare benefits to aliens on grounds that have no direct relationship to the naturalization process. Whether the alien is seeking naturalization is not a consideration under the PRWORA. We find it significant that *Mathews* made no explicit mention of the Naturalization Clause in upholding Congressional authority to establish a residency requirement for aliens to obtain Medicare benefits. * * *

Moreover, the purpose of the uniformity requirement in the Naturalization Clause is not undermined by the PRWORA's grant of discretion to the states with respect to alien qualifications for Medicaid benefits. The uniformity requirement was a response to the widely divergent practices among the states under the Articles of Confederation with respect to the requirements to become a naturalized citizen. One state would have a lenient rule, another a very strict rule; yet the Articles required the strict state to treat as a full citizen anyone admitted to citizenship by the lenient state. Here, the choice by one state to grant or deny Medicaid benefits to an alien does not require another state to follow suit. * * *

* * *

HENRY, J., dissenting.

* * *

In the case at bar, the majority has advanced a deft methodology, but it disregards the Supreme Court's mandate that we apply strict scrutiny to a state's classification of persons on the basis of United States citizenship for the purposes of distribution of economic benefits. Colorado's program undisputedly discriminates between subclasses of legal aliens and classifies a group of legal aliens as ineligible for benefits. The majority holds that, under *Graham* and its progeny, if the federal government expresses a policy that gives the states the option to provide coverage for legal aliens, then we apply rational review to the state's actions. In refusing to apply strict scrutiny to Colorado's classification of legal immigrants as ineligible for Medicaid coverage, the majority compromises this court's equal protection jurisprudence, as Colorado S.B. 03–176 compromises the rights of legal, tax-paying, and military-serving aliens.

* * *

In *Doe,* the Massachusetts Supreme Court applied rational basis analysis to a supplemental benefits program that imposed a residency requirement on qualified aliens applying for benefits. A key difference in the Massachusetts Supreme Court's analysis, noted in the majority opinion only by a parenthetical, is that the program affected in Massachusetts was a *supplemental* benefits program that was open to only aliens and designed *to benefit only aliens;* that is, the program was enacted by the state legislature to supplement federal benefits that had been taken away from Massachusetts aliens by Congress. ("It is undisputed that the Massachusetts Legislature was not required to establish the supplemental benefits program. It is also undisputed that the supplemental program provides no benefits to citizens, and that the only persons eligible for benefits are qualified aliens.").

The court held it axiomatic that the supplemental program crafted to restore benefits to aliens could not discriminate against aliens and in favor of citizens. Thus, noting the "critical differences" between the New York and Massachusetts statutes, and heeding the admonitions of *Nyquist* [*v. Mauclet,* 432 U.S. 1, 97 S.Ct. 2120, 53 L.Ed.2d 63 (1977)] that strict scrutiny applies to a statute that "discriminate[s] only within the class of aliens," 432 U.S. at 8, 97 S.Ct. 2120, the Massachusetts Supreme Court determined that *Aliessa's* strict scrutiny review could not apply. *See Doe,* 773 N.E.2d at 412 (distinguishing *Nyquist:* Unlike the New York statute at issue there, "the Massachusetts statute establishes a program open only to aliens, imposes a residency requirement on all who are qualified to apply for its benefits, and does not harm aliens by barring them from the benefits of the program."); *id.* at 413 (distinguishing *Aliessa:* "Unlike the supplemental program created [by the Massachusetts Legislature], the amended New York State Medicaid program presented ... the very paradigm so definitively addressed in *Graham.*"). It is this distinction between the Colorado and Massachusetts statutes that mandates we view S.B. 03–176 through the lens of strict scrutiny. Thus, the Massachusetts court did not reach a decision inconsistent with *Aliessa;* in fact, the court cited *Aliessa* with approval and carefully distinguished its holding.

* * *

NOTES AND QUESTIONS ON DELEGATION BY THE FEDERAL GOVERNMENT

1. After *Aliessa,* New York extended its new state-funded health insurance program to all noncitizens residing lawfully in the state who show financial eligibility. *See* 78 Interp. Rel. 1600 (2001). More recently, however, and especially after the 2008 financial crisis, some states have reduced or eliminated state assistance programs that had replaced the federal assistance to noncitizens ended by PRWORA. *See, e.g., Hong Pham v. Starkowski,* 300 Conn. 412, 423, 16 A.3d. 635, 641–42 (2011); Santi, *NJ Budget Cuts Health Care for Immigrants, Poor,* Associated Press, Apr. 15, 2010; Goodnough, *Massachusetts Cuts Back Immigrants' Health Care,* N.Y. Times, Aug. 31, 2009, at A17.

2. In *Khrapunskiy v. Doar*, 12 N.Y.3d 478, 487–89, 909 N.E.2d 70, 881 N.Y.S.2d 377 (2009), the New York Court of Appeals rejected an equal protection challenge to noncitizen eligibility rules for a state program limited to noncitizens. Adopting reasoning similar to Judge Henry's dissent in *Soskin*, the court distinguished *Aliessa*. For a similar approach, see *Hong Pham, supra*, 300 Conn. at 428–62, 16 A.3d. at 644–64.

3. What is the relevance of *Hampton v. Mow Sun Wong* for *Aliessa* and *Soskin*?

4. The Court in *Mathews v. Diaz* said: "The real question presented by this case is not whether discrimination between citizens and aliens is permissible; rather, it is whether the statutory discrimination within the class of aliens—allowing benefits to some aliens but not to others—is permissible." This idea—that a line distinguishing among noncitizens is different from a line distinguishing noncitizens from citizens—reappears in *Aliessa* and *Soskin*. Assume that State A has one welfare program that includes citizens and some noncitizens, but excludes other noncitizens. State B has two welfare programs: one is for citizens, and the other is for some noncitizens but not other noncitizens. Is there a constitutional difference between what states A and B are doing?

5. Michael Wishnie has argued that the constitutional immigration power—which he conceptualizes broadly to include both immigration law and alienage law—is exclusively federal and not devolvable by statute to the states:

> Most importantly, devolution would erode the antidiscrimination and anticaste principles that are at the heart of our Constitution and that long have protected noncitizens at the subfederal level. The plenary power doctrine of immigration law inevitably shields governmental action from the level of judicial scrutiny that ordinarily would be applied, distorting constitutional jurisprudence and countenancing what otherwise would be invalidated as arbitrary or discriminatory government behavior. Permitting devolution would amplify this distortion, privileging the plenary power doctrine over equal protection norms at the state and local level. Given the choice, one should reject a constitutional theory that endorses the creation of state and local laboratories of bigotry against immigrants.

Wishnie, *Laboratories of Bigotry?: Devolution of the Immigration Power, Equal Protection, and Federalism*, 76 N.Y.U. L. Rev. 493, 553 (2001). *See also* Romero, *Devolution and Discrimination*, 58 N.Y.U Surv. Am. L. 377, 383 (2002) ("if racism within immigration law and policy is systemic, then devolution will not cure the problem"); Carrasco, *Congressional Arrogation of Power: Alien Constellation in the Galaxy of Equal Protection*, 74 B.U. L. Rev. 591, 626–30 (1994) (arguing that federal authorization for state alienage classifications impermissibly delegates power that is exclusively federal under the Naturalization Clause).

6. In rejecting the *Soskin* plaintiffs' Naturalization Clause argument, the court echoed (but did not cite) similar analysis in Chang, *Public Benefits and Federal Authorization for Alienage Discrimination by the States*, 58 N.Y.U Surv. Am. L. 357, 359–60 (2002):

Rather than creating "laboratories of bigotry against immigrants," to use Wishnie's phrase, we might just as plausibly view federal authorization of divergent state policies as creating laboratories of generosity toward immigrants. If we had bound Congress with a constitutional constraint of uniformity in the political atmosphere of 1996, then Congress might have excluded immigrants from Medicaid or welfare rather than leaving the question of immigrant access up to the states.

Id. at 363.

Assume Chang is correct that a power that is exclusively federal may nonetheless be delegated to the states. Why does it follow—as *Soskin* suggests in part 4 ("There is, however, one significant difference . . .")—that the standard of constitutional judicial review that would apply to a federal enactment must apply unchanged to a constitutional challenge to a law that a state enacts pursuant to that delegation?

7.   In contrast to Chang's "laboratories of generosity" argument, Peter Spiro has observed that even if states are less generous to noncitizens, "state-level authority will allow those states harboring intense anti-alien sentiment to act on those sentiments at the state level, thus diminishing any interest on their part to seek national legislation to similarly restrictionist ends." Spiro, *Learning to Live With Immigration Federalism*, 29 Conn. L. Rev. 1627, 1627 (1997).

8.   Compare the delegation in the 1996 Welfare Act with INA § 287(g), discussed in Chapter Nine, p. 1076, which spells out how federal authority to enforce federal immigration laws may be delegated to state and local governments. Clare Huntington has identified these as the only two instances of express federal delegation to states of federal authority in immigration law and alienage law. *See* Huntington, *The Constitutional Dimension of Immigration Federalism*, 61 Vand. L. Rev. 787 (2008). Do the concerns that Wishnie raises in the alienage discrimination context about the erosion of antidiscrimination and anticaste principles apply equally—or less or more so—to state and local enforcement of federal immigration law pursuant to INA § 287(g)?

SECTION B.   GOVERNMENT AND POLITICS

According to both tradition and doctrine, some alienage classifications are permissible in matters of government and politics. The key modern court decision is *Sugarman v. Dougall*, 413 U.S. 634, 93 S.Ct. 2842, 37 L.Ed.2d 853 (1973). In that case, the U.S. Supreme Court relied on *Graham* in striking down a New York State law that limited state competitive civil service positions to U.S. citizens. Drawing on the concept of political community and discussing the right to vote, *Sugarman* suggested that a narrower U.S. citizenship requirement for only some state public employees would pass constitutional muster:

While we rule that § 53 is unconstitutional, we do not hold that, on the basis of an individualized determination, an alien may not be refused, or discharged from, public employment, even on the basis of noncitizenship, if the refusal to hire, or the discharge, rests on legitimate state interests that relate to qualifications for a particular position or to the characteristics of the employee. We hold only that a flat ban on the employment of aliens in positions that have little, if any relation to a State's legitimate interest, cannot withstand scrutiny under the Fourteenth Amendment.

Neither do we hold that a State may not, in an appropriately defined class of positions, require citizenship as a qualification for office. Just as "the Framers of the Constitution intended the States to keep for themselves, as provided in the Tenth Amendment, the power to regulate elections," *Oregon v. Mitchell*, 400 U.S. 112, 124–125, 91 S.Ct. 260, 263, 27 L.Ed.2d 272 (1970) (opinion of Black, J.); "(e)ach State has the power to prescribe the qualifications of its officers and the manner in which they shall be chosen." *Boyd v. Thayer*, 143 U.S. 135, 161, 12 S.Ct. 375, 382, 36 L.Ed. 103 (1892). Such power inheres in the State by virtue of its obligation, already noted above, "to preserve the basic conception of a political community." *Dunn v. Blumstein*, 405 U.S., at 344, 92 S.Ct., at 1004. And this power and responsibility of the State applies, not only to the qualifications of voters, but also to persons holding state elective or important nonelective executive, legislative, and judicial positions, for officers who participate directly in the formulation, execution, or review of broad public policy perform functions that go to the heart of representative government. There, as Judge Lumbard phrased it in his separate concurrence, is "where citizenship bears some rational relationship to the special demands of the particular position." [*Dougall v. Sugarman*, 339 F.Supp. 906, 911 (S.D.N.Y.1971) (Lumbard, J., concurring).]

We have held, of course, that such state action, particularly with respect to voter qualifications is not wholly immune from scrutiny under the Equal Protection Clause. But our scrutiny will not be so demanding where we deal with matters resting firmly within a State's constitutional prerogatives. This is no more than a recognition of a State's historical power to exclude aliens from participation in its democratic political institutions, and a recognition of a State's constitutional responsibility for the establishment and operation of its own government, as well as the qualifications of an appropriately designated class of public office holders. This Court has never held that aliens have a constitutional right to vote or to hold high public office under the Equal Protection Clause. Indeed, implicit in many of this Court's voting rights decisions is the notion that citizenship is a permissible criterion for limiting such rights. A restriction on the employment of noncitizens, narrowly confined, could have particular relevance to this important state responsibility, for alienage itself is a factor that reasonably could be employed in defining "political community."

413 U.S. at 646–49, 93 S.Ct. at 2849–51.

Consider how the ideas reflected in this excerpt from *Sugarman* are essential to analysis of the two topics in this Section: public employment and voting.

1. PUBLIC EMPLOYMENT

Is it constitutional—or sound policy—to limit public employment to citizens? After *Sugarman*, the Court began to carve out an area where states were allowed to require citizenship in this context. For example, it upheld citizenship requirements for state troopers, *see Foley v. Connelie*, 435 U.S. 291, 297–300, 98 S.Ct. 1067, 55 L.Ed.2d 287 (1978); and public school teachers, *see Ambach v. Norwick*, 441 U.S. 68, 69–72, 99 S.Ct. 1589, 60 L.Ed.2d 49 (1979). But it struck down—as equal protection violations—citizenship requirements that kept permanent residents from becoming lawyers, *see Matter of Griffiths*, 413 U.S. 717, 718, 93 S.Ct. 2851, 37 L.Ed.2d 910 (1973); and notaries public, *see Bernal v. Fainter*, 467 U.S. 216, 219–28, 104 S.Ct. 2312, 81 L.Ed.2d 175 (1984). In the next case, a divided Court explained this "political community" exception to *Graham*.

CABELL v. CHAVEZ–SALIDO

Supreme Court of the United States, 1982.
454 U.S. 432, 102 S.Ct. 735, 70 L.Ed.2d 677.

JUSTICE WHITE delivered the opinion of the Court.

In this case we once again consider a citizenship requirement imposed by a State on those seeking to fill certain governmental offices. California Gov't Code Ann. § 1031(a) (West 1980) requires "public officers or employees declared by law to be peace officers" to be citizens of the United States. California Penal Code Ann. § 830.5 (West Supp. 1981), provides that probation officers and deputy probation officers are "peace officers." * * *

I

Appellees were, at the time the complaint was filed, lawfully admitted permanent resident aliens living in Los Angeles County, Cal. Each applied unsuccessfully for positions as Deputy Probation Officers with the Los Angeles County Probation Department. With respect to two of the three appellees, the parties stipulated that the failure to obtain the positions sought was the result of the statutory citizenship requirement.

* * *

II

Over the years, this Court has many times considered state classifications dealing with aliens. As we have noted before, those cases "have not formed an unwavering line over the years." *Ambach v. Norwick*, [441 U.S. 68, 72, 99 S.Ct. 1589, 1592, 60 L.Ed.2d 49 (1979)]. But to say that the decisions do not fall into a neat pattern is not to say that they fall into no pattern. In fact, they illustrate a not unusual characteristic of legal development; broad principles are articulated, narrowed when applied to new contexts, and finally replaced when the distinctions they rely upon are no longer tenable.

* * *

The cases through *Graham* dealt for the most part with attempts by the States to retain certain economic benefits exclusively for citizens. Since *Graham*, the Court has confronted claims distinguishing between the economic and sovereign functions of government. This distinction has been supported by the argument that although citizenship is not a relevant ground for the distribution of economic benefits, it is a relevant ground for determining membership in the political community. "We recognize a State's interest in establishing its own form of government, and in limiting participation in that government to those who are within 'the basic conception of a political community.' " *Sugarman v. Dougall*, [413 U.S. 634, 642, 93 S.Ct. 2842, 2847, 37 L.Ed.2d 853 (1973)]. While not retreating from the position that restrictions on lawfully resident aliens that primarily affect economic interests are subject to heightened judicial scrutiny, we have concluded that strict scrutiny is out of place when the restriction primarily serves a political function: "[O]ur scrutiny will not be so demanding where we deal with matters resting firmly within a State's constitutional prerogatives [and] constitutional responsibility for the establishment and operation of its own government, as well as the qualifications of an appropriately designated class of public office holders." *Sugarman v. Dougall*, 413 U.S., at 648, 93 S.Ct., at 2850. We have thus "not abandoned the general principle that some state functions are so bound up with the operation of the State as a governmental entity as to permit the exclusion from those functions of all persons who have not become part of the process of self-government." *Ambach v. Norwick*, 441 U.S., at 73–74, 99 S.Ct., at 1593. And in those areas the State's exclusion of aliens need not "clear the high hurdle of 'strict scrutiny,' because [that] would 'obliterate all the distinctions between citizens and aliens, and thus depreciate the historic value of citizenship.' " *Foley v. Connelie*, [435 U.S. 291, 295, 98 S.Ct. 1067, 1070, 55 L.Ed.2d 287 (1978).]

The exclusion of aliens from basic governmental processes is not a deficiency in the democratic system but a necessary consequence of the community's process of political self-definition. Self-government, whether direct or through representatives, begins by defining the scope of the community of the governed and thus of the governors as well: Aliens are by definition those outside of this community. Judicial incursions in this area may interfere with those aspects of democratic self-government that are most essential to it. This distinction between the economic and political functions of government has, therefore, replaced the old public/private distinction. Although this distinction rests on firmer foundations than the old public/private distinction, it may be difficult to apply in particular cases.

Sugarman advised that a claim that a particular restriction on legally resident aliens serves political and not economic goals is to be evaluated in a two-step process. First, the specificity of the classification will be examined: a classification that is substantially overinclusive or underinclusive tends to undercut the governmental claim that the classification serves legitimate political ends. The classification in *Sugarman* itself—all members of the competitive civil service—could not support the claim that it was an element in "the State's broad power to define its political community," 413 U.S., at 643, 93 S.Ct., at 2848, because it indiscriminately swept in menial occupations, while leaving out some of the State's most important political functions. Second, even if the classification is sufficiently tailored, it may be applied in the particular case only to "persons holding state elective or important nonelective executive, legislative, and judicial positions," those officers who "participate directly in the formulation, execution, or review of broad public policy" and hence "perform functions that go to the heart of representative government." *Id.*, at 647, 93 S.Ct., at 2850.[7] We must therefore inquire whether the "position in question ... involves discretionary decisionmaking, or execution of policy, which substantially affects members of the political community." *Foley v. Connelie*, 435 U.S., at 296, 98 S.Ct., at 1070.

The restriction at issue in this case passes both of the *Sugarman* tests.

III

Appellees argue, and the District Court agreed, that Cal. Gov't Code Ann. § 1031(a) (West 1980), which requires all state "peace officers" to be citizens, is unconstitutionally overinclusive: "Section 1031(a) is void as a law requiring citizenship which 'sweeps too broadly.' " 490 F.Supp., at 986. The District Court failed to articulate any standard in reaching this conclusion. Rather, it relied wholly on its belief that of the more than 70 positions included within the statutory classification of "peace officer," some undefined number of them "cannot be considered members of the political community no matter how liberally that category is viewed." The District Court's entire argument on this point consisted of just one sentence: "There appears to be no justification whatever for excluding aliens, even those who have applied for citizenship, from holding public employment as cemetery sextons, furniture and bedding inspectors, livestock identification inspectors, and toll service employees." In believing this sufficient, the District Court applied a standard of review far stricter than that approved in *Sugarman* and later cases.

We need not hold that the District Court was wrong in concluding that citizenship may not be required of toll-service employees, cemetery sextons, and inspectors to hold that the District Court was wrong in striking down the statute on its face. The District Court assumed that if the statute was overinclusive at all, it could not stand. This is not the proper standard. Rather, the inquiry is whether the restriction reaches so far and is so broad and haphazard as to belie the State's claim that it is

---

7. * * * [A]lmost every governmental official can be understood as participating in the execution of broad public policies. The limits on this category within which citizenship is relevant to the political community are not easily defined, but our cases since *Sugarman*—*Foley v. Connelie*, 435 U.S. 291, 98 S.Ct. 1067, 55 L.Ed.2d 287 (1978), and *Ambach v. Norwick*, 441 U.S. 68, 99 S.Ct. 1589, 60 L.Ed.2d 49 (1979)—suggest that this Court will not look to the breadth of policy judgments required of a particular employee. Rather, the Court will look to the importance of the function as a factor giving substance to the concept of democratic self-government.

only attempting to ensure that an important function of government be in the hands of those having the "fundamental legal bond of citizenship." *Ambach v. Norwick*, 441 U.S., at 75, 99 S.Ct., at 1593. Under this standard, the classifications used need not be precise; there need only be a substantial fit. Our examination of the California scheme convinces us that it is sufficiently tailored to withstand a facial challenge.

The general requirements, including citizenship, for all California peace officers are found in Cal. Gov't Code Ann. § 1031 (West 1980). That section, however, does not designate any particular official as a peace officer; rather, Cal. Penal Code Ann. § 830 (West Supp. 1981) lists the specific occupations that fall within the general category of "peace officer." Even a casual reading of the Penal Code makes clear that the unifying character of all categories of peace officers is their law enforcement function. Specific categories are defined by either their geographical jurisdiction or the specific substantive laws they have the responsibility to enforce. Thus, not surprisingly, the first categories listed include police officers at the county, city, and district levels. This is followed by various categories of police power authorized by the State: *e.g.,* highway patrol officers, the state police, and members of the California National Guard when ordered into active service. After this, the statute includes a long list of particular officers with responsibility for enforcement of different substantive areas of the law: *e.g.,* individuals charged with enforcement of the alcoholic beverage laws, the food and drug laws, fire laws, and the horse racing laws. Finally, there are several catchall provisions that include some officers with narrow geographic responsibilities—*e.g.,* park rangers, San Francisco Bay Area Rapid Transit District police, harbor police, community college police, security officers of municipal utility districts, and security officers employed in government buildings—and some with narrow "clientele"—*e.g.,* welfare-fraud or child-support investigators, correctional officers, parole and probation officers.

Although some of these categories may have only a tenuous connection to traditional police functions of law enforcement, the questionable classifications are comparatively few in number. The general law enforcement character of all California "peace officers" is underscored by the fact that all have the power to make arrests, and all receive a course of training in the exercise of their respective arrest powers and in the use of firearms. *Foley* made clear that a State may limit the exercise of the sovereign's coercive police powers over the members of the community to citizens. The California statutes at issue here are an attempt to do just that. They are sufficiently tailored in light of that aim to pass the lower level of scrutiny we articulated as the appropriate equal protection standard for such an exercise of sovereign power in *Sugarman*.

IV

The District Court also held that the citizenship requirement was invalid as applied to the positions at issue here—deputy probation officers. In reaching this conclusion, it focused too narrowly on a comparison of the characteristics and functions of probation officers with those of the state troopers at issue in *Foley* and the teachers in *Ambach*. *Foley* and *Ambach* did not describe the outer limits of permissible citizenship requirements. For example, although both of those cases emphasized the communitywide responsibilities of teachers and police, there was no suggestion that judges, who deal only with a narrow subclass of the community, cannot be subject to a citizenship requirement. Similarly, although both *Foley* and *Ambach* emphasized the unsupervised discretion that must be exercised by the teacher and the police officer in the performance of their duties, neither case suggested that jurors, who act under a very specific set of instructions, could not be required to be citizens. Definition of the important sovereign functions of the political community is necessarily the primary responsibility of the representative branches of government, subject to limited judicial review.

Looking at the functions of California probation officers, we conclude that they, like the state troopers involved in *Foley*, sufficiently partake of the sovereign's power to exercise coercive force over the individual that they may be limited to citizens. Although the range of individuals over whom probation officers exercise supervisory authority is limited, the powers of the probation officer are broad with respect to those over whom they exercise that authority. The probation officer has the power both to arrest, and to release those over whom he has jurisdiction. He has the power and the responsibility to supervise probationers and insure that all the conditions of probation are met and that the probationer accomplishes a successful reintegration into the community. With respect to juveniles, the probation officer has the responsibility to determine whether to release or detain offenders, and whether to institute judicial proceedings or take other supervisory steps over the minor. In carrying out these responsibilities the probation officer necessarily has a great deal of discretion that, just like that of the police officer and the teacher, must be exercised, in the first instance, without direct supervision.

* * *

One need not take an overly idealistic view of the educational functions of the probation officer during this period to recognize that the probation officer acts as an extension of the judiciary's authority to set the conditions under which particular individuals will lead their lives and of the executive's authority to coerce obedience to those conditions. From the perspective of the probationer, his probation officer may personify the State's sovereign powers; from the perspective of the larger community, the probation officer may symbolize the political community's control over, and thus responsibility for, those who have been found to have violated the norms of social order. From both of these perspectives, a citizenship requirement may seem an appropriate limitation on those who would exercise and, therefore, symbolize this power of the political community over those who fall within its jurisdiction.

Therefore, the judgment of the District Court is reversed, and the case is remanded for further proceedings consistent with this opinion.

So ordered.

JUSTICE BLACKMUN, with whom JUSTICE BRENNAN, JUSTICE MARSHALL, and JUSTICE STEVENS join, dissenting.

Appellees Jose Chavez–Salido, Pedro Luis Ybarra, and Ricardo Bohorquez are American-educated Spanish-speaking lawful residents of Los Angeles County, California. Seven years ago, each had a modest aspiration—to become a Los Angeles County "Deputy Probation Officer, Spanish-speaking." Each was willing to swear loyalty to the State and Federal Governments; indeed, appellee Chavez–Salido declared his intent to become a citizen. By competitive examination, two of the appellees, and possibly the third, demonstrated their fitness for the jobs they desired. Appellants denied them those jobs solely because they were not citizens.

The Court today concludes that appellees' exclusion from their chosen profession is "a necessary consequence of the community's process of political self-definition." The Court reaches this conclusion by misstating the standard of review it has long applied to alienage classifications. It then asserts that a lawfully admitted permanent resident alien is disabled from serving as a deputy probation officer because that job "go[es] to the heart of representative government."

In my view, today's decision rewrites the Court's precedents, ignores history, defies common sense, and reinstates the deadening mantle of state parochialism in public employment. I must dissent.

I

* * *

Since *Sugarman*, the Court consistently has held that in each case where the State chooses to discriminate against permanent resident aliens, "the governmental interest claimed to justify the discrimination is to be carefully examined in order to determine whether that interest is legitimate and substantial, and inquiry must be made whether the means adopted to achieve the goal are necessary and precisely drawn." *Examining Board v. Flores de Otero*, 426 U.S. 572, 605, 96 S.Ct. 2264, 2282, 49 L.Ed.2d 65 (1976). "Alienage classifications by a State that do not withstand this stringent examination cannot stand." *Nyquist v. Mauclet*, 432 U.S., at 7, 97 S.Ct., at 2124.

* * *

Under the *Sugarman* standard, a state statute that bars aliens from political positions lying squarely within the political community nevertheless violates the Equal Protection Clause if it excludes aliens from other public jobs in an unthinking or haphazard manner. The statutes at issue here represent just such an unthinking and haphazard exercise of state power. The District Court found, and the Court does not deny, that some of the more than 70 "peace officer" positions from which aliens have been barred "cannot be considered members of the political community no matter how liberally that category is viewed." 490 F.Supp., at 987. At the same time, California has long permitted aliens to teach in public schools, to be employed on public works, and to serve in most state, city, and county employment positions—all positions arguably within the political community.

Thus, exactly like the statute struck down in *Sugarman*, California's statutory exclusion of aliens is fatally overinclusive and underinclusive. It bars aliens from employment in numerous public positions where the State's proffered justification has little, if any, relevance. At the same time, it allows aliens to fill other positions that would seem naturally to fall within the State's asserted purpose. "Our standard of review of statutes that treat aliens differently from citizens requires a greater degree of precision." [*Sugarman*, 413 U.S., at 642, 93 S.Ct., at 2847.]

Nor can the Court reconcile its new notion of a "substantial fit" with the stringent standard of review the Court long has applied to alienage classifications. Every time the State requires citizenship for a single "peace officer" position, it excludes permanent resident aliens from hundreds or even thousands of public jobs. The Court's novel standard of review condones a legislative classification that excludes aliens from more than 70 public occupations although citizenship cannot be even rationally required for a substantial number of them. The fact that many of those positions may involve law enforcement cannot justify barring noncitizens from any of the positions that plainly do not. Today's decision thus defies the Court's earlier holdings that the States may not exclude aliens from any "harmless and useful occupation" for which citizenship cannot rationally be required. *Yick Wo v. Hopkins*, 118 U.S., at 374, 6 S.Ct., at 1073; *Truax v. Raich*, 239 U.S., at 41, 36 S.Ct., at 10.

II

* * *

I read *Foley* and *Ambach* to require the State to show that it has historically reserved a particular executive position for its citizens as a matter of its "constitutional prerogativ[e]." *Sugarman*, 413 U.S., at 648, 93 S.Ct., at 2850. Furthermore, the State must demonstrate that the public employee in that position exercises plenary coercive authority and control over a substantial portion of the citizen population. The public employee must exercise this authority over his clientele without intervening judicial or executive supervision. Even then, the State must prove that citizenship "bears some rational relationship to the special demands of the particular position." *Id.*, at 647, 93 S.Ct., at 2850, quoting *Dougall v. Sugarman*, 339 F. Supp. 906, 911 (S.D.N.Y.1971) (Lumbard, J., concurring).

Without such a rigorous test, *Sugarman*'s exception swallows *Sugarman*'s rule. Yet the Court does not apply such a rigorous test today.

Instead, it "look[s] to the importance of the [governmental] function as a factor giving substance to the concept of democratic self-government." Applying this nebulous standard, the Court then concludes that Los Angeles County probation officers perform three "important sovereign functions of the political community." Yet on inspection, not one of those functions justifies excluding all permanent resident aliens from the deputy probation officer position.

First, the Court declares that probation officers "partake of the sovereign's power to exercise coercive force over the individual." Yet the Court concedes that "the range of individuals over whom probation officers exercise supervisory authority is limited." Even over those individuals, a probation officer's coercive powers are carefully conditioned by statute. Probation officers cannot carry guns. They may arrest only those probationers under their jurisdiction, and even then only for the purpose of bringing them before the court for a determination whether they should be held or released. State statutes authorize probation officers to detain juveniles only in emergencies and, even then, for only brief periods.

The Court claims that § 1031(a) "limit[s] the exercise of the sovereign's coercive police powers over the members of the community to citizens." Yet other statutes belie that assertion. The State gives the power of arrest to a number of public employees who are not peace officers, but does not require that those employees be citizens. Moreover, California authorizes any "private person," including permanent resident aliens, to arrest others who have actually committed felonies or who have committed or attempted public offenses in their presence. The Court's hollow assertion that the legislature has reserved its sovereign coercive powers for its citizens ignores the reality that the State has already bestowed some of those powers on all private persons, including aliens.

Second, the Court asserts that probation officers necessarily have "discretion that ... must be exercised, in the first instance, without direct supervision." Yet to say this is to say very little. Almost everyone who works in the government bureaucracy exercises some discretion that is unsupervised in the first instance. The Court itself observes that probation officers have discretion primarily to investigate, to supervise, to evaluate, and to recommend. Their primary duties are preparing presentence reports, supervising probationers, and recommending sentences and probationary terms.

While I do not denigrate these functions, neither can I equate them with the discretionary duties of policemen, judges, and jurors. Unlike policemen, probation officers are not "clothed with authority to exercise an almost infinite variety of discretionary powers." *Foley v. Connelie*, 435 U.S., at 297, 98 S.Ct., at 1071. Unlike jurors who deliver final verdicts and judges who impose final sentences, the decisions of probation officers are always advisory to and supervised by judicial officers. California probation officers cannot by themselves declare revocation of probation. Furthermore, the investigative and reporting duties of a probation officer are extensively regulated by statute. The fact that probation officers play an integral role in the criminal justice system does not separate them from prison guards, bailiffs, court clerks, and the myriad other functionaries who execute a State's judicial policy.

More significantly, California's inflexible exclusion of aliens from deputy probation officer positions is inconsistent with its tolerance of aliens in other roles integral to the criminal justice system. * * *

* * * [A] criminal defendant in California may be represented at trial and on appeal by an alien attorney, have his case tried before an alien judge and appealed to an alien justice, and then have his probation supervised by a county probation department headed by an alien. I find constitutionally absurd the Court's suggestion that the same defendant cannot be entrusted to the supervised discretion of a resident alien deputy probation officer. In the Court's own words, a statutory scheme that tolerates such a result is sufficiently "haphazard as to belie the State's claim that it is only attempting to ensure that an important function of government be in the hands of those having the 'fundamental legal bond of citizenship.' "

The Court's third and final claim is that a probation officer acts as an actual and symbolic "extension" of the judiciary's authority to set conditions of probation and the executive's authority to coerce obedience to those conditions. Yet, by so saying, the Court simply concedes that the ultimate authority for a probation officer's acts lies elsewhere. In *Griffiths*, we held that aliens are not constitutionally disabled from serving as "officers of the court." 413 U.S., at 722–727, 93 S.Ct., at 2855–2857. Given the size of the State's judicial and executive bureaucracy, little would be left of *Sugarman*'s holding if a State could invoke the *Sugarman* exception to exclude probation officers from any position which "extended" judicial or executive authority.

Nor am I convinced by the Court's claim that a probation officer personifies the State's sovereign powers in the eyes of probationers and the larger community. This justification knows no limit. Surely a taxpayer feels the State's sovereign power when the local tax collector comes to his door; the larger community recognizes the sovereign power of the government when local firefighters put out a fire. The State could not also demand citizenship for those jobs, however, without thoroughly eviscerating *Sugarman*. Nor does the Court deny that the sight of foreign-born individuals not merely following, but encouraging others to follow, our laws is an equally powerful symbol of respect for our society's social norms.

In the end, the State has identified no characteristic of permanent resident aliens as a class which disables them from performing the job of deputy probation officer. The State does not dispute that these appellees possess the qualifications and educational background to perform the duties that job entails. Indeed, the State advances no rational reason why these appellees, native Spanish-speakers with graduate academic degrees, are not superbly qualified to act as probation officers for Spanish-speaking probationers, some of whom themselves may not be citizens.

The State cannot challenge the appellees' lack of familiarity with local laws or rules. Such a consideration might disqualify nonresident citizens, but not permanent resident aliens who have lived in California for much of their lives. Nor can the State presume that aliens as a class would be less loyal to the State. The Court's rulings in *In re Griffiths*, 413 U.S., at 726, n.18, 93 S.Ct., at 2857, n.18, and *Hampton v. Mow Sun Wong*, 426 U.S. 88, 111, n.43, 96 S.Ct. 1895, 1909, n.43, 48 L.Ed.2d 495 (1976), clearly state that one need not be a citizen in order to swear in good conscience to support the Constitution. When these appellees applied for their jobs, they expressed their willingness to take such oaths. One later declared his intent to become, and then became, a citizen. Finally, the State cannot claim that by enacting § 1031(a), it seeks to encourage aliens to become citizens. That objective is an exclusively federal interest.

I only can conclude that California's exclusion of these appellees from the position of deputy probation officer stems solely from state parochialism and hostility toward foreigners who have come to this country lawfully. I find it ironic that the Court invokes the principle of democratic self-government to exclude from the law enforcement process individuals who have not only resided here lawfully, but who now desire merely to help the State enforce its laws. Section 1031(a) violates appellees' rights to equal treatment and an individualized determination of fitness.

I would affirm the District Court's ruling that § 1031(a) is unconstitutional on its face and as applied.

NOTES AND QUESTIONS ON CITIZENSHIP REQUIREMENTS FOR PUBLIC EMPLOYMENT

1. Is *Cabell* faithful to *Sugarman*'s original articulation of cases in which a state may require U.S. citizenship? Is the dissent correct to say that the majority has construed *Sugarman*'s exception so broadly that it swallows *Sugarman*'s rule?

2. Has *Cabell* adequately explained the distinction between the economic and the political? Why isn't public employment economic? Notice that the majority seems to see the issue as *public* employment, while the dissent seems to see the issue as public *employment*. And if it matters that the plaintiffs were excluded from work, is it because access to work has constitutional significance? *See generally* Karst, *The Coming Crisis of Work in Constitutional Perspective*, 82 Corn. L. Rev. 523 (1997).

Assuming that one can find a principled distinction between the economic and the political, is the economic versus political typology undercut by recognizing, as the opinion seems not to, that permanent residents are of course clearly included in the community of the governed? Can you construct a better rationale that would allow the states to exclude noncitizens from voting and holding high public office, yet retain a strong shield against oppressive state statutes? Or to put it another way: what does Justice White mean by "membership in the political community"?

3. What is the relationship between *Cabell* and *Mathews v. Diaz*? Is *Cabell* the state analogue to *Diaz*, in that each case upheld an alienage classification that was within the government's competence to define a certain community? Linda Bosniak has written:

> [T]he membership interest at stake in this context is unlike any we have seen so far because it is not embodied in the federal immigration power. The community's concern here is not to regulate admission to the national territory or to formal citizenship status, but rather to regulate political—and perhaps, one senses, spiritual—admission to the "community of the governed and thus of the governors as well." Having affirmed states' authority to regulate such admission, the Court effectively treated membership questions as extending beyond matters of national immigration control and policy to include states' rights to ensure a "fundamental . . . identity between a government and the members, or citizens, of the state."

Bosniak, *supra*, 69 N.Y.U. L. Rev. at 1112 (quoting *Cabell*, 454 U.S. at 439, 102 S.Ct. at 740; and *Sugarman*, 413 U.S. at 641, 93 S.Ct. at 2847). *See also* Motomura, *Whose Immigration Law?: Citizens, Aliens, and the Constitution*, 97 Colum. L. Rev. 1567, 1599–1601 (1997).

EXERCISE: NONCITIZENS AS SCHOOL TEACHERS

Ling Chen is a permanent resident from China who has lived in Fredonia (a hypothetical state of the United States) for about ten years. Having met all of the educational requirements, Ling has applied for a certificate that would qualify her to teach Chinese in the public high schools. She is married to a U.S. citizen and is eligible to naturalize, but she isn't interested in doing so. Under Fredonian law, state authorities will issue a teaching certificate to a permanent resident who has filed a declaration of intent to become a citizen, see INA § 334(f), but will revoke the teaching certificate if the teacher does not naturalize when eligible, or if she becomes ineligible to naturalize. Applying the analysis in *Cabell v. Chavez–Salido*, what are the arguments for and against its constitutionality? Does the statute reflect sound policy?

Does it matter if a noncitizen is not a permanent resident, but a nonimmigrant? Does it matter if a noncitizen seeks a professional license instead of a government job? Does it matter if the profession is law?

EXERCISE: NONIMMIGRANTS AS LAWYERS

Beatrice Jarry is a French citizen initially admitted to the United States on an L–2 spousal visa, but currently present as an H–1B temporary worker. She holds a law degree from Tulane University School of Law in New Orleans and is currently employed as a paralegal. She wants to take the Louisiana bar exam, but Louisiana law requires that "[e]very applicant for admission to the Bar of this state shall . . . [b]e a citizen of the United States or a resident alien thereof." The Louisiana Supreme Court has held that the term "resident alien . . . appl[ies] only to those aliens who have attained permanent resident status in the United States." This interpretation effectively prohibits noncitizens who are lawfully in the United States as nonimmigrants from sitting for the Louisiana Bar. Is the Louisiana law constitutional?

---

2. VOTING

Should permanent residents be allowed to vote in state or federal elections? Central to *Cabell* is the idea of membership in a *political community*—a group of human beings united by, and for, self-governance. If this view accurately captures the essence of citizenship, then it is understandable why we, as a society, seem to have a consensus that denies noncitizens the right or privilege of voting in state and federal elections. To guarantee noncitizens a right to vote, so the argument might run, would destroy one of the few remaining distinctions between noncitizens and citizens and would fatally undermine our understanding of a nation as a self-governing political community.

Counterarguments are possible. In *Minor v. Happersett*, 88 U.S. (21 Wall.) 162, 22 L.Ed. 627 (1875), the Supreme Court upheld a Missouri state law that denied women the right to vote. The Court made it clear that, at least in the nineteenth century, the terms "voter" and "citizen" were not coterminous. The Court's reasoning rested on the idea that not all citizens were voters:

> As has been seen, all the citizens of the States were not invested with the right of suffrage. In all, save perhaps New Jersey, this right was only bestowed upon men and not upon all of them. Under these circumstances it is certainly now too late to contend that a government is not republican, within the meaning of this guaranty in the Constitution, because women are not made voters.

Id. at 176. And, the Court explained, not all voters were citizens:

> Besides this, citizenship has not in all cases been made a condition precedent to the enjoyment of the right of suffrage. Thus, in Missouri, persons of foreign birth, who have declared their intention to become citizens of the United States, may under certain circumstances vote.

The same provision is to be found in the constitutions of Alabama, Arkansas, Florida, Georgia, Indiana, Kansas, Minnesota, and Texas.

Id. at 177. Only in 1920 did the Nineteenth Amendment provide, in part: "The right of citizens of the United States to vote shall not be denied or abridged by the United States or by any State on account of sex." U.S. Const. amend. XIX, § 1.

a. Historical Background

To begin our inquiry, the next excerpt discusses the rise and fall of noncitizen voting in the nineteenth and early twentieth century.

JAMIN B. RASKIN, LEGAL ALIENS, LOCAL CITIZENS: THE HISTORICAL, CONSTITUTIONAL AND THEORETICAL MEANINGS OF ALIEN SUFFRAGE

141 U. Pa. L. Rev. 1391, 1401–16 (1993).

It is crucial to see that the early spirit of political openness toward aliens was perfectly compatible with the exclusionary definition of "the American people as Christian white men of property." Indeed, when properly cabined within the existing rules of suffrage, alien voting subtly reinforced the multiple ballot exclusions of the time. To exclude aliens from voting would have given rise to the dangerous inference that U.S. citizenship was the decisive criterion for suffrage at a time when the majority of U.S. citizens, including almost all women and substantial percentages of men without property, were categorically excluded from the franchise. On the other hand, alien enfranchisement reflected the assumption that the propertied white male alien voter would be sufficiently similar to other electors so as not to threaten fundamental cultural and political norms.

If alien suffrage in the early years of the Republic reflected the states' power to define their own electorates and their elevation of race, gender, and property over citizenship, the United States Congress used alien suffrage in an instrumental way to produce immigration in the northwest territories. In 1789, the first Congress to convene under the Constitution reenacted the Northwest Ordinance of 1787 to provide for the governance of the territories northwest of the Ohio River. The Ordinance gave freehold aliens who had been residents for two years the right to vote for representatives to territorial legislatures, and gave wealthier resident aliens who had been residents for three years the right to serve in these bodies. This remarkable willingness to welcome aliens *qua* aliens into the nascent political enterprise of the new nation continued as Congress supervised the organization of the territories and oversaw their passage into statehood. In the various congressional acts authorizing the election of representatives to statewide constitutional conventions in Ohio, Indiana, Michigan and Illinois, Congress deliberately extended the right to vote to aliens. This policy placed its stamp on the political culture of the states that would emerge from the territories. In 1802, for example, the new State of Ohio enfranchised all "white male inhabitants" twenty-one years old who had lived there for one year.

* * *

[T]he War of 1812, which produced a militant nationalism and suspicion of foreigners, heralded the end of the Revolutionary period of liberal attitudes toward noncitizen voting. In 1812, beginning with Louisiana, most newly admitted states, including Indiana (1816), Mississippi (1817), Alabama (1819), Maine (1820), and Missouri (1821), confined the franchise to citizens. Meanwhile, a number of early states which had permitted alien suffrage, revoked the practice during this same period, changing the "constitutional definition of voters from 'inhabitants' to 'citizens.' " In addition to the effects of the " 'rise of national consciousness' engendered by the War of 1812," Rosberg suggests that the turn away from alien suffrage may have been due to "the increasing public dismay at the arrival of large numbers of new immigrants who were not of English stock and who were thought incapable of ready assimilation." [Rosberg, *Aliens and Equal Protection: Why Not the Right to Vote?*, 75 Mich. L. Rev. 1092, 1096–1098 (1977).]

Another factor may have played a role in the eroding commitment to noncitizen voting in this period. If early alien suffrage was ideologically consistent with the property qualification, the "agitation for the abolition of property qualifications ... [, which] began shortly after the [War of 1812] ended [,]" [J. Shklar, American Citizenship: The Quest for Inclusion 46 (1991)] may have undermined popular support for alien suffrage. The abolition of the property qualification would have meant that, in states with alien suffrage, all male aliens, not simply the property owners and the wealthy, would have the right to vote. Thus, for the first time, alien suffrage states would be extending political membership to a different, and obviously more threatening, class of aliens—those generally deemed unworthy of the ballot.

* * *

* * * Wisconsin's admission to the Union in 1848 revived and transformed the practice of alien suffrage. The framers of Wisconsin's Constitution adopted a modified form of alien suffrage, extending full voting rights only to so-called "declarant aliens"—"[those] White persons of foreign birth who shall have declared their intention to become citizens, conformably to the laws of the United States on the subject of naturalization." As Neuman notes, this provision took advantage of federal naturalization law, which since 1795 had required aliens seeking citizenship to "first declare under oath to a competent court their intention to apply subsequently for citizenship (known colloquially as 'taking out first papers'), and had postponed eligibility for actual naturalization ('second' or 'final papers') until three years after the declaration." [Neuman, *"We Are the People": Alien Suffrage in German and American Perspective*, 13 Mich. J. Int'l L. 259, 297 (1992).] Neuman observes that such declaration, under federal law, did not deprive the alien of his original nationality, did not legally obligate him to complete the process of becoming a citizen, and did not even require an oath of allegiance to the United States. The Wisconsin plan would later come under attack for these reasons.

Nonetheless, the declarant alien qualification succeeded in weakening the force of nationalist opposition to alien suffrage by recasting the practice of alien suffrage. It now became, much more clearly, a pathway to citizenship rather than a possible substitute for it: noncitizen voting became pre-citizen voting. Thus, declarant aliens in Wisconsin, those presumably on the "citizenship track," won the right to participate in local, state, and national elections.

The Wisconsin formula of enfranchising aliens, but only those who had declared their intention to become citizens, proved popular as the country continued to push westward in the nineteenth century. The desire for immigration carried noncitizen voting along. Less than three months after Wisconsin's admission, Congress passed an organic act for the Oregon Territory which embodied the same terms on alien voting. It was followed in 1849 by a parallel provision in the organic act for the Territory of Minnesota. Although Congress did not extend voting rights to aliens in the territories of Utah, New Mexico, and California (lands won during the Mexican War), it did include provisions for declarant alien suffrage in the enabling acts of the territories of Washington, Kansas, Nebraska, Nevada, Dakota, Wyoming, and Oklahoma. After achieving statehood, some of these territories preserved the practice of declarant alien suffrage in their state constitutions; others decided to abandon the practice entirely; and a few dropped it but made provisions for grandfathering in noncitizens who were already voting.

* * *

During the period of the 1850s and 1860s, alien suffrage played a growing role in the struggle between north and south, with southerners trying to reduce and northerners trying to expand the political influence of immigrants, who were overwhelmingly hostile to slavery (if not necessarily friendly to blacks). The issue of noncitizen voting became a bone of contention in congressional debate over the laws governing new territories and states. * * *

After the Civil War began, the Union's military manpower needs caused the armed forces to turn to aliens for help, and the "foreign-born" came to constitute "nearly 25 percent of the Union Army." [J.W. Chambers II, To Raise an Army: The Draft Comes to Modern America 49 (1987).] Not all alien soldiers were there voluntarily. In confronting the thorny question of aliens and conscription, the government gradually chose voting as the crucial dividing line between draftable and undraftable aliens. On July 17, 1862, Congress passed the Militia Act, which called for the nine-month enrollment of "all able-bodied male citizens between the ages of 18 and 45, to be apportioned among the States according to representative population." The Act empowered the President "to draft citizens into the state militia if that state failed to fill its quota through voluntarism." In August, Wisconsin Governor Edward Salomon wrote to Secretary of War Edwin M. Stanton, informing him that approximately half of his state's able-bodied men were aliens, but pointing out that they had already declared their intentions to become citizens and were eligible to vote. Governor Salomon urged that these men not be exempted from the draft. In his answer, Stanton took the position that the mere declaration of intent to become a citizen did not subject these men to the draft but that declarant aliens who had in fact voted would be draftable.

* * *

The inadequacies of the Militia Act eventually led Congress to pass the Enrolment Act of March 3, 1863. This Act, often described as the first precedent for the modern selective service system, included in the draft males between the ages of twenty and forty-five "of foreign birth who shall have declared on oath their intention to become citizens." Suddenly, many aliens who had declared their intentions to become citizens now wanted to renounce their plans. On May 8, 1863 President Lincoln issued a proclamation giving such persons sixty-five days to exit the country or, at the lapse of this period, face the draft. Significantly, however, all declarant aliens who had already voted were excluded from this offer and could not renounce their declarations of intent. Thus, any alien who had voted in the United States was subject to the draft immediately, along with U.S. citizens. Aliens trying to escape military service were required to appear before their draft enrollment boards and show "that they had never voted in this country."

While the North mobilized aliens to fight for the Union at the outset of the war, southern opposition to alien suffrage deepened. Delegates to the Confederate constitutional convention in Montgomery, Alabama in 1861 chose to do what the original American Founders had not: ban alien voting as a matter of constitutional law. * * *

* * *

After the Civil War, noncitizen voting recaptured its lost ground as an electoral practice. At least thirteen new states adopted declarant alien suffrage, "all of them in the South or West and all of them evidently anxious to lure new settlers." [Rosberg, *supra*, 75 Mich. L. Rev. at 1099.] A number of the former Confederate states formed part of this trend as the Reconstruction governments of Alabama, Florida, Georgia, South Carolina, and Texas included provisions for declarant alien suffrage in their Constitutions. There are a number of plausible explanations for this phenomenon which await treatment by a historian to determine their relative weight. Some of the southern states may have been motivated by the progressive attitudes of Reconstruction and a corresponding eagerness to inject new blood into the post-slavery South. This desire to encourage immigration would have constituted a fairly typical motivation for alien suffrage, although designed more for political than economic purposes.

A second and related possibility is that it was seen as only fair to grant the vote to white male aliens, many of whom had fought for, and indeed been drafted by, the North during the Civil War. Shklar explains that suffrage history is repeatedly marked by returning soldiers demanding and obtaining the right to vote as the just reward for their services and "the most basic and characteristic political act of the citizen-soldier." [Shklar, American Citizenship, *supra*, at 45.] Surely this logic, operating fiercely at the time with regard to blacks, did not escape the notice of alien veterans, who had fought for the blacks' freedom. Finally, a more sobering interpretation of the move to alien suffrage is that the South had a great need to attract a cheap immigrant labor force in the wake of slavery's abolition.

At any rate, the spread of noncitizen voting after the Civil War renewed the vitality of the practice. In 1894, a political scientist hostile to alien voting attributed recent statewide election results in Wisconsin and Illinois to "the weight of a foreign element" and also described foreign newcomers as the heart of the Tammany political machine which "names a president, and in some degree controls an administration." By the time the nineteenth century came to a close, according to Rosberg, "nearly one-half of the states and territories had some experience with voting by aliens, and for some the experience lasted more than half a century." [Rosberg, *supra*, 75 Mich. L. Rev. at 1099.]

The late nineteenth century revival of alien suffrage, launched by Wisconsin and accelerated by the defeat of the Confederacy, came to a halt at the turn of the twentieth century, when anti-immigration feeling ran very high. Alabama stopped allowing aliens to vote by way of a constitutional change in 1901, followed by Colorado in 1902, Wisconsin in 1908, and Oregon in 1914. "With the quickening tempo of war, the enlightened tactic of education for immigrants steadily gave way to the harsh technique of repression." [D.M. Kennedy, Over Here: The First World War and American Society 66 (1890).] The demise of alien suffrage was hastened by the "frantic and overreactive days of the First World War when attitudes of parochialism and fear of the foreigner were the order of the day." [*Ambach v. Norwick*, 441 U.S. 68, 82 (Blackmun, J., dissenting).] Just as the nationalism unleashed by the War of 1812 helped to reverse the alien suffrage policies inherited from the late eighteenth century, the hysteria attending World War I caused a sweeping retreat from the progressive alien suffrage policies of the late nineteenth century.

In 1918, Kansas, Nebraska, and South Dakota all changed their constitutions to purge alien suffrage, and Texas ended the practice of noncitizen voting in primary elections by statute. These changes apparently came on the heels of great and, as one observer remarked wryly, quite belated agitation in the press about the horrors of aliens voting. The momentum for cleansing state law of alien suffrage provisions continued as Indiana and Texas joined the trend in 1921, followed by Mississippi in 1924 and, finally, Arkansas in 1926. * * *

For further discussion of the history of noncitizen voting, see R. Hayduk, Democracy for All: Restoring Immigrant Voting Rights in the United States 15–40 (2006).

b.   Noncitizen Voting and the Constitution

Does the Constitution *allow* noncitizen voting? Historical practice suggests that the answer must be "yes," but Gerald Neuman has grounded this answer in an analysis of how one might define "political community."

> The move toward universal citizen suffrage, in the sense of overturning restrictions of class, property, race, religion, and gender, has been a great achievement. It could, however, mislead us into concluding that questions of electoral qualification always have unique right answers. Modern legal doctrine on voting rights could have a similar tendency. In the United States, restrictive voting qualifications, with a few traditional exceptions, are now subject to "strict scrutiny" under the Equal Protection Clause. When the permissible qualifications are cumulated, they define a constitutionally privileged category of citizens (nonfelonious residents over the age of eighteen, and so on), which I will call the core electorate. The breadth of this core electorate is a measure of the success of the egalitarian reforms. Members of the core electorate have not infrequently succumbed to the temptation to identify the core electorate with the political community and to regard any enfranchisement of others as a dilution of their votes and a violation of their rights.

G. L. Neuman, Strangers to the Constitution: Immigrants, Borders, and Fundamental Law 141 (1996). Pointing to various U.S. Supreme Court decisions that upheld the expansion of voting rights beyond this core electorate, for example by allowing non-residents to vote in certain elections, *see, e.g., Spahos v. Mayor of Savannah Beach*, 371 U.S. 206, 83 S.Ct. 304, 9 L.Ed.2d 269 (1962) (per curiam), Neuman went on to conclude:

> [T]he Constitution does not provide a single "conception of a political community" that uniquely determines the electorate of each governmental unit, resulting in a neatly nested hierarchy of political communities, towns within counties within states within a nation. Rather, it affords government some discretion to supplement the core electorate with a variety of optional electorates, consisting of categories of persons who have interests implicated in the community's political process.

Id. at 143.

Does the Constitution *require* noncitizen voting? The next excerpt addresses this question.

GERALD M. ROSBERG, ALIENS AND
EQUAL PROTECTION: WHY NOT
THE RIGHT TO VOTE?

75 Mich. L. Rev. 1092, 1127–1135 (1977).

* * * Immigrants who have arrived recently in the United States may know little about this country's institutions of government or about the issues on which election campaigns are fought. They can certainly learn about these matters, and it would not take very long for many of them to gain this knowledge. But in all likelihood many immigrants are also largely ignorant of this country's values and traditions and therefore cannot have developed an appreciation of or commitment to them. The naturalization requirement for voting could be seen as responsive to this concern in two different ways. First, the durational residence feature gives the immigrant an opportunity to develop a feel for American values and traditions. Second, the act of naturalization itself represents a formal and solemn commitment to the country, its values, and its institutions. The testing of a prospective citizen's loyalty, knowledge, and character is critical, under this view, not so much because it screens out the undeserving candidate but rather because it makes the attainment of naturalization difficult and meaningful. The judicial setting and the oath of renunciation and allegiance (with its grand language about foreign princes and potentates and bearing true faith and allegiance to the United States) drive home to the new citizen the significance of the occasion. It all adds up to a very deliberate and ritualized act of opting into the community and accepting its values and traditions as one's own.

In my view, this argument is the most substantial one that can be made in defense of the citizenship qualification for voting. And yet it is by no means free of difficulty. If everything is going to turn on a sense of commitment to the country's values and traditions, it would seem important to know exactly what values and traditions * * * we have in mind. * * *

The very fact that neither candidate in an election wins all the votes is in itself a good indication that the electorate is already divided on fundamental value questions. Political analysts typically assume that different segments of American society—Catholics, Chicanos, blue-collar workers, Polish–Americans—have their own values and traditions that influence their voting behavior. To which set of values and traditions are the aliens expected to commit themselves? Do we exclude them from the polls until they have narrowed the choice to two—the Democratic tradition and the Republican tradition—and then turn them loose to make a free choice between Alexander Hamilton and Thomas Jefferson? Or is it rather that the central value and tradition of this country is that there is no central value and tradition? Perhaps aliens are entitled to hold whatever views they want, but they cannot be allowed to vote until they have come to understand and cherish the fact that they may hold whatever views they want. One has an intuitive sense that an alien who has not been socialized in the United States will lack certain characteristics or attitudes that are fundamentally American. But given the diversity of socialization experiences available in the United States, this intuition would seem a rather treacherous foundation on which to build an argument of compelling state interest.

Instead of trying to determine the substantive content of the country's values and traditions, one might do better to focus on the act of commitment to the United States that naturalization apparently involves. In terms of values, culture, and language, resident aliens may be indistinguishable from at least some group of American citizens. And their loyalty may be beyond question, at least in the sense that they think well of the country and wish it no harm. But what may be lacking is a willingness on the part of resident aliens to identify themselves with the country and its people and to give up once and for all their attachment to the countries in which they were born. The unnaturalized alien is perhaps holding something back, refusing to join in. * * *

[But] it is simply not correct to say that unnaturalized aliens have made no commitment to the United States. In contrast to native-born citizens, whose commitment, if any, is tacit, resident aliens have committed themselves knowingly and voluntarily. They have all had to make considerable effort to qualify for an immigrant visa, which is ordinarily a good deal harder to obtain than a certificate of naturalization. Even after proving themselves qualified, they have had to wait months and even more often years for a visa to become available. And they have given up their homes in the countries of their birth and resettled in the United States. Moreover, most resident aliens had ties to the United States even before they arrived, for they have tended to follow their countrymen and kinsmen in chains of migration. * * *

* * *

* * * We have come to accept and even cherish the fact that many citizens will retain what Justice Frankfurter called "old cultural loyalty" to another country, and the line between cultural matters and political matters is known to be indistinct. The internment during the Second World War of persons of Japanese ancestry—citizen and alien alike—is a powerful reminder of how far we have been willing to go on the supposition that national origin may be much more accurately predictive of loyalty than is citizenship. In short, it is hard to see what it is about resident aliens that makes us insist on excluding them from the polls for want of the necessary commitment to the United States.

Yet it may be objected that the net effect of this kind of argument is to deny the existence of any distinction at all between the citizen and the alien. If the alien is indistinguishable from the citizen in terms of knowledge of affairs in the United States, loyalty, and commitment to the people and institutions of the United States, and if for that reason the alien has a constitutional right to vote, then it may appear that the concept of citizenship has been robbed of all its meaning. Plainly, nothing that I have said would jeopardize the distinction between the citizen and the nonresident alien. But one might insist that under the view presented here resident aliens would in effect be naturalized as of the moment they take up residence in the United States. Much of the difficulty arises, however, from the assumed equation of citizenship and voting. My argument is not that resident aliens look like citizens, so therefore they must be citizens. It is rather that in pertinent respects resident aliens are enough like citizens that it may be unconstitutional to distinguish between them in allocating the right to vote.

Citizens have historically enjoyed certain rights and undertaken certain obligations that resident aliens did not share. Every time one of those rights or obligations is passed on to aliens the gap between citizens and aliens narrows. If we are determined to maintain a gap, to preserve a sense of "we" and "they," we could disqualify aliens from owning land or deny them welfare benefits or make them all wear green hats. The imposition of these disabilities on aliens may seem intolerable. But why should it be any more tolerable to make the burden of preserving the distinction between citizens and aliens fall exclusively on the right to vote, the most precious right of all?

Moreover, extending the franchise to aliens would not, in fact, completely close the gap between citizens and aliens, since voting is not the only distinction between the two that survives the Supreme Court's recent decisions on the rights of aliens. By the terms of the Constitution itself aliens are ineligible to hold certain offices in the government of the United States. Aliens do not have the same right as citizens to gain admission to the United States. Citizens born abroad can take up residence in this country whenever they desire. Citizens can abandon their residence in the United States without fear of losing their right to return. Aliens, on the other hand, gain the right to reside in the United States only upon compliance with the stringent terms of the immigration laws. And resident aliens who abandon their domicile in this country will not necessarily be readmitted. When citizens travel outside the United States they carry American passports, and they expect and ordinarily receive the diplomatic protection of the United States when the need for it arises. Aliens, even resident aliens, have no right to call upon the United States for that protection and would not receive it in any case. Citizens are entitled to have the government represent their interests in international tribunals. Aliens have no such right, and under international law the government would be barred from representing them even if it had any interest in doing so. Citizens are generally free from any obligation to register with the government or to inform the government regularly of their whereabouts. Aliens are subject to rather elaborate reporting requirements. Citizens can be held to account in American courts for conduct overseas in some circumstances where aliens apparently cannot. Citizens can confer an immigration preference on their relatives overseas in a considerable number of situations where aliens cannot.

* * * [C]onsidering the primacy of the right to vote one could reasonably argue that it is distinctions like these that should bear the burden of differentiating citizens from aliens, and not the distinction between voting and not voting. We could, in other words, grant the right to vote to resident aliens and still leave them readily distinguishable from citizens. Yet that result would remain unacceptable to those who believe that allowing aliens to vote would eviscerate the concept of citizenship. Their assumption must be that political rights are inherently and properly rights of citizenship, whereas civil rights have no necessary connection with citizenship and properly belong to "persons." In the earliest part of the country's history, however, the assumption was precisely the reverse: citizenship "carried with it civil rights but no political privileges." [Start, *Naturalization in the English Colonies in North America*, in American Historical Assn., Annual Report for the Year 1893, at 319 (1894).] Citizenship, and in particular naturalization, was thought important because it determined whether or not a new settler would be able to own and convey land. Even today, * * * the Supreme Court insists that citizenship as such confers no right to vote. Indeed, it would seem anomalous to equate citizenship with voting so long as we separate the power to make persons citizens from the power to make persons voters. The former power inheres in the national government, the latter in the states.

Yet I cannot deny the existence of a widespread assumption that the right to vote is not only a right of citizenship, but the quintessential right of citizenship. And the conferral of the right to vote on aliens would undermine that assumption. But where does the assumption come from, and why should we insist on preserving it? Intuitively, it seems that there must be some explanation for the assumption. After all, the very fact that it is so widespread may be an indication that it responds to some important inner need of citizens to distinguish themselves from what are perceived to be outsiders, even where the outsiders are their neighbors. But I do not believe that it is possible to articulate an explanation for this assumption without moving the discussion to a level of extremely high abstraction and without putting a great deal of weight on symbolic values. To sustain the disenfranchisement of aliens on the strength of that kind of reasoning would be fundamentally inconsistent, it seems to me, with our ordinary approach in determining which state interests are compelling. I am reluctant to conclude that, because I have so much difficulty articulating the state's interest, it must be less than compelling. But I am confident at least that the validity of laws denying aliens the vote is by no means self-evident. It is surely not enough to tip one's hat at the state interest in having knowledgeable and loyal voters and let it go at that.

NOTES AND QUESTIONS ON NONCITIZEN VOTING

1. Addressing whether the Constitution requires noncitizen voting, the Colorado Supreme Court rejected an equal protection challenge to a state statute that required citizenship to vote in school elections. *See Skafte v.*

Rorex, 191 Colo. 399, 553 P.2d 830 (Colo.1976), *appeal dismissed for want of a substantial federal question*, 430 U.S. 961, 97 S.Ct. 1638, 52 L.Ed.2d 352 (1977). The court, relying heavily on *Sugarman*, explained: "The state has a rational interest in limiting participation in government to those persons within the political community. Aliens are not a part of the political community." Voting in school elections, the court explained, "involves participation in the decision making process of the polity." 191 Colo. at 402–03, 553 P.2d at 832–33.

2.   Today, noncitizen voting is rare. Noncitizen parents of schoolchildren may vote in school elections in Chicago, as they could in New York City school board elections from 1970 until the school boards were disbanded in 2002. Residents, including some noncitizens, may vote in local elections in several Maryland communities.

Proposals for local noncitizen voting continue to surface, but none have been adopted recently. In 2004 and again in 2010, San Francisco voters defeated ballot initiatives that would have allowed noncitizens regardless of immigration law status to vote in school board elections if they have children in the public schools. In 2010, voters in Portland, Maine, rejected a proposal to allow residents who are "legal immigrants" to vote in local elections. On previous proposals for noncitizen voting in cities throughout the United States, including Los Angeles and Washington, D.C., see R. Hayduk, Democracy for All, *supra*, at 109.

3.   Federal law has moved in the other direction. The 1996 Act added new inadmissibility and deportability grounds for voting unlawfully. *See* INA §§ 212(a)(10), 237(a)(6). It also amended 18 U.S.C.A. § 1015 and added 18 U.S.C.A. § 611, which generally make it a federal crime for a noncitizen to falsely claim citizenship in order to register to vote, or to vote in a federal election.

4.   Even assuming the Constitution allows noncitizen voting, is it a good idea? Does it matter if the elections in question are local elections? Does noncitizen voting at federal, state, or local levels devalue citizenship, or rob it of meaning? Among the differences between U.S. citizens and permanent residents, just how significant is it that citizens have the right to participate in political affairs through voting, and permanent residents do not?

To return to the three views of immigration suggested by Hiroshi Motomura, see Chapter Seven (p. 669) and earlier in this chapter (p. 1348), most arguments in favor of noncitizen voting are based on viewing immigration as affiliation. The idea is that noncitizens, after a period of residence, should have the right to vote based on their ties with U.S. society. But most long-time resident noncitizens are eligible to naturalize, so can't we expect them to acquire the franchise through naturalization? For permanent residents who have not been here long enough to naturalize, immigration as affiliation lends much less support.

5.   Some proponents of noncitizen voting point to Europe, where it is practiced in certain circumstances. *See, e.g.,* Raskin, *supra*, 141 U. Pa. L. Rev. at 1458–60. Perhaps most prominently, the Treaty on European Union provides: "Every citizen of the Union residing in a Member State of which he is not a national shall have the right to vote and to stand as a candidate at

municipal elections in the Members State in which he resides, under the same conditions as nationals of that State." Treaty on European Union, art. 8b, Feb. 7, 1992, art. G(C) 86, 31 I.L.M. 247 (1992). Note that this provision does not guarantee voting rights for all resident noncitizens—only for those who are citizens of an EU member country who are now residing in another EU country. Seventeen European countries have laws potentially allowing some lawfully present noncitizen residents who are not citizens of EU member countries may vote in local elections, but some of these laws are very restrictive. *See* K. Groenendijk, Local Voting Rights for Non–Nationals in Europe: What We Know and What We Need to Learn (2008).

Does it make sense to compare Europe and the United States? Where, as in Europe, naturalization is generally more difficult, viewing immigration as affiliation may support noncitizen voting more persuasively than it does where, as in the United States, naturalization is more commonplace. European developments suggest that some policymakers have seen easing naturalization as an alternative to noncitizen voting. *See* Groenendijk, *supra*, at 7. On the other hand, Kees Groenendijk, commenting on studies of naturalization rates in countries with local voting rights, concluded: "Local voting rights . . . are not a barrier, but rather function as an incentive to be become naturalized. Therefore, policymakers should see local voting rights and naturalization as complementary measures." *Id.*

6. Compare the following proposal, described by its authors as "a modified form of the current effort to make noncitizens eligible to vote":

> We would add two twists. First, we would allow noncitizens to vote for the five-year period during which they are statutorily ineligible to naturalize. Under this system, recently immigrated permanent residents would be able to obtain a five-year voter registration card (transferable across jurisdictions, but not extendable). After the five years, they would no longer be eligible for permanent resident voting privileges, but would be able to naturalize. Recognizing that [processing of applications for immigration benefits] suffers from frequent backlogs, we would allow some provision for extending the temporary privileges while the application is on file. Although the authors of this discussion do not fully agree on whether voting should be limited to local elections (de la Garza) or should include all elections (DeSipio), we both advocate the extension of noncitizen voting privileges to local elections at a minimum.

> The second twist is that naturalization applicants who can show that they voted in most primary and general elections during the five-year period of noncitizen voter registration would be exempt from the naturalization exam. The exam is designed to test good citizenship through indirect measures such as knowledge of American history and civics. We propose that voting is an equally good measure of commitment to and understanding of the American system.

de la Garza & DeSipio, *Save the Baby, Change the Bathwater, and Scrub the Tub: Latino Electoral Participation After Seventeen Years of Voting Rights Act Coverage*, 71 Tex. L. Rev. 1479, 1522–23 (1993). *See also* Motomura, *Americans in Waiting*, *supra*, at 193 (linking the de la Garza–DeSipio proposal to the historical practice of voting by intending citizens).

7.   Assuming that only citizens may vote, may noncitizens participate in politics in other ways? Does the absence of noncitizen voting suggest that it is constitutional to forbid other forms of participation? Assuming that noncitizens are entitled under the first amendment to debate issues that are pivotal in the election context, and to seek to persuade others to their point of view, what about making campaign contributions? Section § 319 of the Federal Election Campaign Act, 2 U.S.C.A. § 441e, bars foreign nationals from contributing to political candidates' campaigns, with the express exception of lawful permanent residents. What does the idea of political community suggest on this question? In *Bluman v. Federal Election Commission*, a three-judge panel of the U.S. District Court for the District of Columbia held that this provision does not violate the First Amendment, ___ F.Supp.2d ___, 2011 WL 3443833 (D.D.C. 2011), *statement as to jurisdiction in the U.S. Supreme Court filed*, 80 USLW 3119 (Sept. 1, 2011).

CONCLUDING EXERCISE: NONCITIZEN VOTING AND THE IDEA OF POLITICAL COMMUNITY

You have been asked to prepare members of a state legislative commission on equality in representation before the state legislature, county boards of supervisors, and city councils. You are aware that with regard to the U.S. House of Representatives, section 2 of the Fourteenth Amendment provides in part: "Representatives shall be apportioned among the several States according to their respective numbers, counting the whole number of persons in each State, excluding Indians not taxed." Pursuant to this clause and Article I, § 2, cl. 3, which requires an "actual enumeration," congressional districts are apportioned to achieve equal population based on the census, which counts all inhabitants, regardless of immigration status.

In the context of apportionment of districts for state and local offices, courts have consistently rejected the argument that the U.S. Constitution requires the counts on which districts are based to be limited to citizen population rather than including noncitizens. *See, e.g., Chen v. City of Houston*, 206 F.3d 502, 522 (5th Cir. 2000). As a consequence of including noncitizens, a citizen's vote in a district with many noncitizen residents has greater influence in an election than a citizen's vote in a district with fewer noncitizens.

Sociologist Marta Tienda views this situation as problematic and analyzes two possible solutions to "align democracy with demography," as she puts it. The first is "to equalize the voting power across districts" by disregarding noncitizens in redistricting. The second is "to strive for truly equal representation by allowing noncitizens to vote." Tienda, *Demography and the Social Contract*, 39 Demography 587, 600 (2002).

According to a Ninth Circuit decision addressing district lines for the Los Angeles County Board of Supervisors, drawing districts without considering noncitizen residents would mean that elected office-holders in districts with more noncitizens would serve larger constituencies. This "would dilute the access of voting age citizens in that district to their representative, and would similarly abridge the right of aliens and minors to petition that representative." *Garza v. City of Los Angeles*, 918 F.2d 763, 775 (9th Cir. 1990). The court cited *Yick Wo v. Hopkins*, 118 U.S. 356, 368, 6 S.Ct. 1064, 1070, 30 L.Ed. 220 (1886), for an "equal protection right ... to allow political participation short of voting or holding a sensitive public office."

Is it wise, as a policy matter, to count noncitizen residents in drawing district lines for elected representatives? What would you recommend to the commission members on how they should respond to this situation, which creates a form of inequality either way that districts are apportioned? Which method of apportionment better accords with the principle of "one person, one vote"?

INDEX

References are to Pages

†